Work Motivation in Organizational Behavior

Second Edition

Work Motivation in Organizational Behavior

Second Edition

Craig C. Pinder
*University of Victoria,
British Columbia*

Ψ Psychology Press
Taylor & Francis Group

NEW YORK AND HOVE

Published in 2008
by Psychology Press
711 Third Avenue
New York, NY 10017

Published in Great Britain
by Psychology Press
27 Church Road
Hove, East Sussex BN3 2FA

First issued in paperback 2014

Copyright © 2008 by Psychology Press

Psychology Press is an imprint of the Taylor & Francis Group, an informa business

Typeset by RefineCatch Limited, Bungay, Suffolk, UK

Cover design by Lisa Dynan

Library of Congress Cataloging in Publication Data
Pinder, Craig C.
  Work motivation in organizational behavior / Craig C. Pinder. — 2nd ed.
    p. cm.
  Includes bibliographical references and index.
  ISBN 978–1–1388–3820–8 (pbk)
  1. Employee motivation.   2. Organizational behavior.   I. Title.
  HF5549.5.M63P56 2008
  658.3′14—dc22

                                           2007050237

ISBN 978–0–8058–5604–0 (hbk)
ISBN 978–1–1388–3820–8 (pbk)

To my parents, Charles and Gertrude Pinder, who taught me my earliest lessons about the value and importance of work motivation and to Pat Pinder, my wife, life-partner, and best friend, who has helped me to focus my energy and direction in applying what I learned from my parents.

Contents

Foreword

Those of us who have pretensions as academic scholars in the field of work motivation in organizations owe the author of this book, Craig Pinder, a great debt of gratitude. The reason for this is because finding, critically reviewing, and integrating the vast scientific literature on this topic – and making overall sense of it – is a daunting and demanding challenge. As I have said elsewhere, "work motivation is . . . a sort of Rubik's Cube of many interesting facets and components, but also extremely difficult to put together in a meaningful whole with all of the pieces lined up appropriately." The author, in both earlier incarnations of this book, and in this revised second edition, has done exactly that: He has brought order and understanding to an excessively jumbled and disparate set of scholarly studies. To repeat: For this, we owe him!

The present and prior editions of this book represent a substantial feat of scholarship. The result is that the "Pinder motivation book," as it is commonly referred to in the field of organizational behavior, has become *the* essential volume to have if one is interested in studying or researching this topic. There are at least three major reasons why it has achieved this status in the field.

First, it is, without question, extremely comprehensive. Its 15 chapters blanket the subject of work motivation. It is not just that within these chapters well over 1000 references (and, who among us can claim that we have read and digested this many articles and books on *any* topic?) are cited, which they are. It is also the fact that this sprawling, often tangled literature is organized into meaningful clusters and subsections that give coherence to the array of theories and empirical findings that abound throughout the book. If a topic in the subject of work motivation is not covered in this book, it is probably not important.

A second reason for the lofty status of this book in the OB field, and perhaps even more important than the first reason, is that the author provides interpretative evaluations to the literature he reviews. The book is replete throughout with observations and commentaries on particular theories and studies as well as on whole bodies of literature pertaining to major topics in the subject matter of work motivation. Although knowledgeable readers may find themselves disagreeing with Pinder's viewpoints from time to time – although probably not *too* often – they are seldom in doubt where the author stands on a particular issue. This refreshing candor and willingness to take a stand clearly adds value to the book and provides a stimulus and direction for the reader on how to move ahead on making further scholarly advances in this domain.

Another reason for the book's deserved standing in the field is that it is written in a sprightly and frequently engaging style not often found in books of this type. After all, a scholarly-oriented book with a chapter titled "Power, Love, and Sex at Work," cannot be considered dull. More specifically, all through the book the author provides pithy and entertaining examples and explanations to highlight his points. Two among my favorites can be illustrated by the following. In Chapter 11 ("Equity, Fairness, and Justice Motives Related to Work"), when talking about equity theory and distributive justice: "Professional athletes often make the news by demanding that their contracts be torn up before their terms expire. The reason for this apparent lack of respect for contract law usually involves feelings by these athletes that the previously agreed upon rates of pay are, by some standard, no longer 'fair'." Also from Chapter 11, in discussing how individuals can restore equity: "The author has known colleagues who have proclaimed that their employers 'seem able to afford less of my time every year'."

For all of these reasons, and also because this newest edition has been extensively updated with coverage of the literature since the previous 1998 edition, this book remains – as stated earlier – "essential" for anyone interested in the subject. It demonstrates how a lot of motivation on the author's part can lead to a superior outcome.

Lyman W. Porter
University of California, Irvine

Preface

It was 10 years ago this month (June, 1997) when I wrote the preface to the first edition of this book (Pinder, 1998). Issues related to work motivation are at least as important today as they were then. Indeed, they have been important throughout the history of our species. As an academic who has devoted a career to the study of work motivation, I am often asked the question: "So, what motivates people?" I usually try to dodge this question because I have learned from decades of experience that those who ask it usually expect a 60- to 90-second answer. Their eyes glaze over when I become more detailed than what 90 seconds permits, so it is easier – in casual settings, at least – merely to change the subject. (I rarely tell people to "buy my book" to get their answer, although I have been tempted on occasion to do so.)

Sometimes I am asked a different question by more knowledgeable friends, colleagues, and acquaintances: "So, what's *new* in work motivation?" Although, I confess, I frequently try to sidestep this question as well, I am usually more inclined to try a polite, sophisticated answer structured in the lexicon of the field. As I look back on my answers to this second question, I notice that my typical answer has varied over the years. A quarter-century ago, my answer to this second question (what's new?) was "Not much, really" (see Pinder, 1984).

However, I am proud to report that, more recently, I have become more sanguine with my answer to the same question (see Pinder, 1998) because by 2000, progress had been made in a few substantive areas that had not been well established by the 1980s (e.g., social cognitive theory, the role of affect in work motivation, and the understanding of cross-cultural differences). In addition, by the year 2000 there had been an increase in the level of sophistication of the research methods employed to develop and advance theory and technique. More and more frequently, old (and newer) theories were being put to empirical testing by methodologies more appropriately suited to the true tenets of those theories. Meanwhile, some older theories (such as need-based and expectancy-valence models) had gone into dignified retirement, having demonstrated their respective validity, utility, and their roles in the puzzle of understanding work-related human behavior, within Western culture, at least. The lack of recent empirical interest in these theories does not mean they are not valid or useful; to the contrary, they have had their years under the looking glass and have shown their merit. Others were moving along gracefully (such as goal-setting theory), while still others had been subsumed or had morphed (e.g., equity theory had become an integral part of the justice theory movement, and cognitive evaluation theory had become part of the broader framework of self-determination theory).

My friend and colleague – Dr. Gary Latham – and I reviewed the literature on work motivation in 2005 for the *Annual Review of Psychology*, examining the progress that had been made since the previous *Annual Review* chapter devoted to the subject (Korman, Greenhaus, & Badin, 1977). In our review, Gary and I reached many of the conclusions summarized earlier: Incremental improvements have been made over the previous 30 years but there have been very few fundamentally-new insights such as those offered in the early days of organizational science, such as by J.S. Adams, Frederick Herzberg and his colleagues, James March, Abraham Maslow, Douglas McGregor, Lou Pondy, Herbert Simon, B. F. Skinner, Frederick W. Taylor, to mention but a few.

In this volume, I have expanded and updated a number of areas, such as those related to job design, affect, equity, fairness and justice (especially the latter), and international differences in values and culture. I have also tried to promote the recent attempts of scholars such as Denise Rousseau and Gary Johns to advance an appreciation of the nature, importance, and functioning of *context* in work motivation and behavior. In psychology, this is not new insight but we in organizational science have been slow to take it seriously in our research.

Throughout, I have attempted to acknowledge the interplay and tradeoffs between the oft-competing goals in science between parsimony (such as is usually sought by people who ask the first of the two questions mentioned earlier) and the requisite complexity that is required for deeper scientific understanding, although not necessarily applied utility.

In the final chapter, I raise a question of my own: What are the real reasons for the field's apparently new interest in cross-cultural differences in work values and cultures? Given that there are more human slaves alive today than at any time in recorded history, and that there are countless unemployed and underemployed people working in borderline (and worse) conditions not much better than slavery, what can we do about them, and to what end? I suggest that hierarchical need theories that have largely been abandoned by Western work motivation theorists might usefully be reconsidered if and when the field seriously undertakes to study human work motivation rather than simply the motivation to work in Western civilizations and economies.

I would like to acknowledge a number of special people who have provided inspiration, encouragement, and material support throughout my career pursuit of work motivation as well as during the preparation of this particular book. Professor Bikhu Parekh of the University of Hull was an early inspiration for me to consider the political nature of human action. Professors Bill England, George Milkovich, Karl Weick, and Lawrence K. Williams provided me with quality graduate-level education and training at the University of Minnesota and Cornell University to make my career in social science both possible and rewarding.

I thank Professors Philip Bobko, Robert House, Gary Latham, Murdith McLean, Larry Moore, T. K. Peng, Ana Maria Peredo, Lyman Porter, Robert Roe, and Claire Ward for their encouragement over the past 30 years. I also give my sincere thanks to Dean Ali Dastmalchian, Vice President Academic and Provost Jamie Cassels, and President David Turpin at the University of Victoria for their unconditional support – in all its forms – during the personally-challenging period of nearly 4 years it took me to write this revision. I have never worked for better bosses!

Ms. Inba Kehoe, my star-librarian at the McPherson Library at the University of Victoria provided me with invaluable assistance over the years, both teaching me to find things myself, and, when I failed, for digging up things I could not locate on my own, notwithstanding her tutelage. She has become a good friend and my go-to person when I am lost in the ocean of literature.

I also thank the people at Lawrence Erlbaum Associates/Psychology Press, notably Anne Duffy and Arthur Brief for their patience and trust in me to deliver this manuscript, albeit 2 years late.

Finally, and most of all, I thank my wife and best friend, Pat, for her unending love and support for more than 36 years, especially for her strength and devotion over the past 4 years of my health difficulties while this project was underway.

I have required and received gifts from many wonderful people. I humbly thank them all.

Craig Pinder
Victoria, B.C.
June 2007

PART ONE

How Theories of Work Motivation are Developed

Work Motivation, Productivity, and the Economy

1

The principal object of management should be to secure the maximum prosperity for the employer, coupled with the maximum prosperity for each employee.
F. W. Taylor

"Hope. Vision. Action."

These three words comprised the theme of the convocation address that Frank O'Dea delivered to the audience attending the June 2005 graduation ceremony at Royal Roads University at Victoria, B.C. Mr. O'Dea, who had just become Dr. O'Dea after receiving the university's doctor of laws degree *honoris causa*, was telling the story of how he rose from living on the streets in downtown Toronto in the late 1960s to a position of prominence in Canadian business and society. He described how he and his friends would panhandle on Yonge Street, spend their money on cheap wine, and, if it were cold at the time, on a thin bed in a flop house that night. If it was relatively warm, he said, they would sleep on park benches. Every day, he and his friends would promise one another to improve their lives "tomorrow . . . tomorrow . . . tomorrow." For a long time, tomorrow never came.

Eventually, in 1968 when O'Dea was 23 years of age, he began to turn his life around. He joined Alcoholics Anonymous and has not had a drink since. By 1974 he ran a successful political campaign for a local politician and co-founded The Second Cup in 1975, which is today Canada's largest chain of gourmet coffee and tea stores. He has created and sold a number of businesses and become a major Canadian philanthropist. In the mid-1980s, he helped to raise more than $2.5 million to create an animated film for educating destitute children in Africa about HIV-AIDS. He helped found Street Kids International, War Child (Canada), The Canadian Landmine Foundation, and an airline to transport people from remote regions who are in need of medical care. In May 2004 he was recognized for his many contributions to the poor of Canada and abroad by being named an Officer of the Order of Canada by the Governor General.

The secret of his success, O'Dea repeated many times during his convocation address, was found in the three concepts: *Hope*, *vision*, and *action* – three concepts that capture much or most of the essence of work motivation, the topic of this book. Hope is one of many energizing internal forces that can arouse an individual toward action (Luthans, 2003). Vision provides direction(s) for the person's actions as well as the sense of conviction and tenacity to persist when the going gets tough (Senge, 1990). Finally, action itself is what brings about change in a person's circumstances, such as those of Dr. Frank O'Dea when he realized that he would not survive long unless he radically changed his life and, along the way, the lives of countless beneficiaries in Canada and abroad. Dr. Frank O'Dea, in the parlance of this volume, is full of work motivation, and he is infectious when he tells his personal story.

PURPOSE OF THIS BOOK

This book is about the multiple reasons people work. It examines the origins of the impulse to work and the many reasons people either enjoy their work or hate it. It explores the scientific and humanistic insights into why work is such a central – even defining – characteristic of human activity. This is not a book intended to instruct second and third parties on how to "motivate" others to work, although applied implications of the analysis will be presented where appropriate. Hence the content and tone of most of the text is descriptive rather than normative and critical as well as comparative rather than of a proselytizing nature. My goal is to be dispassionate in my treatment of current theories related to work motivation and behavior. A key purpose in all that follows is to entice others to explore theories, models, and hypotheses that shed light on work motivation, one of the most central, most important, and most researched topics in the organizational and social sciences (Miner, 2003).

The topic of work motivation is popular in the media although it frequently appears in disguised forms as authors, consultants, social critics, and management theorists explore real or putative trends in people's work behavior and habits, job satisfaction levels, entrepreneurial activity, leisure behavior, or career turbulence. Because work is such an important institution in everyday life, it is certainly a topic of considerable discussion and even controversy. In many ways, most people believe themselves experts when any aspect of work is raised for examination and discussion. We frequently read newspaper opinions or the results of studies purporting to demonstrate that people don't work as hard as they used to (or that they work harder), that the desire for leisure is driving out the desire to work and prosper, that "today's" employees aren't as eager as were their ancestors, or that people in other countries are collectively outworking those of us here in North America.

For example, *The Economist* (2006) magazine recently published a secondary report of a working paper released by the Federal Reserve Bank of Boston (see Aguiar & Hurst, 2006). The research examined the validity of the commonly held belief that Americans are working harder these days than they did in previous decades and generations. Aguiar and Hurst (2006) concluded that this belief is largely a myth but the existence of the original research and its reportage in *The Economist* reflect the popular importance of the issue in daily discourse. Nevertheless, the cover story of the October 2, 2005 edition of *Business Week* (see Mandel, Hamm, Matlack, Farrell, & Therese, 2005) claimed that "more than 31% of college-educated male workers [in the United States] are regularly logging 50 or more hours a week at work, up from 22% in 1980." The article also claimed that "Forty percent of American adults get less than seven hours sleep on weekdays . . . up from 31% in 1980." The same *Business Week* article reported that since 1991, average annual work hours have dropped in Japan by 11%, in France by 10%, by 6% in Germany and Britain, and 5% in South Korea (Mandell et al., 2005).[1] It is the Koreans who have been seen as the most highly motivated among the world's workforce in recent years. By contrast, Germany and France are often accused of not being particularly devoted to their work, in part because of the shorter work week and employment laws in the European Community. A study reported in Sweden – and cited in the *Times Colonist* (September 18, 2004, p. A12 via American Press) – found that 40% of the population there believe it is okay to stay away from work (and seek sick-leave compensation) when they are tired or having a difficult time getting along with their colleagues.

It is important to state at the outset that most of the ideas to be presented in this book are either theory or derived from theory. There are virtually no laws or solid facts pertaining to human behavior. The complexity of human behavior is something most of us are quick to acknowledge in some settings, but equally quick to forget when we seek solutions to behavioral problems in other

---

[1] In the previous edition of this book (Pinder, 1998), the author commented that the Koreans appeared by conventional wisdom to be the hardest working!

settings. Some of the theories to be presented contradict one another, either conceptually or in application. That is the state of the science related to work motivation as it is of the art of management. This is something that the reader will simply have to accept. The pithy advice offered by many of the airport paperbacks we mention later notwithstanding, there are no simple, single "quick fixes" that have withstood the scrutiny of the social scientist and the intelligent manager over the long haul. As we will see throughout this book, many old ideas from social science have appeared and reappeared more than once, usually with new names and buzzwords, since World War II.

In short, this book is about the nature of differences among people in their motivation to work, whether it is working for oneself, a small employer, a government agency, or some part of a large multinational conglomerate. It seems that we must, collectively, be willing to put our feet on the floor on cold, rainy mornings to work if we are to survive and flourish as individuals and as a safe, comfortable, and stable economic society. Individually, we *must* be productive; collectively, we *must* be productive. Yet, as we will see shortly, the productivity mentality that has characterized the concepts of work and working since the beginning of the Industrial Revolution may have, ironically, become a portent of the doom of many millions of people while being the indicator of success for only a selected few. What is productivity, and how is it related to work motivation? We address these questions in the following sections.

PRODUCTIVITY: A RELATIVE CONCEPT

In his 2005 budget speech in front of the Canadian House of Commons, then-finance minister Ralph Goodale stated:

> A nation's ability to achieve higher levels of prosperity is a function of two ingredients – a steadily growing work force and steadily improving productivity . . . We need to encourage that work force to be as smart and skilled as possible – to beat its international competition and to adapt to changing times.
>
> (*The Globe and Mail*, October 3, 2005, p. B6)

Indeed, the competitive economic edge and subsequent well-being of countries such as Canada, the United States, Sweden, and Switzerland in recent decades has largely been a result of the high comparative levels of productivity in the economies of those countries over the past few generations. High productivity and comparatively high increases in productivity have permitted high wages, inexpensive goods and services, abundant public amenities and social services, and a generally high standard of living for all (Hall & Jones, 1999; Mahoney, 1988). High productivity has long been both a measure of, and a contributing factor to, the quality of life we can enjoy. It is important to note that a considerable amount of the attention devoted to issues of who works harder than whom (as discussed in the previous paragraphs) is frequently sparked by reports of comparative productivity between and among national economies. This is the first of many examples to appear in this book of the importance of being precise when discussing inter-individual differences on the grounds of concepts and constructs such as motivation and productivity. Indeed, individual motivation is only one component – albeit an important one – among the forces that determine a nation's productivity and attendant economic well-being. In short, cross-national comparisons of productivity (or cross-industry or cross-organizational comparisons, for that matter) must not be confused with cross-unit comparisons of work motivation. That said, we turn now to a short discussion of productivity, per se, because of the role that work motivation plays in determining productivity levels, increases in productivity levels, and, consequently, economic well-being.

In its simplest terms, productivity is the value of the economic output achieved in an industry or economy per unit of human labor and fixed capital required to attain it. It is a measure of how much work people accomplish at their jobs, divided by the amount of time they spend doing those jobs – time spent collecting salaries (or wages) and benefits. It is usually measured in terms of the gross domestic product (GDP) produced per person in a given year. When the level of economic output per unit of input increases, more people can enjoy more goods and services without causing others to consume less (Rees, 1980). Using Germany's GDP per person as its base of 100 points, the State Secretariat for Economic Affairs (Economic Promotion Geneva, 2003) reported that the United States had the highest productivity index (at 152), followed by Ireland (131), Switzerland (125), Belgium (116), France (115), Great Britain (107), Italy (106), Austria (104), and the Netherlands (103). By way of extolling the high standing of Switzerland in this largely Western-European analysis, the Swiss State Secretariat credited that country's liberal labor laws, few regulations, consistent social stability in its labor markets (i.e., comparatively few strikes and lockouts), and the fact that its social insurance system is jointly funded by employers and Swiss workers.

Mahoney (1988) pointed out that increases in *production* are accomplished through either or both of two means: (1) increased use of production inputs (for example, capital, land, water resources, and labor); and (2) increased efficiency in the transformation of inputs into usable outputs (such as goods or services). For Mahoney and most economists, productivity has to do with the second of these two approaches – getting more goods and services for a given or fixed level of input factors. Moreover, productivity has meaning only in relative terms: "There is no ideal level of productivity, and judgments are limited to 'more' or 'less' comparisons" (p. 14). Therefore, we can reasonably compare the productivity of a given firm or economy with its own level from a previous time, and/or we can make comparisons among firms or entire economies for a common time period.

Economists, business executives, shareholders, and public leaders are constantly concerned with the productivity problem, and make both of the two types of comparison described by Mahoney (1988). Productivity is measured by a variety of indicators, such as profit, customer satisfaction, reduced costs, units produced, and so on. Productivity ratios, such as return on investment, net earnings per share and output per employee are other examples. There is no "one best way" to measure productivity: Different types of measure are required for different contexts and purposes. Moreover, regardless of how it is measured, increases in one's own productivity over time are universally seen as good, as situations where one's own level of productivity is either higher than someone else's level or higher than their own particular rates of increase in productivity. To repeat: "[C]omparative level and rate of change are the key aspects of productivity measurement" (Mahoney, 1988, p. 22). The range of disparity across nations in output per worker is shocking: In 1988, for example, output per worker in the United States was more than 35 times higher than that of workers in Niger (Hall & Jones, 1999)!

Sometimes the wages, salaries, and benefits paid to a nation's workforce rise faster than its productivity. Hence, when we speak of declining productivity, we mean that it is taking comparatively more human labor to accomplish the same amount of economic output as before – fewer goods and services for the same investment as in the past. The consequence, in part, is that the benefits an economy can deliver cost everyone more than in the past – a phenomenon referred to as cost-push inflation (Blair, 1975). Traditional economists (e.g., Malkiel, 1979) see declining productivity (or a failure to increase productivity as much as other countries increase theirs) as the most serious threat to the health of the economies of the Western world. It seems that most concerns about productivity and analyses related to it focus on the private and manufacturing sectors. But productivity is also an important issue in the service sector (cf. Schneider, Ehrhart, Mayer, Saltz, & Niles-Jolly, 2005), as well as in government (Crane & Jones, 1991), affecting the quality of life enjoyed by all of us.[2]

---

[2] See the *Editors' Forum* on the role of management scholarship in the public sector published recently by the *Academy of Management Journal* (2005).

DETERMINANTS OF PRODUCTIVITY

What determines the level of productivity in an industrial economy? A traditional answer to this question might begin by observing that there are many contributing factors, and that it is possible to categorize them into two major groups.

Large-Scale, National-Level Influences on Productivity

The first group consists of large-scale factors generally beyond the control of individual managers, executives, corporations, or governments. In fact, some of them, as we will see, may eventually be responsible for an ironic, cataclysmic redefinition of the very nature of human work. Hall and Jones (1999) have argued on the basis of comparative analyses of the productivity of 127 national economies that a cluster of factors they refer to as *social infrastructure* explains the vast variance among economies in productivity. Social infrastructure is defined as:

> [T]he institutions and government policies that determine the economic climate within which individuals accumulate skills, and firms accumulate capital and produce output. A social infrastructure favorable to high levels of output per worker provides an environment that supports productive capacities and encourages capital accumulations, skill acquisition, invention, and technology transfer. Such a social infrastructure gets the prices right so that . . . individuals capture the social returns to their actions as private returns.
>
> (Hall & Jones, p. 84)

Hall and Jones (1999) cite thievery, squatting, and Mafia protection as examples of social infrastructure forces that can divert resources away from productive output. They note that governments can be either a boon for productive output or, paradoxically, they can be a major source of difficulties, through laws and legal practices of expropriation, confiscatory taxation, and corruption. Legislation that restricts the natural workings of the marketplace also limits productivity, according to some economic critics who desire a return to a laissez-faire framework for conducting business. Guidelines and regulations concerning equal employment opportunity, health and safety, minimum wages, antitrust, and rates that may be charged for services (as was the case in the airline industry until a few years ago) are examples cited by these critics. An article in the November 11, 2006 edition of *The Economist* (p. 61), for example, discussed the resistance on the part of Britain to the massive encumbrances imposed by membership of the European Union. But, while regulations of this type do contribute to the cost of production, it is also important to consider the economic (and social) benefits they contribute in return. For example, if the aggregate cost of a regulation is greater than the net value it generates, that regulation might be judged dysfunctional from a strict social and economic perspective. (Notice the convergence between macro-level factors and the factors cited earlier by the Swiss State Secretariat for the high level of performance of that country's economy.)

One key determinant of economic productivity is the level of investment made in fixed capital, such as new plants, refineries, office buildings, and other operating sites – places that help to make more efficient the way the work gets done (Freund, 1981). The amazing levels of productivity in postwar Germany and Japan can be partially explained by the new industrial facilities constructed in those nations following 1945, although other factors have caused low productivity and inflation to infest those countries more recently (Bowen, 1979). Investments in technology and high levels of capital investment are other examples of large-scale determinants of high national productivity: Indeed, the superior national output per worker enjoyed by the United States can be attributed in large measure to the comparatively high levels of technological innovation and investment in that economy (see Hall & Jones, 1999; Taylor, 2007). Taylor (2007) claims that the steadily increasing gap in productivity and prosperity between the United States – as well as South Korea, Australia, and Japan – and Canada, for example, has been driven largely by the comparatively low level of investment by Canadian companies in technology and innovation per worker (see also Unsworth and Parker, 2003).

Finally, scarcity of many raw materials contributes heavily to the cost of production of goods and services. The continuing increases in energy costs over the past three decades are a major example with which all of us are too familiar.

In short, there are many large-scale economic and political factors that have traditionally been blamed for combining and interacting to restrict productivity, thereby fuelling price inflation and compromising the quality of life that is possible for us to achieve in Western society. These factors are beyond the control of the vast majority of managers and executives in industry. For example, not many chief executives can immediately cause a rollback in government regulations (although a few have tried). Likewise, not many first-line supervisors can initiate major changes in the basic physical design of work plants, so as to make their employees significantly more productive. The point is that executives and managers who wish to influence the productivity of the workforce must find alternatives to the means described earlier. The question becomes: What sources of productivity are there which fall within the grasp of individual employees and employers?

SMALL-SCALE, LOCAL INFLUENCES ON PRODUCTIVITY

If we turn our attention away from the issue of national levels of comparative productivity toward the issue of the productivity of individual workers, we discover that there are a number of productivity determinants that are much more amenable to control by individual managers in an economy. The central concern of this book will be to explore the nature of one of these more manipulable factors – the level of motivation of the workforce and of the individual worker. In so doing, we will examine and evaluate the effectiveness of a variety of managerial techniques aimed at boosting ability and motivation.

There are at least two major factors that determine the level of productivity in any given organization, industry, or economy which can be influenced (within limits) by executives, managers, and first-line supervisors: The level of *ability* of people who are assigned to work and the amount of *effort* these people expend doing that work (Campbell et al., 1988).

Employee Ability

Some critics (who are often advanced in age) claim that the postwar workforce is less skilful and less devoted to hard work than were the workforces of previous times. It is a simple fact of demographics that today's worker is, on average, younger and less experienced than the workers of previous generations. But today's average employee is generally better trained and/or educated as well, so it is difficult to make summary statements about the comparative net levels of skill of the employees of various eras. (The reader may wish to hash out this subject with his or her parents, children, or other family members who have views on the matter.) Indeed, in the face of an ongoing shortage of skilled labor across Canada in recent years, many employers are hiring erstwhile-retired people, who return to the workforce, bringing with them their wisdom and experience (Galt, 2006). The point is that individual supervisors can sometimes have considerable influence on the level of job-related ability of the people they assign to particular tasks on a daily basis. Training programs, job redesign, and merely making careful person–job matches are means that, within limits, enable supervisors in many work settings to gain leverage on the problem of productivity in their organizations.

Employee Motivation

The second factor over which effective supervisors can often have some control is the level of motivated effort expended by those below them in organizational hierarchies, not always, but often. Motivation it is a popular topic that relates directly to all of us, particularly to those of us whose job it is to accomplish organizational goals through the effort of other people. We widely believe in the importance of a widespread desire to work, and many critics are quick to blame slumps in such a desire for social and (especially) economic decline. The constant importance of work values and the "work ethic" was thoughtfully summarized in the following:

> So ingrained is the work ethic as an explanation for the success of the U.S. economy that managers reflexively attribute declines in productivity and increases in worker recalcitrance and discontent to the decline of the work ethic. For example, in analyzing unrest in the workplace in the early 1970s, Deans (1973) observed, "Corporation executives seem no less puzzled than any other Americans as to why young people entering the labor force – even in a time of scarcity-are less enchanted with the so-called Protestant ethic of hard work and upward striving than their parents and grandparents" (pp. 8–9). Thus, it is evident that the tenets of the Protestant work ethic . . . are still taken seriously by managers, scholars and policy makers. They are viewed as central to the development and functioning of capitalism.

> (Nord, Brief, Atieh, & Doherty, 1988, p. 8)

In both its general connotation and as it relates to work, motivation is a topic about which many people claim to have some degree of knowledge, even expertise. "Motivation" is a buzzword in virtually all work settings and educational institutions. Folklore on the topic dates back at least as far as the literature on any other managerial topic, and, as noted already, newspapers and magazines regularly feature stories and essays on it. Countless self-help books have been published to provide managers and executives with quick insights into what makes themselves and their subordinates work (or not work). Airport bookstores are replete with books offering quick fixes of this variety.

But there is also a vast scientific literature on work motivation, the content of which only sometimes relates to the wisdom imparted to managers through the popular materials they read. Nevertheless, work motivation is one of the most important topics in organizational science: No other issue in the discipline has more significance for our general economic well-being, and few, if any, other topics command more attention in the journals and textbooks of the field (Miner, 2003; Steers & Porter, 1991, pp. xii, 3). Moreover, in view of the intractability of many key determinants of productivity, we can expect work motivation to be at least as important an issue in organizational science and management in the future as it has been in the past, although the reasons may be considerably different from those offered in the past (cf. Pinder, 1984, 1998).[4]

In the remaining sections of this chapter, we will define and examine the meaning of work motivation and other key concepts related to it. It will be argued that individual managers are

---

[3] Hill (1999) has provided a fascinating history of work and people's attitudes toward working, going back to ancient times, on the internet at http:www.coe.uga.edu/workethic/historypdf.pdf

[4] Economists often argue that the large-scale factors such as those discussed here are much more important in their impact on productivity than are the human factors to be discussed throughout the rest of this book. For example, Freund (1981) claimed that capital investment is the most important determinant of productivity, and that human factors are far less influential. It is hard to separate the contributions made to productivity by these various factors, but it is important to note that, even when they are working side by side in the same factory, plant, or office, different employees produce widely differing amounts of work output. Years ago, Lawler (1973) noted that the ratio of output produced by the best worker to that produced by the poorest worker in many work settings can be three-to-one or greater. Clearly, micro-factors play an important role in the productivity of individual employees, organizations, and entire national economies.

generally less able to observe their employees' work motivation, per se, than they are to observe their levels of job performance. More specifically, we will begin the discussion by providing a definition of work motivation and delineating a number of features and implications of that definition. We will then focus on the meaning of job performance, and show why the difference between the two concepts is so important. As we will see, other factors in addition to motivation determine an employee's level of job performance. One of these other factors is ability. Accordingly, we will discuss the nature and significance of work-related ability in a later section of the chapter. So then, what is work motivation?

WHAT IS WORK MOTIVATION?

It is only a slight exaggeration to say that there have been almost as many definitions of motivation offered over the years as there have been thinkers who have considered the nature of human behavior (Kleinginna & Kleinginna, 1981, reported and categorized 140 definitions!). One classic textbook (Atkinson, 1964) deliberately sidestepped the definitional problem until almost 300 pages of material on the topic were presented. Another major textbook (Cofer & Appley, 1964) presented the definitions of a number of scholars without offering a simple definition of its own. Other books (e.g., Erez, Kleinbeck, & Thierry, 2001; Korman, 1974; Locke & Latham, 1990a) have discussed the issues that motivation is seen as dealing with, but do not tell what the concept is, per se.

There are many reasons for the apparent difficulty in defining motivation, although a full treatment of these reasons is beyond our purpose. Suffice it to say that there are, paradoxically, few singular definitions of motivation because there are so many aspects of it. There are also many philosophical orientations toward the nature of human beings and about what can be known about people. Some theorists deny the usefulness of the concept altogether, and concentrate primarily on the consequences of behavior as its causes. Some writers view motivation from a strictly physiological perspective, while others view human beings as primarily hedonistic, and explain most of human behavior as goal oriented, seeking only to gain pleasure and avoid pain. Others stress the rationality of people, and consider human behavior to be the result of conscious choice processes. Some thinkers stress unconscious or subconscious factors. The multiplicity of the views on the fundamental nature of human motivation and behavior is reflected in the diversity of chapters found in modern anthologies such as those of Levine (1975) or Petrie (1991).

The interested reader is referred to those sources as well as to the works of Atkinson (1964) and Cofer and Appley (1964) for thorough treatments of the historical and philosophical perspectives which have been offered over the years. There has been quite a variety.

Definition of Work Motivation

Where does this leave the student or manager who wants to learn about motivation and job performance in the workplace? Since the topic of this book is *work* motivation, attitudes, and behavior (as opposed to general human motivation, attitudes, and behavior), a traditional definition will be offered and used throughout. The definition draws heavily upon those of a number of previous writers, and attempts to provide some balance in the philosophical assumptions that underlie those definitions. The work of Jones (1955), Vroom (1964), Locke, Shaw, Saari, and Latham (1981), and Steers and Porter (1979) are of particular importance in giving rise to the following definition of work motivation:

Work motivation is a set of energetic forces that originate both within as well as beyond an individual's being, to initiate work-related behavior, and to determine its form, direction, intensity, and duration.[5]

Implications of the Definition

A number of features of our definition deserve highlighting. First, it attempts to be both specific enough to relate primarily to work-related behaviors, but general and eclectic enough to avoid many of the basic issues that have divided previous writers who have concerned themselves with the origins of human behavior, particularly work behavior. For example, it is intended to apply to behaviors such as joining or not joining an organization for employment purposes; being late or on time for work on a given day; obeying or rejecting a supervisor's orders to work harder; accepting or rejecting a directive to relocate to another city; conceiving of better and smarter ways of performing one's job; and even retiring or resigning from an organization. Implicit in the foregoing is that our definition sees work motivation as a middle-range concept (cf. Merton, 1968; Pinder & Moore, 1980) that purports to deal only with events and phenomena of work, careers, and the management of people at work. It does not presume to be a general definition of human motivation that transcends all contexts, such as that of Ford (1992).

Second, the concept of *force* is central to the definition. This makes it consistent with Vroom's (1964) definition of motivation, without necessarily adopting the cognitive orientation or the elements of decision making that are so important to his theory (see Chapters 9 and 12 of this book). The notion of force also makes our definition consistent with the hydraulic metaphors found in Freud's work in psychoanalysis. The definition allows for motivation levels to be either weak or strong, varying both between individuals at any particular time, as well as within a given individual at different times, and under different circumstances.

Our definition states that there is a set of energetic forces, implying the *multiplicity* of needs, drives, instincts, and external factors that have been considered over the years regarding human behavior, without necessarily accepting the primary importance of any of these sources. The idea of force suggests that motivation will manifest itself through effort. In fact, the concepts of effort and motivation are frequently treated as identical. In other places, effort is used as an operationalization of motivation. In this book, effort will be treated as a consequence and primary indicator of motivation, but not identical with it.

The definition implies the notion of movement, in recognition of the Latin root of the word motivation (*movere*, to move). Recognition of both internal and external origins acknowledges the merits of the philosophical positions of both those who believe in free will and those who believe in determinism (cf. Joad, 1957; Chapters 7 and 14 of this book). This feature of the definition permits recognition of the importance of characteristics of the work environment that can arouse behavior (such as the nature of the work being performed or the style of leadership being applied), without ruling out certain work behaviors originating primarily from within the employee (such as staying home when ill). More will be said on this critical issue shortly.

Our definition does not stress hedonism as a primary force in work motivation, but neither does it rule it out. It does not preclude consideration of a number of other human traits either, such as fear, lust, greed, or jealousy in the context of work behavior.

Blau (1993), following on some of his own earlier work with Katerberg (Katerberg & Blau, 1983), examined some of the various components of the definition of work motivation to determine whether and how they each contribute to job performance. In a study of 115 bank tellers, he

---

[5] This definition was offered in an earlier version of this book (Pinder, 1984; see also Pinder, 1998) and is not changed here. Although it was developed with the thinking of a number of earlier theorists in mind at the time, as described here, the definition has also been adopted by or been consistent with definitions used by other writers since 1984 (e.g., Ford, 1992; Landy & Becker, 1987; Latham & Pinder, 2005).

operationalized "effort" by observing them on video cameras and then generating ratings of the degree to which they were actually working at tasks related to their jobs, as opposed to being engaged in non-work activities. To assess direction of effort, Blau asked the tellers to indicate the frequency with which they engaged in 20 different legitimate behaviors related to the tellers' jobs. These 20 items were reduced to two factors, financial behaviors and customer behaviors. Next, Blau sought relationships between both his effort and direction indicators with two different criteria of job performance, controlling for a variety of other variables that might otherwise have confounded or confused the results. The two criteria of performance were: (1) raw productivity, which was the percentage of time on the job the teller actually engaged in one or more of the legitimate activities; and (2) the number of referrals of customers the tellers made for opening new accounts. Blau (1993) found that both effort and direction contributed to performance on the tellers' jobs, although they were more predictive of productivity than of sales referrals. Of particular interest was the finding that, aside from individual contributions of effort and direction, an interaction term that combined the two motivational components was also effective for explaining variance in the productivity dependent variable.

Studies such as Blau's (1993) make a tremendous contribution to our understanding of the nature of work motivation, of the relationships among the components of this tricky construct, and of the relationships between work motivation and other important variables such as job perform- ance. It is one thing for theorists to posit and postulate the existence of constructs such as work motivation and how it relates to people's lives. It is another matter for researchers such as Blau to go to the field, develop valid measures, and then test for the expected relationships among the con- structs of interest. More work of the quality shown by Blau will be needed for us to understand fully the empirical qualities of the work motivation construct.

Another element of our definition of work motivation has also received focused attention in recent years – the *intensity* dimension. Brehm and Self (1989) made a distinction between *potential motivation* and *motivational arousal*. For them, needs, values, and the person's perceptions about whether effort will result in need satisfaction determine, in some multiplicative way, the amount of motivational effort that is available. This, however, is not a sufficient set of conditions to determine actual arousal of the person. In addition, the person must be engaged in some degree of behavior thought to be instrumental for the sake of meeting the needs in existence. The amount of energy is assumed to be no greater than what is needed to produce the required instrumental behavior. So, when little effort is needed, motivational arousal will be low, no matter how great the need is or how valuable the potential outcome (p. 111). Intensity is then defined as the momentary magnitude of motivational arousal (p. 110). In other words:

> [P]otential motivation is created by needs and/or potential outcomes and the expectation that per- formance of a behavior will affect those needs and outcomes. Motivational arousal occurs, however, only to the extent that the required behavior is difficult, within one's capacity, and is justified by the magnitude of potential motivation. When the difficulty of the instrumental behavior surpasses one's capacities or outweighs the value of the potential gain . . . there will be little or no mobilization of energy. The greater the potential motivation, the greater is the amount of energy that a person will be willing to mobilize.
>
> (Brehm & Self, 1989, p. 111)

And, to repeat, intensity is defined as the momentary magnitude of actual motivational arousal, regardless of the available potential.

The *direction* toward which motivated force is focused also appears in the definition. Inclusion of this feature recognizes that it is not sufficient merely to consider the intensity and duration of work motivation. Rather, one must allow for the specific goals toward which motivated energy is directed to fully understand it (Katerberg & Blau, 1983). The "vision" component of the mantra of Frank O'Dea that opened this chapter speaks to the importance of vision, focus, goals and a sense of mission and purpose as key elements of work motivation.

The notion of *duration*, found in the definition, implies that goal attainment may be a possible (but not a necessary) outcome of behavior at the job, keeping the definition not inconsistent with goal-oriented theories of early writers, such as Murray (1938) and Dunnette and Kirchner (1965), and more recent goal theorists such as Locke and Latham (1990b). Persistence is a major element of work motivation.

Our definition accommodates three of the five "behavior patterns" identified by Maehr and Braskamp (1986) and Maehr (1987): Choice (as it relates to absenteeism behavior); persistence (length of service); and continuing motivation (voluntarily upgrading one's work skills).[6] Likewise, the definition takes into account work behaviors described by various authors – "willingness to cooperate," "innovative and spontaneous behavior," "prosocial behavior," and, most recently, "personal initiative" (Frese, Kring, Soose, & Zempel, 1996) – all of which imply working in a way that goes above and beyond the call of duty (see Dalal, 2005; LePine, Erez, & Johnson, 2002).

Another feature of the definition is that it does not imply that motivation is the sole source of human behavior, or that work motivation is the sole source of work behavior, per se. Rather, it readily accommodates the fact that forces other than motivation also contribute to human action, whether on the job or off. This matter is critical in view of a recent, highly critical attack by Ford (1992) on traditional theories of motivation. Among other claims, Ford (p. 10) has argued that, in order to be of value, the concept of motivation must be limited to account only for the "*psychological* processes in the direction, energization and regulation of behavior pattern*.*" While Ford sees motivation as strictly psychological and separate from other forces such as biology, environmental and "non-motivational psychological and behavioral influences," our definition admits the role of many biological factors in energizing and controlling behavior. It also permits the possibility that features of the environment can trigger motivational (even primarily psychological) forces. Hence, we differ somewhat with Ford on these counts. Nevertheless, we do not imply by our definition that all behavior is motivated. Much human activity is non-motivated, compulsive, and habitual. The definition also accommodates the assumption that not all behavior results from conscious phenomenological states. Instead, as Brody put it (1980) "behavior may be influenced by motive states which are not in awareness, and that certain motive states will not exert a particular influence on behavior unless they are out of awareness" (p. 156).

But the most important feature of the definition is that it views motivation as an invisible, internal concept, or what may be called a hypothetical construct (MacCorquodale & Meehl, 1948) – a concept representing an assumed physical process that is, as yet, unobservable directly. We cannot actually see motivation, per se, or measure it directly. Instead, we assume it exists and rely on the theories we have to guide us in measuring what they suggest are its manifestations. Hypothetical constructs of this sort abound in psychology (e.g., personality, perceptions, beliefs, attitudes, and so on), as well as in virtually all other sciences at one time or another during their development. For example, adrenaline was originally an inferred variable. These days it is administered regularly in medical and clinical settings. Nevertheless, while there are countless examples of hypothetical constructs in the sciences, the reliance on invisible internal processes such as motivation constitutes an important point of controversy. In Chapter 14, for example, we will discuss a school of thought that rejects the use of such hypothetical constructs in favor of focusing only upon observable behavior.

In short, the definition offered here is intended to apply to work behaviors of all sorts, while at the same time avoiding many of the ontological and epistemological issues that have led to most of the debates and confusion we have already mentioned. Motivation is an important factor in job performance and human productivity. It is the central concept of interest in this book, and when the term is used in subsequent chapters, it will denote the definition provided earlier.

---

[6] The definition does not, however, fit with two of their categories, "activity level" and "performance," because they are related to performance, not motivation, per se. This is a major distinction that will be discussed at length later in this chapter.

HAS WORK MOTIVATION BEEN DECLINING?

Earlier, we briefly observed that there are sometimes disagreements – even heated quarrels – between members of different generations over the issue of work motivation. The question becomes: Are "today's employees" any more or less motivated than those of past times?

Whether for purposes of work motivation, per se, or because of strong gains in our desire for the material and non-material things money from work can buy, Americans believe they are working longer hours and enjoying less leisure time than they did a few decades ago. Recent evidence, however, indicates this is not the case. A recent study by Aguiar and Hurst (2006) showed that, depending on the type of measurement used, Americans are devoting, on average, between 4 and 8 hours a week more on leisure than they did 40 years ago! Americans generally work longer hours than employees in many first-world countries, but a primary reason for that is that the work week has been reduced in many of those other countries (e.g., Germany).

Now we might ask: Do people, in fact, place greater or less *value* on work and working today than they did "in the old days?" A study reported by Statistics Canada in 2006 concluded that "aging Canadians" (those aged 55 and older) were working longer in life than were their counterparts in a similar study conducted 15 years earlier (*Times Colonist*, July 27, 2006, p. A6).

Hill (1999), Brief et al. (1988), Tausky (1995), and Erikson and Vallas (1990), among others, have sketched how work values have evolved from the days of the ancient Greek philosophers (when work was viewed as a waste of time), the ancient Hebrew and Roman philosophers and theologians (who believed that, in addition to being a waste, work comprised a sort of punishment for original sin), right through to current times, when there are many secular and non-secular views of work and work values. When measured by such a broad brush, it is clear that work, the meaning of work, and what is to be of value in work have changed dramatically. The study of work values and the meaning of work, therefore, must always be placed in the socio-historic times of the analysis.

For example, a study conducted nearly a quarter of a century ago compared data from two matched samples – one gathered in 1982, the other in 1989 – examining the degree of change that had occurred in over 41 different values related to work (England, 1991). Four general factors underlay the 41 specific items. They were: (1) the importance and significance of work and working in one's life; (2) the normative beliefs and expectations that people held about their obligations and entitlements at work; (3) the relative importance of achieving various work goals [alternatively called work values, work needs, and incentive preferences]; and (4) the bases used by people to decide whether an activity is considered work or non-work. The findings of the study were interesting. In such a short period of time as 7 years, it was clear that there had been significant shifting of American values related to work. While there was no single factor among the 41 studied which had altered dramatically, collectively the findings were that Americans had changed their views of work and working. Statistically significant shifts were observed on 21 of the 41 specific items studied. Economic goals had become more important while "comfort" goals seemed to be less important. This reflects what England reported as an instrumental reaction to the economic realities during the time between the two studies. Yet the importance of working as a life role declined over the same period. For many people in the second study, work seemed to be less intrinsically valued and more a means to instrumental ends. Finally (and contrary to the general trend of change), people's beliefs about their entitlements and obligations showed virtually no change over the period studied.

England's study was not the final word on the matter nor should it be accepted as the sole grounds for the payment of wagers between fathers and daughters (or mothers and sons, for that matter). The study does remind us, however, that values *do* change with time and that values, beliefs, and attitudes regarding work are subject to large-scale movement over relatively short periods of time. Considerably more will be presented in this book (see Chapters 3, 9, and 10) on the topics of job attitudes and work values.

Current Intergenerational Differences in Work Ethic and Work Values

Earlier, we observed that people of any generation frequently make claims about the work ethic and work values of the generation(s) that follow them. Usually, of course, the older people of any age claim that they, as a generation, worked harder and had more difficult working lives than their successors. In many cases, these claims may be true! The popular novel by Coupland (1991) on the values and work-related anxieties of his so-called "Generation X" implies that people born in North America between 1963 and 1981 see things related to work and careers differently from the perspectives of older North Americans. The sheer success of the novel implies that it struck a chord among both Generation Xers and the Baby Boomers they abhor. Adherents to the Generation X phenomenon claim that the work values of previous generations are of little value to them. This is in part because the benefits of work and traditional careers are not, and will continue not to be, available to them because Baby Boomers are clogging organizational hierarchies, driving up the prices of consumer goods and services, mortgaging the Xers' futures by current deficit spending, and other transgressions. In keeping with the tradition, the Boomers make claims about Xers, usually based on stereotypes that have all the validity of most stereotypes (i.e., there is probably some basis in reality for them, but they are subject to countless exceptions to the rule).

The upshot, for older managers and people in power, is that Xers are simply too hard to manage. In the current edition of the drama, Boomers frequently claim that Xers are viewed as lazy, selfish, disloyal, and simply out for themselves (Tulgan, 1995). They have dreadfully short attention spans and high needs for stimulation and fast action. They whine about their jobs, their bosses, and their working conditions and make unreasonable demands of the organizations in which they work. They are not prepared to "pay their dues" as older workers had to do before they could enjoy the fruits of their contributions to their employers and to society as a whole. Xers are alleged to be too much in a hurry, demanding fast payoffs, challenging work, constant feedback about their performance, and constant opportunities for personal and professional development through their jobs (Tulgan, 1995). They abhor authority and are cynical about most things. Mostly, however, it is their alleged lack of loyalty that seems to be the most irritating characteristic of Generation Xers in the eyes of their elders – they simply take jobs and employment for granted and when their employers don't provide enough of what they want, they pull up stakes and move on to other work. They are far less concerned with social justice than their parents were; they are out for themselves. According to Tulgan (1995), they don't rely on others; they look out for themselves.

In an interview study of 85 young American professionals – aged between 21 and 31 years – working in banking, law firms, and the like, Tulgan (1995) found a number of coherent allegations and perceptions among his sample. Indeed, four consistent themes emerged from the interviews. Research participants placed very heavy emphasis on: (1) belonging (to a work unit in which they can make meaningful contributions); (2) learning personal and professional development through access to sufficient information for self-development and involvement in decision making; (3) entrepreneurship (i.e., to work in a context where they define their own work problems, develop solutions at their own pace, and produce their own results); and (4) security (will they be able to provide for their long-term security, whether by remaining in one or a few organizations or by moving when it suits them as they define their careers to provide for their own long-term best interest). Tulgan develops a summary of the historical and sociological differences between the experiences Xers had as children in America and those of their forebears. Details of that summary are beyond our scope here.

More current insight into the inter-generational matter was recently reported by Universum (2006), a Swedish polling firm. Consistent with the thrust of much of the common press, Canadian undergraduate students stated a preference for "balance" between their work lives and their personal lives. In the end, however, a careful reading of Tulgan's findings reveals that the working conditions valued by his respondents are really not that much different from what most people want at their work (it may be that they are simply more vocal about demanding and/or getting these things). Indeed, the ingredients of the job itself are almost completely in line with prescriptions that emerge from job design research of the 1960s (see our discussion in Chapter 2 of the motivator-hygiene theory and the job characteristics model of job design in Chapter 7). As mentioned, they demand high levels of feedback on how they are doing. They demand jobs that are meaningful. They require autonomy and self-determination in their work. They demand respect and desire to be accepted by work teams in which their contributions are acknowledged. They don't like it when bad planning by their superiors or associates requires them to waste their own time in idleness. They expect diversity in action, not just in policy. They detest being micro-managed by bosses and technical specialists. They also hate being driven and threatened by fear-mongering superiors.

The point is that most people in our society, regardless of age or generational identity, like and dislike the same things as listed here. The tenets for appropriately designing and managing an organization to suit Xers are, for the most part, little different from the tenets of enlightened management of motivation and reward principles, most of which are explained in detail throughout this book. A heading in the book reporting the study reads (Tulgan, p. 93) "The best way to demotivate Xers is to make us feel that we are not getting the rewards we deserve." Amen for all of us!

The key difference, in the opinion of this author, is that younger people have, in fact, learned a great deal by observing the work experiences of their elders and developed career and work values that do not as commonly include organizational commitment (see Chapter 10) and blind devotion to one or a few employers for the duration of their careers (cf. Loughlin & Barling, 2001). As a group, they claim to be smarter than that. More recently, some social observers claim that the so-called *Generation Nexters* (sometimes called "Generation Y" or "Echo Boomers," who were born later than 1980) comprise yet again a different breed who possess different views and values pertaining to work and careers.

Work Motivation and Job Performance are NOT the Same Thing!

One of the most important distinctions that needs to be made early in this book is the difference between job performance and motivation. The difference is much more than a matter of semantics. It is one that has powerful implications for both the understanding and the application of the theories and ideas which will constitute the rest of this book. It is a distinction noted by Vroom (1964) in his early book on work motivation, and one that has been acknowledged frequently since (cf. Cummings & Schwab, 1973; Lawler, 1973; Porter & Lawler, 1968; Terborg, 1977). What is the difference between the two concepts?

Managers are primarily concerned with the accomplishment of work through other people. They are responsible for seeing to it that others accomplish the work assigned to them. Therefore, a manager is effective when her staff of subordinates accomplishes their respective work goals. But the successful accomplishment of one's work goals is normally the result of an interaction among a number of factors, only some of which can be controlled by the employee himself (such as the amount of effort he invests in the task). Another critical factor, for example, is the level of ability the employee possesses to do the particular job assigned to her. (We will return to the issue of ability shortly.) Still other factors are external to the employee, such as the amount of support she receives from her supervisor and from her own staff (if she has one).

A massive study of American workers reported by Hall (1994) detailed how the vast majority of people wish to work and perform well at their jobs, but are prevented from doing so by restrictive practices of their supervisors and limited policies of their companies.[7] Characteristics of the physical work environment, such as the lighting and noise levels, temperature, and air quality (Baron, 1994), and the availability of materials needed to perform the job, will limit the degree to which she can convert all of her well-intended effort into what her organization would call effective job performance. In short, *we can define job performance as the accomplishment of work-related goals, regardless of the means of their accomplishment.*[8]

The importance of the distinction between motivation and performance

When we think of poor employee performance, we implicitly or explicitly assume that some sort of goals exist, having been set either by the individual in question or by some group or other person (Mitchell & O'Reilly, 1983). We also implicitly assume that it is possible to measure performance to see whether the goals have been reached. Therefore, what is judged to be poor performance will depend heavily upon who sets the goals, whether there is more than one goal in place at a given time or whether there are multiple goals and, if there is more than one goal, whether they are mutually exclusive. (In Chapter 13, we will discuss the theory of goal setting more thoroughly.)

Also of importance in considering alleged "poor performance" is the issue of how and when the performance is measured, and by whom. Finally, there is the issue of whether the performance is measured in some absolute sense or whether it is measured vis-à-vis performance levels attained by other people, either in the present or in times past. Hence, *poor performance* can be an arbitrary thing – very much a matter for the eye of the beholder (Mitchell & O'Reilly, 1983).

A common mistake made by managers who notice poor job performance by their subordinates is automatically to attempt to remedy the problem as if it were the result of low motivation. Thus, for example, a sales manager may notice a slump in the average monthly sales figures (low job performance) for a key sales person and react by increasing the rate of commission that will be paid to that sales rep for future sales. The manager's reaction is an explicit attempt to increase the sales rep's motivation level – as might be reflected in the degree of effort the rep will spend selling the firm's products. The manager assumes that the rep is not trying hard enough for some reason – that the rep has lost interest or has simply turned lazy (cf. Mitchell, Green, & Wood, 1981).

But in many cases the problem might better be attributed to any (or all) of a number of the types of external factor that were mentioned earlier (a superb review was provided by Baron, 1994). For instance, it may be that the sales rep is now facing stiffer competition in his sales region from representatives of other companies with superior products to sell. It may be that the rep has lost a few traditionally held accounts and that he is struggling to recapture them. Or, it may be that he is not fully aware of new company policies that are reflected in the firm's marketing strategies. Social psychologists refer to the natural tendency humans have to attribute cause and effect to internal factors (such as ability or motivation) rather than to external, contextual factors, as the *fundamental attribution error* (see Ross, 1977).

In short, apparent performance problems must be considered from the perspective of the person who alleges that the work is not up to standard. We must take into consideration the possibility of outside, situational factors – factors which are, in part at least, beyond the employee's control. Even if the person is the primary source of the difficulty, attributing the blame to motivation work

---

[7] It is interesting to note that a similar observation was published on the basis of large-scale studies decades ago by Likert (1961, pp. 97–103) and others, and that the solutions provided at that time were virtually the same as those offered by Hall (1994).

[8] Staw and Boettger (1990) pointed out that traditional definitions of performance are limited in scope because often it is in the best interests of an employer, an employee, or both, for the individual to deviate from the directives of a predefined task role and to alter the nature of the job. They refer to this form of behavior as *task revision* and argue that there are many instances in which rigid adherence to formal tasks and goals is not in the best interest of anyone involved, such as when, for example, instructions become inappropriate or outdated, circumstances change or when new alternatives present themselves. We suspect that such elasticity and innovativeness will become more relevant and important in work settings of the future.

attitudes problems can be a mistake. To apply strategies that are implicitly (or explicitly) designed to increase motivation levels when motivation is not the problem can result in a self-fulfilling prophesy – the employee responds to the new threats or incentives, but still cannot perform up to standard (for the same reasons as before), becomes frustrated, and withdraws. He may ultimately quit trying altogether. (We will take a more complete look at the problem of frustration in Chapter 8 of this book.)

Diagnostic errors of the sort made by our fictitious sales manager are common and easy to make. Parents often make a similar mistake when they notice a decline in the performance of their children in high school or college. Many students find they can achieve acceptable standards in high school with a certain level of effort, their natural level of mental ability, and a minimum amount of charm. However, once in college, these same students often find that greater ability is required (which sometimes they don't have) and/or higher levels of effort are necessary. Charm is usually helpful as well. Parents who attempt to apply motivational strategies to children who simply do not have the native ability, or a sufficient level of acquired skills, are not usually able to help their children perform more effectively. In fact, the sort of pressure that parents can apply in these cases can result in resentment, fear, and withdrawal by the now frustrated student. The author has known of cases of student suicide that have resulted from this sort of pressure. Success in college, like success on most jobs, requires a blend of ingredients, only one of which is motivation. Ability is another. And there is usually a host of other factors which function to either magnify or attenuate the effects of motivation and ability on successful performance (cf. Baron, 1994).

In short, the point here is this: It can be a serious mistake to automatically assume that poor performance is the result of low motivation. Other factors in addition to motivation interact with it to determine job performance. One of these is the level of the individual's ability for the task in question. Therefore, let us take a look at what is meant by the term "ability."

Ability in the Workplace

As the preceding examples have suggested, employee ability is an important factor in effective job performance. Some psychologists, in fact, have argued for years that ability is more important to job performance than is motivation (e.g., Dunnette, 1972). A person might be highly motivated to lift a heavy weight from the floor onto a table (after being offered $100 for doing so), but may not have the physical strength (a type of ability) to do it. The result: High motivation, no ability, no performance.

Defining ability

But what is ability? We run into almost as much difficulty finding a simple definition for ability as we did earlier when we sought to define motivation. The reason for the difficulty this time seems to be that ability is a word which includes and represents a number of other concepts, such as skill and aptitude, for instance. In its simplest form, we might define ability as the capacity of an individual to accomplish tasks, controlling for her level of motivation to attempt those tasks. But this merely begs the question by substituting capacity for ability. One author defines ability in terms of the perform-ance people can achieve on tests designed to assess ability (Cronbach, 1970). In other words, ability is what ability tests measure. The circularity is not very helpful.

One way to approach the problem is to define ability by looking at definitions of those things that collectively constitute it. One of these is aptitude, which is defined by the *Oxford English Dictionary* (1961, vol. 1) as: "Natural capacity, endowment, or ability; talent for any pursuit." We can dodge the circularity in this definition, by focusing on two of its key terms – *natural* and *talent*. This suggests that aptitude consists of that part of ability that is innate in people, or which seems to develop naturally in them, without explicit training. An example would be spatial intelligence.

Another element of aptitude is skill (Dunnette, 1972). Again, the *Oxford English Dictionary* (1961, vol. 9): "Capability of accomplishing something with precision and certainty; practical knowledge in combination with ability; cleverness, expertness." (The reader should be developing a sense of appreciation for the difficulty in defining these terms independently of one another!) The essence of skill is the capacity or capability resulting from raw, natural aptitude (as we defined it earlier), as well as from the capability that people gain through both explicit training and development of their aptitudes. Development of this sort can be deliberate and active, and it can also occur passively as the individual grows and learns (see Chapter 14).

In sum, we are left with a definition that is similar to, but not identical with, that reached by Lawler (1973): *Ability is an aggregation of natural aptitude plus the capacity to behave which results from the application of training and experience to one's aptitude.* That is:

Ability = Aptitude + Aptitude (Training and Experience)

Defined as such, ability subsumes common concepts such as wisdom, sagacity, and competence – words we often hear attributed to people in work settings.

The point is that natural talent and the skill that one develops over time are major determinants of effective job performance. Highly motivated people working at jobs for which they lack the necessary ability are not generally capable of performing the job.

Types of ability

There are many forms of human ability. Guilford (1967) claimed that *there may be as many as 120 distinct varieties of basic mental ability alone*! When combined in various proportions with the many sensory and psychomotor abilities humans possess (cf. Guion, 1965) we are left with virtually an infinite number of possible combinations, or sets of abilities any employee might bring to the workplace (see McCall, Lombardo, & Morrison, 1988, for a specific treatment of managerial skills and abilities).

This seems like an obvious point, in principle, but it requires explication because of the tendency of so many of us to make remarks such as "Jones has no skill," or "Smith is incompetent." It is true that some people are more richly endowed with skill sets than others. But in organizational settings we must ask: "Competent for what?" (cf. Warr & Conner, 1992). Highly competent people who are assigned to jobs for which their ability sets are not appropriate are generally no more effective in organizations than are people with less impressive ability sets who are assigned to jobs for which they have some of the basic requisite abilities (Dawis & Lofquist, 1984). Hence, we appreciate the importance of careful personnel selection, placement, and job design.

It is interesting to note that people are not always aware of the limitations to their own abilities. That is, people can frequently overestimate their own social and intellectual abilities (which are a bit less directly observed than other abilities, such as physical strength). A fascinating set of studies by Kruger and Dunning (1999) found that Cornell University undergraduates frequently overestimated their ability on tasks requiring humor, logical reasoning, and English grammar in relation to objectively set standards. The researchers also found, as predicted, that the study participants generally lacked the "metacognitive skills" to understand that they lacked abilities in the areas being studied. In other words, people frequently don't know what they don't know.

The world's economies are increasingly dependent on what has come to be known as "knowledge work," – a term that implies work that requires people to "use their heads more than their hands to produce value" (cf. Horibe, 1999, p. xi). Davenport (2006) estimated that between a quarter and a half of the workers in the Western world qualify for this moniker, particularly in the service sector. The management of knowledge workers requires a different set of skills and techniques from the traditional methods used to manage work that hitherto has relied more on brawn than on brains (Davenport, 2006), but that discussion is beyond our present purposes (although, in Chapter 13, we discuss the relatively new literature on *learning goals*, as opposed to performance goals in the goal-setting literature).

The concept of job competence

In recognition of the increasing importance of mental abilities for job performance in many (most?) modern job settings, Warr and Conner (1992) offered a broad definition of what hitherto might have been considered ability, but what they refer to as *job competence*, which they defined as follows:

> A job competence is a set of behaviors, knowledge, thought processes, and/or attitudes, which are likely to be reflected in job performance that reaches a defined elementary, basic or high-performance standard. Statements about job competence may refer to one or a number of jobs, at one or several job-levels. Measurement of specific types of job competence may be undertaken either in job settings or through observation of behavior in other controlled situations.
>
> (Warr & Conner, 1992, p. 99)

Warr and Conner focused attention on the fact that competence may be broad or narrow, relating to merely one task or to a variety of tasks in a large number of job settings. They also stressed the critical importance of mental skills, including intelligence, cognitive style, and cognitive complexity for the effective performance of work in today's work settings.

Motivation, Ability and Job Performance

Empirical studies which have explicitly examined the role of ability in task performance have generally tended to affirm and reaffirm its importance, although the exact ways by which it combines with motivation are still not exactly clear. Some early studies suggested the relationship is interactive, such that high levels of one factor can compensate for low levels of the other (Fleishman, 1958; French 1957). This view, for example, would predict that a person with twice as much ability but only half as much motivation as another individual would be approximately of equal effectiveness on the job. Moreover, if either factor were essentially absent (i.e., the person has no ability for the job and/ or has no motivation to engage in it), performance would not be possible. Studies by Locke (1965) and Terborg (1977) supported the importance of ability as a determinant of performance, but challenge its interactive relationship with motivation. That is, they would conclude that it is not necessary for both factors to be at least somewhat operative for performance to result. Borman, White, Pulakos, and Oppler (1991) and O'Reilly and Chatman (1994) confirmed the role of ability and its interactive effect with motivation in yielding employee performance. On one level, the necessity for both ability and motivation seems obvious. There is now sufficient evidence and impressive theory to put an end to the debate.

The history of industrial and organizational psychology has witnessed the coming and going of the view that mental ability is the most important form of ability for the performance of most jobs. It makes sense that as less work is done by simple physical strength and more is performed by humans equipped with technology in various forms, mental capacity is critical (cf. Herrnstein & Murray, 1994; Warr & Conner, 1992). The argument then concerns which of the types of mental ability is most critical. Psychologists have long been interested in the concepts of *general intelligence*, or what they call *g* for short, and specific abilities (which they refer to as *s*, of course), and in the relative importance of general and specific mental capacities. In brief, the question is one of whether a general, overarching level of more mental ability is most important for effective human functioning, or whether a larger number of more focused skills, each of which relates to particular types of problems and issues, is more effective for explaining human mental competence. There are impressive bodies of evidence and argument for both sides on the matter. The interested reader is referred to summaries of the debate by Herrnstein and Murray (1994) and Ree, Earles, and Teachout (1994). Our purpose here is not to adopt a position on the debate, but merely to draw attention to it. For our purposes, it is clear that mental ability, regardless of how broadly it is considered, is of major importance in human functioning and in job performance. Hence any analysis of work performance must consider mental ability as well as work motivation, especially when our purpose is to award credit for good work or to make attributions of blame for poor performance.

Before leaving our discussion of employee ability and its role in job performance, it is worth noting one type of ability that is an especially important factor in job performance in many organizations. We might refer to this sort of ability as *savoir faire*, or simply "savvy." For college students, savvy is knowing which classes they can afford to skip in order to go skiing. It is having a feel for which professor's assignments can be turned in late and which ones stand tough by their deadlines. For the junior employees in an organization, savoir faire involves a host of things, such as knowing the clique structure of the workgroup and knowing the people with whom they should or should not exchange rumors. It is knowing how to read their supervisor's facial expression and the mood of the boss's secretary. It is being acquainted with the ropes. A delightful and highly instructive treatment of these matters – one that can be very useful to the new college graduate – is Ritti's (1994) book.[9]

In brief, both ability and motivation are required by employees in order to perform most jobs, although the exact form of the relationship between motivation, ability, and performance is not clear. In addition, myriad external factors can either enhance or inhibit the impact of motivation and ability – a key point that will receive plenty of attention throughout this book. Regardless of the precise nature of this relationship, however, the important point is that not all performance problems in the workplace are a consequence of low levels of motivation to work, so the supervisor or manager in charge must be careful in diagnosing the causes of whatever performance problems are observed. As we will see in Chapter 7 of this book, there are a host of other factors in most work settings that can either magnify or attenuate the effects of both motivation and job-related ability on task performance. Tactics to increase motivation, when it is not the problem, may make matters worse, both for the individual employee and for the organization.

Ability: Dispositions and Contexts

We have mentioned on more than one occasion already that a major issue in our consideration of work motivation is whether the force that comprises it originates solely from inside the individual in question, or whether outside, environmental factors are at least partially responsible as well. In the previous section of this chapter we saw how the debate over the predictive power of general intelligence (g), in relation to the need for specific factors, rages on. It appears that general intelligence has considerable capacity to explain job performance in jobs requiring mental skill, at least, *regardless* of the job or organizational settings involved (Anastasi, 1986; Schmidt & Hunter, 1977, 1984, 1993).

On the other hand, this author (Pinder, 1984, 1998) and many others (as we will see in the following chapter), have argued the importance of "situational factors" in our understanding of work motivation (and of organizational behavior more generally). Some authors claim that the dispositional/situational issue may be as old as the traditional "nature vs. nurture" debate as it relates to the development of human personality, aptitude, and mental health (Mitchell & James, 1989). The parallel between the two sets of issues is both interesting and suggestive. In her summary and review of the matter of the relative importance of dispositional and situational factors, Anastasi (1986) concluded that situational factors are more important in determining *personality differences* than they are in determining differences in people's *abilities*.

---

[9] In a later chapter, we will examine the concept referred to as emotional intelligence as well as the debate on the issue of whether this currently popular construct has anything to offer in addition to a blend of general intelligence (g) and a number of personality factors.

For example, a person may be quite sociable and outgoing at the office, but rather shy and reserved at social gatherings. Or a student who cheats on examinations may be scrupulously honest in handling money . . . individuals exhibit considerable situational specificity in several nonintellective dimensions, such as aggression, social conformity, dependency, rigidity, honesty, and attitudes toward authority.

(Anastasi, 1986, pp. 9–10)

By comparison, the effectiveness of a person's abilities, especially mental skills, seems to be more consistent *across situations*. In other words, a person with superior intelligence is likely to be able to apply her gift in many dissimilar task settings. Anastasi (1986) suggested that it is our basic school curricula and our experiences as young people in formal settings that develop:

[B]roadly applicable cognitive skills in the verbal and numerical areas. Personality development, in contrast, occurs under far less uniform conditions. Moreover, in the personality domain, the same response may elicit social consequences that are positively reinforcing in one type of situation and negatively reinforcing in another. The person may thus learn to respond in different ways in different contexts.

(Anastasi, 1986, p. 10)

Further discussion of this debate is beyond the purpose of this chapter, but we return to the disposition vs. context debate in Chapter 2. Suffice it to say here that the author's position is an interactionist one. Theories of work motivation and behavior, employee skills, aptitudes and abilities, and job performance offer more intellectual muscle and predictive validity when the theorist and the practitioner admit that both personal and contextual factors may be relevant. A dogmatic posture that precludes, a priori, the possibility that either individual traits or environmental conditions are not likely to be relevant is foolish and shortsighted.

SUMMARY

In this chapter, it has been argued that productivity is an issue of major economic concern in Western civilization. Our ability to live in comparative economic affluence depends, in large measure, upon the productivity of the workforce in all sectors of the economy. Many of the most powerful determinants of productivity in any economy are well beyond the influence of individual managers and executives. Indeed, many politicians and heads of state claim that world forces related to economic prosperity are beyond their reach (they make these claims most frequently during bad economic times). Nevertheless, the levels of motivation and ability of the workforce are two factors that can, within limits, be influenced by enlightened managerial practices. The importance of human productivity in economic well-being is a topic that has been written about and studied many times (e.g., Campbell et al., 1988; McClelland & Winter, 1969; O'Toole, 1981; Thurow, 1980). The purpose of this book is to provide a scientifically based treatment of our scientific knowledge of work motivation and its role in job performance, and, ultimately, the overall level of productivity in Western economies and the quality of life we can expect to enjoy.

OUTLINE OF THE BOOK

Now that we have dealt with a few basic concepts and definitions, we can begin the major task of this book, which is to examine current knowledge pertaining to work motivation. A major theme of the book is that what we know about work motivation consists of theory. *Theory* is an aversive word in some quarters, but a failure to recognize that most social and behavioral science knowledge is merely theory can lead to a number of disappointments for the student or manager who tries to utilize this knowledge and who then finds it limited in what it can provide. Therefore, Part One of the book will conclude with Chapter 2, in which we will present a framework that illustrates how theories of work motivation are developed. Understanding the framework will be important for comprehending much of the analysis that follows in subsequent chapters, where specific details about current theories of work motivation are presented. Chapter 2 will also more completely address the matter of the interaction between individuals and contexts in the cause and explanation of work motivation and behavior.

When we speak of human motivation, we necessarily speak about human nature. To understand why people behave the way they do, we must have some understanding of the essential nature of human beings. Therefore, a number of alternative models of human functioning will be presented over six chapters in Part Two. Chapter 3 provides a groundwork for the presentation of theories of work motivation that examine specific human needs, one at a time, in the five remaining chapters of Part Two. It will become clear as the book develops that different theories of work motivation rest upon entirely different assumptions concerning human nature. The bulk of Chapter 3 will then begin the analysis of work motivation by looking at theories that assume human beings are wanting animals, driven by sets of basic needs and values. For the most part, we will not address the proposition that much of human work is undertaken to provide people with the resources to meet their most basic, biological needs for food, water, and shelter. These "lower-level" needs are clearly highly important in all human behavior, but we will not spend much space studying them here,[10] although, in Chapter 15, we will briefly discuss the limitations of this assumption when one takes a more global view of the human condition.

The emotional side of human nature is the focus of Chapter 4. We will examine a variety of theoretical views of human emotions and emotionality and discuss the resurgence and current significance of emotions in behavioral science, paying particular attention to the role of affect in current thinking about work motivation.

In Chapters 5, 6, and 7, we will build upon the general concepts of Chapter 3 by focusing on a variety of specific human needs that have more recently been shown to be relevant to the study of work motivation. Thus, human needs for intimacy, love, sex, and power will be examined, along with a discussion of how these needs may or may not account for aspects of the behavior of people in the workplace.

A dominant theme throughout Part Two is that much of the most interesting behavior in organizations arises from the fact that humans are gregarious, social creatures, who must interact with others of their kind. Chapter 6 will look in depth at the human needs for affiliation and esteem. We will examine how people not only frequently elect to be around others while working, but that the sheer presence of others can influence what they perceive and believe about their work and how they behave in the workplace. Chapter 6 will also look at the human need for esteem – to be thought well of by others.

Chapter 7 builds on a major section of Chapter 3, dealing with human needs for growth, competence and self-determination. Specifically, Chapter 7 examines a variety of theoretic and applied approaches to job design, most of which are intended to appeal to these particular human needs. Then, to finish Part Two, Chapter 8 will explore the meaning and significance of frustration – the phenomenon that occurs when needs are blocked from satisfaction. Taken collectively, Chapters 3 through 8 will provide a current summary and critique of the hundreds of research-based statements of the role of human needs, particularly socially based human needs, in the workplace.

---

[10] If the doomsday scenarios about the end of jobs and the end of work as we know them come to be as portended by Rifkin (1995) and Bridges (1994), lower-level needs for sheer survival in tough, unending times of unemployment may take on much greater importance in the motivation to work.

Again, the assumption underlying all of this work is that hypothetical concepts called needs are useful lenses through which to study work motivation: This assumption will be relaxed (or replaced) in Parts Three and Four.

Part Three consists of five chapters dealing with concepts of work motivation that assume that people's beliefs, attitudes, and intentions are the ultimate determinants of their behavior. Accordingly, Chapter 9 will discuss some of the more popular[11] views of the nature of human beliefs, attitudes, and intentions, and provide the basic concepts needed to understand the cognitive theories that follow in Chapters 10 through 13. Chapter 10 extensively examines three particular types of human belief and attitude that are especially relevant to work motivation. Chapter 11 will focus on human perceptions and beliefs about fairness, justice, and equity, and their places in the study of work motivation. This is the largest and most detailed chapter of the book, largely because the author believes that the core concepts contained in it (such as perceptions of equity, fairness, and justice) are among the most potent and important forces in the behavior of people at work.

In Chapter 12, we will examine the popular expectancy-valence models of work motivation, paying special attention to the notion of human agency – the issue of people's beliefs about their capacity to perform particular tasks. Chapter 13 presents the nature of human intentions and their role in human goal-setting processes, followed by a treatment of the formal theory of goal setting, and control theory, which, at first blush appears similar to goal-setting theory but that, on second inspection, differs from goal theory in some fundamentally important ways. The chapter continues with a study of self-regulation processes that are founded at least in part in goal-setting concepts and techniques. Management by objectives, a popular managerial technique that has its main roots in the theory of goal setting, is the final topic of Chapter 13.

Chapter 14 is the sole chapter in Part Four, where we will deal with views of "work motivation" that, to varying degrees among their adherents, deny the importance of the concept altogether, preferring to focus instead on work *behavior*. This chapter will feature a historical treatment of the role of behaviorism in psychology, organizational behavior, and work motivation in particular. It will conclude with a presentation of the currently popular social cognitive theory and discuss the applied techniques called "self-regulation." The feature that theories in this part (and chapter) have in common is that they assume a learning approach to work motivation.

In Part Five, we will attempt to provide a summary and evaluation of the progress made in recent years in the study of work motivation as well as an exhortation to organizational scholars to become more global as well as more systems oriented in their approach to motivation issues. The chapter closes with suggestions for future research and theory.

To begin then, because most of what is to follow in this book is theory, Chapter 2 will explain the meaning of theory, and show how the theoretic nature of our knowledge of work motivation is an important feature of that knowledge, for both the student and the practicing manager.

---

[11] We refer to these selected theories of attitudes here as among the most popular. To be more precise, the theories that comprise most of the focus are those that have been the most useful and popular to organizational and social psychologists in their study of work motivation. A complete survey of the theory of attitudes is far beyond the scope of this book.

Methods of Inquiry in Work Motivation Theory and Research

2

No way of thinking or doing, however ancient,
can be trusted without proof.
H. D. Thoreau

In Chapter 1, we argued that managers might benefit from an understanding of human work motivation because such knowledge can help them to contribute to workforce productivity in their respective organizations and, indirectly, to the aggregate level of economic prosperity of the nation. Most managers are aware of the need for some knowledge of employee motivation and, as will be argued in Chapter 3, most managers hold implicit mental models as to "what makes employees tick." In response to the widespread desire for solutions to the problem of employee motivation, many consultants, academics, and business people have developed and promulgated numerous theories of work motivation. Some of these theories have merit, others do not, and still others offer useful ideas without being adopted holus bolus. Some have enough truth and insight into these matters that people pay attention to them and attempt to apply them. Sometimes, these applications are valuable, other times they are less valuable.

The purpose of this chapter is to provide the reader with an understanding of the means by which theories of work motivation are developed and made available to practitioners for application in organizational settings. A model is presented that represents the cyclical process through which research and theory development often proceed as new ideas about work motivation are generated and refined for application. It is important for the reader to understand the nature of this process to appreciate or apply the theoretic notions presented throughout the remainder of this book and in other books dealing with human behavior in organizations. This cyclical process is illustrated through a detailed summary of the development and promulgation of one of the most influential and controversial theories of work motivation, Herzberg's classic (and contentious) motivator-hygiene theory. We discuss the general problem of the ways that a practitioner can determine the readiness for application of any theoretical framework that has its roots in behavioral and social science. We look at theory and technique into work motivation from the perspective of the history and sociology of knowledge, noting that "the times" often make certain topics more interesting to managers, policy-makers, and social scientists. We examine how research and theory of work motivation have been subjected to tugs-of-war between constituent groups who have demanded either simplicity or enhanced realism and applied utility. We then explore at greater length the issue of context and how the introduction of moderator variables and mediating mechanisms into work motivation theories for the sake of better understanding has complicated many of them in recent years.

The issues and concepts introduced in this part of the chapter have relevance for the discussion elsewhere in the book, where various theories and techniques of employee motivation are presented in greater detail.[1] To begin, let's look at the cycle of events that is typical during the development of

---

[1] Readers may find that the content of this chapter is different from that in the rest of the book. Those who wish to get to the particular details of the various theories we examine, disregarding the caveats and considerations developed in this chapter, may do so by moving directly to Chapter 3. In fact, some readers may find it most useful to do just that and once having acquired a working knowledge of the major tenets and features of the various theories discussed in the book, return

most new theories in behavioral science – a cycle that is particularly common in the development of theories of work motivation.

DEVELOPMENT AND ADOPTION OF THEORIES

Where Do Theories Come From?

The knowledge base of most social and behavioral sciences results from a cycle of activities, a cycle that many practitioners (and scientists) either are not aware of or tend to ignore. Our base of knowledge about work motivation is no exception to this cycle, so it is important for the student or manager who wishes to apply these theories to understand the nature of their origins.

For the sake of discussion, the cycle is illustrated graphically in Figure 2.1. Although the

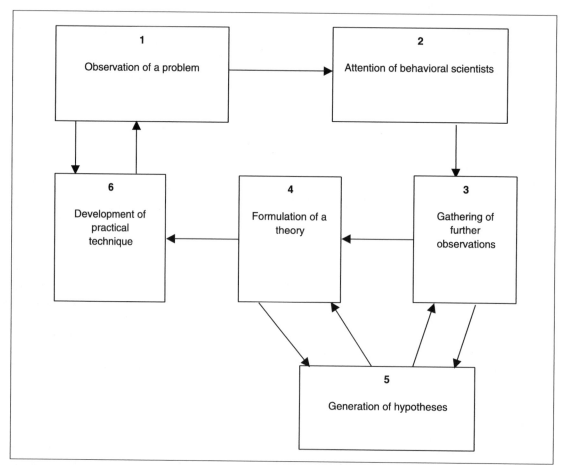

FIG. 2.1 Cycle of events leading to development and refinement of theories of work motivation and applied techniques.

to Chapter 2. Our suggestion, however, is that the reader carefully work through the points contained in the current chapter, because aside from being of intrinsic importance, they provide an understanding of the approaches and values that we apply in our treatments of the theories and techniques that comprise the rest of the book.

sequence of events varies considerably from one case to another, it is common for the cycle to begin with the observation of a problem or a phenomenon of concern to someone (such as a manager or administrator) who is responsible for dealing with it (see Box 1 in Figure 2.1).[2] Low job performance, absenteeism, tardiness, insubordination, or the occurrence of wildcat strikes are a number of examples that are of particular relevance to us here. At some time or other, the problem may come to the attention of a behavioral scientist, at which stage any of a number of things may occur (see Box 2). In some cases the scientist may set about to explore the phenomenon of interest, gathering more preliminary observations related to it, relying, sometimes, on only a few more observations (see Eisenhardt, 1989; and Box 3 in Figure 2.1).

In other cases, the scientist may already have a number of hypotheses or hunches that can be tested with the data already in hand. Regardless, once a phenomenon comes to the attention of a social or behavioral scientist, a cycle of scientific activity gets underway, leading sooner or later to a formal theory to explain it. In most social scientific disciplines, attempts are made to apply the implications of theories for the amelioration of problems. If successful, the loop illustrated in Figure 2.1 is closed and the cycle continues as new "problems" emerge. Frequently, there is a direct reciprocal connection between Boxes 1 and 6 (in Figure 2.1), as techniques are applied, modified, and then tried in revised form. This means that – in principle at least – there is a strong, reciprocal, mutually interdependent relationship between theory and practice and, therefore, between social scientists and practitioners, as was illustrated nicely by Latham (2001a), in his description of the evolution of the theory of goal setting and the applied techniques that emerged from it over a period of three decades. (See also the entire issue of *Applied Psychology: An International Review*, Volume 50, April 2001, for Latham's article and the comments of a number of other organizational psychologists on the reciprocity issue.)

A Critical View of the Process

The mutualistic model of progress presented in Figure 2.1 is idealized and stylized to make a general point. In actual practice, however, there are frequently long and troublesome disconnections along the way. Latham[3] and Latham (2003) recently characterized the two parties to the relationship (practitioners and scientists) as "two solitudes" between whom communication is often non-existent or strained. They propose a set of eight recommendations to facilitate the transfer of knowledge between the two camps.

Klimoski (2005) and Ghoshal (2005) have also recently addressed the mutualistic relationship between social science theory and managerial practice, and the attendant reciprocal dependency between social scientists/teachers and business executives. Klimoski claimed that "there is nothing so dangerous as a bad theory," while Ghoshal (2005) raised a number of strong arguments to the effect that the primary norms and practices of science, such as those featured in modern "social science" and throughout this book, are largely inappropriate and, indeed, dysfunctional for application in many cases. While most of the examples Ghoshal (2005) cited to make his argument are found in – and relevant to – the more "macro" levels of analysis of the organizational and management sciences, his points are fundamental and bear attention.

One of Ghoshal's key concerns was that such management theories start from a gloomy set of ideologically based assumptions regarding the nature of humans and of institutions, proceed to only partial analysis of problem-based phenomena, using methods and assumptions that deny any role for human (read managerial) choice and intentionality, resulting in "bad practices" that reinforce the

---

[2] It is not always the case that real-world problems are the origins of theories (Ziman, 1987), but we restrict our discussion here to cases in which this is so.

[3] Dr. Gary P. Latham's name will be used many times throughout this book. For the sake of simplicity, he will be referred to merely as "Latham." On very rare occasions, members of Dr. Latham's family have co-authored work with him: on those occasions, their personal initials will be indicated (e.g. S. D. Latham, Professor Latham's spouse).

negative assumptions social scientists make as the cycle continues. Along the way, moral and ethical considerations are ignored or abandoned. Whereas the venerated social psychologist Kurt Lewin (1945, p. 129) stated famously "nothing is as practical as a good theory," Ghoshal (2005, p. 86) countered with the argument that: "Nothing is as dangerous as a bad theory ... [and] that bad management theories are, at present, destroying good management practices." Further exploration of the arguments behind, and resulting from Ghoshal's (2005) provocative position, are beyond our scope and purpose here. The interested reader is referred to the March 2005 edition of *Academy of Management Learning & Education* (Volume 4, No. 1).

Implications for teaching and education

The issue of the degree of connectedness between scientists and practitioners has major implications for the relationship between both of those parties (on the one hand) and the process of teaching students of management and administration (on the other). In her 2005 presidential address to the Academy of Management, Rousseau (2006a) raised the question: "Is there such a thing as evidence-based management?" (see also Rousseau, 2006b; Rousseau & McCarthy, 2007). In his opening statement of a special issue of *Academy of Management Learning & Education*, Ashkanasy (2007) summarized evidence-based management (EBM) as a movement that believes that "managers, like health and education professionals, need to understand that their decisions ought to be based on valid evidence founded in the scientific model of research, coupled with dispassionate practice-based feedback and reflection" (p. 6). In short, EBM is a nascent attempt in the organizational sciences at the time of this writing to bring practitioners and theorists/researchers closer together than has been the case heretofore, closing the gap between Latham and Latham's (2003) "two solitudes" and enable a mutualistic relationship more in line with the idealized one presented in Figure 2.1. The interested reader is referred to the March 2007 edition of *AOML&E* for more discussion on EBM.

Meanwhile, we proceed with our discussion of the development and application of social and behavioral science theory and practice, particularly as they pertain to issues of work motivation and employee performance, because, points raised by Ghoshal (2005) and the others mentioned in the previous paragraphs notwithstanding, there is a voluminous and influential body of research and practice on these matters that bears critical study and exploration – the primary purpose of this book.

What is a Theory?

The term *theory* is often viewed with suspicion by practical people, so many academics and consultants avoid using it when dealing with them. Nevertheless, virtually all of our knowledge of business, organizations, and the behavior of people in organizations consists entirely of theory. There are few irrefutable *laws* pertaining to human behavior. This point has a number of important implications for anyone who wishes to permit behavioral science to influence the policies and practices of a manager of human resources. In later sections of the chapter we deal with some of these implications, but since the bulk of the ideas presented in this book consist of or derive from theory, it is important that we define the term and begin to understand it.

As usual, definitions abound, but in this case they tend to converge. One popular definition from a major philosopher of science – one that seems to represent most others – holds that "theories are nets cast to catch what we call 'the world'; to rationalize, to explain, and to master it" (Popper, 1968, p. 59). A second definition is that a theory is "an ordered set of assertions about a generic behavior or structure assumed to hold throughout a significantly broad range of specific instances" (Sutherland, 1975, p. 9). Another defines theory as "a system of constructs and variables in which the constructs are related to each other by propositions and the variables are related to each other by hypotheses" (Bacharach, 1989, p. 498).

Theories are like templates that are fashioned as representations of reality: Sometimes they are accurate reflections of that reality; sometimes they are not. When a theory truly represents the part of reality it purports to represent, it is said to be *valid*. Proposing a theory can be easy; proposing a valid theory can be much more difficult, and proposing a theory that will be truly useful to managers and social scientists requires imagination and nonlinear thinking (Weick, 1989). But validity is not an all-or-nothing phenomenon (neither is it the only criterion by which to assess a theory, as we discuss shortly). Rather, it is possible for some aspects of a theory to be more valid than other aspects. Moreover, as the phenomenon of interest changes, the theory that purports to represent it may become less valid unless it is changed accordingly (see Cronbach, 1975), and the value of any social theory must be assessed in relation to the sociopolitical environment in which it is offered (Nord et al., 1988).

There has been considerable debate – some of it colorful and heated – in the organizational sciences about the processes of theorizing and about the criteria that one can, or should, use to evaluate a theory. Much of the polemics results from the fact that participating scholars represent fundamentally opposing philosophical views about human nature, social events, the ontological meaning of "organizations," and the meaning of life in general (Gioia & Pitre, 1990). Some of the difference is rooted in differing political ideologies (Nehbrass, 1979). A complete discussion of these issues and of the various positions related to them is beyond our scope and purpose here.[4] Rather, we restrict our discussion to a relatively conventional view on the matter: What makes for a good theory (of work motivation).

Criteria for Evaluating Theories of Work Motivation

One author has proposed that the two major criteria for evaluating a theory are *falsifiability* and *utility* (Bacharach, 1989). This means that a theory must be constructed such that it is possible for someone to gather (valid) data by observing the phenomenon of interest (e.g., work motivation) and then to demonstrate that the information gathered conflicts in important ways with the tenets of the theory or with hypotheses legitimately derived from the theory. This criterion has been widely popular in the social and physical sciences for many years (see Popper, 1968). The utility criterion implies that the theory should permit us to both explain and predict events with better-than-chance regularity and accuracy.[5] Nevertheless, it is sometimes possible to predict events (such as the likelihood of a wildcat strike), but it is not as easy to explain *why* they happen.

To return to the typical cycle of events portrayed in Figure 2.1, we see that theories result from observations and are intended to make sense of those observations, to explain them There is usually a prolonged sequence in which scientists gather observations through the conduct of formal research, formulate propositions based on those observations, and then gather more data to confirm, modify, or reject the propositions. Often, many scientists are involved: Some gather and report data; others criticize the data or the inferences derived from them; still others may be responsible for integrating the ideas of several researchers into a theoretical formulation. The iterative relationships between the collection of observations, the casting of propositions, and the refinement of theory are represented by Boxes (4) to (6) of Figure 2.1.

---

[4] The interested reader is referred to special issues of the *Academy of Management Review* (e.g., October 1989, July 1991, July 1992) and *Academy of Management Learning & Education* (March, 2005) for representative treatments of the various positions and the controversies involved.

[5] It also sometimes implies the managerial value of using the theory in applied problems over and above what can be accomplished without the assistance of the theory. We have more to say later in the chapter about this second interpretation of the utility concept.

Varieties of Validity

One of the most important criteria applied throughout this book in our comparative assessment of research and theories is *validity*. The validity criterion is a difficult standard to apply. Moreover, there are many varieties of validity (Cook & Campbell, 1979). The four forms that we adopt for our purposes are internal validity, construct validity, statistical conclusion validity, and external validity. It is important that the reader be basically familiar with all these forms. We provide only an outline of them here; the interested reader is referred to Cook and Campbell (1979) for complete details.

Internal validity deals with the following question: Do the putative causal variables in a research study really account for the variation we observe in the putative outcome variables of the research, or are other factors at work that better explain the effects we see on the dependent variables? Sometimes research designs are not careful enough to rule out plausible alternatives to the cause-and-effect relationships that researchers offer at the end of a study to explain their results.

Confounding variables and alternative explanations

For example, assume that a field experiment on work motivation is conducted in the forests of British Columbia into the relationship between reward systems and levels of individual worker motivation. Two types of pay system are used: One a flat salary system and the other a piece-rate pay plan. Assume that the people studied in the salary group are older and better educated than the people who work under the piece-rate plan. If there are differences in performance between the two groups and the experimenter concludes that, indeed, the piece-rate program produced higher levels of motivation than the salary system did, a critic may challenge these results, saying that they may not be internally valid. Why? The critic can point out that the differences in age and/or education between the two pay groups may both be feasible explanations for the observed performance differences. In other words, the critic may say that the results argue just as strongly that education, or age, or both, is the cause of differences in motivation, not the pay system being used.

The burden of proof is on the researcher: He or she is required to rule out "confounding" factors such as age and education by whatever means, so that there can be one and only one reasonable explanation for any observed differences in the dependent variable – in this case, the planned independent variable, reward systems. If there are such alternative explanations, there is no reason to think that we have learned anything from this research about the link between pay and motivation (or performance). There are many other generic ways that research can be poorly designed so as to permit *threats to internal validity* (or what we have here called confounds, or alternative explanations) to cast a shadow of doubt on the conclusions of a study (see Cook & Campbell, 1979, pp. 50–58).

This leads to a second concern: *Construct validity*. In the foregoing example, the researcher planned to study the link between pay systems and work motivation but measured "motivation" by *performance rates*. We saw in Chapter 1 that motivation and performance are not the same phenomenon. So if there are differences between the two pay groups it would be a mistake to conclude that pay affects motivation: Again, *motivation is not performance*.

As a second example of a problem of construct validity, suppose we held a theory that overly strict supervision is a cause of employee aggression. Testing that theory would require distilling this general proposition into testable hypotheses using real-world indicators that reflect both *overly strict supervision* and *employee aggression*, gathering data on both of these sets of indicators, and conducting analyses of the data to determine whether the indicators are related in the way suggested by the theory. Problems abound, however, in finding indicators that are *construct valid* – that represent all of what we mean conceptually by the term *overly strict supervision*, and that do not include elements of other constructs as well (Schwab, 1980). Similarly, we would have to find real-world indicators that represent all of what we imply by the term *aggression* – nothing more and nothing less. If these real-world indicators do not meet the test of construct validity (e.g., if we measured employee behavior that really does not represent aggression and/or excluded from our empirical observation supervisory behavior that should have been included under the umbrella of overly strict supervision), any conclusions that we draw at the conceptual level about the validity of the theory would be false. Finally, we would have to design our study so as to validly test our hypotheses that the relationship between supervisory style and aggression was causal and in the direction we anticipated. Again, failure to do so constrains our ability to say that we have validly and fairly tested our theory.

Now: Suppose that the researcher managed to gather data using construct valid measures of both the independent variable (reward system) and the dependent variable (e.g., supervisory reports of employee effort) but failed to find any differences between the effort levels of the two pay groups. The conclusion may be that there is, in fact, no differential effect on motivation by pay systems. On the other hand, a closer look might reveal that the researchers made mistakes in the use of the inferential statistics that they gathered on pay structures (which would be unlikely in this example) and effort levels. There are a number of ways that such *statistical conclusion* errors can be made. The researchers may not have studied enough people in the two pay systems to have had enough *statistical power* to find systematic differences that did, in fact, exist; or perhaps the variables used to measure the constructs were not measured reliably. (If they are not measured reliably they cannot possibly be construct valid.) The reader is referred to Cook and Campbell's (1979, especially pp. 39–50) classic treatment of these matters for further explanation and examples.

A fourth validity concern has to do with the generalizability of the results of a study. *External validity* is the issue of the degree to which the results can reasonably be generalized to populations other than the one used in the study, to periods of time other than the present, and to settings other than the one studied. In our pay and motivation example, we would be interested to know whether any results that we might find could be generalized from the British Columbia forest products industry to mining, fishing, and manufacturing, for example; we would hope that the results gathered today would be of value for planning compensation systems in the future; and we would want to know whether the results of our study would generalize to American and Asian workers, whether in their respective forest products industries or even more broadly than that. Notice that a study must be internally valid to be externally valid: Before we can safely generalize a finding (such as how pay systems affect work motivation), we must be sure that we actually have an internally valid conclusion to generalize!

We refer to the various forms of validity as we discuss theories and techniques of work motivation throughout the book, especially in Chapter 12. Generally, our concern is with internal validity: The issue of whether the conclusions that researchers report are justified given the research design and execution on which those conclusions are based.

Our point is this: Validity is a necessary criterion for us to take a theory seriously, yet it is extremely difficult to demonstrate the validity of a theory. In addition, validity is not enough; the theory must be useful and falsifiable. Jacques (1992) even proposed that we adopt an "ethic of caring," which would require that we take into account the social conditions of power and authority and would raise questions about whether a theory is likely to be used to strengthen the grip of those who hold power in society or whether the theory may be useful in furthering the case of disadvantaged groups, such as women and minorities (Jacques, 1992, p. 601).

A second point here is that theories ultimately rest on the more or less structured observations of scientists (gathered during their research activities). It stands to reason that mistakes made in the way a problem is formulated or conceived (Weick, 1989), in the way constructs are operationalized, and in the means by which data are collected and analyzed can all result in theories that are less valid (and/or less useful) than they might otherwise be. Although a full treatment of research methodology is not our purpose here, the reader should recognize that faulty scientific methods can lead to inaccurate and useless theories and/or make it difficult to assess the level of validity of extant theories. There are countless ways to err in the research process, some of which are more common than others (see Cook & Campbell, 1979). Nevertheless, the reader is reminded that virtually all of the ideas concerning work motivation presented in this book consist of or are derived from theory, and the true level of validity of these theories is often open to dispute. Accordingly, managerial techniques rooted in these theories are likely to be of limited value. In fact, they may even be harmful (Pinder, 1977).

Summary

In closing this section, we express our support for a view proposed over 20 years ago by Fry and Smith (1987, pp. 129–130), who wrote: "The driving force behind our quest for theory is the need to impose order on unordered experiences, and thereby solve real-world problems that require collective effort. Grounding our theories in everyday problems is all important because it is the logical relation to a problem situation which makes a theory interesting and meaningful, and gives it power to solve existing problems and to illuminate new ones."

In the following section, we illustrate the cycle described earlier and represented in Figure 2.1 by relating the story of the development of one of the most widely known theories of work motivation, proposed over 50 years ago by Frederick Herzberg and his colleagues. In addition to illustrating the cycle of activities that commonly occurs in the development of a science, the following section should serve to introduce the first of the major theories of work motivation described in this book. Later in the chapter we discuss the general validity of theories of work motivation and introduce other criteria for theory evaluation that have been applied to the assessment of these theories in recent years.

THE MOTIVATOR-HYGIENE THEORY AS EXAMPLE

On the basis of an exhaustive review of hundreds of early studies of the causes, correlates, and consequences of *job attitudes*, Herzberg and his colleagues (Herzberg, Mausner, Peterson, & Capwell, 1957) developed the preliminary hypothesis that the factors which cause positive attitudes toward one's job are different from the factors that generate negative job-related attitudes. This hypothesis was revolutionary at the time because it implies that job satisfaction is not simply the opposite of job dissatisfaction, as had commonly been assumed. Instead, the new hypothesis held that feelings of job satisfaction and job dissatisfaction are independent of one another, such that an employee can be happy about some aspects of his job while being unhappy about others. Using the terms shown in Figure 2.1, the problem of interest in this case was employee work attitudes, and the observations that led to the preliminary hypothesis were actually the observations of hundreds of other researchers and behavioral scientists – a much wider and more justifiable base for offering a hypothesis than is usually the case in behavioral science.

Herzberg's Own Research

To test the two-factor concept, Herzberg and his colleagues (Herzberg, Mausner, & Snyderman, 1959) gathered their own original data (observations) from a sample of 203 engineers and accountants who worked for a variety of organizations in the Pittsburg area. Using a semi-structured interview technique (meaning that both the researcher and the interviewee influenced the direction taken during the interview), the researchers asked the employees, one at a time, to think of an occasion when they felt "exceptionally good" or "exceptionally bad" about their jobs. Interviewees were permitted to recall such critical incidents from their current jobs or from any held previously. They recorded two or three incidents of this sort, on average, from each employee. For each incident, detail was requested concerning three things: (1) a description of the objective conditions surrounding and causing the incident; (2) a description of the reasons why the employee felt a particular way at the time of the incident; and (3) a summary of the consequences of the incident for the employee and the job.

Analysis of the Incidents

Once the data in a research project are gathered, they must be analyzed. (As we saw earlier, both the collection and analysis phases of such a project are potentially problematic.) Herzberg and his colleagues broke each interview down into almost 500 separate thought items and then classified these items into categories based on the degree of similarity that appeared among them. Notice that the researchers allowed the nature of the items to determine the categories to emerge from this analysis rather than sorting them into predefined categories. Care was taken to assure that independent researchers could agree on the classification of particular items into the various clusters that resulted. The items were also categorized as having either long- or short-term effects on the employees at the time.

Sixteen separate groups of items, or factors, emerged from this exercise – 16 sets of items that were related in one way or another with instances of extremely satisfying or unsatisfying job experiences. The next step was to see whether any of these groups or factors seemed to be more closely associated with instances of positive job attitudes than with instances of negative job attitudes, and, similarly, whether certain factors appeared more frequently in stories of negative incidents than in stories of positive job attitudes.

Further detail on the data analysis techniques employed is well beyond the scope of this book; the interested reader is referred to the original report (Herzberg et al., 1959). What is important to the present discussion is a summary of the results, and, even more important, the way the results have been interpreted, misinterpreted, and fought over ever since by pro- and anti-Herzberg factions.

The *Motivators*

In fact, certain patterns did seem to emerge from the data. As had been the researchers' hunch before the data were collected, one set of factors appeared more frequently in stories of positive job attitudes than in stories of negative job attitudes. For example, reports of achievement appeared in 41% of the instances of positive job attitudes, making it the single feature most frequently related to job satisfaction experiences. (An example from the study is the case of a marine engineer who described an instance when he succeeded in designing a propeller for a new boat design.) Similarly, recognition appeared in 33% of the positive stories; challenging, varied, or interesting work appeared in 26%; responsibility appeared in 23%; and advancement was an element of fully 20% of the stories of high job satisfaction.

By the same token, 10 of the 16 factors that were identified previously appeared in fewer than 7% of the job satisfaction episodes, suggesting, as had been expected, that they were not usually related to job satisfaction experiences. Because the interviewees indicated that the occurrences of these highly favorable periods of job attitudes tended to result in greater job performance. Herzberg labeled these as sources of satisfaction *motivators*. A number of special features emerged from a close look at the five most frequently mentioned satisfiers/motivators. First, positive stories that featured one of these factors tended to include elements related to one or more of the other four – they seemed to go hand in hand in producing job satisfaction. Further, the researchers noted that compared to the negative feelings, the positive feelings tended to be relatively long-lasting rather than short term in effect. They also tended to be related to aspects of the content of the job and to the personal relationship between the worker and the job. It was eventually determined that these five factors were associated with job satisfaction because they tended to cause feelings of growth and personal development.

The *Hygiene Factors*

The researchers then looked at the stories that referred to instances of job dissatisfaction and found that the 11 remaining factors revealed in their earlier analysis seemed to appear most frequently in them. Thus, company policy and administration were blamed at least partially for 31% of the reported cases of job dissatisfaction. Similarly, unhappy relationships with the employee's supervisor appeared in 20% of the stories, and poor interpersonal relations with one's peers was the critical factor in 15% of the instances of poor job attitudes. Unhappiness with technical aspects of the employee's supervisor was a critical factor in 20% of the stories of low job attitudes, while bad relations with the supervisor on a personal level appeared important in 15% of these stories. Two other factors that figured predominantly in the episodes of low job attitudes were poor working conditions and unfriendly relationships with one's peers, which appeared in 11% and 8% of the stories of dissatisfaction, respectively. Compared to the frequency with which this second set of factors appeared in stories of job dissatisfaction, they were not frequently related to instances of high job attitudes.

Herzberg and his colleagues (1959) named the second set of factors *hygienes* because, analogous to the concept of mental hygiene in psychiatry, these items were seen as necessary, but not sufficient, for healthy adjustment. (In this case, they are necessary for preventing job dissatisfaction but are not capable of generating either job satisfaction or motivated behavior.) The researchers noted a number of features shared among the hygiene factors. First, they all tend to be related to the context of the work – the circumstances within which the person performs the job. (Recall that the motivators were more closely linked to the content of the work.) Second, the hygiene factors tended to be associated with shorter-lasting job experiences than were the motivators. Herzberg (1981) argued that providing decent working conditions and cordial interactions on the job, for example, may serve to move people in the short run, but that their zero point escalates, so that people quickly take these things for granted, and become likely to ask, "What have you done for me lately?" Contrariwise, the provision of motivator factors in the employee's work is seen as having a much longer-lasting effect on the individual, resulting in motivation rather than simple movement.

The predominant reason given by the respondents in the original study (Herzberg et al., 1959) to explain why the lack of hygiene factors was associated with dissatisfaction was that their absence tended to cause feelings of being unfairly treated. So whereas the provision of motivators led to feelings of growth and development, a sense of injustice seemed to explain the link between the absence of hygienes and job dissatisfaction.

Overlap Among the Factors

There was at least one other important aspect of the hygiene factors noted by Herzberg and his colleagues, a feature that is highly relevant to the controversy sparked by the theory. There were a number of stories of job dissatisfaction that featured elements of some of the motivator factors, especially recognition, work itself, and advancement. For example, failure to receive recognition was said to be the principal cause in 18% of the stories of job dissatisfaction. It is important to acknowledge that the researchers recognize these deviations from the basic split in their original book.

All the basic satisfiers, recognition, achievement, advancement, responsibility, and work itself appeared with significantly greater frequencies in the highs (stories of job dissatisfaction). However, some of these factors also appeared with some frequency in the low stories: Recognition, 18%; work itself, 14%; and advancement, 11%. Evidently these three satisfiers are not as unidirectional in their effect on job attitudes as the factors that cause job dissatisfaction. From these results it would appear that a better statement of the hypothesis would be that the satisfier factors are much more likely to increase job satisfaction than they would be to decrease job satisfaction but that the factors that related to job dissatisfaction very infrequently act to increase job satisfaction (Herzberg et al., 1959, p. 80).

Anyone who has ever worked at a dull or disagreeable job knows from experience that the nature of the work, by itself, can be a very powerful cause of job dissatisfaction, as can instances in which either recognition for accomplishment is hard to come by or employees are not advanced at a rate that is deemed fair. Quite clearly, if absent from an employee's job, these motivators can be great sources of frustration and dissatisfaction.

Two issues require highlighting here. The first is a technical point but one with significance for the argument being presented in this chapter. Notice that in their well-intended acknowledgement of the lack of perfect symmetry between the causes of job satisfaction and dissatisfaction, Herzberg and his colleagues indicated the possibility that the three motivators in question could also decrease job satisfaction. The problem lies in the fact that their data, as well as their own theoretical interpretation of data, imply that satisfaction and dissatisfaction are not opposite sides of the same emotion. Instead, they are held to be entirely independent and different from one another – but not opposites[6] (see Bobko, 1985). To be consistent with the rest of the theory, what the caveat should have said about the three common crossovers is that like the major hygiene factors, these motivators are capable of causing job dissatisfaction (as opposed to decreasing job satisfaction) among people. The difference is important, because it illustrates the ways by which misinterpretations and misunderstandings can arise as a theory is developed and then passed from one researcher to another in the cycle of testing and modification shown in Figure 2.1.

The second point is that although they drew attention to the fact that their data featured these (as well as other) crossovers, both Herzberg and others who followed him seemed to lose sight of this acknowledgment in the original statement of the theory. In popularized interpretations of his own theory, for example, Herzberg himself (1968, 1981) listed his basic motivators as associated with motivation and satisfaction, and his hygienes as causative only of dissatisfaction, failing to mention the reversals in the data that originally gave rise to the theory. In short, these two points illustrate how the refinement of a theory can encounter snags and delays, making the process shown in Figure 2.1 less precise than one might wish it to be.

The role of pay

The most ambivalent of the 15 factors found in the stories of satisfaction and dissatisfaction was salary. It appeared in almost as many stories (proportionately) of job satisfaction as it did in stories of dissatisfaction. However, because it was related to more stories of long-term negative attitude shifts than to long-term positive shifts, Herzberg and his team classified salary in the hygiene category.

The Two-Factor Theory in a Nutshell

Briefly, the two-factor theory proposes that human beings have two basic sets of needs and that different elements of the work experience can serve to meet them (Herzberg, 1966). The first set of needs is devoted to *basic survival* or maintenance. They are characterized as being concerned with

---

[6] Later, Herzberg (1966) described how the motivators are responsible for meeting growth needs, whereas the hygienes are needed only to provide basic survival.

avoiding pain and discomfort and as providing for primary drives such as sex, thirst, and hunger. The second set of needs, called *growth needs*, expresses itself in attempts by people to become all that they are capable of becoming, by exploring and conquering challenges posed by their environments. (See Chapter 3, where the notion of growth needs is discussed in greater detail.) Minimum levels of the hygiene factors (e.g., salary) are necessary for fulfillment of the survival needs, but when they are present, they do not cause feelings of job satisfaction; they merely prevent feelings of job dissatisfaction. Hygienes can be useful motivators, according to the theory, only until the survival needs are somewhat provided for. Then they lose effect.

To produce positive job attitudes and to motivate employees, the theory claims that items originally identified as motivators must be built into all types of job. The content of the work rather than the setting in which it is conducted is the important thing. The work must provide opportunities for the employee to achieve, and the person must receive recognition for that achievement. The work should be interesting, provide for advancement, and require responsibility. When jobs are designed according to these principles (or "enriched"), motivation and positive attitudes will be forthcoming. When these factors are missing, however, no dissatisfaction results, simply an absence of satisfaction. The original study revealed a number of other findings, but those already mentioned are the most important as well as the most controversial and the most relevant to the present discussion.

The Ensuing Controversy

The cycle shown in Figure 2.1 indicates that newly developed theories are usually put to the test of reality either by their original proponents or by others interested in confirming, refining, or refuting them. Accordingly, the motivator-hygiene theory quickly drew a lot of attention. Within a few years, dozens of attempts were made to interpret the theory, to develop measures of the various factors included in it, and to gather data and compare the results found in the data with predictions that followed from the theory. As is often the case, the results were highly mixed. Some studies seemed to support the two-factor concept, others did not. As evidence accumulated on both sides of the ledger, a dispute between pro- and anti-Herzberg factions developed, generated in part by a number of allegations that Herzberg's results (and therefore the theory itself) could be explained primarily by the methods he and his colleagues used to both gather and analyze the data! This point is crucial. A theory of work motivation is supported to reflect the true underlying nature of just that – work motivation. Such a theory should not, in fact, be merely an artifact of the methodology used to generate it.

The argument was that the storytelling technique (described earlier) naturally tended to cause the interviewees to link instances of satisfaction to their own accomplishments, and – not wanting to look bad – caused them to associate instances of negative feelings with factors that were somewhat beyond their control or responsibility. So, for example, it was alleged that the engineers and accountants quite understandably blamed company policies, their supervisors and peers, and other contextual factors for the negative events reported in their stories. This criticism was a serious challenge to the validity of the theory because it cast fundamental doubt on the very meaning of the data. Moreover, the criticism grew in seriousness when it was noted that studies using the Herzberg methodology tended to support the theory, whereas those that used other methods to gather and analyze data tended not to support it (Behling, Labovitz, & Kosmo, 1968).

A complete history of the Herzberg debate is beyond the scope of this book. Interested readers are referred to papers by Bockman (1971), Grigaliunas and Weiner (1974), House and Wigdor (1967), and Whitsett and Winslow (1967) for summaries of the controversy and insight into the many fine points that are involved. Briefly, however, by 1970 enough data had been gathered that cast doubt on the theory for Korman (1971) to conclude that that research had "effectively laid the Herzberg theory to rest" (p. 149). Subsequent pronouncements of the demise of the theory have been plentiful. But more than a decade after the two-factor theory was formally proposed, some of its proponents claimed that it was seldom tested fairly, so that the conclusion that it is invalid is itself not well founded (Grigaliunas & Weiner, 1974). For example, these writers argued that virtually none of the studies that were conducted to test the theory used measures of job satisfaction and job dissatisfaction that represented two separate and independent continua, as the theory would demand. Moreover, data are presented that imply that the social desirability explanation for the original data (as discussed already) is not tenable. Grigaliunas and Weiner also pointed out that critics of Herzberg's theory tended to ignore the substantial evidence that has accumulated to support the theory's prescriptions for job design. In short, these authors argued that it may not be possible to test the theory fairly and that attempts to do so before 1974 failed to provide sufficient grounds to conclude that it is not valid. (One study (Ondrack, 1974) that employed the methodology that Grigaliunas and Weiner proposed failed to support the theory.)

Herzberg himself has alleged at times that he has been misinterpreted (e.g., Herzberg, 1976). The problem is that for the self-correcting cycle of scientific activity shown in Figure 2.1 to occur, it is first necessary that the theory in question be interpreted accurately, without biases or nuances that are not founded on the basis of the observations that gave rise to it initially. To the extent that Herzberg and his codefendants are correct in their position that the theory has been misinterpreted and tested with inappropriate instruments, there is no way that anyone – including academics, students, or practitioners – can be sure that the theory has anything to offer to help them understand and/or influence work motivation.

Aside from the allegation that inappropriate instruments have been used to examine the motivator-hygiene theory, it has been demonstrated by King (1970) that there have been as many as five different interpretations of the two-factor notion, and that none of these interpretations enjoys much empirical support that cannot be attributed to methodological artifact, as was alleged of the original study. To illustrate, one interpretation suggests that all the motivator factors combined contribute more to job satisfaction than to job dissatisfaction, and that all hygienes combined contribute more to dissatisfaction than to satisfaction. A different interpretation holds that all motivators combined contribute more to satisfaction than do all hygiene factors combined, and that all hygiene factors combined contribute more to dissatisfaction than do all motivators combined. Remarks made in Herzberg's 1966 book suggest that this is what the theory implies. Regardless, King (1970) showed that only studies that used the Herzberg method were successful at replicating and supporting the theory and that the various interpretations fail, as tested, to provide unequivocal support for the two-factor feature of the theory.

On balance, when we combine all the evidence with all the allegations that the theory has been misinterpreted, and that its major concepts have not been assessed properly, we are left not really knowing whether to take the theory itself seriously, let alone whether it should be put into practice in organizational settings. There is support for many of the implications the theory has for enriching jobs to make them more motivating. But the two-factor aspect of the theory – the feature that makes it unique – is not really a necessary element in use of the theory for designing jobs per se. One need only believe that building jobs to provide responsibility, achievement, recognition for achievement, and advancement will make them satisfying and motivating. There is no need to assume that failure to provide these 28 factors will not lead to job dissatisfaction, or that the provision of certain hygiene factors in the workplace cannot also be motivating, in the true sense of the word.

Implications of the Herzberg Controversy

Why have we devoted so much attention to the details surrounding development of the two-factor theory and to the controversy it generated? One obvious purpose was to explain the theory, because it remains one of the best-known approaches to work motivation among practitioners today, despite the decades of doubt and controversy that have surrounded it.[7] But there are several other reasons for examining it so closely. First, the Herzberg story permits us to illustrate a number of important problems and issues that relate to the development of new theories in behavioral science as we introduced them earlier in the chapter. In fairness, these problems and issues are certainly not unique to the case of the motivator-hygiene theory; rather, it is the one theory of work motivation that seems to have been exposed to the closest criticism on grounds of methodology.

The foregoing story illustrates the difficulty of developing tools or instruments for assessing hypothetical concepts such as motivation. As was noted both in Chapter 1 and earlier in this chapter, we must *infer* the existence of motivated force from the observation of effort or by asking people what is going on inside them. We cannot directly weigh or measure concepts such as attitudes and motivation as we would physical objects (Hughes, Price, & Marrs, 1986; Schwab, 1980). This means that we must worry about whether our crude proxy measures (such as Herzberg's interview technique) really allow us to measure those things we think we are measuring, nothing more and nothing less. This is the problem of construct validity described earlier (Schwab, 1980), a constant issue in assessing nonphysical entities and a major limitation on our capacity to establish fairly the validity of theories of work motivation.

To make matters worse, we must also worry about the possibility that the measurements we make vary from one time to the next (when in fact we know that the entity being measured has not changed). That is, do our measures fluctuate or are they relatively stable? This is referred to as the problem of *reliability of measurement*. Clearly, we cannot develop or test a theory with instruments that give us inconsistent assessments of the concepts that must be calibrated, yet the stability of measurement in behavioral science when interviews and/or questionnaires are used is usually a problem (Nunnally, 1967).

Further, consider the possibility that the very process of asking people how they feel toward their jobs may itself influence the type of response. Some critics (e.g., Salancik & Pfeffer, 1977, 1978) claimed that it is virtually impossible to assess job attitudes without changing those attitudes merely by asking about them. This is referred to as the problem of *reactivity of measurement* (Webb, Campbell, Schwartz, & Sechrest, 1966). It too is endemic in behavioral research and figures heavily in the problem of measurement reliability. In the case of Herzberg's research, the allegation that his results could be accounted for by the ego-defense (or social desirability) motives of the interviewees provides an example of how difficult it is to assess attitudes and motives without influencing them simply by asking about them.

The Herzberg example also shows that there are many ways to make observations, and that once a theory has been proposed, there are many ways to test its validity (i.e., to determine whether it actually reflects reality). The story shows how theories are sometimes not tested appropriately, and as a result may either be confirmed or rejected for the wrong reasons. Hypotheses that are supported by poorly conducted research (when, in fact, they should be rejected) can accumulate, resulting in theories that misrepresent the nature of things. Alternatively, valid hypotheses that do not pass the scientist's test (as a result of poor research) may be ignored and forgotten. The result is that potentially useful knowledge is discredited. The Herzberg case also illustrates what can happen when a theory, once developed, is oversimplified, misinterpreted, or misrepresented. In Chapter 3, we will see that Maslow's famous theory of needs has suffered similar treatment, as has the expectancy theory of motivation, discussed in Chapter 12. If a new theory is not interpreted accurately, how can its true level of validity be determined and how can either the scientist or the practitioner decide whether it has any value in understanding and/or influencing the world?

In short, the story of the development of Herzberg's theory and the controversies that followed it help to illustrate many of the difficulties involved in the advancement of new theories of work motivation. It helps us understand the potential for error on the part of any new theory that

---

[7] Very few general textbooks in organizational behavior treat work motivation without discussing the two-factor theory, its dubious validity and all the controversy we have reviewed here notwithstanding.

purports to reflect the nature of work motivation. It also suggests that because of difficulties inherent in operationalizing them for testing, certain theories may be more valid than scientists are able to demonstrate, a proposition advanced repeatedly in later chapters. By way of contrast, however, the story shows that as in other sciences, progress in organizational science is a nonlinear affair, such that new theoretical developments can earn widespread attention and influence despite – rather than because of – the quality of the research on which they are based. We hope that the Herzberg story will help the reader understand the necessity for caution on the part of behavioral scientists as they generate new theories. But, more importantly, we hope that the reader with applied interests will learn to be somewhat discriminating and cautious in the adoption of new managerial techniques and programs that are grounded in theoretical ideas that are, in turn, based on more or less rigorous scientific methods of observation, analysis, and interpretation.

A Perspective from the History and Sociology of Knowledge

Now that we have looked at the views of a number of thinkers on the criteria by which we should evaluate work motivation (and other behavioral and social) theories, we must step back and take a broader perspective by recognizing, as we mentioned earlier, that there are other bases for evaluation, bases that are either ascientific, such as interest value and even beauty, or that recognize that concepts such as relevance and usefulness are socially constructed notions, rooted in the sociology of the times and in the eyes of the beholder.

Social and ideological issues

It is important to keep in mind that science (especially social and behavioral science) is a social institution and set of social processes (see Merton, 1973; Mitroff, 1983). This implies that social science is fraught with all or most of the phenomena that characterize social institutions of other sorts, including processes of politics, status and power, tradition, and the like (Mayhew, 1971). An implication of this is that as we discussed in Chapter 1, it is necessary to keep in mind the social and historical contexts within which any body of research or theory emerges and becomes popular (or unpopular). As social beings, motivation theorists and other social scientists have ideological belief systems, and these ideologies can (and do) influence the perception of what is "good" or "useful." Keeley (1983) observed that "scientific and ethical criteria can complement one another – not *substitute* for one another – in the evaluation of alternative views [regarding organizations and the management of people]. Social science can indicate only whether a model yields good (factual) solutions to specific problems. Ethics, on the other hand, can indicate whether a model yields good (worthwhile) problems to begin with. Although neither scientific nor ethical tests are apt to be conclusive, only if both show reasonably acceptable results should much trust be placed in the *general* validity of a social model" (p. 384).

A specific example of Keeley's (1983) point in the areas related to work motivation was furnished by Nehbrass (1979), who described how an ideological belief in the inherent virtue of human nature has fostered the promulgation of many management techniques, particularly those pertaining to worker participation – techniques that could not otherwise be supported or justified by cold, objective analysis: "The central belief of the ideology in question is a faith in the inherent goodness of humanity. People by nature are [seen as] good but they find themselves in an organizational (and societal) system that often distorts their nature and prevents the goodness from showing. In the face of this dehumanizing organization environment it is the role of the theorists to design new . . . management techniques that will capture the natural worth of workers. Although not always identified as such, the adherents of this belief system could be termed 'humanists' " (p. 427).

Nehbrass (1979) cited scientific reports from that time period which claimed that workers were alienated from their jobs, dissatisfied in massive numbers, and uncommitted to their work. He compared these popular reports with data from surveys at the time that failed to support such conclusions. At the time, quality of work life (QWL) was the management technique in vogue – every decade has one. Proponents of the movement at that time claimed that the North American worker was thoroughly alienated from work and that the "new worker" was rebelling at the lack of variety, autonomy, and challenge that characterized so many of the jobs in the economy at that time. For Nehbrass (1979), such sentiments were the informal, popular signs of the times – the stuff managerial literature was made of – but, he reported, these beliefs were not supported by the scientific evidence of the day that dealt with such matters.

Singling out the case of the argument at that time in favor of participative management, Nehbrass noted how the fervor of the managerial theorizing of the 1960s and 1970s was based largely on dated empirical studies of small groups of boys in contrived laboratory situations 30 years earlier. Nehbrass wrote:

> The impression the reader is intended to come away with is clear: Participation is a *proven* management tool; it is "extremely motivational" [Carlisle, 1976, p. 478]; it "fosters commitment" [Scanlon, 1973] . . . and it is, indeed, "probably the most widely recognized motivational technique in practice today" [Trewatha and Newport, 1976].
>
> What is surprising about so many discussions of the positive nature of [participative decision making] is that there is no mention of the plethora of research [he cites five studies] that does not support the authors' ideological stance. Practicing managers can find numerous reason for not sharing decision-making authority with subordinates and when they encounter these Utopian and one-sided views supported by research that is two and three decades old, it is little wonder that they view academics with skepticism and perhaps a bit of condescension.
>
> (Nehbrass, 1979, pp. 428–429)

Interestingly, a similar case was made throughout the 1980s, 1990s and since in organizational science by a new generation of scholars who, although using new terminology and research methodology, have embraced the same basic beliefs as those expressed by Nehbrass: Science is a social-political process and the knowledge of the day is a socially constructed artifact, subject to change as times change (see *Academy of Management Review*, July 1992; Berger & Luckman, 1966; Merton, 1973; Nord et al., 1988). But academics and theorists are not alone in the effects that social structures can have on them. Managers and administrators are heavily influenced by the ideologies and prevailing value structures of the times. Managerial programs and techniques cycle into and out of popularity in much the same way as fads and fashions in other arenas of life. Recent decades have seen the ascendancy and decline of such managerial techniques as employee participation, MBO, job enlargement, job enrichment, quality circles, management by walking around, employee empowerment, and organizational reengineering. We will examine many of these techniques in later chapters.

To summarize, the prevailing ideological values and belief structures of a given age determine the most appropriate problems to investigate and place boundaries around the nature of scientific enquiry that is imaginable or possible. The same values and beliefs will then heavily influence the nature of the criteria that are used to determine what is deemed to be "good," "useful," or "valid." In fact, they may even foster sentiments in favor of discarding such traditional standards and replacing them with entirely new sets of criteria for the evaluation of theory and social scientific activity (see Brief & Dukerich, 1991; Jacques, 1992).

APPLYING WORK MOTIVATION THEORY

The preceding analysis raises a number of questions. First, if it is accepted that caution is required in the application of new theories of motivation, how can an enlightened manager know when it is safe or advisable to adopt and begin applying new theories to human resource problems? What criteria or standards are available to suggest that such applications are appropriate? Further, just how valid are our best theories of work motivation? Simple answers to these questions are not possible, but in the following sections we shed some light on the issues involved.

Field Testing Versus Commercial Application

When we consider the issue of the application of new theories of motivation in real organizational settings, it is important to keep in mind a distinction between two different types of application. The first type is that done by behavioral scientists, whose purpose is to examine the validity of the new theory in real settings. The second type of application is that conducted by practitioners, who (more or less) assume that the theory being adopted holds some probable value for them in dealing with actual organizational problems.

The first type of application is a necessary step in the appropriate refinement and ultimate scientific adoption of a theory of motivation. Scientists simply cannot determine whether a theory represents reality without comparing it to samples of that reality (Garner, 1972). As we will see in subsequent chapters, some theories (such as equity theory) have, on the one hand, shown promising levels of accuracy when tested in contrived artificial settings but have failed to hold up to the scrutiny provided by testing in the field. Goal-setting theory, on the other hand (see Chapter 13), has benefited considerably by research conducted to examine it in real settings (Locke & Latham, 2002). In short, application of the first type is advisable and necessary in the development of new theoretic ideas.

But when is application of the second type warranted? In other words, when is it safe and reasonable for a new theoretical idea to be distilled into formalized commercial packages and programs for use by practitioners in their respective organizations? Too frequently it has been the case that new applied motivation-oriented programs, based on behavioral science, have been widely disseminated among practitioners with unrealistic expectations for what they could accomplish (Pinder, 1977; Walter & Pinder, 1980). Two important examples are job enrichment and management-by-objectives (MBO) programs. As we will see in Chapter 13, MBO (which has some of its theoretic underpinnings in the very successful goal-setting theory just mentioned) has failed in most organizations in which it has been installed. Years after so many failures, more complete understanding of the organizational circumstances necessary for it to succeed became understood (Halpern & Osofsky, 1990; Jamieson, 1973). Similarly, only after several years of difficulties with formal job enrichment programs has it been learned what organizational preconditions are necessary for these programs to succeed (see Chapter 7; Heckscher, 1988; Oldham & Hackman, 1980; Yorks, 1979).

The point here is not that motivation theories have no applied utility, neither is it that they should not be implemented in real organizational settings. Rather, too often the urgency of applied managerial problems, such as employee motivation, has occasioned the premature widespread commercial application of new behavioral science technology in situations where it has not been appropriate and, consequently, where it has failed. Why does this happen?

Managers tend to be practical people who seek practical tools to deal with urgent organizational problems. They tend to process information very quickly, looking for the essential elements of the problems they face as well as of the solutions they consider in their decision making (Mintzberg, 1973). Often, however, managers' preferences for practicality translate into demands for simplicity – managers often seek and expect relatively simple solutions to problems that they openly recognize as complex. They often prefer nuts-and-bolts solutions stripped of most cautions, caveats, and reservations that might appropriately accompany the advice they seek from others. In response, people with managerial programs (such as motivation-oriented techniques) willingly cater to the managerial preference for simplicity by offering or advocating scientifically based procedures stripped of all the "ifs, ands, and buts" that are justified by the research finds that underlie the procedures.

In her recent presidential address to the Academy of Management, Dr. Jone Pearce (2004) admitted to the forces she has experienced to sell "snake oil" based on management myth and lore rather than scientifically based knowledge to her MBA students because, in large part, that is frequently what they want. Indeed, this author has sat through countless highly entertaining, yet oversimplified presentations at conferences for human resources practitioners – clever routines offered by witty "motivational experts" and speakers who have offered half-truths, oversimplifications, and simply false assertions about human work behavior. The humor and simplicity of these acts make them the *sine qua non* of many practitioners' conferences. They do little to enhance the status and reputation of scholars and professors who are serious in the pursuit of knowledge about work motivation and behavior. Our advice here is borrowed from Alfred North Whitehead: "Seek simplicity and distrust it." In short, complex phenomena such as human work motivation are often oversimplified to make them palatable to practical people. Techniques that require unrealistic and oversimplifying assumptions are doomed to be ineffective when installed in complex, real settings (cf. Kanter, 2005). We will return to the issues of complexity and simplicity later in this chapter, offering the observation that recent theory and research into work motivation have pursued a path toward more complex models to capture the complexity of the phenomena involved, the pressures for simplicity we have discussed in this section notwithstanding.

Potential Risks of Premature Application

Repeated instances of failure of hastily applied behavioral science are costly and unfortunate. Changes implemented on the basis of such techniques can have a profound influence on both the job satisfaction and life satisfaction of people in organizations – especially so for the lower-level participants whose jobs are changed in accordance with the theory being applied. Organizational change is necessary for effectiveness and survival, but changes that are ill advised and inappropriate are disruptive and unfair to those affected (e.g., Pringle & Longenecker, 1982). But premature and ill-advised applications are costly in other ways as well (Pinder, 1977, 1982; Walter & Pinder, 1980). Organizations that adopt programs such as MBO, job enrichment, or flex time (to cite three examples) must invest considerable amounts of money and managerial effort in the installation and operation of these programs. When the programs fail, management groups are justified in investigating the soundness of the advice in which they have invested. In cases where it becomes clear that the technique in question was really not appropriate, disappointment and/or hostility toward behavioral science and behavioral scientists is understandable. Alienation of this sort is unfortunate in view of the absolute necessity for science to interact with practitioners for the sake of solving real problems (Fry & Smith, 1987; Garner, 1972; Pinder, 1982).

If managers and behavioral scientists are mutually dependent on one another in the ways already described, how can a progressive management group decide in favor of formal attempts to install behavioral science-based programs and engage in application of the second type described earlier? One obvious basis for deciding that a theory is ready and safe for application is the level of scientific validity the theory has demonstrated in research-oriented applications of the first type just described and explained in detail earlier in the chapter.[8] By way of contrast, there may be a case against reliance on validity alone, as we see in the following section.

Application: Validity or Marginal Utility?

In response to a paper written by the author (Pinder, 1977), Bobko (1978) suggested that the absolute level of validity of a theory of motivation is an inappropriate basis for determining whether

---

[8] The reader will recall that we also described other, nonscientific criteria for the adoption of theories, such as interest value and the caring ethic. The focus here is on an issue related only to validity per se.

formal application of that theory is warranted or justified. He argued that managers must make decisions on a day-to-day basis, using implicit theories of human nature and motivation to guide them (see Chapter 3 of this volume). The decisions reached on the basis of these implicit, informal theories result in more or less value (or utility) for their respective organizations. Bobko (1978) argued that whether a manager should employ a formal theory of motivation to guide human resource-related decisions should depend on the marginal utility (or extra value) added by application of the theory. (Cronbach and Gleser, 1965, made the same argument with regard to the use of psychological tests for the selection of personnel.)

Bobko's argument was compelling, but as argued elsewhere, the application of his marginal utility criterion for determining whether or not to apply a formal theory of motivation is impractical (Pinder, 1978). To follow Bobko's advice, a manager would be required to estimate the base rate of effective motivation-related decisions (or influence attempts) between him- or herself and each employee prior to the application of a particular theory. The manager would then have to estimate the value of decisions (or influence attempts) that are made with the assistance of the particular theory in question and determine whether the value added as a consequence of the advice provided by the theory is sufficient to justify its use. This would be impractical, if not impossible, in view of the many difficulties associated with assessing individual job performance (see Latham & Wexley, 1981) and the fact that a particular supervisor's success would vary from one subordinate to another as well as across time and across circumstances for all employees. Moreover, in view of the complexity of organizational events, it would be very difficult to rule out explanations other than the application theoretical principles if changes in decision-making effectiveness did seem to occur.

On balance, utility may be a reasonable criterion, in principle, for deciding when a theory is ready for application, but the practical difficulties it poses make it hard to employ. The enlightened manager is left, therefore, with the validity of a new theory as the only "objective" basis for deciding on its formal adoption in practice. This raises the next questions we address in this chapter: How valid (and useful) are our major theories of work motivation, and are we capable of knowing the answer?

WORK MOTIVATION THEORY: VALID, UNBIASED, AND VALUE FREE?

We introduced some of the many varieties of validity early in this chapter as a basis for evaluating social science theory and research. Now we return to the issue of validity and other criteria that have been applied to the assessment of theories of work motivation, the principal concern of this book. The question of the absolute validity of current work motivation theory is difficult to answer with much certainty, for a variety of reasons. Some of these are a matter of measurement and statistics; others are much more basic, having to do with fundamental issues in the philosophy and sociology of organizational science. We examine the matter, therefore, at several levels.

Measurement Issues

First, the very means by which the concept of motivation itself is measured are limited and problematic. The reader will recall that we defined work motivation as dealing with issues of intensity, direction, and duration; it is, by definition, a multidimensional concept. Typically, however, only the concept of intensity is operationalized for the sake of representing the entire concept. This comprises a problem of construct validity, as we have discussed already (see Schwab, 1980). To make matters worse, researchers have typically measured only some of the components of the various theories, applied the various sorts of arithmetic formulas dictated by the theory in question (such as addition or multiplication of component scores), and come up with a total "score" representing the predicted level of motivation for individuals. Then some sort of correlation is conducted between these predicted levels and another outside measure or criterion variable. Often, perhaps usually, the same sort of problem occurs: What is used as the outside criterion, the basis that will be used to validate the theoretical predictions made by the theory?

Sometimes variables such as supervisory rating are employed. Sometimes individual levels of *performance* are used as the criterion. (In Chapter 1, we discussed the error of confusing motivation with performance; they simply are not the same thing.) Aside from the fact that many of these outside criteria are inappropriate by their very nature, they are frequently subject to measurement problems of their own (such as unreliability). As a result, it can be very difficult to find significant and meaningful correlations between the levels of motivation predicted by the components of a theory (and as measured by the tools of the researcher) and external criteria that are supposed to verify (or validate) the theory under examination. For this reason, many of the theories available to us may in fact be more valid than we as social scientists are capable of demonstrating with our crude tools. The good news is that continuing development of more valid scales for the measurement of organizational and individual constructs has alleviated some of these problems in recent years (e.g., Fields, 2002) and the development of more appropriate research designs such as within-person, repeated measures approaches (cf. Hormuth, 1986) has also helped considerably.

The Validity and Usefulness of Work Motivation Theories

Just how valid are current theories of work motivation? There have been a number of attempts over the past two decades to answer this question. In most cases, the issue addressed is the judged *comparative* value of the theories in question, not their absolute levels per se. The people making the judgments are typically "experts" in the field, and the criteria used are not normally comparative validity, utility, and influence in the field. We summarize two of these studies in detail to illustrate the usual procedure.

In 1984 a senior academic industrial psychologist reported a study that examined the importance, validity, and usefulness of 32 established organizational science theories, the most common of which were theories of work motivation (Miner, 1984). The purpose of the study was to see whether there was any relationship among the three variables of interest. Miner solicited the "importance" ratings from a panel of key journal editors and former journal editors, asking them to nominate theories on the basis of their usefulness in understanding, explaining, and predicting organizational behavior. The nominations were also to take into account whether the theories had clear implications for practice and applications in management settings and whether the theories had generated significant research. (Notice the similarity between the criteria Miner used with his judges and the criteria we discussed earlier in this chapter.) In short, then, independent experts rated the *importance* of theories. The theories that were culled from those nominated in this fashion were then rated by Miner himself on the basis of two other criteria. One was his estimate of the *scientific validity* of each of the theories; that is, whether scientific tests had been carried out on them and had been supportive of some or all of the major tenets of each theory. Miner's third criterion (again, as rated by himself) was one that we discussed earlier in this chapter – the theories' estimated *usefulness*, "the extent to which the theory had contributed applications that could be put to use in practice to achieve stated goals" (Miner, 1984, p. 297).[9]

Then, using simple statistics of association, Miner examined the relationships among the three rating criteria over the 32 theories of organizational behavior. His findings were interesting:

---

[9] The notion of usefulness was mentioned earlier; we return to a discussion of it toward the end of the chapter.

1. No relationship was found between ratings of importance and scientific validity (despite the fact that his independent raters had been asked to consider validity in their determination of the theories' importance).
2. Similarly, there was no relationship between ratings of importance (by the outside panel) and Miner's own ratings of the theories' usefulness (again despite the fact that usefulness was one criterion the external judges were asked to use to rate importance).
3. There was only a slight relationship between the criteria of validity and usefulness (the two criteria by which Miner judged the theories himself).
4. Of most significance for our discussion here, there was a highly significant clustering of theories of work motivation (as opposed to other areas of management and organizational science) in the high-validity/high-usefulness cell. In other words, it was the various theories of work motivation that had been disproportionately rated as high in importance by the judges and at the same time rated as high in scientific validity by Miner himself.

Miner (2003) replicated his study 20 years later and reached fundamentally the same conclusions, with a few interesting exceptions. In the earlier study, the various criteria failed to inter-correlate highly among themselves, indicating that the different evaluative dimensions were tapping different values or underlying dimensions. In the 2003 study, however, the ratings provided on the importance dimension were moderately correlated with ratings on validity. Similarly, importance and usefulness were correlated positively. Of particular interest to our present purpose is that theories and models of work motivation were among the most highly rated in importance and validity. Miner (2003, p. 259) concluded: If one wishes to create a highly valid theory, which is also constructed with the purpose of enhanced usefulness in practice in mind, it would be best to look to motivation theories' (p. 259).

By now, the reader is probably wondering: Aside from all these considerations, which are the most valid theories of work motivation today? We answer this question gradually as we present, discuss, and evaluate the various perspectives throughout the book. But for the curious, we will side for the time being with those reviewers who cite goal-setting theory and social cognitive theory as probably the most valid theories of work motivation available today. These two theories are presented in Chapters 13 and 14, respectively.

The *Relevance* Criterion

Miner's (1984, 2003) work suggests another criterion for the evaluation of work motivation theory (or any organizational theory). Actually, as discussed by Thomas and Tymon (1982), the relevance criterion is related more directly to the evaluation of the research on which the theories are based, but nevertheless, their concepts of research relevance have a major bearing on the "value" of the theory that emerges from such research. Thomas and Tymon (1982) see relevance as consisting of five key components. For them, to be relevant a theory should be:

1. As concerned with generalizability as it is with tight, internal standards of scientific rigor.
2. Focused on problems that managers and administrators actually have to deal with, even if these are not obvious or hard to measure and conceptualize. Researchers have tended to work on problems (or dependent variables) that are tractable or interesting from a scholarly perspective, as opposed to problems that are "real" to the average person regardless of how slippery these problems may be.
3. Capable of being applied and implemented by manipulation of the independent variables contained in the theory.
4. *Non-obvious*: The theory should offer the practitioner insights that are not readily available by mature common sense or everyday experience.

5. *Timely*: The theory should be available to deal with problems when the problems are, in fact, problematic, not too late to be of value, after events have run their natural courses.

The *Usefulness* and *Practicality* Criteria

Earlier we mentioned that Miner (1984, 2003) assessed theories of organizational behavior on the basis of their usefulness. Following Miner's first review, Brief and Dukerich (1991) addressed the issue of usefulness and have argued that it is not a reasonable or appropriate basis on which to evaluate theories in the organizational sciences. Whereas Miner defined usefulness as "the extent to which the theory had contributed applications that could be put to use in practice to achieve stated goals" (p. 297), Brief and Dukerich (1991) conceived of usefulness as "a theory's prescriptive value in terms of the degree to which it contains actionable solutions to 'real world' problems" (p. 328). They then differentiated between usefulness and *practicality*, which they defined as follows:

> A practical theory is an idea generator – it is capable of stimulating practitioners to view their worlds in ways they might not otherwise have. A practical theory can suggest courses of action but, unlike a prescriptive ("useful") theory, it is not an advocate of one particular course of action.
>
> (Brief & Dukerich, 1991, p. 341)

Brief and Dukerich put forward a conservative argument embraced by this author (Pinder, 1977). Their argument has many strands, the most important of which for our purposes is that all knowledge in the social and behavioral sciences has limited generalizability; it is bounded by the nature of the people on whom it is founded and by the contexts in which it is generated. They use a specific example from the literature on goal setting – one of the major theories discussed in this book – to illustrate their point. They believe that the best organizational scientists can and should offer is to develop and advance practical theory, not useful theory. They point out that we can never really take into account all the contextual variables that are at play when a research project is undertaken to yield or to test a theory, so to presume to make predictions and prescriptions on the basis of research done in the present or the past is risky. They argue that the best thinking on a matter of organizational behavior at a given point in time may become obsolete with the passage of time and with the further "discovery" of new variables and "boundary conditions" as further research is conducted. Brief and Kuderich believe that the best we can expect from organizational science is description and explanation, but not prediction, and certainly not prescription. They state that "usefulness as a criterion for evaluating organizational behavior theories would appear to be threatened by such failure to expect generalizability or, at least minimally, by the inability to specify a priori, in any certain way, the likelihood that a prescription will hold in a given context . . . What *might* work is different from saying it either will work or should work in a probabilistic sense" (Brief & Dukerich, 1991, p. 337).

The distinction between *useful* and *practical* is adopted in this book, along with the conservative implications the distinction implies. Again, quoting Brief and Dukerich (1991): "Present theory may be the best we have *to raise people's consciousness*, not to specify particular actions in particular contexts. Since we cannot be sure what specific parts of any theory may be fallible or not, we assert that it is inappropriate to make authoritative statements based on the theory" (p. 346).

COMPLICATING MODELS OF WORK MOTIVATION

In Chapter 1, we discussed the tension that has often occurred in the application of work motivation theory between those who want simple solutions (one- or two-factor models, for example) and those who insist on developing, testing, and offering models that seek to capture more of the complexity of human motivation, attitudes, emotions, and behavior in complex organized settings. A recent review of the literature by Latham and Pinder (2005) offered 10 major conclusions about the development of theory and research in work motivation over the past 10 to 30 years. In a nutshell, the authors concluded (among other things) that models have become more complex and, presumably, more realistic, cautions offered by critics such as Brief and Dukerich (1991) notwithstanding. Therefore, in this section, we examine the forms and means by which work motivation theories and models have become more complex and we attempt to derive some principles for future development of the field.

Occam's Razor vs. Requisite Variety: Context and Mediating Factors in Work Motivation Theory and Research

Our definition of work motivation (see page 11) indicates that it is "a set of energetic forces that originate both within *as well as beyond an individual's being*" (emphasis added). Hence, contrary to prevailing beliefs of just 50–60 years ago, we view work motivation as an internal psychological process *resulting from the interaction between the individual and the environment, or context in which the individual exists*. Indeed, in their *Annual Review of Psychology* chapter devoted exclusively to work motivation in the late 1970s, Korman, Greenhaus, and Badin (1977), consistent with Cronbach (1975), warned against the potentially ephemeral nature of moderator variables in human affairs. (Context variables would be categorized as moderators in this view.) As mentioned in Chapter 1, the fields of psychology and organizational behavior underwent a round of controversy and debate during the 1980s over the relative importance of dispositions (the force of main effects attributable to stable human characteristics) and contexts (cf. Chatman, 1989; Edwards, 1994; Pervin, 1968; Schneider, Smith, & Paul, 2001).

This debate notwithstanding, the majority position of scholarly reviews of work motivation theory and research since Korman et al. (1977) has been to support the necessity of considering context to increase our understanding of work-related motivation, attitudes, and behavior (e.g., Mowday & Sutton, 1993; O'Reilly, 1991; Pinder, 1998). *Moderator variables spell out the contexts in which psychological factors operate, or are magnified or attenuated, and/or they identify the types of people who can be expected to react to particular types of contextual circumstances, such as enriched jobs, for example.* (See Baron & Kenny, 1986, for a formal treatment of moderator and mediator variables.)

Mediating Mechanisms

Simultaneously, there has been increased attention paid in recent decades to *mediating variables*, which purport to facilitate our understanding of *why* independent variables affect outcome variables (cf. Baron & Kenny, 1986). For example, if we hypothesize that a certain type of leadership style affects employee behavior through the effects that that style has on employee trust, then employee trust would be cast in the role of a mediating variable, or mediating mechanism, to explain the observed effects of leader style on employee behavior. As we examine the bulk of the literature on work motivation since the late 1970s, we observe a proliferation of more complex models than those of earlier times, models that postulate the effects of moderator variables or mediating mechanisms, or – in some cases – both (cf. Latham & Pinder, 2005).

A masterful piece of research by Timothy Judge and Daniel Cable (2004) illustrated the development and testing of a model using mediating variables. The basic proposition that initiated their research is interesting: Tall people do better in life than shorter people. Using meta-analysis, Judge and Cable reviewed the extant literature linking the proposition that taller people do better in careers and life than shorter people. The meta-analysis established that there is indeed a main effect: Tall people are more successful in many endeavors than shorter people. They then constructed a model, based on diligent theory and previous work, to hypothesize *why* tall people may have more successful careers. Hence, the key players in their model are as follows: Independent variable, a person's height; the dependent variable: Career success. Next, they proposed a modification to the simple model by hypothesizing that a person's height influences his or her career success through the effects of the influence of the person's height on a number of mediating variables such as social esteem and self-esteem. They then tested the possibility that this effect has different impacts on men, as opposed to women (so gender played the role of a potential moderator variable in the expanded model). Using fresh data sets, they supported their model: Height affects a person's social esteem and self-esteem, which, in turn, both have impacts on career and life success. The trick in constructing and testing such models, of course, is the diligent use of theory and reason as one posits mediating (and moderated) causal mechanisms.

A Glance Ahead

In the remaining sections of this chapter, we will: (1) examine the notion of context and discuss generic ways by which it has been used to make work motivation models more elaborate than they were in previous years; (2) report on the research of a few specific approaches to contextualizing motivation models – including studies that have included dimensions of organizational structure, climate and culture, and social support; (3) revisit the role that mediating variables have played, providing a specific example from a recent empirical study as an illustration. In short, our purpose is to promote an examination of the importance of elaborating motivation models (without over-doing it!) and to provide examples and suggestions for how this trend may be pursued beneficially in the future.

Moderator Variables: What *is* Context?

Johns (2006) defined context as "situational opportunities and constraints that affect the occurrence and meaning of organizational behavior as well as functional relationships between variables" (p. 386). He pointed out that context (such as, for example, a type of reward system), can serve as either a main effect or a factor that interacts with individual-level or dispositional variables in determining outcomes such as motivation, performance, and so on. In the workplace, the most common features of context that scholars have examined include the following categories of variables: The design of jobs; leadership styles; organizational policies and practices (especially with regard to human resources management); group processes; personal networks; psychological contracts; organization structures, cultures, and climates; and even the demographic characteristics of cohorts. Later in this chapter, we discuss the increasingly important role that national culture is playing in the study of all social sciences, including the study of work motivation. To paraphrase Johns (2006), researchers have certainly studied the main effects of these and other contextual variables on work motivation, but too seldom have researchers considered the joint or interactive effects of such variables with individual-level variables such as, for example, the individual's age, growth-need strength, or ability. But there is more to context than this!

Time Setting as Context

The *time* in which a study is conducted or during which an event occurs is an important but frequently overlooked context variable. Careful specification of the time during which independent variables are manipulated or measured and when measures are taken on dependent variables is necessary for organizational researchers to establish valid causal relationships among variables (Mitchell & James, 2001). Time is also important when considered over longer terms as we attempt to develop a cumulative social science of work motivation because, as noted by Cronbach (1975) decades ago, fundamental changes in the relationships among human and social variables are likely to occur from one generation to another. His observation may have particularly strong relevance when we consider the study of human events on work settings while the very nature of work and/or work organizations is changing so rapidly (see Rousseau & Fried, 2001).

Type of Person as Context

Sometimes researchers develop theories about relationships between independent and dependent variables and find that relationships hold among only certain types of person. In Chapter 7, for example, we will review the history of the study of enlarged and enriched jobs, and learn that theorists in different decades argued that job redesign may have valuable outcomes for only certain types of person (the challenge was to find reliable ways of determining which people these were).

Roles Played by Variables is (Somewhat) Arbitrary

A final note requires emphasis here. Any researcher may generate and test any of a number of models that assign particular variables to any of a number of roles. So, for example, organizational climate may serve in one research model as an independent variable (e.g., climate causes retention/turnover rates), a mediating variable (leadership style affects retention/turnover through its effects on climate), a moderator variable (e.g., leadership style affects retention/turnover in only certain types of organizational climate), or even as a dependent variable (retention/turnover rates determine organizational climate characteristics). It is a mistake to assume that any particular variable, particularly those highlighted in this chapter in our discussion of contexts, moderators, and mediators must be exclusively assigned to any particular role in research models.

In this chapter, as well as in later chapters, we examine research and theory involving many of these contextual factors. We will see that particular theories and models that include moderator/context variables generally offer idiosyncratic explanations for the "boundary effects" they imply, but only recently has there been a systematic attempt to develop a general view of the effects of context variables in the organizational sciences. Therefore, to set the stage for our study of specific theories of work motivation that explicitly include moderator variables, we summarize the recent work of Johns (2006) and Rousseau and Fried (2001).

How Does Context Influence Work Motivation?

Johns (2006) provided a typology of the means by which contextual factors can influence organizational behavior research. Seven of his categories are most significant for our purpose here – of understanding the causes and consequences of work motivation.

First, contexts can provide opportunities for, or constraints against, human effects. Sometimes these constraining or facilitating effects are strong; other times they are weak. Sometimes they don't appear significant at all until or unless they are at such a level as to create a "tipping point" (Gladwell, 2000), then effects occur. An apparently not-so-critical remark by a domineering supervisor, for example, may be the "straw that breaks the camel's back" for a disgruntled employee who has bottled up her anger for months in the face of other, similar remarks (e.g., see Harlos & Pinder, 1999).

A second variety is the means by which variables at one level of analysis influence variables at another level of analysis. In motivation theory and research, this usually takes the form of situational or context variables (such as the design of a job or the culture of an organization) affecting variables at the individual level. It is possible for the causal effects to flow in the opposite direction however. For example, a particularly salient leadership style of an individual executive can have a powerful impact on organizational climate or culture. Third, sometimes management practices or policies, when considered as a package, can have interactive effects on individual factors when the context variables, taken alone, have no effect, a reduced effect, or a magnified effect. Rousseau and Fried call this "configuration" (2001, p. 4). Hence the effects of a particular form of monthly pay system may have quite different effects on employee satisfaction and performance depending on the nature and variety of benefits offered, the levels of compensation that are paid, and so forth.

Fourth, sometimes a single event (such as a strike or a lockout, for example) can influence organizational behavior in interesting ways that might not otherwise occur. Fifth, contexts can influence the interpretation applied to events or to the relationships among variables. Johns (2006) offered the example of how being an individualist in a primarily individualistic culture may engender different attitudes and behavior than would be the case for someone with an individualistic orientation who is operating in the context of a collectivist culture (more on this later).

Finally, because most research is conducted using cross-sectional designs, frequently involving only single levels of analysis, many assumptions are made about how relationships among these variables would be altered with the passage of time or with the relaxation of other variables that are considered "other things equal" or not considered at all. Rousseau and Fried stated: "One person's context is another person's taken-for granted assumption" (2001, p. 3).

In short, both Rousseau and Fried (2001) and Johns (2006) have delineated a variety of generic ways by which contextual variables can influence the design, results and the interpretations applied to the results of organizational research. Their work reminds us of the belief held by many scholars that the design of useful research is really an art. It also encourages us to be cautious when we read and consider the research of other scholars who may not delineate completely the contexts in which their variables of primary interest are manipulated and/or measured. Johns (as well as Rousseau & Fried, 2001) would suggest that, in many cases, researchers themselves may not be aware of contextual effects and that greater and greater importance falls on the tenets of good research design (see our discussion earlier in this chapter) to ensure that new findings about work motivation comprise valid knowledge about it.

How to Contextualize

Rousseau and Fried (2001) offered three general approaches to assist researchers in their attempts to contextualize their work. The first, generally, is to engage in "rich description," through focusing more heavily than otherwise on the settings in which research is conducted, to draw comparisons of one's research with that of earlier studies, to explicitly consider how events and phenomena in a particular study might be interpreted differently in different settings, by different people or at different times, considering whether the range of variation in the independent variables included in one's research represents the full range potentially covered, and evaluating the role that time plays (as mentioned earlier).

A second set of approaches is more active than the first. It involves actually measuring or observing context factors and deliberately building them into one's research model as mediators, moderators, or independent variables. One might also simply focus on events as the phenomena of interest or study configurations of practices or features of the context simultaneously. (We discussed configurations earlier.)

The third general approach recommended by Rousseau and Fried (2001) for contextualizing research is to conduct comparative studies in which individuals and/or organizations in different times, places or circumstances are explicitly studied in juxtaposition with one another.

Contextualizing and External Validity

In short, one might conclude that contextualizing research sets an additional layer of challenges for social scientists as they conduct their craft. On the other hand, we remind the reader that the external validity of research requires, in addition to internally valid results (results that cannot be realistically interpreted by hypotheses other than those posed by the researcher), generalizability of these findings across actors, settings, and times (see Cook & Campbell, 1979). In this light, the requirement to contextualize is no more than a requirement to conduct research that has a chance of enjoying some degree of external validity once it is completed and reported.

Summary and a Glance Ahead

During his April 1, 2005 "Fireside Chat" at the 2005 Annual Meeting of the Western Academy of Management in Las Vegas, venerated motivation scholar Lyman Porter observed that the field of organizational behavior in general "has featured far too much 'B' and not enough on 'O' " – meaning that there has been far too little concern for the organizational contexts within which "organizational behavior" occurs. We agree with Dr. Porter. In the following sections of this chapter, we turn to a number of the more successful attempts that have been made to contextualize work motivation, beginning with what are known as "goodness of fit models."

Goodness of Fit Models

By definition, so-called "person–environment fit" or "goodness of fit" models simultaneously consider individual and contextual variables to understand human motivation, attitudes, and behavior. The basic notion underlying these models is that the relationship between individual characteristics (such as need or abilities, for example) and both individual and organizational outcomes is contingent upon characteristics of the task or the organization as a whole (Kristof, 1996). Models of this variety originated with the seminal work of Patterson, Darley, and Elliott (1936). Later, Shaffer (1953) used Murray's (1938) definition and typology of needs to develop a goodness of fit model that takes into account individual differences in needs of employees and the different characteristics of jobs. The relationship between individual characteristics (e.g., need or abilities) and both individual and organizational outcomes is contingent upon characteristics of the job or the organization as a whole (Kristof, 1996). Thus goodness of fit models consider individual and contextual variables simultaneously.

The concept of fit, itself, has been dimensionalized and classified into subcategories. For example, Muchinsky and Monahan (1987) distinguished between *supplementary congruence*, the degree of fit between an individual and a group of people comprising the "environment," and *complementary congruence*, the degree of correspondence between a person's talents and the needs of the environment. Cable and DeRue (2002), through a confirmatory factor analysis, found that employees differentiate between three varieties of fit: (1) person–environment fit; (2) "needs–supplies" fit; and (3) job demands–abilities fit. The first of the two forms of fit result in benefits for both persons and organizations. Similarly, at the individual level, Holtom, Lee, and Tidd (2002) found that matching employees' preferences for full- or part-time work status benefited job satisfaction, commitment, retention as well as extra-role and in-role behaviors. Kristof-Brown, Jansen, and

Colbert (2002) showed that three varieties of person–context fit can have simultaneous positive effects on job satisfaction. Edwards (1994) compared two versions ("supplies/values" and "demands/ abilities") of fit models. He found that the former was more effective in predicting job dissatisfaction while the latter was better at predicting individual tension among graduate business students performing a managerial task. Both models were related to both forms of strain. Hollenbeck and Wagner (2002) developed a model expanding notions of fit across several levels of analysis at once and found that there is benefit in studying both the degree of fit between individuals and groups simultaneously with the degree of fit between those groups and their task environments.

Theory of Work Adjustment

One of the field's earliest and most successful goodness of fit models was the University of Minnesota's *theory of work adjustment* (TWA) (Dawis & Lofquist, 1984). One major feature of that work is that it postulated and demonstrated that two mediating variables, job satisfaction and "satisfactoriness" (performance), linked person–occupation match, on the one hand, with longevity on the job (their primary dependent variable), on the other. Note that the primary focus of TWA was not on work motivation, per se, but the quality of the theory, including its conceptual base, psychometric sophistication, and practical applicability to the rehabilitation of injured workers make it more than worthy of consideration here.

The model hypothesizes that a person is satisfied with his or her occupation to the extent that there is a match between the individual's needs and the *reinforcers* offered by that occupation, assuming that the individual is performing satisfactorily at the work. By the same token, a person was hypothesized to be proficient at a job to the extent that there is a match between the individual's abilities and the ability requirements of the job, assuming that he or she is satisfied with the job. In short, employee satisfaction is necessary but not sufficient for satisfactory performance, and satisfactory performance is necessary but not sufficient for employee satisfaction. In order to understand either employee satisfaction or satisfactoriness, it was necessary to take into account the other variable as well as the goodness of fit between the person's needs and abilities as well as the ability requirements of the job and the rewards it offers.

TWA provides a theoretically rich and practically useful model for understanding the two most studied variables in organizational behavior, satisfaction and performance, as well as the relationships between them, in large part because of the central role played in the model by intelligent moderator and mediating variables.[10] Work adjustment theory set an early and high standard for subsequent goodness of fit models to emulate.

Attraction–Selection–Attrition

One of the most comprehensive models of P–E fit is that of Schneider and his colleagues (see Schneider et al., 2001, for a summary). In brief, their theory is based on an "attraction–selection– attrition" (ASA) model that hypothesizes that organizations attract and retain individuals who are similar to those already employed by the organization. The model places heavy emphasis on the importance of the personal characteristics of founders who begin the process of attracting employees who are similar to themselves. Unlike most other goodness of fit theories, Schneider's explicitly addresses the dysfunctions of interpersonal homogeneity (such as the dangers of limited perspectives for decision making, groupthink, etc.) as well as the putative benefits (such as high levels of interpersonal harmony and job satisfaction). Most of the work done with this approach has been

---

[10] TWA would be classified by Cable and DeRue (2002) as an example of a combined needs–supplies model and a job demands–abilities model.

conducted at the level of individual organizations. However, Schneider, Smith, Taylor, and Fleenor (1998) found high levels of homogeneity among the personalities of managers within enterprises and even across organizations within industries. Schneider's ASA model offers a fascinating meso-level approach that integrates individual, organizational, and industry-wide parameters, including plausible hypotheses to explain mediating mechanisms.

Social Cognitive Theory

Among the most sophisticated current theories of work motivation that is predicated on person-by-context interactions is Bandura's (1986, 2001) *social cognitive theory*. Although not really a goodness of fit model that predicts positive outcomes for close matches between people and their environments, as in the case of the other theories discussed already, its major tenet is that human behavior (including human work behavior) is a joint function of the interaction between the individual, his or her behavior, and the environment in which the individual is situated. The author has declared this theory to be one of the most valid and useful among the many theories of work motivation available today (Latham & Pinder, 2005). We will discuss this theory at length in Chapter 14, so no more will be presented at this point.

Criticisms of Goodness of Fit

Fit models have long been plagued by the traditional difficulties related to the use of difference scores (cf. Johns, 1981). Edwards (1994) proposed an alternative method based on a polynomial regression procedure that avoids those difficulties. Accordingly, O'Reilly, Chatman, and Caldwell (1991), and Chatman (1991) developed and tested the "organizational culture profile," which is based on a Q-sort methodology to assess goodness of fit. They found that similarity of values between the individual and the organization at the time of hiring as well as the strength of the socialization an employee experiences after being hired were critical in predicting job satisfaction and tenure.

Another criticism of goodness of fit theory and research is that the interaction between the person and characteristics of the job or organization are usually treated as a steady state rather than dynamic. (Recall what Johns, 2006, had to say about this.) Moreover, there are no agreed-upon ways of assessing dynamic interactions (Borman, Klimoski, & Ilgen, 2003).

In a recent review, Hulin and Judge (2003) concluded that the conceptual advantages of goodness of fit models have not yielded significant gains in understanding of workplace affect or behavior. We hold a more positive position, expecting that improvements in measurement, especially in the definition and calibration of "fit," and the inclusion of time variables into fit models may help to advance the goodness of fit cause (cf. Fried & Slowik, 2004; George & Jones, 2000; Katz, 1980). Clearly, a return to main-effects or dispositional models will not move the field forward substantially.

SOME SPECIFIC AND IMPORTANT CONTEXT VARIABLES

A key purpose in this book is to highlight the means by which researchers and theorists have responded to the call of critics for increased attention to context (hence our focus on moderator variables and boundary conditions) and to fleshing out the means through which causal factors influence outcome variables (in other words, including mediating mechanisms in their work). The foregoing treatment has introduced some of these ideas in general terms and provided a few of the more notable generic approaches that have been attempted. There is a nearly limitless number of contextual factors one might consider (hence the point made by Brief & Dukerich, 1991, referenced earlier), so it is difficult to know where to stop listing them and where to proceed with a discussion of the major theories of work motivation – the primary purpose of this volume. So we have decided to break the task from here on into pieces. In the following sections of this chapter, we will examine recent developments in which organizational characteristics have played roles of moderators or mediators and delay until later chapters our discussions of other classes of variables that have played these roles – notably national culture (which will be examined in Chapter 3 as part of our discussion of needs and values) and job characteristics (which will be examined in relation to our discussion of intrinsic motivation in Chapter 7). Therefore, given that context variables are usually (or at least often) those that occur at one level of abstraction higher than individual variables, we turn to a focus on the roles played by three important organizational variables in our study of work motivation: Organizational structure, organizational climate, and organizational culture.

Organizational Structure

The organizational sciences have devoted considerable attention over the years to various formally and informally defined features of work organizations. For example, researchers examined a long list of formal characteristics of organizational structure (cf. Hall, 1991). Dimensions of structure have included, among other things, the degree of division of labor, the number of hierarchical levels in the structure, the span of control (average number of people supervised by managers and executive), formalization of procedures, standardization of procedures (from one location to another), and even organizational size. For the most part, empirical attempts to find relationships between these various dimensions and outcome variables, such as employee satisfaction and performance, were disappointing: Where relationships were found between structural variables and outcome variables, they were weak and of limited practical value to either managers or academics (see Berger & Cummings, 1979, for a review). However, little empirical attention was directed at relationships between structural variables and work motivation, the phenomenon of major interest in this book.

Organizational Climate

By the early 1970s, perhaps in part because of the disappointments with the study of formal structure, organizational scholars turned attention to a newer concept, referred to as *organizational climate* (see Litwin & Stringer, 1968). (Much earlier than that, Fleishman, 1953, discussed the effects of leadership climate in organizations, but our focus here will be on organizational climate, per se, as a manifestation of context.) Different teams of researchers generated different lists of dimensions of climate and, naturally, found differing relationships with outcome variables. As often happens when a new construct is introduced, there was more chaos than meaning.

Ultimately, Ostroff (1993) successfully proposed and supported a 12-dimension model of climate that she factor analyzed into three primary components: (1) an affect component that concerns interpersonal and social relationships among coworkers; (2) a cognitive component that deals with the individual's relationship with the work; and (3) an instrumental component that deals with the involvement of people and the orientation toward getting things accomplished in the organization. Her work provided a solid empirical and conceptual base upon which other work has been based. For example, a significant meta-analysis by Carr, Schmidt, Ford, and DeShon (2003) has demonstrated how Ostroff's (1993) three facets of climate relate to individual job performance, psychological well-being, and withdrawal through the mediating effects of organizational commitment and job satisfaction. This is one of only a few solid demonstrations that climate deserves a place in causal models as a mediator between antecedent and outcome variables.

An example of a consciously managed climate is found in one of Canada's leading fast-food chains, A&W. Founded in 1956, A&W has continued to grow successfully across Canada and the United States; in 2002, the company opened its 600th restaurant. Total revenue in 2003 was $475 million, based on a total workforce of 18,000 employees. In large part because of its "climate goal process," the company was named as one of "Canada's 50 best-managed companies" in both 2002 and 2003. The climate goal process is a program that sets out the attributes, values, and behaviors it embraces and encourages its personnel to pursue. This program has been an explicit part of A&W's strategic planning model since 1977. The company claims the practice of rewarding and practicing these seven styles has provided the company a competitive advantage that is reflected in lower staff turnover as well as high levels of commitment and motivation. The seven climate goals are the following: Listening, trust, self-responsibility, appreciation, teams, getting better, and being extraordinary.

Climate strength

A considerable amount of work on climate has been produced by Schneider and his associates, with service management as its major concern (e.g., Schneider, White, & Paul, 1998). A newly emerging construct in this tradition is *climate strength*, a notion analogous to *culture strength* in the culture literature reflecting the degree of within-unit variability/homogeneity of climate perceptions (Klein, Conn, Smith, & Sorra, 2001; Schneider, Salvaggio, & Subirats, 2002). In one large bank study (Schneider & Salvaggio, 2002), climate strength was found to moderate the relationship between one measure of employee perceptions of service climate and customer satisfaction, although it failed to perform as anticipated in the case of three other service climate scales. In other words, the degree of homogeneity of employee beliefs about managerial practices accounted for significant variance in customer satisfaction after the main effect for managerial practices was accounted for. Gonzáles-Romá, Peiró, and Tordera (2002) found that intra-group social interaction and the degree to which leaders kept employees informed were related to two of three elements of climate strength studied (goals orientation and innovation, but not social support). Likewise, as predicted, climate strength strengthened the relationship between climate innovation levels and both job satisfaction and organizational commitment. But climate strength did not serve as an effective mediator, as predicted, between antecedent and outcome variables – once climate quality level was taken into account – in a study of nearly 1200 employees from 180 organizations (Lindell & Brandt, 2000).

Specific climates for specific purposes

On balance, it appears that climate strength may be an important concept in climate research although more work is required to flesh out a nomological net for it. Meanwhile, Schneider and Salvaggio (2002) have proposed that the general, broad concept of climate be differentiated and defined in reference to specific activities or concerns, such as customer service, safety, etc. Accordingly, Zohar (2002) has demonstrated the potential of this differentiated approach, reviewing the literature on safety climate, while Amabile (1998) has described how to design and manage organizations to foster creativity, Schneider, Bowen, Ehrhart, and Holcombe (2000) have explained in detail their concept of the "climate for service," Yang, Mossholder, and Peng (2007) have studied a construct referred to as *procedural justice climate* (see Chapter 11 of this book) and Dastmalchian (in press) has advanced his concept of "industrial relations climate" which is defined as "the perceptions of organizational members about the norms, conduct, practice, and atmosphere of union-management relations in the workplace" (Blyton, Dastmalchian, and Adamson, 1987; Dastmalchian, in press, p. 1). On the darker side, Ashforth and Anand (2003) have described climates and cultures that encourage corruption, cheating and illegal behaviors (see Chapter 5).

Lawler (1992) provided the benefit of years of research and experience in the design of organizational climates for enhancing the attraction and retention of employees, as well as for encouraging motivation, performance, skill development, the reinforcement of organizational climate and culture, and minimizing cost. For example, reward systems that link formal rewards to performance provide a strong endorsement about what is valued and what is not valued in an organization. Paying relatively high wages, salaries, and benefits can foster employees' beliefs that they are working for an elite, top-flight company. Innovative pay systems foster beliefs that the organization is, in general, innovative. And having employees participate in pay decisions can foster feelings of high employee trust, innovativeness, and involvement, which may foster commitment to the organization (see Chapters 7 and 12; and Lawler, 1992). The key point here, again, is that these dimensions, and many others not discussed, all comprise elements of the context within which we can best study and understand work motivation.

Organizational Culture

Organizational culture consists of the shared beliefs, norms, values, knowledge, and tacit understandings held by members of an organization or organizational subunit (e.g., Ashkanasy, Wilderom, & Peterson, 2000; Frost et al., 1991; Maehr, 1987; Sackman, 1992; Schein, 1985; Schneider, 1990). In fact, values (shared values in particular) are the very essence of cultures and of organizational cultures specifically (Meglino, Ravlin, & Adkins, 1989; O'Reilly, Chatman, & Caldwell, 1991):

> Research on culture usually begins with a set of values and assumptions . . . These values, whether conscious or unconscious, typically act as the defining elements around which norms, symbols, rituals and other cultural activities revolve . . . In this vein, basic values may be thought of as internalized normative beliefs that can guide behavior. When a social unit's members share values, they may form the basis for social expectations or norms . . . Thus, researchers who investigate culture by focusing on norms . . . are studying social expectations that are based on underlying values. Others who study culture through rituals, stories, or myths . . . are examining phenotypic outcroppings that reflect underlying beliefs and values.
>
> (O'Reilly et al., 1991, pp. 491–492)

Strong cultures

Directly analogous to the concept of "strong climate," discussed earlier, the concept of *strong culture* concerns the degree of consistency among employees' belief structures, values, and general assumptions about life. If there is limited agreement among workers regarding the relative importance of specific values in a social unit, a strong culture does not exist (Meglino, Ravlin, & Adkins, 1989; O'Reilly et al., 1991).

What are the benefits of strong organizational culture? There is some evidence that homogeneity among the value structures of organizational actors can be a source of job satisfaction, commitment, job proficiency, and long tenure (see Brown, 1976; O'Reilly et al., 1991; O'Reilly, Caldwell, & Mirable, 1992). Further, value homogeneity among employees enables managers to make better-than-chance predictions about the behaviors of their subordinates when other forms of control, such as rules or direct supervision, are not in place (Adkins, Ravlin, & Meglino, 1992; McDonald & Gandz, 1992). By standardizing the premises that organizational members use for information processing and decision making, managers can attain higher degrees of control over their personnel and greater predictability about the ways that employees will behave when not under direct supervision (Stackman, Pinder, & Connor, 2000).

What about possible benefits for employees? Adkins et al. (1992) concluded that value congruence among coworkers helps to make social cues, including information about the importance of exerting effort, and seeking to improve quality on the job, as well as the importance of attendance more salient. Van Maanen and Kunda (1989) noted that shared or *appropriate* emotions are also part of an organization's culture and that many organizations stage more-or-less formal rituals and ceremonies for the sake of teaching employees how to emote "properly." (More will be said about this in Chapter 4 when we focus directly on the role of emotions in work motivation.)

In short, proponents of strong organizational cultures claim that such cultures can be sources of positive job attitudes for workers and at the same time, powerful managerial control devices in the absence of more direct measures. If the benefits are so great, why aren't all organizations characterized by high value homogeneity?

Curiously, there has been very little empirical work conducted on the relationship between organizational culture and work motivation. Why would one expect such a connection? First, values are, after all, motivational by nature and they are one of the most central concepts in considerations of culture (see Chapter 3; and Weiner & Vardi, 1980). Second, cognitive anthropologists believe that needs, motives, and goals (as conceived of by psychologists) are insufficient to explain human behavior. They argue that a more fruitful approach is "to investigate how cognitive schemas learned in specific cultural contexts are linked to one another and to goals for action . . . [they] can have motivational force because these [schemas] not only label and describe the world, but also set forth goals (both conscious and unconscious) and elicit or include desires" (D'Andrade, 1992, p. 23). In other words, one might expect the development of schemas representing an organization's predominant beliefs, values, traditions, and mores also to develop goals with motivational properties of their own. (On this logic, there is no reason to necessarily assume that these motivational forces will be in line with those of management – they might, instead, instigate and direct behavior counter to the organization's official goals.) Nevertheless, there would seem to be sufficient conceptual reason to expect a cultural approach to organizational behavior to shed light on work motivation independent of that which results from an exclusive reliance on needs, goals, values, and other traditional psychological constructs.

Although interest in organizational culture has existed since the famous Hawthorne Studies (Roethlisberger & Dickson, 1939), the modern era of research on the topic began two decades ago (cf. Frost et al., 1985), and serious research into the *consequences* of culture in organizations was not undertaken until the early 1990s (Wilderom, Glunk, & Maslowski, 2000). The focus of most of this work has been on organizational *performance* (as opposed to work motivation (recall the distinction we made earlier between these two constructs), testing the implied hypothesis implied or declared in popular writings such by Peters and Waterman's (1982) in their early claim that "excellent" companies feature strong internal cultures. A recent rigorous review of this work has concluded that "evidence regarding the claimed predictive effect of organizational culture on organizational performance/effectiveness appears to be there, but not very convincingly so" (Wilderom et al., 2000, p. 201).

Weiner and Vardi (1980) adapted an earlier model by Fishbein and Ajzen (1975) and one that was later to emerge from Weiner (1982) to propose a conceptual model linking organizational culture to work motivation and behavior. Pivotal in their adaptation is the joint influence of commitment and instrumental beliefs in creating intentions to act. Commitment results from the shared norms and values that characterize the organization's culture. Once intentions are formed, behavior follows, subject – presumably – to the constraints imposed by Ajzen's (1991) theory of planned behavior. But no data were provided to test the model.

Are Climate and Culture Distinct?

Since the popularization of the notion of organizational culture there has been considerable discussion about the differences between this construct and the older notion of organizational *climate* (cf. Litwin & Stringer, 1968), discussed earlier in this chapter. Two papers (Denison, 1996; Payne, 2000) and at least one book (Schneider, 1990) come to grips with the supposed differences between them, generating a number of distinctions, most of which are epistemological and methodological rather than of sufficient substance, we suspect, to matter significantly to organizational participants. Reichers and Schneider (1990), for example, attempted to explain the coexistence of the two constructs in terms of a model of construct evolution, admitting that the two concepts are very similar. Since then, others have participated in the debate as empirical research on culture accelerated while that on climate seemed to diminish for a decade. Nevertheless, it still seems premature to declare that the constructs are redundant. Climate relates more to people's perceptions of formal structures, rules, and procedures whereas culture is rooted more in the informal values, language, beliefs, and traditions shared by members of a group. At the 2005 meeting of the Society for Industrial and Organizational Psychologists (SIOP) in Los Angeles, Benjamin Schneider, one of the leading scholars of these concepts, concluded (Schneider, Ehrhart, Mayer, Saltz, & Niles-Jolly, 2005) that culture offers an interpretation of the *source* of organizational behavior while climate offers a focus on the *meaning* of organizational behavior. This conclusion is consistent with the view offered by Payne (2000), who argued that scales and methods used to measure climate may be useful in the service of expanding our understanding of culture.

Popularized Concepts of Climate and Culture

The popular managerial literature has seen a boom of books and magazine articles that deal with features of organizational climate and culture and the putative benefits of having positive climates/cultures while avoiding negative ones. Business periodicals make annual lists of the "best" employers[11] and we often see that the criteria on which employers are rated and ranked are dimensions of both internal tone and texture of the organization (what academics would refer to as features of climate and/or culture) and, sometimes, to the external image of the organization in the broader community.

"Toxic" workplaces

While a comprehensive review of this literature is beyond our purpose here, we highlight for interest the idea of "toxic" workplaces – work contexts (where we think of them as cultures or climates) that feature a number of characteristic symptoms, such as: Reward systems based on mediocrity and favoritism, management by fear, constantly high stress levels among executives, restricted hiring practices that homogenize the workforce and reinforce the demographic status quo, stagnant leadership ranks, terrible public image, a view that employees are costs rather than assets, a lack of corporate vision, and a prevalence of individual egos over organizational mission and goals. Frost (2003) described the emotional pain that he claimed is an inevitable and universal byproduct of everyday organizational life. He referred to these negative emotions as *toxicity*, and described at length how, even unwittingly, the behavior of people in organizations can create negative emotions and pain for others, and how some people whom he refers to as the "toxic handlers" incur the extra cost of witnessing and attempting to assuage the toxicity suffered by others.

While some toxicity is unavoidable simply because of events that are beyond the control of even well-meaning executives and coworkers, there is a variety of other features of organizational contexts that are more deliberate, certainly more pernicious. For example, some people we work with are simply mean spirited and intentionally behave in ways that hurt their coworkers. Simple incompetence in dealing with people, Frost noted, can also create negative, hurtful emotions and generate a climate that is toxic for everyone involved. Sometimes, organizational members betray one another, break confidences, and erode the trust that has been built up between people for long periods of time. Sometimes, people can become so committed to the vision and actions of leaders or coworkers

---

[11] For example, *Maclean's* magazine publishes an annual article on the 100 best employers in Canada.

that they are seduced into an unhealthy situation in which failure and disappointment are unavoidable, especially if the person being emulated leaves the organization or abandons the causes that seduced others to follow. In short, Frost (2003) described in vivid detail how toxins are generated in organizations and how they, like the biological toxins on which his metaphor is based, can make individuals sick, in extreme cases, literally killing them. We discuss further the creation and handling of toxic emotions in Chapter 4.

Social support

As mentioned earlier, social support has been subsumed by some researchers as an element of organizational climate (e.g., Kopelman, Brief, & Guzzo, 1990). As such, it is seen as having motivational value through the effects it has on the valence of interactions between an employee and another individual who is held in high regard because of the support s/he provides. Pinder and Schroeder (1987), for example, found that high levels of perceived support facilitated the speed at which transferred employees attained satisfactory levels of performance following a particular geographic relocation. On its own right, however, social support has enjoyed increased attention in recent years. A meta-analysis by Rhoades and Eisenberger (2002) found that three categories of beneficial treatment (fairness, supervisory support, and organizational rewards and favorable job conditions). In turn, perceived support was found related to a number of significant individual (job satisfaction, positive mood) and organizational (affective commitment, performance, and lessened withdrawal behavior) outcomes.

Section Summary

In the foregoing section of this chapter, we have argued that considerable progress has been made in recent years in our understanding of work motivation because of the trend toward contextualizing in research and theory on the subject. We believe that further progress will require even more and better contextualizing than has been practiced over the past 30 years. The seductive simplicity of models based on main effects no longer appears warranted: The most powerful main effects appear to have already been studied. As Rousseau and Fried state in relation to this point: "Simplicity and parsimony are not the same when that simplicity is achieved by misrepresenting the complexity of the underlying phenomena . . . The common demands for clean (read: simple) models do not always fit with the messy reality of contemporary and organizational life" (2001, p. 3). The trick will be, in large measure, for researchers to balance the truth value of this position with the necessity of losing the traditional value attained by Occam's razor by throwing into research designs and conceptual models everything but the proverbial kitchen sink.

CHAPTER SUMMARY AND A LOOK AHEAD

It has been argued in this chapter that, on the one hand, our knowledge of work motivation consists largely of theory and that much or most of that theory is of limited or unknown validity. Moreover, it has been argued that there are risks to the premature application of work motivation theory – risks that can result in costs for the organizations that engage in such premature application, as well as for the future prospect for organizational scientists to contribute to the economic well-being of our economy. On the other hand, we have found that theory and research of the past two or three decades have withstood the demands by many practitioners for simplicity in application and have begun to develop models that are more complex than those of previous decades (see Latham &

Pinder, 2005). In short, work motivation is an important issue, about which our current knowledge is still limited. But that knowledge base is growing, and the purpose of this book is to examine and evaluate it. In Chapter 3, we explore a variety of basic assumptions that underpin current approaches to work motivation and behavior, setting up our subsequent presentations and discussions of the most important current theories available today.

PART TWO

Alternative Models of Human Functioning

Human Nature: Needs and Values as Motives at Work 3

*It is a characteristic of man that the more he becomes involved in complexity,
the more he longs for simplicity; the simpler his life becomes, the more
he longs for complexity; the busier he becomes, the stronger is his desire
for leisure; the more leisure he has, the more boredom he feels, the more
his concerns, the more he feels the allure of unconcern, the more his unconcern,
the more he suffers from vacuousness; the more tumultuous
his life, the more he seeks quietude; the more placid his life, the lonelier
he becomes and the more he quests for liveliness.*
Shin'ichi Hisamatsu (1965)
The Zen understanding of man, *The Eastern Buddhist* (n.s.), l(1)

"To some extent, almost all of us harbor beliefs about the nature of human beings, about what makes people 'tick.' To some extent we all tend to be amateur philosophers and 'naive psychologists' " (Heider, 1958). In fact, the pursuit and discovery of the basic "essence of man" has occupied thinkers since the days of early philosophy (see Fromm & Xirau, 1968; Mitchell, 1972) and continues today. It should come as no surprise that philosophers and psychologists have failed to reach unanimity on the issue of human nature. By the same token, an analysis of many of the attempts made to grapple with the problem reveals that there has been some convergence concerning a number of essential attributes of human beings (where essential attributes are seen as elements common to all people but that do not themselves comprise the essence of humanity per se). The most common of these attributes is rationality. Human beings are commonly thought of as more or less rational beings. Second, there is wide agreement that we are gregarious creatures. We tend, more or less, to exist in the presence of others. A third essential attribute of human beings is that we tend to be producers. Although many lower animals are also producers, only human beings produce according to plans developed in their own minds, and only humans are effective producers of tools, which in turn are used for further production. A final commonly agreed-upon attribute is that human beings are symbol-making creatures. We generate, acknowledge, and make use of countless symbols, the most important of which are words (Fromm & Xirau, 1968).

People tend to assess other individuals and behave in their presence according to beliefs they have about their essential characteristics, whether or not the specific set of beliefs they hold matches the set identified earlier. Nowhere is this more the case than in work and organizational settings (Knowles & Saxberg, 1967; McGregor, 1960; Tead, 1929; Urwick, 1967). To quote McGregor (1960): "Behind every managerial decision or action are assumptions about human nature and human behavior" (p. 33).

This chapter has three major purposes. The first is to examine a variety of widely held sets of assumptions about human beings that are particularly relevant when we consider work motivation and how it might be influenced. Second, we introduce a typology of human functioning – fundamental sets of assumptions we often make about the nature of human beings. This typology will serve as a major framework for organizing the various theories of work motivation throughout the book. Therefore, as theories of work motivation are presented in later chapters, the reader should bear in mind that each theory is predicated on certain sets of assumptions regarding human nature. Then, in the remaining sections we discuss two major sets of concepts that have served to help us understand the essentials of a considerable amount of human nature: Needs and values. We begin with a survey of beliefs about the underlying nature of human beings, particularly as they relate to the motivation to work.

THEORY X AND THEORY Y

One of the most insightful and enduring observations ever made by behavioral science concerning work is that of McGregor (1960). McGregor was acutely aware of the pervasiveness of a set of assumptions held by managers and administrators in particular concerning human beings at work. He referred to this set of assumptions as Theory X, the key elements of which are the following:

1. Average human adults are by nature indolent – they work as little as possible.
2. They lack ambition, dislike responsibility, and prefer to be led by other people.
3. They are inherently selfish and indifferent to organizational needs and goals.
4. They are resistant to change, by their very nature.
5. Finally, they are gullible, not very intelligent, and are easily duped by manipulators.

McGregor claimed that the importance of this implicit theory of human nature is that it lies behind much of what we observe in the practice of management. If managers believe that human nature is inherently as described by Theory X, they will formulate policies and utilize motivational and control strategies designed to tame people and coerce work effort from them. The direct result of policies, practices, and procedures of this sort is that they often cause the very behaviors that reinforce managers' beliefs that people are in fact like the Theory X model – a self-fulfilling prophesy of the sort diagrammed in Figure 3.1. Managers caught in this cycle believe that the problem lies in the basic nature of human beings. McGregor recognized that low interest, resentment, embezzling, sabotage, tardiness, and absenteeism are, in fact, commonly observed in organizations. The wisdom in his analysis lies in his recognition that these behaviors are frequently *caused* by managerial practices, which, in turn, are based on Theory X beliefs about human nature: A case of chicken and egg, with powerful implications for the design of motivation and reward systems. In practice, who can blame managers for holding views of the Theory X variety when they regularly observe behavior that reinforces those beliefs?

McGregor proposed an alternative view of human nature in work organizations which he called, simply, *Theory Y*. The main tenets of Theory Y are:

1. People are not passive by nature. They have become so as a consequence of the way they are usually treated in organizations.
2. People possess, by nature, the potential to develop, assume responsibility, and behave in accordance with organizational goals. Management's responsibility is to recognize these potentials and to make it possible for employees to develop them themselves.
3. To do this, management should structure organizational policies so that human beings can achieve their own goals while pursuing the goals of the organization.

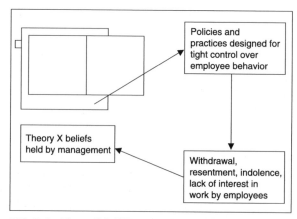

FIG. 3.1   The self-fulfilling prophesy of Theory X assumptions.

When McGregor put his observations forward more than four decades ago, he noted how difficult it would be to see Theory X supplanted by Theory Y as the basic model of human nature underlying organizational policies and procedures and managerial behavior. Belief systems are very hard to change, especially when the person holding a set of beliefs (such as those of Theory X) constantly observes behaviors that reinforce them. McGregor's pessimism seemed well founded at the time. If he were alive today, one wonders whether he would be any more optimistic. We still see an abundance of time clocks, highly differentiated and boring jobs, close supervisory practices, and "carrot-and-stick" reward systems (e.g., Kohn, 1993).

Clearly, as employees enter the lower ranks of organizational hierarchies and observe behaviors around them (including their own) that support Theory X views, they naturally tend to believe in Theory X and to accept the organizational structures and policies that are needed to control people – even as these employees are promoted up the ranks. People become socialized to, and take as natural, those practices with which they are familiar. Breaking free to different views of human nature and how organizations should be designed is difficult after so much socialization to Theory X beliefs and methods. The negative view of human nature continues to characterize a considerable amount of managerial behavior and organizational policy, the wide familiarity with McGregor's work among practitioners notwithstanding (cf. Miner, 1984) and the constant exhortations in management best-sellers to adopt philosophies of a Theory Y nature (e.g., Covey, 1989; Kouzes & Posner, 1995; Pfeffer, 1994). Old habits die hard.

A TYPOLOGY OF HUMAN FUNCTIONING

Walter and Marks (1981) offered a theory of how human beings change and develop. As they note, if you wish to understand something, try changing it (or, to gain an understanding of human beings, try changing them). Drawing from the works of Levy (1970), Maddi (1976), and others, Walter and Marks have compiled a typology (or classification scheme) that summarizes the models of human nature that have been developed and studied by more than 60 behavioral and social scientists. Their typology is especially useful as a means of setting the stage for a presentation of the most popular theories of work motivation because the assumptions about human nature underlying most of these theories correspond with various categories in Walter and Marks' typology. Let's look briefly at the major categories they have identified, emphasizing those most often underlying current theories of work motivation.

First, there are the *fulfillment* models (Maddi, 1976, 1980). Representing these views are the theories of Maslow (1943, 1954) and Rogers (1959). These theories share the notion of human beings as unfolding, as developing their innate potentialities. They see people as experiencing pressure "that leads to the direction of their becoming whatever it is in their inherited nature to be" (Maddi, 1980, p. 90). Different people hold different types of potential on the basis of their unique sets of abilities, interests, and genetic characteristics. In the case of Maslow (1955, 1962), fulfillment motivation is less urgent in the short run as a motivating force behind behavior than are the forces directed at assuring the continued existence of the person – first survival, then fulfillment. We have more to say about Maslow's theory of motivation later in the chapter.

Consistency models of human nature (Maddi, 1980; Walter & Marks, 1981) emphasize "that there is a particular kind of information or emotional experience that is best for persons, and hence, that they will develop personalities which increase the likelihood of interaction with the world such as to get this kind of information or emotional experience" (Maddi, 1980, p. 156). The critical aspect of this set of models is that human nature is the result of people's interactions with their environments rather than the result of inherited attributes of the people themselves (a position similar to that of the philosopher John Locke). These theories are more concerned with consistency among the acts, beliefs, and predispositions that reflect human nature than with understanding the precise nature of the content of those acts, beliefs, and predispositions. They see people as driven to be consistent and to seek circumstances that are compatible with their previous experiences. Korman's (1970, 1976) theory of work motivation is predicated largely on this model of human nature.

The *cognitive-perceptual* models (Levy, 1970; Walter & Marks, 1981) see human beings as information-processing systems. In this view, human behavior results from the interpretation of events in the environment rather than from the strict, objective nature of the events themselves. This model does not deny the existence of an external reality, but views human action as caused by the way in which reality is perceived and understood. Work motivation theories predicated on this assumption of human nature are presented in Chapters 8 through 14.

The *learning* models of human functioning are composed primarily of the various brands of behaviorism that were first put forward in the 1940s (see Hull, 1943) and that have since evolved in the work of B. F. Skinner (1953, 1969, 1971). This view avoids recourse to internal states and processes such as those used in cognitive-perceptual models (such as beliefs and expectations). Instead, they tend to see behavior as determined solely by its consequences. Underlying this perspective is Thorndike's (1911) *law of effect*, which states that people will be more likely to do those things which experience has shown to be rewarding. They will be less likely to do things they have found aversive. Behavior is a function of its consequences – period. Application of this model in the form of motivation-oriented programs in organizations is presented in Chapters 13 and 14.

The *contextual* models of human nature (Levy, 1970; Walter and Marks, 1981) focus primarily on the social and gregarious aspects of human beings. There are no current theories of work motivation, per se, that derive exclusively from this perspective. However, many of the theories treated in this book include social needs and/or social comparison processes as part of more general need-oriented perspectives to work motivation. Finally, although it has not yet been articulated into a theory of work motivation per se, the social information processing approach to job attitudes developed by Salancik and Pfeffer (1978) is entirely consistent with the contextual models of human nature described by Levy (1970) and Walter and Marks (1981), although it also places heavy reliance on the cognitive and perceptual assumptions already described.

Walter and Marks' typology includes two other categories of theory: The conflict and life sciences models. The conflict views share an orientation toward intrapsychic and social conflict, in which life is seen as a process of compromise and balancing. The life science models are biological in nature, drawing most heavily on ethology, sociobiology, and neuroscience. Whereas these three disciplines are active in their own right, they have yet to enter any formal theories of work motivation. The author is also not aware of any theories of work motivation that have their philosophical roots in the conflict model.

Recapitulation

Five of the seven major categories in Walter and Marks' (1981) typology of models of human functioning underlie the many theories of work motivation that have appeared during the past half-century. Three of these – the fulfillment model, the cognitive-perceptual model, and the learning model – have been most dominant to date. Although evidence is presented throughout the book concerning the validity of the various motivation theories discussed, it will not be possible to conclude which of the five sets of assumptions concerning human nature is "correct" or most valid. For as Walter and Marks (1981) conclude: "Each of the models of human functioning has [its own] implications . . . when used in combination their explanatory power is increased – the whole is greater than the sum of its parts" (p. 57). Hyland (1988) agrees: "Motivational research is now at a stage when different theories need to be brought together" (p. 650). Later in the book we take a look at Hyland's (1988) suggestion for integrating a number of popular theories.

In later sections of this chapter, we examine two major work motivation theories that rest primarily on the fulfillment model of human functioning. Before we do, however, more detail is required about the basic view that human beings are acquisitive, self-fulfilling creatures. In particular, we need to gain an understanding of the exact nature of human needs and values. Let's take a closer look at the fundamental elements underlying this perspective.

NEEDS AND HUMAN BEHAVIOR: HUMANS AS WANTING ANIMALS

The model of human nature implied by this statement (Maslow, 1954, p. 24) has underpinned a great deal of the scientific work by psychologists into the nature of human motivation. It reflects a set of assumptions that whatever else we might be, people are always in need of something, and that much or all of our work behavior (and other forms of conscious behavior) is directed toward the fulfillment of our needs. This raises a question concerning the nature of the energetic force (see Chapter 1) that actually constitutes motivation – what is it?

Over the years, psychologists have studied a number of concepts that have represented the essential energetic force that constitutes human motivation. Among the earliest of these concepts was *instinct*. It was thought that like most animals, people are born with certain inherent behavioral capacities. McDougall (1923) defined an instinct as "an innate disposition which determines the organism to perceive (or pay attention to) any object of a certain class, and to experience in its presence a certain emotional excitement and an impulse to action which find expression in a specific mode of behavior in relation to that object" (p. 110). Instincts were invoked to explain acts of all varieties. But by explaining everything, the concept really explained nothing. Before long there were lengthy lists of instincts attributed to human nature. They were cumbersome, ascientific, and somewhat ludicrous. For example, an early book by Tead (1918) discussed the role of 10 instincts (such as parental, sex, workmanship, and pugnacity) in employee behavior in industry. As we see later in this chapter, some modern critics (e.g., Ford, 1992) believe that the concept of human needs (and perhaps values as well) is as cumbersome, scientifically vague, and of as little practical use as instincts were deemed to be 50 years earlier.

After publication of the book *Dynamic psychology* (Woodworth, 1918), the notion of instinct gave way to the concept of drive as the explanation for why people do things. According to drive theorists, people have primary and secondary drives. *Primary drives* arise either from deficiencies of substances necessary for survival or from excesses in substances that are harmful to survival. For example, Hull (1943) listed the following primary drives: Hunger, thirst, air, temperature regulation, defecation, urination, rest, sleep, activity, sexual intercourse, nest building, care of the young, and avoidance of, or relief from, pain. *Secondary drives* are seen as being learned through association with primary drives. For instance, fear is associated with the pain of bodily injury and itself comes to be learned as a source of energy that can arouse behavior. A detailed treatment of the historical and scientific development of instinct and drive theories is beyond the scope of this book. The interested reader is referred to Atkinson (1964) and Cofer and Appley (1964). Our focus in this chapter is on two other concepts: The meaning and nature of human needs and values, which have been among the most commonly invoked concepts in theories of work behavior.

What Needs Are

Again, we have a problem of definition. The reader is referred to Atkinson (1964), Cofer and Appley (1964), or Sheldon, Elliott, Kim, and Kasser (2001) to gain an appreciation of the multitude of uses and interpretations the concept of need has assumed over the years. For the purposes of this book,

Murray's (1938) definition will be adopted because it is most compatible with the need-oriented theories that have been developed to explain work motivation. For Murray, a need is:

> [A] construct (a convenient fiction or hypothetical concept) which stands for a force . . . in the brain region, a force which organizes perception, apperception, intellection, conation and action in such a way as to transform in a certain direction an existing unsatisfying situation. A need is sometimes provoked directly by internal processes of a certain kind . . . but, more frequently (when in a state of readiness) by the occurrence of one of a few commonly effective presses (or features of the environment) . . . Thus, it manifests itself by leading the organism to search for or to avoid encountering, or when encountered, to attend to and respond to certain kinds of press. Each need is characteristically accompanied by a particular feeling or emotion and tends to use certain modes . . . to further its trend. It may be weak or intense, momentary or enduring. But usually it persists and gives rise to a certain course of overt behavior (or fantasy) which changes the initiating circumstance in such a way as to bring about an end situation which stills (appeases or satisfies) the organism.
>
> (Murray, 1938, pp. 123–124)

A number of elements of this definition deserve highlighting. First, notice that like the concepts of instinct, drive, personality, interest, or ambition, a need is a hypothetical entity (recall Chapter 1). We cannot assess it directly or determine its color. It has no physical mass, density, or specific gravity. We must *infer* its existence by indirect means such as by observing the behavior of the person said to have a particular need. Second, notice the use of the "force" metaphor, making it consistent with the definition of work motivation given in Chapter 2. The organizing function of needs is something with which most of us are familiar. It underlies the concepts of perceptual vigilance and perceptual defense in psychology (see Zalkind & Costello, 1962). For example, an employee's need state may make her more likely to notice a job opportunity at another organization, an opening that may have existed long before the employee reached the particular need state that she was in when she read the advertisement. The emergence of a need makes a person more likely to notice things that may satisfy the need.

Third, notice the possibility for needs to be induced by characteristics of the environment. In much the same way as seeing an attractive member of the opposite sex may arouse one's sexual needs, for example, being promoted into a job with supervisory responsibilities can arouse an erstwhile dormant need for power in an upwardly mobile employee. A fourth feature of Murray's definition of need is that it helps us understand approach behaviors as well as avoidance behaviors. An example from the work setting is the preferences that employees develop for particular types of job and the aversion they have to other jobs.

One very important feature of the definition is that needs are seen as either strong or weak and as either momentary or enduring. Thus, some employees are constantly gregarious and seeking social interaction on the job, whereas for others, working in groups may be less important. People not only differ among themselves but the same person can experience increases and decreases in the strength of various needs. For example, consider the avoidance of further fatigue that motivates certain employee behaviors toward the end of a tedious day in an office setting.

Murray (1938) claimed that particular needs are accompanied by particular emotions. This point has attracted some attention and controversy. At least two positions have evolved on this matter since the time of Murray's work (see Zurbriggen & Sturman, 2002). One view is that all or nearly all emotions can be associated with any human need. Another view, championed by McClelland, a student of Murray, is that there is a more focused connection between particular needs and emotions, as implied in Murray's definition. Indeed, McClelland (1985) believed that there is a small set of fundamental human needs and a small set of basic human emotions and that there are relatively close associations among the members of the two sets. (We will discuss the matter of the number and classification of emotions in Chapter 4.)

Using two samples of United States' psychology students and two different experimental methods, Zurbriggen and Sturman (2002) found considerable, but not total, support for McClelland's (and Murray's) side of the debate. That is, they found that people who had experienced specific instances associated with one of three motives of interest (achievement, power, or affiliation) were most likely to report a limited range of emotions in association with those experiences. Specifically, there were strong associations between power motivation and anger but anger was not associated with either achievement or affiliation intimacy. The results for happiness and sadness were as predicted but not as strong as those related to anger. That is, happiness was associated more with affiliation intimacy than with power, as expected. However, happiness was also associated with achievement experiences. It appears that some need–emotion connections are stronger and more one-to-one than others. Happiness, for example, clearly appeared to be associated with motives other than simply affiliation intimacy. We will examine the role of anger as a primary and important human emotion in other chapters of this book.

A final feature of Murray's (1938) concept of needs is that they give rise to behavior (or fantasy) aimed at reducing the force behind the needs. A number of points need elaboration here. First, not all need-driven, goal-oriented behavior is successful in reaching the goals sought. The result is defined as *frustration*, a topic discussed in Chapter 8. Notice the possible role that fantasy can play, especially when behavior itself is not feasible. At one time or another, most people fantasize about what they would do if they won a lottery. Similarly, many frustrated workers fantasize about the regimes they would administer if, magically, they were promoted to powerful managerial positions.

Throughout the remainder of this book, the term *need* will imply all that is involved in Murray's definition. A solid grasp of that definition and the implications that arise from it will be essential to understanding the rest of the material to be presented, particularly in the remainder of this chapter and in Chapters 3 through 8.

The Relationship Between Needs and Behavior

Consider the difficulty involved in making inferences about the need(s) that determine a person's behavior. First, most motivated[1] behavior is said to be *overdetermined*, meaning that deliberately or inadvertently, behavior is driven by the force to satisfy more than one need (Maslow, 1954).

For example, an employee may seek a promotion for the sake of meeting several needs (although the person may be more conscious of the importance of some of them when seeking promotion). Second, the same need may be satisfied by any of a variety of acts. So our upwardly aspiring employee may in part be seeking greater satisfaction of esteem needs. Notice that gaining a promotion is one way – but only one way – to meet esteem needs. Volunteer service after hours or becoming president of the employees' union are alternative behaviors that might be employed. In short, there is no one-to-one relationship between the force of a particular need and the type of behavior that one will observe. To complicate matters, there is a common tendency for people to *project* their own need behavior styles into their interpretations of the behavior of others (Zalkind & Costello, 1962). For example, in attempting to infer why their subordinates frequently exaggerate the stress levels of their jobs, supervisors are apt to come to reasonably sound understandings of why they themselves might make such exaggerations.

The importance of all this lies in the difficulties and risks it implies for the application of need theories to an understanding of employee behavior. Remember, we cannot observe needs directly, so we must make inferences about the role of needs in behavior by observing that behavior. This lack of one-to-one correspondence between needs and behavior and the natural tendency to impute our own behavior motivation styles onto others make explanation very difficult after the fact. It makes precise predictions of employee acts almost impossible, except in cases involving the simplest

---

[1] We recognize that not all behavior, indeed not all behavior in the workplace, is motivated behavior. Many of the acts that people perform are habitual, impulsive, or compulsive, based on little or no thought or sense of drive (Landy & Becker, 1987).

behaviors (see Bandura, 1977; Ford, 1992). Yet managers do it all the time, especially those who consciously attempt to "motivate" their employees. Indeed, these problems of explanation and prediction notwithstanding, of scientific imprecision and applied usefulness, the concept of needs seems to have a certain appeal to both scientists and practitioners. Research into needs and reliance on the concept in theories of work motivation have both enjoyed long and popular traditions.

The Role of Needs in Work Motivation

Locke (1991, p. 290) provided a succinct summary of the nature of human needs, a summary that concludes that needs are the basic set of factors underlying human behavior, including human work behavior. In particular, he noted nine features of needs that social science and everyday observation and experience support:

1. Needs operate cyclically; they are never satisfied permanently.
2. Needs can be only partially satisfied habitually, either by choice (e.g., by sleeping) or involuntarily (e.g., by imprisonment).
3. Need frustration is experienced as pain, discomfort, or illness.
4. Different needs signal different degrees of urgency.
5. Needs exist whether or not we are aware of them.
6. People can plan in advance to provide for their needs.
7. A given need can instigate many different behaviors.
8. Any particular act may satisfy more than a single need.
9. Problems such as errors, irrationality, and practical circumstances frequently prevent human acts from resulting in the need satisfaction intended.

Finally, for our purposes here, Locke (1991) also saw needs as lying at the very base of human and organizational behavior. Needs give rise to and help shape other concepts we discuss in this book, such as values, intentions, and, ultimately, action. In the remaining sections of this chapter, we take a closer look at human values and their role in understanding work motivation.

Need Satisfaction

Most people tend to view need satisfaction as the state that a person feels after the tension associated with a need has been removed (such as the pleasurable feeling of a full stomach, for example). In the case of certain needs, however, satisfaction may consist more of the experience one has while in the process of *reducing* the tension (Murray & Kluckhohn, 1953). Again using the example of eating, this principle would suggest that satisfaction consists more of the joy of eating than of the joy of having eaten. Moreover, greater satisfaction seems to occur when more tension is reduced, implying that people may be motivated to deprive themselves of gratification (within safe limits) so as to be able to experience greater subsequent satisfaction from the process of need fulfillment. Sexual foreplay illustrates this principle, as does the notion of skipping lunch to assure that one has a sharp appetite for a special dinner.

In work settings this principle would imply that employee satisfaction results from the process of interacting with one's peers, for example, rather than from having done so. As we will see in Chapter 10, job satisfaction has typically been equated with the satisfaction of one's needs on the job, particularly with the experience of having met one's needs. It may be that researchers have overlooked the importance of the fulfillment process itself in their understanding of job satisfaction.

A newer perspective on satisfaction

Experimental work on human emotions has yielded an *emodynamic* view of human satisfaction. We touch on this view again later in the book, notably in Chapter 10, where we examine job satisfaction, and again in Chapter 14, where we discuss the self-control of human emotions. For our purposes here we simply summarize this new approach (see Salovey, Hsee, & Mayer, 1993, for an extended summary of this perspective). According to the emodynamic view, people experience satisfaction (which is viewed as a set of positive emotions) when they attain higher levels of outcomes (e.g., goods or rewards) than they possessed previously. The rate or *velocity* at which they acquire these additional levels is the key. A person whose pay increases by 30% over a period of 7 months will experience greater satisfaction than will a person who receives the same increase over a longer period. Eventually, however, people become used to their new levels of satisfaction. A person who wins a lottery is much happier immediately after receiving the good news than she is months later. This approach suggests that *changes in the rate of improvement* are also important. If things become better more and more quickly, a person experiences even greater joy.

Now that we have examined the general concepts of need and need satisfaction and have a brief understanding of the emergence of that concept in the history of psychology, we discuss some of the most important theories of work motivation – theories that have invoked needs as the concept representing the force behind employee behavior. In the terms of Campbell, Dunnette, Lawler, and Weick (1970), we will be dealing with the question of what determines work motivation – a question of content (hence these theories are labeled *content* theories). We deal with how and why motivation occurs later (Chapters 10 through 14 in particular) when we look at a number of *process* theories.

MASLOW'S HIERARCHICAL THEORY OF NEEDS

The hierarchical theory of human motivation developed by Maslow (1943, 1954, 1968) is the most paradoxical of all the current approaches to work motivation. On the one hand, it is one of the most familiar theories among academics and practitioners (see Miner, 1984). On the other hand, it is probably the most misunderstood and the most frequently oversimplified and misrepresented. Further, despite its widespread popularity, it is a theory which enjoys very little scientific support and suffers from the same shortcomings of weak explanatory accuracy and negligible predictive power as lamented by Ford (1992) – but it is popular nevertheless.

Rudiments of the Theory

Maslow's theory holds that there are basically five categories of human needs, and that these needs account for much or most of human behavior but not all of it. The needs vary in their relative prepotency or urgency for survival, arranging themselves in a sort of hierarchy. As the most prepotent needs become reasonably satisfied, the less prepotent ones (referred to as the higher-order needs) become increasingly important in causing behavior.

The most prepotent category of needs in the theory is *physiological* in nature. They function in a homeostatic fashion, such that imbalances or deficiencies in certain physiological substances instigate behavior aimed at restoring the balance by filling the deficiencies. Hunger, sex, and thirst are three examples. The physiological needs correspond closely to the primary drives in the drive theories discussed earlier. According to Maslow, when someone lacks satisfaction of physiological needs, the person becomes obsessed with acquiring whatever is needed to satisfy these needs and thus restore equilibrium. In short, deficiency dominates behavior, and no other need set is more dominating than the physiological needs when unfulfilled. According to Maslow (1954), "if the physiological needs are relatively well gratified, there then emerges a new set of needs, which we may categorize roughly as the safety needs (security; stability; dependency; protection; freedom from fear, from anxiety and chaos; need for structure, order, law, limits; strength in the protector, and so on)" (p. 39). Next to the physiological needs, the safety needs are the most prepotent determinants of behavior. When unfulfilled, they possess the same sort of potential for dominating behavior as do the physiological needs.

Problems of (mis)interpretation

It is worth stopping at this point to consider one of the ways that Maslow's hierarchical theory has been oversimplified and misrepresented. The theory is often interpreted as if all of the force motivating a person's behavior at a given time originates in one and only one need state and that this total domination continues until satisfaction is experienced, at which time that need state somehow shuts off, or goes away, while the next set of needs clicks on to take its place. (This discrete shutting off/clicking on image is fostered by the staircase-like pictures often used in management textbooks to represent the hierarchy.)

Instead, Maslow (1954) saw most behavior as multimotivated or overdetermined (p. 55). Any particular behavior will tend to be the consequence of simultaneous functioning of more than one need, perhaps several. It is a matter of relative deprivation or satisfaction (as stated in the passage just quoted) and relative influence of the various needs in determining behavior. Clearly, when a person faces an emergency such as extreme hunger, desperate thirst, or an onrushing assailant, one need set does dominate until gratification occurs. But once gratification is achieved, that need does not disappear as a factor in behavior. It does, however, account for less of the total force working on the person, because other needs then take on relatively more importance than before. Maslow (1954) wrote: "In actual fact, most members of our society . . . are partially satisfied in all their basic needs and partially unsatisfied . . . at the same time. A . . . realistic description of the hierarchy would be in terms of decreasing percentages of satisfaction as we go up the hierarchy of prepotency . . . As for the concept of emergence of a new need after satisfaction of the prepotent need, this emergence is not a sudden, salutary phenomenon, but rather a gradual emergence by slow degrees from nothingness" (pp. 53–54).

The author has chosen to quote directly to emphasize that Maslow never intended to portray the emergence of new need states in the crisp, all-or-nothing, lockstep fashion adopted by so many of his interpreters. Human behavior is clearly not that simple, and Maslow never portrayed it as such. Nevertheless, many managers, teachers, parents, counselors, and administrators over the years have demanded simplistic models and streamlined interpretations of Maslow's work. Sadly, many textbook authors and other academics have been more than willing to provide such oversimplifications. Let's return to the hierarchy.

Love, esteem, and self-actualization

The next most prepotent set of human needs, according to Maslow, are the *love* needs. They take on comparatively more influence in behavior as the physiological and safety needs are reasonably well gratified. The person desires relations with other people and will feel more compelled than before to achieve such relations. Feelings of loneliness, ostracism, rejection, and friendlessness will be experienced much more than before. Maslow (1954) claimed that the thwarting of the love needs "is the most commonly found core in cases of maladjustment" (p. 44). A person who suffers frustration of these needs becomes ill, although the illness is mental rather than physical. It is important to note that the theory claims that people need both to give and receive love, and that social interactions need not be cordial to satisfy these needs.

The *esteem* needs, the next most prepotent category in Maslow's hierarchy, are grouped into two sets. One set includes desires for strength, achievement, adequacy, mastery and competence, independence, freedom, and a fundamental confidence in facing the world. Gratification of these needs for self-esteem leads to feelings of self-confidence, capability, and worth, whereas frustration of them results in neurotic feelings of weakness, inferiority, and even helplessness. The second subset of esteem needs are for prestige and reputation – the esteem of others. This motivates people to seek recognition, praise, dominance, glory, and the attention of other people. When people fail to achieve these outcomes in sufficient quantity, they suffer the same sort of feelings that result when the need for self-esteem is thwarted.

The esteem needs are seen as less prepotent than the highest set of needs on the hierarchy – the need for *self-actualization*. Maslow himself seems to have given differing interpretations of the meaning of this need (see Maslow, 1943, 1954, with Maslow, 1968), but the clearest and most widely accepted view is that it consists of a requirement to fulfill one's potential, to become all that which one is capable of becoming. Amateur athletes who are already well established economically and who have many friends and all the prestige that being world champions has earned for them will still be motivated to continue to improve their performance. Why? Because they feel that they are capable of running faster or jumping higher than they have in the past. The force behind this urge to become even more of what they are capable of becoming is referred to as the need to self-actualize. (Note that some of the lower needs could help explain the athletes' continued striving for further excellence, such as a fear of losing their championship status, the esteem of their admirers, or their contracts for the commercial endorsement of athletic equipment. Remember that most behavior is overdetermined. The U.S. Army has used a catchy tagline for decades: "Be all that you can be – in the Army," an appeal to the self-development and actualizing needs of prospective soldiers.)

An important feature of self-actualization needs is that they express themselves in different ways in different people. For example, one person may seek fulfillment through the refinement of musical skills, while another may seek to develop talents as a father. Moreover, the satisfaction of self-actualization needs tends to increase their importance rather than reduce it (Maslow, 1962) – they become somewhat addictive. This is an important difference between self-actualization and the other needs in the hierarchy, all of which are seen as losing their capacity to motivate behavior once they are relatively well fulfilled.

Fine Points of the Theory

With a background now in the primary elements of Maslow's theory, let's look at some of the less frequently recognized features of the theory, features that when dropped lead to many of the misinterpretations and misrepresentations mentioned earlier. First, Maslow recognized that there are many differences among people in the relative prepotency of their needs (although the order described earlier is held to be the most common). He referred to variations from the basic ordering as *reversals*, and he acknowledged several common varieties. For instance, many people seem to place self-esteem ahead of love, seeking respect rather than affection from others. As another example, some people are innately creative and seem to pursue self-actualization despite the fact that their lower-level needs have not been met (as in the starving artist syndrome). Still others, who have been deprived of social interaction for extended periods, seem to lose the capacity to respond to the affection of others. Maslow (1954, pp. 51–52) notes other reversals, but the point is that the basic hierarchy was never intended to be totally universal and invariant, either across individuals or within the behavioral styles of any one person over time.

Another important point in the theory is that not all behavior is seen as resulting from the force provided by basic needs. Much of human behavior can be determined by forces outside a person (recall Murray's notion of environmental press, discussed earlier). In addition, some behavior is obsessive-compulsive, and some behavior is simply expressive of personality (e.g., the random movements of a child or smiles made by a happy person when alone). In fact, Landy and Becker

(1987) suggested that we should consider a sort of continuum, ranging from simple reflexive behavior, to consciously initiated acts, to over-learned or automatic patterns and habits.

A third fine point of the theory is that the needs are seen as neither necessarily conscious nor unconscious, but that, on the whole, most people are not consciously aware of their needs at the time they behave. This point will be important in subsequent chapters when we discuss the issues of designing jobs and reward systems to match employee needs.

The key factor here is that Maslow's theory, as seemingly well known as it is, is much more complex and much less mechanistic than is implied in many management and human relations textbooks. The importance of acknowledging the details lies in the implications they have for both understanding human behavior and for attempts to influence it. For example, supervisors who assume that their subordinates are constantly conscious of their own needs and are therefore under total control of their acts will probably give them far too much credit or blame for these acts (Mitchell, Green, & Wood, 1981). Similarly, reward and punishment systems which assume implicitly that employees are motivated by single needs, one at a time ("George is into security needs"), will be misguided and quite ineffective. Finally, assuming that everyone seeks to satisfy their needs according to the same strict order will foster the development of managerial policies that will frustrate as many employees as they will satisfy.

How Valid is the Theory?

It was stated earlier that Maslow's theory is paradoxical – most people in organizations think they know about it, while many tend to oversimplify it. An additional aspect of the paradox centers on the fact that there has been very little evidence to attest to its scientific validity, and these results have been mixed, at best. In other words, the theory has been popular despite limited evidence that it is valid. To make things worse, most of the research conducted to test the theory – until recently – has not been conducted appropriately (Mitchell & Moudgill, 1976), although most studies that have been done have resulted in negative conclusions (see Huizinga, 1970; for an early, relatively supportive summary with Wahba & Bridwell, 1976; also see Wicker, Brown, Wiehe, Hagen, & Reed, 1993, for a summary of these issues).

Some critics have argued that Maslow's theory and, indeed, all theories based on concepts such as needs and instincts are destined to be of only limited value in understanding human behavior. They claim that these theories are capable only of making uncertain, after-the-fact explanations of human action. They are far less capable of making precise *predictions* of behavior before the fact (see Ford, 1992). Moreover, these critics argue that a sort of "conceptual confounding" occurs in which, as Ford (1992) put it, "the evidence for a need or instinct [is] identical with the behavior it was designed to explain" (p. 9). This is related to the problem of overdetermination we discussed earlier and to the human tendency to project one's need state onto others when we attempt to explain the needs behaviors connections of other persons.

These criticisms and shortcomings are hard to refute. Nevertheless, Maslow's theory remains very popular among managers and students of organizational behavior, although there are still very few studies that can legitimately confirm (or refute) it. It may be that the dynamics implied by Maslow's theory of needs are too complex to be operationalized and confirmed by scientific research. If this is the case, we may never be able to determine how valid the theory is or – more precisely – which aspects of the theory are valid and which are not. Thus, one attempt that used techniques that were more appropriate than most (Rauschenberger, Schmitt, & Hunter, 1980) failed to support the theory.

More recent work, however, has been somewhat more encouraging. Ronen (1994) applied different data analysis techniques than most studies before his and found support for the taxonomic categories in Maslow's model in 15 different cultures (see also Kluger & Tikochinsky, 2001). Confirming the number and nature of the categories is probably the most basic test of the model (cf.

Mitchell & Moudgill, 1976) because if it is not valid, it makes little sense to consider the dynamics of deprivation and prepotency that build on the categories. Hence, Ronen's (1994) work comprises a major contribution to the viability of the theory, years after many critics had written it off! About the same time Ronen was publishing his work, after summarizing the mixed and largely negative empirical support for the theory, Wicker et al. (1993) provided a cogent summary of many of the methodological problems that had plagued testing of the theory. They also offered some fresh empirical evidence that supported one of the key dynamic aspects of the model – the proposition that a person's intentions to satisfy certain needs increases as those needs are more deprived, especially in the case of the lower-level needs. At the time of this writing, it may be best to conclude that the demise of Maslow's famous hierarchy is premature. As has been the case many times in the history of the scientific study of work motivation, problems of interpretation, measurement, and empirical testing of new theories often bias the results and conclusions pertaining to the validity of these theories (cf. Kluger & Tikochinsky, 2001). We make this observation many times throughout this book.

Modifications of the hierarchy

Since Maslow's last writings on the subject of his hierarchical theory of needs, there have been a variety of modifications. Two of these propose a reduction in the number of levels in the hierarchy and converge, accordingly, with the suggestion by Maslow in some of his later work that we might fruitfully consider only two basic levels of human needs (Maslow, 1968). One of these modifications (Lawler & Suttle, 1973) resulted from an unsuccessful attempt to support the original five-level theory empirically. Another modification (Alderfer, 1972) resulted from a deliberate attempt to develop and test a model with fewer need levels, referred to as "existence," "relatedness," and "growth."

EXISTENCE, RELATEDNESS, AND GROWTH

For the most part, Maslow's theory of human needs was based on induction from his own clinical observations rather than from empirical research conducted in organizational settings as such. Nevertheless, as suggested earlier, it provided an attractive and intuitively acceptable perspective to writers in the human relations movement of the time (e.g., Argyris, 1957; McGregor, 1960). One of the earliest empirical attempts to generate and test an alternative to Maslow's theory was that of Alderfer (1969, 1972), who proposed an existence, relatedness, and growth (ERG) model of his own. Alderfer's theory has its roots in Maslow's work as well as in the theory and research of a number of earlier psychologists concerned with human motivation.

The theory posits three general categories of human needs. These categories are similar to and partly derived from those in Maslow's model but are not identical. Each of the needs is seen as primary, innate to human nature rather than learned, although learning can increase their strength. The theory concerns itself with the subjective states of need satisfaction and desire and how satisfaction of certain needs influences the strength of the desires of other needs. *Satisfaction* refers to the internal state of a person who has obtained what he is seeking to quell his desires. It is synonymous with getting or fulfilling (Alderfer, 1972, p. 7). *Desire* refers to an internal state that is synonymous with concepts such as want, need strength or intensity, or motive. Let us take a look at the three categories of needs.

Existence Needs

The first set in the model is referred to as the existence needs. They correspond closely to Maslow's physiological needs as well as to those aspects of Maslow's category of security needs that have to do with physical (as opposed to interpersonal) security. Typically, the substances required to satisfy existence needs are concrete in nature. Moreover, these substances are often scarce, such that more satisfaction for one person will tend to result in lower potential satisfaction for others. In work settings, pay and fringe benefits are examples – the more money that is paid to the office staff, the less is available to pay the shop workers. The types of outcome (such as money) instrumental for gratifying Maslow's physiological needs are basically the same as those required to provide for physical safety; and according to Alderfer, Maslow's physiological and physical safety needs are approximately equal in importance in a person's existence. For example, people who are threatened with physical violence quickly abandon all behaviors that are not intended to provide for their safety. There are logical grounds, at least, for gathering them in a single class.

Relatedness Needs

Similarly, the goals typically sought by people to satisfy what Maslow calls love needs are basically those that are necessary to provide for the need for prestige or for the esteem of others as well as for the interpersonal security needs included in the second level of Maslow's hierarchy. Successful satisfaction of each of these Maslow needs requires interaction with other human beings and the development of meaningful relationships with others. Moreover, each of these three varieties of social needs, on a logical level at least, seems equally important.

The interaction among people needed to satisfy this category of needs, referred to as relatedness needs by Alderfer, does not necessarily have to be positive or cordial. In fact, the expression of hostile feelings toward others is seen as an important aspect of developing meaningful interpersonal relationships. Unlike the zero-sum aspects of the satisfaction of existence needs, relatedness need satisfaction by one person tends to be positively associated with the same sort of satisfaction for others, by virtue of the very nature of social interaction. Therefore, Alderfer's theory combines all of Maslow's need categories pertaining to social interaction into a single class called relatedness needs. We will see shortly that relatedness continues to be studied as a major need in humans, the satisfaction of which is critical for well-being (see Chapter 6; and Reis, Sheldon, Gable, Roscoe, & Ryan, 2000).

Growth Needs

The third category of needs in Alderfer's model is referred to as the growth needs. They are similar to the needs for self-esteem and self-actualization in Maslow's theory, but not identical. Whereas Maslow saw self-actualization as consisting of the fulfillment of innate potential (a potential that may have a unique form for a given person), Alderfer's growth needs consist of desires to interact successfully with one's environment – to investigate, explore, and master it. As the person's environment changes, so will the expression of growth needs, according to Alderfer. Nevertheless, the highest-level needs on Maslow's hierarchy are similar enough to the needs classed as growth needs by Alderfer (if for no reason other than the fact that self-actualization activities tend to enhance one's self-concept) to justify combining them into a single class.[2] Shortly, we will examine research

---

[2] The theory of intrinsic motivation advanced by Deci and his colleagues (presented shortly) extends considerably the notion of mastery of one's environment.

and theory pertaining to achievement motivation, a variety of growth need that is conceptually and empirically similar to Maslow's views of self-actualization and Alderfer's growth category.

Differences between Maslow's and Alderfer's Theories

Whereas Maslow posited five major groups of human needs, Alderfer's model is more parsimonious, suggesting only three discrete categories, although the two models often dovetail. Aside from these similarities, however, there are a few key differences between the two theories. For instance, ERG theory holds that all three sets of need are active in all human beings, although the notion of hierarchy and general prepotency found in Maslow (his reversals notwithstanding) is absent in ERG theory. Alderfer's model does not require that a person be satisfied at the level of existence to witness a shift upward in importance from relatedness to growth needs. It would be possible for employees who work under short-term contracts with their employers to derive sufficient satisfaction of their relatedness needs that they could experience an increase in the importance of gaining growth experiences through their work.

Another important feature in ERG theory that does not appear in Maslow's work is what Alderfer refers to as the *frustration–regression hypothesis*. As we will see in Chapter 8, frustration is defined as a situation in which individuals' behavioral attempts to satisfy their needs are blocked or thwarted (by forces that lie either inside the people themselves or beyond their control). ERG theory posits that failure of a person to satisfy growth needs can result in an increase in the importance of the person's relatedness needs. Similarly, a failure to satisfy one's relatedness needs can result in an increase in the importance of existence needs. In hierarchical terms, these two propositions imply a movement downward in the face of frustration. We have more to say about the causes and consequences of frustration in Chapter 8.

Initially, Alderfer proposed seven basic propositions that summarized how the satisfaction or frustration of needs at a particular level influence the satisfaction and the strength of desires at that level as well as at other levels. He subjected his theory to a 4-year study involving hundreds of research subjects and several different types of organization. By most standards, the research was reasonably well conducted. Some of his original propositions received empirical support, but others did not. Some were revised based on the evidence gathered. The reader is referred to Alderfer (1969, 1972) for more complete detail concerning the total set of propositions both before and after the research was conducted.

Needs and Need Hierarchies: Some Conclusions

Is there such a thing as a hierarchy of needs? Evidence reviewed above suggests that different needs exist and that they can be measured (Alderfer, 1972; Mitchell & Moudgill, 1976; Williams & Page, 1989) and that there is some degree of consistency among North American samples about the relative importance of needs (Sheldon et al., 2001), although evidence on this latter point is relatively new and in need of much further confirmation. Nevertheless, recent work by Sheldon et al. (2001) and Ronen (2001) also provides some preliminary support for the proposition that, when certain research methods are used, evidence may be found for considerable (although not complete) cross-cultural similarities in the structure and relative importance of human needs. Again, more work is needed, and this work must employ the same level of care in the choice and application of methodology that these more recent studies have employed.

Indeed, a comparison of results from early studies on the hierarchy issue with those from more recent studies offers an object lesson of the sort we discussed in Chapter 2. The methods used in early studies would have led to the conclusion that a hierarchy of needs is just a fanciful idea not worthy of being taken seriously. Later studies, those using different methods, have led to a more lenient conclusion (see Pinder, 1998).

In short, while it is unwise to advocate a theory unabashedly in the absence of any proof that the theory has empirical validity (recall Chapter 2), it is equally irresponsible to abandon a theory that has yielded primarily negative results when those results come from empirical tests that have been largely inappropriate or unfair. As stated earlier, it may be that many of the theories presented in this book are, in fact, better representations of the nature of work motivation than organizational researchers are capable of demonstrating. Indeed, in the case of hierarchical theories of need satisfaction, we will argue that, when we consider the human condition on a global scale, there is considerable evidence that people's needs do emerge according to an order of prepotency (see this argument in the American case as presented by Lindsey, 2007). We return to this point in Chapter 15.

ACHIEVEMENT MOTIVATION

Henry Murray (who provided us with the general definition of need that we examined earlier in this chapter) generated numerous lists of human needs. One of these needs is the *need for achievement*, which he defined as a need to "accomplish something difficult. To master, manipulate, or organize physical objects, human beings, or ideas. To do this as rapidly and as independently as possible. To overcome obstacles and attain a high standard. To excel oneself. To rival and surpass others. To increase self regard by the successful exercise of talent" (Murray, 1938, p. 164). As mentioned earlier, the overlap between this need and Maslow's notion of self-actualization is apparent, although not complete. The essence of achievement motivation might be seen as a struggle *against one's own standards of excellence*, which clearly is consistent with the idea of becoming all that one is capable of becoming. But the element of achievement motivation having to do with mastering objects and overcoming obstacles and challenges is not necessarily part of self-actualization, although the two can, in practice, go hand in hand. Kanfer and Heggestad (1997) noted that the majority of the research and measurement work that has taken place in relation to achievement motivation has stressed the mastery component and under-emphasized the component dealing with competitive excellence and comparative performance.

The aspects of the need for achievement pertaining to mastering and organizing the environment are clearly consistent with White's (1959) concept of *competence motivation* and de Charms' (1968) notion that people prefer to be responsible for their outcomes rather than merely being pawns. In short, these various growth needs are not identical, in large measure because they have been identified and studied by scholars working more or less independently of one another, but they do converge considerably in terms of the types of behaviors they instigate. David McClelland, a student of Henry Murray, devoted much of his career to developing our understanding of achievement motivation and the role it plays in entrepreneurial behavior and the economic prosperity of nations (Stewart, 1982). His work is far too extensive to be summarized completely here, so the reader is referred to some of the original sources (e.g., McClelland, 1961, 1962, 1965, 1985; McClelland & Winter, 1969). But a number of features of this work of particular relevance to our understanding of employee work motivation will be discussed here.

The Origins of Achievement Motivation

McClelland argued that all motives are learned from experiences in which certain cues in the environment are paired with positive or negative consequences. Accordingly, the need for achievement is learned when opportunities for competing with standards of excellence become associated with positive outcomes. Hence, childrearing practices that encourage youngsters to tackle challenges independently and to do well are critical. In fact, McClelland (1961, pp. 340–350) believed that childrearing practices are the most important determinants of the level of a person's achievement motivation. McClelland has also shown that deliberate programs of training that involve the development of an achievement-oriented mentality can induce entrepreneurial behavior among adults where it did not previously exist (McClelland, 1965; McClelland & Winter, 1969). In other words, adults can be trained to create and respond to opportunities to strive against challenges and to behave in the ways described in the definition above.

Gender and Achievement Motivation

It is important to recognize that most of McClelland's research evidence pertains to boys and men. Similarly, most of the early work on the matter failed to address gender differences (as was the case in most of behavioral science in the early years). Some research studies intended to generalize the theory to women and girls have been attempted, but many were flawed, as is often the case in research on human motivation (recall Chapter 2). After a thorough review of studies that did investigate gender differences in how achievement motivation is aroused among women, what forms it takes, and what consequences it has among females, Stewart and Chester (1982) concluded: "It seems . . . that an intellectual and cultural climate of unconscious sexism has led researchers to adopt untested assumptions, ignore evidence, and make interpretations that depend on attending to only some of the data" (p. 184). Until a sufficient number of valid studies have been designed, executed, and reported on the matter of gender and achievement, there is no reason to conclude that either the need or its arousal, force, or goals is different among men and women. That leaves us with the question: What does achievement-oriented behavior look like?

Characteristics of Achievement-Motivated Behavior

As we mentioned earlier, we can sometimes detect the existence of many particular needs in a person by observing the person's behavior and drawing inferences from it. Accordingly, the behavior of achievement-motivated persons is commonly characterized by three features. First, achievement-motivated people prefer tasks of moderate levels of difficulty. Second, achievement-motivated people prefer tasks for which successful performance depends on their efforts rather than on luck. Finally, achievement-motivated people demand feedback and knowledge about their successes and failures to a far greater degree than do people who are low in achievement motivation.

Moderate perceived task difficulty

The preference for tasks of moderate levels of difficulty deserves special attention. According to Atkinson (1964), the total achievement-oriented force affecting a person who confronts a task is determined by three variables. Further, the three combine multiplicatively, so that if one of them is inactive, or "zero," there is no psychological force to engage in the task. The first factor is the strength of the person's underlying need for achievement. This remains constant from one day to the next, although as already suggested, it can be developed among adults using focused training procedures. The second factor is the level of difficulty of the task, as the person perceives it. Whether a particular task will be viewed as easy or difficult depends on a host of variables, such as the person's perception of his or her ability to perform the task, for example. The third factor that determines the strength of achievement-oriented motivation is the degree of intrinsic reward (or feelings of accomplishment) that the person expects to experience by accomplishing the task. Naturally, meeting a difficult challenge will bring a person greater feelings of accomplishment than will achieving a task thought to be simple. Therefore, the value of this third factor is related inversely to the second factor, the perceived level of difficulty of the task. Symbolically,

$$\text{T.A.F.} = \text{Nach} \times \text{P.S} \times \text{I.S.} \quad \text{and} \quad \text{I.S.} = 1 - \text{P.S.}$$

where

    T.A.F. = total achievement-motivated force
    Nach = strength of the person's underlying need for achievement
    P.S.   = perceived probability of task success
    I.S.   = intrinsic feeling of accomplishment

To illustrate how this works, consider the net force operating on an employee if (1) he has a very low level of the need for achievement, (2) he perceives the task to be too difficult for him to succeed, or (3) he perceives the task as very easy. In all three cases, we would not expect much achievement motivation in the person contemplating the task. His level of effort toward performing the task would be determined by the strength of other needs and incentives he believed would result from task success (such as recognition by a woman he was trying to impress).

Notice that insofar as a person's level of underlying need strength is constant in the short run, the net level of achievement-related force acting on the person to engage in a particular task will be determined by the perception of the level of difficulty of that task. The implication of this for the design of jobs and for the assignment of people to jobs is clear: To arouse motivational force associated with achievement needs, a supervisor must structure jobs and assign people to them so that employees see their chances of job performance as 50/50: Not too low, but not too high. A moderate level of challenge must be perceived. In practice, application of this principle can be difficult, because it requires that a supervisor be capable of accurately perceiving the difficulty level of a task as the employee sees it. A supervisor who overestimates or underestimates an employee's ability vis-à-vis a task will probably fail to arouse and take advantage of a certain amount of the natural achievement motivation of that worker. In theory, the principle is relative simple: Applying it effectively can be another matter.

In the following sections, we turn to a body of theory and research dealing with a phenomenon called *intrinsic motivation*. Although, as we will see both in this chapter as well as in Chapter 7, there are a number of approaches to understanding the nature of intrinsic motivation. They converge to provide an evolving theoretical base for understanding a considerable amount of employee work behavior, job attitudes, preferences for career choices, psychological well-being and wisdom for the design of jobs. We will also see that an important element of intrinsic motivation is found in the dynamics associated with learned needs such as Alderfer's (1969) "growth" category as well as those from Maslow (1954) – especially self-actualization and self-esteem (which we study more carefully in Chapter 6) as well as in McClelland's (1961) theory, as summarized here.

INTRINSIC MOTIVATION

Imagine that you are walking with a friend through your neighborhood on a warm summer evening. As you walk, you notice a 9-year-old boy pushing a lawn mower in erratic circles and strips around the grass on his parents' front yard. The boy has his head lowered between his straight, extended arms, and he is bent over at the waist as he runs and pushes the mower. Upon getting closer, you hear him making sounds like an engine – an airplane engine. You stop and ask the young man what he is doing and learn that he is pretending to be a pilot flying an airplane. The young pilot seems friendly enough, so you stop to chat for a while. The conversation reveals that the boy is having fun with his fantasy Beechcraft and that he did not consider his activity to be work. Further probing on your part informs you that the boy receives no pay or other form of direct compensation from his parents for cutting the grass (or flying his airplane). You part company, wishing him a safe flight.

Is the boy in this example working (cutting the lawn), or playing (flying his aircraft)? Or does it matter what you call it or how you classify his behavior? For the boy, the behavior clearly was playing. The boy's father, by way of contrast, would view it as work – a chore that he would now not have to perform himself. It may simply be a matter of one's perspective, as seemed to be the case when Tom Sawyer managed to lure his friends into whitewashing his Aunt Polly's fence. Using some of the concepts from Maslow and Alderfer, described earlier, we can look a bit deeper behind the reasons for our young pilot's behavior, asking, for example, what motivated him to behave the way he did. We can probably rule out existence and relatedness needs as explanations for the boy's action, because he was not deriving monetary rewards for his play, neither did he seem to be seeking social interaction from it. If we assume that the boy's behavior was, in fact, motivated (as opposed to being simply random or compulsive), we are left with the conclusion that the boy must have been motivated largely by growth needs. What, you may ask, has growth got to do with the erratic flight of a low-altitude lawn mower?

The purpose of the following sections is to examine further a set of needs that we classified earlier as growth needs, and then study the role of growth needs in a phenomenon called *intrinsic motivation* or *intrinsically motivated behavior*. We then move to an analysis of alternative perspectives on intrinsic motivation and present some of the controversy that has surrounded this fascinating concept.[3]

What is Intrinsic Motivation?

Current thinking in work motivation would define the boy's behavior as *intrinsically motivated*. Or we might say that each was "intrinsically motivated to do what he or she was doing." Intrinsically motivated behavior can be defined, loosely, as behavior that is performed for its own sake rather than for the purpose of acquiring any material or social rewards. But there is much more to it than that. One scholar who has investigated intrinsically motivated behaviors extensively defines them as those "which a person engages in to feel competent and self determining" (Deci, 1975, p. 61). More recently:

> Intrinsic motivation is based on the innate, organismic needs for competence and self determination. It energizes a wide variety of behaviors and psychological processes for which the primary rewards are the experience of effectance and autonomy. Intrinsic needs differ from primary drives in that they are not based on tissue deficits and they do not operate cyclically, that is, breaking into awareness, pushing to be satisfied, and then when satisfied, receding into quiescence. Like drives, however, intrinsic needs are innate to the human organism and function as an important energizer of behavior. Furthermore, intrinsic motivation may interact with drives in the sense of either amplifying or attenuating drives and of affecting the way in which people satisfy their drives.
>
> (Deci & Ryan, 1985, p. 32)

Feelings of interest and enjoyment – even excitement – characterize intrinsic motivation, accompanied by what Deci and Ryan call a "sense of flow" of the sort that the young lawn mower pilot must have been sensing. Yet, even though feelings of competence and interest in the task are central

---

[3] Later, in Chapter 7, we will focus on a number of theories of job design that attempt to stimulate and engage intrinsically motivated behavior.

to intrinsic motivation, a person must also feel free of pressures such as rewards or potential punishments. The person must feel that her behavior is autonomous and not under the control of outside forces (Gagné & Deci, 2005). Hence, the notion of *choice* is central to the concept of self-determination – the person must be in control of the alternatives for action and be able to choose among them. Although choice is also a possibility in many extrinsically motivated activities, it is central to the concept of intrinsic motivation.[4] In addition, the person must feel challenged: Experiencing, finding, or creating situations that will provide opportunities for mastery, as in the case of the boy with the lawn mower we described earlier.

The intrinsic needs for competence and self-determination motivate an ongoing process of seeking and attempting to conquer optimal challenges. When people are free from the intrusion of drives and emotions, they seek situations that interest them and require the use of their creativity and resourcefulness. They seek challenges that are suited to their competencies, that are neither too easy nor too difficult. When they find optimal challenges, people work to conquer them, and they do so persistently. In short, the needs for competence and self-determination keep people involved in ongoing cycles of seeking and conquering optimal challenges (Deci & Ryan, 1985, pp. 32–33).

Exploratory and inquisitive behaviors are common among animals as well as human beings (see Harlow, Harlow, & Meyer, 1950). It is adaptive. If members of a species did not explore and take risks in seeking new places to live and new sources of food, they would surely perish. Psychologists have argued that such behavior is not only innately human, but that it is also characteristic of many cultures – such as those found in Canada and the United States – that emphasize individualism, self-fulfillment, and freedom (e.g., Eisenberger & Cameron, 1996).

The reader will notice from the passages quoted above that Deci and Ryan (1985) sometimes wrote of the *needs* for competence and self-determination as if they are equivalent, or at least two elements of a single concept. Skinner and her colleagues took exception to the idea that competence and self-determination are one and the same thing. Building on de Charms (1968), Skinner wrote that "the need for self-determination, or autonomy, is the desire to be the origin of one's own behavior, to be free, to choose one's course of action for one's self" (Skinner, 1995, p. 10). By comparison, *competence* refers to the "connection between behaviors and outcomes; it is the extent to which a person feels capable of producing desired and preventing undesired events; its opposite is helplessness." *Autonomy* refers to the connection between volition and action; it is the extent to which a person feels free to show the behaviors of his choice; non-autonomous behaviors include both compliance and defiance, which have in common that they are reactions to others' agendas and not freely chosen" (Patrick, Skinner, & Connell, 1993, cited by Skinner, 1995, p. 11).

Intrinsic or Extrinsic (Part One): The Bifurcation

The distinction between internal and external work motivation originated with Herzberg, Mausner, and Snyderman's (1959) study of the determinants of job satisfaction (recall Chapter 2). Although the concepts of intrinsic and extrinsic motives, rewards, and outcomes have not always been understood and used consistently (Dyer & Parker, 1975), the distinction has been seen as critical in the motivation literature, if for no reason other than the expectation that intrinsic motivation (and hence the intrinsic rewards required to satisfy it) may well become increasingly important as the workforce becomes more highly educated and less threatened by challenging jobs.

For years following Herzberg's research, adherents to the field seemed to fall into a trap of binary thinking on these matters: A motive or an act was either intrinsic *or* extrinsic. Intrinsic outcomes were seen as relating to either the satisfaction or frustration of higher-level or growth

---

[4] The theme of the English poem "Invictus," which opens Chapter 7, expresses the notions of self-determination and internal control of one's activities and outcomes.

needs. Examples of intrinsic outcomes include positive feelings of accomplishment or a sense of diminished self-esteem. Intrinsic outcomes occur immediately upon the performance of the acts that produce them. They are, in a sense, self-administered by the person rather than distributed by others. By contrast, if not merely via the logical process of elimination, extrinsic outcomes have been seen to relate more to the gratification and frustration of the existence and relatedness needs we examined in Chapter 2. They include such things as pay, promotions, and social interaction with one's colleagues. Moreover, they tend to be mediated by outsiders, such as one's supervisor or peers. Controversy ensued for more than two decades about the distinction and even about whether it should be abandoned altogether (cf. Billings & Cornelius, 1980; Dyer & Parker, 1975; Ford, 1992; Guzzo, 1979; Thierry, 1990). Cameron and Pierce (1994) found that different "extrinsic" outcomes (such as money and praise) have different effects on people receiving them so lumping praise and pay into the same category may be more convenient than valid from a scientific perspective. By 1985, Deci and Ryan (1985, Ch. 2) reported that there had been at least 20 conceptualizations of intrinsic motivation and intrinsically motivated behavior.

Alternative Explanations of Intrinsic Motivation

Three of these approaches – those first discussed at length by Deci (1975) – have attracted the most attention and bear the most interest for those concerned with work motivation. In the interest of space, we focus on the three viewpoints that Deci (1975) first identified, as well as a theoretical link with self-efficacy, a concept presented in Chapter 6 and elsewhere in this volume. In short, what are some useful ways of understanding intrinsic motivation when work is our primary interest?

The optimum arousal approach

The first approach, represented by the work of Hebb (1955), posits that human beings seek preferred or optimum levels of arousal (where arousal is seen as the stimulation of the brain and central nervous system). Arousal levels result primarily from stimulation found in a person's environment. If the arousal level is too low in comparison with someone's desired level, the person will be motivated to behave so as to increase it. For example, an employee who is used to a fairly hectic work pace but who finds things slower than usual on a particular day will be motivated to seek out other people for conversation, set new tasks to be accomplished, or do something simply to "stir things up." Contrariwise, if the person's level of arousal is greater than the level preferred, the person will attempt either to withdraw from the highly arousing circumstances or take steps to slow things down toward the level desired (e.g., by turning off a noisy radio or moving into a job that is less demanding). In this view, then, intrinsically motivated behavior is behavior intended to increase or decrease the physiological stimulation that a person experiences, to bring it into line with the levels desired. The implications of activation/arousal theory for the motivation of employees through the design of work have been reviewed by Gardner and Cummings (1988) and Scott (1966). We return to their work later in the book when we address job design issues explicitly.

The optimum incongruity perspective

A second approach (which is similar to the first) posits that people desire and behave to achieve an optimum level of uncertainty or incongruity, where incongruities consist of psychological inconsistencies in a person's beliefs, thought, perception, values, or behaviors (Zajonc, 1960). Unlike Festinger (1957), who posited that people find cognitive dissonance aversive and that they are motivated to minimize the number of inconsistent cognitions they hold, this approach claims that people vary in the number and intensity of the disparate beliefs, acts, and perceptions they prefer in their lives. When a person is experiencing either too little consistency ("Things just don't add up") or too much consistency ("The world is in total harmony with itself"), behavior is instigated either to reduce or increase the level of congruity in the person's mind. Whereas the optimum arousal approach described earlier is physiological in orientation, the optimal congruity approach stresses the level of psychic comfort or discomfort that a person experiences as a consequence of his or her acts and perceptions. The work of Hunt (1965) and Berlyne (1973) represents this second approach to explaining the origins of intrinsically motivated behavior. More recently, Amabile (1988) has shown how high levels of intrinsic motivation can contribute to creativity and innovation in work organizations. In Chapter 13, we will see that goal-setting theory postulates an analogous process wherein individuals set goals (states or accomplishments that are initially beyond reach), strive to achieve those goals (bringing about some degree of satisfaction), then set new goals, whether achievement oriented or learning oriented.

The need for competence and self-determination approach

The third approach to intrinsic motivation identified by Deci (1975) is best represented by White's (1959) concept of competence (or *effectance*) motivation and de Charms' (1968) notion of personal causation. According to White (1959), competence refers to a person's capacity to master and deal effectively with the surroundings – to be in charge of them. The exploratory behavior of children characterizes a desire to be competent, as do adult behaviors that are intended to enquire, to manipulate, and to learn about things. Competence motivation represents a need that is always available to instigate and direct behavior, although this need is less urgent (or *prepotent*, to use Maslow's term) than are the types of existence needs we examined earlier in this chapter. Once aroused, however, competence motivation causes people to seed out challenging situations in their environments and then to conquer those situations, leading to feelings of competence and efficacy.

Similarly, according to de Charms (1968), Burger (1992), and Skinner (1995), people desire to be the origin of their own behavior rather than the pawns of circumstances beyond their control. People strive for personal causation, to be in charge of their own lives and for the outcomes that accrue to them. Similar to Deci's concept of self-determination is Burger's (1992) concept of *desire for control*. This is defined as "the extent to which people generally are motivated to see themselves in control of the events of their lives" (p. 6). Burger views the desire for control as a personality trait, one that is generalized through the various arenas of a person's life. Therefore, if a person has a strong desire for control in his marital relationship, he probably has a strong desire to be in control of his work situation, his social activities, and his friendships. Whereas Burger is concerned with a desire for control that he views as a stable personality trait, Skinner (1995) is concerned with *perceived control*, seen as a "flexible set of inter-related beliefs that are organized around interpretations of prior interactions in specific domains . . . [T]hey are open to new experiences and can be altered" (p. 4).

Another, less well-known approach to intrinsic motivation was advanced by Weick (1969), although he did not use the term. For Weick, the very process of organizing consists of the activities associated with the removal of *equivocality* and the construction of procedures and systems to make this possible. Equivocality implies multiple meanings and mixed and confusing messages. It is represented by puzzles; in humor, by puns. For Weick, people tend to enjoy the process of organizing through removing uncertainty from their environments as well as the processes of planning to continue to deal with these uncertainties. Being somewhat enjoyable in themselves, these activities will motivate a person to be productive in one way or another: Planning, sense making, and resolving uncertainties. Therefore, as long as productivity is a path to the removal of uncertainty, we will see people being both highly motivated to engage in tasks and deriving pleasure from the process (Weick, 1969, p. 99). In many ways, Weick's concept of equivocality removal is similar to Deci's concepts of self-determination and control: In fact, they have common roots in the theoretical work of White (1959), discussed earlier.

In short, then, intrinsically motivated behaviors are those behaviors that a person engages in to feel competent, self-determining, and in command of the situation at hand. They are enjoyable and they are instigated and sustained by the enjoyment they create for the actor. These behaviors are of two general types: Those intended to find or create challenge and those intended to conquer it. Hence, the adult who deliberately takes a clock apart merely to see how it works, or who learns a foreign language simply for the sake of learning it, are two examples of intrinsically motivated behavior from this third perspective.

Intrinsic or Extrinsic (Part Two): Can They be Combined?

Earlier, we noted that the rise in interest in intrinsic motivation, assisted by the bifurcation of results purportedly found in the research of Herzberg et al. (1959), created a two-bucket world that generated considerable heat along with much of the light it shed on human work behavior. Edward Deci and Michael Ryan were criticized considerably for their stream of research, particularly for their studies that found, under certain circumstances at least, that the addition of extrinsic rewards (such as money) can have the effect of reducing the intrinsic motivation of the individual to perform the behavior in the future while in the absence of any extrinsic inducement.

Briefly, to help us explain the controversy, let us return to the example of the boy and the lawn mower that opened this chapter. Consider what would happen if the boy's father elected to compensate him for cutting the lawn using pay or some other form of extrinsic reward. Further, assume that the father agreed to pay the boy some amount of money for cutting the grass each time, thereby making the receipt of the money contingent upon his cutting the lawn. What would happen to the boy's net level of motivation to cut the lawn, and what would happen to the amount of fun the boy would have in cutting the grass/flying his imaginary airplane?

Common sense, widespread practice, and considerable theory and research evidence (Lawler, 1971) support the proposition that compensation systems that tie pay and other rewards to the performance of an activity can *increase* the level and rate of performance of a task. It would stand to reason, therefore, that paying the boy to "fly" the lawn mower would add considerable extrinsic motivation to the level of intrinsic motivation the boy already has for that task. In other words, the boy's net level of motivation to cut the lawn should now be greater than before, because the extrinsic motivation provided by the money will somehow combine with his prior level of intrinsic motivation, resulting in a greater overall level of motivation than the boy had before he started to receive the pay. Again, common sense would support this reasoning, as do some formal theories of work motivation (e.g., Galbraith & Cummings, 1967; Porter & Lawler, 1968).

However, a series of experiments conducted more than 30 years ago by Deci (e.g., 1971, 1972) and others (e.g., Condry, 1975; Greene & Lepper, 1974; Pinder, 1977; Pritchard, Campbell, & Campbell, 1977) suggested that intrinsic and extrinsic motivation may not always "add up" (in a psychological sense) the way that common sense would have it. Instead, these experiments suggested that in some circumstances, the addition of an extrinsic, contingently paid incentive (such as money) to a work context in which the employee is intrinsically motivated to do the work may result in a loss of some (or all) of that employee's prior level of intrinsic motivation toward the task, and perhaps also toward other tasks perceived as similar.

The possibility that intrinsic and extrinsic incentives may not be additive generated considerable research activity in the 1970s and 1980s. Scientists (especially in educational settings) pursued the idea that rewards may diminish people's propensity to engage in an otherwise-attractive activity once the rewards are discontinued. Also investigated was the possibility that rewards might be detrimental to individual creativity and innovativeness.

The results of these studies, most of which were experiments conducted in laboratory settings, were mixed. Sometimes extrinsic rewards appeared to reduce intrinsic motivation; other times the opposite effect seemed to occur – the contingent reward enhanced the intrinsic motivation

(Wiersma, 1992). A number of attempts were made to build theories that would reconcile these contradictory results, some of which we review briefly here. Staw (1976) reviewed the evidence regarding the *overjustification hypothesis* to that point and concluded that whether extrinsic rewards enhance or reduce intrinsic motivation[5] depends on at least five factors: (1) the degree of saliency of the reward; (2) the prevailing norm regarding the appropriateness of payment for the activity in question; (3) the prior level of commitment of the person to the task; (4) the degree of choice the person has to perform, or not to perform, the task; and (5) the existence of potential adverse consequences.

Cognitive Evaluation Theory (CET)

Deci and his colleagues (e.g., Deci, 1975, 1980; Deci & Porac, 1978; Deci & Ryan, 1985) proposed the *cognitive evaluation theory* (CET) to reconcile the contradictory evidence pertaining to the relationship between intrinsic and extrinsic motivation. According to the theory, rewards can bear at least two fundamental features for the person receiving them. The first of these is referred to as *feedback*, meaning that rewards given for performance of a task can convey information to the individual concerning *how well* she is doing at the task.

According to CET, a second feature of rewards can be the messages, if any, they have for the individual about *why* she is performing the task. Deci refers to these as *control* perceptions (i.e., "Why am I doing this job? For the reward, of course!"). The theory states that which of these two features is more salient serves either to enhance or to reduce a person's intrinsic motivation toward it. If control perceptions are more salient, they may cause a shift in the person's perceived *locus of causality*, such that she attributes her reasons for engaging in the task to the external inducements surrounding it rather than to any internal satisfaction provided by the task itself.

This notion also draws on self-perception theory (Bem, 1967), which states that people examine their own behavior, much as they do the behavior of other people, and make attributions about their motives for behaving as they do. In CET theory, control perceptions arising from a reward are said to shift from self-perceptions of intrinsic motivation ("I am cutting the lawn because it is fun") to extrinsic self-attributions ("I am doing it for the money"). As the perceived locus of causality shifts, the person's intrinsic motivation to do the task diminishes. Highly contingent rewards (such as in a piece-rate of commission payment system) seem more likely to imply control perceptions, and thereby reduce intrinsic motivation, than do less contingent pay systems (such as monthly salaries or hourly wages), largely because they are salient and undeniably connected with behavior.

According to CET, feedback perceptions may either enhance or reduce intrinsic motivation. If the feedback indicates to the person that he is doing well at a task it is increased (because, for Deci, competence and self-determination are the essence of intrinsic motivation). But if the person perceives that he is doing poorly as a result of the feedback implied by the rewards (or lack of rewards), his feelings of competence will be diminished, as will his intrinsic motivation, and the person will be less likely to engage in the task in the future without some form of extrinsic incentive.

A major shortcoming of CET was that it failed to specify the conditions under which either of the two facets of reward (feedback or control) will be more salient for a particular person in a given situation (Guzzo, 1979; Wiersma, 1992). In one statement of the theory, Deci and Porac (1978) stated only that " 'individual differences and situational factors' are related to the way people interpret the meaning of the rewards they receive" (pp. 163–164). Arnold's (1976) work suggested that when a person's prior level of intrinsic motivation for a task is very high, feedback perceptions may be more salient, although one experiment failed to confirm this hypothesis (Pinder, Nord, & Ramirez, 1984). Another problem with the theory is that it is imprecise about

---

[5] Notice that the focus here is on intrinsic motivation, not on performance.

the exact *types* of reward that may diminish intrinsic motivation (Eisenberger & Cameron, 1996). That is, rewards can be provided merely for engaging in a task, or they can be provided only for completing the task. Similarly, quality of performance may or may not be a basis for receiving rewards. Cognitive evaluation theory is not sufficiently developed to make sharp differential predictions about the effects of various rewards on intrinsic motivation (Eisenberger & Cameron, 1996).

Validity of CET in real workplaces

We have noted that the majority of the research that led to the advancement and subsequent testing of CET was conducted in contrived (or artificial) work settings or in educational settings where the focus was on children's intrinsic motivation to continue or engage in play behavior (see Cameron & Pierce, 1994).

But what about the process of tying extrinsic rewards to employee behavior and performance in real work settings?[6] The major applied implication of the theoretical "Deci effect" for industrial work settings is that pay for performance may offset whatever intrinsic motivation workers experience as a consequence of initiatives such as job enrichment or employee programs. There is still only limited empirical evidence that this occurs in practice, despite our common, everyday encounters with surly employees who refuse to perform duties that are not strictly within the formal definitions of their jobs ("I'm not paid to do that"). Rigby et al. (1992) proposed that field research into intrinsic motivation may better be focused on feelings of competence self-determination. In fact, one study had already pursued that suggestion (Deci, Connell, & Ryan, 1989).

The research was an 18-month field study of nearly 1000 technicians and field managers working for a large office machine corporation examined the effects of supportive leadership styles on employee job attitudes (Deci et al., 1989). The experimental manipulations were designed to influence the degree of self-determination the employees would experience. The hypothesis was that higher levels of felt self-determination, brought about by supportive supervision, would yield higher levels of satisfaction and trust. The results largely supported the hypotheses, especially when the general economic condition of the company was favorable (when times were not good, the supervisory support had little impact on the satisfaction variables). As impressive as this experiment was, we must keep our attention on the fact that it was self-determination that was manipulated and it was a set of attitudinal variables (rather than performance or motivation) that served as the dependent variable of interest. Although self-determination is a critical element of intrinsic motivation according to CET, there is more to it than that, as already described.

Conclusions on CET

Three and one-half decades have elapsed since Deci's (1972) early work, and more than two have passed since theories – particularly CET – appeared for the sake of reconciling contradictory conclusions about the effects of rewards on intrinsic motivation, task interest, and creativity (cf. Deci & Ryan, 1985). As often occurs, researchers have conducted meta-analyses[7] of previous, independent studies, hoping that combining results across many studies might provide greater statistical power and more definitive answers. Such was the case with the "Deci effect," particularly as regards the alleged effect of rewards of various kinds on intrinsic motivation and other outcomes.

One of the first meta-analyses found that when the concept of intrinsic motivation was

---

[6] In the discussion that follows, keep in mind the distinctions we made in Chapter 1 between motivation and performance. It may be that extrinsic rewards have negative effects on performance whether or not decreased intrinsic motivation per se can explain such effects.

[7] As we have seen in previous chapters, a *meta-analysis* is a study in which the results of many earlier studies are combined, especially when the earlier studies have been yielding inconclusive or mixed results. The procedures used in meta-analysis are beyond the scope of this book; the interested reader is referred to a book by Hunter, Schmidt, and Jackson (1982).

operationalized by whether research participants continued to "work" or play at the experimental task in what they believed was "free time" following the termination of the study, extrinsic rewards did seem to reduce intrinsic motivation. In other words, when experimental subjects were rewarded with an extrinsic payment that varied with their performance levels, their propensity to engage in the task during a free interval was lower than the same propensity among the control participants, who received either no reward or a flat payment unrelated to their behavior or performance. The results suggested that we still cannot be sure whether extrinsic rewards actually have a deleterious effect on intrinsic motivation. Rather, all that could be concluded was that *withdrawing a previously administered extrinsic reward may have such an effect* (Wiersma, 1992, p. 110). By way of contrast, when the researchers operationalized intrinsic motivation as performance levels during the experiment itself, the payment of contingent external rewards combined to *increase* overall levels of motivation (Wiersma, 1992). The overall findings again remind us of the importance of carefully defining motivational constructs. They also provide another example of how the experimental procedures used by researchers can influence the content of the theory that results from their research (recall Chapter 2).

Another meta-analysis, this one based on a larger number of studies, was even less supportive of the proposition that rewards diminish intrinsic motivation (Cameron & Pierce, 1994; see also Eisenberger & Cameron, 1996). These researchers made an interesting observation about the effects of differing paradigms and theoretical perspectives on the findings that had emerged *prior to their analysis*: "The overjustification effect, cognitive evaluation theory, and the recent behavioral explanations each attempt to account for the disparate effects of reward and reinforcement on intrinsic motivation . . . [R]eviewers on all sides of the issue tend to be highly critical of research designed outside their own paradigm, and, more often than not, findings from studies in opposite camps are not considered relevant" (Cameron & Pierce, 1994, p. 372).

These meta-analyses addressed three fundamental questions:

1. What is the effect of reward on intrinsic motivation?
2. What are the effects of specific features of reward on intrinsic motivation?
3. What is the effect of reinforcement[8] on intrinsic motivation?

The study included the findings of 96 experiments that had focused on four different operationalizations of intrinsic motivation: Free time spent on a task once reward is removed, self-reports of attitude, performance during the free time period, and willingness to volunteer for more of the same type of work.

Cameron and Pierce's (1994) meta-analysis concluded that rewards do not have a negative effect on intrinsic motivation in terms of any of the four dependent variables studied. In fact, they concluded that "people who receive a verbal reward spend more time on a task once the reward is withdrawn; they also show more interest and enjoyment than non-rewarded persons" (p. 391). The only decremental effect of rewards on intrinsic motivation, across studies, seemed to have occurred when expected rewards (as opposed to unexpected rewards) were administered simply for engaging in a task (as opposed to being based on performance at the task). In this case the decrement was on the "free time spent after reward withdrawal" measure of intrinsic motivation. Cameron and Pierce (1994) noted that this effect is consistent with CET:

> According to cognitive evaluation theory, competence and self-determination underlie intrinsic motivation. Rewards can facilitate or hinder competence and self-determination depending on whether they are perceived as informational, controlling or ainformational. From this perspective,

---

[8] The concept of *reinforcement* comes from a body of theory presented in Chapter 14. For present purposes, the term has two major interpretations: (1) it is a consequence of an act that increases the rate of probability of the occurrence of the act; or (2) it is something deemed positive that is provided as a consequence of an act.

results from the meta-analysis would suggest that verbal rewards increase a person's intrinsic motivation because of their informational value. Verbal praise would be seen to lead an individual to feel competent in performing a task; hence, intrinsic motivation. Contrariwise, rewards offered to people for participating in a task, in spite of how well they perform, would be perceived as controlling and would decrease intrinsic motivation (p. 395).

But that was about all the support the meta-analysis revealed for CET: It was based on a single indicator of intrinsic motivation. The theory was not supported when attitudinal measures of intrinsic motivation were used, although Cameron and Pierce (1994) acknowledged that many of the studies included in their analysis may not have used valid measures of task attitudes (p. 396).

This meta-analysis raised serious questions about intrinsic motivation as well as about the effects of rewards on intrinsic motivation. Although it is true that many laboratory experiments have individually suggested that rewards have a negative effect, the size of the effects in most of those studies now appears not to have been substantial enough to lead to major policy conclusions against the use of rewards in either the workplace or the classroom. Rigby, Deci, Patrick, and Ryan (1992; cited by Cameron & Pierce, 1994, p. 396) suggested that the simple dichotomy between intrinsic and extrinsic motivation may be *too* simple and that a shift of emphasis is in order toward further development of the concepts of competence and self-determination.[9] As in the case of most theories in social science (and most theories of work motivation), the theories related to the effects of rewards on intrinsic motivation are scrutinized and supported, rejected, or altered (recall Chapter 2).

The meta-analysis by Cameron and Pierce (1994) was not the end of the debate on the additivity or non-additivity of intrinsic motivation and extrinsic rewards. Five years later, a meta-analysis of 128 studies reported by Deci, Koestner, and Ryan (1999) found results largely supportive of their hypothesis, although the effect varied in strength across populations and circumstances.[10] Nevertheless CET has rarely been taken seriously as a viable theory of work motivation since these meta-analyses because of a number of its shortcomings. The most significant of these were recently summarized by Gagné and Deci (2005) and Latham (2007):

1. Most of the research that originally spawned and developed CET was conducted in laboratory settings that lacked the ecological validity necessary to make it of interest to people in real work settings.
2. It was difficult to reconcile many of the major tenets of CET into the dominant theories of work motivation when CET was being developed.
3. Work assignments are usually just that, assignments, so in most work settings the concept of electing or rejecting to work at most tasks is not a matter of choice; there is no choice involved if the individual wishes to continue his or her employment; moreover, many (most?) tasks for most workers really offer little chance of offering much fun.
4. Pay is expected by people for their work and organizations must compete, largely on the basis of comparative rewards, to attract and retain workers. Hence, the issue of mixing external rewards, particularly pay, with intrinsic motivation is a moot point.
5. Different types of extrinsic reward (such as pay, recognition, and deadlines) seem to have different effects on intrinsic motivation, making it clear that the concept of extrinsic motivation is not a monolithic construct.
6. The view of individual determinism that underlies the theory may be highly restricted to Western cultural settings.

---

[9] Nevertheless, Amabile, Hill, Hennessey, and Tighe (1994) developed the notion that people may have a trait orientation that is oriented more toward intrinsic (or extrinsic) rewards.
[10] The interested reader may wish to read the critique leveled at the Deci et al. (1999) meta-analysis and a neutral decision on the matter proffered by Lepper, Henderlong, and Gingras (1999).

Self-Determination Theory (SDT)

In the face of these and other criticisms, Ryan, Connell, and Deci (1985) developed *self-determination theory* (SDT), which, among other things, disassembled the notion of extrinsic motivation (refer to point 5 in the last list). The key was to adopt the concept of *internalization* which "refers to 'taking in' a behavioral regulation and the value that underlies it" (Gagné & Deci, 2005, p. 333). This approach recognizes that there are varying degrees of autonomy (as opposed to externally imposed control) available to people working for extrinsic rewards. SDT also accesses research findings related to personality differences in causality orientations (Deci & Ryan, 1985).

Autonomous and controlled motivation

The core of SDT is the distinction between autonomous motivation and controlled motivation (Gagné & Deci, 2005). Autonomous motivation implies "acting with a sense of volition and having the experience of choice (Gagné & Deci, p. 333). Intrinsic motivation is an example of autonomous motivation. Such activities are fun for the persons involved, they engage in them entirely as a consequence of voluntary choice and desire. By contrast:

> [B]eing controlled involves acting with a sense of pressure, a sense of *having to* engage in the actions . . . SDT postulates that autonomous and controlled motivations differ in terms of both their underlying regulatory processes and their accompanying experiences, and it further suggests that behaviors can be characterized in terms of the degree to which they are autonomous or controlled. Autonomous motivation and controlled motivation are both intentional, and together they stand in contrast to *amotivation* [emphasis added], which involves a lack of intention and motivation.
>
> (Gagné & Deci, 2005, p. 334)

In short, there are three broad categories of motivation in SDT: (1) amotivation (which is a lack of motivation and features an absence of intentional regulation); (2) extrinsic motivation (that may have as many as four different levels that vary in the degree of autonomy vs. control they entail for the individual); and (3) intrinsic motivation, which is inherently autonomous, and enjoyable for the person (see Gagné & Deci, 2005).

Three universal needs

Another key tenet of SDT is the notion that "something is a need only to the extent that its satisfaction promotes psychological health and its thwarting undermines psychological health" (Gagné & Deci, 2005, p. 337). According to SDT, the three needs for competence, autonomy, and relatedness are necessary for the psychological health of all humans. Recent work by Sheldon et al. (2001) used these three needs as well as needs postulated in other dominant theories, yielding a list of 10 in total for further examination: Autonomy, competence, relatedness, physical thriving, security, self-esteem, self-actualization, pleasure/stimulation, money/luxury, and popularity/influence. In three studies, they asked samples of both Korean and American students to rate the 10 "need candidates" as most present or most salient during their most satisfying experiences. They also asked their research participants to assess "Which qualities of experience best predict variations in positive and negative affect with the event described" (2001, p. 327). Readers will notice (recall Chapter 2) that this sort of "critical incident" method is the one used by Herzberg and his colleagues (1959) during their original empirical studies that resulted in their two-factor theory.

For our purposes, the key findings across the three studies can be summarized as follows:

1. Participants were able to distinguish among 10 distinct categories of need.

2. There was high consistency across studies and culture about the nature of the most satisfying and dissatisfying events.
3. The needs most consistently related to events of high satisfaction and high dissatisfaction were self-esteem, autonomy, competence, and relatedness (the consistency of these results provide strong support for SDT as well as for the importance of models that stress the importance of self-esteem (see Chapter 6).
4. The need appearing to be most important to satisfy in the United States was self-esteem, whereas relatedness was the most important need among Korean subjects.

The authors speculate that the three key needs found in SDT (autonomy, competence, and relatedness) may provide the core for a unified theory of needs analogous to the popular "Big Five" theory of personality (see Barrick & Mount, 1991). More recently, a study of psychology students found that the degree to which these three needs (autonomy, competence, and relatedness) are satisfied had a direct bearing on the students' sense of well-being (Reis et al., 2000).

A final observation on self-determination and intrinsic motivation

SDT is broader than CET (although the former subsumes the latter) and has applications in a variety of settings such as education, sports, and work. Indeed, much of the early work in this area (e.g., Lepper & Greene, 1978) and some of the later work (e.g., Ryan et al., 1985) was conducted in educational settings. As has been the case in many other theories of work motivation to be discussed in the book, CET and SDT represent an evolving body of work-in-progress that, its adherents claim, are consistent with various elements of other leading theories of work motivation (Gagné & Deci, 2005) such as goal setting (see Chapter 13), job characteristics theory (see Chapter 7), the needs theories of Maslow and Alderfer (as discussed earlier in this chapter), organizational commitment (see Chapter 10) as well as others not featured here. In the same manner as equity theory gave way to justice theories (see Chapter 11), behavior modification evolved into social cognitive theory (see Chapter 14), and Maslow's elaborate hierarchical theory of needs gave way to more simplistic models (as described earlier in the current chapter), Deci's early work on the overjustification effect evolved into CET and then SDT (see Ryan & Deci, 2000). Critics such as those summarized by Latham (2007) may be correct in concluding the SDT is not yet ready to be taken seriously as a stand-alone theory of work motivation. But, as Gagné and Deci pointed out recently (2005), it is consistent with many other important theories and helps these other theories explain work motivation more effectively. Stay tuned.

VALUES AND WORK MOTIVATION

Related to the tradition that has focused on human needs as the basis for understanding work behavior is a similar tradition that has focused on human *values*. To consider values in the workplace is to probe the very reasons that people work and why they behave the way they do in their jobs (Posner & Munson, 1979; Sikula, 1971). A person's values lie at the core of his or her conscious career decisions (Judge & Bretz, 1992) and the affective reactions people have to their jobs, defining for us the concepts of job satisfaction and job dissatisfaction (Locke, 1969).

In fact, some studies suggest that merely subscribing to certain values in the course of a career contributes to satisfaction with one's work (Blood, 1969; Merrens & Garrett, 1975).[11] Values and value similarity between managers and their subordinates can also interfere with the legitimacy of day-to-day human resource management, as in the case of the validity of performance ratings made

---

[11] Merrens and Garrett (1975) specifically studied the "Protestant ethic," where "hard and steady work is valued" (p. 125).

by superiors of their employees (Senger, 1971). In fact, the degree of perceived similarity between one's own values and those of one's leader has been shown to predict a person's satisfaction with the leader (Meglino, Ravlin, & Adkins, 1991). In short, values play a key role in human behavior in general and in the world of work in particular. We turn now to defining values and distinguishing them from needs.

Some Definitions of Values

Although needs and values are related concepts, they are distinct from one another both conceptually and empirically. It is also critical to distinguish between values and *attitudes*, a concept that we examine later in the book. What are values, and how are they related to the human desire to work or not to work? According to Kilmann (1981), values are objects, qualities, standards, or conditions that satisfy or are perceived to satisfy needs and/or that act as guides to human action. Subsequently, Connor and Becker (1994) defined values as "global beliefs [about desirable end states or modes of behavior] that underlie attitudinal processes. In particular, they serve as the basis for making choices" (p. 68). Hence, conceived of as global beliefs, values are neither attitudes nor behaviors. Instead, values are the very building blocks of the behavior of and choices made by individuals.

In much of the organizational literature dealing with values, the framework and definition advanced by Rokeach (1969) has been particularly popular: "[A]n enduring belief that a specific mode of conduct or end-state of existence is personally and socially preferable to alternative modes of conduct or end-states" (p. 160). For Rokeach and those who have adopted his conception, values entail attention to both means (such as acts) and ends (such as outcomes of various sorts). Examples of *instrumental* values for Rokeach are: Ambitious, capable, broadminded, clean, logical, and loving. Examples of his *terminal* values are: A comfortable life, a world of beauty, pleasure, and wisdom (Rokeach, 1973).

Needs vs. Values

As we defined them earlier in this chapter, needs represent forces in the brain region and central nervous system (Murray, 1938). These forces, aroused internally or by outside factors, compel a person to search for or avoid certain things thought to be useful to reduce the force(s). As we saw earlier in this chapter, *press* is a feature of the outside environment that can arouse or strengthen the force of a need, such as a plate of aromatic food presented at a time when a person may or may not otherwise have felt hungry.

Values enter the picture through their effects on the choices a person makes in selecting among commodities, events, or outcomes to satisfy needs. In fact, Rokeach (1979) claims that values "can be regarded as the cognitive representations of internal 'needs' mediated by external 'presses' " (Murray, 1938). Put another way, values may be conceived of as cognitive representations of underlying needs – whether social or antisocial, selfish, or altruistic – after they have been transformed to also take into account institutional goals and demands. In this way, "all of a person's values, unlike all of a person's needs, are capable of being openly admitted, advocated, exhorted, and defended, to oneself and to others, in a socially sanctioned language" (p. 48). For example, a person may have a strong need for other people's esteem, which he seeks to satisfy by purchasing expensive clothes, cars, and other toys. Such a person would be said to *value* expensive clothes, cars, and other toys, but it could not be said that he needs them per se. A second person, by contrast, might seek to satisfy an equally strong need for esteem through community service and a humble life of spirituality and clean living. The second person may be well able to articulate a desire to provide such service or to live in such a manner but may not be able to identify the needs that underlie these stated values and behaviors. Same need but different instrumental and terminal values.

If we set aside the distinction between needs and values, it is clear that both are critical in understanding work motivation. Most theories in this area assume that people have basic, underlying needs but that it is their values that most directly influence the preferences people express for how they desire to be rewarded (and punished) in the workplace. Similarly, managers who wish to influence, reward, and/or punish employee behavior at work need to be most keenly aware of employee values, because at one level or another, we all share the same ultimate set of needs, to varying degrees.

Attitudes are cognitive and affective *orientations toward specific objects and situations*, as we will see in detail in Chapter 9. For values theorists, behavior is the manifestation of a person's fundamental values and corresponding attitudes. The relationships among these concepts are depicted in Figure 3.2.

Terminal and Instrumental Values

Rokeach (1969, 1973) made an important distinction between terminal and instrumental values, as suggested earlier. Terminal values represent ultimate end goals of existence, such as wisdom, equality, and family security. Instrumental values represent the behavioral means of achieving various end goals, such as being honest, ambitious, or logical (Rokeach & Ball-Rokeach, 1989).

Values Versus *Work Values*

One issue of major contention in the values literature has to do with a distinction between values (in the general sense) and *work values*, a concept that implies the particular set(s) of values that govern employee work behavior in all its forms. Most conceptions and definitions of *work values* per se are consistent with most general definitions of values in the broader sense, but their focus is on work, work behavior, and work-related outcomes (e.g., Wollack, Goodale, Wijting, & Smith, 1971). One typical definition was provided by Pine and Innis (1987), who conceived of work values as "an individual's needs and priorities and consequent personal dispositions and orientations to work roles that have the perceived capacity to satisfy those needs and priorities" (p. 280). Another definition was provided by Nord et al. (1988): "We define work values as the end states people desire and feel they ought to be able to realize through working" (p. 2).

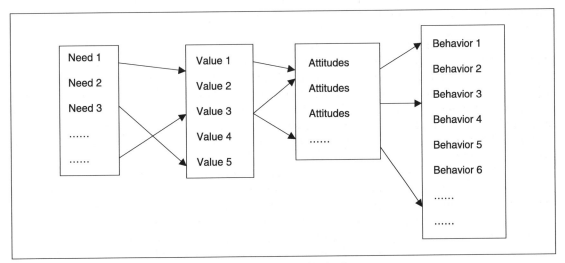

FIG. 3.2   Relationships among needs, values, attitudes, and behavior.

The controversy has to do with whether there is any benefit added – such as conceptual clarity, applied insights, or academic usefulness of any sort – in distinguishing between values in general (as Rokeach and his followers did, for instance) and values related to the workplace. Critics of the generality distinction claim that work values are, or should be conceived of as, subsets or derivatives of general values and that the distinction is bogus and muddies the water, adding nothing that is really new. The other side argues that finer analysis and understanding of the workplace and of problems and successes in the workplace and in people's careers can be gained by thinking of sets of less general/more specific values that pertain to the world of work. One popular typology of work values includes concepts such as pride in work, activity preference, job involvement, attitudes toward earnings, and upward striving.

The role of work values

The point may be obvious but is probably worth stating nevertheless. The values approach to work motivation assumes that people will pursue through work those things, states, conditions, activities, and outcomes that they value. The job of managing or of motivating someone is, by this view, to arrange jobs, working conditions, and organizational policies in a way that appeals to workers' values. Whether this is possible is an interesting issue. We return to the matter shortly after we examine the question of the stability of human values. If values are not more or less stable, it will be virtually impossible for managers, teachers, parents, and others to influence human behavior by appealing to them.

Do work values change?

Nord et al. (1988) described how work values (as opposed to values in general) have evolved since the time of the early Greeks, for whom work was seen as a waste of time (such a view is feasible in a society where there are slaves to do the work). Later, Roman and Hebrew philosophers and clergy added to the Greek position the belief that work was a form of atonement necessary for humankind to pay for original sin. Much later, the emergence of the *Protestant work ethic* (Weber, 1930) expounded the virtue of work as "in itself the end of life, ordained as such by God" (p. 159). Clearly, if one stands back to examine the prevailing nature of work values over the millennia, change is abundantly apparent.

But what about value change over shorter periods of time? A study by Inglehart (1981) found that U.S. employee values remained remarkably stable over the 13-year period 1968–1981. The top six and bottom six values in this research did not vary by more than one rank over the period of the study. About the same time, England (1991) reported the second phase of a large-scale study of values among the U.S. workforce. Specifically, comparing data from two matched samples, one gathered in 1982, the other in 1989, England examined the degree of change that had occurred in over 41 *work values*. Underlying the 41 specific items were four general factors: (1) the importance and significance of work and working in one's life; (2) the normative beliefs and expectations that people hold about their obligations and entitlements at work; (3) the relative importance of achieving various work goals (alternatively called work values, work needs, and incentive preferences); and (4) the bases used by people to decide whether an activity is considered work or non-work.

England found statistically significant shifts of U.S. work values over the 7 years of the study. Although no single factor among the 41 he studied altered dramatically, collectively the findings suggested that economic goals had become more important and "comfort" goals seemed less important, reflecting what England sees as an instrumental reaction to the economic realities during the period between the two studies. Nevertheless, the importance of working as a life role declined over the same period. For many people, work seemed to be less intrinsically valued and more a means to certain ends than it had been previously. Between 1982 and 1989, no significant change was observed in the beliefs that Americans held about their entitlements from employers or about their obligations to the organizations for which they worked.

Value Change at the Individual Level

Studies by Inglehart (1981) and England (1991) suggested that people's values can and do change, particularly values related to working. Large-scale studies of this sort are interesting, but they failed to shed much light on the dynamics related to the change in individuals' values. Few studies, in fact, have tried to do this. An exception is a fascinating, classic study by Lieberman (1956), which demonstrated how natural changes in workplace roles altered the attitudes of a sample of workers as they moved from rank-and-file jobs into either foreman's or shop steward's positions, and back again.[12] The attitudes in question were the employees' views regarding management and officials of management, their views regarding unions and union officials, their attitudes toward the management-sponsored incentive system, and finally, their attitudes regarding the union-sponsored seniority system. The results of the study, somewhat simplified, can be summarized as follows: The expressed attitudes of the employees studied correlated directly with the roles they occupied at given points in time. As their work roles changed and then changed back again, so did their attitudes (and presumably their work values) in accordance with their roles.

A second, rare, longitudinal study conducted by Armon (1993) adopted an unusual approach based on the concept of moral development (Kohlberg, 1981, 1984). Armon asked 50 people, ranging in age from 23 to 70 years, "What is good work?" She followed these people and asked them the same question four times over a 12-year period. Armon found that many of the participants in her sample matured through a five-stage developmental sequence in which what they valued in work became less visceral, less instrumental, and directed more heavily toward the pursuit of higher values, such as ethical conduct, assisting other people, and having a positive impact on the world in general. She also found that those people who did progress toward higher philosophical standards of work values did so through a common developmental sequence, and that there were no differences between the men and women in her sample. In fact, progression through the stages was related to education. Those people who advanced toward less selfish, more worldly values were more highly educated than those who did not. They also tended to have experienced more critical life events – mostly work-related events – that featured ethical problems or dilemmas that had to be dealt with or that required them to address issues of their own self-identity and integrity.

Despite the empirical studies cited here, very little is known about *how* values actually change in individuals, particularly their values about work and working, yet it seems clear that they do change (Connor & Becker, 1994; Stackman et al., 2000). Moreover, we know that many (most?) work organizations attempt to gain varying degrees of control over employees by the standardization of individual values. In fact, recent emphasis on the concept of organizational culture relates to these issues, as academics and practitioners alike have sought to understand and manipulate the homogeneity of individual values in North American workplaces. We will examine the concept of organizational culture as it relates to work motivation and control shortly. First, however, we visit the issue of whether North Americans belonging to different age groups value different things at work, as is frequently claimed in the popular press and some management literature.

---

[12] We emphasize that Lieberman was studying certain work-related *attitudes*, not values per se. Values theorists such as Rokeach (1969) and Connor and Becker (1994) would argue that the apparent changes in attitudes were instigated by corresponding changes in values, since values underlie and are consistent with attitudes.

Values and the Concept of Fit (Again)

As we saw in Chapter 2, the key link between dimensions of organizational culture and work motivation, performance and other work-related outcomes seems to be through the strength and homogeneity of values within a culture. (Recall our discussion of goodness of fit models in that chapter.) The question arises: How do organizations achieve homogeneity among the values of their employees? There are two basic strategies: To select people who appear to possess the "appropriate" values in the first place and/or to socialize employees, once hired, to conform to a set of value standards that management desires. McDonald and Gandz (1992) concluded that, for the sake of securing managerial control, the optimal strategy is to combine "make-value" with "buy-value" strategies. They reported that virtually all the Canadian executives they interviewed on the matter agreed with the importance of value congruity among their employees, and many described a variety of techniques they employed to encourage and reinforce the sharing of common values among their workers. McDonald and Gandz (1992) also demonstrated how human resource management programs of recruitment, selection, training, counseling, and support systems can create and nurture adherence to key organizational goals. For example, a study by Ashforth and Saks (1994) found interesting empirical support for a conceptual model proposed nearly 30 years ago by Van Maanen and Schein (1979), dealing with the various means by which organizations attempt to "socialize" employees (Ashforth & Saks, 1994). These researchers demonstrated how, to varying degrees, employers used six basic tactics with their new recruits (all business school graduates of Concordia University in Montreal) for the sake of making them malleable.

Common institutionalized socialization tactics, conducted in a fixed sequence of steps and with a fixed timetable for completion – rather than a series of idiosyncratic or individualized experiences – were related to lower levels of role innovation (i.e., higher levels of compliance) by the new hirees. The findings also showed that segregating newcomers from existing employees by designating them as initiates also made them more compliant. Also effective was the use of designated, experienced role models as trainers and mentors.

Although we have abundant everyday and anecdotal experience with organizational socialization tactics, procedures, and programs, only a few systematic studies such as that by Ashforth and Saks (1994) are known to this author. Army and Marine boot camps, the training sessions and codes of conduct prescribed by strong culture firms such as McDonald's, IBM, and Mary Kay, and even the early weeks in law school and graduate schools of business provide examples of the anecdotal and everyday experience of organizational socialization. Clearly, some employee work values are malleable, and it would appear that the work values of some people are more malleable than those of others.

Later we address the notion of *organizational values* and claim that the term is inappropriate. In the meantime, however, it is worth noting one study that sought to show that higher levels of "personal investment" (i.e., motivation) would result among employees whose personal incentives (or values) matched the rewards and espoused cultural values of an organization than among employees for whom such a match was lower or did not exist. Contrary to expectations, the results showed that a highly salient organizational culture in which goals are clear, a work ethic is emphasized, and employees are evaluated and rewarded for their accomplishments had beneficial effects on the investment levels of most employees. The degree of match between the employee and the company did not seem to matter (Mayberry, 1985, reported by Maehr, 1987).

The ethics of strong cultures

It appears that most North American employers implicitly assume that they have a right as part of the employment contract to attempt to alter employee values. Similarly, many or most employees seem to share, tacitly at least, that assumption – that the company has a right to alter their values, within limits, in ways that will increase managerial control and employee uniformity and predictability. This is a moral issue that students of work motivation should consider. At some point, a question arises as to the limits of the rights of employers (as well as administrators in organizations such as graduate schools of business) to attempt to socialize, homogenize, deindividuate, and standardize the values and behaviors of managers, workers, clients, and students. Basic questions concerning the limits to the loss of individual rights and freedoms that can reasonably be expected or accepted in the greater context of a free society should be raised.

As discussed earlier, a central element of managerialism[13] has been the development of a shared culture or corporate value system. This feature, Heckscher (1988) observed, is antithetical to some very fundamental beliefs of North American society:

> This aspect is the source of some of the strongest emotions that have been aroused by managerialism. Our society retains a deep suspicion of social values from its historical struggles against religious oppression. The right to believe in whatever we please is one of our most cherished freedoms. We tend to emphasize impersonal and rational values because they protect us from arbitrary uses of personal power. *Thus any attempt to build shared values arouses suspicion* [emphasis added]. On the other hand, there seems to be an equally deep social longing for the sense of community that has been shattered by bureaucracy, a longing that creates an unresolved tension in many of our institutions.
>
> (Heckscher, 1988, pp. 95–96)

There may be fundamental ethical issues related to achieving value homogeneity by manipulating employee values and belief structures. Similarly, it is deemed unethical, and in many cases illegal, to *select* employees on the basis of their personal traits, such as gender, race, or age. One might ask why it is ethical, by the same token, for employers to presume to select from among job applicants on the basis of their apparent value structures. It seems that we take for granted that such practices are fair, reasonable, and morally justifiable. Yet as long as a selection device is related to a performance criterion, employers regularly select and reject prospective employees on their apparent values. As in the case of value manipulation after hiring, what are the limits to which an individual's values should be used as a basis to hire, fire, or transfer to a new job at a different location within a company? Is there nothing sacred about a person's values?

To our knowledge, such questions are seldom raised by managers and students of work motivation. Rarely are such practices examined objectively from the point of view of ethics, informed consent, freedom, and human dignity. It is obvious that by their very nature and definition, organizations require control and predictability. But where are the limits, and who is to decide how much managerial control used to "motivate" employees by tampering with (or appealing to) their values is legitimate in a democratic society?

Do Organizations have Values?

Do organizations have values? The discussion earlier in this chapter may have implied that they do. Certainly, we often hear people speak of organizational values. There are even books published with these words in their titles (e.g., Woodcock & Francis, 1989). In fact, Rokeach, one of the great scholars in the domain of the study of values, wrote the following:

> The value concept is an especially powerful one for all the social sciences because it can be meaningfully employed at all levels of social analysis . . . [I]t is just as meaningful to speak of cultural, societal,

---

[13] *Managerialism* is an umbrella term used by Heckscher (1988) to refer to a range of managerial techniques that go back decades, most of which have had as their goals increased employee satisfaction and productivity, usually through some form of work redesign or participation scheme.

institutional, organizational, and group values as it is to speak of individual values. If individual values are socially shared cognitive representations of personal needs and the means for satisfying them, then institutional values are socially shared representations of institutional goals and demands.

(Rokeach, 1979, p. 50)

It is a logical error many of us make when we anthropomorphize the organizations in which we work and with which we interact. To *anthropomorphize* something is to attribute to it characteristics of individual human beings – organizations are thought and spoken of as having, in a sense, minds, memories, hearts, and other distinguishing properties of *homo sapiens*. For example, we may hear people speak of "loving" the Air Force or of hoping that Baton's will remember them when they are due for a raise. When people cry while chopping onions, it is not because they are sorry for inflicting pain on the onions. It is true that organizations are comprised of people and can be defined *as* systems of interactions and events linking people (Katz & Kahn, 1966), but it is a logical error to attribute, other than metaphorically, human properties to aggregations of individuals (Stackman et al., 2000). Organizations do not have minds, memories, or hearts. Organizations do not possess aspirations, loves, or fears.

Nevertheless, in the paper cited earlier, Rokeach (1979) outlined five methods by which institutional values can be measured. Four of these methods require assessment of the value structures of individual "gatekeepers" or "special clients" related to the institutions in question. (The fifth method is to apply content analysis to the instrumental and terminal values reflected in formal documents and publications produced by the institutions for public consumption (1979, pp. 53–54).) Hence, although Rokeach claims that aggregations of people have values, he recognizes that operationally, one must assess the values of key players to make sense of the concept.

There are many problems with these practices. First is the matter of determining whose individual values are to be assessed and then aggregated to yield a composite definition of the organization's values. Second is the issue of how, arithmetically, such values or value profiles (see Connor & Becker, 1994) are to be aggregated. Third, there are the possible ethical problems of (mis)leading lower-level participants and interested outside parties (such as customers, clients, and others) about the "values" of the organization, as if these values possessed the same qualities as those possessed by single persons (e.g., trustworthiness, loyalty, and honesty). Finally, there is a major practical problem here, one that should concern practitioners and scholars alike. We must assume that there is a degree of coherence or agreement among the value structures of the gatekeepers. Modern theorists in organizational culture openly and readily admit that organizations of any size are likely to feature multiple cultures, varying across various functional, ethnic, age, or professional groups, for example. Hence, to portray a single organization as having a strong culture implies that value congruence exists, in abundance, throughout the organization. To the extent that this is not so, then it becomes meaningless to speak of an organization's (singular) culture, and hence, of its values. Therefore, the transporting of an individual-level trait or concept (in this case, values) to a level of analysis higher than that of single individuals is, at best, a metaphorical use of the terms involved. At worst, it is a logical error that will only confound analysis and our study of how organizations work (Stackman et al., 2000). The key point here is that it is critical to keep individual-level concepts (such as needs and values) focused on and devoted to the understanding of individual-level problems and phenomena, and to create, invoke, and utilize other terms, representing other concepts, to deal with group, organizational, and institutional issues, as appropriate.

What do Employees Value?

Now that we have examined at length the concepts of employee needs and values and some of the important theoretical and applied issues related to them and to their roles in work motivation, we turn briefly to two questions: What, then, *do* North American employees value? What do they seek from their work?

Actually, these questions have been the focus over many decades of countless surveys conducted by journalists and social scientists. Often, the focus is on reported *changes* in employee work values (as discussed earlier). Often, the focus is specifically on the issue of the relative importance of money vis-à-vis other outcomes. In fact, the revelation that employees value more than merely money and economic security was probably the most socially significant findings of the famous Hawthorne studies, which precipitated the human relations movement of the 1940s (see Roethlisberger & Dickson, 1939). In virtually every study of this variety (in affluent societies) money is found not to be the most important motivator for most groups of employees.

Sometimes the focus is on international similarities and differences in values. An example of this line of inquiry was provided by Schwartz (1992) and Schwartz and Bilsky (1987). These researchers propose that, for example, there are seven distinctly different motivational values which transcend many international boundaries: Achievement, enjoyment, maturity, prosocial, restrictive conformity, security, and self-direction (Schwartz & Bilsky, 1987). Another vein of attention has been on gender differences. Do men and women value the same things from their work? Kovach's (1987) research suggests that there are few significant gender differences these days, although it appears from his work that women may place slightly higher emphasis on "full appreciation of work" than men do and that women also place greater importance on interpersonal relations and communications.

A study by Konrad and Langton (1991) tended to support these conclusions. These researchers surveyed a total of 42 empirical studies that were published in the North American management and organizations literature in the late 1980s and early 1990s and found that certain "job outcomes," such as prestige, autonomy, leisure, avoiding pressure, and influence, appear not to be valued differently by men and women. By way of contrast, certain other work values (or job preferences, as they call them) – money, advancement, leading others, and taking responsibility for risks – were more or less important to men than to women. They also found that six work-related outcomes were more important to women than to men: Achievement, intrinsic job aspects, relationships on the job, working conditions, balancing work and family, and helping others. Interestingly, of the 32 studies Konrad and Langton (1991) surveyed, 17 showed that men placed a higher value on money than women did and no studies reported that women valued money more highly than men.

Torbert (1994) provided a personal assessment of the concept of "good work." For him, good work is four personal values that, for him, collectively comprise a good life. In addition to good work, Torbert drew attention to the importance of "good money," good friends, and good ideas. Of these, good ideas are the highest value because, in Torbert's integrated scheme, they are most likely to emerge in the context of good work with good friends, all enabled by the earning of good money. Good work:

> [M]eans work that invites the development of craft-like skills and judgment (whether in the realm of materials or language). Such work calls for a kind of mastery that is never fully achieved, in the sense that it can thereafter be exercised in a rote, repetitive or mechanical fashion. Instead, good master-work requires and reflects an active attention by the masterworker at each moment to the interplay between one's own body in action and the material . . . This active attention integrates knowledge and application. Prior experience and future ideal, disciplined sobriety and spontaneous responsiveness. In short, good work raises the consciousness of the worker. It integrates mind, body, and good health.
>
> (Torbert, 1994, p. 61)

Good money does not necessarily means lots of it, according to Torbert's values. Rather, good money is enough money to enable a person to achieve and blend the other three values (good work, good friends, and good ideas). A person who doesn't earn enough to pursue these other values is earning too little money. A person who is driven to make lots of money often must do so at the expense of not attaining good friends, enjoying good work, or pursuing good ideas. Torbert's notions about the good life are provocative, coherent, and clearly the result of many years of existential insight and experience. The reader is urged to read the original essay to get a complete appreciation of this fascinating concept of one person's values, especially as they relate so closely to a person's motivation to work.

A large-scale study of employees in the unionized sector of the United States found that workers want more "say" (meaning influence and participation) in the workplace than they currently have, believing that greater participation will benefit both their own welfare as well as the prosperity of the organizations that employ them (Freeman & Rogers, 1999). This "Worker Representation and Participation Study" (WRPS) found that participation was sought both for individual workers as well as for groups. One-third of the respondents wanted more cooperative relations with management groups and to be treated with more respect and trust by management (recall our earlier discussion of Theory X and Theory Y belief systems). The greater "say" and improved relations were hoped to result through varying forms of collective representation, whether that be in the form of labor management committees and councils (European style) or through certified unionization, complete with collective bargaining. The workers believed that although most of the management for whom they worked were technically competent, these managers were seen as unwilling to share power in the decision-making and policy-setting processes. Unionized employees in the sample generally supported their unions and often believed, incorrectly, that many management acts that they see as unfair are often not illegal. In other words, many workers overestimated their statutory rights.

In many ways, these desires for power sharing are not surprising, particularly in the context of North American society, where individual rights and freedom are so predominant. Indeed, the need for self-determination is the central topic of Chapter 7 of this book.

The Value of the Values Concept

In a review of values and the workplace, Connor and Becker (1994) were quite critical of the state of our collective understanding of individual values. They cite a list of reasons for their assessment, some of which are methodological and many of which sound similar to the sorts of criticisms raised by theorists such as Ford (1992) of motivation theory based on needs. Connor and Becker (1994) decried the limited capacity of knowledge of a person's values to enable us to predict that person's behavior. They criticized values researchers who use only parts of existing values instruments or rapidly compose their own ad hoc measures. The problems of unreliability that this causes mean that there is unknown validity in the measures that are taken, so it becomes impossible for values theorists to accumulate a coherent body of knowledge. Finally, Connor and Becker (1994) argued that researchers frequently neglect to consider values as a feasible set of factors to take into account when trying to understand organizational behavior, even, in some cases, after values data are collected. In short, Connor and Becker (1994) issued a plea for more and better inclusion of the values concept in our thinking about work organizations. Their cry is acknowledged by this author, who believes that values have, in fact, been underdeveloped, badly conceived of, and poorly measured in the particular context of the study of work motivation. Researchers and theorists interested in work motivation could – and should – do better with values.

NATIONAL CULTURE AS A CONTEXT FOR STUDYING WORK MOTIVATION

In Chapter 2, we explored the meaning and significance of the concept of "contextualizing" organizational research (cf. Johns, 2006; Rousseau & Fried, 2001), recognizing that, to this point, we have largely restricted our discussion of context to considerations contained *within* individual national and cultural boundaries and that the default assumption of the discussion has been that our knowledge about work motivation and related concepts is Western, primarily North American. It is time to relax this assumption and broaden the argument for contextualizing theory and research on work motivation.

The future of understanding work motivation is rapidly requiring greater understanding of global differences in work motivation (Erez & Earley, 1993; Erez, Kleinbeck, & Thierry, 2001) regardless of the role that values and differences in values play. So, in the remaining sections of this chapter, we discuss the work that has been accomplished so far in the fascinating field of international and cross-cultural differences in work motivation (Latham & Pinder, 2005).

An early study (Williams, Whyte, & Green, 1966) comparing the job attitudes of American and Peruvian workers indicated that at least some organizational scholars recognized the importance of cross-cultural differences years ago, although the issue was not extensively studied until recently. More recently, Steers and Sanchez-Runde (2002) stated that societal culture determines three key sets of distal sources of motivation: (1) people's self-concept including personal beliefs, needs, and values; (2) norms about work ethic and the nature of "achievement," tolerance for ambiguity, locus of control, etc.; and (3) "environmental factors" such as education and socialization experiences, economic prosperity, and political/legal systems. These distal factors influence self-efficacy beliefs, work motivation levels and goals, as well as the nature of incentives and disincentives to perform.

Accordingly, Huang and Van de Vliert (2003) studied how national characteristics moderate the relationship between job characteristics and job satisfaction – a topic of central importance in the area of work motivation. On the basis of a huge sample (107,202 employees working in 49 countries), they found that the link between intrinsic job characteristics (such as autonomy, for example) and job satisfaction is stronger in richer countries, and in countries in which there are better social welfare programs. Similarly, the relationships were higher in nations where the culture is more individualistic than collectivistic and where the norms for power distance are smaller (characteristics discussed later). In addition, they found that although extrinsic rewards are positively related to satisfaction in all countries, "motivating satisfaction" was more strongly related to intrinsic job characteristics in countries with good governmental social welfare programs, regardless of the degree of power distance.

Following a review of the literature, Markus and Kitayama (1991) found that whether an individual has an independent or an interdependent self-concept has major implications for cognition, emotion, and motivation. They argued that most of what is known scientifically about "human nature" is based on a "Western view of the individual as an independent, self-contained, and autonomous entity who (a) comprises a unique configuration of internal attributes (e.g., traits, abilities, motives and values) and (b) behaves primarily as a consequence of these internal attributes" (p. 224). Consequently, motives such as (a) individual achievement, (b) avoidance of cognitive conflict, and (c) enhancement of one's self-esteem are more frequently found in Western countries than are motives such as deference, affiliation, and abasement. The latter are more salient among people with interdependent concepts of self, such as employees in Asia, Latin America, and parts of Africa. The implications of this hypothesis for understanding work motivation in cross-cultural settings is profound.

Similarly, Erez and Earley (1993; see also Earley, 2002; Erez, 2000) have developed a "model of cultural self-representation" to guide individual behavior and managerial practice in cross-cultural settings. They argued that people strive to fulfill values for self-enhancement, efficacy, and self-consistency. Their model is based on two dimensions frequently used to characterize national cultures: Individualism–collectivism,[14] and power distance.[15] Three principles are advanced to assist the design and interpretation of motivation and reward systems: (1) identify the cultural characteristics of a country regarding collectivism/individualism and power distance; (2) understand yourself and the cultural values you represent; and (3) understand the meaning of various managerial practices (such as differential vs. flat salary reward distribution and top-down vs. two-way communication styles) in each country (Erez, 2000, pp. 419–425).

Projecting values onto people from other cultures that differ in these two key dimensions can create dysfunctional consequences in terms of employee motivation, interpersonal communication, and overall performance (Earley, 2002; Steers & Sanchez-Runde, 2002). On the other hand, research shows that taking such cultural considerations into account can be effective from the point of view of work motivation and performance. For example, a cross-cultural study by Roe, Zinovieva, Diebes, and Ten Horn (2000) found differential relationships between context variables and outcome variables in a comparative test of a motivation model in Bulgaria, Hungary, and the Netherlands. Similarly, Man and Lam (2003) showed how individualism/collectivism moderated the relationship between job complexity and autonomy, on one hand, with group cohesiveness, on the other (the link was stronger in the context of an individualistic culture). In two case studies conducted in widely dissimilar cultures (Morocco and Mexico), d'Iribarne (2002) demonstrated how standard, North American-style motivational techniques were effective only when modified to take into account cultural characteristics of the two countries.

In a conceptual analysis of the issue, Leung (2001) argued that: (1) Work teams in collectivistic cultures have higher levels of unconditional benevolence and positive social identity which, in turn, lead to higher levels of in-group involvement than is the case of groups who value individualism; (2) productivity and performance levels are more homogenous (not necessarily higher or lower) in collectivistic cultures than in individualistic cultures; (3) motivational strategies by superiors have more effect on subordinates in cultures with high levels of power distance than in cultures low in power distance; and (4) negative reactions from supervisors in high power distance cultures generate more negative reactions among workers than is the case in low power distance cultures. An experiment comparing Israeli and Chinese college students in Singapore supported the hypothesis that people from low power distance cultures, the Israelis, set higher goals and reach higher performance levels than people from a high power distance culture, the Chinese (Kurman, 2001).

Earley (2002) proposed a three-level construct of "cultural intelligence," in which a person's self-efficacy vis-à-vis social discourse in cross-cultural settings plays a key role in the effectiveness of such interactions. High self-efficacy resulted in individuals' initiation of cross-cultural interactions, persisting in the face of early failures, and engaging in problem solving as a way of mastering necessary skills.

Other Important Cross-Cultural Values and Variables of Interest

Earlier, we discussed Erez and Earley's (1993) model of "cultural self-representation" and the roles played in that model by two of the most familiar dimensions in the cross-cultural literature on management and organizational behavior: Individualism/collectivism and power distance. We now

---

[14] Individualism–collectivism pertains to the degree to which people in a culture are autonomous individuals or embedded in their groups (see Gelfand, Bhawuk, Nishii, & Bechtold, 2004, for a recent review of the literature on this construct).

[15] This dimension relates to the degree to which "a community accepts and endorses authority, power differences, and status privileges" (Carl, Gupta, & Javidan, 2004) among its members.

briefly review a variety of other important parameters that social scientists have used in cross-cultural research that have a bearing on employee relations and work motivation: Performance orientation, future orientation, gender egalitarianism, assertiveness, humane orientation, and uncertainty avoidance. A wonderful recent source of research on these parameters is the *GLOBE* study reported by Robert J. House and a host of international scholars (House, Hanges, Javidan, Dorfman, & Gupta, 2004).

Performance orientation

This dimension reflects the degree to which a community encourages and rewards innovation, high standards, and performance improvement (Javidan, 2004). According to Javidan (2004), the roots of this concept can be found in Max Weber's (1904/1930) writings about the so-called Protestant work ethic, mentioned earlier in this chapter. It also has roots in the early thinking of Martin Luther and John Calvin and their notion of work as a *calling* (see Chapter 15; and Elangovan et al., 2007; Hall & Chandler, 2005). Briefly, for Luther, this idea implies that work is not a distraction from a godly life. For Calvin, having a calling implies that primary purpose for the world's existence is the glorification of God, and every individual is responsible to contribute to this cause through their daily work and other activities (Javidan, 2004). At its core, however, performance orientation is about the degree to which a society places real value on hard work, even though societies may vary in the ways by which they assess differences in work accomplishment.

Future orientation

Although this concept has been conceived of in a variety of ways over the years, in the context of cross-cultural analysis it is taken to mean "the degree to which a collectivity encourages and rewards future-oriented behaviors such as planning and delaying gratification (Ashkanasy, Gupta, Mayfield, & Trevor-Roberts, 2004).

Cross-cultural differences in gender egalitarianism

Some societies are more egalitarian in the roles they expect men and women to play than others. Hofstede (1997) referred to this dimension as the "taboo" dimension of national cultures. Some societies have strict and even codified rules about the roles and activities that women (in particular) can play, whereas other societies make fewer or no such distinctions.

Assertiveness

This dimension deals with whether the people in a culture are generally encouraged to be assertive, aggressive and tough, as opposed to nonassertive, non-aggressive, and tender in their social relationships (Den Hartog, 2004).

Humane orientation

The roots of this concept lie in many of the world's religions, such as Judaism, Christianity, and Islam. Orders from God include specific duties and prohibitions that are associated with goodness and humanitarian behaviors such as giving alms to the poor or, at least, not harming one's fellow humans. Societies strong in humane orientation feature strong attachment to values such as altruism, benevolence, kindness, love, and generosity. Therefore, societies high in humane orientation will find people typically to be (in comparison to societies low in humane orientation): Other-focused, altruistic, and responsible for one another's well-being. Members of extended families take care of one another across generations and the state is not expected to enact laws to assure that the weak and infirm are provided for – the social norms of the people enforce these patterns. Low humane orientation societies feature much more self-interest and devotion to personal luxury and pleasure. The state is expected to enact laws to protect minorities and people in need because it does not expect such individuals to be taken care of automatically by the natural goodwill of its citizens.

Uncertainty avoidance

This parameter "involves the extent to which ambiguous situations are threatening to individuals, to which rules and order are preferred, and to which uncertainty is tolerated in a society" (de Luque & Javidan, 2004). Societies high on this dimension feature orderliness, consistency, structure, formalized procedures, and laws to cover day-to-day life situations. At the individual level, it is closely related to the concept of *tolerance for ambiguity* (see Budner, 1962). Cyert and March (1963) developed this construct at the organization level to discuss the mechanisms organizations use to minimize the need for predicting uncertain events in their task environment. Hofstede (1997) discussed this construct as a national characteristic that varies across societies.

Not all motivation-related values vary across cultures. A study of more than 19,000 participants from 25 countries (Scholz, Dona, Sud, & Schwarzer, 2002) found a high degree of consistency in the psychometric properties of a scale assessing general self-efficacy, an important concept in the mechanisms related to goal setting and self-regulation.

Other-Orientation *within* Western Cultures

Our brief foregoing review of cross-national research on work values makes it clear that collectivism is a key component of the values structures of many non-North American cultures. Indeed, we have seen that the dimension of individualism–collectivism is a major construct used to contrast Western and many non-Western (most frequently, Asian) cultures. Hence, it would be easy to conclude that a values orientation toward the welfare of collectives or, at least, of other people, is strictly a non-Western characteristic.

But that would be an oversimplification. Meglino and Korsgaard (2004) have recently drawn attention to the value of other-orientation *at the individual level*. They view other-orientation as a general trait that varies among people within cultures as well between populations of people at the cultural level. Indeed, they have shown that individual differences in this general trait, which they treat as a value, are predictive of differences in behavior similar to those differences observed when groups from different national cultures are compared. For example, in one study, they showed that self-ratings of performance, which are usually upwardly biased in Western culture, are far less prone to such biases among Westerners who are other-oriented (Korsgaard, Meglino, & Lester, 2004). While there are a variety of explanations for the tendency of some individuals within an individualistic culture to be more other-oriented than others (see Korsgaard, Meglino, & Lester, 1997 for a review), they believe that variance on this trait can help to explain a number of other organizational behaviors that seem at odds with an ironclad assumption that all Westerners are driven by self-interest and, instead, place relatively high importance on helping others. Examples from the workplace and organizational behavior literature include prosocial behavior (cf. Organ, 1990) and even engaging in occupations that are primarily directed to serving other people, often at risk to one's self. Such individuals are simply not as prone to engage in complex calculations of personal costs and benefits as others when they process social information (Simon, 1995). They will act far less consistently than others in accordance with predictions of many work motivation theories, such as those presented elsewhere in this book (because virtually all of these Western-grown models assume a "rational," self-interest model of human functioning). They will also be far less likely to escalate their commitment to failing courses of action (cf. Staw, 1976) or be influenced by job design factors of the sort we discuss later in this book to enhance employee motivation and job satisfaction.

Accordingly, Lam, Schaubroeck, and Aryee (2002) found that perceptions of organizational justice had stronger effects on satisfaction, performance and absenteeism among U.S. research participants who, *as individuals*, scored relatively low on power distance – the same parameter that has been used so successfully as a cross-national variable to differentiate countries from one another (see Hofstede, 1997; Leung, 2001), and Turillo et al. (2002) found that some people find that virtue is its own reward, and are prone to making decisions that require some degree of self-sacrifice for the benefit of others. (We will return to some of these issues about virtue, selflessness, and deontic morality in Chapter 11.)

As Ronen (2001) points out, although much of the recurrent interest in groups, teams, and other collectivities found in Western culture (and management literature) can be explained by noting that collectives are often useful for promoting individual goals, there are also other, non-selfish, non-instrumental values associated with the promotion of the welfare of others, independent of concern for self-interest. Interestingly, while we are frequently cautioned against allowing Western values and mentality from inappropriately influencing our study of the motivation of people from other cultures, we have here an example of how a major cross-cultural variable (individualism–collectivism) is shedding new light on otherwise anomalous organizational behaviors among Westerners.

The Limitations of Values as a Lens for Cross-Cultural Analysis

The preceding studies show that progress has been made in understanding cross-cultural differences in work values and motivation. In short, national culture can be a powerful explanatory factor in understanding employee differences in work motivation, behavior, and attitudes, either as a main effect or as a moderating, context factor (Rousseau & Fried, 2001). Moreover, different mediating mechanisms explain why motivational strategies vary in effectiveness in different countries. Recently, a number of scholars have challenged the value of the values concept as a dominant lens through which cross-cultural work should be undertaken fruitfully. Rather, a broader set of factors – including values – has been proposed by Gelfand, Nishii, and Raver (2006). *Cultural tightness*, a macro-level concept directly analogous to the notion of organizational culture strength (discussed earlier in this chapter) is proposed as a potentially useful parameter for studying cross-cultural differences. A complete discussion of cultural tightness and its consequences for the study of cross-cultural differences in work motivation is beyond our current scope. The interested reader is referred to Gelfand et al. (2006).

SUMMARY AND A LOOK AHEAD

The purpose of this chapter has been to introduce a number of perspectives on human nature that are relevant to the study of work motivation. The assumptions we make about the essence of human nature affect the ways employees interact with one another, the ways managers and supervisors treat subordinates, and the ways organizational policies are promulgated and administered (McGregor, 1960). The assumptions that students and scholars make about human beings underlie the various theories of work motivation that come from social science (see Sullivan, 1986).

Clearly, there are many, many perspectives that we might have taken to examine human nature, but given the primary focus and topic of this book, in this chapter we focused most heavily on popular views of human nature that feature needs and values. People have been characterized by many popular theories of work motivation to be driven by their needs and guided by their values – in life as well as in their work. By comparison, the emotional side of human functioning has, until recently, received insufficient attention. Accordingly, in Chapter 4 we examine theories of human affect and the growing literature on the role of emotions and mood in work motivation and organizational behavior. In subsequent chapters, we will adopt different models of human nature and pursue the implications they offer for understanding work motivation. First, we examine humans as affective, emotional creatures.

Human Nature: Affect and Emotions as Motives to Work

4

*No man, for any considerable period, can
wear one face to himself and another to
the multitude, without finally getting
bewildered as to which may be the true.*
Nathaniel Hawthorne

Whatever else it may be, work is an emotional experience, a major part of the emotional lives of most people (Waldron, 2000). Strangely, however, emotion was largely ignored as a source of organizational behavior and employee motivation until only a few years ago. Previously it seemed that both managers and organizational scientists wanted to keep emotion and work organizations separated by a wall of denial and ignorance. At best, managing was viewed in large measure as an attempt to keep human emotion under control (Rafaeli & Worline, 2001). Unpleasant managerial decisions were best made, it seemed, by managers who could keep their emotions under control as well. More recently, however, both the scientific and applied literature have seen a proliferation of research and theory into the emotional dimensions of work and work organizations: Indeed, emotion has become a hot topic in the discipline (see Brief & Weiss, 2002; Latham & Pinder, 2005; Rafaeli & Worline, 2002).

It is obvious that *people have feelings at work* and that *they have feelings about their work*.[1] They brag with pride about their work successes and complain about their frustrations at work. Consider the joy people feel when they are promoted or when they succeed in a difficult task at their work. Consider the anger they feel when colleagues or coworkers frustrate their efforts. Consider the envy that many people feel when their peers are rewarded and they are not for work they judge to be of equal value. Consider the fear that people feel when there are rumors about layoffs. Consider the resentment when an employee is disciplined by management for breaking a company rule. Consider the excitement that a person feels when s/he falls in love with an employee in the office or in the factory. By nature, people are emotional creatures, and they take these emotions to work with them. Moreover, many of the emotions that people feel are formed, shaped, and experienced in the workplace. Lazarus and Lazarus (1994) claim that human beings are the most emotional animals on earth.

A BRIEF HISTORY OF AFFECT IN ORGANIZATIONAL SCIENCE

Ironically, some of the earliest theories of organizational behavior (e.g., Barnard, 1938; Likert, 1967; Mayo, 1933; Roethlisberger & Dickson, 1939; Whyte, 1948) were laced with observations about the

---

[1] Sandelands and Boudens (2000) also claim that many people have feelings *of* their work, i.e., they become "in an entirely non-mystical sense, one with the work . . . Feeling and doing are co-existent, codeterminous, and coordinate" (p. 53).

emotional side of work and working (Ashforth & Humphrey, 1995; Lord, Klimoski, & Kanfer, 2002; Wright & Doherty, 1998). Then emotions seemed to go out of style in North American behavioral science, and the dominant assumption for decades was that cognition is the primary cause of behavior (Derryberry & Tucker, 1994; Ross & Nisbett, 1991). Behaviorism also had a period of hegemony (see Skinner, 1953); there was no room for emotion in understanding the origins of human action in behaviorism (see Chapter 14).

Then in the mid-1970s, Locke (1976) defined job satisfaction as an *emotional reaction* that people feel after they appraise their jobs vis-à-vis their values (see Chapter 12 for more detail). It was a start, but Locke's definition was about all the emotional content in the field, even though the necessity to bring emotion back into organizational theorizing was being acknowledged. Indeed, one of the scholars whose work has raised the attention paid to affect has observed that job satisfaction does not capture the full range of affect [in the organizational sciences]" (Weiss, 2001). A conclusion reached by Sandelands and Buckner (1989) seems nearly as true at the time of this writing as it did 15 years ago. They wrote: "There is a lot to learn about work feelings. Despite a reconnaissance by literally thousands of studies . . . the territory of work feelings remains largely uncharted, beyond the frontier. Questions about why people feel as they do when working find superficial answers. It is said that the work is interesting, or challenging, or stressful, or dehumanizing. Or it is said that the match between the worker and work is a good or a bad one. Such answers betray little of the subtle texture and dynamics of the work itself, and even less of the intricate psychology of its apprehension and appreciation" (p. 106).

But the tide turned sometime in the mid-1990s: Since then, emotions have been taking on more importance in psychology and other disciplines (for example, see Meyer & Turner, 2002, on how emotion has been "discovered" in classroom settings and in educational psychology more generally). Nobel laureate Herbert Simon (1995) called for an increased emphasis on "affect" as part of his plan for further advancement of cognitive psychology. Emotions are even being recognized in economics and decision analysis (see Pieters & Van Raaij, 1988). Organizational scientists have responded to the call, and research and theory construction is underway in organizational behavior (see Rafaeli & Worline, 2001, for a more detailed historical review of the ascendancy and recognition of emotion in organizational life). One leader in the resurrection of interest in affect has suggested that the massive increase in attention being paid to it may cause a fundamental change in the domains claimed to be part of the discipline of organizational behavior (Brief, 2001). Accordingly, the purpose of this chapter is to explore the role of human emotionality in matters related to work motivation and behavior.

FORMS OF AFFECT: EMOTIONS, MOODS, FEELINGS, TEMPERAMENTS, AND PREDISPOSITIONS

A competent discussion of "emotions" or the role of emotions in work motivation requires that we distinguish among a number of concepts, all of which describe some aspect of human affect. Frequently, the term emotion is used in common parlance as an umbrella term to cover affect or some or all of the manifestations or forms of affect, but we must be more precise here.

What are Emotions?

Two leading authorities define *emotions* as:

> [C]omplex reactions that engage both our minds and our bodies. These reactions include: a subjective mental state, such as the feeling of anger, anxiety, or love; an impulse to act, such as fleeing or

attacking, whether or not it is expressed overtly; and profound changes in the body, such as increased heart rate or blood pressure. Some of these bodily changes prepare for and sustain coping actions, and others – such as postures, gestures, and facial expressions – communicate to others what we are feeling, or want others to believe we are feeling. An emotion is a personal life drama, which has to do with the fate of our goals in a particular encounter and our beliefs about ourselves and the world we live in. It is aroused by an appraisal of the personal significance or meaning of what is happening in that encounter. The dramatic plot differs from one emotion to another, each emotion having its own particular story.

(Lazarus & Lazarus, 1994, p. 151)

Emotions can be thought of as "communications" to oneself and to others (Oatley & Jenkins, 1992). In this view, they are readouts, some of which are communicative (Buck, 1985), although there are frequently "substantial differences between a person's conscious awareness and behavioral or physiological indications of emotions. Hence communications of emotion, which are picked up from behavioral signs, need not be consciously recognized by the person emitting these signs" (Oatley & Jenkins, 1992, p. 59, summarizing work by Lang, 1988).

Emotions can signal the occurrence of events relevant to important goals. They are changes of action readiness (Frijda, 1986). Emotions are mental states, or processes, that are usually elicited by external events. They are phasic; they have a "defined onset, perhaps rising to one or more peaks of intensity, and a decline" (Oatley & Jenkins, 1992, p. 59, citing work by Frijda, Mesquita, Sonnemans, & van Goozen, 1991). Emotions are determined by the personal meanings we attach to things and events, and hence depend on what is important to us and the things we believe about ourselves and the world.

Emotions often indicate intentions or changes of intentions. They affect other people's actions, tending to set pairs or groups of people into particular modes of interaction (Oatley & Jenkins, 1992). At any moment, an emotion can be experienced internally, behaviorally, and have varying degrees of intensity. They can be registered physiologically or by self-report. Emotions are usually elicited by evaluating events that concern a person's goals or needs. Sometimes these evaluations are innate or subconscious (Oatley & Jenkins, 1992). As noted in the Lazarus and Lazarus definition, most emotions usually include a distinctive subjective experience and physiological accompaniments, which Oatley (1992) calls "distinctive phenomenological tones" (p. 20). Thus, sadness feels different from joy or fear; love different from anxiety (although they may go hand in hand). Similarly, emotions are usually also associated with compulsive thoughts and, on many occasions, distinct facial expressions and bodily reactions.

For Oatley (1992) and Frijda (1986) an emotion is a "mental state of readiness for action . . . or a change of readiness" (Oatley, 1992, pp. 19–20) that is usually based on an evaluation of something in a person's life space that affects the person's goals or concerns. Moreover, these evaluations are not necessarily conscious but operate to specify a possible range of actions the person might take to protect personal concerns. For example, when we are frightened, we might consider acts such as fighting, fleeing, or submitting to the source of fear.

An ongoing controversy among psychologists and other interested scientists is whether some emotions are more "basic" while others are best considered blends or hybrids. The bases upon which the basic vs. non-basic battle has been fought has varied. The nuances of these debates are beyond our present scope: The interested reader is referred to Ekman and Davidson (1994). We provide only a few examples on the matter to illustrate the point. For example, Ekman and Friesen (1975) cited happiness, surprise, anger, and fear as examples of basic emotions. Oatley's (1992; Oatley & Johnson-Laird, 1987) list of basic emotions is restricted to happiness, sadness, anger, fear, and disgust. An important means for determining whether an emotion is basic is whether the facial expression associated with it is recognized across cultures (Oatley & Johnson-Laird, 1987). In comparison, blended emotions such as wariness may consist mostly of interest and moderate fear (Frijda, 1986). Hence, categorizing emotions can be a problem, and there are, in fact, many different taxonomies of emotions with only some overlap or agreement among theorists regarding which emotions are basic and which are mixes or composites of others (see Russell, 1991). Nevertheless, eventually we must adopt a taxonomy of emotions that has some degree of apparent academic merit as well as practical utility. We will do so shortly.

Of critical importance is the fact that common events or circumstances may result in different emotions for different people because the events or circumstances are interpreted differently. For example, a flip comment by a supervisor may generate anger in one employee because of a history of conflict between the supervisor and the employee, whereas the same comment may not be significant to another employee and therefore have no emotional consequence. This lack of one-to-one connection between events and emotional reactions often makes it difficult for outsiders to understand a person's emotional reaction to events such as comments made by others or even to more powerful events such as accidents or deaths.

Emotions as Internal Commodities

A short article in *Maclean's* (May 22, 2006, p. 41) reported that a restaurant in the Philippines helps its customers relieve their frustration by permitting them to throw plates "and other breakables" against its "wall of fury." The restaurant charges a nominal fee for this activity. People may yell epithets and even write statements of fury on the wall. The restaurant even offers more expensive breakables, for those individuals who don't receive enough relief from breaking a simple 33c plate.

In common parlance, many emotions are often *reified* – spoken of and considered as if they are physical entities within people, much as one might contain gallstones, a quart of beer, or even a goldfish (Tavris, 1982). Anger is a good example, as when people say: "She is full of anger" or "Henry was filled with jealousy." One implication of this conception of an emotion is that it is possible, even desirable, for the person *to get the thing out of themselves*, like a badly digesting meal. This raises the issue of voluntary control of our emotions. Some early thinkers, including Charles Darwin, extrapolated their observations of lower animals to the case of human beings. Dogs might be seen or thought of as becoming angry in response to threats or danger – their animalistic response is instinctive. Although Darwin was a brilliant ethologist, he is accused of being a poor psychologist: "[Darwin's] account of anger was oversimplified: someone offends you, so you dislike him; your dislike turns to hatred; brooding over your hatred makes you angry" (Tavris, 1982, p. 33).

Since the days of Darwin (and Freud), there have been schools of thought that people are healthier if they do *get their anger out*, because keeping it bottled up inside is bad for us. These "ventilationists" believe that not expressing our emotions causes pain and interpersonal conflict. They believe that we should openly express anger, love, sympathy, and other emotions openly and honestly – that high blood pressure, ulcers, depression, sexual problems, and substance abuse are probable consequences of withholding the expression of our emotions. As early as the 1960s we heard stories of Japanese companies providing their employees with rubber dummies and baseball bats so that they could give vent to their bottled-up emotions. A leading engineering firm in Calgary has established and furnished a quiet room for similar purposes, a place where emotional employees may go to cry, shout, or merely work through their emotions in private. The room is *very* popular.

At least one theorist rejects the value of the view that emotions are something locked up inside us, and that processes and devices aimed at "getting them out" are beneficial. She argues that although: "[S]uch views get people ventilating and agitating . . . they rarely recognize or fix the circumstances that make them angry in the first place. When Aesop's lion roared, no one thought the lion had a hostility complex or a problem with temper control; they knew a net had trapped him. No amount of chanting or shouting or pillow pounding will extricate us from the many nets of modern life" (Tavris, 1982, p. 45). Tavris's point has major implications for the management of many emotions in the workplace, particularly as they relate to frustration. No number of silent rooms, baseball bats, or ersatz supervisors will themselves rectify the dysfunctional policies and practices that give rise to human emotionality in organizations. People may feel better after cathartic sessions of violence, tears, or brooding, but their return to similar circumstances is likely to occasion recurrences of the emotions. The debate about the therapeutic value of expressing one's emotions – anger in particular – and of the possibility of controlling them completely is not resolved. The interested reader is referred to Tice and Baumeister (1993) for a summary of the history and contending positions in that debate. Their summary position is that "anger can be controlled and regulated and channeled to a substantial degree. But it cannot be eliminated" (p. 396). We will take a closer look at anger as a particular emotion later in this chapter.

Emotions and Feelings

A critical aspect of emotion is that it entails activation (Kitayama & Niedenthal, 1994). An emotional person is activated and prepared to act, depending on the strength of the feelings aroused and the potential objects of the aroused energy. Oatley and Duncan (1992) found that 77% of the emotions of happiness, sadness, anger, and fear included a subjective inner feeling of emotion; 77% included a bodily sensation; 81% came with involuntary thoughts; and 90% involved a "consciously recognized action or urge to act emotionally. Most episodes of emotion included all these features, but in some one or several features were absent" (Oatley, 1992, p. 21).

When we emote, we witness one or more bodily stimulations. When we say "love hurts," the expression has more than metaphorical meaning. Similarly, the condition we refer to as having a "broken heart" is actually characterized by pain and aching in one's heart and stomach, often accompanied by sadness and dread that one *feels* at the visceral level. Depending on which of many different philosophical perspectives one has, there are any of a wide number of emotions recognized by various camps. Accordingly, there are many different visceral feelings associated with emotional states, and there is not necessarily a one-to-one correspondence between emotions and their physical symptoms. The emotional feeling associated with the death of a friend may be similar to that associated with the absence of a loved one, even for a temporary period. The first emotion is usually referred to in our culture as grief, but in many ways it is similar to the longing and pining experience related to the absence of a loved one.

Two organizational scholars emphasized the feeling aspect of emotion in their definition:

> Emotions are ineffable feelings of the self-referential sort. They index or signal our current involvements and evaluations. Like sight and hearing, emotion provides a communication channel between the world and its moments and our assessments of just how we are gearing in and out of this perceptual world. They may be intense or subtle, fluctuate wildly or show stability within a narrow band. *What is certain, however, is the fact that we have no scientific or otherwise privileged access to feelings as either states or processes beyond that provided by self-reports. The validity of an emotion for those who feel it is a given, is subject to no known truth test, and is neither right nor wrong . . .* They are self-referential feelings an actor experiences or, at least, claims to experience in regard to the performances he or she brings to the social world [emphasis added].
>
> (Van Maanen & Kunda, 1989, p. 53)

Sometimes, emotions instigate other emotions and feelings. For example, people who exhibit what they quickly decide are extreme levels of joy and happiness may then immediately express embarrassment for their lack of self-control. People who catch themselves publicly engaging in extreme displays of pride (e.g., after a conquest) may quickly feel episodes of shame (or of guilt if their pride display offends the vanquished). The sensations of jealousy or envy can often trigger hatred toward those who would take a loved one from us or who possess things we covet. We may even accuse people of being "emotional" as a way of denigrating them, when, in fact, these people may be feeling the same emotion we feel, or are capable of feeling, in similar circumstances. Many men in our culture feel ashamed of their inability to control their spontaneous expressions of "soft" emotions, such as love or sadness, especially when tears confirm the feeling. In short, emotions often come in clusters and sequences, and the many combinations available are often difficult to predict and informative to witness.

Moods, Temperaments, and Affectivity

When emotional states are enduring and "have no specific objects to which the emotion is directed, they are called *moods*" (Kitayama & Niedenthal, 1994, p. 7; see also Salovey & Mayer, 1990). Moods can begin and last beyond exposure to an event or an agent in a person's life space. Moods tend to persist in the absence of specific events and stimuli (Frijda, 1986, p. 59). "The focus of a mood is broad rather than being centered on a single, narrow goal or event. Acute emotions usually are provoked by some event that sets them going, whereas moods express existential concerns that are apt to be diffuse" (Lazarus & Lazarus, 1994, p. 84). A person may have a general mood of anger or anxiety and carry it around for a period of 2 or 3 days, attaching it to all elements of her life. "Behaviorally, moods are configurations of activity that are not centered around an object or event, but in that fleeting manner attach now to this object, then to that; or similar configurations of activity easily evoked by a multitude of relatively insignificant events" (Frijda, 1986, p. 59). In one study of more than 200 sales personnel, for example, it was found that people's moods were negatively related to their absenteeism behavior (George, 1989). So in a sense, moods are not well focused but are generalized feelings that may attach to any and all events and people in a person's life as long as the mood is activated.

By contrast, a *temperament* is defined as a predisposition to an emotion (Oatley & Johnson-Laird, 1987). In other words, if someone has a predisposition toward the emotion of anger, for example, we say that the person "has an angry temperament." Psychologists use the terms *negative* and *positive affectivity* to describe people's characteristic tendencies to view the world either negatively or positively. One might expect that a person who has a basic negative affectivity would not often display a positive temperament or positive affectivity toward life's events. In fact, the two dimensions appear to be independent of one another; most of us are capable of projecting either affective state (George, 1992; Warr, Barter, & Brownbridge, 1983; Watson, Clarke, & Tellegen, 1988). As we will see later in this chapter, many authors believe that possession of a generally positive mood, backed by a characteristically positive affectivity, can be the source of many good things for both individuals and organizations. The currently popular "Positive Organizational Behavior" movement is predicated in large measure on the assumption that happiness, hope, forgiveness, and other positive moods and emotions have widespread beneficial effects for work motivation and employee behavior (cf. Cameron, Dutton, & Quinn, 2003; as well as a debate in the April 2006 edition of the *Academy of Management Review* devoted to the validity of this assumption).

PERCEPTIONS, COGNITIONS, AND EMOTIONS

An ongoing debate in psychology that has lasted for decades concerns the relationships among what people perceive, what they think and believe, and how they feel. In fact, the basic dualism between thinking and feeling dates back at least as far as Descartes: Thinking was thought to be the key activity of the mind, whereas emoting was one of several roles associated with the body (see Damasio, 1994; Goleman, 1995). One issue is whether a person's feelings or emotional state influence what is seen and believed. Another is whether, to have an emotional reaction to agents and events, a person has to perceive and think about events and impinging stimuli or whether emotions can affect a person directly, without being filtered through cognitive processes or accompanying them. Consider a person who is experiencing blockage in attempts to perform well on the job by the unavailability of subordinates. Is this manager likely to experience negative emotions (such as anger) immediately, without a clue as to the causes of employee absences? Or will the manager have to gain some insight, accurate or otherwise, into the motives and circumstances of the staff before emotion occurs?

Some of the earliest and most interesting work on this matter was reported by Schacter and Singer (1962) in what is called the *cognition arousal theory* of emotions. The key hypothesis in this theory is that emotional states result from an interaction of two factors: Physiological arousal and cognition about the causes of the arousal. The arousal is perceived of as being emotionally nonspecific; that is, the person merely feels stimulated and immediately becomes prepared to make sense of the cause of the stimulation, but the stimulation itself is experienced initially in the same way for all emotions. Once arousal has occurred, the person seeks clues as to its cause. The theory holds that both arousal and cognitive activity are *necessary* for an emotion such as happiness, fear, or shame to occur, *but they are not sufficient, taken together*, because the person must make the link between the arousal and those features of the environment associated with the arousal. This theory dominated the social psychology of emotion for many years. A review of the empirical support for the theory was provided by Leventhal and Tomarken (1986).

Considerable theory and controversy in the field of emotions has its roots in issues raised by cognition arousal theory. The central issue is whether people can have emotional reactions and, indeed, even behave exclusively on the basis of their emotions, before and without engaging in conscious thought about the circumstances they face. For example, consider a debate by two leading protagonists in an issue of the *American Psychologist* in 1984. One of these theorists, Lazarus (1984), summarized his position as follows: "Cognitive activity is a necessary precondition of emotion because to experience an emotion, people must comprehend – whether in the form of a primary evaluative perception or a highly differentiated symbolic process – that their well-being is implicated in a transaction, for better or worse" (p. 124). Thus, a person would not experience jealousy until realizing that the developing friendship between his sweetheart and the new employee in the office was based on more than business matters. He would have to recognize that there was an amorous interpersonal attraction developing between the two.

Somewhat more recently, Lazarus (1991) repeated and expanded his earlier position slightly. He claims that "cognitive activity causally precedes an emotion in the flow of psychological events, and subsequent cognitive activity is also affected by that emotion" (p. 127). For instance, consider a supervisor who is being blocked in attempts to improve the performance of her unit. The frequent absence of her employees is not likely to generate negative emotions (such as anger) until she gains some understanding of the situation. She will seek to determine whether her personnel are deliberately avoiding her (in which case anger is possible), or whether they are overworked and unable to come to her assistance. If it appears that there is some degree of insubordination afoot, the supervisor may immediately become angry and express that anger. In turn, the expressed anger will affect the way the supervisor perceives the subsequent attempts of her staff either to be more available or to continue not to be available when needed. However, if the supervisor perceives that it is a matter of overwork for her team, no emotion, or a different emotion, may be expressed. In fact, such a conclusion might yield positive influences on her beliefs about the value of her staff.

For many years, some people thought of emotions as "drive" variables, similar to hunger, fatigue, and thirst. According to the Lazarus school of thought, the difference between drives (or needs, as we have defined them) and emotions is that the latter require assessment by the person of what is happening. Emotions imply consciousness, an assessment of the situation. So although a person may become more and more thirsty the longer he is without water, an emotion such as fear occurs "only if a person appraises a situation as dangerous or fearful" (Averill, 1982, p. 10).

Representing the other side of the debate is Zajonc (1980, 1984). He believes in the "primacy of affect" and its independence from cognition. In his words, "preferences need no inferences." He believes that affect (emotion) can occur before, after, or simultaneously with cognition, and he adopts a slightly different definition of cognition than that of Lazarus. For example, Zajonc believes that it is possible for an employee to have an emotional reaction such as fear in response to the appearance of a supervisor without actually thinking about the supervisor and their relationship.

Much of the debate on the primacy of either emotion or cognition hinges on the difference between the two theories in their definitions of cognition. Zajonc (1984) claimed that his position is irreconcilable with that of Lazarus (1984) because of the way Lazarus defined cognition, a definition that Zajonc called narrow and limited. He argued that it is impossible to refute Lazarus's position, and "all distinctions between cognition, perception, and sensation disappear" (Zajonc, 1984, p. 121). These nuances and the semantics they involve are beyond our purposes here. The interested reader is referred to a helpful summary of the debate by Leventhal and Scherer (1987).

Physiological Evidence on the Debate

Damasio's (1994) and Goleman's (1995) summaries of research on the brain help to clarify some of the central debates related to the primacy issue and the issue of whether emotions help or hinder rational decision making. Goleman (1995) presented many cases of human behavior (often related to parents with children in peril) where the "passions overwhelm reason time and again" (p. 5). He speaks of human beings as having "two minds": A rational mind (which is centered in the cerebral cortex) and an emotional mind, whose functions are centered in other brain regions, such as the *limbic system.* In many or most day-to-day circumstances, the two minds work in harmony, with the emotional mind considering circumstances and the rational mind electing choices from alternatives available to the person for action.

But Goleman (1995) reminded us that from an evolutionary perspective, the emotional mind preceded the cortex. Our species developed the capacity to sense and feel long before we refined the capacity to think and reason. Sociologist George Simmel (1950) agreed: "If one arranges the psychological manifestations in a genetic and systematic hierarchy, one will certainly place, at its basis, feeling (though not *all* feelings), rather than intellect. Pleasure and pain, as well as certain instinctive feelings that serve the preservation of the individual and species, have developed prior to all operations with concepts, judgments, and conclusions. Thus, the development of the intellect, more than anything else, reveals the lag of the social behind the individual level, whereas the realm of feeling may show the opposite" (pp. 34–35).

Whether it is this primacy in evolutionary history that makes it happen is not clear, but human beings often act on the basis of emotion (after there has been perceptual activity) before the mind enters the decision. Goleman refers to such instances as "emotional highjacking" and offers many examples of cases where people perform extreme acts on the basis of their emotions – acts they regret (or appreciate) later, upon reflection. Goleman cites an incident involving himself as an example. He was fast asleep when he was suddenly wakened by a loud crashing sound in his bedroom. He leaped out of bed and hurried from the room, pausing only once he was outside to peer back in to see that the noise was caused by a stack of boxes that was falling in the corner of the bedroom. Goleman concluded that his flight from the room resulted from a simple connection between his perceptual apparatus (in this case, his hearing) and his amygdala (part of his limbic system). There had not been enough time for his cortex to get into the act until after the fact. He provides many similar stories to make the point that our emotional side can, in emergencies and on occasion, trigger behavior before the mind cuts in, but that human decision making is at its best when both the cognitive and the emotional systems are involved. (See Damasio, 1994, for similar evidence.) We return to this issue shortly.

At the time of this writing, the most comprehensive and convincing body of evidence on the debate has been offered by Zajonc (2000), who summarizes a number of experiments he and his colleagues have conducted since the 1984 exchange with Lazarus (1984) to demonstrate that affect and cognition are, indeed, independent. The evidence is quite convincing. It shows that a person can have their preferences (which Zajonc uses as his principal benchmark for affect) altered by experiences of which they are not cognitively aware. He writes (2000, p. 55):

Repeated stimulus exposures result in the growth of positive affect toward that stimulus, even when the stimulus is not accessible to awareness. Moreover, under some conditions, especially degraded stimulus access, affective ratings of stimuli are better indicators of the individual's past experience with these stimuli than recognition memory.

In short, affect may function independently of cognition. The challenge, Zajonc noted, is for researchers to note affective reactions as they collect cognitive judgments and to collect cognitive judgments even when we are studying affect. These conclusions bear major significance for the research and theory development remaining to be done in the study of work motivation that focuses on cognition and emotion, as is the case, for example, in further development of models such as affective events theory (which we will examine later in the chapter).

Emotionality and Rationality

A number of myths about emotions bear rejection. One is that emotions are irrational and do not depend on thinking and reasoning (Lazarus & Lazarus, 1994). Nevertheless (or at least to indicate how strongly people feel about the relationship between emotionality and rationality), consider an empirical investigation of Georgetown University students reported by Parrott (1994). He found that when his students were asked to recall a time when they were "emotional" and to describe what it felt like, the most common interpretation provided was that they were "irrational": Unable to think clearly, to cope effectively, or to appreciate others' points of view (Parrott, 1994). People seem to think of emotionality and rationality as incompatible. It may simply be a matter of language; that is, what people believe to be states of irrationality may simply be labeled or thought of as states of emotionality, when in other cultures or in other languages the same phenomenological state may not be thought of or defined as "emotional" (see Russell et al., 1994).

It may have been the pervasiveness of this "myth" that has caused the field to ignore emotions and emotionality to the extent that it did for so long (Ashforth & Humphrey, 1995). So much writing and theorizing about organizations operating under "norms of rationality" (see Thompson, 1967) has affected not only the academic study of work and motivation but the very practice of management. To be rational has been the goal; to be emotional or to be seen as emotional has not been in vogue for many decades. As noted earlier, the venerable Herbert Simon indicated his belief that even cognitive psychology will now have to embrace emotionality in order to proceed as an academic science (Simon, 1995).

Another myth is that emotionality gets in the way of human adaptation. Emotions are seen as "intimately connected with the fate of our struggles to adapt to life in a world that is not very forgiving of adaptive failure" (Lazarus & Lazarus, 1994, p. 3). For example, in their discussion of the sources of error that can arise when people are taking tests, Cooper and Emory (1995, p. 147) stated that "respondents may also suffer from temporary factors like fatigue, boredom, *anxiety*, or another distraction; these limit the ability to respond carefully and fully. Hunger, impatience, or *general variations in mood* may also have an impact." Thus, emotions and emotionality are seen as pesky problems that need to be contained and controlled, or they may yield an unreliable assessment of human nature and functioning.[2]

Nevertheless, there is considerable evidence that emotions affect what we *perceive and how well and quickly we perceive things* (see Oatley & Jenkins, 1992, for a summary of the evidence). Thus, people have been found to identify words and emotion-bearing faces more quickly when these words and faces are consistent with the emotions they are experiencing at the time (Niedenthal, Setterlund, & Jones, 1994). Do our emotions influence our capacity to act rationally? Damasio (1994) claims that "there never has been any doubt that, under certain circumstances, emotion disrupts reasoning"

---

[2] The author thanks Martin Martens (1995) for bringing Cooper and Emory's (1995) statement to his attention.

(p. 52). Hence people advise one another not to respond immediately to someone who has offended or caused the person injury. "Stay cool," we advise, "sleep on it." This line of thought implies that emotion can only hurt intelligent reasoning. Contrariwise, drawing on work that combines neuro-psychology and decision analysis, Damasio (1994) argued that reductions in emotions can constitute an equally important source of irrational behavior. As we saw earlier, the actions of certain brain regions are closely related to reasoning and decision making, on the one hand, *and* to human emotional processes, on the other.

Forgas (1995) and, more recently, Forgas and George (2001) have offered an "affect infusion model" that proposes that whether affect (both moods and emotions) affect people's judgments and behaviors depends on the type of information-processing strategy they adopt in particular situations. Affect infusion is defined as "the process whereby affectively loaded information exerts an influence on and becomes incorporated into the judgmental process, entering into the judge's deliberations and eventually coloring the judgmental outcome" (Forgas, 1995, p. 39). To the extent that a cognitive task requires active generation of new information, as opposed to the passive processing of familiar information, affective states may affect a person's judgment (Forgas, 1995). Moreover, if the person has a pre-existing goal in mind, affect is less likely to influence judgment than in cases where no motivational force is present. Forgas and George (2001, p. 4) propose:

> Tasks that require elaborate, substantive processing are most likely to be influenced by affect, as mood will selectively prime affect-related thoughts and memories to be used when constructing a response. In contrast, tasks that can be solved using more simple and directed processing strategies should show little or no affect infusion.

In short, the affect infusion model proposes that affect impacts on organizational behavior two ways: (1) it influences *what* people think (i.e., the content of their cognitions), and (2) it influences *how* people think – the process of cognition. How people process information can magnify, eliminate or even reverse the effects of transient mood states on people's thinking and behavior. The model also includes consideration of the nature of the task, the individual, and the context. A complete description of the model is beyond our present scope; the interested reader is referred to Forgas (1995) for complete detail.

Of particular relevance to our purposes in this book are the implications of the model for work motivation. Theoretical work by George and Brief (1996) and Seo, Barrett, and Bartunek (2004) as well as empirical evidence provided by Staw, Sutton, and Pelled (1994) have demonstrated that positive moods *can* have positive influences on work motivation (as we mentioned earlier in this chapter and discuss in Chapter 12). It may also be the case that positive *changes* in a person's mood can enhance motivation and that, in some circumstances, negative moods may have the same effect (Forgas & George, 2001).

George and Jones (1997) argued that whether moods have positive or negative (or no) effects on motivation requires a holistic assessment of an individual's values, attitudes, and moods. They proposed that a complete understanding of "the work experience" requires that one consider retro-spective insight that generally relies on a person's attitudes, prospective expectation of what work experience will be like, which is based on a person's values (see Chapter 2), and a contemporaneous component, which are captured best by the individual's work moods. Of the three elements that capture the work experience, work moods are the most fluid – the most susceptible to change. In addition, the three components interact with one another. Of particular interest here is the proposition from the model that work moods, if sustained for extended periods of time, can affect a person's job attitudes and work values. In other words, work moods may change a person's retrospective evaluation of work and color the expectations he or she places on future job experi-ences. Therefore, a person's work moods may have an effect on the likelihood that they will engage in extra-role behaviors (such as citizenship behaviors, which are not part of a person's formal job description). Finally, depending on a person's configuration of job attitudes and values, moods may have a partial effect on turnover, absenteeism, and social loafing behavior.

Emotionality and Gender

We have suggested that emotions and emotionality are closely linked to culture and to language, making it difficult for us to nail down a pan-cultural, classically determined definition of emotion. Aside from cultural differences, there is the question of gender differences. Within our Western culture, women are often stereotyped as being more "emotional" than men.

This stereotype is problematic for a number of reasons (Fischer, 1994). There is no solid empirical evidence that women experience the most prototypical emotions more often than men do (recall our earlier discussion of the prototype approach to defining emotions). That is, there is no evidence that women are more susceptible than men to anger, happiness, sadness, or disgust. By the same token, there is some evidence that women may experience certain specific emotions, such as sadness, fear, and uncertainty, more frequently and more intensely than men do (Fischer, 1994). Interestingly, it is the latter class of emotions that is most commonly associated with the "person-on-the-street" concept of emotionality in our culture:

> Someone who is sad, crying, or terribly afraid is more likely to be called emotional than a man (or woman) who is angry. An important characteristic that links these so-called "feminine" emotions is powerlessness: The belief that nothing can be done about the negative situation and that one is helpless. We may *speculate* [emphasis added] that the relatively frequent or intense experience of these emotions by women may also lead them to have knowledge of this domain. On the basis of their larger experience, they may know more about the causes, characteristics, and consequences of these [female] emotions.
>
> (Fischer, 1994, pp. 459–460)

There is some evidence that the differences in the ways in which boys and girls are socialized can result in significant differences between men and women in their "emotional expertise" (Fischer, 1994, p. 472). Females in our culture learn to talk about and express emotions more than males do and thus become more familiar with the emotional side of human existence. Men and women may also apply different emotion words (or labels) to the same phenomena because of differences in their early experiences. One recent study provided some empirical evidence for the common stereotype that women *recognize* benign or socially constructive emotions in others more quickly than do men (Williams & Mattingley, 2006). Interestingly, however, the same study also found that, among the emotions studied (happiness, sadness, surprise and disgust, fear and anger), anger was the one most quickly identified by both men and women, and it was identified more quickly by male observers than by female observers (Williams & Mattingley, 2006). The researchers argue that the human capacity to detect anger so quickly probably has evolutionary and survival value for the species. It appears more work is needed on sex differences in emotional intelligence, which we address later. Whatever differences do exist, however, they appear not to be major and should not be overstated. In Chapter 8, we will see how gender differences in emotional responses to frustration may be responsible for some of the stereotypes that exist about the effectiveness and suitability of women for managerial jobs. It will be important to keep these developmental, cultural, and linguistic dimensions about the meaning and expression of emotions in mind when we consider people's responses to frustration in the workplace.

CATEGORIZING EMOTIONS

We have seen that the broad concept of affect contains several varieties of human experiences: Emotions, moods, feeling, temperaments, and – some would argue – cognitions. Our intention to this point in the chapter has been to define and sort out these various concepts, setting the stage for a set of more focused analyses of the role of affect (in all its various forms) in work motivation. Before we can do that, however, we need to become more precise about the nature of specific emotions, per se, because so much of what follows in the chapter pertains to emotions. So, it is time to define our terms even more precisely: While we may have an understanding of what they are, collectively, we must grapple with understanding the various forms they come in. The following section reveals that it has not been a simple matter for the field to agree on methods for categorizing emotions, let alone agreeing on the nature of the differences between and among specific emotions. Nevertheless, we try here to do so.

The Prototype Approach to Defining Emotions

Some theorists believe that taking a "classical" approach to defining emotion in general or particular emotions such as love, anger, or fear is not possible (Fehr & Russell, 1991; Russell, 1991). The classical approach requires that a concept (such as emotions) be defined by articulating all the necessary and sufficient conditions for an object or event to be considered an example of that concept. Using this approach, the boundaries between concepts (e.g., between fear and anger) are clear, and we would have no trouble distinguishing between the two emotions (Fehr & Russell, 1991; Russell, 1991). But this is not the case, according to Russell and his colleagues, who believe that in practice, the boundaries between emotions are not clear for people. Rather, it is more useful to think of emotions as "prototypes," that is, to think of and define particular emotions in terms of the everyday language and experience of people within a certain culture. The prototype approach considers the boundaries between emotions to be fuzzy rather than crisp and distinct, so that any one emotion may feature a number of characteristics and it is not necessary for all these features to be in place for a set of perceptions, feelings, and actions to be categorized as a particular emotion.

For example, anger may be seen as comprising a sequence of events such as the following. A person is offended by another, after which the person scowls at the offender, and then feels internal agitation and tension. Next, the person feels his heart pounding and muscles tensing. Finally, the offended person may (or may not) strike back at the offender. By the prototype approach to emotions, a sequence such as this would be defined as the experience of anger, but not all the elements need to be in place to so qualify.[3] This approach to defining emotions acknowledges that the same "emotion" may not be witnessed the same way from one time to another by the same person, or in the same way between any two people, because the specific blend of experiences and events may vary somewhat from time to time or between people. It is seen as especially relevant as one moves "downward" from the broad category of emotion (in general) to increasingly specific forms and types of emotion (e.g., down to "anger"), then to even more specific forms, such as rage, wrath, annoyance, and so on (Russell, 1991).[4] Hence, defining emotions and emotionality is accepted as difficult and somewhat objective by this approach. Yet it is not seen as totally subjective as it is in the subjectivist view.

---

[3] This example, cited by Russell (1991), is attributed to Lakoff's (1987) analysis of anger. Moreover, it bears repeating that anger is an emotion that may or may not emerge or express itself in predictable ways. It may be controlled, deflected, repressed, or channeled in idiosyncratic ways that are hard to predict or to understand (see Tice & Baumeister, 1993). But it is quickly recognized in the facial expressions of the male human (Williams & Mattingley, 2006).
[4] Fehr and Russell (1991) illustrated how love can be viewed from a prototype perspective.

Socially Constructed Emotions

Another body of thought claims that we should think of emotions as *"socially constituted syndromes (transitory social roles)* which include an individual's *appraisal of the situation* and which are *interpreted as passions, rather than as actions"* (Averill, 1982, p. 6). This approach "assumes that any given emotional state is best regarded as an associative network in which specific types of feelings, physiological reactions, motor responses, and thoughts and memories are all interconnected . . . The linkages tying the various parts of the emotional network vary in strength, and the arousal of any one component is not necessarily accompanied by an arousal of the other subsystems to the same degree . . . Nevertheless, to the extent that they are linked together, the activation of any one subsystem in the network (or syndrome) will tend to activate the other components with which it is associated" (Berkowitz, 1993a, p. 9). As Averill (1982) puts it, "no *single response, or subset of responses, is a necessary or sufficient condition for the attribution of emotion"* (p. 7).

As the concept applies in medicine, *syndromes* consist of many interrelated symptoms, no one of which by itself determines the existence of a particular disease. A relatively new disease that is thought of as a syndrome is fibromyalgia (Ediger, 1991). The major symptoms associated with this syndrome are widespread pain, especially in the joints and muscles, fatigue, morning muscular stiffness, troubled sleep, a propensity to allergies, chest pains, irritable bowels, numbness and tingling, and loss of memory. Any of these symptoms can occur alone, or they can affect a person a few at a time as a result of other diseases or disorders. When they come as a package, however, each with more or less force, they are referred to as a syndrome, with a name that identifies them as a collectivity – fibromyalgia. Similarly, for Averill (1982) and Berkowitz (1993a), emotions are syndromes of reactions.

By defining emotions as socially constituted syndromes, Averill means that people learn, through their own experiences and by observing others, what acts, reactions, facial expressions, and utterances are appropriate, within a given culture, to express particular emotions (see Harré, 1986). That is, according to Armon-Jones (1986): "[E]motions are characterized by attitudes such as beliefs, judgments and desires, the contents of which are not natural, but are determined by the systems of cultural belief, value and moral value of particular communities: 'the capacity to experience either shame or guilt . . . involves cultural knowledge and reasoning conventions (Coulter, 1979); . . . our capacity to experience certain emotions is contingent upon our learning to interpret and appraise matters in terms of norms, standards, principles and ends . . . judged desirable . . . or appropriate' " (Pritchard, 1976).

For example, when we are angry, we express tenseness, a stern or severe facial expression, and an abrupt manner to those around us. We may also become loud and boisterous, or quiet, withdrawn, and sullen, but whatever combination of reflections we put together, it will have been learned from experiences within our culture as well as those of others. The same emotion may, for example, be expressed by a different combination of signals and affectations in another culture at another time even though the basic emotions are defined as those whose facial manifestations are pan-cultural (Oatley & Johnson-Laird, 1987). To some degree, then, expressing an emotion is playing a role for a short period of time (Sarbin, 1986). An anthology edited by Harré (1986) contains many chapters that illustrate the role of cultural and temporal contexts in our understanding of emotions and their role in human behavior.

Thus, for social constructionists, there are an infinite number of emotions because of the varying social and life events that can interact, all of which are subject to the interpretations of those involved.

DISCRETE EMOTIONS AND WORK MOTIVATION AND BEHAVIOR

When we discussed the concepts of instincts and needs in Chapter 3, we saw the difficulty of achieving typologies that don't boil down to tautological lists associated, one to one, with every distinctly possible human act. There is a similar danger when we contemplate categories of emotions. There are a variety of categorical schemes, or typologies, of emotions, and there are even different approaches to making such typologies (see Frijda, 1986, pp. 72–73; and the debate between Russell, 1991, and Clore & Ortony, 1991). Moreover, as noted earlier, because of the way they conceive of emotions as formed and enacted by people within unique social and situational settings, social constructionists believe that there are countless emotions. While such a position may be intellectually satisfying (or at least intriguing), it is not particularly helpful in our attempt to study the role of emotion in work organizations, so something more tractable is required – a typology of some sort.

That said, the author is not aware of any typology of "discrete" emotions that deals exclusively with human work motivation or organizational behavior. Neither is there any apparent reason that such a typology should be sought or created. Nevertheless, there are a number of useful general typologies of discrete emotions that shed light on human affect in both work and non-work settings. Later in the chapter, we will review a few popular general models of affective reactions to workplace events and the consequences of those reactions, but, first, it seems useful to examine a number of discrete emotions, up close and one at a time.

Indeed, Ashkanasy et al. (2002) proposed that the most exciting new work on affect will be that in which researchers move away from general mood states and focus instead on specific emotional states. One interesting example is found in a series of three studies by Raghunathan and Pham (1999) who manipulated two negative mood states (anxiety and sadness) and showed that these different affective states had different effects on people's choices among alternatives in a gambling situation that varied in terms of risk and reward conditions. In all three studies, participants who had been induced with anxiety preferred alternatives featuring low risk and low probable reward combinations. By contrast, participants who were sad opted consistently for high risk/high potential reward choice alternatives.

The reason? According to Raghunathan and Pham (1999), the different specific mood states created different sets of motives among participants. Anxiety may have the effect of heightening people's preoccupation with risk and uncertainty, whereas sadness may heighten people's preoccupation with reward and the chances to improve their circumstances. A key point demonstrated by this set of studies is that although sadness and anxiety are both considered negative moods, they can have quite opposite effects on people's goals and behaviors. Together, these studies also shed light on the simplistic and negative hypothesis that affect necessarily has predictable deleterious effects on rational thinking and decision making. This trio of studies provides an instructive object lesson in methodological sophistication, theory building and – most important for our purposes – insight into the value that can accrue by focusing research on specific affective states. As Raghunathan and Pham (1999, p. 56) state: "All negative moods are not equal."

A fascinating study by Basch and Fisher (2000) illustrated the precise role that specific affective events can have on specific employee emotional reactions. Building from the popular affective events theory (Weiss & Cropanzano, 1996) – which we will explore in greater detail later – and the cognitive appraisal tradition, which claims people will feel the same emotional reactions only if their evaluations of the stimulus situation is the same (Lazarus, 1966), Basch and Fisher (2000) explored the connections between specific affective events, which they defined as "[incidents that stimulate] appraisal of and emotional reaction to a transitory or ongoing job-related agent, object or event" (p. 37) and the specific emotions people experience in reaction to these events and circumstances.

Indeed, they created two matrices that cross-categorized specific affect events with specific, discrete emotions (one matrix for positive emotions and one for negative emotions). That is, they developed an event-emotion matrix that shows the relationships between categories of affective job events and the particular positive emotions people experience in response to them as well as a matrix linking events to negative emotions. (Prior research had considered only the effects of global experiences on global reactions, such as overall job satisfaction or dissatisfaction, in the tradition of Herzberg et al., 1959 – see Chapter 2.) The researchers examined 20 different emotions, selected because of their particular relevance to experiences in the workplace. Then, starting with 736 specific event types that emerged from interviews with their 101 Australian respondents, they formed 14 positive and 13 negative events categories using a classification system developed by Bitner, Booms, and Tetreault (1990). Forty-five percent (45% – 332 events) were experienced in conjunction with positive emotions, while 404 (55%) were related to negative emotions. For example, the positive emotion *enthusiasm* was linked to positive events such as "winning business for the company," while the experience of *frustration* (classified as a negative emotion), was linked to events in which employees had to work with poor-quality resources.

Functions of Discrete Emotions

Discrete emotions, particularly negative emotions, are thought to create specific action tendencies: Hence fear is related to a specific urge to escape, anger is related to desires to attack, and so on (see Fredrickson, 2001). A central tenet of theory on discrete emotions is that they can have adaptive qualities, i.e., they focus the individual to engage in behaviors that protect the species and enable it to survive and flourish. Or so it is with negative emotions. Here, one-to-one connections between thoughts and actions are frequently required for safety and survival.

But many specific *positive* emotions do not have simple one-to-one connections with specific actions. For example, joy is linked with a number of action tendencies including behaviors as diverse as aimless activation, interest with attending, and even contentment with inactivity (Frijda, 1986). The vagueness of the connections between specific positive emotions and specific actions has led one theorist to propose a "broaden-and-build theory" of positive emotions (Fredrickson, 1998). In a nutshell, this theory holds that some positive emotions, such as joy, interest, contentment, and love can be functional for humans because they function to broaden the individual's repertoire of connections between thoughts and actions, which, in turn, contributes to the person's physical, intellectual and social resources for coping with the challenges of the world (Fredrickson, 1998, 2001). Because positive emotions are usually aroused in benign or non-threatening circumstances, it is not dysfunctional for quick one-to-one connections with behaviors (such as escaping or attacking). Rather, positive emotions may generate a range of behavioral tendencies. Pride, following a personal accomplishment, for example, may generate a propensity to notify loved ones and to imagine further personal achievements in the future. Moreover, the relatively broad array of behavioral possibilities developed in response to positive emotions may endure and be available for use in subsequent occasions.

Discrete Emotions, Fairness and Injustice

Harlos and Pinder (2000) reported the results of a qualitative study of 33 Canadians who identified themselves as having been treated unjustly at work. Their purpose was to identify common emotional reactions to eight different varieties of interactional and systemic injustice, two of the four major forms of injustice earlier identified by Harlos and Pinder (1999).

Interactional injustice, which they defined as *mistreatment that occurs in the course of workplace relations between employees and one or two authority figures with whom a reporting relationship exists*

(p. 258), appeared in eight interrelated but conceptually distinct forms, viz., (1) physical, verbal or emotional intimidation; (2) degradation – communicating, either verbally or nonverbally in a disrespectful, hurtful manner; (3) criticism – frequently finding fault with the employee's ideas, work performance, personal habits, etc.; (4) abandonment, neither inquiring about nor responding to the employee's needs; (5) inconsistency, i.e., arbitrarily changing direction, focus or standards for employee performance and/or poorly communicating changes to the individual; (6) inaccessibility – restricting physical and/or emotional availability, discouraging contact with the employee; (7) surveillance, which was defined as closely monitoring and directing employees, allowing little or no autonomy or authority; and (8) manipulation – managing the employee's skills, hopes, values, and emotions for personal or work-related outcomes. Systemic injustice was defined as *"perceptions of unfairness involving the larger organizational context within which work relationships are enacted . . . and where allocation decisions are made and/or implemented"* (p. 259).

Emotions were investigated as playing any or all of three roles in the analysis: As causes of perceived injustice, as consequences of perceived injustice, and as feelings that accompanied the participants' experiences of injustice.

In brief, supervisors' anger and their lack of apparent emotionality toward subordinates were the emotions that most frequently emerged from the analysis as *causes* of participants' unjust experiences. As consequences, fear, anger, hopelessness, sadness, excitement, and decreased emotionality were reported by participants most frequently. The emotions most frequently reported as accompanying unjust treatments, as they occurred, were fear, irritation, rage, anger, desire for revenge, shame, embarrassment, dread, guilt, hopelessness, and cynicism. Of particular interest is that anger emerged so predominantly in all three roles studied in the research, i.e., as cause, as effect, and as accompanying feeling.

Cropanzano, Weiss, Suckow, and Grandey (2000, Ch. 4., pp 49–62 of Ashkanasy et al., 2000) have also examined the linkage between organizational events and emotions, building on the traditions of justice theory (see Chapter 11), fairness theory (see Folger & Cropanzano, 2001; and Chapter 11), and affective events theory. They argue, using the various mechanisms of fairness theory, that a person may employ any of a number of cognitive processes to evaluate organizational events and/or physiological processes to modulate the emotional responses that result from the appraisal of the event(s). So, for example, an individual who feels slighted by a coworker may downplay the significance of the event by attempting to influence its future occurrence, by reducing the significance of the event by believing that the coworker had little choice to say what she or he said, given the circumstances. If these cognitions don't reduce the arousal caused by the event, the employee may then resort to physiological modulation by taking a deep breath, laughing it off, smoking a cigarette, or going for a jog. Finally, the offended person may engage in a bit of false expression of emotion by smiling at the offender, and engaging in one or more of the various levels of acting associated with emotional labor (as discussed later in this chapter). In short, this model assumes that emotions result from how people think about events, so understanding how people react emotionally to workplace events, we must learn more about the way people think, about both events and emotional displays.

Later in this book, we will examine the literature on self-management. Meanwhile, it is worth mentioning research on impulse control that shows that people in emotional distress may have a particularly hard time controlling their impulses, especially if they believe that impulsive acts can improve their bad moods. When people do not believe that letting go and following their emotional impulses will improve their mood, they are less prone to give in to their impulses (Tice, Bratslavsky, & Baumeister, 2001). The point is that the model advanced in fairness theory may require further elaboration to appreciate the organizational circumstances under which impulse control is easy or difficult for people in emotional distress in work settings.

A Typology of Discrete Emotions: Implications for Work and Work Motivation

Many of the emotions to be discussed here come from a list of 15 emotions offered by Lazarus and Lazarus (1994). They begin with three "nasty" emotions: Anger, envy, and jealousy. *Anger* occurs over a broad range of intensity, as reflected by the range of nouns used to represent it, such as *rage, fury, wrath, ferocity, indignation*, and *outrage. Hostility* is seen as a predisposition to become angry at someone, although it is not itself an emotion.

Anger can have either positive or negative consequences, although we normally tend to think of the latter. Lazarus and Lazarus (1994) state the following: "The dramatic plot for anger is a *demeaning offence against me or mine.* When we have been slighted, we all have a built-in impulse to retaliate, to extract vengeance for the slight so that our wounded egos can be restored" (p. 20). Thus, anger results from frustration only when the frustrated person believes that the actions of the person who causes the situation are avoidable, deliberate, or arbitrary (Averill, 1982).

Anger is one discrete emotion that has gathered some attention in research directed at the workplace. For example, one Australian study found that the exact features of episodes of anger in the workplace vary as a function of the relative power of the actors involved. For example, superiors were more frequently angered by morally reprehensible acts or job incompetence of subordinates, whereas coworkers were angered by morally reprehensible acts and public humiliation. By contrast, subordinates were most frequently angered by acts of others, particularly superiors, that they viewed as unjust (Fitness, 2000). Subordinates who experienced such injustices are also likely to develop hate toward the superiors who perpetrate the injustices, especially when there is also some element of public humiliation involved. In addition, anger seemed to last longer among subordinates than among superiors, if only because of the general tendency of higher-powered people not to spend a lot of time thinking about people lower in power.

Anger is not aggression as such; rather, it is the impulse to aggress. In work settings, anger is one of the primary emotions that accompanies need frustration: The blockage of goal-directed behavior that is intended to satisfy one or more of our needs. In fact, as we will see in Chapter 8, the anger that accompanies frustration can be responsible for many acts of aggression, including homicide. Anyone who has been employed for even a short period of time knows that anger is a common emotion experienced in the workplace, because the workplace is usually very central to our lives in general and, therefore, a forum where our best interests are so often at stake.

Envy is an especially interesting emotion that entails wanting something that someone else has or possesses (Lazarus & Lazarus, 1994, p. 31). The subjective state is a yearning to have or possess the article or item in question. It results from the "negative comparison of oneself with others" (Lazarus & Lazarus, 1994, p. 29). The experience of envy entails both feelings of discontent brought on by another person's superiority (or possession of prized items) and feelings of hostility directed toward the envied person (Smith, 1991). Envy can be a source of obsession and compulsion or simply a mild, passing phase in which we desire an article of someone's briefly and then forget about it.

People can develop envy over any of a number of things, material or otherwise. Nonmaterial things such as status, education, opportunity, good looks, talent, and youth are examples of traits or characteristics of others that some people covet and envy. To envy is to be human, which is why people often experience a lot of envy in the workplace. In fact, as we will see in detail in Chapter 11, people are constantly comparing themselves with others, especially in terms of the relative value of the exchange relationships they have with one another and with their employers. Frequently, of course, an employee will believe that she doesn't have as good a deal as someone else, and a sense of injustice or inequity may develop. Smith (1991) would argue that the primary emotion that accompanies perceptions and beliefs of injustice is envy. Before we look at envy in the workplace, we examine the third "nasty" emotion, which is related to but somewhat distinct from envy.

Jealousy is similar to envy in many ways, and sometimes the two terms are used synonymously in common parlance (although, strictly speaking, the two are not the same). The critical difference is that envy is a two-person emotion, whereas jealousy "is a three-way triangle in which someone threatens or has taken what we consider ours, most often the affection of a third party" (Lazarus & Lazarus, 1994; Salovey, 1991). Research summarized by Vecchio (1995) suggests that envy is normally accompanied by a sense of inferiority, self-criticism, and a desire to improve (presumably so that the person will become capable of attaining the coveted item). By contrast, jealousy is more likely to be characterized by feelings of suspicion, fear of loss, anger, rejection, and a desire to get even. Envy can exist without jealousy, but jealousy is often accompanied by feelings of envy (Lazarus & Lazarus, 1994; Vecchio, 1995).

Van Sommers (1988) summarized the relationship and the differences between the two emotions by noting that envy is concerned with what we don't have, whereas jealousy concerns what we have but are afraid we might lose. It would seem that both envy and jealousy would have generally negative effects in the workplace, although it is possible to imagine how each of them might help to mobilize positive reactions: For example, employee coping responses such as taking on more responsibility, developing more realistic assessments of people about whom the jealousy exists, seeking support and collaboration with peers, and so on (Vecchio, 1995).

It is clear to this author that envy and jealousy frequently result from unfortunate social relationships in the workplace and, in turn, result in many other unfortunate consequences. For example, envy may cause a person to denigrate the work or status of coworkers. Jealousy (such as of a supervisor) may generate disingenuous behavior, ingratiation, and political behavior that is intended to win the three-way game rather than to pursue legitimate work goals. The reader will readily imagine the difficulties that obsessive envy and jealousy might cause in any social setting, particularly work settings. Preliminary work reported by Vecchio (1995) reveals that a majority of people with work experience either have encountered envy or jealousy as third parties or have been involved directly as players. To varying degrees, we are all subject to the experience and effects of fundamental human emotions. Nasty emotions are as universal in experience as more pleasant ones. The relevance of envy and jealousy will readily be apparent in many places throughout the book, particularly in Chapter 11, where we examine concepts of fairness, equity, and justice.

Although it is not included in Lazarus and Lazarus's (1994) typology, *fear* – defined by Aristotle as a *sense of impending evil* (Frijda, 1986) – is a powerful human emotion witnessed intermittently by all of us (Oatley, 1992). Fear is one of the most important instruments civilizations use to maintain social control. Fear of punishment can be more effective in maintaining or altering behavior than punishment itself (Crawford et al., 1992, p. 92). Naturally, the same dynamics occur in the workplace, so fear frequently plays an important role in human work motivation. In fact, much motivated work behavior is driven by fear: Fear of not being able to find a job that one's parents will approve of, fear of not making enough money to sustain a decent living or to pay off one's debts, fear of a supervisor, fear of being revealed as uncommitted to one's company, fear of being fired or laid off, fear of being disciplined or punished for real or alleged violations of company or union rules. Despite the obvious role of fear in work, few, if any, modern theories of work motivation include fear as a factor in explaining human work behavior, so there is little empirical evidence to cite. Nevertheless, we know that many people are driven by fear in many aspects of their work lives. Fear is certainly rampant among illegal immigrant laborers and countless people working at minimum wage in sweatshops everywhere and is the primary motive that keeps millions of people bound in slavery today, around the world (see Chapter 15; and Kapstein, 2006). Fear is the predominant emotion that motivates adherence to organizational rules and regulations. By extension, it is the principal emotion instigated when organizational discipline and punishment are administered for rule violation (see Chapter 11). Fear has been moving nation states to form economic alliances for decades, perhaps even for centuries. It is commonplace, even trite, to observe that the world marketplace is getting smaller and that fewer trading blocks with varying arrangements of free trade will characterize the economic and social structure of the decades to come. It seems only a matter of time until the world is divided into three economic–social–military sectors of the sort that George Orwell described in his prophetic novel *1984*. On a global level, fear has compelled nation states to align with each other for the impending competition among these massive economic forces. Not to align with some other state has been portended to result in cataclysm.

A former premier of the province of British Columbia was once quoted as saying that "all human behavior is motivated by just two things: greed and fear." The author suspects that Premier W. A. C. Bennett was not the originator of this pithy insight because it has appeared in a variety of places. Regardless of its source, however, the point is important. In many ways, people work to acquire wealth, and greed causes the accumulation of as much material wealth by any person as possible. Meanwhile, the person develops mortal fear that someone else will take away that wealth, someone who, in turn, is driven by the forces of his own greed. Like all generalizations, the aphorism oversimplifies reality, but its very existence requires that we consider the powerful forces of fear, envy, and jealousy in human behavior, especially as they are enacted in the workplace.

Anxiety, guilt, and *shame* are three "existential" emotions discussed by Lazarus and Lazarus (1994) – existential in the sense that "the threats on which they are based have to do with meanings and ideas about who we are, our place in the world, life and death, and the quality of our existence" (p. 41). *Anxiety*, which they link with the notion of *fright*, involves our personal security, our personal identity as individuals, as well as concerns about life and death. Symptoms of anxiety are apprehension, unease, concern, worry, and a sense of insecurity. The anxious person has a vague sense that there is something wrong with her life but is uncertain as to what the problem is. She is unable to relax, not knowing if and when harm will befall her and, if it does, what form it will take.

One of the more common sources of anxiety in work settings has to do with changes in work procedures or in one's job. Lazarus and Lazarus (1994) observed: "Anxiety is provoked when the meanings on which we have come to depend are undermined, disrupted or endangered. If the threat to these meanings seems great, and the endangered meanings are fundamental to our being, the resulting anxiety can be intense and constitute an important personal crisis" (p. 47). Consider the anxiety a person faces upon being hired into a new job or being transferred to a new location: New faces, new people, new role expectations, new political structure, few or no work friends (see Louis, 1980a; Pinder & Walter, 1984). A great deal of information seeking occurs (Ashford, 1986; Ashford & Cummings, 1983, 1985; Feldman & Brett, 1983; Miller & Jablin, 1991), and usually, it is only a matter of time until the newcomer "learns the ropes" at the new job or location, and things work out well. The social support provided by new coworkers and supervisors plays an especially important role until the newcomer adjusts and can become productive (Pinder & Schroeder, 1987).

One study found that newcomers both watched established employees and questioned them to acquire five types of information intended to help assuage the newcomers' anxiety: (1) technical information (about how to perform their jobs); (2) referent information (i.e., information about the demands of their roles and the expectations that people place on them); (3) normative information (about expected behaviors and attitudes); (4) feedback about their performance; and (5) feedback about their acceptability regarding the social, non-task aspects of their behavior at work. The results also showed that positive job attitudes, better job performance, and lower levels of intention to leave the job were related to the amount of information that newcomers sought (Morrison, 1993).

There are many other work-related and career situations that can generate fear and anxiety among people, the most traumatic of which is job loss or its possibility and the prospect of long-term unemployment (see Chapter 11). Part-time and temporary workers face constant, although varying levels of uncertainty about their employment status, never being quite sure how long they will remain employed, or if they lose their current employment, whether and with whom future employment opportunities might arise. In short, anxiety is a universally distributed and experienced emotion, one that plays a central role in the attitudes, feelings, and behavior of people at work.

For Lazarus and Lazarus (1994), *guilt* is similar to anxiety, and may sometimes even be seen as a form of anxiety. They state that "guilt is as much a product of what is going on in our minds as it is about what is happening in our lives" (p. 52). Guilt centers on our moral lapses, fueled by our consciences. "To experience guilt, people must feel that they have transgressed a moral code that has been accepted as part of their own set of values, whether they have or have not done anything wrong – it is the believing that matters" (p. 55). "Guilt feeling is characterized as . . . painful self-evaluation due to some action evaluated negatively and for which action the person holds himself responsible" (Frijda, 1986, p. 201). For example, a person who claims to believe in religious precepts such as the Ten Commandments will experience guilt whenever he believes he has violated one of them. At the societal level, guilt is a useful emotion because it helps restrict socially undesirable behavior. It helps prevent people from breaking laws or moral codes. People who are prone to guilt are generally more honest.

In Chapter 8, we will see how frustration at the workplace often results in violent behavior and/ or aggressive acts against the organization, such as theft and sabotage. Other things being equal, guilt-prone employees would be less likely to engage in such acts. In fact, the author speculates that susceptibility to feelings of guilt must lie behind much of the loyalty that highly committed employees display toward their employers (see Chapter 10). People who are raised to embrace work values such as the "Protestant work ethic" seem especially prone to feeling guilty about work. Fear of guilt feelings may help explain a considerable proportion of their commitment to work in general, in addition to their loyalty to their employers. The author knows of no research to support these conjectures, but they seem plausible. In short, guilt hurts those who experience it but benefits those with whom the guilt-prone person interacts.

What about the emotion we refer to as *shame*? It consists of varying degrees of feelings of mortification, embarrassment, ridiculousness, and/or humiliation (Lazarus & Lazarus, 1994, p. 63): "Shame is caused by some act that should have been left undone (or done so as not to be noticed)" (Frijda, 1986, p. 168). Because it is similar in many ways to guilt, psychologists avoided drawing distinctions between the two emotions until relatively recently.

Like guilt, shame is most likely to be experienced when a person fails to live up to a standard. In the case of shame, the standard may or may not be a widely held or espoused value. The standard arises from the ego ideal of the person involved. If the person has an image of herself as courageous, street smart, a bold warrior, and tough minded, acting in ways that violate that ideal may result in shame (the examples are taken from Lazarus & Lazarus, 1994). Ego ideals are the characterizations we might like to have said about us, or written in our obituaries, after we are dead. Being caught violating our ego ideal brings us shame, and we tend to hide it. The threat underlying shame is criticism, rejection, or abandonment (Lewis, 1992, cited by Lazarus & Lazarus, 1994, p. 64). A person who transgresses may feel guilt even if no one is aware of the failure. He may also feel shame when others are aware of the misdeed or when he believes that others are aware.

As we have suggested, one of the common means used to cope with shame is denial. The person merely denies that he has done anything wrong, externalizing the causes for anything that has obviously gone wrong (Lazarus & Lazarus, 1994, p. 66). People who do this will become angry with others who charge them with miscreance and imply that the guilty party is, in fact, guilty. By contrast, guilt is more likely to compel us to seek publicity that will allow us to atone for our sins (p. 64).

How does shame enter our thinking about work motivation? In practical terms, it is so closely related to guilt that many of the ideas we expressed in relation to guilt could also be related to shame. Clearly, small doses of either emotion, or low to moderate tendencies to experience either one of them, may be healthy for any of us. But to be guilt or shame ridden is dysfunctional, and people so afflicted are not likely to be able to communicate effectively or be taken seriously by those around them. Large doses and frequent intervals of shame, in particular, are likely to result in mistrust, a lack of trustworthiness, and ineffective work behavior.

Lazarus and Lazarus (1994) discussed a number of emotions that are provoked by unfavorable life conditions, including, hope, sadness, and depression. *Hope* is an emotion that involves promise, expectation, and anticipation. Lazarus and Lazarus (1994, p. 72) describe hope as an "antidote to despair." "Hope may be sustained when there is some possibility that the outcome you wish for might occur, when you have not given up . . . and start despairing" (p. 72). Again: "The personal meaning of hope is that one believes that there is a possibility that things will get better, however, bleak they may seem at the moment" (p. 72). These authors claim that the usual provocation for an emotional experience of hope is an unfavorable life condition whose outcome is uncertain, yet in which there is a chance that there will be a reversal of fate – an increase in the odds that things will improve.

A broader view of hope is offered by Snyder (e.g., 2002), who postulates an elaborate "hope theory." A major tenet of Snyder's approach is that the Lazarus and Lazarus (1994; see also Lazarus, 1999) approach tells only part of the story. For Snyder (2002), one should consider two types of hope-related goal. The first are positive, or approach goals (such as occur when a person wants to purchase a car for the first time, to keep one's retirement savings intact, or wanting to support oneself as a writer after having sold a first book). In all cases, the baseline is something benign or positive and the goal is an improvement or maintenance of positive circumstances.

The second category of goals in Snyder's hope theory is what he refers to as "forestalling of a negative goal outcome" (p. 250). This can consist of preventing something from ever happening or of deterring an outcome so that its appearance is delayed. Snyder characterizes the Lazarus approach to hope as the "repair" definition of hope "in which the only appropriate goals are those that fill a profound void in a person's life" (p. 250). In short, Snyder (2002, p. 250) defines hope as "a positive motivational state that is based on an interactively derived sense of successful . . . goal directed energy, and . . . pathways (planning to meet goals)" (p. 250).

Hope theory shares many common or similar insights with other theories, some of which are described elsewhere in this book, such as self-efficacy (Chapters 6 and 13), goal setting (Chapter 13), expectancy theory (Chapter 12), and frustration theory (see Chapter 8). Snyder (2002) presents evidence based on years of his own research and that of other scholars that "high-hopers" (people who are characteristically high in hope) fare better in many arenas of life than low-hopers, such as academic performance, athletic accomplishment, and physical and mental health. Luthans (2003, pp. 183–184) explores nuances related to the similarities and differences among these concepts in detail, so we will not attempt to do so here. Suffice it to say that the differences among them are likely of more interest to academics than to those with applied interests.

What is the role of hope in work motivation? The question seems almost not worth asking. People hope that they will be able to find jobs after periods of unemployment, they hope that they will be able to improve their relationships with coworkers and superiors, they hope that they will be promoted and/or given a chance to enter programs that will develop their skills, they hope that they will be able to earn enough money and pension funds to be able to retire comfortably. Hope springs eternal in almost all aspects of work for most people. In Chapters 12 and 13, where we discuss expectancy-based theories of work motivation and goal setting, respectively, we examine a number of cognitive concepts such as expectancy and self-efficacy whose experience must be accompanied by the emotion of hope. Lest we forget during that discussion, we make the point here: Work motivation is a matter of more than needs, beliefs, cognitive events, and values. Emotions are collateral events that are very human and that provide much of the color of motivation to work. Hope can be a strong emotional factor in work motivation (see also Luthans, 2003). In short, a strong argument that, as an emotion (or as a trait, as Snyder would have it) hope could easily be slotted in the positive emotions category in the Lazarus and Lazarus (1994) typology – to which we turn shortly.[5]

Sadness and *depression* are two more emotions that figure largely in the picture of work motivation. Sadness is an emotion that is felt following the loss of something significant that we think cannot be retrieved or restored (Lazarus & Lazarus, 1994, p. 78). Probably the most extreme example comes with the death of a loved one, but the same emotion occurs, to varying degrees, in reaction to the loss of other valued commodities or elements of one's life, such as a job. Earlier, we saw that

---

[5] Ehrenreich (2007) claims that hope can be pathological, especially for people who are seriously ill and who are showered with well-intended messages of hope when, realistically, the sick person has no reasonable chance of expecting to recover and survive.

sadness can affect people's preferences when faced with alternatives involving differing combinations of risk and reward (Raghunathan & Pham, 1999). In Chapter 11, we discuss job loss at length, including the emotional and attitudinal reactions of both victims and survivors of job loss, both as it occurs "for cause" – as a matter of dismissal for poor performance, insubordination, or rule violation – or for the sake of downsizing by an organization trying to cut costs.

Grieving is defined by Lazarus and Lazarus (1994) as the process of coping with a loss (p. 79), although they suggest that the concept is used most commonly in reference to loss due to death of a loved one. Nevertheless, organizational downsizing and reengineering result in tremendous losses to millions of people. Sadness has been felt by many people as their hopes have been dashed and they have been faced with serious uncertainty concerning themselves, their careers, and the safety of their dependants.

Depression is defined as emotional but not as a specific emotion itself (Lazarus & Lazarus, 1994, p. 82). Instead, it is a composite of a number of other emotions, including anger, anxiety, and guilt. We know that depression is a serious emotional condition that can result from job loss and unemployment and that can lead to severe consequences, including suicide (Ahlberg, 1986; Ahlberg & Shapiro, 1983–1984).

Positive emotions

Adherents of a new movement in psychology have observed that the discipline had been largely concerned with the causes and consequences of pathology and with healing the human condition, particularly since World War II (Seligman & Csikszentmihalyi, 2000). This new movement, appropriately called "positive psychology," recognizes that the full range of human functioning cannot be accounted for within purely negative (or problem-focused) frames of reference (Sheldon & King, 2001); hence it is devoted to studying and building the positive qualities of human existence. Its focus is on valued subjective experiences: Well-being, contentment, and satisfaction (in the past); hope and optimism (for the future); and flow and happiness (in the present)" (Seligman & Csikszentmihalyi, 2000, p. 5). It focuses on individual traits such as the capacity for love, courage, interpersonal skill, aesthetic sensibility, perseverance, originality, wisdom, and hope. At the group level, it is about civic virtues and the institutions that will foster human conditions such as responsibility, nurturance, altruism, civility, tolerance, moderation, and work ethic (Seligman & Csikszentmihalyi, 2000). A central pillar of the positive psychology movement is a focus on positive emotions. In fact, adherents of the movement argue that positive emotions not only serve as *indicators* of well-being but that they also *produce* well-being (Fredrickson, 2001, 2003) in various forms, including, among others, optimism, happiness, self-determination (see Chapter 8), and physical health. A fascinating study by Ilies and Judge (2002), for example, demonstrated how positive mood states contributed to positive job satisfaction, when considered both across individuals as well as within individuals, over time (we will discuss this research later, in Chapter 10).

Fredrickson (2003) goes further to argue that the possession of positive emotions by individuals can actually create and foster "upward spirals" that benefit entire organizations. In this regard, a recent Australian study that followed individuals over time (a "within-subjects" design) found that people's interest in their work, their perceived skill at their jobs, and the effort that they put into their jobs were positive predictors of positive emotions and negative predictors of negative emotions (Fisher & Noble, 2004). Results also showed that people's emotions about their work varied considerably over time, as did their levels of job performance. However, the results did not support the hypothesis that prior positive emotions would predict current performance levels or the hypothesis that prior negative emotions would predict current performance levels (Fisher & Noble, 2004).[6]

---

[6] The ineffable and elusive relationship between employee job satisfaction and employee job performance has intrigued, beguiled, and challenged both managers and academics since the early days of the field. We will explore this relationship more completely in Chapter 12.

Another longitudinal study found that positive affect reduced employee absenteeism and that negative affect increased both absenteeism and turnover (Pelled & Xin, 1999).

(A complete review and critique of positive psychology is beyond the scope of this book. The interested reader will find a readable source in the January 2000 issue of the *American Psychologist*.)

Remember that there are many different typologies of emotions; the one by Lazarus and Lazarus (1994) generally being followed here is only one of many that might be invoked for an exploration of the affective side of work motivation. We now continue by turning to a set of emotions that they describe as the "happy" emotions. What is happy about work?

Happiness is a strong emotion that many of us witness through our work and our careers. Aristotle argued that the pursuit of happiness is the major aim of human existence. Indeed, studies have shown that the pursuit of happiness is a universal goal in most cultures (see Lyubomirsky, 2001, for a review). Like the others, this emotion can vary in intensity and duration. Hence we see a wide range of synonyms for happiness, all the way from terms such as *joyous* and *jubilant* to less extreme feelings such as *carefree* or *amused* (Lazarus & Lazarus, 1994, p. 89). Different things make different people happy, although there are some events that seem to be widespread as sources of happiness, such as when we are paid a compliment, when we are shown that we are loved, when we are promoted, or when we see our loved ones doing well. Happiness can be conceived of as a temporary emotional state and as a more long-term mood which stands for a sort of calculation of how well we are doing in life in general. It is a general assessment of our quality of life (Lazarus & Lazarus, 1994, p. 89). Nevertheless, some people seem to be generally happier (or unhappier) than others, regardless of the "objective" circumstances of their lives. Lyubomirsky (2001) has offered a "construal approach" to happiness which holds that "happy individuals construe naturally occurring life events . . . in ways that seem to maintain and even promote their happiness and positive self-views, whereas unhappy individuals construe experiences in ways that seem to reinforce their unhappiness and negative self-views" (p. 241).

Work can lead to happiness in many ways. It can result from the sheer experience of working (in which case we would think of the phenomenon referred to as *intrinsic motivation* (see Chapter 3); it might result from the joyous interactions we have with the people at work, in which case we think of the gregarious side of our beings and the social needs discussed in Chapters 5 and 6). We might find that happiness comes from the satisfaction of our needs for power, sex, or esteem. Lazarus and Lazarus (1994, p. 96) cite evidence that positive, happy moods contribute to our thinking effectiveness as well as to our relationships with other people. We tend to be more considerate and helpful toward others. We feel more inclined to see problems as challenges rather than as hassles, and we are somewhat less inhibited. By the same token, unhappy moods can make us self-centered and defensive. The point is that work can be a very happy and satisfying experience for people, subject to only minor and infrequent interludes of unhappiness. In fact, national surveys continue to show that most North Americans are, in fact, satisfied with their jobs (see Maich, 2005; and Chapter 10). Nevertheless, as discussed at length in Chapter 10, job and career dissatisfaction can be extremely aversive states that can spill over into the rest of our lives. Interestingly, happiness is one of the few emotions that has been taken seriously in the modern literature on work motivation, figuring into the widely adopted definition of job satisfaction advanced by Locke (1969). We return to a summary of the benefits of positive affect later in this chapter.

Pride is another (generally) positive human emotion that accompanies work experiences and affects the motivation to work. Pride entails the "enhancement of one's ego identity by taking credit for a valued object or achievement, either our own or that of someone or of a group with whom we identify – for example, a compatriot, a member of the family, or a social group" (Lazarus, 1991, p. 271). Pride is different from happiness in that pride entails a confirmation of personal worth, a boost to our egos that is missing from the emotion we typically call happiness (Lazarus, 1991, p. 271). Pride (as well as happiness) typically compels us to become expansive and to share the experience with other people. In this way, it is somehow the opposite of shame, which compels us to hide from others. As with all emotions, it is the personal meaning that a person attaches to an event that determines whether pride is experienced. The objective truth of a person's circumstances is only part of the picture.

Lazarus and Lazarus (1994) pointed out that pride is a sort of "competitive" emotion "because it centers on the need to protect and enhance our personal identity" (p. 101). As a result, pride can sometimes be a negative emotion, because it can amount to stubbornness, preventing people from apologizing for mistakes they make or from forgiving the mistakes made by others. How does pride figure into work motivation? There are a variety of possible roles for pride at work. Pride can be experienced when we receive compliments on our work, or when we perform well and simply know that we did, without the help of praise from outsiders. Pride can be instigated when a person's ability is challenged, doubted, or denigrated. Pride can be hurt when we are disciplined or punished on the job. Pride can be dashed when we are dismissed from our jobs.

We often hear the phrase *pride of workmanship*. The English author John Galsworthy (1867–1933) told a poignant story of a young man who purchased his boots from a German bootmaker who believed in quality (Galsworthy, 1927). Once when the boy ordered a pair of custom-made boots from the old craftsman, he asked: "Isn't it awfully hard to do, Mr. Gessler?" The older man gave the lad a sudden smile and replied "Id is an Ardt!" The good boots lasted a long time and later the boy returned to the German's shop, only to find that the old man had recently died. The new occupant of the shop reported that the German bootmaker had starved to death because he wouldn't allow anyone else to participate in making boots for his customers, he spent untold hours making each pair, and he simply could not compete with mass producers who easily made a profit at the trade. In response to the competition, the old man simply redoubled his efforts and cut his costs by cutting off the heat in his shop and, ultimately, the nourishment he provided his own body.

Hubris is an extreme form of pride that is not completely justified by one's accomplishments. It can often lead to the downfall of the prideful person. For example, an employee who brags at length about the quality of his work may bring undue attention to the work – attention that reveals that it is flawed.

Love is another (generally) happy emotion that is also conceived of as a need, as we saw in the early part of the chapter. Since we discuss love and intimate relationships in the workplace extensively in Chapter 5, we will not go into the matter here. It suffices to note only that love happens frequently in the workplace, as does the heartache that comes with the withdrawal of love and from unrequited love.

Gratitude is an interesting emotion discussed by Lazarus and Lazarus (1994) and others. It is provoked when one receives material help in the form of money, information, assistance, advice, or some other form of social support. Park and Peterson (2003) defined it as "being aware of and thankful for the good things that happen." It is generally a mildly felt emotion rather than a strong passion. People feel gratitude when others around them provide such resources without apparent personal motive. That is, the motives of the provider must be experienced as selfless or empathic. Gratitude may be experienced when one person performs a job for another at a level above and beyond the call of duty. Gratitude has received considerable attention as a virtue in the history of ideas (see Emmons, 2003). Kant saw it as a duty – people must honor those for the benefits they provide us. Thomas Aquinus viewed it as a "secondary virtue associated with justice, which entails rendering to others that which is their right or due" (Emmons, p. 83). Indeed, gratitude was a primary emotional rationale lying behind many of the tenets of the old human relations movement. A "law" of that movement has always been that satisfied employees are more productive employees, presumably in part because satisfied employees are grateful to employers who treat them well. We will see that the simple belief linking satisfaction and performance is just that – oversimplified – unless we define the concept of "performance" broadly to include more than just individual productivity (see Brief & Motowidlo, 1986, for a discussion of a variety of "prosocial organizational behaviors," as well as Chapter 10). Similarly, gratitude is probably one of the most important emotions that accompanies (and/or causes) loyalty and commitment to an employer. In Chapter 10, we discuss organizational commitment at length. It will be good to keep emotions in mind at that point, as well as the more cognitively oriented aspects of organizational commitment.

Many of the devices and rituals that an organization's management can use to build commitment among employees may work because they are effective at generating feelings of gratitude on the part of employees. On the other hand, it follows that such tactics may backfire and result not in gratitude but in cynicism among workers if they believe that the kindnesses of management are *intended* to build commitment (see Isen & Baron, 1991; Van Maanen & Kunda, 1989). A manager may elect not to displace (or "outplace") a worker at a time of economic exigency out of a sense of compassion for the worker, so feelings of gratitude may be in order as long as it is clear that the manager's decision was intended primarily to benefit the worker in question. In such a case it is clear that gratitude on the part of the worker is an understandable and justified emotional reaction that may, in fact, result in redoubled effort and increased loyalty and devotion. Similarly, work above and beyond the call of duty may generate feelings of gratitude in the heart of the manager overseeing the work, because she believes that the extra effort and attention to excellence is offered by the workers as a selfless act, intended to make the manager look good to her superiors. Gratitude would seem to be called for in such cases.

The author's position on the matter is that in times of severe competition and downsizing, gratitude to an employer becomes an especially interesting and complicated matter. It is up to the person to decide on a day-by-day basis whether he chooses to be grateful to any particular coworkers, whether they are peers, superiors, or subordinates. But caution must be exercised if and when a person begins to feel gratitude (or any other emotion) in relation to an organization. The reason for caution is that to emote toward an organization as one would toward a human being is to anthropomorphize the organization – to attribute human qualities to it, qualities that an organization does not possess. It is a mistake to anthropomorphize organizations, to think about and relate to them as if they are human beings with minds, hearts, and memories. All the recent theory about "organizational memory" (see, e.g., Walsh & Ungson, 1991) and "organizational learning" (see Fiol & Lyles, 1985; Pennings, Barkema, & Douma, 1994; Senge, 1990) notwithstanding, it is *individuals* who treat one another well or badly. It is individual people who should be the recipients of our gratitude or our rage in relation to our work experiences. A person who "falls in love" with or becomes angry toward an organization is fooling herself: No organization has a mind, a memory, a conscience, or a heart. Specific individuals within organizations possess these human traits, but it makes no more sense to emote toward an organization than it does toward a piece of iron. The necessary properties of human nature are not contained in an organization per se any more than they are contained in the iron. We say more on this matter in Chapter 10.

Lazarus and Lazarus (1994) refer to *compassion* as a "uniquely human emotion" (p. 122). Similar to compassion are concepts such as sympathy, pity, and empathy, although they are not the same. When a person is compassionate, he understands that another human being is suffering and deserves help. Awareness of the plight and suffering of another is what triggers compassion. The emotion is particularly strong when the person doing the emoting has had experiences similar to those of the person perceived to be suffering. Compassion may also be more readily instigated when the person in trouble is someone we love. Things are more complicated when the troubled person is a stranger (Lazarus & Lazarus, 1994).

In Chapter 3, we briefly introduced Frost's (2003) work on toxic organizations and the "toxic handlers" found in some organizations – people who work to assuage the pain toxic work environments create. In fact, his work is emblematic of the positive organizational scholarship movement we encounter throughout this book. According to Frost, compassion is the key component of efforts to make organizations less toxic and more human. Specifically, the skills of compassionate managers include the capacity to read emotional cues and anticipate their effects in work settings (this requires considerable emotional intelligence – a topic discussed elsewhere in this chapter); to keep people connected, engaging people regularly in a personal and human way; to empathize with people who are victims of toxicity; to act to alleviate their pain, while mobilizing people to be able to deal with their own pain and building a team environment in which acting compassionately toward others is encouraged and rewarded (2003, pp. 24–25). Frost cited the empirical evidence of other scholars who have demonstrated the importance of humane human resource management policies in developing mechanisms for dealing with organizational toxicity while contributing to the bottom-line performance of business firms.

Earlier in this chapter we discussed the issue of whether cognitions precede emotions or whether emotions can be experienced independently of cognitions. We also noted that in the debate between Lazarus (1984) and Zajonc (1980, 1984) on the matter, the issue may depend primarily on how we define *cognition*. Nevertheless, when we consider compassion as an emotion and its role in instigating human behavior, the question of the primacy of either cognitions or emotions comes to the fore.

Examples of the relationship between compassion and work motivation are common. Compassion must enter a person's decision-making process during the early stages of selecting an occupation and pursuing an education to realize that occupation. It is relatively easy to imagine that compassion figures into the decisions that people make to pursue healthcare, social work, education, law enforcement, and other careers where helping other people is a (or *the*) primary goal. Indeed, the final two sentences in the story Tilda Shalof (2004) tells of her lengthy career in a Toronto hospital's intensive care unit read:

> One thing I know for sure is that at times when our wisdom falters, compassion always abounds. That is what nursing has taught me above all: compassion is the greatest wisdom.
>
> (Shalof, 2004, p. 337)

Shalof's book is replete with stories that demonstrate the central role compassion plays in healthcare service, especially nursing.

Compassion may also account for many of the instances of *prosocial behavior* we observe in work settings, instances in which people work above and beyond the call of duty in the service of customers and clients (see Organ, 1990). Two studies shed partial light on this possibility. Although these studies did not examine compassion, as such, they did address the role of emotion in prosocial organizational behavior. The first of these studies (Organ & Konovsky, 1989) failed to find a link between employees' "typical mood states" and the occurrence of prosocial acts. The second study (George, 1991) *did* find that when mood was assessed as a transitory state rather than as an ongoing, stable trait, there was a connection between affect and prosocial acts. The author is not aware of any work that addresses the specific effects of compassion (or of any other specific emotion, for that matter) on the willingness or tendency of workers to provide services that exceed the formal expectations of a job. For that matter, we have noted repeatedly the paucity of empirical work that deals with the role of any emotions in work motivation. As we will see shortly, evidence has been collected that supports the idea that positive mood states are beneficial for organizational functioning, largely through the favorable impact they can have on cooperation and communication in the workplace (Isen & Baron, 1991). Finally, compassion may be an emotion that we can develop after having held positions in careers where we see people suffer and experience difficulty. In this sense, compassion may be both a cause and a consequence of our work experiences.

A final category of discrete emotions in Lazarus and Lazarus's (1994) typology is referred to as *aesthetic experiences* on the job. This category is different from most of the others we have examined because there is no single emotion related to our contact with beautiful music, good food, a stirring screenplay, or a spectacular sunset. In fact, the particular emotion(s) that is/are aroused after experiencing something aesthetically appealing will depend primarily on the particular meaning the person places on it (much as in the case of other emotional events, but more so in this case). Hence, when we encounter something that is aesthetically appealing, any or many of the other emotions we have listed and discussed earlier may come into our experiences, either alone or in sequence. Again, the particular emotions felt will vary from person to person as well as within the same person on different occasions, depending on the meaning attributed to the stimulus at any given time. For example, a favorite song may bring joy when it is experienced by a young man when he is in the company of his sweetheart, but the same song may bring heartache and sorrow when he hears it after she has left his life. The meaning depends on the circumstances and people involved.

We have observed the lack of attention by researchers to the emotional aspects of work motivation and organizational behavior. Aesthetic experiences associated with work and motivation are perhaps the least well understood. Sandelands and Buckner (1989) have attempted to begin to fill the void by drawing associations between aspects of work and the work process, on the one hand, and art, on the other. They cite literature from history, management, and organizational behavior in an attempt to explore what work feels like to people who perform it. The issue for them is not one of "How do you like your job?" rather, it is one of "How do you feel when you are on your job?" It is a matter of work feelings rather than of feelings about work (p. 125). For Sandelands and Buckner, aesthetic experience is not antithetical to the experience of everyday work life, with all of its typically practical values and goals. They claim that the practical and the aesthetic can be experienced simultaneously, especially when the work is done well. They cite Henri (1923), who wrote: "Art . . . is the province of every human being. It is simply a question of doing things, anything, well. It is not an outside, extra thing. When the artist is alive in any person, whatever his kind of work may be, he becomes an inventive, searching, daring, self-expressing creature . . . He does not have to be an artist. He can work in any medium. He simply has to find the gain in the work itself, not outside it" (Henri, 1923, p. 15, cited by Sandelands & Buckner, 1989, p. 118).

Sandelands and Buckner (1989) also argued that the passion for "excellence" that was a popular management theme during the 1980s and early 1990s (see Peters & Waterman, 1982) had an artistic, aesthetic quality. In Chapter 3, we explored the meaning of concepts referred to as *intrinsic motivation* and *intrinsic satisfaction*. These are motivational forces and sources of satisfaction that emerge from the performance of work for its own sake. There is an element of play or playfulness related to these concepts that is somewhat distinct from the instrumental satisfactions and emotions that derive from the recognition and rewards from outside sources. There is also a strong element of feeling of control over one's fate and of making things happen according to one's preferences that feels good when we are working (see Deci & Ryan, 1985; and Chapters 7 and 13 of this book).

THE MANAGEMENT OF EMOTIONS AT WORK

In the foregoing sections, we discussed the possible relationships between a variety of human emotions distilled and listed by Lazarus and Lazarus (1994) and the motivation to work. Many aspects of work and work motivation were brought to bear in the analysis, such as the motivation to seek and hold a job or career, the motivation to start one's own business, the desire to perform one's job well and with excellence and pride, and the notion of performing above and beyond the call of one's formal job requirements. We also considered how emotions can originate in either one's work life or outside of it and then follow the individual from either of these to the other. We have seen how emotions may help to cause and explain work motivation and organizational behavior or result from motivated effort and work experience. To this point, however, most of the discussion has cast emotions in a passive light, as if their occurrence happens naturally and without much focus on how they can actively be controlled, influenced, or manipulated. In this section, we turn attention to the management of emotions in work organizations. We start with emotional intelligence, a set of skills that enables those who have it in high degrees to recognize their own emotions and those of others as well as to control their emotions or, at least, their display of emotions. We then discuss emotional labor, a term used to describe the deliberate projection of affect by people in jobs where their emotional appearance is defined as a formal job requirement.

Emotional Intelligence

Earlier, we explored the question of possible gender differences in the experiencing of discrete emotions and in the relative capacity of men and women to recognize discrete emotions in other people. Aside from gender differences, it seems that well-educated people with high IQs may or may not be equally competent in dealing with the emotional aspects of their lives. Goleman cites the poor statistical connections between indicators of cognitive skill (e.g., SAT scores, high school grades) in making valid predictions of people's ultimate success in life. In other words, "making it" requires more than simple cognitive intelligence. Goleman (1995) argued that if people are to function effectively with others and to succeed, *emotional intelligence* may be just as important as the more traditional indicators, which are largely cognitive in nature. He defines emotional intelligence as follows: "[A]bilities such as being able to motivate oneself and persist and persist in the face of frustrations; to control impulse and delay gratification; to regulate one's moods and keep distress from swamping the ability to think; to empathize and to hope" (p. 34).

An earlier definition of emotional intelligence was offered by Salovey and Mayer (1990): "[T]he subset of social intelligence that involves the ability to monitor one's own and others' feelings and emotions, to discriminate among them and to use this information to guide one's thinking and actions' (p. 189). For these authors, social intelligence has several dimensions. As we consider these dimensions (or categories), it is worth keeping in mind how the various forms of abilities must contribute to effective performance in most work settings, that is, how possessing or not possessing these skills might make a difference in the way that organizational members get along with one another and are likely to succeed in their careers:

1. *Knowing one's emotions*: Self-awareness, recognizing a feeling as it happens.
2. *Managing emotions*: Handling feelings so they are appropriate in the circumstances; being able to soothe oneself, to shake off gloom, and to generate positive feelings when necessary.
3. *Motivating oneself*: Being able to energize oneself, to get "into the flow state," to delay gratification, and stifle impulsiveness.
4. *Recognizing emotions in others*: Being empathic, able to sense the feeling states that others are experiencing.
5. *Handling relationships*: Being able to generate constructive relationships with others, being popular, exerting leadership or support, being able to be a friend.

More recent models of emotional intelligence have evolved during the past decade, some of which view the concept primarily as a mental ability (cf. Mayer & Salovey, 1997) while other, broader models (such as Salovey and Mayer's original model – described earlier – and Goleman's (1995) popularized version) view it as a broader *combination* of mental skill and a set of adaptive emotional traits and dispositions (Schutte et al., 1998). A recent empirical investigation by Warwick and Nettlebeck (2004) supported this distinction.

Regardless of which model one considers, there is no denying the importance of cognitive intelligence in leadership and effective job performance, but the point here is that without minimum levels of these and related emotional abilities, personal effectiveness in work relationships is likely to be attenuated (see Ashkanasy, Hartel, & Zerbe, 2000; Cherniss, Extein, Goleman, & Weissberg, 2006; Matthews, Zeidner, & Roberts, 2002, Chapter 12). According to Salovey and Mayer (1990), people with high emotional intelligence may be more creative and better able to plan flexibly, because their periodic mood swings can cause them to "break set" and move their concentration from one issue to another more easily than can people with lower emotional intelligence. People in happy mood states appear to be more successful at creative problem solving and at tasks involving inductive reasoning. People in sadder mood states may be more effective at deductive problem solving, so the capacity to alter one's own emotional state may be a skill that makes some people more creative and productive than others (Salovey, Hsee, & Mayer, 1993). We return to this possibility in Chapter 14, where we examine notions of self-regulation more broadly. In short, people who possess high emotional intelligence "can be thought of as having attained at least a limited form of positive mental health. [They] are aware of their own feelings and those of others. They are open to positive and negative aspects of internal experience, are able to label them, and when appropriate, communicate them. Such awareness will often lead to the effective regulation of affect within themselves and others, and so contribute to well being" (Salovey & Mayer, 1990, p. 201).

It seems that most people *believe* that they possess adequate degrees of emotional intelligence and that they can correctly identify emotions in themselves and in others. We tend to assume that we are able to diagnose the emotional events occurring in other people. We believe that we can tell whether they are sad, happy, or fearful, in large part because certain facial and vocal expressions have interpersonal effects that are registered independently of any words spoken (see Oatley & Jenkins, 1992). Despite these beliefs, there is considerable evidence to show that adults differ considerably in terms of these interpersonal sensitivity skills, even though many children do develop them early in life (see Matthews et al., 2002; Salovey et al., 1993). A meta-analysis reported by Elfenbein and Ambady (2002) found that many emotions are recognized universally, but that people with common cultural backgrounds recognize each other's emotions more readily than do those from different cultures.

Aside from being in touch with one's emotions and being able more or less accurately to perceive the emotions of others, a major component of emotional intelligence consists of the ability to regulate one's own emotions. The simple hedonistic hypothesis that people are happier when they possess more of things they like has been challenged by a series of studies which show that in addition to the possession of desired outcomes, the rates at which we receive such outcomes and the changes that these outcomes imply over our baseline experiences are also critical in determining our satisfaction and pleasure (Salovey et al., 1993). That is, we compare the level of outcomes we have at a given moment with the levels we have had in the past. Positive additions of good things bring pleasure, but after we have grown used to the new level of our circumstances, the pleasure level drops. An employee who receives a sudden 10% pay increase may be ecstatic at first, but the joy will probably subside as he grows used to the new level of income. Similarly, when we lose valued commodities, the initial anger tends to diminish with the passing of time. So far, so good: People adapt to their new circumstances more or less readily. In addition, the *faster* things improve, the greater our satisfaction and the happier our mood. If pay increases come quickly, they bring more satisfaction than if they take longer. A person whose house increases in value by $10,000 over a year's time will be happier than a person whose house increases in value by $10,000 over 2 years (Salovey et al., 1993). So, in addition to positive changes from a baseline position, the rate at which the positive changes occur also makes a difference in our satisfaction (Salovey et al., 1993). Researchers refer to this phenomenon as the *velocity* of change.

There is more. In addition to a high velocity of change, people appear to gain even greater satisfaction when the velocity itself changes from negative to positive. That is, people are happiest when the desired value first decreases and then increases, and they are unhappiest when the velocity changes from positive to negative: "That is, when the desired value first increases and then decreases" (Salovey et al., 1993). We gain most pleasure from watching our favorite sports team win a game after falling behind and then making a valiant comeback to score the winning goal late in the match. By contrast, the pain we feel for our team is especially acute when they blow a lead and lose late in the game.[7] Salovey and his colleagues (1993) conclude: "This dynamic – indeed *emodynamic* view suggests that we are acutely sensitive to the pattern over which outcomes accrue in time,

---

[7] It is tempting to think of the notions of velocity and increases in velocity in mathematical terms, such as first and second derivatives. In these terms, neohedonism hypothesizes that satisfaction is greatest when both the first and second derivatives of the curve relating a person's level of desired outcome acquisition are both positive, and that dissatisfaction is at its worst when both mathematical terms are negative.

especially to their rate and shifts in that rate" (p. 269). We return to the self-control of emotions in Chapter 14, where we examine the broader notion of people's capacity to self-regulate their behavior.

Controversy and Emotional Intelligence

As discussed in Chapter 2, it is natural that the emergence of a new concept in social science will be followed, sooner or later, by close scrutiny by scholars and critics who take issue with the conceptual basis for the new concept, who claim that it is not really that new, or who dispute the rigor of the research upon which the new concept candidate is based. So it has been with emotional intelligence. One of the earliest issues to be sorted out (as mentioned earlier) was whether there is more than one construct justifiably named emotional intelligence. Eventually, peace has been made by recognizing that there are probably (at least) two concepts of interest here: The first one being primarily an ability (as was first proposed by Salovey, Mayer, and their colleagues) and the second, either a trait and disposition or a blend of abilities, traits, and a disposition.

As we saw in Chapter 2, it is critical, eventually, to establish the construct validity of new concepts and the measures attached to them. Another, related, issue, concerns whether the ability form of the construct offers anything that cannot be explained by a combination of general intelligence and one or a few standard, well-established personality variables, such as "agreeableness." Controversy and investigation are healthy although they ought to reflect somewhat on the presumptive readiness of the concepts and associated measures for wide-scale commercial application (recall the argument presented in Chapter 2). In this case, the *prima facie* validity of the idea of multiple human abilities, particularly abilities that pertain to one's "emotional intelligence," has seen a meteoric rise in acceptance over the past decade. Several scales have been developed and validated to measure emotional intelligence and related constructs (e.g., see Gowing, 2001; Salovey, Brackett, & Mayer, 2004; Schutte et al., 1998), and techniques have been advanced to instruct adults how to develop higher levels of emotional intelligence (cf. Cherniss et al., 2006).

In many ways, the popular and commercial interest we have seen may have sustained the serious ongoing scientific investigation of its scientific integrity (e.g., Matthews et al., 2002; Salovey, Brackett, & Mayer, 2004). Indeed, Muchinsky (2000) goes so far as to suggest that the discipline's newly revived interest in emotions may serve as an important vehicle in bridging the gap between academics and practitioners. The particular interest shown toward emotional intelligence by both sides may be the spearhead of that coming together. That would be a good thing.

EMOTIONAL LABOR

It is widely recognized that the forced expression of happiness, pleasure, and joy is a job requirement for thousands of employees in many modern work settings, especially those who work in boundary-spanning roles (Rafaeli & Sutton, 1987; Wharton and Erickson, 1993). Using Disneyland as an example, Van Maanen and Kunda (1989) provided colorful detail about how young employees must "put on a happy face" under virtually all circumstances while running the rides at the theme park and serving its visitors on a daily basis. They describe how internal police forces assure that the happy faces are always engaged and that the young people representing the Disney experience are always at their most (apparent) cheerful emotional best. The authors detailed how this enforced and contrived joy and effervescence is maintained, guarded, and disciplined. How often or for how long, for example, can a 22-year-old woman express the same uniform joy and vicarious excitement while witnessing families from around the world discovering the thrills of *Pirates of the Caribbean*?

In private-sector businesses, customer satisfaction is the immediate goal. Long-term economic survival is the ultimate goal. Employees who conform to the practices of contrived emotional display are rewarded. Those who do not comply are typically dismissed (see Van Maanen & Kunda, 1989). In fact, many formalized management rituals and events, such as parties, retreats, and picnics, have as their major goal the expression and development of the set of emotions that management wishes workers to adopt. In the case of professional employees, masking of one's emotions is critical, and violations of this norm are patently unprofessional (see Wharton & Erickson, 1993). A matter of managing "organizational culture," these formal functions are intended to teach employees what to emote, as well as when and how to emote (Isen & Baron, 1991; Van Maanen & Kunda, 1989). People who must project one range of emotions in their personal lives and a different range of emotions when they are at work must be especially flexible in order to be effective in their various life roles (Wharton & Erickson, 1993).

A 22-year-old student told the author that he was holding down two part-time jobs. During the day he worked for a store that sells hiking gear, clothing, and equipment. It is a sales-driven job in which the clerks are supposed to help customers with friendly sales pitches and helpful, smiling advice about what equipment to buy, how to use it, and so on. After his shift at the store was finished, the student worked as a server at a steak and beer restaurant noted for its emphasis on suggestion sales, friendly *smiling* service, and close pseudo-personal attention to diners' needs. "Some days, I just can't do it," he said. There is only so much you can smile and put on a phony face. Sometimes, I'm actually too tired or bored or pissed off at the world to pretend I am happy, but my jobs both require that I pretend that I am really happy, all the time."

In any other circumstances, such behavior would be called manipulation, intimidation, duplicity, phoniness, even unethical. For our purposes it is often a matter of required work behavior, driven by reward and punishment schedules that assure that all patrons and customers go home happy and harbor desires to return for more of the same (contrived) treatment. The bind that manipulated emotions place on employees who must return to their lives outside the workplace, often facing emotion management roles and expectations of their own at home, can be pernicious (Wharton & Erickson, 1993). Hochschild (1983) noted that workers in such situations lose more control of their work and of themselves than do most employees. As we will see in Chapter 7, feelings of self-control and self-determination are critical elements of both work motivation and people's self-esteem.

More than two decades ago, Hochschild (1983) coined the term *emotional labor* to represent "the management of feeling to create observable facial and bodily display; emotional labor is sold for a wage and therefore has exchange value" (p. 7). This is the sort of contrived emotion and emotional expression that Van Maanen and Kunda (1989) described. Hochschild (1983) made great use of the emotional labor demanded by airline managers of their flight attendants to illustrate the concept. Attendants are told to smile, smile, smile:

> Now girls, I want you to go out there and really *smile*. Your smile is your biggest *asset*. I want you to go out there and use it. Smile. *Really* smile. Really *lay it on.*
>
> (Hochschild, 1983, p. 4)

These smiles are not a genuine indicator of the flight attendants' actual beliefs about their jobs or about how they feel with regard to serving passengers. The smiles are *on* the workers, not *of* them (p. 8).

Hochschild estimated at that time (in 1983) that approximately one-third of all American workers had jobs that expose them to "substantial" demands for emotional labor and that the proportion is closer to one-half among working American women (p. 11). A more recent estimate claims that "services account for approximately three-fourths of the gross national product and nine out of every ten jobs the economy creates" (Zeithaml, Parasuraman, & Berry, 1990, cited by Wharton, 1993). Hochschild referred to the false presentation of emotions in emotional labor as a *transmutation* of one's emotional system. She discussed at length the individual and social costs of this process when it is conducted widely and regularly. Her complaints concerned the loss of people's privacy, their sense of credibility and genuineness vis-à-vis the world, self-concepts, and sense of personal worth. In short, for Hochschild, emotional labor is akin to exploitation and the sort of alienation portended by writers such as Jean-Jacques Rousseau and Karl Marx – not a good thing. (The quotation from Nathaniel Hawthorne's famous novel *The Scarlet Letter* (1850), which we featured at the top of this chapter, "No man, for any considerable period, can wear one face to himself and another to the multitude, without finally getting bewildered as to which may be the true," is consistent with this concern.)

Ten years later, another empirical study of bank employees and healthcare workers provided partial support for Hochschild's claims (Wharton, 1993). This survey found greater levels of emotional exhaustion and strain among employees in occupations that Hochschild had classified as high risk than those she had classified as low risk. Wharton (1993) did not find, however, greater levels of emotional exhaustion among workers in emotional labor job categories who were either women or who had partners at home. In fact, she found that women who perform emotional labor were significantly more satisfied with their jobs than were their male counterparts in similar types of work. Finally, Wharton found that the effects of emotional labor may be somewhat mitigated by the degree of an employee's level of job involvement, autonomy on the job, and capacity to self-monitor.

Does Emotional Labor Necessarily Affect Employees Detrimentally?

As is often the case when a main effect hypothesis emerges in a new area of research (in this case, the proposition that emotional labor has generally detrimental effects on employees), subsequent studies emerge that report either contrary results or modified results. This has been the case with the emotional labor hypothesis. It appears that the effects are not always simple and of the nature Hochschild (1983) suggested. Indeed, one review suggested that emotional labor can have positive effects on workers in some circumstances (see Morris & Feldman, 1996).

Varieties of emotional labor

On the basis of a number of studies (e.g., Kruml & Geddes, 2000), it appears that if a job requires an employee to engage in simple "surface acting," it can cause them *emotional dissonance*, meaning a clash between what he or she actually feels and the feelings they project outwards for the sake of performing a job. If conducted long enough, this dissonance can be harmful to employees in terms of a number of outcomes, including alienation from customers, burnout, and reduced job involvement. By the same token, if the employee is capable of *actually feeling* the emotion that the job circumstances require (from a management perspective), there may not be such harmful consequences. Behavior of this sort is referred to as *passive deep acting*. In short, one can conceive of a dimension referred to as "dissonance" that ranges from surface acting (or "faking it") to passive deep acting.

A second dimension, referred to by Kruml and Geddes (2000) simply as *effort*, reflects the degree to which employees try to change their internal feelings to match those they must express on the job. Hochschild (1983) conceived of these terms, which are based on a dramaturgical metaphor.

Results suggest that employees who engage in *active deep acting*, i.e., those who engage in considerable effort to actually alter their emotions to align with required circumstances, experience more personal accomplishment, higher levels of job involvement (see Chapter 12), and more personalized relationships with their customers. By contrast, employees who engage in passive deep acting ("faking their emotions") and who portray emotions they don't really feel are more prone to emotional exhaustion than those who reflect emotions they really feel, either naturally or as a consequence of the effort required to project the "appropriate" emotions.

This emerging hypothesis has a number of interesting (and ethics-related) implications for the management of people in service settings. In a nutshell, it implies that employee adjustment is a matter of two independent dimensions (dissonance and effort) rather than a single, bipolar dimension as had previously been assumed. It also suggests that the healthiest emotional laborers are those who are allowed or taught to express their true feelings in the workplace. However, ethical issues arise when the individual's true feelings are not naturally appropriate, so effort is required to develop such appropriate emotions.

More recently, Côté (2005) has offered a conceptual model that places acts of emotional labor – emotion regulation – in a social interaction framework, hypothesizing that whether an individual suffers strain as a consequence of enacting false emotions will depend, at least in part, on the reactions of others at whom the regulated emotions are directed. Côté argued that surface acting that, by definition, entails inauthentic displays are usually bound to increase the strain on the senders of such displays. Contrariwise, displays that are more authentic as a result of deep acting (see earlier) may have either positive or negative effects on the strain of the sender, depending on the reactions of the receiver(s) of the emotional display. Côté's (2005) work is the most important recent breakthrough on this topic as of the time of this writing. It holds promise for further development.

Our discussion of the management of emotions would not be complete without noting that it has been the cultural norm for decades for people to control their (and others') negative feelings and emotions in most contexts, but in organizational contexts in particular. To the same degree that it has been the norm to behave rationally because of the belief that rationality is optimal for decision making, it has been against the norm to express negative feelings such as rage, hatred, and jealousy in the workplace. (It is not acceptable to express positive emotions too vociferously either!)

Controlling negative emotions

Ashforth and Humphrey (1995) noted that negative emotionality is generally contained through one or more of four basic methods. First, they describe *neutralizing*, a tactic that relies on emphasizing the virtues of the norms of rationality, as we have described them. This is accomplished through simple socialization processes, bureaucratic procedures, and the use of subtle (or not so subtle) rewards and punishments.

A second tactic is referred to as *buffering* (Ashforth and Humphrey, 1995). The essence of this approach is that emotionality is contained and allowed to appear only in prescribed, well-organized settings and times, such as at office parties, retreats, and the like (see Van Maanen & Kunda, 1989). A third approach used to deal with emotions is what Ashforth and Humphrey (1995) call *prescribing emotion*. This is the method that we discussed at length earlier: People are trained, even required, to express emotion on the job (usually positive affect backed up with a contrived smile).

Finally, organizations and individuals often have to deal with emotion that simply escapes the other constraints listed before. They "normalize" emotionality, recognizing that sometimes emotionality is inevitable and unstoppable (Ashforth & Humphrey, 1995). Hence people are expected to apologize to one another after displaying sufficient lack of control over their emotions. Humor is often used, especially to dispel emotions such as fear. Police officers make jokes about dangerous and frightening situations, and pathologists engage in crude or light remarks in reference to the ghoulish tasks they must perform.

The point here is that the norms of rationality in our culture have dominated the desire to be emotional and to express emotionality, especially in the extreme. These norms have resulted in a variety of characteristic managerial and bureaucratic styles and mechanisms to control emotionality, and when it cannot be stopped, to cover it up, rationalize it, or minimize its effects. Management has also developed many tactics to motivate and enforce norms of false or contrived positive emotionality in many industries and job categories where their businesses interface with customers and the community. It seems to the author that these devices for suppressing emotionality where it is not desired and for encouraging it where it is deemed necessary are so common and pervasive and so powerful in effect that we neither notice them nor object to them on a day-by-day basis. Given the power and ubiquity of these emotion management procedures, it is high time that organizational researchers began to pay more attention to them.

Emotionality and Partial Inclusion

If we are to begin to admit consideration of emotions and emotionality into our thinking (and feeling) about work motivation, we must bear in mind that people are generally only partially included in their work and in the organizations for which they work (Weick, 1969). In other words, they have lives outside their jobs (although we often suspect that some people have too little life other than that found in their work) and they bring elements of their makeup from the outside with them into the job. A person who holds certain values about life in general will bring those values to work (see our discussion of values and work values earlier in the book). If a person places a strong general emphasis on loyalty, for example, he may be more likely to develop strong commitment to his employer.

People's emotions and moods are evidenced similarly. The emotions that may play significant roles in our motivation to perform well or to quit a job or to join a union or to pursue a romantic relationship with a clerk in the purchasing department do not reside solely within the confines of the work setting. It is important to recognize that emotions (and more so, moods) that we feel on the job can follow outside the job, and vice versa. As George and Brief (1996) put it: "Workers are people too." Therefore, adopting emotions and moods as lenses through which to study or influence human work motivation requires that we take a holistic view of the individual, recognizing that people's perceptions, beliefs, attitudes, intentions, values, needs, and emotions reside and have influence both within and outside the bounds of the work setting (see Wharton & Erickson, 1993).

LOCATING EMOTIONALITY IN THE MOTIVATION TO WORK

Our purpose in much of the preceding has been to discuss possible linkages between emotions (and emotionality) and work experience, especially with the motivation to work. To this point, however, the precise role of emotions in motivation has not been located, ordered, or described systematically. Sometimes, emotions result from performance that was motivated by other factors, such as intrinsic or extrinsic incentives. Sometimes, emotions seem to serve as a precursor to motivational experiences. Other times, emotions seem to accompany and occur with motivated effort simultaneously. In short, we are lacking firm rules of thumb as to where in the cycles of experience related to the motivation to work emotionality resides.

Some help is offered by Buck (1985), who argued that:

> [E]motion is a readout mechanism associated with motivation. Emotion is generally defined in terms of subjective experiences or feelings, goal-directed behaviors (attack, flight), expressive behavior (smiling, snarling) and physiological arousal (heart rate increases, sweating) . . . [E]motion has evolved as a readout mechanism carrying information about motivation . . . in a kind of running progress report . . . Motivation is *the potential* for behavior inherent in the neurochemical structure, and emotion involves the means by which that potential is realized or read out, when activated by challenging stimuli. The relation of motivation and emotion in this view is analogous to the relation of energy and matter in physics: Just as energy is a potential that manifests itself in matter, motivation, as seen here,

is a potential that manifests itself in emotion. Thus motivation and emotion are seen to be two sides of the same coin, two aspects of the same process.

(Buck, 1985, p. 396)

Of concern here is the possibility that work motivation theory will find itself in yet another conundrum of the chicken-and-egg variety, similar to the one we discussed earlier in the context of the primacy of cognitions over affect (or vice versa). This risk notwithstanding, if we wish to include emotions in theory and research, it may be useful at this stage to consider the possible range of "roles" that emotions may play in the work motivation process. If we adapt Buck's (1985) approach, it would seem that emotions and emotionality are virtually omnipresent and become more or less salient as people become more aroused (by their needs, values, or cognitions) by work experiences. Buck's (1985) view also suggests that emotions serve a readout function, providing people with information about the state of motivation to engage in and gain experience from work events.

Carver and Scheier (1990a) suggested a similar, consistent notion. Adopting a self-regulation perspective (of the sort that we discuss in Chapter 14), they suggest that a person's affective state is in part determined by the observation the person makes about his or her progress in pursuit of goals and objectives. The emotions that people experience and display follow from their own assessments of their success at goal accomplishment. To the extent that this is the case, emotions would seem best to be studied at all stages of the motivational sequence. Hence, although the theoretical perspective Carver and Scheier (1990a) adopt is different from that embraced by Buck (1985), the implications for a wide-ranging role for emotionality in work motivation theory seems to result from their approach as well.

AFFECTIVE EVENTS THEORY

The most comprehensive and well-reasoned attempt to locate emotions in the spectrum of workplace experience was provided by Weiss and Cropanzano (1996). They developed a conceptual model called *affective events theory* (AET). Represented here as Figure 4.1, this model shows that people have emotional reactions to work events. These affective responses, in combination with the influence of objective features of the work environment, determine an employee's work attitudes.

In addition, affective reactions to work events can result directly in job-related behavior, which, in turn, may also affect work attitudes, although this linkage is not central to the model as it is portrayed in Figure 4.1 (H. M. Weiss, personal communication, July 15, 1997).

Weiss and Cropanzano's (1996) model has provoked and guided a number of empirical investigations since it was published more than a decade ago. The creative study that resulted in the affective *events–emotions matrix model* (summarized earlier) provides a fine example (see Basch & Fisher, 2000). Another study by Fisher (2002), employing a within-subjects design, found considerable

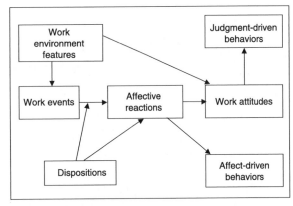

FIG. 4.1 Affective events theory.

Source: Weiss, H. M., & Cropanzano, R. (1996). Affective events theory: A theoretical discussion of the structure, causes and consequences of affective experiences at work. In B. M. Staw & L. L. Cummings (Eds.), *Research in organizational behavior* (Vol. 18). Greenwich, CT: JAI Press. © Elsevier, 1996.

support for affective events theory. For example, it demonstrated, as hypothesized, that different factors predicted positive and negative affective reactions: Job characteristics were predictive of positive affective reactions but not negative reactions. By the same token, as hypothesized, role conflict predicted negative affective reactions but not positive reactions. The relationships proposed by the theory between affective reactions and job satisfaction received mixed support. This study was a bold early attempt to introduce methodological refinements necessary to provide fair and reasonable tests of dynamic relationships among variables such as those postulated in AET, including the use of within-person, real-time (as opposed to retrospective) longitudinal assessment of key parameters, consideration of moderated and mediating relationships, and – as specified in the model – the measurement of both affective and attitudinal variables.

A study of the effects of managerial communications and change management procedures during a period of downsizing adopted an AET framework to study the effects of job loss on employee anxiety (Paterson & Cary, 2002). Specifically, this study found that procedural justice and change anxiety explained the effects of change management procedures on employee acceptance of downsizing, while interactional justice and change anxiety explained the effects of the quality of change communications on trust in the managers charged with affecting the downsizing.

AET at the group level

Although AET was proposed to explain individual-level phenomena such as job attitudes and performance, there has been some interest in applying the core concept to the functioning of teams in organizational settings. For example, a longitudinal study of 53 research and development teams investigated how certain critical events, or obstacles, impact the "collective sense of affect" in teams – or what the authors also referred to as "team climate" (Pirola-Merlo, Hartel, Mann, & Hirst, 2002). As hypothesized, obstacles did have a negative impact on team climate, but facilitating and transformational leadership styles by team leaders offset some of this impact. Moreover, the strength of teams' climates was strongly related to their respective performance levels. In short, the potentially negative impact of exogenous events on team climate and, consequently, team performance, can be buffered by the appropriate use of effective leadership styles by R&D team leaders.

In short, affective events theory (Weiss & Cropanzano, 1996) has stimulated a number of substantively creative and elaborate empirical studies that have demonstrated varying degrees of support for the model. It is an impressive corpus of work, although more remains to be done.

A BRIEF PAUSE FOR REFLECTION ON THE ROLE OF AFFECTIVE VARIABLES

It may be that affect is the most ubiquitous category of factors related to work motivation that we can profitably study. A recent article by Seo, Barrett, & Bartunek (2004) showed how core affective feelings people experience in the workplace can influence work motivation via (at least) three different channels. First, affect can influence the levels of goals people seek to achieve as well as their commitment to those goals (see Chapter 13). Second, affective states can also influence people's perceptions of expectancies and utility judgments (see Chapter 12), as well as of their rates of goal-related progress (see Chapter 13). They may enter the work motivation process at the beginning, at the end, or throughout the entire work motivation cycle (Pinder, 1998), influencing the direction, intensity, and persistence of work-related behavior (see Seo et al., 2004; and our definition of work motivation in Chapter 1). Indeed, Ashkanasy, Hartel, and Daus (2002) observed the ubiquitous role that affective states have played as mediating mechanisms and as moderator variables in recent models of organizational behavior (recall Chapter 2; see Latham & Pinder, 2005). The author takes all these current and recent observations as evidence that employee emotions, moods, and dispositions have come of age in the study of work motivation and organizational behavior. As we stated at the beginning of this chapter, whatever else it may be, work is an emotional experience, a major part of the emotional lives of most people. As this book proceeds to examine many different theories of work motivation and behavior, we will see that affective variables, especially short-term emotions, play a significant role in virtually all of them!

SUMMARY AND A LOOK AHEAD

Approximately a decade ago, the author (Pinder, 1998) wrote that theory and research in the domain of human affect and work motivation was relatively new and unexplored terrain and that much work was needed. Since then, a vast amount of work has been undertaken linking affect to organizational behavior and to work motivation in particular (cf. Latham & Pinder, 2005). Aside from the fact that general theories such as affective events theory and the affect infusion model have been fleshed out and modified, a considerable amount of research has been conducted into the causes and consequences of discrete emotions. The currently popular "positive organizational scholarship" movement (Cameron et al., 2003) has been responsible for much of this work and shows promise of provoking considerably more investigation. The affective side of human nature remains as strong as it ever was, so understanding and managing one's own emotions (as well as those of other people) will continue to become a major challenge for practitioners of all sorts.

In the following three chapters in Part Two, we return our focus to human needs and explore more closely a variety of specific needs and how they relate to work motivation. It will behoove us to remember that the boundaries we erect around these concepts for the sake of exploration and discussion are largely arbitrary and very fuzzy. The reason is, of course, that human nature is ultimately much more than a sum of the various "parts" social scientists examine – a few at a time – to understand the totality of persons.

Power, Love, and Sex as Motives at Work

5

*What's affection, but the power
we give another to torment us?*
Edward Bulwer Lytton

*Power when wielded by
abnormal energy is
the most serious of facts.*
Henry Brooks Adams

*The omnipresent process of sex, as it
is woven into the whole texture
of our man's or woman's body, is the
pattern of all the process of our life.*
Havelock Ellis

In the foregoing four chapters, we have argued that most work and work organizations provide opportunities for the expression and satisfaction of most human needs and emotions. In this chapter, we examine the role(s) played by three basic human needs and the emotions that accompany them: Power, love, and sex. Aside from reviewing the social scientific literatures on these needs and emotions, we will examine their relevance for understanding a number of elements of organizational behavior. We will find that, as powerful origins of human impulses, these needs can explain a great deal of what we observe in motivated work behavior as well as in management policies designed to constrain the human beast.

The first half of the chapter will look at power – as a need, as a goal, and as an attribute of organizations that motivate much human behavior in work settings. Then, in the second half of the chapter, we conduct a similar analysis of the human needs for love and sex: They too can be thought of as playing many roles, including needs, emotions, goals, and sources of some fascinating organizational behavior and management attention.

THE NEED FOR POWER AND THE MOTIVATION TO WORK

What is Power?

There are many conceptions of power from a wide range of humanities and social sciences. Because the term *power* is used as a descriptor of both persons and positions, we will take some care here defining our basic terms. Careful distinctions between power as a need and power as a goal will be necessary for an understanding of the role of power in work motivation, particularly in Chapter 8 where we discuss frustration.

The most basic and perhaps parsimonious definition comes from Dahl (1957, 1986), who defined power as the capacity of one individual (or social unit) to change the probability that another individual (or social unit) will or will not do something. For example, if an office supervisor's orders result in her work crew spending more time cleaning their desks and work spaces than they spent previously, we would conclude that the supervisor has power over her subordinates and that she has successfully exercised her power. This formulation of power is meant to apply to social units of all levels: Individuals, groups, organizations and even nation states (Dahl, 1986).

Similarly, Winter (1973) defined social power as "the ability or capacity of [one person] to produce (consciously or unconsciously) intended effects of the behavior or emotions of another person" (p. 5).

The need for power

In these definitions, power is a characteristic of a person-in-context, but it is different from the power motive, per se. The power motive is a more basic trait of an individual that transcends contexts and settings. For Winter (1973), the power motive is "a disposition to strive for certain kinds of goals, or to be affected by certain kinds of incentives." People who have the power motive, or who strive for power, are trying to bring about a certain state of affairs – they want to feel "power" or "more powerful than." Power is their goal. Therefore, a person may possess power by virtue of his social status, his physical prowess or his superior reasoning skills. Whether the person uses that power is another matter. Most critically, whether the person *wants* to attain and retain the power and use it is at issue. A person may be in a position of power but not have the desire or craving for power. *Our focus here is on the need for power* (or the power motive).

Winter and Stewart (1978, p. 393) defined the power motive as:

> [T]he quest for power, the desire for power, or the seeking of power (or the subjective feelings associated with power). This motive is not always conscious, nor does it always lead a single behavior or set of behaviors . . . Moreover, the power motive may be in conflict with other motives such as affiliation, play, autonomy, or being taken care of.

Elsewhere, Winter defined the power motive as "a concern for having impact on others, arousing strong emotions in others, or maintaining reputation and prestige" (Winter, 1988, p. 510).

Power and Anger

In Chapters 2 and 4, we discussed Heider's (1958) and McClelland's (1985) beliefs that particular needs tend to be accompanied by particular feelings and emotions. Also in Chapter 4, we reviewed a study by Zurbriggen and Sturman (2002) that tested just how exclusive the linkages are between specific need states and specific emotions. Among the most striking findings of that research for our present purpose was the finding that, as hypothesized, there were much stronger relationships among college students between their imagined successes at power-related goals and the specific emotions of anger, confusion, and disgust. In one experiment, for example, students wrote stories about times when they experienced four particular emotions: Happiness, sadness, anger, and feeling challenged. As predicted, 55% of the stories reporting anger had some form of power theme. Interestingly, even though the Heider (1958)/McClelland (1985) hypothesis of exclusive linkages between needs and emotions did not show up in Zurbriggen's and Sturman's (2002) data as neatly as the original hypothesis would have predicted, the specific association between anger and power was the most robust of the researchers' findings. Linkages between power, anger, and dysfunctional organizational behavior have been found and reported in a variety of real and simulated research settings, as we will see.

In addition to being conceived of as a need, per se, it is possible to think of power as an attribute of certain roles and positions. For much of our purpose in this book, we will do so. The focus in this section is upon power as a motivating force, a need that is subject to and characterized by all of the aspects of needs described in the previous chapter.

Power behavior is another useful concept, but one that must be distinguished from the idea of power motive. Power behavior is any act by one person to attempt to alter or change the behavior or emotions of another person. The danger in confusing the two concepts is that power behavior may be motivated by needs or desires other than power motives (such as a desire to affiliate or make friends).

Similarly, we must distinguish between power motivation and *feeling powerful* (Winter & Stewart, 1978, p. 408). People high in the power motive often strive for positions in life that offer formal power, prestige, and symbols of potency. In fact, attaining such positions is often the way a person manages to achieve the end state of a high need for power – feeling powerful! However, there is not necessarily a one-to-one connection between the power motive, on the one hand, and the *goal* of formal positions of power such as found in political office or senior executive positions, on the other. *Indeed, the power motive can cause an individual to seek feelings of power by means such as alcohol use, drug consumption, exploitation of loved ones, risk taking, and even exposing oneself to physical challenges.*

The point here is this. We must be careful to understand that a strong power motive usually has the same end goal – feelings of power and influence. However, there are countless means people may use to attain that psychological feeling of power that have nothing to do with formal position, status or authority, or with the conquest of other individuals. A person can seek and pursue influence or reputation. While it is true that becoming known by others or influencing their emotions can be powerful, so can providing help or advice (see Frieze & Boneva, 2001, for a discussion of helping power motivation as well as a scale for assessing various outlets for the expression of power needs). Indeed, there is a considerable literature on the non-selfish use of power motivation. David McClelland was among the first to recognize this in modern social science.

Two "faces" of power

Decades ago, McClelland (1970, 1975) distinguished between what he called two varieties (or two "faces") of power. The first type of power (he called it *personal power*) is characterized by a desire to dominate and defeat other people. It causes people to behave as if life is a zero-sum game: If I win, you lose. "The imagery is that of the 'law of the jungle' in which the strongest survive by destroying their adversaries" (1970, p. 36). People with this form of power motive are more likely to engage in fights, excessive drinking, and interpersonal dominance. They seek out symbols of prestige to display and announce their personal power motives and accomplishments. They are not interested in the welfare of others. Instead, they use others for their own benefit.

The second variety of power identified by McClelland (1970) is called *socialized power*. "It is aroused by the possibility of winning an election. At the fantasy level it expresses itself in thoughts of exercising power for the benefit of others and by feelings of greater ambivalence about holding power" (1970, p. 36). People with this form of power motive are more concerned about the possible negative consequences, for others, of their own use of power. They seek office for the sake of serving other people, not for their own self-aggrandizement.

Power Motivation and Effective Management

McClelland (1975) argued that effective managers are characterized by high levels of the need for power, but that power of the second variety – socialized power – is the more important. Such managers are effective because they use their power to energize and empower those around them. They do not dominate or intimidate. Instead, they generate energy and enthusiasm among subordinates for working effectively. They delegate. As opposed to managers who are high in the need for achievement (as discussed in Chapter 3), managers high in socialized power motivation succeed in large part by getting goals accomplished through other people. Managers high in achievement motivation, by the same token, get things done themselves. They also have a strong desire for feedback on how well they are doing, so they often set short-term goals that may or may not be appropriate for the well-being of the company.

One study found that managers who scored high on a self-report measure of need for power also reported lower levels of stress from their work. The explanation provided by the researchers was that the higher levels of power needs among some managers allowed them to deal more effectively with stressors in their environment through the control they attained by their power-seeking behavior. Managers who were lower in reported power needs experienced higher job stress, presumably because they were not able to acquire the same degree of control over their work environments. Interestingly, the same study found no relationship between power needs and stress among the non-managers studied (Hendrix & Stahl, 1986).

A more recent study found that interactions between the strength of managers' social power bases (as introduced by French & Raven in 1959 – to be described shortly) and the needs of their subordinates, including their need for power, were significant in explaining variance in a number of the primary dimensions of organizational climate. In this study, climate was used as an operational surrogate for managerial impact. The results showed that the person × situation interaction (managers and the contexts provided by subordinates' salient needs) contributed to managerial effectiveness.

Frieze and Boneva (2001) have updated McClelland's (1970, 1975) "two faces of power" and discussed how power motives can instigate helping behavior by people who possess it in the service of others. Power motivation need not express itself in the domination or control of others. Accumulating influence, developing a reputation, or offering advice to others are other outlets for this need. In accord with this theory, Schmidt and Frieze (1997) developed a scale to assess *helping power motivation*.

To summarize, effective managers, according to McClelland's research, must be motivated by a strong need for power, combined with considerable self-control. This power must be socialized power, not personalized power. These managers must be more driven by a socialized need for power than by a need for achievement or a high need for affiliation. They must be devoted more to the welfare of the organization than to having warm personal relationships with subordinates. They must want to empower other people so they can get the job done through those people rather than by their own direct efforts (McClelland, 1975).

Gender, Power Motivation, and the Expression of Power Through Leadership

For many years, nearly all the empirical research on the power motive was conducted with male samples. Most of what we "knew" about the power motive among women was based on folklore and intuition. Social scientists tended to conclude that women were generally lower in power motivation than men. In those cases where women had strong power motivation, it was somehow seen as different from the male variety, perhaps because it was frequently expressed differently through different actions toward different goals (Stewart & Chester, 1982). More recently, however, abundant evidence has been accumulated to suggest that there are no systematic sex differences in the ways by which the power motive is aroused, in average levels of the need for power, or in relationships between the need for power and attaining formal social power, power-related careers and prestige (Maroda, 2004; Winter, 1988). "The need for power is a human trait, not a gendered one" (Maroda, 2004).

However, there *are* systematic differences in the ways men and women *express* their power needs.

Winter (1988) defined a dichotomy of power of his own – it is strikingly parallel to that of McClelland, detailed earlier. Winter referred to one form as *egoistic dominance*, reflecting verbal and physical aggression, rough play, and attention seeking. He referred to the second category as *responsible nurturance*, which is manifested in providing help and support to others, prosocial dominance, physical contact. Men are more likely to exhibit the egoistic variety; women the responsible nurtuance variety. Winter observed that people of both sex groups move from the egoistic variety to the more prosocial variety as they age. Although Winter's (1988) work is a bit old, it has been extended and updated with insights for the interpretation of the 20th-century images of women, power, and feminism (Maroda, 2004).

An interesting issue related to sex differences in the need for power is whether men and women differ in the styles of leadership they employ in the workplace. Just as stereotypes have been developed and maintained about sex differences in the power motive (described elsewhere in this chapter), there is a rich North American tradition in stereotypes about the ways in which men and women lead other people. This stereotype has it that women employ a much less autocratic style than men, featuring instead more of a tendency toward interpersonal and supportive styles. In one study representing this line of thought, a researcher found among a sample of effective women managers a greater tendency than among men to use "transformational" styles, by which they motivated others to transform their own self-interest into the goals of the organization (Rosener, 1990). Although she didn't make reference to McClelland's (1970) distinction between personal and socialized power, Rosener's findings were clearly consistent with the stereotypes about men and women as managers. They provide an interesting parallel between the stereotypes as they pertain to power motives and to leadership styles. The stereotypes about women's leadership styles are entirely consistent with the parallel stereotypes about their power motives, and it would be easy to confound or equate the two concepts. Clearly, leadership positions can serve to satisfy power motives. It is also true that people high in the power motive may be more likely to seek out positions of formal power and authority. But it is a mistake to assume a one-to-one correspondence between power motivation and leadership style. McClelland (1975), among others, has shown us often that seeking leadership and the expression of leader behavior are driven by more than simple power motives. In addition to the need for power, other motives (such as affiliation and achievement, for example) can explain leader behavior and differences in leadership style.

What are the similarities and differences in leadership between men and women, especially in view of the interesting parallels between them in the need for and expression of power?

One study investigated possible sex differences in the use of the two varieties of power by managers (Chusmir & Parker, 1984). Consistent with the researchers' hypotheses, the women managers displayed higher overall need for power than the male managers. Most of the difference between the two groups was found in the socialized power category, where the women showed significantly stronger needs for the "desirable" variety of power than the men. There was no significant difference between the two groups on the less socially desirable form of power from McClelland's dichotomy.

A comprehensive review of the empirical evidence on the matter reveals that male and female leaders are no different on a systematic basis when they are studied *in real organizational settings*. However, when researchers have examined the matter in laboratory studies or in hypothetical circumstances in which the participants were not in a leadership context, stereotypic gender differences have been observed. That is, in these two generally contrived research contexts, there has been a tendency for women to be more interpersonally oriented and for men to be somewhat more task oriented in their leadership styles (Eagly & Johnson, 1990). The study by Rosener (1990), just described, that found apparent gender differences is an example of this sort of artifact. Rosener asked people to self-report on their leadership styles rather than actually observe the leaders in action. As Eagly and Johnson (1990) found, Rosener's data suggested that men and women differ as managers in their relative use of interpersonal styles and task orientation (see the debate between Rosener, 1990, and others).

Bases of Personal Power

There have been a variety of conceptual models forwarded over the years in the social sciences to explain the bases on which people can generate power (here we are talking about the capacity to change the probability of an event occurring, not the human motive for doing so). Two of these are most popular and are presented here.

The French and Raven typology

One of the most influential theories from 20th-century social psychology is the typology of personal bases of power advanced by French and Raven (1959). They proposed that people have a set of sources of power available to them in social affairs. A person can have power by dint of his personal attractiveness or desirability. Called *referent power*, other terms such as charisma come to mind. So, if John likes and admires Mike, Mike has a basis of potential power over John (i.e., he has the possibility of altering the probability of certain of John's behavior). Interestingly, Mike may not realize he possesses this power.

John may have expertise, talent, experience or information that Mike needs or admires. In such a case, John is said to have *expert power*.

If John can make things difficult for other people, he is said to have *coercive power*. He can threaten sanctions to gain compliance with his wishes. Alternatively, if John is able to provide special rewards or benefits to other people, he may be in a position of *reward power* relative to other people.

Finally, Mike may be the boss or in a formal position of authority that enables him to change other people's behavior. In such cases, Mike is said to have *legitimate power*.

In any situation, an individual may have any or all of these bases of personal power available. They may be used one at a time, or in combination, and sometimes they may be used unwittingly.

Dependency relationships

A second, more fundamental approach to understanding the means by which people acquire power in social contexts was offered by Emerson (1962), a sociologist. The essence of Emerson's approach is *dependency*: Power is based on the dependency one person can establish in another for the first person's resources.[1] That is, for Emerson (1962), A has power over B to the extent that:[2]

1. A has resources B requires.
2. B does not possess resources A requires (which limits the potential for trade).
3. B does not have alternative sources for the resources A possesses.
4. B cannot coerce A.

It follows, therefore, that power accrues to those who hold or acquire scarce resources and who make other people (or groups, or social units at any level) dependent upon their supply of those resources. The best advice available for any newcomer in a work group, by this perspective, is to develop a unique set of skills that is in short supply within the group in question! Indeed this model provides the conceptual underpinnings for many of the more modern approaches to understanding power-related behavior in organizations. Academic and practitioner books on power flourished during the 1970s, 1980s and 1990s, many of them, at core, making use of the wisdom found in French and Raven's (1959) and Emerson's (1962) models, although the original works were not always credited sufficiently. Notice that many of French and Raven's categories of personal power can be subsumed under the

---

[1] "Resources" is a broad term implying such things, for example, as money, talent or skill, water, land, information, etc.
[2] In these terms, A and B are social units, such as individuals, groups, departments, racial groups, or even nation states.

more generic framework offered by Emerson, inasmuch as a person's charisma, expertise, and capacity to grant rewards can be conceptualized as "resources" in Emerson's framework. At the nub, however, the key to this dependency of some actors on the resources lies in the possession by other actors. Pfeffer (1981a), Pfeffer and Salancik (1974), and Salancik and Pfeffer (1974), expanded on the many ways people attempt to accumulate power over those around them by building networks of dependencies. Again, the fundamental strategy is to provide resources of various kinds that co-workers need to pursue their careers and do their jobs. Possessing and distributing such resources can make the recipient dependent on the one who has the resources to dispense, thereby giving the latter bases of power.

A popular management book entitled *The 48 laws of power* (Greene, 1998) is replete with practical tips for the use of power to accomplish one's own ends. The lessons offered in Greene's book come from a variety of traditional and classical sources, and many of them, while they appear pernicious and devious, actually have reasonable explanations (if not justifications) in more modern social science, including the wisdom of French and Raven and Emerson and others. Indeed, many of the themes related to power that we discuss in this chapter and elsewhere in this book are readily reconciled with many of Greene's (1998) suggestions. The most central example is his Law #11: *Learn to keep people dependent on you.* This is a direct adaptation of Emerson's (1962) major tenet of power. In his overview of this law, Greene (1998, p. 82) wrote:

> To maintain your independence you must always be needed and wanted. The more you are relied on, the more freedom you have. Make people depend on you for their happiness and prosperity and you have nothing to fear. Never teach them enough so that they can do without you.

Another "law" augments the wisdom found in Law #11. Numbered by Greene (1998, p. 115) as Law 16, it is as follows: *Use absence to increase respect and honor.*

Too much circulation makes your price go down: The more you are seen and heard from, the more common you appear. If you are already established in a group, temporary withdrawal from it will make you more talked about, even more admired. You must learn when to leave. Create value through scarcity.

In summary, power is the capacity a person has to change the probability of acts occurring (Dahl, 1957). It is based on the possession and judicious use of scarce resources, the capacity to keep control of those resources, and to maintain their scarcity. As we have seen, much of the literature written for both academics and practitioners on the topic of power in recent decades rests on these fundamental tenets.

USES AND ABUSES OF POWER IN THE WORKPLACE

Power can be useful and put to positive ends (Pfeffer, 1981a). It can sometimes also be pernicious and dysfunctional. Kanter (1979) distinguished between *productive power* and *oppressive power*. The former comes from having open channels to valued organizational resources, whereas the latter is derived from these channels being controlled and manipulated. Kanter's two varieties are reminiscent of another dual concept of power offered by McClelland (1970) which we discussed earlier.

In the following sections of this chapter, we focus on three particularly intriguing organizational phenomena that have many of their roots in power motivation and its expression through work: Political and territorial behavior; ingratiation; tyrannical, bullying and harassment behavior by superiors; and systemic, institutionalized corruption.

Abuses of Power in Work Organizations: Power, Political Behavior, and Territoriality

Although there is lack of total agreement on a definition, the active acquisition of power and the pursuit of blatant self-interest is usually defined as *political behavior* (cf. Drory & Romm, 1990; Frost & Hayes, 1979). This label often makes political activity *sound* inherently evil and, in many cases, political activity can be disruptive, even toxic for those who get caught in its web (Frost, 2003; Greene, 1998; Kacmar, Bozeman, Carlson, & Anthony, 1999). Countless popular paperbacks dealing with the art and strategies of organizational politics and power acquisition have been published and sold to North American managers over the years (e.g., Greene, 1998). Tactics for building power and maintaining it are a popular skill taught in schools of business (cf. Whetten & Cameron, 2007). Whether it is good, evil or benign, *the need for power* motivates a great deal of organizational behavior that is intended to acquire and maintain power as a commodity, tool or weapon.

Another dynamic that is similar to and often influenced by political and power motives is *territorial* behavior in organizations, defined as "an individual's behavioral expression of his or her feelings of ownership toward a physical or social object" (Brown, Lawrence, & Robinson, 2005). On this definition, an "object" is broadly defined to include things other than simple physical things. Hence, a person can become territorial toward physical space as well as toward intangibles such as ideas, roles, and responsibilities, as well as social entities such as individuals or groups. Hence, in common political parlance in many organizations, a statement such as "I was only defending my turf" may apply to one's behavior that was intended to protect access to information, to a powerful other person, a parking spot, or even a responsibility, such as being the group's social convener.

As pointed out by Brown et al. (2005), the relationship between territorial behavior, on the one hand, and power and political behavior, on the other, is a complex one, but it does exist, and there is no doubt that a considerable amount of turf warfare in organizations is motivated by the desire to maintain or enhance one's power, influence, and share of scarce resources. Encroachment of one's putative "territory" can trigger emotional reactions such as jealousy as well as conflict, at either a latent or open level. In addition, the territorial acts of "marking" one's territory – attempting to make it clear to all concerned that ownership of objects belongs to one person or another – can also be disruptive, particularly when there is disagreement about who "owns" what. Like political behavior designed primarily to acquire and maintain scarce resources, territorial behavior that is driven by needs for identity, control, and other motives is a fascinating phenomenon that can, in many cases, preclude conflict by making it clear whose turf is whose (Brown et al., 2005). It may be that territorial behavior can also contribute positively to organizational commitment, although evidence on most of these hypotheses about territoriality in organizations is scarce.

Abuses of Power in Work Organizations: Ingratiation

Most of us are aware of the phenomenon variously called "brown-nosing," "sucking up," and other euphemisms. Organizational scientists refer to this activity as *ingratiation*. Ingratiation is considered to consist of three types of interrelated acts: (1) self-presentation/promotion, (2) opinion conformity, and (3) the enhancement of other people[3] (Jones, 1964; Kacmar, Carlson & Bratton, 2004). *Self-presentation* is "behaving in a manner perceived to be appropriate by the target person (i.e., person being ingratiated) or in a manner to which this individual will be attracted" (Ralston, 1985, p. 477). *Opinion conformity* is defined as "expressing an opinion or behaving in a manner that is consistent with the opinions, judgments, or behaviors of the target person" (Ralston, p. 477). *Other enhancement* "is expressing favorable opinions and evaluations of the target person by the ingratiat-

---

[3] Many of Greene's (1998) 48 laws of power can be found to relate to these three elements of ingratiation.

ing individual" (Ralston, p. 477). Although the categories of ingratiation cited by Kacmar et al. are similar – they offer four – they note that some are directed more toward oneself while some are directed toward other people. Regardless of the categories used, the key principles are the same, so we adopt Ralston's (1985) typology here for exposition.

For example, if a subordinate is aware that a superior is constantly trying to lose weight, ingratiation may take the form of a compliment about the superior's "robust build" (p. 477). Wortman and Linsenmeier (1977, p. 134) add that:

> The ingratiator tries to behave as though the issue at hand were his only concern, when in fact he is also interested in enhancing himself in the target person's eyes. An ingratiator may seek attraction because he is personally gratified by liking and approval from others, or he may value attraction or positive evaluation not as an end in itself, but because it is instrumental to achieving other goals.

Ralston (1985, p. 477) observes that ingratiation has a long history of use, citing the story of Adam, Eve, and the snake: "The bite from an apple in the Garden of Eden resulted from the snake's skillful use of ingratiation for its own self-interests."

An ingratiator may employ a variety of tactics to impress a supervisor. One is simply by doing well on the job. While it is true that being the star performer may bring on the wrath or indignation of coworkers, bosses generally like subordinates who perform well, including in particular those people who are good organizational citizens (see Chapter 10).

Probably the most blatant tactic is for the ingratiator to openly express liking or admiration for the target person: "Gee, Boss, I really like your new car!" Simple balance theory from social psychology (Heider, 1958), as well as a considerable amount of evidence, shows that if one person (Stanley) believes that another person (Huntley) likes him, then Stanley is probably going to like Huntley. If Stanley has low self-esteem, he may be suspicious of the ingratiation attempt, so it could backfire on Huntley (cf. Wortman & Linsenmeier, 1977, p. 143). The lesson is that the ingratiator should avoid making statements about the target person that are inconsistent with the target's self-concept.

Balance theory also helps to explain why espousing attitudes similar to those of a target person can be successful in getting the target's attention and affection. Similarly, doing favors for a target person can yield positive feelings, as long as the helper's intention seems genuine and that she *intended* to be helpful.

Ingratiation may be unsuccessful in situations where the ingratiator's motives are transparent or when he generally lacks credibility for other prior reasons. A husband who agrees that his wife's choice of dress for an evening out is terrific has much more credibility if he has a reputation for speaking honestly on earlier occasions when he thought the wife's taste or choice was lacking. It follows that a tactic for an ingratiator to employ is to be on record with both positive and negative commentary and opinions, establishing a bank of credibility for occasions when she wants to attempt false flattery. But, again, if the ingratiator is in an obvious position of subordination to the target, his motives may be questioned and the attitudinal structuring attempt can backfire (Wortman & Linsenmeier, 1977, p. 161).

Ralston (1985) noted that ingratiatory behavior is influenced as readily by organizational context factors as by the characteristics of the individuals involved. He proposes that autocratic bosses (who tend to make decisions unilaterally and not allow subordinates to exercise their own skills and abilities) are more likely than non-autocratic bosses to produce ingratiatory acts among their workers. He does not propose that democratic bosses will be associated with particularly low levels of such influence attempts, but simply that autocracy *will* yield high levels. Ralston also suggests employees in task settings that are generally ambiguous, where they are not clear regarding what is expected of them, are most likely to attempt to influence their bosses through ingratiation, especially when the employees want to do well and move ahead in the organization.

A third organizational context factor likely to foster ingratiation, according to Ralston (1986), is resource scarcity. When there is scarcity of money for supplies and expenses, raw materials, equipment, information, or access to the attention of one's superior's time and attention, for example, people are likely to use whatever means are available to acquire these resources, including ingratiatory behavior.

In summary, Ralston (1985) hypothesized that more than simple personality predispositions of organizational actors will determine the use of ingratiation in work organizations. The policies and practices of management may also contribute through the leadership styles used by managers, the degree of uncertainty about the nature of the work, and the level of scarcity of resources needed to get the organization's work accomplished.

A recent empirical investigation found that different antecedent factors were related to different forms of ingratiation behavior. This study, which employed a person × situation interaction model, found that different combinations of person variables (such as need for power and self-esteem, for example) and different contextual factors (such as role ambiguity) interact to predict ingratiation behaviors that are either self-directed or other directed (Kacmar et al., 2004).

The point here is that ingratiation is a deliberate attempt by people to misrepresent themselves for the sake of gaining personal advantage. Whether there is anything inherently wrong with such deception is a matter decided by one's values. To the extent that we value integrity and honesty, we cannot condone false presentation of our values or our beliefs and attitudes in work settings. Beware the entire set of declarations and opinions that come from those whom we have seen spin false praise when it seems to serve their ends. The desire for power and influence can motivate people to misrepresent themselves and undermine a climate of honesty and trust. It is fitting to bolster this point by citing another of Greene's (1998) "48 laws," viz.:

> Use selective honesty and generosity to disarm your victim. One sincere and honest move will cover over dozens of dishonest ones. Open-hearted gestures of honesty and generosity bring down the guard of even the most suspicious people. Once your selective honesty opens a hole in their armor, you can deceive and manipulate them at will. A timely gift – a Trojan horse – will serve the same purpose.
>
> (Greene, 1998, p. 89)

Does power corrupt people?

Popular culture is replete with stories in the forms of movies and novels about mean-spirited – even sadistic – bosses and supervisors. *The Devil wears Prada, Working Girl, Nine to Five*, and *Glengarry Glen Ross* provide four examples from recent years of wide-screen yarns about how people are downtrodden by tyrants at work and how they often (although not always, as in the case of Mamet's *Glengarry Glen Ross*) rise up and overthrow the tyrants! Perhaps the reason this theme is so recurrent in our entertainment and popular culture is because it is so universal in our working lives. The revenge Dolly Parton and her cohorts extracted from their nasty and conniving boss, played by Dabney Coleman, in *Nine to Five* serves as a fantasy escape for those of us – in this case, particularly office women who work for male chauvinist bosses – and speaks volumes to the almost perverse mass appeal of this genre of story. At the time of this writing, Donald Trump's *The Apprentice* is soaring in North American television ratings. Enough said.

So, the question is: Is there something inherent in people and in power that makes the former susceptible to intoxication and evil-doing when in possession of the latter? Kipnis (1972, p. 33) observed that Hobbes, in *Leviathan*, claimed that: "Men formed societies as a means of limiting the exploitive consequences of the unequal division of power." Following on this possibility, Kipnis and his colleagues reported two fascinating studies over three decades ago which suggest that power may have a corrupting influence on some people (Kipnis, 1972; Kipnis, Castell, Gergen, & Mauch, 1976). On the basis of these two projects, the researchers concluded that the possession and use of power over other people can cause power holders to devalue the worth of the work of less powerful people, to increase their attempts to use their power, to take personal credit for the efforts provided by the less powerful, and to express a preference to keep a social distance from those over whom they use their power. In a later publication, Kipnis (2001) documents evidence that shows that power-dependency relationships in other contexts (such as psychotherapy, for example) can have the same detrimental effects on the evaluation of non-powerful by people who hold and exert power, even when that power is intended to benefit the non-powerful.

Seemingly countless trade books have appeared in the popular media to showcase the extreme exercise of power in work organizations. Books entitled *Corporate abuse*, *Bullying at work*, and *Psycho-bosses from hell* have enjoyed considerable commercial success. Why is that? Is it because most of us who hold jobs have been subjected to abusive bosses? Is it because many of us desire to confirm that we are not the only bosses who are abusive? Whatever the cause, the popularity of these managerial books suggests that North Americans are once again (or still) acutely interested in the use and abuse of power in organizations. Let's take a brief look at the proposition that the need for power, or the possession of power, or both, can cause people to behave in ways that would otherwise be unacceptable.

Abuses of Power in Work Organizations: Tyranny, Bullying, and Harassment

In their startling book *Corporate abuse*, Wright and Smye (1996) summarized a variety of forms of abuse that people suffer in modern organizational settings. They note that some abuse results from strict adherence to bureaucratic norms and rules, while other abuse follows from the "wrenching changes in industrial and economic structures that put an entire company under pressure" (p. 55). These two sources of abuse are common and frequently beyond the control of any individual: They are natural costs of life in modern work organizations.

Another form of abuse, however, is less innocent and less acceptable. This is the abuse dished out by "bullies," people who flaunt and abuse their personal and/or administrative power. In a recent book by two experts on the subject, Namie and Namie (2003) defined bullying as "the repeated, malicious, health-endangering mistreatment of one employee (the Target) by one or more employees (the bully, bullies)" (p. 3). Bullies exercise power through the fear they generate in other people. They apply a mix of psychological violence, and verbal and strategic assaults intended to prevent their targets from accomplishing their work. Bullies can be either male or female, although Namie and Namie (2003) reported that the majority of advice seekers who seek their guidance are women who claim to be bullied by other women. They taunt and ridicule their coworkers, particularly their subordinates. Their "leadership styles" are reminiscent of those of military commanders, as associated and depicted in the movies with General George Patton, as depicted by the late George C. Scott in the movie *Patton*.

Citing *Bullying at work* (Adams, 1992), Wright and Smye (1996) listed a number of ways in which we can recognize bullies in the workplace. They include acts such as displaying uncontrolled anger, including the use of loud, vulgar language; humiliating other workers, either alone or in public; persistently using sarcasm and criticism; setting impossible deadlines; changing instructions in midstream, making failure for others inevitable; resisting delegation of authority to others; taking credit for other people's work and success; and undermining other people's attempts to get ahead. Namie and Namie's (2003) "top 10 bullying tactics" are similar. Their book, along with another by three English authors (Rayner, Hoel, & Cooper, 2002) are commended as comprehensive treatments of bullying in the workplace.

Ashforth (1994) explored the "petty tyrant" syndrome. There may be many personal and situational factors associated with this form of behavior, but a few factors are particularly interesting. Ashforth suggests that some people of this sort may, in fact, be low in self-esteem, using their formal authority as a sort of compensatory device.[4] Petty tyrants often fit a mold that includes

---

[4] Petty tyrants can also be people with *high* levels of self-esteem (Ashforth, 1994).

authoritarianism and dogmatic belief structures and *Theory X* beliefs about workers (recall Chapter 3). They place high importance on conformity and order and low value on treating other people with respect. They have a preference for action and a relatively low tolerance for ambiguity. But petty tyranny may be caused by factors other than a person's personality predispositions. Highly controlling institutional factors such as those found in prisons and many hospitals may give rise to this sort of behavior as well. And, ironically, people who actually have relatively little institutional power may behave tyrannically, lording what power they do have over others around them. For example, a low-level office clerk who keeps the keys to important conference rooms may exhibit a haughty, indifferent style that reminds others who need access to those rooms that *he* determines who gains access and who does not.

Adopting an interactional justice framework (see Chapter 11), Harlos and Pinder (1999) reported a study of what it is that tyrannical bosses actually do to earn the label. Their typology found eight major categories of acts that employees found unjust: Intimidation, abandonment, inconsistency, degradation, criticism, inaccessibility, surveillance, and manipulation. Interestingly, a large proportion of the tyrannical deeds perpetrated by the supervisors reported in this study were conducted in public!

What are the effects of petty tyranny? Ashforth (1994) suggested that this sort of style results primarily in bad things for the organization, including the rejection of supervisors by their subordinates; heightened stress among its victims; emotional reactions normally associated with frustration, such as fear, anxiety, and irritation; reactance *against* the directives and preferences of the tyrant (as the victim asserts defiance and self-control); feelings of helplessness and alienation; a reduction in individual initiative; reduced self-esteem; and diminished work performance. Finally, the hostility and aggressive behavior of petty tyrants can undermine work group cohesiveness.

Petty tyranny also has serious dysfunctional consequences for employees. In a recent longitudinal survey of 362 Americans, Tepper (2000) studied the experiences and consequences of abusive supervisory behavior. Among those people who had not quit their organizations following his first contact with them, Tepper found the very results hypothesized by Ashforth's conceptual model. Abusive supervision was related to voluntary turnover between the first and second phase of the sample. Among those who remained with their organizations for the second phase of the study, abusive supervision was associated with lower job and life satisfaction, lower normative and affective commitment to their organizations (see Chapter 12), higher continuance commitment, conflict between work and family, and psychological distress. Tepper (2000) interpreted his results using an organization justice-based model – specifically, demonstrating how abusive supervisory styles adversely affect interactional justice, which, in turn, adversely affect individuals. (See Chapter 11 for our treatment of organizational justice and injustice.)

As we discussed in the context of Theory X supervisory styles in Chapter 3, tyrannical behavior by managers can result in a vicious circle: Employees react with fear, low initiative, and low performance, triggering a continuation or escalation of tyrannical behavior by the manager.

What is the point here? Over the long term, by making life miserable for those around them, bullies are usually not good for the organizations they work for. Although this sort of style *can* achieve short-term results, the longer-term effects on the attitudes, emotions, and withdrawal behavior of other people are usually dysfunctional. The work of Ashforth (1994), Wright and Smye (1996) and Adams (1992) continues the tradition in organizational science that shows that power *can* corrupt those who hold it in organizational settings. Power may be one of the great motivators, as McClelland and Burnham (1976) observed. It can arouse, direct, sustain, and explain much of the motivated work behavior we observe every day.

In Canada, both government and the courts have recently begun to weigh in on the issue. "Judges started to rule that if a boss was so mean to an employee that he got sick or quit, the boss, or his company, should have to compensate the target [of the misuse of power] for the abuse" (Scott, 2007, pp. 40–41). Some payouts had been in the order of one million dollars during the 2 years before the *Maclean's* article in which this story was published (Scott, September 3, 2007). The province of Quebec outlawed workplace bullying in 2004. There, it is referred to as *psychological harassment* and defined as "any vexatious behaviour in the form of repeated and hostile or unwarranted conduct, verbal comments, actions or gestures, that affects an individual's dignity or psychological or physical integrity that results in a harmful work environment for the employee" (Scott, p. 41). Another form of regulation by government and legal authorities appears to be required when norms of civility are not observed continuously in Canada's workplaces. It's a shame that people cannot control their incivility and aggression as they work for all the motives discussed herein. We discuss at length both incivility (see Chapter 6) and aggressive workplace behavior (in Chapter 8) at length elsewhere in this volume.

Sexual harassment

One of the most pernicious ways power is misused in organizational settings is via sexual harassment. In the United States, sexual harassment "takes place when one person engages in sexual behavior toward another but the other person is unwilling to reciprocate and work rewards are attached to the bargain" (Mainiero, 1989, p. 34). In Canada, two forms of sexual harassment are recognized, and both are illegal. The first form is called *quid pro quo* harassment, which occurs when a sexual act is requested or extorted from an individual in exchange for a promotion, pay increase, or any other form of work-related outcome. This form of harassment can be either subtle or blatant in its expression, but it amounts to simple extortion in either case. It is both unethical and illegal. As Mainiero (2003) put it: "The problem is that sex is a commodity that can be traded for power" (2003, p. 3).

The second variety is referred to as systemic or environmental harassment. Again, this variety can be either subtle or blatant. It consists of requiring employees to work in an environment that is in some way permeated with sexual innuendo, pictures, themes or other features. "Girlie calendars" on the wall, jokes with sexual overtones, and verbal or nonverbal overtures that are unwanted by the recipient comprise this second form of harassment. The employing organization is legally responsible for the conduct of its management group and therefore liable in the case of charges successfully brought against the organization by an employee who has been exposed to either form of harassment. The laws in the United States are virtually identical to those in Canada.

Sexual harassment is a power issue, not a matter of love and innocent sexual desire. Simple romance between consenting partners of comparable organizational status levels is a different matter from situations in which one person demands sex or behaves sexually in regard to someone who does not want such attention, *particularly when there is a disparity in the power and status levels of the players involved.* Not surprisingly, therefore, sexual harassment has been particularly rampant in military settings, where power differentials are much more salient and sacrosanct than they are in most other types of organization (cf. Branswell, 1998; Caproni & Finley, 1997; Carlson, 1995; Geddes, 1998; Office of the Inspector General, 1993; O'Hara, 1998a, 1998b; Pinder & Harlos, 2001). Almost always, harassment cases in the military involve abuse of junior female personnel by ranking male personnel, often officers (see O'Hara, 1998a, 1998b). Expressing voice in military settings to complain of mistreatment is rare, although it does occur. Fear of retribution and further victimization by superiors holding power differentials is the usual reason for this silence (Hotelling, 1991; Morrison & Milliken, 2000), especially among women (Rudman, Borgida, & Robertson, 1995). Building on a series of cases of sexual harassment in the Canadian military as well as original field data from non-military settings, Pinder and Harlos (2001) proposed an inductive model of employee silence in response to such maltreatment. Some positive news on the harassment front in the military is that the U.S. Naval Academy has recently unveiled a new mandatory sexual harassment prevention program "to teach midshipmen in a structured setting what is and is not permissible in today's military"[5] (Kelly, 2007). Bravo!

---

[5] http://www.hometownannapolis.com/cgi-bin/read/2007/10_26–37/NAV (October 22, 2007).

In the past, many managers have had difficulty distinguishing between romance and harassment, in part because the form the latter takes has *surface* similarities in appearance with the former. Companies can clamp down on harassment by promulgating and enforcing policies prohibiting it, but they cannot prevent the occurrence of natural romantic love. Nevertheless, managers are missing the point when they cannot distinguish between the two phenomena (cf. Berdahl, 2007). We discuss further the issues of love and sex in the workplace later in this chapter.

The domain of research and theory on sexual harassment is voluminous and beyond the scope of this volume. Nevertheless, a study of the work we examined earlier in this chapter on tyranny and the abuse of power provides a start in understanding sexual harassment. A more complete treatment is offered by O'Donohue (1997).

Normalization of corruption

To close this section, we observe some promising new theoretical work by Ashforth and Anand (2003) who have developed a conceptual model of how corrupt behavior can become normalized in organizations. Following on Sherman (1980), Ashforth and Anand (2003) defined corrupt acts "as the misuse of authority for personal, subunit, and/or organizational gain" (p. 2). Their model describes a three-stage process, involving: (1) institutionalization, "the process by which corrupt practices are enacted as a matter of routine, often without conscious thought about their propriety"; (2) rationalization, "the process by which individuals who engage in corrupt acts use socially constructed accounts to legitimate the acts in their own eyes," and (3) socialization, "the process by which newcomers are taught to perform and accept the corrupt practices" (p. 3). While Ashforth and Anand offered many real-world examples, fans of the television series *The Shield* witness the cycle of normalized corruption in every episode. The organizational processes that lead to normalization of corrupt practices would seem to apply to all of those we have reviewed in this chapter, although empirical work is needed to test and confirm the generalizability of the normalization phenomenon.

Whether or not power corrupts people, some individuals often behave as if it *does* corrupt; *other* people, that is. Lust for power is often attributed as a motive (and sometimes *the* motive) for the acts of other individuals. A recent Canadian example occurred when Ms. Belinda Stronach, Conservative MP and heiress to an auto-parts fortune, crossed the floor of the House of Commons on May 17, 2005 to immediately take on an important cabinet position in the then-faltering minority Liberal government of Prime Minister Paul Martin (*Globe and Mail*, 2005; *Maclean's*, 2005; *Times Colonist*, 2005). Ms. Stronach, who had run unsuccessfully for leadership of the newly formed Conservatives, claimed that the reason for her joining the Liberals was a principled one: She could not in good conscience stand with the opposition Conservatives, in league with the separatist Bloc Québécois, to bring down the government on any of a number of non-confidence motions that were pending in the House of Commons. At the time, every vote counted: The Liberals eventually had to rely on a tie-breaking vote by the Speaker of the House to survive the crisis that was underway when Ms. Stronach switched sides. Even though she had harshly criticized Mr. Martin and the way he was running the government only a few months earlier, Ms. Stronach was adamant that her motives had nothing to do with power (a chance to immediately take on a key cabinet post). (To make the story even juicier for the Canadian media, Ms. Stronach forsook her boyfriend, who was the second-in-command in the Conservative caucus when she crossed the floor.)

The point here is that the media had a field day for weeks, accusing Ms. Stronach of merely being power hungry, and that her espoused principled motives concerning keeping the government from falling at the feet of the separatists (and the Liberals) were specious. From an attribution theory perspective (Hewstone, 1983), power appears to provide a salient, ready alternative to external attribution for human behavior. In other words, the Stronach story shows that if a person acts a certain way when there is potentially a gain of power in the offing, that power can quickly displace other explanations for the person's behavior. Power appears a very powerful causal factor in the eyes of many people when they seek to understand and explain the behavior of others.

The hypothesis that power corrupts individuals, therefore, has a number of interesting and compelling classical, social-scientific and everyday experiential roots. Yet recent work suggests that the power–corruption hypothesis may be an oversimplification, and that a number of factors enter into the equation. We examine some of these recent developments here.

Power and self-construals

People develop perceptions of who they are, referred to as *self-construals* (Lee & Tiedens, 2001). Whereas the term *self-system* is used to refer to the entire range of views we have about ourselves, self-construal is a narrower term and concept, related to limited aspects of one's being. Self-construals are malleable, heavily influenced by the roles we adopt and play and by the contexts in which we find ourselves.

A key distinction here is whether a person views herself as highly *independent* of others or *interdependent* with others. Independent people (on this distinction) define themselves in their own terms (e.g., "I am a terrific swimmer"), whereas interdependent individuals will think of themselves in terms of their roles vis-à-vis other humans (e.g., "I am a terrific swimming coach"). These images play an important role in our social lives, affecting the way we think, emote, and behave toward other people and even toward inanimate objects. Individual characteristics that, within a given cultural context, are associated with power (such as age, gender, or ethnicity) tend to develop independent self-construals in people. (In Chapter 6, we will examine a related body of theory referred to as status characteristics theory, which lays out the mechanisms by which certain personal characteristics are associated with higher levels of status and power.)

Generally, most people are prone to self-enhancing biases, but this tendency is especially acute for people who construe themselves as independent of others and who hold higher levels of power. They are also more positive about their own future; they make self-serving attributions, believe they are better than others, and have higher overall levels of self-esteem (see Chapter 6). They also tend to be higher in power motivation than people who construe themselves as interdependent with other people.

Lee and Tiedens (2001) reviewed a number of interesting parallels between the holding of power (whether based on personal traits or one's circumstances) and the nature of one's self-construal. High-power individuals are more prone to self-enhancing biases. High socioeconomic individuals have higher levels of self-esteem and self-confidence than people in lower SES categories. High-power people also rate themselves as more competent, more likeable, more desirable, and even better looking than people in low-power positions (Lee & Tiedens, 2001). When things go wrong, high-power people blame others rather than themselves, particularly people in lower-power positions. They also engage in more in-group favoritism than do low-power individuals. In summary, there are some uncanny parallels demonstrated in the literature among a number of dimensions related to the holding (or not holding) of power, to whether one construes one's self as interdependent or not with other people, and a variety of behavioral tendencies. In the standards of most North American social circles, the syndromes described by this literature are not particularly socially desirable.

A paradox?

Ironically, however, there is also considerable evidence that people in high-power positions have more relational ties with other people (rather than fewer, their self-construals notwithstanding). (Again, see Lee & Tiedens, 2001, for a review.) According to *this* body of research, they are better communicators and are generally better at developing and maintaining relationships with other people. How can this be the case? Lee and Tiedens (2001) offer a number of explanations for what, at first blush, may be seen as a serious contradiction between the bottom-line conclusions of two streams of research. Among the solutions they offer, two stand out and must be used in combination. First, they suggest that independent and interdependent self-construals are not mutually exclusive, not opposite ends of a single continuum (as so often occurs during construct development in social science). Rather, they posit that the two traits are independent of one another so that any individual can be characterized as either, or both, and quite possibly, change in style from one context to another.

Second, they propose that acquiring power and using it are two separate, distinctly different phenomena, in which the use of an interdependent orientation may be required for building the relationships, networks, and communication links necessary for a power base, but that once power is established within a context, persons are capable of adopting a much more independent self-construal! In the words of Lee and Tiedens (2001, p. 67): "Once power is attained, self-construals become more independent. The power holder now receives cues from others and the situation that she is different from and better than others, and that others need her more than she needs them. As a response to attaining power, self-construals may become more independent." Finally, Lee and Tiedens (2001) suggested that certain personality variables (which we will discuss later) may moderate the relationship between the degree of power a person has and the primary construal one has of one's self as well as upon the way that people exercise that power.

In a similar vein of research and theory, Lee-Chai, Chen, and Chartrand (2001) have concluded that: "Contrary to the popular notion that power acts as a corrupting influence, for some it is a cue for heightened social responsibility" (p. 57). They cited some of their own empirical work (Chen, Lee-Chai, & Bargh, 2001) that demonstrated that *the nature of an individual's goals* helps to determine whether power corrupts. After inducing power in three simulated laboratory settings, and gathering psychometric measures of participants' primary relationship orientation, they showed that, when in power, "communals" (people who characteristically prefer to benefit one another in response to each other's needs, without any expectation of a personal return, in exchange) volunteered to take on more voluntary work than they left for the other participants to undertake.

By contrast, when they were not in positions of power, the communals volunteered to perform less work than did the no-power "exchangers." Why? Because the low-power circumstances in the second condition dampened the communals' tendency to behave in a socially responsible manner. In other words, for communals to behave in a manner consistent with their fundamental personality orientation, they had to believe they were in positions of power in which to do so was appropriate. So, on balance, does power corrupt? According to the interaction between persona and situation found in this series of experiments, it depends on both personality and context, in the way we describe elsewhere when discussing person × situation interactions. Lee-Chai et al. (2001) reviewed other literatures that support the same conclusions in other contexts (including situations involving sexual aggression and harassment). They have also developed a scale to assess individual differences in people's attitudes toward the misuse of power.

In summary, although there are a number of research traditions that indicate that power *does* corrupt individuals, it seems safer to conclude at this point merely that power *can* corrupt people, but that not all people are as easily corrupted as others. Individual differences, as usual, factor into the equation. Whether because of a person's self-construal as independent or interdependent with others (as Lee & Tiedens, 2001, would have it), or whether because of a person's characteristic goal orientation – as either a communal or an exchanger (as Lee-Chai et al., 2001, would have it) – it appears safe to conclude that power is not always an intoxicant with pernicious effects. When in the right hands, power (which is merely the capacity to alter the odds of events occurring, after all) can be a wonderful force for the betterment of people. This is no less the case in work organizations than it is in other social contexts (Kanter, 1979; Pfeffer 1981a). By the same token, bullying and other forms of power abuse remain common phenomena, both inside work settings as well as in life in general. The reason? They are frequently very effective for those who employ such tactics (Namie & Namie, 2003; Rayner et al., 2002; and see Chapter 8).

CONCLUSIONS ON THE USE AND ABUSE OF POWER

To conclude this section, we borrow directly a statement made later in his life by a leading social scientist (Kipnis, 2001, p. 3) who spent much of his career studying the use and abuse of power:

> The Hobbesian . . . assumption that we are programmed by our desires, and by our dependence on other people to satisfy these desires, provides an important perspective for understanding the use of power. At times, our desires override our obligations to help others, to be decent, to be charitable, and to be what society considers civil. We want things from others from the moment of birth until death. We want affection, material goods, services, information, to be loved, to dominate, the chance to do better than others, to be treated fairly, and to be left alone, to name but a few of the many desires that impel us to influence others. There is no end of our dependence on others, because there is no end to the things we want. The dismal observation of Hobbes that people's motivations consist simply of endless streams of appetites appears as true today as when he wrote Leviathan . . . in the 17th century. If we accept these assumptions, then it follows that everyone must exercise influence and power on a day-to-day basis. Thus, the critical question is not whether people exercise power, but *how* [emphasis added] we exercise power.

LOOKING FORWARD

In the foregoing sections, we have examined the human need for power. We saw that the same noun, *power*, is used to represent both the need as well as one of the most important goals associated with that need: The capacity to make things happen that otherwise might not happen. The need for power, the pursuit of power, and the exercise of power are all commonplace in work organizations. They are, indeed, ubiquitous forces in organizational dynamics, some of which are useful and constructive, and some of which can be less so.

In Chapter 6, we will focus in part on the human needs for esteem and belonging. That discussion will bring us back to forms of uncivil behavior that are often manifested in work organizations. The foregoing analysis of bullying and petty tyranny will be germane to that discussion as well. Meanwhile, in the remaining sections of the current chapter, we will look at two more ubiquitous and interrelated needs – love and sex – that instigate fascinating and important determinants of motivated behavior in work settings.

LOVE, SEX, AND WORK MOTIVATION

Maslow (1954) and other need theorists include love as a basic human need. He proposed that if a person's physiological and safety needs are fairly well gratified:

> [T]here will emerge the love and affection and belongingness needs . . . The person will feel keenly, as never before, the absence of friends, or a sweetheart, or a wife, or children. He will hunger for affectionate relationships with people in general, namely, for a place in his group or family, and he will strive with great intensity to achieve his goal. He . . . may even forget that once, when he was hungry, he sneered at love as unreal or unnecessary or unimportant. Now he will feel sharply pangs of loneliness, of ostracism, of rejection, of friendlessness, of ruthlessness.
>
> (Maslow, 1954, p. 43)

Maslow (1954) claimed that deprivation of the love need early in one's life is frequently associated with neuroses. Unless the condition has progressed so far as to be irreversible, the administration of affection and kindness can be an integral part of treating such neuroses. Healthy adults, he believed, may need less love than maladjusted adults because, presumably, they have already enjoyed enough of it.

More recent work has viewed love as having psychological, biological, social, and physiological dimensions, all of which have demonstrated validity (see Fisher, 1992, 2004; Jankowiak, 1995). Historical analysis of the phenomenon suggests that until recently, Western cultures assumed that only they have been capable of experiencing romantic love (or romantic passion, as some authors call it):

> Indeed, it has become axiomatic among Western literati that the experience of romantic passion is a mark of cultural refinement, if not obvious superiority, and that the less cultured "masses" are incapable of such refinement; lust, yes; romance and love, no. The hidden inference of this assumption may be that romantic love is the prize or reward of true culture.
>
> (Jankowiak, 1995, p. 2)

Research has shown this is not so. Two anthropologists found romantic love to be a reality among 146 of 166 cultures in which they investigated it (Jankowiak & Fischer, 1992). The way it is manifested may depend in part on socioecological, political, or economic conditions and the stress that they can cause during a person's childhood (Chisholm, 1995). This multidimensional nature of love makes it particularly unusual among human needs and emotions, but humans and other animals share many features of the experience of being in love (Fisher, 2004).

Defining the Many Types of Love

The nature and force of love must be one of the most dominant themes in the histories of art and literature. Countless individuals have observed that there are many types of love, although there is little agreement on the issue of how many types there are (see Fehr & Russell, 1991). For example, the American author C. S. Lewis (1960) suggested that there are four main categories or types of human love: Affection, friendship, erotic love, and the love of God. Lazarus and Lazarus (1994) distinguished between two types: *Romantic love* and *companionate love*. Sexual intimacy may accompany the former type but not the latter. Modern social scientists use a variety of terms to refer to this general variety of love, defining it as: "[A]ny intense attraction involving the idealization of the other within an erotic context. The idealization carries with it the desire for intimacy and the pleasurable expectation of enduring for some unknown time into the future" (Jankowiak, 1995, p. 4).

Companionate love features many of the same feelings and emotions as romantic love, but is detached from sexual impulses. This category includes the filial love among family members, such as that between parents and their children, as well as the friendship that occurs between people of either the same or opposite genders. Women can have strong loving relationships with other men or women without sexual impulses or implications. According to Lazarus and Lazarus (1994), men in our culture often prefer to speak of their *friendship* for each other rather than their *love* for each other because of their definition of maleness and, presumably, fear of the stigma associated with homosexuality.

Prototypical love

To this point, we have considered several attempts to define two or three broad types of love. We have yet to come to grips with a general definition of love as a concept or phenomenon, for good reason.

As we saw in Chapter 4, many emotional states defy definition by the classical approach to defining objects and entities. The classical approach requires that we specify a set of necessary and sufficient conditions and characteristics for an object or concept to have in order to qualify for a definitional category (Russell, 1991).

Instead of trying in vain to form hard-and-fast distinctions among human emotions, Russell (1991) and others have advanced the idea of using prototypes: Classifying human emotions with fuzzy boundaries on the basis of their resemblance to prototypic examples and instances of a particular emotion. For example, there are variations and "shades of grey" among the various forms of anger, such as annoyance, wrath, rage, and so on.

The reader is referred to Chapter 4 for a more thorough treatment of the prototype approach to defining emotions. In this chapter our attention is on *love as a need*, while not denying that it is also an emotion and, for some, an attitude as well (Fehr & Russell, 1991). This approach helps us get around the difficulty of defining love by the classical approach. Indeed, philosophers, social scientists, poets, and anthropologists have had a very difficult time coming up with a single definition of love that seems to be universally acceptable. Perhaps the very elusiveness of the concept is one feature that makes love so fascinating. Regardless, a prototypical approach helps us understand the many elements of the phenomenon that people in our culture have in mind when they think about love.

Studies conducted at the University of Winnipeg used students to generate all of the types of love they could think of (Fehr & Russell, 1991). The students generated an average of 8.69 varieties. As the song says, "Love is a many-splendored thing!" A total of 20 varieties were selected by the researchers on the basis of the students' brainstorming. The rank ordering by which the students rated each form as "an extremely good example" vs. "an extremely poor example" of love is as follows: Maternal love, paternal love, friendship, sisterly love, romantic love, brotherly love, familial love, sibling love, affection, committed love, love for humanity, spiritual love, passionate love, Platonic love, self-love, sexual love, patriotic love, love of work,[6] puppy love, and infatuation.

The researchers conducted a series of further investigations to delineate the ways by which these categories could be clustered into smaller families. Eight different criteria emerged, eight different ways by which it appears that people seem to think of categories of love as more or less similar to one another. One of these criteria, for example, was the number of features each type had in common with other types. A second criterion was "T" (for "True") or an "F" (for "False") when each of the 20 varieties of love was flashed on the screen and they were asked if, for example, "Infatuation is a type of love."

The complete mapping of the relationships among the various varieties of love studied by Fehr and Russell (1991) is beyond the scope of our purpose. The interested reader is referred to the original research report. It is fascinating. Suffice it to say that there are many types of love and that, in our culture, some of these types seem more closely related to the core concept of love – whatever that is – than others. There is still plenty of room for philosophers, novelists, and poets to have fun with the concept of love.

Experiencing Romantic Love

The feeling of romantic love is one of tenderness and affection. If it is going well, it features feelings of joy, elation, satisfaction, and even ecstasy. There is a desire to be close to the loved one, to touch and embrace him or her. The loved person is seen as special, as beautiful or as wonderful in some way or another (Harris, 1995). What we see as beautiful or wonderful is culturally determined (Lazarus & Lazarus, 1994).

---

[6] Inclusion of work as a commonly held object for love, in the company of other objects such as mothers, fathers and sisters, is of particular interest to us here with our focus on work motivation.

Harris (1995) identified seven *mind-centered attributes* or *core properties* experienced by people who are in romantic love with one another in most cultural settings:

1. the desire for union or merger
2. idealization of the beloved person
3. exclusivity of the relationship
4. intrusive thinking about the loved one
5. emotional dependency
6. a reordering of the individual's goals and priorities
7. a strong sense of empathy and concern for the beloved person.

Leading American anthropologist Helen Fisher (2004) has recently added to this list. In addition to the elements of the love experience listed by Harris, Fisher adds that people in love also:

1. attribute special meaning to the loved person; she or he becomes "all important"
2. focus attention on the loved one
3. experience a sort of "emotional fire"
4. lose sleep and appetite as tremendous energy is expended in love
5. witness wild mood swings, raging from exhilaration to anxiety, despair, and fear of rejection
6. become hyper-sensitive, looking for clues about whether love is mutual
7. develop feelings of lust and an expectation of exclusivity in sexual relations
8. suffer pangs of jealousy when a third party is seen as entering the scene.

Finally, as many a poet has observed with sadness, love can be transient.

Fisher (2004) claimed that romantic love is often unplanned, involuntary, and seemingly uncontrollable. In addition, adversity heightens the passion of love, according to Fisher (2004). Known as the "Romeo and Juliet effect," we witness a redoubling of the effort to be near and to attract the loved one when barriers get in the way. Love generates hope – one of the powerful emotions we discussed in Chapter 4 and that Frank O'Dea claimed was partially responsible for his elevation from the gutters of Toronto (see page 3 of this book).

Interestingly, Fisher's (2004) research has demonstrated that emotional union trumps sexual union. Eighty-three percent of respondents to her research in Japan and the United States agreed with the following statement: "Knowing that _____ is in love with me is more important to me than having sex with him/her."

There are some universal differences between men and women in the bases for romantic attraction – differences that can make things interesting as well as difficult and painful from time to time. Women tend to show more interest in men's social status or in understanding a man's character, whereas (it may come as no surprise) men are more immediately attracted by the physical attributes of a woman (Jankowiak, 1995). As a result, women often appear to take longer to develop and to show romantic interest because character and social status usually take longer to gauge than do a person's physical attributes. Nevertheless, Fisher (2004, Ch. 2) provides considerable evidence that, when it comes to love and sex, people really are animals – homo sapiens exhibit many of the same physiological and emotional reactions in the course of romantic love that "lower" mammals experience and exhibit.

Rejection and unrequited love

As mentioned, love can be ignored and/or lost. Separation or detachment causes distress and depression (Lazarus & Lazarus, 1994). Having one's love not reciprocated is also very painful and can sometimes cause obsessive behaviors such as stalking the loved one. Doubtless, this form of harassment has existed for as long as people have loved each other romantically, yet stories of the stalking of public figures such as Anne Murray and Madonna captured the attention of both the media and the public at large. Without doubt, it is our capacity to identify with either public icon as victim or with the stalker as the unloved one that fosters our identification with these stories. The pain of unrequited love is as universal as the experiencing of romantic love itself. There is a "Society for the Study of Broken Hearts" in India. This society sets aside May 3 as a special day on which people whose hearts have been broken by unrequited or lost love can commiserate with each other (Jankowiak, 1995).

The frequency of rejection and of the occurrence of love that is not mutual are some features of this need that make its manifestation in the work setting difficult. In our culture, love usually results in one of two ultimate outcomes: Marriage and happiness (for some time, anyway), or rejection. Rejection by a lover can be a great source of pain, embarrassment, loss of face and reputation, and inner sorrow. It is definitely a powerful form of frustration (see Chapter 8). A natural consequence of frustration is aggression. People will often strike back one way or another at either the source of their frustration or at other more convenient targets. Unrequited love in the relatively small world of most workplaces can be a common and awkward source of difficulty, not only for the players involved but also for many people around them. When we turn our attention directly at love and sex in the work setting, the odds and the costs of love breaking down must be kept in mind.

With our focus on motivation in the workplace, the following observation from Maslow is germane:

> [The] feeling of pleasure in contact and in being with, shows itself also in the desire to be together with the loved one as much as possible in as many situations as possible; *in work* [emphasis added], in play, during aesthetic and intellectual pursuits.
>
> (Maslow, 1954, p. 182)

Thus, for Maslow, a person in love can be consumed with the desire to be in the presence of the loved one, perhaps regardless of the context involved. As we will describe later, the workplace is both an arena for the establishment of love relationships and a forum for their pursuit and fulfillment.

A need AND an emotion

While love can be defined and understood as a need, we noted in Chapter 4 that it is strongly tied to and considered to be an emotion. In both practice and theory, it is hard to disentangle one from the other. Lazarus and Lazarus (1994) noted that a difficulty of considering love from an emotional perspective is that the passion associated with it "waxes and wanes and cannot be sustained moment by moment over the long haul. Long-term relationships are not conducive to constant passion or the acute emotion of love, but the meanings required for active loving feelings surface from time to time . . . when other considerations in the relationship take a back seat" (p. 112).

The Relationship Between the Love and Sex Needs

The human need for love is related to, but must be kept distinguished from, the need for sex. Maslow (1954) was one of the first need theorists to discuss the relationship between these two needs. He wrote:

> One thing that must be stressed at this point is that love is not synonymous with sex. Sex may be studied as a purely physiological need. Ordinarily sexual behavior is multi-determined, that is to say, determined not only by sexual but also by other needs, chief among which are the love and affection needs.
>
> (Maslow, 1954, pp. 44–45)

Henry Murray, the psychologist whose concept and definition of human needs underlie most of the discussion on needs in this book, defined the sex need simply as the need *to form and further an erotic relationship, to have sexual intercourse* (Hall & Lindzey, 1970, p. 177). There is no mention of love in this definition, making it at least partially supportive of Maslow's perspective on the matter.

While it may be easy for the author to exhort the reader to keep the notions of romantic love and sex disentangled, the close and often-confusing link between the two needs is understandable. Jankowiak (1995, p. 6) wrote:

> They are organized around different cultural and psychological criteria, which puts them, in several ways, in direct competition with one another, and this competition raises important implications for understanding their origins and manifestations in everyday life.

As a result, it appears that most cultures have highlighted the importance of either sexuality or love, but seldom both at the same time. This is especially true of the intellectual history of the Western world, which has repeatedly shown a continuous and pronounced ambivalence toward sexuality and love (Jankowiak, 1995, p. 6). Ovid[7] believed that "love is essentially a sexual behavior sport in which duplicity is based in order that a man might win his way into a woman's heart and subsequently her boudoir" (Murstein, 1988, p. 59).

A physiological explanation

Fisher's (2004) research has provided a much more straightforward explanation for the connection between love and lust: Dopamine, a hormone that becomes particularly plentiful and active in the caudate (a region near the center of the brain) when a person is experiencing romantic love, can stimulate testosterone, the hormone of sexual desire. The tight linkage and "direct competition" between them is part of what makes understanding and dealing with amorous relationships in the workplace difficult, as we will see.

Romantic Love and Sex in the Workplace

In the spring of 2005 the CEO of a major aerospace manufacturer was fired by his employer for allegedly having "an affair" with another company executive who was 20 years his junior. Ironically, the executive had been a co-author of the very policy against company romances that ultimately led to his dismissal. His paramour did not lose her job (*Times Colonist*, March 13, 2005, p. C11). The company made it clear that it would not tolerate workplace romance and that further instances of such relationships were open to the reportage of whistleblowers who wished to reveal violations of the company's policy on the matter.

Later in 2005 the world's largest retailer, Wal-Mart, found that simply imposing company rules that prohibit sexual relations among coworkers is not as easy in some countries as it may be in the United States. Indeed, their 28-page "ethics manual" that sought to prohibit a variety of human behaviors the company found objectionable was rejected vociferously by German Wal-Mart employees. Aside from being a violation of German's labor laws (that require consultation with works councils), the do's-and-dont's of the manual were seen as too heavy handed, according to the March 18, 2005 edition of *Workers' Independent News*.[8]

It appears that what is acceptable policy on romance at work varies as a function of many factors, not the least of which are employee perceptions and expectations of what is fair (Foley &

---

[7] The Roman poet Ovid was a self-styled expert in matters of love and sex. It was his poem entitled "Ars amatoria" (which is about the art of making love) as well as his alleged knowledge of a scandal involving the Emperor Augustus' daughter that had him exiled to remote territory that is now in Romania.
[8] See also *Associated Press* article of June 16, 2005: "Update 2: Court rules against parts of Wal-Mart code."

Powell, 1999). According to a survey reported by the Society for Human Resources Management in the United States (reported by Fisher & Welsh, 1994), few organizations in the U.S. have formal policies to deal with workplace romance. In the U.S., laws that pertain to the issue vary from state to state (Foley & Powell, 1999).

The workplace is a rich forum for the expression and satisfaction of love and relatedness needs (recall Chapter 3). Many (perhaps most) of us find friendships there and enjoy going to work for the social interaction and, romance and/or sexual encounters the workplace provides. The offices and factories in which we work also provide venues where many of us encounter our love interests, sexual partners, and spouses.

Although "love and sex in the workplace" have been popular topics in tabloids and everyday magazines for years, little social scientific work was done on them until the 1980s and 1990s, and there appears to have been a decline of scientific interest in more recent years. It may be that the fundamental principles established 25 years ago are seen as relevant today. In addition, the very nature of the topic itself, no doubt, makes it difficult to research. Nevertheless, more scientific work has been completed on the matter since the mid-1980s.

An exhaustive discussion of love and sex in the workplace is beyond our purpose here. Nevertheless, a summary will be provided because love and sex are human motives that express themselves at work and that can have effects upon not only the players immediately involved, but also upon others in the organization.

Workplace romances are "relationships that occur between two individuals who work for the same organization and experience enduring erotic or romantic interest in one another that is known to observers" (Brown & Allgeier, 1996). At least one definition (Pierce, Byrne, & Aguinis, 1996) limits the focus to heterosexual relationships, so it is not presented here. These relationships may be instigated by more than simple love, however. Quinn's (1977) early study into the matter concluded that romance at work can help to satisfy as many as three motives: Love needs, ego gratification, and job advantage. The needs for love or sex may even be major determinants of a person's decision to work, where to work, which hours to work, and so on. What do we know about this hitherto taboo subject?

According to Mainiero (1989), who has been one of the most active researchers on this topic, there are a variety of factors that make interpersonal attraction, and amorous relationships in particular, more likely to occur at work. The first is physical proximity (cf. Pierce et al., 1996). People working in close proximity for extended periods are more likely to become attracted to each other. A study by Gutek, Cohen, and Konrad (1990) supported this hypothesis. Second, Mainiero (1989) argued that intense task accomplishment also fosters attraction. She cited the characters in the Hollywood movie *Broadcast News* to illustrate this hypothesis. Working together with high stakes involved can encourage people to cooperate and reciprocate favors, help, assistance, and admiration.

Third, similarity between the players also contributes. "Birds of a feather" do seem to "flock together" (see Chapter 6; and Byrne, 1971). Similarities of interests and pastimes are especially important because they at least provide the prospective couple with a basis for conversation, social comparison, and shared activities (Pierce et al., 1996). Traveling together on work assignments is an interesting aid to attraction, in part because it is exciting, requires proximity, and, by definition, assures that the individuals have at least one thing in common – their destination. Opportunities to explore possibilities with coworkers are generally safer when one is away from home. Hence, shared travel combines elements of many other factors Mainiero (1989) identified. In fact, there is something inherently sexy about travel, she claimed.

Similarly, people who have attended mixed-sex office retreats may have witnessed how employees "get together" during the meetings and after hours. Travel is frequently necessary for the work group *as a whole* to get to a place away from the office and its interruptions. Once on site, it is common for formalities to be temporarily abandoned and for people to engage in joint problem-solving sessions for hours at a time, often with other individuals with whom they don't normally work. Games, entertainment, good food, and liquor are frequently provided to promote good feelings and a party atmosphere – one intended, largely to diminish people's inhibitions. Travel in general and office retreats in particular are fertile occasions for interpersonal and amorous relationships to develop. The author has witnessed on many occasions how participants on multiple-day retreats become more and more "tired" as the event progresses. Homesickness, hard work during sessions, and the burdens of travel and meeting new people can explain some of this common fatigue, but not all of it. No more need be written by way of explanation for the rest of the fatigue.

Much of the early work on love and sexual relationships in the workplace treated these topics as taboo. It generally seemed bad taste for people to become intimately involved with coworkers (cf. Mead, 1980). The reason for this position, naturally, consists of the many risks that can be involved for the individuals in the relationship. According to one interpretation of Mead's (1980) position, these risks are likely to exist in all intimate relationships at work, whether they are between mentors and protégés, superiors and subordinates, or even between organizational peers (Colwill & Lips, 1988). Relationships can destabilize legitimate working relationships and isolate individuals from their coworkers (cf. Collins, 1983; Kennedy, 1992; Quinn, 1977). The gossip associated with relationships can disrupt work flow and distract people's attention. Real or imagined favoritism can upset norms of fairness of treatment and equity (Mainiero, 1986). Sometimes innocent sexual attraction and activity can lead to serious cases of harassment (which we discussed earlier).

A survey conducted on a sample of personnel managers in the United States found widespread concern for the issue and a general lack of consensus on what companies can or should do about love and sex in the workplace (Ford & McLaughlin, 1987). Nearly 40% of the respondents believed that the romantic interests of employees should be of no interest to employers, while 70% agreed that: "There is really nothing the organization can do to stop romantic attractions between men and women working together" (Ford & McLaughlin, 1987). Another survey of the same sort (Fisher, 1984) found a strong continuation of these trends. Nearly three-quarters of the executives polled in the 1994 survey (conducted for *Fortune* magazine) believed that romances between workers are none of the employers' business, although they acknowledged that such relationships can increase the risks of sexual harassment suits against employers. Foley and Powell (1999) suggested that a policy that deals with romantic situations on a case-by-case basis may be more "realistic" than attempting to prevent them with global organizational policies prohibiting them. A key determinant of coworkers' reactions to management intervention, they claim, is whether the intervention is consistent with their perceptions of distributive justice. So, when coworkers perceive that a relationship is disruptive and/or particularly egregious from a power exploitation perspective, a heavier hand is favored (Foley & Powell, 1999).

Potential benefits of romantic relationships at work

So far in our treatment, it may appear that there is nothing good about workplace romances. There are, in fact, arguments that claim they may have beneficial effects (cf. Dullard & Miller, 1988). For example, a study of 1044 American executives and managers examined three varieties of *non-sexual* interpersonal attraction at work: Deep emotional bonds, mutual interest and respect, and willingness to devote time and energy to another person on a strictly voluntary basis (Lobel, Quinn, St. Clair, & Warfield, 1994). The researchers found that people who are involved in any of these intimate varieties of relationships were more supportive of each other at work, sharing career information, working toward task goals, and providing work-related feedback. They also found people in such relationships were more committed to their work, to their employers, and to their own spouses. The women in the study reported higher levels of intimacy in their workplace relationships than did the men and that these relationships provided greater amounts of the work-related social support described earlier.

It must be repeated that this study (Lobel et al., 1994) looked only at non-sexual relationships. Nevertheless, the findings were overall much more balanced and less negative than those of earlier studies that reported only bad outcomes from intimacy at work. On the negative side were some of the usual caveats: Romance at work *can* result in non-work-related activities, down time, gossip, conflicts of interest, and reduced morale among observers who believe that special treatments are accruing to one or the other of the partners.

A study of graduate students at an American university found that the marital status of the people involved in an office romance was especially important in determining the reactions of third parties to such affairs (Brown & Algeier, 1996). The same study revealed that third parties are more likely to accept an office romance if the two parties are of equal status (rather than being in a superior–subordinate relationship), when the affair didn't seem to negatively affect the job performance of the male (the same was not found in relation to the female's job performance), and when the partners behaved "in a professional manner" – not flaunting their relationship at work. Students in this study were more accepting of office romances if they had been engaged in one themselves and when they perceived that the motives of the couple were love oriented rather than driven by ego needs or job leverage (cf. Quinn, 1977).

A model by Foley and Powell (1999) supports and extended these findings. In addition to the genders of the participants, Foley and Powell claim that whether third parties are bothered by workplace relationships depends, in part, on the apparent motives of the lovers, on their perceptions of whether the relationship in question is disruptive of the working environment and/or creates conflicts of interest. Superior–subordinate relationships (as in the case of the aerospace executive mentioned at the beginning of this chapter) seem to bring about the concern of third parties. Clearly, when people fall in love in work settings, other people around them frequently become aware of the relationship and are likely to form attitudes about them. Whether these attitudes are positive or negative seems to depend upon the marital and organizational statuses of the lovers and the blatancy of their amorous acts.

By far the most positive treatments of office romance have been provided by Mainiero (1989, 2003) and by Fisher and Welsh (1994). While acknowledging all of the potential risks and cost factors described by earlier students of the topic, Mainiero (1989) identified an interesting list of potential benefits of romance at work. Some observations are based on her own research, while some are inferred from the research of others. Her list of good things that *can* result from romance in the workplace includes the following: Energizing of general workplace morale ("love is in the air"); increased motivation and improved attitudes among the particular employees involved; encouragement of creativity and innovation; improved teamwork, communication and cooperation; enriched personal relationships; and stabilized workforces.

This final item is particularly interesting. Permitting married or involved couples to work in the same workplace can help reduce the loss of good employees. Why? Because it can reduce the odds that one member of a couple will seek or accept employment opportunities in other organizations. To leave for greener pastures would entail leaving behind a sweetheart. Interesting: The ties that bind people to their work. Any analysis of the motivation to work must include love and sex needs and the attendant goals that the workplace usually provides.

Many authorities interviewed by Fisher and Welsh (1994) made the same claims about the energizing positive effects love can have in the workplace, although the vast majority of the executives surveyed in the *Fortune* study she reported believed that office romances can increase the possibility of favoritism or the appearance of it, and that they can create "un-businesslike" appearances. Fisher concluded her analysis with these words:

> As the old lifetime employment guarantee fades into history, employees – particularly the best and the brightest ones – are less willing to let a company dictate the terms of their private lives. Even with the divorce rate [as high as it is], a marriage these days is likely to last longer than a job . . . The 1.5% of employers still struggling to wrestle Eros to the ground will find, if they haven't already, that they can no more stamp out sex than they can enforce rules about gossip, daydreaming, or wine with lunch.
>
> (Fisher & Welsh, 1994, p. 144)

To summarize, whereas early writings typically rejected romance in the workplace as an inherently harmful and disruptive phenomenon, more recent work reports that some benefits can accrue from intimate and amorous relationships at work as well. Still, many of the truisms and caveats from the past still seem worth keeping in mind. Nevertheless, humans are inherently sexual by nature, pursuing love and sex wherever they find opportunities to do so, subject to the social, religious, and administrative restraints in force. Consequently, dogmatic rules and regulations designed to prevent or to punish such activities are doomed to resistance, subversion and/or outright failure. Love and sex are powerful human needs that seek expression (consider the list of physiological and psychological "symptoms" of the romantic experience presented earlier). It's that simple.

A second point follows from the first. Management should leave well enough alone, unless relationships can be shown to be detrimental to the performance of the workplace. Managers' jobs are to produce goods and services through the efforts of other people. There is not (nor should there be) an inherent right for any manager to interfere with the human dignity and freedom of others who express their humanity in any form (here, through pursuing romance). If the romance of a couple can be shown to interfere with organizational effectiveness, steps can and should be taken. The law and some common practice seem to have adopted this principle. It should be enacted in all work settings.

Finally, intimate relationships at work can be risky and dysfunctional – for both the immediate participants as well as for the organization – when there is an imbalance of power between the lovers. The reason? Superior/subordinate relationships *can* evolve from romance to harassment, which, as we have discussed, is a matter of power and status, not sex (Berdahl, 2007; Pierce, Byrne, & Aguinis, 1996) and unless the participants marry or otherwise commit to life together, someone, usually the subordinate (and most frequently a woman), will suffer personal and/or professional consequences.

GENERAL SUMMARY AND A GLANCE AHEAD

In this chapter, we have examined two fundamental human needs that comprise two very interesting elements of human nature and that can explain significant degrees of behavior of people in work organizations. Of necessity, our treatment was brief. Countless thinkers and observers of the human condition have produced endless insights and observations about both the human need for power and the propensity for people to love each other. Our purpose here has been to reveal some aspects of power and love (and sex) that seem to the author to have particular relevance for a comprehensive understanding of human work motivation. In the following chapter, we will focus attention on three more categories of human needs that share with power and love the important gregarious nature of our species: The needs for affiliation, self-esteem, and what social scientists now call *social motivation*.

Social Motives and Self-Esteem as Motives at Work

6

No man is an island.
John Donne

Advice columnist and family therapist Rhona Raskin published the following letter from a teenage girl in the September 11, 2007 edition of the Victoria *Times Colonist* (and other newspapers across Canada):

> I'm a 13-year-old girl and I've been a school outcast since I walked into preschool and no kids wanted to sit by me. I'm now in high school. This year, I wanted to make new friends (my one friend dumped me) so I started sitting with a different group at lunchtime. They started whispering to each other and walked away from me. They gave me dirty looks and obviously didn't want me around them. I cry myself to sleep every night and I'm scared to talk to people because everyone thinks I'm so weird. I always have a sad look on my face but I can't be happy if I don't have any friends. I'm always depressed and I've even thought of suicide but I've never attempted to do so.

Psychologists such as Maslow (1954), as well as countless social scientists, poets, novelists, historians, and others have discussed at length since antiquity the importance of interpersonal relations among human beings for their health and survival (see Battle, 1990; Branden, 1969). People are gregarious creatures by nature, and to be and remain healthy they must interact with one another (Baumeister & Leary, 1995; McAdams, 1988). Evolutionary psychologists such as Buss (1999) have claimed that much of the success of our species to evolve and survive can be attributed to our highly developed capacity to cooperate and interact with one another. Indeed, current thinking in the area called social motivation holds that homo sapiens' ability to cooperate and interact with others is a defining characteristic of the species (see Forgas, Williams, & Laham, 2005). Although need satisfaction is only one of a number of explanations for social interaction, it is clearly an important one, and some theorists – such as Murray (1938), whose definition of need we have adopted in this book (see Chapter 1) – believe that social interaction may serve to satisfy as many as 11 different needs: Abasement, affiliation, aggression, dominance, exhibition, nurturance, order, play, sex, succorance, and understanding, all of which contribute to our evolution and survival (Buss, 1999). Some argue that the desire to keep conscious knowledge of our mortality in check is largely responsible for a variety of defensive social behaviors such as maintaining high self-esteem, creating strong cultural bonds and embracing others of our species (Forgas et al., 2005).

By definition, work organizations consist of two or more persons, making human interaction immediately and inherently possible and, usually, necessary. Even in the case of single-person enterprise, the individual must interact with others to permit the business to survive. We take these points as obvious and will not belabor them. The major point here is that work organizations of all sizes are *more or less capable* of providing social interaction between and among people. Moreover, as we will see in this chapter, there are certain features of many or most organizations that actually compel or motivate their members to affiliate with one another, in many cases with people we either don't know or don't know well (cf. Forgas, Williams, & Wheeler, 2001; Goffman, 1972). Finally, work organizations frequently provide numerous opportunities for people to get to know one another on a friendship or more intimate basis. These interpersonal dynamics in the workplace can be addressed and understood from the perspective of need theory, and are so examined in this chapter.

We begin with an examination of the need for affiliation and discuss various ways that affiliative motives are relevant for an understanding of work motivation and organizational behavior. Then we look at the literature on social motivation – the effects that people can have on one another's motivation to perform (even without trying). We examine a number of ways that the mere presence of other people can inadvertently, and without awareness, affect a person's motivation. Finally, we study another social need, the need for esteem, and examine the role that esteem needs play in work motivation.

AFFILIATION MOTIVATION

Consider the following letter that appeared in a national women's magazine and consider its similarity to the sadness, fear, and distress expressed by the 13-year-old girl cited earlier:

> My coworkers hate me. Ever since I joined the company 3 years ago, these cliquish women have treated me like a pariah. At meetings, I'm rarely addressed, and when I speak up, they don't seem to listen. I tell a joke and they roll their eyes, but if someone else tells the same joke, it's hilarious. They all go out for lunch together, buy each other birthday cakes and cards . . . and forget about me. During my down time, I've offered to assist a few of them with their work; that favor has yet to be returned. The rudest thing is, when I'm in the middle of a conversation with an employee from another department, the ring-leader of the group invariably interrupts, ignores me, and talks to the other person as if I'm invisible. I realize we're not at work to socialize, but their nastiness is affecting my morale. I do have a great relationship with my boss, who says the offensive employees are probably jealous because I'm vivacious and talented. From the beginning, he's always advised me to ignore them and focus on my job. But how can I do that when we're working in such close quarters?
>
> (*Cosmopolitan*, September 1995, p. 48)

The poignancy of the two statements presented here helps to emphasize just how important being accepted or rejected by other people is to most of us, including people of all ages. A recent study of the causes of 15 shootings in U.S. public schools revealed that acute or chronic rejection, such as shunning and ostracism, bullying, or romantic rejection played a major role in all but two of the cases examined. The study concluded that these rejection experiences had motivated the shooters to behave with violence. Why? Either to achieve retribution from those who had offended them or to attempt to gain some degree of social respect for having taken action (Leary, Kowalski, Smith, & Phillips, 2003).

Indeed, as we will see in Chapter 8, a considerable amount of interpersonal violence occurs as a consequence of social rejection, frequently among employees by their coworkers (Murphy, 2004). It hurts to be rejected, and the pain can often motivate action. According to a story in the August 7 (2006) edition of *Maclean's* magazine (Whalen-Miller, 2006), a number of schools in Labrador are banning the distribution of birthday party invitations by gradeschool children on school property because of the hurtful impact not being invited to someone's party has on the ostracized children. As one leading scholar in the area of affiliation motivation wrote: "The motivation for social contact can be considered a central influence on human behavior" (Hill, 1987a, p. 1008). In fact, recent work has shown that ostracism can affect many motives, including needs for control (including self-efficacy and power, which we discuss elsewhere in this book, especially in Chapter 5), self-esteem, and motives related to maintaining the belief that one's life is meaningful in a broader social context (Warburton & Williams, 2005). A series of six experiments contributed to supporting the hypothesis that excluding people from their relevant social groups can hamper people's attempts to regulate their behavior (Baumeister, De Wall, Ciarocco, & Twenge, 2005; see Chapter 13 for more on this).

Ostracism and social isolation are particularly problematic for lesbian, gay, and bisexual employees (who comprise between 4% and 17% of the American workforce). Whether they are actively shunned by coworkers after they make their sexual orientations known, or whether they maintain social distance from coworkers in order to keep their identities private, gay, lesbian, and bisexual employees are frequently deprived from social interaction, social networking, mentoring, and the joy of belonging that is a fundamental human need (Ragins, 2004).

In addition, the two letters we saw earlier remind us vividly that emotions are a major manifestation of need states (see Murray, 1938; and Chapters 3 and 4 of this book) and that these emotions can be powerful, visceral, and very real. Both the teenager and the older woman revealed potent blends of loneliness, bitterness, anxiety, envy, and a touch of anger. At some point in our lives, most of us will witness the sort of isolation, loneliness, and bitterness expressed in the two letters. These periods of isolation can be among the most unhappy and unhealthy facets of a person's life.

What is the Need for Affiliation?

Henry Murray (1938) originally defined the need for affiliation as follows: "To draw near and enjoyably cooperate or reciprocate with an allied other (an other who resembles the subject or who likes the subject). To please and win affection of a cathected[1] object. To adhere and remain loyal to a friend" (from Hall & Lindzey, 1957, p. 176). Murray's definition makes sense; it fits with most common, everyday connotations of affiliation.

Hill (1987a) suggested that we can gain a better understanding of affiliation motivation if we distinguish among four different subtypes of the motive while maintaining an appreciation for the common features they share. Hill proposed that the desire for social contact can originate with one (or more) of four social rewards that may be associated with affiliation, enabling us to differentiate among the following subtypes of the motive: "(1) positive affect or stimulation associated with interpersonal closeness and communion, (2) attention or praise, (3) reduction of negative affect [specifically fear and stress] through social contact, and (4) social comparison" (p. 1008). The first dimension is close in meaning to what we normally refer to as *love* (Buss, 1983). We will not explore this subtype here because it is dealt with at length in Chapter 5. However, each of the other three categories of social reward (and corresponding variety of affiliation motive) has implications and value for our study of work motivation.

Attention and praise

The second social reward Hill (1987a) discussed is the attention and praise that people can provide one another. Work organizations are arenas in which people are constantly evaluating one another and providing praise, criticism, approval and disapproval, and feedback in its various forms (see Ashford, 1993). Although it is true that many people thrive on the feedback *they administer to themselves* (so to speak) as they master tasks and accomplish goals (see Ashford, 1989; Hanser & Muchinsky, 1978; and Chapter 7 of this book), the attention and praise that we receive from others, such as peers and supervisors, is also very important for understanding the mechanisms by which affiliation motives are aroused and satisfied. Of course, the feedback that people send and receive in work settings is usually intended to influence the work behavior or performance of another; the primary purpose of the feedback is rarely the satisfaction of affiliation needs, as such. Nevertheless, such feedback may serve other functions, such as satisfying part of people's need for affiliation. Ashford (1993) reported a study in which it was found that regardless of a person's seniority, the feedback provided by the company and supervisor was seen as more important than that emanating from peers and self-assessments.

---

[1] *Cathexis* is a term from psychoanalytic theory that refers to the "accumulation of mental energy on some particular idea, memory, or line of thought or action" (Drever, 1952, p. 35).

Positive feedback is a mainstay in the arsenal of tools used in operant conditioning, organizational behavior modification programs, and self-regulation programs in work organizations (see Chapter 14). Similarly, the provision of praise and attention is a key component of many current *employee empowerment programs* (see Eylon, 1994; Eylon & Pinder, 1995). Although work settings can be fora for the distribution and receipt of criticism of one's work and one's worth as a person, they are also certainly places where people regularly receive attention and praise, two elements of one of the main social rewards that meet people's need for affiliation (Hill, 1987a).

Reduction of fear and stress

Hill (1987a) claims that a third social reward that can stimulate and satisfy the need for affiliation is the reduction in difficulties that people encounter through the provision of support by others. Generally, the literature refers to this form of interaction as dealing with *social support*, which can be defined as "an exchange of resource between at least two individuals perceived by the provider or the recipient to be intended to enhance the well-being of the recipient" (Shumaker & Brownell, 1984, p. 13).

Cohen and Wills (1985) have suggested that there are four basic types of resource that one person can provide another in the form of support: Emotional, informational, companionship, and instrumental. *Emotional support* (which has also been referred to as *esteem support*) is information provided to a person that s/he is esteemed and accepted. This form of support enhances self-esteem (which we discuss at length later in the chapter) by communicating to others that they are valued for what they are, for their own worth, including any difficulties or personal flaws. *Informational support* is assistance provided to a person to help define, understand, and cope with problems. *Social companionship* is "spending time with others in leisure and recreational activities" (Cohen & Wills, 1985, p. 313). It seems to work simply by providing contact and affiliation and by distracting people from their problems and difficulties. The fourth category, *instrumental support*, consists of the provision of financial aid, material resources, and needed services. It can work directly by addressing and removing the other's problems, or it can work by providing the person in difficulty with extra time and reduced pressure for performance.

The value of social support for offsetting some of the dysfunctions of work contexts that offer low social interaction was demonstrated by a study reported by Wiesenfeld, Raghuram, and Garud (2001). The focus of the research was on employees engaged in some form of "virtual work" – work that occurs away from the primary workplace (such as work done at home, "telecommuting," on the road, or otherwise removed from the central locus of the organization and one's coworkers). This is an interesting problem because of the challenges it can pose for such individuals and the negative impact it can have on the capacity of the workers to identify with the employer. They are often "out of sight, out of mind" and incapable of enjoying some (or most or all) of the social interaction that working in groups makes possible. According to Wiesenfeld et al. (2001), 51% of North American companies have some form of virtual work program, so the management of remote individuals can be problematic, particularly those employees whose motivational basis for working is social (see also Allen, Renn, & Griffeth, 2003).

Wiesenfeld et al. (2001) hypothesized (and found) that remote employees high in need for affiliation were, other things equal, more likely to identify with their work organization. (This hypothesis was based on plenty of prior research in the field.) They also found that perceived levels of social support were positively related to organizational identification. Their third hypothesis – the one of key interest here – was also supported: Wiesenfeld et al. (2001) found an interaction between need for affiliation and perceived social support, such that the latter can attenuate the deleterious effects of virtual work on organizational identification. In other words:

> Among virtual workers who were relatively high in the need for affiliation, organizational identification remained fairly high even when perceived work-based social support was low. However, among

virtual workers who had low need for affiliation, the relationship between perceived level of work-based support and strength of organizational identification was much stronger and positive.

(Wiesenfeld et al., 2001, p. 222)

As more work organizations become "virtual" in nature and remote work (such as telecommuting) becomes more prevalent, the impact on remote employees as individuals will become more of a challenge through the negative impact this form of work can have on the satisfaction of social needs. Moreover, coordinating and managing work in such contexts will also become more problematic for managers. Allen et al. (2003) offer a comprehensive review of the literature on these matters, particularly as they relate to telecommuting, and advance a conceptual model to encourage research and theory on the challenges involved.

There has been some debate over the mechanisms by which social support has benefits for people. One position has it that support works only to the extent that it assuages the effects of stress. This is referred to as the *buffering hypothesis*: Support "buffers" the effects of stress. The second position holds that support has beneficial effects on people whether or not they are under stress. This is referred to as the *main-effects hypothesis* (Cohen & Wills, 1985). One comprehensive review of the matter concluded that there is empirical support for both positions, depending on the circumstances. In a study of the length of time it took a sample of Canadian managers to "get up to speed" following geographic transfers, Pinder and Schroeder (1987) found that the levels of social support the transferees received from their supervisors and coworkers were critical. In fact, social support had the greatest beneficial influence on the time to job proficiency among those transferred employees whose moves entailed the most radical changes in the work they had to do following their transfers, as opposed to before the transfers.

Mentoring is a powerful organizational process designed for the development of junior employees by more senior employees through the provision of both social support and career-related support (see Wanberg, Welsh, & Hezlett, 2003, for a recent review). Mentoring relationships may be formalized, as when a newcomer is assigned to the care and attention of someone who has more experience in the organization, or they may be informal, as when one person helps another out often enough and in sufficiently meaningful ways that the recipient eventually recognizes that, de facto, s/he has been mentored. For Kram (1985), one of the earliest to study and describe formal mentoring relationships in work organizations, mentoring requires that the mentor provide all or most of a set of 10 different varieties of service, such as sponsoring, exposure and visibility, role modeling, and personal counseling. Schroeder (1988) argued that it is not necessary for a person to receive all these forms of support from one other person; it is only necessary that s/he receive them from any of a number of other people. Hence, to enjoy the benefits of mentoring it is not necessary that one have a formally designated mentor. Schroeder's work demonstrated that employees who receive these varieties of support, regardless of the number and nature of the sources, demonstrated higher levels of skill development, promotion success, and other job-related outcomes, such as salary increases and job satisfaction. Dreher and Ash (1990) concluded that mentored individuals receive higher levels of income, although Wanberg et al. (2003) questioned whether other factors, besides mentoring, might have accounted for these results. Likewise, there is preliminary evidence that mentors benefit from mentoring relationships, although that evidence is still scanty and mixed (Wanberg et al., 2003).

Hill (1987b) demonstrated that different types of support can have different effects on the well-being of people, depending on the strength of their need for affiliation. He collapsed the four varieties of support just mentioned (positive affect, attention and praise, reduction of fear and anxiety, and social comparison) into two basis forms: Material and socio-emotional. He found that material support was of benefit for all the people included in his study, regardless of their need for affiliation. However, only those people with low affiliative needs benefited from socio-emotional support.[2]

---

[2] In fact, there was some suggestion from this study that socio-emotional support may even have a deleterious effect on the physical health of high-affiliation-need persons.

Social Comparison and Affiliation

In Chapter 4, we discussed the emotions fear and anxiety. Many people face new work assignments with a certain amount of trepidation (or dread), and these emotions can be very strong. More broadly, people in strange and uncertain circumstances naturally experience some degree of anxiety, if not fear. One of the ways that we cope with these emotions is to seek the social support of other people; this is not less true on the job than in any other arena of life (see Festinger, 1954; and Chapter 11 of this book).

The hypothesis linking social affiliation to the experiencing of anxiety was first offered by Schacter and Singer (1962) in a series of clever experiments in which women students were recruited and told that they would be exposed to either mild or severe electric shocks as part of their involvement in the research. The students were then provided alternative ways to wait until the experiment was to begin; the options included staying alone in a room or staying in another room in the presence of other students. The results of the study suggested that those people who were induced into the higher levels of anxiety about what was about to happen to them preferred to be in the company of others, especially, it was found in subsequent research (Schacter & Singer, 1962), other students who were "in the same boat" they were in. On the basis of these studies, social psychologists concluded and have believed for years that "misery loves company" and that "miserable people love miserable company." People affiliate to help reduce anxiety and fear.[3] A recent study among male coronary bypass patients demonstrates the continued relevance of this hypothesis. Patients who were assigned to a presurgical room with a roommate who had been through surgery fared better than those who had not. Those whose roommate had had heart surgery fared better than those whose roommate had other types of surgery. Finally, those patients who had no roommates recovered the most slowly (Kulik, Mahler, & Moore, 2003).

Louis (1980a) described the process of "sense making" in a new career situation: New faces, new roles, new local politics, new supervisors and peers, and new tasks are frequently encountered when a person undergoes a career transition. Clearly, different types of transition will feature more or less novelty than others (see Louis, 1980b), but entering, leaving, or moving around inside an organization can be stressful and can cause the people involved to seek out the social support and information available from others at the scene. In fact, Katz (1980) suggested that interpersonal needs may be the most critical at the time of career transitions, and that existence and growth-related needs may become salient only after there has been sufficient affiliation for the sake of reducing anxiety and helping those in transition to make sense of what is happening to them and around them (see Festinger, 1954; Pinder & Walter, 1984; Schacter & Singer, 1962).

In summary, Hill (1987a) suggested at least four varieties of social reward that can be involved in affiliation behaviors; four different, albeit interrelated, types of comfort, enjoyment, and pleasure that can arouse the need for affiliation and then serve to satisfy that need. The strength of the need and the strength of the pleasure that the various rewards provide can vary, of course, as in the case of any need. We examine that issue next.

Intensity of the Affiliation Need and Related Emotions

In Chapter 4, we saw that people vary in the degree of intensity with which they experience emotions (Diener, Larsen, Levine, & Emmons, 1985) and that the tendency to experience emotions strongly

---

[3] From time to time, researchers replicate the original Schacter and Singer (1962) experiments for the sake of finding different explanations of the results. One such attempt was made by Rofe and Lewin (1988), who sought to demonstrate that a simple utility argument could explain the results – that is, that by affiliating under conditions of high anxiety, it is a matter of practical mutual assistance rather than anxiety through sense making that occurs. Their results were mixed and suggested that there may be gender differences in the phenomenon.

generalizes across the range of human emotions; similarly, if a person tends to experience some emotions only mildly, s/he probably experiences other emotions only mildly. Other research has found that affiliation motivation may be related to the strength of people's feelings. In fact, one study showed that the strength of people's emotions is related to all four of the varieties of affiliation motivation that we have just discussed (Hill, 1987a). In other words, it seems that people who experience emotions intensely are more likely to seek higher levels of positive stimulation, emotional support, attention, and social comparison (Blankenstein, Flett, Koledin, & Bortolotto, 1989). In a similar study, Hill (1991) found that people with high needs for affiliation were more likely to seek social support from others than were those with lower levels of affiliation need. Interestingly, neither of these studies found gender differences in the strength of the correlations: Neither the link between affiliation motives and intensity of affect nor that between affiliation motivation and desire for social support was stronger for men than for women (or, as a common stereotype might have it, the other way round). What does this mean? Only that people who tend, by nature, to feel emotions strongly seem more motivated to seek out others with whom they might interact for the sake of getting the optimal level of emotional arousal they desire.

When we discuss the strength of people's motives, we must consider those persons who tend not to be particularly "emotional" as well, and we must also keep in mind that motives and motive strength are only partly responsible for human behavior. In the specific context of affiliation motivation, for example, one study in India found that interpersonal similarity was much stronger than people's need for affiliation in predicting interpersonal attraction (Shaikh & Kanekar, 1994). In other words, needs do, as we have discussed at length, account for a considerable amount of motivated effort, in both work settings and in other settings, but needs are not the sole instigators of action. Rather, needs should be considered only as a class of variables among sets of other factors that can account for human behavior, such as perceived similarity between people in the case of the Indian research (Shaikh & Kanekar, 1994).

Affiliation Motivation and Managerial Effectiveness

Next we can ask about the value to people of having strong affiliation motivation in the context of their work. Some interesting research has been devoted to studying managerial and executive needs, including the need for affiliation and the findings of much of this work have been consistent and of practical importance. One study found that affiliation motivation had virtually no relationship with the financial success of a sample of chief executive officers of top American corporations (Chusmir & Azevedo, 1992). Using the lead researcher's own definition of need for affiliation as "a concern for establishing, maintaining, or restoring positive or love relationships with other persons" (Chusmir, 1985), a negative correlation was in fact expected between the strength of the executives' affiliation needs and business success measures such as sales growth, profits, return on equity, and return on sales. Although no significant negative relationship was found between business performance and affiliation needs of the executives, there were, as predicted, significant positive relationships between the executives' power and achievement needs and patterns of the success indicators.

Findings of this sort are consistent with writings of McClelland (1970, 1975; and see Chapter 3 of this book) and his colleagues, who have developed a *leadership motive profile*, a profile of needs associated with effective leadership. Specifically, the effective leader is most likely to have a strong need for power and what is referred to as *activity inhibition*, a capacity to use power to achieve institutional goals rather than personal goals. At the same time, however, the leadership motive profile is characterized by a *low need for affiliation* (see McClelland & Boyatzis, 1982; McClelland & Burnham, 1976). Finally, strong need for achievement is hypothesized to be related to success in small, entrepreneurial organizations in which the person can be responsible directly for the growth and success of the enterprise, but it is not expected to be a factor in larger organizations where success or failure is determined by many people working in harmony (McClelland & Boyatzis, 1982, p. 738).

In their study, Chusmir and Azevedo (1992) reasoned that the need for power can motivate an executive to pursue growth and profits, while a strong need for achievement is likely to induce a concern with immediate growth in sales. Having a strong need for affiliation, however, "is normally not a desirable motive for top-level managers since the effort to please others may get in the way of needed hard decision making" (Chusmir & Azevedo, 1992, p. 610).

House and his colleagues reported some fascinating research on the personalities of 39 U.S. presidents and the varying degrees of success these presidents accomplished while in office (see House, Spangler, & Woyke, 1991; Spangler & House, 1991). In one analysis they examined the inaugural addresses of the presidents and found that references and imagery related to power, affiliation, and achievement were predictive of their rated success in office; although consistent with prior work on the leadership motive profile, affiliative tendencies were generally related to lower effectiveness (Spangler & House, 1991). Although being affiliative by nature may have helped the presidents to become nominated and elected, once in office it seems that affiliative tendencies have been detrimental to the effectiveness of U.S. presidents (House et al., 1991).[4]

In summary, the need for affiliation has an interesting role in current theory and research about employee work motivation, managerial performance, and organizational behavior. It is clear that affiliation motivation is one of the central motives of people as they live with other people and that the workplace can be a rich venue for arousing, directing, satisfying, or thwarting the desire to affiliate. It also seems clear that strong affiliation tendencies may not be instrumental to those who seek positions of power and authority in management because people who like people (too much) may not be very successful at placing the interests of organization above those of their personal friendships; they may not be capable of making the tough decisions that positions of leadership and authority require for managerial and executive success.

Next we turn to another fascinating feature of the relationships among people in work settings: The ways by which people can influence one another's work motivation and performance without even consciously trying to do so. We explore the phenomena referred to collectively as *social motivation*.

SOCIAL MOTIVATION AND WORK BEHAVIOR

The somewhat ambiguous phrase *social motivation* has emerged and gained some use in the social sciences in recent years. We describe it as "ambiguous" because there is only partial agreement among scholars regarding which social phenomena are included under this rubric (see Brody, 1980; Geen, 1991; Pittman & Heller, 1987; Reykowski, 1982). In fact, one reviewer has implied that the very notion of social motivation may be somewhat redundant, inasmuch as most human motivation and behavior occur within the company of other people and are determined at least in part by the existence of these people in our lives (Reykowski, 1982). Nevertheless, one reviewer has offered guidelines, or criteria, for determining which human processes are and are not appropriately seen as social motivation (Geen, 1991, p. 178):

> First, the conditions of social motivation [are] defined as those in which the person is in direct contact with another person or group of persons, such as an audience, a group of co-actors, or a partner in interaction. Second, the effect of the social presence [is] defined as *nondirective* [emphasis added; the

---

[4] Similarly, achievement motivation was also negatively related to many of the measures of presidential performance, presumably because of the sheer size of the organization the president must manage.

social entity does not provide specific cues to the individual about how to act in the situation]. For example, direct social influence, persuasion, or attempts at attitude modification fall outside the . . . definition of a social motivational phenomenon. Third, this socially engendered effect on the individual is considered an intrapsychic state capable of initiating and/or intensifying behavior.

On the basis of the criteria delineated in this definition, Geen (1991) isolated three particular phenomena for study, albeit recognizing that other topics had been considered part of "social motivation" by other authors at other times. Each of these three phenomena – social facilitation, social loafing, and social anxiety – has implications for our study of work motivation, so we examine each in this section. In addition, we examine *incivility* – a construct that has attracted some attention in recent social science and that also has particular relevance for work motivation and organizational behavior.

Social Facilitation

Modern interest in the social facilitation effect was kindled nearly 50 years ago by Zajonc (1965). In brief, this effect takes the form of increased task motivation (and often performance) when people work "in the sheer presence of other individuals" (Zajonc, 1965, p. 269), as opposed to working in isolation. The effect was reported to occur over a broad array of activities and over a wide number of animals. Pigs eating, ants working, human beings solving problems: In all cases, performance increases, according to Zajonc, when it is conducted in the presence of others.

   Among human beings, it is not clear whether the mere presence of others can stimulate heightened motivation or whether the observer in question must be perceived to be in the position of evaluator of the performance for the effect to occur (Geen, 1991). Regardless, it does seem that the mere presence of others may trigger apprehension about one's performance being negatively evaluated. Moreover, it appears that the degree of the apprehension grows as the perceived status of the group members present grows. Two explanations that have been offered for the effect are that the person is distracted by the presence of others, or that the person desires to "look good" in front of observers. Either way, it appears that having other people observe us at a task – people who are not part of the task activity themselves – frequently increases the levels of uncertainty and anxiety we experience, and this elevated anxiety, in turn, explains the increase in motivation to perform well (Geen, 1991). Whereas social facilitation can occur when one person watches another perform a job, the presence of more than one person actually involved in doing the job (as in a team) may work the other way. This seemingly opposite phenomenon is referred to as *social loafing*.

Social Loafing

In 1913, a scholar named Ringlemann observed that individual output in a wide variety of tasks often decreases as the size of the group performing the task increases.[5] As Geen (1991, p. 384) noted: "When a person is a member of a group, subjected to social forces, the impact of those forces on each person in the group is diminished in inverse proportion to the strength (e.g., status, power), immediacy, and number of persons in the group." The social loading effect (Latané, Williams, & Harkins, 1979) has been observed among task groups working at maze performance, writing, swimming, problem solving, and a host of other activities. In a meta-analysis of the phenomenon, Karau and Williams (1993) defined social loafing as "the reduction in motivation and effort when individuals work collectively compared with when they work individually or coactively" (p. 681). Working collectively means that people are working together in the real or imagined presence of others, with whom their

---

[5] The original paper has been discussed and described in detail by Kravitz and Martin (1986).

inputs will be combined to yield a single product. Working coactively, by contrast, implies that people are working in the real or imagined presence of other people but that their inputs are not pooled or combined to yield a single product. Collective effort seems to foster social loafing, whereas coactive work does not.

Several explanations have been offered for social loafing behavior (see Karau & Williams, 1993; Levine, Resnick, & Higgins, 1993). One early explanation held that there can be a coordination loss, in which the individual efforts of group members interfere with one another. More recent explanations, however, discount the coordination explanation and have offered more psychological reasoning. For example, one study derived an equity explanation: Individuals expended more effort when they were told that their group partners were going to expend more energy (Jackson & Harkins, 1985). Another explanation looks to the inherent level of interest the participants may have in the task itself. If the task is seen as boring or lacking in fun, people may attempt to "hide in the crowd" (Kerr & Brunn, 1981) and permit their team members to bear the brunt of the work (see Geen, 1991, pp. 385–386).

It appears that social loafing is also likely to occur in settings in which there is no chance of being evaluated for one's individual performance and/or when there is no stated standard for performance. Kerr (1983) proposed a *free-rider effect*, which may occur when a person believes that some other member of the group will do the work, solve the puzzle, or whatever is required, and that *his or her own contributions to the success will not be differentiated from those who actually contributed.*

Geen (1991) observed: "Social loafing may be due not so much to a group-engendered loss of motivation as to the facilitation of performance decrements motivated by other conditions. For various reasons, individuals may not be motivated to exert effort on a group task. Believing their efforts to be unnecessary, they may be content to let others do the work. They may wish to avoid putting out more than their fair share of effort. The task may be uninteresting. When subjects believe they are safely anonymous in the group, they will, given such low motivation to perform, become loafers" (p. 389). Since Geen's (1991) interpretation of social loafing, the meta-analysis of earlier studies conducted by Karau and Williams (1993) concluded that a theoretical model they call the *collective effort model* explains a considerable amount of the phenomenon that earlier researchers had reported. They concluded that social loafing "appears to be moderate in magnitude and generalizable across tasks and subject populations." It occurs "because individuals expect their effort to be less likely to lead to valued outcomes when working collectively than when working coactively" (p. 700).

The collective effort model has its roots in the popular and influential expectancy theories of work motivation that we examine in detail in Chapter 12. It is necessary to foreshadow that discussion briefly to report an interesting study of how social loafing can be affected by threats of punishment. In a nutshell, the expectancy theory (or theories) of motivation hold that a person's work motivation is maximized to the extent that she believes three things: (1) that if the person expends effort at a task, task success is likely; (2) that if task success is achieved, positively valued outcomes will be received; and (3) that negative outcomes such as punishment will be avoided. However, a number of studies indicate, collectively, that things are not that simple.

First, a study reported by George (1995) found that contingent rewards administered to individuals in sales groups in an American retailer successfully reduced social loafing. On the other hand, contingent punishment of individuals had no noticeable effect on the phenomenon. In some ways, this finding is counterintuitive for those who believe that individual punishment that is tied to particular behavior will reduce the incidence of that behavior. But, as we will see in a later chapter, punishment can have any of a number of unusual effects on individuals, including the enhancement of their desire for self-determination (see Chapter 14), which, in turn, may motivate them to carry on as before the punishment to establish that self-determination.

Social loafing and punishment

Miles and Greenberg (1993) reported a study of a high school swimming team of 120 members to demonstrate social loafing and how threats of punishment may reduce its effect. First, they established a standard performance goal for swimming speed that team members found difficult but reasonable. They then had some of the students swim as teams, in relay, in which their performance would be determined by their combined efforts. Other swimmers swam alone. The coaches manipulated the threat of punishment three different ways for poor-performing swimmers. There was a "severe" punishment condition, a "moderate" punishment condition, and a control group in which no punishment would be contingent upon poor swimming performance. (The punishment took the form of extra laps.)

As expected by social learning theory (Chapter 14), and consistent with the expectancy theory-based collective effort model, individuals in groups performed more poorly than individuals performing alone under conditions in which punishment threats were not in place. In other words, "whereas adolescent swimmers attempting to meet a group relay goal time swam slower than comparable individuals attempting to meet an analogous individual goal time, [the] social loafing effect did not occur when the coaches threatened the swimmers with relay laps for failing to meet their goals" (Miles & Greenberg, 1993, p. 259).

The point here is that social loafing is more likely to occur when people believe that they are part of a group effort and that their individual efforts will not be rewarded directly to themselves, or when their restrained effort will not result in direct punishment to themselves. By the same token, as shown in the swimming example, when reduced effort is expected to result in punishment for the entire team for poor performance, the social loafing effect was reduced, and team members performed as well as they would in working alone conditions. Pooling appears to bring out social loafing.

Comer (1995) observed that unlike the case of the swimming experiment, much of the theory of social loafing arises from laboratory experiments conducted with students performing contrived tasks. There is nothing inherently wrong with laboratory research, as long as the phenomena being studied are considered to be independent of the contexts in which they occur (Runkel & McGrath, 1972; and see Chapter 2 in this volume). In the case of social loafing, however, *a key factor is the reality of the evaluations that are made – if any – of individual and group performance.* Comer noted that such evaluations and the attributions that people make about success and failure are much more meaningful in real, ongoing work groups than they are in artificial laboratory research groups. Accordingly, she offered a somewhat more complex model of the causes of social loafing than those discussed earlier.

A complete description of Comer's (1995) model is beyond the scope of this chapter. The interested reader is referred to the original article. For our purposes, however, a few important factors deserve attention. One of these is the perception by a group member that the group is not doing well, and that, therefore, s/he has little influence over task performance. This may cause the person not to contribute as heartily as s/he otherwise might contribute to subsequent group performance. (Reduced self-efficacy beliefs would explain this phenomenon.) The same effect might occur, according to Comer (1995), if the person felt that s/he didn't have sufficient task ability, regardless of the apparent success of the group. Persons who believe that they possess comparatively high levels of task ability might engage in "self-effacing" behavior, hoping not to diminish the spirits of others whom they perceive as less competent. Again, Comer's (1995) model deserves to be considered in its original formulation, and field experimentation must yet be conducted to test its validity.

Concepts similar to social loafing

In contrast to Geen's (1991) position and the work of Karau and Williams (1993), Kidwell and Bennett (1993) asserted a set of sharp distinctions among definitions of social loafing, *shirking*, and *free riding*. For Kidwell and Bennett (1993, p. 430):

In the shirking process, a person can withhold effort for various reasons, such as monitoring difficulties, self-interested behavior, and opportunism . . . In the social loafing process, a person withholds effort as he or she moves from an individual performing alone to individuals performing in groups of increasing size. Perhaps because a collective task is involved, individuals can hide in a crowd, and their performance becomes less identifiable, and, they believe, more dispensable . . . In the free riding process, a person withholds effort when invisible public goods [Olson, 1965] are involved, and it is rational to reduce effort because the free rider believes he or she can receive the goods by letting others do the work.

In short, according to Kidwell and Bennett (1993), it is important to distinguish among these three categories of phenomena, although collectively they comprise the *propensity to withhold effort*. Although the author sides with Kidwell and Bennett on this issue, believing that clarity and precision of constructs is critical, the reader may prefer merely to conclude that the important thing is that for whatever reason(s), people frequently expend less energy while working in groups with other people than they would while working alone.

Social Anxiety

We mentioned earlier that Geen (1991) identified a third class of social motivation that may be of interest to our study of work motivation and behavior. He refers to this phenomenon as *social anxiety*, the state created in a person when he or she is motivated to make a certain impression on other people but believes that s/he is unable to make that impression (see Geen, 1991; Schlenker & Leary, 1982). It involves that feeling we all experience from time to time, and in varying degrees, of being out of place or of not projecting the kind of attitude, aura, or image that we would optimally elect to project. Public speaking affects many people this way. This author is not aware of any work that examines the effect of social anxiety directly on work motivation, although the concept would seem to have relevance for at least two other dynamics that we have examined in this book: The expression of emotions (see Chapter 4) and the desire to project an image of fairness (Chapter 13).

In Chapter 4, we discussed at length the concept of emotional labor – the requirement made in many jobs and occupations for people to emit and control certain emotions. Required friendliness, obligatory smiling, and carefully controlled sadness or upset are examples: Many jobs require that we emit or inhibit the expression of emotions. To the extent that a person suffers from social anxiety, the person will harbor self-doubts about his or her capacity to do what is expected. In the terms of expectancy theory (see Chapter 12), this would imply that the person would be less likely to undertake such task assignments or to engage in jobs where emotional labor is required.

In Chapter 11, we will see that there appears to be a cultural norm that motivates people to project an image of fairness; that is, that it is generally the case that people prefer to be viewed as fair in their interactions with others rather than unfair, dishonest, or exploitive (see Greenberg, 1990a). Hypothetically at least, it would seem that managers (or even work peers) who experience social anxiety may be quite frustrated in their attempts to generate, instill, and foster an image of fairness in the eyes of others, frustrating their attempts to make friends or to be judged as fair supervisors or honorable people. If Greenberg (1990a) is correct that people in our culture favor a norm for projecting an image of fairness to others about themselves, occupying a job where perceived fairness is critical would be very difficult and discouraging for people who frequently experience social anxiety.

We include the notion of social anxiety for two purposes; first, for the sake of completeness in reporting on Geen's (1991) scholarly typology of social motivation effects, and second, for the sake of stimulating research into the possible or likely relationships between social anxiety and the motivation to engage in work that requires emotional labor.

Incivility

It seems an unofficial law of collective human behavior that any (and every) social group, be it a class, an office cohort, a production team or even an informal group of tourists traveling together will include at least one individual who "rubs people the wrong way" with behavior deemed to be rude. (Of course, rudeness is in the eye of the beholder, so there may not be agreement among the members of any such group who the culprit is, but the hypothesis is worth considering.)

Incivility is a form of human activity that fits the criteria for social motivation forwarded by Geen (1991), although he did not mention it, per se. Whereas the demonstration of civility is the demonstration of interpersonal respect (Carter, 1998), the core of incivility is "rudeness and a disregard for others that violates norms for respect" (Pearson & Porath, 2005, p. 8). For our purposes, Andersson and Pearson (1999) defined *workplace incivility* as "low-intensity deviant behavior with ambiguous intent to harm the target, in violation of workplace norms for mutual respect . . . [they are] characteristically rude and discourteous, displaying a lack of regard for others" (p. 457). It is conceived of as a form of workplace deviance. When there is a particular target for the behavior, it is little different from psychological aggression, which we discuss in Chapter 8. Moreover, there are fine lines between incivility and the many manifestations of bullying, petty tyranny, and interactional injustice that we examine in Chapter 5. Therefore, many instances of incivility are not intentional: They result merely from instigator insensitivity or ignorance. The harm done to the target, however, can be substantial, especially if the uncivil behavior is frequent.

Incivility is also to be distinguished from physical aggression (see Chapter 8) and interactional injustice, although interactional injustice (which is involved in the manner by which organizational policies and procedures are interpreted and delivered – see Chapter 11) is, virtually by definition, uncivil. Moreover, interactional injustice usually involves relations between superiors and subordinates (see Harlos & Pinder, 1999), whereas incivility applies to any players in an organizational setting, although the two concepts are clearly very similar. Finally, we distinguish incivility from petty tyranny and bullying, which we discussed in Chapter 5, because the latter are intentional, whereas the former is defined as unintentional.

Pearson and Porath (2005) claimed recently that incivility is increasing in North American society. A survey they conducted in Canada indicated that as many as 25% witness incivility every day and that half claim to have been targets within the previous week. A similar survey in the United States found similar results, although the percentages were not has high. Studies summarized by Cortina, Magley, Williams, and Langhout (2001) suggested that incivility may be more common in Scandinavian countries than in North America.

A "me-first" attitude fostered by the fast pace of modern work in competitive times is a favorite explanation for this sort of workplace behavior. Frost (2003) described incivility as a major component of "toxic workplaces," and argued that toxicity must be managed to reduce its spread and impact. Pearson and Porath (2005) have also claimed that incivility tends to spread in the same way that aggression spreads through the aggression–aggression hypothesis and the principle of displaced aggression (see Chapter 8).

Summary on Social Motivation

In summary, it appears that social motivation effects are very real and that they can have varying degrees of impact on human work motivation and performance. It seems obvious to state that the presence of other people will influence the ways we work, how hard we work, when and where we work, and so on. The central point in the foregoing section is that much or most human work activity is conducted in social settings and it is important to remember that aside from the deliberate attempts of bosses, managers, and peers to influence our work motivation, there can also be subtle, inadvertent, and unconscious social influences as well. In this section of the chapter, we have looked briefly at the last category of social influences: The mechanisms through which human beings subconsciously or unknowingly affect the motivation of one another.

The author feels that more empirical research is required to gain an estimate of the relative strength of social influence effects, in comparison with the more direct and intentional forms of social influence on work in work organizations. The powerful rewards and punishments that people can deliberately apply to one another for influencing work motivation and performance have been studied for years (e.g., Roethlisberger & Dickson, 1939); the results are reported in myriad places dealing with topics such as group dynamics (see the early paper by Roy, 1952), and leadership and supervision (e.g., Bass, 1981). How powerful are the effects of social motivation in relation to the formal and conscious forces? Considerable empirical work needs to be done to provide the answer.

ESTEEM NEEDS, STATUS, AND WORK MOTIVATION

The nature of the work that people do (or do not have to do) has long been a principal basis for the determination and definition of one's social class – of one's comparative status within society as a whole (Parker, 1981; Pfautz, 1953; Striker, 1988). Among modern thinkers, Karl Marx was probably the most influential student to this concept. However, long after the death of Marx and the wane of Marxism, there is still a strong relationship in most cultures between work (or non-work) and a person's status in the greater scheme of things (Clegg, 1990).

To bring the concepts of this chapter closer to home, consider the psychological impact of being demoted by one's employer. Consider the effects of having another employee take over a job or assignment that you were in charge of previously. Consider the effect on a person of being "disciplined" by a supervisor. Consider the effect on a person's emotions of being told that she is not longer deemed able to hold a job or to continue working for an employer. Consider the effects on a person's feelings of watching a rival in an organization being trained, advanced, and promoted ahead of the person who may have thought that she deserved the promotion and the adulation that goes with it. Consider the effects on a person's emotions when a client or a customer degrades or complains about the person's work. Especially consider the impact when a person is berated for a job into which she or he has invested a lot of time, energy, devotion, and care, particularly when comparisons are made between the person's worth and that of another employee.

In Chapter 4, we discussed positive emotions such as happiness, hope, pride, and a sense of accomplishment. In contrast to this, we studied negative emotions such as anger, fear, depression, envy, and jealousy, to mention but a few. These are some of the most powerful emotions people take home with them after a day's work. Whether these work-related emotions are positive or negative is critical to a person's general well-being (as we will see in more detail in Chapter 12). On occasion, a person's self-esteem can be either elevated or challenged and diminished at work. Because of the central role work plays in people's lives, as we have discussed already, enhanced self-esteem at work can contribute to an overall elevation of one's more general self-esteem (Pierce, Gardner, Cummings, & Dunham, 1989). Conversely, that same centrality assures that when self-esteem is damaged at work, there is often a contagion effect on the individual's broader sense of personal worth. When this happen, it hurts; it really hurts.

Some Key Definitions

The discussion in the following sections could be difficult to understand unless a few concepts and terms are made clear at this point. The *need for esteem* is the central concept in what follows: It is a need of the sort defined in Chapter 3. Maslow (1954, p. 45) claimed that:

> [All] people in our society have a need or desire for a stable, firmly based, usually high evaluation of themselves, for self respect, or self esteem, and for the esteem of others. These are, first, the desire for strength, for achievement, for adequacy, for mastery and competence, for confidence in the face of the world, and for independence and freedom. Second, we have what we may call the desire for reputation or prestige (defining it as respect or esteem from other people), status, fame and glory, dominance, recognition, attention, importance, dignity, or appreciation. [. . .]
>
> Satisfaction of the self esteem needs leads to feelings of self-confidence, worth, strength, capability, and adequacy, of being useful and necessary in the world. But thwarting of these needs produces feelings of inferiority, of weakness, and of helplessness.

A more recent argument of the thesis that self-esteem is a need has been provided by Locke, McClear, and Knight (1996, p. 1). They argued that:

> [S]elf esteem is a profound psychological need. It is impossible for a human being to tolerate the full, conscious conviction that he is fundamentally no good, that is, evil, worthless, inefficacious, without going insane or committing suicide. A person with low self esteem experiences self-doubt, anxiety, self-contempt and ultimately depression . . . One with high self esteem experiences the serenity that comes from the conviction that he is fundamentally "ok" and not on trial with himself. Self esteem has two closely related dimensions: efficacy and worth. By efficacy here we mean general efficacy – the ability to deal effectively in principle with life and the world. By worth we mean the conviction that one is morally good.

Whereas we can talk about and define a person's *need for esteem*, we can also consider the individual's *level of self-esteem* as that person's perception of his or her own worth (Battle, 1990, p. 22). Self-esteem is a *multifaceted set of beliefs*, one that grows and changes gradually, evolving as the person ages and has experiences with the world. Maslow (1954), among others, viewed self-esteem as a syndrome – an interrelated set of beliefs and attitudes that give rise to limited sets of behaviors. When a person can be influenced to act in certain ways that demand more strength and force, that person's entire belief structure about his worth may improve accordingly (Maslow, 1954).

"High" and "Low" Self-Esteem

Traditionally, self-esteem has been considered in dichotomous terms – for any individual, it has heretofore been considered as either "high" or "low" (Kernis, 2003). In addition, it has generally been assumed that high self-esteem is preferable to low self-esteem. As we said, people with high levels of self-esteem are generally healthier than those with lower levels; they are less anxious and demonstrate fewer symptoms of depression. High self-esteem is associated with higher levels of happiness with life in general. People with high self-esteem engage in fewer self-defeating acts and tend to be far more optimistic about themselves and their opportunities.

But high self-esteem is not a monolithic construct. Multiple forms of self-esteem exist, and some are better understood by psychologists than others. The concept usually implies a global view of one's self, but it is also possible to consider more specific, focused forms (cf. Pierce et al., 1989). In addition, a simple aggregation of the specific forms is not equivalent to the global self-assessment

(Kernis, 2003). Global self-esteem seems to be more closely linked to affective responses than specific self-esteem, which appears to have a more cognitive nature.

High self-esteem as a mixed blessing

Nevertheless, while all people *need* to feel good about themselves and to have others respect them and to feel good about them, it may be that, for some people, having particularly high levels of self-esteem (as a set of beliefs about one's self) is not as unequivocally beneficial as has been previously assumed (cf. Baumeister, Campbell, Krueger, & Vohs, 2003; Kernis, 2003; Schutz, 2001). Recent theory and research suggest, for example, that some (not all) people of higher self-esteem present themselves socially in markedly different ways than people of relatively low self-esteem. Members of the former group frequently act in self-enhancing ways, conveying the impression that they want to be admired and deemed competent. In contrast, the latter group (people with low self-esteem) frequently present themselves more protectively, behaving in ways to win approval or to become regarded as "nice" persons. In addition, high self-esteem frequently bears implications for the way people evaluate other individuals: In other words, having an especially high regard for one's self can be tantamount to having a relatively low regard for others, often giving the high self-esteem people the appearance of possessing beliefs of their own superiority relative to others. This can create a gap between the perceptions a person has of his or her social attractiveness and the evaluations others make of them. In some cases, this can influence high self-esteem people not to accept their requisite share of the blame for interpersonal conflict. So, while it may be true that high levels of self-esteem (as a belief about one's self) are frequently associated with generally higher levels of mental health and happiness, some of this positive self-regard may be illusory or unfounded, and – at times – dysfunctional in other ways, particularly in social relations with other people (Baumeister et al., 2003; Schutz, 2001).

Individuals whose high self-esteem results in these and other unfortunate outcomes have been referred to as people with "fragile" self-esteem. By contrast, some people with higher self-esteem are able to accept failures in certain domains of activity and not allow it to diminish their overall reactions to themselves. These more "secure" individuals are also less likely to demonstrate the superior attitudes and demeanor of the fragile group and are less self-deluded (Kernis, 2003). On the basis of a thorough review of the literature, Baumeister et al. (2003) concluded, among other things, that:

1. High self-esteem does not reliably cause any improvement in academic performance.
2. People with high self-esteem do better than other people on some jobs and tasks, although most laboratory studies and many field studies have found no difference. Quite possibly, occupational success leads to high self-esteem rather than the reverse.
3. People with high self-esteem regard themselves as better liked and more popular than others, but most of these advantages exist mainly in their own minds. In some cases, such as after an ego threat, people with high self-esteem are actually disliked more than others.
4. People with high self-esteem sometimes perform better than people with low self-esteem in groups. They speak up more and are recognized by their peers as contributing more. (There are only weak relationships between high self-esteem and leadership skills.)

Baumeister and his colleagues (2003) also found either no relationships between the possession of high self-esteem and antisocial behavior, delinquency, or the capacity to form and maintain close relationships. The most consistent positive outcome associated with high self-esteem was personal happiness, although the order of causality was not strongly established. They also concluded that high self-esteem is sometimes hard to distinguish from conceit, narcissism, and defensiveness, "as opposed to accepting one's self with an accurate appreciation of one's strength and worth" (p. 37).

Sources of Self-Esteem

Recent research has indicated that there is a large genetic influence on people's self-esteem levels (see Neiss, Sedikides, & Stevenson, 2002, for a review). Postnatal sources (which are not independent of the effects of early childhood experiences, as just discussed) include self-perception of performances, social feedback, and social comparison (see Schutz, 2001, for a review of the literature). Hence, it is common to observe that a person's early childhood can have a huge impact on the formation of his or her self-esteem because children are constantly attempting new tasks and challenges as they develop into adulthood while receiving feedback from parents, peers, teachers, and other significant people. In addition, they are constantly involved in comparing their own opinions, beliefs, and abilities with those of other people, including – again – other children, their siblings, and so on.

Sometimes, positive self-esteem may develop *despite* the quality of a child's upbringing. For example, in February 1996, CBC Radio conducted an interview with a woman named Karen who was raised in a series of miserable and sometimes brutal foster homes. Eventually, she was transferred to a family in which her new mother instructed her to call herself "Suzie [Smith]," not the mother's real surname. The young Karen refused and proclaimed that her name was Karen, not Suzie. Years later, when she learned that she had so asserted herself in such a high-risk situation, the adult Karen rejoiced at how noble she thought the youngster had been. She reasoned to herself that if she liked and admired the youngster for having such courage and self-control, she was also proud of herself as an adult. She pursued an education and became a successful professor of English literature.

What is "Low" Self-Esteem?

There have also been recent challenges to our traditional understanding of low self-esteem. In the past, it was assumed that low self-esteem is comprised of general unhappiness and low satisfaction with one's self, with one's value. A newer view is that these individuals merely have a confused and uncertain view of themselves. They often act inconsistently, reflecting unstable self-assessments, sometimes acting with confidence and other times with anything but confidence (Baumeister, Tice, & Hutton, 1989). But the thinking on the meaning of low self-esteem seems as confused as the people about whom this hypothesis is based. It is clear that people with *very* low self-esteem are, indeed, prone to mental illness, even suicide. The bulk of individuals who respond with relatively low scale scores on self-esteem are "low" mostly in relation to those with "high" self-ratings, so it seems to be a relative matter, not an absolute one. At the time of this writing, it is clear that there is more to self-esteem than was previously assumed by both lay people and professionals. The key matter for our present purposes is that – whatever its exact nature (belief or affective reaction, fragile or secure, etc.) – self-esteem is a critical element in a person's motivational and emotional structure and one which must be taken into account in any analysis of work motivation. One of the easiest ways to dash an individual's desire to focus sustained energy to a task or commitment to a cause (such as an organization) is to assault his or her self-esteem in a meaningful manner. On a more positive note, as we saw in Chapter 3, events that entail the enhancement of one's self-esteem are closely related to instances of job satisfaction for many, many people (Sheldon, Elliott, Kim, & Kasser, 2001).

In many ways, self-esteem is related to the concept of self-determination that underlies so much of what we can call intrinsic motivation (see Chapter 3). It is the sum of one's self-confidence and self-respect (Branden, 1969). For Branden, self-esteem is the most important value judgment a person makes. It is about his or her value vis-à-vis the world (p. 103). Maslow (1954) explained how the satisfaction of esteem needs is central to the social and mental adjustment of people in our society. He pointed out, however, that the most valuable and most healthy self-esteem is based on the *deserved* respect from other people, rather than from false external fame or unwarranted celebrity. Branden (1969) asserted that the need for self-esteem is so powerful that people who don't really enjoy its satisfaction often engage in faking behavior: They pretend to like themselves and to be more proud of themselves than they really are. Such inauthentic self-esteem is an irrational pretence, maintained by the use of defense mechanisms (such as by rationalizing one's failures or making excuses and attributing defeats to external causes). Branden (1969, p. 103) stated:

> Man experiences his desire for self esteem as an urgent imperative, as a basic need. Whether he identifies the issue explicitly or not, he cannot escape the feeling that his estimate of himself is of life-and-death importance.

Self-Esteem as a Need; Status as a Goal

To this point, we have considered self-esteem as *a set of beliefs, attitudes, and emotional reactions a person holds about one's self*. But the term self-esteem also refers to a need; indeed, the need for esteem is internal to a person's need structure – some have stronger needs for esteem than others. The concept of self-esteem is a cognitive construct, a belief having to do with one's self-worth and how others appraise the person.

Now, consider the concept of *status*. Status is not a need, it is a goal (recall Chapter 3). The term *need* refers to a force internal to a person. Status is a designation ascribed to a person by other people. A person may have a high need for esteem but may or may not enjoy status. The social setting in which a person exists is the source of her status. As we will see later, status is a socially constructed concept and reward that others place on a person. Whereas esteem is a potent, universal need, status is a social designation from others. Our discussion in this chapter deals with how work organizations (as outside sources) either help to frustrate or to satisfy people's need for esteem. It is critical that the reader keep these distinctions in mind for the concepts in this chapter to be useful in understanding this element of work motivation.

Facets of Self-Esteem

Earlier, we mentioned that a number of scholars have suggested that it may be important to distinguish between a person's global view of his or her self-esteem and self-esteem that is related more directly to specific tasks and activities (cf. Baumeister et al., 2003). The former idea has to do with a person's total view of herself. As in the case of any attitude we hold, however, it is possible to have a positive overall attitude (such as "I like the city in which I live"), while having more discordant attitudes toward facets of the object (such as "but I wish it wouldn't rain so much!"). Rosenberg, Schoenbach, Schooler, and Rosenberg, et al. (1995) showed that it is also possible to have specific attitudes about particular facets of one's self. In a massive study of more than 1800 boys, they showed that global assessments of self were related to, but conceptually and empirically distinct from, the boys' "academic self-esteem." Moreover, they found that the former concept – global self-esteem – was positively related to a variety of measures of psychological well-being but not to the boys' actual academic achievement. On the other hand, the measure of academic self-esteem was strongly associated with the boys' actual performance in school.

Facets of self-esteem at work

Similarly, Pierce et al. (1989) proposed a three-level construction of self-esteem. The first is a global concept, similar to that of Rosenberg et al. (1995). They also have an organization-based concept, which they defined "as the degree to which organizational members believe they can satisfy their needs by participating in roles within the context of an organization" (Pierce et al., 1989, p. 625). Finally, Pierce et al. (1989) delineated a concept of task- and job-based self-esteem, which is concerned with a person's views about his capacity to perform particular tasks.

Of particular interest to our purposes is their second construct, *organization-based self-esteem*. They state:

> Employees with high organization-based self esteem [OBSE] perceive themselves as important, mean-ingful, effectual and worthwhile within their employing organization . . . [T]he determinants of OBSE may include managerial respect, organizational structure, and job complexity. Factors influenced by organization-based self esteem may include not only global self esteem but also job performance, intrinsic motivation, general satisfaction, citizenship behavior, organizational commitment, and gen-eral satisfaction.
>
> (Pierce et al., 1989, pp. 643–644)

On the basis of many years of research on the topic of self-esteem in the workplace, Brockner (1988a, p. xi) observed that self-esteem influences employee behaviors and attitudes in two funda-mental ways. First, employees bring to work with them their various levels of self-esteem, which in turn influence how they feel and behave on the job. Second, because of the powerful human need for esteem, much of what people do and feel on the job is at least partly related to their desire to satisfy that need, through seeking and mastering assignments, being promoted and advanced, and by developing their work skills. These two dynamics are in a sense circular and mutually reinforcing, and they lie behind a considerable amount of organizational behavior.

Korman (1970, 1976) argued that a person's level of self-esteem even has a heavy influence on the nature of the careers and jobs the person seeks to enter. Korman's theory holds that people are largely motivated to behave consistently with themselves; that is, people tend to prefer to engage in acts that are consistent with their beliefs and attitudes and – in particular – with their self-concepts. Therefore, a person who consciously espouses certain values and beliefs will be heavily affected by those values and beliefs as s/he seeks areas to study and careers to pursue. A person's self-esteem (which, we saw earlier, is a type of belief – see Chapter 9) plays a critical role. People with high self-esteem will shoot for the stars in tracking jobs and careers; people with lower self-esteem will tend to have much lower aspiration levels with regard to their working (and non-working) lives. Movie fans may recall that the two down-and-outers played by Mickey Rourke and Faye Dunaway in the movie *Barfly* illustrate low self-esteem and low career aspiration levels.

Brockner (1988a) consistently found support for the main tenets of Korman's theory, finding that people with high self-esteem tend to believe that their careers will be successful in satisfying their life goals and that they possess the right skills and abilities to be successful in their chosen careers (p. 17). The significance of employment for people's self-esteem was vividly demonstrated in a recent longitudinal study of more than 11,000 American high school graduates. The researchers found that periods of unemployment and job dissatisfaction were detrimental to people's self-esteem. Com-pared with graduates who had been employed over the 7-year period between 1980 and 1987, those who had been employed in dissatisfying jobs, and those who had experienced great periods of unemployment showed less development of their self-esteem over that period than did grads who had been employed in satisfying jobs. Moreover, the greater time of unemployment, the harsher were the effects on the students' self-esteem (Dooley & Prause, 1995).

Self-Esteem and Organizational Culture: "Organizational Respect"

In Chapter 2, we examined the important roles organizational climate and culture can play in determining both individual and organizational outcomes. These two dimensions of the context within which organizational behavior is determined hold powerful implications for employee consequences such as job satisfaction, work motivation, and even burnout. For example, a recent longitudinal study reported by Ramarajan, Barsade, and Burack (2006) found that organizational respect was predictive of burnout rates – even after the usual effects of job demands and people's positive affectivity had been taken into account – among a panel sample of nursing assistants in the New York City region. *Organizational respect* was operationalized by five self-report questions: "Staff members respect each other"; "Staff members are treated with dignity"; "Cultural diversity of the staff is valued"; "Supervisors pay attention to staff members' ideas"; and "Staff members are encouraged to be creative when solving problems."

Self-Esteem vs. Self-Efficacy

The past 30 years in psychology have seen the emergence and study of a concept that is similar to, but slightly different from, self-esteem. This newer concept, *self-efficacy*, plays a major role in a number of the formal theories of work motivation discussed later in the book (see Chapters 9, 12, 13, and 14 especially). Its similarity to and tendency to become confused with self-esteem, especially self-esteem in the context of work motivation and performance, requires that it be introduced at this point.

Self-efficacy is a concept from *social cognitive theory* (which is examined in detail in Chapter 14), a theory that posits that human behavior, human cognition, and the environment all interact in a mutually causal manner to determine one another (Bandura, 1977, 1986, 1997). It is a person's belief about his or her capacity to succeed at a specific task, or "a judgment about task capability that is not inherently evaluative" (Gist & Mitchell, 1992, p. 185). Therefore, whereas a person may believe that she is not very competent at a specific task or job, such as painting, painting may not be important enough to the woman to affect her evaluation of herself in broader terms; that is, her low self-efficacy with regard to painting is unlikely to diminish her overall self-esteem. Again, self-esteem is a basic belief a person holds about his or her worth as a person, spanning a wide variety of situations (Brockner, 1988a). Hence, self-esteem is not likely to be influenced by a person's feelings and perceptions of self-efficacy unless the person lacks skill and ability at almost every task contemplated.

Creative self-efficacy

Beliefs about one's self-efficacy are multifaceted: It "should be measured in terms of particularized judgments of capability that may vary across realms of activity, under different levels of task demands within a given activity domain, and under different situational circumstances" (Bandura, 1997, p. 42). So, for example, Tierney and Farmer (2002) tested Ford's (1996) proposition that self-efficacy perceptions can influence employee creativity. They adopted Gist and Mitchell's (1992) model of self-efficacy development, introducing a new construct, *creative self-efficacy*, which they defined simply as "the belief one has the ability to produce creative outcomes" (Tierney & Farmer, 2002, p. 1138). In a study involving two disparate samples of American workers, Tierney and Farmer (2002) found that job tenure, job self-efficacy, supervisory behavior (in the form of modeling and persuasive behavior) and job complexity all contributed to creative efficacy beliefs. In addition, they found that scores on this new construct added variance explained in supervisory ratings of creative job behavior, over and above that explained by simple job efficacy alone.

Self-efficacy has repeatedly been shown to predict task success (Bandura, 1986; Stajkovic & Luthans, 1998). Moreover, self-efficacy may have an interesting relationship with social facilitation and social loafing, two other concepts we examined earlier in the current chapter. Experimental research reported by Sanna (1992), for example, suggested that people with high self-efficacy beliefs, working together but for individual goals (co-acting), may work more effectively than high-efficacy people who work alone. This is what Sanna (1992) found, supporting the social facilitation hypothesis (described earlier in this chapter). In addition, when people had beliefs of low self-efficacy, they performed better when working toward group goals than when working toward individual goals. Sanna (1992) cited this as support for the social loafing hypothesis.

In short, self-efficacy may help to explain and reconcile the fascinating effects of people on one another's work motivation through social facilitation and social loafing. More work is required on this possibility. Aside from its lack of clear effects on job performance, however, it seems that high self-esteem is positively related to other aspects of work performance, such as "prosocial" work behavior (good citizenship and work above and beyond the call of duty (Brockner, 1988a; and see Chapter 10)).[6]

Controversy over the breadth of self-efficacy

Although Bandura (1997) conceived of self-efficacy as a belief about one's self that is particular to a task and a context, other researchers have attempted, with varying degrees of success, to develop and advance other, similar constructs. For example, some confusion between self-esteem and self-efficacy beliefs (as constructs related to one's beliefs about one's self) resulted from attempts to develop the concept of *task-related self-esteem*. Brockner (1988a), among others, claimed that the notion of task-specific self-esteem is synonymous with the concept of self-efficacy. However, since the emergence and acceptance of self-efficacy, the idea of task-related self-esteem has received little attention, aside from that reflected in the work of Pierce et al. (1989). Somewhat later, Parker (1998) introduced the concept of *role breadth self-efficacy*, which "refers to employees' capability of carrying out a broader and more proactive set of work tasks that extend beyond prescribed technical requirements" (p. 835).[7]

Further confusion resulted from the introduction of *generalized self-efficacy*, which is viewed as a broad view about one's competence *across tasks and settings*. This construct has enjoyed some success (cf. Chen, Gully, & Eden, 2001; Locke, McClear, & Knight, 1996). One empirical study differentiated between general self-efficacy (GSE) and self-esteem, concluding that the former is more highly related to motivational variables than the latter, whereas self-esteem is more highly related to affective variables than is GSE (Chen, Gully, & Eden, 2004).

Higher-Order Constructs Related to Capability Beliefs

In a previous edition of this book, the author (Pinder, 1998) called for more work on the distinctions between and among these highly interrelated constructs, claiming that the distinctions among them are probably of more interest and value to psychometricians than to anyone with applied interests. In other words, there have probably been more distinctions among concepts than is practically or even theoretically necessary. Occam's razor (recall Chapter 2) dictates simplicity and parsimony in the development and advancement of theory, so why proliferate more and more constructs than we can possibly differentiate from one another in our measurement and science making and that are of value to our understanding of human (work) behavior?

In accord with that reasoning, a number of efforts have been made to propose higher-level concepts that subsume and integrate many of the lower-level, more specific constructs itemized in the foregoing paragraphs. Many of these higher-level constructs incorporate self-efficacy along with other personality and affective states.

---

[6] Later, in Chapter 12, we will see that self-efficacy is similar to another construct in the popular expectancy-valence models of work motivation; we will deal with that apparent overlap at that point.

[7] We return to this construct in Chapter 7.

Core self-evaluation

The first of these, referred to as *core self-evaluations* was introduced by Judge, Locke, and Durham (1997). It is a broad, latent, higher-order trait composed of four elements: *Self-esteem* (as discussed in this chapter), *generalized self-efficacy* (cf. Locke et al., 1996), *neuroticism* – a personality style that causes people to hold generally negative cognitive and explanatory styles and to focus on the most negative aspects of one's self, and *locus of control* (beliefs about the causes of events in one's life, i.e., whether a person generally causes his or her own consequences, or whether external forces determine one's outcomes) (see Judge, Erez, Bono, & Thoresen, 2003).

A study based on 12 different samples of people, comprising approximately 15,000 individuals, reached the conclusion that these four traits do, in fact, inter-correlate enough to be considered a higher-level construct worthy of investigation (Judge, Erez, & Bono, 1998). (This implies that a person high on one of these four individual dimensions is likely also to score highly on all or most of the other three.) The researchers then advanced a cogent set of conceptual arguments, using many of the theories of motivation presented in this book, to explain how and why levels of this trait would be associated with high levels of work motivation and performance. Their overall conclusion was that being positive is a good thing from the perspective of work, working, and work motivation.

Indeed, a subsequent review of studies reported by Erez and Judge (2001) found that people's standing on this new construct was positively related to many motivation and performance indicators. Another study found that scores on core self-evaluation were positively related to life and job satisfaction in three samples from the Unites States and Israel (Judge, Locke, Durham, & Kluger, 1998). More recently, an impressive longitudinal study of unemployed people found that core self-evaluation was related to job search intensity. That is, unemployed individuals who were assessed as higher on core self-evaluation tried considerably more frequently to find new jobs than did those who scored lower on the trait (Wanberg, Glomb, Song, & Sorenson, 2005).

Core confidence

Most recently, Stajkovic (2006) has proposed a similar higher-order construct combining hope, self-efficacy, optimism, and resilience, referring to the new construct as *core confidence*. He claims that his new construct is somewhat different from that of core evaluations; he argues (2006, p. 1216) that the essence of his construct is confidence, whereas the essence of the core evaluations construct is neuroticism (Judge, Erez, Bono, & Thoresen, 2003). Stajkovic (2006) generates conceptual arguments to predict that his construct will be related to job performance, job satisfaction, well-being, and educational and career success.

Too many constructs?

It remains to be seen whether the introduction of either or both of these higher-order constructs – core evaluation and core confidence – will help to advance our understanding of work motivation dynamics. This author believes that higher-order constructs hold the potential to shed light but that a proliferation of them could result in a battle among nomological nets that will be of more interest to psychometricians and theorists than to people with applied interests. Time will tell.

In the remaining sections of this chapter, we turn our attention away from the individual worker and his or her esteem motivation to examine the contexts within which esteem-driven persons live and work: We examine status systems, particularly status systems within work organizations.

SOCIAL AND STATUS SYSTEMS

The acclaimed British zoologist Desmond Morris (1969, p. 21) once observed that:

> In any organized group of mammals, no matter how cooperative, there is always a struggle for social dominance. As he pursues this struggle, each adult individual acquires a particular social rank, giving him his position, or status, in the group hierarchy. The situation never remains stable for very long, largely because all the status strugglers are growing older. When the overlords, or "top dogs," become senile, their seniority is challenged and they are overthrown by their immediate subordinates. There is then renewed dominance squabbling as everyone moves a little farther up the social ladder. At the other end of the scale, the younger members of the group are maturing rapidly, keeping up the pressure from below . . . The general result is a constant condition of status tension. Under natural conditions this tension remains tolerable because of the limited size of the social groupings. If, however . . . the group size becomes too big . . . then the "rat race" soon gets out of hand, dominance battles rage uncontrollably, and the leaders . . . come under severe strain. When this happens, the weakest members of the group are frequently hounded to their deaths, as the restrained rituals of display and counter-display degenerate into bloody violence.

Note that for Morris (1969) these dramatic and very serious rituals of status, domination, and power are universal in the mammal kingdom. They are certainly universal in the world of work, having profound implications for our understanding of work motivation and organizational behavior.

The Nature of Social Status

What is social status? Sociologists offer a variety of definitions, and they tend to converge. For Faunce (1982), social status is a location in a hierarchy resulting from the unequal distribution of anything that is valued and that produces relations of deference, acceptance, or derogation (p. 172). Hence, status implies differences among people or social units in terms of honor, esteem, respect, and prestige (Zeldich, 1968). Troyer (2003, p. 149) defined status as "the perceived value of an actor in a social system." Locke (2003) claimed that when people think about relations among individuals, two general dimensions characterize their thinking. The first of these relates to comparative status, power, and agency. (The second dimension has to do with solidarity, intimacy, friendliness, or communion.)

The differences that exist among categories of working people are powerful indicators of their relative status, both at work and outside the work context. Hence, it is common practice upon meeting a newcomer in Western culture to inquire immediately about the person's occupation. The labels and categories that come as answers are symbolic, significant, and value laden. Inherent in them are distinctions with status implications. We have work-related distinctions between manual and non-manual employees, supervisors and non-supervisors, "productive" versus "nonproductive" labor, professionals versus nonprofessionals, managers and routine workers, and credentialed versus uncredentialed workers (Burris, 1990). These days it may not even be polite or politically correct to refer to someone as a "worker," the preferred term being "employee," perhaps.

Genetics, occupational achievement, and social status

If people's occupational achievement is the primary determinant of their status in Western society, what is it that determines a person's occupational achievement? A complete answer is beyond the scope and purpose of this book, but one factor that may not come to mind readily but is worth mentioning is genetics.

Elsewhere we have noted that some scholars have suggested that biology may play a role in certain aspects of human work motivation and behavior (e.g., Arvey & Bouchard, 1994). Interestingly, there is preliminary evidence to suggest that biology, notably in the form of the male hormone testosterone, may influence the relative occupational achievement (and hence, social status) of North American men. In a large-scale study of Vietnam war vets conducted by the Centers for Disease Control, Dabbs (1992) found that higher levels of testosterone were correlated with lower levels of occupational achievement. The sample studied comprised a representative cross-section of the U.S. population at large. The explanation offered was that higher levels of the hormone among young males led to higher levels of antisocial behavior, lower levels of intelligence, and lower levels of education, resulting, eventually, in fewer or lower levels of marketable job skills. Dabbs (1992) observed that the effects were small in statistical terms but important enough to be taken seriously, because testosterone levels are heritable and virtually fixed at the time of birth. The point here is that occupational status may be determined by a variety of factors, at least one of which is beyond the control of the individual.

For the concept of social status to have much psychological effect on people or to serve as an incentive for people to "get ahead" in life, it seems reasonable to expect that there be some degree of consensus among the people of a society regarding the comparative status of occupations. Such has not always been the case, however (e.g., Powell & Jacobs, 1983). In fact, a study by Guppy and Goyder (1984) found that although there was considerable consensus among people of high socio-economic status (SES), there was much less agreement about occupational prestige among people of both mixed and lower SES levels. There was comparatively low consensus about occupational status among the black participants of the study as well.

The measurement problem notwithstanding, there has long been a powerful connection between work, working, and the status of people. The workplace is a potent *potential* forum for the satisfaction or the frustration of esteem needs and for the very definitions we apply to ourselves and to others. To denigrate the working category of a person is usually taken as insulting, and it becomes important for many people that they are seen as belonging to one of the more prestigious status groups (professionals, executives, entrepreneurs, etc.). More will be said on these matters shortly. In the following section, we will briefly review some of the knowledge related to esteem need satisfaction and the powerful role that work and work organizations can have in the satisfaction or frustration of esteem needs. The need for positive self-regard from others and for having a positive view of one's own worth motivates a lot of human behavior; it is certainly a powerful source of work motivation. Before we begin, we take a brief look at the nature of status systems in general terms, to explore what they are, why they exist, and how they function.

The Nature and Functions of Organizational Status Systems

One early organizational scholar defined status with the workplace in mind as "the condition of the individual that is defined by a statement of his rights, privileges, immunities, duties, and obligations as well as the restrictions, limitations, and prohibitions concerning his behavior" (Barnard, 1946). Why do status systems exist? A first, simple answer is found throughout the current section of this chapter: Status systems provide for the possible satisfaction of human needs (such as the esteem needs). But what else do they do? What other functions are served by status systems?

Status as reward

First, they can serve as incentives and, for those who hold status and the rewards it brings, a form of gratification Zeldich (1968). In such cases, to lose status is a deprivation. According to Zeldich (1968, p. 253):

Opportunities to improve status are seized by almost everyone, even in societies that are not achievement-oriented . . . When status is threatened, its loss is resisted.

High-status positions can be rewarding for their own sake, and they can also be instrumental for the attainment of other rewards and benefits (Barnard, 1946).

Status and control

Second, status systems can help develop and maintain a sense of responsibility and decorum among people. The threat of a loss in one's status can be a considerable impediment in work settings, causing people to adhere to company codes of conduct as well as the mores of society at large. The author knows of professional accounting firms that have strong informal rules about the conduct of their employees outside the workplace, after working hours. Violation of these rules can be costly to the status and subsequent treatment and career advancement prospects of those who dare to violate them. Reducing a person's status officially can be one of the most dramatic and traumatic acts in organizational life. Having to discipline an employee is a dreaded part of most managers' jobs, and being the recipient of organizational discipline can be even more traumatic for the employee involved (see Chapters 11 and 14). Having to lay off people for economic reasons is bad; having to fire an employee for cause is the stuff of nightmares for most bosses and executives. Status can be thought of as a cherished commodity, in life in general and particularly in the context of one's work. To be stripped of one's status is, therefore, a consequence of organizational behavior dreaded by most people. Hence, the maintenance of a strong status system makes control, reward, and punishment powerful managerial tools.

Status and communication

There is a mixed and complex relationship between status and interpersonal communication. On the one hand, status systems can expedite communication (Barnard, 1946). A junior officer who receives an order from a commander has no legitimate reason to ask about "why's and wherefore's" – an order is an order. The uniform worn by the commander immediately lets the junior officer know that what the former has to say is to be taken seriously and acted upon. Communication is thereby expedited. Further, the recognition of rank by both parties determines the sort of language and decorum that is appropriate. People tend to speak and write to others in terms that are appropriate to the status of both the sender and the receiver of the message. Again, communication is enhanced by status. On the other hand, status differences between people can inhibit the open communication of ideas if the lower-status person is afraid to be frank, open, honest, and complete in what s/he communicates, or if the "superior" person resents being addressed by a status inferior.[8] Similarly, high-status persons may withhold information that is sensitive, classified, or beyond "the need to know."

The theory of status characteristics and expectation states that when members of a group are arranged in a certain rank order by their status, they will tend to have the same relative standing among group members in terms of the amount of interaction they have with other group members (Berger, Cohen, & Zeldich, 1972; Berger, Rosenholtz, & Zeldich, 1980). A massive field test of three key hypotheses from the theory supported it (Cohen & Zhou, 1991). The researchers investigated 2077 respondents representing 224 research and development teams from 29 large corporations. They assessed all team members on a variety of "external" status indicators (education, gender, status within the company as a whole, seniority, and whether the person was a formally designated leader)

---

[8] Porter (1962) tells the story of the invention of the spindle found in many restaurants. According to Porter, differences between highly skilled cooks and lesser skilled waiters and waitresses (called "servers" these days) were not culturally acceptable in many restaurants. Low-status people should not be in a position to initiate orders with persons of higher status. The introduction of the spindle on which a diner's order can be placed and then rotated into the view of the cook obviates the need for cross-status communication.

as well as on two "internal" indicators (expert status and team status). The findings revealed that the external indicators all had a major impact on the scientists' status within their respective teams, and that this team status, in turn, was significantly predictive of the amount of formal interaction involving each person. The study suggests the pervasiveness and importance of society- and organization-level status systems and shows how they can affect the interaction of people inside formally designated work groups.

Status and Emotional Displays: A Vicious Cycle?

There is some evidence that a person's formal social status can influence the range of emotions they feel and display and that these emotional displays, once witnessed by others, can reinforce the status of the people who exhibit them (Tiedens, 2000). Thus, as we mentioned in Chapter 4, a vicious cycle, or self-fulfilling prophesy linking emotion to social standing, can operate in formal social systems – such as work organizations – cycles that can serve to reinforce the status quo.

For example, when there is a bit of uncertainty about the causes of positive or negative work outcomes in mixed-status work groups, three types of causal attribution (or *agency evaluation*) are possible, and the emotions people feel at the time vary as a function of their perceived social status. The three causal explanations are: (1) "I am responsible," (2) "someone else is responsible," or (3) "no one is responsible" (Ellsworth & Smith, 1988). When work outcomes are negative, both high- and low-status people tend to attribute the failure to the low-status partners in groups. The former group expresses anger while the latter group expresses guilt for the failure. By contrast, when the outcome is favorable, the high-status players feel pride while the low-status participants feel appreciative (see Tiedens, 2000, for a more complete treatment of this research).

Differences Among Occupations in Status and Prestige

An issue of longstanding interest to sociologists has been the comparative status of various occupations in the economy. Historians and political scientists can use the relative comings and goings of status differences as a means of tracking "the times," the importance of various current events, and the general values of the culture at large. For example, the author vividly recalls the tremendous negative impact that the Watergate hearings had on the social status of attorneys in the United States in the late 1970s and early 1980s. Negative stereotypes about lawyers as a population of professionals are at least as strong in the new millennium as they were during the Watergate years. Nevertheless, the point is that societies typically stratify members of the workforce on the basis of the occupations to which people belong. There is rarely a case where all occupations are viewed as equally prestigious.

The traditional bases for determining inter-occupational status differences are the power, income, and/or necessary educational levels associated with the occupations (Abbott, 1981). Accordingly, the professions are usually ranked in the higher echelons of a society's status hierarchy, and the issue becomes one of deciding and agreeing upon which occupations are professions and which are not. Another issue that emerges quickly has to do with the comparative status of the professions: Are nurses more prestigious as a group than school teachers? Are physicians of higher status than accountants? But that's not all: We also have a keen tendency to differentiate among ourselves within occupations.

Stratification within *occupations*

The human desire to stratify usually also causes stratification consciousness to occur within particular occupations. Among the members of any profession, for example, stratification occurs.

All physicians are not seen as equal within the population of people accepted as physicians. In Britain, for example, general practitioners have been regarded as the lowest-status doctors for many years, making it hard for the government and private agencies to recruit and retain GPs. The reason? General practitioners have not been able to supplement their incomes by providing hospital services to private patients, as have hospital doctors, who may do so. Recently, the British government has intervened by increasing the annual salaries of family doctors by approximately 50% in just over 2 years (*The Economist*, May 14, 2005, p. 61). It is too early to tell whether this dramatic increase in their pay will result in higher social status for family doctors among their medical associates.

In Canada, homeopaths are held in low regard and high suspicion by much of the rest of the "medical establishment." Similarly, not all lawyers are perceived as equally prestigious among members of that profession. Interestingly, it seems that the lawyers (or physicians, etc.) who are seen as the most prestigious by the outside community are held in much lower regard by members of the inside group of lawyers (or physicians). In other words, the eminent scientist who takes her work to the people by popularizing and making intelligible the current knowledge of her field via television or radio is likely to be held in relatively low regard by members of the same subdiscipline who prefer not to go public. Rarely do highly successful university professors whose claim to fame is their classroom appeal rise in academic ranks in large North American universities without a commensurate record in the publication of cutting-edge research in elite periodicals – often the less accessible to the public, the more status they enjoy.

Abbott (1981) attempted to explain this paradox by arguing that professionals prefer to keep themselves "pure," unencumbered by what he called nonprofessional issues or irrelevant professional issues arising from practice. Anything that entails human complexity, problems, or reality despoils the state of purity, and accordingly, denigrates the status of the professional engaged in the activity. Hence the judge holds superior status to the district attorney because the former can maintain professional purity through the buffering rules of the courtroom. The theoretical engineer who works in a university lab is likely to enjoy much less status in the eyes of the general public than the famous engineer who is publicly acknowledged for constructing large public projects such as bridges or dams.

Inside the profession, however, Abbott (1981) would predict that the comparative status of these two engineers would be quite the opposite. Biopsychologists enjoy higher status in the profession than social psychologists, who in turn look down on the industrial psychologist (whose work has the most to do with problems of real people in messy organizational settings). It seems that dealing with people and the real problems that people drag along with them, such as illness, laws, crimes, or troubles of any sort, creates an opportunity for an erstwhile professional to lose her purity and, with it, some of the status she enjoys within the culture of her peers.

Status Assignment Systems

But what determines the emergence of status differentials within a group? The mechanisms by which status differentials are created and enforced are variously referred to as "status organizing processes" or "status assignment systems." A comprehensive summary of Western thinking in social science related to status assignment systems is offered by Webster (2003), so the interested reader is referred to his chapter. Among the more intriguing notions discussed by Webster is referred to as *expectation states*. Webster illustrates the concept as follows:

> [T]he higher the relative expectation states associated with one individual as compared to another, the more likely the first person is to attempt to solve a group's problem, the more likely this problem solving attempt is to receive positive evaluations and agreement, the less likely he is to accept influence in case of disagreement, and the more likely he is to enjoy all the subjective assessments such as perceived ability and leadership potential. Expectation states arise through interaction, primarily

through differential participation rates and evaluation processes. Whatever results in positive evaluations increases the chances that high expectations will get associated with an individual, and whatever results in negative evaluations increases the chances that low expectations will become attached to him or her. Expectations are not necessarily conscious, though they may be accessed through questionnaires and interviews.

(Webster, 2003, p. 177)

In simple terms, those members of a group who appear to be able to deal with the group's most pressing problems (or task at hand) will, by trying at least, initially generate high expectation states for themselves. If successful, a cycle begins that can result in the accrual of power and prestige to the individual. (Recall our discussion of the relationship between power and dependency in Chapter 5.)

Status characteristics

Whereas expectation states have their genesis in what a person does or can do, status characteristics are based more on features of the person herself (Troyer, 2003). Hence, if a characteristic (such as intelligence or an outgoing personality) carries social advantages in the broader society, this advantage can often be imported into a group as a primary basis for differentiation among its members. Recall from Chapter 2 how Judge and Cable (2004) reported how physical height seems to be a characteristic valued in Western society that eventually can have great benefit for people in terms of their life earnings!

There are two general categories of status characteristic: Specific and diffuse. Specific status characteristics refer to particular abilities or traits, such as, for example, physical height or interpersonal skills. So, if members of a social group value height, then taller members will initially be accorded more status than shorter members. By contrast, diffuse status characteristics are less related to specific traits or abilities. One contentious example is sex: In North American society, some economists argue that our business culture values men more highly than women, in the aggregate, as judged by gender-based pay differentials. A recent Dutch study of more than 2000 employees found that emotional stability – a personality trait – was positively associated with higher wages for both men and women, while another trait – agreeableness – was negatively correlated with wages among women (Nyhus & Pons, 2005). *Within* specific organizational contexts, characteristics that are valued form the basis of the organization's culture, and, as we saw in Chapter 2, these cultures can be powerful contexts for work motivation, rewards, and punishments.

Things become particularly interesting within this model when it comes to combining two or more status characteristics (Webster, 2003). How does one compare the status of a short male with that of a tall woman, extending the hypothetical examples introduced earlier?

Status assignment systems

The concept of status assignment systems helps us understand the ubiquity of inter- and intra-occupational status comparisons (Faunce, 1982, 1989). For Faunce (1989, p. 384), the basic elements of status assignment systems:

[A]re a set of persons or positions being evaluated, a set of people doing the evaluating, a set of values, and a resulting hierarchy of persons or positions. Any social encounter that includes relations of deference, equality, or derogation involves an explicit or implied status-assignment system.

Moreover, these status assignment systems occur within boundaries of varying size and degrees of inclusion. So, as we have seen already, an occupational status assignment system may be circumscribed by the boundaries of a work group, office, firm, occupation, or set of corporations in a community or society (Faunce, 1989, p. 385). "Having a very rich brother-in-law may locate one differently in a family status hierarchy from having a highly educated brother-in-law" (Faunce, 1982, p. 168). The problem is moot, of course, when the same brother-in-law is both highly educated and rich!

One study found that members of a common occupation will differ from one another in status on the basis of whether they match the dominant gender composition of the occupation in question (Powell & Jacobs, 1984). For example, the study found that women in female-dominated occupations (e.g., nursing) were regarded as having higher prestige than male nurses. Similarly, women truck drivers were regarded as having lower prestige than male truck drivers, the driving of trucks being a predominantly male preserve. Moreover, the gap in prestige between males and females within any given occupation was correlated with the degree to which the person was "misplaced" in comparison to the population at large.

In a related study, the same researchers sought to determine whether there is an inherent gender-related status for occupations or whether the gender of typical occupants in the various occupations also played a role (Jacobs & Powell, 1985). They found that the general status of occupations seemed to reflect the prestige normally attributed to the gender-typical jobholders (men in male-dominated occupations, women in female-dominated occupations). The researchers concluded that "the seemingly sex-neutral concept of occupational prestige incorporates strong sex-linked assumptions . . . [T]he prestige accorded to an occupation reflects the sex-typical incumbent – men in male-dominated occupations and women in female-dominated occupations" (pp. 1069–1070). Clearly, the relationships between gender, gender role stereotypes, and the actual distribution of men and women across occupations are complex and subject to change as the nature of the workforce changes. Aside from how complex or tricky these relationships are, they do matter to people in the workplace.

The point here is simple: People, by nature, will stratify. Much of the desire to do so (not all of it) is driven by a universal need for esteem. The nature of work that people perform is a ready, handy, and common basis for forming horizontal layers between people, and as we have seen, there is almost no end to the fineness of the gradations people conjure or create to assure that some persons are superior to others while receiving less status and prestige than others.

Status Symbols in the Workplace

An integral part of virtually all status systems is any number of tangible and intangible symbols that serve to reflect the status of the people who use or possess them. Office size and decoration are an example. One study found that employees who were temporarily relocated to higher-status offices increased their work performance. Conversely, employees in the same study who were temporarily relocated to offices of lower-status values than they were used to occupying demonstrated a reduction in work performance (Greenberg, 1988a). Many organizations invest considerable trouble, time, and expense to assure that there is a close relationship between the quality of the office space a person occupies and that person's status. Corner officers are coveted, for example, because they often tend to be larger and have more windows. Occupants of corner offices may claim that the extra space is appreciated because it permits easier access, more storage, or larger meetings; the real value, however, usually lies in the fact that there is a limited number of large corner offices and the recipients of these spaces are the higher-status members of the organization. People often go to great lengths to deny the sociological facts of status symbols ("The extra space is functional" really means "Look at me, I have arrived!"). Their corner offices are used for the firm's library, conference and meeting rooms, and for other purposes. Despite the firm's desire to deny status differences, other bases emerge, usually based on the subspecialty of the employees themselves.

What is seen as a status symbol varies from culture to culture, from group to group and with time. Status symbols are generally commodities that are rare and take on value in part because of the cultural belief that they are rare and valued. Possessing one's own price marker was a jealously sought-after and protected status symbol in the culture of a grocery store in which the author once worked. To possess one's own price marker implied that the person was of high status. It was especially "cool" to possess one's own belt holster in which to carry the marker.

Status symbols need not be tangible objects. Privileges – to come and go at will, for example, or to set one's own work schedule – are non-tangible indicators of status that people can grow to cherish, protect, maintain, and covet.

Job titles

The fuss many people make over their job titles is a fascinating example: Consider the character Dwight Schrute in the currently popular NBC television program *The Office*. Poor old Dwight's actual job title is Assistant to the General Manager, Michael Scott, although Dwight refers to himself on every possible occasion as the Assistant Manager. There is a world of difference, so Michael and all of Dwight's political coworkers (and political rivals) correct the poor fellow every time he misrepresents his true status in the hierarchy of the office. It is hilarious on television but ubiquitous and very real and very powerful for people engaged in careers in hierarchical organizational structures.

Equipment: Optional or required?

The author recalls the status attributed to any individual in many work organizations 15 years ago who carried a cell phone or a pager while on the job. To carry one of these devices, in the early days at least, implied high status for the person carrying and using them. Not too many years later, in many organizational cultures, these electronic trappings seemed to lose their luster: University presidents and university janitors all carry pagers and/or cell phones, so in some cultures being required to carry such paraphernalia on the job may be seen as carrying an electronic chain that denotes lack of autonomy on the job and, therefore, low status. In short, "the times" can change the value of status symbols.

Status in the military

Military and paramilitary organizations place especially heavy importance on status symbols. Stars, stripes, chevrons, pins, badges, and other insignia are carefully assigned to officers and troops of various levels with the strictest of control and regimentation. That the symbols of military rank are taken seriously was vividly illustrated in two fascinating cases.

The first case involved Admiral Mike Boorda, who was the U.S. Chief of Naval Operations when he took his own life in the spring of 1996. A veteran of 40 years' service, Boorda was distressed when questions were raised about the appropriateness of his wearing two small bronze V pins among the considerable collection of decorations on his uniform. These insignia designate that the wearer saw combat in the war zones represented by the V's. Although Boorda had served in combat zones during the Vietnam War and had earned two commendations for his service there, he had not actually earned the V's, the wearing of which implied that he had been exposed to personal hazard due to direct hostile action by the enemy. When he realized his mistake, Boorda stopped wearing the pins, but by this time there were journalists and other people who were curious about his ever having worn them. Rather than permitting his error to cause a denigration of the symbolic value and meaning of the medals, Admiral Boorda killed himself immediately before a meeting with the curious journalists. For Boorda and other members of the U.S. military culture, it was a matter of honor (Zoglin & Thompson, 1996).

In the second case, Otto ("Dutch") Bischoff, aged 97, was awarded the U.S. Military's Silver Star for his "great coolness and courage" during action against the German Army at the Battle of the Argonne Forest in early 1918. For whatever bureaucratic reasons, the Army failed to award the Silver Star in due course, and it took the Fraternal Order of Trench Soldiers to research the case and to rectify the oversight. The medal was awarded to Mr. Bischoff in June 1996, 78 years after he had earned it. After all the intervening years, the Silver Star was still deemed of sufficient value to be awarded, and the military still believed in the symbolic importance of awarding it (*Vancouver Province*, June 27, 1996, p. A26).

There are countless other examples of status symbols, their importance, and the functions they serve. Anyone old enough to have held a job, seen a movie, or read a book about work will recognize the point here. Status systems require and are defined by status symbols. To possess these symbols implies high status. Not to possess them implies lower status, and to have them taken away is usually a source of great embarrassment and humiliation for the person involved.

A theoretical caveat

Most of the examples just provided to illustrate status symbols in work settings probably have a familiar ring for most readers. Yet for those who are concerned with theory development and the refinement of concepts of status, status symbols, and their potential for appealing to people's needs for self-esteem, a precaution was sounded by Faunce (1982).

Using the specific substantive example of status and self-esteem, Faunce criticized modern sociology for the slapdash way by which complex concepts (such as social status) are operationalized and interpreted without careful connections to theory. As examples, he noted that we might be tempted to equate status differences between occupations with the levels of pay they receive, or with the educational levels that they require, or with whether the work involved is manual or conceptual, and so on. In practice, these various "indicators" of status may be correlated among themselves (such that high-paying jobs tend to require greater training and education and tend to be conducted by people in white collars, using their minds rather than their hands, for example), but neither are these connections perfect and always predictable, and neither do the choices among the indicators find theoretical justification in a carefully articulated conceptualization of social status. Faunce (1982, p. 160) wrote:

> [M]any of the presumed consequences of occupational status differences rest on the assumption that people care about these differences. The assumption that occupational status influences self esteem without further specification of the mechanisms through which this may occur [is] an example of chain saw sociology. A theory explaining this relationship would have to identify various types of occupational status hierarchies, specify the conditions under which these hierarchies are more or less likely to become relevant to social experience, and detail the ways in which social evaluation involved in the experience of status differences influences self esteem.

In many ways, Faunce's observations and lament are related to those that we see in psychology and micro-organizational behavior under the general heading of *construct validity* (see Schwab, 1980; and Chapter 2 of this book). The point is that sometimes our desire to make practical (managerial?) use of social scientific concepts induces us to grasp at handy, salient, or obvious indicators of those concepts, for the sake of getting on with practical matters, such as running a school or a business, raising a family, or providing assistance to those in need. The problem, according to Faunce (1982), is that such quick and loose interpretations of concepts by practitioners can obscure the essential meanings of the concepts themselves and inhibit the development of theoretical disciplines such as sociology. In addition to the meanings of the concepts is the problem of understanding why and how the various concepts are connected.

This author offered a similar lament three decades ago in relation to the "premature application" of theories of work motivation (Pinder, 1977). The reader with applied intentions may benefit from the wisdom regarding status symbols and self-esteem that was offered earlier in this section, but Faunce (1982) cautioned that the connections between the "obvious" indicators of status and status differences and the true meaning of the concepts they purport to represent (in this case, social status) are only partial, imperfect, and without much in the way of conceptual wholeness. Point well taken, although we will see shortly that Faunce (1982, 1989) offered a *constructive* example of how theoretically based connections can be made between concepts in social science, again using the specific substantive case of the relationship between status and self-esteem.

Status Assignment and Denigration

Status can be achieved through ascription, by effort, by merit, or by accomplishment. When a person has earned the right to a higher level of status, there is often some form of ceremony involved to mark the event (see Trice, Belasco, & Alutto, 1969). The greater the transition in status, the greater and more extravagant the event tends to be (Ritti, 1994). Work organizations make frequent use of ceremonials in the more or less well-managed realities of status in the workplace. Promotions are advertised, demotions are kept hush-hush (unless the purpose is to damage the demoted person's pride and self-esteem), and retirements are frequently feted by lavish gifts and testimonials.

Interestingly, lateral career moves are seldom free of status implications (Pinder, 1989). It seems that as long as two jobs are somehow different from one another in terms of content, location, or mission, they are held not to be of equal status in most organizational status systems. Geographic moves within a company are similar. Moving from Toronto to Chicago in one company may be widely interpreted as a promotion ("She's really on the fast track"), whereas the same move in another company (other factors being equal) may widely be held as a demotion – that the person is being "put out to pasture" (see Pinder, 1983).

An issue of common concern in many companies these days is caused by the fact that most companies' formal structures are pyramidal and the demographics of the work population are uneven. This means that many people (especially in the Baby-Boomer generation and in Generation X – see Chapter 3) are confronted with limited opportunities for upward movement within their organizations. Their bosses are still far from retirement. One solution that has been proposed is downward movement of people for the sake of keeping them interested and motivated in their work, and committed to the employer (see Hall & Isabella, 1985). Naturally, this solution meets with only limited success because of the traditional association in work organizations between career advancement, increased status levels, and *upward* movement in the hierarchy. Status and status consciousness are ubiquitous in work settings.

The Role of Occupational Status in Self-Esteem

Now that we have discussed the need for esteem and the potential of work and work organizations for either satisfying or denying these needs, we can directly ask the question: Does working in a putatively high status role necessarily result in the satisfaction of esteem needs? Faunce (1982, 1989) claimed that the answer is no; the relationship is not so simple. According to Faunce (1989), the empirical research on the relationship between occupational achievement and self-esteem is confused, mixed, and ambiguous. He argued that "the effects of status on self esteem occur not simply as a result of *knowledge* of one's location in a status hierarchy but, more important, as a result of the frequency with which one is *reminded* of that location." In other words, Faunce suggested that merely possessing a superior position in a status hierarchy does not assure that a person will experience high self-esteem; rather, the system must frequently remind the person of his or her rank through any of a variety of means.

For example, frequent encounters with persons of apparently lower or higher status, frequent use of the perquisites of one's status, or frequent recognition by others of one's status are characteristics of status systems that can make one's status meaningful or central to one's definition of self. Faunce (1989) referred to this notion as *self-investment*: Different activities or attributes of a person's life take on different levels of significance for the way the person defines his or her value or success in life: "Self-investment is defined as a commitment to achievement with regard to an activity or attribute based on the relevance of that activity or attribute for self-esteem. High self-investment in work, for example, means that occupational achievement in some form is necessary to maintain self-esteem; those with low self-investment can fail in this area with impunity" (pp. 381–

382). Moreover, the more frequently a person is evaluated by others in terms of an activity or attribute, the higher will be the centrality of that activity (such as one's work) or attribute (Dubin, 1956), or in Faunce's terms, if a person is not heavily self-invested in work, the attainment of status at any level will probably have no impact, good or bad, on the person's self-esteem.

Work is a major determinant of status for many of us, although not for all of us (Faunce, 1989). Among those of us for whom work is a central life interest, however, the status systems found related to work at all levels can be critical determinants of our self-esteem. If work is important to us and we fail to achieve sufficient status, we expect the person's self-esteem to suffer, to be frustrated. Work achievement for these people, by the same token, will contribute greatly to their sense of self-worth. However, if a person does not have a high degree of self-investment in work, his success or failure in work-related pursuits may have no impact on his self-esteem. Other areas of his life (such as his family, religion, or leisure accomplishments) may be much more critical for the determination of self-esteem.

GENERAL SUMMARY AND A GLANCE AHEAD

In this chapter, we continued our explicit examination of the human needs for social interaction and of the motivational consequences of those needs and interactions for organizational behavior. Whereas in Chapter 5 we looked at power motivation and the human desires for love and sex as they appear in work settings, in this chapter we explored the human desire for affiliation and for the esteem of others and of one's self. We also explored the ways by which the needs for affiliation and esteem may be aroused and then either satisfied or frustrated by work settings and experiences.

In the following chapter, we turn our attention toward the design of jobs in work organizations, with a particular interest in how job design represents a critical contextual factor (recall Chapter 2) for the generation or frustration of many of the human needs we have been examining in Part Two of this book (Chapters 3 through 6). A strong grasp of the material discussed in Chapter 3 is particularly useful for understanding the material presented in Chapter 7.

Job Design as a Contextual Source of Work Motivation

7

It matters not how strait the gate
How charged with punishments the scroll
I am the master of my fate
I am the captain of my soul.
W. E. Henley

In Chapter 3, we saw that intrinsic motivation consists of energy expended to increase and then to reduce a person's levels of arousal, challenge, and incongruity for the sake of generating feelings of mastery and self-determination. People are viewed as seeking levels of stimulation in their environments that provide degrees of both physiological and psychological arousal that are neither too low nor too high for their personal preferences. In Chapter 6, we studied major elements of the social/gregarious side of human functioning by examining the human needs for self-esteem and many of the social mores associated with work. In this chapter, we build heavily on the theoretical bases provided in Chapters 3 and 6 – particularly Chapter 3 – to explore the design of jobs from the point of view of human work motivation. We will see that the immediate connection between people and the work they actually perform comprises one of the most powerful contextual factors determining work motivation and behavior. The job is right there, often, in many cases, even when we are not officially at work.

OVERVIEW OF THE CHAPTER

The chapter begins with a physiological model of human functioning to assist an understanding of job design. A physiological approach is desirable from a scientific point of view because it permits an objective, quantifiable insight into the impacts of jobs on people, without the necessity of relying on subjective self-report explanations by employees. Contrariwise, there are a variety of difficulties associated with a strictly physiological approach – difficulties that make such an approach difficult to put into managerial practice. Accordingly, we then move through a number of cognitive approaches as well as approaches that attempt to appeal to the human needs for self-determination, self-esteem, and social interaction that, as mentioned, were the foci of previous chapters. We conclude the chapter with a brief study of some relatively new theoretical frameworks for the design of jobs that assume a much broader, systemic understanding of the workplace of the future. So, we begin with activation arousal theory as originally proposed in the organizational scientific literature by Scott (1966) and expanded later by Gardner and Cummings (1988).

ACTIVATION AROUSAL THEORY

The principal thrust of the activation theory approach to job design is that jobs are themselves sources of activation for the people who perform them. *Activation* is ultimately conceptualized as "the degree of excitation of the brain stem reticular formation" (Scott, 1966, p. 11). Certain properties of any stimulus object or setting (such as a job) generate greater levels of activation and arousal. In particular, the intensity, variation and variety, complexity, uncertainty, novelty, and meaningfulness of objects and situations are of special importance. Therefore, a job that has little variety, few component tasks, little novelty, and no uncertainty or unpredictability, will be less activating than a job that features the opposite characteristics. That is, jobs that feature elements of novelty and change, unpredictable requirements, and multiple tasks, other things being equal, should be comparatively quite capable of generating arousal.

Notice that the theory does not suggest that more activation is better. Instead, it suggests that these characteristics of work determine the overall levels of arousal experienced by the employee. But the level of arousal most comfortable for a particular employee is the critical issue. Again, too much stimulation is dissatisfying, as is too little. When an employee encounters a work situation in which the stimulation level is either slightly higher or slightly lower than her preferred level, she will enjoy it. For example, a spontaneous gathering of colleagues in a person's office, followed by an unusually brisk flurry of telephone calls, may be viewed as exciting and pleasurable. By the same token, extreme deviations from a person's optimum arousal level are aversive and instigate efforts to restore normality by either generating or reducing stimulation. Daydreaming, clown play, and kibitzing on the job are common examples of the former, while escape behaviors such as tardiness or malingering are examples of the latter (cf. Noon & Blyton, 2007). Employees can often increase or decrease the stimulation of a job situation by modifying the content or flow of the work itself.

For example, ways of increasing stimulation would include informally trading jobs with other employees, reversing the sequence of certain tasks, or designing new techniques for performing tasks. Alternatively, breaking complex jobs down into constituent elements, or simply postponing or ignoring certain parts of a job, are examples of means of reducing job-related stimulation. The point is that workers can often adjust the level of activation provided by a job or create means of magnifying or reducing the degree of arousal a job provides. As a result of the efforts that a person expends to adjust stimulation levels closer to what is "normal," that person's performance at whatever other tasks he is doing usually suffers. In balance, therefore, the relationship between activation level and task performance is best summarized by an inverted-U, such that performance of a job is compromised when the job is either too dull or too hectic for the person involved (Yerkes and Dodson, 1908).

Individual Differences in Arousal Preference

People differ in at least three separate ways in the amount of stimulation and arousal they prefer (Korman, 1974). First, for a given time of day, some people desire greater stimulation and resultant activation than other people. Students who share housing accommodations with friends who seem perversely "night people" or "morning types" are aware of the fact that people vary considerably among themselves as to when they seek and enjoy stimulation and activity from their surroundings.

Second, a given person varies across the period of a day in the level of stimulation he or she finds desirable. A common pattern is for people to prefer relatively low levels of noise and commotion early in the morning, before a sufficient quantity of caffeine has been ingested. Later in the day, greater levels of excitement are desired until bedtime approaches, when, again, less excitement is preferred. But this pattern is not universal by any means.

A third form of individual difference that pertains to activation arousal theory is a tendency for people to adapt, within limits, to progressively higher or lower levels of stimulation at particular times in a day. Whereas a junior clerk comes to accept relatively little stimulation from his entry-level position, he manages to desire and seek increasing levels of stimulation as he is promoted upward through a series of jobs that involve increasingly higher levels of stimulation, and as a result, higher levels of overall arousal.

In short, people vary a great deal, both from others and within themselves, in terms of their preferred levels of stimulation. These differences are of vital importance in understanding how to use arousal theory to design jobs, but as discussed in the next section, they make formal, precise application of the theory by managers virtually impossible.

The Value of the Optimum Arousal Approach

Although it has proven virtually impossible to empirically validate activation arousal theory[1] because of the necessity for measuring variables in people's central nervous systems and accounting for all the inter-individual and intra-individual factors we have described, the theory provides a number of very simple suggestions for job design. Specifically, this approach suggests that job-related motivation is maximized when the job is neither too complex nor too simple for an employee; therefore, jobs should be designed to feature optimum, balanced levels of complexity, novelty, and stimulation. But applying this advice in practice is far from easy, for a number of reasons.

First, it is not possible for job design specialists (let alone line supervisors) to gain precise measures of either the level of stimulation that a job generates or of the effect that particular objective stimulation levels (even if they could be determined) have on a particular employee. Moreover, the between- and within-person differences in arousal preferences add to the problem: How are managers to appreciate the differences among their employees in their preferred levels of arousal for particular times of the day? Further, how can a job be designed such that it arouses greater activation in the employee at precisely those times of day that match the person's preferences for more or less arousal? Finally, how can a manager accurately measure the changes that occur for particular people in their preferred levels of arousal as they change and adapt to sequences of job assignments, as described earlier? In brief, the precise adoption and application of this approach to job design seems impossible in practice. However, it would be a mistake to discard or ignore it altogether, for several reasons.

One reason is that the optimum arousal approach provides a relatively sound physiological basis for understanding why and how other approaches to job design function as they do. As we show in the following sections, a variety of other general strategies for job design have been advanced, most of which offer concrete detail concerning how jobs should be designed for the purpose of making them intrinsically motivating, but there have been few explanations of *why* their prescriptions can be motivating for employees. Although the optimum arousal approach is not fully consistent with all other approaches, it does provide us with some biological insights into how the design characteristics of jobs may influence people.

A second major value of the optimum arousal approach is that its principles can be kept in mind by managers for their use on an informal day-to-day basis, as both a guide to the assignment of people to jobs and a basis for understanding effective and ineffective job behaviors and attitudes. In other words, although it is impossible for managers to calibrate stimulation and arousal levels precisely (as argued already), it is possible for managers to pay attention, in a less formal fashion, to the differences among their people in the levels of challenge, excitement, and activity they seem to desire. Moreover, it is desirable for managers to fully appreciate the differences among the jobs that

---

[1] The theory was developed inductively by integrating research evidence from other, earlier models of the relationships between stimulation and arousal variables and outcome variables such as performance and satisfaction.

fall under their purview in terms of the types and amounts of challenge, excitement, and activity they entail, especially for an employee newly assigned to perform them.

A third point of value of this theory (one that is related to the second) is that the concepts it provides can be useful both for explaining certain personnel problems after they occur, and/or in preventing problems before they occur. For example, the so-called *Peter principle* (Peter & Hull, 1969) suggests that promotion systems in organizations tend to advance people upward in hierarchies until they are ultimately assigned to jobs at which they are not competent. There is little scientific evidence in support of this proposition, but it does fit the observations of many of us and therefore holds some intuitive appeal. To the extent that the Peter principle has any validity, the mechanisms described in the optimum arousal approach help us understand it. Translated into the terms of the theory, the Peter principle might be paraphrased as follows:

> There is a tendency in many organizations, in which promotions and transfer are based on merit, for employees eventually to be moved into jobs in which the level of physiological and psychological stimulation featured in these jobs is high enough to arouse activation levels that are sufficiently too great in comparison to employees' preferred levels. When this happens, these employees are motivated to reduce activation through avoiding or reducing the net stimulation generated by the job, thereby limiting their effective performance of these jobs.

A related example concerns the use of job transfers as a means of fostering experiential learning for the sake of developing employees so as to prepare them to take over senior-level positions in geographically dispersed organizations. It may be that the stimulation and traumas associated specifically with undergoing a move (see Brett, 1981) can add to the increment in arousal that normally accompanies a job reassignment (such as a promotion) that does not entail geographic mobility, thereby resulting in net levels of activation that are dysfunctional for experiential learning to occur (Pinder & Schroeder, 1987; Pinder & Walter, 1984).

To summarize, the two preceding examples illustrate that a manager need not be a physiological psychologist to benefit from the key concepts provided by Scott's (1966) activation theory approach to job design. As we will see in the following sections, managers who attempt to follow the explicit guidelines of other, more subjective, formal theories of job design will inadvertently be adhering to much of the advice that activation theory would propose. These subjective theories of job design seem easier both to researchers who wish to construct theories without monitoring brain activity and to managers who simply wish to match people and jobs in an enlightened fashion. Accordingly, in the following sections we present the central ideas found in three of the most popular and well understood of these subjective approaches: Herzberg's two-factor theory, Hackman and Oldham's job characteristics model (JCM), and Staw's expectancy theory approach. Less emphasis is placed here on Herzberg's model because it received so much attention in Chapter 2.

TWO-FACTOR THEORY AND THE JOB CHARACTERISTICS MODEL

The motivator-hygiene (or two-factor) theory of work attitudes and motivation was presented and discussed in detail in Chapter 2, where it was argued that the asymmetry posited to exist between the origins of job satisfaction and job dissatisfaction has made the theory very controversial, so much so that it fell into disrepute with many critics decades ago. But it was also argued in Chapter 2 that it is not always necessary to adopt or reject a theory of work motivation holus bolus to be influenced by it; sometimes it is wise to accept certain elements of a theory while reserving judgment on or rejecting other, less defensible elements. This seems to be the case for Herzberg's motivator-hygiene theory. Specifically, it is not necessary to accept Herzberg's notions of the independence and asymmetry of positive and negative job attitudes to accept (and benefit from) the advice provided by the theory for job design.

Herzberg (1966) was among the first industrial psychologists to consider and write explicitly about the notion of human growth needs (recall Chapter 3). Although his theory borrowed somewhat from Maslow (1943; and recall Chapter 3), it was not identical to Maslow's theory and made substantial additions to it. (For example, Herzberg rejected Maslow's notions of hierarchical differences in prepotency among human needs.) The point is that Herzberg's theory argues that jobs must feature a number of characteristics to permit them to arouse and then satisfy growth needs. To repeat in part the discussion of Chapter 2, jobs should permit achievement as well as recognition of that achievement, they should be interesting to perform, they should permit feelings of growth through advancement, and they should provide feelings of responsibility on the part of the employee executing them.

In short, jobs should feature those factors that Herzberg et al. came to call the *motivators*. It is not necessary to assume that the absence or removal of these job characteristics does not result in low job attitudes. But there is some evidence that when jobs are changed so as to build in higher levels of these factors, positive consequences can accrue for both the employee and the organization (Ford, 1973; Paul, Robertson, & Herzberg, 1969). Few of Herzberg's toughest critics denied this.

THE JOB CHARACTERISTICS MODEL

Perhaps the most popular current perspective on job design is one developed by Hackman, Oldham, and their associates. Their approach is similar to Herzberg's insofar as it proposes a set of features that should be built into jobs in order that they be satisfying and motivating, although the two approaches differ somewhat with regard to the specific characteristics of work that make it desirable. The interested reader is referred to the early work of Turner and Lawrence (1965), Hackman and Lawler (1971), and especially to Chapter 3 of Hackman and Oldham's (1980) book. The theory is generally referred to as the *job characteristics model* (JCM).

Elements of the Theory

According to Hackman and Oldham (1980), an employee will experience *internal motivation* (which is taken to mean the same as intrinsic motivation, as discussed in Chapter 3) from a job when the job generates three critical psychological states. First, the employee must feel personal *responsibility* for the outcomes of the job (such as its levels of quantity and quality). Second, the work must be experienced as *meaningful*; that is, the employee must feel that his efforts "count" or matter somehow, to someone. The third critical state is knowledge of the actual results of the person's work efforts. In other words, an employee should be aware of how effective he is in converting his efforts into performance (see our discussion of VIE theory terms in Chapter 12): He should have *feedback* – a knowledge of the results of his efforts. In short, jobs should be designed to generate experiences for the employee of meaningfulness, responsibility, and a knowledge of the results of one's effort.

Notice that Herzberg's model of job design would agree completely with Hackman and Oldham's requirement for feelings of responsibility, and that Herzberg's achievement and advancement for achievement factors are consistent with Hackman and Oldham's suggestion concerning knowledge of results, insofar as knowledge of one's success is necessary for feelings of achievement to occur, and that, in addition, advancement often serves as a formal recognition of positive results. There is thus some degree of consistency between the two approaches with regard to the role of responsibility and knowledge of results in the design of motivating work. The question remains: How can jobs actually be designed to make it possible for employees to experience these three critical psychological states?

Generating Experienced Meaningfulness

For Hackman and Oldham, three specific core factors of jobs are particularly important for making work feel meaningful. The first factor, referred to as *skill variety*, is defined as "the degree to which a job requires a variety of different activities in carrying out the work, involving the use of a number of different skills and talents of the person" (Hackman & Oldham, 1980, p. 78). The need for competence (White, 1959) expresses itself, in part, by behaviors that involve exploring and investigating the environment, as explained earlier in the chapter. One aspect of this searching and exploring entails the use and development of the person's various skills and abilities. Accordingly, Hackman and Oldham proposed that jobs which require the use of multiple talents are experienced as more meaningful, and therefore more intrinsically motivating, than jobs that require the use of only one or two types of skill. Also notice that the exercise of numerous skills would probably result in the stimulation of a greater number of the employee's senses, thereby resulting in higher overall levels of activation and arousal. (See Schwab and Cummings, 1976, for a discussion of the issue of the stimulation of multiple sensory modalities when designing jobs.)

Hence, the inclusion of task variety as an element of job design is consistent with the concept of growth need satisfaction as well as with the more physiological approach taken by activation theory. It is not consistent, however, with Herzberg's approach, which refers to the simple addition of tasks as horizontal job loading or job enlargement (as opposed to job enrichment). This difference between the Hackman–Oldham approach and that of Herzberg is crucial because, as will become evident in the following sections, the addition of varied tasks to a job can be one practical means of generating some of the other key features prescribed by both theories.

A second job characteristic that is seen as contributing to experienced meaningfulness, referred to as *task identity*, is defined as "the degree to which a job requires completion of a 'whole' and identifiable piece of work ... doing a job from beginning to end with a visible outcome" (Hackman & Oldham, 1980, p. 78). Over the years the popular press has paid considerable attention to worker *alienation*, which results from repetitive jobs in which employees perform the same simple operations hundreds or thousands of times every day with only a minimal understanding of how the work they do relates to the "bigger picture." For example, auto assembly workers who install the same three or four parts in the hundreds of partially constructed cars that pass their workstations every month have little understanding of how those few parts fit in with the effective functioning of the completed vehicle. Work is experienced as more meaningful, according to Hackman and Oldham, when employees are capable of gaining a greater understanding of how their jobs fit in with those of other employees and with the effective functioning of the completed vehicle. For example, the famous curvilinear assembly lines used in Scandinavian auto assembly plants are designed, in part, to permit employees to participate in much larger subsections of finished automobiles than is possible in conventional straight-line assembly plants in North America (Gyllenhammar, 1977).

How does the notion of task identity fit with the other viewpoints presented here? On the surface, simply providing task identity does not seem particularly relevant for the satisfaction of the major growth needs we have examined. By the same token, insofar as stimulus complexity and meaningfulness determine the stimulating capacity of objects and events (Fiske & Maddi, 1961; Scott, 1966), a job with task identity should be more stimulating from the point of view of activation theory. Finally, Herzberg's approach would probably admit that task identity contributes to the motivator factor referred to as *interesting work*.

The third factor that makes work more meaningful, referred to as *task significance*, is defined as "the degree to which the job has a substantial impact on the lives of other people, whether those people are in the immediate organization or in the world at large" (Hackman & Oldham, 1980, p. 79). For example, munitions employees during World War II worked long, hard hours in miserable production plants, maintaining high levels of motivation and morale because of the important contribution they knew they were making to the war effort (Turner & Miclette, 1962). The *task significance* component of Hackman and Oldham's experienced meaningfulness concept is harder to relate to other job design approaches than are the skill variety and task identity components, with the possible exception that performing work perceived as significant might contribute to the satisfaction of esteem needs (both the need for the esteem of others and for a positive regard of one's self). Grant (2007) has recently proposed a number of methods by which jobs can be designed to enhance the beneficial effects their work can have on the quality of the lives of the beneficiaries of their work.

In summary, Hackman and Oldham's (1980) theory suggests that experienced meaningfulness is important for a job to arouse intrinsic motivation and that it, in turn, requires that the work be integrated, important, and demanding of the use of multiple skills and abilities.

Generating Experienced Responsibility

Whereas three core job factors are seen as contributing to feelings of meaningfulness, only one factor – autonomy – is required for an employee to experience the psychological feeling of responsibility. *Autonomy* is defined as "the degree to which the job provides substantial freedom, independence, and discretion to the individual in scheduling the work and in determining the procedures to be used in carrying it out" (Hackman & Oldham, 1980, p. 79). Autonomy and responsibility have long been recognized as important facets of employee motivation and satisfaction. They are explicitly recognized in Herzberg's two-factor theory (see Chapter 2), McClelland's (1961) theory of achievement, and de Charms' (1968) thinking about pawns and origins (recall our earlier discussion). Moreover, autonomy was treated as a separate category of higher-order need by Porter (1962, 1963) in his early adaptation of Maslow's need hierarchy for studying managerial job attitudes. From the point of view of activation theory, it is reasonable to assume that people who are responsible for their own job outcomes will be more fully activated than people who share with others responsibility for success or failure on the job. Hackman and Oldham's suggestion that autonomy (and the responsibility feelings it fosters) is motivating is quite consistent with the other perspectives and approaches we have considered.

Generating Knowledge of Results

The third critical psychological factor in Hackman and Oldham's model is referred to as *knowledge of results*. They see two basic types of feedback as the essential determinants of the degree to which an employee understands how well he is doing on the job. The first type of feedback comes from the job itself, such as that which occurs when a worker assembles an alarm clock and tests it to see whether she has put it together properly. The second type comes from other people, such as one's superior, who informs the worker how well he is doing on the job. Hackman and Oldham recognize the role that both forms of feedback can have for providing knowledge of results, but stress the importance of designing jobs so that they regularly provide the former type, feedback from the job.

Why would we expect that feedback from the job itself would be more motivating than feedback mediated by other people, such as one's supervisor? One reason is that when the feedback comes from the person's own observation of how well she is doing, it often comes immediately after the employee has done the work. Second, this form of feedback is not as susceptible to the interference that can result from a variety of social-psychological processes, such as those that have to do with the perceived credibility of the source of the message or the relative power of the sender of the message. In short, feedback from the task itself is simple, direct, and impersonal, and seems to be a more powerful means of providing motivating information than is feedback from outside sources (Ilgen, Fisher, & Taylor, 1979; Ivancevich & McMahon, 1982).

The importance of feedback for intrinsic motivation is recognized explicitly in Deci's cognitive evaluation theory (Chapter 3), in which it was seen as critical for either enhancing or reducing a person's feelings of competence and subsequently the person's level of intrinsic motivation, or alternatively, affecting the person's locus of causality and subsequent intrinsic motivation. Similarly, a strong desire for task-related feedback is one of the most important traits displayed by males who are high in achievement motivation (McClelland, 1961). Feedback can clearly affect a person's level of self-esteem as well, depending on whether it is favorable or unfavorable. Feedback to a person about her goal accomplishment (or failure) is a key feature of both goal-setting theory and control theory, as we will see in Chapter 11. Finally, from the perspective of activation theory, feedback from a task may contribute to both the complexity and novelty of that task for the individual. A full summary of the critical-psychological states as well as the major core factors seen as producing them is illustrated in Figure 7.1.

Measuring the Dimensions of JCM

Hackman and Oldham developed an instrument called the job diagnostic survey (JDS), which is used to assess what they refer to as the overall motivating potential score for a particular job.

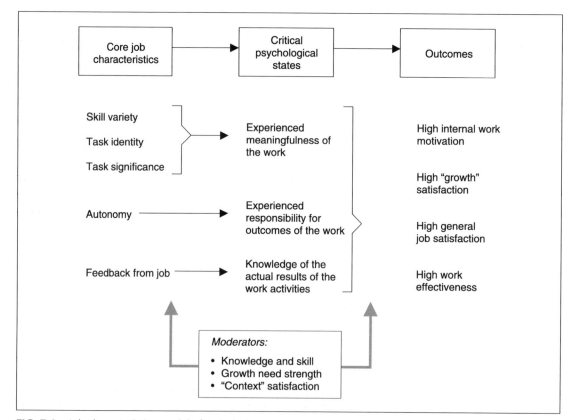

FIG. 7.1   Job characteristics model of task design.

Source: Hackman, J. R., & Oldham, G. R. (1980). *Work redesign* (Figure 4.6, p. 90), © 1980. Reprinted with permission of Pearson Education Inc., Upper Saddle River, New Jersey.

Perceptions of the job incumbent are used to calculate the amount of skill variety, task identity, task significance, autonomy, and feedback found in a job. When combined, scores on these dimensions enable a job analyst to assess the degree to which a job may be capable of arousing intrinsic motivation for particular individuals. Detail concerning the content and psychometric properties of the JDS is beyond the scope of this book. The interested reader is referred to Hackman and Oldham (1975, 1976, 1980) and Hackman, Oldham, Janson, and Purdy (1975) for more detail on the development of the theory and the instrument, and to Aldag, Barr, and Brief (1981) for a positive assessment of the JDS itself.

Research Evidence on the JCM

Drawing on some of their own work as well as that of other researchers, Parker, Wall, and Cordery (2001, p. 415) reached two conclusions about the scientific validity of the Hackman–Oldham model:

1. The collective efforts of the core characteristics on affective responses (satisfaction and motivation) have been largely supported, but those for behavior (i.e., work performance, turnover, and absence) less consistently so (Parker & Wall, 1998).
2. The more particular features of the model remain unproven. For example, the specified links between job characteristics and the critical psychological states have not been confirmed (Johns, Xie, & Fang, 1992), and the job characteristics have not always been found to be separable aspects of jobs (Cordery & Sevastos, 1993).

EXPECTANCY THEORY AND THE JOB CHARACTERISTICS APPROACH

More than three decades ago, Staw (1976) proposed a model for job (re)design that applies a formulation of VIE theory[2] that had previously been proposed by House (1971) and House and Mitchell (1974). In essence this model explicitly recognizes the fact that overall work motivation can be determined by both intrinsic and extrinsic factors. More important, the model delineates the separate effects of two specific types of intrinsic motivation: (1) that which is associated with simply doing a job, and (2) that which is associated with effective achievement of the job. Specifically, the House et al. (1974) expectancy model can be represented as follows:

$$M = IV_a + (P_1)(IV_b) + \Sigma (P_{2i})(EV_i)$$

where

M = total task motivation
IV_a = intrinsic valence associated with task behavior
IV_b = intrinsic valences associated with task accomplishment
EV_i = extrinsic valences associated with outcomes for task accomplishment
P_1 = perceived probability that one's behavior will lead to task accomplishment
P_2 = perceived probability that one's task accomplishment will lead to extrinsically valent outcomes

---

[2] The reader is referred to Chapter 12 for a complete treatment of this theory of work motivation.

A number of features of this model deserve highlighting. First, the reader is reminded of the crucial distinction between valence and importance: It is the expectation of the satisfaction associated with an outcome that attracts a person to engage in a task. Second, the strength of the valence associated with task behavior for a person (IV_a) rests largely with the strength of the person's need for competence. It consists of the enjoyment that people anticipate receiving from merely attempting a task, regardless of how successful they expect to be at it. The reader is reminded of Murray's (1938) belief (see Chapter 3) that satisfaction consists of pleasure of the process of reducing need-related tension, in addition to the pleasure of the feeling that one has once the need has been satisfied. The first component of the House et al. model is consistent with the element of satisfaction.

Furthermore, the strength of the intrinsic valence associated with task accomplishment (IV_b) is determined largely by the strength of the person's need for achievement. Therefore, the net force attributed to the achievement component of the model is seen as being determined by the mechanisms described in the discussion earlier in the chapter: Overall achievement-oriented motivation is determined largely by the person's *perception* of the probability of task success. Tasks that are anticipated to be either too easy or too difficult arouse little achievement motivation, because the intrinsic thrill of mastering an easy goal is small, whereas difficult goals are judged to be unattainable, thereby discouraging a person from attempting them. In short, the achievement-related component of the Staw–House et al. model requires consideration of both the anticipated probability of success and the anticipated thrill from succeeding. Moreover, because of the inverse relationship between perceived probability of task success and this form of valence, the net motivational force associated with achievement outcomes will be maximized when the person perceives the odds of success as moderate.

The final component in the equation consists of the person's *expected value* from various extrinsic outcomes that might be available. It is determined by the strength of her belief (or perceived probability, P) that performance, if it occurs, will result in outcomes such as pay, recognition, promotion opportunities, discredit with coworkers, and so on. Valence is the expected level of satisfaction or dissatisfaction with each of the extrinsic outcomes. As described by the formula, the perceived probabilities are multiplied in the person's mind by the expected levels of satisfaction or dissatisfaction and the mathematical products summed across the various outcomes that the person considers relevant. We explore the intricacies of these types of motivation model in greater depth in Chapter 12.

Independence of the Intrinsic Components

As presented here, the model implicitly assumes that the two forms of intrinsic motivation are independent of one another. For example, it suggests that a person could continue to expect to derive pleasure from engaging in a task even if he constantly fails at it. Hall's theory of career success experiences (Hall, 1976) and the impact they can have on feelings of competence and self-esteem suggests that this may not in fact be the case (see also Bandura, 1982). Instead, Hall suggested, repeated success experiences at a task may, up to a certain limit, serve to increase a person's attraction for a task, whereas continual failures eventually reduce the person's affinity for it. Nevertheless, Staw's adaptation of the House et al. (1974) expectancy theory to job design provides a theoretical rationale for a number of prescriptions for the design of work.

Design Implications from the Expectancy Model

The equation just examined suggests that overall task motivation can be influenced if a job is designed to affect the intrinsic valence of doing it, the intrinsic valence associated with succeeding at it, and the person's perceptions of her chances of succeeding. Specifically, the equation suggests that jobs featuring a variety of tasks, jobs that are not overly routine, and jobs that require the employee to interact a great deal with others will, *ceteris paribus*, have a greater likelihood of appealing to employee needs for competence: That is, they will foster relatively high levels of the intrinsic valence associated with doing the task. In other terms, such tasks will tend to be comparatively enjoyable, and satisfaction will result from the very act of doing them and reducing the tension associated with the need for competence.

The model also suggests that the valence associated with success at a job will be comparatively high when the person sees it as comparatively high in Hackman and Oldham's (1980) task identity and task significance dimensions and when the person expects that he will be largely responsible for his success or failure at the job. In other words, a person will expect a greater thrill from accomplishing a job goal when he believes that his efforts (as opposed to luck or the efforts of other people) determine success or failure and when he is able to see how his accomplishments fit into the larger picture and are of value to the organization or to someone associated with it. Intuitively, this argument makes sense. But recall that net achievement-oriented motivation also depends heavily on the person's judgments about whether he will be able to perform the task. The equation illustrates that a host of factors in the job itself, or in the context of the job, can serve to influence the employee's views about his ability to perform it. The interactive nature of the valence associated with achievement (IV_b) and the perceived probability of achievement (P_1) in determining the individual's overall achievement-oriented motivation are the remaining elements of the model, as summarized in the equation presented above.

INDIVIDUAL DIFFERENCES AND JOB ENRICHMENT

We know that people differ considerably in terms of the strength of their growth needs – the learned needs that, when aroused, account for what is called intrinsic motivation. In addition, in an earlier section we discussed the complexity of the differences, both between people and within a single person, in terms of the levels of stimulation desired from the environment (including jobs). To the extent, therefore, that individual differences exist in the strength of the needs and preferences that people have for the outcomes that job enrichment can provide, it should follow that enriched jobs will be more attractive to (and more highly motivating for) some people than to others. In other words, we would logically expect considerable individual differences between people in their attitudinal and behavioral reactions to enriched work. In fact, many theories of job design explicitly recognize the fact that many people view their jobs as secondary sources of need satisfaction and simply do not wish to work in jobs that feature high levels of challenge and responsibility. Let's take a brief look at the role attributed to individual differences in the theories discussed so far.

Herzberg has often been criticized for ignoring the role of individual differences in the motivation styles that people display, although later statements of his theory readily acknowledge that certain people are abnormally preoccupied with the satisfaction of hygiene needs, for various reasons (see Herzberg, 1976; see also Chapter 2). Similarly, early research reported by Turner and Lawrence (1965) on the motivational characteristics of jobs suggested that employees from rural backgrounds respond much more positively and favorably to job enrichment than do employees with urban backgrounds. The work of Hackman and Lawler (1971) followed directly from that of Turner and Lawrence, although Hackman and Lawler attempted to measure the strength of the growth needs of each person in their study, reasoning that a more precise prediction of the effect of job enrichment could be gained by considering individual need states rather than a person's general sociological-geographic background. Their reasoning made logical sense and their empirical results provided support. There were higher correlations between the existence of enriched job characteristics and outcomes such as intrinsic motivation, job satisfaction, and attendance among employees with high growth need strength than among employees who were low in growth needs. Later studies by Wanous (1974), Brief and Aldag (1975), and Giles (1977) supported Hackman and Lawler's conclusions, and the model forwarded by Hackman and Oldham (1980, described earlier) includes provisions for assessing the strength of employee needs for growth before implementing changes in their jobs (Hackman & Oldham, 1980, p. 118).

But as is often the case, the matter is not so simple. A review of the evidence by White (1978a) concluded that the majority of studies in which employee responses to job design were found to depend on employee traits of some form or another failed to hold up in replication studies. That is, sometimes a particular variable (such as the strength of employee growth needs) determined the effect of job characteristics on work outcomes, but sometimes those same variables failed to make any difference. White (1978a) concluded that individual difference factors that influence the impact of worker responses to job characteristics are situation specific. In other words, certain variables may be important in some situations, whereas other variables may be important in other situations, where jobs are designed to be enriched. A separate review of the evidence by Pierce and Dunham (1976) reached essentially the same conclusion. White added strength to his argument by showing in a vast study of his own (White, 1978b) that not one of 73 individual variables that he investigated consistently affected the impact of job characteristics on employee responses.

Other researchers, including Dunham (1977) and Sims and Szilagyi (1976), attempted to show that organizational factors (as opposed to individual factors) may determine whether job enrichment has positive consequences for employees. Still, the results are very inconsistent and inconclusive. It may be that the most accurate and most practical way of predicting whether job enrichment will have a positive benefit for a particular person is simply to ask the person, as Cherrington and England (1980) once did, how much he desires enriched work, rather than relying on less direct predictors such as work values or need states. There is abundant evidence that not everybody desires to work at jobs that feature the enriching characteristics proposed by the theories described in this chapter. But it is still very difficult to predict which categories of people will or will not benefit from and enjoy job enrichment. Surrogate measures such as assessments of individual needs and personality traits are unreliable predictors, although simply asking the people involved directly about their desire for job enrichment may be useful.

PRACTICAL ISSUES IN JOB DESIGN FOR ENRICHMENT

Now that a number of theoretical approaches to job design have been discussed, there are a variety of practical issues that deserve attention, issues that are important for understanding how job enrichment can be applied to real settings, as well as in explaining some of the successes and failures that job enrichment has had in the field.

Where might Enrichment be Attempted?

A number of clues, most of which can be gathered from documents such as union contracts, personnel manuals, organization charts, and organizational folklore, can sometimes help to identify situations in which job enrichment may be of value (Drake, 1974).

Repetition of functions

If an operation is performed at one point in a workflow and repeated by someone else later in the same flow, it may be that the two jobs involved are not sufficiently different to justify their separation into two jobs. Perhaps the jobs can be combined into a single job that features more stimulation, variety, meaningfulness, and feedback than is possible in either of the separate jobs.

Unusual reporting relationships

People whose jobs require them to report to more than one supervisor will encounter role conflict and probably not enjoy as much autonomy as they might otherwise experience from their jobs. By the same token, a high frequency of one-to-one reporting relationships may suggest that many employees are expected to perform the menial and unmotivating tasks that are neglected or discarded from the jobs of their superiors.

Layering

Some organizations feature multiple levels of authority among jobs in which the work performed is basically identical. For example, allowing low-level employees to provide refunds to customers up to a certain maximum amount, and requiring successively higher amounts to be passed upward in the organization's structure, limits the potential for employee feelings of responsibility, autonomy, and to a lesser extent, knowledge of results. Similar-sounding job titles, such as junior file clerk, intermediate file clerk, file clerk, and senior file clerk, may signal the existence of layered functions that might be rearranged for the sake of job enrichment.

Super-gurus and troubleshooters

The smooth functioning of many work settings often relies heavily on the existence of a small number of gurus, who seem to know virtually everything about the company, its customers and suppliers, and all other aspects of the operation. Such people are, of course, very important and usually very powerful as a consequence of their wisdom. Moreover, they are often quite jealous about their roles and unwilling to share their knowledge. But their monopoly often robs other employees of responsibility, meaningfulness, and autonomy in the work they perform, while leaving the organization as a whole vulnerable to their departure.

Special checking or inspection jobs

Investigation may show that special inspections are unnecessary. Permitting employees to check the quality of their work adds potential task meaningfulness, autonomy, and knowledge of results to their jobs.

Excessive number of job titles

Drake (1974) suggested that if the ratio of people to job titles in a work setting is not at least 5:1, it may be the case that the work is too fractionated and that enrichment may be appropriate.

Pools

Drake (1974) also suggested that the existence of pools of people performing similar work, such as typing, keypunching,[3] or word processing, is a signal that certain people in the organization are casting off the routine (and boring) parts of their jobs onto other people. Conversely, operators in such a pool may receive more variety and task identity than do operators who work for only one or a few persons.

---

[3] Although keypunching is now obsolete, the general principle behind Drake's (1974) example is worth considering.

Liaison personnel

Highly differentiated organizations often require special people to coordinate and integrate activities that involve more than one group (Lawrence & Lorsch, 1969). Whereas entrusting such special functions to particular people may facilitate integration, it may also impoverish the motivational potential of those jobs being integrated, depriving them of task significance, task identity, and skill variety.

Existence of several jobs requiring the same equipment

Duplications of equipment use suggest that the work being done on these jobs is too highly special-ized and fractionated. Is it possible that a single job (with many incumbents) might be created that combines all the tasks that were previously assigned to many different jobs, thereby providing potential for higher levels of skill variety and task identity?

There are a variety of characteristics of organizational structure that may suggest places in which jobs might benefit from enrichment and/or restructuring. After noting such clues, the inter-ested manager would have to proceed to investigate more thoroughly the potential for and feasibility of job redesign. Some aspects of this feasibility assessment are the topic of the next section.

Implementing Job Enrichment

Two of the leading proponents and developers of the theory and practice of job enrichment recog-nized from the outset that taking the theory and putting it into effective practice can be very difficult because of the constraints that are often encountered in real organizational settings (Hackman & Oldham, 1980). Changes in job design cannot usually be implemented without changes in (or at least accommodation to) other elements of the organization and its various programs and procedures. In fact, many early failures of job redesign programs can be blamed on failure to recognize these other organizational considerations.

Obstacles in Implementation

What, then, should be attended to in addition to the diagnosis of jobs and people for the sake of installing job enrichment successfully? Oldham and Hackman (1980) identified a number of constraints to the effective installation of such programs, including the following:

1. The technological system (i.e., the basic nature of the production or work process) can drastically curtail the degree to which jobs can feasibly be enriched. The assembly line is a classic example of such a technology. Any type of work process that depends heavily on the use of particular machinery will typically be very expensive to modify, perhaps prohibitively so (see Anderson, 1970a).
2. Personnel systems, such as job analysis and the development of more or less rigid job descrip-tions, which are often enshrined in labor management collective agreements, can limit the feasibil-ity of job enrichment. Enriching jobs means changing jobs, and seldom only one or two at a time. Tradition, bureaucratization, and formal agreements can make this sort of change very difficult.
3. Control systems (such as budgetary and accounting systems or production and quality control reporting systems) can also impede job redesign efforts because by nature they are often designed to limit individual discretion, autonomy, and flexibility. Groups that traditionally have been responsible for these control functions are often quite resistant to giving them up. Training programs must be available that can permit whatever levels of effort are induced by the enriched

work to result in useful performance. Otherwise, the motivated effort created by the work will be frustrated and result in employee frustration (see Chapter 8).

4. Career development practices must also be appropriate. For example, we noted earlier that job enrichment may not be appropriate for all employees; some people neither want nor are capable of handling the challenge and responsibility that enrichment entails. Without career development strategies (such as transfers or reassignments) to accommodate or deal effectively with employees unsuited for job enrichment, frustration, job dissatisfaction, and resentment can be expected and one can anticipate limited benefit from job enrichment programs.

5. The levels of pay and the methods of payment are also important. Equity theory (see Chapter 11) would predict that increased levels of pay would be expected by employees who perceive the increases in responsibility that result from enrichment to constitute additional inputs they must make to their jobs. Alternatively, employees who perceive enrichment as resulting in greater satisfaction (or in greater outcomes) may not make such pay demands. One practitioner with considerable experience in job enrichment has suggested that if the redesign of jobs is done properly, employees do not necessarily demand more money for the responsibility added to their position. In fact, he notes that most job evaluation programs in organizations are designed to deal easily with the added levels of responsibility and skill levels that can result from enrichment, should the issues be raised (Caulkins, 1974). Nevertheless, very little research has been directed toward the issue of pay-level implications of job enrichment, although there is some theoretical basis to worry that the form of payment is important. Recall from our earlier discussion that Deci's (1975) cognitive evaluation theory claimed that contingently paid money (as in piece-rate pay plans) may, in some circumstances, undermine intrinsic motivation, the very goal sought by enrichment programs. Finally, whether the pay is distributed on an individual, group, or organization-wide basis must be compatible with the means by which the work is accomplished (i.e., by individuals, by groups, or by overall organizational performance).

Similarly, Sirota and Wolfson (1972) noted other obstacles to the installation and success of job enrichment. While these other factors are a bit more subtle than those noted by Oldham and Hackman, they are no less critical. For example, it is often very difficult to overcome the longstanding biases and beliefs held by many managers concerning the virtues of job design according to the classical principle of previous times (see Massie, 1965). But even when traditional beliefs are challenged successfully, it is still necessary to educate managers in the theory and techniques of job enrichment so that they can provide the types and amounts of support that are necessary for success.

Many managers who have considered job enrichment for their organizations have expected to see real returns on the financial investments involved in unrealistically short periods of time. Demanding evidence of return on investment is fine, but the payoffs that are possible (although not guaranteed) from enrichment interventions seldom appear immediately. Moreover, an honest "sales job" by someone proposing that an organization venture into job enrichment cannot *promise* meaningful return on investment, whether in the long or the short run. Such promises simply are not well founded, especially today, after so many attempts have been observed to fail. It is no wonder that many managers concerned with costs and profitability are skeptical about allowing enrichment changes in their organizations. To make matters worse, unless top management is at least somewhat enthusiastic, any new enrichment attempt is bound to fail – a sort of self-fulfilling prophesy of disaster. This has been the experience with the implementation of management by objectives programs as well, as we will see in Chapter 13.

Another barrier to effective installation of job enrichment can be generalized fear of the unknown among those who will be affected most heavily, especially middle managers, who often expect that such programs will undermine their authority and possibly make them redundant. ("If I give away all my power to my subordinates, what need will there be for me in this organization?") There is also a natural tendency on the part of many managers to accept the idea of enrichment in abstract terms but to deny that it might be feasible, or even necessary, in their organizations. Sirota and Wolfson (1972) also noted a tendency among many enrichment specialists to be dogmatic in the techniques they employ either to diagnose or to install enrichment strategies. There are many cases where the particular problems facing an organization require eclecticism on the part of the interventionist (Sandler, 1974), but successful applications brought about by a method often encourage continued use of that method alone.

Unions and job enrichment

There is at least one other set of factors that can influence the effective installation of job redesign: Labor unions and the collective bargaining process. Although the majority of formal job enrichment programs have been conducted in nonunion settings or among only the nonunion personnel in organizations where unions are represented (Schlesinger & Walton, 1976), there have been a number of instances where formal enrichment has been attempted in the midst of unionized settings. It would be an oversimplification to say that labor unions have a typical or unitary attitude about such programs (Donahue, 1982), but there are a number of issues that normally must be dealt with when a union is involved.

First, it is often the case that union leaders are wary about job enrichment (and other formal programs aimed at improving the quality of work life). This wariness comes from the concern that their own positions may be undermined. That is, to the extent that the enrichment design entails greater responsibility and autonomy for dealing with job-related problems, union stewards may fear that their traditional role as representatives of the rank and file may be diminished. A second common concern for labor officials is that the union membership may perceive any joint union–management cooperation over the planning and installation of enrichment with suspicion that they are "in bed" with management.

Unions are often suspicious that programs such as job enrichment are simply newfangled methods of "speed up" designed primarily to extract higher levels of productivity per hour of labor. Often, this sort of suspicion has been well founded. Unions may accept managerial prerogatives to redesign work so as to make more efficient use of capital equipment and other resources, but they rarely agree to programs they perceive as designed primarily to increase productivity through exploitation of their membership (Schlesinger & Walton, 1976). But perhaps the biggest difficulty in installing programs such as job enrichment successfully in unionized settings is the fact that by its very nature (in North America, at least), the labor–management relationship is adversarial rather than cooperative – hardly the sort of relationship to foster collaboration and joint decision making (Ephlin, 1973).

It is commonplace to argue that organizations are systems and that change in certain of their parts necessitates change in other parts (e.g., Katz & Kahn, 1978). Oldham and Hackman (1980) and Sirota and Wolfson (1972) have provided specific illustrations of the meaning of this concept: Job enrichment cannot be implemented effectively without regard to various subsystems in the organization's structure, policies, and practices. Pursuant to the discussion presented in Chapter 2, it is, unfortunately, the case that the precise nature of the interdependencies among new managerial techniques (such as job enrichment) and other organizational considerations are not appreciated until a significant number of costly and disappointing failures are experienced. This raises the question of the validity of the theory (or theories) of job enrichment and of their "track records" in applied organizational settings.

VALIDITY AND VALUE OF JOB ENRICHMENT

In Chapter 2, the twin issues of validity and applied utility were introduced as they relate to theories and techniques from behavioral science. It is timely now to inquire into the scientific validity and applied utility of the predominant approaches to job enrichment. Just how good are they? Sadly, there is no simple answer to this question, although there are a variety of answers pertaining to the different approaches that are available. First, the author is not aware of any empirical tests or applied applications of the Staw–House et al. model presented earlier, although there are myriad tests of various expectancy theories, if not the precise one underlying Staw's model. The reader is referred to Chapter 12 for a summary of the evidence concerning expectancy (or VIE) theory.

Similarly, there are no specific empirical tests of the activation/arousal theory approach to job design per se, with the possible exception of a study reported by Standing (1973), who found that steel mill inspectors who were particularly high or low on a measure of cognitive complexity (which may be a surrogate measure for preferred activation levels) were more satisfied with various aspects of their jobs than were inspectors (performing virtually the same job as the others) who attained moderate scores on the cognitive complexity scale. More direct tests of Scott's theory have not been conducted, in large measure because of the obvious difficulties involved in operationalizing it.

The bulk of the research and applied evidence is old, and it pertains mostly to Herzberg's approach and the job characteristics model of Hackman, Oldham, and their colleagues. A complete study-by-study review of the evidence is beyond the scope of this chapter, but a brief summary of the evidence is appropriate here. The interested reader is referred to the following sources for more detail: Cummings, Molloy, and Glen (1977); Davis and Taylor (1979); Fein (1974); Gyllenhammar (1977); Hackman (1977); Hackman and Oldham (1980); Luthans and Reif (1974); and Yorks (1979).[4]

Before the mid-1970s, the majority of job enrichment programs attempted in North America were based on Herzberg's motivator-hygiene theory or on some variant of the socio-technical approach of Davis and his colleagues (see Davis and Taylor, 1979; Kelly, 1978). The early literature reported these projects as generally quite positive and encouraging (e.g., Ford, 1973; Paul, Robertson, & Herzberg, 1969), although it is probable that most of the failures and disappointments were less likely to be reported. Nevertheless, Herzberg-inspired job enrichment programs have enjoyed a reasonable track record, despite the limited and/or unknown validity of the theory behind them (recall Chapter 2). As stressed earlier, the concept of asymmetry between what Herzberg calls motivators and hygiene factors is less important for the practical purposes of job redesign than the fact that jobs which feature the motivators seem to result in more favorable consequences than those that do not. Since the mid-1970s, new theories, such as the job characteristics model, described earlier, have emerged and have influenced organizational development via job enrichment.

How valid is JCM? As has been the case so many times in this book, the best answer to this question is that the scientific validity of this theoretical model is unknown, despite the considerable amount of research that lies behind it. Why? Much of the research that attempted to study the theory's validity was flawed in either design or execution (Arnold & House, 1980; Roberts & Glick, 1981). For example, the theory holds that *changing* jobs so as to build in higher levels of the core factors (task identity, skill variety, etc.), will result in increases in intrinsic motivation and job satisfaction and reductions in employee withdrawal behavior such as absenteeism. Yet the majority of the research pertaining to the theory has not, in fact, shown that changes in job design at one time result in changes of the sort predicted later. Instead, most studies have been synchronous, or cross-sectional, meaning that measures of job characteristics have been gathered and correlated with measures of employee reactions that were gathered at the same time. Thus, although the evidence based on data of this sort has revealed encouraging simultaneous associations between the strength of the core factors and favorable employee reactions, it cannot itself support the type of causal claims made by the theory.

In addition, the research has featured a number of other shortcomings which collectively reduce

---

[4] The reader should note that these empirical assessments of job enrichment are old, many being published approximately three decades ago. This is another indication that scientific interest in job enrichment has declined sharply since the publication of Hackman and Oldham's (1980) major book.

the conclusiveness of the findings and leave uncertainty about the actual validity of the job characteristics approach. Nevertheless, theories often gain popularity, even hegemony, despite weakness in the research on which they are based (Bourgeois & Pinder, 1984), and it is important to remember that failure to support a theory of this sort unequivocally does not necessarily imply that it is wrong. Hackman, Oldham, and their colleagues have made a contribution, and time and further research will reveal how valuable that contribution is.

Putative Benefits of Job Enrichment

It was stated earlier that the most important goal of job enrichment is to increase and sustain intrinsic motivation among employees. Presumably, higher levels of intrinsic motivation will be accompanied by higher levels of performance and job satisfaction as well as reduced levels of withdrawal such as absenteeism and turnover. What is the evidence in this regard? Does job enrichment deliver the sorts of benefits that it was hoped it might deliver?

With some exceptions, the research that might have provided an answer to this question has not been as well conducted as one might have hoped. It is very difficult to establish sufficient experimental control in real organizational settings to permit either a researcher or a manager to rule out all possible explanations for observed changes in employee behavior when an experiment has been attempted. Moreover, as suggested earlier, there is more chance that we will see and hear about the supposed successes than about applications of job enrichment that have failed. These considerations aside, what evidence there is on the matter suggests that job enrichment is probably much more useful for influencing employee attitudes than it is for improving performance levels (e.g., Orpen, 1979). Thus, enriched work may contribute to organizational effectiveness indirectly through the impact it has on the consequences of healthy work attitudes much more than directly through increases in employee productivity per se (Dowling, 1973).

Although research into the matter has tended to be of questionable quality (Griffin, Welsh, & Moorehead, 1981), positive changes in work attitudes do not usually seem to be accompanied by increases in productivity as a consequence of job enrichment. There may be a number of reasons for this, but two seem most plausible. First, the reader is reminded of the tenuous relationship that exists between beliefs, attitudes, intentions, and behaviors (see Chapter 9). Changing jobs so as to change employee perceptions of task characteristics (as proposed by Herzberg, Staw, Hackman, and Oldham) can be expected to have only very indirect impact on employee effort levels, because beliefs must be positively evaluated and then converted into specific intentions to act. As we will see in Chapter 9, for any given person, some beliefs about particular stimulus objects will be positive, whereas others will be negative. In the case of job redesign attempts, this means that employees may perceive many things about enriched jobs, some desirable, some adverse. Presumably, it was hoped that individual differences in growth need strength would be important; people high in these needs were assumed to assess their beliefs about enriched jobs favorably. But models such as that of Hackman and Oldham (1980) fail to take into account the possibility that employees will hold beliefs about enriched jobs other than those pertaining only to their capacity to satisfy growth needs. As a result, it may be that not all beliefs that are generated by enriched work are evaluated positively. Consequently, there is a diminished likelihood that net perceptions of enriched work will lead to the types of intention that are necessary to instigate the sort of behavior that is required for higher levels of performance. In short, any model that tries to build predictive bridges between employee beliefs and employee behaviors overlooks the important intermediary roles of attitudes and intentions (Fishbein & Ajzen, 1975) and will result in only limited predictive effectiveness.

A second reason why enrichment may not easily result in increases in job performance has to do with the fact that many factors can operate to dampen the conversion of employee effort (even if it is increased by enrichment) into performance. A number of the specific impediments that can interfere with enrichment programs have been identified already. In conclusion, one can argue that increased job satisfaction and possibly reduced levels of withdrawal may be the major benefits that are potentially attainable from enrichment efforts; and that these positive benefits seem attainable without accompanying cost in productivity to management (e.g., Dowling, 1973). Accordingly, one might argue that job enrichment is a desirable strategy for management to adopt. But there remains too little solid evidence to claim that enrichment results in higher levels of effort of job performance per se.

CRITICISMS OF JOB ENRICHMENT

We have argued that a healthy skepticism must accompany any assessment of the success of job enrichment, because of the difficulties that researchers and managers naturally encounter when trying to gain the sort of rigorous experimental control that is necessary to demonstrate that observed changes in employee attitudes and behavior can be attributed to enrichment attempts. In addition to this set of criticisms, however, a number of others have been aimed at job enrichment in general, based on a variety of considerations of a nonscientific nature. One of these has to do with the problem of individual differences as we discussed them earlier in the chapter. Briefly, the argument is that job enrichment is not for everyone: Some workers would much prefer increases in pay or job security, better working conditions (Fein, 1974), or more social interaction (Reif & Luthans, 1972) from their jobs rather than the more amorphous things attributed to job enrichment.

Further, Katz (1977, 1978, 1980) has argued that some people will benefit from enrichment much more at some stages in their careers than they will at others. For example, newcomers to a job setting will be oriented primarily toward establishing social ties that will assist them in becoming established and making sense of their new surroundings, whereas employees who have been at their jobs for long periods of time will be oriented toward pay, security, and other factors that Herzberg would refer to as satisfying hygiene needs. For Katz, only those employees who have been established in their jobs for moderate periods of time will be likely to benefit from the potential outcomes offered by enrichment.

Another criticism concerns the application of job enrichment, the argument being that this technique has been treated as only one of a series of programs distilled from behavioral science for application to management problems as a sort of panacea (Hackman, 1975; Pinder, 1977, 1978, 1982, 1984). When this occurs, management groups are prone and/or susceptible to adopting job enrichment without first establishing that the problems being addressed, if any, are the sorts of problems for which the technique might be appropriate.

Finally, some critics have suggested that job enrichment is doomed to failure as a means of really increasing the quality of working life because like most or all other management techniques, it takes as given the very socioeconomic conditions that give rise to organizational problems for human beings – the nature of the fundamental means of ownership and distribution of wealth. This radical attack (Jenkins, 1975; Nord, 1977; Nord & Durand, 1978) held that no managerial technique will cure the ills caused by work designed according to the principles of classical management and scientific management, because they do not address the most basic cause of these ills, the fundamental assumptions made by the capitalist system itself.

CONCLUSION ON JOB ENRICHMENT

Job enrichment was once one of the most popular and most written about of the applied motivational techniques based on behavioral science. However, much of the scientific and managerial experience with job enrichment has not been as impressive or as encouraging as its proponents had anticipated. It is clear that any hope that job enrichment would help make work universally more humane, and help make the workforce more productive, simply has not been fully realized. But it is also clear that much of the research done to develop and test new approaches to job redesign has not been of sufficient quality to permit an accurate estimate of either the validity of the scientific theories involved or the applied utility of the techniques that arise from those theories (Hackman, 1977).

The reader must not be too critical of either the theories or the scientists who have attempted to develop them. As we saw in Chapter 2, it is extremely difficult to conduct research in real organizational settings that permits us to generate unequivocal evidence in support of the validity or utility of behavioral science ideas. As has been the suggestion in many other parts of this book, it may be that the theory (or theories) of job enrichment is, in fact, more valid and of more potential applied utility than we are (and have been) capable of demonstrating.

EMPLOYEE EMPOWERMENT

The degree of power people have available to them to effectively perform their work is an important determinant in their satisfaction with their work. Kanter (1977, 1979) was among the first to make this observation: She wrote that both formal job characteristics (such as those described throughout this chapter) as well as informal alliances and relationships people maintain in their work settings contribute to employee "empowerment" (cf. Laschinger, Finegan, Shamian, & Wilk, 2004). People feel empowered, Kanter (1977) wrote, when they have access to information, support, and other resources, *including access to the decision-making processes that concern them*. We discussed the major importance of feelings of control and self-determination in work motivation in Chapter 3 (recall self-determination theory) as well as in Chapter 2, and also in previous paragraphs in this chapter in relation to the motivator-hygiene model.

Following Kanter's (1977) lead, Laschinger, Finegan, Shamian, and Wilk (2000) hypothesized that both the structural characteristics of the workplace as well as the psychological experiences a sample of nurses had about their level of empowerment would explain variance in their job satisfaction. Indeed, they supported their hypothesis. In fact, their data showed that perceptions of psychological empowerment mediated the relationship between structural characteristics of the work and the nurses' job attitudes. However, the researchers observed that because they had used a cross-sectional design, cause-and-effect conclusions could not be drawn with confidence. Subsequently, in a second study – this time with a longitudinal design – the same research team found that nurses' perceptions of structural conditions in their work (such as opportunities to succeed, access to information, formal power, and access to key resources) had direct effects upon both psychological empowerment and job satisfaction. (This time, there was no evidence for a mediated model as had been suggested by the first study.)

In the following sections, we will examine the concept of employee empowerment, stopping along the way to review various forms of work organization practices that have in common the goal of utilizing the decision-making capabilities and potential of employees, often in the context of work groups and teams, for the sake of increasing employee motivation, commitment, productivity, and quality. Although the literatures on lean production systems and high-involvement work practices do not necessarily employ the concept of employee empowerment, per se, they do share many of the goals included in the job enrichment techniques discussed earlier in this chapter. We begin with an examination of empowerment as a construct and then take a tour of a variety of specific work design models. Before we finish the chapter, we will also briefly consider the concept referred to as *disempowerment*.

Employee Empowerment Systems and Methods

The past few decades have seen the emergence of a concept referred to as *empowerment* in a wide range of disciplines (e.g., Weil & Kruzich, 1990). With its origins in religion, where it initially meant the sharing among people of real power, the meaning of the term evolved as it was picked up in other disciplines (such as social work, sociology, and psychology) to imply acts that foster human welfare through providing people with knowledge and other resources required to develop and sustain themselves. More recently, the term was adopted in the management literature and its meaning drifted considerably: In most management parlance, to "empower" someone implies making it possible for them to be more productive for the best interests of the organization (Bartunek & Spreitzer, 2006).

Following on the tradition sparked by Kanter (1977) in the management literature, workers are said to be "empowered" when they take on more responsibility at work, becoming more accountable for their jobs. Such empowerment is particularly likely to come from greater involvement in decision making through suggestion systems, quality circles, and work teams. "Management articles . . . emphasize the benefits organizations would likely accrue through empowerment – more efficient workers, higher productivity, less need for close supervision" (Bartunek & Spreitzer, 2006, p. 268). Conger and Kanungo (1988) proposed that empowerment functions to enhance employee feelings of self-efficacy (see Schwartzer, 1992; and Chapters 6, 12, and 13 of this book).

Subsequently, Thomas and Velthouse (1990) advanced a model of empowerment that hinges on the concept of intrinsic motivation as we discussed the concept earlier in the chapter. They claimed that if a person becomes "empowered," she witnesses changes in what they call *task assessments*, which represent increases in a sense of *impact, competence, meaningfulness, and choice*. The overlap and similarity between these cognitive elements and the essence of intrinsic motivation as we described it earlier should be apparent, as should the overlap among the four factors and the psychological mechanisms thought to mediate the relationships between job design and employee outcomes in Hackman and Oldham's (1980) theory of job design. To empower someone means to give them power, and that power can be of *at least* two varieties. One form is legitimate authority; the other is represented by energy. It is this notion of energization through task assessments that lies at the core of the Thomas and Velthouse concept of empowerment. It is critical to keep in mind that these internal cognitive states come about through perceptual interpretation of a person's context (such as a job or any other situation).

Objective work context factors and circumstances (such as the level of trust, information, and resources actually available to a person) are contributing factors, but it is one's *perception* of the availability of these resources that will determine whether the person will assess the situation as providing possible impact, competence, and so on. As Parker et al. (2001, pp. 416–417) put it:

> The state of psychological empowerment is defined as a motivational state involving an assessment of meaning, impact, competence, and choice (or self-determination). These cognitive-motivational assessments overlap considerably with the critical psychological states in the job characteristics model.[5] Thus, meaning is similar to meaningfulness; impact is similar to knowledge of results; and self-determination/choice is similar to experienced responsibility. Indeed, evidence suggests that work characteristics result in psychological empowerment, which in turn results in affective outcomes such as work satisfaction (Liden, Wayne & Sparrowe, 2000). *However, where the psychological empowerment approach is distinct from the JCM is that it recognizes that the psychological states of empowerment can arise from influences over and above work characteristics, such as peer helping and supportive customer relationships (Corsun & Enz, 1999). In this respect, it has some parallels with the earlier social-information processing perspective* [emphasis added].

---

[5] We examined this more closely earlier in this chapter.

A final note: As Corsun and Enz (1999, p. 206) reminded us, supervisors can play an enormous role in empowering employees: "A new partnership between management, customers, and employees based on honesty, trust, caring, support, dignity, and mutual respect is at the heart of employee experienced empowerment."

Empowerment in Services Management

Employee empowerment has been the focus of considerable attention in the context of services management in recent years. Two leading authorities define it as "increasing workers' level of responsibility and autonomy; it involves pushing the level of decision making in an organization to increasingly lower levels" (Schneider & Bowen, 1995, p. 140). More specifically, it involves pushing downward in an organization four key commodities that are normally held in the hands of senior managers and employees, viz.:

1. Power to make decisions that influence organizational direction and performance through the use of quality circles, employees' suggestion systems and self-managed work teams.
2. Information about the company's performance, one's own work groups and directions the organization is contemplating.
3. Rewards that are allocated on the basis of the organization's performance, such as via profit sharing, gain sharing, or stock ownership programs.
4. Knowledge that makes it possible for employees to understand and contribute to the organization's performance. This may entail training in a wide array of topics such as economics and accounting, group leadership skills and data analysis (Schneider & Bowen, 1995, p. 250).

The design of jobs, organizational structures, and policies, rules, and procedures is key: They can collectively provide opportunities for empowerment or constraints against it (Spreitzer, 1996). Thus, one would expect higher levels of empowerment in organizational structures with wide spans of control, requiring employees to take on more initiative with less supervision from their supervisors (Spreitzer, 1996). Similarly, people who work in jobs in which they are unclear about what is expected of them will feel less empowered, according to Spreitzer. Such people will not be confident of their level of authority and may be hesitant to act.

In a cross-sectional study of a sample of Fortune 500 executives, Spreitzer (1996) found that managers who experienced clear goals, a wide span of control, sociopolitical support from their peers, access to information, and a positive work climate reported higher levels of perceived empowerment than did those who did not experience these features in their jobs.

Employee Disempowerment

Spreitzer (1995a, 1995b, 1996) and Kane and Montgomery (1998) developed a model of the antecedents and consequences of employee empowerment and disempowerment (see Figures 7.2 and 7.3). The reader will notice some striking similarities between this model and the job characteristics model of job design presented earlier in the chapter (cf. Hackman & Oldham, 1980). As shown, Spreitzer's (1996) "organizational antecedents" are seen as responsible for creating psychological states of either empowerment or *disempowerment*. These core psychological dimensions (which include *meaning, competence, self-determination,* and *impact*) are familiar to us after a reading of the theories of intrinsic motivation at the beginning of this chapter. The organizational antecedents that give rise to these psychological states are factors such as low role ambiguity, low supervision, sociopolitical support, access to information (see Eylon, 1994), and a participative climate (Spreitzer, 1996).

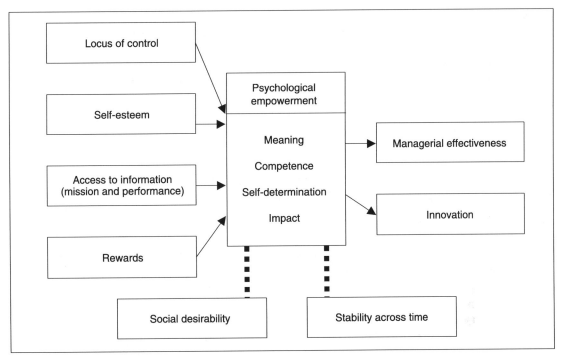

FIG. 7.2 Partial nomological network of psychological empowerment in the workplace.

Source: Spreitzer, G. M. (1995a). Psychological empowerment in the workplace: Dimensions, measurement, and validation. *Academy of Management Journal, 38*, 1442–1465. Reprinted with permission. This work is protected by copyright and it is being used with the permission of Access Copyright. Any alteration of its content or further copying in any form whatsoever is strictly prohibited.

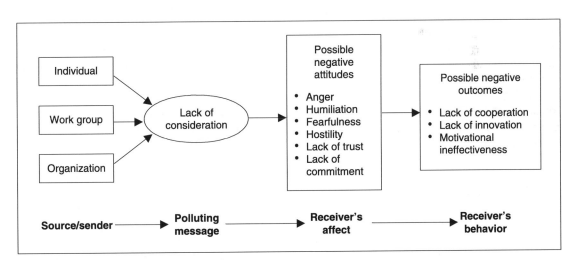

FIG. 7.3 Model of disempowerment.

Source: Kane, K., & Montgomery, K. (1998). A framework for understanding disempowerment in organizations. *Human Resource Management, 37*(3–4), 263–275. Reprinted with permission of John Wiley & Sons, Inc.

Disempowerment is defined as "an interruption with an individual's motivation to perform a work role, manifested in one or more affective reactions in an individual employee to the receipt of certain types of negative messages from another organizational actor" (Kane & Montgomery, 1998). Hence, the origins of disempowerment consist of negative information, originating from another employee, the work group, or the organization itself. The core of the phenomenon is the receiver's emotional reaction to such messages. The medium of the message can be either verbal or nonverbal. Disempowering information may be transmitted either deliberately or inadvertently (Kane & Montgomery, 1998). Such messages are harmful to work motivation because they convey a lack of consideration of the person's dignity and well-being, either personally or professionally. They may have tones of distrust, insincerity, rudeness, disrespect, disinterest, and tactlessness. Their effect is to deflate the recipient's work-related energy, in part through the effect they have on his or her perceptions of fairness, justice, and trust (Kane & Montgomery, 1998).[6]

EMPOWERMENT AND RELATED CONCEPTS

A fundamental assumption underlying the concept of employee empowerment is that people need and desire control, to be in charge of decisions that affect them, and to be equipped to make things happen. Theoretically, it is rooted in much of what we discussed earlier: People's needs for feelings of control and self-determination, to be origins rather than pawns, and so on (Burger, 1992; de Charms, 1968; Deci, 1975; Deci & Ryan, 1985; Skinner, 1995). As we have noted, the mechanics of the empowerment process (in a work motivation setting, cf. Bartunek & Spreitzer, 2006) are similar to those found in the job enrichment movement of the late 1960s, 1970s, and 1980s (cf. Hackman & Oldham, 1980). Indeed, the roots of employee participation programs go back to the earliest days of the scientific study of work and motivation in the discipline (see Coch & French, 1948; Vroom & Yetton, 1973; and a review by Strauss, 1982). Nevertheless, whether employee empowerment is old wine in new bottles or really a newer tool for understanding and managing organizational behavior, it has been applied with vigor in recent years and appears to be here to stay for a while.[7] Thus, Hanson, Porterfield, and Ames (1995) reported that between 60% and 80% of Fortune 500 companies have either implemented empowerment programs or were experimenting with them at that time. More recently, Cox, Zagelmeyer, and Marchington (2006) have argued that the degree of *embeddedness* of employee involvement and participation is critical: The broader and the deeper the involvement, the better, for both the employee and the organization.[8] Embeddedness, a concept attributed to Granovetter (1985), relates to the number and strength of ties an individual has within a social-economic system. Ties can include jobs, family connections, history in a location, commitments made for the future – any social or economic linkages a person may have within the social and economic milieu or context in which he finds himself. Cox et al. (2006) reviewed previous literature on employee involvement and participation and found that most research has examined the binding effects of only one or two forms of employee involvement within organizations at a time. Here is a statement by Cox and her colleagues (p. 253) about the mechanisms through which a variety of employee involvement and participation practices may help to embed them in an organization:

> For example, downward communication practices could be used to promote or instill organizational [sic] values. The improvement of product or service quality via EIP [employee involvement and participation] could increase employees' sense of pride in their work and thereby their employer. Lastly, the cumulative benefits of EIP practices in terms of enhanced autonomy, greater understand-

---

[6] The tones of contempt and exasperation with which some parents address their children are disempowering; they imply a fundamental lack of respect, patience, and trust.

[7] The concept of employee empowerment is a standard prescription in bestsellers addressed to management audiences, although it is often referred to by other terms (e.g., Kouzes & Posner, 1995, suggest that managers *enable* others to perform effectively, and Covey, 1989, suggests that successful people *synergize*).

[8] We will return to the concept of embeddedness in Chapter 10 when we consider employee responses to job dissatisfaction, turnover in particular.

ing of managerial plans and opportunities to express views about the organization could enhance feelings of loyalty. These arguments are supported by research evidence.

Cox and her colleagues presented data from a large United Kingdom database to illustrate how small the effects are of single involvement practices, applied one at a time, on employee commitment and satisfaction, whereas the combined effects of such practices yielded significant effects on the same employee outcomes (although the effects were not large in absolute size). Another English study (Axtell & Parker, 2003) found that employee involvement in "improvement groups, combined with relevant training, adequate workplace communication, as well as job enlargement and task control combined to enhance 'role breadth self-efficacy' – 'an employee's confidence in performing proactive, interpersonal tasks that go beyond traditional boundaries' (p. 113).[9] Finally, results from a study of a large Australian database revealed that 'high-quality' work – meaning, in this case, work for which people were well trained and that was characterized as entailing variety and autonomy – resulted in lower levels of occupational injuries. The effects of the high-quality work on injury rates were both direct as well as indirect, mediated by high levels of job satisfaction (Barling, Kelloway, & Iverson, 2003).

We will have more to say about high-involvement workplaces in Chapter 10, in connection with our discussion of employee commitment, satisfaction, and withdrawal behaviors.

BEYOND THE JOB CHARACTERISTICS MODEL

Now that we have studied the concept of empowerment, we turn to a discussion of a variety of production processes that, to varying degrees and using varying design tactics, attempt to make work empowering for employees. These are *lean production systems*, *high-involvement work systems* and *interdisciplinary systems* (of varying degrees of scope, as we shall see).

Lean Production: Progeny of Mass Production Systems

Womack, Jones, and Roos (1990) traced the history of production processes in North America (focusing on auto manufacturing) from the early days of small-scale craft production through the rise and decline of mass production technologies to the post World War II period when the Japanese (lead by Eiji Toyoda) began to invent ways to modify the American mass production model in ways that would cut costs, reduce waste, improve quality, and develop employees in ways that would benefit the employer through the lifetime of the worker's career in the company. It is an interesting book. Although complete detail of the technology is well beyond the scope of this book, the reader is referred to the story told by Womack and his colleagues and their descriptive and normative treatment of lean systems – one of the first varieties of "job design" models to emerge from the growing discontent in North America (and elsewhere) with the tedium, alienation, and withdrawal consequences of the Tayloresque assembly line.

A key element of lean production systems are semi-autonomous work groups (Applebaum & Batt, 1994, cited by Parker, 2003; Womack et al., 1990) that perform both production as well as non-production tasks, to varying degrees. This means that, in many settings, groups are responsible for varying degrees of planning, quality control, and problem solving. It "transfers the maximum number of tasks and responsibilities to those workers actually adding value to the [product]" (Womack et al., p. 99). Other features of lean production systems can include (or have included at one time or another):

---

[9] Recall our broader discussion of self-efficacy in Chapter 6.

1. Rapid changes in dye stamps for small production runs, as required, these changes being conducted by the assembly workers rather than by specialists.
2. Lifetime employment for workers.
3. Responsibility for problem solving and quality control by work teams.
4. Development and use of (what we call in North America) "quality circles."
5. Development of relationships with suppliers of materials to improve reliability of delivery of materials while minimizing the costs of in-company inventory control and management.
6. Job rotation.
7. Highly specialized procedures for specific tasks, in the tradition of scientific management.
8. Creation of career paths that encourage individuals to become proficient at multiple stages of the design and production cycle, rather than keeping these functions separated in functional silos.
9. Application of the foregoing features (with others) to allow the company to respond more quickly to changing consumer demand than was possible in traditional mass production facilities.

Again, complete detail of lean production systems is beyond our scope here. Suffice it to say that in practice, not every production site had, in fact, all the features of the ideal type (Kochan, Lansbury & MacDuffie, 1997; Liker & Morgan, 2006), but the fundamental ideas spread to North America and elsewhere, as detailed in an article published in the periodical *Organizational Dynamics* in 1973 by its editor. Another classic paper, written by Adler and Cole (1993), compared and contrasted the Japanese-style lean production Toyota plant in Fremont in California with two Swedish plants that produced Volvos during the 1980s – which they referred to as a more "human-centered" model, with a special focus on the relative capacity of the two systems to continuously stimulate improvement while, at the same time, maintain employee morale. Their conclusion was that the Japanese-style New United Motor Manufacturing Company, Inc. (NUMMI) was superior on both counts. Given that the NUMMI plant utilized smaller work groups and more highly prescribed assembly procedures, it is interesting that they fared better on the morale dimension.

Criticisms of lean production

Lean production has been controversial, spurring some critics to characterize it as a neo-Tayloristic, exploitive form of production that may be detrimental to employee satisfaction, health, and organizational commitment. The lack of standardization of elements-in-practice where putative lean production programs have been implemented has made them hard to assess scientifically. Recently, however, a quasi-experiment in Australia has developed and tested a longitudinal model of the effects of lean production techniques on employee outcomes, using the following work characteristics as mediating variables in the model: Job autonomy, skill utilization, participation in decision making, and role overload. The employee outcomes included in the model were organizational commitment, job anxiety, job depression, proactive motivation, and role breadth self-efficacy (which we discussed earlier). The three features of lean production manipulated were lean teams, assembly lines, and workflow formalization. Workers in all the lean production groups were adversely affected, especially those on assembly lines, in terms of reduced commitment, reduced role breadth self-efficacy, and increased job depression (Parker, 2003).

Elements of the entire package of lean production systems are common in both manufacturing and service settings these days. Liker and Morgan (2006) have recently described the "Toyota production system" – a systems-based model of lean production that has proven efficient in many settings in North America and elsewhere,[10] although the negative effects of these methods on employee welfare

---

[10] Although Friel (2005) provides a case illustration of how lean production methods that are "successful" in some cultural settings may not be as successful in different cultural and regulatory environments.

(such as limited potential for creativity and innovation, narrow professional skills, worker isolation and harassment, dangerous working conditions, and excessive overtime) continue to be reported by critics of the Toyota model (cf. Mehri, 2006).

High-Involvement Work Practices (HIWP)

Lawler and Mohrman (1991, p. 27) defined high-involvement management as "an approach to management that encourages employee commitment to the success of the organization. Employees at all levels . . . are given the right mix of information, knowledge, power and rewards so that they can influence and be rewarded for organizational performance." More recently, Benson, Young, and Lawler (2006) defined it as "a specific set of human resource practices that focus on employee decision-making power, access to information, training, and incentives" (p. 519). In various combinations and styles, these human resource practices have been available, practiced, and advocated for years because they have been assumed to contribute to employee motivation, efficiency, and quality of work (cf. Lawler, 1992).

There has been considerable evidence, gained from many field studies and case studies, that, indeed, these practices, particularly when applied in combination, do contribute to positive individual and organizational outcomes (see Benson et al., 2006, for a review). There is also evidence that these practices are positively related to financial performance in many organizations, although not always (Benson et al., p. 522). Combs, Yongmei Liu, Hall, and Ketchen (2006) recognized that the lack of unanimous support for the connection between application of high-performance practices and financial performance may have resulted (as is often the case) from the fact that the various earlier studies into the matter used different indicators of the various "practices" as well as different outcome measures. Accordingly, they conducted and reported a meta-analysis of 92 studies and found an overall estimated correlation of 0.20. The results were stronger when the practices were used in combination rather than one at a time (as is the case in lean production settings), and the results were consistent across the different performance measures they studied. In short, it appears that human resources practices that encourage power sharing in decision making, teamwork, incentives, and training, especially when used as integrated systems, have the hypothesized beneficial consequences, largely mediated, presumably, by the effects they have on work motivation.

Broader, multidisciplinary approaches for the "new world of work"

Since the mid-1990s, spurred by the common recognition that the world of work is changing, a number of theorists have proposed models to accommodate and anticipate these changes. For example, Noon and Blyton (2007) have identified a host of shifting parameters that characterize the changing context of work. These include:

- political contexts
- deregulation
- privatization
- economic context
- globalization
- competitive strategies
- industrial structures
- workforce composition
- part-time employment
- self-employment
- location of employment

- job insecurity
- redundancy
- unemployment.

They might have added other factors such as immigration and cross-border flows of human resources, shortages of labor, especially in the context of seasonal work, the continued practice of slavery (at numbers higher than at any time in the past), nationalization of industries, and so forth. Theory, research and practice have begun to respond to these changes but it appears much more needs to be done.[11] Thus, Parker et al. (2001) have recently observed that current approaches to job design have failed to step back far enough in the causal sequence to study the antecedents of work content. They also state that more research is required to isolate factors other than job characteristics (such as supervisory supportiveness, as demonstrated by Corsun and Enz, 1999) that foster psychological empowerment, as well as moderator variables that may moderate the job characteristics → outcomes connection(s).

Interdisciplinary Approach to Job Design

In 1993 Campion published an award-winning doctoral dissertation that proposed a broader, more multidisciplinary approach to job design than had been considered in the organizational behavior literature, or in the cognate literatures of a number of other disciplines, either. Specifically, he surveyed the published literature to that time dealing with work motivation, industrial engineering, biomechanics, and perceptual/motor skills. He went on to identify nearly 700 "job design rules" among the four bodies of work and established a four-way typology among these rules, establishing reliability in how they are categorized. Then, consulting the same literatures, he identified a range of job outcomes that were sorted into four categories (Campion & Thayer, 1985):

1. Satisfaction (affective, motivational, and attitudinal outcomes (such as job satisfaction, job involvement, and intrinsic motivation)).
2. Efficiency (such as the percentage of people who could perform a job, the average time it takes to train someone to perform the job).
3. Comfort (such as the fatigue associated with a job, risks such as muscle strain, hearing loss, etc.).
4. Reliability (safety, accident rates, accident-prone situations, error rates, and attitudes toward equipment involved, among others).

Using a sample of American hourly production workers in five wood products plants of a single organization, the researchers developed a four-category questionnaire, the *multimethod job design questionnaire* (MJDQ) and tested preliminary hypotheses that showed that variance in each of the four sets of dependent variables was typically best explained by job design items that were found in the corresponding literatures. The authors concluded:

> This study demonstrates that different approaches to job design can be reliably measured in a field setting, and they relate to important outcomes for both the individual and the organization. As no single approach can fully explain all outcomes, an interdisciplinary approach is suggested . . . Although there is some overlap between the job design approaches [the traditional bodies of literature with which they started the research], there are also some basic conflicts. Most of these differences are between the motivational approach and the perceptual/motor and mechanistic approaches [as they had expected] . . . Clearly, each approach has a different orientation. The perceptual motor approach

---

[11] For example, Hall et al. (1996; Hall & Chandler, 2005) and Arthur and Rousseau (1996) have offered fundamentally new insights into the nature of careers and the relationships people now have with organizations.

strives to develop equipment and jobs that are simple, safe, reliable, and minimize the mental demands required of workers. Conversely, the motivational approach stresses that the more complicated and challenging jobs are more rewarding and should be encouraged.

(Campion & Thayer, 1985, p. 39)

Table 7.1 summarizes the outcomes typically associated with each of the four main job design approaches.

A replication and extension of the Campion and Thayer (1985) study was reported by Campion (1988). In this research, he tested the applicability of the model to a much wider range of jobs, altered the MJDQ so it could be self-administered (the original instrument relied on the observation of second parties, such as an employee's supervisor), found that the model could be tested and supported at the level of the individual worker, as opposed to the aggregated level of jobs – as was done in the original work – and examined the robustness of the model against individual differences – that is, he looked for possible moderating influences on the main effects. Campion's (1988) results were impressive. Aside from providing additional validity to his model, he showed that the model is not susceptible to effects of the moderator variables he examined, that it could be tested with a self-report instrument, that the validity of the model extends far beyond the restricted blue-collar jobs used in the first study, and that the results were consistent, regardless of whether they were computed at the level of the job or the level of the individual worker.

Later, on the basis of a few methodological and conceptual concerns they had with Campion's model, Edwards, Scully, and Brtek (1999, 2000) challenged Campion's four-factor structure and

TABLE 7.1   Summary of hypothesized outcomes from four approaches to job design

JOB DESIGN APPROACH	POSITIVE OUTCOMES	NEGATIVE OUTCOMES
Mechanistic	Decreased training time Higher utilization levels Lower likelihood of error Less chance of mental overload and stress	Lower job satisfaction Lower motivation Higher absenteeism
Motivational	Higher job satisfaction Higher motivation Greater job involvement Higher job performance Lower absenteeism	Increased training time Lower utilization levels Greater likelihood of error Greater chance of mental overload and stress
Biological	Less physical effort Less physical fatigue Fewer health complaints Fewer medical incidents Lower absenteeism Higher job satisfaction	Higher financial costs because of changes in equipment or job environment
Perceptual/motor	Lower likelihood of error Lower likelihood of accidents Less chance of mental overload and stress Lower training time Higher utilization levels	Lower job satisfaction Lower motivation

Source: Adapted from Campion, M. A. (1988). Inter-disciplinary approaches to job design: A constructive replication with extension. *Journal of Applied Psychology, 73,* 467–481.

proposed a 10-factor model, one that does not replicate the same simple alignment of work design principles and work outcomes that characterized the results of Campion's work. Nevertheless, Edwards et al. (1999) suggested that their 10-factor solution can be conceptually reconciled with the four a priori categories that instigated Campion's research (Campion & Thayer, 1985).

The 10 factors emerging from the analysis of the MJDQ in Edwards et al. (1999) are the following:

1. feedback
2. skill
3. rewards
4. specialization
5. task simplicity
6. physical ease
7. work conditions
8. work scheduling
9. ergonomics
10. cognitive simplicity.

A later study by Edwards, Scully, and Brtek (2000) provided additional support for their 10-factor model and reaffirmed the value of the MJDQ as a comprehensive instrument for assessing jobs from a multidisciplinary perspective that is more comprehensive than any of the four traditional approaches (motivational/psychological, industrial engineering, human factors, and socio-technical). The point is that the works of Edwards and his colleagues does not diminish the importance of either the MJDQ or the value of the original insights made by Campion and Thayer. It merely restructures the way the instrument is scored for use in scientific and applied settings. Collectively, the work of Campion and Thayer and that of Edwards and his colleagues comprise a very valuable advance in the conceptualization and measurement of work, suitable for the "new world of work" we now face (cf. Noon & Blyton, 2007).

An Even Broader, "Elaborated" Model

Parker et al. (2001) presented a very broad "elaborated" model that includes macro-level antecedents such as environmental uncertainty, political and labor institutions, labor markets, management style, and other factors (see Figure 7.4). These macro factors are seen as causes of an "expanded" list of work characteristics that include factors found in the JCM as well as a number of group-level and interactional variables, which, in turn, are hypothesized to affect a wider range of both individual and organizational outcomes than have been studied in most research conducted in the past. As seen in Figure 7.4, this "elaborated model" recognizes the potential influences of a host of individual-, group-, and organization-level moderator variables. Finally, employee motivation, the central focus of this book, is treated in the elaborated model as a mediating variable.

In short, the ambitious elaborated model proposed by Parker and her colleagues takes into account the knowledge gained over previous decades by more micro- and meso-level approaches and expands to include a much wider array of environmental antecedents as well as an intelligent selection of plausible mediators and moderators and a comprehensive set of outcome variables.

The authors concluded:

Anyone contemplating work design in a call centre, a high-technology plant, among hairdressers, for teleworkers, for knowledge workers, for virtual teams, or in a multitude of other contexts, and armed with only existing work design theory, cannot feel other than inadequately prepared. Those theories, though providing a window, do not speak to the reality and complexity of the situation. Reducing

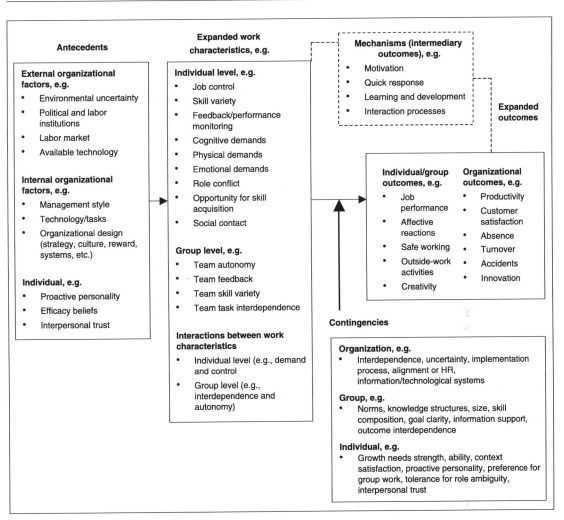

FIG. 7.4   Elaborated model of work design.

Source: Parker, S. K., Wall, T. D., & Cordery, J. L. (2001). Future work design research and practice: Towards an elaborated model of work design. *Journal of Occupational and Organisational Psychology*, *74*, 413–440. Reproduced with permission from the *Journal of Occupational and Organisational Psychology* © The British Psychological Society.

work design theory to a handful of universalistic prescriptions in respect of work characteristics and outcomes might be convenient, but it is not realistic.

(Parker et al., 2001, p. 433)

The elaborated model cannot realistically be tested holus bolus, and that is not the intention of the authors. It does, however, offer the possibility of the invocation of a variety of extant theories (most of which are discussed in this book) and theories-still-to-come for the construction of middle-range theories (Pinder & Moore, 1980) that will eventually allow a better informed, much more systemic understanding of the distal and proximate causes of work design, as well as of its consequences, boundary conditions, and mediating mechanisms (see Chapter 2). The elaborated model sets a daunting research agenda, but is well advised.

SUMMARY AND A GLANCE AHEAD

In this chapter, we have focused on job enrichment and employee empowerment, two latter-day concepts that have both philosophical and conceptual roots in the theory of intrinsic motivation (recall Chapter 3). The essential goals that all these managerial programs have in common are to make work more interesting and a source of dignity and self-determination for the people who perform it.

Ubiquity of Self-Determination in Job Design and Work Motivation Models

Perhaps the most recurrent theme to emerge when all these various theories are compared simultaneously is *control* and, more especially, *self-determination*. This concept enters the picture under different rubrics in elements of need hierarchy theories (Chapter 3), self-determination theory, activation theory, Staw's (1976) expectancy theory approach, as well as in the three newer models of work design just discussed: Lean production, high-involvement work practices (Benson et al., 2006), and the "elaborated" model proposed by Parker and her colleagues (2001). Indeed, self-determination and having some degree of "say" about one's work is not only ubiquitous among formal theories of work motivation and job design, autonomy on the job continues to emerge as a critical issue in the demands being made by today's highly educated and highly mobile workforce in North America, Europe, and other affluent national economies (recall Chapter 3). Bandura's (1997, 2001) concept of *personal agency* is similar to that of self-determination, and will be examined in Chapter 11.

Still a way to go

All the foregoing theory and research evidence favoring employee self-determination in the North American workplace notwithstanding, there are still countless examples of high-control, suppressive work environments where employees are virtually (if not literally) chained to their workstations. For example, an October 31, 2005 article in the Victoria *Times Colonist* reported allegations that workers in an Alberta meat-packing plant are not permitted to leave their places in the production line to take bathroom breaks "even if it means wetting their pants." It seems that we still have a long way to go, even in otherwise civilized parts of the world.[12]

What prevents all these good things from happening?

We turn in the next chapter to the problem of need frustration – situations in which people are prevented from attaining the goals they pursue to satisfy the needs we have been studying throughout Part Two.

---

[12] In Chapter 15, we will examine slavery as it persists and grows in the 21st century.

Causes and Consequences of Frustration at Work

8

Perseverance is more prevailing than violence; and many things
which cannot be overcome when they are together,
yield themselves up when taken little by little.
Plutarch

The Canadian Centre for Justice Statistics recently reported "nearly one-fifth of violent victimization, including physical assault, sexual assault and robbery, occurred in the victim's workplace in 2004" (Statistics Canada: *The Daily*, February 16, 2007). More than 356,000 incidents were reported across Canada that year, 71% of them classified as physical assaults. Men and women were equally likely to have experienced workplace violence, although the men were more likely to be injured by it. A disproportionate frequency of the violence occurred in social assistance or healthcare facilities such as hospitals, clinics, and nursing homes.

Violence is not a new phenomenon in Canadian workplaces (neither is it a uniquely Canadian problem). One of the country's most high-profile instances of workplace violence occurred on the afternoon of August 24, 1992, when Professor Valery Fabrikant of Concordia University in Montreal entered the ninth floor of the engineering building where he worked, carrying a briefcase containing three handguns and many rounds of ammunition. He proceeded to shoot the president of the Concordia Faculty Association three times, killing him. He then shot two colleagues who had entered the scene, wounding one in her leg and fatally wounding the other. He then deliberately crossed through a maze of aisles and corridors, fatally shot the head of the electrical and computer engineering department, and fell into a scuffle with another colleague who was visiting the department at the time. Losing his first gun, Fabrikant shot to death another engineering professor while his previous two victims were tending to one another's traumas. Fabrikant finally grabbed another professor and a security guard and locked them away in an office with him while he called 911 and sought access to a television reporter. Eventually, the captive professor and the security guard overpowered Fabrikant and ended the crisis (Wolfe, 1994). Ultimately, four people died in the incident.

The Concordia University massacre shocked the Montreal community at large and the academic community all across Canada. How could such a terrible and unpredictable horror occur, especially in the otherwise safe and benign context of a university? After a period of time, investigations revealed that Dr. Fabrikant, a mechanical engineer with an international reputation, had been repeatedly frustrated by the university and by his colleagues and superiors, ultimately reaching the point where he felt he had to take control of his career by his own means. The means he used was violence. The event is still highly salient to academics and administrators in Canada and elsewhere.

Otherwise civilized and highly educated people are quite capable of resorting to violence in response to continued frustration in their lives and in their workplaces in particular. Fabrikant was known as a loner but also as a highly prolific scholar (Wolfe, 1994). He placed heavy demands on department heads and other superiors for resources and research support and never seemed satisfied with what he received as a result of his demands. In the spring of 1991, for example, he was awarded a merit pay increase, the highest granted in his department. But he continued to demand more and was constantly in the "bad books" of most of the key players in his group. Eventually, an

237

administrator examined his personnel file, found "minor discrepancies" (Wolfe, 1994, p. 18) in his resume, and asked Fabrikant for proof of his academic qualifications. This led to an escalation of conflict between Fabrikant and the rest of his colleagues, who met to discuss disciplinary actions against him. One sanction applied was an increased teaching load, including courses Fabrikant claimed were beyond his area of expertise. The case started to receive media coverage outside the university's boundaries and again, the conflict escalated. A former student alleged that she had been raped by Fabrikant. Meanwhile, Fabrikant was writing letters to at least two colleagues, demanding that they acknowledge that they had not made sufficient contributions to some of his papers to have earned the credit received, threatening them with lawsuits. Fabrikant was frustrated in the court battle and was charged with contempt. Eventually, he managed to obtain the three guns that allowed him to relieve his stress and frustration by murdering four colleagues.

Although it is hard to document, an impression the author holds is that cases of workplace violence have become more frequent since the Concordia University event or, at least, more widely reported by the media and familiar to the public. For example, in 2002, a public servant in Kamloops, British Columbia, killed three coworkers after receiving an unfavorable performance review and then took his own life (Douglas, 2002). In 2005 a dismissed paper plant worker in Romulus, Michigan, shot both the supervisor involved in the firing as well as a translator who attempted to mediate the dispute between the dismissed employee and his erstwhile supervisor. The mediator died of her wounds (*Milwaukee Journal Sentinel*, Associated Press, February 20, 2005). The U.S. Bureau of Labor Statistics reported 1062 work-related homicides in 1996, making homicide the second leading cause of death in the workplace that year (Toscano & Windau, 1998, cited by Glomb, Steel, & Arvey, 2002; see also Capozzi & McVey, 1996).

In earlier chapters we discussed a number of human needs that may be gratified through working. This chapter is about frustration: It deals with situations in which people's behaviors fail to result in the attainment of sought-after goals. In the sections that follow, we examine some common causes and a number of predictable consequences of need frustration in work settings. At the outset, it is necessary to make clear that violence, especially homicide, is not the only consequence of workplace frustration, and that factors other than frustration can cause violent human behavior. Nevertheless, it appears that aggression, in its many forms, and employee frustration are often associated in modern work settings.

ONCE AGAIN: NEEDS AND GOALS

Before we begin it is essential to remind the reader of the meanings of two key terms: *Needs* and *goals*. Successful understanding and application of our knowledge about frustration depend largely on keeping the distinction between the two concepts in mind. As we have discussed at length in previous chapters, *needs* are hypothetical concepts that represent the basic internal forces posited to explain motivated behavior (recall Chapter 3). They are characteristics of individuals and are relatively fixed, at least in the short run. *Goals*, by way of contrast, are things that people seek and try to attain for the sake of fulfilling their needs. Goals such as food and sleep are necessary, respectively, for satisfying the human physiological needs called hunger and fatigue. In work settings, pay, promotions, recognition from one's superior, and a chance to show one's skill are examples of goals that people may seek to satisfy their existence, relatedness, and growth needs on the job and through their work. The frustration model that follows is of value only if we keep the distinction between needs and goals in mind: Needs are internal to a person, part of the personality; goals are external agents or states.

As we noted in Chapter 3, different people often pursue different goals to satisfy the same need. For example, relatedness needs may be expressed by a gregarious employee through constant chitchat during work hours, whereas another employee may attempt to satisfy that same need by seeking election to the organization's social committee. Further, a given goal, if achieved, may satisfy several needs simultaneously. A promotion, for instance, may be instrumental for the fulfillment of a person's existence, relatedness, and growth needs. In short, there is no one-to-one correspondence between needs and goals, and it is essential to keep the two concepts separate when we consider the causes and consequences of frustration. The complex theoretical relationships between needs and goals are represented in Figure 8.1.

MOTIVATION, FRUSTRATION, AND BEHAVIOR

Before we explore the nature and consequences of frustration in the workplace, we examine briefly the formal theory of frustration presented by Maier (1946, 1961), an American psychologist whose early work still figures prominently on this subject. The reader will see some basic similarities between the definition of motivation and motivated behavior offered by Maier and the definitions offered earlier in the book. The key point in what follows is to understand how motivated behavior differs from instinctive behavior and frustration.

For Maier (1946), motivated behavior is controlled by both internal and external conditions. The internal condition is a need, desire, or emotion. The external condition is a goal: "Either condition may be present without the other and produce a stimulus–response behavior, but both are essential for creating the state of motivation which selectively arouses behavior that may be goal oriented. Behavior called forth by the state of motivation tends to relieve the internal condition and this in turn leads to satisfaction. So-called 'adaptive behavior' is characterized by the fact that it leads to a reduction in need" (Maier, 1961, p. 96).

To be adaptive, of course, the behavior must be aligned appropriately with the nature of the need, and learning occurs over time – learning that associates the accomplishment of certain goals with particular need states. Maier defined instinctive or innate behavior as acts that occur in the presence of both need states and goals but without the learning of associations between need states and goal acquisition. Jumping back in the presence of a sudden loud noise is an example. Whereas motivated behavior indicates a choice among alternative possible goals, there is no goal orientation in frustration behavior.

When frustration is experienced, behavior is a terminal response to frustration and not a means to an end. No need is satisfied because no goal is involved. Any satisfaction that occurs must be in the form of relief, not in the form of consummation. We must distinguish, therefore, between two possible forms of satisfaction: Relief from frustration, and the removal of a need through the attainment of a goal:

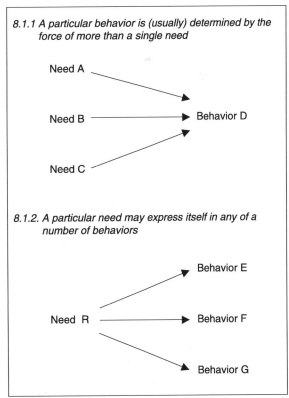

8.1.1 A particular behavior is (usually) determined by the force of more than a single need

8.1.2. A particular need may express itself in any of a number of behaviors

FIG. 8.1 Relationships between needs and goals.

Frustration, although it may be set up through need deprivation, initiates behavior which may be unrelated to the conditions that lead to the frustration . . . Goals no longer serve as guides, so that frustration-instigated behavior is behavior that is forced by the condition of the organism. In this sense all frustrated behavior has the character of a compulsion.

(Maier, 1961, p. 99)

Defining Frustration

Leonard Berkowitz (1989) spent much of his career studying frustration and its consequences, especially aggression (to which we turn shortly). After surveying the set of possible definitions of frustration, he noted that this term is used frequently in everyday speech. People are always claiming to be "frustrated" for some reason or another. However, Berkowitz (1989) adopted a precise scientific definition of frustration for his work, a definition that was first advanced in 1939 by a group of Yale psychologists. For them, *frustration* is "an interference with the occurrence of an instigate goal-response at its proper time in the behavior sequence" (Dollard, Doob, Miller, Mowrer, & Sears, 1939, p. 7).

Berkowitz (1989, pp. 60–61) pointed out that this definition implies a number of things, including: an impediment to a goal is not a frustration unless (1) the person involved is striving, implicitly or explicitly, to reach the goal; and (2) the person involved anticipates satisfaction of a need through the attainment of the goal in question. Therefore, Berkowitz observed, poor people lacking the good things in life need not be defined as frustrated unless they are actually pursuing goals and are prevented from attaining them. In concert with Berkowitz (who has reaffirmed and updated his early work – see Berkowitz, 1997) we adopt the Yale University definition he adopted in his work (see Dollard et al., 1939) along with the nuances he identified as following from it.[1]

Causes of Frustration

People tend to associate certain goals with satisfaction of their particular needs (although there is not always a one-to-one correspondence). Each of us tends to find certain things satisfying and other things less so. A simple example is the act of going to the refrigerator for a cold drink (the goal) for the sake of quenching one's thirst (the need). The more frequently a particular goal object proves successful in meeting a need, the more likely the person is to seek that same goal in the future when the need arises. To some extent, we form habits (although Maier is careful to distinguish between habits and fixated behavior – one common response to frustration that we discuss shortly).

What happens when a traditionally successful behavior fails to reach the goal being sought? What happens when, for whatever reason, the behavior itself is not possible? Or what happens when a person's behavior tends to make goal accomplishment more difficult rather than easier? Situations of this sort are common in virtually all job settings. They are often difficult to identify and difficult to ameliorate. Nevertheless, the behavior that tends to occur in response to frustration is common in organizational settings and is usually (although not always) dysfunctional. Managing frustrated behavior is a major challenge for supervisors, and it is not always done effectively (see Figure 8.2).

What types of thing block a person's learned behavior from reaching work goals? In other words, what causes frustration in work settings? We can classify causes of frustration into two

---

[1] In everyday usage, people frequently claim that they are "frustrated." But statements of this sort are usually inaccurate from a technical point of view. Although people who make such statements are, in fact, frustrated, what they usually mean by their statements is that they are angry or depressed as a result of not being able to accomplish their goals. Frustration is formally a *situation*, not an emotional reaction. See Chapter 4 for a complete discussion of emotions in the workplace.

categories for the sake of discussion. The first includes factors that are, for the most part, external to the person, although they may or may not be beyond her control. Examples abound in organizations. The structure of the organization is a common cause of need frustration, because hierarchies, which tend to be pyramid shaped, prevent most of us from reaching the top. Other examples are policies that prevent people from interacting with one another on the job, that stipulate when a person may take a rest, or that prevent people from taking a vacation when they want. A job that is boring and repetitive is another

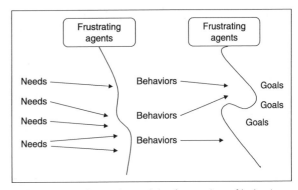

FIG. 8.2   Needs, goals, and the frustration of behavior.

example, one faced by many. A supervisor who will not cooperate and help an employee can frustrate that employee. Similarly, low-performing employees constitute barriers that prevent supervisors from achieving their job goals. Coworkers who exclude a newcomer and ignore his attempts to be friendly, and situations of ongoing conflict between coworkers, are other examples. People may attempt myriad behaviors to meet their needs, and there are countless potential barriers external to a person that can interfere with those behaviors, preventing her from meeting her basic needs at work (see Peters & O'Connor, 1980; Peters, O'Connor, & Eulberg, 1985).

Neuman and Baron (1997) suggested that the very nature of the American workplace – in which organizational climates are leaner and meaner as a result of globalization – and competitive international marketplaces may be a factor. Reductions in workforce levels, demands for higher productivity, and dramatic alterations in the nature of the employment relationship may all be contributing to contexts in which frustration and aggression may be more likely than they were in the past. We return to their model and others similar to it shortly.

A second general category of potential frustrators consists of characteristics of the person being frustrated. A lack of ability to do the work (where work accomplishment is the goal) can block a person's attempts and leave his needs unfulfilled. Similarly, characteristics such as gender (Bartol, 1978; Larwood & Wood, 1977), age (Rosen & Jerdee, 1976), or departmental affiliation (Dalton, 1959) are other factors that can pose barriers and prevent people from getting jobs, promotions into new jobs, or even access to information that they need to be effective in their jobs. Disabled employees provide a powerful example of how a personal characteristic or set of personal characteristics can prevent a person from reaching work-related goals.

It tends to be easier to identify causes of frustration external to the person being frustrated than it is to identify internal causes, and people often blame factors other than themselves for their frustrations at work (Harvey & Albertson, 1971; Mitchell, Green, & Wood, 1981; Vroom, 1964). Diagnosing the root causes of an employee's frustration can be difficult, for many reasons. First, frustrated people are not always aware of the barriers to their goal achievement, especially when these barriers are internal to themselves or when they are rooted in organizational factors that are beyond their cognizance. An employee with unusual religious beliefs is an example of the former; a company's advertising campaign that projects an unfavorable image of the product he is attempting to sell illustrates the latter.

Second, the behavior that results from need frustration will vary from person to person. There is no universal one-to-one correspondence between the force of particular needs and the behavior that results (Figure 8.1). Also recall the human tendency to project our own need behavior linkages to others, even when they are not appropriate. A supervisor who observes frustrated behavior by one of her subordinates may have difficulty both in diagnosing the need(s) seeking satisfaction and in detecting the nature of the barrier(s) responsible for the frustration of the behavior aimed at those needs – complex problems indeed.

It is generally easier to talk about and understand the frustration of existence and relatedness needs than to understand and identify the frustration of growth needs. This is in large part because the goals typically sought for the satisfaction of existence and relatedness needs are usually relatively concrete and tangible. But as noted in Chapters 3 and 7, growth needs are responsible for a considerable amount of the behavior we observe at work, and they may become even more important in the future. The goals that people seek to satisfy their growth needs are more often amorphous and idiosyncratic, making their attainment difficult at times. In fact, most of the jobs we perform in our economy do not readily satisfy human growth needs. As a result, the frustration of growth needs is a major problem in organizations, one that manifests itself in job-related boredom and dissatisfaction (as we will see in Chapter 10). There are limits to the degree to which jobs can be structured to allow the ongoing satisfaction of human needs for competence, self-esteem, and self-actualization, although, as we noted in Chapter 7, several formal managerial programs have been advanced to try to ease the situation and to make it more possible for people to satisfy their growth needs through their work.

Consequences of Frustration

Need frustration tends to result in any of a number of typical classes of behavior, although, as we have noted, people manifest these classes of behavior in different ways. In fact, Maier noted decades ago (1961, p. 100) that motivated and frustrated behavior processes may appear simultaneously, in equal strength. In these cases, some of a person's behavior may be goal oriented and some of it may simply be driven by the inner state, with no particular goal in mind. Sometimes the frustration may be relieved and the person's behavior becomes almost (or entirely) goal oriented (a good scream or the utterance of an epithet are common means by which this occurs). Alternatively, goal-oriented behavior is not possible and most of the force driving the person is frustration – no goal is in mind or in sight.

The most constructive reaction to frustration is exploration and *problem solving*, by which the person sets about (with or without the help of others) to diagnose the cause, or barrier, and to remove it (Wong, 1979). This sort of behavior occurs regularly in our lives, so much so that we usually take it for granted. Problem solving in response to frustration can contribute to the satisfaction of most human needs. A second constructive adaptation to frustration is the *adoption and pursuit of alternative goals*. Rather than seeking to increase her income through a promotion or a raise in pay, a single working mother might take on a part-time job. Similarly, an employee who works in physical isolation from his coworkers may seek fulfillment of his social needs by pursuing friendships off the job. The need(s) remains the same, but the goal(s) changes.

But there are many less functional classes of human responses to frustration that deserve highlighting, including sabotage, theft, the intentional withholding of output, and – as we have noted – aggression and violence (to name just a few). Spector (1997) has advanced a revision of an earlier model (Spector, 1978) linking frustration at work to the behavioral reactions one might expect from a frustrated employee. In keeping with other definitions, he sees a frustrator as "an environmental event or situation that interferes with or prevents an individual from achieving or maintaining a personal goal at work" (Spector, 1997, p. 3). His model, shown in Figure 8.3, indicates that the entire frustration–reaction cycle is a bit more complicated than was reflected in the earlier theories, such as that by Dollard et al. (1939).

As shown in Figure 8.3, in order for an individual to actually experience frustration, she or he must make a cognitive appraisal of the environmental conditions at hand. Following Peters and O'Connor (1980), Spector (1997) proposed eight categories of common frustrator, including: Job-related information; tools and equipment; materials and supplies; budgetary support; required services and help from other people; task preparation; time availability; and positive self-image. But an environmental situation can become a frustrator only if the individual experiences it as such (recall how cognitive appraisal processes intervene in the interpretation of events in some cognitive

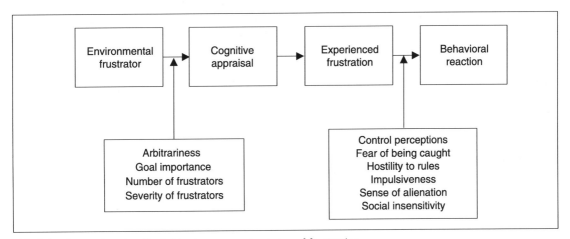

FIG. 8.3   Determinants of individual responses to states of frustration.

Source: Spector, P. E. (1997). The role of frustration in antisocial behavior at work. In R. A. Giacalone & J. Greenberg (Eds.), *Antisocial behavior in organizations.* Thousand Oaks, CA: Sage. Reprinted with permission of Sage Publications, Inc. This work is protected by copyright and it is being used with the permission of Access Copyright. Any alteration of its content or further copying in any form whatsoever is strictly prohibited.

evaluation models of affect and emotion, discussed in Chapter 4). A number of features affect whether a potential frustrator actually is appraised as a frustrator, including, among other things: (1) the number and relative importance of the needs being blocked from satisfaction, (2) the degree of deprivation and/or its duration, (3) the extensiveness of the blocking and the completeness of the frustration that results (i.e., whether it is constant or intermittent), (4) the perceived motives (if any) of the source of the frustration, (5) the person's prior experiences of success and failure in using various reactions to frustration, and (6) the probable threats or costs perceived to be associated with the various response alternatives.

For example, if a person is prevented from seeing her boss for a scheduled appointment because the boss's busy schedule of morning meetings is running late, the subordinate may be slightly disappointed but is more likely simply to seek an alternative meeting time than to threaten her boss or to withhold the ideas she was planning to share. In this case there is little urgency to the meeting: There are few goals at stake, they are not urgent, and it will be only a matter of time until the worker can see her boss on another occasion. Hence, little or no frustration is experienced. Likewise, more passive responses (such as fixation and/or resignation) are more likely when, for whatever reasons, aggression is impossible or is seen as too risky.

In short, we can go back to Berkowitz (1989, p. 68) who raised the question of what makes a frustration situation aversive and more likely to result in aggressive responses. He wrote: "Frustrations can give rise to aggressive inclinations because they are aversive [and] only to the extent that they are unpleasant to those affected" (p. 68).[2] If the blockage is aversive, aggression is likely to occur. If the blockage is not experienced as aversive, the connection between frustration and aggression is attenuated. What makes a frustration aversive? As we noted earlier, one key factor is the assumed intentions of the parties who cause the blockage. If we believe that there has been a capricious, unwarranted, or malicious intention driving the actions of other people to thwart us, the experience is aversive, and aggressive impulses are more likely to result. Similarly, if the blockage represents the failure to attain something we wanted badly, the experience is likely to be more aversive than otherwise and therefore more likely to produce aggressive desires. But, again, there are no simple, direct connections between experienced, aversive frustration, and the choice of a behavioral reaction.

---

[2] One theorist denies a simple link between the choice of a response to frustration and the severity of the frustration itself (see Gloria, 1984).

People who typically believe they have little or no control over their outcomes (so-called "externals" in the parlance of locus of control theory), impulsive people who are poor at controlling and regulating their own behavior (see Chapter 12), people who lack social sensitivity and/or who feel alienated from their surroundings are also likely to resort to more assertive and possibly less socially acceptable responses to frustration. Figure 8.3 also shows that a person's beliefs about the odds of being caught for antisocial acts also may inhibit or enhance the selection of a forceful response to felt frustration.

Frustration and Aggression Up Close

As mentioned earlier, aggression is a common and highly predictable reaction to need frustration. The connection between frustration and aggression is so strong that 70 years ago the Yale psychologists mentioned earlier pronounced that "aggression is always a consequence of frustration" and "the occurrence of aggressive behavior always presupposes the existence of frustration" (Dollard et al., 1939, p. 1, quoted by Berkowitz, 1993, p. 59). Since then we have learned that there are more causes of aggression than only frustration, and that frustration can result in consequences other than aggression. Nevertheless, the connection between the two concepts is still regarded as powerful.

Usually defined as some form of attack accompanied by anger (Maier, 1973, p. 73), *aggression* can be open and aboveboard, or more covert and less obvious. Berkowitz (1989) adopted the view that there are two varieties of aggression: Hostile and instrumental. *Hostile aggression* is intended to hurt or to cause damage. *Instrumental aggression* is intended to attain an objective, such as money, land, the affections of a mate, or another commodity (p. 62). Examples of hostile aggression might include bawling out a subordinate or hitting a coworker. Less obvious examples include gossiping about someone behind his back or voting against a colleague's project proposal in an executive committee meeting. Overt or covert, hostile aggression is intended to somehow damage, hurt, or frustrate its target.

The majority of our focus here is on hostile aggression and its causes and consequences for work motivation and the workplace.[3] More recent definitions are in concert with the early Berkowitz definition. For example, Neuman and Baron (1997) employ the term workplace aggression to refer to "efforts by individuals to harm others with whom they work, or have worked, or the organizations in which they are currently, or were previously, employed" (p. 38). Following Buss (1961), workplace aggression can be physical or verbal, active or passive, and either directly or indirectly aimed at the source of the frustration. The key thing is that workplace aggression is intended to harm someone or something related to the workplace experience.

Individual Differences and Propensity Toward Aggression at Work

When and under what circumstances does frustration lead to aggression? Spector's (1997) model, as we have seen, provides a number of clues (see Figure 8.3). Current thinking continues to follow that of Berkowitz (1989) and others (e.g., Neuman & Baron, 1997), adhering quite closely to the original frustration–aggression formulation advanced by Dollard et al. (1939), but has been modified in recent years to include a variety of cognitive, dispositional, and affective factors.

Fox and Spector (1999), for example, developed and successfully tested a multivariate model in which individual dispositions (locus of control beliefs about one's work, negative affectivity, and trait

---

[3] Hostile aggression is one of many antisocial and frequently dysfunctional forms of behavior we discuss in this book. The key thing is that hostile aggression is intentional, designed to harm another person or an organization. This makes it different from uncivil behavior, procedural and interactional injustice, which are discussed in other chapters.

anger), as well as a key situational variable – the perceived likelihood of being caught in the expression of aggression – interacted to determine the frequency of aggressive responses to organizational frustration. Trait aggressiveness was found by Bushman and Wells (1998) to be predictive of penalty minutes served by hockey players for aggressive penalties (such as fighting), as opposed to penalty minutes for more passive infractions (such as delay of game). Similarly, Douglas and Martinko (2001) found that trait anger, negative affectivity, self-control, and attitudes toward revenge were related to self-reports of workplace aggression among samples of transportation company employees and employees of a public school system.

Finally, a study by Greenberg and Barling (1999) found that different individual and contextual factors were associated with aggression against different victims in the workplace. Specifically, in a sample of nonacademic employees in a Canadian university, these researchers found that individuals with a history of violence and the amount of alcohol consumed predicted aggression against coworkers, whereas aggression against one's supervisor was predicted by perceived procedural injustice and the use of workplace surveillance techniques. However, none of these personal or workplace factors was predictive of aggressive acts against subordinates.

In short, recent work in the person × context paradigm (recall Chapter 2) has demonstrated that the old frustration–aggression syndrome is not a simple main effect: There are many personal and organizational factors that interact to determine the occurrence of aggression in work settings.

Displaced Aggression and Scapegoating

The targets of aggressive acts are often not the actual causes of the frustration. This phenomenon is referred to as *displaced aggression* or *scapegoating*. In organizational settings, a middle manager who is disciplined or frustrated by a superior may in turn vent his frustration on his own subordinates. Similarly, employees whose education levels are blocking them from receiving further promotions may turn their aggression against their supervisors or coworkers, none of whom is responsible for causing their frustration. Finally, assembly line employees who deliberately sabotage the products they build (e.g., Dubois, 1979; Jermier, 1988) can be seen as taking out the aggression caused by the monotonous nature of their jobs on a handy, convenient scapegoat.

It was clear to Maier (1961) that behavior of this sort is not motivational because goal orientation is not involved, there is no apparent attempt to solve problems, to remove barriers, or to make things right again. Aggression of this sort is a product unto itself, not a means to another end (the accomplishment of a goal). Relief comes (or can come) merely through the expression of the act. It is, by definition, frustration-instigated behavior. The *principle of availability* is a potent predictor of the targets against which a person may select to aggress. People or objects nearby and unable to strike back are frequently the objects of a frustrated person's aggression. Wife beatings and child abuse by chronically unemployed workers are examples.

One reason that aggression so commonly results from frustration is that it often works to remove the frustrating barriers. A bully who usually wins through intimidating others soon learns that intimidation and the threat of force are quite effective in helping him achieve his goals. People do those things they find to be rewarding (see Chapter 14). Moreover, aggressive styles may evolve as a person ages and advances from the simple use of brute force to the use of less physical, but equally forceful tactics such as sarcastic verbal attacks. Employee behavior ranging from theft and pilfering to the formation of a union (cf. Stagner, 1956) may be seen as aggressive responses against organizational realities that perpetually frustrate human needs. Employees who feel locked into their jobs have limited constructive means for dealing with their frustration and as a result are more likely to resort to either aggression or displaced aggression in their jobs.

WHY ALL THE MAYHEM AT WORK?

A variety of factors contribute to the shocking rate of workplace violence (Capozzi & McVey, 1996; Elliott & Jarrett, 1994; Glomb et al., 2002; Johnson & Indvik, 1994). Some characteristics of people's jobs seem to be associated with the incidence of violence in organizations.

Job Design and Personal Circumstances

For example, LeBlanc and Kelloway (2002) have identified 22 job features (such as requirements to handle weapons, to provide for the physical or emotional care of others, to work alone during the evening or overnight, or to enter clients' homes – to name a few) that are related to higher incidence of workplace violence. (They have developed and validated a scale to assess the potential of jobs for violence based on these 22 factors.) Some workplace violence is caused by frustration that originates outside work, such as in the home or family setting. The general crime rate in the community in which a workplace is located may affect the violence that occurs within that workplace (Dietz, Robinson, Folger, Baron, & Schulz, 2003). Some of it is triggered when events at work dredge up suppressed violence that people witness as children. Perceptions of unfairness and inequity in the treatment of employees enter into the frequency of violence in work settings (Leck, 2005).

Indeed, the workplace is a forum of hierarchy, frustration, and real and imagined threat for many people. Job insecurities based on organizational changes such as mergers, acquisitions, work redesign, and the introduction of new technology can pose threats and opportunities for aggression to be expressed. In fact, a combination of economic factors, including the tough economic times we have been having, combined with high rates of competition for fewer and fewer good jobs, immigration, and the multiculturalism and diversity brought about by immigration, can comprise real or imagined barriers for career advancement in the minds of many North Americans who are willing to take up arms against their coworkers or bosses (Elliott & Jarrett, 1994; Leck, 2005; Neuman & Baron, 1997). The dynamics associated with layoffs, particularly perceptions of justice (and injustice) by employees, are treated in Chapter 11. The current discussion will be of particular importance then.

Breech of Psychological Contracts

One factor that seems to underlie many of these sources of threat and frustration is violation of psychological contracts between workers and employers (Robinson & Rousseau, 1994; Rousseau, 1989; Rousseau & Parks, 1993). When agreements and promises appear to have been broken, career expectations are dashed. Persons seen as the cause of such events can quickly become the targets of aggression of the sort and scale described earlier. Another factor that seems associated with violence and aggression is interactional injustice: People are more likely to lash out when they believe they are being treated badly (see Folger & Skarlicki, 1998; and Chapter 13).

Sabotage

A less dramatic form of aggression in the workplace is sabotage: A deliberate action or inaction intended to damage, destroy, or disrupt some aspect of the workplace environment, including the organization's property, product, processes, or reputation, with the net effect of undermining goals of capitalist elites (Giacalone, Riordan, & Rosenfeld, 1997; LaNuez & Jermier, 1994 p. 221, following Taylor & Watson, 1971). We normally think of sabotage as perpetrated by unskilled or semiskilled personnel. In fact, sabotage is frequently the tactic of choice among managers, professionals, and "technocrats" (Jermier, 1988; LaNuez & Jermier, 1994). Besides obvious acts of sabotage such as shutting down production lines, damaging equipment and supplies, or generally "throwing a wrench in the works," managerial and professional personnel can conduct sabotage by deeds such as divulging company secrets, circulating bogus rumors, erasing company computer files, blowing the whistle on questionable practices, and/or litigating – suing the employer for alleged wrongdoings (see Giacalone & Greenberg, 1997). Anything that hurts the company's best interests qualifies as sabotage, and anyone may participate.[4]

Other Non-Aggressive Responses to Frustration

In our discussion of Alderfer's ERG theory, the concept of frustration–regression was introduced. *Regression* consists of the use of behaviors that are less sophisticated and less mature than those befitting a particular person (Maier, 1961, p. 107). They are childlike, or at least characteristic of behaviors learned during one's earlier developmental stages, or alternatively, simply less mature, even if they were not practiced and learned by the frustrated adult when he was younger (Maier, 1961). Common manifestations of regression include behaviors such as horseplay, swearing, humor (Duncan, Smeltzer, & Leap, 1990), crude and cruel joking (especially in male-dominated workplaces; see Collinson, 1992; Kahn, 1989), and, among women, crying. Women are as capable as men at most forms of regression (see Collinson, 1992). For example, a female employee of Deere and Co. of Moline, Illinois, was caught several years ago photocopying her bare bottom on a company copier and was dismissed as a result. The concept of availability also pertains here. People may tend to engage in regressive acts that are easiest to accomplish or that more readily cause relief. Again, this is behavior without a goal other than the expression of the behavior itself. It may reduce tension, but it is not motivated by the attainment of an external goal.

Crying represents a particularly complex example, as does the use of foul language or physical violence. On the one hand, these styles of behavior represent adaptive responses that a youth or adolescent might employ in reaction to frustration. They may even have been useful during a person's younger years for removing frustrating barriers. When employed as a response to frustration by adults, on the other hand, regressive acts often function to increase the intensity of the frustration. For example, a woman who characteristically cries in response to frustration or attack in board meetings can inadvertently increase the tendency of her male colleagues to discount her managerial "cool" and ability. Similarly, a foul-mouthed male may add to his own exclusion from the inner circles of a management group simply by reconfirming that as an immature lout with a dirty mouth, he deserves to be excluded. Regression sometimes works to assist in the removal of the barriers that cause employee need frustration, but it can boomerang and make the frustration worse.

Fixation is another common behavioral response to need frustration. It involves repeated use of the same goal-seeking behaviors despite their ineffectiveness. For example, a student who continually approaches a mathematics problem using only one or two strategies, despite evidence that those strategies are not appropriate, is engaging the fixated behavior. Repeated failures breed even greater feelings of futility and make the adoption of more adaptive behaviors less likely. In work settings, fixated behavior can be pathetic because unlike aggression or regression, which sometimes result in goal accomplishment, it cannot, by definition, lead to success. Resorting to fixated behavior can be damaging to one's self-concept because of the image of helplessness it entails (see Korman, 1970, 1976; Hall, 1976; these articles discuss the importance of success experiences for one's self-esteem).

---

[4] Jermier's (1988) treatment of sabotage assumes that it is based on inherent conflictual forces in the workplace, where the interests of various groups such as owners, executives, managers, professionals, and production workers cannot be assumed to be in harmony merely because they are all associated with a common "organization." Jermier's chapter is rich with examples.

It is worth noting at this point that one reason behind the oft-noted resistance to change in organizations (Zaltman & Duncan, 1977) is that change can make learned and familiar behaviors by employees obsolete and frustrating. In other words, change (such as a redesigned organizational structure or a new work process) can generate very real barriers to the behaviors that employees have used in the past, barriers to the behaviors associated with goal accomplishment, and, with it, need satisfaction. There are many examples of how the introduction of new computer technology (e.g., Mann & Williams, 1972) has been seen by workers as a threat and source of frustration, resulting in considerable unhappiness for them as well as reduced effectiveness of the new technology.

Another response to frustration that has particular relevance to work behavior is *resignation*. In simple terms this amounts to "giving up" – becoming docile, uninspired, and nonchalant. In many ways it is a nonresponse, insofar as the frustrated person merely continues to show up for work, performing to a minimum expected standard, obeying the rules, and getting by. This style of adaptation is in essence the style that reinforces belief in Theory X, according to McGregor (1960). Argyris (1957) claimed it is the natural response that one can expect when employee needs for growth collide with organizational structures and procedures designed to achieve efficiency and control. It accounts for much of the half-hearted service we observe from workers in service industries and much of the apparent lack of intelligence and creativity exhibited by many people in various industrial settings. People adapt to the frustration caused by their job experiences by simply bringing their bodies to work and leaving their hearts, minds, and souls at home. We return to resignation and other forms of withdrawal from the job (such as absenteeism and turnover) in Chapter 10 when we examine work-related beliefs and attitudes in detail.

SUMMARY

There are a variety of responses to frustration, and the one chosen in a given circumstance will be affected by the frustrated person's interpretation of the frustration situation. The foregoing examples suggest that cool problem solving is not always the reaction of choice to frustration situations. There are a variety of other, less constructive ways of responding to frustration – forms of behavior that are often found in organizational settings, such as that of Professor Fabrikant of Concordia University.

The reader is encouraged to use the frustration framework for viewing, understanding, and dealing with dysfunctional employee behaviors ranging from tardiness and absenteeism to poor quality and low levels of work effort. The insights into employee attitudes, emotions, behavior, and performance that this model can reveal are among the most useful available at present for understanding work motivation (or the lack of it) from the perspective of need-based models. The frustration model is especially useful for understanding deviant, aberrant, and antisocial behaviors such as theft, lying, tardiness, sabotage, whistleblowing, and litigating against one's employer (Giacalone & Greenberg, 1997). When we think of it, most human behavior occurs in states of relative deprivation, so frustration, in varying degrees, is the normal condition for most of us most of the time.[5]

---

[5] The principles of frustration here will be especially important as background when we explore problems of equity, fairness, and justice in the workplace in Chapter 11.

OVERVIEW OF NEED-BASED THEORIES AND A GLANCE AHEAD

This concludes Part Two of the book, our treatment of need-based approaches to work motivation. It is critical to note at this point that need-based theories of work motivation comprise only one general approach to the issues discussed in this book, albeit one of the most popular approaches in the history of the organizational sciences. The activity devoted to studying these theories of work motivation has declined dramatically among social scientists since approximately the mid-1970s. The attack on need-based theories of job satisfaction (and of motivation and related concepts) by Salancik and Pfeffer (1977) seemed to precipitate a shift in emphasis in the field away from needs and toward models that are predicated on different root assumptions regarding human nature.

This author believes that a total abandonment of need-based models is inappropriate. It is true that need-based models have limitations and ambiguities. Many of them (such as Maslow's theory) are hard to operationalize for scientific testing, but the more recent use of more appropriate methodologies than were used in the past has proven promising (e.g., Ronen, 1994). Others, such as Herzberg's motivator-hygiene theory (Chapters 2 and 7), simply seem to be at least partially wrong (at least in their too-literal, oversimplified, and commercialized versions) or severely limited in validity. On the other hand, many elements of the motivator-hygiene theory, considered in isolation, have proved very useful for the design of jobs and the structuring of enlightened human resources practices (e.g., Pfeffer, 1994; and see Chapter 7). There is also the problem of the complex connections between and among needs and behaviors (as illustrated in Figure 8.1), making it difficult to predict precise behaviors on the basis of knowledge of a person's predominant need states, or for that matter, to interpret the need states in the first place.

Cognitive theories such as those we examine in Part Three have similar difficulties in subjectivity. We are left with the question: "Are people need-driven, goal-seeking creatures?" The many difficulties of extant need-based models notwithstanding, the author's answer is: Yes, indeed, we are, at least in part. The difficulties scientists have had in testing the validity of need theories are as important as the disappointing results usually yielded in scientific tests. Meanwhile, human needs such as power, love, sex, achievement, and self-esteem continue to manifest themselves constantly in human affairs, especially in the workplace (see Chapters 5 and 6).

In Part Three, we turn our attention toward theories of work motivation that are predicated on the root assumption that human beings are information processors, and that their work motivation and behavior can best be understood by reference to their beliefs, attitudes, intentions, and goals. These theories have been dominant for three decades among organizational scholars. Their ascendancy can be explained in part, but not completely, by the problems inherent in need-based models. Early forms of many of the cognitive theories to be discussed in Part Three were developed in the 1950s and 1960s, when need-based theories were dominant in the field as well as in practice among managers.

PART THREE

Concepts of Work Motivation and Ultimate Determinants of Behavior

Beliefs, Attitudes, and Intentions

9

He that complies against his will is
of his own opinion still
Samuel Butler

The purpose of this chapter is to examine in general terms the meaning and importance of beliefs and attitudes and how they are related to human behavior, setting the stage for a discussion in subsequent chapters of many particular beliefs and attitudes that are of special interest in the context of work and work motivation (such as job satisfaction, organizational commitment, job involvement, equity, and fairness, among others). Given that the body of research and theory on human attitudes is voluminous in its own right (see Pratkanis & Greenwald, 1989), we must restrict our focus somewhat. We refer the reader who wants a comprehensive treatment of the psychology of attitudes to scholarly reviews such as those of Eagly and Chaiken (1993) and Olson and Zanna (1993). Here, we focus on the work of Ajzen (1991), Ajzen and Fishbein (1977), and Fishbein and Ajzen (1975), along with a little help here and there from other sources and scholars as needed.

The current chapter also serves as a sort of transition point in the book as a whole: It will turn our attention away from models of human functioning that are primarily need-based and toward a set of theories that assume human beings to be information-processing creatures. As is the case when we adopt a need-based model of behavior, there is plenty of controversy about the relevance and usefulness of relying on hypothetical constructs such as attitudes, beliefs, and the like (recall Chapter 2). Nowhere has the debate on this matter been more heated than in the organizational sciences, and it has been underway for years (see, for example, Karmel, 1980). There are some camps in the discipline that, following schools of behaviorism in psychology (see Chapter 14), do not deny that people hold attitudes toward objects and phenomena, but they do dismiss as unnecessary the invocation of concepts such as attitudes for explaining or predicting work behavior. So, to begin, what are attitudes?

THE NATURE OF HUMAN ATTITUDES

People have attitudes. People hold attitudes toward many or most of the other people in their life spaces. They also tend to form attitudes in relation to tangible as well as intangible objects, causes, concepts, acts, and other phenomena with which they are familiar. The holding of attitudes is clearly one of the characteristics of human beings. Much of a person's identity is definable and understandable in terms of the attitudes s/he holds, how firmly the attitudes are held, and how easily changed his or her attitudes are.

But this is a book about work motivation and behavior. Accordingly, it is also about people's attitudes regarding their work, their careers, their occupations and professions, and toward the companies and other employers for whom they work. In other words, a comprehensive treatment of work motivation and behavior requires a thorough understanding of human attitudes in a generic sense because attitudes play a central role in much of the most important current thought about specific attitudes regarding why and how people work.

253

THE NATURE OF ATTITUDES IN GENERAL

To get things started, we borrow a straighforward definition of *attitude* from Eagly and Chaiken (1993):

> Attitude is a psychological tendency that is expressed by evaluation of a particular entity with some degree of favor or disfavor . . . [P]sychological tendency refers to a state that is internal to the person, and evaluating refers to all classes of evaluative responding, whether overt or covert, cognitive, affective, or behavioral.
>
> (Eagly & Chaiken, 1993, p. 1)

Olson and Zanna (1993) claimed that there are a variety of definitions of attitudes and no single commonly accepted definition. (This is a familiar theme throughout this book: A failure of social scientists in general and motivation theorists in particular to agree on definitions of common terms.) Nevertheless, there appear to be three common themes or elements that run through the most common definitions, according to Olson and Zanna (1993).[1]

The first element is that attitudes generally involve an *evaluative* component. An attitude doesn't normally form until a person has made some evaluation of an attitude object (such as toward her car, her boss, or her job). A second common component of definitions of attitudes is that they are often conceived of as *links between belief structures and knowledge structures*, such that the invocation of one attitude often triggers other mental events. When topics are somehow inter-related for a person (such as long working hours and the comparative willingness of supervisors to grant days off for sick leave), thinking about one of these matters can quickly lead to thought of the other.

The third common element of definitions and conceptualizations of attitudes is that *they entail cognitive, affective* and *behavior components*, and *"correlates."* As we detail later, the cognitive component might be a piece of information, a simple fact about some subject ("That house is painted blue"). Not only can cognition of this sort be part of an attitude, but such a cognition can trigger attitudes (Olson & Zanna, 1993, p. 120). Thus, the very blueness of a newly painted house may cause a person to form an attitude about blue houses for the first time ("I've never considered whether I like blue houses until now. I sort of like them, I guess").

Similarly, all attitudes have long been seen as having *an affective component*, usually some degree of emotional reaction based on a person's values ("I hate the color blue"). Such an affective reaction may trigger an attitude, similar to the way the cognitive fact about the blue house may cause a newly formed attitude. Finally, attitudes have generally been seen as including a *behavioral intention* ("I plan to paint my house blue next summer"). Again, it is believed currently that being exposed to such a behavioral intention may initiate an attitde that wasn't there previously. ("If McPhillips is going to paint his house blue, maybe that's a good color for a house; in fact, I think I actually like blue houses.")

In short, current thinking about attitudes by social psychologists is that the traditional components of attitudes – the cognitive, the affective, and the intention – not only continue to comprise the three key elements of an attitude but can also be antecedents of attitudes, although "these domains will not necessarily all apply to a given attitude" (Olson & Zanna, 1993).

---

[1] The "tripartite" definition of attitudes is popular and has dominated thinking in the literature on attitudes for centuries, but it is not the only view. A review of radical criticisms of the tripartite view is provided by Tesser and Shaffer (1990).

The Functions of Attitudes

Attitudes serve many functions for human beings, some of which may be judged as positive, others as not so positive. Pratkanis and Greenwald (1989) have identified the following list of uses of attitudes as a heuristic in conceptual processing:

1. Attitudes can help us interpret and explain social events.
2. Through their formation of *halo effects*, attitudes can bias the expectations and inferences we make about people simply on the basis of our knowledge that they belong to certain groups or categories.
3. Attitudes toward the conclusions of syllogisms can have an influence on whether we accept the conclusions as valid or not valid.
4. Whether a person's attitude toward a person or object is positive or negative can influence whether the person offers counterarguments against attempts by other people to persuade them into believing things about the object in question.
5. When people encounter others with attitudes similar to their own, there is a positive influence on the interpersonal attraction between them.
6. When people hold a certain attitude toward another person, they tend to believe that that person holds attitudes similar to their own.
7. People sometimes believe that the attitudes they hold are more popular and more widely held than is actually the case.
8. Holding an attitude can lead to the selective reconstruction and recollection of past events.
9. A person's recollection of her past attitudes and behavior can be revised to be consistent with her current attitudes toward the same attitude objects.
10. Through a mechanism referred to as an information error technique, people will be biased in selecting among bits of false information to choose those that are most consistent with their own current attitudes.
11. Holding an attitude can influence the predictions we make about future events. Wanting something to occur because we have a positive attitude toward it causes us unduly to expect it to occur.

Functional perspective

One way we can think of attitudes is to examine them from a functionalist perspective, asking: What services (or disservices) do attitudes perform for us? What are the functions of attitudes? Pratkanis and Greenwald's (1989) compilation of the scientific evidence suggests that there are many answers to these questions: Attitudes serve a variety of functions in the way people perceive and behave toward the social world. Interestingly, many of these functions are driven by the human tendency toward consistency: To varying degrees, people prefer their attitudes, beliefs, and behaviors to be in concert (Cialdini, 1993). It will be important to keep both this list of functions of attitudes and the principle of attitudinal consistency in mind in subsequent chapters when we examine people's beliefs and attitudes about such things as their employers, their coworkers, and the treatment they receive at work.

THE THEORY OF REASONED ACTION

For the purposes of this book, in which the focus is on work motivation and employee attitudes, we rely most heavily on the theory of attitudes that is still the most commonly used when the issue is the connection between attitudes and behavior (Olson & Zanna, 1993), called the *theory of reasoned action* (TRA) (Fishbein & Ajzen, 1975). If this book were devoted purely to social psychology, a variety of formulations would have to be presented. Because we are interested here primarily in employee attitudes and the relationships between employee attitudes and behaviors (e.g., perform-ance, absenteeism, and prosocial acts in the workplace), TRA, although more than 30 years old, is the most useful tool for our purposes (Olson & Zanna, 1993; Tesser & Shaffer, 1990):

> [TRA] is based on the assumption that human beings are usually quite rational and make systematic use of the information available to them. We do not subscribe to the view that human social behavior is controlled by unconscious motives or overpowering desires, nor do we believe that it can be charac-terized as capricious or thoughtless. Rather, we argue that people consider the implications of their actions before they decide to engage or not engage in a given behavior.
>
> (Ajzen & Fishbein, 1980, p. 5)

Figure 9.1 is a schematic representing the theory of reasoned action. It is offered as a visual guide to our explanation of how beliefs and attitudes may or may not result in employee behavior.

The reader will note that this is an entirely different perspective on the origins of human behavior than we featured throughout Part One (Chapters 3 through 8). No reference is made to forces such as needs or environmental pressures, although this theory makes use of hypothetical constructs of its own, such as beliefs, values, and expectancies. We adopt here the definition of attitude that Fishbein and Ajzen offered in 1975.

Definition of TRA

Fishbein and Ajzen (1975) defined attitude as the degree of positive or negative feeling (or affect) a person has toward a particular attitude object, such as a place, thing, or other person. (This is readily reconcilable with the definition provided earlier, as borrowed from Eagly & Chaiken, 1993.) Thus, when we speak of positive job attitudes, we mean that the people involved tend to have pleasant internal feelings when they think about their jobs, although different aspects of one's job are bound to cause different sorts of feelings. On one level, this concept of attitude makes intuitive sense and fits with our everyday understanding of the meaning of the concept. On another level, we must still address the question of the origins and causes of these affective

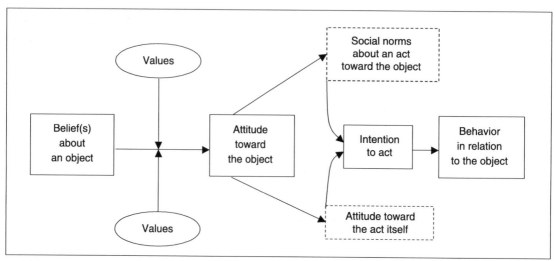

FIG. 9.1   Representation of the theory of reasoned action.

Source: Adapted from Ajzen, I., & Fishbein, M. (1980). *Understanding attitudes and predicting social behavior.* Upper Saddle River, NJ: Prentice-Hall.

reactions. In other words, what causes us to feel particularly good or bad about specific things or people?

The Nature of Beliefs

Part of the answer to the question regarding the origin of affective reaction lies in the beliefs we hold about the objects, persons, or things in question. A *belief* is a person's "subjective probability judgment concerning a relation between the object of the belief and some other object, value, concept, or attribute" (Fishbein & Ajzen, 1975, p. 131). It is a mental linkage tying an entity to a property in a probabilistic manner. For example, we might hold the belief that a certain occupation is challenging. The attitude object here is the occupation. The attribute is the property of being challenging. The strength of a person's belief about an attitude object consists of the magnitude of the probability in her mind that the object is associated with the attribute (Fishbein & Ajzen, 1975, p. 134).

How are beliefs formed? According to Fishbein and Ajzen (1975), we can think of three different types of belief, each formed by a different means. These are called descriptive beliefs, inferential beliefs, and beliefs formed on the basis of information from outside sources. Let's take a brief look at these. *Descriptive beliefs* are formed on the basis of a person's own observations. For example, an employee may notice that his supervisor keeps his office neat and form the belief that his supervisor is generally a tidy person. *Inferential beliefs* result from logical connections that people make in their minds between certain thoughts. For example, consider a person who holds antiunion attitudes and also believes that promotions should be based on merit rather than seniority. Assume further that this person has never considered the possible link between these two concepts (unions and the various bases for promotion). When asked to indicate whether he believes that unions normally favor seniority or merit as the primary basis for promotion, it is likely that the person would reply that unions probably favor seniority. The person would reach such a conclusion for either of two reasons. First, because it is inconsistent for a person to hold conflicting or unbalanced perceptions and beliefs about objects and issues (Heider, 1958), it is unlikely that he would associate something he positively evaluates (promotion on the basis of merit) with something else that he evaluates negatively (unions). Therefore, out of a desire to be internally consistent, he would probably conclude that unions favor promotions on the basis of seniority rather than merit. A second reason for his probable conclusion has to do with probabilistic reasoning on his part, such as the following: (1) anti-management groups naturally tend not to favor promotions on the basis of merit; (2) unions are generally anti-management; therefore, (3) unions probably favor promotions on the basis of seniority rather than merit. In short, inferential beliefs result from either the desire to be internally consistent and/or any of a number of logical processes.

A third source of beliefs consists of other people or outside information sources, such as newspapers. Once they are accepted, beliefs originating from external sources are similar in nature to beliefs formed through personal observation (Fishbein & Ajzen, 1975).

Several important points follow from Fishbein and Ajzen's concept of belief. Notice that beliefs may or may not be valid, depending on the accuracy of the information on which they are based. Descriptive beliefs are less prone to the influences of a person's prior beliefs and attitudes than are inferential beliefs (Fishbein & Ajzen, 1975). In other words, people are much less likely to formulate false beliefs based on their personal observation of events than they are when their beliefs are based on any of the types of inferential processes just described.

Second, notice that because of the potential role of personal bias in the formation of inferential beliefs, it is quite possible for any two people to hold differing beliefs about the same attitude object, even when they share common experiences. For example, two students may both spend a summer working as interns in the same accounting office. One of them may conclude that accounting is a dull occupation, but the other may have the opposite belief. Even descriptive beliefs vary between people when they pay attention to different aspects of their experiences with attitude objects.

A third point worth emphasizing has to do with the important influence that outside sources can have in the structuring of beliefs (see Salancik & Pfeffer, 1978). This phenomenon is particularly powerful for newcomers to work settings, who must learn new jobs, become acquainted with new colleagues, and assimilate myriad other details about aspects of that work setting (see Graen, 1976; Van Maanen, 1977; Wanous, 1980).

A fourth point concerns the number of beliefs that people hold about attitude objects. Because of the natural limits to human cognition, it is likely that most attitudes are formed on the basis of no more than five to nine beliefs concerning an attitude object. Of course, many people seem to desire fewer than five pieces of information about another person or object. Beliefs differ in the salience as well as in the importance they hold for people, such that individuals formulate their attitudes about objects because of those characteristics that stand out for them or seem most crucial. For example, an employee who is acutely aware of his low rate of pay is likely to mention it early in any conversation he has about his job.

A final important feature of beliefs is that they tend to be internally consistent with one another. For example, there is evidence that people tend to link personal attributes of other people in predictable clusters, such that a belief that a person is poised will lead to the assumption that the same person is also calm, composed, and nonhypochondriacal (Fishbein & Ajzen, 1975). Clusters about attitude objects other than people also tend to go hand in hand, largely because human beings tend to prefer consistency among their beliefs, actions, and attitudes (Festinger, 1957; Heider, 1958).

Combining Beliefs and Attitudes

As suggested earlier: "An attitude represents a person's general feeling of favorableness or unfavorableness toward some stimulus object . . . [A]s a person forms beliefs about an object, he automatically and simultaneously acquires an attitude toward that object. Each belief links the object to some attribute; the person's attitude toward the object is a function of his evaluations of these attributes" (Fishbein & Ajzen, 1975, p. 216).

To return to our previous example, one summer intern may have a positive attitude about accountancy because he believes that it is interesting and because he evaluates positively the property of being interesting. Similarly, an employee may dislike his job because he believes that he is underpaid for the work he does, and he evaluates negatively the condition of underpayment he perceives. In this view, attitudes are the affective (emotional) reactions people hold about attitude objects based on the way they evaluate the attributes they associate with those objects.[2]

The general attitude a person has toward an object is seen as an aggregation of all the beliefs that she holds about it, each weighted by the positive or negative evaluations she places on the various beliefs. Therefore, two employees may have the same set of beliefs about a job ("It's repetitive") but hold different attitudes toward it because one of them prefers routine work whereas the other desires more uncertainty. Alternatively, the same two employees may have differing beliefs about an object or person (such as their common supervisor) but have similar attitudes toward him. For example, one employee may be aware of the supervisor's prowess at the pub after work and admire him for it, whereas the second employee may positively evaluate the supervisor for what he believes to be his characteristic fairness.

To summarize, we can say that the connection between beliefs and attitudes is the following: If a person approves of or positively evaluates the attributes that he associates in his belief structure with an object, he will tend to hold a positive general attitude toward that object. Contrariwise, if the attributes he connects in his beliefs with an object are characteristics he evaluates negatively, he will

---

[2] The reader is reminded, however, that people differ in the degree of incongruity and inconsistency they tolerate in their minds (recall Chapters 3 and 7, where we discussed intrinsic motivation).

hold a negative overall attitude toward the object. So to influence a person's attitudes about an object (say a job), we might introduce new information about that job that links the job with attributes that the employee evaluates positively (such as its variety and status). Alternatively, we might attempt to change the employee's assessment of the desirability or undesirability of the attributes the employee now associates with a job.[3]

Stability and change of beliefs and attitudes

How stable or susceptible to change are human beliefs about attitude objects? Traditional thought on this matter has held that attitudes (and the beliefs on which they rest) are relatively permanent predispositions of people toward attitude objects (other people, jobs, organizations, or whatever). More recent thinking (e.g., Fiske, 1993; Fiske & Taylor, 1991; Levine, Resnick, & Higgins, 1993) recognizes that attitudes – particularly attitudes that people form and hold about one another – are heavily influenced by the social contexts in which people exist; that is, how people feel about attitude objects is heavily influenced by the descriptive and evaluative information they acquire through their social interactions with other people. This alternative view, however, fails to recognize that there is some consistency and stability to attitudes over time – they do not swing wildly from one social setting to another. Therefore, a third view has been advanced that balances both the "attitudes as fixed dispositions" position and the "attitudes as socially constructed beliefs" position. For the sake of discussion, we refer to this third position as the information-processing approach (Calder & Schurr, 1981).

For Calder and Schurr (1981), an attitude is an integration of the evaluative meaning of sets of thoughts that a person holds in memory (p. 287; see also Olson and Zanna, 1993). Thoughts are similar to beliefs, as we discussed them earlier. Thus an attitude might be reflected in statements such as the following: "I think the company's transfer policy is quite liberal" or "I think the people I work with are dull and uninteresting." These thoughts need not be uttered in any way; they can be held privately by a person. (Notice the role of evaluation in this conception of attitudes. It corresponds with the evaluative nature of attitudes in the Fishbein and Ajzen model presented earlier.)

The concept of storage in memory is important (Olson & Zanna, 1993). Olson and Zanna (1993) consider both long- and short-term memory. The former serves two functions: The ongoing storage of information pertaining to an attitude object, and the interpretation of new information that is being processed in a particular setting by the person's short-term memory. As a person interacts with his surroundings, information is gathered about attitude objects. This information is processed with the assistance of information stored by the person in long-term memory, the contents of which help the person make sense of new information, as it were. For example, if an employee hears a manager promise to redistribute workloads to make it possible for her staff to get away early on a long weekend, she will process this promise while remembering other promises made by the supervisor on past occasions. As new information is interpreted through the perceptual apparatus provided by memory, it, in turn, enters long-term memory and modifies or updates the contents of the memory bank. Thus, attitudes are influenced by the characteristics and nuances of the settings in which attitude objects are considered, but they are also heavily subject to the interpretive assistance provided by past experiences; thereby featuring some degree of stability over time. We might say that the information-processing approach sees attitudes as structured and developed according to a type of dynamic equilibrium process.

A study by Griffin (1982) illustrated that one type of belief that is of particular interest to this book is in fact relatively slow changing – the nature of the perceptions people have about the capacity of their jobs to bring about intrinsic motivation and satisfaction. In Chapter 7, we

---

[3] Notice again the potential role of inaccurate beliefs for the formation of attitudes. Propaganda programs designed to change people's attitudes toward enemy groups focus heavily upon introducing to the populace belief-structuring information about the enemy more than upon trying to make the populace evaluate differently the information they hold.

examined job design and redesign models, the most popular of which, the job characteristics model, relies heavily on employee beliefs that their jobs possess motivating qualities. Griffin's research suggested that these beliefs are relatively stable over time, although people's affective reactions to these beliefs (their attitudes) may be less stable.

Attitudes, Intentions, and Behavior

There has been considerable debate over the years concerning the nature of the relationship between attitudes and behavior. As mentioned earlier, it seems to make intuitive sense to many people that attitudes are major causes of the way we feel about them. An alternative view has it the other way around: That people's behavior toward objects and other people may help shape their attitudes toward them (Bem, 1967, 1972). A few explanations are available for this possibility (Olson & Zanna, 1993; Tesser & Shaffer, 1990). The first is that sometimes an individual's internal states such as emotions and attitudes are weak and ambiguous, so they must infer these states by referring to knowledge about their overt behavior and the contexts in which the behavior occurred. Cialdini (1993, especially Chapter 3) provides several powerful examples of how even the smallest of acts committed by people can lead to major shifts in espoused attitudes.

A second explanation is based on dissonance theory (Festinger, 1957), which claims that people experience an aversive psychological force when they say and do things that are logically inconsistent with one another, or when they find that their various beliefs, attitudes, and values are logically out of sync. The management of cognitive dissonance has been discounted somewhat as an explanation of attitude change toward consistency (Tesser & Shaffer, 1990).

Therefore, a third explanation is possible: That people are concerned about the impressions they make on others, especially when they are accountable for their views. When a person is not expecting to be accountable to others but only to himself, he may readily change his attitudes to be consistent with his behaviors. If he expects to be accountable, however, he may be less quick to change his attitudes; rather, he may formulate "publicly defensible" opinions after carefuuly considering the issue at hand (Tesser & Shaffer, 1990).

On balance, and theoretical explanations aside, it seems that both causal arguments are valid: Attitudes can be both the antecedents and the consequences of behavior. According to the theory of reasoned action (see Ajzen & Fishbein, 1980), how do attitudes influence behavior? *Attitudes affect behavior only to the extent that they influence a person's intentions to act.* (Recall the earlier example: "I plan to paint my house blue next summer.") That is, attitudes can create a set of possible intentions to behave in certain ways toward the object in question, although a particular attitude usually does not relate to any single intention on a one-to-one basis. For example, an employee may have a generally positive attitude toward her new supervisor following a transfer. That generally positive attitude may predispose her to act in a variety of positive ways toward the supervisor, although it will not be useful as a predictor of any specific behavior (such as volunteering to help the supervisor on a special project without pay during off-hours). Nevertheless, it is possible that the generally favorable attitude will create an intention to do such free overtime work should the occasion arise. The point is that attitudes foster sets of intentions that are consistent with one another as well as consistent with the tone of the attitude itself. But single attitude–intention connections can seldom be predicted in advance.

By way of contrast, every intention, once formed, is associated with specific behaviors. To the extent that behavior is volitional (as opposed to being strictly reflexive or coerced by the environment), people will attempt to do those things they intend to do (Ryan, 1970). Therefore, although the employee likes his new supervisor (because he positively evaluates the beliefs he holds about her), that general attitude may foster several positive intentions. When a specific behavioral opportunity presents itself, the positive attitude may (or may not) translate into an intention to act in a positive or helpful way toward the supervisor. The key is whether the person develops a positive or negative attitude toward the act in question (as we discuss shortly). Nevertheless, once an intention is formed to act in a way that is in keeping with the positive attitude, the employee will strive to behave in the way intended.

To summarize: "[A]ttitude is viewed as a general predisposition that does not predispose the person to perform any specific behavior. Rather, it leads to a set of intentions that indicate a certain amount of affect toward the object in question. Each of these intentions is related to a specific behavior, and thus the overall affect expressed by the pattern of a person's action with respect to the object also corresponds to his attitude toward the object" (Fishbein & Ajzen, 1975, p. 15).

The specificity of intentions

To fully understand the connection between attitudes and intentions, it is necessary to understand more about intentions themselves, particularly about the importance of the specificity of the intentions involved. According to Fishbein and Ajzen (1975), intentions consist of four elements: The particular behavior being considered; the target object toward which the behavior might be directed; the situational context in which the behavior may be performed; and finally, the time at which the behavior is to occur. Each of these elements can vary in terms of how specifically it is considered. The more specific situation involves an intention to perform a clearly defined act toward a specific target in a highly specified place and time. For example, "I intend to walk off the job tomorrow morning after nine o'clock, as soon as I have convinced the rest of the gang to join me!"

Intentions are more closely connected to behavior when they are *specific* (Ajzen & Fishbein, 1977; Jaccard, King, & Pomazal, 1977). In other words, the more any of the four elements of an intention is left general, the weaker the connection to subsequent behavior (Ajzen & Fishbein, 1977). For example, an employee might indicate that she intends to be more punctual in reporting to work. Left at this low level of specificity, we might expect this intention not to result in real punctuality as much as an intention of the form: "I intend never to come to work later than nine o'clock again this year." In the second case, the particular behavior was more specifically articulated than it was in the first case (as was the time involved). Similarly, if the target object of an intention is left general rather than specific, behavior is less probable. Statements such as "I would never vote for a union" may prove to be poorer predictors of actual behavior than statements such as "I will never vote for the Sheepherders' Union, Local 123." The more specific the target of the intention, the more likely it will be associated with behavior that is consistent with the intention.

What about the specificity of the time element? Ajzen and Fishbein (1977) would suggest that statements such as "I plan to go on a diet" will not be as likely to lead to a loss of weight as a statement such as "I'll plan to start a diet in the New Year" (although we are all familiar with the fate of most New Year's resolutions). Finally, we can consider the specificity of the situation. If an employee says he intends to stop smoking on the job, we can expect to see less smoking on his part than if he were simply to say "I will stop smoking." The point is that increases in specificity with regard to the behavior, the target, the time, or the situation involved, will be associated with a higher likelihood that an intention will result in actual behavior that is consistent with it (Ajzen & Fishbein, 1977).

Intentions and Behavior

The final step in understanding why and how attitudes result in behavior requires that we examine how intention, once formed (at whatever level of specificity), leads to behavior. According to Fishbein (1967), there are two important factors that determine intention once attitudes have been formed toward an object. The first of these is itself an *attitudinal factor*, and the second is a *normative factor*. The attitudinal factor has to do with the person's feelings concerning the act being considered. In other words, it consists of the person's attitude toward performing the behavior in question under a particular set of circumstances. Moreover, this attitude (toward the behavior) is determined by both the person's perceived consequences of the behavior and his evaluations of those consequences.

Caution! It is important not to confuse the attitude a person has toward an object (such as one's company) with the attitude he holds toward behaving a certain way toward that object (such as leaking the company's trade secrets to a competitior). The first of these attitudes, as we have said, consists of the individual's evaluations of the beliefs he holds about the object itself. Whether he develops an intention to act in a way consistent with that attitude depends on his attitude toward the aciton implied by the intention. This second attitude, in turn, is determined by the person's beliefs about the probable consequences of his action and his evaluation of those consequences.

To return to our earlier example, the new employee may hold a positive general attitude toward his supervisor and may therefore be generally predisposed to act positively toward her. Suppose the employee learns that the boss requires help at the office after hours on a particular night but that he would have to work without pay and therefore be violating the union contract if he were to volunteer. Will the employee's positive attitude translate into the specific act of offering assistance? Fishbein (1967) would suggest that the employee will form an attitude about the act of volunteering to help. That attitude will be determined by the consequences of the person's evaluation of those consequences. On balance, whether our friend decides to volunteer for the job will depend, in this view, on whatever consequences he expects might result from volunteering and how favorably or unfavorably he evaluates those consequences. Again, we have an evaluation of a set of beliefs, although, to repeat, these beliefs pertain to the likely consequences of behavior, not to the supervisor per se. The theory predicts that if the employee believes that consequences he evaluates positively will outweigh consequences that he evaluates negatively, he will volunteer. If the employee believes that most of the consequences of volunteering will be negative (such as being reprimanded by the shop steward), he will not intend to volunteer and, accordingly, will not do so.

The second determinant of whether an attitude results in an intention, the normative component, concerns the influence of the social environment. That is, it has to do with the person's beliefs about what significant others around him expect him to do. Different people will be sensitive to the expectations placed on them by various people, such as one's spouse, one's coworkers, and so on. A person in a particular situation may consider the expectations of a variety of reference groups in the context of considering a particular behavior. So it may be that helping the supervisor without pay is something members of the work group expect of their youngest member, regardless of who it is and the fact that such work violates the union agreement. By the same token, the employee's new spouse may have a different view of the situation, leaving the employee with some ambivalence and causing the generally positive attitude toward the boss not to result in an offer to work at night.

The self-prophesy effect

Building on earlier work by Sherman (1980), Sprott, Spangenberg, and Fisher (2003) have shown that asking a person whether he or she will undertake a particular behavior increases the probability that they will, indeed, perform that behavior, particularly when the behavior in question is deemed socially desirable or appropriate. In other words, if the individual believes that the target behavior is socially desirable or "the right thing to do," asking them in advance whether they would actually engage in the behavior increases the likelihood that they will, indeed, attempt to perform the act when the circumstances to do so arise. This is referred to as the *self-prophesy effect*.

To summarize, whether an attitude toward an object results in a specific intention to behave in a certain way toward the object depends on the person's attitude about the behavior itself and on his beliefs about the expectations of relevant others regarding the behavior (see Figure 9.1). Notice two or three things about this theory. First, consider the important role played by the person's beliefs both about the attitude object and about the probable consequences of specific acts toward that object. Clearly, beliefs are not always accurate or valid, and they are certainly subject to change. Moreover, beliefs either about an attitude object or about the consequences of certain acts toward it can be heavily influenced by other people as well as by one's personal experiences. Notice, too, that a generally positive (or negative) attitude toward an object may not result in certain behaviors related to that object (such as helping one's supervisor at night) but may result in other behaviors that seem to outsiders to be quite similar (such as volunteering to help the supervisor with a special project during regular working hours).

Perhaps the most important thing to remember about using the theory of reasoned action is that it is highly unlikely that we will be able to predict a person's actions on the basis of our knowledge only of her attitudes toward an attitude object (Ajzen & Fishbein, 1980). Therefore, if we know that a small store owner does not generally like members of a particular ethnic group, it would be very risky to predict whether she would or would not hire a member of that group to work for her on the basis of that fact alone. There may be many reasons in her head for hiring such a person: It is her attitude toward the act of hiring such a person, combined with the power of the subjective social norms that she perceives about hiring her, that will determine her intention, one way or the other. As we have said, the more specific the intention in her mind, once it is formed, the more likely it is that she will (or will not) hire someone from that ethnic group.

Criticisms of the Theory

One of the main limitations of the theory of reasoned action is that it restricts itself to volitional or voluntary behavior, behavior(s) that people perform because they decide to perform them (Eagly & Chaiken, 1993). Therefore, the theory is limited in its capacity to predict behaviors that require skills, resources, or opportunities and conditions that are not available to people. Further, introducing intentions into the model between attitudes and behaviors, strictly speaking, precludes the possibility of understanding categories of behaviors that require little or no thought. Eagly and Chaiken (1993) cite examples such as spontaneous impulses that lead to violence against a hated minority group, behavior that results from a strong craving for a drug, and impulse buying that is driven by brand loyalty and plenty of practice. Similarly, some habitual behavior, such as smoking or fastening one's seat belt upon getting into a car, frequently requires no conscious thought. Merely possessing a well-ingrained attitude may be sufficient to provide a basis for predicting behavior (Eagly & Chaiken, 1993).

A study by Bagozzi and Yi (1989) demonstrated that intentions may sometimes not need to play a role in connecting attitudes and behavior. They conducted an experiment with a sample of marketing students. The task they used was of a voluntary nature, to review and report on a marketing case. Half the students were given a warm-up exercise that was very similar to the case analysis they were asked to perform. The other half of the group was given a bogus exercise that had nothing to do with the marketing case. The researchers used these initial exercises to manipulate the strength of the intentions of the students vis-à-vis performing the voluntary case analysis. As they had hoped, the "relevant" preexercise caused the students' intentions to be much stronger than did the bogus preexercise. The researchers then observed the strength of the connections in the two groups between their attitudes about the case and their actual behavior. The results were interesting. The data from the students whose intention had been manipulated to be the stronger of the two sets revealed that their intentions did come into play in explaining their actual behavior on the case. Among the students whose intentions had been weaker, however, the connection between their attitudes and actual behavior was not affected by those intentions by nearly the same degree. In short, the researchers concluded that when intentions are weak and the task is not something that takes much thought, attitudes and behaviors may be quite closely linked without a role being played by intentions. If results of this sort are replicated, we could see an interesting modification to the theory of reasoned action.

The formal theory deliberately restricts itself to reasoned actions. This restriction seems to be both a basis for the success of the theory in predicting many behaviors (very well, as we shall see shortly) as well as its primary drawback. It cannot be used as a general theory of attitudes for the prediction of all human behavior (Eagly & Chaiken, 1993). Another criticism of the theory is based on the belief that there are many more determinants of people's intentions than one's attitude toward the behavior and subjective norms. For example, Schwartz and Tessler (1972) have suggested that people's personal beliefs about right and wrong, their sense of moral obligation, may also influence their intention to act in a certain way. This set of factors is internalized in a person's value system, independently, conceptually at least, from the subjective norm factor that Ajzen and Fishbein (1980) discuss. Similarly, some people will act in certain ways that are consistent with their self-identities. For example, if a person views herself as helpful by nature, she is more likely to form intentions to act in prosocial helpful ways at work than if her self-identity did not include such a feature.

The upshot of these criticisms is not that they deny the critical, final role of intentions in inducing and directing behavior. Rather, they share the argument that the theory of reasoned action oversimplifies the matter of how intentions are formed in the first place. They claim that the theory overlooks many factors and forces by restricting the focus to attitude toward the act and the perception of social norms. Eagly and Chaiken (1993, Chapter 4) review these and other criticisms of the theory found in the literature.

Finally, some students and managers who wish to understand human behavior or work behavior and attitudes simply find the long, rocky road from beliefs, through attitudes, to intentions via attitudes toward behaviors (and social norms) counterintuitive and difficult to comprehend at first. Nevertheless, when we stand back and think carefully about life experiences in which we have seen people behave in ways that seem contrary to their attitudes toward other people or things (attitude objects), the theory of reasoned action takes on more credibility. This leads us to the question of the predictive validity of the theory.

Validity of the Theory of Reasoned Action

Criticisms and shortcomings of the theory notwithstanding, how valid is it? Two different reviews of the scientific tests of the theory both conclude that the theory is very valid as a predictor of people's actions and, in addition, of the outcomes of people's actions (Eagly & Chaiken, 1993; Sheppard, Hartwick, & Warshaw, 1988). Sheppard et al. (1988) conducted a massive summary of the evidence related to the validity of the theory, beginning with this statement to remind us of what the formal theory does and does not purport to do for us: "[A] behavior intention measure will predict the performance of any voluntary act, unless intent changes prior to performance or unless the intention measure does not correspond to the behavioral criterion in terms of action, target, context, time-frame and/or specificity" (p. 325). They then observe that the theory has frequently been applied to situations in which any or all of three conditions that violate the theory's assumptions are in place. One is that the target behavior is not completely under the person's control (see the discussion of the *theory of planned action*, later).

A second condition that is inappropriate to the formal assumptions of the theory is where "the situation involves a choice problem not explicitly addressed by the theory itself." Finally, there have been cases where the theory has been used to predict people's acts in situations where they did or could not have sufficient information to make a completely confident intention. In short, there have been many studies that have attempted to test the theory "unfairly."[4]

Using the technique of meta-analysis (which has been used in many other studies reported in

---

[4] Recall our discussion in Chapter 3 of how Maslow's theory of needs has similarly been treated unfairly. We will run into this problem again and again.

this book; see Hunter, Schmidt, & Jackson, 1982), Sheppard et al. (1988) surveyed 87 previous empirical studies and came up with an average correlation of 0.53 for the connection between intentions and behaviors. The corresponding correlation between attitudes and subjective norms, and intentions, was 0.66. Each of these results was based on work that included many thousands of participants in a variety of settings and in relation to a wide variety of intentions and behaviors. By any standard, these results were spectacular. Even more impressive is how the results remained strong when Sheppard et al. (1988) included in the analyses studies conducted more or less inappropriately, or unfairly, given the formal terms and conditions spelled out in the theory. The specific details of how they did this are too complex to be detailed here. The interested reader is referred to the article by Sheppard and his colleagues (1988). The point is that TRA appears to be one of the best predictors of human behavior available in the social sciences. It is applicable to many behaviors and contexts and is remarkably robust to violations of some of the major tenets specified by the theory itself.

Recapitulation

Let's stop for a minute and review where we have been. So far we have seen that beliefs are the core of attitudes. They consist of perceived linkages between attitude objects and attributes. Strong beliefs consist of high subjective probabilities that particular objects are characterized by particular attributes. People tend to emphasize the most salient and most important beliefs they hold about objects as they form attitudes toward them. Attitudes are evaluative reactions that people have concerning the beliefs they hold about objects. The connection between attitudes and behavior, however, is unpredictable, for many reasons. For an attitude to result in behavior that is consistent with it, the attitude must result in an intention to act. For an intention to be developed, the person must hold a positive attitude toward the act itself and must believe that significant others would see the act as appropriate. Even then, the holding of a particular intention will result in a specific behavior only if the intention is somewhat specific regarding a variety of factors, including the exact nature of the behavior itself, the precise target toward which the behavior will be directed, the circumstances within which the act is contemplated, and finally, the time at which the act is to take place.

There is virtually never a simple connection between the holding of a particular attitude toward a person, a job, or some object, and specific behaviors toward that person, job, or object. Using attitudes to predict specific behaviors is a risky business. For example, an employee may like his job because he positively evaluates those things he believes about it (that it pays better than comparable jobs, that he can trust his coworkers, and that it may provide him with long-term security). On the basis of this attitude alone, we cannot predict whether he will work hard, seek promotions, take training courses, or help to organize a union. To make such behavioral predictions we would need a great deal more information about the employee's beliefs about the consequences of these particular acts as well as about his evaluative attitudes toward those beliefs and his understanding of what is expected of him by significant others. Conversely, we can make predictions, in advance, that because an employee holds a generally positive attitude toward his job, positive job behaviors are more likely to result from him than are negative job behaviors, although the specific acts cannot be foreseen.

THE THEORY OF PLANNED BEHAVIOR

Before leaving our discussion of the theory of reasoned action, we note briefly that Ajzen (1991; Ajzen & Madden, 1986) modified the theory slightly to take into account the possibility that, although a person may (1) be positively disposed to perform an act, and (2) believe that the act is socially desired or expected, s/he may also have doubts about the feasibility of performing the act in question. (We alluded to this possibility earlier.) For example, a person may wish to drive to the store to buy groceries but find that his car doesn't work or be uncertain about whether the store will be open for business by the time he gets there. There may be forces beyond his control that limit the possibility of the act. Sometimes, according to the theory of planned behavior, a person may lack behavioral control. Ajzen refers to the additional construct as *perceived behavioral control*. The mitigating factors that cause perceptions of low behavioral control might be internal to the person, such as perceptions of low self-efficacy, or in the context in which the act would otherwise occur (e.g., a shortage of materials needed to make the task possible).

Ajzen and Fishbein (1980) demonstrated how the addition of people's perceptions of behavioral control to the other two key factors in determining intentions – attitude toward the act and the social norms regarding the act – better explains the variability among people in the strength of their intentions to act. In other words, whereas TRA claims that two factors determine intentions, the *theory of planned behavior* claims that three variables determine intentions – it adds the person's perception of his or her control over the circumstances that will make an act possible.

Research investigations of the predictive validity of the theory of planned behavior were summarized by Ajzen (1991) himself and by Olson and Zanna (1993), who observed that although the evidence is mixed, most comparative tests of the two theories conclude that the later, expanded theory enjoys more empirical support than the original theory, as impressive as that is.

Theory X and Theory Y Revisited

Before leaving our discussion of the relationship between beliefs, attitudes, and behavior, it is worth recalling from Chapter 3 two particular sets of beliefs commonly held by many managers concerning the nature of human beings. These beliefs, called Theory X and Theory Y, are seen as resulting in managerial behaviors that are consistent with the view either that people like to work, can be trusted with responsibility, and so on (Theory Y), or that they are lazy, dislike work, and cannot be trusted with responsibility (Theory X). According to McGregor (1960), Theory X beliefs are the cause as well as the result of apathetic and withdrawal behavior – a *self-fulfilling prophesy*. Although there is no claim that either Theory X or Theory Y beliefs are connected on a one-to-one basis with specific managerial behaviors, McGregor believed that these underlying beliefs are associated with managerial acts and policies that tend to be self-reinforcing. This association between a set of beliefs and a set of behaviors is entirely consistent with the model of beliefs, attitudes, and behaviors presented earlier (Ajzen & Fishbein, 1980; Fishbein & Ajzen, 1975).

Now that we have examined the general nature of human attitudes, at least from the perspective of one major and successful theory, we turn our attention to the more specific issues of people's beliefs, attitudes, and emotional reactions concerning their work, their jobs, and the organizations for which they work.

Human Reactions to Work, Jobs, and Organizations

10

As part of a research interview reported by Harlos and Pinder (2000, p. 255), an office clerk named Brenda reported:

> There are good days, mostly when he [the boss] is not in . . . I think things are picking up, maybe I'm starting to fit in, maybe I was imagining all the bad stuff and I don't have to look for a new job . . . But then the next day is terribly bad and I just scream in my car on the way home.

Anyone who has ever held a job can relate (to some degree at least) to the visceral and emotional experiences that are the focus of this chapter; it is about people's beliefs, attitudes, and feelings (emotions) toward their work. Positive attitudes about what we do for a living make a tremendous difference in the way we feel about life in general. To have a job that is annoying, frustrating, or that regularly causes fear and conflict can be a terrible experience, as reported by Brenda in the foregoing statement.

This chapter is about such job-related attitudes and emotions. Although the discussion is sometimes scientific and esoteric, the reader should keep in mind the human experiences of the joy that comes from having a "good job" or "good career" and the worse, painful, private agonies that come from having to perform work that is dissatisfying, illegal, boring, or humiliating. This chapter, more than most others, appeals to the human, emotional side of work motivation. Job satisfaction, organizational commitment, and the identification that people have with their work are all at the very core of the issue of work motivation. It is here (as well as in Chapter 4) where the mind and the heart meet in this book more than in any other chapters: Work can be a major source of pleasure for people or the primary source of their own private hell.

A PRECAUTION

A point of semantics is in order before we begin. Although much of the discussion in this chapter is about "job attitudes," it is important to recognize that, in fact, attitudes (as we have defined them in Chapter 9) are only part of what this chapter is about. As we will find shortly, much of our experiencing of job attitudes in life and in common discourse deals, in fact, with job-related beliefs and, ultimately, emotions. So, as often happens in organizational science, terms from common parlance are often used to represent concepts that have different technical meaning in the discipline. We clarify the distinctions among job-related beliefs, attitudes, and emotions by the end of the chapter.

WHY AN INTEREST IN WORK ATTITUDES?

Since the early days of the organizational sciences, academics and other researchers have spent considerable time researching the nature, causes, and correlates of a variety of work-related attitudes, for a variety of reasons. Why is this so?

Many years ago, Smith, Kendall, and Hulin (1969) provided four commonly accepted answers to the question. First, it has long been assumed by many managers, parents, teachers, and people in general that attitudes influence behavior. The importance of this assumption for our present purposes lies in the possibilities that it holds for managers and supervisors who wish to influence employee motivation and job performance. It has long been assumed that work-related attitudes must somehow be related to work behaviors (see Brayfield & Crockett, 1955; Fisher, 1980). Early forms of this belief held that higher levels of job satisfaction are associated with higher levels of job performance: "A more satisfied employee is a more productive employee." Although years of research have shown that the relationship is not so simple (Judge, Thoresen, Bono, & Patton, 2001), there is still some basis for believing that attitudes and behaviors are related to one another in some circumstances (Ajzen & Fishbein, 1977; Cialdini, Petty, & Cacioppo, 1981). Accordingly, it remains important to develop a precise understanding of what attitudes are, the factors that influence them, and whatever connections they may have with behavior.

Second, Smith et al. (1969) pointed out that a great deal of management's activities with regard to personnel selection and placement, training, career counseling, and so on, are based in part on a concern for employee attitudes and, in turn, for employee behavior. Third, Smith and her colleagues noted that improving employee job satisfaction is a desirable goal in its own right, for humanitarian reasons. In other words, one need not expect some form of managerial payoff to justify attempts to understand employee work attitudes. Finally, understanding the nature of job attitudes may be beneficial for the greater scientific concern of understanding attitudes in general: Work is only one arena in which human attitudes are formed and altered, albeit an important one. Social scientists are interested in the nature and change of attitudes for political reasons, for marketing research, and for a variety of other social purposes. Things that are learned about job attitudes contribute to this greater stock of knowledge about human attitudes in general.

After decades of theory, research, and practice relating job attitudes to individual and organizational outcomes, an impressive study published by Harrison, Newman, and Roth (2006) demonstrated that higher-order constructs representing job attitudes held powerful statistical relationships with individual and organizational relationships – much more powerful than the typical bivariate studies that have been conducted since Smith and her colleagues (Smith et al., 1969) made their observations of the importance of job attitudes so many years ago. As observed by Dormann and Zapf (2001): "Job satisfaction is placed as a central concept in work organizational psychology, which mediates the relation between working conditions on the one hand and organizational and individual outcomes on the other hand" (p. 483). Accordingly, we are interested in the study of job attitudes because they are believed to relate to work behavior, because a great deal of managerial activity is concerned with positively influencing them, for humanitarian reasons and for general scientific purposes. The purpose of discussing them in this book is influenced by each of these reasons.

Job Attitudes of the Most Interest

Without doubt, the most commonly studied variety of job-related attitudes is *job satisfaction*, often defined as the degree to which a person's work is useful for satisfying her needs. (A more rigorous treatment of job satisfaction will be presented shortly.) Job satisfaction is widely viewed as a multidimensional concept, such that a person may be satisfied with certain aspects of her work ("I like my supervisor") while simultaneously being unhappy with other aspects of her work ("The pay and working conditions are terrible").

A second construct that has received considerable interest in research and theory is referred to under the general rubric of *commitment* (or, recently, *attachment*). This concept is also multidimensional and has to do with the attachment or adherence of persons to any or all of the following: To the work ethic in general, to one's occupation or profession, to one's actual day-by-day work experiences, and/or to one's employer (Morrow, 1993). As detailed by Morrow (1993), each of these four approaches to commitment has a number of variations that differ conceptually among themselves by minor degrees, and each is accompanied by one or more sets of scales and measures for their assessment. The interested reader is referred to Morrow's (1983, 1993) careful analyses and evaluations of the many nuances in meaning and measures of these concepts; we limit our discussion here to two of the major dimensions of commitment, those usually referred to as organizational commitment and job involvement.

The third concept treated in this chapter is referred to as *job involvement*. This construct has to do with people's devotion to their work per se, independent of the particular jobs they hold or the particular organization they work for. Job involvement concerns a person's views about the centrality of work to his life. For example, a person may enjoy being a machinist but may or may not be satisfied with his current job as a machinist and he may or may not have a sense of commitment to his employer.

In summary, then, the purpose of this chapter is to examine the theory and research related to job satisfaction, organizational commitment, and job involvement, considering their place in a broader study of work motivation.

JOB SATISFACTION

According to a recent article in *Maclean's* (September 19, 2005, p. 38), Canada's national weekly newsmagazine, the labor movement in North America is in trouble; membership is declining in both public and private sectors and in both Canada and the United States. The putative reason, according to business writer Steve Maich, is that "working people" are doing very well, thank you very much, so the advantages traditionally attributed to union membership – higher wages, job security, safe and pleasant working conditions, to name a few – are no longer urgently required by working people. According to Maich, who cited studies carried out in 2005 by the American Enterprise Institute (in the United States) and a poll conducted by Environics (a leading national pollster in Canada), satisfaction of the vast majority of American workers with their jobs is very high, so union membership is in decline. In the U.S. study, 91% of respondents claimed they either liked or loved their jobs, approximately the same proportion as 4 years earlier. About four in five claimed that they were satisfied with their pay and about the same number said they were not worried about losing their jobs. Maich (2005, p. 38) wrote:

> Decades ago, those forces [fear of losing one's job and anger over social inequality] helped create things like overtime, minimum wage and protection from arbitrary firing. But now, thanks in part to past union victories, North American workers no longer see themselves as part of any movement of the downtrodden.

Meanwhile, in the local Victoria, B.C., newspaper, the *Times Colonist* (*TC*), a story appeared on September 3, 2005 (p. B3), claiming that, compared to the "glass is four-fifths full" analysis reported by Maich's summary in *Maclean's*, the glass is still one-fifth empty (the metaphor is adopted by this author, not by any of the sources cited here). In the *TC* report (which summarized survey data based on national samples similar to those summarized by Maich and *Maclean's*), the text read as follows:

> Nearly one in five Canadians dreads going to work each day, and another one in three feel their job is just a job . . . [suggesting] a lot may want to spend this Labour Day holiday reassessing their careers . . . Nearly one-third of the 10,000 respondents also admit to faking a sick day in the last year . . . A lot of workers feel their current job isn't giving them enough opportunity for advancement, skill development or new experiences.

Finally, on the same page in the *TC* (September 3, 2005, p. B3), a separate report, attributed to a survey conducted by the Canadian Labour Congress, read as follows: "Strong job growth and low unemployment have not made workers feel more secure about their jobs, nor has it translated into significant wage gains."

As a matter of fact, the proportion of people in North America who report being satisfied with their jobs has not changed a great deal over recent decades. Over a decade ago, Firebaugh and Harley (1995) reported that about 85% of U.S. workers were happy with their jobs and that men and women were approximately equal in this regard. Older workers tended to report higher levels of satisfaction than were reported by younger workers, in part because they tend to hold better jobs. In addition, the expectations of older workers may not be as high as those of younger employees because many older workers were raised during economic times when things were not as abundant as they have been more recently (Firebaugh & Harley, 1995). These figures are very similar to data reported 30 years earlier.

In short, things haven't changed much in the level of job attitudes among North American workers over the past two generations, yet it is still the focus of considerable media attention and managerial interest. An article in the June 19, 2006 edition of *Maclean's* magazine focused on the current issue referred to as "work–life" balance: Providing means and time for employees to get away from their jobs so that they don't become burned out and, in the longer term, be more productive *and* satisfied with their work. Alcan, one of the world's largest producers of aluminum, head-quartered in Canada, found through employee surveys that "staff were grossly overworked and turnover rates were swelling, especially in the all-important finance departments." The company implemented a "work–life effectiveness strategy" that included "coaching for top executives, mandatory no-work hours, and on-site massage sessions" (p. 35). In the end, most employers have now dropped specious high-sounding principles to explain their concern for fostering work–life balance for their employees and openly admit that programs such as these do contribute good things to the "bottom line." A recent study by Greenhaus and Powell (2003), for example, showed that personality differences (such as self-esteem) and the relative strength of an individual's identification with work and with family may play key roles in the dilemmas faced by working people concerned with keeping balance in their lives.[1] Most large urban and airport bookstores are replete with paperback books dealing with the issues of job blues, getting more out of life through one's work, etc.

What's the point here? The point is simply to demonstrate that as old as the concept is, job satisfaction (particularly job dissatisfaction) is a matter of timeless concern for anyone who works or for anyone who must interact with working people. In fact, it is not unfair to state that most people believe themselves to be experts on the issue. Nevertheless, we turn attention to examining what this construct represents in the organizational sciences.

---

[1] See also a book by Blyton, Blunsdon, Reed, and Dastmalchian (2006), which presents a range of scholarly papers on a variety of issues related to work–life balance.

The Nature of Job Satisfaction

Many implicit and explicit definitions of job satisfaction have been offered over the years. The definition that has probably had the most influence in the field has been that of Locke (1969, 1976). For Locke, *job satisfaction* is an *emotional* reaction that "results from the perception that one's job fulfills or allows the fulfillment of one's important job values, providing and to the degree that those values are congruent with one's needs" (Locke, 1976, p. 1307). Unless otherwise indicated, this definition will be the one intended whenever the term *job satisfaction* is used in the present volume, and its obverse will be intended whenever the term *job dissatisfaction* is used. It is interesting to note in relation to our discussion in Chapter 4 that, although job satisfaction is widely seen as an attitude, Locke's definition defines it in terms of an *emotional* reaction. While introducing their affective events theory (recall Chapter 4), Weiss and Cropanzano (1996) gave emotion greater emphasis in their definition than Locke (1976, p. 2) did. They defined job satisfaction as:

> [A]n evaluative judgment about one's job that partly, but not entirely, results from emotional experiences at work. It also partly results from more abstract beliefs about one's job. Together, affective experiences and belief structures result in the evaluation we call job satisfaction.

Neither Locke (1976) nor Weiss and Cropanzano (1996) speculated about the particular emotions that are involved, but considerable scientific progress has been made to discern the nature of the range of emotions associated with both job satisfaction and job dissatisfaction (recall Chapter 4).

What about the emotions that accompany *job dissatisfaction*? Of those that we reviewed in Chapter 4, a few likely candidates come to mind, including anger, fear, jealousy, and envy (see also Lazarus & Lazarus, 1994). So in keeping with the general tradition of the field, job satisfaction and dissatisfaction are discussed here primarily as if they are attitudes, although it is clear that emotions are also heavily involved in the experiences that people witness on the job.

Locke noted that job satisfaction is not the same thing as morale. Although satisfaction has to do with a retrospective assessment of one's job, morale is seen more as concerned with a positive desire to continue to work at one's job. Further, the term *morale* is often used to describe the overall attitudes of a *work group* rather than of a single individual. Both Locke's and Weiss and Cropanzano's definitions of job satisfaction are conceptual. In practice, researchers and managers often operationalize job satisfaction as having to do with the gratification of one's needs on the job or through the work setting. (Recall the discussion in Chapters 3, 4, 5, and 6 of the multitude of needs that might be considered in such a context, and see Fields, 2002, for examples.) Moreover, interest is often directed at the satisfaction one has with a variety of *specific aspects* of one's job and the circumstances surrounding it. For example, the *theory of work adjustment* (Bretz & Judge, 1994; *Journal of Vocational Behavior*, 1993; Lofquist & Dawis, 1969) concerns itself with employee satisfaction and dissatisfaction with 21 aspects of work and organizations, ranging from creativity and recognition to social status and working conditions. Thus, as noted by Locke (1976) and confirmed by Ben-Porat (1981), the list of potential causes of job satisfaction and dissatisfaction that have been investigated includes both *agents* (such as pay levels of one's supervisor) and *events* (such as the level of responsibility that one is usually permitted to assume on the job).

Moreover, different writers over the years have tended to contrive their own measures of satisfaction, making what is learned from one study difficult to compare with the results of other studies, although this situation has improved somewhat (Cranny, Smith, & Stone, 1992; Fields, 2002). Consequently, progress toward general agreement in the field on the nature of the construct was impeded somewhat, although the needs-based approach to job satisfaction dominated the thinking and research of scholars and practitioners alike (see Stone, 1992), at least until a decade ago, when the affective events theory (Weiss & Cropanzano, 1996; and our discussion of AET in Chapter 4) was introduced to the literature.

Traditionally, those interested in measuring job satisfaction would seek an *overall* assessment of an individual's job ("How do you like your job?") or, alternatively, assessments of particular facets of the job, such as the pay, job challenge, or supervision, for example. A newer approach suggested the assessment of the levels of satisfaction that people have with the various *tasks* that comprise their jobs. Allowing the 573 study participants (who represented a variety of different jobs) to define "tasks" according to their own definitions, Taber and Alliger (1995) concluded that global and facet measures of satisfaction were "consistent with, but only partially predictable from," the properties of the component tasks of jobs. The value added by this approach over the traditional approach has not been demonstrated particularly well since it was first proposed.

Causes/Antecedents of Job Satisfaction

What is known and agreed upon in relation to job satisfaction? As indicated earlier, most authors see job satisfaction as resulting from the fulfillment of needs through the activities one performs at one's job and from the context in which the work is performed. In other words, in this approach, job satisfaction is a function of, indeed the same thing as, need satisfaction, or at least the degree of correspondence, congruence, or complementarity between a person's needs and the need-gratifying capacity of the work setting. Characteristic of this work is that of Betz (1969), Fredericksen, Jensen, Beaton, and Bloxom (1972), Lofquist and Dawis (1969), Mathieu, Hofmann, and Farr (1993), Ostroff (1993), Pervin (1968), Porter (1962, 1963), Seybolt (1976), and Tuckman (1968).

Other authors, including Ilgen (1971) and McFarlin and Rice (1992), conceived of job satisfaction as resulting from the size of the *discrepancy* a person perceives, if any, between what he expects to receive from his work and what he perceives he is receiving. Thus, large differences between the amount of pay an employee perceives he is receiving and the amount he expects to receive would result in dissatisfaction with pay, no reference being made to needs per se. Within this tradition is the issue of whether people are more or less concerned with various facets of their workplaces (e.g., the pay, the supervision, the working conditions) or whether overall, global satisfaction is more important. One pair of studies, for example, found that discrepancies between what employees perceive they are receiving on the job and what they want from their jobs were critical when the comparative importance of the various facets was considered. Employees who placed high value on a specific facet were more satisfied with a small discrepancy and more dissatisfied with large discrepancies than those who placed lower importance on the same facets (McFarlin & Rice, 1992; see also Rice, Gentile, & McFarlin, 1991).

As we saw in Chapter 3, satisfaction results from at least three general types of perception. First, the person must see that there is a positive increment in the level of desired outcomes he or she receives. Second, the shorter the period over which the improvement occurs, the greater is the feeling of satisfaction (called the *notion of velocity*). Third, positive increases in the rate of positive change also add to the sensation of satisfaction: People want to see things get better for themselves over time, and the faster the improvement, the better (Salovey, Hsee, & Mayer, 1993). To the knowledge of this author, no empirical work has investigated this so-called *emodynamic theory* as it pertains to job satisfaction and dissatisfaction.

The importance of global measures, reflecting overall satisfaction with the work, was discussed by Cranny et al. (1992), who believed that global satisfaction may be both a contributing cause and a partial effect of facet satisfaction and that global satisfaction may make workers more receptive and cooperative in reaction to management-initiated changes to the workplace. In other words, it may be that as people become satisfied with one or a few aspects of their jobs, they tend to form positive global attitudes about those jobs. By way of contrast, a person may have, for whatever reason, a generally positive view of her job and will therefore tend to report satisfaction with specific aspects of it (e.g., the promotion opportunities), if only because her general attitude is positive – a halo effect.

A third approach considers employee *values*, which are defined as those things that a person sees as conducive to his or her welfare. Recall from Chapter 3 that it is important to distinguish between needs and values: Needs are basic forces that initiate and guide behavior for the sake of the preservation and health of the individual. People are not aware of the operation of many needs: They frequently function at the subconscious level. By contrast, values are conscious beliefs about what is good and bad for the individual's well-being. Thus, whereas the author might place a high value on a new sports car, he might have trouble convincing his wife that he really needs one. Locke (1976) emphasized the role of values being met as the key determinant of job satisfaction, at least to the degree that these values are congruent with one's needs.

Still another approach centers around the issue of whether a person's expectations are met or thwarted. In other words, the concern here is with whether the individual believes that psychological (or literal) contracts, promises, and expectations are honored in the workplace (see Rousseau, 1995).

Another view sees satisfaction or dissatisfaction resulting from comparisons that a person makes between herself and others around her. In this view (see Chapter 11) a person is most likely to be dissatisfied when she perceives that the relationship between the contributions she makes to the organization and the benefits she derives in return is less satisfactory than the relationship she perceives between the inputs and outcomes derived by some other person or group of persons. Feelings of inequitable treatment have been shown to be predictive of intentions to quit organizations.

Finally, the most recent and currently influential view on what causes job satisfaction and dissatisfaction (particularly the latter) is found in the burgeoning literature on justice theory. As we will see in the next chapter, perceptions by people that they are victims of injustice cause them many negative reactions toward the job and the employing organization, as well as toward the individual(s) who is seen as the proximal deliverer of the injustice. Being treated unjustly hurts. A more thorough treatment of equity theory and several issues related to justice and injustice is presented in Chapter 11.

Situations, dispositions, and job satisfaction

For many years, much of the debate on the origins and nature of job satisfaction hinged on the issue of whether it is determined by situations (i.e., the contextual factors of the workplace, such as organizational climate and culture, reward systems, leadership style) or by stable traits and dispositions of individuals. Brief mention was made of this issue earlier in the book (see Chapter 2), and a full discussion of the matter is beyond the scope of this chapter as well (cf. George, 1991, 1992; Gerhart, 2005), except note here that the position one adopts on this matter may have applied consequences aside from theoretical import. Although the dispositional approach does not rule out the potential effects of contexts (such as job design and organizational structure), it does propose that people may have characteristic predilections toward positive or negative emotional states and toward jobs in particular that might limit the power of interventions in the work context.[2] Gerhart (2005) discussed these potential applied implications and concluded that an assumption on the side of dispositions implies that there is wisdom in hiring people who have generally positive personalities; on the other hand, there may, theoretically, be limits in the degree of benefit that can be attained by improving working conditions for people with a generally negative view of the world. On the basis of his analysis of the matter, Gerhart concluded: "within-person consistency in attitudes and behaviors can coexist with mean-level changes in [both] attitudes and behaviors induced by situational changes in the workplace" (p. 79).

Researchers in the late 1980s and into the 1990s investigated two streams of enquiry. One stream, basing their analyses largely on research involving monozygotic twins, successfully identified

---

[2] In the extreme, the dispositional approach would significantly reduce the emphasis placed on contextual factors such as job design, organizational policies, climates and culture, and leadership styles (Dormann & Zapf, 2001).

statistical relationships between people's genetic structures and their reactions to jobs (e.g., Arvey & Bouchard, 1994; Arvey, Bouchard, Segal, & Abraham, 1989; Arvey, McCall, Bouchard, Taubman, & Cavanaugh, 1994).

The second stream examined the relationships between individual personality traits and job reactions. For example, some scholars started with the premise that human beings vary in a general trait toward happiness (*positive affectivity*) or unhappiness (*negative affectivity*), a disposition that accompanies and influences them in many different aspects of their lives, predisposing them toward positive or negative emotional reactions, even toward otherwise-neutral stimuli (cf. Watson, Clark, & Tellegen, 1988; Watson, Wiese, Vaidya, & Tellegen, 1999). Soon, connections between these traits and employee reactions to jobs were sought in empirical studies: A meta-analysis by Connolly and Viswesvaran (2000) reported an adjusted overall correlation between positive affectivity (PA) and job satisfaction of 0.40 and a corresponding correlation between negative affectivity (NA) and job dissatisfaction of -0.33.

Until recently, however, the reason for a two-way relationship between genetic composition and job attitudes was a matter of speculation (e.g., Judge & Larsen, 2001). Then, two investigations by Timothy Judge and his colleagues (a meta-analysis by Judge, Heller, & Mount, 2002, and an original study by Ilies & Judge, 2003) supported the hypothesis that a (or *the*) missing link between genes and job satisfaction/dissatisfaction is *personality*; that is, genes heavily influence an individual's personality structures and that they, in turn, influence a person's predisposition toward job satisfaction or dissatisfaction. While the meta-analysis of Judge et al. (2002) found moderate-to-mixed correlations between the *Big Five* (Barrick & Mount, 1991) personality traits and job satisfaction, the two personality dimensions mentioned earlier (positive affectivity and negative affectivity) did a better job than did the Big Five of explaining the mediated relationships between genes and job reactions by working people.[3]

Finally, a meta-analysis of previous studies of test–retest estimates of the stability of job satisfaction (as measured by standard scales for this purpose) was reported by Dormann and Zapf (2001). The purpose of the study was to estimate the extent to which stable personality traits, as opposed to organizational contextual factors, can explain job satisfaction. In a clever research design, the researchers separated samples of employees into "stayers" (those who did not shift jobs between the occasions when their job satisfaction was measured) and "changers" (those who shifted jobs). They found that job stayers and job changers did not differ significantly in the test–retest stabilities of their job attitudes, at least in part because people who shift from one job to another are bound to seek considerable levels of similarity between their former jobs and their new jobs. Why? Because their stable personality traits contribute to the preferences they have for any and all jobs. In other words, as people change jobs, they do not normally find themselves moving to entirely different job circumstances than they leave behind; rather, their (stable) preferences will cause them to seek new jobs that share many core features with their former jobs. Thus, support was provided for the argument that, although dispositions may contribute a significant proportion of the cause of job attitudes, contextual factors also play a significant role. Once more, as we discuss in Chapter 2 and elsewhere throughout this book, both individual and contextual factors are involved in explaining work motivation, work behavior, and other phenomena related to them.

The Nature and Causes of Job *Dis*satisfaction

Traditional thought on the matter has always held that job dissatisfaction is simply the opposite of job satisfaction, such that if an employee becomes more satisfied with her job, she necessarily

---

[3] For the current author, these two streams of work – introducing genetic research into organizational behavior and reintroducing personality dimensions with construct-valid measures to investigate mediated relationships – separately and in combination, comprise some of the most interesting and significant advances made in the general domain of work motivation in more than a decade.

becomes less dissatisfied, and vice versa. In Chapters 2 and 7, Herzberg's challenge to this assumption was presented and discussed at length. To review it briefly, Herzberg, Mausner, and Snyderman (1959) argued that the concepts of job satisfaction and dissatisfaction are not the opposite of one another; rather, they are independent of one another.

The reader will recall from that discussion that this asymmetrical aspect of the motivator-hygiene theory is the one responsible for much of the so-called Herzberg controversy.[4] Because of the lack of clear and consistent support for the two-factor approach that has *not* been based on questionable research, the perspective adopted here is the traditional one: Satisfaction and dissatisfaction represent opposite ends of the same continuum. Nevertheless, it is clear that jobs have multiple facets, so it is recognized that people can be satisfied and/or dissatisfied with different aspects of their jobs simultaneously (Rice, Gentile, & McFarlin, 1991). (See Mahoney, 1979, for an approach that reconciles the two-factor approach with the more traditional one.)

Job Dissatisfaction as Need Frustration

It is important to note as well the connection between what was presented in Chapter 8 as need frustration and what is commonly viewed as job dissatisfaction: When dissatisfaction is conceived of as an emotional reaction to the blockage of attempts on the job to satisfy one's needs, job dissatisfaction amounts to the same psychological state of frustration as we discussed in Chapter 8, and we can expect any of the usual human responses to it (see Spector, 1978).

What causes such blockages? Organizational policies that prevent people from being effective, despite their best efforts. Fellow employees who don't cooperate. Too much work to be done in the time permitted, such that none of it can be accomplished effectively. Shoddy machinery or supplies. A supervisor who doesn't listen or who fails to provide assistance when it is needed. An organizational structure that prohibits rapid advancement or promotion. One's gender (being the wrong one), or lack of abilities. Inconsistent expectations from one's bosses or members of one's job environment. Being assigned to undesirable working hours, such as the night shift. In short, frustration results from a blockage of one's effort in pursuit of goals, and the blockage can emanate from any of a countless number of sources in an organization. The emotional reaction to frustration on the job is job dissatisfaction, although as we noted earlier, the specific emotions felt during job dissatisfaction have received little empirical attention and may, in fact, vary widely from person to person. Work is required on this issue.

To understand job dissatisfaction as a specific form of frustration, we must understand the nature of the needs that can be blocked on the job. Remember from Chapter 3 that there are a variety of human needs in addition to those for existence and relatedness. The various forms of growth needs have become more important to members of the modern workforce than they were in previous times, in large measure because of the relatively high levels of education and economic abundance enjoyed by Western society over the past generation. The point is that the modern workforce demands greater challenge and stimulation, greater opportunities to self-actualize on the job, more chances to feel competent and efficacious, and more frequent opportunities to achieve and develop than did previous generations (Universum Communications, 2006). But there are not enough jobs in business and industry that provide sufficient challenge and stimulation to make this sort of universal need satisfaction possible from work. People seek alternative activities to meet their needs for challenge and stimulation.

Earlier, we focused on Locke's (1968) definition of job satisfaction as an emotional reaction to one's work. It follows that job dissatisfaction is also an emotional reaction, although the blend and intensity of the emotions involved have not received systematic study. Nevertheless, the concept

---

[4] In fairness to Herzberg, and as noted in Chapter 2, much of the research that purports to refute the motivator-hygiene theory was also flawed (Grigaliunas & Weiner, 1974).

of *emodynamic* satisfaction (and dissatisfaction) must be mentioned here again. From this view a person's emotional experience of job dissatisfaction will be greatest when she loses desired outcomes, when the loss occurs suddenly rather than gradually, and when the rate of loss increases over time (see Salovey et al., 1993). Empirical research into this dynamic, temporal perspective on job dissatisfaction remains to be conducted, although the fertile and relatively new affective events theory (Weiss & Cropanzano, 1996) introduced in Chapter 4 may prove useful in such research.

Social Information Processing and Job Satisfaction/Dissatisfaction

Throughout this book, we will periodically encounter the hypothesis that people's reactions to and interpretations of organizational events are heavily influenced by the social contexts within which the events occur. That is, people can be heavily influenced by the cues they receive from others (such as their coworkers, their supervisors, and even their loved ones) in forming beliefs about the meaning and significance of events that occur around them. In the following chapter, for example, time and again, we will see that these social cues play a huge role in people's interpretations of whether they are being treated equitably and justly in their work. Interestingly, this *social information processing* approach made its first notable appearance in the domain of organizational behavior theory and research in the context of job attitudes (see Pfeffer, 1981b; Salancik & Pfeffer, 1977, 1978). Indeed, the proponents of this view have been among the harshest critics of needs-based models of job attitudes (see Salancik & Pfeffer, 1977; and a reply by Alderfer, 1977).

Again, the basic tenet of this school of thought is that a person's reactions to his or her job are heavily influenced by the interpretation of cues provided by other people and other sources. Employees make use of the nouns and verbs as well as of the nonverbal cues provided to them by the social contexts of the workplace to describe and to think about their jobs. They learn about the relative desirability of the work by watching and speaking with coworkers and other people. Two proponents of the social information processing approach describe it this way:

> Social information refers to comments, observations, and similar cues provided by people whose view of the job an employee considers relevant. It may be provided by people directly associated with the job, such as co-workers, supervisors, and customers, or it may be provided by people not employed by the company, such as family members and friends.
>
> (Thomas & Griffin, 1989, p. 65)

Social information from these sources provides the employee not only with ideas about what things are important in the workplace but also about the relative importance of these features (Pfeffer, 1981b). In addition, they can provide insight into formation of the employee's evaluation of these features – are they favorable or aversive? Hulin (1990, pp. 455–456), who is a harsh critic of the social information processing view, wrote:

> An extreme version of this approach argues that individuals experience little affect about their job satisfaction until they are *asked* (usually by social scientists). This view argues that social attitudes and affect are latent and unrecognized until some event triggers an evaluation. The nature of the triggering event (e.g., an attitude survey) may influence the resulting expressed and experienced attitudes as much as the events that presumably formed the latent attitudes. If asked, the respondents will produce an answer *because they are expected to*; they will then search their environments for information to justify their response – they enact subjective environments that provide a justification for their response.

As is usually the case in the social sciences, the introduction of new approaches to a sacred tradition sparked a number of studies that attempted to pit the old theory against the new one. In this case the question was: Which is correct, the belief that objective features of the work environment are responsible for people's attitude, or are job attitudes merely the result of socially constructed realities? The reader is referred to Griffin (1987), Griffin, Bateman, Wayne, and Head (1987), and Thomas and Griffin (1989) for summaries of these studies. As often occurs in situations such as this – the debate between competing views on a matter – the conflicting data that result from research studies cause someone to proclaim that there is an element of truth in both viewpoints. Hence, Griffin et al. (1987) concluded: "The conclusions of researchers seeking to validate the social information processing model notwithstanding, it appears that perceptions of tasks are, in fact, partially determined by their objective properties and partially determined by social cues in workplaces" (p. 505). This author still concurs with this conclusion (cf. Pinder, 1998).

In summary, there is a variety of theoretical perspectives on the nature and experience of job dissatisfaction. The reader is encouraged to consider the proposition that all the models we discussed here have elements of truth: None is more "right" or "wrong" than the others, so perhaps the most important thing to remember is that job dissatisfaction can be a terrible drain on the spirits and health of people, both when they are at work and when they are trying to be away from it. We turn now to a look at some of the consequences of disliking one's job.

Some Consequences of Job Dissatisfaction

It is instructive to consider what job dissatisfaction *feels like* to those who are experiencing it. It often carries feelings of gloom and despair, sometimes anger and resentment, sometimes futility. A study employing affective events theory (cf. Weiss & Cropanzano, 1996), for example, found that negative experiences on the job caused employees to develop "emotion composites" and that three specific emotions – disappointed, unhappy, and depressed – were most significantly related to employees' intentions to leave the job (Grandey, Tam, & Brauburger, 2002). Jobs that are frustrating tend to make people tired and more mentally fatigued than they would otherwise be. Dissatisfying jobs can fill up lives, such that people feel depressed off the job as much as they do while at work, making the pursuit of leisure activities more critical, yet often less rewarding at the same time (recall Chapter 4). Moreover, job dissatisfaction can be a major contributor to poor mental health as well as to poor physical health (Herzberg, 1976; Jamal & Mitchell, 1980; Kavanagh, Hurst, & Rose, 1981).

In a nutshell, job dissatisfaction hurts. Discussing it in black and white offers a limited means of portraying how powerful an emotion it can be for those who suffer personally from it, not to mention how powerful the consequences can be for coworkers and loved ones associated with people suffering it. In extreme cases, such as those reported in Chapter 8, job dissatisfaction can, at times, be a matter of life and death.

Satisfaction and Dissatisfaction in Jobs and in Life

It should come as no surprise, then, that the relationship between job satisfaction (dissatisfaction) and life happiness (unhappiness) has been a topic of considerable study for decades in the social sciences, although the strength of the relationship has been challenged from time to time (Tait, Padgett, & Baldwin, 1989), as has the nature of the causal relationships between the two constructs, if they do exist (e.g., Heller, Judge, & Watson, 2002). The primary implicit hypothesis has traditionally been that of a form of "spillover effect": Because work plays such a central role in our lives, experiences on the job produce either positive or negative attitudes and emotions and these are carried by the individual into the home setting. Tait and her colleagues (Tait et al., 1989) conducted a meta-analysis of the studies reported through the mid-1980s on the matter and concluded that, indeed, the correlation between life and job satisfaction is significantly higher than zero and that, interestingly, the correlation among male samples in studies before 1974 (corrected r = 0.40) was significantly higher than that among female samples during that same time period (corrected r = 0.20). However, in the individual studies conducted *after* 1974, the difference between the correlations found in the two sex groups diminished to non-significance although the overall relationships between the two forms of satisfaction remained significantly greater than zero.

As opposed to the relatively simple one-way causal model assumed to link job happiness (the putative cause) with life happiness (the putative consequence), alternative models have been explored. For example, Judge and Watanabe (1993) tested and supported a reciprocal causal model and, still more recently, Heller et al. (2002) have provided support that the long-observed correlations between life and job satisfaction may be spurious; that is, it is possible that people's dispositional happiness/unhappiness (as we discussed it earlier) may account for much of the common variance observed in happiness in the two arenas.

The diversity of conceptual and operational definitions of job satisfaction (and dissatisfaction) used by investigators and managers (cf. Fields, 2002; Wanous & Lawler, 1972) makes it somewhat difficult to generalize the findings of research into the organizational consequences of holding favorable or unfavorable job attitudes. It has been assumed for many years that job attitudes may be more closely related to employee decisions to participate in organizations than they are to employee decisions concerning performance levels (see March & Simon, 1958). In others words, job satisfaction and dissatisfaction have been assumed to be much better predictors of attendance (or absenteeism), tardiness (as opposed to punctuality), and turnover than they are of performance levels. In the following section, we focus on the evidence behind these conclusions and discuss the costs and benefits of the consequences associated with unfavorable job attitudes.

Job Dissatisfaction and Withdrawal Behaviors

Withdrawal in response to job dissatisfaction takes a number of characteristic forms, sometimes together or in sequence. Tardiness, absenteeism, and turnover are the three most commonly acknowledged forms of withdrawal, but psychological withdrawal consists of passive compliance and minimal attempts to perform on the job, demonstrating a general lack of desire to excel, to be creative, let alone to perform "above and beyond the call of duty" (see George, 1991; Organ, 1990). It sometimes manifests itself as laziness, sometimes as stupidity. Hanisch and Hulin (1990) developed a scale of withdrawal behaviors that includes self-report items such as leaving work early, letting others do my work for me, making excuses to go somewhere to get out of work, and being absent when not really sick. While tardiness, absenteeism, turnover, and psychological withdrawal are separate phenomena, they do tend to be related to one another and to appear hand in hand or sequentially (Beehr & Gupta, 1978; Boswell & Olson-Buchanan, 2004; Edwards, 1979; Hanish & Hulin, 1990; Stumpf & Dawley, 1981). It is important to distinguish between voluntary and involuntary absenteeism, tardiness, and turnover, and to realize that job attitudes can be predictive only of withdrawal behaviors that are voluntary in nature (Steers & Rhodes, 1978). Many times, employees are late for work, absent from work, or must quit their jobs for reasons that are somewhat or totally beyond their control. For example, many employees find they must quit their jobs to accompany their spouses to new job sites in other cities following transfers. It would be unreasonable to include turnover of this sort in any analysis of the connection between job attitudes and turnover.

Research evidence suggests that job satisfaction will be conducive to lower levels of absenteeism (Breaugh, 1981; Dittrich & Carrell, 1979; Ilgen & Hollenbeck, 1977; Mirvis & Lawler, 1977; Nicholson, Wall, & Lischeron, 1977), higher levels of motivation to attend work on a given day (Smith, 1977; Steers & Rhodes, 1978), lower levels of tardiness (Adler & Golan, 1981), and lower levels of voluntary turnover (Arnold & Feldman, 1982; Dunnette, Arvey, & Banas, 1973; Karp & Nickson, 1973; Nicholson et al., 1977), possibly including early retirement (Schmitt & McCune, 1981).

A number of other studies have shown that employees' expressed intentions to leave an organization are more closely correlated with actual subsequent turnover than are other indicators of job dissatisfaction (Hom & Griffreth, 1995; Kraut, 1975; Mitchel, 1981). Note that this finding is entirely consistent with the theory of reasoned action presented in Chapter 9. Intentions, once formed, are more closely connected to behavior than are attitudes (see Ajzen & Fishbein, 1980; Fishbein & Ajzen, 1975; and recall Chapter 9).

Absenteeism from work: A costly proposition

Absenteeism from work is a major expense to employers. For example, a study conducted in 2000 by William M. Mercer Ltd., a large management consulting organization specializing in employee compensation and benefits, found that Canadian organizations, in both the public and private sectors, are spending between 2% and 8% of their payroll on staff who do not come to work.[5] That number does not include the costs of wages, salaries, and benefits (aside from less visible costs such as reduced productivity) paid to replacement workers. The Mercer study reported that the "vast majority" of employee absences are not work related (such as a result of injury or work-related illness). A similar study conducted in Canada and reported by Watson Wyatt, another large management consulting firm, found converging results: The direct costs of disability and absence management were estimated at 7.1% of organizations' payrolls. A more recent study by Watson Wyatt in Canada[6] found that mental health claims are on the rise and comprise a growing source of absence from work. Stress, depression, and anxiety disorders were cited by 56% of the employing organizations that participated in the survey.

Another study, conducted by Harris International in 2002 for CCH Incorporated, a widely known provider of human resources and employment law information, found strikingly similar results in a sample study of 333 human resource executives who worked for U.S. companies of all sizes and industries.[7] Among the findings of the American study was an estimate that the average cost of absenteeism per employee had climbed to $789 per year in 2002, up from $755 in 2001. The aggregate cost to small companies was estimated at $60,000 annually; for large companies, the aggregate costs were as high as US $3.6 million. Personal reasons, such as family issues, were the most frequent immediate cause of last-minute absence (24%), while stress accounted for 12% of cases. An "entitlement mentality" was reported as the immediate cause of 10% of absences.

In Europe, a 2004 survey reported by the National Social Insurance Board of Sweden[8] found that 40% of the population believe it is acceptable to stay away from work on any given day because they feel tired or are having difficulty getting along with their coworkers. According to the report, sick leave compensation tripled from 15 billion kronor (Cdn $2.6 billion) in 1997 to 45 billion (Cdn $7.8 billion) in 2002. The point is simple: Absenteeism is a very expensive cost item for employers, worldwide.

Finally, the issue of gender differences in absenteeism rates among men, as opposed to women, has been in the news in Canada recently. Statistics Canada (*The Daily*, February 23, 2007) reported a study of absenteeism and quitting rates among men and women over the 5-year period 1998–2003. As part of that study, it was found that, on average, men took 2 days of paid sick absence per year while women took about 4 days of paid sick absence annually. On the other hand, there were no gender differences in terms of other paid and unpaid absences, with the exception of women who have young children. These mothers took 2 more days, on average, than women who did not have young children.

---

[5] Reported by Elizabeth Church, *The Globe and Mail*, February 3, 2000.
[6] Reported by Eric Beauchesne, CanWest News Service, *Times Colonist*, September 30, 2005, p. D2.
[7] Absenteeism costs companies more than ever. Howard Kettner's BenefitsWorld.com. October 16, 2002.
[8] *Times Colonist*, September 18, 2004, p. A12.

Absenteeism and job attitudes

It has long been an article of faith among both researchers and managers that a primary cause of absenteeism behavior is low job satisfaction, low organizational commitment, or some other blend of unhappy attitudes toward one's work and the workplace. Although it may be true that, on the margin, unhappy workers are less likely to report to work than happier ones, there is much more to the absenteeism phenomenon than job attitudes, and the research evidence shows that the connection between absenteeism and job satisfaction/dissatisfaction is not very strong.

For example, Johns and Nicholson (1982) argued many years ago that there are several different reasons for people to be absent from work, and the psychological factors related to absence behavior should be treated case by case. In fact, two meta-analytic studies of the matter have reported that facets of job satisfaction count for less than 5% of absence behavior. Another meta-analysis of 31 at about the same time (Hackett & Guion, 1985) concluded that the relationship between the two concepts was very small and weak, the apparent appeal of the belief that people who dislike their jobs are more likely to stay away from those jobs notwithstanding. A decade later, Martocchio and Judge (1994) formed clusters of employees who worked for a large university on the basis of the common origins of their absenteeism behavior. Factors such as personal illness, the illness of others in one's household, community activities and hobby or leisure activities, and having children were considered. The results suggested that, following Johns and Nicholson (1982), there are many reasons, and combinations of reasons, for people to be absent from work. Of interest to our purposes here, job dissatisfaction was a statistically significant factor, but the effect was not large, particularly compared to some of the other factors included, such as personal illness.

Employee turnover and job attitudes

Two very thorough meta-analyses of the empirical literature on the antecedents and consequences of employee turnover have found a consistent although only moderate linear relationship between job satisfaction/dissatisfaction and employee turnover (Griffeth, Hom, & Gaertner, 2000; Hom & Griffeth, 1995). Although absenteeism does not appear to have many redeeming qualities, there is considerable theory and research to suggest that employee turnover entails both costs and benefits both for individuals and for organizations (Mitchell, Holtom, & Lee, 2001). As in the case of absenteeism and other withdrawal behaviors, it is critical to distinguish between voluntary and involuntary quitting behavior.

First, let's consider the costs of turnover for organizations. First, departing employees frequently take with them valuable expertise and knowledge acquired at the organizations they leave. This is especially problematic when they have developed profitable and positive relationships with some of the organizations' customers and clients. There are costs associated with recruiting and placing new people, training them, and waiting until the costs they represent are offset by the value they contribute once they are up to speed. Estimates of the aggregate costs of replacing an employee vary (with the skill level sought, the supply and demand for labor in the marketplace, and other factors). A survey by New York-based William Mercer Inc., found that 45% of companies in their sample reported turnover to cost more than $10,000 per employee. Twenty percent estimated the costs at $30,000 or higher.[9] A study of the tourism industry (where turnover is approximately 30%!) estimates that the cost of replacing an employee is between $1500 and $4500 (*Personnel Today*, January 2, 2007, p. 19). When turnover occurs among top performers in senior organizational ranks, the costs to the organization can be particularly acute: The value contributed by higher-paid individuals is usually higher than that contributed by people at lower organizational levels and,

---

[9] This information was taken from c20011948, "What are the costs of employee turnover?" by Entrepreneurial Edge, Edward Lowe Foundation. http://www.celee.edu/publications/edinfo/ED01-07.html

frequently, it can be more difficult to locate and recruit suitable replacements at high levels than at lower levels. Finally, the loss of senior people, especially higher-performing ones, can mean the loss of future leadership talent for the organization as a whole (Trevor, Gerhart, & Boudreau, 1997).

What are some benefits to organizations of employee turnover? In some cases, an organization can reap real dollar cost savings through turnover, especially in cases where those who leave can easily be replaced by newcomers who are compensated at lower rates of pay and benefits (Dalton, 1981; Dalton & Todor, 1982a). In addition, turnover can help introduce new ideas, new "blood," and the potential for change and adaptation of the organization involved, a necessity for organizations facing even moderate levels of change in their environments (Aldrich, 1980; Gross, 1965). People who leave tend to be the ones who withdraw in other ways, so turnover may help reduce absenteeism, tardiness, psychological withdrawal, and their associated costs (Mobley, 1982).

Turnover may also be the only solution in cases of extreme conflict between organizational members, as often occurs following mergers and other forms of reorganization (Mobley, 1982). For the individual, moving to a new organization can serve as an adaptive escape from a job that is stressful or conducive to marital discord, alcohol and drug abuse, or general life maladjustment (see Hulin's 1990 discussion of withdrawal behaviors of all sorts as adaptive responses to job dissatisfaction and frustration). From a societal point of view, turnover helps cross-organizational institution building, as ideas and techniques developed in some organizations are taken into others, often at the cost of individual organizations but often for the benefit of entire industries or networks of organizations. (See McKelvey, 1982, for a discussion of the transmission of "genes" among organizations.)

Second, although job dissatisfaction may generate a desire to leave one's organization in favor of employment elsewhere, we cannot assume that low levels of turnover are indicative of generally positive work attitudes in a workforce. A number of factors can lock in disgruntled employees, preventing them from leaving dissatisfying work settings (Flowers & Hughes, 1973; Hershey, 1973). For example, while an employee may be very dissatisfied with some aspects of her job (such as the nature of the work itself), she might be quite unwilling to leave it and lose the high levels of pay it brings her. The availability (or unavailability) of alternative employment has been recognized as a major factor in determining whether an unhappy employee will actually leave a paying job voluntarily (cf. March & Simon, 1958; Mitchell & Lee, 2001). Sometimes a generalized fear of the unknown, often based on real or imagined self-perceptions of obsolescence, prevents dissatisfied employees from quitting. That said, a recent study by Maertz and Campion (2004) found that people who leave a job with no alternative lined up tend be much more dissatisfied than those who have alternatives available. Another study found that people who feel they have been mistreated are more likely to quit than others (Boswell & Olson-Buchanan, 2004). Finally, Côté and Morgan (2002) found that employees whose jobs require them to suppress unpleasant emotions suffer decreased job satisfaction, which is, in turn, related to intentions to quit (recall our discussion of emotional labor in Chapter 4).

Many organizations inadvertently prevent their employees from leaving them because of the "golden handcuffs" they manage to lock onto their workforce over the years through pension plans, health insurance plans, and other benefits. The importance of this point is that although there is no necessary connection between job attitudes and individual job performance, disgruntled employees are often those who perform their jobs at the minimum levels required and who seldom demonstrate any desire to be creative or to excel "above and beyond the call of duty" when the occasion to do so presents itself. Moreover, there is evidence, presented earlier, that dissatisfied personnel are more likely to be absent and tardy, disrupting the normal flow of events for their employers, customers, and coworkers (Wright & Bonett, 1993). Hence, an organization may benefit from ridding itself of those who are dissatisfied.

This raises the following question: Is voluntary turnover higher among an organization's poor performers or its high performers? At first blush, one might hypothesize that workers who voluntarily leave are often the most competent and (therefore) the most marketable. But Steers and Mowday (1981) suggested that low performers are probable candidates for turnover because of their low satisfaction with intrinsic elements of their jobs, motivating them to leave for more satisfying pastures. What does the research evidence say? It is mixed.

The results of three meta-analyses reported uncorrected linear correlations in the range of -0.16 to -0.24 (MacEvoy & Cascio, 1987; Bycio, Hackett, & Alvares, 1990; Williams & Livingstone, 1994): *Turnover and performance tend to have a small inverse linear relationship.* A study of employee files in a large U.S. insurance company, using logistic regression rather than the more frequently used OLS technique, came to the same conclusion (Morrow, McElroy, Laczniak, & Fenton, 1999). By way of contrast, Jackofsky (1984; see also Jackofsky, Ferris, & Breckenridge, 1986) proposed that there may be more to the story than a simple (inverse) linear relationship. Building on some of the conceptual arguments presented earlier, he proposed that there may be a curvilinear relationship, such that both high and low performers may be more likely to quit work voluntarily than people who are "average performers." Indeed, a large-scale study by Trevor et al. (1997) found support for such a curvilinear relationship,[10] as did the meta-analysis by Williams and Livingstone (1994).

Whether turnover occurs among an organization's high performers and low performers may depend on its reward system. Trevor et al. (1997) summarized their findings this way:

> [P]erhaps the most important result from this study concerns the moderating influence of salary growth. We found that low salary growth resulted in a more pronounced curvilinear relationship, relative to the high salary growth condition, as top performer turnover probabilities approximated the high turnover tendencies of poor performers. Conversely, because the negative effect of salary growth on turnover probability increased in magnitude as performance increased, paying for high performance defused this tendency as high performer turnover probabilities resembled the relatively low turnover tendencies of average performers.

In other words, both high- and low-level performers are more likely to quit voluntarily when pay and other rewards are contingent on performance, whereas they are more likely to leave when rewards are not distributed in accordance with performance (see also Dreher, 1982). Whether the relationship is linear and inverse or curvilinear seems to depend on moderator variables still to be discovered. At this point, the key consideration for the retention of top performers is to recognize their excellence with positive rewards, as would be prescribed by most theories presented elsewhere in this book (see especially Chapter 12).

The focus of all the work examined here in relation to the connection between performance and turnover has been on individuals. There has been less research conducted at the level of work groups or formal organizational units. An exception is a study reported by McElroy, Morrow, and Rude (2001) which found that three varieties of turnover at the unit level were all related to reductions in profitability among a sample of 31 geographically separated units of an American insurance company. The three forms were involuntary turnover (dismissals), voluntary, and reduction in force (layoffs). All three types of turnover had detrimental impacts on organizational performance, although the effects of layoffs were the strongest.

Finally, while job dissatisfaction is a contributing factor to voluntary turnover, it is not responsible for most cases of involuntary quitting. Hence, turnover may be beneficial for the employee who leaves and for the organization to which he goes. And turnover may be either beneficial or detrimental to the organization that suffers it, depending on the costs associated with the economic and noneconomic considerations discussed earlier. An exhaustive analysis of the causes, costs, and benefits of turnover is beyond the scope of this chapter; the interested reader is referred to recent reviews by Griffeth, Hom, & Gaertner (2000) and Mitchell & Lee (2001).

---

[10] This project is an admirable example of the combination of good theory, common sense, and rigorous empirical study, one that has interesting theoretical and applied implications.

The unfolding model of voluntary turnover

Employee turnover has been the subject of countless empirical studies over the past 50 years (Mitchell & Lee, 2001). As suggested in the foregoing discussion, most of the research and the theory related to it has focused on attitudinal factors (such as those discussed in Chapter 9) – the idea being that dissatisfying experiences will result in negative job attitudes that, in turn, will generate intentions to quit, followed by, when alternatives were perceived to be available, actual quitting behavior.

Mitchell and Lee (2001) introduced a fundamentally new model of voluntary turnover, one that introduces new constructs called *organizational attachment* and *job embeddedness*. (Embeddedness is a newly coined term for a construct that includes an individual's links to other people, teams, and groups; perceptions of their fit with the job, organization, and community; and what they say they would have to sacrifice if they left their jobs.)

Although this new model does not replace the traditional dissatisfaction-search-quit paradigm, it augments it by recognizing that there are a variety of sequences that explain the quitting behavior of different people. Specifically, they recognize that certain events in a person's life, either related to their jobs or not, can cause an individual to take stock of his or her job attitudes and, in some cases, consider whether the event (which they refer to as "shock") bears significance for their decision to search for alternatives or not. For example, the death of a loved one may cause an individual to consider whether s/he should leave a job and move abroad to be closer to one's children. The takeover by one's employer by another organization is a second example: The event may cause a person to stop and reflect about the wisdom of staying or leaving the company. Mitchell and Lee (2001) proposed four general "paths" that people tend to follow toward quitting (or staying) in a job in the aftermath of a shock. The path(s) people follow toward quitting or staying "unfold" as they consider a variety of factors, including the availability of alternative jobs, the goodness of fit they perceive between themselves and the circumstances they anticipate by either leaving or staying, the degree of embeddedness they have in their current work, and life-in-general circumstances.

Mitchell and Lee (2001) described two early studies they conducted with their colleagues to help launch the unfolding model, and a number of other studies have followed to develop the model (e.g., Holtom, Mitchell, Lee, & Inderrieden, 2005) and, in subsequent studies, found that job embeddedness explained variance in intentions to quit as well as actual quitting behavior (Lee, Mitchell, Sablynski, Burton, & Holtom, 2004; Mitchell, Holtom, Lee, Sablynski, & Erez, 2001).

Complete detail of the unfolding model is beyond our present scope. The point is that job dissatisfaction is not the only cause of the various types of withdrawal behaviors that we have discussed here, although it does contribute to many people's decisions to quit.

Suffice it to say that this new model offers a much more realistic description of the processes in voluntary turnover than earlier models and, as research and further validation proceed, it will enhance our capacity to predict and perhaps control voluntary quitting (cf. Mitchell, Holtom, & Lee, 2001).

Turnover and gender in Canada

In the study mentioned earlier in this chapter, Statistics Canada (2007) has recently reported that the traditional gap in turnover rates of men and women has virtually closed over the past two decades. The annual percentage of the male workforce in Canada that voluntarily quit their jobs in 1984, 1994, and 2002 were, respectively, 5.5%, 5.5%, and 7.6%. The corresponding figures for working Canadian women were 7.0%, 5.6%, and 7.5% – now, virtually no different from the male data.

A closing note on the strength of the forces to withdraw: The case of the military

A powerful and poignant portrayal of the forces that cause individuals to be voluntarily absent from their work and/or to quit it altogether is provided by Dobie (2005) in her discussion of the problems of AWOL (absent without leave) and desertion in the U.S. military. According to her analysis, the number of desertions in the U.S. Army has risen from 1509 in 1995 to 4739 in 2001. When one considers the severity of the punishment for being caught in either of these two forms of withdrawal (court martial and imprisonment), the magnitude of misery soldiers face is placed in stark relief. Knowing the personal costs of being caught and punished for being AWOL or for desertion, increasing numbers of military personnel "withdraw" anyway. This author suspects that the traditional dissatisfaction → withdrawal model as well as the unfolding model featuring "shocks" can both contribute to the experiences of soldiers who take the risks of escape from life in the military.

Job Satisfaction and Individual Productivity

At least since the beginning of the human relations movement in the 1940s, it has commonly been assumed that employees who are more satisfied with their work tend to be more productive than those who are not as satisfied. Among many managers, politicians, and social critics, it makes intuitive sense to assume that "a more satisfied employee is a productive employee." Fisher (2003) has offered evidence of the strength and universality of this belief as well as a number of explanations for its widespread acceptance, while Judge et al. (2001) identified seven different belief structures people hold to portray the satisfaction–performance relationship (see Figure 10.1). For the current author, this "truism" (that happy workers are more productive workers) is the surest way to debunk naive ideas students and newcomers to the field have about the limitations to the argument that OB is simply a matter of common sense!!

The intuitive appeal of this idea notwithstanding, after countless studies into the relationship between these two variables, it can be concluded that there is only a small statistical bivariate relationship between job attitudes and individual performance, where "performance" is conceived as short-term productivity and task accomplishment (see Fisher, 2003, for a review).

Recall from our discussion in Chapter 9 that it is seldom the case that attitudes lead to specific behaviors in a predictable fashion. Sometimes, high levels of satisfaction are associated with high levels of productivity; other times, the opposite is the case. It may be, for example, that a dissatisfied employee will become quite productive if she perceives that high performance levels may help her earn a promotion, a raise in pay, or even a chance to attain a job elsewhere. Alternatively, highly satisfied employees can become complacent, resting on their reputations and assuming that contributions made in the past have earned them the right to "coast" on the job, perhaps until retirement or layoff.

Why do general attitudes about one's work *not* predict job performance? Fisher (1980) observed years ago that it is unreasonable to expect *general* attitudes (such as a generally positive attitude toward one's job) to be predictive of *specific* acts (such as performing at a high level of productivity). Fisher points out that we can reasonably expect only *specific attitudes* to predict *specific actions*. More to the point – using concepts from the theory of reasoned action (recall Chapter 9) – rather than expecting to predict a specific behavior (such as expending high job effort) with a global attitude toward one's job, we should attempt to use people's *attitudes toward the act in question* (expending high levels of effort on the job) to predict that behavior. Fisher (1980) observed that until attitudes and behaviors are conceptualized and measured at the same levels of specificity, it is hopeless to expect job satisfaction to predict individual job performance. The wisdom of Fisher's insight was to be resurrected years later to help OB researchers get the genie out of the bottle on the satisfaction–performance hypothesis. We return to her insight shortly.

One intriguing theoretical approach suggests that satisfaction may be responsible for high levels of individual productivity only when the person believes that productivity will be successful as a means of removing "equivocality" (Weick, 1969, p. 99). Equivocality is disorder, ambiguity, multiple meanings, and a touch of chaos. We noted in Chapter 7 that people are frequently motivated to increase and then reduce the amounts of uncertainty in their lives. The energy expended in creating these cycles is called, in one view, intrinsic motivation. The actual behavior associated with increasing and removing uncertainty is called intrinsically motivated behavior. Weick (1969) suggested that there is pleasure in the removal of equivocality from one's environment, and so if an employee believes that equivocality can be mastered through high energy expenditure and that pleasure occurs in the removal process, performance and satisfaction will covary: As one increases, so does the other. Historically, it is interesting to note that Weick's hypothesis was apparently derived, at least in part, from some of the same intellectual roots that inspired Deci and his colleagues, although the latter two authors do not acknowledge one another. The common roots are found in White's (1959) writing about *effectance motivation* (see Chapter 7). Direct comparison of Weick's thinking and that of Deci (1975; Deci & Ryan, 1985) would require us to equate the concept of equivocality (Weick) with that of uncertainty (Deci).

Katzell, Thompson, and Guzzo (1992) advanced a complex theoretical model summarizing a great deal of the then-existing evidence on the complex relationship between job satisfaction and job performance. In the research that followed, they found, as had other researchers before them, that the simple bivariate connection between positive job attitudes and high levels of performance is either low or nonexistent, depending on whether employees or their supervisors

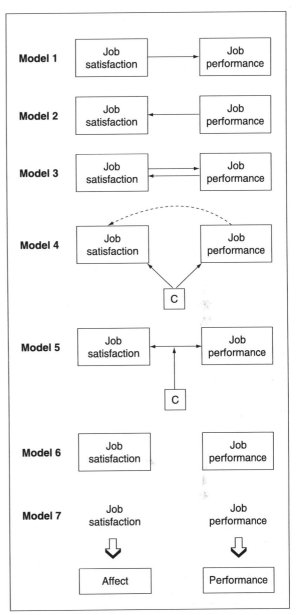

FIG. 10.1 Models of the relationship between job satisfaction and job performance.

Source: Judge, T. A., Thoresen, C. J., Bono, J. E., & Patton, G. K. (2001). The job satisfaction–job performance relationship: A qualitative and quantitative review. *Psychological Bulletin, 127*(3): 376–407. (Note that in Models 4 and 5, C denotes a third variable.) Reprinted with permission.

provide the performance data. They also concluded that both performance and satisfaction are probably best thought of as consequences of many other organizational and attitudinal factors, and that when they are connected with one another, it is usually very indirectly, through the effects of other such variables. For example, the work must yield intrinsic rewards. There must be highly valued extrinsic rewards tied to performance and administered equitably. Job involvement must be high, and clear, challenging, and acceptable goals must be set (Katzell et al., 1992). Their conclusions were reminiscent of much earlier formulations presented by Porter and Lawler (1968) and by Locke and Latham (1990b).

The between-persons–within-persons issue (again)

Since the last time this author reviewed this literature (Pinder, 1998), significant innovations have occurred in both conceptual clarity and research methodology directed to the satisfaction–performance relationship. One more time, we find that research evidence is frequently a joint product of the actual relationships among parameters and the nature of the methodology we use to find those relationships. At this point, the reader is reminded of the "between–within" dilemma in research methodology we first discovered in Chapter 2 and that will reappear in Chapter 12.

Here is the core of the matter: Do we believe that:

(a) Persons who are happier with their jobs than other people are also likely to be more productive at their jobs than those other people?
(b) As a particular individual becomes happier with her job, she will become more productive at it?
(c) As a person becomes more productive at her job (and receives intrinsic and/or extrinsic rewards for this improvement), she will become more satisfied with that job?

Interpretation (a) has been the most traditional throughout this long debate, and the evidence to support it has been very weak – see Fisher (2003) for a summary of the reviews on the matter. Why would one suppose that because John is happier (for any of a number of reasons) with his job than Mary is with hers he should be more productive than Mary? The correlation and possible causal connection between a person's attitudes and motivation or behavior is a private affair, not a social one. Therein lies the wisdom of Fisher's insight.[11]

Experience-sampling procedures

Interpretations (b) and (c) discard the across-person comparisons and adopt a more appropriate within-individual person approach and have found much stronger connections between the two parameters than have been isolated by the between-persons approach. The technique of choice for undertaking research with the within-individual conceptualization of the satisfaction–performance hypothesis is *experience sampling methodology* (ESM), described here by Ilies and Judge (2002, p. 1120):

> In an ESM design, participants are required to report their momentary experiences or subjective feeling states, or to record momentary measures of physiological variables (e.g., heart rate, body temperature, etc.). The ESM measurement approach eliminates the process of recall or summarization, which can be problematic due to selective memory processes . . . Measurement occurs in the natural environment and the data collection process is intensive, typically involving multiple observations per person.

In short, this method allows the researcher to study the covariation between two (or more) variables, over time, within a single person, permitting the study of within-person dynamic relationships among those variables. Of most interest to our present purposes, of course, this method allows us to study whether increases in positive mood experienced at Time 1 by a person are associated with subsequent increases in performance at Time 2. Notice that data collected through this method also

---

[11] The interested reader may enjoy a debate instigated by Wright and Staw (1999), who resurrected the happy–productive worker hypothesis for further study by examining the relationship between people's mood states and trait dispositions, successfully seeking relationships with supervisory ratings. Ledford (1999) and Wright and Staw (1999) then exchanged papers to advance the resurrection of the hypothesis.

enable a search for across-person covariations (of the traditional sort as well). The interested reader is referred to a paper by Hormuth (1986) for greater detail about this data-collection technique.

Using this technique, Ilies and Judge (2002) tested a model that an individual's personality (neuroticism, extraversion, positive affectivity, and negative affectivity) would predict his or her average mood, and that mood would, in turn, predict job satisfaction between and within individuals. They tested their model using 27 Americans whose jobs ranged from secretarial to professional, each person recording his or her momentary mood and job satisfaction four times per day for 19 working days. This meant that the maximum number of observations per person was 76, and the maximum number of observations across individuals and time periods was 2052. (In fact, they managed to record a total of only 1907 ESM ratings of mood and job satisfaction.) Among their findings was that "for the average individual, job satisfaction ratings vary across time almost as much as average levels of job satisfaction vary across individuals. To be more precise, 36% of the differences in job satisfaction ratings were due to differences within individuals" (p. 1132). Note that Ilies and Judge were not concerned with the satisfaction–performance link in their study but, rather, were employing the ESM technique to study relationships among personality, mood and satisfaction, largely supporting their model.

A study more germane for our present purposes was reported by Fisher and Noble (2004), who, using the ESM method, both hypothesized and found significant within-person correlations among a host of variables, including task skill, task difficulty, task interest, effort, performance, and positive and negative emotions. A total of 4507 responses were gathered from a sample of 1221 people. Complete detail of their elaborate model is not provided here; the interested reader is referred to the original research report. Nevertheless, while causal connections among variables could not be justified by the cross-sectional nature of the data collection and analysis, the researchers estimated a strong within-person correlation ($r = .47$) between task performance and positive emotions and a strong inverse correlation ($r = −.43$) between task performance and negative emotions.[12]

Conclusions on job satisfaction and individual job performance

A thorough and scholarly review of the literature on this subject was conducted by Judge et al. (2001). Noting that thousands of previous studies as well as a number of earlier meta-analyses had failed to reach much in the way of satisfying conclusions, they conducted a fresh meta-analysis that included 312 samples and a combined number of 54,417 research participants. As mentioned earlier, they organized their thinking around seven different conceptual models that previous researchers had employed, either explicitly or implicitly. (Judge and his colleagues cite a general lack of clarity in model articulation and accumulation as a source of much of the confusion they found in the literature.) Using the various procedures for adjusting parameter estimates employed in meta-analysis, they estimated the "mean true correlation" between overall job satisfaction and job performance to be .30. On the basis of their review, they propose a hybrid model to guide future research that is, for the most part, a blend of five of the models they identified at the beginning of their research. In many ways similar to the early theoretic model of Porter and Lawler (1968), the hybrid model proposed by Judge et al. (2001) contains the following features:

1. A circular relationship between individual satisfaction and individual job performance; that is, each is a contributing cause of the other.

---

[12] As mentioned in Chapter 4, another ESM study by these researchers found that people's interest in their work, their perceived skill at their jobs and the effort that they put into their jobs were positive predictors of positive emotions and negative predictors of negative emotions (Fisher & Noble, 2004). Results also showed that people's emotions about their work varied considerably over time, as did their levels of job performance. However, the results did not support the hypothesis that prior positive emotions would predict current performance levels or the hypothesis that prior negative emotions would predict current performance levels (Fisher & Noble, 2004).

2. In the case of the satisfaction-causes-performance connection, several mediating variables are proposed, including the individual's behavioral intentions and possessing a positive mood state. This model is also seen as subject to the effects of a number of moderator variables, the person's self-concept, autonomy on the job, norms of the workplace as well as methodological factors such as the means by which data are aggregated and the level of analysis used in the research.
3. In the case of the performance-causes-satisfaction connection, mediators such as the person's self-efficacy and positive mood may be invoked to explain the relationship. Moreover, the main bivariate relationship may well be moderated by characteristics of the person's job, the strength of the relationship between rewards and performance, and personality factors such as need for achievement.

Finally, Judge et al. (2001) identify nearly 20 research questions that follow from their analysis to inspire and guide other researchers who wish to join the ranks of countless others before them who have sought the solution to the problem: "What is the relationship between employee performance and satisfaction?"

Job Satisfaction and other Forms of Performance

So why are positive job attitudes important if they are so modestly related to bottom-line indicators of performance? Farrell (1983), Fisher and Locke (1992), and Smith (1992), among others, have provided some answers. Although it is true that positive job attitudes are not reliably predictive of the performance levels of individual employees (as detailed earlier), *job satisfaction may be related to a variety of other outcome variables that have largely been ignored until recently.* An alternative way of stating the same thing is that current thinking requires a broader definition of performance than has traditionally been used in the past by organizational scientists – a definition that equates "performance" with "individual productivity."

Unit-level analyses

Throughout the 1990s, the Gallup Organization conducted and reported a series of studies on job attitudes and copyrighted a 13-item scale to assess job satisfaction and employee engagement, which, for Gallup, refers to an individual's involvement and satisfaction as well as enthusiasm for work. The items were identified through focus groups and other, more traditional approaches. The particularly interesting thing about these items is that they focus on issues that managers and supervisors can influence, such as the degree of clarity a person has about what is expected of her at work and the degree to which the person feels pride in the organization's vision. When results collected by Gallup's instrument are combined to the work unit level, they are generally positively associated with positive unit-level dependent variables, including profit. A meta-analysis reported by Harter, Schmidt, and Hayes (2002) summarized and supported the satisfaction–performance link at the unit level, with the implication that the causal flow was in the satisfaction/engagement → performance direction. An early study by Ostroff (1992), involving nearly 300 public schools and more than 13,000 teachers, showed that, collectively, positive job attitudes (including attitudinal commitment) among the teachers was significantly correlated with a range of school-level performance measures.

Building on the work of Farrell (1983), for example, Fisher and Locke (1992) constructed a typology of outcomes that can result from negative job attitudes. These categories include avoidance acts such as quitting one's job outright, avoidance by minimizing effort or dodging difficult tasks, psychological adjustments (e.g., using drugs or other substances), constructive problem solving or forming a union, defying authority and resisting managerial directions, and outright aggression, such as acts involving sabotage, rumor mongering, and the like. Fisher and Locke's categories include many other specific examples, but their point is made: "Performance" consists of much more than simple efficiency and measures of individual productivity, as has usually been construed in the past (see Staw, 1984).

On the positive side, an entire set of prosocial behaviors (or what Fisher and Locke, 1992, call "helping behaviors") often result from positive employee attitudes. Originally conceived of as work that lies outside the individual's formal job description (Katz, 1964), four more specific forms of work above and beyond the call of duty have been studied in recent years, usually in relation to positive job attitudes. These positive behaviors have been referred to as extra-role, prosocial, altruistic, and citizenship behaviors (see Organ, 1990).

Clearly, most organizations would rather have their employees engage in such acts than not do so: We have all experienced the chill of the bureaucratic employee who prefers not to extend himself beyond minimal service, and a few of us have actually enjoyed the relief and satisfaction that can occur when an employee extends himself beyond normal expectations to be especially helpful. Good citizenship behavior by employees becomes particularly important in service industries, where courtesy, sympathy, and energetic creativity and positive attitude toward customers' problems can mean the difference between profit and loss (George, 1991).

Job Satisfaction and Life Satisfaction

There may be other reasons to be concerned with generating and fostering positive job attitudes – having more to do with mental and physical health and personal well-being than they do with corporate profit and individual job performance. As suggested earlier, there is a renewal in the belief that positive attitudes in one forum of a person's life "spill over" into positive mental health and happiness in other arenas of life. This idea was first proposed decades ago but has continued to receive attention from job satisfaction theorists such as Smith (1992), who wrote about general feelings of happiness and trust that people may generate and enjoy through their work. Their feelings of happiness and joy also contribute to similar emotions in non-work settings, such as in their family lives, recreation activities, and so on (see Schmitt & Bedeian, 1982; Schmitt & Pulakos, 1985). A general sense of joy and a predilection toward being happy fosters positive job attitudes as well, so the causality between general happiness and context-specific happiness prevails. According to Smith (1992), people blessed with such feelings of happiness and trust are much more open to change in their lives, particularly changes in their work situations. Their generally positive disposition tends to transcend time and situations, although as we noted earlier, they too are subject to negative feelings. It is a matter of relative rank order among their peers who don't possess the predisposition. At work, they are less resistant to managerial initiatives and approach new work procedures more constructively and with minimum supervision.

A longitudinal study conducted in the mid-1980s involved a sample of full-time employees of a private U.S. university. This study illustrated the concept of spillover and the statements that Cranny et al. (1992) have made about the benefits of positive general life satisfaction. The study also extended previous work to examine the effects of two (rather than just one) dimensions of emotionality: Negative affectivity and positive affectivity (Levin & Stokes, 1989; Watson & Slack, 1993). Each of these moods can be experienced either as a passing state or as stable traits, although the focus in this project was on the trait forms of affectivity. People who have strong negative affectivity tend to view the world from a negative, pessimistic perspective. They witness higher levels of distress and dissatisfaction in most settings in which they find themselves. On the contrary, people high in positive trait affectivity have fun in life, viewing things positively and with a generalized optimism. They may even have heightened capacities to enjoy positive stimuli.

In their study, Watson and Slack (1993) gathered data on both positive and negative affectivity at two points in time, spanning 2 years. They controlled for a number of other variables relating to their participants' work and assessed job satisfaction at the end of the 2-year period. A total of 82 of the original 151 employees stayed with the project to provide complete sets of data. The results confirmed that both positive and negative trait measures of emotionality were related to at least some dimensions of job satisfaction. Thus, negative trait affect was associated with lower satisfaction with one's work and one's coworkers; positive trait affect was predictive of positive assessments of employees' work, promotions, and overall job satisfaction. They also found that these traits/predispositions remained stable over the 2 years of the project. The authors concluded that job satisfaction can reasonably be understood "in the context of the broader emotional lives of employees." It is not just a result of organizational policies, procedures, and job design; it is a reflection of the greater, more general degree of individual happiness or unhappiness of the person. To the extent that this is true, there is plenty of reason to study job satisfaction, aside from the relentless quest for its elusive link to productivity, performance, and other aspects of organizational effectiveness.

Another study examined the notion that job and life satisfaction are related to one another using a large survey database from the early 1970s (Judge & Watanabe, 1993). These researchers found a strong cross-sectional link between the two variables but a much smaller connection between job satisfaction and life satisfaction when the latter was measured 5 years later than the former.

In contrast to the argument that job satisfaction and life satisfaction are related to one another (Cranny et al., 1992) presumably in the sense that one is responsible for much of the other (i.e., that job satisfaction causes some or much of life satisfaction), there is another possibility. A study of 631 people in their homes, combined with data analysis techniques appropriate for the purpose, suggested that any relationship that does exist between job and life satisfaction is due, at least in large measure, to the effects of one or more other variables (Frone, Russell, & Cooper, 1994). In other words, it may be that the oft-observed bivariate relationship between satisfaction at work and satisfaction with life in general (or, alternatively, dissatisfaction in both arenas) is spurious. This means that the correlation between them may be because some other variable(s) is driving both of them, although life and work satisfaction may not actually be causally related. Indeed, a more recent study by Hart (1999) found that job satisfaction and non-work satisfaction, although related to one another directly, both contributed to the variance in life satisfaction reported by a sample of police officers and a within-individual study by Heller, Watson, and Ilies (2006) found that both marital and job satisfaction were positively correlated with the life satisfaction of a sample of married Americans under the age of 65.

Measurement of Job Satisfaction

Perhaps the construct of most interest over the 70-year history of social scientific attention to work, employees, and related matters, job satisfaction has been measured countless times by countless managers, consultants, and researchers. As is usually the case, hasty scales and single-item measures were often slapped together for quick-and-dirty analyses. However, perhaps more than any other construct of interest in the organizational sciences, job satisfaction has enjoyed some of the "best" (recall Chapter 2) measurement available to us. A recent compendium of organizational measures compiled by Fields (2002) lists many scales of proven validity. Indeed, even some of the scales that brag the best early psychometric properties continue to undergo scrutiny (e.g., Kinicki, McKee-Ryan, Schriesheim, & Carson, 2002). There is no longer any excuse for researchers to construct home-made measures of job satisfaction.

Conclusions on Job Satisfaction and a Glance Ahead

In the foregoing sections of this chapter (as well as in parts of Chapter 4), we have seen that job satisfaction (and dissatisfaction) are complex motivation-related phenomena, containing both attitudinal and affective elements. We have seen that both are influenced by a range of individual and organizational variables and they, in turn, can have significant effects on a range of other individual as well as organizational variables. The history of the study of job attitudes is as old as the history of the organizational sciences and history has seen a cyclical pattern of attention being paid to people's feelings about their jobs. The frustrated attempts through the 1980s to find the widely anticipated causal connections between job attitudes and individual performance portended a decline in scientific interest, even though practitioners seemed to believe that "a satisfied employee is a productive employee." The connections between job attitudes and nonperformance variables, especially withdrawal behaviors, never lost their value in the eyes of either researchers or practitioners. Then, with the introduction of more appropriate conceptualizations of job attitudes (as within-individual phenomena) in the 1990s, research on job attitudes and all of its antecedents and consequences enjoyed a renaissance and the topic is now again "popular" in the academic literature.

Aside from the historical significance of the phenomena, the more important issue, for this author, is the tremendous significance they have as experienced by working people. Those who have experienced the joys of working know what this means, as do those who have suffered the frustrations of job and career dissatisfaction: They really hurt, and they deliver significant impacts on our daily lives, both while we are actually at work as well as when we are not.

A glance ahead

Whereas Part Two of this book approached the motivation to participate and the motivation to perform from a needs perspective, Part Three looks at these two elements of work motivation from the perspective of people's attitudes and beliefs. In short, the purpose here is to understand how certain job-related attitudes may or may not be related to the desire of people to participate in organizations and to perform well for those organizations. Now that we have examined job satisfaction in detail, we turn our attention to work commitment, a set of attitudes, beliefs, and intentions that people form in reference to their employers, as opposed to their jobs per se.

WORK COMMITMENT

Whereas job satisfaction generally has to do with the degree to which one's needs or values are satisfied by one's job, work commitment is a multidimensional construct that is somewhat broader in scope. Specifically, *work commitment* is currently seen as comprising several dimensions, such as adherence to a work ethic (see Chapter 1 of this book), commitment to a career or a profession, job involvement (the degree of daily absorption in everyday work experiences), and organizational commitment (the degree of loyalty a person holds for a particular employer) (see Blau & Paul, 1993; Morrow, 1993). Space limitations here require that we focus primarily on the third and fourth varieties of work commitment identified by Morrow (1993): Organizational commitment and job involvement. The interested reader is referred to Morrow (1993, Chapter 1) and to Chapter 1 of this volume for a discussion of the issue of the Protestant work ethic, and to Morrow (1993, Chapters 2 and 3) for an examination of a relatively new concept, career commitment. We examine organizational commitment in the following sections and conclude the chapter with job involvement.

Varieties of Organizational Commitment: What is It?

Organizational commitment has attracted more attention among organizational scientists than any other variety of work commitment, and it has been conceptualized in a variety of ways, although there is some convergence among the best-developed perspectives (Morrow, 1993). For example, Porter, Steers, Mowday, and Boulian (1974) saw organizational commitment as consisting of three interrelated (although not identical) attitudes and intentions: (1) a strong belief in, and acceptance of, the organization's goals and values; (2) a willingness to exert considerable effort on behalf of the organization; and (3) a definite desire to remain a member of the organization (Porter et al., 1974). The Porter approach, which has been the predominant one for three decades, has come to be referred to as an *affective* view of the concept (e.g., Meyer & Allen, 1997; Meyer, Paunonen, Gellatly, Goffin, & Jackson, 1989). "Employees with a strong affective commitment continue employment with the organization because they *want* to do so" (Meyer & Allen, 1991, p. 67).

A second component of organizational commitment is referred to as *normative commitment* (Meyer & Allen, 1991). It consists of "the totality of internalized normative pressures to act in a way that meets organizational goals and interests" (Weiner, 1982). In this approach, commitment causes individuals to behave in ways that they believe are morally right rather than in ways that are going to be instrumental for their own goals. It involves a belief that *a person simply ought to be loyal*; it is a matter of intrinsic responsibility. Beliefs and values of this sort are believed to originate in one's family and culture and through organizational socialization (Meyer & Allen, 1991). People who are normatively committed to their organizations are more likely to make sacrifices for them, to persist in their attempts to serve them, and to be preoccupied with them, devoting a considerable proportion of their time and energy to the pursuit of the objectives of their organizations. It is seen simply as the right thing to do.

A third approach to organizational commitment has been referred to as *calculative* (Morrow, 1993) or *continuance commitment* (Meyer & Allen, 1997; Meyer et al., 1989). Originating with Becker (1960), this form of organizational commitment is concerned with the individual's attachment to an employer by virtue of transactions that occur between the employee and the organization, resulting in various forms of side-bets and investments over time (e.g., seniority rights, personal attachments to other workers, pension plans, company-specific work skills). In this view an employee is committed to an organization because the costs of leaving become too high. A person's attachment is not based on emotion or good feelings toward the company (as in the affective view), or upon any normative beliefs about the inherent goodness and value in being loyal (as in the second approach). Rather, this third understanding of commitment is based upon sheer economics and pragmatic consideration: It simply becomes too expensive for the person not to adhere to the company or other employer.

In short, we can think of organizational commitment as a form of extreme loyalty to one's organization. The important aspect of this construct for our present purpose is that the attitude object here is the organization per se, not the person's particular job, department, work group, occupation, profession, or career. Meyer and Allen (1997), two of the leading scholars in this area, suggest that we think of the three dimensions of commitment just discussed as components (of an underlying construct) rather than as types of commitment (which would imply less underlying unity of the construct).

Distinctive forms of commitment?

Research directed to empirically distinguish among the three forms of commitment has not always succeeded in verifying that they are distinct from one another. While continuance commitment has had no trouble differentiating itself from affective and normative commitment, the last two frequently are found to be very highly intercorrelated in empirical studies (cf. Meyer, Stanley, Herscovitch, & Topolnytsky, 2002). A recent conceptual paper by Bergman (2006) has examined the nature of the three forms conceptually and has raised issues concerning the different antecedents and consequences that should be associated with each form as well as a number of different moderator variables that could be investigated in connection with the operations of each of the three forms. She also provides advice for better measurement of the constructs that have occurred in the past and offers a research direction for the future.

Is Organizational Commitment a Trait, a Value, or a Propensity?

Earlier in this chapter we touched briefly upon the notion that job satisfaction and job dissatisfaction may represent personal dispositions among people – that some people possess a propensity toward either positive or negative affective states that influence the way they evaluate their jobs and their general work lives. Similarly, some researchers think of organizational commitment, or at least certain aspects of it, as parts of a person's personality or personal value system (e.g., Angle & Lawson, 1993). In one study, a sample of 400 employees who were transferred en mass by their employer more than 1000 miles for a corporate relocation were measured for organizational commitment twice, both at the time of the relocation and then again 2 years later (Angle & Lawson, 1993). The researchers found that affective and continuance commitment were only modestly related to one another, but more important, they tested and supported a model that treated normative commitment as a personal value that predisposes a person toward possessing high affective and continuance commitment (Angle & Lawson, 1993). By this view, then, normative commitment is a more or less stable trait – a value – that people bring with them to any and all workplaces. Although a person's values are subject to change over time (see Chapter 3), normative commitment is seen by this perspective as being more or less constant: Either a person values commitment or does not, regardless of the circumstances.

Another early study, this one with a sample of U.S. Air Force cadets, investigated Mowday, Porter, and Steers' (1982) concept of *commitment propensity* (Lee, Ashford, Walsh, & Mowday, 1992). This concept is seen as representing all the personality factors, experiences, expectations, and values that a person brings to bear when considering going to work for an employer (Mowday et al., 1982). Commitment propensity is a summary concept that reflects the likelihood, in advance of being employed by an organization, that the person will become committed to the organization after being hired. It also takes into account the degree of volition a person has in choosing to work for a particular organization. The Air Force study showed that the various experiences (situational factors) and the cadets' varying degrees of commitment propensity both had an effect on their survival in the Air Force. Specifically, preentry commitment propensity was related to initial commitment, which, in turn, was related to organizational commitment in the longer term, as measured by lower levels of voluntary withdrawal from the academy.

The Lee et al. (1992) study was important for several reasons. First, it provided an early example of the new variety of research that attempts to disentangle the various effects of personal variables from situational variables (recall the discussion in Chapter 1; and see Judge, 1992; Organ, 1990; and Schneider, 1983). Second, it provides another illustration of the critical importance of early experiences for a person after he enters an organization or new job setting for the first time. Earlier in this chapter, for instance, we saw how important it is for newcomers to have challenging first assignments, participation in the decisions about their jobs, and a chance to be "heard" about the work itself for satisfaction and commitment to the organization. This same effect has been well documented among engineers (Badawy, 1982).

Psychological Bases for Organizational Commitment

O'Reilly and Chatman (1986) built upon an earlier typology of attitude change proposed by Kelman (1958) to delineate three distinct psychological bases that can underlie organizational commitment. The issue is: What, psychologically, forms the basis for a person's commitment to an organization? The three bases are referred to as compliance, identification, and internalization. *Compliance* occurs when a person is attached for the sake of gaining rewards or advancement of some sort. It is an instrumental form of commitment that has little or nothing to do with adherence to the organization's mission or the values of its key members. *Identification* occurs when a person accepts influence to establish or maintain a satisfying relationship (see also Pratt, 1998). This may entail pride in membership in a group, "respecting its values and accomplishments without adopting them as his own" (O'Reilly & Chatman, 1986, p. 493). Affiliation with another person or group, for the sake of affiliation, is the key.

The third basis for commitment that O'Reilly and Chatman borrowed from Kelman (1958) is referred to as *internalization*. In this case, the person accepts a group's attitudes and behaviors as congruent with his or her own. There is commitment that goes beyond mere identification: Internalization means the closest association between one's own motives and the motives of whatever group or organization is at issue. In two different studies, O'Reilly and Chatman (1986) found that identification and internalization forms of commitment were positively related to prosocial behaviors and negatively related to both intentions to quit and actual quitting behavior. Commitment based on compliance was not related to prosocial behaviors or actual quitting behavior, but it was correlated with people's expressions of an intention to leave. The distinctions among these three "bases" for commitment are important and have roots in organizational science from many years past. We will see shortly that keeping the psychological bases for organizational commitment disentangled from one another allows for even further refinement of the general concept of organizational commitment (see Becker, 1992).

Why is Commitment Thought to be Important?

Why has there been so much interest in organizational commitment among managers and academics? There are a number of reasons, some of which have legitimate scientific grounding, and some of which have been shown to have little or no basis in reality. On an intuitive level, it has been believed that high commitment is beneficial for both employers and employees. From the individual's perspective, high commitment provides a sense of identity and perhaps even status and prestige (Romzek, 1989). High commitment provides an opportunity for the person to receive both intrinsic and extrinsic satisfactions through their association with the employer, the other employees, and the business or industry in general. An employee who is committed to his employer may suffer less anxiety about the prospect of losing his job and may generally feel much more secure and content as a result. Commitment is accompanied by feelings of nurturance and mutual trust and fosters a generally positive outlook in life. For those who have it, commitment can be a source of comfort, identity, and security (Mowday et al., 1982).

Commitment and identification

Ashforth and Mael (1989) described the value to people of *identifying* with an organization. While committing to an organization is related to identifying with it, the concepts are slightly different:

> According to SIT [social identity theory], people tend to classify themselves and others into various social categories, such as organizational membership, religious affiliation, gender, and age cohort ... Social classification serves two functions. First, it cognitively segments and orders the social environment, providing the individual with a systematic means of defining others ... Second, social classification enables the individual to define *him- or herself* in the social environment.
>
> (Ashforth and Mael, 1989, pp. 20–21)

It is possible for a person's social identity to adhere to a work group, a department, or a union (Ashforth & Mael, 1989), but our focus here is on the identification that comes with high organizational commitment. Once a focus for the identification has been selected ("I am an employee of the University of Nebraska's Alumni Association"), the person will derive a sense of pride and self-concept, defined in part through that association. In short, identification that comes with commitment can be beneficial to a person (cf. Pratt, 1998; Whetten & Godfrey, 1998).

In the years since Ashforth and Mael's (1989) observations about the propensity to identify with an organization and how it is similar or different from being committed to one, organizational researchers working under the tradition of the commitment banner have devoted increasing attention to the matter of identification and its conceptual and empirical relationship(s) with commitment. Two other constructs – *attachment* and *embeddedness*[13] – have also come onto the scene, causing some skeptics, with good reason, to wonder whether the distinctions among these many concepts have more to offer theorists than practitioners and whether it is even possible to differentiate among them.

Most recently, a special edition of the periodical *Journal of Organizational Behavior* (cf. Van Dick, Becker, & Meyer, 2006) was devoted to these matters in late 2006. In that issue, Herrbach (2006) gathered data from a sample of engineers to provide some evidence for a distinction between identification and affective commitment, as they related to people's attachment to either (or both) their workgroup or their organization.[14] Elsewhere in the same *JOB* issue, Van Knippenberg and Sleebos (2006) concluded that identification represents a sense of oneness between an individual and an organization whereas commitment implies a relationship between two distinct entities (the person and the organization), while Meyer, Becker, and Van Dick (2006) proposed that literatures pertaining to commitment and those related to identity might be useful in informing one another.

A "discursive essay" by Brooks and Wallace (2006) provided a very readable summary of the various facets, factors, and nomological nets that pertain to the theory and research on organizational commitment. It is clear from their essay that there has been considerable convergence on the nature of the constructs themselves, conceptually, at least, and individuals in organizational settings will be "committed" to many different facets of the organization and its constituent elements (such as coworkers, bosses, workmates, the work etc., and the union). On the basis of their summary, however, Brooks and Wallace (2006) concluded: "More research endeavor is required before a complete understanding of the specific antecedents and consequences (and their directional connections) relating to the concept unfolds" (p. 236). This author agrees with their conclusion and would issue a caution that the proliferation of constructs relating to the connections between people and organizations has reached its limits: The conceptual hairs have been frequently split, perhaps enough.

Management's Stake in Commitment

What is important about commitment from an employer's perspective? Organizations value high levels of commitment on the parts of their employees for a number of reasons (Randall, 1987). It has been widely believed that highly committed employees perform better on the job and are less likely to be absent, late, or to leave altogether. Such people are assumed to be more likely to engage in good citizen behaviors or work above and beyond the call of duty (Katz & Kahn, 1978; Mowday et al., 1982; Organ, 1990; Organ & Konovsky, 1989). At a societal level, high commitment may be associated with lower rates of overall mobility, higher levels of stability, greater national productivity, and higher aggregate levels of quality of life (Mathieu & Zajac, 1990). On the face of it, then, intuitive reasoning suggests that high levels of organizational commitment will benefit both individuals and employers: Everyone wins.

In the following sections, we examine the ways in which organizations attempt to build commitment for the sake of gaining the benefits it is thought to produce. We then look closely at the evidence on the matter: What are the actual costs and benefits of high commitment?

---

[13] We encountered the embeddedness concept earlier in this chapter in relations to its association with voluntary employee turnover.

[14] We return to issue of multiple foci for commitment shortly.

Organizational Socialization and Commitment

From the time they enter the employment of organizations, most people witness attempts to make them committed and devoted to those organizations. Again, the purpose of these attempts is based on the hope and belief that highly committed workers are likely to be more effective. Thus, organizational rules are designed to assure that employees behave according to the norms and expectations of the organization. Often, an attempt is made to impress the newcomer with the merit of the organization's mission and major goals as well as to provide a sense of the history and traditions of the organization (Pondy, Frost, Morgan, & Dandridge, 1983).

For example, induction programs and other socialization rituals attempt to inculcate the employee with an understanding of, and an appreciation for, "our way of doing things" (Feldman, 1977, 1981). Pensions and other benefit plans sometimes constitute so-called "golden handcuffs," which make it increasingly difficult for employees to consider leaving (see Angle & Perry, 1981, 1983). Organizational logos and insignia, off-the-job social functions, and programs for employees' spouses are all designed, in part, to build loyalty. (See Becker, 1960, on the role of social involvement in commitment building.) Company newsletters are common in large organizations, serving more to build a sense of loyalty and commitment than to communicate real news.

It has been suggested that even certain formal personnel transactions conducted upon employees once they are "onboard" facilitate commitment, binding them to the organization as a primary source of emotional and social support. For example, Edstrom and Galbraith (1977) suggested that the transferring of employees to positions at the various operating sites of geographically dispersed organizations functions, in part, to make them less likely to build connections outside the organization that may be distracting or that may serve to compromise their complete and undivided devotion. Finally, there is some evidence that reward systems (including promotions and merit pay) that link performance to rewards will tend to make employees more committed (Dreher, 1982). Many of these commitment builders are more deliberate than others, and some of them can be very subtle. The point is that organized activity requires commitment among organizational members (Katz, 1964), so organizational procedures are necessary to generate and sustain such loyalty.

Several researchers have shown that in addition to active and deliberate organizational procedures for building commitment, other factors can contribute to it as well: Factors related to the employees themselves, to their jobs, as well as to other elements of the work environment (e.g., Angle & Perry, 1981; Morris & Sherman, 1981; Steers 1977).

For example, in a study of scientists, engineers, and hospital employees, Steers (1977) found that individual needs for achievement, education, and age were associated with commitment to their organizations. (Education was inversely correlated: Higher levels of education were related to lower levels of commitment. This is a common phenomenon among professional employees, whose loyalty is devoted to the profession first and to the employer second.) Pro-organizational attitudes of the person's work group were associated with greater commitment. Jobs that permitted the employee greater degrees of voluntary interaction with coworkers, and jobs that permitted employees to understand how their work related to the jobs done by others in the organization, also seemed to be conducive to commitment (probably through the satisfaction these job characteristics fostered). However, Steers' (1977) results showed that certain work-related experiences were more powerful as predictors of commitment than were the personal, job, or other organizational factors considered. Specifically, Steers found that positive group attitudes among one's peers, feelings that the organization had met the person's prior expectations, feelings that the organization could be relied on to carry out its commitments to its personnel, and feelings that the individual was of some importance to the organization collectively seemed to be the most important influences on commitment levels. Similar results were found in separate studies by Angle and Perry (1981), Buchanan (1974), and Morris and Sherman (1981).

A number of work-related experiences have been shown to foster organizational commitment, such as confirmation of preemployment expectations (Arnold & Feldman, 1982), job satisfaction (O'Reilly & Caldwell, 1981), participation in decision making (Rhodes & Steers, 1981), role clarity and freedom from conflict (Jamal, 1984), and organizational dependency or concern for employees (Steers, 1977). As pointed out by Meyer and Allen (1988), however, most of these early studies were cross-sectional, so the direction of the causality is hard to determine. In other words, such research designs do not permit us to discern whether job satisfaction causes organizational commitment, or vice versa. (Another possibility is that both variables are the consequences of one or more other systemic variable, such as organizational policies, leadership style, or whatever.)

One work-related experience that seems to have definite positive impact on organizational commitment early in a person's career is the nature of the early assignments they are given on being hired. Two related studies of Canadian university graduates by Meyer and Allen (1987, 1988), for example, found that measures of self-expression (being allowed to be one's own person), participation in decision making, and confirmed preentry expectations during the first month after being hired were positively related to organizational commitment later (after 6 and 11 months). These two studies both employed longitudinal designs, allowing for more confidence in the causal conclusions reached than is the case with cross-sectional designs. Other, earlier studies that tried to link early experiences with commitment much later in employees' tenure with employers failed to find such an effect, so the impact may erode after a year on the job (Meyer & Allen, 1987, 1988). The critical thing, then, seems to be that managers must be clear about what employees can expect on the job, before they are hired, and then assure that early job assignments both fulfill those expectations and permit the employee to express herself in the planning and execution of her work, especially during the critical first month or two of employment (Meyer & Allen, 1987, 1988; Wanous, 1980).

Evidence on Organizational Commitment

Earlier we noted that employers attempt to generate and sustain high commitment because many of them believe that high commitment yields high business benefits. Is this actually the case? Since an earlier examination of the matter (Pinder, 1984), considerable effort has been invested to confirm or disconfirm the validity of people's beliefs about the benefits of high commitment. As might by expected the evidence does not support most of the popular beliefs and expectations (Mathieu & Zajac, 1990).

Commitment and performance

First, there is mixed evidence for positive relationships between organizational commitment and a variety of forms of organizational performance (see Brooks & Wallace, 2006, for a recent review), although the link between organizational commitment and individual productivity has been hard to establish reliably. When the general notion of commitment is disassembled, there is some support for the notion that certain varieties of commitment may have different relationships with different varieties of employee performance (see the discussion above of varieties of commitment). Hence, Meyer et al. (1989) found, as they had hypothesized, that affective commitment (that which is characterized by positive beliefs and attitudes about the organization) was correlated with performance, whereas continuance commitment (which is based on economic necessity and side-bets) was inversely correlated with performance. Affective commitment is also positively related to organizational citizenship behavior (see Organ, 1990). Moreover, as service industries grow to become a more significant element of many economies, it is interesting to find that positive organizational culture can positively influence employee satisfaction, organizational commitment, and the delivery of better services to customers (cf. Mowday, 1998; Paulin, Ferguson, & Bergeron, 2006).

Commitment and withdrawal

A number of attempts were made during the 1990s to link different types or elements of organizational commitment to different types of withdrawal behavior. An example was provided by a study by Somers (1995), who found that affective commitment was the best predictor of the various forms of withdrawal considered (which included intentions to withdraw, turnover, and absenteeism). By comparison, normative commitment was associated only with intentions, and continuance commitment had no direct effects on any of the withdrawal variables studied. (The reader is referred to our earlier discussion of the three psychological bases of commitment.) However, most of the correlations found between commitment and leaving behavior have varied in size and strength and have depended in part on how one defines organizational commitment – as normative, affective, or continuance (Jaros, Jermier, Koehler, & Sincich, 1993), leading to at least two closer examinations using meta-analysis (Cohen, 1993; Mathieu & Zajac, 1990).

In one of these meta-analyses, as expected, Cohen (1993) found that the relationship between commitment and turnover was much stronger when the two variables were measured relatively close in time: When the time between the measurement of commitment and the observation of departure was longer, the relationships have been weaker. The reader will recall that we discussed this matter in Chapter 9 in relation to the theory of reasoned action. In short, it seems clear that organizational commitment, in some of its various forms (as was discussed earlier), is predictive of employees' staying with or leaving their organizations. The effects of commitment, however, appear to be indirect (Jaros et al., 1993). That is, the effects of high or low commitment on turnover behavior seem to work through the person's *intentions* to withdraw (see Jaros et al., 1993; and recall the theory of reasoned action in Chapter 9). If the intention to leave is not formed, the likelihood of leaving is low.

Mathieu and Zajac's (1990) meta-analysis confirmed the conclusions reached a decade earlier by Mowday et al. (1982), that there is very little relationship between organizational commitment and individual worker performance (see Mathieu & Zajac, 1990, p. 184). As in the case of Cohen's (1993) meta-analysis, there is very little relationship between organizational commitment and lateness, turnover, and intention to turn over. High commitment was also associated with attendance. Although significant in statistical terms, none of the relationships in Cohen's study between commitment and withdrawal and attendance behaviors was large in magnitude.

In a summary of the link between commitment and withdrawal behaviors, Meyer and Allen (1997, p. 26) concluded:

> On the basis of these findings, it might be tempting to conclude that if an organization's goal is to develop a stable workforce on whose continued membership it can count, any form of commitment will suffice . . . [H]owever, we caution strongly against this conclusion unless employee retention is the organization's *only goal*. An emphasis on employee retention to the exclusion of performance is unlikely to characterize many organizations. Indeed, it is now widely recognized that some voluntary turnover is helpful, rather than harmful, to the organization in that it includes resignations from employees who perform poorly or are disruptive . . . Most organizations – and most managers – want much more from committed employees than simply their continued membership in the organization.

A comparison of the general findings of studies that consider constructs at the most general, undifferentiated levels (e.g., Mathieu & Zajac, 1990) with more fine-grained analyses such as that of Meyer et al. (1989), which look at the more precise subconstructs, highlights the importance of defining constructs carefully and precisely before expecting to find relationships among variables, such as commitment and performance (Schwab, 1980). We saw the same issue arise earlier in this chapter in connection with the long-sought-after linkage between job satisfaction and job performance (see Fisher, 1980). Morrow (1983) is responsible for first pointing out the multidimensionality of commitment; the wisdom of her observation and argument set the stage for the deliberate examination of *elements* of the overall construct in relation to performance by Meyer et al. (1989). There is a lesson to be learned.

Costs to employees of high commitment

In the foregoing sections, we examined the value of high worker commitment from the organization's point of view. What about the individual's perspective? People who become highly committed often tend to anthropomorphize or reify their organizations. We noted earlier in this book that although organizations are made up of human beings, they are not themselves human beings. Organizations are complex social systems that structure themselves and behave so as to survive. They do not have memories, and they do not have hearts. Senior managers and executives may be capable of remembering who deserves support and loyal treatment for jobs done well in the past, but senior executives come and go. Loyalty earned during one era can lose all value as new managerial regimes evolve. The survival of the organization is tantamount; if it is expedient to continue to support the faithful servants of the past, they will be supported. But when economic or other exigencies arise to threaten the survival or effectiveness of an organization, the highly committed individual's loyalty is often unrequited, and the individual may be left with organization-specific skills that are limited and that restrict her mobility to find new employment (Randall, 1987).

The author was personally acquainted with the senior executive of a large foreign airline who devoted most of his adult life to the profitability and effectiveness of the firm. The executive's hard work led to a stroke at age 46, although he eventually recovered most of his physical abilities and all of his mental skills. The company kept him on, but organizational policies requiring that he have his health examined by corporate doctors (rather than local doctors) precipitated a second stroke 12 years later. Obeying the firm's orders rather than acting according to his own best interest, the executive undertook to travel halfway around the world for a medical check, despite his protestations that his health was poor at that time and that it would be further threatened by a trip of such demanding proportions. His local doctors were able to perform the necessary work, making the journey unnecessary. The trip killed the executive, and his wife was granted a small settlement. The high levels of commitment the executive had to the airline and the obedience that derived from that commitment compelled him to pursue corporate advice that was not in the best interest of his health.

Aside from the possibility that commitment may not be reciprocated by one's organization, leaving the person abandoned in hard times, there is the issue, of course, of the nature of the organizational goals to which individuals commit themselves. Clearly, if a person becomes enthralled by the goals of an organization, the legality and the morality of those goals have important implications for the committed employee (Weiner, 1982). Many cases of corporate corruption and crime have been perpetrated by highly committed employees whose zealous pursuit of their employer's goals required them to engage in illegal and immoral activities in which they probably would not have otherwise engaged.

Twenty years ago, Schaef and Fassel (1988) advanced the idea that work organizations can be seen as addictive substances, and that adherence to the goals and work expectation of these organizations can result in a condition of process addiction for employees (Schaef & Fassel, 1988, p. 119). According to these authors:

> Nothing in and of itself is addictive. *Anything* can be addictive when it becomes so central in one's life that one feels that life is not possible without the substance or process. Organizations function as the addictive substance in the lives of many people. We recognized [in our work] that for many people, the workplace, the job, and the organization were the central foci of their lives. Because the organization was so primary in their lives, because they were totally preoccupied with it, they began to lose touch with other aspects of their lives and gradually gave up what they knew, felt, and believed.

The point is this: Organizations require the commitment of their members in order to survive, so they do what they can to develop and foster it. But economic necessities can force even the most benevolent of employers to lay off, or otherwise abandon, those who have helped to make them effective. Even in Japan, where loyalty to one's organization is an inherent part of the culture, managers, and employees at all levels have been laid off, North American style, as the economic advantage previously enjoyed by Japanese industry has declined over the years (e.g., Rifkin, 1995, p. 105; Watanabe, 1996). In short, although commitment is necessary for the organization's survival, it may or may not be best for a person's long-term interests, all the things our parents told us notwithstanding.

Romzek (1989) pursued the old hypothesis that beneficial experiences at one's work can "spill over" and have a positive influence on a person's non-work life (as we discussed earlier in this chapter in connection with the linkage between job satisfaction and life satisfaction). She has reported a study in which she followed a panel of 485 employees through two waves of data collection, in 1982 and then again in 1984. Of interest to Romzek in this longitudinal project was whether the consequences of employee commitment on non-work and career satisfactions are positive or negative. Although the effects were not strong, she found consistent support for the proposition that organizational commitment has positive benefit for people's lives outside the employment relationship, in areas such as satisfaction with their families, the cities in which they live, their friendships and hobbies, and so on. She also found that high levels of organizational commitment as measured in 1982 were predictive of high levels of job satisfaction and career satisfaction 2 years later. One of the interpretations Romzek placed on her findings is that people tend to possess a disposition toward either positive or negative attitudes in life in general, and that these predispositions cover most or all aspects of a person's life, including work and non-work activities. This dispositional hypothesis was discussed earlier in this chapter; there is no need to review it again here (see George, 1992; Judge, 1992).

Multiple, Conflicting Commitments

One interesting consequence of extreme levels of organizational commitment may be reduced levels of commitment to other sources of support (as mentioned earlier). Sometimes this can be dysfunctional for the organization involved. For example, Rotondi (1975) found that research and development engineers who were more committed to their organization tended to be less creative and innovative, probably because devotion to one's scientific discipline can often clash with devotion to one's employer (see also Shepard, 1956).

On the other hand, some feel that work organizations represent arenas for multiple forms of commitment for the employees involved. Hence, according to Reichers (1985), many employees experience allegiance to the goals, products and services, values, or people associated with multiple constituencies associated with their workplaces, such as unions, suppliers, customers, managers, professional associations, and so on. Therefore, the nature of the "commitment" experienced by any one person is likely to be entirely different from that experienced by another, because the foci of the commitment(s) vary from person to person. "Thus one individual's 'organizational commitment' may be primarily a function of the perception that the organization is dedicated to high quality products at a reasonable price: another person's commitment may depend to a great extent on the individual's belief that the organization espouses humanistic values towards [its] employees" (Reichers, 1985, p. 473).

Taking the multiple constituencies concept a step further, Becker (1992) argued that we should differentiate between the foci of commitment, meaning the various individuals and groups to whom an employee might be attached, and the bases of commitment, the motives that explain the attachment (recall the three bases mentioned earlier: Compliance, identification, and internalization). The reason for the argument is that attachment to foci may be predictive of different organizational outcomes than is attachment, which is predicated on different psychological "bases."

In fact, Becker was able to demonstrate that this may be the case. He found negative correlations between people's commitment to their organizations, work groups, and supervisors, and their intentions to quit. In other words, attachment to the various groups tended to reduce a person's desire to leave an organization. At the same time, he found positive correlations between these interpersonally based bonds and job satisfaction and the occurrence of prosocial behaviors of the sort we discussed earlier in the chapter.

Different results were found when the focus turned to the psychological bases for organizational commitment. Becker assessed the employees' levels of compliance, identification, and internalization (see O'Reilly & Chatman, 1986). As predicted, when the basis for commitment was either identification or internalization, higher levels of job satisfaction and prosocial behavior resulted, while commitment based on compliance was associated with higher levels of intention to leave the organization. In short, it appears that the global concept of organizational commitment is, in fact, a blend of attachments to various groups and individuals, on the one hand, and an array of psychological dynamics, on the other – a sort of apples and oranges concept in totality. The work of Reichers (1985) and, particularly, of Becker (1992) points to the wisdom of disentangling the foci of commitment (the people to whom we are committed) from the bases of the commitment (the psychological motives for the attachments). For as O'Reilly and Chatman (1986) demonstrated, different psychological bases for one's attachment to an organization can result in entirely different outcome dynamics for people.

The Past, Present, and Future of Organizational Commitment

It was an article of faith among many people of previous generations that being committed to one's employer was wise and a proper thing to do (Randall, 1987). The virtues of organizational commitment seemed self-evident – again, if not for the instrumental benefits that would accrue, but also because it was somehow inherently virtuous. This sentiment was summarized in an important book of the mid-1950s, *The organization man* (Whyte, 1956).

A few generations of experience in North America of intermittent recessions and the attendant layoffs, cutbacks, downsizing, and "right-sizing" that comes with recessions have seen a change in the common values as they pertain to organizational commitment. Twenty-five years ago, for example, three influential American scholars in the area of work motivation and commitment wrote that *they anticipated a marked decrease* in the commitment of North American employees to their companies. Among the reasons they cited to back their prediction were that more people would be wanting jobs, more people would be wanting *good* jobs, increasing demands for personal growth and personal freedom, greater expectations for immediate need gratification, demands for more than work in their lives, better awareness of job alternatives than in the past, and, interestingly, a sort of acceptance at societal levels that low commitment is legitimate: If it were to become a cultural norm to reject high organizational commitment, more people would feel free to do so (Mowday, Porter, & Steers, 1982).

A few years later, Baruch (1998, p. 136) wrote an essay that reiterated this argument, claiming that, indeed, the aggregate experiences of working people had dashed the traditional values favoring organizational commitment: "Recent processes and developments in the way organizations treat their employees raise doubts about whether the traditional concept of OC fits the new age of management and industrial relation [sic] systems." First, he noted that organizational commitment to employees (from the organization) is a major causal factor in the commitment organizations can expect in return from employees. Moreover, as the former declines – as it had appeared to be declining in the years before Baruch wrote his essay – the latter (employee commitment to organizations) will decline as well, and he predicted that both would continue to decline downward for years to follow. On the basis of this argument, Baruch (1998) concluded that organizational commitment would reduce in importance as a determinant of positive individual and organizational outcomes.

He cited the results of three meta-analyses conducted by other researchers to show that the apparent impact of OC on organizational outcomes was lower among studies conducted in the late 1980s than those conducted in either the early 1970s or the early 1980s. For Baruch (1998) "recent actual practice [had] put the developments of OC on a dead end track." It was not that organizational commitment was not inherently important, but that it had become much less useful in explaining organizational outcomes than it had been in previous decades: Survival requirements had trumped the softer values of loyalty.

In part a response to Baruch (1998), one of the key academics in the early work on commitment, Mowday (1998) wrote an essay that, in part, acknowledged that organizational commitment by employees is a critical contributing factor to organizational success and that, in spite of the fact that many organizations continue to lay off people during good times as well as bad times, the underlying importance of the commitment factor will not be diminished. He added that recent advances in what have come to be called "high-performance management systems" (see Chapter 7), the purpose of which is to create employee commitment and engagement, have proven to be effective for organization-level performance (cf. Benson, Young, & Lawler, 2006; Combs, Yongmei Liu, Hall, & Ketchen, 2006; Pfeffer, 1998).

Meyer and Allen (1997), two scholars who have championed the commitment construct over the past 20 years, noted that most small organizations are particularly dependent on core groups of devoted people who will offer the energy and citizenship behavior required for their survival and success. Second, even though many organizations are outsourcing much of their work to other organizations, they must be concerned about the commitment of the personnel in these other organizations. "Admittedly, the commitment may be different, perhaps being of a shorter duration and with a focus on a contract of project rather than on the organization itself" (Meyer & Allen, 1997, p. 5). Finally, Meyer and Allen (1997) claimed that commitment develops naturally in people. Not to be committed to *something* is to be alienated. So workers who do not commit to employers will naturally seek commitment with some other source of gratification, such as a hobby, a church, a friend, a job, or an occupation. Hence, even if *organizational commitment* itself declines, it will remain important for social scientists to pursue an understanding of commitment in its varied forms.

Conclusion: The Ebb and Flow of Organizational Commitment

The author has been teaching students in several North American business schools for more than 35 years, observing the changing attitudes of students regarding life's important issues. It is true that values swing like a pendulum on most issues, the issue of commitment being no exception. Thirty years ago, it was heretical to suggest to business school students that to become committed to an employer was foolish. In recent years, young people who are leaving college and joining the workforce for the first time seem to be fully aware of the issues of loyalty and commitment. Many or most of these students have known someone who was the victim of harsh or inconsiderate treatment at the hands of an organization. Most have known people who were laid off because of downsizings, mergers, and other corporate necessities for survival. Regardless of whether it is wise or noble for a person to expect commitment from an employer, and whether it is fair of an employer to expect loyalty from its workers, are matters of opinion, rooted in the values each of us hold.

For their part, North American employers seem to be trying to recapture the commitment of employees as they had in years gone by. Management texts and journals these days rarely use the word commitment however – these days terms such as employee *attachment*, *engagement*, and *identification* are used – but, to a large extent, these notions are old wine in new bottles: Their primary purpose is to keep (good) employees locked in, happy at their jobs, creative and less willing to be absent, late for work or likely to leave. (See a scholarly paper by Mitchell et al., 2001, for a summary of some of these newer constructs.) The author hopes only that the foregoing discussion will bring the matter of commitment, its costs and its benefits, to a conscious level for consideration by readers of this book.

We turn next to a study of a similar work-related attitude – job involvement.

JOB INVOLVEMENT

A third psychological construct related to work behavior that has received considerable attention is referred to as *job involvement*. There have been a number of attempts to define this concept and to differentiate it from related constructs such as job satisfaction and intrinsic motivation (Lawler & Hall, 1970; Lodahl & Kejner, 1965; Saleh & Hosek, 1976). *Job involvement*, loosely defined, has to do with the strength of the relationship between a person's work and his or her self-concept.

Definition of Job Involvement

Specifically, a person is said to be involved in her job if she:

- finds the job motivating and challenging
- is committed to her work in general, to her particular job, and to her organization, making her less likely to consider leaving her position
- engages closely with coworkers in such as way that she can get feedback about her work and performance (Brown, 1996).

A recent study in Sweden (Hallberg & Schaufeli, 2006) confirmed the separate identity of job involvement, as distinct from organizational commitment, which we discussed in the forgoing sections, and *work engagement* (which is defined as a positive feeling of energy and joy in working).

People who are highly job involved can be obsessed with their work. When they perform poorly, they feel poorly. They like others to know them for their work and to know that they do it well. For a highly job-involved person, work is one of the most important aspects of life, if not the most important. There is some evidence that job-involved people tend to be more satisfied with their work (Gorn & Kanungo, 1980) and more intrinsically motivated (Lawler & Hall, 1970), but it is important to repeat that involvement, satisfaction, and intrinsic motivation are distinct constructs (Lawler & Hall, 1970). *Moreover, this construct has to do with one's commitment to her job, not to her employer per se*, and these two forms of commitment are only slightly related to one another (Stevens, Beyer, & Trice, 1978; Weiner & Vardi, 1980).

Causes/Antecedents of Job Involvement

What determines the level of involvement a person has in his job? A number of studies have suggested that, as in the case of the determinants of commitment, characteristics of both the individual and of the organization must be taken into account. For example, Rabinowitz and Hall (1977) found that job involvement was correlated with the strength of the person's growth needs (see Chapter 7) and with the strength of one's belief in the "Protestant work ethic." In addition, the length of time the person was on the job, as well as the scope provided by the job, were positively associated with involvement. Another study found that employees whose jobs served to satisfy their most salient needs (regardless of whether these were intrinsic or extrinsic) were higher in both involvement with the particular jobs they held at the time, as well as with work in general (Gorn & Kanungo, 1980). In a third study, it was found that employees who participated more in the decision making related to their jobs were more involved in those jobs (Siegel & Ruh, 1973).

In short, the level of involvement people feel with regard to their jobs is determined by the interaction of their own needs and values with a variety of features of the job and the job setting. Consequently, we might assume that job involvement may be somewhat manipulable through the enactment of appropriate organizational policies and procedures.

Consequences of Moderate Job Involvement

As we did in our discussion of commitment, we can suitably ask whether job involvement is a good thing; and as before, we must conclude that the answer may depend on who provides it. There is some evidence that job-involved employees tend to be more satisfied with their jobs than are employees who are less job involved (Cheloha & Farr, 1980; Gannon & Hendrickson, 1973; Gorn & Kanungo, 1980; Lawler & Hall, 1970). Similarly, there is suggestive evidence that job-involved employees are likely to be somewhat happier with their organizations (Schwyhart & Smith, 1972), as well as more committed to them and less absent from them (Cheloha & Farr, 1980), although as mentioned earlier, the relationships are mixed and of only moderate strength (Gorn & Kanungo, 1980). This means that it is quite possible for employees to enjoy their jobs but not feel fully involved in them. Or it is possible for people to be attached to their jobs and to enjoy them but not be very committed to their employing organization. This is often the case with managerial, professional, technical, and other highly skilled employees. Physicians working under terribly constrained budgets and limited resources in equipment and supplies often are terribly unhappy with their jobs, totally uncommitted to the hospitals in which they function, yet remain unflaggingly committed to their chosen profession of medicine.

Is there any relationship between job involvement and employee effort and performance? Very little research has been reported on this issue, so caution is necessary. One study found moderately strong linkages between involvement and self-report measures of effort and performance (as measured by salary) among a group of insurance sales representatives who worked on commission (Gorn & Kanungo, 1980). It is critical to note that virtually all of the studies reported earlier were conducted in a cross-sectional manner, making it impossible when there were relationships observed to determine which variables were causal and which were the results of the workings of others.

For example, are highly involved employees more likely to devote higher levels of effort to their jobs because of the fulfillment it provides them? Or is it the other way around: Could more highly involved employees become more satisfied with their jobs because their devotion to them results in mastery and feelings of achievement and competence? What seems most plausible is that certain characteristics of employees, their jobs, and their organizations are likely to be responsible for causing levels of commitment, satisfaction, and involvement; these in turn both influence, and are influenced by, the person's performance level. Therefore, managers may be able to affect this cluster of events and associations by thoughtful application of enlightened policies and practices, but it is probable that the characteristics of their employees will limit (or magnify) the impact that they can have on these various outcome variables.

In simple terms, the job involvement construct has to do with how seriously people take their work. Therefore, it would follow that people who are characteristically high in job involvement may be more prone to permit the stressors they encounter on their jobs to "get to them," to be more deleterious to their well-being, than would be the case for people who are lower in job involvement. In fact, a study by Frone, Russell, and Cooper (1994) suggested this may be the case. After controlling for a set of sociological variables that are normally associated with poor health, the researchers found that job involvement exacerbated the relationship between job stressors and employee health. Although the results were mixed across the various dependent variables studied (such as depression, alcohol use, and physical symptoms), they were consistent with our understanding of the job involvement construct as well as with common sense. People who "eat, breathe, and sleep their work" seem more susceptible to health difficulties, particularly if they do not engage in practices that are designed to assuage tension and relieve the stress that their work entails for them. What about people who are exceptionally committed to their work? We turn next to an examination of people who become addicted to their work, commonly referred to as *workaholics*.

Work Addiction: Involvement and Commitment in the Extreme

Before we leave our discussion of the benefits of job involvement, we should ask whether extreme levels of job involvement, like extreme levels of commitment, might have any unfortunate consequences for the employee. The person on the street often uses the term *workaholism* to refer to the construct labeled job involvement by students of organizational science. What is workaholism?

Aziz and Zickar (2006) have concluded that workaholism can legitimately be conceived of as a *syndrome*, consisting of at least three factors:

1. excessive work involvement
2. a high drive to work (intrinsic motivation)
3. lack of work enjoyment.

Individuals classified as workaholics were more likely to label themselves as such, more likely to have acquaintances think of them as workaholics, and more likely to have relatively low life satisfaction and low work–life balance.

In early work on the issue, Killinger (1991) pointed out that not everyone who works hard is a workaholic. She noted that "work is essential for our well-being. Through work we define ourselves, develop our strengths, and take our places in society. Work gives us satisfaction, a sense of accomplishment, and mastery over problems. It provides us with a sense of direction, and gives us goals to reach and hurdles to overcome" (p. 5). Further to this point, Friedman and Lobel (2003) suggested that "happy workaholics" are people who legitimately love their work so much that they are merely being authentic to their values when they put in long hours. The notion of work–non-work "balance" should be replaced by a norm of such authenticity, whereby people should be encouraged, within limits, of course, to apportion their time to work and non-work activities in accordance with their own values.

For Killinger (1991), work *addiction* is a different matter. It usually happens to middle-class people who are necessarily driven by economic necessity. A workaholic is "a person who gradually becomes emotionally crippled and addicted to control and power in a compulsive drive to gain control and success" (p. 6). Such people are competitive and driven to acquire the "fix" of fame, recognition, and success that comes with hard work and long hours. Without this fix, the workaholic feels pain in the form of anger, hurt, guilt, and fear. Working becomes a state of mind more than simply a job. Working permits people an overly inflated sense of responsibility and an escape from intimacy with other people (Killinger, 1991).

Workaholics are people who live to work. They plan their work during periods when they are otherwise at play, such as during holidays and vacations (Killinger, 1991). Machlowitz (1980) estimated that about 5% of the adult population are workaholics, but that the proportion of the workforce who are workaholics is probably higher since, almost by definition, these people tend not to be unemployed. Although not all hard workers are workaholics, all workaholics are hard workers. They plan their lives round their jobs and love it. Both men and women can be workaholics, although the difficulties faced by female workers are different (and sometimes worse) than those faced by male workaholics. Many workaholics contribute to the effectiveness of their organizations at levels that are detrimental to their own health (Caplan & Jones, 1975) but don't mind doing so and are often not aware that they are doing so (Killinger, 1991).

The author is not aware of any research that has attempted to apportion workaholic tendencies between people's organizational commitment and their job involvement, as we have defined these phenomena here. Research on workaholics suggests that people who work too hard for their own good can be driven by either high commitment to their institutions, or to their occupations, or to some blends of both. The precise origins of the phenomenon are less important than the consequences of workaholism for the people who are afflicted as well as for those who love them or work with them.

Types of work addiction

According to Fassel (1992), there are at least four categories of workaholics. The reader will notice the similarities among the names of the categories, the characteristics of the people in the categories, and the nouns and verbs that are used in common reference to addictions and addicts related to other substances and processes. There is the *compulsive worker*, the person who is simply driven to work all the time. This is the category we usually associate with workaholism. They keep long and strange hours, they never plan vacations, and they seldom make plans in their outside lives because they are always concerned about what might come up for them at work. But these people are not the only category or type of workaholic, according to Fassel (1992).

There are also *binge workers*, people who work with high intensity when they work, even if it is only at intervals. When work has to be done, they are obsessed and driven to get it done. Fassel likens the patterns of these people to those of binge drinkers, who "save it up" and then go on working with nothing else in their lives for short, sharp spurts of it.

A third category consists of what Fassel (1992) refers to as *closet workers*. People in this category have "a niggling awareness" that something is dysfunctional about their work style (p. 20). They tend to make promises to reform themselves but seldom keep their promises. They hide work-related files and problems away similar to the ways that alcoholics hide bottles of liquor in closets, basements, and nooks and crannies. They often pretend not to be working, as when they are on "vacation," but they are thinking, dreaming, and making plans about their work. They are the types of people who take cellular telephones with them to museums, libraries, and gymnasiums, into places and into activities where, otherwise, they might be thought of as relaxing or not working. They are basically dishonest about their priorities and cheat in the way they relate to others about those priorities.

A fourth category of workaholic identified by Fassel (1992) are people whom she refers to as *work anorexics*. They are people who act as if the way to get out of their problems (analogous to overeaters) is by not doing anything at all. Their theme, according to Fassel (1992, p. 23), is "I'm darned good at what I do, but I seldom do it." Work becomes such an addiction to these people that they do everything they can to avoid it, to pretend that it is not a problem for them. They procrastinate and then feel guilty about their procrastination. So they place themselves in positions of lateness, deadlines, and pressures where they must produce to survive and to save face. They force schedules upon themselves because pacing and spacing of assignments fail to provide the thrill of an emergency in which the work must get done at once. They like to "slip under the gate just as it is closing," according to Fassel (1992, p. 24).

Is there a problem? In an economy worried about the motivation of its workforce to sustain itself and be competitive, we can ask: Is workaholism a good thing? A quarter of a century of research and writing on the issue has brought mixed answers (see Fassel, 1992; Killinger, 1991; Machlowitz, 1980; Oates, 1971). Without workaholics, many organizations could not function as effectively as they do (Oates, 1971). Workaholics are always there to backstop the errors made by others. (Of course, they are also often the cause of many of these errors themselves.) They often make up for the low commitment of others. They can be counted on to perform the jobs others avoid, and generally, to attack them with passion. They work hard; they provide management more "bang for the buck." Every person reading this volume must be familiar with at least one workaholic, as well as with how others around that person have grown dependent on him, or her, in the job setting.

There has been disagreement over the years among people who have studied workaholics on the issue of whether they are healthy or normal. One early authority, for example, claimed that workaholics are generally healthy and happy people (Machlowitz, 1980). By the same token, it is common to pity workaholics, or even to look upon them with disdain, as if they are afflicted with some form of social or occupational disease. For example, Schwartz (1982) defined involvement as a manifestation of neurotic obsession/compulsion, while Schaef and Fassel (1988) and Fassel (1992) cast overly involved work as an addiction, a "process addiction that features all the common characteristics of other addictions." According to Schaef and Fassel (1988) and Fassel (1992), these symptoms include confusion, self-centeredness, dishonesty, perfectionism, a preoccupation with control, frozen feelings, ethical deterioration, stress, low self-esteem, an inability to relax, depression, negativism, and a variety of other forms of maladjustment. Workaholism is a major source of marital breakdown. It is a substitute for normal religious experiences for many who are afflicted by it (Killinger, 1991).

Most commonly, addicts of all types make great use of *denial*: They claim steadfastly that there is nothing wrong with them, that they have no problems (Fassel, 1992; Killinger, 1991). An interesting comment once made by a friend to this author about work addiction is that "people are workaholics who work harder than I do." In other words, for many hard-working persons, the pace they set and the goals they accomplish are, to them, defined as somehow "normal." Anyone else who significantly exceeds these standards is typically defined by anyone else as being abnormal, as being a workaholic.

Workaholics typically come from dysfunctional families, families in which behavior and interpersonal relations deviate from normal. Frequently, these families feature addiction to substances such as alcohol or drugs or to processes such as sex, perfectionism, or orderliness (Killinger, 1991). In fact, workaholism is often "the addiction of choice" of adult children of alcoholics (Schaef & Fassel, 1988). Typically, these people are better at work than they are at personal relationships, so they fill their lives with work – too much of it. Therefore, employees who are addicted to their work, in the extreme, are anything but healthy, according to Fassel (1992) and Schaef and Fassel (1988).

Machlowitz (1980) claimed that while they spend long hours of intense effort at their jobs, workaholics are often very poor performers, for a variety of reasons. One reason is that they have an inherent aversion to delegating responsibilities to other people. They insist on maintaining control and would generally rather do everything themselves. As a result, they often spread themselves too thinly and take on so many tasks that they simply cannot be effective at all of them, despite the long hours they spend at their work. Workaholics often try to create and foster the impression that they are indispensable (due to their reluctance to delegate, this is often the case). But much of the flurry surrounding them is artificial rather than truly warranted. Moreover, workaholics tend to intimidate and annoy others around them who are not so completely obsessed with work. As supervisors, they push their subordinates with impunity, often causing high levels of stress and low levels of job satisfaction among them, and sometimes driving away talented people. There is no cause to believe that the high levels of energy they expend necessarily result in greater levels of performance efficiency than would be attainable by working at more "normal" speeds. Workaholics often lose sight of work priorities; in their attempts to get everything done, they often get little actually accomplished. Their obsession with their own time and time schedules means they frequently fail to honor the time requirements of others; they are characteristically late for meetings and frequently leave in the middle of meetings. Cast in the terms we discussed in Chapter 8, workaholics can be major sources of frustration for people around them, both on the job and off.

Fassel's work indicated that workaholics become hooked on both a physiological (or "substance") level and a process or activity level, making this form of addiction especially pernicious. The substance is adrenaline; the rush comes when the person is under pressure. The process aspect comes from the acts of applying effort, of spending the hours and of feeling the thrill of accomplishment when (and if) it arrives, just in time. Like others writing on this topic, Fassel (1992) used the terms *workaholism* and *work addiction* interchangeably because they categorize the condition as they do other forms of addiction, as sharing many of the characteristics and problems seen in other addictions. What are some of these symptoms of work addiction that are so similar to other addictions to substances and processes?

Fassel argued that like other addictions, workaholism can be a one-way slide toward person destruction. Combinations of the symptoms listed earlier can ultimately result in hospitalization, physical illness, and death. Workaholics can kill themselves via stomach ailments, alcoholism, accidents brought on by physical fatigue, excessive smoking and eating, insomnia, and even suicide. Fassel (1992) argued that in our society, the syndrome can be especially perilous for women, especially women who try to establish and maintain occupations outside of the home: "A woman's work is never done" (p. 53). She acknowledged that work addiction is gender neutral, however, in the sense that many men also become victims, although the specific tasks and role expectations placed on them (or which they place on themselves) are different in type, although not in ultimate effect. For many men in our culture, the self-concept of innate superiority must be fulfilled and maintained, according to Fassel (1992), so the drive to produce, to provide, can be constant and unrelenting. Space limitations prevent a full treatment of the theory and research evidence here; the interested reader is referred to Fassel (1992), Schaef and Fassel (1988), and Schor (1991).

So the prevailing current answer to the question "Is workaholism a good thing?" seems to be a resounding "No!" Perhaps a more appropriate position is the one proposed recently by Friedman and Lobel (and discussed earlier): People should be authentic and true to their values, adopting a "live-and-let-live" approach for themselves and for others.

SUMMARY

Employees' job attitudes (and emotional reactions to their work) are important both to the people who hold them and to the organizations that employ those people. Although the connections are somewhat unpredictable, attitudes can result in behaviors that can have either positive or negative consequences for both people and organizations (recall Chapter 9). Managers often assume that the connection between employee attitudes and behaviors is stronger than in fact it is, sometimes overreacting to what they see as extreme attitudes of either positive or negative tone. Up to a certain point, both organizational commitment and job involvement are necessary and potentially beneficial for both employees and employers. In the extreme, however, too much commitment may make employees emotionally and occupationally vulnerable, and too much job involvement may result in the sorts of human consequences associated with workaholism. To date, however, there has been nothing to indicate that too much job satisfaction has any harmful effects, but we seem to be a long way from reaching the stage where, on a macro level, this will ever be the case. In the foreseeable future, a vast number of undesirable jobs will continue to need to be done.

The various job-related attitudes discussed in this chapter are not the only ones that have been investigated by organizational scientists. Job satisfaction, organizational commitment, and job involvement were singled out for discussion here both because they have been the subjects of considerable research over the years and because they are important. In other words, these three constructs do not exhaust all the possible forms that employee attitudes may take. Identified and articulated in the ways they have been presented here, these constructs represent only three of an infinite number of mental and visceral reactions people may have toward their work. In many ways, these concepts are arbitrary: Who is to say that they represent the most common or even the most important attitudes that can be found in the minds and hearts of working people? In short, the careful reader will pay attention to these three constructs as important but will realize that in many ways they represent the mental events of the researchers and scholars who have identified (created?) and discussed them (see Schwab, 1980).

RELATIONSHIPS AMONG THE CONCEPTS

Although the various forms of work-related attitudes are thought of as conceptually distinct from one another, empirically they tend to be inter-correlated: A person who tends to be high on one of these dimensions will tend to be relatively high on the others (Blau & Paul, 1993; Morrow, 1983, 1993). One study of more than 700 U.S. men and women found that job satisfaction had a significant effect on job involvement, but the obverse was not the case (Mortimer & Lorence, 1989). Although the researchers failed to show that satisfaction at one time may predict levels of involvement 4 years later, their cross-sectional analysis did support a weak but significant satisfaction-causes-involvement connection. This particular paper is cited because it is typical of the many that have been conducted on these matters, as are the findings reported.

In fact, the empirically observed relationships among job satisfaction, organizational commitment, and motivation are so consistent (although not overwhelmingly high) that two reviewers suggested that the three variables "may be conceived of as rather specific aspects of a more generalized affective response to the work environment" (Mathieu & Zajac, 1990). On the other hand, the more recent Swedish study mentioned earlier (Hallberg & Schaufeli, 2006) concluded that job involvement is in fact distinct from organizational commitment, and work engagement.

Some working people may not be able or willing to disentangle their feelings about their jobs from their beliefs and attitudes regarding their employers. That explanation may have a lot of merit; not everyone we study is as cerebral or as contemplative about work-related matters as organizational researchers wish them to be.[15] Another explanation is that organizational researchers may simply not be able to measure these various dimensions with sufficient validity and precision using the particular time sequences in longitudinal designs that are appropriated to the phenomena involved, to find any relationships that actually exist among these variables. Difficulties of this sort were introduced and discussed at length in Chapter 2.[16]

The author suspects that the truth lies in some combination of these two explanations. There are plenty of intuitive grounds to believe that people who are satisfied with parts of their jobs may become committed to their employers, out of gratitude or for no particular reason, such that we would expect satisfied employees to be more committed employees. The causal connection may work the other way: People who, for whatever reason, are committed to their employers may tend to see their work as satisfying (Mathieu & Zajac, 1990). As is the case on many points throughout this book, the author suspects that the intuitive truth about matters related to work motivation may not be totally discernible by the crude tools of behavioral researchers. Hence, in this case, there is still just cause to expect causal relationships between motivation, commitment, and other job attitude variables, although the relationships may be complex and circular.

Before we leave our extended discussion of job satisfaction, organizational commitment, and job involvement, it is worth considering briefly how these concepts might interact in practice.

---

[15] Nevertheless, at least two studies, involving different categories of workers, found that measures of job involvement, organizational commitment, and job satisfaction are distinct from one another; that is, that the people studied did differentiate among the three forms of work-related attitudes (Brooke, Russell, & Price, 1988; Mathieu & Farr, 1991).

[16] Some progress has, however, been made: A study examined four possible causal models linking commitment and satisfaction (satisfaction causes commitment; commitment causes satisfaction; the two are related reciprocally; and that there is no simple bivariate relationship between the two constructs). The evidence supported the "commitment causes satisfaction" alternative (Vandenberg & Lance, 1992).

Consider what it may be like for someone who is high in job involvement (meaning they live to work) but who is exceptionally dissatisfied with her company or with conditions of her current job. Consider the case of the person who is high in job involvement but who has no job or who is capable of holding only part-time work. People of this sort are commonplace; in the next few years they may become the norm. There will then be major consequences for people to redefine the concept of careers as we have known them, and for many people, there may be a regression to an increased importance to simple survival needs, to do "whatever work needs to be done" (Bridges, 1994).

LOOKING AHEAD

In Chapters 9 and 10, we introduced the cognitive approach to understanding work motivation and behavior. In Chapter 9, we studied the general nature and functioning of human beliefs and attitudes and their connection to behavior. In the current chapter, we surveyed the scientific literature dealing with three important types of work-related attitude: Satisfaction, commitment, and involvement. While attitudes are not motivation, per se, attitudes can instigate behavior: Job attitudes can instigate work-related behaviors such as joining an organization, leaving it, staying with it, forming a trade union, working hard, stealing from the organization, and so on. Attitudes are slippery and hard to discern or observe directly. But job attitudes are common, powerful precursors to employee work behavior. They provide an important conceptual basis for an understanding for work motivation and behavior that complements the need-based theories presented in Chapters 3 through 8.

In the following three chapters, we present three separate bodies of formal theory of work motivation, all of which rely on the cognitive model of human functioning introduced in Chapter 9.

Equity, Fairness, and Justice Motives Related to Work

11

You remember Thurow's answer . . . you never expected justice from a company, did you? They have neither a soul to lose, nor a body to kick.
Reverend Sydney Smith

Judge not, that ye be not judged. For with what judgment ye judge, ye shall be judged; and with what measure ye mete, it shall be measured to you again.
Matthew 7: 1–2

There is nothing so finely perceived and so finely felt, as injustice.
Charles Dickens

Consider the following scenario (it might be hypothetical for some, but very real for others): You are a small child sitting in your high-chair or at the table in the kitchen and your younger sibling – let's say a younger sister – is sitting opposite you; you are both waiting for your Mom to bring you glasses of orange juice. You receive your glass of juice. Then, within 20 seconds of the delivery by your Mom of your sister's glass of juice, you stop to consider. What is the first thing you do, after your sister has received her juice?[1]

Systematic interdependencies among people and social units following a norm of reciprocity are critical in keeping a society together. That is, *exchange* is the essence of social interaction. At some level, sooner or later, people expect to receive from one another goods, services, and social benefits commensurate in value with those they contribute and provide (Gouldner, 1960; Parsons & Shils, 1951). People like to be treated fairly in their exchanges with one another and develop norms concerning what is fair and what is unfair treatment.

The workplace is an important forum in which people experience the joys and miseries of fairness and unfairness in the exchange for their talents, efforts, and ideas for economic and non-economic benefits. The norms of reciprocity and fairness that function in the greater society are critically important in the functioning of economic organizations such as businesses, government agencies, and other employment settings. According to one leading theorist in this area (Greenberg, 1990), people have a strong urge to see themselves and to be seen by others as fair. They will go to great lengths of self-image management to attain and maintain these perceptions. In fact, Greenberg (1988b) found that managers deemed it more important to be seen as fair by coworkers than actually to be fair.

---

[1] Many children will check to see whether their sibling has received more or less juice than was served to them. See Chapter 3 of Damon (1977), McGillicuddy-DeLisi, Watkins, & Vinchur (1994), and Thorkildsen and White-McNulty (2002) for discussions of the early development of norms of justice in young children.

THE RATIONALE FOR FAIRNESS IMPULSES

Why is fairness so important to human beings? Cropanzano, Rupp, Mohler, and Schminke (2001) suggest there may be at least three separate (yet interrelated) classes of reasons that people are concerned with norms of equity and fairness in social exchange. The first set has to do with norms of instrumental self-interest; that is, people tend to adhere to such norms because in the long term, at least, it is in their economic and social best interest to do so. People expect to receive goods and services as a consequence of ongoing exchange relationships. A second category of reasons – slightly similar to the first, has more to do with the very social nature of our species, viz., it is in our nature to interact on the basis of interpersonal trust to help one another survive and flourish. On this view, there is something about the exchange process itself in addition to the mere consequences of the exchange (see Organ, 1990).

A third "road to justice" – as Cropanzano et al. (2001) called it – is rooted in another fundamental feature of the species – our characteristic requirement for a sense of fairness, dignity, civility, and decency. This third strand rests on abstract moral principles and values that go beyond instrumental values and selfish motives – it is based on a human tendency toward "doing the right thing, for its own sake," a deontological view of morality that has been recognized by philosophers as far back as Kant. Cropanzano, Goldman, and Folger (2003, p. 1019) summarized this view:

> Justice includes treating others as they *should* or *deserve* to be treated by adhering to standards of right and wrong. In other words, justice is in part a judgment about the morality of an outcome, process, or interpersonal interaction. It is concerned with what people view as ethically appropriate, and not merely what serves their economic self-interest or group-based identity.

Thus, for example, a study by Turillo, Folger, Lavelle, Umphress, and Gee (2002) demonstrated how people can sometimes make self-sacrificing decisions in the name of what is right, even when dealing with others who may not subscribe to the belief that virtue may be its own reward. Bies and Moag (1986) and Cropanzano et al. (2003) have provided reviews of this rationale for fairness and justice while Cropanzano et al. (2001) provide a thorough review of all three fundamental bases for norms of equity, fairness, and justice.

Lind and Van den Bos (2002) offered another rationale explaining the importance of fairness, proposing that fairness is functional for people in managing the uncertainties they face in life. They propose that:

> Fair treatment helps people manage their uncertainty . . . both because it gives them confidence that they will ultimately receive good outcomes and because it makes the possibility of loss less anxiety-provoking or even, as in fair gambles, enjoyable. Conversely, unfair treatment under conditions of uncertainty gives the uncertainty a particularly sinister complexion, and makes people even more uneasy.
>
> (Lind & Van den Bos, 2002, pp. 195–196)

Lind and Van den Bos (2002) outlined a comprehensive argument that is beyond our present scope. At its core, however, their argument provides a basis for understanding how the benefits of fair treatment are especially pronounced among people who are facing high levels of uncertainty, as occurs when they face being disciplined, laid off, fired, or reassigned to a new job in an organization.

Some Common Consequences of Unjust and Unfair Treatment

The literature shows that treating people unfairly *or in a way that they perceive to be unfair or unjust* can lead to a wide array of dysfunctional consequences for the victims, for the perceived perpetrators of unfairness, and for the organization within which the unfairness is believed to have occurred.

For example, perpetrators of workplace violence frequently believe that they have been victims of injustice (Folger & Skarlicki, 1998; Leck, 2005). There is evidence that the experience of long-term, sustained injustice is dysfunctional for one's health – contributing to burnout (van Dierendonck, Schaufeli, & Buunk, 1998), mental ill-health (Tepper, 2001), and even coronary heart disease (Kivimäki et al., 2005). Employee perceptions of inequitable or unjust treatment by the employer have been shown to be major contributing causes of theft (e.g., Greenberg, 1993a, 2002), sabotage (Ambrose, Seabright, & Schminke, 2002) and myriad other intentional deviant behaviors[2] that cost U.S. business and industry billions of dollars every year (Aquino, Lewis, & Bradfield, 1999). Employee withdrawal behaviors, ranging from silence (Pinder & Harlos, 2001), absenteeism, and tardiness to turnover can all be influenced by employee perceptions of unjust or unfair treatment in the workplace (Boswell & Olson-Buchanan, 2004; de Boer, Bakker, Syroit, & Schaufeli, 2002). Some theorists and researchers have suggested that problems with distributive justice (the distribution of rewards and punishments among actors) are most closely associated with effects on personal outcomes (e.g., individual job satisfaction), whereas perceived problems with organizational rules and procedures (procedural injustice) are more closely associated with the evaluation by employees of the systems in which they work, including organizational authorities (see Colquitt et al., 2001; McFarlin & Sweeney, 1992).[3] We return to finer distinctions among these constructs shortly; our purpose for using the terminology associated with varieties of (in)justice somewhat loosely at this point is to attract the reader's attention to the fact that *justice-related phenomena are among the most pervasive and important in the domain of work motivation theory and research.*

Being treated unfairly hurts

Anyone who has been demoted, reassigned, fired, "downsized" or even treated shabbily, unfairly (in their view), by an organization will appreciate that the analysis, while attempting to be scientifically grounded, may miss much of the point. Being treated unfairly at one's workplace hurts, it really hurts:

> I was getting really tired, very tight, irritable. I was getting a lot of headaches and tightness in my stomach from feeling confused and not understanding what was going on . . . I wasn't sleeping very well and I didn't want to go to work.
>
> (Harlos & Pinder, 2000, p. 267)

And it affects job performance:

> My wife could see it at home. I was depressed all the time. I was doing my MBA part time and my marks were slipping. Instead of handing them in ahead of time I was handing them in three weeks late.
>
> (Harlos & Pinder, 2000, p. 266)

Unfair treatment by the major systems in which a person works, as we will explore in this chapter, hurts people, emotionally, physically, and in the devotion they have to the work that they do.

---

[2] Robinson and Bennett (1995, p. 556) defined employee deviance as "voluntary behavior that violates significant organizational norms . . . threatens the well-being of the organization, and its members, or both."
[3] Colquitt et al. (2001) provided a thorough review of the history of the evolution of justice theory in organizations, including a meta-analysis of the consequences for both individuals and organizations of justice/injustice.

Justice of treatment is an imperative for civilizations to survive and, on a more micro level, for organizational behavior to progress to the mutual advantage of employees and employers. The requirement and expectation of justice is the domain of international law and jurisprudence, far beyond the scope of this volume. Nevertheless, we take a quick look at the importance of justice in the international arena, for those of us who believe that our concepts of justice are irrelevant in understanding Western organizational behavior, or that, if relevant, may apply to the understanding of the work motives of people in other countries, in other cultures (see Erez & Earley, 1993; Erez et al., 2001).

International differences and moderated relationships

At the very top of this chapter, we cited the "Golden Rule": Do unto others as you would have them do unto you. The reader may be interested to learn that the essence of this rule is found in the writings of the sacred books, scriptures, and documents of many different creeds and religions.[4] Indeed, a survey of the literature reported by Lam, Schaubroeck, and Aryee (2002) concluded, as noted earlier, that although distributive justice has tended to be more closely related to personal outcomes than has procedural justice, and that procedural justice has tended to be more closely related to "evaluations of institutions and employee contributions" (p. 2), "Studies of the effects of procedural and distributive justice do not provide consistent and mutually supportive conclusions as to generalizability across cultures" (p. 2). A study by Fields, Pang, and Chiu (2000) set in Hong Kong provided an example. These researchers hypothesized that it might have been that the values of collectivism/individualism and power distance (recall Chapter 3) were the source of some international differences in the relationship between perceptions of injustice and withdrawal behavior in their research. As in most cases of research of this sort, values such as collectivism/individualism were assumed to exist at common levels among all research participants from a common national grouping.

Lam et al. (2002) extended this reasoning in samples of bank tellers drawn from both Hong Kong and the Unites States, assessing research participants' personalities directly rather than relying on a more distal assessment of cultural influences (which account for only some of the differences we observe between people on a one-on-one basis). That is, they measured employees from both national samples on both power distance and individualism–collectivism directly, rather than merely categorizing them into broad national groupings and assuming homogenous standing among the employees with each of the two groupings on these two key values.

The findings were mixed but suggestive. Specifically, Lam et al. (2002) found that, whereas justice perceptions were related to job satisfaction, performance, and absenteeism in both societal cultures, only partial support was found for the anticipated interaction (moderated) effects. The work outcome variables did not appear to be affected by individual differences in individualism (whether measured at the group level or the individual level) but power distance did seem to make a difference. In this case, there was a more positive effect between distributive justice perceptions and work outcomes among persons having low power distance scores (i.e., among those who value a more egalitarian distribution of status and power among people). The moderating effect of power distance on the strength of the connection between procedural justice and the work outcomes was similar. The researchers explain these effects in terms of met expectations: "For low power distance individuals, a more equitable workplace permits the exercise of self-determination at work. Although high power distance individuals are supposed to be more reverential towards their superiors and they may be more accepting of more arbitrary treatment from their superiors, the findings indicate that such individuals also appreciate equitable treatment and outcomes" (p. 15). Interesting! As anticipated, there was considerable overlap on power distance scores between members of the American and Hong Kong samples.

---

[4] http://www.teachingvalues.com/goldenrule.html (July 27, 2006).

Konovsky (2000) has provided a brief summary of other research into international similarities and differences in justice effects across cultures and concludes, quite appropriately, that more work is required in this area.

PREVIEW OF THE CHAPTER

This chapter deals with a variety of issues related to fairness, equity, and justice in the workplace: It comprises five main sections. We begin with a study of the traditional body of theory and research on *equity* and *distributive justice*. These concepts have to do with the distribution of benefits and sanctions among people and deal with questions such as who is to receive how much and how fairly are these outcomes distributed?

In the second section, we move to an examination of *procedural justice*, which is concerned with the fairness of the policies and procedures by which people interact. We will see that not only are the official practices used to distribute rewards and punishment in organizations important, but that the nature of the interpersonal relationships during the administration of justice is important as well. This is the domain of *interactional justice*, the focus of the third major section of the chapter. The fourth major section of the chapter will deal briefly with fairness theory, a relatively new perspective on these matters that provides different insights into matters of fairness and equity.

The final major section provides an evaluation of the corpus of work collectively referred to as "justice theory," and sets the stage for Chapter 12 in which we will examine expectancy theories of work motivation that share the fundamental assumptions of other chapters in Part Two concerning the cognitive, information-processing model of human functioning introduced in Chapter 1.

As we proceed through Chapter 11, we will introduce and discuss a number of significant social and organizational issues that pertain to the various varieties of fairness and justice, as appropriate, including topics such as comparable worth, employment equity and affirmative action, organizational downsizing, firing, and employee discipline. A key theme throughout the chapter is that *people's perceptions and beliefs about fairness are heavily influenced by the social contexts* in which these perceptions and beliefs are formed. To begin, then, what is meant by the terms *fairness*, *justice*, and *equity*?

EQUITY, FAIRNESS, AND DISTRIBUTIVE JUSTICE

According to Cohen (1991), justice is thought to exist when people receive those things they (and others around them) deserve or are entitled to. These receipts can be either benefits (such as pay increases) or burdens (such as a transfer to an undesirable city or region). Injustice involves a violation of a moral contract for goods, services, opportunities, or treatment. An employee who is hired by a large bank with the clear expectation that she will be moved quickly through a series of new and challenging jobs will feel a sense of injustice if these reassignments are not forthcoming (see Robinson & Rousseau, 1994, for an empirical example of the violation of such contracts). Generally, we follow the practice of Sheppard, Lewicki, and Minton (1992) and most others, who use the terms *justice* and *fairness* interchangeably. The notion of equity has been the most researched justice-related topic in the organizational sciences as well as the focus of the earliest work, so we begin our discussion with it.

Equity Theory: Historic Roots of Distributive Justice Concepts

Professional athletes often make the news by demanding that their contracts be torn up before their terms expire. The reason for this apparent lack of respect for contract law usually involves feelings by these athletes that the previously agreed-upon rates of pay are, by some standard, no longer "fair." But these considerations are not unique to professional athletes. A recent article in the *The Economist* magazine (June 18, 2005, p. 31) reported that judges in the Unites States were feeling inequitably compensated for their work. According to the article, many first-year lawyers earn more pay than the judges they appear before in court!

People hold beliefs about the value of their contributions at work and how well these contributions are recognized and rewarded. These beliefs are formed in a social context in which people compare how well they are being treated with how well they believe others are being treated. When people believe that, relative to others, they are being under-compensated or somehow under-recognized, they become unhappy and motivated to do something about it. Smith (1991) argued that the primary emotion experienced at times like these is envy (see Chapter 4). Professional athletes have been known to sit out entire seasons over contract disputes of this sort, and labor unions in many non-sports industries go on strike every year for similar reasons. In this section we describe a collection of theories generally and collectively referred to as *equity theory*. There are a variety of theories that fit under this general heading. Due to limitations of space, the discussion here will be general and relevant to all of them rather than devoted to a precise analysis of the nuances of each of the differences between them.[5]

Key Elements of Equity Theory

Equity theory rests on three main assumptions (Carrell & Dittrich, 1978). First, the theory holds that people develop beliefs about what constitutes a fair and equitable return for their contributions to their jobs. Second, people tend to compare what they perceive to be the exchange they have with their employers with what they perceive to be the nature of the exchange *other individuals* have with their employers (although the employers being considered need not be one and the same). Finally, the theory holds that when people believe that their own treatment is not equitable relative to the exchange they perceive others to be making, they will be motivated to do something about it, as in the examples of the millionaire athletes mentioned earlier.

The theory states that individuals hold perceptions about the number and value of the contributions they make to their work, usually referred to as *inputs*. For example, people may consider the education and training they bring to their jobs, the number of hours they work, and how hard they try to perform. Different people tend to pay attention to difference inputs, and there is a tendency for people to place greater emphasis on the inputs they have to offer (e.g., Cummings, 1980). For example, highly educated people tend to place great importance on their schooling, even in work contexts where what they have learned in college is not related to the nature of the work they do. The college graduate with a major in German literature, for example, may become frustrated when she learns that her degree is discounted by prospective employers seeking to hire computer operators. Equity theory assumes that people aggregate their perceived inputs into a sort of psychological total, representing the net value they believe they contribute to their jobs.

People also hold beliefs about the nature and quantity of the consequences or *outcomes* they receive as a result of doing their work. Pay, fringe benefits, job satisfaction, status, and opportunities

---

[5] The interested reader is referred to Adams (1963, 1965), Homans (1961), Jacques (1961), and Patchen (1961) for treatments of many of the specific versions of early equity theory. It is acknowledged that the following discussion is influenced most heavily by the work of Adams (1963, 1965), because his version seems to have been the most influential in the research and theoretic work among organizational scientists interested in work motivation and behavior (Pritchard, 1969).

to learn, as well as physical outcomes such as company cars, represent the range of things people might consider as outcomes. Different people tend to recognize different outcomes, depending on what their own jobs provide. For 125 years, members of Canada's prestigious Royal Canadian Mounted Police have enjoyed tremendous status and respect from the citizenry, somewhat offsetting what many of them believed to be comparatively low pay levels. Similarly, junior professors at highly prestigious universities are often expected to work for lower starting salaries than they might receive elsewhere, in part because of the status they are expected to derive from being affiliated with these institutions, a phenomenon known as "eating ivy."

Equity ratios

Equity theory holds that people evaluate their outcomes relative to their inputs and form opinions about how well they are being treated. Most (but not all) versions of the theory stress that this evaluation often takes place in a comparative, social sense, such that people consider their inputs and outcomes relative to the inputs and outcomes they perceive other people contribute and take away from their work. The crucial aspect of this social comparison process is the belief that inputs and outcomes are considered in ratio terms rather than absolute terms.

For example, the reader may believe that Karen earns twice as much money as he does. Whether or not that belief results in annoyance will depend on his beliefs about the value of the contributions Karen makes to her work compared to the value of the contributions he believes he makes to his own job. People can tolerate seeing others earn more money and other benefits than they do if they believe that the others also contribute more in the way of inputs. When we see other people making a lot more money (or other forms of outcome) than we do but not appearing to be contributing more in the way of relevant inputs, a tension results that the theory says will motivate behavior to equalize the ratios. The tension is particularly strong when the other person's outcomes are perceived as higher than ours but that person's inputs are simultaneously perceived to be lower (Adams, 1963).

Symbolically, we can represent these two ratios for a hypothetical person (named Richard) as follows:

$$\frac{\text{Richard's beliefs about } \textit{his own outcomes}}{\text{Richard's beliefs about his own inputs}} \quad \overset{?}{=} \quad \frac{\text{Richard's beliefs about } \textit{someone else's outcomes}}{\text{Richard's beliefs about the other person's inputs}}$$

If Richard perceives that, psychologically, his ratio of outcomes to inputs compares favorably with that of some other person with whom he compares, the theory suggests that he will be content. Tension builds, however, when Richard perceives that the ratio of outcomes to inputs of his comparison person is more favorable than the ratio he attributes to his own situation. However, life is rarely so simple, as we shall see shortly. Meanwhile, we digress slightly from our treatment of classical equity theory, per se, to introduce a particularly insightful conceptualization of *fairness*.

Fairness

About 16 years after the work of Leventhal (1976) and his colleagues, Sashkin and Williams (1990) identified nine facets of *fairness*[6] and showed how differences in employee perceptions on these nine dimensions were related to the differences in employee sickness rates and accident compensation

---

[6] The reader will note that some of these dimensions of fairness might be classified as perceived outcomes from the employment process, as much as they reflect procedural processes. Nevertheless, the entire list is presented here for the sake of coherence in relating the work of Sashkin and Williams (1990).

costs among 20 outlets of a large retail organization, 10 in each of two regions of the United States. The nine dimensions were:

1. *Trust*: Confidence that employees have in management and the degree to which employees believe what management tells them.
2. *Consistency*: Regularity, steady continuity, or predictability of management action such that employees are not surprised by management actions.
3. *Truthfulness*: Management's fidelity and sincerity in action.
4. *Integrity*: Management's adherence in action to values, ethics, or a moral code.
5. *Expectations*: Provision of clear statements by management as to what task activities are desired of employees and what consequences will result.
6. *Equity*: Demonstration through action that all employees are treated alike in terms of rewards and punishments for similar behaviors and results.
7. *Influence*: Provision of authority to employees equal to their responsibility, so that employees have a sense of "ownership" of their actions and achievements.
8. *Justice*: Adherence to a code of standards that is perceived as appropriate and administered impartially.
9. *Respect*: Management's expression of concern, consideration, and regard for employees.

Sashkin and Williams (1990) developed scales to measure perceived fairness in terms of their nine dimensions (as well as a final scale to assess overall fairness). They asked the store manager to rate their own fairness on these scales. Similarly, they had the department managers rate themselves in terms of the 10 fairness dimensions. Finally, they had the employees use the rating scales not to assess themselves, but to assess their bosses in terms of fairness. The reader may anticipate the findings. The store managers in both the high-illness/accident-cost stores saw their own behavior as fair, as did the managers from the stores with the lower illness rates and accidents costs. By their own admission, then, all of the store managers were equally fair. Similarly, when the researchers compared the department managers' ratings of their own behaviors, there were no systematic differences related to whether they were from high- or low-accident/illness stores. Finally, when the researchers compared the ratings provided by department managers of their store managers, a different picture emerged. Fairness ratings on two dimensions were related to the health statistics: Expectations and influence. Even more interesting were the differences between the high- and low-health statistics stores when the researchers compared the ratings of fairness provided by the non-supervisory employees (who had assessed their bosses). There were differences across all 10 dimensions of fairness, five of them statistically significant. In a nutshell, the results showed that employees who worked in the stores with the lowest accident rates and health costs systematically and consistently rated their supervisors as lower in fairness.

The factors that were especially critical in differentiating among the two groups of stores were what the authors referred to as "warm and fuzzy" factors: Factors of fairness such as trust, truthfulness, integrity, and justice. On the basis of these findings, Sashkin and Williams concluded that fairness does make a difference – even on hard bottom-line-outcome variables such as employee sickness (and, therefore absenteeism) and accident compensation costs. The point of this simple, relevant study is that treating employees fairly is important. It can make a difference to do so, not only in terms of soft-attitudinal measures but also in terms that managers frequently care about the most: The bottom line.

Returning to formal equity theory: The eye of the beholder

Let's get back to Richard and his perceived ratios: They represent Richard's view of the world, but they may not be shared by other people, such as Richard's supervisor, or the person with whom Richard compares himself (the "referent other"). Therefore, any two people could compare themselves with each other and each conclude that the other has the better deal. It depends entirely on the degree to which their beliefs about how closely each other's (and their own) inputs and outcomes are matched. Often, supervisors get themselves into considerable trouble by distributing rewards and punishments in a way they perceive to be *equal* among employees – so that the norm of equity is immediately at risk if the recipients don't perceive their inputs to be equal. Alternatively, supervisors who attempt to recognize a norm of equity can err by distributing rewards (or punishment) in doses that the various parties don't perceive to be commensurate with the efforts, performance, seniority, or other inputs they have provided. Hence, distributing rewards and punishments among subordinates is widely acknowledged as an anguishing task among parents, teachers, and supervisors in many diverse settings. Sometimes it can be a matter of "damned if you do and damned if you don't!" That justice and fairness can be a matter of "the eye of the beholder" was illustrated by a simple study. The employees of a company were asked how they thought *a lump sum* of money should be divided among members of their organization. Highest-level executives thought organization-wide equity should be used; departmental managers suggested intradepartmental equity; lowest-level employees did not differentiate between equity and equality of distribution as bases for distributing the money (Lansberg, 1984).

Bazerman (1993) suggested three mechanisms, or standards, by which people may be seen as irrational in their judgments of fairness. The first is caused by any deviation from what would normally be considered rational by broad economic standards. The second criterion is based on any outcome or circumstance that can be judged to be Pareto inefficient. "An agreement is defined as Pareto efficient when there is no other agreement [between two parties] that would make one party better off without decreasing the outcomes to any other party" (Bazerman, 1993, p. 190). This implies that either an equal or an unequal distribution of resources or outcomes may be best for the society at large, depending on prior circumstances. Deviations from such decisions are irrational by this criterion. The third basis for a person's fairness judgments to be seen as irrational is when they are inconsistent. The inconsistencies may result from ultra-sensitivity or be based on irrelevant concerns. Or if a person changes his decisions about outcomes on the basis of irrelevant data, he would be seen as irrational.

The current view: Social influences on the eye of the beholder

Many years ago, Deutsch (1983) claimed that the approach taken to assess fairness in equity theory and research to that point in time had been too psychological and far too little social-psychological in nature. That is, too much attention had been devoted to the choice of a referent other(s) a focal person uses to establish his or her equity beliefs, and too little attention had been devoted to the possibility that these equity perceptions and beliefs are social constructions, heavily influenced by the social context in which an individual is working. In a nutshell, people make conclusions about the fairness of their treatment by the systems within which they live and work upon the basis of both their own experiences as well as upon those of others around them, whom they deem to be relevant comparison others. As Lamertz (2002) put it:

> [P]erceptions of fairness are subject to social influence through social comparison and interpersonal validation of reality . . . employees experience uncertainty about their relationship to the organization and use fairness judgments about the way the organization treats its members as a heuristic for evaluating the quality of that relationship . . . An employee responds to this uncertainty by seeking information about procedures to confirm the trustworthiness and neutrality of organizational decision makers and validate his or her standing as a valued member . . . However, ambiguity exists about the meaning of formal organizational procedures . . . particularly among . . . newcomers . . . because formalization and implementation of rules are removed from the every day experience of employees by several layers of organizational hierarchy . . . the ambiguity of organizational rules and the normative nature of justice make perceptions of organizational fairness prone to social influence processes when employees seek to reduce uncertainty about their relationship to the organization . . . social cues

from, as well as social comparison with, peers and managers to whom an employee has social relationships will influence his or her justice perceptions.

(Lamertz, 2002, pp. 20–21)

The reactions people have about the reported injustice experiences of others can be complex, however. For example, a study of tenure decisions in an academic setting found that both procedural and distributive justice enter into faculty attitudes about their employers and that the passage of time is a key variable (Ambrose & Cropanzano, 2003). Specifically, perceptions of procedural justice had their greatest impact on employee attitudes prior to and soon after tenure decisions were made and distributive justice perceptions were most influential a year later.

Degoey (2000) has proposed the adoption of a "contagion model," a metaphor rooted in epidemiology, representing the spread of diseases to characterize how active and how social the sense making of justice is among coworkers. Thus, Lind, Kray, and Thompson (1998) found that individuals rely on both personal and vicarious experiences with authority figures in forming their individual beliefs about justice. They indicated, however, that people tend to place considerably more weight on their own experiences than upon those of others who report having been treated unjustly.

Kray and Lind (2002) found that a number of situational/contextual variables can moderate the effects of reports of injustice by alleged victims to others i.e., to third-party observers. Of key importance is whether the coworker-observer (as opposed to the victim of injustice) has had personal experiences that are similar. In other words, personal experiences of injustice may make other people's reports of injustice more credible, especially when the observer has had negative personal experience with the alleged perpetrator of the injustice (such as a particular supervisor). In these situations, the observer is more likely to respond with empathy to the victim. However, if the third-party observer does not perceive the evaluation standards used to assess victims as unfair, then the report of injustice may backfire, causing the observer to derogate the victim rather than feel empathy for him or her (cf. Skarlicki, Ellard, & Kelln, 1998). The odds that derogation, rather than empathy, will result from a report of injustice may also be higher when the injustice is reported as severe rather than mild. Finally, a study by Korsgaard, Roberson, and Rymph (1998) showed how the circular relationship between an employee and his or her supervisor can provide a dyadic version of social information processing. In two studies, they showed that a subordinate's communication style can affect a supervisor's fairness behavior during decision making, and that it, in turn, can influence the subordinate's attitudes concerning the decision, the manager, and the organization!

Social information processing on fairness and justice in groups
A series of studies in recent years has shown how *groups* can affect the perceptions of justice/injustice among group members. In a pair of studies using student populations *working in groups*, Colquitt (2004) demonstrated how procedural justice had beneficial effects on individuals' role performance and on their conflict perceptions. Moreover, as hypothesized, the beneficial individual effects of individuals' own justice perceptions were stronger when they perceived that their team members also received high levels of procedural justice. In other words, *consistency of treatment* by supervisors of all team members amplified the benefits of positive procedural justice experienced by individual team members. It appeared that individuals learn both personally and vicariously (via the experiences of team members) about the justice of the treatment within the system, so consistency of fairness and justice may be just as important as maintaining an overall high level of justice.

A Dutch study shed some light onto why procedural justice may have beneficial effects in group effectiveness. Tyler and Blader (2002) developed and tested a model to illustrate how people attribute higher levels of status to groups that they believe exercise high levels of procedural fairness than to groups in which procedures are not deemed to be fair in their internal operations. Fair procedures "communicate an important message regarding relational concerns, leading group members to think: (1) that their group is of high status and (2) that they are of high status within the group. Both of these evaluations are believed to play a role in the construction and maintenance of a positive social identity, which is itself an important psychological objective" (Tyler & Blader, 2002, p. 814).

Subsequently, De Cremer, Tyler, and den Ouden (2005) hypothesized and found support for the proposition that when members of a team are treated in ways that they deem just, they develop stronger identification with the team (or merging of the self with the team) and, as a consequence, are more likely to be cooperative to help the team succeed in reaching its goals.

In short, there is considerable evidence that people do not form their judgments of justice and injustice in social vacuums. Rather, as in the case of the formation of equity beliefs (as we discussed earlier in this chapter), considerable vicarious learning via the experiences of the apparent justness of the treatment other people receive – or report to have received – augments an individual's assessments of personal justice experiences. In Chapter 12, we will see how social information processing can also play a large role in personal assessments of job satisfaction–job dissatisfaction as well.

Beliefs, attitudes, inequity, and behavior

Another key point in equity theory is that it deals with people's beliefs and attitudes. The beliefs consist of thoughts such as "Richard has a key to the executive washroom and I don't." Attitudes consist of evaluations of these beliefs ("Who cares about having a key to the executive washroom, anyway?"). Beliefs and attitudes about equity are formed and modified in the same manner as other beliefs and attitudes (see Chapter 9). Moreover, the beliefs and attitudes of equity theory are related as unpredictably to employee behavior as are all beliefs and attitudes. To result in relevant behaviors, they must be converted into specific intentions.

Consequences of inequity perceptions

Nevertheless, the theory claims that people find conditions of perceived inequity uncomfortable or dissonant (Festinger, 1957), and when the tension becomes great enough, the person will do some-thing to redress it.[7] States of perceived inequity are seen as constituting a need of the sort examined in Chapter 3, possessing all the characteristics of needs discussed there. Notice that it is possible for a person such as Richard to perceive that he is being overly well treated in relation to his comparison person. The theory states (and research supports the contention) that people have a greater tolerance for this sort of inequity situation than for cases where they believe they are being poorly treated. However, the theory predicts that eventually they will be motivated to equalize the ratios as they perceive them (Adams, 1963; Andrews, 1967; Weick & Nesset, 1968).

Theoretically, how is equity restored? First, remember that equity is in the eye of the beholder. The theory states that people will be motivated to change elements of either (or both) of the ratios they perceive. For example, Richard might demand a raise from his boss if he feels he is being poorly treated compared to his coworker. Or he might demand some other form of increased outcome, something he values enough to feel that justice has been done. Alternatively, Richard might attempt to change the nature of the denominator of his own equity ratio by, for example, reducing the quantity or quality of his work. ("Fine, if that's all you wish to pay me, you won't be seeing me around here on Sundays anymore.") The author has known colleagues who have proclaimed that their employers "seem able to afford less of my time every year!"

Adjusting effort to restore equity
It is important to note that the theory makes different predictions about whether an employee (who believes she is being inequitably treated) will increase or decrease her effort level, depending on the

---

[7] Greenberg (1984) argued on both empirical and theoretical grounds that "inequity distress" is "apocryphal" and that, even in cases where it may exist, it is not strong enough to motivate the types of response hypothesized by equity theory.

nature of the payment system under which she is working. If the employee is working for a piece rate, for example, the theory predicts that feelings of underpayment inequity (as a result of a belief that the rate of payment per unit produced is too low) will lead to attempts to increase productivity levels, thereby maximizing the net level of pay earned overall. By the same token, underpayment inequity is predicted to result in reduced performance levels in situations of hourly pay. Similarly, equity theory predicts perceptions of overpayment under a piece-rate pay plan to result in restricted output and increased quality, thereby limiting the net amount of overpayment the person earns while providing greater input to the exchange. Finally, overpayment perceptions under an hourly compensation plan would be expected to result in increased performance levels, because higher productivity is one means of increasing one's inputs and restoring balance. Reference to the equity ratios represented earlier helps explain why different behavioral reactions are predicted in the various underpayment and overpayment conditions.

Notice that Richard might be able to restore equity in the ratios he perceives by influencing either the numerator or the denominator (or both) of the ratio he attributes to his comparison person. If Richard were brash enough, for example, he might enquire about the inordinately high level of pay being earned by his coworker. More likely, Richard might attack the numerator of his coworker's ratio; he may behave in such a way as to assure that his comparison person actually earns his fancy salary and key to the executive washroom.

The point is that perceptions of inequitable treatment generate motivational forces (using the terminology of Chapter 9, we would call them *beliefs* and *attitudes* with the potential to become *intentions*) that instigate behavior to reduce tension, and that often a variety of behaviors is available for correcting a situation of perceived inequity. But we know from Chapter 8 that not all goal-directed behavior is successful – people do not always succeed at what they attempt to do. Moreover, it is not always feasible even to try certain acts. For example, it would be quite risky in most circumstances for Richard to attempt to have his coworker's pay cut or to try to get the other person to contribute more to the organization. Consequently, people in Richard's position often find that they have more control over elements of their own perceived ratios, particularly over the level and quality of inputs they provide. In other words, the theory predicts that people like Richard may deliberately reduce the level of effort they put into their jobs. But even this can be difficult or risky at times. What if Richard's job is machine paced, so that it is not possible for him to reduce the quantity of work he performs? What if Richard cuts back on the quality of his work? If he did so and were caught by his boss, his frustration would become even greater.

An interesting study by Greenberg and Ornstein (1983) is relevant here. These researchers employed undergraduate students in a proofreading task. Each of two groups of students received a "high-status job title," one group on the basis of what they thought was their superior performance on the job, the other for no apparent reason. Both groups were asked to contribute more work to the proofreading project for no additional pay. The people who believed they had actually earned their elevated titles sustained their performance at the task for no extra pay. In the group granted the higher status for no stated reason, the performance level increased for a short period, then fell off dramatically. (The employees who were given added responsibility but no title reduced their performance over time.)

Cognitive reevaluation of outcomes

If behavior to influence the value of any of the four main elements of the two equity ratios in Richard's mind is impossible, what can Richard do to reduce the motivational force? Remember that the elements of the two ratios are simply Richard's *perceptions* of the nature and quantity of his own and his partner's inputs and outcomes. The theory says that when reality cannot be changed, the perceptions that give rise to the motivational force will be changed. Hence Richard may reevaluate any (or all) of the beliefs he holds about either the numerators or the denominators he has in mind. For example, he may investigate and learn that his apparently overpaid coworker has a better set of credentials than Richard initially thought he had. Richard may notice that the other person actually works harder than he had given him credit for previously. Or Richard may decide that his own Ph.D. in anthropology really is not a material input to his job as a dishwasher. Finally, Richard may reevaluate his beliefs about his outcomes, noticing that the people he works with are very congenial, and that low paying as it is, at least his job is clean.

Greenberg and Ornstein (1983) demonstrated that people can and do alter their beliefs about the value of the outcomes they receive in their exchange ratios vis-à-vis their employers. In a study of 114 salaried clerical workers whose pay was cut by natural circumstances, Greenberg found support for equity theory in the form of an increase in the perceived importance of non-salary rewards as a means of reducing feelings of inequitable treatment. He had the employees rate the value of a number of physical features of their working environment, such as the amount of floor space, desk space, privacy, the number of coworkers who shared their offices, the number of windows in their offices, and so on, both while their pay was below normal and after their salaries had been reinstated to normal levels. As hypothesized by equity theory, the clerical employees attributed higher value to these physical amenities during the period when their pay had been reduced than they did many months later, after their regular salary levels had been restored to normal levels. In summary, when behavior is not possible to restore a perception of equity, the theory predicts that the person will try to change his beliefs about his equity ratios and/or his evaluative reactions to those beliefs.

What if it is simply not possible to change one's beliefs about equity matters sufficiently? The theory predicts that when behavior is not possible, and when it is not possible to change perceptions sufficiently to restore feelings of equity, people will respond with denial, repression, or withdrawal, as they do when faced with other types of frustrating circumstance (recall Chapter 8). Hence, perceptions of being inequitably treated contribute to job dissatisfaction (Pritchard, 1969), which in turn results in higher rates of absenteeism and turnover (Carrell & Dittrich, 1978; Telly, French, & Scott, 1971) and other forms of withdrawal, such as silence (Cohen, 1990; Pinder & Harlos, 2001).

There is evidence that both distributive and procedural justice have an effect on employee attitudes toward work but that the two forms of justice may affect different types of attitude. One study of 188 public utility engineers, for example, found that perceptions of distributive justice were more closely related to what the authors called personal-level outcomes such as pay satisfaction, whereas procedural justice was more closely linked to organizational-level outcomes such as organizational commitment (Sweeney & McFarlin, 1993; see also McFarlin & Sweeney, 1992). This particular model of the findings was the most effective of four alternative theoretical approaches studied by the authors. We discuss the matters of procedural justice and interactional justice later in the chapter.

Dysfunctional reactions to perceived inequity

Greenberg demonstrated in both laboratory (1993a) and field (1990b, 2002) settings that one reaction that people may have to being treated inequitably is to *steal* from their employers. In the simple terms of the equity ratios discussed earlier, theft of property, money, ideas, or information from one's employer constitutes an increase in the outcomes that a person takes away from the employment exchange, albeit perhaps not an outcome or benefit that the employer had in mind (Greenberg & Scott, 1996). According to Dr. David Hannah, an expert on employee theft issues (cf. Hannah, 2006), estimates of the aggregate cost of employee theft vary and are sometimes unreliable (Hannah, 2006, personal communication with the author), although it is clear that theft of property by employees is a huge national (and international) problem. A 2000 report by the National Retail Security Survey claimed that U.S. retailers lost 1.75% of their total annual sales to "shrink." In that study, it was found that retail security managers attributed more than 46% of their losses to theft by disgruntled employees. The total cost of this theft was estimated to be $14.9 billion, annually, approximately 50% more than the cost attributed to shoplifting by customers![8] The story in Canada

---

[8] http://retailindustry.about.com/od/statistics_loss_prevention/1/aa011124a.htm (July 30, 2006).

is similar, on a proportional basis. A survey conducted by the Retail Council of Canada claimed that internal theft was the leading cause of retail losses at 48%, compared to 31% due to external theft, and 19% due to administrative error (*Star-Phoenix* – Saskatoon, 2005).[9]

In an early study, Greenberg (1990b) observed the theft rates among employees who worked for a Midwestern U.S. company at three different manufacturing plants. Because the company lost two major contracts, it cut the employees' wages by 15% in two of the three plants. In one of the two plants, management explained to the employees in advance that their pay was going to be cut for a temporary period, outlining the causes of the pay cut and expressing regret that such action had to be taken. Management took great care to make the employees believe that the pay cuts were unavoidable and that they were sorry. In the second plant, a brief meeting was held and minimal information was provided about the cuts. Management expressed little or no sorrow or regret. No pay cuts were required in the third plant. There was no significant change during the experiment among the control (no-wage-cut) employees. However, there was an increase in theft rates among both wage-cut plants during the period of the cuts. The increase was particularly dramatic among the employees who had received only a brief explanation of the necessity for the cuts. The results of this study are among the few available *from field settings* that demonstrate how employees can be motivated to restore equity in their exchange with their employers. They also illustrate the importance of interactional justice, a concept we focus on later in the chapter.

Silence

In a landmark book, Hirschman (1970) offered one of the most useful models for understanding employee reactions to unfavorable treatment by employers. He advanced a typology of three reactions: Exit, voice, and loyalty. *Exit* implies withdrawal from the company. *Voice* implies speaking up: Complaining, protesting, or initiating action intended to make things right. *Loyalty* implies accepting the inequity and remaining more or less committed to the company, despite the circumstances. One consequence of perceived injustice that has received some recent attention might be seen as the flipside of voice mechanisms – employee silence. That is, one reaction that people can have to injustice is remaining silent, neither protesting nor attempting to make their views heard. They withdraw but stay onboard. This sort of silence might be interpreted by management as a sign of contentment: After all, if no one is complaining, things must be all right. Ironically, in many cases it is the most disadvantaged of groups who choose to remain silent about injustice, even when formal procedures for action are available (Pinder & Harlos, 2001).

By its very nature, silence in the context of justice and injustice is hard to discern and understand. Cohen (1990) has argued, for example, that silence may be seen as support for, and endorsement of, the status quo, or it might be a reflection of objection. Silence might also reflect a lack of information or means for expression. Employee silence might indicate that voice mechanisms are bogus or ineffectual. Finally, silence may reflect fear of speaking up. Therefore, both voice and silence may be signs of either justice or injustice (Cohen, 1990; Pinder & Harlos, 2001).

Pinder and Harlos (2001) defined employee silence as: "The withholding of any form of genuine expression about the individual's behavioral, cognitive and/or affective evaluations of his or her organizational circumstances to persons who are perceived to be capable of effecting change or redress" (p. 334). They proposed a number of causes and consequences of silence, and identified two varieties of employee silence: *Quiescence* and *acquiescence*, the latter deeper than the former in the likelihood of employee expression of change. Inspired by original research by Harlos (1998), the model expanded to observations of abuse of soldiers in the Canadian and American military. In military or quasi-military organizations, rank, decorum, and, ultimately, fear, suppress the expression of wrongdoings to one's self as well as of abuse to others. When people are afraid to speak out to register complaints or to propose corrections to the policies and practices of an organization, the potential for changes in policy and practices is diminished (Morrison & Milliken, 2000). Since the

---

[9] See Jim Jamieson (October 11, 2005). Employee theft plagues small business. CanWest News Service.

early work of Morrison and Milliken (2000), there has been a marked increase in interest in silence dynamics in recent years: The interested reader is referred to the entire September 2003 edition of the *Journal of Management Studies*.

Individual differences and reactions to inequity

Many years ago, Tornow (1971) suggested that researchers and theorists should take individual differences into account when testing predictions from equity theory. He based his suggestion on the observation that some people tend to classify certain elements of their work experiences as inputs whereas others may classify the same elements as outcomes (responsibility on the job is an example). Subsequent work tried to improve the predictive accuracy of the theory by considering the possibility that different types of people may have characteristically different cognitive and emotional reactions to conditions of perceived inequity and, if they do, taking into account these characteristic reactions when making predictions in equity research.

Accordingly, Huseman, Hatfield, and Miles (1985, 1987) and Miles, Hatfield, and Huseman (1994) proposed that we consider an individual trait they referred to as *equity sensitivity*, which would have us classify people into one of three categories. One group, called *benevolents*, comprises people who can tolerate having their own perceived equity ratios in a disadvantaged position relative to others. A second group, the *equity sensitive*, is posited to adhere to the traditional predictions of equity theory, responding with a degree of discomfort to positions of either felt overpayment or felt relative deprivation. The third category is comprised of *entitleds*, people who prefer to have things imbalanced in their favor.

One study demonstrated that members of the three groups may place greater emphasis or importance on different types of work-related outcome in equity/inequity circumstances (Miles et al., 1994). Four different factors (or groupings of outcomes) were created statistically after 20 specific outcomes were rated for importance. Some examples of the specific outcomes included "sense of accomplishment," "using one's abilities," "pay," "appreciation from others," and "job security." Factor analysis resulted in four clusters of outcomes. The entitled placed greater importance than the other two groups of employees on extrinsic, tangible outcomes such as pay, fringe benefits, and job security. There were no systematic differences between the three groups in terms of the importance they placed on extrinsic intangible outcomes such as recognition for good work and friendships on the job. Finally, the results revealed that, of the three types, the benevolents placed the highest importance on strictly intrinsic outcomes from the work, items such as "a sense of accomplishment," "doing challenging work," and "a feeling of achievement."

One of the key criticisms of equity theory over the years has concerned its predictive validity – a general weakness in making accurate, better-than-chance predictions of individual behavior and attitude changes (Mowday, 1991). As we will see later in the chapter, there may be a number of reasons for this failure. The attempt made by Huseman, Miles, and Hatfield to introduce an individual differences variable into the model was a useful step in the right direction. Moreover, there is something to be said in favor of tailoring such a new moderator variable to the theory itself rather than attempting to increase validity by subgrouping people on the basis of a common demographic variable such as age or race.[10] On the other hand, the use of such idiosyncratic constructs for the sake of improving the predictive validity of any theory – constructs that have little or no relevance or use in other scientific constructs – is a costly proposition. Taken too far, this approach could result in a proliferation of single-use, single-context variables, cluttering the landscape, and militating against the development of useful middle-range theories. At the limit, approaches such as this can border on tautology. Nevertheless, at least one new independent test and application of the equity sensitivity construct has proven useful (King, Miles, & Day, 1993), so it is too early to be critical of the idea.

---

[10] This is similar to the strategy used almost 30 years ago by Cherrington and England (1980) in the context of making better predictions about people's reactions to job redesign after previous attempts using large-scale sociological variables proved to be relatively ineffective (e.g., Hulin & Blood, 1968).

Inequity and individual reactions: The research evidence

As with the case of every other major theory of work motivation presented in this book, equity theory has come under a great deal of scrutiny and criticism from researchers and theorists. In fact, in its early years, this particular theory received some of the most voluminous and fine-grained inspection among most of the theories in this book. Perhaps one reason for this is that equity theory has been of interest not only to organizational psychologists interested in motivation and job attitudes, but also to social psychologists interested in social exchange dynamics in contexts other than the workplace (e.g., Walster, Berscheid, & Walster, 1976).

There have been many summaries of the findings and apparent validity of equity theory in the workplace over the years (e.g., Campbell & Pritchard, 1976; Carrell & Dittrich, 1978; Goodman & Friedman, 1971; Pritchard, 1969; among others). One of the most comprehensive reviews was that provided by Mowday (1991), who concluded that there was generally positive support for most predictions made by the theory but that a host of research design issues and concerns in many of the most important supportive studies of the theory raised a number of doubts about the various forms of validity we discussed in Chapter 2 of this book (particularly construct validity, internal validity, and external validity). The interested reader is referred to Mowday's (1991) work for a careful discussion of the scientific problems that plagued so much equity theory research and that, the appearance of high validity notwithstanding, leave a careful reader worried about the net validity of the theory as it applies to work motivation and employee attitudes.[11]

About the time the evidence on equity theory was being critically evaluated, other schools of thought in social psychology and other disciplines were advancing notions of fairness and justice that did not require many of the key tenets and assumptions of equity theory (see Reis, 1986, cited by Greenberg, 1987). Soon, fresh research on equity theory declined sharply and the basic substantive concerns and issues it dealt with were subsumed by justice models (see Colquitt et al., 2001; Greenberg, 1987). Accordingly, the language used henceforth in this chapter will refer increasingly to the concept of *distributive justice* and less to equity, per se.

Organizational Causes of Perceived Inequity (Distributive Injustice)

What creates feelings of inequity among employees? Most answers to this question involve the sensitivity and responsiveness of organizational reward systems. Feelings of inequitable treatment tend to occur when people believe they are not receiving fair returns for their efforts and other contributions. To prevent this sort of perception from developing, an organization must structure its reward system so that it distributes rewards in accordance with employee beliefs about their own value to the enterprise. In practice, this is very difficult. One reason is the difficulty of achieving agreement among people concerning what constitutes value ("Is your MBA degree really relevant to the work you perform here? I don't think so . . ." or, "Who cares if you held several other farm laboring jobs before coming to this one? I can train someone much younger than you are to pick as many berries as you can; probably more").

Measurement problems

Another problem is the difficulty of recognizing good performance when it occurs. Performance appraisal is a very complicated process that is fraught with potential for errors and the creation of inequities, either real or imagined. Union contracts often require that seniority be rewarded. For

---

[11] The author also discussed the problems and promises of equity theory as they appeared 15 years ago in more depth in an earlier edition of this volume (Pinder, 1998).

those who are senior, such provisions seem very equitable, because they tend to see their seniority as valuable experience (a type of input) that should be compensated. By way of contrast, junior employees often do not agree, especially when they also believe that they contribute more or better job performance to the organization than do their older colleagues. Favoritism – whether real or imagined – in all its manifestations, tends to generate feelings of inequitable treatment. Nepotism is a particularly interesting example. Members of the boss's family are often in the difficult position of making sure their coworkers see that they deserve any and all benefits they receive, sometimes to the point where the boss's family members feel they are maltreated in relation to other employees. Finally (although this list is intended to be illustrative rather than exhaustive), idiosyncratic employment agreements between an employer and an employee, whether to accommodate the employee's particular life circumstances or his or her unique skill set, can also raise concerns about fairness and equity within a work organization (Greenberg, Roberge, Ho, & Rousseau, 2004).

Alternative distribution rules

People also develop perceptions of inequity because their managers make no attempt to exercise reward and punishment systems according to the tenets of a norm of equity. Equity is only one of many "distribution rules" possible for allocating rewards and punishment in organizations (Leventhal, 1976; Sheppard et al., 1992). Depending on other goals and priorities, reward systems may be based on norms of *equality* rather than equity. The norm of equality deliberately avoids most of the intrapsychic subtleties and risks of managing by the norm of equity (see Leventhal, 1976). Equality may be chosen to maximize harmony and minimize conflict among employees. Equal treatment is easier to manage than equitable treatment because, in part, no one is required to try to imagine the perceptions of relative inputs and outcomes held by other people. Further, a norm of equality may be highly justified when there is a considerable amount of interdependence and cooperation among members of a work group. Whether by intention or through lack of courage, tacit equality norms influence many decisions made by managers and authorities in work organizations: Somehow, for some people, treating people by this norm seems so much easier and less emotionally demanding than relying on norms of equity!

Social responsibility

Sometimes a norm of *social responsibility* is the guiding principle used by management. Under these conditions, people are deliberately treated according to what they need rather than on the basis of what they deem to be fair. This principle for distributing rewards may be best when one is dealing with a friend or with someone for whom the manager feels responsible. This type of standard may be deemed more paternalistic than norms of equity or equality. It can certainly be open to problems of real or alleged favoritism. Nevertheless, it is an alternative basis for the distribution of work-related outcomes, both positive and negative, that can result in feelings of inequitable or unfair treatment by employees (see Leventhal, 1976; Sheppard et al., 1992). The point is that there are myriad practical factors in most work settings that contribute to feelings of inequity among employees. Many of these factors are difficult for managers to control. One particularly intractable problem is caused by the clash between internal norms of equity and the cost of labor in the external marketplace.

Internal and External Equity in Formal Compensation Systems

Most large organizations (as well as many smaller ones) employ some form of job evaluation system, designed to assure that there is a relationship between the amount of pay provided to incumbents of its various jobs and the value of those jobs to the organization. Although plans of this sort are often capable of providing reasonable degrees of pay equity within an organization at a particular time, they generally do not account for fluctuating labor market conditions, which can heavily influence the compensation levels necessary to attract new employees from outside. Sometimes there is a tradeoff between internal and external equity considerations. This can make it very difficult to maintain perceptions of equity inside an organization while permitting it effectively to recruit new employees from the labor market.

One solution often adopted, in part to deal with the internal versus external equity tradeoff, is to keep pay levels secret throughout the organization – people are not told how much money others earn (Miner, 1974). Pay secrecy policies have a number of interesting features. First, people often talk informally about salaries and wages, sometimes about their own and sometimes about the compensation earned by others. Often the "rumor mill" on the issue of money is not accurate, as people knowingly or inadvertently distort figures they associate with themselves and with others. There is also evidence that managers may tend honestly to underestimate the compensation levels of their superiors and overestimate the compensation levels earned by their peers and subordinates. When this occurs people are likely to feel that there is underpayment inequity vis-à-vis their subordinates. Furthermore, the belief that higher organizational levels don't fetch that much more compensation may tend to reduce the incentive value of promotions (Lawler, 1965, 1967; Milkovich & Anderson, 1972). As a result, it has been suggested on theoretical grounds that compensation levels should not be kept secret (Lawler, 1972), but that they should be opened up to the scrutiny of all concerned, despite the initial difficulties the opening-up process may create. This is a thorny issue.

The author was once part of a two-person consulting team asked to intervene in a number of personnel management problems being tackled in a small federal government agency. Central to these problems was a pay structure that had grown willy-nilly without much rationalization. There was evidence of pay discrimination on the basis of gender and a host of other anomalies that had emerged slowly over time as people's jobs had changed and as the traditions and customs of the small office prevailed over the best principles of compensation management. The author and his partner suggested (among other recommendations) that the new pay structure being proposed be opened up and made public to all members of the office. The agency's board of directors flatly refused, largely because of the opinion of one retired career personnel administrator who was afraid the roof would come off immediately after employees became aware of the proposed new realignment of salaries. The management group agreed that changes had to be made, and they realized that gossip and rumors would quickly flourish among the staff about "who makes how much now." Despite being warned about the likelihood and risks of false rumors, the managers refused to implement an open salary system. Parenthetically, they quickly accepted and adopted the many suggestions made by the author's lawyer partner in relation to other matters in the office, presumably because so many of his recommendations were shrouded in Latin terminology.

In short, the fact that organizations must recruit and retain a labor force from external markets can make the maintenance of equitable internal compensation plans a tricky problem for which no easy solution seems available. Moreover, plans of this sort can deal only with the equitable distribution of pay. They have virtually nothing to do with the equitable distribution of other forms of compensation (such as fringe benefits) or informal rewards (e.g., recognition, praise). It is very difficult, in practice, to administer rewards in a manner that will be perceived as equitable by everyone concerned.

COMPARABLE WORTH: AN ISSUE, A MOVEMENT, AND A DOCTRINE

Matters of fairness, equity, and distributive justice take on major significance when we cast them in the light of one of the major social and economic movements of the past four decades in North America (Kelly & Bayes, 1988; Killingsworth, 1990). This movement is referred to as *comparable worth* in the United States and as *pay equity* in Canada. The movement's focus is on the pay that employers provide to people who perform jobs of varying degrees of similarity, especially, as we shall see, when the workers involved are of mixed genders.

Definitions of Comparable Worth

The movement itself rests on a doctrine whose essential meaning was described by Mahoney (1987) as "equal pay for jobs of comparable (equal) worth," or in terms of the 1957 doctrine adopted by the European Community in the 1957 Treaty of Rome "equal pay for equal work" and later, in the Equal Pay Directive, for "work to which equal value is attributed" (Baker & Fortin, 2004). The surface similarity of the jobs in question is of minor importance; neither do the jobs need to be from the same organization. Therefore, comparable worth ignores (or even counteracts) the effects of the marketplace on wage rates on the grounds that entire classes of apparently dissimilar jobs have been undervalued by the market forces of supply and demand because they have traditionally been held by women. For example, if the services that a public nurse provides are considered equal in value to those provided by a person who trims trees in the same community, the doctrine of comparable worth would have the two incumbents paid the same compensation by their common employer. Quite simple *in principle*, really. There are a variety of categories of policy and practice that deal with the comparability of remuneration between and among jobs. The practical and policy implications vary significantly among them. To make our discussion of these matters as clear as possible, let's examine a few of these categories. The least-debated category is referred to as *equal pay for equal work* (Moore & Abraham, 1992, p. 456). Under the terms of the Equal Pay Act of 1963, there are four basic factors on which jobs are to be compared to determine equality or inequality: Skill, effort, responsibility, and working conditions. When these four criteria (or "compensable factors") are applied to two or more jobs and the jobs are found not to differ very much on these factors, they are deemed to be substantially equal. When two jobs are believed to be similar in terms of the four factors but still not seen as substantially equal, we have the case of *equal pay for similar work* (Moore & Abraham, 1992, p. 456). Comparable worth advocates argue that differences in pay are not justified in such cases. A second category is referred to as pay parity: "This requires that the average salary for women must equal the average salary for men, aggregated on a national basis . . . This is the most extreme view" (Moore & Abraham, 1992, p. 456). Finally, comparable worth is the category in which we have equal pay for equal work: "This means that jobs that are dissimilar, but equal in terms of value or worth to the employer, should be paid the same" (Moore & Abraham, 1992, p. 456). Any variety of job evaluation scheme or formula may be used to determine "value" and "worth," but when two or more jobs somehow are deemed to have a similar number of points of value as measured by these schemes, they should be paid the same. Of the (various) levels or standards for comparison just described, this one – comparable worth – is the most controversial (p. 456).

As noted earlier, simple notions of equality and equity are represented in varying forms and degrees within each of the four categories. We focus our discussion here on the fourth of these because it has resulted in legislation and a great deal of resistance and controversy in organizational practice. Before we begin, we note that most of the work conducted on comparable worth issues has been concerned with distributive justice – a matter of the perceived fairness, or lack thereof, of the distribution of remuneration among people and across gender groups. We recognize there are several issues concerned with *how* pay is distributed that also have relevance for the concept of comparable worth. The interested reader is referred to a paper by Greenberg and McCarty (1990) for a discussion of the relationship between procedural justice and comparable worth. The primary orientation here will be to view comparable worth as a matter of distributive justice.

Origins of the Doctrine and Movement

A number of interrelated origins provided the impetus for the comparable worth movement: the emergence of greater numbers of women in the workforce, the rise of the feminist movement, the observed disparity between the earnings made by men and women, and the powerful association of certain types of work with men and other types of work with women (Kovach & Millspaugh, 1990; Mahoney, 1987). The translation of the doctrine into legislation and practice is a major political struggle. By and large, the struggle consists of finding gender-unbiased methods for determining wages and salaries in occupations filled primarily by women, even though, in principle, the doctrine of comparable worth is a gender-neutral concept (Mahoney, 1987).

The Gender Pay Gap: The History of its Size and Importance

We have alluded to the traditional gap existing between the earnings made by men and by women. This gap, referred to here as the *gender pay gap* and *gender earnings gap* is an interesting and durable social phenomenon. Marini (1989) traced the history of the size of this gap and contributed significantly to our understanding of its origins (see also Bayes, 1988; Mahoney, 1987; Moore & Abraham, 1992, 1994). The gap is usually referred to or calibrated as a ratio of the average earnings made by women compared to the average earned by men. The figure hovered around 60% during the 1970s and began to grow in the 1980s. By 1995, the ratio stood at approximately 72% (*The Economist*, June 8, 1996) depending on how certain factors were taken into account, such as the precision of the estimates of actual wages paid, whether wages from more than one job per person were considered, the inclusion of self-employment income, the age range over which the estimates were made, and the amount of reporting error that entered into the estimate (Marini, p. 344).

Current data on the pay gap

The gender wage gap changed very little in the United States between 1920 and 1980, hovering around 60%, sometimes rising, sometimes falling. Nevertheless, recent data show that the gap continues, a number of legislative and labor economic phenomena that might have been expected to cause it to diminish notwithstanding (such as those discussed in the previous paragraph).

A large-scale study by Statistics Canada (2006) revealed that, in 2003, women working on a full-time, full-year basis had earnings that amounted to only 71% of what their Canadian male counterparts earned. A primary reason for this ongoing situation is that women make up a disproportionate share of the population in low-income jobs. The gap is even greater for unattached and single-parent income earners. A comparable study published by the Women and Work Commission (WWC) in Britain found similar results there as well as in European Union countries. The pay gap in Britain between full-time male and female workers there was estimated at 17% (*The Economist*, March 4, 2006, p. 51). The WWC study reported the comparable figures to be gaps of 15% in Europe and 20% in the United States. In short, the gap persists.

Causes of the Gender Pay Gap

Why does the gap exist? Several explanations have been offered. Early in the debate, McDonald (1977) suggested that approximately half the gap was attributable to the fact that women tend to occupy lower-paying jobs than men (as reported in the Statistics Canada report of 2006 and the British WWC report, as cited in *The Economist* in 2006) and that the other half can be attributed to discrimination against women, meaning that women are simply paid less than men even when they do the same jobs (see Konrad & Langton, 1991). On the other hand, England and McLaughlin (1979) argued against the simple discrimination explanation. They suggested that the gap exists because in addition to occupying lower-paying jobs, women tend to be at the lower pay brackets within the jobs they occupy because so many of them have entered the labor market only recently (see also Farrell, 2005). In this section, we take a look at two sets of theory that have been offered to explain the earnings gap between men and women. The first set comes largely from economics and sociology; the second comes primarily from psychology.

Economic perspectives on the pay gap

Marini (1989) categorized the causes for the wage gap into two groups, labeled supply- and demand-side causes. *Supply-side explanations* focus on the "characteristics and decisions of individual work-ers" (p. 348), including such things as the qualifications, intentions, and attitudes that women and men bring to the workforce, factors lumped under the heading of *human capital*: "To the extent that men possess greater education, skill and experience than women, they would be expected to earn more than women," and in fact, such has been the case in North America (Mahoney, 1987, p. 221). For example, some writers note that compared to men, women frequently have more discontinuous careers, dropping out of the job market more frequently and spending, overall, a smaller percentage of their lives working for remuneration. Similarly, women tend to take on a much larger share of the domestic duties than that of men. Even when women try to pursue upwardly mobile jobs where more pay might be earned, they are frequently limited in the amount of time and energy they can devote to pursuing their careers (see Mahoney, 1987; Moore & Abraham, 1992).

Demand-side explanations focus on the differential value that members of a society place on different goods and services, tradition, discrimination, and systemic features of the marketplace that perpetuate the effects of discrimination: Factors such as prejudice, differential performance expec-tations, and unjust assessment procedures (see Marini, 1989). These forces are the sort that psycholo-gists and students of organizational behavior typically offer as explanations. Mahoney (1987) observed that every society places differential degrees of value on different types of skills and services. He reported, for example, that the U.S. Census found that physicians were paid 6.5 times as much as nursing aides and orderlies.

The reason? Americans place more value on what physicians can do than on what nursing aides and orderlies can do. To the extent that men tend to occupy the more highly valued occupations, they will earn more money; and such is the case (see Moore & Abraham, 1992). Men and women tend to work in different types of job and occupation, the women's movement and other social forces and norms of egalitarianism notwithstanding. The North American labor force has virtually always been segregated by gender, and, it would seem, a pernicious self-fulfilling prophesy prevails in which one of the reasons that women and men continue to hold certain types of job is because they have always held those jobs (see more on this later and Mahoney, 1987).

There are also industry factors that affect the demand for (and therefore the value of) different forms of labor. In brief:

> Certain industries appear better able to pay than do others, and exploit this ability by offering higher wages. In a very real sense, a given occupation is worth more in one industry than in another (Mahoney, 1987).

There are also a number of institutional factors that can account for some of the observed earnings gap. One of these is trade unions. Women are proportionately underrepresented in industries in which trade unions organize workers and bargain for collective agreements with management, and other things being equal, unionized employees tend to earn more money than do nonunionized employees (Freeman & Medoff, 1984). Certain organization-level factors may also contribute. Ironically, since there are typically fewer senior women managers and executives in most organizations, there are fewer people available to serve as role models and mentors for less senior women. Therefore, women are less able to build and use networks than men, and the cycle is reinforced (see Moore & Abraham, 1992, p. 457).

In summary, there are a number of powerful "big picture" factors that can be cited as contributing to the systematic differences that we observe between the earnings of men and women in North America. The sheer intractability of these forces helps explain why and how they have continued to perpetuate the gender wage gap – they are not easily turned around or overruled. Although they may not be as big by nature, there are also many other factors of a more micro nature that may be just as difficult to change when we consider pay inequality in the workplace. We look at some of these phenomena next.

Psychological perspectives on the gap

Thirty years ago, Bartol (1978) provided an early examination of a phenomenon she referred to as the "sex-structuring of organizations" – the tendency of men to occupy the higher-status, higher-paying jobs within most North American organizations. Although somewhat similar to the arguments advanced by economists and sociologists, Bartol's reasoning adds a different perspective, based largely on the psychology of beliefs and attitudes, primarily the former (refer to Chapter 9). Although Bartol's analysis is 30 years old, it still sheds considerable light on the matter.

First, many women simply do not enter labor pools in search of jobs that are traditionally male dominated, in part because of the cultural norm just mentioned and the socialization of females that fosters it (Stein & Bailey, 1973). In addition, the lower-starting salaries offered women by some organizations discourage them from seeking employment in male-dominated occupations. (It is hard to estimate how common this practice is today because it is illegal in most Western jurisdictions.) Selection tests and procedures that are biased in favor of men and have an adverse impact on women, when applied, can reinforce the exclusion of women from applying for work in many occupations.

At the time of Bartol's (1978) analysis, there was also evidence that when they compete for jobs, women are frequently offered lower-paying positions, often of the clerical variety or some type that is consistent with the gender-labeling norm (Cash, Gillen, & Burns, 1977; Cohen & Bunker, 1975; Rosen & Jerdee, 1974a, 1974b). Moreover, women who are admitted to managerial jobs are often not provided with challenging early task assignments that give them a chance to demonstrate their competence and get off to as fast a start as their male counterparts (Rosen & Jerdee, 1974b; Rudman & Glick, 1999; Terborg, 1977). Personality traits generally associated with being "male" have traditionally been more closely related to those associated with being a manager than are "female" traits, by both males and females (Schein, 1973, 1975; Rudman & Kilianski, 2000), reinforcing the tendency to exclude women from managerial positions. Studies of women who have succeeded in climbing the corporate ladder suggest that females may have to demonstrate traits that are usually defined as male in our culture (Stein & Bailey, 1973; Van Der Merwe, 1978). Sometimes "token" women are hired into responsible positions for the sake of window dressing, often when they are not really qualified for these positions. The failures that result tend to further reinforce the prior beliefs about the competence of women for male-type (read *managerial*) positions.

During the summer of 2006, three events dealing with the status of women in business appeared in the Canadian media within a single month. First, Ms. Indra Nooyi, a woman born in India, was promoted to the position of Chief Executive Officer of PepsiCo, making her the 11th woman running a firm in the current Fortune 500 list of America's largest companies (*The Economist*, August 19, 2006, p. 51). In Canada, in the same week, the Executive Director of *REAL Women of Canada* (a conservative social movement) claimed in the national media that it is time to abolish a branch of the Canadian government named the *Status of Women Canada*, a service established approximately 30 years ago to help with the advancement of women's rights in the country. Ms. Gwendolyn Landolt, the ED, stated that the existence of the branch is:

> [B]ased on the premise that women are allegedly victims of a patriarchal society and need support and special recognition . . . Our view is that the vast majority of women are not victims, and quite capable of making decisions in their lives.
>
> (*Times Colonist*, August 25, 2006, p. A9)[12]

And, coincidentally, *Catalyst* (2006), a nonprofit research and advisory organization with the goals of "building inclusive environments and expand[ing] opportunities for women at work" reported that the glass ceiling[13] is not eroding very much or very quickly. Based on the career progress of Fortune 500 women executives, the *Catalyst* study found that, in the previous three years (2002–2005), the average growth in the percent of corporate officer positions held by women fell to 0.23 percentage points per year, the lowest annual gain in a decade. During that 3-year period, the total number of women corporate officers increased by only 0.7 percentage points to 16.4%! The study concluded that, at this rate of progress, it could take four decades for women to achieve parity with men among the ranks of top corporate positions in America (see Tallarico & Gillis, 2007). CanWest News Service recently reported an internal study conducted by the Royal Canadian Mounted Police (RCMP) that found female officers in the force continue to believe that their rights are too-frequently violated and that they do not earn the respect they deserve from the male-dominated culture in which they work (*Times Colonist*, October 29, 2007, p. A1). The paucity of women in senior ranks in the RCMP was one example cited; another was the high incidence of sexual harassment they endure. Alleged unfairness and rights violations, as we saw in Chapter 5, are particularly frequent in military (and paramilitary) organizations.

Again: Women often hold the same sex-role views about the suitability for men and women to hold certain types of job as men hold. Rudman and Kilianski (2000) have reviewed three competing (yet converging) hypotheses to explain this ongoing phenomenon. One is the gender role hypothesis, which holds that, to the extent that people associate men with career roles and women with domestic roles, they will tend also to view women in authority as somehow violating the basic division of roles. A second hypothesis, the gender authority hypothesis, "posits that labor divisions within the workplace signify different status expectancies for men and women" (Rudman & Kilianski, p. 1316). In other words, males are afforded greater status simply by virtue of being male.

Finally, the gender stereotype hypothesis "posits that different trait expectancies for men and women underlie negative attitudes toward female authority" (p. 1316). Using both a measure of implicit attitudes as well as a conscious measure, Rudman and Kilianski (2000) found that both male and female college students revealed preferences for having men in authority positions rather than women, although the women were more egalitarian toward female authority when an explicit measure (in the form of a self-report questionnaire) was used to solicit their responses rather than a response latency technique that has often been used in research to reveal attitudes and beliefs. In an earlier study, Rudman and Glick (1999) showed that these biases may cause women to be evaluated as lacking in social skills (i.e., niceness) when they act in agentic (culturally male) ways. This can lead to discrimination against the hiring of women in jobs, especially when the jobs in question are "feminized" – i.e., require "niceness."

Eagly and Karau (2002) also demonstrated that there is still a considerable bias against women

---

[12] The Canadian government followed this sentiment a month later, cutting the budget for the *Status of Women*.
[13] The metaphorical term *glass ceiling* refers to the forces that systematically inhibit the upward movement of women in work organizations.

in leadership roles in our society. Somehow, it is still the case that women are perceived less favorably as leaders than men and that women's leadership behaviors are too-frequently evaluated less favorably than those enacted by men. Moreover, work done by women is often not as highly evaluated as work done by men, *even when women evaluate the jobs*. Using role congruity theory to explain these prejudices, Eagly and Karau (2002) observed that it is still the case that many in our culture view concepts of leadership and womanhood as incongruous.

The role of context (again)

There is a temptation for many of us to conclude that the sex discrimination tendencies described here are solely a result of people's traits and personality predispositions. Glick and Fiske (in press) have argued, consistent with the importance we have placed on contextual factors throughout this book (see Chapter 2, especially), that "acts of discrimination are not committed only by obvious bigots . . . discrimination . . . is a situation-dependent social phenomenon" (p. 4). Hence the norms of an individual's immediate work group provide an example of proximate contexts that can influence discriminatory acts while more distal forces, such as the types of sex role stereotypes that are found throughout our society, can also exert powerful influences. The reader is referred to Glick and Fiske (in press) for a further explication of these arguments. Regardless of the causal factors involved (personalities or traits, proximate or distal contextual effects), the fact remains that men and women in our culture still hold beliefs about men and women and about the nature of work each sex group is better suited to pursue. The research cited in the previous two paragraphs reveals that things have not changed much since the pioneering work of Schein (1973, 1975) on the tendency to associate men with agency and authority and to associate women with niceness and nurturing, and that, somehow, violations of these expectations are not natural. Moreover, even though Bartol's (1978) theory of the sex-structuring of organizations was solidly predicated on theory, research, and practice that were current when she published it nearly three decades ago, many of the factors Bartol identified, such as childrearing practices and difficulties in job evaluation and performance appraisal techniques, for example, are slow to change. A recent assessment of the social costs and benefits of affirmative action policies and programs in the United States (Crosby, Iyer, Clayton, & Downing, 2003) confirms that, even if things have improved in America since Bartol's (1978) time, there is still plenty of room for further improvement.

Criticisms of the Comparable Worth Doctrine

Reference was made earlier to the resistance that comparable worth has encountered by people who have to implement it and manage it as policy. Let's take a brief look at the sources of this resistance with the help of Waluchow (1988) (see also Moore & Abraham, 1994). One of the key sources of difficulty, Waluchow claimed, is that some people adopt the position that it is not clear that the reason for the gap is discrimination; rather, the main causes are legitimate human capital factors of the sort reviewed earlier (e.g., women are less educated than men, or have less seniority in many cases).

A second source of resistance is fear of the very high cost that businesses and government would incur if the pay gap is closed. A third, related concern held by some critics is that closing the pay gap would decrease the demand for labor, especially in those sectors of the economy dominated by women employees. According to this view, well-intentioned policies designed to bring about social equity and fairness would backfire, hurting the very people the policies are designed to help.

There is also the problem of deciding how to determine when work of equal value is, in fact, of equal value. In other words, how can we decide which jobs are of equal value? Whose criteria are to be used? Who is to decide? This puzzle has been cited by a number of authors over the years, but few have addressed it other than to state that "the market" will determine relative value. Nevertheless,

Waluchow (1988) listed eight possible answers to the question: How does one determine the worth or value of someone's work so as to compare it with the work of others? He generated the following list:

1. By whatever value the existing market (i.e., an employer) will pay for it.
2. By whatever a fair market would pay for it.
3. By what she deserves for doing it.
4. By how much her work contributes to the success of the firm.
5. By how much her work contributes to the community.
6. By whatever the going rate is in "the industry" for people who perform the same work.
7. By whatever value her work is assigned by her employer's explicit wage policy.
8. By whatever value her work is assigned by her employer's implicit wage policy.

Kelly and Bayes (1988) identified another fundamental source of disagreement that is somewhat hidden in our eight-point list. There is a simple lack of agreement among interested parties concerning who should *implement* comparable worth policies even if they are accepted in principle: Legislatures, unions, courts, or executives?

In summary, there are many ideological and practical sources of resistance to the doctrine of comparable worth, how acceptable it might seem at face value notwithstanding. The resistance is often quite passionate and even hostile. Consider, for example, the following excerpts from a column by Barbara Amiel (1985), a right-leaning critic who appears in a number of magazines around the world, including *Maclean's* in Canada. The title of her column was "The dangerous cost of equal pay." In accordance with the market value concept (Smith, 1937, cited by Mahoney, 1987), Amiel (1985, p. 9) wrote:

> Of all the concepts that the totalitarian instinct of our times has bequeathed to society – including racial and gender job quotas and laws against free speech – the seemingly harmless slogan "equal pay for work of equal value" is potentially the most destructive to a free society . . .

> The value of a job is determined by nothing but supply and demand. Value depends upon how many people require a service and how many others are willing to provide it. Nobody in his right mind would decide that a performer of pop tunes is a more skilled musician than the concertmaster of a symphony orchestra, but the demand for one outstrips the other and often so does the pay. My own classical preference may be for a classical violinist, but that is a minority view; most people want to hear Madonna . . .

> To stop this steamroller policy will require fighting shortsighted and narrow-minded feminists as well as cowardly politicians. But if our society wishes to retain equality of opportunity and liberty, the fight must be won.

Although written more than 20 years ago, Amiel's position continues to be embraced by many other critics; for them, the entire process of equating jobs that are inherently different amounts to replacing the natural forces of supply and demand in a democratic, capitalist society with a contrived, arbitrary set of wages and salaries of the sort found in controlled economies.

Comparable Worth and Pay Equity Over the Millennia

One of the earliest manifestations of the doctrine of comparable worth can be found in the Old Testament:[14]

---

[14] The author acknowledges the scholarship of Michael Evan Gold (1983) for drawing his attention to this passage.

And the Lord spoke to Moses, saying, Speak unto the children of Israel, and say unto them: When a man shall clearly utter a vow of persons unto the Lord, according to thy valuation, then thy valuation for the male from twenty years old even unto sixty years old, even thy valuation shall be fifty shekels of silver, after the shekel of the sanctuary. And, if it be female, then thy valuation shall be thirty shekels.

(Leviticus 27: 1–4)

Although the author is not a Biblical scholar, a Jew, or even an adherent of the dictates of the Old Testament, the power of this passage reflects the importance of the comparable worth doctrine when we take into account the point made by Mahoney (1987) on the phenomenological significance of pay equity and, with it by extension, employment equity. Mahoney wrote:

In other words, there is more to comparable worth than fairness in economic treatment of people by their employers. There are issues of human dignity and self-esteem deeply associated with the simply pay aspects of the work relationship.

(Mahoney, 1987, p. xxi)

The very age of the passage is also important in its own right: It demonstrates that people have been concerned with these matters for a long time! Nevertheless, a cursory scan of current business magazines and the popular press in Canada over recent years yields the impression that pay equity and employment equity (more broadly) are less contentious as social issues than they were 15 to 25 years ago, when gender-based employment inequities were "hot" social and political topics. That is, it seems that it was much more popular and acceptable to speak and write about employment equity, affirmative action, and minority rights 25 years ago (e.g., Pinder, 1984) than it is now, in the early years of the new millennium. Yet, the evidence presented in the previous section indicates that the problem persists. How can we explain this apparent paradox?

David McPhillips, a leading British Columbia labor arbitrator and Professor Tom Knight, a labor management scholar and practitioner at the Sauder School of Management at the University of British Columbia, believe that this may be true and that there may be a number of reasons for the decline in popular interest in Canada.

First, McPhillips noted that employment equity was installed as formal, official policy in only a few jurisdictions and industries in Canada – largely in the public sector and government, such as the federal government and Bell Canada – while other jurisdictions that had expressed early interest in the doctrine (e.g., Ontario and Manitoba) backed away from implementing it, largely due to considerations of cost. Nevertheless, the high profile of the doctrine and its application has had a large spillover effect into the consciousness of many practitioners in other sectors in recent years. Second, he observes that many labor markets these days are so tight – so much in demand of talented labor – that few employers can afford to discriminate on the basis of sex.

Third, both Knight and McPhillips have stated that years of media content and coverage, formal education, law suits, high-profile arbitration hearings, immigration policy, and management training and development have simply caused a decline in the social acceptability of unfair discrimination practices – on the basis of any demographic characteristic. Knight observed: "Continuing developments in human rights litigation are pushing out the boundaries of employment equity . . . Various challenges to employment requirements [and] tests are effectively increasing opportunities for those formerly (and questionably) prevented from entering certain fields" (personal communication, 2006). He cited the particular, recent legal case brought by a woman challenging the traditional tests that favor males over females applying for jobs as firefighters in the province of British Columbia. Knight continued: "All this ties into the concept of '*bona fide* occupational requirements' – a test that puts the burden on employers to justify their employment requirements on business grounds." In addition, McPhillips suggested that fairness may have become more socially expected or even more often viewed as inherently the right thing to do (the deontic view – justice as inherently worthwhile – as we discussed earlier in this chapter). Finally, he cited the massive influence of globalization in all its manifestations: People in business may be becoming more color blind, if only for instrumental reasons and practicality (recall our discussion of the philosophical underpinnings for norms of justice, addressed early in this chapter).

McPhillips' insights notwithstanding, a recent economic analysis of the effects of comparable worth legislation in Ontario (Canada's largest province) attested to the failure of the law in that jurisdiction. There were two key findings: First, that there were widespread lapses in the application of the law, especially among small organizations in the private sector (where the majority of the workforce are employed); second, the law had no noticeable effect on the aggregate wages paid to men and women (Baker & Fortin, 2004).

Dr. Faye Crosby, a leading U.S. academic who has studied these matters for many years has stated that if, indeed, the attention paid to matters of equity, fairness, and justice in the American workplace has declined in recent years, it may be because of the marginal gains that have been achieved through legislation, litigation, education, and the other processes cited by Messrs Knight and McPhillips.[15] Besides, she observes, the media tend to like new things to cover, so injustice (in all its forms) in the workplace may now be "old news" relative to other current social issues.

American author and critic Warren Farrell (2005) recently offered some fascinating insights in a recent book *Why men earn more*. Although Farrell does not dispute the aggregate gender gap in pay cited by other authorities (and reported here), Farrell observed that women are actually paid, on average, considerably more than men in many diverse occupations (e.g., sales engineering, radiation therapy, agriculture and food science, meter readers, library technicians, and funeral service workers). The crux of his analysis to explain the overall wage gap, however, lies in his argument that people, men or women, earn more when they adhere to one or more of 25 different tactics in choosing work and careers. A few examples reported in Farrell's (2005) book include:

- Choose a field in technology or the hard sciences rather than in the arts or sciences.
- Choose work where you get hazard pay without the real hazards.
- Among lower-paying jobs, choose those that expose you to the outdoors and bad weather rather than indoor, office settings.
- Choose jobs with higher levels of emotional risk.
- Choose jobs that require more working hours, travel, and long commutes.

Another factor that makes a difference in a person's chances to move to the top of pay scales and organizational hierarchies, according to Farrell, is the capacity to stay on the job, without interruptions to one's career. An article in *The Economist* (July 23, 2005, p. 11) made the same point. Farrell analyzed the work that men and women typically perform (we discussed work role stereotypes earlier) and observes that because of the choices men and women make in the tradeoff between work and other pursuits (such as childrearing), it is natural that men, in the aggregate, earn more than women. Farrell's (2005) book is a fascinating and well-documented analysis that leads him to adopt a position that has generally been politically incorrect for many years. It bears close scrutiny.

On balance, when one considers all the economic, historical, sociological, and psychological factors that come to play on the issue, this author expects the aggregate gender pay gap to continue for at least another quarter century. The only question will be whether the gap widens, stays fixed, or somehow manages to continue to close, slowly.

---

[15] The opinions of Mr. McPhillips, Dr. Knight, and Dr. Crosby (cf. Crosby, Iyer, Clayton, & Downing, 2003) were gathered through personal communications with the author in the summer of 2006.

Summary and a Glance Ahead

To this point in the present chapter, we have taken an extended look at the key principles of equity theory and distributive justice, focusing particular attention on the applied social issue of comparable worth. The key point underlying the discussion is the fact that people develop perceptions, beliefs, attitudes, and emotional reactions to the ways by which valued resources such as pay are *distributed* among people. We have also indicated, using a quasi-historical approach, how traditional equity theory from the 1960s (e.g., Adams, 1963) came to be subsumed as one key element of the broader body of justice theory (cf. Colquitt, Le Pine, & Noe, 2000; Greenberg, 1987).

This conjoining of theory does not provide grounds to ignore simple notions of equity, however. Indeed, equity remains a central strand in theories of rewards and compensation, psychological contracts, and even organizational change. For example, a recent study of downsizing in Finland found that the effects of past downsizing experiences and employees' expectations of future downsizing affected their health and well-being as well as their job attitudes and thoughts about retirement. The key parameter mediating the effects of downsizing concerns on the dependent variables was employees' perceptions of equity in the exchange relationships they had with their organization (Kalimo, Taris, & Schaufeli, 2003). In short, whether it is called equity or distributive justice, this form of fairness is critically important in work organizations and in the lives of working people.

In the two remaining sections of this chapter, we direct our attention away from the outcomes of distribution decisions and toward matters of fairness and justice related to the *means by which rewards and punishments are distributed in a society (or a workplace)*. We will see that attention can be paid to both (1) the formal procedures that an organization prescribes for the administration of justice, and (2) the informal, interpersonal dynamics that actually characterize the delivery of rewards and sanctions. The first of these topics is referred to as *procedural justice*. The second issue is referred to as *interactional justice*. We now deal with research and theory pertaining to both phenomena in sequence.

PROCEDURAL JUSTICE IN THE WORKPLACE

The procedures by which managers distribute work-related outcomes have justice implications that are different from the actual decisions themselves. That is, as early as the 1970s, researchers were finding that "the distribution of rewards was not always as important as the process by which they were allocated" (Cohen-Charash & Spector, 2001). Accordingly, the last 25 years have witnessed considerable theory and research under the rubric of *procedural justice*. This new school of thought has not supplanted the earlier focus on distributive and equity matters, but it has provided fresh insights into matters of fairness and justice at work (Greenberg, 1987, 1990c).

Definitions of Procedural Justice

Folger and Greenberg (1985) "conceive of procedural justice as the perceived fairness of the procedures used in making decisions" (p. 143). They noted that regardless of "whether the outcomes are pay raises to be distributed to employees, labor disputes to be settled, or performance evaluations to be recorded, a key determinant of these decisions involves *how* they are made" (p. 143).

In a book devoted exclusively to the importance of justice in the management of human resources, Folger and Cropanzano (1998, p. 26) wrote:

"Procedural justice" refers to fairness issues concerning the methods, mechanisms, and processes used to determine outcomes. For example, these issues might involve considerations about the proper way to conduct a decision-making process, a dispute-resolution process, or an allocation process.

Two common elements of procedurally-just practices are those in which employees have some degree of participation in decision making, or "voice" (Folger, 1977, 1987) and the degree to which they have an element of process control (Thibault & Walker, 1975). The earliest focus of procedural justice in organizational behavior and human resources management was on the procedures used to resolve disputes in the workplace (see Thibault & Walker, 1975, 1978; Colquitt et al., 2000). Since then, scholars have broadened their attention to the procedural justice issues related to a variety of workplace matters, such as personnel selection (Arvey, 1979; Singer, 1992), reward allocation (see Leventhal, 1976, 1980), performance evaluation procedures (Folger, 1987), organizational change (Beer, Eisenstat, & Spector, 1990), discipline, compensation systems, and participatory decision-making systems (see Greenberg & Cropanzano, 2001; Konovsky, 2000, for two recent reviews).

Antecedents of Procedural Justice

One of the earliest attempts to define distributive justice in social psychology identified six dimensions in the construct (Leventhal, 1980). By this view, procedures are fair if they are made:

- with consistent procedures
- without self-interest
- on the basis of accurate information
- with opportunities to make corrections
- with the interests of all legitimate parties taken into account
- while observing moral and ethical standards.

For the sake of emphasizing the distinction between procedural and distributive justice, notice that none of these six criteria (or dimensions) mentions the nature of the outcomes of decisions. Rather, they all deal with the nature of the formal procedures used. As we see later, the wisdom in discerning these six dimensions – sometimes referred to in the later literature as the "Leventhal criteria" – was profound and robust (cf. Colquitt, Conlon, Wesson, Porter, & Ng, 2001).

Consequences: The Importance of Procedural Justice

Adhering to the tenets of procedural justice and avoiding the pratfalls of procedural injustice has been demonstrated time and again to be a key element in attaining good things for employees and organizations while avoiding bad things. Several researchers have shown that employees are much more willing to accept less-than-favorable distributions of outcomes (which would otherwise be viewed as distributional injustice) when procedures are perceived to be fair and equitable (Brockner & Siegel, 1996; Colquitt et al., 2001). *In other words, solid procedural justice can assuage, offset, or mitigate some of the normal dysfunctions of distribution problems.*

One of the key reasons procedural justice can have beneficial effects is that it engenders trust – it helps people form beliefs about the future behaviors of other people. Brockner and Siegel (1996, p. 401) wrote:

> In deciding whether the party is trustworthy, individuals draw on information about the party that is perceived to be stable – that is, in which the past is believed to be a good predictor of the future . . . Thus, when current procedures are fair (or unfair), it is reasonable to believe that future procedures

also will be fair (or unfair). Trust, in short, is affected by people's estimates of the future level of procedural justice.

Procedural Justice and Job Performance

For many years, there were mixed data on the question of whether procedural justice yields benefits in terms of employee job performance. However, a thorough meta-analysis conducted on the issue by Cohen-Charash and Spector (2001) found that, indeed, procedural justice *does* tend to be positively correlated with job performance, whereas distributive justice and interactional justice do not (on a consistent basis).

Procedural justice is important to people for a number of other reasons as well. With procedural fairness comes trust, as mentioned, and that can provide the basis for ongoing social exchange, which is believed by some social scientists (e.g., Blau, 1993) to be a primary basis for interaction among people (recall Chapters 5 and 6). Procedural justice can also facilitate instrumental or economic exchange among parties; again, largely through the trust it engenders. In short, for people to interact over the long haul, they must trust one another so the provision of fair and just procedures for their exchange relations is critical. Harmonious relations within organizations are no different, so there must be minimum levels of trust among coworkers, especially superiors and subordinates, in order for collective work to be accomplished (Kramer & Tyler, 1996).

Balance, Correctness, and the Eye of the Beholder (Again)

For Sheppard et al. (1992; see also Minton, Lewicki, & Sheppard, 1994) a decision is perceived as fair if the outcomes are seen as *balanced* and *correct*. Their concept of balance is central to distributive justice, which we dealt with earlier. By *balance*, they mean that an act by (for example) a manager "is compared to similar actions in similar situations. If the act is seen as roughly equivalent to actions in these situations, it is seen as fair; if it is seen as not equivalent, it is judged as unfair . . . [T]he same punishment should be applied to all who commit the same crime" (Minton et al., 1994, p. 139).

Their concept of *correctness* also gets at the nub of the matter of procedural justice. Minton and colleagues argue that perceptions about the correctness of the procedures followed in decisions are as important as perceptions about the outcomes of those decisions. "By 'correctness,' we mean that quality which makes the decision seem right – a determination that the decision seems to be compatible with qualities of consistency, accuracy, clarity, procedural thoroughness, and compatibility with the morals and values of the times" (Minton et al., 1994, p. 140). For example, an employee may be unhappy about the absolute amount of pay increase he receives, but he may ultimately feel that he was treated fairly if the procedures used to determine that amount are explained to him and are seen as appropriate. In other words, "perceived procedural fairness may help mitigate the effects of perceived unjust outcomes (i.e., low raises, missed promotions, or small budgets)" (Sheppard et al., 1992, p. 17).

Levels of justice

In addition to the issues of balance and correctness, fairness perceptions are seen as operating on at least three different *levels*, referred to as outcome, procedure, and system: "At the outcome level, judgments are made about the balance and correctness of particular results, for example, a pay raise, a layoff, or a dismissal. At the procedural level, judgments are made about the balance and correctness of the procedures and processes by which decisions are made: How a raise is determined or how a layoff decision is implemented. Finally, at the systemic level, judgments are made about the broader organizational systems in which procedures are generated and embedded" (Minton et al., 1994, p. 141).

This three-way distinction implies that judgments about the fairness of the system must usually be based on the observation of a number of treatments and decisions by some people about others. For example, an employee may feel that a coworker has been treated harshly and unfairly by a supervisor upon coming to work late for the first time. The observer may have feelings about the balance and correctness of the outcome (a verbal reprimand) and even about the procedure used (the supervisor decides that the employee was late even though there was a misunderstanding about the starting time). But a decision about the fairness of the system as a whole must be based on the observation of *many* instances of lateness and disciplinary acts for lateness, as well as upon occurrences of other forms of crime and punishment.

In short, the concepts of balance are seen as independent (Folger & Greenberg, 1985) of the levels of the judgment. Perceptions of either or both balance and correctness may be made by an employee about specific outcomes ("I didn't get a raise"), about procedures ("The boss didn't refer to my performance review before she denied me a raise"), or about the broader system that governs decisions ("I think the company should refer to our formal performance reviews before making decisions about our raises!").

The goals of decision making

For Sheppard and his colleagues (Minton et al., 1994; Sheppard et al., 1992) perceptions of balance and correctness can also be affected by the *goals* of a person or an organization in decision making. One goal is *performance effectiveness*. A second goal is a concern for a *sense of community*. Here the goal and the basis for assessment of fairness is whether people manage to coalesce, to form groups, and to work in harmony. A third goal involves a concern for *individual dignity* and *humaneness*. If the purpose of decision making has implications for these goods, the assessment of fairness (via balance and correctness) takes on yet another frame of reference.

Sheppard and his colleagues (1992) pointed out that the goals associated with decision making can often be in conflict. For example, if rewards and punishments are distributed with performance as the primary goal, individual or group achievement will be rewarded, possibly undermining the sense of esprit de corps of those who did not do so well (thereby compromising the community goal). Yet if rewards are distributed *equally* among employees for the sake of maintaining harmony, the incentive value of the rewards is diminished and the goal of performance effectiveness is compromised. These clashes among goals are especially common in work settings where different parties may favor different goals, such that any set of decisions about reward distribution may alienate all but a few people (whose own goals have been served at the expense of the goals of those who are not rewarded).

To make matters even more complex, perception plays as big a role in the determination of procedural justice as it does in assessments of distributive justice, as discussed earlier. For example, a manager may distribute rewards and sanctions according to a strict norm of equality because she wishes to serve a goal of community and harmony. Her employees may or may not understand that the benefits are being distributed equally, even if they all accept the wisdom of her choice of goal. As a result, many of the employees may be disgruntled and lose faith in the manager. As in the case of distributive justice, fairness is in the eye of the beholder when we consider the procedures by which decisions are made.

Procedural Justice and Downsizing

Downsizing is the planned elimination of positions or jobs. It can entail the elimination of whole groups, departments, or levels of an organization, usually necessitated by economic exigencies or organizational redesign. People are laid off permanently and involuntarily (although in some cases, people are called back to work if and when economic conditions improve). Downsizing is different from firing people for cause, although principles and considerations of procedural justice are definitely relevant in the case of firing for cause as well, as we will see later. The authors whose work is cited here all have based their suggestions on real experiences with downsizing in major North American enterprises. Before we begin, we must note that there are at least two major groups affected by downsizing and layoffs: The victims and the survivors. We concern ourselves here with the motivational effects of downsizing on both groups, beginning with the victims.

The interactive effects of outcome and procedural fairness were illustrated more than a decade ago in a study of the fallout effects from company layoffs (Brockner et al., 1994). Following Folger's (1986) *referent cognitions theory*, Brockner and his colleagues reasoned that: "The joint presence of negative outcomes and low procedural fairness will elicit particularly negative reactions. To state the predicted interaction differently, when procedural justice is low, outcome negativity should have an adverse effect on individuals' reaction" (p. 398). Studying three different groups of employees who had been affected one way or another by layoffs by their employers, they supported their hypothesis. One group consisted of 218 layoff victims who were applying for the first time for unemployment benefits. Most of them had worked in the service sector. The second group (of 150 people) was referred to as layoff survivors: They had kept their jobs in a financial services organization that had undergone layoffs about half a year earlier than the study. The third group studied were 147 employees who were about to be laid off from a large unionized manufacturing plant in the southern United States. Because the people in each of the three groups were in entirely different circumstances, the researchers used different measures of what they called outcome negativity as their dependent variable. The researchers were especially interested in the role played by advance notice among those who had been laid off (group 1) and who were about to be laid off (group 3).

Without getting into the nuances of the different measures for the different groups, we can summarize the findings by reporting that, as predicted, the employees reported lower levels of outcome negativity (such as low levels of organizational trust and commitment) when they perceived that appropriate steps had been taken to treat them fairly in the context of the various layoff experiences they had had. It seems that perceived fairness in process helped to assuage some of the bitterness and dissatisfaction that employees experienced, whether they had been laid off, survived a layoff, or were about to be laid off.

The key role of trust

One possible explanation for the interaction of distributive and procedural justice on employee attitudes was proposed by Siegel, Brockner, and Tyler (1995). They suggested that employees who have experiences that they perceive to be fair in terms of process and procedures will be more likely to develop feelings of *trust* toward their employers. These positive feelings may then serve to make the effects of harsh or undesirable outcomes (to use disappointing pay increases as one example) less damaging to their feelings toward the employer.

In other words, procedural justice may help to build trust, which in turn may help to offset or assuage the negative impact of distributive decisions. Siegel and her colleagues also suggest that the procedural justice–trust development connection is probably not as strong during times of scarcity of resources (Siegel et al., 1995). Nevertheless, a subsequently published conceptual model proposed that employee trust in management is key. That is, "When [there is] trust in management (because survivors believe that management is competent, reliable, open, and concerned about all stakeholders) a perceived just implementation of the downsizing . . . will reduce threat assessments and, in turn, will lead to more cooperative survivor responses" (Mishra & Spreitzer, 1998, p. 568).

On that point, a recent paper by Elangovan, Auer-Rizzi, and Szabo (2007) demonstrated in German and Austrian samples that trust can be eroded by trustees (those of whom we make expectations) when they repeatedly violate the trust held by trustors (those who make the expectations).

The erosion of trust is particularly strong when the trustor attributes the failure to meet expectations to causes internal to the trustee. ("It was her fault; she has no excuses for disappointing me.") Elangovan et al. (2007) also found that the degree of erosion of trust increases with successive breaches. That is, a person is much more willing to overlook a first breech of trust than he is to overlook a second breech (by the same trustee). The aphorism "Fool me once, shame on you; fool me twice, shame on me" seems to apply here (Elangovan et al., 2007).

The implications of this research are that organizations that institute major changes should be careful in assuring victims and survivors that further rounds of change and attendant violations of psychological contracts may or may not be forthcoming. The worst-case scenario is to disrupt these contracts and imply (or promise) that no further disruptions will occur, only to do it again to employees. For example, successive waves of downsizing are bound to make employees anxious, angry, and feel betrayed. Once this has happened, trust stands no chance as a basis to generate cooperation with subsequent management decisions. Once lost, trust is hard to regain (cf. Elangovan & Shapiro, 1998; Kramer & Tyler, 1996; Morrison & Robinson, 1997).

The Motivational Effects of Downsizing on Victims

The involuntary loss of a job can be one of the most stressful events in a person's life. Even if the person is placed out of work because of economic necessity as seen by the company (as opposed to being fired for "cause," which we discuss later), the impact on the person's sense of worth and self-esteem can be devastating. Many people witness depression, decreased life satisfaction, increased social isolation, and feelings of powerlessness. Some people also experience a loss of their sense of time and the development of feelings of apathy, passivity, and resignation. Many studies have reported that people experience a degeneration of their physical health and well-being. Suicide is not unusual (see Ahlberg, 1986). Although it is true that some people experience more positive reactions, such as a sense of relief and hope that they can restore more hope into their lives (Leana & Feldman, 1994), the vast bulk of the work in social science has been devoted to the negative effects on people and the means they use to cope with the emotional and physical damage caused by job loss.

The first reaction is usually to assess the seriousness of the job loss for the person's own life and circumstances. The more intensely the loss is experienced, the more the person attributes the cause to herself, the less reversible the loss is seen to be, the higher is the short-term stress experienced by the person (Leana & Feldman, 1994). In the longer term, people who lose their jobs can suffer difficulties of financial hardship, strains on marital and familial relationships, increasingly greater isolation from friends and acquaintances, and new or renewed careerist attitudes (i.e., less willingness to commit to an employer while adopting a mercenary attitude about working). Frequently, when unemployed people manage to find new jobs, they accept positions of lower quality and value than the ones they originally lost, and the diminished sense of pride and self-esteem may not rebound to levels that existed before the layoff. Simply finding a new job may not end the emotional and physical damage that result from job loss; these problems may become chronic conditions (Leana & Feldman, 1994).

Earlier, we said that being the victim of downsizing can have deleterious effects on victims' attitudes toward work and working. One study suggested that these negative effects tend to dissipate over time, and that people who are earlier in their careers may be affected more negatively than employees who are at more advanced career stages when they are outplaced (Allen, Freeman, Reizenstein, & Rentz, 1995). The types and amounts of social support offered by the company during layoffs is critical to the severity of the initial impact on the victim as well as upon his or her success in dealing with the longer-term considerations of adjustment and finding reemployment. Accordingly, let's look at what experience has taught us about the policies and procedures that have been used to assuage some of the negative effects of layoffs. As we do, let us keep in mind the three dimensions of outcomes, procedures, and systems and how they all may have elements of both balance and correctness in how we view them. (We will also keep in mind that different goals are served by managerial decisions on downsizing, although the continued survival of the enterprise is usually paramount in these cases.)

Employer policies and practices in layoffs: Implications for victims

First and foremost, advance notice of layoffs is clearly an important managerial tactic when down-sizing is required (see Baker, 1988; Feldman & Leana, 1989; Settles, 1988). There is virtual agreement on this policy among all authors and practitioners. Notice that we are talking here about multiple or mass layoffs caused by economic exigency facing the organization, not dismissal for cause. Some authors have stressed the importance of adequate severance pay and extended health benefits (Feldman & Leana, 1989; Settles, 1988). Outplacement assistance in the form of office space, secretarial help, personal counseling, and job search training has been offered by many organizations that have laid people off (see Feldman & Leana, 1989; Settles, 1988). Severance pay, one of the most frequently used corporate interventions to mitigate the negative effects on laid-off workers may have a deleterious effect on coping behavior, however (Leana, Feldman, & Tan, 1998).

It is important to make the *reasons* for the layoffs clear to people and to make the criteria used to select among victims and survivors explicit and honest (Feldman & Leana, 1989; Fisher, 1988). This is a matter of interactional justice: If sound reasons are offered for the bad news, the bad news is easier for recipients to take (Greenspan, 2000). If management wishes to use performance as its criterion, it becomes especially critical that performance appraisal procedures be valid, regular, and perceived as fair. One study of the criteria favored by unions and management for selecting among employees found that seniority, not job performance, was preferred by both management and union respondents, presumably out of a shared norm of fairness and respect for employees who have given more of their time to their companies (McCune, Beatty, & Montagno, 1988).

Treating layoff victims with dignity and respect, both at the time of the layoffs and afterward, is important (Brockner, 1988b; Feldman & Leana, 1989; Fisher, 1988; Greenspan, 2000). This means that disparaging comments about the departed after they have left must be discouraged (see Bies & Moag, 1986). Settles (1988) suggests the use of exit interviews with departing employees and a system of employee tracking that can be used in case of callbacks. It is usually recommended that layoffs be conducted all at once rather than a few at a time (Feldman & Leana, 1989). Feldman and Leana (1989) stress the importance of working with whatever unions are involved in a worksite to determine the procedures to be used, although the evidence related to this suggestion is sparse (see Baker, 1988, for a discussion of some of the issues involved). Regardless, open and honest communication to employees about the reasons for the downsizing, the criteria being applied to determine who is to be let go and who is to survive, and careful execution of procedures are necessary for downsizing with the dignity of employees in mind (Greenspan, 2000).

Some authors discuss how companies can develop reputations from the unfair methods they use during layoffs (Feldman & Leana, 1989; Greco & Woodlock, 1989; Newman, 1988) and how these reputations can affect the capacity of the company to attract new employees in better times. Presumably, reputations for being unfair can result from perceptions that layoff decisions are not balanced or correct, that they rely on capricious decisions by biased managers, and/or that there are either no policies or misguided policies in place to guide layoff decisions (see Minton et al., 1994; Sheppard et al., 1992). Again: Procedural justice is a matter of perception, and large, public organizations are under the scrutiny of many observers, both inside their boundaries and beyond those boundaries.

Earlier in the chapter we referred to a study by Brockner et al. (1994), which demonstrated in three different samples how perceptions of procedural fairness among layoff victims helped offset the negative impact of the experience on victims. Translating the general principles of procedural justice into active organizational policies is the trick. Principles of fairness such as those identified by Sashkin and Williams (1990), mentioned earlier, must be made to come alive and have real meaning for layoff victims if the motivational and other consequences of the trauma of job loss are to be minimized.

Motivational effects of layoffs on survivors

For a variety of reasons, downsizing often fails to yield the types and amounts of economic benefit that are intended (Cascio, 1993). Downsizing can have drastic effects on employees who are not cut, the "survivors." Survivors often find themselves in new, strange, and frequently anxiety-laden work environments, hardly the optimal type of environment for healthy work motivation to flourish (see Cascio, 1993, for evidence on this point). Survivors often change their expectations about future promotions and career advancements and may lose much or all of the trust they previously placed in their superiors. The performance and organizational commitment of those who remain can be diminished, especially depending on their perceptions of the fairness received by the victims (e.g., Brockner, Grover, Reed, De Witt, & O'Malley, 1987). Dashed morale can be harmful to organizational attempts to increase or maintain high-quality service and a positive image in the eyes of customers (recall our discussion in Chapter 12 of the consequences of low satisfaction). Frequently, the amount of work to be accomplished is not reduced, so more work is placed on the shoulders of those who remain.

About the effects of layoffs on survivors, Cascio (1993) wrote: "From the perspective of the individual, the implications of all of this can be summarized succinctly: Our views of organizational life, managing as a career, hard work, rewards, and loyalty will never be the same. Unfortunately, far too many senior managers . . . seem to regard employees as 'units of production,' costs to be cut rather than as assets to be developed. This is a 'plug-in' mentality – that is, like a machine, plug it in when you need it, unplug it when it is no longer needed. Unlike machines, however, employees have values, aspirations, beliefs – and memories" (p. 101). Cascio (1993) predicted that downsizing would continue in North American business as long as overhead costs remain uncompetitive with those of domestic and foreign competitors. Although the frequency and rates of downsizing are not as high as they were when Brockner made his prediction, it is still a commonly used managerial procedure for keeping organizations competitive with one another.

But are all the motivational effects negative? Brockner (1988b), who has done a considerable amount of work on the effects of downsizing, reports anecdotal accounts of how downsizing has sometimes resulted in positive effects on employee motivation, morale, and productivity. For example, *relief* (that one has managed to survive the cuts) is one of many psychological states that can result from downsizing. Similarly, the anxiety that downsizing produces may serve to heighten the activation and motivation of survivors (see Brockner, 1988b; Gardner & Cummings, 1988; Yerkes & Dodson, 1908) and may even result in increased effort through the forces of perceived over-reward inequity that were described much earlier in the chapter (see Adams, 1963).

The point is that layoffs have the *potential* to generate either positive or negative (or both) psychological states among survivors. Accordingly, Brockner has developed and tested a theoretical model that enables us to make both predictions and prescriptions in regard to the downsizing process, especially as it affects survivors. A full treatment of Brockner's model is beyond the scope of this chapter. Suffice it to say that a number of variables are involved, such as the person's self-esteem (see Chapter 5), the degree of interdependencies in the work flow between those laid off and those who remain, the types and amounts of social support offered by both the formal organization (i.e., management policies) and the informal organization (the friendship networks among the employees themselves). Building on their earlier conceptual model (Mishra & Spreitzer, 1998), Spreitzer and Mishra (2002) demonstrated that employee perceptions of the trustworthiness of management, procedural justice, distributive justice, and empowerment were positively related to survivors' affective commitment to the organization – the degree to which they identified with it.

Recapitulation: Downsizing and procedural justice

To summarize, there is considerable although not perfect convergence in the advice offered by authors addressing the layoffs of people from work organizations. Of primary concern here are the implications of these procedures for the perception, by all parties involved, of the procedural and interactional justice involved (we discuss interactional justice shortly). The reason for the concern, again, is that people want to be treated fairly and with dignity, especially at times when their very self-identity is at risk, as is often the case when terminations are being experienced, be they general layoffs or firings for cause (which we examine next).[16] Procedural and interactional justice matter to the job attitudes of survivors, to the self-concepts of the victims, and to the motivation and goals of the victims to continue with their working lives.

Procedural Justice, Discipline, and Punishment

One of the areas of management and work motivation that has strong associations with the concepts of justice discussed in this chapter is employee discipline and punishment (see Chapter 14). Our purpose here is to look at discipline and punishment from the perspective of *perceived* justice, particularly as assessed in the eyes of third parties, such as coworkers of the individual(s) punished. To begin, let us define our terms. Although they ultimately decided to use the two terms interchangeably in their analysis of the matter, Arvey and Jones (1985) drew a distinction between punishment and discipline as they are found in work settings. For them, following Kazdin (1975, pp. 33–34), *punishment* is defined as "the presentation of an aversive event or the removal of a positive event following a response which decreases the probability of that response" (p. 369). This definition has its roots in the school of operant conditioning (which we examine in Chapter 14).

Although the roots of their adopted definition may lie in behaviorism,[17] Arvey and Jones acknowledged that there are social cues associated with punishment and that the concept of *discipline* differs from it in a number of ways. First, punishment implies negative motives on the part of the person using it. The punishment itself has the connotation of retribution, or payback. Discipline, by way of contrast, is more future oriented. The goal of discipline is to point the way to new, anticipated behavior. There is also a distinction based on the formality or informality of the act: "Typically, employees use the term discipline to refer to the *formal* sanctions delivered by the organization (e.g., write-ups, formal warnings, etc.) whereas punishment implies aversive stimuli delivered in a less formal fashion. It is not necessary that punishment occur within the actual structural confines of the organization; it could occur in outside social settings which include organizational members" (Arvey & Jones, 1985, p. 370).

A Brief Aside on the Basic Issue

In the context of an extended discussion of equity, fairness, and justice in supposedly voluntary work situations in a free society, one might ask a number of fundamental questions about the right of any employer to "discipline" or "punish" an employee. The existence of discipline procedures in the workplace in Western societies implies something about the unstated rights of employers and the unstated appropriateness of the use of discipline by one party over another.

---

[16] Gopinath and Becker (2000) have shown how adherence to the principles of procedural justice discussed in this section is also beneficial in the context of divestiture, fostering trust, and organizational commitment among affected employees.
[17] A non-behaviorist definition was offered by Trevino (1992, p. 649): "Punishment is defined as the manager's application of a negative consequence or the withdrawal of a positive consequence from someone under his or her supervision." No mention is made of the punishment's effects on the future probability of the occurrence of the punished act. In the behaviorist model, discipline amounts to punishment, by definition, only when it alters the probabilities of future behaviors.

What about human freedom and dignity? What about people's rights under the eyes of their gods or under the legal constitutions of the countries in which they live? How often does an employee challenge the right of a boss, supervisor, or enterprise owner to apply sanctions of any kind? Clearly, company policies, social standards of judgment, and even the decisions of arbitrators place limits on the types and degrees of sanctions that are tolerated in work settings. The fundamental fact of their existence, however, goes unstated in Western business practice. Seldom do students of management think such thoughts about the fundamental nature of the work relationship; not until, perhaps, they themselves have been on the receiving end of retribution for violating some organization's formal or informal rules. We seem to take it for granted.

Social Effects of Discipline and Punishment at Work

Let's return to the basic point. People frequently witness the administration of discipline and punishment in work settings, the sentiments raised in the preceding paragraph notwithstanding. Through the dynamics of social learning, modeling, and vicarious reinforcement and punishment (see Chapter 14), employees other than those upon whom the sanctions are delivered learn something about the rules and about the consequences of running afoul of those rules (see Trevino, 1992). In earlier times, punishment by the state or by the church was deliberately administered in public for all to see, presumably to allow the powerful effects of social learning to obviate the need to administer punishment to any and all who might otherwise sin, left to their own devices and personal tendencies.

Previous reviews of the work on punishment in the workplace have tended to focus on the consequences of the punishment for the behaviors and attitudes of the victims. The results of these studies have been mixed and inconclusive (see Arvey & Jones, 1985). Nevertheless, interest in the topic remains and may in fact be growing, in part because the field is increasingly turning away from behaviorism toward social cognitive theories such as that of Bandura (1986; see also Kreitner & Luthans, 1991; and Chapter 14). A question for today's workplace is: What are the effects on other people of the administration of organizational discipline and punishment?

More recent thinking that abandons the behaviorist perspective (e.g., Ball, Trevino, & Sims, 1994) throws organizational punishment in a somewhat different light, suggesting a number of potential *positive* consequences of its use (Trevino, 1992): "For example, punishment may serve to uphold social norms within a group, signal appropriate and inappropriate behaviors to observers . . . deter misconduct in . . . group embers, and create perceptions of the supervisor and the organization as just or unjust" (Trevino, 1992, p. 674). Observers of punishment form opinions about its fairness when it is administered, and they base these judgments on several factors (Arvey & Jones, 1985). These factors include many considerations, such as their own knowledge about the alleged offense, whether the punishment seems to fit the crime, and whether other people had committed similar offenses and gone unpunished. These factors sound quite similar to many of the factors contained in the theory of procedural justice of Sheppard et al. (1992), described earlier.

Trevino (1992) pointed out that another key factor determining the reactions of observers is whether they view the "misconduct" as being, in fact, misconduct. An act may violate company rules but still be seen as acceptable by employee-observer. Other issues that may enter a person's assessment of the fairness of discipline include employee characteristics (such as gender, age, and race), the consequences of the rule infraction or crime, the person's disciplinary history, and even the person's skill or ability to do the job properly in the first place (Mitchell, Green, & Wood, 1981; Shingledecker, 1983, cited by Arvey & Jones, 1985, p. 393). Individual assessments of the severity of the punishment, taking into account the severity of the crime, are also important (from an equity perspective).

Lest it be thought that employee reactions to the application of discipline to their peers is always negative, we must observe that there is a norm in Western society for rule violation to be dealt with by retributive justice in some form or other, and the workplace is no exception. Thus, workers who all live under a set of rules and procedures that are more or less well accepted grow to expect the authorities to apply some form of punishment to those who seriously violate the rules (Trevino, 1992). Violation of the rules with the strongest general support tends to motivate the strongest desire among group members for severe retribution. By these norms, when an important rule is violated and the perpetrator is not punished, others in the group will feel a sense of injustice. When punishment is not meted out in such circumstances, the "group's belief systems, norms, and values are open to question and may be viewed as degrading" (p. 654) to those people who suffered the effects of the rule transgression. A model based on interviews of 77 American managers proposed by Butterfield, Trevino, and Ball (1996) builds on Trevino's earlier work, offering hypotheses about the effects of punishment on the actors involved, the organization, from a manager's perspective.

Another key factor is the degree to which the accused person is seen as actually having been responsible for the crime, or whether there were external or extenuating factors beyond her control. Similarly, if the offensive behavior is viewed by observers as intentional, and if the consequences of the offending act are seen as severe, there tends to be a greater desire among observers for retribution (Trevino, 1992). There is some evidence that the severity of a witnessed punishment affects the probability that an observer's own misconduct behavior will be affected. The more severe the outcome, the more likely it is that observers will pay attention to the occurrence of the punishment and then be discouraged from committing the punished deed themselves. However, this seems to be the case only when the perceived costs of the punishment are believed to outweigh the perceived benefits of the misconduct in question (Trevino, 1992). It also seems that one of the most influential forms of punishment in the workplace is sanctioning and disapproval by one's peers – rejection by one's coworkers.

Summary

Because discipline and punishment are social events, witnessed by observers other than the direct recipients, a considerable amount of learning about such a culture occurs – people learn either vicariously or personally just what *is* valued, believed, and felt by the organization's key players. This learning can have major effects on the willingness and tendency (i.e., motivation) of employees to engage in particular forms of behavior in the context of their work (see Cropanzano, 1993, for an alternative review).

Dismissal: Firing for Cause[18]

Before we leave our discussion of the effects of job loss on people, we take a brief look at another traumatic event that occurs in many careers – one that also has serious implications for procedural justice. We are referring to situations in which people are released from their jobs when *the reason for the termination is not broad, general economic circumstances facing the organization but rather, the particular behavior of the individual*. This is organizational discipline in the extreme, and may be one area of human resource management in which the acuity of perceptions of balance and correctness is especially critical.

According to Morin and Yorks (1992), the reasons for firing people often vary with the level of employee involved. Lower-level employees are most frequently "let go" because of poor job

---

[18] Discussion of firing and layoff can often be cast against the doctrine referred to as *employment at will*. This doctrine is defined as "the right of an employer to fire an employee without giving a reason and the right of an employee to quit when he or she chooses" (Fulmer & Casey, 1990, p. 102), or "the absolute right to discharge an employee for whatever cause he might choose, without incurring liability" (Coulson, 1981, p. 111). Space limitations prohibit a detailed discussion of this doctrine; the interested reader is referred to Coulson (1981), Fulmer and Casey (1990), and Youngblood and Bierman (1994) for thorough treatments of the matter.

performance, failure to comply with company rules and regulations, and/or insubordination. Senior managers and executives are more likely to be fired for reasons of personality or a judged lack of fit between them and the organization's goals (p. 33). Other reasons for firing people include "up-or-out" policies, in which a number of junior people are hired and developed with the explicit understanding that many of them won't make it. Professional accounting and law firms have made great use of this form of survival-of-the-fittest strategy over the years when there was an abundance of eager young talent in tough labor market situations. Significant deviations from one's prescribed job duties is another reason often used to justify firing, as are instances of flagrant ethical misconduct (Morin & Yorks, 1992).

Morin and Yorks (1990) reported that, in practice, terminations for cause tend to have a number of common features. For example, they are often executed on Friday afternoons, providing the fired person with little or no guidance about what to do next. Many people are treated so vaguely and "with so many euphemisms that they don't know they are being let go" (p. 7). For example, some people are told that they have been working too hard and that they need to take a break. Other people are treated with "excessive cruelty" (p. 7): Their personalities are attacked, they are yelled at, and they are roughly escorted out of the building, violating every tenet of interactional justice we will consider shortly. Sometimes people are fired over the telephone. (In an age of email and fax, the possibilities here are endless.) The author knows of executives who were fired from a Minneapolis-based corporation long distance, while they were on vacation in Florida ("Reach out and touch someone!"). Perhaps the worst cases are those in which the victim hears about the firing secondhand, via public media or by rumor. Professional athletes often complain of such treatment.

The psychological effects of being fired are similar to those that occur when a person is laid off for economic, non-cause reasons. On the widely noted Holmes and Rahe (1967) scale, being fired ranks eighth out of the 43 events considered by the scale. Grieff and Munter (1980) (quoted by Morin & Yorks, 1990) wrote:

> It doesn't matter what you call it, fired, axed, socked, canned, kicked upstairs, or allowed to resign. They are all the same. The only certainty about losing a job is that it hurts. It threatens everybody – the family, peers, even the executive who has to do the firing.
>
> (Grieff & Munter, 1980, p. 117)

Employers have had to increase the care and attention they devote to their firing practices for a number of reasons. First, there is often a fear of discrimination charges if the victim is a woman or member of a visible or "protected" minority group. Even if the victim is not a member of one of these groups, litigation over unfair dismissal can be costly if it is undertaken. In response to this concern, many employers pay huge severance packages, hoping to obviate suit. Morin and Yorks (1990) reported that common practice is to provide a middle or senior manager with as much as a year's salary in a lump sum.

There are other reasons for paying close attention to the procedures an organization uses to terminate people (Morin & Yorks, 1990). One of these has to do with the organization's reputation and the effect it can have on the capacity of the organization to recruit new employees. The problem is especially acute in the context of recruiting senior executives, among whom there is often a small community of friendships and acquaintanceships. People talk, compare notes, and share experiences. In most cities and, indeed, in most industries, the population of senior people is a relatively small community, so word gets out about how companies treat their executives. At any level of the organization, if the firing victim's peers and colleagues view the treatment of the victim as having been unfair, morale can suffer among the survivors, who may develop fears that they too could be treated capriciously and fired. Finally, there are cases of vengeance in which fired people extract retribution by violence, even murder (Allen & Lucero, 1996; and see Chapter 8 of this book).

Procedures for Dismissal with Justice in Mind

So with all of these psychological, economic, and organizational considerations in mind, how should employers deal with the termination of employees for cause? Morin and Yorks (1990, p. 69) observed that "consistency in the handling of firings requires a well-defined policy, *consistency of treatment* being one of the standards of fairness in procedural justice" (see Sashkin & Williams, 1990). Clearly, Sheppard and his colleagues (1992) would endorse this suggestion. The organization's dismissal policy should make it clear that terminations will not be used for vague or unsubstantiated reasons. This means that managers must keep records, documenting instances of poor performance, insubordination, and rule violations. This also means that valid performance appraisal procedures must be in place and used appropriately. It is the author's experience and the insight of countless authors in the human resources management literature that this is easier said than done. Performance appraisals take time and can be a source of hassle and embarrassment for everyone involved. Hence, in practice, this may be one of the least-well-performed activities in the management and supervision of workers by bosses. The point is that when it comes time to fire someone, both the law and human decency require that there be substantiated evidence that a firing is just and called for. (Consider how the principles of balance and correctness fit in here, as they apply to the assessment of the fairness of the organization's procedures and systems; see Sheppard et al., 1992.)

There has been some disagreement among the experts about the style and speed of execution of the firing once it has been decided that a dismissal is to take place. Coulson (1981) suggested that before firing takes place, the problematic employee should be told clearly that problems are perceived regarding his work. There should be counseling by the supervisor or other official to seek ways to sort things out. If this fails, there should be a written reprimand, followed, if necessary, by a "final warning." The final warning should contain copies of previous warnings, identification of specific areas in which the employee must improve, a period of time within which the employee has a chance to show improvement, and a statement that this is the person's final opportunity to bring performance up to standard. It should be made clear that this *will be* the final warning. A copy of the warning should be given to the employee and another placed in his file. If all these procedures fail, the person's immediate supervisor should perform the firing.

All these procedures are consistent with the advice of Sheppard and his colleagues (1992; Minton et al., 1994). But here is where they depart from Coulson's (1981) advice. Coulson claims that the message should be direct, fully explained, unequivocal, and leave no cause for the employee to believe that further chances are possible: There is no turning back (Coulson, 1981). On the other hand, Minton et al. (1994) favor the person's right to a hearing, including adequate time for the employee to prepare for it. The person may also have the right to representation at such a hearing and, ultimately, the right to appeal. At first blush, the two sets of prescriptions seem equally fair. At a second glance, they seem irreconcilable.

An organization's formal dismissal policy should also clearly spell out the nature of the support package that will be provided to terminated employees, if any. For example, it should be clear how much money will be awarded, and the terms and criteria for the amount should be spelled out in writing and provided to the person when he is fired. The person should be told whether he may use any of the company's employees as referees for future employment and, if so, who these people are. Provisions for counseling and outplacement support, such as the use of an office, a shared office, secretarial support, and the assistance of professional recruiters, should also be specified if they are to be provided at all (Morin & Yorks, 1991).

The rationale underlying these guidelines for the firing of employees is partly legal, motivated by the goal of protecting the organization from lawsuit. Aside from legal considerations, these types of procedure and policy should be grounded in principles of procedural justice as detailed by Lewicki and his colleagues (Sheppard et al., 1992). Life goes on after a firing,[19] for both the victim and the other employees of the organization, so it seems imperative that life be made as civilized and as pleasant as possible for everyone concerned. Keeping an eye on the basic principles of fairness as well as the legal issues concerned seems to be the most humane and business-wise way to proceed.

A final note: Those who have had to do it report that dismissing another employee can be among the most stressful assignments they have to perform as managers or supervisors. It would seem that some degree of comfort would be more available to those who bear the message when policies are structured with the principles of procedural justice in place than in situations where there are no policies or where the policies are ill planned, inconsistent, and inhumane. Translating the principles of procedural fairness and interactional justice into explicit policies of discipline may not be easy, because to some degree, every case requiring dismissal may have its own idiosyncrasies and nuances. Moreover, investing the time to adhere to carefully designed policies can also be demanding on supervisors and managers who have other duties to perform. Nevertheless, a certain portion of every manager's pay is (under normal circumstances) provided for executing policies of discipline, including the intermittent need to dismiss other employees. The norms of *distributive justice* we examined at the beginning of this chapter require that those who are paid more because they bear these responsibilities must be willing and able to perform them, unpleasant as they may be.

INTERACTIONAL JUSTICE

Since the mid-1970s, the vast majority of research on theorizing about fairness in organizations has been devoted to distributive and procedural justice, as described in the foregoing sections of this chapter. Over the past two decades, however, organizational theorists have offered a distinction between procedural justice – which refers to the bureaucratic systems that make decisions about people – and another form of justice, *interactional justice*, which has to do with the quality and content of person-to-person interactions as people relate to one another:

> Concerns about the fairness of interpersonal communication are representative of a set of issues dealing with what we refer to as interactional justice. By interactional justice we mean that people are sensitive to the quality of interpersonal treatment they receive during the enactment of organizational procedures.
>
> (Bies & Moag, 1986, p. 44)

Hence, it is one thing to have formal rules and procedures that are more or less fair. The interpretation and enactment of these procedures is what interactional justice is about. How a boss relays bad news based on a new organizational policy may have as much impact on an employee's perceptions of justice as the nature of the news itself and the perceived fairness of the policies being enacted.[20]

Bies and Moag (1986, p. 46) suggested that procedural justice and interactional justice are related to perceptions of the fairness of outcomes in a causal, sequential manner in the following way:

Procedure → Interaction → Outcome

They stated: "Each part of the sequence is subject to fairness considerations and thus, every aspect of an organizational decision (procedure, interaction, outcome) may create a potential justice episode"

---

[19] Actually, job loss and/or extended periods of unemployment can lead to death, either indirectly through the natural physiological impact of the experience or through suicide (see Ahlberg, 1986).

[20] Donovan, Drasgow, and Munson (1998) developed and validated a scale to assess two components of interactional justice in the work setting: that which emanates from (1) supervisors and from (2) coworkers.

(p. 46). This means that it is possible for an employee to believe that the rules and procedures that result in a layoff, a cut in pay, or a disciplinary action are fair, but that somehow, the entire experience is taken as unfair. It is not the decision that is unfair: It is not the outcome that is unfair. As we saw earlier in the context of downsizing and dismissal for cause, *it is the way the bad news is delivered that matters*. The message must be delivered in a way that is seen as candid and truthful. It must be respectful to the receiver rather than rude or condescending. And it must be seen as appropriate and justified (Bies & Moag, 1986). In fact, the justification factor is often especially critical. We return to this point shortly. First, we observe the emergence of two subcategories of interactional justice: Interpersonal and informational.

The Role of Accounts and Justifications

One of the key factors influencing whether people view relationships to be fair in interactional justice terms is whether apparent violations of justice norms are accompanied by justifications, or causal accounts. If there is a causal account – an explanation – provided for instances of apparent mistreatment, a person who is treated unfairly is less likely to be unhappy with the treatment. But the existence of a causal account by itself seems not to be enough. The explanation offering details about extenuating circumstances must be seen as adequate; merely offering an excuse is not as effective as offering an explanation that is viewed as adequate or reasonable (Bies, 1987; Bies & Shapiro, 1987).

Let's look at an example that is particularly relevant to the lives of students. Suppose that a professor is late or absent from her office hours and many students are kept waiting for her to arrive to help them with ideas for their term papers. If the professor eventually shows up and tells the waiting students that she was late because she "was delayed," she will not satisfy the annoyed students nearly as much as if she honestly explains that the reason she was late was because her daughter was ill and had to be taken to the doctor for medical attention. If no explanation is given, the students will perceive low interactional justice. If they are told that the professor "had a delay," they may feel less interactional injustice. If they learn that there was a valid reason for the lateness – the illness of the professor's child – the students will perceive much more interactional justice and be more likely to excuse the professor for her tardiness.

When people in organizations feel unfairly treated, there is a tendency for them to experience feelings of anger, resentment, and moral outrage (Bies, 1987). People who feel they have been treated badly may be motivated to "get even," to seek revenge in some form or another. They can also experience diminished self-esteem (Koper, Van Knippenberg, Bouhuijs, Vermunt, & Wilke, 1993). But provision of a social account – an excuse, an explanation, or a rationale – may mitigate feelings of resentment on the part of the maltreated party. Specifically, a social account is "an explanation containing a reason to mitigate the harm doer's responsibility for some action, or as it is more commonly referred to, an excuse" (Scott & Lyman, 1968, cited by Bies, 1987, p. 298). Providing a social account can mitigate the sting associated with the delivery of bad news, even when that news is fair by strict procedural standards. So a manager who lays off employees and cites a downturn in profits and revenues will generate much less ill will and moral outrage than a boss who provides no such explanation. In fact, a manager who fails to provide explanations for the delivery or the enactment of bad news is likely to lose authority and respect in the eyes of subordinates (Baron, 1993; Bies, 1987).

The importance of treating people with respect (one of the two major elements of interactional justice) at the time of a downsizing was illustrated in a near-unique field study of Russian military officers who were facing being dropped from the army. Hamilton (2000) interviewed nearly 1800 officers in such a position and found that those who reported they had been treated with interactional justice, both in the form of respect and in the provision of information, reported lower levels of stress and anxiety and higher levels of organizational commitment than those who felt they received less interactional justice. Perceptions of distributive justice were also correlated with organizational justice among those officers who were to be let go.

A study by Brennan and Skarlicki (2004, p. 1321) showed that the personality variable angry hostility moderates the relationship between perceptions of interactional justice at the time of downsizing and survivors' levels of commitment and intentions to leave the organization:

> Specifically, the relationship between interactional justice and both organizational commitment and intention to leave was significant only when angry hostility [among survivors] was low. For employees who scored low on angry hostility, however, perceptions of interactional justice were not related to either organizational commitment or intention to quit.

Brennan and Skarlicki's (2004) study was one of the first of what is bound to be a number of empirical investigations of the role of individual differences – personality in particular – in justice/injustice-instigated outcomes.

Recently, Greenberg (2006) demonstrated in a field experiment how training nursing supervisors in the skills of providing social support (see Chapter 2) to subordinates who felt underpaid following a change in compensation helped to assuage stress and improve subordinates' insomnia problems. This is another example of how simply providing people with information pertaining to the details and the rationale for the changes that are taking place in their work settings can help to offset some of the normal negative reactions to what are otherwise seen as arbitrary and – in many cases – totally unjust decisions made by authorities.

Trust (Again)

A key element of violations of interactional injustice is the perception of violation of *trust*. (Recall that trust is one of the key mechanisms that explain the effects of distributive justice as well.) When one person feels that another has betrayed him, changed the rules on him, broken a promise, breached a contract, committed a lie, stolen an idea or a material object, disclosed a confidence, or publicly slandered him, the sense of injustice can be acute. Notice that many or most of these misdeeds involve interactions rather than outcomes or the execution of legitimate procedures. In other words, interactional justice (or injustice) lies at the heart of violations of interpersonal trust and the violation of trust. Trust is an interpersonal value that is earned slowly and over time, yet it can be lost or broken quickly, by only seemingly minor violations or transgressions (see Kramer & Tyler, 1996). People whose trust has been violated typically react in any of a number of ways, including withdrawing from the offender, denying the claims made, or striking back, seeking revenge (see Allen & Lucero, 1996; Bies & Tripp, 1996).

A fascinating set of three studies has shown that a climate of interactional justice can influence the natural tendency for people to regard a disproportionately large share of resources for themselves as fair in negotiation contexts (Leung, Tong, & Ho, 2004). Combining the two components of interactional justice for the purpose of these studies, the researchers proposed and found that the demands of others whom they had previously found to be fair in their exchange relationships were trusted more than those who had proven less fair. In short: Social exchange in all its forms is frequently an ongoing affair, so it behooves participants to treat each other respectfully and according to norms of interactional justice. As the aphorism states: "What goes around, comes around," and the dynamics of memory, trust, trustworthiness, and equity are critical in the cycles of exchange.

Other Sources of Interactional Injustice

In a useful summary of the emergence of interactional (in)justice and its struggle to earn its place alongside procedural (in)justice, Bies (2001) has outlined a number of other common sources of injustice (or "profanities") that violate people. Briefly, his list includes acts such as derogatory judgments, deception, the invasion of privacy (including the disclosure of the confidences and secrets of others), disrespectful acts in the form of inconsiderate actions, abusive words or actions, public humiliation, and coercion.[21] For Bies (2001), justice theory was facing a new challenge to grow as a contender at that time: A requirement for it to become concerned with moral issues as much as with statistical and scientific purity.

FAIRNESS THEORY

The notion of accountability has been introduced into the justice literature by Folger and his colleagues (cf. Folger & Cropanzano, 2001). This theory has three primary elements. The first is that some form of unfavourable event or situation must occur or be present in a social setting such as a workplace. Second, the event must be caused by some volitional, discretionary acts of an individual – the person(s) whose accountability is to be questioned. Finally, the act must be seen as violating an ethical norm or standard of conduct. In short, accidents, events that are not particularly harmful and/or that do not violate some code of conduct, are not situations in which fairness theory is relevant. So there is a large role played by judgments – perceptions (of events) and beliefs (about responsibility and norm violations) – in making the theory go.

The judgment process consists of deriving answers to three fundamental questions. The first is: "What else might have happened if the situation at hand had not developed or happened?" Hence, being demoted at work during a time of retrenchment might not been seen as harmful when one considers that many of her peers were laid off altogether. Again, it is critical for the person making the judgment to believe that at least some damage has occurred to her, regardless of what has happened to her now-unemployed colleagues. One tricky aspect of this judgment is the point of reference the individual adopts when making the assessment. So the demoted employee may not feel bad relative to those who were laid off, but she may feel badly done by if she were to compare herself with others she knows whose careers have advanced during the tough times that occasioned the cutbacks. These judgments concern outcomes, or matters of distributive justice. Fairness theory also holds that people pass judgments about the fairness of the procedures that were used to bring about their circumstances and, again, they form these judgments of fairness in relation to the procedures they have seen applied to others in similar circumstances. In short, judgments about "would" establish for the individual a belief regarding whether harm has occurred.

According to fairness theory, a second question is involved in determining overall fairness. Folger and Cropanzano (2001) referred to this as the "could" question; viz., could the person seen as responsible for the state of affairs (such as my being demoted) have behaved any differently? In other words, was the act volitional, within the power of the person to have acted differently (or not at all), or were constraints or superior forces at play that left the person little or no choice? In this case, the question becomes: Could my boss have avoided demoting me? Or did she have alternative courses of action available? As Folger and Cropanzano put it (2001, p. 13): "It makes no sense to hold people morally responsible for the implications of events that they could not control or could not reasonably be expected to have anticipated." In relation to judgments made about the question of "could," it is possible to assess sins of omission as well as sins of commission – people might be held responsible either for acting one way or for failing to act in other ways. Folger and Cropanzano explored in detail the ins and outs of the decision-making processes involved.

---

[21] Research by Harlos and Pinder (2000; and see Chapter 4 of the current volume) found many of these "profanities" and forms of interpersonal abuse related to reports of injustice experienced by their research participants. Also see Chapter 5 to review our discussion of the dysfunctions of abusive relationships and incivility in the workplace.

In summary, the "would" question is intended to address whether harm has occurred. The "could" question is intended to assess whether key actors had any choice in bringing about the events or circumstances in question. So far, the multiple-stage social assessment process has not established whether an injustice has occurred, so a third question follows – the "should" question, as in "should things have occurred in ways other than the way in which they have occurred?" Again, standards and norms are involved, but in this case, these are moral or ethical. Judgments about whether something else should have occurred are queries into the morality of the decisions that were made or into the circumstances within which the harm has occurred and whether the relevant actors had alternative courses of action available to them. If one believes that things should have been different, a judgment of unfairness is reached.

It is critical to note, again, that fairness (or justice/injustice) is in the eye of the beholder, although – as we have noted earlier at length – social cues-in-context can play a huge role in determining the judgment of fairness/unfairness. At any of the three stages in the assessment process, two people with essentially the same facts available may ultimately reach differing conclusions about the fairness of the outcomes. They may differ on the matter of whether any harm occurred, whether any real damage was done (considering the alternatives). Even if they reach accord on the first issue, they may also differ, because of differing standards for comparison, on whether things could have been different, i.e., whether alternative consequences could have arisen, given the will and ability of key players. Again, the two people may differ on their perceptions of key parameters regarding the choices available, the power and ability of key decision makers, and so forth. But even if, after reaching similar conclusions to the "what" and "could" questions, they may still differ widely on the matter of the morality involved in the events that led to the circumstances they face. Here, different people may, for purely legitimate reasons, apply different standards of morality or codes of ethics to assess the third question – the "should" question – and thereby reach widely different views on whether they have been fairly treated.

Further detail about the rudiments of fairness theory is limited here by space considerations. In a nutshell, this work is a natural extension of the burgeoning and largely successful tradition of justice research begun by Greenberg and his colleagues (cf. Greenberg, 1990c) approximately two decades ago. Indeed, Folger and Cropanzano (2001) have explored the linkages in some detail. One key point deserves highlighting here, nevertheless: The logic of *would*, *could*, and *should* assessments apply to all three categories of justice/injustice in the "traditional" justice theory: Distributive, procedural, and interactive matters.

ASSESSMENT OF ORGANIZATIONAL JUSTICE THEORIES

As theory and research on justice in organizations has progressed over the past 30 years, there has been a gradual process of construct splitting and the differentiation among various forms of justice. Originally, as we have noted, critics believed that simple notions of equity were insufficient to cover all elements of fairness issues in the workplace. Then, as we have reported in this chapter, equity was reconceived as distributive justice and the strong case was made that procedures also matter, hence procedural justice emerged as a viable and fruitful research topic. It took some time to show that there was substantial benefit to be gained by the joint consideration of two constructs (distributive and procedural justice) rather than just one.

Not long afterward, in similar fashion, people became concerned with the notion of interactional justice (Bies & Moag, 1986), and – as before – there was some debate for a few years about whether there were reasonable scientific and applied grounds to admit this third member. (Some critics held that interactional justice was really not sufficiently distinct from procedural justice to warrant special attention as a construct of equal standing; rather, they argued, interactional justice is most reasonably and parsimoniously considered a subset of procedural justice.) Each of these cycles took time.

Interpersonal and Informational Justice

Subsequently, Greenberg (1993b) offered yet another distinction: This time a differentiation between two forms of interactional justice. One form, *interpersonal justice*, reflects the degree to which people are treated with dignity, respect, and politeness by others. A second form, *informational justice*, is concerned with the explanations provided to people to inform them about why certain procedures were used to make decisions or about why outcomes such as rewards and punishments were distributed in a particular fashion. This final distinction sets the stage for an understanding of why accounts and justifications can be so critical in fostering climates of justice in work settings. It is one thing for procedures to adhere to standards of procedural justice, it is another for people to be informed about the rationales for these procedures, to be told why things are happening the way they are.

This author has been impressed by the care with which scholars have considered the entry and acknowledgement of each new construct: The fanciful proliferation of putatively new constructs into the field has been a problem for decades – too many cases of ersatz "new wine" in old bottles (see Chapter 2). Indeed, there have been some disagreements along the way among key proponents of the theory (for example, over the matter whether distributive and procedural justice were sufficiently distinct in the minds of ordinary people to justify differentiating among them and, similarly whether interactional justice is best considered a subset of procedural justice). On the basis of qualitative work by Harlos (1998; see also Harlos & Pinder, 2000) as well as impressive scaling and construct validation work by Colquitt (2001) and a convincing set of meta-analyses by Colquitt et al. (2001), this author believes there are sufficient scientific grounds to differentiate among distributive justice, procedural justice (as represented by the six so-called "Leventhal criteria" explained earlier in this chapter), and both of the two forms of interactional justice cited by Greenberg (1993b): Interpersonal and informational.

New Directions: Justice at Higher Levels of Analysis?

Other scholars have opened the door for even further expansion and differentiation of justice forms. For example, Mossholder, Bennett, and Martin (1998), consistent with Greenberg (1990c), argued that, aside from the personal perceptions and beliefs individuals have about procedural justice, the "procedural justice context" within which people work can also influence employee attitudes and behavior. As they observed: "[O]rganizations involve multiple levels of nested relationships . . . [so] many organizational constructs may operate at more than one level" (p. 132).

To test this hypothesis, Mossholder et al. (1998) collected data from more than 300 employees in an American financial services organization, measuring individual justice perceptions as well as participants' perceptions of the organization's "overall fairness of facets central in the organization's human resources system: performance appraisal, raises, benefits, and working conditions" (p. 135). They found that this measure of procedural justice context accounted for significant variance in employees' job satisfaction, even after their individual perceptions about justice had been accounted for.

Similarly, Harlos and Pinder (1999) found that employees who had reported they had been unjustly treated by their organizations identified a category of sources the researchers categorized as *systemic (in)justice*. Distinct from the more familiar categories of distributive, procedural, and interactive justice, Harlos and Pinder (1999) defined systemic injustice as "perceived unfairness in larger organizational contexts within which relationships, procedures and distributive decisions occur, for example, organizational inconsistency ... abandonment ... discrimination and organizational overwork" (p. 106). It stands to reason that the overall cultural and climatic conditions within an organization will provide a backdrop against which general norms of fairness and justice (or unfairness and injustice) develop and that these will influence specific procedures, leadership styles of managers and supervisors, and the general tone of civility in interpersonal relations. As Harlos and Pinder (1999) found, consistent with Frost's (2003) concept of toxic work environments (recall Chapter 2), Degoey's (2000) concept of *contagious justice* (which we introduced earlier in this chapter), and Ashforth and Anand's (2003) model of how corruption becomes the institutionalized norm in some organizations (see Chapter 5), there seem to be elements in organizational settings that transcend and influence (and are influenced by) the more micro procedures, interpersonal interactions, and distributive decisions made on a day-by-day basis by individual actors.[22] Researchers who undertake to study organizational justice issues at group and organizational levels must be cautioned (recall Chapter 2), that there is more to morphing individual-level constructs to higher-level constructs than meets the eye (cf. Klein et al., 2001).

Elsewhere, with Latham (Latham & Pinder, 2005), the author has concluded that organizational justice theory – broadly defined – comprises one of the three most important new contributions to the corpus of theory and research in work motivation during the previous three decades.

Indeed, the work is impressive in many of the most important ways: In construct development and articulation, in the development of measures and scales for measuring constructs, in the design and execution of both experimental and non-experimental research studies to develop and test key tenets of the theory (theories), and in the articulation of the applied, social, and managerial implications of its key points. It has been cumulative, collective, and coherent and, at times, it has been self-critical. Of special interest to us is that it also has many significant and interesting implications for the development of other bodies of theory and practice related to work motivation and managerial practice, and these are highlighted in many places throughout the current volume. These other bodies of theory, research, and practice include (but are not limited to): Affect and emotion, the design and management of reward and discipline systems, power-related behavior, organizational structure and redesign, job design and redesign, and career management.

Seven Canons of Organizational Justice

Accordingly, we close this section with an assessment of organizational justice theories by summarizing a thoughtful essay written by Jerald Greenberg, one of the early and most influential architects of this body of knowledge. Greenberg (2001) warned us of "seven loose canons of organizational justice." After acknowledging the difference between a canon, which is a "body of rules, principles, or standards, accepted as axiomatic and universally binding in a field of study" (*Random House Unabridged Dictionary*, 1993), and a loose cannon, which is "a person whose reckless behaviour endangers the efforts or welfare of others" (same dictionary), Greenberg (2001) highlighted seven potential pratfalls that must be recognized and dealt with so that the field of organizational justice can continue to grow and be useful rather than causing people to reach "premature and misleading conclusions about organizational justice" (p. 245). In keeping with the caveats we expressed in Chapter 2 of this volume, we applaud Greenberg's explication of his seven caveats.

First, Greenberg pointed out that justice issues are possible in any and all organizational settings but that they may not come to the surface unless people feel badly treated, unless some form of significant change is underway, and/or when resources are scarce. He also noted that power

---

[22] In Chapter 5, we reviewed at length the dysfunctions associated with the abuse of power by individuals. The concepts of procedural, interactive, and distributive injustice are the crux of much of these forms of power abuse by tyrants in organizational settings.

differentials found in all organizations can provide fertile grounds for justice concerns. Although he didn't make the point explicitly, these power differentials are most likely to generate concerns of injustice when some or all of the earlier three conditions prevails. In our view, his point is well taken, but his concerns may be too conservative on this score, given the universal nature of power differentials, resources scarcity, constant change, and the inevitability for people to maltreat one another in social settings.

Greenberg's second concern was that others interpret his own and his colleagues' scientific efforts as being a campaign in favor of organizational justice. For the most part, this body of work has been concerned with building descriptive theories through a particular lens. It is much less intended to be a normative prescription for the dissemination of just practice. That said, he recognizes that this literature has been adopted and applied to the betterment, or potential betterment, of organizations and the people who work in them.

Third, Greenberg (2001) dispelled the belief that favourable outcomes are necessarily fair outcomes. As we have said many times in this volume, largely on the basis of justice theory and its predecessors, fairness is in the eye of the beholder. A distribution of good things deemed favorable by one individual has only a modest chance, in most circumstances, as being deemed favourable by everyone else present. That said, there is work that has shown that single-minded self-interest is not universal; indeed, Meglino and Korsgaard (2004) have argued that unmitigated self-interest can usefully be seen as a human disposition, subject to individual differences, complicating matters considerably. And, as we have seen, classical equity theory has shown a propensity for some people to be motivated to restore equity from situations which hitherto advantaged themselves.

Fourth, Greenberg warned, people's reactions to injustice are unpredictable, even idiosyncratic in some instances. The consistency of hypothesized results in organizational research into organizational justice can be explained as much by the constraints and opportunities available to research participants as they are to natural tendencies of unjustly treated people in naturalistic settings. Moreover, even in such natural settings, people often disguise their reactions, repress them, or express them in ways far too complex and multitudinous for us to predict, given the state of our theory and research. The point is that Greenberg urged caution in any presumptions we might have, either as managers or as scientists, in predicting individual responses to just or unjust circumstances.

A fifth point is more subtle and conservative, in our view. Greenberg cautioned that, the considerable evidence related to the interaction between distributive and procedural justice notwithstanding (in which perceptions of fairness in the latter can mitigate otherwise unfavorable reactions to the former),[23] it is not always the case that "fair" procedures enhance the odds that people will accept organizational outcomes. For one thing, he noted, fair procedures matter more to people when the distribution of outcomes is judged negative than when judged positive. In addition, this work has shown that "more is not always better" when it comes to distributive justice. Granting people voice may enhance their acceptance of outcomes (cf. Pinder & Harlos, 2001) but granting them more voice may not have even greater positive effects. Finally, again on the matter of voice, the opportunity to participate in decision making or even to be apprised of the procedures used in managing reward systems must be seen as sincere. Indeed, advice sought but ignored can backfire.

A sixth point is methodological as much as it is substantive, although it has major implications for the furtherance of the work on justice (recall our Chapter 2). It is simply this: Care must be taken to develop valid measures and manipulations of justice constructs. Otherwise, ad hoc approaches will yield weaknesses in internal validity and attenuate the capacity of the literature to continue to accumulate at the rates accomplished since work began on organizational justice a quarter century ago (see Greenberg, 1990, for more on this point).

Greenberg's final point was particularly critical at a time when cross-cultural psychology and cross-cultural management are becoming so critical. It involves acknowledging the powerful moderating role of cultural differences in understanding justice dynamics. While it may be true that

---

[23] See Folger (1987) and Brockner and Siegel (1996) for reviews of the interaction between distributive and procedural justice.

concern about social justice is a universal human trait, cultural and national boundaries occasion considerable differences in the way justice is operationalized, particularly distributive justice. Moreover, there may be much more universal agreement about the structural determinants of procedural justice than there are about the international styles by which procedures are administered. In a nutshell, the point is that we Westerners must be careful not to permit our zeal for promoting universality to cloud the fact that people in different cultures have different standards for the operationalization of procedures and the person-to-person distribution of rules, rewards, and sanctions – a lesson not learned by many conquering armies who wish to spread Western notions of freedom and democracy!

The Paradox of Occam vs. Requisite Variety in the Justice Theory Domain

Only a few years old, in relative terms, "justice theory" has earned its place as a major player on the stage of importance in understanding work motivation – the topic of this book. Although we have not yet reviewed a number of other theories of work motivation (and behavior), we have, to this point, considered many of the most important ones.

The author states here that justice concepts have not only been the most provocative and fertile new concepts for research and theory over the past 20 years in the area of work motivation, but also the most important from an employee's interest perspective. Indeed, they contain many ideas for the benefit of both employees and their overlords. Justice concepts are the most rounded and grounded in liberal egalitarian, religious, and moral bedrock. They provide the basic foundation for the legal systems and jurisprudence of most civilized nation states (cf. Rawls, 1971). Of most relevance here is that justice concepts (of all the sorts we have described in this chapter) have served well in many roles in causal models of work motivation and organizational behavior. That is, they have served as independent variables, dependent variables, and mediating variables in hundreds of studies of organizational phenomena (cf. Cohen-Charash & Spector, 2001; Colquitt et al., 2001). They have been well researched, insightful, and useful. Sometimes, the insights have been counterintuitive; sometimes they have merely confirmed the truth value of what many of us, in most cultures and nations of the world, learned as children (see Footnote 1 of this chapter). The concepts of justice help us to understand human behavior and work motivation, whether it is coming from a needs theory perspective (see Chapter 3), an affect (emotions and moods) perspective (Chapter 4), a frustration–aggression perspective (recall Chapter 8), a learning theory viewpoint (to come in Chapter 14), or an expectancy theory perspective (to be presented in the next chapter). Justice is a norm universally; it is no wonder that it plays a massive, pervasive role in work motivation and organizational behavior.

Occam's offer: The Golden Rule

Nevertheless, for this author, there is a paradox when one sits back and juxtaposes the vast and ever-growing literature on organizational justice concepts, in all the roles they play in causal models of organizational behavior (on the one hand), versus the simplicity of the insight of the Golden Rule, which has been cited on occasion throughout this chapter (on the other).

Here is the question: Is it necessary for social scientists, professors, and others who would wish to publish what may seem obvious (i.e., that people should treat one another with dignity and humanity) for all of us to internalize these beliefs and values and to treat people in our work settings in accordance with these values? The proliferation of management-oriented books over the past 20 years dealing with "spirituality in the workplace" (e.g., Burkett, 1998) and the more recent emergence of "positive psychology" and "positive organizational scholarship" (cf. Cameron et al., 2003) suggests that, for some people, it may be necessary for a social science base or the voices of putative authorities to make it "okay" for superiors to treat people below them in power structures with humanity. The voices or human and egalitarian treatment of employees have been around for many years.

The *law of requisite variety* requires that we generate a complexity of solutions commensurate with the complexity of the phenomena we have to deal with (recall Chapter 2). Yet the counter-vailing force and argument to consider, especially when one contemplates issues of equity, fairness, and justice – the theme of this chapter – is that it may be necessary to shed all the highly energized social-scientific justifications for treating people and running organizations according to norms of fairness: It is likely that there is a far simpler solution, not only to understand a considerable amount of both positive and negative organizational behavior, but also to make prescriptions, in a normative manner, to those who wish to make things work. There is profound, universal insight in the essence of the Golden Rule: Do unto others as you would have them do unto you. People in starvation conditions in the Third World, and even countless others in the "First World" who do not know where they will sleep on a given night or whether they can survive long enough to see their children grow up and graduate from high school, really have no reason to care about the differences between self-esteem and self-efficacy, distributive and procedural justice, performance goals and learning goals, instrumentality and expectancy (see Chapters 12 and 15), or among anger, rage, and pique (recall Chapter 4). Just think about the simplicity in the elegant and universally acknowledged aphorism: *Do unto others as you would have them do unto you.*

One does not need to be religious to acknowledge the wisdom of this insight. Perhaps that is all there is to the mountain of research and theory on fairness, equity, and justice. Perhaps Occam's value should prevail here.

TAKING STOCK: LOOKING BACKWARD AND FORWARD IN OUR ANALYSIS

A recent article in the British magazine *The Economist* (June 17–23, 2006, pp. 28–32) opened with the following paragraph:

> Americans do not go in for envy. The gap between the rich and the poor is bigger than in any other advanced country [it is bigger in Brazil], but most people are unconcerned. Whereas Europeans fret about the way the economic pie is divided, Americans want to join the rich, not soak them. Eight out of ten, more than anywhere else, believe that though you may start poor, if you work hard, you can make pots of money. It is a central part of the American dream.

The foregoing paragraph, along with the opening paragraph in a companion piece in the same edition of the journal, provide an apt bridge between key concepts of the present chapter on fairness, equity, and justice (along with implicit concerns for equality) and a major theme of Chapter 12, which follows.[24] There, we will explore theories of work motivation that rest heavily on people's beliefs (recall Chapters 9 and 10) about what it takes to "get ahead" and about the value of doing so. As we saw in the present chapter, reward systems – whether at the macro or the micro level – are rooted in the value structures of society (the community, the organization in question) and will either encourage or discourage hard work, upward mobility, and inequality among individuals. Accordingly, if the micro- and macro-reward systems of a culture foster a justified belief that merit, hard work, and the development of one's personal skills and social capital will be instrumental for attaining a more heterogeneous distribution of wealth, one that favors those who try harder than

---

[24] We will present the second paragraph at the beginning of Chapter 12.

others, then an ethos supporting inequality of rewards and wealth prevails and people may either envy those who are "doing better" and try to "soak them" (as *The Economist* put it) under the rules, or attempt to emulate them, to join them. Traditionally, of course, American ethos has been predicated on the value of *equality of opportunity* – opportunity to create unequal classes of wealth, power, and influence. However, as *The Economist* paragraph states: Inequality is a central part of the American dream, at least as it applies to the *distribution of economic success*. Adherence to differing views on this matter can be observed among individuals within cultures as well as between cultures, and we often observe how the prevailing views of both individuals and cultures sometimes shift as their personal circumstances advance or decline over time.

On the other hand, if individuals and the companies in which they work (not to mention the greater societies in which both operate) believe that equality of treatment and distribution of rewards is appropriate, then certain norms for behavior are established and certain natural limits are placed on the degree to which merit, hard work, upward striving, and self-development are encouraged. Consequently, the distribution of wealth and quality of life will be closer to that experienced in social democracies such as Sweden, Norway, Denmark, and Canada and even France and Germany (recall Chapter 3, where we discussed such matters, particularly intercultural differences in *performance orientation*).

Here is a reminder as the reader moves forward through this text: People require to be treated with norms of justice, in all its forms. For our purposes, unfair treatment of employees by their bosses is one of the most significant sources of job dissatisfaction, low commitment to the employer, impulses to strike and to strike back at the organization. For academics, job satisfaction and other job-related attitudes are among the oldest foci of attention in the social sciences. For real people (even academics when they dislike their jobs or feel unjustly treated), job dissatisfaction really hurts, as we saw in Chapter 10.

Next, in Chapter 12, we study the structures of people's beliefs about (1) the degree to which effort and personal development are linked with performance, (2) the degree to which performance is associated with outcomes that will (3) either satisfy their needs and correspond to their values or, alternatively, thwart them. While following the scientific trails, cognitive analyses, and arguments about other theories examined in this book, it is critical for the reader to understand that job satisfaction is massively important in people's lives.

Expectancy-Valence Theories of Work Motivation

12

PROCESS

Never is there either work without reward,
nor reward without work being expended.
Livy (Titus Livius)

Toward the end of Chapter 11, we cited a paragraph from a recent edition of *The Economist* magazine, one that started with the sentence: "Americans do not go in for envy" (*The Economist*, June 17, 2006, p. 28). In an earlier piece in the same edition of the magazine, the opening paragraph read as follows:

> More than any other country, America defines itself by a collective dream: the dream of economic opportunity and upward mobility. Its proudest boast is that it offers a chance of the good life to everybody who is willing to work hard and play by the rules. This ideal has made the United States the world's strongest magnet for immigrants; it has also reconciled ordinary Americans to the rough side of a dynamic economy, with all its inequalities and insecurities. Who cares if the boss earns 300 times more than the average working stiff, if the stiff knows he can become the boss.
>
> (*The Economist*, June 17, 2006, p. 13)

Coincidentally, at virtually the same time as *The Economist* issue was published, *Maclean's* magazine, Canada's primary national magazine, released a number of findings from sociologist Reginald Bibby's latest national survey of Canadian (and Canadian vs. American) beliefs and values (Bibby, 2006; George, 2006). Among the findings of interest to our study of work motivation was the belief reported by 50% of Canadians that *working hard will not necessarily get them to the top*.

In this chapter, we focus on a variety of theories of work motivation that are variously and collectively referred to as *expectancy theory*, *expectancy valence theory*, or – our preferred term – *valence-instrumentality-expectancy* (VIE) *theory* – one of the most popular, useful, and robust bodies of thinking about work motivation over the past century. Each of these theories has its modern roots in Victor Vroom's (1964) landmark book on work motivation, although earlier theory in psychology relating to general human motivation quite clearly predated Vroom's interpretation for organizational science (e.g., Atkinson, 1958; Davidson, Suppes, & Siegel, 1957; Lewin, 1938; Peak, 1955; Rotter, 1955; Tolman, 1959), and an early study by Georgopoulos, Mahoney, and Jones (1957) demonstrated the relevance of the theory for work behavior.[1] As we will see, the core elements of VIE theories are expectations people hold about being able to perform well at their work, about whether working hard will enable them to succeed at their work (or make appropriate work-related decisions more generally), and whether, if they do accomplish their work, their high performance will result in work- and non-work-related outcomes from which they expect to gain utility.

---

[1] One notable expectancy valence theory is Fishbein and Ajzen's *theory of reasoned action*, which we examined in Chapter 9 (Ajzen & Fishbein, 1980; Fishbein, 1980; Fishbein & Ajzen, 1975). This theory proposes that a person's attitude toward performing a behavior (an act) can be estimated by the summed products of beliefs (b_j) about the outcomes of performing that behavior and the evaluations (e_j) of those outcomes (i.e., $Aact = \Sigma_{ij}b_je_j$). While its similarity to VIE theory is evident, the theory of reasoned action has spawned a large body of work in areas outside of work motivation (e.g., Ajzen & Madden, 1986; Bagozzi, 1986; Budd, 1986; Crawford & Boyer, 1985; Craychee, 1987; Critchlow, 1987; Fisher, 1984; Hewstone & Young, 1988, Hughey, Sundstrom, & Lounsbury, 1985; Miniard & Cohen, 1983; Oliver & Bearden, 1985; Shimp & Kavas, 1984; Toneatto & Binik, 1987).

The relevance of the juxtaposed statements from *The Economist* about Americans and from *Maclean's* about Canadians is that they suggest, as a nation, Americans tend to believe more strongly than do Canadians that hard work will lead to good things in life, including ascending "to the top." VIE theory could shed some light on this hypothesis and help to explain, in part at least, why the standard of living in the United States has outpaced that in Canada for many years, and why the gap seems to continue to grow.

We will attempt to accomplish two things in this chapter. First, we will discuss at length the most important versions of the VIE theories of work motivation. As in the case of most other approaches to work motivation in this book, we will address the theories' weaknesses, methodological and scientific limitations as well as present the theories in their pure form. We will also discuss some of the most important implications they have for leadership in real work settings.

VROOM'S ORIGINAL THEORY

Vroom's theory assumes that "the choices made by a person among alternative courses of action are lawfully related to psychological events occurring contemporaneously with the behaviour" (1964, pp. 14–15). In other words, people's behavior results from conscious choices among alternatives, and these choices (behaviors) are systematically related to psychological processes, particularly perception and the formation of beliefs and attitudes. The purpose of the choices, generally, is to maximize pleasure and minimize pain. Like equity theory, then, VIE theory assumes that people base their acts on perceptions and beliefs, although, as we saw in Chapter 9, we need not anticipate any simple one-to-one relationships between particular beliefs and specific behaviors (such as job behaviors). More specifically, VIE theory proposes that behavior is instigated and directed to the extent that: (1) people believe that the behavior will lead to outcomes such as job performance; (2) people believe that such outcomes will be rewarded; and (3) people value those rewards. In the following sections, we examine the three key mental components that are seen as instigating and directing behavior. Referred to as *expectancy*, *instrumentality*, and *valence*, respectively, each of these components is, in fact, a *belief* (using the terminology developed in Chapter 8).

The Concept of Valence

VIE theory assumes that people hold preferences among various outcomes or states of nature. For example, the reader probably prefers, other things equal, a higher rate of pay for a particular job over a lower rate of pay. Here, pay level is the outcome in question, and the preference for high pay over low pay reflects the strength of the reader's basic underlying need and value structure. Likewise, some people hold preferences among different types of outcome (as opposed to greater or lesser amounts of a particular outcome). For example, many employees would seem to prefer an opportunity to work with other people, even if the only jobs featuring high levels of social interaction entail less comfortable surroundings, lower pay, or some other tradeoff. The point is that people have more or less well-defined preferences for the outcomes they derive from their actions. (Notice that these outcomes correspond roughly with what we referred to as goals in the discussion of employee frustration in Chapter 8, as well as to the outcomes we examined in the previous chapter, in the context of equity theory.) Preferences, in short, relate to a person's relative desires for, or attraction to, outcomes. (The reader is referred to Chapter 3 where the issue of intergenerational differences in preferences for work-related outcomes is discussed. See also Randstad, 2004.)

Vroom uses the term *valence* to refer to these affective orientations that people hold with regard to outcomes. An outcome is said to be positively valent for an individual if she would prefer having it to not having it. For example, we would say that a promotion is positively valent for an employee who would rather be promoted than not be promoted. Likewise, we say that an outcome which a person would prefer to avoid has negative valence for her, or simply that it is negatively valent. For example, fatigue, stress, and layoffs are three outcomes that are usually negatively valent among employees. Finally, sometimes an employee is indifferent toward certain outcomes; in such cases, the outcome is said to hold zero valence for that individual.

Valence is expected *satisfaction, not actual value*

The most important feature of people's valences concerning work-related outcomes is that they refer to the level of satisfaction the person *expects* to receive from them, not from the real value the person actually derives from them. So, for example, the reader may be enrolled in a program of business management because she expects that the outcomes to follow (an education and a diploma, among others) will be of value to her when she is finished. It may be the case that when the student graduates there will be little or no market demand for the services she has to offer the world of business and administration, so the degree may have little real value. The point is that people attribute either positive or negative preferences (or indifference) to outcomes according to the satisfaction or dissatisfaction they expect to receive from them. It is often the case that the true value of an outcome (such as a diploma) is either greater or less than the valence (expected value) it once held for the individual who was motivated to pursue it. As a final example, consider the individual who fears being fired, but learns after actually being dismissed from a job that she is healthier, happier, and better off financially in the new job she acquired after having been terminated by her former employer. In this case, being fired was a negatively valent outcome before it occurred, but eventually turned out to be of positive value after it occurred. One more time: Valence is the value a person expects to achieve from an outcome; it is what contributes to the motivation to act. The actual value of an outcome is usually not known until after the fact, so it has little motivational power.

Performance as an Outcome

The most central outcome of interest in the context of VIE theory is job performance. In most organizational settings, besides being an outcome in itself, performance is likely to result in additional outcomes, such as pay, promotions, satisfaction, keeping or losing one's job, and so on. Performance can be thought of as a *first-level outcome*, and outcomes that result from performance as second-level outcomes. *Second-level outcomes* are directly associated with valences, while performance has valence through its connection with second-level outcomes. As we shall see shortly, the strength of the connection in the mind of the employee between effort and the performance level achieved is central to Vroom's theory. Performance is the most direct outcome of effort and usually the most important for understanding work motivation from a VIE theory perspective.

The Concept of Instrumentality

Instrumentality is the term used by Vroom to describe the connection between performance on the job and outcomes that result from it; that is, between first- and second-level outcomes. This connection is what determines the valence associated with performance. A given level of performance is positively valent if the employee believes that it will lead to second-level outcomes and that those second-level outcomes are positively valent. In other words, if an employee believes (through all the belief construction processes we discussed in Chapter 9) that a high level of performance is instrumental for the acquisition of other outcomes that he expects will be gratifying (such as a promotion, for example), and/or if he believes that a high performance level will be instrumental for avoiding other outcomes that he wishes to avoid (such as being fired), then that employee will place a high valence upon performing the job well.

Consider the meaning of the adjective *instrumental*. The author's word processor at the present time is instrumental in the preparation of this book. It contributes to the job; it helps. Something is said to be "instrumental" if it is believed to lead to something else, if it helps achieve or attain something else. Hence, studying is commonly seen by students as instrumental for passing exams. In turn, passing exams is often believed instrumental for the acquisition of diplomas, which, in turn, are believed to be instrumental for landing jobs in tight labor market conditions.

Vroom (1964) suggested that we consider instrumentality as a probability belief linking one outcome (performance level) to other outcomes, ranging from 1.0 (meaning that the attainment of the second outcome is certain if the first outcome is achieved), through 0 (meaning that there is no likely relationship between the attainment of the first outcome and the attainment of the second), to −1.0 (meaning that the attainment of the second outcome is certain without the first and that it is impossible with it).

For example, bonus pay that is distributed at random would lead to employees' having perceptions of the instrumentality between bonus pay and performance equal to zero. ("Performance and pay have no connection around here!") By the same token, commission pay schemes that tie pay directly to performance, and only to performance, are designed to make employees perceive that performance is positively instrumental for the acquisition of money. (A recent longitudinal study by Sturman, 2006, confirmed one more time that when pay is directly related to employee performance, the performance level increases, whether through merit pay that is added to base salary or through bonuses.)

Finally, an employee who has been threatened with dismissal for being drunk on the job may be told by his supervisor, in effect, that lack of sobriety at work is negatively instrumental for continued employment, or, alternatively, that further imbibing will be positively instrumental for termination. (The notion of negative instrumentalities makes Vroom's original formulation of VIE theory somewhat more difficult and cumbersome than it might otherwise be, so subsequent versions of the theory have avoided using it, choosing instead to speak only of positive instrumentalities.)

Consider the case of an employee who perceives that high performance will not lead to things he desires, but that it will be more instrumental for attaining outcomes to which he attributes negative valences. High performance will not be positively valent for such a person, so we would not expect to see him striving to perform well. As a further example, an employee might perceive that taking a job as a travelling salesman will be instrumental for attaining a number of outcomes, some of which he expects will be positive, some of which he believes will be negative. On the positively valent side, meeting new people and seeing the countryside may be appealing to him, because he expects that these outcomes will be instrumental for satisfying his relatedness and growth needs, while the possible threat to his family life may be aversive to him.

In short, the "I" in VIE theory stands for instrumentality: The belief about the way in which performance and other first-level outcomes are related to second-level job outcomes. It serves as the connection between performance and valence. A first-level outcome is positively valent if the person believes that it holds high instrumentality for the acquisition of positively valent consequences (goals or other outcomes), and the avoidance of negatively valent outcomes. That is, in order for a first-level outcome to be positively valent, the outcomes to which the person believes it is connected must themselves, in turn, be seen as positively valent. If an employee anticipates that high levels of performance will lead primarily to things he dislikes, then high performance will not be positively valent to him. Likewise, if the individual perceives that high performance is generally rewarded with things he desires, he will place high valence on high performance and, other things being equal, he will strive for high performance. Of course, the valence of such second-level outcomes is determined by the nature of the person's most salient needs and values.

At this point, the reader may be seeing the implications for the design of reward systems in organizations. If management wants high performance levels, it must tie positively valent outcomes to high performance and be sure that employees understand the connection. Similarly, low performance must be seen as connected to consequences that are of either zero or negative valence.

Expectancy and Related Concepts

(a la cause-d-effect)

The third major component of VIE theory is referred to as *expectancy*. Expectancy is the strength of a person's belief about the degree to which a particular first-level outcome is the result of his or her actions. This author, for example, would place very little expectancy on the prospect of becoming an astronaut. The reasons are, of course, personal, but the point is that he doesn't believe that any amount of trying on his part will see him aboard the space shuttle! If a person believes that he can achieve an outcome, he will be more motivated to try for it, assuming that other things are equal (the other things, of course, consist of the person's beliefs about the valence of the outcome, which, in turn, is determined by the person's beliefs about the odds that the outcome will be instrumental for acquiring and avoiding those things he either wishes to acquire or avoid, respectively).

Vroom (1964) spoke of expectancy beliefs as action–outcome associations (beliefs) held in the minds of individuals, and suggested that we think of them in probability terms ranging from 0 (in the case where the person's subjective probability of attaining an outcome is psychologically zero – "I can't do it") through to 1.0, indicating that the person has no doubt about his capacity to attain the outcome. In practice, of course, people's estimates tend to range between these two extremes. (The reader will recall from Chapter 3 that achievement-oriented individuals tend to prefer tasks that are neither too difficult nor too easy, such that, for example, we might say they prefer tasks with perceived expectancy values near 0.5, meaning that there is a 50/50 perceived chance of success in performing the task.)

A variety of factors contribute to an employee's expectancy beliefs about various levels of job performance. For example, his level of confidence in his skills for the task at hand, the degree of help he expects to receive from his supervisor and subordinates, the quality of the materials and equipment available, and the availability of pertinent information and control over sufficient budget, are common examples of factors that can influence a person's expectancy beliefs about being able to achieve a particular level of performance. Previous success experiences at a task and a generally high level of self-esteem also strengthen expectancy beliefs (Lawler, 1973; and see Chapter 6 of this book). Previous success is the essence of "enactive mastery," which Bandura (1982) argued is the predominant influence on *self-efficacy*, or "one's belief in one's capability to perform a specific task" (see Gist, 1987, p. 472; and refer to Chapter 6 for more on self-efficacy).

"ENACTIVE MASTERY"

Expectancy beliefs vs. self-efficacy beliefs

During our discussion of self-esteem in Chapter 6, we encountered the concept of *self-efficacy*, in part because it is frequently confused with self-esteem, although, as we noted then, the two concepts are only remotely related. In similar fashion, it is appropriate to reintroduce the concept of self-efficacy at this point because it is also frequently confused with the notion of expectancy, or expectation. Clearly the concept of self-efficacy expectations is closely related to the concept of effort–performance expectancy.

Self-efficacy is, however, a somewhat broader construct. According to Daniels and Mitchell (1995), self-efficacy has to do with a person's judgment about whether s/he *can* do something; it is an estimate of ability relative to a task. If someone asks you if you can make a perfect martini and you answer with honest confidence "Of course!," you are reflecting high self-efficacy for this exquisite task. Inasmuch as self-efficacy beliefs have to do with a person's confidence about her capability to perform a particular task in a particular context, then deliberate training for that task-in-context ought to increase the strength of self-efficacy beliefs. Indeed, one study conducted at the U.S. Naval

Recruit Training Command demonstrated that this is the case. More than 1000 Navy recruits were assessed on the basis of their commitment, self-efficacy, and motivation levels both before and after rigorous socialization training. Comparison of pre- and post-training self-ratings of self-efficacy showed significant increases as a result of the training (Tannenbaum, Mathieu, Salas, & Cannon-Bowers, 1991). We return to the concept of self-efficacy in a number of places in this book, especially in Chapter 14 (and see Chapter 6).

But merely having such high self-efficacy for this task can actually stimulate you to engage in it: Thus, self-efficacy is said to have *generative* properties – it can actually stimulate the behavior in question.[2] It *is* possible to have high self-efficacy with regard to a task but not be motivated to perform it, however, so, while high self-efficacy can be a major contributing factor to task motivation, it is not necessarily generative or predictive of work motivation. The point is that self-efficacy concerns the question: "Can I do it?" By contrast, expectancy perceptions concern the issue of how a person believes s/he will actually do at a task (Daniels & Mitchell, 1995). Kanfer and Ackerman (1989) referred to this judgment as "predicted performance," whereas Henry (1994) calls it a *performance prediction*. So, if "self-efficacy can be thought of as a 'can do' construct ... then an expectation can be viewed as a 'will do' construct" (Daniels & Mitchell, 1995). Expectancies do not have any generative power as self-efficacy beliefs are thought of as possessing.

Gist (1987) suggested that self-efficacy may predict non-performance of a task as a result of a person's belief that he is unmotivated. Gist and Mitchell suggested (1992, p. 185):

> [T]hat self-efficacy may represent a more comprehensive formulation of the rationale underlying the expectancy theory construct [expectancy]. For example, the most frequent conceptualization and empirical assessment of [expectancy] is in terms of the relationship between effort and performance ... By contrast, Bandura asserted not only that self-efficacy subsumes variables typically not included in [expectancy] (such as mood), but also that "[s]elf percepts of efficacy are not simply inert predictors of future behaviour" (1984: 242). Though both constructs involve forethought, self-efficacy is viewed as having *generative* capability: it influences thought patterns, emotional reactions, and the orchestration of performance through the adroit use of sub-skills, ingenuity, resourcefulness, and so forth (Bandura, 1984, 1986).

The distinction between expectancy and self-efficacy notwithstanding, the other influences on self-efficacy that Bandura proposed likely apply to expectancy as well. To the extent that this is so, expectancy will be influenced by vicarious experience (observing a successful model, preferably one who is similar to the observer), verbal persuasion aimed at convincing a person of her capability, and physiological arousal (such as when anxiety is interpreted as debilitating fear) (Gist, 1987). The point is that an employee's subjective estimate of the odds that he can achieve a given level of performance is determined by a variety of factors, both within his own control and beyond it. A recent paper by Nebeker and Pon (2004) provided both theoretical and empirical evidence that the overlap between the two constructs is significant and that both are valid predictors of performance. They conclude that self-efficacy and expectancy "likely measure the same construct" and that formally integrating the two concepts, if not the theories behind them, is a reasonable proposition. This author believes there is considerable merit in the suggestion by Nebeker and Pon (2004), particularly for applied purposes.

---

[2] There have been a number of attempts to postulate and define a concept of *group efficacy*, which has been defined by one team of authors as a "group's (or organization's) collective belief that it can successfully perform a specific task" (Lindsley, Brass, & Thomas, 1995). Noting that self-efficacy beliefs can link up with high performance into spirals, such that these beliefs become both a contributing cause of high performance as well as a consequence of such performance, over and over, the notion is that groups can generate and enjoy such spirals. Moreover, spirals linking efficacy and performance can also work in a downward direction: Once things start going badly for a group, self-efficacy beliefs decline and further poor performance becomes more likely. The author understands and appreciates the concept, such as it is, but would prefer that a concept other than self-efficacy be used in such analyses. Self-efficacy is an individual-level concept, so that linking it to group-level phenomena constitutes anthropomorphism (see Chapter 3).

Efficacy Spirals

As'bevief

There is a particularly interesting feature about self-efficacy beliefs that can have major importance for both people who work as well as people who oversee the work of others. Individuals can often become engaged in efficacy spirals – periods in which successful performance of a task will fuel higher beliefs of self-efficacy that, in turn, raise an individual's confidence and facilitate further successful performance: The better one becomes at a job, the more confidence she feels, and the better still she does at the job. Within human and technological limits, things just keep getting better and better!

These spirals can work in the opposite direction. If an individual experiences one or two significant failures at a job, and if those failures are taken seriously, she may witness feelings of self-doubt, performance anxiety, and lowered beliefs of self-efficacy. The author has a young friend (a former student) who works in a Human Resources Department in a large Canadian food retail company. Over the period of only a few days, this woman made two or three simple yet innocent *adding mistakes* in the process of completing and submitting a report for her boss. The boss detected the errors and made mention of them. The woman took these errors to heart and the concern expressed by her boss crushed her. She reported to the author that she felt her supervisor would no longer trust her and that she was beginning to doubt whether she was capable of performing her job satisfactorily. She was convinced, in fact, that she had been performing below standard since the event, and that it was only a matter of time until she would be detected as an incompetent and fired. The "spiral" in this case worked in the opposite direction: The worse things became, the worse still they became. This is a true story about a woman who was president of her graduating class at university, who had a first-class average in her courses, who managed to find a professional job (during a time when it appeared that there were no jobs), and who had performed at least to standard during the first 18 months following her graduation. This woman is a leader, a "winner." *The I hate my job handbook* (Tien & Frankel, 1996) is full of case stories of this variety. Few people who begin to slip into one of these spirals of poor performance → self doubt → further poor performance may think of these situations as involving problems of self-efficacy, but that is what they are called in the organizational behavior literature.

The Pygmalion and Galatea Effects

Readers who are fans of Greek and Roman mythology may be amused to learn that two heroes from the classics lend their names to psychological effects related to the notions of expectancy and self-efficacy. The Israeli professor Dov Eden is largely to credit for bringing these effects some personality by advancing and describing the so-called *Pygmalion* and *Galatea* effects.

For the Romans, Pygmalion was the sculptor of Cyprus. He hated women and was determined that he would never be married. In spite of his resolve, working on the beautiful statue enthralled him and he fell in love with it. He was distraught that his love object was merely a stone idol, and prayed to Venus (who was in charge of love) to provide him with a real-life version of the statue. The maiden who resulted from the statue was Galatea (Encarta, 1993a). For the Greeks, Galatea was a sea nymph who was loved by the Cyclops Polyphemus, who was an ugly fellow with a single eye in the middle of his forehead. Galatea rejected his advances and mocked him, then teased him into believing that maybe she could love him. But he never won her affection for real. Meanwhile, Galatea fell in love with Acis, a young prince. Poor Polyphemus killed Acis in a jealous rage (Encarta, 1993b).

In the realm of modern work motivation theory, the *Pygmalion effect* is a general increase in an employee's performance that results from raising a manager's expectations about the possible performance levels of employees (Eden, 1984). Managers who truly believe that people working for them are capable of high performance act in ways that instil confidence and that result in high performance. This sort of effect has been demonstrated time and time again in classroom settings. Teachers in controlled experiments who believe that their students are superior eventually end up with superior-performing students, when, in fact, the students are randomly chosen and assigned. Believing that someone can excel seems to make us cause them to do so, even when we are not aware of doing so. This is the Pygmalion effect. The early research on this effect found support for the hypothesis generally among male samples only. However, two experiments reported by Davidson and Eden (2000) extended the findings to females samples. A meta-analysis reported by Kierein and Gold (2000) confirmed the strength and consistency of this effect across 13 different samples of research participants.

By contrast, the *Galatea effect* is a performance gain that results from an employee's expect-ations about her own performance (Eden, 1988; Eden & Kinnar, 1991). One interesting field experi-ment involved Israeli military inductees. In the usual approach, pre-screened recruits who were eligible for special forces on the basis of aptitude and motivation are provided with information about the special forces and then solicited to volunteer. The purpose of the experiment was to entice a number of these young soldiers into serving in special forces units by manipulating their self-efficacy beliefs. After they pre-screened recruits who were eligible for special forces on the basis of aptitude and motivation, they provided the eligible ones with information about the special forces and then solicited them to volunteer. This was the usual approach before the experiment was undertaken.

In the experiment, the inductees were split into two groups. Each group was exposed to a veteran member of one of the special forces who told the candidates about life in these forces. In the "experimental group," the veterans making the presentations stressed that they had once been raw recruits and had wondered whether they would have had the ability to succeed in the special forces. In other words, the presenters attempted to manipulate the self-efficacy beliefs of the experimental soldiers, influencing them to believe that they were capable of doing well in these elite groups. The "control" soldiers received the same stories from the veterans, but no mention was made by the veterans about the similarities between themselves when they were younger and the new recruits in the audience. In short, this simple experimental manipulation, aimed at creating an association in the minds of the new recruits between themselves and the successful soldiers, was used to boost the self-efficacy beliefs of half of the recruits. Self-efficacy was measured among all the recruits after their exposure to the veterans.

As expected, the self-reported self-efficacy scores of the experimental inductees were signifi-cantly higher than that among the control inductees. More importantly, 84% of the recruits exposed to the experimental induction volunteered for service in the special forces, compared to only 16% – a ratio of about 5:1. The reason was they believed that they too could perform well in special units (because they believed they were similar in ability to the successful special forces soldiers who presented the special forces option to them).

The experimenters concluded that this special induction was successful in increasing the young soldiers' beliefs that they had "the right stuff" to make it in the especially demanding roles of the special forces, so they volunteered to sign up (Eden & Kinnar, 1991). In Chapter 14, we will revisit the development of self-efficacy beliefs and see that there are a variety of general approaches available. Eden and Kinnar's (1991) powerful early demonstration of the Galatea effect has recently been reinforced and extended by McNatt and Judge (2004).

Empowerment (again)

In Chapter 7, we examined the concept referred to as *empowerment* – a buzzword of the 1980s that survives until this day. While the concept has applications and relevance for a variety of settings and disciplines (Eylon, 1994; Spreitzer, 1995a, 1995b), it has particular relevance for the management of people in work settings. Conger and Kanungo (1988) were the first to define empowerment for the

Def empowerment

organizational literature; for them, it is merely *the motivational concept of self-efficacy*. Thomas and Velthouse (1990) argued that empowerment is a multidimensional construct that includes elements of four cognitions related to a person's beliefs about her work: Its meaning or purpose; the person's competence to perform the task; her degree of self-determination in how to approach the task; and *impact* – the degree to which she can influence the strategic, administrative, or operating outcomes at the workplace (Spreitzer, 1995a, 1995b):

> Together, these four cognitions reflect an active, rather than a passive, orientation to a work role and context. The four dimensions are argued to combine additively to create an overall construct of psychological empowerment . . . the lack of any dimension will deflate, though not completely eliminate, the overall degree of felt empowerment.
>
> (Spreitzer, 1995a, p. 1444)

By this view, empowerment is not a trait that transcends settings; rather, it is a set of beliefs held by a person *in a particular work setting* (Thomas & Velthouse, 1990; recall the discussion in Chapter 1 of this book). Spreitzer (1995b) developed and validated scales to assess this conceptualization of empowerment and found some encouraging empirical results connecting empowerment to effectiveness and innovativeness among two samples of employees.

Recapitulation

The purpose of the foregoing sections has been to explain the major elements of Vroom's (1964) original VIE theory, by exploring the meaning of valence, instrumentality, and expectancy. The last few paragraphs have taken us somewhat off-course because our discussion of expectancy naturally leads us into a discussion of other concepts similar to expectancy, such as self-efficacy and empowerment. We now return to our treatment of Vroom's (1964) major concepts by examining what he meant by *force*.

The Concept of Force in VIE Models

"Force"

Vroom (1964) argued that expectancies, instrumentalities, and valences interact psychologically to create a motivational force to act in those ways that seem most likely to bring pleasure or to avoid pain: "Behavior on the part of a person is assumed to be the result of a field of forces each of which has a direction and magnitude" (p. 18). Vroom likened his concept of force to a variety of other metaphorical concepts, including things such as performance vectors and behavior potential.

FORCE AS INTENTION

Force as intention

In keeping with the terminology developed in Chapter 9, we can think of the force as representing the "strength of a person's intention to act in a certain way." For example, if a person elects to strive for a particular level of job performance, we might say that the person's beliefs cause the greatest amount of force to be directed toward that level, or that he intends to strive for that level rather than for other levels.

Symbolically, Vroom (1964, p. 18) summarizes his own theory as follows:

$$F_i = f\left(\sum_{i=1}^{n} E_{ij} V_j \right) \text{ and } V_j = f\left(\sum_{j=1}^{n} I_{jk} V_k \right)$$

where

F_i = the psychological force to perform an act (i) (such as strive for a particular level of performance)

E_{ij} = the strength of the expectancy that the act will be followed by the outcome j

V_j = the valence for the individual of outcome j

I_{jk} = the instrumentality of outcome j for attaining second-level outcome k

V_k = the valence of second-level outcome k

Or, in his words:

$$F_i = f\left(\sum_{i=1} E_{ij} V_j\right) \text{ and } V_j = f\left(\sum_{j=1} I_{jk} V_k\right)$$

The force on a person to perform an act is a monotonically increasing function of the algebraic sum of the products of the valences of all outcomes and the strength of his expectancies that the act will be followed by the attainment of these outcomes.

So people choose from among the alternative acts the one(s) corresponding to the strongest positive (or weakest negative) force. People attempt to maximize their overall best interest, using the information available to them and their evaluations of this information. In the context of work motivation, this means that people select to pursue that level of performance that they believe will maximize their overall best interest (or subjective expected utility). Notice from the formula that *there will be little or no motivational force operating on an individual to act in a certain manner if any of three conditions hold*: (1) if the person does not believe that acting in that manner will have any result (that is, if her expectancy is effectively 0); (2) if she believes that there is no association between the result of her behavior and any second-level outcomes (if her instrumentality is effectively 0); (3) if she does not value the second-level outcomes (if her valence is 0).

Choice of Performance Level

When we think of the levels of job performance that an employee might strive for as the outcome of interest, Vroom's theory suggests that the individual will consider the valences, instrumentalities, and expectancies associated with each level of the entire spectrum of performance levels and will elect to pursue the level that generates the greatest positive force (or lowest negative force) for him. If the person sees more good outcomes than bad ones associated with performing at a high level, he will strive to perform highly. On the other hand, if a lower level of performance results in the greatest degree of psychological force, we can anticipate that he will settle for such a level. The implication is that low motivation levels result from employee choices to perform at low levels, and that these choices, in turn, are the result of beliefs concerning the valences, instrumentalities, and expectancies held in the mind of the employee. These beliefs are formed and modified in the ways described in Chapter 8, and suggest, accordingly, a number of implications for the management of work motivation. We will address these implications later in this chapter.

REFINEMENTS TO VIE THEORY FOLLOWING VROOM

Since the publication of Vroom's book in 1964, there has been a considerable amount of both theoretical and empirical attention paid to expectancy-type models of work motivation. Aside from attempting to test the validity of the theory in its simple form, most of these efforts have sought to study the characteristics of people and organizations that influence valence, instrumentality, and expectancy beliefs, or to examine the types of condition within which VIE-type predictions of work motivation can be expected to apply. A complete discussion of these refinements could easily constitute an entire book, so it is well beyond our present purposes. (The reader who is interested in pursuing major theoretic advances in VIE theory is referred to the following sources: Campbell, Dunnette, Lawler, & Weick, 1970; Dachler & Mobley, 1973; Feldman, Reitz, & Hiterman, 1976; Graen, 1969; House, Shapiro, & Wahba, 1974; Kanfer, 1990; Kopelman, 1977; Kopelman & Thompson, 1976; Lawler, 1971, 1973; Naylor, Pritchard, & llgen, 1980; Porter & Lawler, 1968; Reinharth & Wahba, 1976; Staw, 1977; Zedeck, 1977. Thorough reviews of the research evidence pertaining to VIE theory are provided by Campbell & Pritchard, 1976; Heneman & Schwab, 1972; Mitchell & Biglan, 1971.)

For the purpose of the present discussion, only one of the many theoretical advancements of VIE theory will be presented, followed by a brief summary of the validity of the theory and a number of difficulties that have been encountered in determining its validity. Finally, as mentioned above, the chapter will conclude with a discussion of the major implications of VIE theory for the practice of management. So, to begin, let's take a look at one of the most important modifications and extensions offered to Vroom's work – the model offered by Porter and Lawler (1968).

The Porter–Lawler Model

Vroom's (1964) statement of VIE theory left a number of questions unanswered. Perhaps the most important of these concerned the origins of valence, instrumentality, and expectancy beliefs, and the nature of the relationship, if any, between employee attitudes toward work and job performance. Porter and Lawler (1968) developed a theoretic model and then tested it, using a sample of managers, and revised it to explore these issues. The revised statement of their model is provided in schematic form in Figure 12.1.

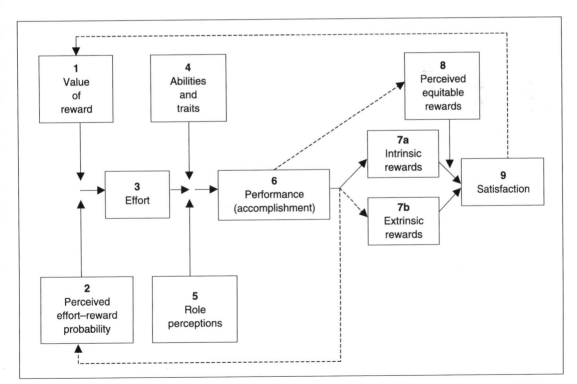

FIG. 12.1   Revised Porter–Lawler model.

Source: Porter, L. W., & Lawler, E. E. (1968). Managerial attitudes and performance. Homewood, IL: Dorsey Press, Division of Richard D. Irwin. Reprinted with permission.

In a nutshell, their theory suggests the following. Employee effort is jointly determined by two key factors: The value placed on certain outcomes by the individual, and the degree to which the person believes that his effort will lead to the attainment of these rewards. As predicted by Vroom, Porter and Lawler found that these two factors interact to determine effort level; in other words, they found that people must both positively value outcomes and believe that these outcomes result from their effort for any further effort to be forthcoming. However, effort may or may not result in job performance, which they defined as the accomplishment of those tasks that comprise a person's job. The reason? The level of ability the person has to do his job, and his role clarity, the degree of clarity of the understanding the person has concerning just what his job consists of. Thus, a person may be highly motivated (putting out a lot of effort), but that effort will not necessarily result in what can be considered performance, unless he has both the ability to perform the job as well as a clear understanding of the ways in which it is appropriate to direct that effort. The student reader is probably familiar with at least one colleague who has high motivation to learn and succeed in university, but who lacks either the ability or the savoir faire needed to direct his energy into what can be considered performance in the academic context: Learning and self-development. In short, all three ingredients are needed to some degree, and if any of them is absent, performance cannot result.

Next, what is the relationship between performance (at whatever level) and job satisfaction? As reflected in Figure 12.1, Porter and Lawler proposed that performance and satisfaction may or may not be related to one another, depending upon a number of factors. First, they noted that it is not always the case that performance results in rewards in organizations. Further, they recognized that there are at least two types of reward potentially available from performance: Intrinsic and extrinsic. (We have dealt with the distinction between intrinsic and extrinsic outcomes earlier in this book; the reader is referred to Chapter 3.) Porter and Lawler also recognized that intrinsic rewards can be much more closely connected with good performance than extrinsic rewards, because the former result (almost automatically) from performance itself, whereas the latter depend upon outside sources (both to recognize that performance has been attained and to administer rewards accordingly).

Porter and Lawler suggested that the level of performance a person believes she has attained will influence the level of rewards that she believes will be equitable (see the discussion of internalized standards of equity in Chapter 11). So, if an employee believes that her efforts have resulted in high degrees of performance in the past, she will expect a greater level of reward than would be the case if she believes that her performance is not as high. As a result, a particular reward, if any is forthcoming, will be assessed in terms of its level of equity in the mind of the employee, rather than in terms of its absolute level. We sometimes hear statements such as "That pay increase was an insult, considering all I do for this company," reflecting Porter and Lawler's belief that *it is not the absolute amount of reward that follows performance which determines whether it is satisfying; rather, the amount, however large or small, must be seen by the employee as equitable in order for it to be satisfying.*

Satisfaction was defined in Porter and Lawler's research as "the extent to which rewards actually received meet or exceed the perceived equitable level of rewards" (p. 31). And, as suggested by the feedback loop at the top of Figure 12.1, the level of satisfaction or dissatisfaction experienced by the person as a result of his treatment by the organization helps determine the value he places in the future on the rewards in question (which we now call "valence"). Moreover, notice the feedback loop at the bottom of the diagram. It suggests that the strength of the person's belief that effort will result in rewards is also determined through experience.

Comments and Criticisms of Porter and Lawler

A number of points must be made about this model. First, the primary focus of the research that accompanied its development was upon pay and the role of pay in employee motivation. Although the authors limited their consideration only to pay outcomes, they argued that the general model should be relevant for consequences other than pay. In addition, since pay was the focus, the emphasis was upon positive consequences only rather than upon both positive and negative consequences (such as fatigue, demotions, or various forms of punishment). Second, Porter and Lawler tested the propositions they derived from their model cross-sectionally (rather than over time), and using only managers from the extreme ends of the distributions on the important variables in that model, excluding those individuals who fell near the middle in each case. This is a common practice in research, but one that causes overestimates of the validity of the model being tested (Taylor & Griess, 1976). Additionally, they measured job satisfaction using a technique that is also commonly used, but one which has subsequently been shown to be inappropriate, probably reducing the apparent validity of the model (Edwards, 1994; Johns, 1981). A third point is that although their model posits the importance of ability as an interactive factor with motivation as a determinant of job performance, Porter and Lawler's own research did not pay much attention to examining the specific role of ability. As was noted in Chapter 1 of the present volume, however, other researchers have addressed this issue, and the results seem to suggest that while ability has an important influence on performance, it may not interact with motivation in the manner believed by Vroom (1964) and Porter and Lawler (cf. Terborg, 1977). Fourth, while Porter and Lawler used the term _value_ rather than _valence_, it seems clear that they had the same concept in mind as Vroom. The reader is reminded again of the importance of distinguishing between valence and value when considering motivation from a VIE theory perspective: It is the anticipated value (valence) of an outcome that is crucial in determining effort, not actual value, per se.

Another point has to do with the way the connection between effort and rewards was conceptualized and measured. Current theories recognize that employee beliefs about the strength of the connection between effort and reward distribution can usefully be broken down into two components: (1) the strength of the belief that a person's effort will result in job performance; and (2) the strength of the person's belief that performance, if achieved, will eventuate into rewards. Porter and Lawler acknowledged the prospect for breaking this overall cognition down into its component parts, and subsequent work by Lawler (1973) and others maintains this distinction.

Performance and Satisfaction (again)

A major contribution of the Porter–Lawler model consists of the implications it holds for the issue concerning the relationship between performance and satisfaction (recall Chapter 10). Consider the diagram in Figure 12.1. According to the theory, will satisfaction and performance be related to one another? If so, when? The figure suggests that these two factors may or may not be related to one another, but that when they are, the order of causality is far from simple. First, how might satisfaction be a contributing determinant of performance levels? A number of conditions must hold:

1. Satisfaction must leave the person wanting more of the same outcome(s). Recall from Chapter 3 that satisfied needs tend to lose their capacity to motivate behavior, although growth need satisfaction seems to increase the strength of these needs.
2. Even if the reward maintains its valence, effort will result only if the person believes that effort results in the attainment of the reward (which, as we have discussed, is not always the case).
3. In order for the individual's effort to result in performance, the person must have the ability to perform, as well as have a clear idea concerning how to try to perform – where to direct his effort.
4. The performance must result in rewards, and these rewards must be perceived as equitable, for the reasons discussed earlier.

In short, in order for satisfaction to be a contributing cause of performance, as was believed during the days of the human relations movement (and as is still commonly believed by managers and people on the street), all of the foregoing individual and organizational conditions must apply. Rather complicated, to say the least.

Can performance be a cause of satisfaction? The model implies that it can. First, as already noted, high performance can be an immediate cause of intrinsic satisfaction, assuming that the job provides sufficient challenge to appeal to growth needs (recall Chapter 7). Second, performance can contribute to extrinsic satisfaction if at least three conditions hold: (1) desired rewards must be tied to that performance (as opposed to being tied to chance or other factors); (2) the person must perceive the connection between his performance and the rewards he receives; and (3) the person must believe that the rewards he receives for his performance are equitable. Again, not a very simple relationship, but Porter and Lawler's model helps explain why the relationships observed between performance and satisfaction have traditionally been so low, although, in their research, the two factors were found to be more strongly connected than is usually the case.

In conclusion, Porter and Lawler provided a useful elaboration of the fundamental concepts of VIE theory as presented only a few years earlier by Vroom. The dynamic features of their model (as reflected in the feedback loops) indicate the ongoing nature of the motivation process, and shed some light on why some employees are more productive than others, why some employees are more satisfied with their work than others, and when we can expect to find a relationship between employee attitudes and performance. The reader may wonder about the age of the Porter and Lawler revision of Vroom's (1964) model: It was published nearly 40 years ago. There have been other, more recent models proposed, but they offer few major innovations over and above that of Porter and Lawler (1968). *The mere age of an idea is not sufficient grounds to reject it.*

VALIDITY OF VIE THEORY[3]

Despite the fact that there have been innumerable tests of the scientific validity of VIE theory, it is unclear whether or not researchers have conducted fair tests of the theory, given the claims made by the theory itself, and problems with the way that studies have been conducted. In their 1976 review, Campbell and Pritchard identified 12 common problems in the many studies conducted to that time. During the more-than 40 years since then some of these have been seemingly resolved, others have not.

The Between/Within Issue

Probably the most widely cited of these problems has had to do with what has come to be called the "between/within issue." It concerns the argument that VIE theory is solely intended to make behavioral and attitudinal predictions within individuals, and not across individuals (Arnold, 1981; Klein, 1991a; Kopelman, 1977; Mitchell, 1974; Nickerson & McLelland, 1989; Wolf & Connolly, 1981). In other words, *is Vroom's theory intended to make predictions about which behavioral alternatives a single individual will choose from among those that confront him, or to make predictions about the relative likelihood of different individuals choosing from among the alternatives confronting them?*

Vroom states that the alternative which is perceived to maximize the individual's overall expected utility and satisfaction will be the one selected. This implies that the theory is concerned

---

[3] Much of the content in this section is technical. It deals with some difficult topics related to measurement and research strategy in the context of VIE theory. Some readers may wish to move directly to our treatment of the path–goal theory of leadership, which accepts VIE theory's basic tenets as valid and offers suggestions for the application of the VIE model.

with choices across alternatives but within individuals. Conversely, many of the investigations purporting to "test" VIE theory computed expected levels of motivational force (or effort) for a number of people using those people's scores on VIE factors, and then correlated these predicted scores, across individuals, with ratings representing actual behavior or attitudes.

To illustrate more completely, suppose we were to compute expected effort scores for a sample of 20 people, using the information these people provide us through interviews or questionnaires. We would calculate these scores using some form of E(ΣVI) formula. Then suppose we rank-ordered these people on the basis of the magnitude of this overall predicted effort level. Next, we gather supervisory ratings of the actual typical effort levels of these same people and rank-order them again, this time on the basis of their supervisory ratings. Finally, assume we correlate the rated effort scores with our predicted effort scores, attempting to determine whether the people with the highest predicted scores tended to have the highest supervisory ratings, and whether those with the lowest predicted scores also had the lowest ratings.

Proponents of the within-individuals approach have argued that the between-persons approach is invalid for two reasons. First, on theoretical grounds, they have argued that it does not test VIE theory per se. Then, on empirical grounds, they have argued that the tendency of findings of between-individual studies to be weaker shows that the between approach is not valid. Here, we will discuss these arguments in terms of three interrelated issues. The first is statistical, concerning the relative ability of the two approaches to show empirical support for the theory. Between-persons versus within-persons research designs have differential power to detect existing empirical relationships. The second issue is a methodological one. It concerns the vulnerability of the two approaches to alternative explanations (recall Chapter 2). The third issue is theoretical, concerning whether or not VIE theory makes between- as well as within-individual predictions.

Using the terms defined by Cook and Campbell (1979) in their definitive work on the validity of propositions, these three issues correspond to concerns about *statistical conclusion validity*, *internal validity*, and *construct validity* (these concepts are presented in Chapter 2 of this book). Our position is that conclusions about the validity of the within- as opposed to between-individual approaches cannot be made on the basis of empirical results (Nickerson & McLelland, 1989) and must, rather, be made on theoretical grounds. Further, we hold that advancements in conceptualization and operationalization of VIE theory concepts make between individual studies valid extensions of Vroom's theory.

Statistical Conclusion Validity

Tests employing the within-individual approach have often been more supportive of VIE theory predictions than those adopting a between-persons approach. That is, they have been more likely to find statistically significant relationships between predictor and criterion measures of VIE concepts. For example, Parker and Dyer (1976) were able to make better-than-chance predictions about the decisions reached by naval officers as to whether or not to retire voluntarily. Likewise, Arnold (1981), Fusilier, Ganster, and Middlemist (1984), and Baker, Ravichandran, and Randall (1989) made predictions supportive of the theory concerning the choices of jobs made by students (see also Wanous, Keon, & Latack, 1983, for a review of within-individual studies of occupational choice); Butler and Cantrell (1989) predicted the research productivity of business faculty; Matsui, Kagawa, Nagamatsu, and Ohtsuka (1977) predicted which of six insurance policies agents would prefer to sell; while Nebeker and Mitchell (1974) and Matsui and Ohtsuka (1978) predicted the leadership styles of supervisors in different settings and in different cultures.

At the same time, while generally finding weaker relationships, the between-individuals approach has also supported VIE theory (see Schwab, Olian-Gottlieb, & Heneman, 1979, for an early review of early between-individuals research). The results of studies that purported to contrast the within- and between-individual approaches were mixed. Snyder, Howard, and Hammer (1978), for example, found that the between-individuals approach outperformed the within-individuals approach in predicting job choice. By contrast, Muchinsky (1977) and Kennedy, Fossum, and White (1983) found that within-individuals predictions of effort were stronger than between-individuals predictions.[4]

In Chapter 2, we introduced the concept of statistical conclusion validity. This issue concerns whether a researcher makes correct inferences about the true relationships among constructs of interest to him (such as, for example, between predicted effort scores and actual effort ratings provided by supervisors in a VIE theory study) on the basis of the statistical measures and statistical relationships he found in his research. Of the numerous threats to this kind of validity listed by Cook and Campbell, three are particularly relevant here: (1) the greater statistical power of within-individuals designs, (2) low reliability of measures, and (3) random heterogeneity of respondents.

First of all, VIE studies employing the within-individuals approach generally have significantly greater power to find relationships than do between-individuals designs. By asking the same individuals to provide repeated measures, the number of observations given the same number of participants is much higher. Baker, Ravichandran, and Randall (1989), for example, conducted a within-individuals study of VIE theory in which they obtained 25,800 observations from 101 participants!

Second, the low reliability of VIE measures (de Leo & Pritchard, 1974) was a problem for both within- and between-individuals studies. However, given the lower ability of between-individuals approaches to find effects for the other reasons given here, and the small proportion of total variance in behavior often explained by VIE measures, the effect of low reliability may have been to attenuate relationships found in between-individuals studies to below traditional significance criteria.

Third, and likely most importantly, one of the reasons that within-individuals tests of VIE theory often outperform between-individuals tests is that they control for differences across individuals, for random heterogeneity. Between-individuals tests require strong assumptions about the comparability of individuals, assumptions that are often not met (Dawes & Smith, 1985; Hammond, McLelland, & Mumpower, 1980; Jaccard, 1981; Nickerson & McLelland, 1989; Wolf & Connolly, 1981). In within-individuals research designs each individual acts as his or her own control, thus differences between people in ability, experience, personality, preferences for different rewards, instrument response tendencies, and various other things are held constant for each individual (Kennedy, Fossum, & White, 1983). To the extent that such things are relevant to what the researcher is trying to predict, as is very much the case for VIE theory, research designs in which they are held constant are likely to show stronger relationships between predictor and criterion measures than those in which they are left to vary. In between-individuals designs the effect of such individual differences is left to vary randomly thus reducing the proportion of the variance in the criterion measure that is predicted by VIE theory constructs.[5] As Nickerson and McLelland (1989) stated: "Possible distortions in the across-persons correlations render meaningless any comparisons between across-persons and within-persons predictions" (p. 266).

In effect, VIE theory is an incomplete specification of employee behavior. For example, ability is an obvious determinant of performance, yet it is not included in VIE theory; if performance is used as the criterion in tests of the theory it will be imperfectly predicted. Similarly, we pointed out earlier that employee self-esteem is likely to have an effect on expectancy beliefs. Indeed, incorporating individual differences improves the predictions of VIE theory (Miller & Grush, 1988). To the extent that these or other relevant variables are not held constant their effect on effort will be counted as error variance, reducing the apparent validity of the theory. The effect of this fact is to make fair comparisons of the between- and within-individuals approaches to VIE theory very difficult.

To state the problem another way, every theoretical proposition contains an implicit *ceteris*

---

[4] Later, we will argue that such comparisons are meaningless.
[5] Nickerson and McLelland (1989) show that, in fact, factors such as response bias can yield higher across-persons than within-persons predictions, depending on how such biases are manifested and how differences between individuals being studied interact with VIE theory measures.

paribus clause. Vroom, for example, hypothesized that individuals will choose outcomes that maximize their overall best interest, *all other things being equal*. Yet most research designs do not hold all other things equal. Within-individuals designs come closest by comparing the behavior of an individual in one instance with his or her behavior in another instance (such as when facing two job choices), thus holding individual differences constant. Between-individuals designs allow individual differences to vary but intentionally randomize this variance. In both approaches, the validity coefficient is the effect size divided by random error. But in between-individuals designs, this random error includes the effect of individual differences whereas in within-individuals designs it does not. Using the magnitude of predictor-criterion relationships to judge the differential validity of the two approaches biases the comparison in favor of within-individuals studies.

Finally, lest we be misunderstood, it is important to note that every theory of human behavior is incomplete. None predicts behavior perfectly, for every person, in every situation. Theorists attempt to build theories that are as descriptive as possible, using as small a number of concepts as can get the job done. It is a truism that theories cannot be simultaneously general *and* parsimonious. Our point is that different research designs account for this incompleteness in different ways. Each has advantages and disadvantages, in terms of such things as the power to detect differences, vulnerability to alternative explanations, realism, practicality, and so on (Runkel & McGrath, 1972). Choosing effectively among them is a matter of managing the tradeoffs among these factors. Evaluating the validity of the within- and between-individuals designs, therefore, requires considerably more than merely comparing the magnitude of empirical results.

Internal Validity

Having concluded that a relationship between a predictor and a criterion measure exists, internal validity concerns the question of whether the effect on the criterion can be correctly attributed to the predictor. That is, having made the decision that repeated measures of VIE concepts are statistically significantly related to repeated measures of choices among alternatives, can we conclude that the latter is a consequence of the former? For a complete review of threats to internal validity the reader is referred to Cook and Campbell (1979), Runkel and McGrath (1972), and Chapter 2 of this book. For our purposes here, the threats that are particularly relevant to the between versus within debate include the effects of repeated testing in within-individuals studies and the interaction of this with the awareness of participants that they are being studied.

When people are asked to respond to similar questions repeatedly, they are vulnerable to testing effects, such as learning and familiarity. Familiarity can "enhance performance because items and error responses are more likely to be remembered at later testing sessions" (Cook & Campbell, 1979, p. 52). As Keren and Raaijmakers (1988) pointed out for studies of utility theory: "[A] likely effect . . . of such repeated stimuli is to evoke the subjects' awareness to provide consistent responses (even if they do not reflect the true preferences)" (p. 237).

Further, when individuals are aware that they are participants in a study, they may behave in ways that introduce bias into experimental results. Their responses may tend to confirm implicit hypotheses rather than reflect their unbiased motivations. They may try to be "good" participants by providing responses that are consistent with what they think the researcher wants. This is true for both between- and within-individuals designs. However, in within-individuals studies, participants may be more likely to guess the experimenter's intent and be more able to act on that. For example, in within-individuals experimental designs participants may be cued by the multiple choices placed in front of them (Greenwald, 1976; Nickerson & McLelland, 1989). In between-individuals designs, participants are usually aware of only one condition. For example, they might be asked to report only one set of measures of expectancy, instrumentality, valence, and choice. In contrast, in within-individuals designs participants are asked to report multiple sets of measures corresponding to a number of alternative choices. These repeated measures may cue participants to the experimental hypothesis. That is, participants may be more able to guess the experimenter's hypothesis and to fulfil their desires to be good experimental subjects (Rosenthal, 1976).

Artifacts of this sort can lead experimenters to avoid within-individuals designs; they also contribute to the ability of such designs to appear to support theoretical predictions. Our point here is that the within-persons approach has advantages (and disadvantages) that affect its ability to claim support for VIE theory quite independent of whether or not VIE theory makes within- or between-persons predictions.

Construct validity

Construct validity concerns the correspondence between empirical operations and the theoretical constructs they are intended to represent (recall Chapter 2). It concerns the very question of whether the comparisons made in VIE studies are appropriate tests of the theoretical propositions of VIE theory as well as the question of whether operational measures of VIE constructs are valid. In other words, do the statistical comparisons made in VIE studies test the form of the relationships specified in the propositions of VIE theory, and do the measures employed validly represent VIE constructs? As we shall see, these two issues are connected.

Most proponents of the within-individuals approach to VIE theory studies have argued that this is the approach that Vroom (1964) intended and that therefore between-individual studies are inappropriate. Yet it must be said that Vroom did not write the last (or the first) word on VIE theory.[6] This is to say that, if we wish to believe that the development of motivation theory is an ongoing, progressive enterprise, we cannot allow ourselves to be ideologically fixed to a single conception of the relationship between expectancies, valences, and behavior. The developments of the past 30 years in VIE theory have been just that, developments. Surely Vroom intended to describe the behavior of employees rather than prescribe one best, unchanging way of making choices about occupations or effort. Advancements and refinements to the theory, such as the addition of constructs and propositions and the development of improved measures, are part of the cycle of theory building and testing that leads to better description and prediction of employee behavior. To adhere to one conception does not assist this enterprise.

Leaving this issue aside, what did Vroom intend? His formulation indicated that individuals will choose from among the alternatives available to them the one that has the highest valence. On the face of it, this is a within-subjects prediction. Yet it is also the case that if two individuals are faced with two identical alternatives and we know that for the first person the first choice has higher valence than the second and for the second person the reverse is true, then VIE theory will predict greater motivational force toward the first choice for the first person and the second choice for the second person. This is clearly a between-individuals prediction. It is, in fact, an example given by Vroom himself (our "first" and "second" persons correspond to persons 1 and 4 respectively on page 192 of Vroom, 1964). He also gave the following example of three individuals: The first has high expected payoffs for both high and low effort, the second has high expected payoffs for high effort but not for low effort, and the third has high expected payoffs for neither high nor low effort. He argued that only the second person is highly motivated to perform effectively and says that these cases "[I]llustrate the kind of predictions that can be derived from the model."

So, it seems that perhaps Vroom's intent may have included between-individual VIE theory predictions. The example he gives shows that between-individuals predictions are possible if we have information about the relative preference *within persons* for choices about alternatives. In other words, if we know the relative preferences of a sample of employees for choosing to expend high as opposed to low effort then it makes sense to correlate those preferences with ratings of their

---

[6] Interestingly, studies of the theory of reasoned action (see Chapter 9), which some researchers do not distinguish from VIE theory (e.g., Nickerson & McLelland, 1989), tend to employ a between-individuals approach without any attendant controversy about its appropriateness.

[handwritten margin notes: EXPECTANCY AT MULTIPLE EFFORT LEVELS / INCREMENTAL VALUE / RETURN ON EFFORT METHOD]

performance (keeping in mind the other factors affecting the relationship between motivation and performance). Critical readers may wish to argue that Vroom's definition of expectancy speaks of preferences for only a single level of effort. Recall, however, that every theoretical proposition contains an implicit "all other things being equal" clause. Thus every theoretical statement about one effort level (or choice) implicitly refers to other choices.

Ironically, the argument that a person's motivational force toward one choice can be meaningfully compared only to that same person's scores for other choices (Dachler & Mobley, 1973; Kennedy, Fossum, & White, 1983; Kopelman, 1977; Mobley & Meglino, 1977) has been used against the between-individuals approach. Yet if this requirement is incorporated into measurement of expectancy concepts the argument is negated.

This brings us to the second component of construct validity: The validity of measurement of VIE theory concepts. As mentioned earlier, Vroom suggested that expectancy beliefs be measured in terms of a person's subjective probability that a particular first-level outcome (e.g., task performance) would result from his or her actions (e.g., effort). As a result, expectancy has been most often operationalized by asking people to provide a rating of the likelihood that, given a high level of effort, they would be able to achieve a given level of performance. There was a steady trend, however, toward incorporating multiple effort levels into the measurement of expectancy. Kopelman (1977) and Staw (1976) proposed that expectancy scores should be calculated by subtracting the likelihood of an outcome given low effort from the likelihood of the same outcome given high effort. The resulting measure would reflect the incremental value of increased effort, rather than just the value of high effort. This has been labeled the return on effort method. A number of researchers claimed that it is superior to the conventional method (Biberman, Baril, & Kopelman, 1986; Kennedy, Fossum, & White, 1983; Kopelman, 1977).

Continuing in this line of thinking, Hollenbeck (1979) proposed a "matrix method" for expectancy research that asks respondents to provide assessments of the likelihood that each of a range of effort levels will result in a range of levels of performance. Instrumentality is similarly measured for combinations of performance levels and various outcomes. Matrix multiplication is applied to calculate the motivational force associated with each level of effort. Hollenbeck (1979) proposed, finally, that a probabilistic approach be taken to relate effort to these multiple force scores in which an individual exerts effort in proportion to the relative attractiveness of each level of effort.

[handwritten margin notes: MATRIX METH. / INSTRUMENTALITY]

Building on Hollenbeck's work, Sussman and Vecchio (1985) proposed a "four-fold" model which also includes the measurement of subjective probabilities associated with combinations of levels of effort and outcome. They point out that their approach resolves the problems associated with traditional approaches to expectancy theory, in which variables measured on interval level scales are subjected to impermissible transformations, such as multiplication (Schmidt, 1973).

[handwritten margin note: 4 FOLD MODEL]

Ilgen, Nebeker, and Pritchard (1981) made an early contribution to the validation of measures of the major VIE theory concepts. They proposed multiple effort, performance, and outcome measures of expectancy and instrumentality and compared these to traditional measures. For example, they constructed both "expected value index" and "covariation" measures of expectancy, the latter corresponding most closely to the approaches advocated by Hollenbeck and Sussman, and Vecchio. They then sought to validate these measures by comparing the scores of respondents who completed work in "high" and "low" objective expectancy conditions. Contrary to their own hypothesis that expectancy is best conceptualized as the covariation between effort and performance, they found that this measure "showed little responsiveness to the expectancy manipulation" (p. 215).

*[handwritten margin note: H₀ * H₁ *]*

The reason for this, we propose, is that the manipulation of objective expectancy did not in fact manipulate the covariation between effort and performance. The researchers sought to create a high expectancy condition by using a relatively easy task and a low expectancy condition by using a relatively difficult task. It is possible, however, for tasks with very different degrees of difficulty to have the same relationship between working hard and achieving outcomes. That is, a person can increase his effort by 10 units, say, and see 10 units of increase in performance in both a relatively easy and a relatively difficult task. Similarly, tasks can create very different relationships between

[handwritten notes at bottom: MOTIVATIONAL FORCE / PROBABILISTIC APPROACH / RELATIVE EFFORT / EXPECTED VALUE INDEX / COVARIATION]

effort and performance yet have the same overall probability of success (Eden, 1988). In sum, task difficulty and expectancy are not necessarily inversely related (Garland, 1984).

The importance of these developments in measurement is that they explicitly incorporate the comparison of multiple levels of effort and performance; they make explicit the within-individuals nature of the theory in the operationalization of VIE theory concepts. In so doing, they make possible between-individuals predictions. This resolves part of the debate between advocates of the within- and between-individuals approaches. On the one hand, by incorporating comparison of multiple effort and performance levels into measurement, it is possible to test hypotheses that individuals with higher motivational force toward particular choices will be more likely to make those choices than will other individuals who have lower motivation toward those choices. On the other hand, this is different from saying that motivational force scores are determined by the particular multiplicative function specified by Vroom. In other words, *the between- and within-individuals approaches test different hypotheses of VIE theory*.

Wolf and Connolly (1981), in their criticism of between-individuals studies, put it bluntly. They say that between-individuals studies have "without doubt, established that individuals commonly shape their work-related behaviors in a manner somewhat responsive to their anticipation of the likely outcomes of those behaviours – a finding we see as less than surprising. They certainly have *not* cast light on the cognitive processes of individuals in regard to their work choices" (p. 44).

Although there has been a sharp decline since the 1980s in research intended to validate, per se, VIE theory (Ambrose & Kulik, 1999), a few studies have been reported and a meta-analysis of 77 studies conducted between 1964 and 1990 was performed and reported by Van Eerde and Thierry (1996). The focus of the meta-analysis was on tests of the original Vroom formulation. Among the results were the following: (1) multiplicative models did not yield greater effect sizes than did analyses of specific components, taken one at a time (valence, instrumentality, and expectancy); (2) within-subjects models using choice preference or effort as the criterion variable fared more strongly than did between-subjects designs; (3) attitudinal criteria, such as intention and preference, were more significantly related to VIE components than were behavioral variables such as performance, effort, and choice.

Other Early Research Difficulties

In addition to the between-within and measurement problems just described, there have been a variety of other problems faced by researchers interested in VIE theory (Campbell & Pritchard, 1976). Most of these have to do with the complex nature of the theory, making the operationalization of measures and research designs so as to be isomorphic with the theory very difficult. For example and as we noted earlier, VIE theory studies often use supervisory ratings of *performance* as the criterion against which predictions of employee force is compared, whereas the theory purports to predict *effort*.[7] Because effort is only one determinant of performance the results of these studies have been negatively biased against the theory.

VIE theory also speaks of *changes*, at one point in time, of V, I, and E perceptions being predictive of *changes of effort* at some subsequent point in time. Yet cross-sectional designs (whether within or between individuals) cannot assess such changes (see Kuhl & Atkinson, 1984; and Mayes, 1978a, for a discussion of this problem; and Lawler & Suttle, 1973; and Kopelman, 1979, for attempts to get around it). VIE theory proposes that valence, expectancy, and instrumentality beliefs combine multiplicatively. This imposes the assumption that these beliefs people hold are independent of one another, then multiplying these scores algebraically. It may be that these three beliefs are not, in fact, independent of one another. People may place higher valence upon outcomes that are

---

[7] Recall from Chapter 1 that employee effort (or motivational force) and job performance are not the same thing. Using performance to measure motivation is an error in construct validity (recall Chapter 2).

believed more difficult to attain. Indeed, many researchers attempted to evaluate the tenability of the multiplication hypothesis (e.g., Baker, Ravichandran, & Randall, 1989; Harrell, Caldwell, & Doty, 1985). Finally, VIE theory assumes a high degree of rationality among employees. Yet we know that people have limited cognitive capacities and that much of human behavior is habitual and subconscious (Locke, 1975; Mayes, 1978b; Simon, 1957; Staw, 1977).

SUBCONS

THE PATH–GOAL THEORY OF LEADERSHIP

many Groups

VIE theory inspired a formal theory of leadership referred to as *path–goal theory*. In a nutshell, this theory suggests ways that leaders can make work groups more effective through the impact they can have on employee beliefs about valences, instrumentalities, and expectancies. More specifically, the theory discusses the ways in which leaders may use any of at least four types of behavioral style to influence employee satisfaction, the acceptance of the leader by employees as well as employee beliefs that effort can result in performance, and that performance will result in desired rewards (House & Mitchell, 1974). The four leadership styles considered are the following:

MGMT SHL STYLE

1. *Directive* – meaning the leader structures the work, assigns tasks, clarifies his or her role with subordinates, and creates and enforces standards of performance.
2. *Supportive* – the leader shows genuine respect for employee needs and status, attempting to make the work more pleasant Such a leader treats subordinates as equals, and is friendly and approachable.
3. *Participative* – the leader consults with subordinates about problems and decisions that must be made, and takes subordinates' suggestions into account when possible.
4. Finally, *achievement-oriented* leadership involves a style in which the leader sets challenging goals, and shows confidence that subordinates can reach their goals.

ADJUST STYLE ACCORDINGLY

Path–goal theory assumes that individual managers are capable of exhibiting more than one of these styles, depending upon the circumstances. In other words, it is a mistake to assume that a particular manager is simply a participative leader, or a supportive type. In fact, the theory specifies the types of condition under which it is more appropriate for a leader to employ each of these various behavioral styles. Based on VIE theory, it is assumed that the effective leader will behave in ways that recognize and arouse employee needs for the types of outcomes that the leader has at his disposal, and then attempt to increase the payoff to employees for successful performance when it occurs. Moreover, the successful leader will try to influence subordinate expectancy beliefs, by assisting with the accomplishment of difficult tasks, and by clarifying ambiguous task assignments. Finally, the effective leader will attempt, where possible, to make the distribution of rewards contingent on the successful accomplishment of work:

> To summarize . . . the motivational functions of the leader consist of increasing the number and kinds of personal payoffs to subordinates for work-goal attainment and making paths to these payoffs easier to travel by clarifying the paths, reducing road blocks and pitfalls and increasing the opportunities for personal satisfaction en route. (House & Mitchell, 1974, quoted by Downey, Hellriegel, & Slocum, 1977, p. 226)

Limitations of space prevent a more elaborate treatment of the path–goal theory here. The interested reader can trace the development of the theory by reading Evans (2002). Nevertheless, VIE theory and the path–goal model provide a number of illuminating suggestions for the management of reward people and reward systems in organizations.

IMPLICATIONS OF VIE THEORY AND THE PATH–GOAL MODEL FOR MANAGEMENT

We noted in Chapter 9 that beliefs about work (or about life in general) are based on the individual's perceptions of the surrounding environment, and that these perceptions are influenced by information stored in the person's memory. It is assumed here that valence, instrumentality, and expectancy beliefs are established and influenced in the same manner as are other beliefs. Therefore, it also follows that because beliefs may not be valid or accurate, the person's behavior may not seem appropriate to observers. And it also follows that because these three beliefs are merely beliefs (as opposed to intentions), they may not result in behavior at all, or at least, they may not result in any specifically predictable behaviors. They should, however, influence an individual's intentions to act in certain ways. Accordingly, a number of implications follow from VIE theory for any supervisor who wishes to try to "motivate" his staff. Many of these suggestions were implicit in the foregoing discussion of the path–goal theory. Moreover, the reader is reminded of the differential reports made about Americans and Canadians we cited at the opening of this chapter – differences pertaining to whether working hard will lead to highly desired outcomes such as promotions and increases in health and well-being.

Expectancy-Related Factors

First, in order to generate positive expectancy forces, the supervisor must assign her personnel to jobs for which they are trained, and which they are capable of performing. This requires that the supervisor understand the skills, strengths, and weaknesses of each of her subordinates, as well as the nature of the skill requirements of the jobs to which she is assigning them. If people are assigned to tasks that they are not capable of performing, according to VIE theory, their expectancy perceptions will be low, and we will not expect to see them trying to perform.

Consider how difficult it is, in practice, for supervisors completely to appreciate the skill requirements of the jobs their employees must perform, and to recognize that it is the level of skills of the employees vis-à-vis the jobs, not their own skill levels, that matter. Jobs often change with time and as incumbents come and go, making it difficult to keep track of what they require. In addition, supervisors who have performed some or all of the jobs under their purview may forget how difficult these jobs are to newcomers, so they may either overestimate or underestimate the difficulty level of jobs for any of these reasons. Finally, it is important to recognize that employees' skills and abilities change over time, both as a result of formal training and education, as well as from the natural consequences of maturation and simple work experiences. But adequate skill levels are not sufficient to assure positive expectancy perceptions. In addition, the employee must believe that the other circumstances surrounding his effort are favorable and conducive to his success. For example, the supervisor must be sure that machinery and equipment are in good repair, and that the employee's own staff, if any, are trained and capable of being of assistance. Likewise, there must be sufficient budget to make successful performance possible. In short, the job must be capable of being performed by an employee if we are to expect the employee to try to perform it, and, more importantly, the person must perceive that it is so. But countless practical factors can combine to make it very difficult for any supervisor to accurately estimate the expectancy beliefs held by particular employees about specific jobs; accordingly, they make it difficult for supervisors to fully implement the implications that follow from the expectancy component of VIE theory.

Of particular importance for supervisors is the structuring of the expectancy beliefs of newcomers to a work setting (Hall, 1976). Managers often take a "sink or swim" approach with new employees, assigning them work duties that are too difficult, given their relative lack of familiarity with the rules, procedures, and myriad other circumstances that must be understood in order to make work efforts successful. An alternative approach is to under-challenge newcomers, requiring them to work through a tedious series of trivial jobs before being given any real challenge. Recent college graduates often complain of this treatment upon landing their first jobs after graduating, and, as a result, turnover among recent graduates is usually very high (Mobley, 1982).

A third approach, the desired one, is to strike a balance using a combination of achievement-oriented, supportive, and directive leadership styles (as defined in the previous section), attempting to make the newcomer's initial experiences challenging and successful. Success experiences are necessary for developing strong expectancy beliefs, and for maintaining a positive self-concept about one's work, a feeling of competence, self-determination, and high self-esteem (cf. Bandura, 1982; Deci, 1975; Hall, 1976; Korman, 1970, 1976).

Instrumentality-Related Factors

In order to operationalize the concepts of instrumentality and valence, supervisors must make sure that positively valent rewards are associated with good job performance, and that their employees perceive this connection. In practice, this also is difficult for a number of reasons. Most supervisors have a limited stock of rewards available to them for distribution to their subordinates. Company policies with regard to pay and benefits are usually restrictive, for the good reasons of control and the maintenance of equity. Further, union contracts are generally quite clear about the bases of reward distribution and often require that pay and other rewards be based on seniority rather than merit, further restricting the capacity of individual supervisors always to know who their meritorious employees are. This problem is especially common among managerial, professional, and technical personnel, in whose jobs good performance is normally very hard to measure, even when someone tries diligently to do so. As a result of these and other practical difficulties, implementing the instrumentality implications of VIE is often (perhaps usually) very difficult.

Valence-Related Factors

Where does the notion of valence fit into practice? VIE theory would prescribe that those rewards which are distributed for good performance should be the types of thing that employees desire. All that we know from common sense, as well as that which we have learned from research into human needs (see Chapters 3 through 8), tells us that different people have different need profiles at different times, so it follows that different outcomes will be rewarding for different people at different times. Hence, even the same outcome (such as a job transfer to another city) may be positively valent for some people, while being negatively valent for others. And to the extent that satisfied needs tend to lose their capacity to motivate behavior (as is suggested by the need theories discussed in Chapters 3, 4, 5, and 6), we can expect certain organizationally distributed rewards to be satisfying and perhaps motivating for a particular individual in some circumstances, but not so in other circumstances. Hence, older employees often have no desire to meet and befriend new employees on the job: Their relatedness needs are already well met and secured by interactions with old friends and acquaintances. In short, implementing VIE and path–goal concepts, with regard to providing valent outcomes for work, can be very difficult in practice.

Individualized Organizations

One leading authority proposed decades ago that people be rewarded for their work with outcomes that are best suited to their individual needs (Lawler, 1973, 1976). His suggestions entailed comprehensive analyses of both the employees and the jobs in organizations, followed by the careful assignment of people to those jobs in which they will find outcomes they desire, especially as a consequence of good performance.

A notable attempt to structure rewards on a more-or-less individualized basis can be found in the concept of cafeteria-style compensation plans, a concept that has been around for a long time (cf. Lawler, 1966; Nealey, 1963; Schuster, 1969) but relatively rarely practiced. The general design of these plans is for the individual employee to be allotted a fixed dollar sum of compensation that she can distribute according to her own preferences across a variety of forms of compensation including salary, and any of a number of fringe benefits, deferred earnings, stock options, and the like.

A problem usually encountered by managerial attempts to individualize employee rewards in a fashion consistent with VIE theory concerns the difficulty of accurately determining the actual needs of individual employees. The reader is asked to recall the discussion in Chapter 3, in which the risks of inferring need states, from observations of another person's behavior, were examined. Managers simply may not be able to accurately determine the needs of their employees, so they must rely on techniques such as attitude surveys and one-on-one discussions to learn about employee values.

The distinction between needs and values may appear academic, but it is more than that (recall Chapter 2 and especially Chapter 3). Rewards may be satisfying, according to Locke (1976), as long as they correspond with employee values and are not inconsistent with employee needs. But when employee values deviate from needs (meaning that people desire things that are not actually conducive to their best interests), organizational reward systems aimed at fulfilling employee values may not be at all beneficial, for either the individuals involved or for the organization as a whole.

Idiosyncratic deals

Rousseau and her colleagues (e.g., Greenberg, Roberge, Ho, & Rousseau, 2004; Rousseau, 2001) introduced a variant of individualization for the modern workplace and for the new "boundaryless career" (cf. Arthur & Rousseau, 1996). An idiosyncratic deal "refers to those features of employment that the individual worker receives that differ from what workers in similar roles receive" (Rousseau, 2001, p. 261). Called "i-deals," these idiosyncratic arrangements result from bargaining between the employee and the employer, the purpose being to find working arrangements that are suitable to both parties. Naturally, they lead to different psychological contracts and can be sources of perceived unfairness or distributive injustice (see Greenberg et al., 2004; and Chapter 11). Nevertheless, the process of bargaining and the i-deals that result offer flexibility that suits the particular needs, values, and life circumstances of the individual employee while remaining beneficial to the organization. I-deals can be negotiated between the organization and prospective employees, or between the organization and already-onboard employees who share a desire to change the nature of the work relationship (Greenberg et al., 2004). I-deals comprise a modern operationalization of the old adage "Different strokes for different folks" and is quite consistent with the applied tenets of both VIE theory and path–goal theory.

CURRENT ASSESSMENT OF VIE THEORY

A recent review of the theory and literature on work motivation by Latham and Pinder (2005) reached the same conclusion regarding VIE theory as an earlier review by Ambrose and Kulik (1999): There have been very few significant theoretical advances in recent years on the VIE theory front, with a few exceptions (to which we return shortly). Most literature that involves VIE has, instead, employed it as a general framework to understand and describe a range of organizational phenomena. Indeed, a computer search of "expectancy theory" yields countless articles in which the theory is employed in myriad office and shopfloor settings in a wide variety of industries. In these studies, the purpose is generally demonstrative rather than theory testing in purpose. There have also been a few attempts to integrate expectancy theory with other theories, the purpose being to provide greater insights through such integration into motivation and/or decision-making processes (see Ambrose & Kulik, 1999, for a summary of these studies).

That said, there have been one or two interesting new wrinkles in VIE theory worth mentioning. For example, Erez and Isen (2002) explored how positive affect (recall Chapter 4) interacts with task characteristics to influence the key components of the VIE framework. These authors surveyed earlier theoretical and empirical work to offer conceptual reasons that would suggest that people who have high positive affect would: (1) evaluate outcomes more positively than people not high in positive affect; (2) "see more and varied ways by which their performance could be linked to rewards" (p. 1057); and (3) see more covariation between levels of effort and task performance. Details of their two experiments are beyond our scope here, but the upshot of the two studies was that positive mood had the anticipated effects on the major VIE components, resulting in higher levels of motivation and performance. Erez and Isen (2002) were careful to rule out the alternative explanation for their findings that the mood states had their effects through a general elevation of the activation of their research participants. This author encourages more work of this variety: Studies that help to integrate the cognitive and affective dimensions of human functioning and their joint effects on work motivation.

Elsewhere, building upon the early "NPI" version of VIE theory (Naylor et al., 1980), Robert Pritchard and his colleagues (Pritchard et al., 2002) have elaborated a "productivity measurement and enhancement" (ProMes) system, that identifies organizational objectives, measures the degree to which these objectives are met, and provides feedback regarding system performance. The program has proved to be an effective means of enhancing productivity in a number of different countries.

SUMMARY AND A GLANCE AHEAD

While VIE theory may be somewhat dormant in mainstream academic organizational behavior arenas, it is alive and doing well in many, diverse applied settings. Ambrose and Kulik (1999) refer to VIE theory as "mature" and as a "standard" motivation theory. We agree: VIE theory, in all its various versions and forms, constitutes a major contribution to our stock of understanding of employee work motivation and performance. Again, the low level of current empirical activity devoted to testing or developing VIE theory does not mean it is no value.

Even those managers and supervisors who understand VIE theory, and who are capable of distilling practical implications from it for application in their jobs, are usually severely handicapped by countless practical features of organizations' work groups, union contracts, standard practices and policies, history, and precedents. More important, however, we must remember that even if managers are able to structure work settings and reward distribution systems so as to comply with the implications of VIE theory and the path–goal model, they will not be successful unless their policies and practices result in beliefs and perceptions, on the part of employees, which are consistent with high performance levels. For example, employees might not realize that rewards are, in fact, distributed in accordance with merit, even if that is actually the case. Likewise, employees may underestimate their chances of succeeding at a task, because they are not aware of the help that is available to them at the time. According to VIE theory, it is people's beliefs that ultimately determine their behavior, so unless managerial practices translate into beliefs that are favorable toward high job performance, beliefs will not result in employee intentions to perform well.

VIE and Goal Setting

One way of conceptualizing VIE theory is to think of it as a model designed to predict a person's behavioral intentions. When we assess a person's beliefs about expectancies, valences, and instrumentalities and combine them in the configurations described by the theory itself, we have a basis for predicting a person's choices or decisions. These decisions may be to select one job rather than another, to retire or not to retire, or to work hard rather than not so hard. In short, VIE theory helps us to understand what lies behind a person's intentions and goals. In Chapter 14 we examine goal-setting theory, a body of work that explicitly starts with intentions – the place where VIE theory leaves off. As we will see, when we are capable of specifying and understanding a person's goals, we are a step closer to being able to predict his or her behavior. Goal setting is therefore a powerful motivational tool and a body of theory that enjoys considerable scientific validity.

Goal-Directed Theories

13

Ah, but a man's reach should exceed his grasp,
Or what's a heaven for?
Robert Browning

The opening pages of this book told the story of Frank O'Dea, whose three-word mantra: "Hope. Vision. Action" summarizes his incredible rise from poverty on the streets of Toronto to a position of prestige and power in Canadian business and society. Using the concepts developed in this book, we can summarize O'Dea's formula by stating that hope energized him, vision provided goals and direction, and action eventually enabled him to get things accomplished. In fact, *all living systems have goals or objectives of some form or other* (Ashby, 1958, cited by Miller, 1978). Survival depends on focus, purpose, and deliberate attempts to achieve goals states (Miller, 1978). In Chapter 10, we saw that, according to the theory of reasoned action, intentions are the immediate precursors of behavior. When intentions take the specific form of goal states, the connection between cognition and action are relatively simple and direct. Accordingly, it should come as no surprise that goal-setting theory, particularly task-goal theory, remains the most powerful and useful model of motivated work behavior extant (cf. Latham & Pinder, 2005). As pointed out by Klein, Wesson, Hollenbeck, and Alge (1999), there are at least four influential bodies of theory in motivation that feature goals as their central feature: Task-goal theory (e.g., Locke & Latham, 1990a, 2002), social-cognitive theory (e.g., Bandura 1986), resource-allocation theory (Kanfer & Ackerman, 1989), and control theory. In this chapter, we review the first and the third of these four models, deferring our discussion of social-cognitive theory until Chapter 14.

This chapter consists of four major sections. In the first section, we will briefly examine the formal theory of intentional behavior proposed by Ryan (1970). The second part of the chapter will review related work on goal setting, as developed by Locke, Latham, and their colleagues (cf. Locke & Latham, 1990a, 2002), the body of work referred to by Klein et al. (1999) as *task-goal theory*. The major tenets of this original formulation of goal setting will be presented as well as more recent attempts to broaden its scope and to increase its predictive power. We adopt a quasi-historical approach throughout this discussion, showing how goal-setting theory has developed from a small set of basic principles to a much larger and more sophisticated corpus of work. The purpose of the historical approach is to be instructive of how good theories can advance, be criticized, respond to criticism through amendments and additions (and subtractions), and then continue to advance further. The approach is similar to one that we adopted earlier in this book (see Chapter 3) in our discussion of intrinsic motivation and its evolution into self-determination theory, as well as in Chapter 11, where we saw how current justice theory emerged from and subsumed equity theory.

In the third section, we will consider control theory, another cognitively based, goal-oriented theory of human behavior and work motivation that came onto the scene in the organizational literature two decades ago (cf. Klein, 1989). We will see that control theory has a number of major elements in common with goal-setting theory, and we will discuss some of the controversy that the ascendance of control theory has instigated.

The chapter will then look at a managerial and performance management system that relies heavily for its theoretical legitimacy on the principles found in goal setting and control theory, particularly the former – management by objectives (MBO). We will address the disparity between the relative success of goal-setting programs per se and MBO.

To begin then: What are intentions, and how are they formed?

THE THEORY OF INTENTIONAL BEHAVIOR

The fundamental theory of motivation underlying current work on goal setting assumes that people's intentions are an important factor in explaining their behavior, although not the only factor, as illustrated in Figure 13.1 (Ryan, 1970). For example, the theory does not reject needs as a force in initiating action, although it assumes that needs influence behavior primarily through the effect they can have on the individual's intentions.

According to the theory, behavior can be broken down into four interrelated stages or levels (Ryan, 1970). Each level helps explain the one that follows. As mentioned, the most immediate level of explanation consists of the intentions people hold. Individuals strive to act intentionally, pursuing whatever goals they have in mind. Whenever circumstances permit, behavior that is consistent with those intentions can be expected.

The second level of explanation consists of three sets of factors that influence the person's intentions. These are: (1) the person's perceptions concerning means–ends relationships (whether the person believes that certain acts will result in certain outcomes, as in VIE theory); (2) the level of intrinsic interest or attractiveness of the act being contemplated; and (3) the appropriateness of the act in the particular social and physical setting in question (Ryan, 1970, pp. 26–27). The person's perceptions with regard to these three factors are the most important determinants of the person's intentions to act.

The reader may notice the similarities between these three factors and the elements of VIE theory discussed in Chapter 12, Fishbein and Ajzen's theory of reasoned behavior (recall Chapter 9), and even the theories of intrinsic motivation presented in Chapter 7. The point is that it is possible to invoke other bodies of cognitive motivation theory to help understand the origins of human intentions to behave in Ryan's theory.

The third level of explanation consists of those factors that influence the three factors comprising level two. Level-three factors consist of explanations for why people perceive things the way they do, why they find particular acts intrinsically interesting, and so on. The theory assumes that people become "equipped with many prepared ways of perceiving, anticipating, and conceiving the world and their own activity" (Ryan, 1970, p. 28). People have ready-made reactions *to stimuli in their environment* that result from past history and learning. Ryan conceives these as repertoires, as stored products invoked in particular settings to make sense of the environment. These products consist of factors such as needs, values, preferences, plans, rules for behaving, and so on. At this third level, understanding behavior consists of understanding both the contents of the person's repertoire and the principles concerning which of its elements will be used in particular situations. It consists of seeking patterns in the person's reactions to situations, in the way the individual perceives

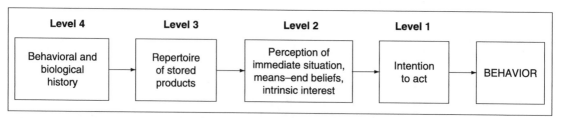

FIG. 13.1   Simplified representation of the four levels of causality of behavior.

means–ends relationships, in the types of activity she finds intrinsically interesting, and in the way she deems particular types of act as more or less appropriate, both practically and socially.

Finally, the fourth level of Ryan's theory consists of the historical and developmental background of the individual that explains why the person's repertoire is formed as it is. For Ryan (1970), this level is the most remotely connected with actual behavior and therefore of least interest in his theory. In short, for Ryan, a person's intentions are the most immediate determinants of her behavior. In view of the critical importance of intentions in his theory, let's take a closer look at the nature of human intentions.

The Nature of Intentions

Fishbein and Ajzen (1975) defined an intention as a special form of belief. For them, an intention is a belief linking a person (the object of the belief) with a behavior (the attribute of the belief). As we saw in Chapter 9, beliefs can vary in strength. Thus, we can speak of an intention's strength as the strength of the person's beliefs (in probabilistic terms) that he will actually behave in a particular manner. In more common terms, an intention is a conviction to act, a predilection to behave a certain way. This conception of intentions has prevailed in most of the social and organizational sciences for many years, often used interchangeably with the concept of *goal*. Intentions and goals were usually considered synonymous. We will return to the issue of the relationship between these two concepts later in this chapter.

According to Ryan (1970), it is possible to consider a number of different dimensions of intentions – aspects that can be used to characterize them. For example, we might consider the degree of freedom of choice (the degree to which people are forced to behave by factors beyond their control, as opposed to the degree to which they feel they will behave in a particular manner, when and where they want) involved in the intention. Similarly, it is possible to consider the content (or direction) of an intention. For example, an intention may pertain to locomotion (going somewhere) or to modifying something (such as baking a pie, firing an employee, or organizing a union). An intention may also pertain to communicating something to someone, seeking a skill, or acquiring new knowledge. The point is that there are many different types of intention people can hold, dealing with convictions to act in an infinite number of ways toward any of an infinite number of objects. The reader is reminded of the importance of the specificity of an intention, however, in making predictions of particular acts (recall Chapter 9; see Ajzen and Fishbein, 1977).

In summary, the basic concept underlying Ryan's theory is that intentions are the most immediate and most important causes of behavior. To understand the origins and nature of people's intentions requires that we understand the way people view the world around them. In turn, to understand why people perceive things the way they do, we must understand the nature of stored products such as their needs, values, norms, and so on. Finally, in order to understand why individuals hold particular repertoires of such products, we must examine their backgrounds. It bears repeating that various other theories discussed in this book can be used to help understand the factors at each of these various levels of explanation, and that, consistent with the model linking beliefs, attitudes, and intentions to behavior (Fishbein & Ajzen, 1975), intentions, once they are formed, are the most immediate causes and predictors of actual behavior.

The foregoing discussion of the basic theory of intentions is brief and considerably oversimplified. The interested reader is referred to Ryan's (1970) book for more detail. Now that the elements of the theory of intentional behavior have been introduced, we can examine the tenets of the theory of goal setting.

GOAL-SETTING CONCEPTS, THEORY, AND RESEARCH

The fundamental tenet of goal-setting theory is that goals and intentions are responsible for human behavior. In this context, goals mean the same thing as they did in Chapter 8, where the concept of frustration was presented. A goal is something that a person tries to attain, achieve, or accomplish; it is the object or aim of an action (Locke & Latham, 2002). In work settings, goals may take the form of a level of job performance, a quota, a work norm, a deadline, or even a budgetary spending limit (Locke, Shaw, Saari, & Latham 1981). Goals in organizations frequently have a time element involved.

We noted earlier that the terms *goal* and *intention* have frequently been used interchangeably. Locke and Latham (1990a) argued that these two concepts should *not* be considered synonymous. They claim that an intention is a person's representation of a planned action, whereas a goal is the object or aim of such an act (Locke & Latham, 2002). By contrast, Tubbs and Ekeberg (1991) advanced an elaborate argument to the effect that people think and plan in such a way that intentions include both the planned action and the objective of the action, making intention a broader concept than goals. Each of these perspectives has merit, but it would be very difficult to pit them against one another in any empirical test to determine which is more meritorious. We will adopt the Locke and Latham (2002) argument here, if only to keep our treatment consistent with the dominant theoretical model extant in the goal-setting literature. For our purposes, a goal is the target of one's intentional acts, while an intention is a person's relationship with, or personal representation of, an act she will undertake to achieve the goal in question. There have been many attempts to develop categories or types of goal, which we will encounter as this chapter develops.

The second major tenet derives from the first. If goals determine human effort, it follows that higher or harder goals will result in higher levels of performance[1] than easy goals. (Later in the chapter, we will see how this basic proposition has been modified to take into account the complexity of the task involved. Specifically, high-performance goals are more effective than low-performance goals only when the person has the ability to do the task. If the task is complex and novel, however, high-performance goals do not surpass self-set goals, or do-your-best goals; rather, learning goals are superior – Locke & Latham, 2002.)

A third tenet of the theory holds that specific goals (such as "reducing employee turnover by 20% within 6 months") result in higher levels of effort than vague goals such as "let's cut back turnover as much as possible." A fourth tenet of the theory is that incentives such as money, feedback, competition, and the like will have no effect on behavior unless they lead to the setting and/or acceptance of specific, hard goals.

Notice that this approach to work motivation relies heavily on the same cognitive/perceptual model of human functioning that underlies both VIE theory and equity theory. In order for a person to have a goal, he must be aware of his surroundings and be fully cognizant of the meaning of what constitutes his goal. Behavior is intentional (Ryan, 1970). It results from the deliberate adoption of one or more conscious choices of action. People engage in acts that are consistent with their intentions and goals.

---

[1] We drew a distinction in Chapter 1 between work effort and performance, an important distinction maintained throughout the book. Although the concept of central interest in this book is *work motivation*, most of the research on goal setting focuses on *task performance*. That is, the success or failure to accomplish tasks is the dependent variable in most of the work in this tradition. The theory discusses both motivation and performance (see Locke & Latham, 1990a). The reader is exhorted to keep the distinction between the two concepts in mind: They are not equivalent and they are not necessarily related to one another in real life.

Goal Difficulty and Task Difficulty

At first blush, these basic elements of goal-setting theory may seem trivial and self-evident. In fact, their simplicity is profound and leads logically to a number of important corollaries for application in work settings. The most important implication of the basic tenets of the theory concerns the most appropriate level of goal difficulty for maximum performance.

A critical distinction must be made between *task difficulty* and *goal difficulty*, however, before we can proceed. According to Locke et al. (1981): "Since a goal is the object or aim of an action, it is possible for the completion of a task to be a goal. However . . . the term goal refers to attaining a specific standard of proficiency on a task, usually within a specified time limit" (p. 126). Therefore, two people could be given the same task (such as to recruit 20 new sales representatives to the firm), but one person could have a much more difficult goal, such as being given half as much time as the other to achieve the goal, for example. Same task, different goals. The theory predicts that to the extent he is committed to it, the person with the harder goal will perform to a higher standard. As Latham and Locke (1991) noted: "Knowing task difficulty . . . does not reveal the person's goals and thus makes it difficult to predict how well a person will perform the task."

The very difficulty of a task may also contribute to performance. For example, one early experiment of chess matches among undergraduate students found that goal difficulty was positively related to performance, as per the theory, but that the difficulty of the task itself contributed positively as well, in large part because it instigated exploration and learning which paid off later on (Campbell & Ilgen, 1976). The early empirical evidence in support of the goal difficulty hypothesis was impressive. Locke and Latham and their colleagues conducted dozens of experiments in both laboratory (Locke, Cartledge, & Knerr, 1970) and field (Latham & Yukl, 1975) settings to show that hard goals result in higher levels of performance than do easy goals (Locke et al., 1981; Locke & Latham, 1990a, 2002). The tasks included in the laboratory experiments have ranged from chess problems to arithmetic problems, card sorting, brainstorming, prose learning, and data coding, among others.

The early field studies were similarly diverse in nature and equally compelling. In one early experiment, for example, Latham and Baldes (1975) had forestry truck drivers set goals for the amount of wood they hauled on each load to their woodyard. Goals were set and measured in terms of the weight of each load, as a percentage of each particular truck's gross vehicle weight. The additional wood hauled over a 9-month period as a result of the goal-setting program would have cost the company $250,000 to purchase the trucks that would have been needed to achieve the same performance increment without the program.

In another early field experiment, Latham and Kinne (1974) showed how a 1-day goal-setting training program resulted in both higher productivity and lower absenteeism among a sample of independent loggers over a 12-week period. In short, there is abundant evidence from advocates of this school of thought that difficult goals result in higher performance than easy goals (cf. Tubbs, 1986). As we will see shortly, the simple hypothesis connecting task difficulty and task performance has been modified over time and as the result of considerable research and thinking since the theory's original promulgation. This prescription regarding the optimum level of goal difficulty appears at first glance to differ from that derived from VIE theory (which, as we saw in Chapter 12, would suggest that motivation is maximized when expectancy beliefs are at a maximum) and McClelland and Atkinson's view (recall Chapter 3) that achievement motivation is maximized when the individual perceives the task to be of a moderate level of difficulty.

Again, *the key is whether we are considering the task or the goal.* McClelland's (1965) work on achievement motivation concerned itself with task difficulty, whereas the goal-setting literature deals with goal difficulty. As mentioned, this is a critical distinction that is useful for theory development and understanding. In practice, however, the distinction may not be so easy to implement or manipulate. A person with low goals confronting a task she finds difficult may encounter many of the same frustrations as a person who has high goals confronting an easy task.

At first glance, the goal difficulty hypothesis seems to be contradictory to a major tenet of VIE theory (recall Chapter 12). VIE theory postulates that expectancy (the belief that effort will lead to the performance required to attain rewards) is positively correlated with motivation, whereas, in goal-setting, there *appears* to be an inverse correlation between expectancy and motivation. As pointed out by Locke and Latham (2002):

> The apparent contradiction between the two theories is resolved by distinguishing expectancy within versus expectancy between goal conditions. Locke, Motowidlo and Bobko (1986) found that when goal level is held constant, which is implicitly assumed by [VIE theory], higher expectancies lead to higher levels of performance. Across goal levels, lower expectancies, associated with higher goal levels, are associated with higher performance.
>
> (Locke & Latham, 2002, p. 706)

Commitment to Goals

The goal specificity and goal difficulty tenets of the theory have assumed (first implicitly, then later explicitly) that the person of interest is *committed* to the goals, that s/he possesses adequate ability and self-efficacy in relation to the task, and that feedback is provided in regard to progress toward the goal (Wood & Locke, 1990). Commitment "refers to the degree to which the individual is attached to the goal, considers it significant or important, is determined to reach it, and keeps it in the face of setbacks and obstacles" (Latham & Locke, 1991, p. 217). In one of their books, Locke and Latham proclaimed that commitment is the *sine qua non* of goal setting: Without commitment, the phenomenon does not exist (Locke & Latham, 2004). People seem most likely to choose and/or commit to them when they believe the goals are attainable and important (Klein, 1991a), so managers may have to use their powers of persuasion, their legitimate authority, and their technical expertise in order to facilitate subordinates' commitment to goals (Latham & Locke, 1991). Yet, as pointed out by Klein et al. (1999), the hypothesis that goal commitment is a necessary condition for goals to influence performance received very little direct empirical evidence as the overall theory was assembled and validated during the 25 years following the theory's earliest appearance in the mid-1960s. Hollenbeck and Klein (1987) concluded that many tests of the major hypotheses of the theory failed to assess commitment directly as part of the research designs, and that goal commitment was frequently offered, post hoc, as an untested factor to explain why hard and specific goals resulted in superior task performance.

Commitment to a goal appears to have a direct as well as an indirect effect on performance. That is, when a person's goals are high, high commitment leads to higher performance than when commitment is low. But when goals are low, "high commitment may restrict performance because committed people will be loathe to raise their goals, whereas uncommitted people may set higher goals (perhaps because they want additional challenge)" (Latham & Locke, 1991, p. 217).

Klein et al. (1999) also addressed this issue.[2] They point out that the moderating effect of commitment on the relationship between goal difficulty and task performance may not be evident unless there is sufficient variance in both commitment and goal difficulty. Indeed, they claim that many empirical studies in the goal-setting tradition featured limited variation on one or both of these two parameters, so the interaction between commitment and difficulty in determining performance has been muted. To test their reasoning, Klein and his colleagues (1999) conducted a very thorough meta-analysis of studies involving goal difficulty, goal commitment, and task performance. Two findings from their analysis are of most significance to the present discussion. First, there was an overall moderating effect of commitment on performance. In other words, regardless of the

---

[2] Later in this chapter, we briefly discuss the concept of vision as a sort of supra-level goal that can be held by individuals, groups, or organizations. Advocates of visioning (e.g., Senge, 1990) also stress the importance of commitment for the sake of being successful.

level of goal difficulty, higher commitment was associated with higher performance. Second, they found that the effect of commitment on the relationship between goal difficulty and task performance was highest when goals were more difficult and lowest when goals were least difficult.

The two key factors that seem to facilitate goal commitment are: (1) those that make goal attainment attractive to people, including the importance of the outcomes that goal attainment is expected to bring; and (2) people's beliefs about whether they can attain the goal – their self-efficacy (Locke & Latham, 2002). Therefore, anything that a person can do to enhance his or her self-efficacy will contribute to goal commitment, including relevant training and assuring that sufficient resources are available to permit the job to be accomplished.

Goal Specificity

In Chapter 9, we noted that higher degrees of *specificity* in an intention will be associated with more accurate levels of prediction of actual behavior (Ajzen & Fishbein, 1977). Similarly, an important tenet of goal-setting theory is that higher levels of performance result when goals are made specific, and specific goals reduce the variance in performance relative to "do-your-best" goals. According to Ajzen and Fishbein (1977), intentions can be made more or less specific with regard to the nature of the act involved, the target of the act, as well as in terms of the time and circumstances in which the intended act might occur. As we will see, managerial techniques based on the goal-setting literature instruct practitioners to be as specific as possible with regard to each of these four dimensions. In short, the theory says that in addition to being difficult, goals should be specific. Again, the evidence is persuasive. Employee performance is consistently higher when goals are formulated in terms such as, "Increase market share 8% per annum," "Sell 30 pounds of peaches by noon," or "Increase my grade-point average by one full grade by final exams," than when the target, the time, or the circumstances are not specified (Locke et al., 1981; Tubbs, 1986).

The Role of Incentives in Goal Setting

If, as the theory states, goals or intentions determine behavior, what about all we know from research and common experience about the influence of incentives (or even threats) on performance? According to Locke (1968), incentives are effective for influencing behavior only to the extent that they influence the goals people strive to achieve. In other words, incentives work only if they change a person's goals and intentions or build commitment to those they already hold. For example, consider the effects of competition as a form of motivational device used by many managers, coaches, teachers, and even parents. Why is competition effective for changing behavior or increasing performance?

According to the theory, there are at least two reasons why competition may result in higher levels of performance. One is that competition may serve to build commitment to the task and to the goal of winning at the task on the part of the individual: Remember that the person must be committed to a goal in order to strive toward attaining it. However, a second feature of competition, particularly when it is "stiff," is that it serves to make the goal (winning) more difficult than it might be otherwise.

What about deadlines? Both common experience and research evidence show that people tend to accomplish a lot more when facing deadlines. In fact, some people seem to thrive under the pressure of meeting deadlines for work! Why might this be so? For the theory of goal setting, the answer is relatively simple: A deadline serves the same function as making a goal harder than it would be without it, and the theory states that harder goals result in higher performance levels. To illustrate, the classic field experiment by Latham and Locke (1975) showed that the performance levels of wood-harvesting crews increased dramatically when restrictions were placed on the number of days during which pulp and paper mills would buy the wood they hauled. In the same way that Parkinson's law (Parkinson, 1957) states that work expands to fill the time that is made available for it, this research, and the goal-setting principle on which it is based, suggest that people's work pace will increase according to the level of difficulty they attribute to the task to be accomplished.

Other incentives seem to influence motivation levels in a similar fashion. Money is probably the most widely used incentive. Goal-setting theory suggests that it will motivate higher levels of performance only to the extent it results in higher levels of commitment by the individual to the task involved. In Chapter 12, we noted the importance, for example, of tying pay to good job performance and of having employees recognize the connection between merit and payment. In Chapter 11, we noted that rewards must be viewed as equitable in order to result in positive attitudes toward work. The relationship between these two principles and the use of incentives, from a goal-setting perspective, should be clear. If a monetary incentive is not seen as contingent on performance, and/ or if it is not seen as equitable, it is less likely to commit the individual to a goal of high performance. In short, principles of equity theory and VIE theory help us understand the role of incentives, of all sorts, from the goal-setting point of view.

One interesting issue related to incentives and goals concerns the intrinsic reward value of attaining goals of differing difficulty levels. There is mixed evidence on the matter, but it may be that people who set and attain low goals may be nearly as happy as people who set high goals and attain them (Locke & Latham, 1990a, 1991). Similarly, a person who sets low goals and achieves higher than planned levels of performance will be even more self-satisfied than an individual who achieves the same high performance standard but started with high goals! More work is required on these relationships before solid conclusions can be drawn.

The Role of Participation in Goal Setting

Should employees participate in the goal-setting process? There are a number of conceptual reasons why higher levels of motivation and performance may result when the employee involved has participated with her supervisor in the setting of work goals (Mitchell, 1973). The traditional reasoning is as follows. First, participatively set goals may sometimes be harder than goals set unilaterally by one's superior. In addition, an employee who has participated in goal setting is more likely to be ego involved in the successful attainment of those goals: Because they are somewhat responsible for the type and levels of the goals they are pursuing, employees will be more desirous of seeing them fulfilled. Thus, most of the early thinking about why and how participation may be beneficial was related to the effects of participation on employee motivation and commitment (Latham, Winters, & Locke, 1994). In other words, participation stimulates motivation and commitment to succeed at one's goals.

In spite of the intuitive appeal of these arguments, the evidence that addresses them is decidedly mixed (Locke, Alavi, & Wagner, 1997; Locke & Latham, 1990a; Shetzer, 1993). For example, Latham, Mitchell, and Dossett (1978) found that although a group of scientists and engineers who participated in setting goals tended to set harder goals than were set for a comparable group by a supervisor, the two groups did not differ significantly in actual performance levels. Moreover, other studies have shown that when the difficulty level of a goal is held constant among groups, people whose goals are assigned to them seem to perform as well, on average, as people who have participated in the setting of their work goals (Latham & Saari, 1979a; Latham & Steele, 1983; Latham, Steele, & Saari, 1982). It may be that the general level of supervisory supportiveness is more important than participation per se (Latham & Saari, 1979b), although the exact nature of the role of supportiveness in the goal-setting process is less well understood than other facets of the theory (Locke et al., 1981).

A series of studies conducted primarily by Latham (and summarized in Locke & Latham, 1990a, pp. 154–166) generated a considerable base for suggesting that participation may not have much of an impact on goal-related outcomes. By contrast, Erez and her colleagues reported a series of their own studies suggesting that participation may have significant salutary benefits (e.g., Erez & Arad, 1986), presumably for the theoretical reasons outlined earlier. In what must be one of the most unusual events in the organizational sciences when two researchers/theorists disagree with each other, Latham and Erez decided to place their differing views head to head by collaborating on the design of four experiments, using a mutually respected third party, Dr. Edwin Locke, as mediator (Latham, Erez, & Locke, 1988; Locke & Latham, 1990a, p. 163). The primary conclusion reached after this dramatic series of experiments was that assigned goals can have as much motivational effect as participatively set goals, as long as other factors are kept constant (variables such as, for example, goal difficulty, and perceptions of self-efficacy).

One of the early hypotheses offered in favor of the participation effect in the success of goal setting was that participation may result in higher performance because *the employee is able to gain a better understanding of task requirements* through participation: She appreciates the reasons behind her goals as well as what to do to attain them (Latham & Saari, 1979b; Mitchell, 1973). This effect is better categorized as a *cognitive rather than a motivational influence*, as such. A recent experimental study by Latham et al. (1994) has suggested that participation in task strategy formulation can affect performance through two cognitive mechanisms – task strategies and the development of beliefs of self-efficacy. That is, participation may foster the development of effective strategies which, in turn influences the individual's beliefs of his or her self-efficacy (which is discussed at several other places in this volume).

In summary, it appears that participation may have weak and indirect effects on task performance. There are both motivational and cognitive explanations for this effect, and these mediating variables may be interrelated in complex ways. Research in this area may be yielding diminishing returns because of the difficulty scientists have in precisely measuring these subtle mediating effects and teasing out the causal linkages among them. The one consistent finding in all this is that the participation effect does exist, but is not very powerful.

Other Forms of Employee Participation

While we are on the topic of the possible effects of employee participation on job performance and employee attitudes, it is worth examining the evidence related to the possible value of employee participation in management involving forms other than direct goal setting. Cotton, Vollrath, Froggatt, Lengnick-Hall, and Jennings (1988) instigated a debate by delineating a variety of forms of "participation," including techniques such as employee ownership and, of more interest here, direct participation in work decisions and a variety of forms of partial and indirect participation.

On the basis of their study, Cotton et al. (1988) concluded that different forms of participation are likely to yield different organizational and employee outcomes. Without going into the details of the debate, Wagner (1994) conducted some meta-analyses and pulled together the results of other scholars on the matter. He concluded that, for the most part, participatory managerial practices have small statistically significant effects on outcome variables, but that the absolute size of these effects is not of practical importance. Wagner's conclusion is persuasive in large measure because he has not been part of any of the "camps" of researchers who may have developed vested interests in the participation phenomenon. He appears to be quite independent and dispassionate in his conclusions: The traditional and ideological rationale justifying it notwithstanding, participation – in any or most of its various forms – is generally not worth the resources required to make it work. The final section of this chapter will address management by objectives, one of the most widely used and recognized formal programs of employee participation of the past four decades.

The Role of Feedback in Goal Setting

Feedback is information. When it is provided to an individual in a goal setting and performance setting, or when a person acquires such information by her own means, feedback interacts with goals to determine performance levels. In an early review of the research on goal setting, Locke and his colleagues concluded that both goals and feedback to people about their performance vis-à-vis their goals are necessary in order to sustain high levels of performance. In other words, neither the provision of feedback nor the setting of goals, taken alone, is as effective in motivating high performance than is the use of both goals and feedback (Locke et al., 1981; see also Bandura & Cervone, 1983; Latham & Locke, 1991). So, how do they work together?

Latham and Locke (1991) described the joint operation of goals and feedback as follows:

> The goal is the object or outcome one is aiming for as well as the standard by which one evaluates one's performance. Feedback provides information to the individual as to the degree to which the standard is being met. If performance meets or exceeds the standard, performance is typically maintained (although eventually the goal may be raised). If performance falls below the standard, subsequent improvement will occur to the extent that: (a) the individual is dissatisfied with that level of performance and, more importantly, expects to be dissatisfied with it in the future; (b) the individual has high self-efficacy, that is, confidence in her ability to improve; and (c) the individual sets a goal to improve over past performance.
>
> (Latham & Locke, 1991, p. 226)

For positive feedback to have its maximum impact on the person's motivation to carry on, it is important that a person believes that it is her own abilities and efforts that result in success (see Thomas & Mathieu, 1994). Greater satisfaction is derived when the person believes that she was responsible for the outcomes of goal-oriented behavior, and the impact on the individual's self-efficacy is stronger than in cases where the person believes that external factors such as luck or the influence of other people were involved in the success. Hence, the nuances contained in the feedback a person receives are especially critical (Thomas & Mathieu, 1994).

Why does Goal Setting Work?

Why is goal setting so effective as a motivational strategy? Recall from Chapter 1 that the concept of motivation is used to explain the arousal, direction, amplitude (level of effort), and duration (or persistence) of behavior. Notice in the following paragraphs how the fundamental tenets of goal setting relate to these facets of motivation (see Latham, 2003; Locke et al., 1981).

First, many goals, especially super-ordinate goals, can appeal to people's emotions, providing a source of arousal and energy. Goals also direct attention and action. They identify the target of intended behavior (Ajzen & Fishbein, 1977), and, if they are stated specifically (as is recommended), the focus of the individual's effort becomes well defined. People can feel a sense of challenge and of accomplishment if and when a goal is achieved. Often, goal attainment is linked with desired rewards or outcomes in addition to the feeling of accomplishment goal success provides. Similarly, the requirement that goals be made difficult relates directly to the effort level and persistence aspects of the motivation concept. If a goal is hard, it will normally require more effort, over a longer period of time, in order to be attained. One element of persistence is tenacity – the refusal to quit trying, in spite of obstacles, until one's goal is achieved. Latham and Locke (1991) believe that commitment is one factor that contributes to tenacity, as does the sheer difficulty of the goal itself.

Finally, Locke and Latham (2004) offered a fourth explanation. They noted that goal setting usually requires the development of a task-related *strategy*. In other words, when people contemplate a goal, they must also consider means for its attainment, especially when that goal is seen as difficult. For example, in the aforementioned study in which truck drivers set higher goals for the capacity at which they loaded their trucks (Latham & Baldes, 1975), many of the drivers involved made recommendations concerning how their trucks might be modified to facilitate their attempts to carry more lumber. It may be that harder tasks are more likely to stimulate more strategy development than easy tasks. Likewise, it makes sense that the more specific the task goal, the more likely it is that people will devise specific techniques to achieve it. Accomplishing learning goals can therefore contribute to feelings of self-efficacy that contribute to successful goal attainment in the future.

Goal Setting and the Theory of Reasoned Action

Recall from Chapter 9 that, according to Fishbein and Ajzen (1975), perceptions influence beliefs, which, in turn, typically result in evaluative attitudes. These attitudes may or may not result in intentions to act, depending upon a number of factors. Nevertheless, in the causal chain linking perceptions, beliefs, attitudes, and intentions with behavior, intentions, once developed, are clearly the cognitive elements most closely connected with behavior. In fact, we can view the others (perception, beliefs, and attitudes) merely as factors that contribute to the development of intentions, but only imperfectly (cf. Mento et al., 1980).

In other words, beliefs and attitudes contribute to the development of intentions, but they do not totally shape or determine them. Therefore, to the extent that beliefs and attitudes are only partially related to a person's intentions (for the reasons discussed in Chapter 9), they will not be as effective as that person's intentions in predicting behavior. To repeat a point made earlier in this chapter, it follows that theories such as equity theory and VIE theory which rely on beliefs and attitudes (which are merely predictors of intentions to act) cannot be as valid as goal setting, which takes intentions per se as its point of departure for predicting behavior.

The linkages between perceptions, beliefs, attitudes, intentions, and work behavior from the three cognitive theories (equity theory, VIE theory, and goal-setting theory) are presented graphically in Figure 13.2. (The reader is urged to refer to Chapter 9 for a more complete discussion of these relationships.) In short, examination of the relationships represented in Figure 13.2 helps explain the limited potential predictive and explanatory capacity of the theories presented in the last two chapters and suggests why goal-setting theory fares better by comparison.

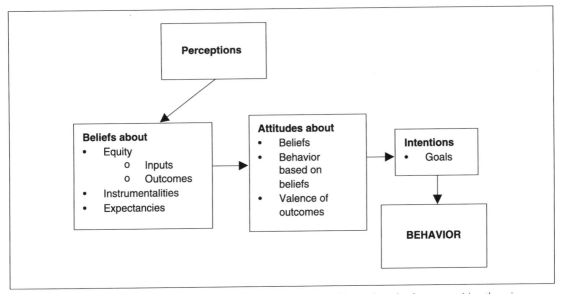

FIG. 13.2   Summary of relationships among beliefs, attitudes, and intentions in three cognitive theories.

How to Set Goals: The Nature of SMART Goals

Latham (2003) has written that in order to be of most value, goals must be specific, measurable, attainable, relevant, and have a timeframe: In other words, they must be "SMART." The goals in question may be directed toward either task performance or task learning. We have already discussed the theory and evidence relating to goal specificity, so there is no need to elaborate further here. Measurement is also important, or at least confirmation in the case of goals that are of a binary success/failure variety. An axiom of management with goal setting is to assure that the goals espoused are those that are measured in a valid way and that these measure be the primary basis for reward distribution (notice a convergence here with the instrumentality concept from VIE theory – recall Chapter 12).

Goals must be attainable. If the individual has little or no belief that a goal can be accomplished, there will be no effort expended and no commitment attached to goal pursuit. Self-efficacy is the key. Likewise, goals must be, and seen to be, relevant. If proposed goals are viewed as capricious or unrelated to the goals of others in the same organization, commitment will again be problematic. Finally, time is of the essence. Goals that are vague with regard to time lose a key element of their specificity. Recall from Chapter 9 and the theory of reasoned action how goal specificity, particularly with regard to time, increases the likelihood that intentions will result in effort.

Early Criticisms and Subsequent Refinements of Goal-Setting Theory

Nevertheless, it is to be expected that popular and robust theories in any social science will be subjected to close scrutiny and frequent attack from critics and scholars who desire to find flaws, weaknesses, and limitations of such theories. Such is the way a discipline progresses (recall Chapter 2). As one of the most successful theories of work motivation over the past two decades, goal-setting theory is no exception.

Scope and Philosophical Underpinnings of the Theory

One of the most thorough critiques of early goal-setting theory and research was provided by Austin and Bobko (1985). Among other things, these authors noted that goal-setting work had been developed in, and relied exclusively upon, logical positivism and has avoided other approaches to the development and accumulation of knowledge. They concluded that goal setting comes from a "narrow, uni-dimensional" view of the world (p. 290) and that it could be informed by other broader approaches, particularly ones that permit constructionist understandings.

Specifically, they cited Royce (1975), who would advocate a different philosophy of science, one that would assume that, among other things: Simple theories are not adequate to represent the complexities of human behavior; complex "pluralism" is necessary for a more complete view; apparent paradoxes and contradictions must be expected and tolerated. Austin and Bobko pointed out that:

> [G]oal setting literature consists mostly of published studies reporting short-term, laboratory experiments that neglect the spectrum of possible dependent measures. They serve more as demonstrations than as attempts to expand the parameters of a theory of goal setting.
>
> (Austin & Bobko, 1985, p. 290)

So, they concluded, goal-setting researchers have failed to explore limitations to the theory. This is pretty tough condemnation of any theory, particularly of one which enjoys such relatively high status in the areas of phenomena with which it deals.

As specific examples, Austin and Bobko (1985) pointed out that, as of the early 1980s at least, the focus had been on uni-dimensional quantity (of performance) goals. Quality goals and multi-dimensional goals had been neglected, as had the prospect that quantity and quality goals can often be in conflict. (For example, the faster a person paints a living room, the poorer is the quality of the work one can expect.) In addition, the focus has been largely on individual-level as opposed to group-level goals. Finally, they complained that goal-setting work had been conducted too frequently in tightly controlled laboratory conditions and not sufficiently often in real-world organizational settings.

Task Complexity and Novelty

Other early researchers and critics found that the simple, original goal-setting formulation was ineffective in situations in which the individual found the task novel or complex (e.g., Campbell, 1984, 1988; Campbell & Gingrich, 1986; Earley, Connelly, & Ekegren, 1989; Wood et al., 1987). One series of experiments reported by Earley et al. (1989), for example, showed that assigning people the task of specific, difficult goals may be the worst thing to do; rather, asking people merely to "do their best" is most appropriate if the task is one that is novel and complex, and for which there may be more than a single best way to approach it.

Responses to the Criticisms

Frankly, as criticisms go in social and behavioral science, these were not that severe and the ledger of research and refinement since the mid-1980s shows that most of these criticisms have been addressed, methodically, and with rigor. For example, on the matter of conflict between a person's multiple goals, Locke, Smith, Erez, Chah, and Schaffer (1994) conducted and reported two studies. One was a laboratory experiment with undergraduate students and the other was a field study of the research productivity of professors. On the basis of these two projects, Locke and his colleagues (1994) concluded that conflicting goals (such as a dilemma between quantity and quality of production or a dilemma between research or teaching goals) can put pressure on people and lead to negative impacts on one of the performance goals under consideration.

Similarly, in response to the allegation of an over-reliance on laboratory experiments, Locke and Latham (1990a) counted and reported the comparative rates of use of field versus laboratory settings. (In fact, the comparative count of lab to field at that time was 239 vs. 156, respectively, although a greater variety of tasks had been used in the field over the years than in the lab – 53 vs. 35, respectively.)

Task complexity, learning, and performance goals

To reply to the issue of the relevance of goal setting for complex, unfamiliar tasks, Wood and Locke (1990) pursued the matter of task complexity. They proposed that as tasks become more complex, the simple focusing mechanisms mentioned earlier (i.e., focus of attention, the devotion of specific energy, and persistence) become less adequate to explain goal-seeking behavior. As tasks become more complex or novel, the person is unable to rely on what Wood and Locke called "stored universal plans" and/or "stored task specific plans" – strategies that have been learned in the past for approaching tasks and challenges. So, task complexity requires the individual to develop *new* task-specific plans – new ways of going about getting the job done. Stored universal plans are exemplified by routine, even mundane activities, such as driving to work in the morning or brushing one's teeth, while universal task-specific plans entail skill development, such as operating a particular software program. The point is that task complexity and novelty can make both of these types of learned routine useless, or even dysfunctional; the person has to discover news ways to act – what Wood and Locke (1990) refer to as *new task-specific plans*.

The joint effects of strategy and goals on a complex task were investigated explicitly to follow up on this line of reasoning (Chesney & Locke, 1991). Using a computer-based business game with a sample of senior undergraduate students, these researchers found that both strategy development and goals had positive effects on performance at the game, but that strategy had the stronger effect. In addition, more difficult goals resulted in a greater use of strategy, so that goal difficulty had both a direct as well as an indirect effect on performance through the strategy process (Chesney & Locke, 1991).

When strategy development is required, learning is taking place. The individual tries to determine, either by trial and error or through other means, how to approach the task. When we speak of learning, we can consider the consequences under which the learning takes place. One critical variable in any teaching/learning context is whether the practice takes place in a massed, single period, or whether there are many practice periods, separated by breaks (Dempster, 1988, 1989).

To pursue this matter, Kanfer, Ackerman, Murtha, Dugdale, and Nelson (1994) had psychology students perform a simulated air traffic control task under the usual "do-your-best" as opposed to assigned specific, difficult goals. The researchers also manipulated whether students worked with intermittent breaks or on single, massed trials to learn the task. As expected, the students who had specific, difficult goals were superior in performance only when they were provided rest periods during the learning and performance exercise; those who were required to learn and perform without the benefits of breaks did far less well.

Types of Goal

Performance goals

This raised the question of the nature of the goals a person attempts to accomplish. *Outcome goals*[3] focus "attention on a specific quantity or quality of something to be achieved (e.g., cut and delimb three trees per hour)" (Winters & Latham, 1996). Goals of this sort have been used predominantly in early goal-setting research and the tasks were usually simple and routine.

Learning goals

But the issue of novel tasks raises the importance of an alternative type of goal, a *learning goal* "which individuals seek to increase their competence, to understand or master something new" (Dwek, 1986, p. 1040). Striving for learning goals, at least initially, "should increase performance when the person lacks the requisite knowledge to master a task. This is because it shifts the focus to task processes in terms of strategy development, and away from task outcome achievement" (Winters & Latham, 1996). When the individual is unfamiliar with a task, a focus on outcome goals can be quite dysfunctional. The more appropriate goal in such occasions is a learning goal which, once accomplished, will facilitate performance in subsequent situations. Latham, Seijts, and Crim (2006, p. 4) stated:

> The primary distinction between a performance goal and a learning goal is the framing of the instructions. With a performance goal, a manager frames the goal so that individuals focus on a performance

---

[3] *Outcome goals* are now usually referred to as *task performance goals* or simply *performance goals*.

outcome (e.g., reduce costs by 10 percent). A search for information to attain the goal is not emphasized. This is because a person's knowledge, skills and ability are treated as a given . . . A performance goal cues the person to draw on extant strategies and/or skills.

In contrast to a performance goal, a learning goal changes one's focus. The requisite strategies or behaviors necessary to perform are not known. Hence, the instructions are framed so that an individual focuses on the acquisition of knowledge or skill (e.g., discover five specific new ways to increase market share). Learning goals thus explicitly encourage the search for, and implementation of, appropriate strategies for increasing one's performance. In short, a performance goal focuses an individual on the end result; a learning goal focuses a person on the process of learning or discovering how to perform a task effectively.

Learning vs. task orientations

Building on a tradition of work in educational psychology (Dwek, 1986), Seijts and his colleagues (Seijts & Latham, 2005; Seijts, Latham, Tasa, & Latham, 2004) and VandeWalle, Brown, Cron, & Slocum (1999) introduced to the work motivation literature the concepts of *learning orientation* (as opposed to task orientation), and the corresponding distinction between *learning goals* and *performance goals*. Learning and performance orientations are seen as personal predilections – essentially traits or personality predispositions. "Goal orientation predicts and explains not only the tasks people choose, but how they behave when the acquisition of knowledge or ability, rather than sheer effort or persistence, is a prerequisite for good performance on a complex task" (Seijts et al., 2004).

A study reported by Zweig and Webster (2004) added weight to the hypothesis that goal orientation, while related to a number of other personality traits such as extraversion, emotional stability, openness to experience, agreeableness, and conscientiousness – the so-called "Big Five" dimensions of personality identified by Barrick, Mount, and Strauss (1993), is both conceptually and empirically distinct from those other concepts. Indeed, they found that goal orientation can mediate the relationship between personality and performance intentions. An experiment conducted recently by Latham et al. (2006) suggested that, in direct parallel to the relationship between goal difficulty and (task) goal performance, there is a positive relationship between the difficulty of learning goals and an individual's task performance. The reason? "[C]onsistent with goal-setting theory, a more difficult goal leads to greater effort and search for task-relevant strategies than an easier goal, given that the individual is committed to goal attainment" (Latham et al., 2006, p. 7).

Another study by Van Yperen and Janssen (2002) found that the traditional relationship between high job demands and job satisfaction was altered when workers' goal orientations were introduced into the equation. Specifically, they found that when an individual's performance orientation was strong and his or her mastery orientation was relatively weak, perceived job demands were associated with declines in job satisfaction. Recent papers by Latham (2003), Seijts and Latham (2005), and Noel and Latham (2006) offer a number of examples from North American business in the correct use and combination of learning and performance goals.

The point here is that this 35-year program of research continues to expand its focus, refine its techniques, and respond to its critics in ways unmatched, in this author's opinion, in the history of the organizational sciences devoted to work motivation. Very impressive indeed.

Personality Differences and Goal-Setting Processes

As mentioned in the previous section, for many years after goal-setting theory was introduced by Locke and Latham, little or no attention was paid to possible individual differences in the model

(Austin & Bobko, 1985). The effects of specific and difficult goals were assumed to apply universally across people of all personality types and predispositions.

Eventually, Barrick et al. (1993) introduced a popular personality construct – *conscientiousness* – to the goal-setting literature. The researchers demonstrated that sales representatives who are high on this variable are more likely to become committed to their goals and, as a result, achieve them. Known as one of the so-called "Big Five" factors of personality[4] to emerge in recent psychological research and theory (Digman, 1990), conscientiousness implies being responsible, dependable, planful, organized, persistent, and – of most importance to us here – achievement oriented (recall our discussion of achievement orientation in Chapter 7).

Barrick and his colleagues (1993) built on the "can do" and "will do" model proposed by Borman, White, Pulakos, and Oppler (1991) to help explain the origins of goal commitment. Recall that the early formulation of goal setting assumed, among other things, that specific and difficult goals are effective only when people are committed to them. The conscientiousness factor of human personality, which may be partially determined by heredity (Digman, 1990), may explain why some people more readily commit to goals. Indeed, a study of undergraduate students conducted by Colquitt and Simmering (1998) found that both conscientiousness and learning orientation (see earlier) were positively related to motivation to learn, both at the beginning of a 6-week course as well as after midterm feedback. By contrast, performance orientation was negatively related to motivation to learn at both time periods.

A caution is in order here. It is possible for a sort of tautology to occur over time as researchers and theorists pursue a theory of work motivation such as goal setting by adding more and more variables into the equation. So, for example, we must be careful not to fall into a loop such as the following: Conscientious people are more likely to commit to goals. Conscientiousness entails a cluster of traits that include being organized, dependable, and strategic. The question arises: Is conscientiousness an independent causal factor that explains one's tendency to commit to goals, or is the tendency to commit to goals merely a defining characteristic of conscientiousness itself? Some thinkers may see goal commitment tendencies as a result of the personality trait, while others may see them as aspects of the same constellation of a person's personality. If we are not careful, we may confuse the two possibilities and lull ourselves into a false belief that we have explained a phenomenon such as goal commitment, when in fact all we have done is to define it as an element of the variables that are its putative causes. If the *definition* of conscientiousness did not sound so much like the tendency to commit to goals (and it does), then we would have more reason to believe we have learned something about the *causes* of goal commitment.[5]

Aside from this possible logical problem, there is evidence other than that presented by Barrick et al. (1993) that need for achievement (see Chapter 3) may predispose people to be more likely to commit to goals. An interesting experiment conducted by Hollenbeck, Williams, and Klein (1989) using college students as participants found that people who are higher in achievement motivation (and those whose locus of control is internal) are more likely to commit to goals. In addition, Hollenbeck et al. (1989) found that people are more likely to become committed to goals when they make their goals public – a finding with plenty of previous support (cf. Salancik, 1977).

---

[4] The so-called "Big Five" personality factors are extraversion, agreeableness, emotional stability, openness to experience, and conscientiousness (Digman, 1990). A paper by Mount and Barrick (1995) summarized the relevance of this taxonomy of personality variables for the theory and practice of human resource management.

[5] A similar problem in the work motivation literature was alleged by Roberts and Glick (1981), who attacked the popular job characteristics model of job design (Oldham & Hackman, 1980) by pointing out that some of the items in the instruments that were used to assess the "causal" elements in the model were the same as some of the items used by researchers to measure elements of other variables in that model. Hence, Roberts and Glick argued, it is no wonder that "perceived job characteristics" were found to be correlated with job attitudes: To a certain extent the concepts and the measures of job characteristics and job attitudes were the same concepts!

The Link with Self-Efficacy

The concept of self-efficacy has already appeared many times in this volume (see Chapters 6, 7, and 12 in particular). The growing body of theory on goal setting has become integrally related to the work on self-efficacy. According to Latham and Locke (1991, pp. 220–221), self-efficacy is "broader in meaning than effort-performance expectancy" (recall our treatment of the two concepts in Chapter 12) in expectancy theory in that self-efficacy includes all factors that could lead one to perform well at a task (e.g., adaptability, creativity, resourcefulness, perceived capacity to orchestrate complex action sequences). It is believed that self-efficacy has not only a direct effect on performance by raising motivation levels, but it also has indirect effects, most notably by affecting people's choice of goals and their commitment to those goals. In other words, the theory holds that people with high self-efficacy beliefs are high performers because they are more likely to undertake difficult goals, to become committed to those goals, and – presumably – work with more intensity to achieve their goals (see Locke & Latham, 1990a, 2002).

Possible New Directions for Goal-Setting Theory

Goal-setting theory has a remarkable 40-year history (see Locke & Latham, 2002) and has become the most dominant, valid, and useful modern theory of work motivation. It is clear that its adherents will continue to pursue its theoretical and applied boundaries. Where else might their efforts be extended?

One interesting issue concerns the emotional experiences associated with goal setting. As we saw in Chapter 4 and elsewhere in this book, emotions and emotionality are areas of renewed interest in psychology and organizational behavior. To the knowledge of this author, little is known about how emotions are related to the various phenomena associated with goal setting, although a few hunches and hypotheses come to mind. Latham (2003), for example, provided a number of well-known examples from 20th-century history to argue that super-ordinate goals (such as the defense of Britain during the bleakest days of WWII) have an emotional component that can arouse the energy needed by people to generate and adhere – in large numbers – to common, large-scale goals.

What types of emotional experience are associated with the goal-setting process? Fear? Anxiety? Joy? What types of emotional state affect the difficulty of goals selected or the degree of commitment a person attaches to a goal? What are the emotional experiences related to participation in goal setting? How does it feel when responsibility for setting goals is delegated to an individual, or removed from her? What emotions usually accompany the feedback process: Seeking feedback, receiving positive feedback or negative feedback? Do positive emotions or what has come to be called a trait of *positive affectivity* (Chapter 4) influence any of the stages and processes of goal setting, including goal determination, participation, feedback seeking, feedback acceptance, commitment dynamics, and/or the experience of goal attainment? Some work on the effects of goal-related progress has been reported by theorists and researchers working in the control theory tradition (e.g., Carver & Scheier, 1990a, 1990b) and in the resurgent literature on the nature of human satisfaction (see Chapter 12), but a systematic expansion of goal-setting theory requires that more research be done that fully integrates emotionality into the various stages of the overall goal experience.

A second area for possible goal-setting work deals with frustration. How does it feel to fail to achieve goals? Some early work by Martin, Tesser, and McIntosh (1993) provided a few clues (such as what they refer to as "passive" and "motivated" activation, depression, and rumination). Here again some interesting theoretical groundwork has been offered. It is time now for empirical research to complete and extend the work.

In a recent summary of their corpus of work, Locke and Latham (2002) summarized future directions they see as useful. One is the joint use of learning and performance goals: Work to this stage has tended to emphasize how individuals pursue one or the other, but it seems reasonable to assume that the pair can be used simultaneously or in sequence as people pursue complex tasks. A second area they identify is how risk and risk strategies interact with goal performance. Considerably more work seems required on the role of personality and trait constructs. It may be that goals (whether performance goals or learning goals) are so strong that they mask the effects of personality differences. Indeed, a recent study found that goal setting can motivate unethical behavior, in large part through the mechanisms of deception and misrepresenting one's performance against their goals (Schweitzer, Ordonez, & Douma, 2004). Finally, Locke and Latham (2002) recognized that more work could be done on the effects of the subconscious as a distal source of human action.

Summary, Conclusions, and A Glance Ahead

This author stated in an earlier book (Pinder, 1984) and in an earlier edition (Pinder, 1998) of this book that it was appropriate to agree with Locke and his colleagues that "The beneficial effect of goal setting on task performance is one of the most robust and replicable findings in the psychological literature" (Locke et al., 1981, p. 145). The same conclusion is warranted today, in the early years of the new millennium, even more so than when Locke and his colleagues made their claim, a quarter-century ago (see also Latham & Pinder, 2005). Like VIE theory, goal-setting theory qualifies for the moniker "mature theory." The primary effects associated with its principal hypotheses are well established. Its theoretical elegance is unusual and being filled in, step by step, now by a much larger cadre of investigators than launched the theory in the 1960s. And its applied utility is manifest.

Before leaving our discussion of goal setting, it is worth noting again the potential this theory has for integrating many of the other theories presented throughout this book (including some approaches and techniques that are still to be presented). Ryan's (1970) theory suggests the important role needs may play in determining the repertoires people develop for interpreting stimulus situations (cf. Locke, 1991). Similarly, the work of Ajzen and Fishbein (1977) and Fishbein and Ajzen (1975) suggests how cognitive theories that rely on beliefs and attitudes (such as equity theory and VIE theory) contribute to the explanation of behavior: Their primary function is to provide a basis for predicting a person's intentions, not the direct prediction of behavior.

It stands to reason that managerial programs that explicitly attempt to influence employee intentions should be more effective for influencing employee behavior than are programs designed to influence beliefs and attitudes. Indeed, evidence about the applied value of the theory continues to amass. For example, a survey of large American businesses found small but statistically significant correlations between organizational profitability and the use of goal setting (Terpstra & Rozell, 1994). The researchers sampled 1000 companies from *Dun's Business Rankings* and received useable responses from 201 of them. They compared the firms' profit margins and average annual growth in profit with replies from senior executives regarding their use or non-use "of Locke's goal-setting theory." Sixty-one percent of the companies responding reported that they used the theory, and the correlations with the two financial indicators ranged from .10 to .54, varying from industry to industry. A more recent paper by Pritchard and Payne (2002) flatly states: "Some form of goalsetting, such as identifying objectives or formal setting of quantitative goals, including management by objectives (MBO), has probably been used by most organizations at some point in time" (p. 22). We focus attention on formal goal-setting programs in work organizations shortly. First, however, we will study a body of theory that has become a rival for goal setting, referred to as *control theory*.

CONTROL THEORY

Although control theory was first proposed a half-century ago (Wiener, 1948), it made its first appearances in the organizational sciences in the early 1980s (e.g., Campion & Lord, 1982). *On first reading*, the theory sounds and looks a lot like goal-setting theory, although some of the relevant nouns and verbs differ. In fact, we will see as this chapter develops that a considerable overlap exists between the two theories and that these similarities have generated controversy and criticism as well as positive attempts at integration between them. Although it appears to have had its origins in Miller, Galanter, and Pribram's (1960) so-called TOTE model[6] (Locke & Latham, 1990a, p. 19), this theory has been offered as a model of human behavior with applications in a variety of human contexts and problem areas, such as motivation, self-management, affective and behavioral reactions to work, stress, goal setting and goal changing, self-appraisal, and feedback seeking (Carver, 1979; Carver & Scheier, 1982, 1990b; Fellenz, 1996). We will discuss self-management later in the chapter, and the relevance of control theory (and goal-setting theory) will be evident.

According to two leading proponents of control theory:

> [I]ntentional behavior [reflects] a process of feedback control . . . When people move (physically or psychologically) toward goals, they manifest the functions of a negative (discrepancy reducing) feedback loop . . . That is, people periodically note the qualities they are expressing in their behavior (an input function). They compare these perceptions with salient reference values – whatever goals are temporarily being used to guide behavior (a comparison process inherent in all feedback systems). If the comparisons indicate discrepancies between reference value and present state (i.e., between intended and actual quantities of behavior), people adjust (the output function) so that it more closely approximates the reference value.
>
> (Carver & Scheier, 1990a, p. 19)

The Genealogy of Control Theory

Control theory has its principal roots in cybernetics, the science of control and communication (Fellenz, 1996). In its most basic form, control theory is concerned with the self-regulation of systems, relying heavily on negative feedback loops that provide information to the system concerning how close it is coming to a desired goal state (Klein, 1989). Like a thermostat that operates a house's heating system, this model implies that a person (or any system) is in a constant state of seeking feedback, adjusting his functioning to accommodate any discrepancies detected between his achieved and desired state, and carrying on. The end-point of the behavior is a still state of retirement, achieved once there is no discrepancy detected between one's goals and one's accomplishments. In simple terms, "when people pay attention to what they are doing, they usually do what they intend to do, relatively accurately and thoroughly" (Carver & Scheier, 1990a, p. 19).

Elements of Basic Control Theory

Lord and Hanges (1987) and Klein (1989) have offered comprehensive theories of control theory that have implications for work motivation. In the interest of space, we will focus here on the model

---

[6] TOTE is an acronym for "test–operate–test–exit" – a sequence of operations by which early cognitive psychologists described how an organism (such as a person) behaves in an environment in pursuit of an end-state, by sensing its progress toward that end-state with the use of feedback, altering behavior on the basis of that feedback, and then, ultimately ceasing the sequence (see Miller et al., 1960, Chapter 1).

proposed by Klein (1989), because it is more recent and includes principal concepts from a variety of other theories in addition to the fundamental notions found in cybernetics.[7]

Klein's (1989) adaptation of the generic theory yields at least 33 testable propositions, although not much empirical work has been reported to this time. The generic model of control theory is presented in Figure 13.3 (adapted from Klein, 1989), and the following explanation is presented in the generic terms used by control theorists.

The elements of this theory are as follows. The most important component of the theory is the feedback loop. As we saw earlier in the chapter, feedback is merely information provided to a person (or any system) about its circumstances. The feedback loop has four parts:

1.   a referent standard (or goal)
2.   a sensor, or input function
3.   a comparator
4.   an effector, or output function.

These four components are all illustrated in Figure 13.2. For the present purpose, we will assume that the terms *input*, *output*, *goal*, and *feedback* are familiar to the reader: They are used regularly in common parlance and elsewhere in this chapter. As Klein (1989) and most other control theorists do, we will return to the example of the typical thermostat controlling the heat of a room:

> [T]he referent standard is the temperature the thermostat is set at, the sensor is the element monitoring the current room temperature, the comparator is the mechanism that compares the current and desired temperatures, and the effector is the furnace or air conditioner.
>
> (Klein, 1989, p. 151)

In its most simple, mechanistic form, the system operates as follows. Some type of input is received by the sensor in the system, which, in turn, sends a signal to its comparator. The comparator tests the signal against the system's current standard or goal. If a discrepancy is found, an error signal is triggered and the system initiates action in its effector to reduce the discrepancy. If there is no discrepancy, then there may be no action taken by the effector (Klein, 1989). This is a description of how control theory works in its most basic, mechanical form.

Human systems are much more complex, of course, although Klein and others have claimed that the fundamental components and processes are similar. For humans, goals can be flexible and multiple. There are often many courses of action that can be selected to close any perceived discrepancies. The information contained in the feedback can be simple or complex, loaded with meaning or ambiguity. It can be subject

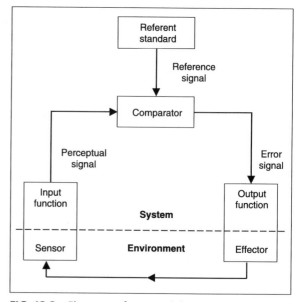

FIG. 13.3   Elements of a control theory system.

Source: Klein, H. J. (1989). An integrated control theory model of work motivation. *Academy of Management Review, 14*, 150–172. Reprinted with permission. This work is protected by copyright and it is being used with the permission of Access Copyright. Any alteration of its content or further copying in any form whatsoever is strictly prohibited.

---

[7] Hyland (1988) also offers a control theory model that integrates other theories of work motivation. In fact, Hyland offers his approach not as a theory of work motivation, as such, but rather "as a meta-theoretic framework for examining the relation between the core ideas of the different motivational programs" (p. 642).

to interpretation and either accepted as valid or rejected as suspicious or misleading. It may be judged as genuine or fallacious and devious. Klein continued:

> Consider . . . a salesperson who has accepted a quarterly sales quota as a personal goal (the standard). The input function would be the information the salesperson perceives about his or her current sales performance. When this information is compared to the standard, the salesperson forms a perception of how well he or she is meeting the quota. If this comparison reveals a discrepancy, the salesperson will take some corrective action, possibly increasing the number of new contacts [he or she initiates with prospective customers].
>
> (Klein, 1989, p. 151)

Control theory includes both cognitive as well as affective elements. The cognitive features hinge around the transmission and interpretation of information. The affective features arise from the perception of discrepancies and consist, at least in part, of the impulses to initiate or terminate action. If the salesperson is satisfied that he has surpassed his sales quota, he will feel a sense of joy and perhaps pride and relief (see Chapter 4 for a discussion of these emotions). If he perceives he has fallen short of his quota, he may experience anxiety, fear, anger, and, possibly, embarrassment or shame. It is easy and tempting to oversimplify control theory by ignoring or forgetting that it includes affective as well as cognitive processes (see Carver & Scheier, 1990a, 1990b).

Unlike most simple mechanical systems, human systems as depicted in control theory consist of hierarchies of feedback loops:

> In such hierarchies, the *means* to reduce discrepancies in higher-order feedback loops become the *standards* of lower-order loops . . . That is, the output function of one feedback loop [as illustrated in Figure 13.2] might consist of a string of other loops, and each of those, in turn, might contain other strings of loops, and so on.
>
> (Klein, 1989, p. 152)

The salesperson introduced earlier continues to serve to illustrate. The output function where we left off was the goal of increasing new contacts. It consists of several actions, such as telephoning current customers to enquire about competitors' needs, checking the Yellow Pages for other companies that might require his products and services, making initial contacts with everyone found by these search tactics, and so on. One output function consists of at least two feedback loops: Finding and contacting. Each of these feedback loops will have the basic elements described earlier – an input function, a sensor, a comparator, and an output function. These hierarchies exist like wheels within wheels until, at the most basic level, there are loops that:

> [Involve] neural signals and changes in muscle tension associated with turning the pages in a phone book. The result is a hierarchical plan for increasing sales through increasing new contacts. Powers (1973) proposed that the human nervous system embodies a detailed hierarchy of such feedback loops.
>
> (Klein, 1989, p. 152)

A Control Theory for Work Motivation

Now that the generic model has been presented, we can look briefly at how Klein interpreted its basic elements for application to our study of work motivation. Klein (1989) substituted *goals* for referent standards and the individual's behavior to replace the notion of effector. *Feedback* represents the sensor. He maintains the notion of comparator. Klein's adaptation of the generic model is reproduced in Figure 13.4.

Some of the boxes in Figure 13.4 contain two labels. The one on top in each case is Klein's term

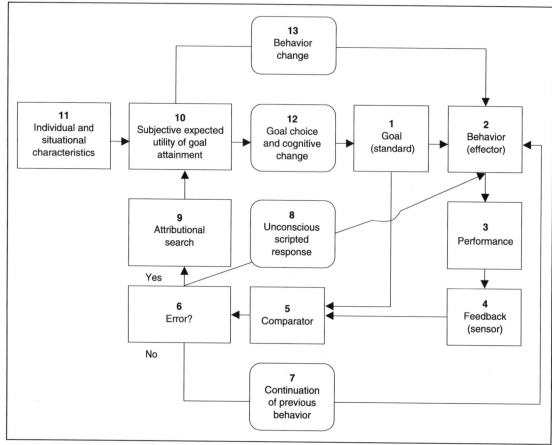

FIG. 13.4   Klein's integrated model of work motivation.

Source: Klein, H. J. (1989). An integrated control theory model of work motivation. *Academy of Management Review, 14,* 150–172. Reprinted with permission.

for the corresponding generic term below it. For example, Box 1 represents the common notion from work motivation of a goal; translated into the generic terms of control theory, the concept represented in that box is a standard. Klein refers to his model as an "integrated control theory model of work motivation" because it incorporates concepts from goal-setting theory (such as goals and feedback), script theory (which will be discussed shortly, and see Lord and Kernan, 1987), and attribution theory (Kelley & Michela, 1980). The reader is directed to Klein's important paper for a complete representation of his integrated model. It is one of the most creative and constructive attempts to integrate what are generally thought of as competing or incompatible theories of work motivation. (See also Klein, 1991a, for an empirical test of part of this model.)

Goal Setting vs. Control Theory

In Chapter 2, we saw how it is part of the development of a discipline for researchers and theorists from one camp in an area to attack and criticize the theories and research methods used by scientists in competing camps. We have surveyed many examples of this sort of controversy throughout this volume. In this section, we will examine some of the controversy that has been directed at control theory, particularly the controversy that has emanated from adherents to the goal-setting camp, notably Locke, Latham, and Bandura. Their attacks have many dimensions and raise a series of issues. We will not deal with them exhaustively here; the interested reader is referred to the original sources as well as to a rejoinder offered by Klein (1991b) as well as the exchange between Vancouver, Thompson, and Williams (2001) and Bandura and Locke (2003).

Is Control Theory too Mechanistic?

Locke and Latham (1990a) claimed that control theory is a modern stepchild of behaviorism, and that it is deficient because it deals only with *discrepancy reduction* by feedback monitoring, completely ignoring initial, natural goal-setting processes they claim are inherently and definitively human. Locke and Latham objected to the motionless end-state that is the logical conclusion of human behavior under the control theory perspective (Locke & Latham, 1990a, p. 19).

The natural state of the organism is seen to be one of motionlessness, or rest. This is true of machines, but not of living organisms which are naturally active. It is, in effect, a mechanistic version of long discredited drive-reduction theory (Cofer & Appley, 1964) (see Chapter 1 of this book).

They continued:

> At a fundamental level, discrepancy reduction theories such as control theory are inadequate because if people consistently acted in accordance with them by trying to eliminate all disturbances [discrepancies], they would all commit suicide – because it would be the only way to eliminate tension. If people chose instead to stay alive but set no goals, they would soon die anyway. By the time they were forced into action by desperate, unremitting hunger pangs, it would be too late to grow and process the food they would need to survive.
>
> (Locke & Latham, 1990a, p. 20)

On the same issue in another place, Locke wrote (1991): "Discrepancy reduction is a consequence of goal-directed behavior, not a cause" (p. 13):

> If tension-reduction or removal of discrepancies were people's major motive, then the simplest action for them to take (short of suicide) would be to adjust the goal or standard to their prior performance, thus obviating the need for any action to reduce the discrepancy. Or better yet, they would choose no standards at all so that any output would be as good as any other. But these alternatives are clearly at variance with how people usually act.
>
> (Locke, 1991, pp. 12–13)

This is clearly a fundamental theoretical difference from the tenet of control theory.

Similarly, Bandura (1989) argued that *goal setting is first and foremost a discrepancy creating process*. (Certainly Deci and his colleagues in the intrinsic motivation theory tradition would agree – see Chapter 7 of this volume and Harackiewicz & Stone, 1991.)

Bandura wrote:

> It [human self-motivation] requires *feedforward control* as well as *feedback control*. People initially motivate themselves through feedforward control by adopting valued performance standards that create a state of disequilibrium and then mobilizing their effort on the basis of anticipatory estimation. Feedback control comes into play in subsequent adjustments of behavior to achieve desired results. After people attain the standard they have been pursuing, they generally set a higher standard for themselves. The adoption of further challenges creates new motivational discrepancies to be mastered ... Self-motivation thus involves a dual cyclic process of disequilibrating discrepancy production followed by equilibrating discrepancy reduction.
>
> (Bandura, 1989, p. 38)

Adherents and defenders of control theory take exception to the allegation that it is too mechanistic a model to represent human processes (e.g., Klein, 1989). "In human control systems, feedback involves much more than the mechanical sensing of environment, goals are not predetermined inflexible standards, and there are several alternatives for reducing discrepancies" (Klein, 1989, p. 151). Carver and Scheier (1981) pointed out that control theory conceives of goals as existing in hierarchies, such that "the standard of comparison for the behavior of a subordinate loop is specified as the output of the loop at the next higher level of analysis" (p. 117). Moreover, human beings usually harbor multiple goal hierarchies (Eckblad, 1981; Fellenz, 1996), and their various goals may be mutually reinforcing, contradictory, or merely compatible and independent. *Human goals* can differ on a number of dimensions, such as their degree of generality, their time frames, whether they are related to activity and process or outcome states, the degree to which they are intended to influence a person's behavior, and the degree to which the person is even conscious of them (Winell, 1987, cited by Fellenz, 1996). The traditional body of goal-setting theory makes it clear that human goals can be manipulated in terms of their specificity, difficulty, and the level of commitment of the person holding the goals (Locke & Latham, 1990a).

In a chapter published at about the same time as the Locke and Latham (1990a) critique, Carver and Scheier (1990a) revealed that they too believed that "human action [is] fundamentally goal-directed" (p. 5). They acknowledged that: "The idea that human behavior – indeed, human personality – is best analyzed in terms of the goals that people adopt is one that has been prominent in the writing for many years . . . the central theme is that human action is defined in terms of the individual's goals" (p. 6). For Carver and Scheier (1990a), the origin of people's goals is their memories: Behavioral knowledge about how people acted and responded in past situations similar to those they face in any given time in the present. People form *schemas*[8] and *scripts*[9] about the nature and sequence of social events – scenarios about the way things work and about how events unfold. These scripts become part of memory, if not a part of a person's repertoire of action in future social situations similar to those in which the scripts were learned. Carver and Scheier (1990a) argued that: "Saying that someone has taken up a behavioral goal is in some sense equivalent to saying that the person wants to manifest in his or her actions a particular quality that is represented in a knowledge structure in his or her memory. Accordingly . . . the behavioral goals underlying human action are specified in memory as elements of behavioral knowledge" (1990a, p. 5).

For this author, the origins and nature of goals, as noted in these published statements, are no

---

[8] More than 70 years ago, Bartlett (1932) introduced the idea of cognitive schemas as follows: " 'Schema' refers to an active organization of past reactions, or of past experiences, which must always be supposed to be operating in any well-adapted organic response. That is, whenever there is any order or regularity of behavior, a particular response is possible only because it is related to other similar responses which have been serially organized, yet which operate, not simply as individual members coming after one another, but as a unitary mass . . . All incoming pulses of a certain kind, or mode, go together to build up an active, organized setting: visual, auditory, various types of cutaneous impulses and the like, at a relatively low level; all the experiences connected by a common interest: in sport, in literature, history, art, science, philosophy, and so on, on a higher level" (Bartlett, 1932, p. 201, quoted by Miller et al., 1960, p. 7). For example, Shetzer (1993) applied the notion of schemas to the processes associated with employee participation in decision making, providing not only a useful lens through which to consider the participation process but also a valuable example of how people form and utilize schemas to make sense of their work environments.

[9] A *script* is a particular type of knowledge schema, which Lord and Kernan (1987) define as follows: "Scripts are cognitive knowledge structures held in memory that describe the appropriate sequencing of events in conventional or familiar situations . . . Scripts are a unique type of knowledge structure because they serve a dual purpose: They not only help one interpret the behavior of others, but they also aid in generating behavior . . . Thus, they guide the planning and execution of familiar or repetitive activities" (p. 266). People develop and make use of scripts for most of the behavioral settings they have encountered more than a few times. So, for example, a student develops a script for taking a midterm examination in a university course – it consists of a series of mental images, concepts, expectations, and ideas associated with taking examinations in the past. The script contains knowledge and ideas about what forms of behavior are appropriate, what the student can expect from the behavior of other students taking the exam, and so on. Scripts are subject to change with the occurrence of new events and experiences. Thus, the occurrence of a fire drill in the middle of a particular examination period teaches the student (and alters her examination-taking script) that fire alarms are a possibility and that certain types of frantic and worrisome behavior can be expected from other students and the professor in charge. In the work setting, people are likely to form scripts that consist of expected and appropriate behaviors and events for a wide variety of occasions, such as meetings with colleagues, performance review interviews with one's boss, a Christmas party, or a labor walkout. Scripts help us organize our thoughts, expectations, beliefs, and behaviors so they can be invoked when appropriate to make our functioning in life efficient.

less vague and no more scientifically helpful than those from Ryan (1970), whose explanation of the origins and nature of goals was presented at the beginning of this chapter. The primary difference appears to be that Ryan's (1970) thoughts relied on a theory of human needs as their bedrock, while those of Carver and Scheier (1990a) relied more on a cognitive, memory-based foundation. It seems ironic that Locke and Latham's (1990a) disapproval of control theory should be so emphatic, given the primarily cognitive basis of their own theory of goal setting.

Whatever the truth, this author contends that the controversy has been more spectacular than the value of the underlying issue: Goals are critical to human behavior and, it follows, to motivation and behavior at work. The origins of these goals must be found in needs, cognitions, memories, and more-or-less specific intentions – "all of the above." Carving up the variance accounted for by each source hardly seems worth the time or trouble.

More recently, Vancouver et al. (2001) reported results of two studies to challenge the basic goal-setting hypothesis that self-efficacy, goals, and performance are all positively interrelated in some circumstances. Bandura and Locke (2003) responded by citing the volumes of literature supporting the hypothesis that self-efficacy has only positive effects on goal attainment for people. The nuances of these opposing positions deserve careful reading by interested parties, in the original periodical articles.

In short, there are many ways that are too simplistic to attack control theory as a mechanical or mechanistic representation of human functioning. There are definite parallels between the operations of human systems and lower-level systems (see Boulding, 1968; Miller, 1978,) but to reject control theory, holus bolus, simply on the basis of those similarities is unreasonable (see Fellenz, 1996, for a far more comprehensive review of the issues). It is possible that moderator variables, such as the personality types proposed by Kanfer and Heggestad (1997; see Chapter 3), might help move the debate forward. Thus, is it possible that people who are particularly high in achievement orientation are more likely to be discrepancy enhancers (as per goal-setting theory), whereas people whose personality is more high in anxiety are more likely to be discrepancy reducers (as in control theory)?

Originality and induction vs. deduction

Locke (1991) also alleged that control theory does not have any original core content of its own. He claimed the central notion – the negative feedback loop – is borrowed from cybernetics, and that all later embellishments of the theory have been ideas borrowed from other motivation theories.

Goal-setting theory, by comparison, comprises a few core, original ideas (such as those pertaining to the setting of difficult, specific goals). The theory started and developed from the "ground up" in an inductive manner, adding variables and amendments as research has progressed over the years. Locke claimed that the inductive approach is the preferred one, citing sociologists Glaser and Strauss (1967), who have extolled the virtues of *grounded theory*. Locke (1991) also criticized the notion inherent in control theory of *goal hierarchies*. Control theory states that the goals a person has that serve as standards when discrepancies are detected are determined by higher-level goals or standards, which, in turn, are determined by still higher-level goals. Locke (1991, pp. 13–14) argued "while it is true that people have goal hierarchies, this only pushes the tension-reduction problem back a step further. If tension reduction is the ultimate ideal, why have any goal hierarchies at all?" In other words, what is the ultimate source of these goals? Locke dismissed both the notion of instincts (as old, discredited theory) and the environment as the principal source of goals and standards, using the same bases that he and other cognitive theorists use to dismiss behaviorist explanations (see Chapter 14). Hence Locke, Latham, and Bandura have discredited control theory as incomplete and lacking in one of the essential features of human behavior.

It is true that induction is a legitimate and appropriate method for theory development. This author believes the organizational sciences have not granted sufficient status and recognition to this approach over the past 40 years. Induction begins with the observation of real behavior by real people in situ and attempts to make sense out of that behavior, offering explanations and predictions, testing those predictions against further experience, and modifying the emergent theory to take into account any reliable differences between the predicted and the observed phenomena. Accordingly, Locke (1991) criticized control theory for starting with the theoretical notions of cybernetics and mechanical systems and "working downward" – filling in the holes and finding explanations for errors of prediction and understanding in other theoretical ideas.

Justifiably, Klein (1991b) defended his approach: There is nothing inherently superior to induction over deduction in the development of new theory. The author's position is that both forms of inference are required, used in combination as theories are promulgated, tested and then modified, reinforced or abandoned. Locke's attack on these grounds seems particularly ironic inasmuch as so many of the current tenets of goal setting were advanced decades ago by Mace (1935) and others. In fact, Locke and Latham (1990a) acknowledged their debt to Mace as follows:

> Another academic influence on our work was the series of experiments conducted in England by Mace (1935). It is not clear what had influenced Mace to do this research, but so far as we know, his were the earliest experimental studies ever done of goal setting as an independent variable. He was the first to compare the effects of specific, challenging goals with goals such as "do your best," and to compare the effects of goals differing in level of difficulty. The results of one of his most successful experiments were reported in Ryan and Smith's (1954) early industrial psychology textbook, which the present first author [Locke] was assigned to read as a graduate student.
>
> (Locke & Latham, 1990a, p. 13)

A historical note on the controversy

It is somewhat ironic that goal-setting adherents are so critical of control theory inasmuch as control theory was offered by some of its early advocates as a means of explaining *why* goal setting works. Campion and Lord (1982), for example, made three suggestions to explain why goal-setting theory, to that time at least, offered little insight into why goal processes work and why the goal literature had not yet integrated with other theories of work motivation. This limited conceptual progress, they argued, was due partly to the inattention of goal-setting advocates to feedback processes, while people studying feedback had not paid any attention to goal setting.

In addition, Campion and Lord suggested there had been too much focus on static rather than dynamic processes in the goal-setting research tradition. Finally, they claimed that the very nature of the goals studied was limited, static, and isolated. They pointed out that, in reality, "goals may be imbedded in complex cognitive or motivational systems, goals may change frequently, and goals may be poorly defined. A comprehensive model of the goal-setting process should be able to handle there types of goals" (1982, p. 266). More recent work by Vancouver and Scherbaum (2002) continued to reconcile the two schools by attempting to explain *why* robust goal effects work; that is, to find the mechanisms that underlie them.

The point for our purposes is that goal theorists have leveled highly critical attacks on the efforts of control theorists and, that, while some of their criticisms are apt, others are less so. Moreover, the similarities between the two theories are more important in practice than the differences between them. Both assume a cognitive human being who pays attention to goals and feedback from his environment and his own consciousness. Both theories provide tremendous insight into processes of self-regulation (Bandura, 1989). In fact, one might claim that the two theories are sufficiently similar that the mere existence of both speaks to the true value they both imply.[10]

In the final section of this chapter, we turn our attention to management by objectives, a popular managerial technique with goal setting as one of its principal theoretical foundations. In Chapter 14,

---

[10] Fellenz (1996) reviewed a number of other criticisms directed at control theory by the Locke and Latham goal-setting school and offers reasonable rebuttals for many of them. The interested reader is referred to his paper for complete detail.

we will study self-regulation, another set of applied techniques with tremendous potential implications for work motivation.

MANAGEMENT BY OBJECTIVES

The applied success of goal setting, even before it was developed and advanced as a formal theory of human behavior, contributed to the birth of a managerial technique that has been in wide usage for half a century. *Management by objectives* (MBO) has been one of the most widely adopted managerial techniques for motivating and rewarding employees in Western economies since the late 1950s. Nearly 30 years ago, one of its first leading proponents claimed that MBO was the predominant form of management in modern business and government organizations, and that this approach to management had been subjected to as much scientific investigation as any other (Odiorne, 1979). A cursory examination of the managerial literature confirms the widespread popularity of MBO, at least in terms of the number of organizations that have adopted it in some form or another. Similarly, as we saw in the first part of this chapter, the scientific literature on goal setting (the major body of research and theory related to a central aspect of MBO) suggests that many of the basic elements of MBO do rest on considerable scientific support. In the following sections, we will briefly examine MBO and discuss a number of related issues.

Origins of Management by Objectives

Although thinkers dating back to the classical philosophers have held that human effort is (or should be) goal directed (Odiorne, 1979), the modern origins of MBO are found in the work of Peter Drucker with General Motors and General Electric (Drucker, 1954; Greenwood, 1981). Whereas earlier management theorists had assumed that objectives are an important part of managing, they placed little emphasis on the origins and consequences of objectives in organizational settings. Drucker (1954) recognized the problematic nature of objectives and built an approach to management centered primarily upon them (Greenwood, 1981). Today, virtually all work organizations of any size have some form of vision statement and/or mission statement to help them guide their activities (cf. Pearce & David, 1987; Senge, 1990). Mission statements are declarations of the nature of the business an organization is in (thereby declaring and delimiting the boundaries of goals and operations they are willing to undertake) whereas vision statements are declarations of a future state the organization wishes to accomplish some time in the future (Pearce & David, 1987). Together, careful preparation of, and adherence to, mission and vision statements can keep an organization focused for limited periods of time, providing a basis for policy decisions and for creating, accepting, or rejecting new ventures.

In practice, however, they are often merely formalities, a form of mandatory requirement that is undertaken by organizations merely because it seems to be the "correct" or fashionable thing to do. Nevertheless, as we saw at the beginning of Chapter 1, we learned of the importance of his personal vision for the renaissance of Frank O'Dea, the Canadian entrepreneur who turned his life of squalor into one of success. An organization's vision is the broadest conceptualization of where it wishes to go and to become. More specific objectives dealing with profit targets, corporate responsibility, and service to the economy are (normatively, at least) distilled from vision statements through a series of levels of increasing specificity until they are operational for individual employees and work units. This is where MBO fits in.

What is MBO?

There is no single, unifying, or dominant *theory* of MBO, a feature that has brought it some harsh criticism (see Halpern & Osofsky, 1990).[11] In practice, there are almost as many varieties of MBO as there are organizations that claim to have adopted it. In other words, the specific elements of MBO and MBO-like programs vary from one organization to another, sometimes causing confusion over just what is and what is not MBO. Nevertheless, one authority defined MBO as:

> A managerial process whereby organizational purposes are diagnosed and met by joining superiors and subordinates in the pursuit of mutually agreed goals and objectives, which are specific, measurable, time bounded, and joined to an action plan; progress and goal attainment are measured and monitored in appraisal sessions which center on mutually determined objective standards of performance.
>
> (McConkie, 1979, p. 37)

This definition will be adopted in this chapter and elsewhere throughout this book.

Some Specific Features of MBO Programs

As noted earlier, the specific characteristics of MBO and MBO-like programs have varied in practice from one setting to another over the years. Goal-setting and objectives-related programs have been incorporated into strategic planning models and programs, where the fundamental mentality is still one of objectives setting and accountability (cf. Crossman, Fry, & Killing, 2002). However, the two most essential features of such programs are usually: (1) a system for establishing work-related goals; and (2) some type of procedure for assessing the individual's performance vis-à-vis those goals after a specified period of time. Beyond these two very basic characteristics, however, there is less unanimity in practice about what constitutes MBO.

Nevertheless, McConkie (1979) reported varying degrees of agreement among a sample of experts concerning the following general statements about the goal-setting aspect of MBO (principles that generally apply to other objective-setting programs):

1. Objectives should be reviewed periodically.
2. The time period for goal accomplishment should be specified.
3. The indicators of results should be quantifiable if possible; otherwise they should at least be verifiable.
4. Objectives should be flexible, changing as circumstances change.
5. Objectives should include a statement of an "action plan" for how they will be accomplished.
6. Objectives should be prioritized, some being agreed upon as more important than others.

MBO usually consists of some combination of procedures for the setting of individual goals on the basis of broader organizational goals and the subsequent evaluation of individual performance in terms of the degree of accomplishment of these goals. The specific nuances with regard to the participation of subordinates in the goal-setting and performance evaluation processes vary across organizations, as well as between units within particular organizations. The most important psychological processes that make MBO potentially successful are those that underlie goal setting, as explained earlier in this chapter.

---

[11] Indeed, MBO is a set of management procedures more than it is a theory. The major theoretical underpinnings of MBO are found in goal-setting theory, if anywhere, even though the practice of MBO was recommended (Drucker, 1954) long before modern goal-setting research was undertaken (in the early 1970s).

Functions (Potentially) Served by MBO

Odiorne (1979) identified a variety of functions MBO might be expected to serve, including the following:

1. Reduction of aimless activity and wasting of time and other resources.
2. Reduction of conflict between superiors and subordinates as a result of greater clarity of each other's responsibilities.
3. Improvement of individual performance and overall organizational effectiveness.
4. Improvements in employee morale, employee development, quality of work, and delegation.
5. Improvement in the capacity of the organization to change and adapt.

Advocates of MBO claim that it can help deal with a number of common problems faced by managers, such as deciding upon who receives pay increases, how many people should report to a particular individual, the types of people who should report to a given manager, the types and amount of information communicated to subordinates, and the amount of delegation and decentralization most desirable in a particular situation. In short, advocates of MBO believe it is more than merely a set of techniques and procedures; rather it is viewed as a total system of management, even as "a way of thinking about management" (Odiorne, 1979, p. 52).

Stages of the MBO Process

The use and administration of MBO can be broken down into four basic steps. First, managers at each organizational level confer and negotiate with each of their subordinates to determine organizational and personal objectives for some upcoming period of time (such as 6 months or a year). In practice, the degree to which the subordinate actually participates in this goal-setting process varies (as mentioned earlier), depending upon the personal styles of both the superior and the subordinate, as well as upon the degree to which they try to adhere to strictly prescribed MBO principles (which normally advocate participation). Second, the subordinate prepares an action plan describing how he will attempt to achieve the agreed-upon goals. The action plan may or may not be reviewed by the superior. Once agreed upon, however, the objectives and action plan guide the employee's work behavior during the following (and agreed-upon) period of time.

The third stage consists of a performance review by the superior and the subordinate of the latter's progress toward the objectives set at the beginning of the period. This performance review, in effect, replaces more traditional methods of performance appraisal practiced in many organizations. In fact, problems with traditional methods were largely responsible for the rapid growth in popularity of MBO and MBO-like programs.

One classic paper, for example, pointed out how traditional performance appraisal systems place supervisors in the untenable position of "playing God" with subordinates. Invariably, the supervisor finds himself passing judgment on the personal worth of the subordinate (McGregor, 1957b). As a result of the unpleasantness that naturally results from such a process, performance appraisal seldom accomplishes its purposes of constructively evaluating an employee's job performance. Instead, it generates defensive reactions on the part of the subordinate and/or attempts by the supervisor to avoid the process entirely. MBO was proposed as an alternative because it requires the superior and subordinate to focus attention on the behaviors and accomplishments of the employee in terms of objectives that the employee helps establish. The result, according to McGregor (1957b), is a more analytic process, which is impersonal and objective, and that makes constructive assessment more possible. McGregor's observations were made more than five decades ago. It is amazing how pertinent they remain to this day.

Finally, the fourth stage of most MBO programs is the setting of new objectives by the superior and the subordinate for the next period of time.

Cascading

One general feature prescribed by advocates of MBO and strategic planning programs is that the goals set at each organizational level should be consistent with the goals set at other hierarchical levels. More specifically, the goals set at the highest level of the organization should be stated in relatively general terms, which can subsequently be translated into increasingly more specific terms at each lower level. The process of distilling increasingly more specific objectives as one moves down the hierarchy is referred to as "cascading" (see Raia, 1974).

For example, an organization might have the objective of increasing profits by 10% over the next 2-year period. This somewhat general objective is then interpreted into more specific goals for managers at lower levels of the firm. The vice-president of administration of the company might generate objectives with his boss (the president) concerning cutting costs, whereas the vice-president in charge of sales may translate the general organizational profit goal into more specific objectives about sales levels and market penetration. Each of these VPs would derive in turn even more specific objectives with each of their own subordinate managers. To continue the example, the VP of administration might collaborate with his employment manager to set goals to reduce cost associated with turnover and the recruitment of new staff. The employment manager would then generate goals with each recruiter and personnel interviewer concerning specific techniques for reducing turnover and recruitment costs. The specific objectives derived at each level will vary from each department, depending upon the type of work performed (e.g., sales, marketing, production, and so on).

Assumptions Underlying MBO

MBO programs rely upon a number of assumptions (Barton, 1981). First, it is assumed that an organization may have more than a single objective. In fact, most organizations have multiple objectives (Gross, 1965). The hypothetical firm in the example just given may have objectives dealing with new product development, the improvement of its corporate image, and diversification into different markets. Similarly, it is assumed that particular employees at each organizational level may have more than one objective, and that objectives at any given level may result in more than one sub-objective at subsequent lower levels.

Second, it is assumed that when they are achieved, the various subgoals at each level cumulatively contribute to the achievement of the goals at each successive higher level, ultimately to the attainment of the organization's goals at their broadest levels (such as increasing profits by 7% over a 2-year period).

Third, the use of an MBO program implies an organization's strategy and tactics are to be found in (and consist of) its goals and the action plans deriving from those goals. The means–ends linkages generated by an MBO program constitute organizational strategy and are the primary basis for organizational policy. It is in this sense that MBO has the potential to be much more than merely a goal-setting and performance appraisal system.

Finally, it might be assumed that, ideally, the goals resulting from an MBO program should be mutually compatible and not counterproductive and mutually antithetical. In practice, of course, this is not normally the case. The opposite is more common: Organizational goals are commonly incompatible (Daft, 1983). For example, the hypothetical organization mentioned earlier may find that its goals of increasing profit and expanding markets interfere with its goal of improving its reputation in the community. Likewise, university students often feel that university goals dealing with research and publication activities are inconsistent with objectives pertaining to quality instruction in the classroom. This is sometimes the case, but not necessarily. Barton (1981) discussed the problem of incompatible goals in MBO settings and has presented an approach for dealing with it.

How Effective is MBO in Practice?

Now that we have looked at some of the claims made in support of MBO and a number of its principal characteristics, it is appropriate to examine the scientific evidence concerning the actual value and effectiveness of these programs. Just how effective is MBO?

One early review of 185 case studies, surveys, quasi-experiments, and true experiments provided a somewhat discouraging conclusion, albeit one that will sound familiar to those who have read the earlier chapters of this book. In a nutshell, this review found an inverse relationship between the level of scientific rigor used in evaluative studies of MBO and the degree of support claimed for the program studied (Kondrasuk, 1981). When researchers employed carefully constructed experiments designed to rule out alternative explanations for their findings, the results tended to be less than favorable for MBO. On the other hand, in one-shot case studies in which no control groups were used and the basic fundamentals of experimental design were violated by the researchers in question, MBO appeared to have been effective. Other surveys found that the form taken by MBO programs varies widely, using different degrees and combinations of the basic elements described already (Carroll & Tosi, 1973). Kopelman (1986) also reported mixed results, not unlike the conclusion reached earlier by Kondrasuk (1981).

A somewhat more recent[12] meta-analysis reported by Rodgers and Hunter (1991) yielded the most positive and encouraging conclusions. In this study-of-studies, Rodgers and Hunter (1991) conducted a thorough search for research reports of other investigators who had examined MBO program effectiveness – reports that had not been included in previous meta-analyses. Their focus was on employee productivity, specifically on productivity gains apparently brought about by MBO programs. They found productivity gains in 68 of the 70 evaluation studies reviewed. The mean percentage increase in productivity across those studies that had used ratio-level (hard) indicators of productivity was 45%. When managerial ratings were used as the basis for assessment of MBO impact, the mean increase was found to be 42% of one standard deviation. No matter how productivity increases were measured, there was solid support for the positive effects of MBO programs (Rodgers & Hunter, 1991).

The Importance of Executive Commitment

Of special interest in this meta-analysis was the significance of the support provided to the MBO programs by the various senior executives in the organizations in which the programs had been installed. The results were strikingly clear: MBO had the greatest impact in those settings where senior executives not only gave positive endorsement, but also practiced the technique at their own level. By contrast, productivity gains were the weakest in organizations in which senior executives neither endorsed nor practiced their MBO programs, and the group in the middle of the support issue – those cases in which there was verbal endorsement but no actual practice of MBO among the executives – fell in the middle of the productivity improvement distribution. The productivity gains were five times higher among those organizations with high executive commitment than among those with low executive commitment (Rodgers & Hunter, 1991).

---

[12] Although goal-setting programs of one form or another have been practiced in most organizations (Pritchard & Payne, 2002), there have been very few, if any, empirical studies reported in the organizational behavior or managerial literature on the effectiveness of MBO-type programs in recent years.

In a meta-analysis of 18 previously reported studies, with their attention on job satisfaction (rather than productivity), similar results were found. The greatest increase in job attitudes was found in studies of organizations in which there were high levels of top management involvement. As before, there was positive improvement in the moderate commitment cases and, finally, a slight *decrease* in job attitudes in MBO installations in which there was very low executive commitment (Rodgers, Hunter, & Rogers, 1993). Only 18 organizations were included in this meta-analysis of job satisfaction effects, so there were not many organizations in any of the three executive commitment-level groups, suggesting the need for some caution in the interpretation of the results. Nevertheless, the two meta-analyses combined (Rodgers & Hunter, 1991; Rodgers, Hunter, & Rogers, 1993) provide impressive empirical evidence to support the almost trite prescription from the managerial and organizational development literature that top management support is necessary for interventions such as MBO to have a chance of reaping positive results.

The Relationship Between MBO Programs and Goal Setting

It was argued earlier in this chapter that goal setting has demonstrated more validity than any other theory of work motivation, and that goal-setting techniques constitute one of the two most common (perhaps universal) features of MBO programs in practice. In view of the success of goal setting per se, one might find the somewhat lower and mixed rates of success among formal MBO programs paradoxical or even contradictory. It is important to repeat that, while goal-setting techniques constitute an integral element of virtually all MBO programs, there is much more to MBO than simple goal setting. As noted earlier, the performance review process is also an important element of MBO, as are the participation of employees in the goal-setting process, the technique of cascading, and the formalization of strategy, tactics, and policy. It may be that the transformation of the relatively simple principles of goal setting (as developed by Ryan, Locke, and Latham, for example) into formal MBO programs can introduce difficulties that may attenuate or dampen the positive effects possible from simple goal setting (cf. Ford, 1979; Muczyk, 1978; Reddin, 1971).[13]

Summary

If the basic principles of goal setting are to have a chance of being successful in work organizations, they must be accompanied by a host of organizational conditions, preparations, and (often) adjustments. The widespread application of MBO during the 1960s and 1970s in ignorance of these necessary organizational preconditions led to failures in the majority of organizations that tried it (Reddin, 1971; Schuster & Kindall, 1974). It would appear that organizational scientists have a better understanding of individual differences and the nature of human intentions to behave than they do of the critical features of organizations in which work behavior takes place. Accordingly, even the more successful theories of work motivation (such as goal setting) will provide limited scientific validity and practical value for managers until more is learned about how organizational variables interact with individual, psychological variables (cf. Mowday & Sutton, 1993).

---

[13] There is reason to believe that the translation of basic mentoring relationships into formalized, organizationally sponsored mentoring programs may have a similar corrupting effect on the value of mentor–protégé relationships (Schroeder, 1988).

What's New in MBO?

Not much. The reader will notice that the bulk of the documents cited in this section are fairly dated, many originating in the late 1960s and 1970s. Only a few refinements have been made to the practice of MBO since then. Most of what needed to be learned had been learned by the time summary reviews of the causes of success and failure in MBO programs, such as that by Kondrasuk (1981), were published. Other than a few details about the significance of top-level executive support (something most people knew intuitively anyway), there have been few lessons of significance to emerge about MBO over the past three decades.

LOOKING AHEAD: ANOTHER CHANGE OF PERSPECTIVES

We have now reached the conclusion of Part Three of the book, a part in which we have examined all the major theories of work motivation. These theories are based primarily on a model of human functioning that assumes that humans are essentially information-processing creatures and that beliefs, attitudes, and intentions can best explain employee work motivation and behavior.

In Chapter 14, which comprises Part Four, we will turn from theories of work motivation that rely primarily heavily on cognitive processes toward a different perspective – one that, in its earliest and purest forms, ignored and even denied the role of mental factors in the causes of behavior in general and work motivation in particular. We will see that this perspective (again, in its original form) enjoyed less success over the past three decades than in the 1960s and 1970s, but that, even so, it has evolved to incorporate some of the insights found in cognitive models, particularly goal setting, and, in this revised form, it does offer considerable applied value to human behavioral problems. Indeed, modern social-cognitive theory, which is the primary focus of Chapter 14, is still one of the most valid and vibrant theories of human behavior and of work motivation that we have at our disposal at the present time (Latham & Pinder, 2005).

PART FOUR

Views of "Work Motivation" and Work Behavior

Learning, Behavior Control, Social-Cognitive Theory, and Self-Management

Men are the sport of circumstances,
when the circumstances seem the sport of men.
Lord Byron

I don't believe in circumstances. The people
who go on in this world are the people who get up
and look for the circumstances they want.
George Bernard Shaw

Different views about the fundamental nature of human beings come and go in the behavioral sciences. We saw, for example, that the idea of instincts was acceptable to psychologists in the early part of the 20th century, and that the concept of needs displaced instincts sometime during the 1930s. During the 1940s, a school of thought that came with a number of headings, but with "behaviorism" as its most common title, gained ascendancy. The single, most basic tenet of behaviorism is that behavior is determined by its consequences: There is no need to refer to mysterious, unobservable inner states such as instincts, needs, emotions, or thoughts. The focus of this school of thought was upon *learning* rather than motivation, per se. It is not that major proponents of this brand of psychology denied the existence of inner states such as emotions, beliefs, or values, for example. Rather, B. F. Skinner claimed in one of his books that "they [internal forces] are not relevant in a functional analysis . . . We cannot account for the behavior of any system while staying wholly inside it; eventually we must turn to forces operating on the organism from without" (1953, p. 35).

Yet, as we will see as the chapter progresses, for many behaviorists, a three-way, reciprocal interaction model, summarized by the formula $B = F(O, E)$ best summarizes the nature of human interaction between persons and the environment. The key elements of "O" (the organism, or person) that matter are the individual's genetic makeup and his or her prior learning experiences. Thus, *at some level*, we see that behaviorism can be reconciled with other theories and models we have studied earlier in this book – models that have repeatedly emphasized the importance of context (or what the behaviorists usually call "environment" – see Chapter 2). But for behaviorists, the "E" (or what we have referred to most on our way to this point as "context") is paramount: "[T]he initiating action is taken by the environment rather than by the perceiver" (Skinner, 1974, p. 73) and "the environment stays where it is and where it has always been – outside the body" (1974, p. 73).[1]

Behaviorism grew in popularity and influence in psychology in the 1950s. By the 1960s it had nearly eclipsed other approaches to modern psychology. By the 1970s, behaviorism had gained a position of hegemony in many of the applied areas of psychology, such as clinical psychology,

---

[1] The author is grateful to Professor Dale M. Brethower of the Instituto Tecnologico de Sonora for his helpful comments on the content of this chapter as they appeared in the first edition of this book (Pinder, 1998).

organizational behavior and management. But by the 1980s, behaviorism seemed to have achieved its zenith and psychology was witnessing the ascendancy of cognitive theories and models of human functioning. A battle was underway in Western science about the relative merits of the behaviorist camp, the cognitive camp, and others. At the time of that writing, behaviorism had, in fact, made a number of contributions to organizational behavior, but it seemed that this school of thought *in its purest, non-cognitive manifestations* had experienced its zenith and, perhaps, it was on the way out of thinking about organizational behavior in general and about work motivation in particular.

What remains of this school of thought today (at least in the realm of work motivation) is a drastically diminished hybrid of the original – one that adopts and incorporates many essential elements from cognitive psychology, such as those we discussed in the previous three chapters. In retrospect, the marriage of the two schools was not as difficult as one might have predicted 20 years ago, given the apparently entrenched ideological differences between the two basic schools of thought (cf. Karmel, 1980; Skinner, 1974).[2]

In what follows, it is important to remember that the focus is upon human *learning* as much as it is on human motivation. In fact, the blend of attention between learning and motivation changes gradually as the chapter develops and we tell the story of how the "radical behaviorism" of the 1950s and 1960s gradually gave way to the hybrid models of social learning theory and social-cognitive theory that have emerged in recent years.

OVERVIEW OF THE CHAPTER

The first part of the chapter deals with the basic tenets of radical behaviorism (or operant psychology). The second part adopts a historical dimension and deals first with behavior modification in general terms and then with *organizational behavior modification* (or *applied behavior analysis*), telling the story of how the behaviorist camp gradually incorporated elements of cognitive psychology into its thinking (see Komaki, 1986; Kreitner & Luthans, 1984). Then, we examine social-cognitive theory, the next body of thought to emerge from this tradition – a school that openly incorporates concepts from goal-setting theory. The chapter finishes with a discussion of self-regulation, a set of applied techniques that people can learn to apply to encourage or discourage aspects of their own behavior.

The Purpose for the Inclusion of Behaviorism at All

If it is true that behaviorism has had its day – for the time being, at least – in the study of organizational behavior, why is it included in this book at all? There are a number of answers. First, although it may no longer dominate thinking about work-related matters, behaviorism has left its legacy in the thinking and writing of much current theory and research in organizational behavior. Second (and related to the first point), there are still a number of people in the field who prefer the root assumptions made by behaviorism: They find it intellectually more reasonable to think about the antecedents and consequences of human action than of black box concepts such as needs, beliefs, expectations, values, and other hypothetical constructs. Finally, there are still a number of the precepts of the behaviorist model that have value in understanding and managing human behavior:

---

[2] There are cognitive theorists such as Locke (1979) who claimed that there was little in the way of blending but that, instead, the operant approach merely gave way to cognitive theory out of necessity. At least one adherent of the behaviorist camp stated a different perspective (Komaki, 1986). She claimed that her approach enjoyed an ongoing, mutually beneficial relationship with the rest of the field, at least through the mid-1980s. This author believes that the truth is found in some blend of their two positions.

While the entire theory has been displaced from its position of hegemony, it is not altogether "wrong" in what it has to say about the human condition. In fact, *functional analysis* (Komaki, 1986, 2003; Komaki, Coombs, Redding, & Schepman, 2000) can be a useful perspective for helping us understand many organizational phenomena, after they occur, by breaking events down into their antecedents, the behaviors that occur, and the consequences of those behaviors (into A–B–C sequences). The current survey and analysis of theories of work motivation would be incomplete without a summary of what the behaviorist camp taught us over the past half-century.

Finally: Who knows when the pendulum may swing back in the direction of a model of human functioning that revitalizes some or all of the tenets of behaviorism? As we will see, elements of it are to be found in the body of work referred to as *social-cognitive theory*, as well as in the applied techniques of self-regulation, which we discuss toward the end of this chapter. With all of these historical issues and rationales in mind, we turn now to a study of the operant conditioning camp in the study of human behavior at work.

We begin by looking at the radical behaviorism of decades ago to provide a basis for understanding the tempered influence it still has in our thinking about work motivation.

BASIC TENETS OF RADICAL BEHAVIORISM

In contrast to the need-based and cognitive/perceptual models of human functioning (Walter & Marks, 1981) that underlie the theories of work motivation presented in the rest of this volume, the major school of thought variously referred to as *behaviorism*, *behavioral learning theory*, and/or *operant conditioning*, avoids reliance upon concepts such as perceptions, beliefs, attitudes, intentions, and motivation for understanding and predicting human behavior. The emphasis is upon human learning, not on motivation. The major tenet of the so-called radical behaviorist approach is simply that behavior is a joint function of human genetic endowment and environmental contingencies. While proponents of this school do not deny that people have needs, beliefs, attitudes, values, intentions, and the like, they do not invoke such concepts, either to study or to influence human behavior. To quote Skinner,[3] the eminent psychologist whose work provides the foundation of this school:

> When we say that a man eats because he is hungry, smokes a great deal because he has a tobacco habit ... or plays the piano well because of his musical ability, we seem to be referring to causes. But on analysis these phrases prove to be merely redundant descriptions. A single set of facts is described by the two statements "He eats" and "He is hungry." The practice of explaining one statement in terms of another is dangerous because it suggests that we have found the cause and therefore need search no further.
>
> (Skinner, 1953, p. 31)

So to state that an employee works hard because she is loyal to her company does not really explain anything; it merely repeats the same information. The important thing is the behavior: The individual either works hard or she doesn't. Skinner wrote:

---

[3] It must be noted at the outset that there is no single, unified school of modern behaviorism, notwithstanding the common tendency to assume that there is (Mahoney, 1974, p. 9). Rather, a continuum of schools of behaviorism exists, representing a number of perspectives differing among themselves in a variety of ways, the most important of which have to do with the role and importance of cognitive processes in human learning and behavior (Kazdin, 1978; Mahoney, 1974). Accordingly, although we draw most heavily from Skinner's behaviorism in this chapter, the reader is cautioned that even by his own admission, Skinner (1974) did not represent the voice of all behaviorism. Our reliance here on his work is based on three things: (1) the fact that it is at least as well known as any other school of behaviorism; (2) its obvious importance in modern psychology during the 1960s and 1970s; and (3) the fact that it, more than any other brand of behaviorism, is most often cited by organizational scientists in particular.

We may . . . be disturbed by the fact that many young people work as little as possible, or that workers are not very productive and often absent [from their jobs], or that products are often of poor quality, but we shall not get far by inspiring a "sense of craftsmanship or pride in one's work," or a "sense of the dignity of labor" . . . Something is wrong with the contingencies which induce men to work industriously and carefully.

(Skinner, 1971, p. 157)

One more time, adherents to this school do not deny that people experience emotions, or that they perceive things in their environments and formulate beliefs. But they consider these hypothetical factors as merely accompanying behavior, not causing it. Hence, an employee may experience what he calls pride in his work or "satisfaction with his employer," but these feelings simply *accompany* the behavior of the individual on his job: They do not cause it, or account for it.

Even the very concept of motivation was questioned by many behaviorists when the term was used to imply an internal causal force that cannot be observed directly (Luthans & Ottemann, 1977). To attribute behavior to motivation as in the statement "Barry works hard at his job because he is a highly motivated fellow," is as redundant as the examples of eating, smoking, and piano playing cited by Skinner. Motivation does not cause behavior – the contingencies of the environment do.

By the same token, behaviorists often use mentalistic terminology out of necessity and convenience, and for descriptive purposes (Skinner, 1974). For example, a behaviorist who says "Barry is motivated," does not mean to imply that any real or physical entity called motivation exists within Barry, causing him to work hard; instead, the behaviorist would be utilizing the term motivated to descriptively summarize Barry's behavior. It is the process of reifying concepts (such as motivation) from descriptive terms into terms that imply the existence of inferred behavior-causing entities that is rejected by behaviorists (Craighead, Kazdin, & Mahoney 1976).

Operant Behavior

According to Skinner and most of those who have followed in his tradition, it is useful to categorize behavior into two general types. One type is referred to as *respondent behavior*, which consists of acts that are reflexive, or unlearned. Sneezing or jerking one's knee when it is tapped with a doctor's hammer are examples. Respondent behavior occurs in response to something in the environment.

The second general category of behavior consists of most of the important acts human beings display. These are learned behaviors that operate on the environment to generate consequences, hence they are called *operant behaviors*. Whereas respondent behavior is elicited by a prior stimulus, operant behavior is emitted to produce a consequence. The environment acts upon the individual to produce respondent behavior, while operant behavior consists of the individual's acting upon the environment.

For example, an employee who is confronted by a hostile supervisor may witness an increase in heart beat, a pair of sweaty palms, and a flight response. The stimulus that caused these behaviors is the boss and the "nervous" reactions are respondent behaviors. Alternatively, the employee may approach his boss with a view to making peace and mollifying him. This action would be classified as operant behavior. It is initiated by the individual to operate on a part of his environment, in this case, his boss.

What is Operant Conditioning?

Operant conditioning is the process of changing the frequency or probability of occurrence of operant behaviors as a result of the consequences that follow them. For example, the employee who successfully applies diplomacy to the problem with his superior will be more likely to try this sort of (operant) behavior again in similar circumstances in the future. Alternatively, the negative consequences of his attempt at diplomacy may teach him not to try it again. The mechanisms through which the future probabilities of operant behaviors are influenced are referred to as *reinforcement* and *punishment*. (We will return to them shortly.)

Functional Analysis and Contingencies

Most of the important behavior we observe in organizations is learned, either before or after individuals enter them. This learning occurs in the context of stimuli, or cues made up of such things as the organization's structure, the work group, the supervisor, the job description, telephone calls, and so forth. Operant learning occurs when people behave in response to these cues in certain ways, and in turn, when consequences follow from their behaviors.

The process of breaking behavioral events down into their antecedents, the behavior itself, and the consequences that follow it is called *functional analysis* (see Komaki et al., 1991). All three elements must be examined in order to understand behavior (Skinner, 1969). Important organizational consequences include the approval or disapproval of coworkers, money, fatigue, promotions, and the many other things that we have referred to as *outcomes* in previous chapters. When consequences such as these are directly tied to certain behaviors, they are said to be *contingent* upon those behaviors. For example, commission is a form of pay that is directly contingent upon the volume of product sold by a sales person. Similarly, fatigue is usually contingent upon hard work. Finally, when consequences bear no relationship to behavior they are said to be non-contingent upon that behavior, as is the case in pay schemes such as salaries under which people are paid simply with the passage of intervals of time. We will return to functional analysis later in this chapter, after we examine in more detail the concepts of contingency and the consequences of behavior.

The Consequences of Behavior

According to the operant conditioning approach, behavior occurring in a particular context can be followed by any of three types of consequence. These are referred to as reinforcement, punishment, and neutral stimuli. *Reinforcement* is defined as a consequence of behavior that increases the probability that an act will occur again in the future. *Punishment* is a consequence of behavior that reduces the probability of further occurrences of the act. Finally, sometimes neither reinforcement nor punishment is contingent upon an act. In other words, there is no change in the person's environment as a consequence of his behavior. When this occurs, the act tends to cease. For example, a person who repeatedly puts a coin into a candy machine and receives nothing in return tends to stop investing in the recalcitrant machine. As a second example, a whining child who is ignored tends (eventually) to stop whining. Finally, an employee who wisecracks about his superior will tend to stop if no one (including his work mates) provides him with any reinforcement. The process of disconnecting a behavior and the consequences that formerly reinforced it is referred to as *extinction* (Craighead et al., 1976).

The law of effect

The relationship between contingent consequences and operant behavior is summarized in the *law of effect*. Although the general gist of this law appeared over a century ago in the writings of Herbert Spencer (1870), its first formal articulation was made by Thorndike (1911, p. 214):

> Of several responses made to the same situation, those which are accompanied or closely followed by satisfaction to the animal will, other things being equal, be more firmly connected with the situation,

so that, when it recurs, they will be more likely to recur; those which are accompanied or closely followed by discomfort to the animal will, other things being equal, have their connections with that situation weakened, so that, when it recurs, they will be less likely to occur. The greater the satisfaction or discomfort, the greater the strengthening or weakening of the bond.

Thorndike was aware that many of his critics would object to his reliance on subjective terms, such as satisfaction and comfort (they sound very cognitive), so he explained further:

> By a satisfying state of affairs is meant one which the animal does nothing to avoid, often doing such things as attain and preserve it. By a discomforting or annoying state of affairs is meant one which the animal commonly avoids and abandons.
>
> (Thorndike, 1911, p. 245)

The law of effect has been subjected to a variety of attacks over the years on numerous logical, philosophical, and empirical grounds. A review of these issues is beyond our present purpose. Suffice it to say that its modern form, the *empirical law of effect* (of which there is more than one version), remains one of the most important tenets of behaviorism today. In a nutshell, the empirical law of effect states that "the consequence of a response is an important determinant of whether the response will be learned" (Wilcoxon, 1969, p. 28). In other words, people tend to do those things that they find positive and they tend not to do those things that they learn to be aversive. Hence, if an employee associates high rates of pay with high levels of job performance, she will tend to behave in ways that she has learned are conducive to high performance.

When a behavior occurs and is followed by a desirable consequence, that behavior is said to be reinforced (meaning strengthened). The odds will increase that the person will behave in a similar fashion on future occasions that are similar. On the other hand, if the behavior results in aversive consequences, that behavior will be less probable in future similar circumstances, and it is said to have been punished. But desirable and undesirable consequences in organizations are only partially contingent upon the behavior or the performance of employees. Accordingly, we can consider a range of relationships that may exist between behavior and its consequences. These behavior–consequence relationships are referred to as *schedules of reinforcement*, and the control of these schedules constitutes the application of operant conditioning in work organizations, educational institutions, clinical settings, and the like.

Schedules of Reinforcement

The simplest type of reinforcement schedule is referred to as *continuous*. When every instance of a particular behavior is reinforced, the schedule is defined as continuous. However, if reinforcement is provided after only some occurrences of an act, the schedule is defined as intermittent, or partial (see Table 14.1).

Continuous and intermittent schedules each have some important characteristics, and some important differences. First, new learning occurs fastest when the behavior being acquired is

TABLE 14.1   Intermittent reinforcement schedules

	BASIS OF DISTRIBUTION OF REINFORCEMENT	
CONSTANCY OF SCHEDULE	*OCCURRENCE OF BEHAVIOR*	*PASSAGE OF TIME*
Fixed	**1** Fixed ratio	**3** Fixed interval
Variable	**2** Variable ratio	**4** Variable interval

reinforced continuously. For example, a new employee who is learning how to set up a jig on a lathe will learn more quickly if he is reinforced every time he does it correctly. By the same token, behavior that is reinforced by a continuous schedule for an ongoing period of time is more susceptible to extinction when, for whatever reason, the reinforcement stops or fails to occur following any particular occurrence of the act. Moreover, once a behavior has been learned, it will occur at higher frequency levels (and perhaps more intensely) when it is reinforced intermittently. So, for example, employees who have been taught to be polite to customers through the use of continuous reinforcement will be more likely to continue being polite if their supervisors decrease the frequency of reinforcement for courteous behaviors to an intermittent schedule.

Types of intermittent schedules

It is possible to administer intermittent reinforcement in a variety of ways. Sometimes reinforcement occurs only after the emission of a certain number of the desired behaviors; in other words, it is possible to assure that the reinforcement is contingent only upon behavior. Such schedules are called *ratio schedules*, because reinforcers are dispensed according to some proportion of the instances when the behavior occurs (such as every fourth time, for example). Alternatively, it is possible to administer reinforcement following the passage of certain periods of time, such that, for example, the first desired response following the designated period (say, 1 hour) produces a reinforcer. Schedules of this sort are called *interval schedules.*

Aside from whether they are granted on the basis of some ratio with the occurrence of behavior or whether certain periods of time must elapse as well, we can also consider intermittent reinforcement on the basis of whether the ratio or the time interval used is constant, or changing and variable. Hence, we can consider the four different types of reinforcement schedule illustrated in Table 14.1.

Let us consider some examples of these various types of intermittent reinforcement. A fixed ratio schedule is one in which the reinforcement follows every nth occurrence of an act. For instance, an employee who is paid a fee after every fourth delivery of materials to a warehouse is being reinforced under a fixed ratio arrangement (see Cell 1). Notice that continuous reinforcement is a special case of a fixed ratio schedule in which the ratio is 1:1. However, if the employee is paid *on average every fourth time, but not every fourth time*, per se, we would say he is being compensated according to a variable ratio schedule (Cell 2 of Table 14.1).

As an illustration of how interval schedules might work, consider a sales representative who is being encouraged by her sales manager to make follow-up visits to her customers. If the sales manager acknowledges only those visits that occur at the beginning of every month, for example, and ignores those visits made by the sales rep during the middle of the month, the manager is using a fixed interval schedule (Cell 3), in which the interval is 1 month. However, if the manager reinforces only those customer visits undertaken by the rep after 1 week, then 3 days, then 4 weeks, then 8 days (and so on), he would be employing a variable interval schedule (see Cell 4). In short, the passage of a particular period of time is necessary for the administration of a reinforcer or punisher under an interval schedule, but it is not sufficient: In addition, once the designated interval has passed, the person must perform the act which is being encouraged or discouraged.

Once a behavior has been learned, it can be encouraged through the careful use of intermittent schedules. Ratio schedules are superior to interval schedules for this purpose (because they are directly contingent upon the occurrence of the desired acts without the necessity of the passage of time), and variable ratio schedules are more effective than fixed ratio schedules. Notice that under a variable ratio schedule (such as what we find in slot machines, for example), the person knows that he will be "paid off" every nth time, on average. But he is never sure whether any specific occurrence of his behavior will be rewarded. Moreover, once the desired act has been acquired and developed, a variable ratio schedule can be made leaner or "stretched," meaning that the ratio of reinforcements to occurrences of the behavior can be reduced. For example, after we train a sales representative to be courteous to customers by using a continuous (or nearly continuous) schedule, we can reduce the ratio of reinforcements to occurrences of polite behaviors by reinforcing, say, every fifth or sixth occurrence on average, and then eventually cutting back on the frequency of reinforcements so that, on average, the ratio of reinforcements to behaviors becomes smaller and smaller. In practice, it becomes increasingly less necessary to reinforce behavior after it is learned.

In summary, we can state the following about reinforcement schedules: (1) new learning is acquired most rapidly when it is conducted under a continuous schedule of reinforcement; (2) however, once a behavior has been acquired, it is best to begin reducing the frequency of reinforcements to some form of intermittent schedule, because they are more resistant to extinction; (3) ratio schedules result in higher levels of performance of an act than interval schedules, because the former are entirely behavior based, whereas the latter are based on both time and behavior; and (4) the highest rates of behavior occur under variable (as opposed to fixed) ratio schedules.

While the foregoing discussion has focused on schedules of reinforcement, we must note that punishment also occurs according to either continuous or intermittent schedules as well, although the effects of punishment under these alternative schedules are different from the effects of reinforcement. More will be said about punishment shortly.

Negative Reinforcement

Organizational scientists and managers often misuse behavior modification terminology and concepts (Heiman, 1975; Mawhinney, 1975). Perhaps the best example of this concerns the misuse of the concept of negative reinforcement.

Negative reinforcement is not punishment. Like positive reinforcement, negative reinforcement strengthens the probability that a person will perform an act. By definition, punishment reduces such a probability. In fact, punishment refers to the presentation of an aversive agent or event, or the removal of a positive agent or event following a response, reducing the probability of that response in similar future circumstances. In order to be considered punishment, however, the act of either adding or removing an agent must result in a reduction in the frequency of occurrence of the act.

Notice that what some people find punishing may be reinforcing for others. For example, some people enjoy an evening at a Broadway musical, whereas, for others . . . But while positive reinforcement involves the application of some circumstance (such as a pat on the back or a Friday afternoon off work), negative reinforcement entails the removal of some circumstance that was previously part of the environmental context. For instance, being permitted to return to day shift as a consequence of good performance on night shift is a negatively reinforcing consequence of effective job behavior for those employees who find night work aversive. Being transferred from a remote outpost as a consequence of good work is another example of negative reinforcement (for many people at least). Notice that the things which are negatively reinforcing for some people may not be negatively reinforcing for others, just as what some individuals find positively reinforcing may have no impact on the behavior probabilities of other individuals. (For example, many people are not bothered at all by the winter weather in Regina or Oshkosh!)

We can classify the concepts of positive reinforcement, negative reinforcement, and punishment quite simply by considering whether the consequence which follows an act increases or decreases the frequency of the act, and whether it is applied or taken away. See Table 14.2.

Reinforcers: The Agents and Events of Reinforcement

Now that we have discussed the nature of reinforcement and punishment and have differentiated between positive and negative reinforcement, let's take a closer look at those consequences that are reinforcing to people – the reinforcers. As will be shown shortly, there are a variety of things that can be reinforcing, although it must be reiterated that different individuals will have their behaviors

TABLE 14.2   Summary of reinforcement and punishment terminology

EFFECT ON FREQUENCY OF BEHAVIOUR	CONSEQUENCE	
	Applied	*Removed*
Increases	Positive reinforcement	Negative reinforcement
Decreases	Punishment by application	Punishment by removal

made more frequent (reinforced) by the administration of different types of positive and negative thing (cf. Dickson, Saunders, & Stringer, 1993).

Primary and secondary reinforcers

An agent or event that increases the probability of an act is referred to as a reinforcer. Many reinforcers (such as food and water) are called *primary reinforcers* because they are reinforcing unto themselves; an individual does not need to learn of their reinforcing value. People who are hungry and thirsty can derive reinforcement from food and water, without having them linked to any other reinforcers. Conversely, certain reinforcing agents and events acquire their capacity to increase the probability of particular behaviors through their learned association with other (primary) reinforcers. These are called *secondary reinforcers*. Money is the most important example in organizational settings. By itself, pay has no primary reinforcement capacity, but people quickly learn that pay can be used to acquire those things that do possess primary reinforcing value (such as food, shelter, status, and so forth). It is important to recognize that not all primary reinforcers will always have the capacity to reinforce behavior. For example, food may lose its capacity to change a person's behavior if the person is not hungry. Likewise, potential secondary reinforcers such as praise may not have the same reinforcing power for some people as they do for others.

Generalized conditioned reinforcers

Some reinforcers are particularly potent for influencing the probability of the occurrence of behavior because they are themselves reinforcing. Again, money is a good example: Because it becomes associated, through learning, with a wide variety of other consequences that have either primary or secondary reinforcement value, it is particularly reinforcing. Attention and the approval of other people are other examples of such generalized reinforcers (Skinner, 1953), because they are usually accompanied by physical contact, praise, kindly remarks, and support of various other forms, including the possibility of the provision of primary reinforcers (such as physical warmth or food).

Behaviors as reinforcers: The Premack principle

The reinforcers discussed to this point have all been stimuli of some sort or other, stimuli that are either provided or removed contingently on behavior. However, it is possible for behaviors to have reinforcing qualities of their own. That is, permitting an individual to work at a favored task contingently upon the completion of a less-preferred task can actually increase the probability that the individual will engage in the former task. This phenomenon is called the *Premack principle* (Mawhinney, 1979; Premack, 1971).[4]

---

[4] We anticipated a variant of this principle in Chapter 4 and again in Chapter 13 where we discussed the issue of self-regulation. Although the treatment in those earlier chapters does not espouse a behaviorist view of the world, the applied implications were virtually the same as those here: people can reward themselves by sequencing the events that impinge upon them, such that their preferred experiences are self-administered as rewards (or, as a behaviorist would call them, as reinforcers).

For example, an employee who dislikes the paperwork associated with inventory control, but who does enjoy using a new inventory to build retail sales displays, might be reinforced to keep better inventory records (and to keep them more up to date) if opportunities to participate in the design and construction of displays were permitted only upon the completion of inventory work. And, like all of the other reinforcers that have been discussed, this activity reinforcer can be administered according to either a continuous reinforcement schedule or any of the intermittent schedules that were discussed earlier.

The multiplicity of reinforcers

It is important to recognize that social situations can include many sources of both reinforcement and punishment for people. Work settings are no exception (Komaki et al., 1991). In fact, the application of behavior modification principles, for either understanding or influencing employee behavior, must recognize that the organization's official reward system (or reinforcement system in operant conditioning terms) is only one of several systems that can dispense reinforcements and punishments for individuals. For example, employees who work in groups quickly learn that coworkers can control both reinforcers (in the form of social acceptance and social status) and punishers (through the removal of approval and status). The point is that managers must remember that they are only one source of reinforcement and punishment for their employees; attempts to shape or influence their subordinates' behavior through the use of formally sanctioned rewards and punishments will be limited to the extent that they are consistent with the reinforcement and punishment contingencies people receive from other sources in the work setting (Jablonsky & DeVries, 1972; Whyte, 1972).

Behavior Shaping

Sometimes the behavior we want to encourage in others is so complex that it does not occur spontaneously, in pure form. Complex behaviors that consist of a number of elements (such as swinging a golf club properly) may be developed, however, if successive approximations to them are reinforced. In other words, we begin by reinforcing behaviors that bear even the slightest resemblance to the behavior we ultimately wish to develop. Continuous and variable ratio schedules are used initially, but the standard required for reinforcement increases as the person proceeds, meaning that behaviors increasingly closer to the final one become required in order for a reinforcement to be earned – a sort of *successive approximations approach*.

So, for example, an employee who has had difficulty interacting with customers would initially be reinforced for even the slightest attempts to be friendly, such as smiling at them, or at least not leaving the room when customers enter. After a while, however, positive reinforcement would be received only for more friendly behaviors, such as asking customers whether they need service. Desirable behaviors are reinforced while irrelevant or inappropriate behaviors are extinguished. Eventually, the employee can be placed on a variable ratio schedule of reinforcement for performing the ultimately desired acts, and the ratio gradually reduced. This process is referred to as *behavior shaping*. Many of the acts we perform every day, such as driving a car, writing a letter, and being a parent, are learned through behavior shaping. They are far too complex to learn all at once.

More on Functional Analysis

It was noted earlier in this chapter that functional analysis explains behavior by looking at both the conditions that precede it and the consequences that follow it. To this point, we have focused largely on the consequences of behavior. What about the antecedents?

Prompts

A reinforcement not only increases the probability of the behavior it follows, but also contributes to bringing that behavior under the control of whatever stimuli are present when the behavior occurs (Reynolds, 1975). In other words, when a particular act occurs and is reinforced in the presence of a certain type of stimulus, the presence of that stimulus, by itself, can increase the frequency of the act (or *prompt* it).

For example, a manager's instructions to a group of employees can set the group in motion. A parent's gesture to her child can often control the child's behavior (but not always, of course). When a particular prompt (or cue) initiates behavior that is subsequently reinforced, it is called a discriminative stimulus. A *discriminative stimulus* sets the occasion for behavior to unfold; it increases the probability that a behavior will follow. It signals the fact that a reinforcement may be following, although, by itself, it does not actually elicit behavior. Nevertheless, after such a stimulus has been associated with enough reinforcement experiences, it can take on reinforcing qualities of its own, permitting the individual to learn elaborate sequences of behaviors called chains.

Chaining

A *chain* is a series of behaviors that are linked together by stimuli that act both as reinforcers and as discriminative stimuli. A chain starts with the presentation of a discriminative stimulus. When the person responds in the appropriate manner in the presence of that stimulus, a reinforcer follows. This reinforcer often serves as a second discriminative stimulus, which makes the next appropriate response more probable (but not definite). Likewise, if the response that results is appropriate, it, in turn, is followed by reinforcement which then prompts a third behavior. The sequence can go on and on until, ultimately, a primary or secondary reinforcer results that is sufficient to put an end to the sequence and to reinforce all of it.

As an example, consider the writing of a business letter to order a shipment of new raw materials for a production shop. The original discriminative stimulus might simply be the time of year (such as the end of September, when orders are normally placed), or a frantic telephone call from a foreman who is worried that the present inventory of materials is close to exhaustion. The chain which follows might be composed of a number of responses, such as booting up a computer, starting a printer, selecting a search engine, entering text that indicates what is being sought on the internet, hitting "Enter" on the keyboard, sitting back with fingers crossed, and then scanning the lists of websites that appear as a consequence of the search. The stimulus that follows each behavior (such as a computer screen with the word "Google" across the top, a list of websites that results from the search, and so on) prompts the next behavior in the chain, each of which, in turn, is reinforced by the stimulus which follows that. Ultimately, of course, the entire chain may be reinforced a week later by the arrival of new materials, and by an end to the incessant reminders of the worried foreman.

Notice that each of the behaviors in the chain can be, by itself, composed of a chain of smaller behaviors. For instance, the very act of putting a fresh sheet of paper in the roller mechanism of a typewriter consists of a sequence of smaller micro-behaviors, tied together in a sequence that has proven more or less successful in the past. Notice also the similarity between these chains and the concept of feedback loops we encountered in connection with control theory in Chapter 13.

Discrimination learning

Not every discriminative stimulus, or prompt, results in reinforced behavior. In the context of some stimuli, a particular behavior may be reinforced, while in the context of other stimuli the same behavior may not be reinforced. For example, uttering a curse may result in the chuckles of one's workmates, but pays off less well when one's spouse is present. People learn to discriminate among stimulus conditions in which particular acts are reinforcing and in which others are punishing. Accordingly, we can make use of this sort of learning by increasing or decreasing the probability of behaviors, by applying or removing the antecedent cues with which they are associated.

Let's look at an example. When a telephone rings (a discriminative stimulus), we are prompted to answer it, because previous experiences of a similar sort have generally been reinforcing. Each sub-act in the chain that constitutes answering the phone sets the stage for the one that follows. For instance, picking up the receiver is reinforced by hearing an open line, which, in turn, prompts the act of saying "Hello," which, in turn, is reinforced by the knowledge of who has called. Notice that the same behavior (lifting the receiver and saying hello) is not likely to occur without the presence of the initial discriminative stimulus (the ringing of the telephone's bell).

In summary, many behaviors consist of chains of less complex behaviors. Each of the elements of each chain sets the stage for, and simultaneously reinforces, other behaviors that follow from them. Functional analysis is the process of breaking an individual's behavior patterns down into a series of antecedent–behavior–consequence (A–B–C) linkages for analysis. Only through a study of the specific cues that prompt a behavior, as well as of the particular reinforcers that follow it, can we understand behavior, let alone influence it.

Stimulus Generalization and Response Generalization

In the foregoing section, it was stated that people discriminate among stimulus conditions before behaving in certain ways. But human learning includes the opposite process as well. This is called *stimulus generalization.*

University students are aware of the virtues of the different pedagogical techniques their professors use to teach them material. It is often said that cases are useful teaching (and learning) devices because they are more realistic or hands on than are lectures or discussions of concepts and ideas. However, the best solution to one case may not be the best solution for any other case, either in reality or in the classroom setting.

Notice that if the process of discrimination went too far, the behavior of students would be idiosyncratic for every different problem they encounter. As a result, many professors try to have their students generalize their learning from one situation to another. In other words, students strive to recognize similarities among stimulus situations (such as case problems) so that they can invoke behavioral solutions that were learned in the context of one problem to deal with problems that are different to varying degrees (e.g., House, 1975). The skills of eating spaghetti are quite similar to those of eating linguini, so a gourmand who learns how to eat the former should also be proficient at eating the latter, through the process of stimulus generalization. Likewise, the behaviors necessary for negotiating with a union steward over an incipient grievance are similar to (but not identical to) those needed to negotiate a raise in pay from one's own boss. Similarity between antecedent contexts is a matter of degree, but effective functioning in our culture requires that we generalize our antecedent–behavior–consequences linkages from one setting to others that are sufficiently similar in important ways.

People also learn how to generalize the responses they make to stimuli. In other words, while stimulus generalization entails learning how to invoke the same behavior in response to a variety of similar antecedent conditions, response generalization entails learning to employ behaviors that are similar to one another in a given situation. To the extent that one behavior is similar to another one (such as smiling and laughing), when one of the acts is reinforced, the other is also more likely to be reinforced.

An example from the work setting might be as follows: A supervisor instructs an employee to act safely when using dangerous equipment. The behaviors associated with "acting safely" are then reinforced. Other behaviors, such as speaking more quietly on the shop floor, keeping the work area clean, or even helping other employees improve the safety of their behaviors may also result. The employee's safety-related skills have generalized in this example to other behaviors that, for some reason, hold some similarity for the individual involved. Research in behavior modification shows that it is not always possible to predict the exact form that response generalization may take for a given individual. Two people may be reinforced for performing the same act, but then generalize that act to entirely different subsequent behaviors. The analysis of operant behavior reveals that learning does not occur in a cue-unique, behavior-unique reinforcement fashion. Rather, people respond to general similarities among stimulus situations using behaviors that have been learned in other circumstances. Likewise, the reinforcement of particular behaviors in situations may result in the reinforcement of other, similar behaviors in the same context.

To this point, the emphasis has been on influencing the probability of behavior through positive means. But we know that punishment also can be used to change the occurrence of behavior. Let us take a look at punishment and the nature of formal discipline procedures typically found in work settings.

Punishment

Of the three types of consequence that can result from behavior, none is more ubiquitous in nature and more controversial in practice than punishment. (Recall from our earlier discussion that reinforcement and extinction are the other two.) We learn a great deal from being punished. Skinner notes, for example:

> A child runs awkwardly, falls, and is hurt; he touches a bee and is stung; he takes a bone from a dog and is bitten; and as a result he learns not to do these things again.
>
> (Skinner, 1974, p. 60)

Likewise, punishment and the fear of it are very common in day-to-day experience in organizations (Arvey & Ivancevich, 1980), largely because it is reinforcing to those who use it (cf. Butterfield, Trevino, & Ball, 1996; George, 1995; Mayhew, 1979). In fact, the heavy reliance on punishment in the usual practice of management provided much of the impetus for the introduction of operant conditioning techniques (with their emphasis on positive reinforcement) into the management literature (see Aldis, 1961; Nord, 1969). Yet, in spite of its ubiquity in work settings, very little work has been done to formally study the nature and consequences of punishment at work (Arvey & Ivancevich, 1980).

Defining punishment

Recall that punishment is defined in terms of the impact it has on behavior. More specifically, punishment is: "[T]he presentation of an aversive event or the removal of a positive event following a response which decreases the frequency of that response" (Kazdin, 1975, pp. 33–34).

It is important to remember that different people find different events punishing, just as differences exist among the things people find reinforcing. "Different strokes for different folks!" As a result, the conscious administration of punishment in organizational settings can be difficult: For example, while some employees find being assigned to night duty punishing, others favor night work. Notice that the simple administration of aversive stimuli does not constitute punishment, according to this definition. Many negative things can occur in the workplace, but unless they are related to behavior and have the effect of reducing the future occurrences of that behavior, they cannot be classified as punishment per se.

The effects of punishment

It was stated earlier that the use of punishment has been controversial. Most of this controversy results from the actual and imagined effects it has on people. Skinner was responsible for giving punishment "a bad name" in some of his early work and many people accepted his position without question for many years, advocating the use of positive reinforcement instead, whenever possible. More recent evidence, however, suggests that punishment, although complex in its effects on behavior, can be effective. In fact, it has been particularly useful in clinical settings as a therapeutic mechanism for dealing with a variety of deviant behaviors (Kazdin, 1975).

One early review of the literature suggested that many of the adverse consequences traditionally attributed to it have not actually been demonstrated in research conducted in work organizations, per se, and that it is premature to discard punishment as a managerial technique (Arvey & Ivancevich, 1980). For example, conventional wisdom has held that punishment results in attempts to get back at the punishing agent or at least to avoid it. In organizational settings, this would imply that punishment will result in deliberate attempts to seek revenge on a punishing supervisor, through acts such as physical aggression toward the supervisor or the work (displaced aggression). Alternatively, the conventional wisdom suggests that a punished employee may withdraw from the work setting either physically or psychologically.

The social context and consequences of the use of discipline

Indeed, in Chapter 11, we observed several times how the formation of justice and injustice perceptions are heavily influenced by the social contexts within which acts among organizational participants transpire. That is, we saw that how people judge the procedures used to mediate rewards and punishments applied to them is influenced not only by their own, individual experiences, values, and perceptions, but also by the vicarious experiences and sense making and social comparison processes they undertake with their coworkers.

A study by Atwater, Waldman, Carey, and Cartier (2001) found that while both recipients of discipline as well as third-party observers can often recognize positive benefit from disciplinary procedures, there is always a risk that both recipients and observers will lose respect for the discipliner and develop negative attitudes toward the organization as a whole, especially when the discipline is perceived to be unfair. In another study, research participants read scenarios of crime and punishment in organizational settings. The details of the scenarios varied from case to case. The results indicated that third-party observers judged that violators with poor prior performance records deserved more punishment than violators with good prior records. In addition, observers believed that lenient punishment was less fair than more severe punishment for poor workers as well as for good workers, but that the fairest treatment was among those hypothetical workers with poor track records and who received the most severe punishment (Niehoff, Paul, & Bunch, 1998).

Finally, as we saw in Chapter 6, a study by George (1995) found that, whereas performance-contingent reward behavior by supervisors helped to reduce social loafing among subordinates (conducting themselves as "free riders" in groupwork conditions), punishment of individuals had little effect. Indeed, when performance *non-contingent* punishment was practiced, there was a significant, positive effect on social loafing. Hence the effects of rewards and punishment are asymmetrical and may be particularly difficult to anticipate in socially charged settings of the sort we find when people work in groups. Again, the point is that superiors risk unanticipated consequences when they apply discipline and punishment in organizational settings, especially when group dynamics related to the formal structure of work and even the informal structure among workers are taken into account (cf. Butterfield, Trevino, & Ball, 1996). The point here is that adopting a more holistic perspective on punishment, particularly one that takes into account the social information processing that occurs when people witness – either personally or vicariously – punishment in organizational settings, may lead to more subtle consequences than had been adopted in early analyses of the phenomenon, such as that by Arvey and Ivancevich (1980).

Finally, another belief about punishment is that its effects generalize to discourage behaviors similar to those being punished, but that are not intended to be discouraged. For example, it would be assumed that punishing an employee for aggressively questioning a client might generalize to reduce the likelihood that the employee will act in such a manner toward suppliers and competitors. A third criticism has been that punishment never totally eliminates a behavior. Rather, it has been assumed that punished behavior tends to disappear only when the punishing agent is present, and that it often reappears when surveillance is discontinued. The implication is that managerial systems based on punishment require close supervision and all of the costs associated with it. (One wonders, for example, whether reformed criminals are ever sorry for their crimes, or whether their sorrow results only from their having been caught and punished!)

The morality of punishment

One interesting criticism raised about the use of punishment concerns its morality: Is it moral to punish another person? It is worthwhile to note that punishment can be of either of two varieties: *Retributional* and backward looking or *corrective* and forward looking. It may be that punishment that is intended to attain revenge is less ethical and less civilized than is punishment intended to prevent the individual from behaving in undesired ways in the future. It is also useful to distinguish between punishment and the use of coercion (Walter & Marks, 1981). Whereas punishment involves the application of aversive consequences or the removal of positive consequences for behavior, coercion goes further. *Coercion* entails the extralegal use of threats, fear, terror, violence, and often the application of naked force. Coercion involves the misuse of power between two people, or between a power figure and his followers (Cook, 1972). For example, the college professor who extorts sexual favors in exchange for grades is employing coercion, as is the supervisor who threatens to systematically assign an employee to unpleasant tasks if that employee participates in union-organizing activities.

It seems that coercion and retributional punishment are generally viewed in our culture as less ethical than punishment – which is administered equitably, within the bounds of legitimate authority, and with a view to preventing further occurrences of dysfunctional or harmful behavior.

Making punishment effective

McGregor (quoted by Sayles & Strauss, 1977) noted many years ago that in order to be effective, punishment should occur in practice, as similarly as possible, as it occurs in nature. In fact, he coined the *hot stove rule* to summarize his belief. According to this rule, the most effective punishment is that which is immediate, contingent upon behavior, intense (meaning not too severe, but not without some pain), consistent, impersonal, and informational. In addition, an alternative to the punished act should be available. Hence, when a person touches a hot stove, what happens? The burn which results is punishing and it is felt immediately. It results from an unfortunate behavior (rather than from the passage of time or random events). If the stove is at all hot, the pain is intense. In addition, hot stoves play no favorites; they are impersonal and consistent, punishing anyone who touches them, every time they are touched. And the experience tends to be informational: That is, people normally infer quickly the cause of their suffering. Finally, there are usually alternatives to touching hot stoves, such as moving away and avoiding them in the future.

In short, according to McGregor, punishment in organizations should have all of these features in order to be effective. The review of the literature mentioned earlier (Arvey & Ivancevich, 1980) reconfirms most of McGregor's wisdom about punishment, and adds that it is most effective when the punishing agent (such as a supervisor) has relatively close and friendly relations with the punished individual, when the agent explains the reason for the punishment to the person, and when the individual understands what the contingencies for punishment will be in the future. Finally, when alternatives to the punished behavior are positively reinforced, it is less likely to occur in the future (Arvey & Ivancevich, 1980).

Alternatives to punishment

Although punishment occurs frequently on a day-to-day basis in organizations, and may be more effective at eliminating behavior than has traditionally been believed, many supervisors would prefer to avoid using it when it is not necessary. Accordingly, a number of alternatives may be effective in some circumstances. One is to ignore the undesirable behavior, and/or remove those aspects of the person's environment that reinforce it, thus bringing about extinction. Another alternative is to positively reinforce behaviors that are incompatible with the undesired ones. For instance, many effective teachers have learned that reinforcing quiet, constructive study and play behavior can reduce the problems created by boisterous students.

Finally, it is often possible to combine these tactics into a careful form of environmental engineering. For example, many organizations in which smoking in particular rooms or offices is unwanted have found it beneficial to provide specially designated areas where smoking is permitted. Rather than displaying signs that say, "No smoking allowed," in restricted areas, they post signs saying, "Smoking allowed in this area," in those places where it is deemed appropriate. Many restaurants make active use of this approach. Likewise, it may be possible to reduce the amount of graffiti that is written on the walls of a washroom, or work area, if paper and pencils are provided in those areas as an alternative. The objective of environmental engineering is to anticipate the types of dysfunctional behavior that might occur in particular settings, and to take steps to make them impossible, or at least, non-reinforcing.

Organizational discipline and punishment

How do formal discipline policies and practices in work organizations compare to the principles of the hot stove? In many cases, not very well. For example, it is difficult in practice to make punishment immediate. This is particularly the case when policies require a series of appeals and quasi-legal investigations after a charge is laid. For example, more than a year and a half passed at a major Canadian university between the time when it was first alleged that a senior professor was misusing government research funds, and the beginning of the period of suspension meted out as punishment for the offense.

Compounding the problem, of course, is the difficulty of distributing punishments so that they are consistent and perceived as equitable and fair (see Chapter 11). Consistency can be difficult to achieve for a number of reasons. One of these is that different people are often responsible for distributing punishment. For example, the same employee may be susceptible to the approval and discipline of more than one supervisor, even though such reporting relationships violate the principle of unity of command. Sometimes an employee is punishable by his own superior, as well as by his superior's boss.

A number of other factors can influence the consistency of the punishment administered by the same individual, including, for example, the mood of the supervisor (Goodstadt & Kipnis, 1970) and the value of the employee to the organization (Rosen & Jerdee, 1974c). Likewise, a variety of factors in the work context can influence the degree to which accidents or mistakes are attributed to the individual employee (as opposed to factors beyond the employee's control). Hence, if supervisors are aware of the consequences of inappropriate employee behaviors, they are more likely to assume that the behavior will occur again, and more likely to assume that the employee is responsible both for the behavior and for the outcome that follows from it (Mitchell & Kalb, 1981). Further, supervisors who have had experience working on a job are more likely to attribute mistakes made on that job to external factors beyond the employee's control.[5] As a result of these and other factors, the same supervisors can make differing interpretations of the culpability of their employees and, as a result, administer different types and amounts of punishment for the same misbehavior (Mitchell, Green, & Wood, 1981). The point here is that although hot stoves may be consistent in the way they punish, supervisors in complex work settings often are not.

Are discipline procedures intense? Generally, formal discipline policies are more progressive than immediately intense. This is commonly the case in unionized work settings, in which collective agreements may restrict the intensity of the punishment that can be meted out by supervisors. One early writer on this topic, in fact, proposed a method of *progressive discipline* that he believed can obviate many of the negative side-effects that have traditionally been attributed to punishment (Huberman, 1964). This approach entails a series of disciplinary measures which are applied following each transgression by a particular employee. For example, the first offense results in a casual reminder of the rules and a "note of correction." The second occurrence results in a private discussion in the boss's office. The third offense also results in a talk with the supervisor, and includes a discussion of possible reassignment. Continued infractions result in suspensions, first with pay, then without. Ultimately, the employee is dismissed.

While programs of this sort are common in organizations, they do violate the purely psychological prescriptions concerning the intensity of punishment. By the same token, they favor the goals of consistency and impersonality, and as a result are more defensible on legal grounds. Finally, they tend to be more readily accepted because of their apparent humanity and reasonableness.

Discipline in arbitration decisions

Issues related to the application of discipline in unionized work settings take on many more levels of complexity originating in labor law. Moreover, the principles and practices vary among jurisdictions to the point where discussing them is well beyond our current purpose. In Canada, the interested reader is referred to the classic text by Brown and Beatty (2006); in the United States, the standard text on the matter is Elkouri and Aspa-Elkouri (1985).[6]

Summary on punishment

Punishment is a major facet of managerial styles employed in work organizations. It can be a very effective means of quickly eliminating undesired behaviors, so it is reinforcing to managers who employ it. A number of unintended side-effects have been attributed to the use of punishment, although there is very little evidence that these occur in work settings among adults. In practice, disciplinary procedures tend to have features that make them only partially similar to the most effective forms of punishment found in nature, and formal organizational policies, as well as arbitrator decisions, seem to support this divergence, probably because nature's style of punishing people is deemed too harsh by civilized people. It must be remembered that, in practice, the use of punishment and discipline occurs within a social context in which norms of fairness are more or less in place and expected by everyone involved. As we saw in Chapter 11, this means that organizational discipline must be administered in a manner that is fair and seen to be fair. It is not a simple issue.

---

[5] For a behaviorist, of course, the mood of the supervisor does not cause his use of discipline. Rather, the evasive behavior of the subordinate is the discriminative stimulus that occasions the use of discipline; the boss's mood is merely an accompanying (or collateral) emotional reaction.

[6] The author is grateful to Vancouver employment lawyer and arbitrator David McPhillips for his advice on this matter.

Operant Conditioning and VIE Theory

At this point it may be instructive to compare and contrast the operant conditioning approach to that of VIE theory.[7] First, we have mentioned many times that the two approaches make entirely different fundamental assumptions about human nature and the causes of behavior. VIE theory attributes behavior to internal beliefs and attitudes, while behavior modification rejects internal constructs in favor of the antecedent stimuli and external consequences of behavior (see Komaki, 1986, p. 301).

Second, both theories include the notion of probabilities, but in different ways (Petrock & Gamboa, 1976). VIE theory speaks of the subjective probabilities in the minds of people in the form of expectancies and instrumentalities. Operant conditioning speaks of the probabilities and frequencies of behaviors occurring as a consequence of the reinforcements and punishments that result from behavior.

Both theories advocate that rewards (or reinforcers) be administered contingently upon behavior, as soon as possible after the desired behavior occurs. Notice, however, that operant conditioning holds variable ratio schedules to be the most motivating in the long run, once a behavior has been learned, whereas VIE theory would suggest that instrumentality beliefs should be strongest when rewards are always tied to performance (as under a continuous reinforcement schedule). Research on this issue involving workers has been largely mixed and inconclusive, if only because of the difficulty of controlling reinforcement/reward schedules carefully in real work settings (cf. Latham & Dossett, 1978; Saari & Latham, 1982; Yukl & Latham, 1975; Yukl, Latham, & Pursell, 1976; Yukl, Wexley, & Seymore, 1972).

To this point, we have used the terms *reward* and *reinforcement* somewhat interchangeably. In fact, however, it is important to differentiate between the two concepts. The term reward implies a set of subjective reactions experienced internally; it is rooted in the cognitive/perceptual model of human functioning. Reinforcement, by way of contrast, implies that a behavior is made more probable, or more frequent, by its consequences; no mention of internal states or perceptions is involved. In short, choice of either term implicitly indicates whether an individual assumes the importance of internal or external factors as the primary causes of behavior.

On the other hand, both theories assume that humans are basically hedonists who seek to maximize pleasure (or at least survival potential) and minimize pain.

In the early years, there was a tendency for operant conditioning to focus on extrinsic outcomes rather than intrinsic ones, if only because the former are objective, measurable, and do not require the invocation of need concepts. VIE theory, however, has devoted considerable attention to the role of both intrinsic and extrinsic rewards, especially since these two types of motivation were both formally recognized in Porter and Lawler's (1968) revised expectancy model (see Chapter 12). Since then, some behaviorists have attempted to provide operant conditioning interpretations of the impact of extrinsic reinforcement on intrinsic motivation (e.g., Mawhinney, 1979).

In balance, we can conclude that the differences between the two approaches are of more theoretical importance than they are of practical significance (Petrock & Gamboa, 1976). Both theories would propose that rewards (or reinforcers) be linked with performance (or desired behaviors). Both schools would suggest that reward/reinforcement contingencies feature outcomes that people desire or value. Finally, both acknowledge the importance of the context of behavior; the behaviorists, because they hold the antecedents and consequences of acts to be their cause, and the VIE theorists (e.g., Lawler, 1973), because they recognize that features of the work environment are important for structuring expectancy and instrumentality beliefs, which, in turn, result in intentions to act.

---

[7] See Chapter 12 of this volume.

A Glance Ahead

Our purpose to this point in the chapter has been to introduce some of the most important traditional principles of operant psychology, laying the foundation for a treatment of the application of these principles to the issues of work motivation and behavior. The purpose in the following sections will be to: (1) examine the general principles of *behavior modification*; then (2) present the specific application of the principles to organizational motivation and behavior – usually referred to as *organizational behavior modification* or *applied behavior analysis*; (3) examine social cognitive theory, one of the most valid approaches surveyed in this book; and finally (4), to explore in detail the principles and practices of self-management (or self-regulation), a currently popular focus of study in the organizational behavior literature.

GENERAL PRINCIPLES OF BEHAVIOR MODIFICATION

On the basis of the diversity of views discussed in the foregoing section, it is not surprising that there is no universally agreed-upon definition of behavior modification. Nevertheless, for the sake of discussion, the following definition is borrowed from Kazdin (1978, p. ix) and adopted for use in this book:

> [T]he application of basic research and theory from experimental psychology to influence behavior for purposes of resolving personal and social problems and enhancing human functioning.

Notice that this definition would imply that knowledge from all branches of experimental psychology constitutes the knowledge base of behavior modification, without regard to the particular schools involved. The definition also implies that behavior modification is not a fixed or final set of techniques. Rather, as new research and theory are developed in the various schools of psychology, the knowledge base and techniques of behavior modification will continue to change accordingly (Craighead et al., 1976). And it should be clear that the principles of operant psychology, as discussed earlier in this chapter, constitute the most important elements of behavior modification.

Addition of Cognitive Processes to Operant Principles

In addition to traditional operant principles, however, modern behavior modification also includes a variety of other principles and processes, *many of which are of a cognitive nature*. Aside from goal setting (which we discussed at length in Chapter 13) and self-management (which will be treated at length later in the present chapter), the most significant other cognitive processes that have been adopted by modern behaviorists are: *Attention, mediation, anticipation, problem solving, attribution, feedback*, and *modeling*. We will briefly examine each of these processes in the following sections.

Attention

Even if we adopt the assumption that behavior has its antecedents and consequences in the environment, we must recognize that people are usually faced with a vast array of environmental events and contingencies, and that we are simply not capable of monitoring them all. Instead, we tend to restrict our focus to subsets of the environment, including subsets of all of the possible antecedents to behavior and subsets of all of its possible consequences. Two people in the same situation may concentrate their attention on different aspects of the environment and behave differently as a result. Therefore, while one employee may be particularly inclined to stay abreast of his supervisor's moods, another may not recognize the fact that the same supervisor tends to have shifts in mood from one day to the next. Likewise, some employees are more susceptible to the reinforcements and punishments they receive via the informal system of the organization, while others concentrate on the rewards and punishment administered by management. In short, it is the environmental events to which people attend that determine their behavior (Craighead et al., 1976, p. 135).

Mediation

As people experience the cues that prompt behavior and the consequences that are contingent upon it, they learn. However, the material that is learned can be organized into symbolic mental structures in an orderly fashion that facilitates recall and recognition, or it may not be so organized. Different people employ different mental techniques for organizing the things they have learned, such as mnemonics poems, and various other types of associations. ("The way I remember the name of my boss's wife is that it is the same as my mother's!") Current behavior modification recognizes the role played by such mental processes in human behavior.

Anticipation

Why do some people take an umbrella to work with them in the morning, even when it is not raining when they leave home? Why do people abandon sinking ships? The answer is that human beings often anticipate events, including those they have already experienced in the past (such as being caught in the rain without an umbrella), as well as those they may not have experienced before (such as going down with a ship). The point is that learning from the past – be it personal learning or vicarious learning – causes people to anticipate reinforcement and punishment from their future behavior.

Problem solving

When an individual behaves in a certain way in response to a challenge or task, the reinforcement or punishment that follows will influence the probability that the person will behave the same way in the future when confronted with the same situation, and we say that a behavior has been learned. By way of contrast, we noted in the previous chapter that it is not necessary for people to experience antecedent–behavior–consequence contingencies for all possible, specific circumstances they may encounter. People develop the capacity to generalize somewhat from one situation to another. In other terms, we tend to develop problem-solving skills which make it possible to consider an array of potential behaviors for dealing with problem situations, as well as select the one(s) that are most likely to be effective.

Attribution

People observe events around themselves and make inferences about the causes of those events. The events may be the antecedents that provide the operant conditioner's prompts or cues for behaving, or they may be the consequences of the operant behaviors that follow the cue. Alternatively, the event may be something that has little to do directly with the individual in question. The point is, people tend to be naive psychologists, trying to determine why things happen the way they do (recall Chapter 3; and see Heider, 1958). In the work setting, managers frequently make attributions about the reasons for the quality of the work of their subordinates, attributing it either to hard work and effort (or a lack thereof), or to factors that are beyond the control of the employees involved (see Mitchell et al., 1981, for a formal theory pertaining to this process).

Feedback

As we have seen on a number of occasions, feedback is the provision of information to a system about its output (recall Chapter 13, in particular). In human terms, feedback consists of telling individuals something about their behavior, in either quantitative or qualitative terms. The provision of feedback is one of the most potent and most common elements of behavior modification, particularly when applied to work settings (Prue & Fairbank, 1980). Often, feedback is combined with the setting of goals, and in fact, the feedback usually consists of information concerning the employee's progress toward those goals (see Ashford & Tsui, 1991; Tsui & Ashford, 1994).

Feedback is usually the most inexpensive and generally the easiest behaviour modification process to employ. It costs little, in most circumstances, to tell employees how well they are doing. Further, feedback is usually a more positive means of gaining behavior control than are punishment and discipline, consistent with the positive orientation of the philosophy of behavior modification. Finally, feedback is usually more feasible than other behavior modification practices in organizations with internal constraints concerning the distribution of rewards and punishments. Union agreements, for example, may limit the use of money as a reinforcer, but seldom prohibit management from telling rank-and-file employees when they are performing well in their jobs. In short, feedback has a number of advantages in behavior modification efforts, accounting in large part for its popularity in such programs (Prue & Fairbank, 1980). It is important to note that while feedback may be reinforcing (i.e., increasing the frequency of behavior), it is conceptually distinct from reinforcement, per se. The reason, of course, is that information fed back can also reduce the frequency of behavior, thereby qualifying for the formal definition of punishment in some situations.

Dimensions of feedback

There are a number of aspects of feedback that must be taken into account when considering its use in behavior modification. Of particular interest is whether the feedback is provided to the individual in public or in private. One summary of the evidence on this matter has concluded that private feedback is desirable when:

1. the performance of the person receiving it is low
2. supervisors have the necessary interpersonal skills to deal with subordinates on a one-to-one basis
3. there are enough resources (such as supervisory time) to provide it
4. workers are in close proximity to their supervisors
5. the individual receiving it is being compared to his own baseline performance or some designated standard (Prue & Fairbank, 1980).

Another consideration is the means used to deliver feedback. It can be provided verbally, in written form, by mechanical or electronic means, or by the individual himself as he keeps record of his own behavior and performance. There are costs and benefits associated with each of these approaches. For example, self-monitoring implies trust of the individual and includes the employee in the intervention program. Verbal feedback can be quick and inexpensive to administer. Written feedback can help with the keeping of records for ongoing assessments of performance improvements.

Also of concern is the content of the feedback, or the standard that is implied in the message (see our discussion of control theory and goal-setting theory on this point in Chapter 13). For example, is the individual's performance to be compared with that of other people (such as her work group), with her own previous performance, or with some external standard or goal? The reader is reminded of the value of specifying hard and specific goals, as we discussed in Chapter 13, and is referred to Prue and Fairbank (1980) and Dickson et al. (1993), who have reviewed a variety of specific issues that should be taken into account when planning the content of the feedback that is to be provided to employees.

The *timing* of feedback is often important. Ideally, feedback should be provided as soon as possible after the behavior about which information is being fed back, although people vary in their capacity to effectively wait to learn how well they are doing at a task. Immediate feedback is particularly valuable when it pertains to a task that the individual is learning for the first time, and/or when the task involved is complex. It would seem that feedback should be made contingent upon behavior rather than the passage of time, per se, as is the case with reinforcement, but there is little research evidence on this point at present.

Who should give the feedback? It stands to reason that the greater the prestige of the person who provides it the more attention will be paid to feedback, although there are circumstances where this may not necessarily be the case. For example, the trustworthiness of the person, his capacity to deliver reinforcers and punishments, his expertise, sincerity, and the nature of the relationship between the person delivering the message and the person receiving it also should be taken into account.

Although the powerful potential effects of feedback on performance have been acknowledged for many years, these effects have only recently been combined into a systematic theory that sufficiently explains these effects (cf. Ilies & Judge, 2005; Kluger & DeNisi, 1996; Locke & Latham, 1990a). Ilgen et al. (1979) provided one of the earliest models; it has served as the theoretical platform for many of the studies conducted into the issue since. But collectively, those studies had been of only limited value, for two principal reasons. First, most of them were either bivariate, cross-sectional designs that neglected to examine the *processes* associated with the effects of feedback on performance (Kinicki, Prussia, Wu, & McKee-Ryan, 2004). A second drawback was that the early studies (which were instigated by the heavily cognitive model of Ilgen et al., 1979) were largely cognitive in nature – affective variables were generally ignored in spite of the fact that, clearly, both the giving and the receiving of feedback, especially about one's work performance, is frequently a highly emotional experience. The most rigorous and elaborate cognitively based model of the mediating effects of feedback on performance was offered by Kinicki et al. (2004).

Adopting an affective events theory (recall Chapter 4) approach, Ilies and Judge (2005) moved the field toward such a theory. In a series of experiments that employed three types of cognitive and problem-solving task, two types of goal (learning and performance) and actual (valid) as well as false (manipulated) feedback, these researchers showed, as hypothesized, that research participants adjusted their performance goals downward following negative feedback and increased the level of their goals over past performance when they received positive feedback (these findings are consistent with goal-setting theory and with social-cognitive theory, which will be discussed later in this chapter). Also, in what the researchers themselves describe as "the most important finding of this research project" (p. 463), emotional reactions to their various forms of feedback mediated the impact of the feedback on the subsequent goal-setting practices of participants. "Emotion" was operationalized as positive and negative affect, as measured by the popular "positive and negative affect schedule" (Watson, Clarke, & Tellegen, 1988).

Clearly, future work to understand the processes relating the receipt of feedback to subsequent goal setting and employee behavior will require the joint examination of both cognitive and affective models. The two studies mentioned here (by Ilies & Judge, 2005; Kinicki et al., 2004) will provide fruitful starting points for such further research.

Modeling

Earlier in this chapter we discussed the development of complex behaviors from simpler ones through the process referred to as behavior shaping. It was noted there that a great deal of human behavior is the result of behavior shaping; in fact, shaping continues throughout our lives, as we become increasingly more sophisticated in dealing with our environments.

Conversely, Bandura (1969, 1977, 1986) and others have noted that many complex behaviors seem not to require the time and ongoing personal experiencing of reinforcement and punishment entailed in shaping processes. Instead, they note that some complex behaviors can often appear all at once for the first time. The primary means by which this occurs, according to Bandura, is through identification processes – we watch others and learn from them.

For example, a new employee in a grocery store may stand beside an experienced clerk to observe how vegetables are trimmed and prepared for display. After watching the several micro-steps involved in efficiently trimming and wrapping a head of lettuce, for example, the experienced clerk may say to the newcomer, "Here, you try." Of course, the rookie may not be as proficient as the veteran upon the first attempt, but a little shaping (of both the lettuce and the rookie's behavior) can normally overcome the problem and, before too long, the entire behavioral sequence has been learned.

Primary modeling mechanisms

There are three basic means through which people model their behavior after others. The first one is called *imitation*, and was illustrated by the example of the lettuce trimmer in the previous paragraph. Notice that the person whose behavior is being modeled need not actually be alive or present for learning to take place. In fact, training films are commonly used in organizations to demonstrate how relatively complex acts are performed.

A second form of modeling involves the use of behavior that already exists in the person's repertoire but that is *cued* (or prompted) by the behaviors of others around him. For example, employees in a work setting may be much more likely to engage in clown play when one of their informal leaders does so than would normally be the case. Although this aspect of modeling is similar to imitation, the difference has to do with whether the behavior being displayed by the individual is new (which is the case in imitation), or whether it is already known by the person but prompted by the behaviors of other people in his environment.

A third modeling mechanism is vicarious identification with the consequences of the behaviors of other individuals. Public punishment in the days of old capitalized on this process: Several people could "learn" about the consequences of illegal acts, without having to perform those acts and incur the costs personally. Thus, if we see others being reinforced for behaving in certain ways, we may be more likely to behave in similar fashion ourselves, almost as if we had experienced the reinforcement firsthand. Notice that it is possible for modeling to result in the learning of behavior (either new behavior or old behavior in new circumstances), without that behavior actually being put into practice. Whether people actually employ the behaviors they observe depends upon a number of things, including who the model is and the consequences that the model incurs as a result of the behavior. Research indicates that people are more likely to imitate the behavior of models who are high in prestige or expertise (Craighead et al., 1976, p. 107).

Goal Setting and Self-Management

Two final cognitive processes included in many behavior modification settings are goal setting (recall Chapter 13) and self-management – a process (or set of processes) by which a person selects, from among those response alternatives that are available at a particular time, those that otherwise would not normally be chosen (cf. Erez & Kanfer, 1983; Mills, 1983; Thoresen & Mahoney, 1974). Self-management consists of overriding one's natural predilections in favor of pursuing goals that are less naturally favored.

We will return to address self-management (or self-regulation) in greater detail later in this chapter, but for the sake of the current discussion, we can describe it as a three-stage sequence in which the individual monitors his own behavior, evaluates that behavior against some goal or standard, and then administers reinforcers or punishment to himself on the basis of the evaluation (Kanfer, 1980). So, for example, an employee who has been instructed by his supervisor to reduce the amount of material he wastes on a construction site might be taught methods for actually measuring the amount of scrap he throws away or the number of times he actively makes use of materials that have been discarded by himself or someone else. The evaluation stage follows closely, of course, as the employee will normally be immediately aware of how well his performance measures up to the standards he or his employer have set for him.

The third stage, the self-administration of either reinforcement or punishment, is somewhat more complex. For example, the person may voluntarily deny himself certain normal pleasures (such as a routine coffee break) if he notices that he is not making progress toward his goal. Alternatively, if he manages to make considerable use of discarded materials on a given morning, he may then administer any of a number of desirable consequences to himself, such as making a phone call to a friend, taking an extra long lunch hour, or merely uttering statements to himself such as, "That's better!"

Summary and Preview

The foregoing discussion has listed a number of processes and techniques that are commonly employed by psychologists in behavior modification settings. When combined with the basic methods of operant conditioning and those of other schools of psychology, these techniques have proven highly effective in influencing a wide array of human behavior in educational, clinical, and rehabilitation settings. When these techniques are applied to organizational and management problems, they are frequently referred to as *organizational behavior modification*. In the following sections, we will examine the key elements of this approach to work motivation and behavior and attempt to leave the reader with an understanding of the current status of this now-hybridized school among the other theories of work motivation discussed in this book.

ORGANIZATIONAL BEHAVIOR MODIFICATION

Aldis (1961) and Nord (1969) were among the first to suggest the application of the principles of operant conditioning to work organizations. As mentioned earlier, the idea caught on and was very popular during the 1970s (Goodall, 1972) and into the 1980s (Komaki et al., 1991; O'Hara, Johnson & Beehr, 1985). The approach was called *organizational behavior modification* (sometimes referred to as *OB mod*, *organizational behavior management*, or *applied behavior analysis*). Two particular journals – the *Journal of Applied Behavior Analysis* and the *Journal of Organizational Behavior Management* – are devoted to disseminating knowledge about the application of these principles to managerial problems and reporting research conducted within the OB mod framework. For historical reasons, it is important to repeat that while operant psychology was originally the most important parent discipline underlying OB mod, the actual techniques applied by its practitioners typically include combinations of cognitive concepts such as those discussed in the foregoing sections of this chapter.

Managing Behavioral Contingencies at Work

Managers who wish to apply OB mod must, in simple terms, learn how to diagnose and influence the antecedents and the consequences of the behavior of their employees. Luthans and Kreitner (1974, 1975) proposed a general sequence for accomplishing this, called *behavioral contingency management*. It consists of five basic steps. First, the manager must identify those employee behaviors which are detrimental to job performance. It is important that the manager be precise about exactly which behaviors are undesirable and need to be dealt with, and, if possible, that they be countable.

The second step is to actually count the frequency of the problematic behaviors, establishing a baseline that can be used to determine the effectiveness of the manager's subsequent intervention. The count may be made by the manager or by the employee himself (recall our earlier discussion of self-monitoring). Often, tally sheets are designed for this purpose, or managers sometimes merely sample the behavior of their personnel, checking how frequently they engage in the behavior in question during randomly selected periods of time. Wrist counters or the judicious application of memory are recommended in cases when it is probable that the employee will change his behavior if he knows that his supervisor is observing and recording it (cf. Whyte, 1972).

The third step is to identify both the conditions that are antecedent to the behavior, as well as the consequences that reinforce it. For example, the author once observed a number of work groups in a plant in which steel containers were manufactured. Foremen in each of the groups often complained that employees of the other groups stole parts and materials for use on their own projects. (The word they used, of course, was "borrowed.") Upon investigation, it was learned that most of the borrowing occurred toward the end of every month. Moreover, the foremen whose workers conducted the informal requisitions managed to keep their cost figures low, while assuring that their project deadlines were met. (The consequences for victimized foremen were exactly the opposite, of course.) Here, the antecedent of the dysfunctional behavior (borrowing) was the time of the month in which it occurred. The consequences? A formal reward system that reinforced the foremen for, in turn, reinforcing staff for raiding the supplies and materials of the other work groups!

The next step in behavioral contingency management is the selection of an intervention strategy (Luthans & Kreitner, 1975). These can include the application of any of the following, alone or in combination: Positive reinforcement, negative reinforcement, punishment, or extinction. The manager tries to make the chosen consequence contingent upon the behavior she is trying to either reinforce or eliminate. There are a variety of factors that can (and should) influence the precise strategy selected, such as the nature of the job, the organization's structure, history and precedents, union contracts, and other, more informal agreements. The manager or the employee continues to record the frequency of occurrence of the behavior in question. If the intervention is effective, the undesirable behavior will decrease in frequency (or cease altogether), and more favorable behaviors will take their place.

The final step is to evaluate the intervention by observing whether the desired behavior actually becomes more frequent, while undesired behavior becomes less frequent. Without evaluation, a manager cannot tell whether her attempt to change her employee's behavior has been successful. If it has not been successful, further remedial steps might then be possible (such as reexamining the antecedents or changing the consequences or the schedules by which they are administered).

Luthans and Kreitner's (1974, 1975) five-step approach follows consistently from the operant conditioners' suggestions for functional analysis, focusing upon the antecedents and consequences of behavior, as well as upon the nature of the behavior itself.

Komaki and her colleagues (1991) reviewed more than 50 applications of OB mod that they felt were well enough controlled to permit valid conclusions. On the basis of their review, Komaki et al. (1991) distilled four steps, or ingredients, that the various researchers and interventionists employed. Their list is similar to that of Luthans and Kreitner (1974, 1975), but has a more positive tone. These four ingredients were the following:

1. Specify the desired behavior (as opposed to identifying behaviors that are not desirable).
2. Measure the frequency of the desired performance [or behavior].
3. Provide frequent, contingent, positive consequences.
4. Evaluate the effectiveness of the ultimate job performance (Komaki et al., 1991, p. 92).

It is worth comparing the advice given three decades ago by Luthans and colleagues (Luthans & Kreitner, 1975; Luthans & Ottemann, 1977) with the techniques actually applied and the results attained by interventionists since then (as summarized by Komaki et al., 1991). They are quite similar, indeed.

Varieties of Consequences

Petrock (1978) suggested a useful means for analyzing the consequences of employee behavior for contingency management. He noted that most on-the-job behavior is of either of two varieties: Job related or non-job related. Moreover, each of these types of behavior can result in either positive or aversive consequences. Finally, regardless of whether they are positive or aversive, the consequences of employee behavior can be classified according to three important dimensions:

1. Whether the impact is on the employee or the organization (or both).
2. Whether the consequences are immediate or delayed.
3. Whether they are certain and highly contingent upon the behavior, or somewhat random and only partially contingent upon behavior.

Therefore, the management of employee behavior requires that the supervisor identify both the reinforcing and the punishing consequences that accrue to the employee, for both those behaviors that are deemed desirable, as well as those that are undesirable (from a managerial point of view). Clearly, individuals will engage in desirable behavior on the job when it results in a positive net balance of reinforcing consequences, rather than a balance of punishing consequences. By the same token, when employees find work demands result in more unpleasant outcomes than positive ones, we can expect that rules will be broken or ignored or that employees will actively engage in practices that are more reinforcing than is compliance with management's desires.

Komaki and her colleagues (1991) reported that five different classes of consequence were in fact used by interventionists in the studies they reviewed through the late 1980s. These were (1) organizational (such as pay raises and special training opportunities); (2) generalized rewards such as cash, frequent flyer coupons, and trading stamps; (3) activities (such as rearranging the order of their tasks, applying the Premack principle); (4) social rewards such as compliments, criticisms, and commendations; and (5) informational, such as feedback, public announcements about progress toward goals, and so on.

According to Petrock (1978), the punishing consequences of desired work behavior are usually personal (rather than organizational), immediate, and directly contingent on those behaviors. For example, wearing safety equipment is often uncomfortable, obeying formal rules can be inconvenient, and doing things by the book is often a "hassle." By way of contrast, the reinforcing consequences of desired behavior are frequently personal, delayed (rather than immediate), and contingent upon behavior, making desirable behavior less attractive in many cases than undesirable behavior. In short, Petrock suggests that supervisors who wish to influence the behavior of their employees must carefully identify and attempt to balance the positive and aversive consequences of both positive and negative behaviors, and then take steps to assure that desired behaviors result in more positive, and fewer aversive consequences than undesired behavior.

It is important to reiterate that many work behaviors are often reinforced informally by the social system of the workplace, in spite of the fact (or often because of the fact) that management officially discourages them.

The Positive Approach in OB Mod

While OB mod makes use of reinforcement as well as punishment, *the emphasis is on the application of positive control measures wherever possible.* Luthans and Kreitner (1975, p. 84) summarized this principle:

> Reinforcement is the key to operant learning theory and the most important principle of behavior modification. The simple fact is that positive reinforcement, contingently applied, can effectively control human behavior . . . With the possible exception of the contingency concept itself, the understanding and appropriate use of positive reinforcement is most important to success in O.B. Mod.

The trick, of course, is to identify those things that people find positively reinforcing, for as has been noted repeatedly, different people find different consequences reinforcing.

Identifying Reinforcers

How can we identify the consequences that particular individuals find positively reinforcing? Strictly speaking from an operant conditioning perspective, the only appropriate way is to conduct functional analyses of people's behavior: That is, to observe the antecedent conditions in which behaviors occur, the specific behaviors themselves, and the consequences of those behaviors, with a particular view to noticing increases or decreases in the frequencies of the behaviors of interest.

For example, if a manager notices that a particular employee engages in clown play when he has too little work to do (the antecedent condition), and that he seems to attract the attention and support of his coworkers when he does so, thereby increasing his propensity to act in such a manner (the reinforcement effect), the manager might infer that the individual's behavior can be influenced by the contingent application (or withdrawal) of interaction with his peers. That is, if social interaction is reinforcing to the employee, chances for social interaction might be adopted by the supervisor as a contingent consequence for encouraging the individual to perform tasks on the job. Just as we can observe the brand of beer people prefer at the pub when they are thirsty, so we can make inferences about the specific nature of other reinforcers of a particular individual's behavior.

In practice, however, it is not possible to observe all the consequences of every employee's acts, and to observe whether these consequences function to increase or decrease the occurrence of specific behaviors. Therefore, other means are more feasible and more frequently used to identify reinforcers. One method is simply to ask people what they desire from their work (recall our discussion of attitude surveys near the end of Chapter 7).

There are a variety of standardized instruments for inquiring about the types of thing people desire from their work. One of these is the *Minnesota importance questionnaire* (Gay, Weiss, Hendel, Dawis, & Lofquist, 1971). Another is referred to as the *job orientation inventory* (Blood, 1973). In common practice, however, employee attitude surveys normally feature a number of tailor-made questions pertaining to the types of potential reinforcer that may be more or less idiosyncratic to the organization involved.

A third approach to identifying reinforcers is through the use of trial and error: The manager simply tries a variety of outcomes contingent upon desired employee behavior and observes whether they actually function to reinforce (make more frequent) the behaviors in question. There are a wide variety of potential reinforcers in some organizations, while in others managers are limited by organizational policies, precedents, or formal agreements (such as union contracts) in the types of thing they can offer employees in return for behavior. Nevertheless, Luthans and Kreitner (1975) suggested several categories of potential reinforcer that might be available in practice. Their categories, with examples, are:

1. *Consumables*: Beer parties, Easter hams.
2. *Manipulatables*: Wall plaques, watches.
3. *Visual and auditory*: Piped-in music, redecoration of work environment.
4. *Tokens*: Money, stocks, vacation trips.
5. *Social*: Solicitations for suggestions, smiles.
6. *Activity based*: Job with more responsibility, time off work on a personal project with pay (recall the Premack principle).

The point is that there are a variety of outcomes creative supervisors might attempt to employ as reinforcers with their staffs, although in virtually all organizations there are constraints of one sort or another. But the desire is to find something positive rather than to rely on negative influences such as punishment or threat of punishment.

OB Mod and Work Motivation [8]

One of its leading proponents stated 20 years ago that the effect of OB mod on the organizational sciences had been "most apparent in the area of work motivation" (Komaki, 1986, p. 299). The most significant contribution, she claimed, was in the way her school of thought emphasized the antecedents and consequences of work performance. As we discussed earlier in this chapter:

> Antecedents are thought to function in an educational or cuing role. Instructions, rules, and goals, for example, are viewed as clarifying expectations for performance, specifying the relationship between behavior and its consequences, and/or signalling occasions in which consequences are likely to be provided contingent on behavior. Consequences, on the other hand, are thought to have the potential of increasing or decreasing the probability of behavior reoccurring.
>
> (Komaki, 1986, p. 300)

In fact, Komaki claimed that the unique feature of the OB mod approach to work motivation is that it places its emphasis on the events that occur *after* the individual's "target behavior." (By contrast, need theories rely on internal states that are operative before, during, and after behavior; expectancy valence models are concerned with prior expectations of a person's likely satisfaction after an act; and goal-setting theory hinges completely around forward-looking intentions.) As we saw earlier, the "consequences" available and useful in this school of thought are varied, although the ones most frequently used and mentioned are recognition, feedback, and incentives.

Earlier we mentioned the notion of antecedents and their role in cuing behavior. Komaki (1986) was careful to emphasize that although they do educate and cue people to act, adherents of OB mod "do not think they [antecedents] are primarily responsible for increasing or decreasing the probability of the behavior occurring again" (1986, p. 301). She cited a number of studies from the 1970s to bolster her point. The common thread among these studies was that antecedents alone were not sufficient either to induce desired employee behaviors (such as attendance or job performance) or to sustain improvements. In most or all cases, there had to be desirable consequences used, either alone or in conjunction with antecedent conditions.

A number of authors have provided reviews of OB mod and its putative value in understanding the management of work performance and a variety of other organizational outcomes, including absenteeism, employee safety, customer service, theft reduction, and the conservation of raw materials by employees (cf. Andrasik, 1979; Hamner & Hamner, 1976; Komaki, 1986; O'Hara et al., 1985; Stajkovic & Luthans, 1997; and, more recently, Stajkovic & Luthans, 2003).

---

[8] The reader is reminded that the terms *functional analysis*, *applied behavior analysis*, and *OB mod* are used interchangeably throughout this discussion.

Controversy and OB Mod

Of the theories of work motivation discussed in this book, Herzberg's two-factor model has doubtlessly been the most controversial (recall Chapter 2). Second in controversy, however, must be the theory and applications that originated with the application of operant psychology to organizations. Soon after the potential relevance of operant conditioning for understanding and managing organizations was first mentioned by Aldis (1961), Luthans and Kreitner (1975), Nord (1969), and others, there was a sequence of controversies ranging from the theoretical and the philosophical through to the operational and ethical. A complete exploration of these controversies was provided by this author (Pinder, 1984, 1998) so we will allude to them here only briefly.

Morality of control

One of the most common concerns directed at operant conditioning and behavior modification pertained to the ethics of controlling human behavior, and the allegation that to do so with the help of applied psychology is denigrating to human beings. Is it moral to apply techniques for the explicit purpose of influencing the behavior of other people? What about the sanctity of human nature and the freedom we have all fought to attain and protect? Who has the right to control another person's behavior, to determine what they can and cannot do?

Answers from the behaviorist camp generally took the following form. Because human behavior naturally can result in only one or more of three possible consequences – reinforcement, punishment, or extinction – all people are both conditioned and conditioners. In Skinner's own words: "We all control, and we are all controlled" (1953, p. 438). From the time we are born and begin to behave, we all find that our acts result in either positive or aversive consequences. The world is a giant Skinner box in which people formally and informally administer rewards and punishments to one another. Control is natural; it is unavoidable, constant, and ubiquitous. To deny that control is everywhere in nature is to ignore reality, so to refuse to exercise control is to defer it to others. So, how can there be organized work effort without some degree of formal control? Employees in a democratic society are free to come and go from one work setting to another, seeking levels of managerial control that are most comfortable, so we are collectively better off by consciously learning about and utilizing the laws of behavior to make life as safe and comfortable as possible (see Rogers & Skinner, 1956, for a classic debate on these issues).

Ethics of observation

A related ethical question concerns the observation of work behavior (Luthans & Kreitner, 1975). Is it ethical to monitor, sometimes surreptitiously, the work behavior of others, with a view either to measure it (for establishing a baseline before intervention) or to watch whether it changes in response to intervention? Still another question concerns whether it is possible to gain reliable measures of the work behavior of employees when they are aware that they are being measured (Whyte, 1972). Let's take these one at a time.

First, it is usually quite difficult in practice to gain realistic assessments of the work rate of employees when those employees realize they are being observed. This is especially so when the purpose of the observation is to set standards for performance and payment under piece-rate pay systems. Therefore, managers who desire to gain reliable information about the rates and levels of employee behavior and performance might benefit, in some settings, from the use of spy-like techniques. Moreover, defendants of OB mod have argued that if the benefit to be gained by the appropriate setting of standards and the fair monitoring of performance is to be conducive to employee welfare, then such observation is justified. In other words, these particular ends justify the means used, within reason, of course (see Luthans & Kreitner, 1975, p. 185). Besides, managers have always observed the work performance of their employees; OB mod merely formalizes the process, and employees should be made fully aware that their behavior will be monitored with a view to managing it.

Dehumanization

Another contentious issue arose from the fact that much of the research that leads to our knowledge of operant and respondent behavior had been conducted upon animals. Critics reacted negatively to the application of animal-based knowledge to human behavior – are we no better than, or different from, animals? Defendants of operant psychology recognized that human behavior is more complex than animal behavior, but argued that much of it is ultimately determined by similar underlying principles. Animals were used merely for the obvious reasons of humanity, cost, and convenience.

Non-rationality

A fourth fundamental attack on operant psychology pertained to the issue of human rationality. To claim that human behavior is merely a function of its consequences ignores the rational side of human nature, and with it, the free will that humans exercise. In other words, critics argued that people have consciousness and the capacity to think, reason, and choose among alternatives. While not denying the importance of the consequences of human acts, these critics proposed that Skinnerian psychology denied any role to human cognition, and thereby treated humans merely as automatons, or mindless creatures, without the capacity to behave with volition. Some critics argued that many of the claims of success made by proponents of behavior modification could be better explained by principles from goal-setting theory (e.g., Locke, 1977, 1978, 1979) – a strictly cognitive model of human functioning. Indeed, as we noted earlier, some modern adherents of behavior modification openly admitted the importance of rational processes (e.g., Craighead et al., 1976; Mahoney, 1974), while others retained the position that internal processes, such as cognition, are useless for understanding behavior: They cannot be observed or measured, so they certainly cannot be influenced (see Ford, 1992, for a review).

The point here is this: The radical behaviorist and cognitive/perceptual approaches constitute two incommensurate sets of fundamental beliefs regarding human nature. *In their pure forms*, they cannot be reconciled. By the same token, a few peacemakers proposed eclectic approaches, claiming that each of these perspectives had something to offer an understanding of human nature – neither is totally correct nor incorrect (e.g., Fedor & Ferris, 1981; Kreitner & Luthans, 1984; Walter & Marks, 1981). Further, it makes little difference to many people with purely applied intentions (such as parents, teachers, therapists, or managers), which theoretical model is being utilized. In fact, the early success of behavior modification techniques that utilized both behaviorist and cognitive concepts illustrates that the difference between the two points of view holds more importance for philosophy, religion, and bar room debate than it does for applied problem solving (cf. Bandura, 1977).

Other, practical criticisms of OB mod

Several other criticisms have been of a practical nature, dealing with the application of behavioral principles in real work settings. One concerned the problems of gaining reliable measurement, as we discussed. Another concerned the difficulty of determining what is reinforcing and punishing for particular employees, and then making it feasible to dispense these reinforcers in such a way that is economically viable and equitable. Another had to do with the heavy administrative procedures and red tape that often accompanies any form of organizational action.

Then there was the language that is used by both the interventionist and the employees involved. On the one hand, precision of communication is necessary in order for professionals to communicate effectively with one another. In fact, one proponent alleged that operant terminology had been particularly subject to misuse and misinterpretation (Mawhinney, 1975). On the other hand, excessive jargon and the use of buzzwords can alienate employees and managers whose cooperation is essential for the success of programs (Murphy & Remnyi, 1979). OB mod had a lingo all of its own, causing it to be rejected by many practitioners.

Still another practical issue concerned the time that is granted by management for change to occur and manifest itself. Management groups are reinforced to participate in enlightened managerial techniques when they show a payoff (especially in dollar terms). Yet because of the many complexities of the dynamics in organizations, positive results sometimes take a while to become evident. While this problem is not unique to applications of OB mod, they certainly do apply to them.

Some early critics claimed that behavior modification proved to be much more effective in settings where the interventionist held a position of high authority and control over those whose behavior was to be modified, as is the case, for example, in prisons, mental institutions, and even school settings (Argyris, 1971). The control over outside influences that can interfere with the strict application of the measurement, reinforcement, and punishment of behavior in these types of setting is most similar to that which is possible in the laboratory settings in which the principles of operant psychology were first developed. But when these techniques were taken to actual work settings in organizations that featured constraints such as traditions, suspicions, unions, budgets, and impatient management groups, they were much less easy to install and make effective (see Murphy & Remnyi, 1979; O'Hara et al., 1985; Repucci & Saunders, 1974).

The Decline of the Behaviorist Camp

It is not hard to find published statements declaring that behaviorism is on the decline in the organizational sciences, but the following observation illustrates the trend and the status of behaviorism (or reinforcement theory) by the late 1980s: "Reinforcement theory, with its emphasis on external incentives and behavioral learning, has been overtaken by goal-setting approaches in which salient outcomes serve as mental targets for behavior" (Staw & Boettger, 1990, p. 534).

At the time of the current writing, radical behaviorism is virtually gone from the organizational sciences. Indeed, in a recent review of the previous three decades of research and theory on work motivation, this author and Dr. Gary Latham mentioned the behaviorist tradition only in passing (Latham & Pinder, 2005, p. 502). The fundamental rejection of behaviorism is reflected in the following quotation from Albert Bandura, one of the most influential scholars in the cognitive camp:

> If human behavior were regulated solely by external outcomes, people would behave like weather vanes, constantly shifting direction to conform to whatever momentary social influence happened to impinge upon them. In actuality, people possess self-reflective and self-reactive capabilities that enable them to exercise some control over their thoughts, feelings, motivation, and actions. In the exercise of self-directedness, people adopt certain standards of behavior that serve as guides and motivators and regulate their actions anticipatorily through self-reactive influence. Human functioning is, therefore, regulated by an interplay of self-generated and external sources of influence.
>
> (Bandura, 1991, p. 249)

Even passionate advocates of OB mod such as Kreitner and Luthans (1984), for example, acknowledged more than two decades ago that the "pendulum" had swung back and forth in the discipline, starting with a preponderance of attention on internal forces such as needs and beliefs, then moving sharply away from internal states to a focus on the consequences of behavior, then settling back in a sort of compromise position, which they referred to as social-cognitive theory (which we will study shortly).

In view of the moribund state of OB mod, the reader may understandably ask why we have included it in this book. The answer is that, as Kreitner and Luthans (1984) observed with their pendulum metaphor, and as we have seen in the cases of other theories throughout this book, theories morph and evolve (recall from Chapter 11 how equity theory was subsumed as part of the broader body of theories related to workplace justice). To write about the broad landscape of work motivation intelligently, this author believes that the historical roots of many theories currently in fashion must be recognized, particularly the central role that learning, per se, plays in these models. We have seen that learning, both direct and personal as well as vicarious learning, plays a central role in many organizational phenomena, such as goal setting, the dynamics of VIE theory, punishment and justice phenomena, and others. Finally, as mentioned earlier, many of the applied implications of the OB mod tradition can still be of value to managers and administrators, who care less about the theoretical and philosophical underpinnings of managerial practices than do academics. For example, Welsh, Luthans, and Sommer (1993) demonstrated the effectiveness of their approach in improving job performance among a sample of 33 Russian textile workers.

Recent reviews of the literature by Stajkovic and Luthans (1997, 2001, 2003) have reminded us of the value of thinking of the consequences of employee behavior as a major determinant of the form, intensity, direction, and continuation of that behavior. Setting aside all the philosophical differences, conceptual baggage, and ideological squabbles the field has witnessed since the early emergence of operant principles on the management scene (cf. Aldis, 1961), one fact concerning human behavior and organizational behavior is obvious: Consequences do matter.

SOCIAL-COGNITIVE THEORY

One of the most dominant and successful bodies of theory in understanding of work motivation and behavior to emerge over the past 30 years is social-cognitive theory (SCT) (Latham & Pinder, 2005). The primary champion of this school is and has been Albert Bandura of Stanford University. At its core, SCT is a theory of human *agency*. Bandura (2001, p. 2) wrote:

> To be an agent is to intentionally make things happen by one's actions. Agency embodies the endowments, belief systems, self-regulatory capabilities and distributed structures and functions through which personal influence [sic] exercised, rather than residing as a discrete entity in a particular place. The core features of agency enable people to play a part in their self development, adaptation, and self-renewal with changing times.

Bandura's theory is (cf. 1977, 2001), in large part, a response to (and rejection of) the behaviorist mentality that dominated psychology for so many years, as we have detailed earlier. Here is how Kreitner and Luthans (1984, p. 54) described the emergence of "social learning theory" (now called social-cognitive theory):[9]

> When Albert Bandura, Stanford's noted behavioral psychologist, was conducting his pioneering experiments on vicarious learning, he became convinced that cognitive functioning must not be overlooked in explaining complex human behavior. He observed that mental cues and memory aids help people learn and retain behavior more effectively than trial-and-error shaping. This challenged operant conditioning as well as radical behaviorism. A practical example of Bandura's position is the salesperson who relies on a mental image of an apple to remember Applegate, the name of a prospective client. In Bandura's view, this way of learning is more efficient than rote memorization of clients' names in a structured training session. But, *unlike the radical cognitive theorists, Bandura gives a great deal of weight to the impact of environmental cues and consequences on actual behavior* [emphasis added].

---

[9] Bandura (1986, p. xii) explained that social learning theory was the name usually given to his early work, but that subtle similarities and differences with other bodies of thought required him to relabel it *social-cognitive theory*: "The social portion of the terminology acknowledges the social origins of much human thought and action; the cognitive portion recognizes the influential causal contribution of thought processes to human motivation, affect, and action."

The Flow of Causality

Whereas most previous theories of human behavior have placed their primary emphases either on internal personal states (such as needs, values, beliefs, or perceptions) or on external environmental conditions (such as antecedents and/or consequences), SCT:

> [E]xplains psychosocial functioning in terms of triadic reciprocal causation ... In this model of reciprocal determinism, behavior, cognitive, and other personal factors and environmental events operate as interacting determinants that influence each other bi-directionally.
>
> (Wood & Bandura, 1989, p. 362)

This triangular relationship is shown in Figure 14.1. What is crucial about this three-way model is that it recognizes that people can have some control over their destinies while, at the same time, the environment sets limits on what is possible (Bandura, 1986, p. xi). The model places heavy emphasis on human thought processes, as is the case with goal-setting theory. Hence, it differs markedly from the behaviorist perspectives discussed earlier in this chapter. Yet this is a theory of learning and one that has been influenced by the powerful roles played by environmental factors – two reasons why it is being presented at this point in the current volume.

Bandura (1986) claimed that because the person, the behavior, and the environment all interact in a series of two-way (or dyadic) interactions, it does not follow that all three sets of factors are of equal importance:

> Reciprocity does not mean symmetry in the strength of bidirectional influences. Nor is the patterning and strength of mutual influences fixed in reciprocal causation. The relative influence exerted by the three sets of interacting factors will vary for different activities, different individuals, and different circumstances. When environmental conditions exercise powerful constraints on behavior, they emerge as the overriding determinants ... There are times when behavior and its intrinsic feedback are the central factors in the interacting system. One example of this would be persons who play the piano for their own enjoyment ... When situational constraints are weak, personal factors serve as the predominant influence in the regulatory system. In deciding what novel to check out from vast library holdings, people's preferences hold sway.
>
> (Bandura, 1986, p. 24)

Simple or Complex Solutions?

On this view, then, it is overly simplistic to accept simple answers to organizational behavior (or human behavior in any context) that rely exclusively on internal human causes.

Consider the following, apparently simple question and the answers it might generate.

Q "Why did Alice join the Navy?"
A "She wanted to see the world."

Inherent in this answer is reference to a set of needs and possibly a set of expectancies. Left out of the analysis is any mention of how the environment might have influenced Alice's decision.

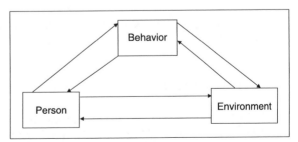

FIG. 14.1 Three-way causal relationships in social cognitive theory.

Source: Adapted from Bandura, A. (1986). *Social foundations of thought and action: A social cognitive theory.* Upper Saddle River, NJ: Prentice-Hall.

For example, has recent Navy policy opened new opportunities for women? Or: What might be the effect of Alice's (and other women's) joining of the Navy? The Tailhook incident of 1994 reminds us that women and men may still expect substantially different experiences in the Navy. Can we seriously stop the answer to our question about Alice joining the Navy with reference to the environment (such as the policies and procedures for the treatment of women sailors in the Navy (i.e, the environment)? No, not according to social-cognitive theory: The environment might have helped to induce Alice's behavior, which, in turn, may affect that environment (suppose Alice became a ranking naval officer and was able to enact new naval policy about hazing activities?).

The one-way causality offered by behaviorism was much easier than all of this: People respond to environmental cues and are reinforced, punished, or ignored for their responses. But it is the environment that matters – the individuals involved are incidental. On the other hand, what about simple, single-cause answers that make reference only to internal personal factors (e.g., "Alice had strong needs for competence and perceived that joining the Navy would help her satisfy those needs")? They are a lot more manageable than gross sets of three factors, interacting in dyadic relationships, two at a time. But are simple, one-way causal models realistic?

Bandura (1986) offered another example of how three-way relationships between a person (and his internal dynamics), his behavior, and the environment all interact: It is an example that most readers of this book will recognize – watching television:

> Personal preferences influence when and which programs, from among the available alternatives, individuals choose to watch on television ... Although the potential televised environment is identical for all viewers, their actual televised environment depends upon what they choose to watch. Through their viewing behavior, they partly shape the nature of the future televised environment. Because production costs and commercial requirements also determine what people are shown ... the options provided in the televised environment partly shape the viewers' preferences. Here, all three factors – viewer preferences, viewing behavior, and televised offerings – reciprocally affect each other. What people watch exerts some influence on their preferences, thoughts, and actions.
>
> (Bandura, 1986, p. 24)

The Social Factor

SCT also places heavy emphasis on the social origins of thought. As we have seen repeatedly throughout this book, people are significantly influenced by the thoughts, beliefs, values, and actions of others around them. We also learn much of what we know vicariously – by observation of the events affecting other people and by identifying with their outcomes in life. Self-regulation is also important. People set goals and behave in ways intended to achieve their goals, monitoring their progress as they go along, adapting and changing their behaviors as the feedback they receive suggests. The reader should see communalities here with goal-setting theory and control theory, as presented in Chapter 13.

The Environment in Social-Cognitive Theory

What is the role of the environment? Whereas behaviorism holds that environmental contingencies are all-important causes of behavior, Bandura's school of thought tempers that view:

> External events may create the occasion for doing something, but, except in simple reflexive acts, they are not the originators of affect and action. External stimuli give rise to courses of action through personal agency.
>
> (Bandura, 1986, p. 12)

Thus, fortuity becomes an interesting phenomenon. Unlike a slavish, deterministic model by which people's behaviors and their fortunes are mechanically dictated by circumstances, the agentic model recognizes that the world flows and offers opportunities and constraints but that people regularly exercise their judgment, their goals, their creativity, their skills and intentions to make whatever they wish to make of the circumstances provided by the environment. "The power of most fortuitous influences lies not so much in the properties of the events themselves, but in the constellation of transactional influences they set in motion . . . People also make chance work for them by cultivating their interests, enabling self-beliefs and competencies" (Bandura, 2001, p. 12).

In other words, people may elect to apply their own skills and abilities when their surroundings present them with opportunities to do so. The notion of triadic causality enters here. People are not assumed to be autonomous agents nor mechanical conveyers of environmental forces. "Rather, they serve as a reciprocally contributing influence to their own motivation and behavior within a system of reciprocal causation involving personal determinants, action, and environmental factors" (p. 12). Moreover, the environment does not influence people's behavior in some sort of mechanical, direct manner; rather, the individual's perceptual and thought processes mediate the impact of the environment: A person may not notice information from her environment and, even if she does, she may or may not elect to act on the basis of that information. "During transactions with their environment, people are not merely emitting responses and experiencing outcomes. They form beliefs from observed regularities about the outcomes likely to result from actions in given situations and regulate their behavior accordingly" (1986, p. 13). In short (Bandura, 1986, p. 15):

> A theory that denies that thoughts can regulate actions does not lend itself readily to the explanation of complex human behavior. Although cognitive determinants are disavowed by radical behaviorism, their causal contributions cannot be excised all that easily. Therefore, adherents of radical behaviorism translate cognitive determinants into stimulus operations, move them outside the organism, and then ascribe their effects to the direct action of the externally relocated events . . . In fact, it is people's knowledge of their environment, not the stimuli, that is changed by correlated experience. Thus, for example, if a given word foreshadows physically painful stimulation, the word assumes predictive significance for the individual, not the painful properties of the physical stimuli.

It seems almost strange that such an obvious point must be asserted, but its necessity at the time, 20 years ago, speaks to the strength of the grip behaviorism once had on modern psychology and the attendant influence it still has on work motivation theory and research.

Distinctively Human Capabilities

In one of his most expansive statements of his theory, Bandura (1986) listed and documented the arguments in favor of a variety of human *capabilities* – inherent features of our humanity that were either ignored or denied by radical behaviorism. These capabilities are self-evident once they are identified but, again, it seems that someone had to describe these human dimensions explicitly in order to foster a shift away from a simplistic, mechanistic psychology of environmental determinism to one that recognized the self-starting, intellective nature of homo sapiens.

The most important of these capabilities for permitting Bandura (1986) to advance his theoretical model are the following: Anticipation and the capacity to form expectations; the capacity to symbolize – to form, manipulate, interpret, and communicate symbols and through symbols; the capacity to learn vicariously rather than only through personal experience; the capacity to self-regulate; and the capacity to reflectively think about one's self. We will briefly look at each of these human capabilities, one at a time.

Anticipation and forethought capability

People form expectancies about the *likely* consequences of their acts, not simply or primarily from the real consequences of those acts. "The notion that consequences influence behavior fares better for anticipated than for actual consequences" (p. 13). The idea of anticipated consequences plays a key role in the cognitively based VIE theory presented in Chapter 12 of this volume. So, in order to know how and whether outcomes will influence a person's behavior, we need to know how the person's cognitive apparatus processes these outcomes. Hence, Bandura rejected the simple, mechanical notion from behaviorism, that "reinforcers" are the primary determinants of individual behavior. He also rejected the necessity of antecedent stimuli by citing work that shows that people are quite able to generate their own thoughts and emotions, not requiring features of their immediate environments to do so.

Symbolizing capability

It bears repeating that this is a thinking person's theory of human behavior, although it does not imply that all behavior results from rational thought, clear thinking, or objective rationality. Biases abound, mistakes are made and human mental aptitudes are not always well developed. Nevertheless, one major implication of this assumption is the observation that people formulate and make use of symbols in their everyday lives, and that symbolic action and the interpretation of symbols are critical in understanding behavior. "Through symbols people process and transform transient experiences into internal models that serve as guides for future action. Through symbols they similarly give meaning, form, and continuance to the experiences they have lived through" (1986, p. 18). People can use these symbols (including scripts and schemas, for example) to devise innovative ways of acting. People are capable of "playing out" scenarios in their minds, imagining the likely consequences of various forms of action. "Through the medium of symbols, [people] can communicate with others at almost any distance in time and space" (Bandura, 1986, pp. 18–19).

Vicarious learning capability

People are capable of learning a great deal via the experiences of other people. In fact, "virtually all learning phenomena, resulting from direct experience, can occur vicariously by observing other people's behavior and the consequences for them" (Bandura, 1986, p. 19). This human capacity is one is of the most important recognized by social-cognitive theory, one of the tenets that makes it so much more realistic than radical behaviorism as a theory of human learning. Individuals and entire species might vanish if it were necessary for every one of us to learn how to deal with the world by trial and error.

Self-regulatory capability

Several times in this book, we have touched upon the human desire for free will, self-determination, and individual freedom. Aside from a desire to be in command of our own acts, human history shows that we have considerable ability to be self-determining, for good or for bad. Nevertheless, one of the key capabilities that Bandura attributed to human nature is the capacity and the desire for what he calls *self-regulation*. "People do not behave just to suit the preferences of others. Much of their behavior is motivated and regulated by internal standards and self-evaluative reactions to their own actions" (1986, p. 20). Considerably more will be stated about self-regulation shortly, particularly in the context of work motivation. Hence we will not dwell on it here.

Self-reflective capability

Bandura (1986) stated: "If there is any characteristic that is distinctively human, it is the capability for reflective self-consciousness. This enables people to analyze their experiences and to think about their own thought processes. By reflecting on their varied experiences and on what they know, they can derive generic knowledge about themselves and the world around them" (p. 21).

Among the types of self-reflection that Bandura considers the most important are the thoughts people have about their own abilities to engage in tasks. We have touched on this notion of self-efficacy at several points in this book: The reader is referred to Chapters 6, 7, 12, and 13 as well as to a later section of the current chapter for treatments of the topic. For our purposes here, the following should suffice: People will be more or less likely to take on tasks, set goals, alter goals, and attempt to master their environments if they positively assess their own capabilities vis-à-vis the world. Lacking self-efficacy beliefs would be terminal because people would be afraid to undertake any action. Overestimating their beliefs about self-efficacy can also have its problems in cases where people place themselves in situations in which they are doomed to fail. Whether our self-reflective beliefs are accurate or inaccurate, the point is that we all spend time thinking about ourselves, our thoughts, emotions, experiences, and desires. This trait makes us particularly human. It is not that behaviorists denied that we had the capacity to think, self-reflect, and emote; they merely denied the importance of these characteristics and processes as causes of human behavior.

Intentionality

Almost implicitly as we consider these other human dimensions of human agency is the concept of intentionality. Intentionality is antithetical, by definition, from a deterministic mindset. It is clear that people form intentions and behave on them, as we saw at length in several earlier chapters of this book (e.g., Chapters 11, 12, and 13, in particular). The point is obvious.

Summary

For Bandura (1986), a defining characteristic of humans is our almost limitless plasticity – our capacity to change ourselves and to be changed, within biological limits. The most important elements of human nature that form a pattern in his model of human functioning are our mental ones – our capacity to think, to plan, to make and use symbols, and our capacity to learn vicariously. It is not that Bandura believes that these mental skills give homo sapiens total hegemony over the world; he does not. He simply gives us, as individuals, much more credit for our capacity to initiate action, to plan our own destinies, to locate ourselves in environments of our open choice and our own making than did the behaviorists who immediately preceded him in the history of modern psychology.

SOCIAL-COGNITIVE THEORY AND WORK MOTIVATION

Wood and Bandura (1989) stated that three aspects of SCT have particular relevance for understanding work behavior. The first relates to the development of people's cognitive, social, and behavioral competencies at work through "master modeling." This has to do with the way people can learn from one another in work settings by observing what other people do (and do not do) and then observing the consequences of those acts. It is not necessary for a newcomer to an organization, for example, to park his car mistakenly in the president's spot in order to learn that this is a "no-no."

This lesson can be learned quite well by witnessing what happens to coworkers who do the same thing.

A second area of relevance of SCT for organizational behavior is "the cultivation of people's beliefs in their capabilities so that they will use their talents effectively" (Wood & Bandura, 1989, p. 362). This has to do with the *development* of self-efficacy beliefs. A third area of direct relevance to us here is the enhancement of people's motivation through personal goal systems (Wood & Bandura, 1989, p. 362). We will focus our attention here on the second and third areas of particular value of social-cognitive theory for work motivation: Self-efficacy and goal systems. We have encountered both of these concepts before, so our treatment here will be brief.

Building Self-Efficacy

We have encountered this concept many times throughout this book, beginning in Chapter 6. The reader is reminded here that self-efficacy:

> [C]oncerns people's beliefs in their capacities to mobilize the motivation, cognitive resources, and courses of action needed to exercise control over events in their lives. There is a difference between possessing skills and being able to use them well and consistently under difficult circumstances. To be successful, one must not only possess the required skills, but also a resilient self-belief in one's capabilities to exercise control over events to accomplish desired goals. People with the same skills may, therefore, perform poorly, adequately, or extraordinarily, depending on whether their self-beliefs of efficacy enhance or impair their motivation and problem-solving efforts.
>
> (Wood & Bandura, 1989, p. 364)

In short, people's self-efficacy beliefs will determine their levels of motivation, which, as we have defined it throughout this book, entails which tasks they undertake, how difficult a goal they will pursue, how much effort they will spend on the task, and how long they will persist in the face of failure or incompletion. A recent study demonstrated, for example, how self-efficacy beliefs mediated the relationship between three personality variables (self-esteem, proactive personality, and conscientiousness), on the one hand, and job search effort, job search behavior, and job search outcomes, on the other (Brown, Cober, Kane, Levy, & Shalhoop, 2006).

Now the question becomes: What determines the strength of self-efficacy beliefs, given that they are so critical for determining the likelihood that a person will undertake tasks? There are four principal ways that efficacy beliefs can be instilled. The first is through "mastery experiences" – performing a task well reinforces a person's belief that she can, in fact, do certain tasks as well as others like it. A second mechanism building self-efficacy beliefs is modeling, which we have mentioned earlier: People learn a great deal by watching others, imitating them, and deriving vicarious rewards and punishments from the consequences of other people's actions.

A third mechanism building self-efficacy is through *social persuasion*. This means having people encourage one another to do well and having other people assign us to tasks that will be challenging yet manageable. The individual does not want to be induced into failure situations that will damage self-efficacy. Encouragements they receive should be realistic. The successes that follow should be against one's own goals, rather than through triumphs over other people (Wood & Bandura, 1989). Finally, people pay attention to their own physical and mental health and fitness. "They read their emotional arousal and tension as signs of vulnerability to poor performance. In activities involving strength and stamina, people judge their fatigue, aches, and pains as signs of physical incapacity" (p. 365). So the fourth way that people can enhance their self-efficacy beliefs is by building their strength levels, reducing stress, and making the most of whatever bad news they receive about their limitations.

Over the years, a number of scholars have addressed the apparent similarity between self-efficacy and other cognitive constructs (such as trait self-esteem or generalized self-efficacy that is a global trait, independent of specific tasks (e.g., Chen, Gully, & Eden, 2004, who have developed a scale of generalized self-efficacy). These other constructs have their roots in theories other than SCT, but they also purport to deal with the issue of people's beliefs about whether they can perform a task, do a job, or reach a goal. We examined this issue in Chapter 6, so we will not dwell on it here. Recall, briefly, however, that self-esteem refers to an individual's degree of liking or disliking of himself or herself – the typical level of self-evaluation the person holds, across time and contexts. Self-efficacy, by contrast, is concerned with the individual's beliefs about whether she or he can execute the behaviors necessary for success in a specific situation (Bandura, 1977). Therefore, it is possible for an individual to have either high or low trait self-esteem while having high or low self-efficacy beliefs in relation to a particular task. In regard to the notion of a concept such as generalized self-efficacy, as proposed by a number of authors such as Chen et al. (2004), Bandura's position is that:

> There is no all-purpose specific self-efficacy scale. It is a contradiction in terms. Specific scales are tailored to particular domains of functioning. An already developed specific scale is usable in other studies only if the activity domain is the same as the one on which the scale was developed.
> (Personal correspondence between Bandura and Latham, cited by Latham & Pinder, 2005, p. 503)

For this author, the specificity requirement may be scientifically valid and therefore justified for research and theory purposes – indeed, there is considerable research evidence that it is (see a meta-analysis by Stajkovic & Luthans, 1998). In such a case, this same specificity makes the construct limiting and perhaps less useful than a more pan-context construct might be (cf. Miner, 2003; and recall Chapter 2 of this book). Presumably, gradients associated with stimulus generalization and response generalization, as discussed earlier in the present chapter, pertain: The gradations of similarity among various forms of human activity can be major or minor, so that the skills learned at one task can frequently be transferred to the successful performance at other tasks and the self-efficacy beliefs a person has in relation to the first task could be expected to correlate with those she holds in relation to the second.

Is high self-efficacy always desirable? Whyte, Saks, and Hook (1997) have suggested that high levels may be dysfunctional for people who are pursuing a losing course of action. Using a business decision-making simulation with graduate students as research participants, these researchers manipulated the apparent success of "decision makers" who had the option of committing more resources to failing courses of action (in order to turn them around) or to withhold further investment; that is, to put a halt to throwing "good money after bad." The researchers also used four different techniques to manipulate participants' beliefs about their self-efficacy for the task(s) involved. (They created three self-efficacy groups: High, low, and a control group.) As hypothesized, students with high-task self-efficacy invested more than control participants, and low-task self-efficacy students invested less than the control participants. Self-esteem was not correlated with the escalation/de-escalation dependent variable, consistent with Bandura's (1977) belief that self-esteem and task-specific self-efficacy are distinct constructs.

Group-Level Applications of SCT

SCT has long recognized that human agency can be exercised in at least three ways: Directly, by the individuals involved, in command of their own goals, beliefs, and values; through proxy measures, by which, for example, we delegate responsibility for getting things done for us by others (such as governments, parents, institutions, spouses, and lawyers, for example); and (3) collectively, meaning through the concerted organization of groups in which individuals deliberately form alliances (teams, work groups, clubs, etc.) to exercise their agency. To this point, we have primarily focused on the first of these three approaches to human agency – actions by individuals.

Recently, attempts have been made to apply variants of social-cognitive theory to group-level performance. Bandura (1997, p. 477) defined group efficacy as "a group's shared belief in its conjoint capabilities to organize and execute the courses of action required to produce given levels of attainments."

In one study, for example, Prussia and Kinicki (1996) examined the role of groups' affective reactions to their own performance accomplishments, group-level goals, and group-level feelings of "efficacy" on task performance. They found that two of the three factors (group-level affect and efficacy) mediated the relationships between feedback and exposure of the groups to films from which they could model effective behavior. Individual motivation also played a role. Interestingly, group-level goals did not have the sort of effects that individual-level goal-setting theory would have predicted. In a more recent study, high school students participated in three-person and seven-person groups in a money-making task. Among the results was a positive correlation between the groups' efficacy for making money with the actual amount of money they earned. In addition, there were stronger relationships reported between group efficacy and group performance than between aggregated values of individual efficacy (among the individual members of each group) and the groups' performance (Seijts, Latham, & Whyte, 2000).

These preliminary results were interesting, although researchers must exercise caution in the ways by which they "translate" individual phenomena into group-level constructs. As Bandura himself (2001, p. 14) put it:

> There is no emergent entity that operates independently of the beliefs and actions of the individuals who make up a social system. It is people acting conjointly on a shared belief, not a disembodied group mind that is doing the cognizing, aspiring, motivating and regulating.[10]

Summary on SCT

In the foregoing sections, we have summarized social-cognitive theory, showing how it emerged from the behaviorism of the 1950s and 1960s, evolving from the application of behavior modification and OB mod in the 1970s, acquiring and admitting cognitive elements as the decades passed. In its current form, SCT is an eclectic theory of human behavior that has subsumed most of the wisdom and contributions offered by these earlier approaches and has, in addition, picked up other useful concepts from cybernetics and goal-setting theory. We adopted an historical approach in this chapter to permit the reader to appreciate the origins of SCT, revealing how it contains and has adapted so many concepts that we have encountered under the umbrellas of other schools of thought. It is critical to see how behaviorism contributed to the blend: Whereas behaviorism may be moribund these days in its pure form, there is no doubt that it contributed, both directly and affirmatively, but also through the backlash that it generated among its critics.

In summary, as noted by Latham and Pinder (2005), we conclude that social-cognitive theory (SCT):

> [S]hows empirically that the effect of environmental antecedents and consequences are mediated by cognitive variables. SCT emphasizes dual control systems in the regulation of motivation, namely a proactive discrepancy production system that works in concert with a reactive discrepancy reduction system ... Thus, people are motivated by the foresight of goals, not just by the hindsight of shortfalls ... Upon goal attainment, people with high self-efficacy set an even higher goal because this creates new motivating discrepancies to be mastered. If the goal is not attained, self-efficacy and goal commitment predict whether people redouble their effort, react apathetically, or become despondent.

(Latham & Pinder, 2005, p. 503)

---

[10] Caution on this point has often been disregarded in the organizational and social sciences, even though scholars (e.g., Katz & Kahn, 1966) have been aware of the issue for years. See Klein et al. (2001) for a thorough discussion.

Indeed, as summarized briefly by Bandura (2001), SCT and the notions of human agency that lie at its core have proven useful in understanding human behavior, including success and failure, in a variety of human and social arenas, such as health, careers, educational achievement and – for our purposes in this book – organizational behavior, work motivation, and job performance.

We will close this chapter by a study of self-regulation, a body of applied techniques that is based upon SCT (and therefore upon elements of goal-setting theory), OB mod, and even control theory (recall Chapter 13).

SELF-REGULATION

One of the most fruitful applications of psychology to everyday life over the past quarter-century has been in the area known as *self-regulation*. In brief, self-regulation is a set of principles and practices by which people monitor their own behaviors and *consciously* adjust those behaviors in pursuit of personal goals.[11] It is a process in which a person consciously elects to behave in ways that, otherwise, he would be less likely to behave (Mills, 1983; Thoresen & Mahoney, 1974). It is a set of techniques that have firm footings in goal-setting theory, social-cognitive theory, and OB mod. In a nutshell, the person learns to recognize situations in which her habits may not serve her best interest, and to select non-habitual options that may even be unpleasant or unfamiliar for her in order to bring about better long-term conditions.

For example, the author may (still) routinely tune into the television program *Law and Order* after dinner on week nights, stretching out on his favorite sofa. Self-management in this case would occasion his continuing to recognize that this comfortable habit is likely less desirable than other ways of spending the evening, such as reading the newspaper, going for a swim, or visiting a friend. Usually, self-management is accompanied by small rewards and punishments that the individual applies or removes after he successfully engages in a consciously selected act that is an alternative to the most probable, habitual one.

Self-management can also entail considerable planning that removes or makes more difficult habitual options: Moving the television set to a drafty basement would continue our example. Most of us have witnessed the attempts that smokers make to kick their habit: They stop purchasing cigarettes, they attempt to eschew others who smoke (except when they want to "borrow" cigarettes), they avoid drinking beverages that have been associated in the past with smoking, and so on. If they succeed and are practicing self-regulation, they may reward themselves by consuming something special (other than tobacco smoke) or by engaging in a favorite activity such as going bowling (now that most public indoor places prohibit smoking!).

Origins and Sources of Self-Regulation Concepts

As might be surmised from the foregoing examples, self-regulation owes much of its history and current status to clinical psychology.[12] In fact, Latham and Locke (1991) and others such as Tsui and Ashford (1994) credit clinical psychologist Frederick Kanfer for his seminal contributions, although Kanfer (1970) himself observed that 4000 years ago, Homer:

> [R]eported some good advice for exercise of self-control through the admonitions of Circe to the sea faring Odysseus. To prevent the disastrous exposure to the bewitching songs of the Sirens, Odysseus

---

[11] Consciousness (cf. Bandura, 2001) is a defining element of self-regulation. Hence any model of human nature or epistemology that denies or does not rely on human consciousness is alien to these principles.
[12] See Pervin (1991) for some examples of self-regulation in the context of compulsions and addictions.

was warned to plug his oarsmens' ears with soft beeswax. For his own control, he let himself be tied to the mast after cautioning the crew not to release him, "shout as he may, begging to be untied."

(Kanfer, 1970, pp. 412–413)

As suggested earlier, self-regulation has been applied in a variety of other human settings and to a number of other human problems, such as personality and social psychology, abnormal psychology and psychotherapy, self-administered health proscriptions (e.g., Bachlin, 2000), and education and learning, to mention a few (Karoly, 1993). In the clinical literature, self-regulation has been referred to as *self-management*, while in the organizational sciences it has also been labeled self-leadership, self-influence, self-management, self-control, and even "substitutes for leadership" (Mills, 1983).[13] Regardless of what it is called, the common feature of these techniques is that "the same person is both object and subject, both the doer and the target of the action" (Kanfer, 1970, p. 412). Our discussions of goal-setting theory and control theory in Chapter 13 and of social-cognitive theory earlier in this chapter will make the following description of self-regulation both familiar and possibly obvious to the reader. The essence of self-regulation is found in the concepts of establishing and planning goals, striving to meet those goals, revising them once achieved (or not), and paying attention to feedback (Kanfer, 2005; Locke & Latham, 2004). Self-efficacy also plays a key role throughout the cycle.

A Formal Definition of Self-Regulation

Karoly (1993, p. 25) defined self-regulation as:

> [T]hose processes, internal and/or transactional, that enable an individual to guide his/her goal-directed activities over time and across changing circumstances (contexts). Regulation implies modulation of thought, affect, behavior, or attention via deliberate or automated use of specific mechanisms and supportive meta-skills. The processes of self-regulation are initiated when routinized activity is impeded or when goal-directedness is otherwise made salient (e.g., the appearance of a challenge, the failure of habitual action patterns, etc.). Self-regulation may be said to encompass up to five interrelated and iterative component phases: 1. goal selection, 2. goal cognition, 3. directional maintenance, 4. directional change or reprioritization, and 5, goal termination.[14]

Self-regulation procedures are intended to maximize the long-term interests of the individual, frequently through simply following rules, delaying gratification, and resisting impulses to act in ways that have become habituated and, in many cases, bad for them (Bachlin, 2000). The many affective, behavioral, and cognitive facets are deliberately undertaken and require energy, volition, and purpose. Indeed, one school of thought (cf. Muraven & Baumeister, 2000) believes that, subject to individual differences, people have finite amounts of *self-control strength* and that this pool of energy can be depleted with use but then replenished – much as a muscle can become tired and of limited use until it is rested to be used again This implies that, in the short term, at least, people can be expected to control their natural and learned impulses only within certain limits, although it is possible that those limits may be increased over time.

---

[13] Manz (1986) provided one of the earliest explications of self-regulation for understanding organizational behavior.

[14] Here is another example in the literature where different terms have been used to represent the same concept or process, or in which a given term may refer to two or more concepts or techniques. This point has been made in several places throughout this book. The term *self-management* in the context of organizational behavior and management has been used by authors such as de Waele, Morval, & Sheitoyan (1992) to refer to a broad set of strategies and tactics that a person might employ to assure that she takes advantage of opportunities to advance her career on an ongoing basis and in a proactive manner rather than allow external events to determine her fate. This is a different use of the phrase "self-management" from the one we are dealing with here.

Self-Regulation, Intrinsic Motivation, and Free Will

In many ways, the goal and gist of self-regulation is similar – perhaps even identical – to the notion of self-determination that we examined in Chapter 3 of this book: The core idea is that people have an innate *need* to be self-determining, to control their own behaviors, to affect their environments, and to be efficacious in those environments. People are driven to be captains of their own ships, masters of their own souls. Binswanger (1991, p. 154) put it this way:

> Since regulation requires the expenditure of energy, self-regulation implies that the entity has its own energy source, one built into its structure. Its self-regulation is accomplished by using this energy source to initiate and steer its own behavior. An entity that is simply pushed and pulled about by external forces is clearly not regulating its motion. When a planet orbits a star, there is no self-regulation because the motion is the direct result of the sum of the external forces operating.

Thus, self-regulation is really no more than a set of techniques that is based on scientifically valid-ated concepts of goal setting and feedback that enable a person to achieve hegemony over her own behaviors, circumstances, and fate. It is a technology designed to utilize what Deci and others (Deci, 1975; Deci & Ryan, 1985) refer to as *intrinsic motivation* (also see Hyland, 1988). Even more so, self-regulation can be seen as a modern behavioral technology intended for humans to pursue the age-old values of *free will* (Karoly, 1993) and it draws heavily on the precepts of agency that lie at the core of SCT (Bandura, 2001), as we discussed earlier in this chapter.

Elements of the Self-Regulation Process

First is the business of goal selection. A defining characteristic of self-regulation, in fact, is that the individual sets his own goals (unlike much of the work done in the goal-setting tradition in which people have their goals set for them or in which they determine their goals jointly with others). So, an individual adopts some goal for himself to accomplish over a set period of time. These goals may be *performance goals* (such as accomplishing so much work in a given period of time) or they may be *learning and mastery goals* (such as acquiring a new set of skills – recall Chapter 13).

For example, a new employee may set mastery goals such as becoming acquainted with the major customers of his new employer within his first 6 weeks on the job (which would represent a mastery goal) and then set other specific goals in terms of dollars of product he will sell each of those customers over the following 2-year period (which would be a performance goal).[15]

Locke and Latham (1990a) reported that self-set goals are as effective as goals that are assigned by other people or participatively set goals, but not *more* effective. Goals may be *distal* or *proximal*; their purpose is to plan the reduction of some discrepancy (as we described in Chapter 13). The goal specifies the nature of the activity as well as the standard that the person desires to accomplish. Once set,[16] a person's goal instigates the three mechanisms underlying human motivation: Effort, persistence, and direction (recall Chapter 1). That is, a person consciously elects to follow one path or another (watch television or visit a friend; eat dessert or have a salad; skip class or attend class), and once chosen, the goal sustains the individual's effort and tenacity until "the

---

[15] Among others, Harackiewicz and Stone (1991) suggested a distinction between *target goals* and *purpose goals*. For them, target goals are specific goals that a person shoots for when undertaking a particular activity (such as, for example, memor-izing a Shakespearean sonnet within 1 hour). A purpose goal, however, is a longer-term goal that is represented by the target goal, but that is more general and of greater and longer-lasting significance. In our sonnet example, a purpose goal might be the development of mental imagery skills, of cognitive focusing skills, or the acquisition of mental command of all of the Bard's work. "Target goals guide an individual's behavior, and purpose goals suggest the reasons for the behavior" (Harackiewicz & Stone, 1991, p. 21).

[16] We are reminded that once identified, a goal must be accepted by the person involved – he must become committed to the goal in order for him to have any hope of attaining it (Erez & Kanfer, 1983).

right thing" has been accomplished, even though it may not have been the preferred or the most pleasurable of the alternatives available. As we saw in Chapter 13, if action results in a failure to reach the goal, some sort of negative self-appraisal occurs and the individual engages in problem solving and further action to reduce the discrepancy. If the initial behavior is successful, the person may set higher or different goals. Generally, the individual provides herself with small rewards or punishments for goal success or failure, just as she would if managing the behavior of some other person.

Self-Regulation of Organizational Behavior

Although self-regulation has an effective track record in dealing with a variety of clinical/behavioral problems such as stopping smoking, reducing weight, and overcoming drug addiction, demonstrations and applications of self-regulation in organized work settings are still not numerous in the literature, but they are becoming more common (Latham & Locke, 1991).

One of the earliest studies of work behavior using social learning theory (now called SCT, as discussed earlier) was a controlled experiment reported by Frayne and Latham (1987) and Latham and Frayne (1989). In this project, the researchers applied a training program in self-management techniques to 20 unionized state government employees with the purpose of reducing their absenteeism from work. The program consisted of eight weekly 1-hour group sessions, followed by eight more weekly 30-minute sessions in which the employees were taught the essentials of self-management. A control group of 20 other employees received no training.

The results of this study were impressive. Employees expressed positive reactions to the training, both immediately after the 8 weeks as well as 3 months later. But more importantly, there was a marked increase in employee presence, the dependent variable of most interest, and it appeared that increases in their self-efficacy were the principal reason. In other words, the trained employees experienced an increase in their beliefs about their ability to overcome the obstacles that had been keeping them away from work, and, as a result, their attendance records improved.

Most impressive, however, was the fact that the effects of the self-management intervention stood up over time. Specifically, Latham and Frayne returned to the same job site studied by Frayne and Latham and monitored the effectiveness of their program on the same 40 employees (20 in the training group and 20 control participants). They found that the program remained effective both 6 and 9 months after the original intervention. Moreover, the employees who had originally served as the control group underwent the same program, yielding similar positive results on their attendance records. Longitudinal research of this sort is rare in the organizational sciences.

Although self-regulation has been demonstrated to benefit human goal accomplishment in a variety of ways (see Frayne & Geringer, 2000, for a brief review), until recently only a few studies have demonstrated the benefit of self-regulation for increasing job performance levels. At least two recent studies have rectified this shortcoming, both focusing on sales performance. First, Frayne and Geringer (2000), using a control group and a training group of insurance sales personnel, demonstrated that a modified version of the training regimen reported earlier by Frayne and Latham (1987) was effective in enhancing sales performance as measured by four different criteria. In addition, the results indicated that self-efficacy, as hypothesized, mediated the effects of self-management training on enhanced performance. More recently, Porath and Bateman (2006) demonstrated that the application of four self-regulation tactics (along with three forms of goal orientation) among a sample of salespeople improved the sales performance among people working from a virtual office for a multinational computer product and services organization.

Porath and Bateman (2006, p. 185) speculate that: "People's ability to self-regulate may be their most essential asset." It may be an important asset in the management of organizations when practiced on a large scale by employees as well, as suggested by a recent study that found that encouraging employees to develop and practice self-regulation habits was superior to command-and-control managerial procedures for the enforcement of organizational policies and rules (Tyler & Blader, 2005).

This raises the question: How natural is the self-management process? There is some evidence that most people do not spontaneously engage in all of these processes (cf. Brief & Hollenbeck, 1985), although the project reported by Frayne and Latham (1987), summarized earlier, makes it clear that problem identification, personal goal setting, the monitoring of feedback, and the self-administration of minor rewards and punishments on the basis of choices made can be taught to (at least some) people (e.g., Frayne & Latham, 1987; Latham & Frayne, 1989). And, although people may not widely engage in these techniques, others do, as illustrated in a study of joint business venture managers (Frayne & Geringer, 1994). These researchers found that executives who made use of self-management techniques enjoyed more success in their ventures. Specifically, the researchers assessed the success of joint ventures with a set of qualitative and financial measures. They found consistently strong and significant correlations between the use of self-management techniques (as described here) and satisfaction with the ventures (in the minds of parent companies' executives) as well as profitability measures. That said, there is some preliminary experimental evidence that suggests that people who feel ostracized and rejected or excluded by their peers may be less likely to engage in self-regulation activity (Baumeister, De Wall, Ciarocco, & Twenge, 2005). Once more, as we have seen repeatedly throughout our analysis (especially in Chapters 5, 6, and 11), the social contexts in which people function may exert considerable moderating effects on human action.

Self-Regulation and Career Management

Two advocates of self-regulation argue that use of these techniques may be especially critical during current times of organizational downsizing, mergers, acquisitions, and other forms of heightened workplace uncertainty. Tsui and Ashford (1994, pp. 93–94) suggested that:

> Under such conditions, it may be impossible and, indeed undesirable for organizations to control managers' behaviors using traditional control mechanisms such as job descriptions, standard operating procedures and static performance appraisal systems . . . Instead, the processes most needed in the ambiguous and complex situations just described would seem to be those of self-regulation and self-control on the part of managers themselves. Managers skilled in self-regulation can respond to the complexity and dynamic pace of their intermediate environment in a timely fashion. In these situations, self-regulation by managers is not only a substitute for other sources of structure . . . it is a necessity if the organization is to survive and to prosper.

Tsui and Ashford (1994; see also Ashford & Tsui, 1991) emphasized the importance for managers under such circumstances to actively seek out information regarding the expectations that key stakeholders place on them (Ashford & Tsui, 1991). This may be a tricky business: Managers must establish specific standards on which to assess their performance, they must learn how to distinguish among the many cues that are available to them from feedback they receive about their performance, and they must also accurately interpret those cues – all very subtle processes, indeed. Additionally, Tsui and Ashford (1994) suggested that managers develop the skill to assess which of the various roles and expectations being placed on them are more important at any point in time (rather than adhering to some predetermined programs or order of priority). They also suggested that managers with strong self-efficacy beliefs are more likely to engage in active feedback seeking (as it relates to their behavior and performance), whereas managers who have low self-esteem (see Chapter 6) will tend to avoid negative feedback and seek positive feedback about their performance.

Their proposed model yielded a number of interesting hypotheses. In fact, an experiment reported by Northcraft and Ashford (1990) found that people with low performance expectations or low self-esteem may engage in low levels of feedback seeking: "Individuals forego inquiry if they believe the feedback will be negative, and especially if others will hear it" (p. 58).

Three-stage process of self-management

The point is that although some early theorists (e.g., Kanfer, 1971) indicated that self-management is a simple three-stage process, involving self-monitoring of one's own behavior, evaluation of that behavior, and the self-administration of rewards and sanctions, Ashford, Tsui, Northcraft, and others have delineated just how subtle and difficult these various stages may be, particularly the monitoring and evaluation of feedback. This subtlety and difficulty must help to explain Brief and Hollenbeck's (1985) finding that these practices are not widely utilized without deliberate intent.

Self-Regulation of Emotions

In Chapter 4, we initially examined the notion of people's capacity to regulate or control their emotions, and in Chapter 8, we paid particular attention to the connection between certain emotions, such as anger, and whether and how controlling anger in the face of frustration is possible or beneficial to human welfare. In these discussions, we encountered the idea of emotional intelligence (Goleman, 1995; Salovey & Mayer, 1990; Salovey et al., 1993) and the purported value to people of maintaining control of their emotions and of their ability to read and respond appropriately to the emotions of other people. We return briefly here to the concept of the control of emotion in the present, broader context of self-regulation.

Emotional intelligence

As we saw in Chapter 4, the concept of *emotional intelligence* appears to have first been presented by Salovey & Mayer (1990) and made popular a few years later by Goleman's (1995) book with the same title. The phrase refers to:

> [A] set of skills expected to contribute to the accurate appraisal and expression of emotion in oneself and others, and the use of feelings to motivate, plan, and achieve in one's life. The emotional intelligence framework suggests that there may be individual differences in people's abilities to exert effective control over their emotional lives.
>
> (Salovey, Hsee, & Mayer, 1993, p. 258)

A person's ability to regulate his own emotions depends upon his capacity to interpret the information that emotional expression – his own as well as that of other people – makes available. The making of "faces" is an example that was cited earlier: Some people are more capable of understanding the meaning of rude or provocative, deliberately projected faces than others (Salovey et al., 1993, p. 260). Likewise, some adults are limited in their ability to express their feelings in words, even though children have been shown to be capable of generating hundreds of words that reflect people's common emotions and of thinking of ways that they could moderate their own emotional expressions.[17] In addition, people vary from one another in their abilities to harness their own emotions for problem solving. For example, changes in a person's mood may open up or suggest new solutions to problems. Creative and inductive reasoning may be served by happy emotional states, which also may cause people to "hang in there" longer when the going gets tough. By contrast, sad states may be most effective in dealing with deductive reasoning tasks (see Salovey et al., 1993). Thus, it

---

[17] Salovey, Hsee, & Mayer (1993) remind us that emotional intelligence includes the capacity to recognize, influence, or regulate the emotions of other people; our focus here will be limited to the interpretation and control of one's own emotions.

appears that possessing the skill to manipulate one's own emotional state may have benefit for the performance of many modern tasks. So, how is this accomplished? As we saw in Chapter 3, evidence from the psychology of satisfaction and affect provides some clues (Salovey et al., 1993).

Simple hedonism implies that people are happier when they possess more of things they like. This simple hypothesis has been elaborated by a series of studies that show that, in addition to the possession of desired outcomes, the rates at which we receive such outcomes and the changes that these outcomes imply over our baseline experiences are also critical in determining our satisfaction and pleasure (Salovey et al., 1993). In other words, we compare the level of outcomes we have at a given moment with the levels we have had in the past. Positive additions of good things bring pleasure, but, after we have grown used to our new circumstances, the pleasure level drops. Thus, an employee who receives a sudden 10% pay increase may be ecstatic at first, but 1 month later the joy will likely subside as she grows used to the new level of pay (cf. Layard, 2005).

Velocity

Likewise, when we lose valued commodities, such as occurs with a cut in pay, the anger initially felt is more acute than that which is likely after time has passed. So far, so good: People adapt to their new circumstances more or less readily. In addition, the *faster* things improve, the greater is our satisfaction, the happier is our mood. If pay increases come quickly, they bring more satisfaction than if they take longer. A person whose house increases in value by $10,000 over 1 year will be happier than a person whose house increases in value by $10,000 over 2 years (Salovey et al., 1993). So, in addition to positive changes from a baseline position, the rate at which the positive changes occur also makes a difference in our satisfaction (Salovey et al., 1993). Researchers refer to this phenomenon as the *velocity* of change.

Finally, in addition to high velocity of change, people appear to gain even greater satisfaction *when the velocity itself changes from negative to positive*. That is, people are happiest when the desired value first decreases and then increases and the most unhappy when the velocity changes from positive to negative "that is, when the desired value first increases and then decreases" (Salovey et al., 1993). We gain most pleasure from watching our favorite sports team win a game after falling behind in the early going and then making a valiant comeback to score the tying and winning goals late in the match. By contrast, the pain we feel for the same team is especially acute when they blow a lead and lose late in the game. Fans of Minnesota Vikings and Vancouver Canucks, such as the author, know whereof we speak![18] Salovey and his colleagues concluded: "This dynamic – indeed *emodynamic* view – suggests that we are acutely sensitive to the pattern over which outcomes accrue in time, especially to their rate and shifts in that rate" (1993, p. 269).

In summary, satisfaction derives not only from the level of one's outcomes, but also from positive changes in that level and from increases in the rate of positive change. The implications of these principles for the self-management of emotions are clear. It becomes a matter of arranging the order of events we encounter in life (and, for our purposes – in our work experiences).

Arranging the sequence of events

Specifically, it follows that a person might regulate, to some degree, his emotional state if he can sequence events and activities so that they bring increasing levels of pleasure and/or create sequences that will minimize feelings of unhappiness and displeasure. Simple examples come to mind: Eat your (dreaded) Brussels sprouts before you turn your attention to your favorite rib eye steak. Organize

---

[18] It is tempting to think of the notions of velocity and increases in velocity in mathematical terms such as first and second derivatives. In these terms, this neohedonism hypothesizes that satisfaction is greatest when both the first and second derivatives of the curve relating a person's level of desired outcome acquisition are both positive, and that dissatisfaction is at its worst when both the mathematical terms are negative. The first derivative concept was successfully tested with Yale undergraduate students by Hsee and Abelson (1991).

your tasks at work on a given day so that the boring and distasteful ones are tackled first and the more pleasurable ones are attempted later. Open your birthday presents in the order that you expect them to bring you pleasure, the one with the most expected value last. We discussed the Premack principle earlier in this chapter. It suggests that people engage in the tasks at work that are "most reinforcing" last, performing the tedious and least reinforcing tasks first – saving the "good stuff" until the end. The final piece of advice is to interact with and, where possible, help other people. There is evidence that helping others is generally a source of pleasure (Salovey et al., 1993).[19] In summary, with some effort given to thinking about the sequence of events we expose ourselves to, we can be capable of managing, or at least moderating, our own emotions and the expression of those emotions.

Scientific Status of Self-Regulation

The standard techniques of self-regulation, as we have noted repeatedly, are well established: It is a behavioral technology that "works" in helping people improve their lives through the deliberate governance of their thoughts, emotions, and deeds. In the terms we used in Chapter 2, self-regulation has established criterion-related validity, but some concern has been expressed recently that not enough is known about *why* self-regulation works; that is, that not enough is known about the construct validity of self-regulation interventions (cf. R. Kanfer, 2005; Vancouver & Day, 2005). Ruth Kanfer (2005), a leading authority on work motivation, observed the ongoing controversy between the goal-setting camp and the control theory camp and the mechanisms by which people are motivated to increase or decrease discrepancies and the role that self-efficacy plays in these processes. Not helping matters toward resolution is the existence of a number of versions of control theory (Vancouver & Day, 2005). It may be that goal setting and social-cognitive models help understand different aspects of the self-regulation process (Kanfer, 2005; Vancouver & Day, 2005) and that they, as Kanfer (2005, p. 188) puts it, "share more common ground than not." Regardless, all of the theories that attempt to explain the mechanisms of self-regulation are multifaceted and so complex that it may be impossible to pit the theories fairly and directly against one another scientifically. Again, quoting Kanfer (2005, p. 188): "From this perspective, theory development in I/O psychology appears to have stalled."

GENERAL CONCLUSION TO PART FOUR

The theories and techniques of work motivation in this chapter had many of their origins in a model of human functioning that is different from those presented earlier in this book. Whereas we examined need-based models in Part Two and cognitive models in Part Three (through Chapter 13) the origins of some aspects of SCT and self-management were predicated on a learning model of human functioning. We adopted an historical approach in this chapter because it seems to be instructive of the ways theories and paradigms come and go in science (recall Chapter 2). Behaviorism was the dominant school of thought in modern human psychology until not long ago (cf. Bandura, 2001). Although it is vastly diminished in importance these days, it is not completely gone from the map and many of its core principles remain useful, particularly in applied settings for practitioners who are not concerned with *why* certain techniques (such as self-regulation, for example) work.

For example, we continue to recognize that behavior is determined – at least in part – by its

---

[19] In fact, a series of experiments found that people prefer to open gifts in such an ascending order of expected pleasure, rather than in the opposite order, which would reflect a sense of impatience to get the fun over with as quickly as possible (see Salovey et al., 1993, for a summary of these studies).

consequences, and limited by biological constraints. The antecedents of behavior also contribute to our understanding – context is supremely important. Moreover, a focus on motivation must include an appreciation for the phenomena related to learning. So it would be foolish to conclude that the behaviorist perspective is gone for good; it may be moribund but it is not dead, not all of it. Still, it is obvious that, even though difficult to manipulate and/or measure scientifically, a number of black box concepts such as self-actualization, expectancy, self-efficacy beliefs, and pride in career progress are extremely important in understanding human motivation and work motivation in particular. But the history of science (cf. Kuhn, 1970) teaches those of us who are willing to listen that world views change and old ones come back, much like Duncan's ghost.

A Final Note: On Common Sense

For this author, no other theory of human behavior (and work motivation and behavior) discussed in this book makes more sense than does SCT, especially as articulated in Bandura's (2001) chapter in the *American Psychologist*. The proactive role it attributes to humans in determining our own behavior and in making the most of environmental circumstances – agency – makes so much sense to this author that it seems absurd that psychology and the other social sciences took so long to get around to recognizing the agentic model of human functioning described by SCT. While it is consistent with at least parts of so many other models and theories discussed in this book, its particular emphasis on self-determination, self-efficacy, forethought, consciousness, and self-awareness transcends other models considered one at a time. Consistent with Latham and Pinder's (2005) recent review of 30 years of research and theory on work motivation, this author believes that SCT is the most intelligent model available at this time. Refinements to its various components will continue apace, as will its further reconciliation with other approaches and its own articulation into the arenas of proxy and collective human agency. Meanwhile, it bears close attention and a considerable degree of respect from workers, managers, teachers, administrators, novelists, and people in most other walks of life interested in a theory of human behavior that enjoys considerable scientific and philosophical legitimacy[20] as well as the intrinsic value of common sense.

---

[20] Concerns expressed by Kanfer (2005) and by Vancouver and Day (2005) notwithstanding.

PART FIVE

Summary and Evaluation of Progress

Profits, Slaves, and Hopes for Strawberry Fields of the Future

15

*The spatial and temporal boundaries
to system analysis are
characteristically interdependent.*
Daniel Katz and Robert Kahn

*Everyone but an idiot knows
that the lower classes must be kept poor
or they will never be industrious.*
Arthur Young

At approximately the time of this writing, the following story came across the worldwide media and was reported online by the *People's Daily Online*:[1]

> Chinese police have rescued 248 people who had been forced to work as "slaves" in brick kilns, while a widespread crackdown is underway.

> Police in central Henan Province have rescued 217 people, including 29 children, and detained 120 suspects after a 4-day crackdown involving more than 35,000 police to check 7000 kilns in the province.

> In the area around Xingiang . . . police raided 20 brick kilns . . . and rescued 23 people including 16 children.

> Laborers had been enticed or kidnapped and transported to the kilns by human traffickers. Upon arrival, they were beaten, starved, and forced to work long hours without pay.

> It is reported that 400 Henan fathers have went [sic] to the remote mountains in Shanxi to track down missing sons who they believe were sold to the kilns.

> There have been raids on coal mines, brick kilns, private contractors and small-sized enterprises after media reports revealed that hundreds of children in Henan Province had been kidnapped and forced work in the kilns of Shanxi.

---

[1] June 15, 2007; see also Eimer, 2007; Ying, 2007.

THE FOCI OF THEORY AND RESEARCH ON WORK MOTIVATION

Such is part of the human work condition in 2007. It has a lot to do with work motivation considered at a global level. Meanwhile, we in the West are relatively comfortable so the focus of a large proportion of the efforts of our work motivation researchers and theorists is toward finding and testing mediating variables, moderating variables, and boundary conditions. The proximate goal of much of this activity is to develop increasingly finer understanding of work motivation in Western work worlds while countless people in all parts of the world are living, working, and starving to death in horrific circumstances such as those of the Chinese brick kilns (and worse).

Many years ago, the late Peter Frost (1980) observed that too much of our attention in organizational science (in general) – and this author would add that Frost's point applies to the case of research and theory on work motivation in particular – has been focused on small, elite populations of (Western) managers and professionals. While it may be the case that more research has now been conducted on lower-level employees in affluent societies, the core of Frost's idea is more significant than ever. In the first edition of this book, the author (Pinder, 1998) cited Frost's (1980) point and added:

> [C]onsider the organizational realities of immigrant laborers (both legal and illegal). They have received virtually no attention during the previous decades of research on work motivation. Likewise, we know very little about the work motivation of the chronically unemployed or chronically under-employed people. What has been learned about the motivation and attitudes regarding the work of seasonal workers (such as farmers and fishers, for example)?
>
> (Pinder, 1998, p. 473)

Workers Required for the Strawberry Fields

The continuing reality and value of the point came alive to this author during the springs of 2006 and 2007 on the Saanich Peninsula on Vancouver Island (north of Victoria, the capital of British Columbia). Owners of farms growing strawberries were having a terrible time attracting workers to pick their crops of the seasonal fruit to bring it to market in time to be saleable and profitable. The weather during the preceding months had been particularly favorable, and the honeybees had done a marvelous job, so the crops in both June 2006 and 2007 were abundant and the berries especially appealing and delicious to consumers. The fruit had to be picked, shipped, and sold within limited windows of time, otherwise, it was of no value: It would rot. Aside from the sad loss of food value and nutrition to people within the marketing area who might otherwise eat and enjoy the strawberries, the cashflow of the farmers and local merchants who would benefit or suffer as a function of the abundance and delivery of the crop was at stake. Farming is a major element of the economy in the local region, so the economy stood to benefit or suffer as a consequence of the success of the profitability of the farming sector. During June of 2006 and 2007, the big issue in the farming community and local economy was the strawberry crop. In short, too few people in the local labor market were willing to work in the fields of the farms to pick the berries in time to get them to market before they spoiled.

Meanwhile, across western Canada, there was an ongoing labor shortage that was affecting all or most sectors of the economy: Fast-food restaurants, coffee houses, and many other small businesses were appealing to the labor of people (young and old!) to do work for minimum wage, or near-minimum wage. Many of the owners/farmers on the peninsula initiated recruitment programs to attract "street people" from the downtown core of Victoria to work for hourly wages slightly above minimum wage, attracting them to pick the berries and to save the crop and the farmers' revenues. As an extra inducement, the farmers offered housing for the workers, in the form of old mobile homes and campers. The work had to be done, the labor had to be attracted and motivated to stay, and so a solution – at least a partial solution – was reached.

At the same time, elsewhere in British Columbia, immigrant farm workers of south-Asian descent were aging and retiring at rates that were worrying the farmers on the Lower Mainland of British Columbia (in the suburbs of Vancouver). The children of these hard-working, largely uneducated people were less willing than their parents to perform hard work in the rainy and muddy fields of British Columbia, for long hours, to sow and harvest the crops of the more affluent people within the market area who benefited from the savings made possible by their hard labor. It's about work motivation and the problems of low-wage earners in B.C. were only a microcosm of the problems of starvation-borderline humans seeking demeaning work in order to survive. There are millions of illegal immigrants in Western countries seeking work, frequently at minimum wages, frequently selling their bodies, if not their dignities and risking their very lives to find and secure work in affluent Western countries. Immigrants from North Africa are flooding Spain via highly risky passage procedures, by the profit of human smugglers, to get them to Europe where they have feint hopes of securing higher standards of life, and in the case of Spain, social security and – most of all – paying work.

Hard, Dirty Work in Difficult Conditions

The author has driven past endless miles of fields of migrant workers performing back-breaking labor to plant, cultivate, and harvest vegetables for the tables of western Canadians. Union involvement is a joke. The wages paid are a joke. The working conditions are primitive. The sun and the rain add extra torment to the workers' efforts. These people work for survival, and, in many cases, with the hope they can bring their families to join them and find better lives than they, themselves, have found here.

Slavery grows globally

Earlier we mentioned slavery conditions in China. The scary fact is that this problem is not unique to China; it is a worldwide scourge. A recent report by the International Labour Organization (cited by King, 2007), claims that there are more people alive in slavery today than at any time in the past – a minimum of 12.3 million individuals. The types of work slaves perform in modern times vary somewhat from those of chattels of 400 years ago, but the point is that their ultimate conditions are the same: "They don't choose their condition and can't get out of it" (King, 2007, p. 64). Traffic in human smuggling is one of the fastest-growing sectors of organized crime, worth billions of dollars annually. As in the past, most people are unaware or conveniently blind to the existence of slavery. People of all ages are bought and sold to work on myriad industries on virtually all continents of the world, such as subcontracting for supply chains, garment manufacturing, agricultural labor, domestic service, camel jockeying, mining, and, increasingly, the sex trade (Joseph Rowntree Foundation, 2007). Kapstein (2006) notes that it took the might of the British Navy more than two centuries ago to force an end to the trade – at least within the realm of Britain's reach. The nation states of today that have the might required to eradicate slavery appear not willing to do much about it. Kapstein (2006) also notes that, aside from the obvious moral issues with slavery as an institution, it has serious economic implications: "The same people who engage in human trafficking also contribute to the deepening criminalization of the world economy overall, often operating in close association with corrupt officials around the world" (p. 104).

Qui Bono?

Corporate profit has been the ultimate goal of much of the research and theory into the scientific discipline called *organizational behavior* since its inception. In his early siren's call to social scientists,[2] Loren Baritz (1960) cited sociologist Thorstein Veblen (1904) as follows:

> It is not a question of what ought to be done, but of what is the course laid out by business principles; the discretion rests with the business men, not with the moralists, and the business men's discretion is bounded by the exigencies of business enterprise. Even the business men cannot allow themselves to play fast and loose with business principles in response to a call from humanitarian motives. The question, therefore, remains, on the whole, a question of what the business men may be expected to do for cultural growth on the motive of profits.

And so it goes, more than 100 years after Veblen's (1904) insight. Business interests fund, fuel, and direct the efforts of most organizational behavior scientists. Along the way, we have become and we have remained the "servants of power" whom Baritz (1960) identified us to be a half-century ago. As already mentioned, too much of the scientific interest in work motivation in the West over the past 60 years has been ethnocentric, biased in terms of sampling procedures, limited in scope and thereby limited in its external validity (as observed nearly three decades ago). Moreover, a significant proportion of the efforts of many social scientists to become international in scope in recent years have been driven by instrumental motives rather than a concern for the welfare of those we have been studying and trying to understand. Perhaps it is time to study human work motivation at a global level, both for three purposes: (1) for its own sake; (2) for humanitarian purposes; and (3) for corporate profit. When we take the life experiences of humans, worldwide, into our laboratories, we will, in scientific terms, increase the variance on our major variables of interest and learn a lot more about our species as a whole rather than merely about our own local and privileged, affluent economies. Along the way, we may create opportunities to simultaneously generate and foster humanitarian goals of world peace *and* economic security. Scandinavian countries have shown the world that productivity, innovation, and social welfare *can* coexist and flourish.

The American Case

In his current bestseller, *The age of abundance*, American author Brink Lindsey (2007) tells the story of how the United States of America evolved from its inception through periods of relative "necessity" and "freedom." For Lindsey (2007), the period of necessity was one of doing everything and anything that was required for people merely to survive. Once accomplished, with a number of perturbations and setbacks along the way, American society clawed its way – for most of its citizens, at least – into a period of relative freedom, wherein survival became taken for granted by most of its citizens. The attention of (most white) people turned to loftier goals, such as making choices about their pursuit of lifestyles, becoming educated and healthy, achieving "growth experiences," and prospering along the lines of the Great American Dream.

At a macro level, and adopting a long historical view, the story and the events Lindsey (2007) documents provide plenty of validation for the notion of a hierarchy of needs, such as that proposed by Abraham Maslow (1943; see Chapter 3). As Lindsey acknowledges, Maslow's theory was generally intended to be a depiction of the motivational forces acting on individuals rather than a theory of economic and social development of entire tribes, nations, or people in the aggregate. Nevertheless, perhaps it is time that we, as organizational scholars, focused some of our time and resources

---

[2] Now organizational behavior scholars.

investigating international differences in values and motivational structures – for the sake of understanding human motivation at a global level, for the sake of helping those whose main concern is their next meal, where they can find potable water, and how they can protect their children and themselves from the ravishes of warlords.

If taken seriously, such an approach – one done at an aggregate level rather than at the individual level – would provide a sort of validation of Maslow's (1943) hierarchy; the one Western scholars have mocked from the relative social and economic security of our affluent academies. We in the West are very quick to give lip-service to the idea that we live in a global community, and social scientists are often quick to study cross-cultural issues – but, again, to what end? What are the goals of Western social science when taken abroad, of theories of organizational behavior, or of work motivation theory in particular? Do we study intercultural differences for the sake of the knowledge, for its own sake? Or do we study them for the sake of providing a basis for conducting business with people at the BOP (bottom of the pyramid) more successfully (whereby "successfully" implies profit for Western interests)? Or do we study intercultural and international differences for the sake of helping people not as fortunate as we are *for the sake of improving their lives*? To what degree are Western social scientists and motivational theorists, especially those who study international business, applied anthropology, and cross-cultural psychology the descendants of the servants of power decried by Baritz (1960) nearly a half-century ago?

Early papers of Professor Walter Nord (1974, 1977) might be of interest to organizational behavior scientists who are serious about becoming global in the scope of their scientific activities. In these papers and others, Dr. Nord challenged the fundamental assumptions made by Western society and its economic systems about the welfare of workers, the nature of job satisfaction, and whether people can ever achieve a world within a capitalist system that would make organizations both productive and humane (cf. Meltzer & Nord, 1981). His thoughts were radical when he wrote them and will probably be viewed with even more political suspicion today.

A Systemic, Global View

A half-century ago, Allport (1954, 1962), noted that the importance of systems concepts in relation to the survival of our (human) species is all encompassing and that systems of life comprise a universe of hierarchically nested and interrelated networks and subnetworks *of human activity* (see also Katz & Kahn, 1966; Miller, 1978). Systems thinking permits us to expand the horizons of our thoughts and become increasingly more inclusive in the scope of the problems and people we care about (Miller, 1978). In the context of work motivation – the core topic of this book – we see this mentality in Bandura's (1986) social-cognitive theory (recall our Chapter 13) as well as in control theory (cf. Klein, 1989; and see Chapter 13). Another example is found in the large-scale holistic model offered by Parker and her colleagues (Parker et al., 2001; and see Chapter 10 of this book) to guide future research on job design. A global concern for human work motivation would require thinking at still-larger levels, encompassing the interconnectedness of human events that influence one another across national and socioeconomic boundaries. Moreover, as suggested earlier, what we learn may provide social science more value for the *simultaneous* advancement of economic and social-welfare goals for everyone, rather than for just the few who hold capital.

In summary, as a student of social science and organizational behavior for nearly 40 years, the author is appealing for a reorientation in research and theory on work motivation in two fundamental (yet interrelated) directions. The first is a hope that we will pay more attention in the future to the working lives of humankind as a whole, rather than exclusively to the limited problems and issues of comparatively well-off workers in convenience samples in affluent countries. The second is a hope that the benefits of scientific activity will benefit the working lives of poor people, such as illegal (and legal) immigrants, displaced individuals, and the growing body of people working in varying degrees of bondage.

With the foregoing pleas recorded, we turn to a summary of the field as it is in the early 21st century and a few more suggestions for new research.

SO: WHY *DO* PEOPLE WORK?

So, what motivates human work behavior? The answer, based on the analyses presented in this book and elsewhere (cf. Latham, 2007), is that many things do. The old economic model that assumed that people work only for money is now terribly dated, in most of the North American context, at least. Indeed, many people prefer not to work for pay in organizations when other life interests and challenges confront them. For example, Statistics Canada (2006) reports that fewer women than before in Alberta and British Columbia are entering the workforce in those provinces: Other needs, constraints, and requirements are causing them to seek family-raising and other activities to meet their needs. In these cases, it is *not* a lack of work motivation; it is a matter of different goals for women to pursue in western Canada.

A Parsimonious Typology of Reasons for Working

While we have taken a research-and-theory-based approach to human motivation and to work motivation, Noon and Blyton (2007) have approached the issue of why people work head on. They offer a simple typology of reasons, all of which can be reconciled with, or explained by, the theories explored in the current book. In brief, their typology includes the following:

1. Working to live: People must work in order to simply survive.
2. Working to consume: People desire material and non-material accoutrements to make life easier than it would otherwise be. We aspire to own automobiles, television sets, and cameras and to engage in non-essential life activities such as taking vacations and going to school.
3. Working for intrinsic satisfaction and a sense of meaning, independent of material requirements or values.
4. Commitment to work for its own sake, even in circumstances when it is not necessary to work for survival or material reason.
5. Working because to do so is a moral necessity. Working is "inherently good," the right thing to do. Being at some form of work is morally superior to being idle or at leisure.
6. Work is an obligation because if one does not work, others will have to provide for his or her existence and other needs. People work so as to provide their fair share of the social contract.
7. Work is a central life activity, second only in importance to family matters. Work defines who and what we are.
8. Work as a conscientious endeavor. This factor focuses on doing a job diligently. Regardless of how menial the task, one must strive to do a good job. "If a job is worth doing, it is worth doing well."

Their list is impressive. It is congruent with all we know, as reported in this book, about why people work. It constitutes a new typology of work motivation – as opposed to general human motivation, à la Maslow (1954) and Alderfer (1972; see Chapter 3 in this book) that must be taken seriously. In the foregoing chapters of this book, although not deliberately following the items on Noon and Blyton's (2007) list, we have attempted to summarize the largely Western-based scientific literature on the origins and essence of work motivation and have run across many of their insights along the way. The author hopes that we have given more insight behind the insights summarized by Noon and Blyton.

THIRTY-YEAR UPDATE AND PROGRESS REPORT

It behooves authors of critical reviews of the literature of the sort represented in this book to offer summary conclusions, including an assessment of the state of the field and suggestions for future directions. In addition to the criticisms of restricted sampling and the overemphasis on affluent populations raised already, the author has recently concluded an assessment of the progress that has been made in theory and research on work motivation with Professor Gary Latham[3] in the *Annual Review of Psychology*. That review contained many of the key points of this author's assessment of progress, so we draw upon it (although not exclusively) here.

First, Latham and Pinder (2005) concluded that behaviorism, in its raw form, is no longer useful, and that models that include cognitive constructs and concepts are far more useful for understanding human functioning, including work behavior (see Chapter 14).

Second, and most importantly, is the rediscovery in psychology and organizational science of the importance of affect, including short-term emotions, longer-term moods, and dispositional character traits (dispositions). It is clear that people are emotional creatures and so, after 20 years of complaining by their critics, organizational behavior theorists have not only recognized emotion but have investigated and documented the major roles that affect plays in behavior, organizational behavior, and work motivation (see Chapter 4). Further advances toward a more complete understanding will have to take into account spiritual, biological, and other factors (the role of genetics in job satisfaction has already been documented, as we saw in Chapter 10).

A significant third conclusion reached by Latham and Pinder (2005) was that researchers have finally started to take the role of context seriously in the understanding of organizational behavior and work motivation, in particular, even though the necessity to do so has been acknowledged in vague terms for decades (cf. Maier, 1946).

Latham and Pinder (2005) also noted how some theories have morphed and evolved into new, more valid and useful theories over the years. This raises a number of points.

First, there is always a risk associated with the movement forward in social science as one theory presumes to gobble up and subsume the terrain of others that went before. For example, while a zeitgeist in the literature focuses on justice models, there is a risk of losing appreciation for the wisdom in equity theory, which has been subsumed under the umbrella of insights into distributive justice (Greenberg, 1987). Similarly, the heat and fury that buried the standing of Herzberg's model (see Chapter 2) notwithstanding, that old theory helped to spawn the popular job characteristics model (see Chapter 7). The two-factor model also enjoyed some vindication in recent findings reported by Basch and Fisher (2000) on the causal connections between discrete emotions and justice/injustice experiences reported by employees.

This raises a second point: As stated many times throughout this book, sometimes good ideas are stronger than are the crude methods we have as social scientists to test and affirm them. The advancement of within-person, experience-sampling designs (cf. Hormuth, 1986) such as those employed so successfully in recent years by researchers such as Fisher and Noble (2004), Ilies and Judge (2002), and others have pumped new life into old hypotheses that were frequently misinterpreted and incorrectly tested with inappropriate methods. We have seen this phenomenon many times throughout this book.

Another issue concerns the problems work motivation theory has had over the years caused by misinterpretations of theory. The history of research and theory on work motivation has been driven by many false and loose interpretations of the theories advanced by their thinkers. The field of

---

[3] In the opinion of this author, Canadian Professor Gary Latham has made more contributions to the theory, research, practice, and leadership on the subject of work motivation than any other scholar. I recommend his recent book (Latham, 2007), which provides a very readable, historically oriented review of the subject.

organizational behavior has, for the most part, been pursuing, testing, and finding false, the tenets of the great minds who proposed to advance the filed. An early example was offered by King (1970), who pointed out the multiple interpretations of the two-factor (motivator-hygiene) model in early empirical testing it faced. Similarly, consider the early years of empirical research on VIE theory (Chapter 12). After years of being (largely inappropriately) tested as a between-persons model, more recent work revealed that it is most appropriately tested as a within-person decision-making model. When so interpreted and tested, the VIE model fared much better under empirical scrutiny (Snyder et al., 1978).

Another point in this digression comes to mind when we consider VIE theory, some 45 years since Vroom (1964) brought it to our attention. Although there has not been much *new* research into the validity of VIE theory (see Chapter 12) in recent years, a major mistake can be made by scholars and practitioners if they conclude that this model is no longer of value. The competition of science making among academics seems to result in the denunciation of, or ignorance of, older models that have had their day in the sun, in part because it is no longer sufficiently rewarding to conduct further research into them. The silence in the recent literature on VIE theory does not mean the theory is not valid or useful; it indicates merely that its value has been established and it has been time for the field to move along to other approaches.

Another point observed by Latham and Pinder (2005) of note here is that the tone of research and theory testing has become less heated than it was in previous years (cf. Pinder, 1998). This is a good thing. Any enlightened practitioner and reader of the social scientific literature on work motivation has been justified if she wonders what all the fuss is about: Where are the main effects?

Still another point is raised by the question: What really matters? Are the distinctions among the constructs spun by academics worth paying attention to? These are good questions and become revealed in their significance as one tries to present them to applied, managerial audiences. So much of the hair-splitting and construct articulation, wrapped in shrouds of construct validity, especially discriminate validity, are of no value to those we serve, as academics, other than other academics (Astley, 1985).

Finally, Latham and Pinder (2005) expressed concern that there have been very few fundamentally new insights into the antecedents and consequences of work motivation over the past 30 years – as significant and as ground breaking as were the insights of Adams (1963), Bandura (1986, 2001), Herzberg et al., (1959), Locke and Latham (2002), Luthans and Kreitner (1974), Maslow (1943), or Vroom (1964).

NEW DIRECTIONS FOR RESEARCH AND THEORY

All that written and taken into account, there are a few possible new directions that offer some appeal. In addition to the author's foregoing appeal for more of a global systems mentality in our study of work motivation, Locke and Latham (2004) have suggested that future research and theory on work motivation should: (1) integrate extant theories for the sake of building meta-theories; (2) eschew traditional barriers among the social and behavioral sciences for the collection and integration of ideas about work motivation; (3) examine how general trait-based constructs, such as personality, interact with short-term, situational variables as mediators or moderator variables (see Chapter 2); (4) study subconscious motives in addition to conscious motives, as well as the relationships among them; (5) use introspection as a basis for research and insight; and (6) continue to acknowledge the role of volition on human action when developing theories.

Steel and König (2006) have recently proposed a new approach to the integration of theory, as proposed by Locke and Latham (2004). Continuing progress in self-determination theory (see Gagné & Deci, 2005; Ryan & Deci, 2000; and recall Chapter 3) is consistent with Locke and

Latham's exhortation for continued emphasis on volition, as might the concept of *I-deals* proposed by Rousseau and her colleagues (cf. Rousseau, Ho, & Greenberg, 2006). Rousseau's (2006a, 2006b) calls for the development of *evidence-based management* will be an important attempt to make theory more accessible to practitioners than it has ever been before. The iterative loops between theory, practice, and research that such a movement would generate could prove fruitful for both social science as well as the humane and productive management of tomorrow's organizations.

Research that eschews the traditional and nearly universal (Western) assumptions of individualistic and hedonistic models of human nature may provide interesting new insights (cf. Shamir, 1991). As we saw in Chapter 3, Meglino and Korsgaard (2004) have generated fascinating new insights of this sort.

Similarly, research that further explores a spiritual assumption about human beings offers promise. Hill and Pargament (2003) have recently reviewed the potential for a spiritual approach to enhance health research. Several articles in the September 2005 issue of the *Journal of Management Inquiry* explore issues of spirituality and the practice of management, while Dobrow (2004), Elangovan, Pinder, and McLean (2008), Hall and Chandler (2005), Wrzesniewski and her colleagues (e.g., Wrzesniewski, 2002; Wrzesniewski, McCauley, Rozin, & Schwartz, 1997), among others, have resurrected the ancient concept of *callings* and explored its potential for understanding a range of organizational behavior phenomena, including work motivation.[4] Finally, Pava and Primeaux (2004) have recently edited a book of original essays that explore the meaning and significance of a construct they call "spiritual intelligence" for understanding human behavior in the workplace.

FINAL THOUGHTS ABOUT WORK MOTIVATION

After considering all the research, theory, and applied insight reported and examined in this book, the author concludes that two insights are the most important at the present time and – probably – for the foreseeable future.

The first of these is the wisdom of Douglas McGregor's (1957a, 1960) observation of the assumptions people make about one another and the self-fulfilling prophesies generated by those assumptions. In a global world, McGregor's insights require more attention than they had when he proposed his theory. As we saw in Chapter 3, McGregor proposed an ideal type comprised of two varieties of these assumptions, calling them *Theory X* and *Theory Y*. In common parlance: *What goes around, comes around*. In the global world, his insight requires expansion and magnification, with appropriate cautions.

The other is the wisdom of the Golden Rule: *Do unto others as you would have them do unto you*. This one requires no qualification. A quick investigation using any current search engine will reveal that this aphorism is universally acknowledged, proffered, and promulgated. It is a wonderful suggestion.

---

[4] Elangovan et al. (2007) argue that although the callings concept has its origins in religion, the notion has evolved over the years to denote secular meanings and interpretations. Further, they argue that callings are not necessarily related to a person's work occupation.

References

A&W. (2007). *The A&W climate goal process*, from www.awincomefund.ca/aboutaw/climate.asp

Abbott, A. (1981). Status strain in the professions. *American Journal of Sociology, 46*, 819–835.

Adams, A. (1992). *Bullying at work*. London: Virago Press.

Adams, J. S. (1963). Toward an understanding on inequity. *Journal of Abnormal Psychology, 67*, 422–436.

Adams, J. S. (1965). Inequity in social exchange. In L. Berkowitz (Ed.), *Advances in experimental social psychology* (pp. 267–299). New York: Academic Press.

Adkins, C. L., Ravlin, E. C., & Meglino, B. M. (1992). *Value congruence between co-workers and its relationship to work-related outcomes*. Paper presented at the annual meeting of Academy of Management, Las Vegas.

Adler, P. S., & Cole, R. E. (1993). Designed for learning: A tale of two auto plants. *Sloan Management Review, 34*(3), 85–94.

Adler, S., & Golan, J. (1981). Lateness as a withdrawal behavior. *Journal of Applied Psychology, 66*(5), 544–554.

Aguiar, M., & Hurst, E. (2006). The land of leisure. *The Economist, 378*(8463).

Ahlberg, D. A. (1986). The social costs of unemployment. In R. Castle & D. E. Lewis (Eds.), *Work, leisure, and technology* (pp. 19–29). Melbourne, Victoria, Australia: Longman Cheshire.

Ahlberg, D. A., & Shapiro, M. O. (1983–1984). The social cost of economic decline: Some earlier evidence. *Journal of Keynsian Economics, VI*(2), 303–304.

Ajila, C. O. (1997). Maslow's hierarchy of needs theory: Applicability to the Nigerian industrial setting. *IFE Psychology, 5*, 162–174.

Ajzen, I. (1991). The theory of planned behavior. *Organizational Behavior and Human Decision Processes, 50*, 1–33.

Ajzen, I., & Fishbein, M. (1977). Attitude–behavior relations: A theoretical analysis and review of empirical research. *Psychological Bulletin, 84*, 888–918.

Ajzen, I., & Fishbein, M. (1980). *Understanding attitudes and predicting social behavior*. Englewood Cliffs, NJ: Prentice-Hall.

Ajzen, I., & Madden, T. J. (1986). Prediction of goal-directed behavior: The role of intention, perceived control, and prior behavior. *Journal of Experimental Social Psychology, 22*, 453–474.

Aldag, R. J., Barr, S. H., & Brief, A. P. (1981). Measurement of perceived task characteristics. *Psychological Bulletin, 90*, 415–431.

Alderfer, C. P. (1969). An empirical test of a new theory of human needs. *Organizational Behavior and Human Performance, 4*, 143–175.

Alderfer, C. P. (1972). *Existence, relatedness, and growth*. New York: Free Press.

Alderfer, C. P. (1977). A critique of Salancik and Pfeffer's examination of need-satisfaction theories. *Administrative Science Quarterly, 22*, 658–669.

Aldis, O. (1961). Of pigeons and men. *Harvard Business Review, 39*(4), 59–63.

Aldrich, H. E. (1980). *Organizations and environments*. Englewood Cliffs, NJ: Prentice-Hall.

Allen, D. G., Renn, R. W., & Griffeth, R. W. (2003). The impact of telecommuting design on social systems, self-regulation, and role boundaries. In J. J. Martocchio & G. R. Ferris (Eds.), *Research in personnel and human resources management* (Vol. 22, pp. 125–163). Amsterdam: Elsevier.

Allen, N. J., & Meyer, J. P. (1990). The measurement and antecedents of affective continuance and normative commitment to the organization. *Journal of Occupational Psychology, 63*, 1–18.

Allen, R. E., & Lucero, M. A. (1996). Beyond resentment: Exploring organizationally targeted insider murder. *Journal of Management Inquiry, 5*, 86–103.

Allen, T. D., Freeman, D. M., Reizenstein, R. C., & Rentz, J. O. (1995). Just another transition? Examining survivors' attitudes over time. In *Academy of Management Best Papers Proceedings*, 55th Annual General Meeting. Vancouver, British Columbia, Canada: Academy of Management.

Allport, F. H. (1954). The structuring of events: Outline of a general theory with applications to psychology. *Psychological Review, 61*, 281–303.

Allport, F. H. (1962). A structuronomic conception of behavior: Individual and collective. I. Structural theory and the master problem of social psychology. *Journal of Abnormal and Social Psychology, 64*, 3–30.

Amabile, T. M. (1988). A model of creativity and innovation in organizations. In B. M. Staw & L. L. Cummings (Eds.), *Research in organizational behavior* (Vol. 10, pp. 123–168). Greenwich, CT: JAI Press.

Amabile, T. M. (1998). How to kill creativity. *Harvard Business Review, 76*(5), 77–87.

Amabile, T. M., Hill, K. G., Hennessey, B. A., & Tighe, E. M. (1994). The work preference inventory: Assessing intrinsic and extrinsic motivational orientations. *Journal of Personality and Social Psychology, 66*(5), 950–967.

Ambrose, M. L., & Cropanzano, R. (2003). A longitudinal analysis of organizational fairness: An examination of reactions to tenure and promotion decisions. *Journal of Applied Psychology, 88*(2), 266–275.

Ambrose, M. L., & Kulik, C. T. (1999). Old friends, new faces: Motivation research in the 1990s. *Journal of Management, 25*(3), 231–292.

Ambrose, M. L., Seabright, M. A., & Schminke, M. (2002). Sabotage in the workplace: The role of organizational injustice. *Organizational Behavior & Human Decision Processes, 89*, 947–965.

Amiel, B. (1985, August 5). The dangerous cost of equal pay. *Maclean's, 98*(31), 9.

Anastasi, A. (1986). Evolving concepts of test validation. *Annual Review of Psychology, 37*, 1–15.

Anderson, J. (1970a). Giving and receiving feedback. In G. W. Dalton, P. R. Lawrence, & L. E. Greiner (Eds.), *Organizational change and development*. Homewood, IL: Irwin.

Andersson, L. M., & Pearson, C. M. (1999). Tit for tat? The spiraling effect of incivility in the workplace. *Academy of Management Review, 24*(3), 452–471.

Andrasik, F. (1979). Organizational behavior modification in business settings: A methodological and content review. *Journal of Organizational Behavior Management, 2*, 85–102.

Andrews, I. R. (1967). Wage inequity and job performance. *Journal of Applied Psychology, 51*, 39–45.

Angle, H. L., & Lawson, M. B. (1993). Changes in affective and continuance commitment in times of relocation. *Journal of Business Research, 26*(1), 3–15.

Angle, H. L., & Perry, J. L. (1981). An empirical assessment of organizational commitment and organizational effectiveness. *Administrative Science Quarterly, 26*, 1–14.

Angle, H. L., & Perry, J. L. (1983). Individual and organizational influences on organizational commitment. *Work and Occupations: An International Sociological Journal, 10*, 123–146.

Appelbaum, E., & Batt, R. (1994). *The new American work place: Transforming work systems in the United States*. New York: ILR Press.

Aquino, K., Lewis, M. U., & Bradfield, M. (1999). Justice constructs, negative affectivity, and employee deviance: A proposed model and empirical test. *Journal of Organizational Behavior, 20*, 1073–1091.

Argyris, C. (1957). *Personality and organization*. New York: Harper.

Argyris, C. (1971). Beyond freedom and dignity by B. F. Skinner: A review essay. *Harvard Educational Review, 41*, 550–567.

Armon, C. (1993). Developmental conceptions of good work: A longitudinal study. In J. Demick & P. M. Miller (Eds.), *Development in the workplace* (pp. 21–37). Hillsdale, NJ: Lawrence Erlbaum Associates, Inc.

Armon-Jones, C. (1986). The thesis of constructionism. In R. Harré (Ed.), *The social construction of emotions* (pp. 32–56). New York: Blackwell.

Arnold, H. J. (1976). Effects of performance feedback and extrinsic reward upon high intrinsic motivation. *Organizational Behavior and Human Performance, 17*, 275–288.

Arnold, H. J. (1981). A test of the validity of the multiplicative hypothesis of expectancy-valence theories of work motivation. *Academy of Management Journal, 24*(1), 128–141.

Arnold, H. J., & Feldman, D. C. (1982). A multivariate analysis of the determinants of job turnover. *Journal of Applied Psychology, 67*(3), 350–360.

Arnold, H. J., & House, R. J. (1980). Methodological and substantive extensions to the job characteristics model of motivation. *Organizational Behavior and Human Performance, 25*, 161–183.

Arthur, M. B., & Rousseau, D. M. (Eds.). (1996). *The boundaryless career*. New York: Oxford University Press.

Arvey, R. D. (1979). *Fairness in selecting employees*. Reading, MA: Addison-Wesley.

Arvey, R. D., & Bouchard, T. J. (1994). Genetics, twins, and organizational behavior. In B. M. Staw & L. L. Cummings (Eds.), *Research in organizational behavior* (Vol. 16, pp. 47–82). Greenwich, CT: JAI Press.

Arvey, R. D., Bouchard, T. J., Segal, N. L., & Abraham, L. M. (1989). Job satisfaction: Environmental and genetic components. *Journal of Applied Psychology, 74*, 187–192.

Arvey, R. D., & Ivancevich, J. M. (1980). Punishment in organizations: A review, propositions and research suggestions. *Academy of Management Review, 5*, 123–132.

Arvey, R. D., & Jones, A. P. (1985). The use of discipline in organizational settings. In L. L. Cummings & B. M. Staw (Eds.), *Research in organizational behavior* (Vol. 7, pp. 367–408). Greenwich, CT: JAI Press.

Arvey, R. D., McCall, B. P., Bouchard, T. J., Taubman, P., & Cavanaugh, M. A. (1994). Genetic influences on job satisfaction and work values. *Personality and Individual Differences, 17*, 21–33.

Ashby, W. (1958). General systems theory as a new discipline. *General Systems Yearbook, 3*, 1–17.

Ashford, S. J. (1986). Feedback-seeking in individual adaptation: A resource perspective. *Academy of Management Journal, 29*(3), 465–487.

Ashford, S. J. (1989). Self-assessments in organizations: A literature review and integrative model. In L. L. Cummings & B. M. Staw (Eds.), *Research in organizational behavior* (Vol. 11, pp. 133–174). Greenwich, CT: JAI Press.

Ashford, S. J. (1993). The feedback environment. *Journal of Organizational Behavior, 14*, 201–224.

Ashford, S. J., & Cummings, L. L. (1983). Feedback as an individual resource: Personal strategies of creating information. *Organizational Behavior and Human Performance, 32*, 370–398.

Ashford, S. J., & Cummings, L. L. (1985). Proactive feedback seeking: The instrumental use of the information environment. *Journal of Occupational Psychology, 58*, 67–79.

Ashford, S. J., & Tsui, A. S. (1991). Self-regulation for managerial effectiveness: The role of active feedback seeking. *Academy of Management Journal, 34*(2), 251–280.

Ashforth, B. (1994). Petty tyranny in organizations. *Human Relations, 47*(7), 755–778.

Ashforth, B. E., & Anand, V. (2003). The normalization of corruption in organizations. In R. M. Kramer & B. M. Staw (Eds.), *Research in organizational behavior* (Vol. 25, pp. 1–52). Kidlington, Oxford: Elsevier.

Ashforth, B. E., & Humphrey, R. H. (1995). Emotion in the workplace: A reappraisal. *Human Relations, 48*(2), 97–125.

Ashforth, B. E., & Mael, F. (1989). Social identity theory and the organization. *Academy of Management Review, 14*(1), 20–39.

Ashforth, B. E., & Saks, A. M. (1994). *Socialization tactics: Dimensionality and longitudinal effects on newcomer adjustment.* Paper presented at the annual meeting of Academy of Management, Dallas, TX.

Ashkanasy, N. M. (2007). From the editor: Evidence-based inquiry, learning, and education: What are the pros and cons? *Academy of Management Learning & Education, 6*(1), 5–8.

Ashkanasy, N. M., Gupta, V., Mayfield, M. S., & Trevor-Roberts, E. (2004). Future orientation. In R. J. House, P. J. Hanges, M. Javidan, P. W. Dorfman, & V. Gupta (Eds.), *Culture, leadership, and organizations* (pp. 282–342). Thousand Oaks, CA: Sage.

Ashkanasy, N. M., Hartel, C. E. J., & Daus, C. S. (2002). Diversity and emotion: The new frontiers in organizational behavior research. *Journal of Management, 28*(3), 307–338.

Ashkanasy, N. M., Hartel, C. E. J., & Zerbe, W. J. (2000). *Emotions in the workplace: Research, theory, and practice.* Westport, CN: Quorum Books.

Ashkanasy, N. M., Wilderom, C. P. M., & Peterson, M. F. (Eds.). (2000). *Handbook of organizational culture & climate.* Thousand Oaks, CA: Sage.

Associated Press. (2005, February 20). Suspect in Detroit shooting ordered held. *Milwaukee Journal Sentinel.*

Astley, W. G. (1985). Administrative science as socially constructive truth. *Administrative Science Quarterly, 30*(4), 497–513.

Atkinson, J. W. (1958). Towards experimental analysis of human motivation in terms of motives, expectancies, and incentives. In J. W. Atkinson (Ed.), *Motives in fantasy, action, and society* (pp. 288–305). Princeton, NJ: Van Nostrand Reinhold.

Atkinson, J. W. (1964). *An introduction to motivation.* Princeton, NJ: Van Nostrand Reinhold.

Atwater, L. E., Waldman, D. A., Carey, J. A., & Cartier, P. (2001). Recipient and observer reactions to discipline: Are managers experiencing wishful thinking? *Journal of Organizational Behavior, 22*, 249–270.

Austin, J. T., & Bobko, P. (1985). Goal-setting theory: Unexplored areas and future research needs. *Journal of Occupational Psychology, 58*(4), 289–308.

Averill, J. (1982). *Anger and aggression: An essay on emotion.* New York: Springer-Verlag.

Axtell, C. M., & Parker, S. K. (2003). Promoting role breadth self-efficacy through involvement, work redesign and training. *Human Relations, 56*(1), 113–131.

Aziz, S., & Zickar, M. J. (2006). A cluster analysis investigation of workaholism as a syndrome. *Journal of Occupational Health Psychology, 11*(1), 52–62.

Azrin, N. H. (1977). A strategy for applied research: Learning based but outcome oriented. *American Psychologist*, *32*, 140–149.

Babb, H. W., & Kopp, D. G. (1978). Applications of behavior modification in organizations: A review and critique. *Academy of Management Review*, *3*, 281–292.

Bacharach, S. B. (1989). Organizational theories: Some criteria for evaluation. *Academy of Management Review*, *14*(4), 496–515.

Bachlin, H. (2000). *The science of self-control*. Cambridge, MA: Harvard University Press.

Badawy, M. K. (1982). *Developing managerial skills in engineers and scientists*. New York: Van Nostrand Reinhold.

Bagozzi, R. P. (1986). Attitude formation under the theory of reasoned action and a purposeful behaviour reformulation. *British Journal of Social Psychology*, *25*, 95–107.

Bagozzi, R. P., & Yi, Y. (1989). The degree of intention formation as a moderator of the attitude–behavior relationship. *Social Psychology Quarterly*, *52*, 266–279.

Baker, A. M. (1988). Plant closings: Lessons from the Maine experience. *Human Resource Management*, *27*(3), 315–328.

Baker, D. D., Ravichandran, R., & Randall, D. M. (1989). Exploring contrasting formulations of expectancy theory. *Decision Sciences*, *20*(1), 1–13.

Baker, M., & Fortin, N. M. (2004). Comparable worth in a decentralized labour market: The case of Ontario. *Canadian Journal of Economics*, *37*(4), 850–878.

Ball, G. A., Trevino, L. K., & Sims Jr., H. P. (1994). Just and unjust punishment: Influences on subordinate performance and citizenship. *Academy of Management Journal*, *37*(2), 299–322.

Bandura, A. (1969). *Principles of behavior modification*. New York: Holt, Rinehart, & Winston.

Bandura, A. (1977). *Social learning theory*. Englewood Cliffs, NJ: Prentice-Hall.

Bandura, A. (1982). Self-efficacy mechanism in human agency. *American Psychologist*, *37*, 122–147.

Bandura, A. (1984). Recycling misconceptions of perceived self-efficacy. *Cognitive Therapy and Research*, *8*, 213–229.

Bandura, A. (1986). *Social foundations of thought and action: A social cognitive theory*. Englewood Cliffs, NJ: Prentice-Hall.

Bandura, A. (1989). Self-regulation of motivation and action through internal standards and external goal systems. In L. A. Pervin (Ed.), *Goal concepts in personality and social psychology*. Hillsdale, NJ: Lawrence Erlbaum Associates, Inc.

Bandura, A. (1991). Social cognitive theory of self-regulation. *Organizational Behavior and Human Decision Processes*, *50*(2), 248–287.

Bandura, A. (1997). *Self-efficacy: The exercise of control*. New York: W. H. Freeman.

Bandura, A. (2001). Social cognitive theory: An agentic perspective. *Annual Review of Psychology*, *52*, 1–26.

Bandura, A., & Cervone, D. (1983). Self-evaluative and self-efficacy mechanisms governing the motivational effects of goal systems. *Journal of Personality and Social Psychology*, *45*, 1017–1028.

Bandura, A., & Locke, E. A. (2003). Negative self-efficacy and goal effects revisited. *Journal of Applied Psychology*, *88*(1), 87–99.

Baritz, L. (1960). *The servants of power: A history of the use of social science in American industry*. Middletown, CT: Wesleyan University Press.

Barling, J., Kelloway, E. K., & Iverson, R. D. (2003). High-quality work, job satisfaction, and occupational injuries. *Journal of Applied Psychology*, *88*(2), 276–283.

Barnard, C. (1938). *The functions of the executive*. Cambridge, MA: Harvard University Press.

Barnard, C. I. (1946). Functions and pathology of status systems in formal organizations. In W. F. Whyte (Ed.), *Industry and society* (pp. 207–243). New York: McGraw-Hill.

Baron, R. A. (1993). Criticism (informal negative feedback) as a source of perceived unfairness in organizations: Effects, mechanisms, and countermeasures. In R. Cropanzano (Ed.), *Justice in the workplace* (pp. 155–170). Hillsdale, NJ: Lawrence Erlbaum Associates, Inc.

Baron, R. A. (1994). The physical environment of work settings. In B. M. Staw & L. L. Cummings (Eds.), *Research in organizational behavior* (Vol. 16, pp. 1–46). Greenwich, CT: JAI Press.

Baron, R. M., & Kenny, D. A. (1986). The moderator–mediator variable distinction in social psychological research: Conceptual, strategic, and statistical considerations. *Journal of Personality and Social Psychology*, *51*(6), 1173–1182.

Barrick, M. R., & Mount, M. K. (1991). The big five personality dimensions and job performance: A meta-analysis. *Personnel Psychology, 44*(1), 1173–1182.

Barrick, M. R., Mount, M. K., & Strauss, J. P. (1993). Conscientiousness and performance of sales representatives. *Journal of Applied Psychology, 78*(5), 715–722.

Barsade, S. G., & Gibson, D. E. (2007). Why does affect matter in organizations? *Academy of Management Perspectives, 21*(1), 36–59.

Bartlett, F. C. (1932). *Remembering: A study in experimental and social psychology*. Cambridge: Cambridge University Press.

Bartol, K. M. (1978). The sex structuring of organizations: A search for possible causes. *Academy of Management Review, 3*, 805–815.

Barton, R. F. (1981). An MCDM approach for resolving goal conflict in MBO. *Academy of Management Review, 6*, 231–242.

Bartunek, J. M., & Spreitzer, G. M. (2006). The interdisciplinary career of a popular construct used in management: Empowerment in the late 20th century. *Journal of Management Inquiry, 15*(3), 255–273.

Baruch, Y. (1998). The rise and fall of organizational commitment. *Human Systems Management, 17*(2), 135–144.

Basch, J., & Fisher, C. D. (2000). Affective events–emotions matrix: A classification of work events and associated emotions. In N. M. Ashkanasy, C. E. J. Hartel, & W. J. Zerbe (Eds.), *Emotions in the workplace: Research, Ttheory, and practice* (pp. 36–48). Westport, CN: Quorum Books.

Bass, B. M. (1981). *Stogdil's handbook of leadership: A survey of theory and research*. New York: Free Press.

Battle, J. (1990). *Self-esteem: The new revolution*. Edmonton, Alberta, Canada: James Battles & Associates.

Baumeister, R. F., Campbell, J. D., Krueger, J. I., & Vohs, K. D. (2003). Does high self-esteem cause better performance, interpersonal success, happiness, or healthier lifestyles? *Psychological Science in the Public Interest, 4*(1), 1–44.

Baumeister, R. F., De Wall, C. N., Ciarocco, N. J., & Twenge, J. M. (2005). Social exclusion impairs self-regulation. *Journal of Personality and Social Psychology, 88*(4), 589–604.

Baumeister, R. F., & Leary, M. R. (1995). The need to belong: Desire for interpersonal attachments as a fundamental human motivation. *Psychological Bulletin, 117*(3), 497–529.

Baumeister, R. F., Tice, D. M., & Hutton, D. G. (1989). Self-presentational motivations and personality differences in self-esteem. *Journal of Personality, 57*(3), 547–579.

Bayes, J. (1988). Occupational sex segregation and comparable worth. In R. M. Kelly & J. Bayes (Eds.), *Comparable worth, pay equity, and public policy* (pp. 15–48). New York: Greenwood Press.

Bazerman, M. H. (1993). Fairness, social comparison, and irrationality. In J. K. Murnighan (Ed.), *Social psychology in organizations* (pp. 184–203). Englewood Cliffs, NJ: Prentice-Hall.

Becker, H. S. (1960). Notes on the concept of commitment. *American Journal of Sociology, 66*, 32–40.

Becker, T. E. (1992). Foci and bases of commitment: Are they distinctions worth making? *Academy of Management Journal, 35*(1), 232–244.

Beer, M., Eisenstat, R. A., & Spector, B. (1990). Why change programs don't produce change. *Harvard Business Review, November–December*, 158–166.

Beehr, T. A., & Gupta, N. A. (1978). Note on the structure of employee withdrawal. *Organizational Behavior and Human Performance, 21*, 73–79.

Behling, O., Labovitz, G., & Kosmo, R. (1968). The Herzberg controversy: A critical appraisal. *Academy of Management Journal, 11*, 99–108.

Bem, D. J. (1967). Self-perception: The dependent variable of human performance. *Organizational Behavior and Human Performance, 2*, 105–121.

Bem, D. J. (1972). Constructing cross-situational consistencies in behavior: Some thoughts on Alker's critique of Mischel. *Journal of Personality, 40*, 17–26.

Bem, D. J. (1974). On predicting some of the people some of the time. *Psychological Review, 81*, 506–520.

Ben-Porat, A. (1981). Event and agent: Toward a structural theory of job satisfaction. *Personnel Psychology, 34*, 523–534.

Benson, G. S., Young, S. M., & Lawler III, E. E. (2006). High-involvement work practices and analysts' forecasts of corporate earnings. *Human Resource Management, 45*(4), 519–537.

Berdahl, J. L. (2007). Harassment based on sex: Protecting social status in the context of gender hierarchy. *Academy of Management Review, 32*(2), 641–658.

Berger, C. J., & Cummings, L. L. (1979). Organizational structure, attitudes, and behaviors. In B. M. Staw (Ed.), *Research in organizational behavior* (pp. 169–208). Greenwich, CT: JAI Press.

Berger, J., Cohen, B. P., & Zeldich, M. (1972). Status characteristics and social interation. *American Sociological Review*, *37*, 241–255.

Berger, J., Rosenholtz, S. J., & Zeldich, M. (1980). Status organizing processes. *Annual Review of Sociology*, *6*, 479–508.

Berger, P. L., & Luckman, T. (1966). *The social construction of reality: A treatise in the sociology of knowledge*. Garden City, NJ: Doubleday.

Bergman, M. E. (2006). The relationship between affective and normative commitment: Review and research agenda. *Journal of Organizational Behavior*, *27*, 645–663.

Berkowitz, L. (1989). Frustration–aggression hypothesis: Examination and reformulation. *Psychological Bulletin*, *106*(1), 59–73.

Berkowitz, L. (1993). Towards a general theory of anger and emotional aggression: Implications of the cognitive–neoassociationistic perspective for the analysis of anger and other emotions. In R. S. J. Wyer & T. K. Skrull (Eds.), *Perspectives on anger and emotion: Advances in social cognition* (Vol. VI, pp. 1–46). Hillsdale, NJ: Lawrence Erlbaum Associates, Inc.

Berkowitz, L. (1997). On the determinants and regulation of impulsive aggression. In S. Feshbach & J. Zagrodska (Eds.), *Aggression: Biological, developmental and social perspectives* (pp. 187–211). New York: Plenum Press.

Berlyne, D. E. (1973). The vicissitudes of aplopathematic and thebematoscopic pneumatology (or the hydrography of hedonism). In D. E. Berlyne & K. B. Madsen (Eds.), *Pleasure, reward, and preferences* (pp. 1–33). New York: Academic Press.

Betcherman, G., McMullen, K., Leckie, N., & Caron, C. (1994). *The Canadian workplace in transition*. Kingston, Ontario, Canada: Industrial Relations Centre, Queen's University.

Betz, E. L. (1969). Need–reinforcer correspondence as a predictor of job satisfaction. *Personnel and Guidance Journal*, *47*, 878–883.

Bibby, R. (2006). *The Boomer factor: What Canada's most famous generation is leaving behind*. Toronto: Bastion Books.

Biberman, G., Baril, G. L., & Kopelman, R. E. (1986). Comparison of return-on-effort and conventional expectancy theory predictions of work effort and job performance: Results from three field studies. *Journal of Psychology*, *120*, 229–237.

Bies, R. B. (1987). The predicament of injustice. In L. L. Cummings & B. M. Staw (Eds.), *Research in organizational behavior* (Vol. 9, pp. 289–320). Greenwich, CT: JAI Press.

Bies, R. B., & Moag, J. S. (1986). Interactional justice: Communication criteria of fairness. In R. J. Lewicki, B. H. Sheppard, & M. H. Bazerman (Eds.), *Research on negotiation in organizations* (Vol. 1, pp. 43–55). Greenwich, CT: JAI Press.

Bies, R. B., & Shapiro, D. L. (1987). Interactional fairness judgements: The influence of social accounts. *Social Justice Research*, *2*, 199–218.

Bies, R. B., & Tripp, T. M. (1996). Beyond trust: "Getting even" and the need for revenge. In R. M. Kramer & T. R. Tyler (Eds.), *Trust in organizatinos* (pp. 246–260). Thousand Oaks, CA: Sage.

Bies, R. J. (2001). Interactional (in)justice: The sacred and the profane. In J. Greenberg & R. Cropanzano (Eds.), *Advances in Organizational Justice* (pp. 89–118). Stanford, CA: Stanford University Press.

Billings, R. S., & Cornelius, E. T. (1980). Dimensions of work outcomes: A multidimensional scaling approach. *Personnel Psychology*, *33*, 151–162.

Binswanger, H. (1991). Volition as cognitive self-regulation. *Organizational Behavior and Human Decision Processes*, *50*(2), 154–178.

Bitner, M. J., Booms, B. H., & Tetreault, M. S. (1990). The service encounter: Diagnosing favorable and unfavorable incidents. *Journal of Marketing*, *54*, 7–84.

Blair, J. M. (1975). Inflation in the United States. In G. C. Means et al. (Eds.), *The roots of inflation*. New York: Burt Franklin.

Blanchard, K., & Johnson, S. (1981). *The one-minute manager*. New York: Berkley Books.

Blankenstein, K. R., Flett, G. L., Koledin, S., & Bortolotto, R. (1989). Affect intensity and dimensions of affiliation motivation. *Personality and Individual Differences*, *10*(11), 1201–1203.

Blau, G. (1993). Operationalizing direction and level of effort and testing their relationships to individual job performance. *Organizational Behavior and Human Performance*, *55*, 152–170.

Blau, G., & Paul, A. (1993). On developing a general index of work commitment. *Journal of Vocational Behavior*, *42*, 298–314.

Blood, M. R. (1969). Work values and job satisfaction. *Journal of Applied Psychology*, *53*, 456–459.

Blood, M. R. (1973). Intergroup comparisons of intraperson differences: Rewards from the job. *Psychology*, *26*, 1–9.

Blyton, P., Blunsdon, B., Reed, K., & Dastmalchian, A. (Eds.). (2006). *Work–life integration: International perspectives on the balancing of multiple roles*. Basingstoke: Palgrave Macmillan.

Blyton, P., Dastmalchian, A., & Adamson, R. (1987). Developing the concept of industrial relations climate. *Journal of Industrial Relations*, *29*, 207–216.

Boal, K. G., & Cummings, L. L. (1981). Cognitive evaluation theory: An experimental test of processes and outcomes. *Organizational Behavior and Human Performance*, *28*, 289–310.

Bobko, P. (1978). Concerning the non-application of human motivation theories in organizational settings. *Academy of Management Review*, *3*(4), 906–910.

Bobko, P. (1985). Removing assumptions of bipolarity: Towards variation and circularity. *Academy of Management Review*, *10*(1), 99–108.

Bockman, V. M. (1971). The Herzberg controversy. *Personnel Psychology*, *24*, 155–189.

Borman, W. C., Klimoski, R. J., & Ilgen, D. R. (2003). Stability and change in industrial and organizational psychology. In W. C. Borman, D. R. Ilgen, & R. J. Klimoski (Eds.), *Handbook of psychology* (Vol. 12, pp. 1–17). New York: John Wiley & Sons.

Borman, W. C., White, L. A., Pulakos, E. D., & Oppler, S. H. (1991). Models of supervisory job performance ratings. *Journal of Applied Psychology*, *76*(6), 863–872.

Boswell, W. R., & Olson-Buchanan, J. B. (2004). Experiencing mistreatment at work: The role of grievance filing, nature of mistreatment, and employee withdrawal. *Academy of Management Journal*, *47*(1), 129–139.

Boulding, K. (1968). General systems theory – The skeleton of science. In W. Buckley (Ed.), *Modern systems research for the behavioral science* (pp. 3–10). Chicago, IL: Aldine.

Bourgeois, V. W., & Pinder, C. C. (1984). *The nonlinearity of progress in organizational science*. Unpublished manuscript, Faculty of Commerce & Business Administration, University of British Columbia, Vancouver, British Columbia, Canada.

Bowen, W. (1979, December 3). Better prospects for our ailing productivity. *Fortune*, *3*, 68–70, 74, 77, 80, 83, 86.

Branden, N. (1969). *The psychology of self-esteem*. Los Angeles: Nash.

Branswell, B. (1998). Pain and pride. *Maclean's*, *111*, 21.

Brayfield, A. H., & Crockett, W. H. (1955). Employee attitudes and employee performance. *Psychological Bulletin*, *52*, 415–422.

Breaugh, J. A. (1981). Predicting absenteeism from prior absenteeism and work attitudes. *Journal of Applied Psychology*, *66*(5), 555–560.

Brehm, J. W., & Self, E. A. (1989). The intensity of motivation. *Annual Review of Psychology*, *66*, 555–560.

Brennan, A., & Skarlicki, D. P. (2004). Personality and perceived justice as predictors of survivors' reactions following downsizing. *Journal of Applied Social Psychology*, *34*(6), 1306–1328.

Brett, J. M. (1981). The effect of job transfer on employees and their families. In C. L. Cooper & R. Payne (Eds.), *Current concerns in occupational stress*. New York: John Wiley & Sons.

Bretz, R. D., & Judge, T. A. (1994). Person–environment fit and the theory of work adjustment: Implications for satisfaction, tenure, and career success. *Journal of Vocational Behavior*, *44*, 32–54.

Bridges, W. (1994). *Jobshift*. Reading, MA: Addison-Wesley.

Brief, A. P. (2001). Organizational behavior and the study of affect: Keep your eyes on the organization. *Organizational Behavior and Human Decision Processes*, *86*(1), 131–139.

Brief, A. P., & Aldag, R. J. (1975). Employee reactions to job characteristics: A constructive replication. *Journal of Applied Psychology*, *60*, 182–186.

Brief, A. P., & Dukerich, J. M. (1991). Theory in organizational behavior: Can it be useful? In L. L. Cummings & B. M. Staw (Eds.), *Research in organizational behavior* (Vol. 13, pp. 327–352). Greenwich, CT: JAI Press.

Brief, A. P., & Hollenbeck, J. R. (1985). An exploratory study of self-regulating activities and their effects on job performance. *Journal of Occupational Behavior*, *6*(3), 197–208.

Brief, A. P., & Motowidlo, S. J. (1986). Prosocial organizational behaviors. *Academy of Management Review*, *11*(4), 710–725.

Brief, A. P., & Weiss, H. M. (2002). Organizational behavior: Affect in the workplace. *Annual Review of Psychology*, *53*, 279.

Brockner, J. (1988a). *Self-esteem at work*. Lexington, MA: Lexington Books.

Brockner, J. (1988b). The effects of work layoffs on survivors: Research, theory and practice. In B. M. Staw &

L. L. Cummings (Eds.), *Research in organizational behavior* (Vol. 10, pp. 213–255). Greenwich, CT: JAI Press.

Brockner, J., Grover, S., Reed, T., De Witt, R., & O'Malley, M. (1987). Survivors' reactions to layoffs: We get by with a little help from our friends. *Administrative Science Quarterly, 32*(4), 526–541.

Brockner, J., Konovsky, M., Cooper-Schneider, R., Folger, R., Martin, C., & Bies, R. B. (1994). Interactive effects of procedural justice and outcome negativity on victims and survivors of job loss. *Academy of Management Journal, 37*(2), 397–409.

Brockner, J., & Siegel, P. (1996). Understanding the interaction between procedural and distributive justice: The role of trust. In R. M. Kramer & T. R. Tyler (Eds.), *Trust in organizations* (pp. 390–413). New York: Sage.

Brody, N. (1980). Social motivation. *Annual Review of Psychology, 31*, 143–168.

Brooke Jr., P. P., Russell, D. W., & Price, J. L. (1988). Discriminant validation of measures of job satisfaction, job involvement, and organizational commitment. *Journal of Applied Psychology, 73*(2), 139–145.

Brooks, G. R., & Wallace, J. P. (2006). A discursive examination of the nature, determinants and impact of organizational commitment. *Asia Pacific Journal of Human Resources, 44*(2), 222–239.

Brown, D., & Beatty, D. (2006). *Canadian labour arbitration* (4th ed.). Aurora, ON: Canadian Law Publication.

Brown, D. J., Cober, R. T., Kane, K., Levy, P. E., & Shalhoop, J. (2006). Proactive personality and the successful job search: A field investigation with college graduates. *Journal of Applied Psychology, 91*(3), 717–726.

Brown, G., Lawrence, T. B., & Robinson, S. L. (2005). Territoriality in organizations. *Academy of Management Review, 30*(3), 577–594.

Brown, M. A. (1976). Values: A necessary but neglected ingredient of motivation on the job. *Academy of Management Review, 1*, 15–23.

Brown, S. P. (1996). A meta-analysis and review of organizational research on job involvement. *Psychological Bulletin, 120*(2), 235–255.

Brown, T. J., & Allgeier, E. R. (1996). The impact of participant characteristics, perceived motives, and job behaviors on co-workers' evaluations of workplace romances. *Journal of Applied Social Psychology, 26*(7), 577–595.

Buchanan, B. (1974). Building organizational commitment: The socialization of managers in work organizations. *Administrative Science Quarterly, 19*, 533–546.

Buck, R. (1985). Prime theory: An integrated view of motivation and emotion. *Psychological Review, 92*, 389–413.

Budd, R. J. (1986). Predicting cigarette use: The need to incorporate measures of salience in the theory of reasoned action. *Journal of Applied Social Psychology, 16*, 663–685.

Budner, S. (1962). Intolerance of ambiguity as a personality variable. *Journal of Personality, 30*, 29–59.

Burger, J. M. (1992). *Desire for control.* New York: Plenum Press.

Burkett, L. (1998). *Business by the book: The complete guide of biblical principles for the workplace.* Nashville, TN: Thomas Nelson Publishers.

Burris, V. (1990). Classes in contemporary capitalist society: Recent Marxist and Weberian perspectives. In S. Clegg (Ed.), *Organization theory and class analysis* (pp. 55–74). New York: Walter de Gruyter.

Bushman, B. J., & Wells, G. L. (1998). Trait aggressiveness and hockey penalties: Predicting hot tempers on the ice. *Journal of Applied Psychology, 83*(6), 969–974.

Business Week/online. (2005). *The real reasons you're working so hard . . . and what you can do about it,* October 3, from www.businessweek.com/print/magazine/content/05

Buss, A. H. (1961). *The psychology of aggression.* New York: John Wiley & Sons.

Buss, A. H. (1983). Social rewards and personality. *Journal of Personality and Social Psychology, 44*, 553–563.

Buss, A. H. (1986). *Social behavior and personality.* Hillsdale, NJ: Lawrence Erlbaum Associates, Inc.

Buss, D. M. (1999). *Evolutionary psychology.* Boston, MA: Allyn & Bacon.

Butler, J. K., & Cantrell, R. S. (1989). Extrinsic reward valences and productivity of business faculty: A within- and between-subjects decision modeling experiment. *Psychological Reports, 64*, 343–353.

Butterfield, K. D., Trevino, L. K., & Ball, G. A. (1996). Punishment from the manager's perspective: A grounded investigation and inductive model. *Academy of Management Journal, 39*(6), 1479–1512.

Bycio, P., Hackett, R. D., & Alvares, K. M. (1990). Job performance and turnover: A review and meta-analysis. *Applied Psychology: An International Review, 61*, 468–472.

Byrne, D. (1971). *The attraction paradigm.* New York: Academic Press.

Cable, J. P., & DeRue, D. S. (2002). The convergent and discriminant validity of subjective fit perceptions. *Journal of Applied Psychology, 87*, 875–884.

Calder, B. J., & Schurr, P. H. (1981). Attitudinal processes in organizations. In B. M. Staw & L. L. Cummings (Eds.), *Research in organizational behavior* (Vol. 3, pp. 283–302). Greenwich, CT: JAI Press.

Caldwell, D. S., & Ihrke, D. M. (1994). Differentiating between burnout and copout in organizations. *Public Personnel Management*, *23*(1), 77–84.

Cameron, J., & Pierce, W. D. (1994). Reinforcement, reward, and intrinsic motivation: A meta-analysis. *Review of Educational Research*, *64*, 363–423.

Cameron, K. S., Dutton, J. E., & Quinn, R. E. (Eds.). (2003). *Positive organizational scholarship: Foundations of a new discipline*. San Francisco: Berrett-Koehler.

Campbell, D. J. (1984). The effects of goal-contingent payment on the performance of a complex task. *Personnel Psychology*, *37*(1), 23–40.

Campbell, D. J. (1988). Task complexity: A review and analysis. *Academy of Management Review*, *13*(1), 40–52.

Campbell, D. J., & Gingrich, K. F. (1986). The interactive effects of task complexity and participation on task performance: A field experiment. *Organizational Behavior and Human Decision Processes*, *38*(2), 162–180.

Campbell, D. J., & Ilgen, D. R. (1976). Additive effects of task difficulty and goal setting on subsequent task performance. *Journal of Applied Psychology*, *61*(3), 319–324.

Campbell, J. P., Campbell, R. J., & Associates. (1988). *Productivity in organizations: New perspectives from industrial and organizational psychology*. San Francisco: Jossey-Bass.

Campbell, J. P., Dunnette, M. D., Lawler III, E. E., & Weick, K. E. (1970). *Managerial behavior performance and effectiveness*. New York: McGraw-Hill.

Campbell, J. P., & Pritchard, R. D. (1976). Motivation theory in industrial and organizational psychology. In M. D. Dunnette (Ed.), *Handbook of industrial and organizational psychology* (pp. 63–130). Chicago, IL: Rand McNally.

Campion, M. A. (1988). Interdisciplinary approaches to job design: A constructive replication with extension. *Journal of Applied Psychology*, *73*(3), 467–481.

Campion, M. A., & Lord, R. G. (1982). A control systems conceptualization of the goal setting and changing process. *Organizational Behavior and Human Performance*, *30*, 265–287.

Campion, M. A., & Thayer, P. W. (1985). Development and field evaluation of an interdisciplinary measure of job design. *Journal of Applied Psychology*, *70*(1), 29–43.

Campion, M. A., & Thayer, P. W. (1987). Job design: Approaches, outcomes, and trade-offs. *Organizational Dynamics*, *15*(3), 66–79.

Capelli, P., & Sherer, P. D. (1991). The missing role of context in OB: The need for a meso-level approach. In B. M. Staw & L. L. Cummings (Eds.), *Research in organizational behavior* (Vol. 13, pp. 55–110). Greenwich, CT: JAI Press.

Caplan, R. D., & Jones, K. W. (1975). Effects of work load role ambiguity and Type A personality on anxiety, depression and heart rate. *Journal of Applied Psychology*, *60*, 713–719.

Capozzi, T., & McVey, R. S. (1996). *Managing violence in the workplace*. Delray Beach, FL: St. Lucie Press.

Caproni, P., & Finley, J. (1997). When organizations do harm: Two cautionary tales. In P. Presad, & A. Mills (Eds.), *Managing the organizational melting pot* (pp. 255–284). Thousand Oaks, CA: Sage.

Carl, D., Gupta, V., & Javidan, M. (2004). Power distance. In R. J. House, P. J. Hanges, M. Javidan, P. W. Dorfman, & V. Gupta (Eds.), *Culture, leadership, and organizations: The GLOBE study of 62 societies* (pp. 513–559). Thousand Oaks, CA: Sage.

Carlson, M. (1995). The louts of discipline. *Time*, *146*(9), 35.

Carr, J. Z., Schmidt, A. M., Ford, J. K., & DeShon, R. P. (2003). Climate perceptions matter: A meta-analytic path analysis relating molar climate, cognitive and affective states, and individual level work outcomes. *Journal of Applied Psychology*, *88*(4), 605–619.

Carrell, M. R., & Dittrich, J. E. (1978). Equity theory: The recent literature, methodological considerations, and new directions. *Academy of Management Review*, *3*(2), 202–210.

Carroll, S. J., & Tosi, H. (1973). *Management by objectives: Applications and research*. New York: Macmillan.

Carter, S. L. (1998). *Civility: Manners, morals, and the etiquette of democracy*. New York: Basic Books.

Carver, C. S. (1979). A cybernetic model of self-attention processes. *Journal of Personality and Social Psychology*, *37*, 1251–1281.

Carver, C. S., & Scheier, M. F. (1981). *Attention and self-regulation: A control-theory approach to human behavior*. New York: Springer-Verlag.

Carver, C. S., & Scheier, M. F. (1982). Control theory: A useful conceptual framework for personality – Social, clinical, and health psychology. *Psychological Bulletin*, *92*, 111–135.

Carver, C. S., & Scheier, M. F. (1990a). Origins and functions of positive and negative affect: A control-process view. *Psychological Reports, 97*, 19–35.

Carver, C. S., & Scheier, M. F. (1990b). Principles of self-regulation: Action and emotion. In E. T. Higgins & R. M. Sorrentino (Eds.), *Handbook of motivation and cognition* (pp. 3–52). New York: Guilford Press.

Cascio, W. F. (1993). Downsizing: What do we know? What have we learned? *Academy of Management Executive, 7*(1), 95–104.

Cash, T. F., Gillen, B., & Burns, D. S. (1977). Sexism and "beautyism" in personnel consultant decision making. *Journal of Applied Psychology, 62*(3), 301–310.

Caulkins, D. (1974). Job redesign: Pay implications. *Personnel, 51*(3), 29–34.

Center for Entrepreneurial Leadership Clearinghouse on Entrepreneurship Education. (June 2001). *What are the costs of employee turnover?*, from www.celcee.edu: EDINFO Number 01–07.

Chatman, J. A. (1989). Improving interactional organizational research: A model of person–organization fit. *Academy of Management Review, 14*(3), 333–349.

Chatman, J. A. (1991). Matching people and organizations: Selection and socialization in public accounting firms. *Administrative Science Quarterly, 36*, 459–484.

Cheloha, R. S., & Farr, J. L. (1980). Absenteeism, job involvement, and job satisfaction in an organizational setting. *Journal of Applied Psychology, 65*(4), 467–473.

Chen, G., Gully, S. M., & Eden, D. (2001). Validation of a new general self-efficacy scale. *Organizational Research Methods, 4*(1), 62–83.

Chen, G., Gully, S. M., & Eden, D. (2004). General self-efficacy and self-esteem: Toward theoretical and empirical distinction between correlated self-evaluations. *Journal of Organizational Behavior, 25*(3), 375–395.

Chen, S., Lee-Chai, A. Y., & Bargh, J. A. (2001). Relationship orientation as a moderator of the effects of social power. *Journal of Personality and Social Psychology, 80*(2), 173–187.

Cherniss, C., Extein, M., Goleman, D., & Weissberg, R. P. (2006). Emotional intelligence: What does the research really indicate? *Educational Psychologist, 41*(4), 239–245.

Cherrington, D. J., & England, J. L. (1980). The desire for an enriched job as a moderator of the enrichment–satisfaction relationship. *Organizational Behavior and Human Performance, 25*, 139–159.

Chesney, A. A., & Locke, E. A. (1991). Relationships among goal difficulty, business strategies, and performance on a complex management simulation task. *Academy of Management Journal, 34*(2), 400–424.

Chisholm, J. S. (1995). Love's contingencies: The development socioecology of romantic passion. In W. Jankowiak (Ed.), *Romantic passion* (pp. 42–56). New York: Columbia University Press.

Chusmir, L. H. (1985). *Matching individuals to jobs: A motivational answer for personnel and counseling professionals*. New York: AMACOM.

Chusmir, L. H., & Azevedo, A. (1992). Motivation needs of sampled Fortune-500 CEOs: Relations to organizational outcomes. *Perceptual and Motor Skills, 75*, 595–612.

Chusmir, L. H., & Parker, B. (1984). Dimensions of need for power: Personalized vs. socialized power in female and male managers. *Sex Roles, 11*(9/10), 759–769.

Cialdini, R. B. (1993). *Influence: Science and practice* (3rd ed.). New York: HarperCollins.

Cialdini, R. B., Petty, R. E., & Cacioppo, J. T. (1981). Attitude and attitude change. *Annual Review of Psychology, 32*, 357–404.

Clegg, S. (1990). *Organization theory and class analysis*. New York: Walter de Gruyter.

Clore, G. L., & Ortony, A. (1991). What more is there to emotion concepts than prototypes? *Journal of Personality and Social Psychology, 60*(1), 48–50.

Coch, L., & French, J. R. P. (1948). Overcoming resistance to change. *Human Relations, 1*, 512–532.

Cofer, C. N., & Appley, M. H. (1964). *Motivation theory and research*. New York: John Wiley & Sons.

Cohen, A. (1993). Organizational commitment and turnover: A meta-analysis. *Academy of Management Journal, 36*(5), 1140–1157.

Cohen, B. P., & Zhou, X. (1991). Status processes in enduring work groups. *American Sociological Review, 56*(2), 179–188.

Cohen, R. L. (1990). *Justice, voice and silence*. Paper presented at the International Conference on Social Science and Societal Dilemmas, Utrecht, The Netherlands.

Cohen, R. L. (1991). Justice and negotiation. In R. J. Lewiski, B. H. Sheppard, & M. H. Bagerman (Eds.), *Research on negotiation in organizations* (Vol. 3, pp. 259–282). Greenwich, CT: JAI Press.

Cohen, S., & Wills, T. A. (1985). Stress, social support, and the buffering hypothesis. *Psychological Bulletin, 98*, 310–357.

Cohen, S. L., & Bunker, K. A. (1975). Subtle effects of sex role stereotypes on recruiters' hiring decisions. *Journal of Applied Psychology*, *60*, 566–572.

Cohen-Charash, Y., & Spector, P. E. (2001). The role of justice in organizations: A meta-analysis. *Organizational Behavior & Human Decision Processes*, *86*(2), 278–321.

Collins, E. G. C. (1983). Managers and lovers. *Harvard Business Review*, *61*(5), 142–153.

Collinson, D. L. (1992). *Managing the shopfloor: Subjectivity, masculinity and workplace culture*. Berlin: Walter de Gruyter.

Colquitt, J. A. (2001). On the dimensionality of organizational justice: A construct validation of a measure. *Journal of Applied Psychology*, *86*(3), 386–400.

Colquitt, J. A. (2004). Does the justice of the one interact with the justice of the many? Reactions to procedural justice in teams. *Journal of Applied Psychology*, *89*(4), 633–646.

Colquitt, J. A., Conlon, D. E., Wesson, M. J., Porter, C. O. L. H., & Ng, K. Y. (2001). Justice at the millennium: A meta-analytic review of 25 years of organizational justice research. *Journal of Applied Psychology*, *86*(3), 425–445.

Colquitt, J. A., Le Pine, J. A., & Noe, R. A. (2000). Toward an integrative theory of training motivation: A meta-analytic path analysis of 20 years of research. *Journal of Applied Psychology*, *85*, 678–707.

Colquitt, J. A., & Simmering, M. J. (1998). Conscientiousness, goal orientation, and motivation to learn during the learning process: A longitudinal study. *Journal of Applied Psychology*, *83*(4), 654–665.

Colwill, N., & Lips, H. M. (1988). Issues in the workplace. In H. M. Lips (Ed.), *Sex and gender: An introduction* (pp. 292–315). Boston, MA: McGraw-Hill.

Combs, J., Liu, Y., Hall, A., & Ketchen, D. (2006). How much do high-performance work practices matter? A meta-analysis of their effects on organizational performance. *Personnel Psychology*, *59*(3), 501–528.

Comer, D. R. (1995). A model of social loafing in real work groups. *Human Relations*, *48*(6), 647–667.

Condry, J. (1975). *The role of initial interest and task performance in intrinsic motivation*. Paper presented at the American Psychological Association, Chicago.

Conger, J. A., & Kanungo, R. N. (1988). The empowerment process: Integrating theory and practice. *Academy of Management Review*, *13*(3), 471–482.

Connolly, J. J., & Viswesvaran, C. (2000). The role of affectivity in job satisfaction: A meta-analysis. *Personality and Individual Differences*, *29*, 265–281.

Connor, P. E., & Becker, B. W. (1994). Personal values and management: What do we know and why don't we know more? *Journal of Management Inquiry*, *31*(1), 67–73.

Cook, S. D. (1972). Coercion and social change. In R. J. Pennock & J. R. Chapman (Eds.), *Coercion* (pp. 107–143). Chicago, IL: Aldine.

Cook, T. D., & Campbell, D. T. (1979). *Quasi-experimentation: Design and analysis issues for field settings*. Boston, MA: Houghton-Mifflin.

Cooper, D., & Emory, C. W. (1995). *Business research methods*. Burr Ridge, IL: Irwin.

Cooper, M. R., Morgan, B. S., Foley, P. M., & Kaplan, L. B. (1979). Changing employee values: Deepening discontent? *Harvard Business Review*, *57*(1), 117–125.

Cordery, J. L., & Sevastos, P. P. (1993). Responses to the original and the revised Job Diagnostic Survey: Is education a factor in responses to negatively worded items? *Journal of Applied Psychology*, *78*, 141–143.

Corsun, D. L., & Enz, C. A. (1999). Predicting psychological empowerment among service workers: The effect of support-based relationships. *Human Relations*, *52*(2), 205–224.

Cortina, L. M., Magley, V. J., Williams, J. H., & Langhout, R. D. (2001). Incivility in the workplace: Incidence and impact. *Journal of Occupational Health Psychology*, *6*(1), 64–80.

Côté, S. (2005). A social interaction model of the effects of emotion regulation on work strain. *Academy of Management Review*, *30*(3), 509–530.

Côté, S., & Morgan, L. M. (2002). A longitudinal analysis of the association between emotion regulation, job satisfaction, and intentions to quit. *Journal of Organizational Behavior*, *23*, 946–962.

Cotton, J. L., Vollrath, D. A., Froggatt, K. L., Lengnick-Hall, M. L., & Jennings, K. R. (1988). Employee participation: Diverse forms and different outcomes. *Academy of Management Review*, *13*(1), 8–22.

Coulson, R. (1981). *The termination handbook*. New York: Free Press.

Coulter, J. (1979). *The social construction of mind*. London: Macmillan.

Coupland, D. (1991). *Generation X*. New York: St. Martin's.

Covey, S. R. (1989). *The 7 habits of highly effective people*. New York: Simon & Schuster.

Cox, A., Zagelmeyer, S., & Marchington, M. (2006). Embedding employee involvement and participation at work. *Human Resource Management Journal, 16*(3), 250–267.

Craig, G., Gaus, A., Wilkinson, M., Skrivankova, K., & McQuade, A. (2006). *Contemporary slavery in the UK.* York: Joseph Rowntree Foundation.

Craighead, W. E., Kazdin, A. E., & Mahoney, M. J. (1976). *Behavior modification.* Boston, MA: Houghton-Mifflin.

Crane, D. P., & Jones Jr., W. A. (1991). *The public manager.* Atlanta, GA: Georgia State University Press.

Cranny, C. J., Smith, P. C., & Stone, E. F. (Eds.). (1992). *Job satisfaction.* New York: Lexington Books.

Crawford, J., Kippax, S., Onyx, J., Gault, U., & Benton P. (1992). *Emotion and gender: Constructing meaning from memory.* London: Sage.

Crawford, T. J., & Boyer, R. (1985). Salient consequences, cultural values, and childbearing intentions. *Journal of Applied Psychology, 16*, 16–30.

Craychee, G. A. (1987). The psychosocial dimension of professional continuing education: Behavioral intentions. *Radiologic Technology, 58*, 529–535.

Critchlow, B. (1987). A utility analysis of drinking. *Addictive Behaviors, 12*, 269–273.

Cronbach, L. J. (1957). The two disciplines of scientific psychology. *American Psychologist, 12*, 671–684.

Cronbach, L. J. (1970). *Essentials of psychological testing.* New York: Harper & Row.

Cronbach, L. J. (1975). Beyond the two disciplines of scientific psychology. *American Psychologist, 30*, 116–127.

Cronbach, L. J., & Gleser, G. (1965). *Psychological tests and personnel decisions.* Urbana, IL: University of Illinois Press.

Cropanzano, R. (Ed.). (1993). *Justice in the workplace: Approaching fairness in human resource management.* Hillsdale, NJ: Lawrence Erlbaum Associates, Inc.

Cropanzano, R., Goldman, B., & Folger, R. (2003). Deontic justice: The role of moral principles in workplace fairness. *Journal of Organizational Behavior, 24*(8), 1019–1024.

Cropanzano, R., Rupp, D. E., Mohler, C. J., & Schminke, M. (2001). Three roads to organizational justice. In G. R. Ferris (Ed.), *Research in personnel and human resources management* (Vol. 20, pp. 1–113). Oxford: JAI Press.

Cropanzano, R., Weiss, H. M., Suckow, K. J., & Grandey, A. A. (2000). Doing justice to workplace emotion. In N. M. Ashkanasy, C. E. J. Hartel, & W. J. Zerbe (Eds.), *Emotions in the workplace: Research, theory, and practice* (pp. 49–62). Westport, CN: Quorum Books.

Crosby, F. J., Iyer, A., Clayton, S., & Downing, R. A. (2003). Affirmative action: Psychological data and the policy debates. *American Psychologist, 58*(2), 93–115.

Crossman, M., Fry, J., & Killing, J. P. (2002). *Strategic analysis and action* (5th ed.). Toronto: Prentice-Hall.

Cummings, L. L. (1980). The brother-in-law syndrome: Inequity in everyday life. In L. L. Cummings & R. B. Dunham (Eds.), *Introduction to organizational behavior* (pp. 142–144). Homewood, IL: Irwin.

Cummings, L. L., & Schwab, D. P. (1973). *Performance in organizations: Determinants and appraisal.* Glenview, IL: Scott, Foresman.

Cummings, T. G., Molloy, E. S., & Glen, R. A. (1977). A methodological critique of fifty-eight selected work experiments. *Human Relations, 30*(8), 675–708.

Cyert, R. M., & March, J. G. (1963). *A behavioral theory of the firm.* Englewood Cliffs, NJ: Prentice-Hall.

Dabbs, J. M. (1992). Testosterone and occupational achievement. *Social Forces, 70*, 813–824.

Dachler, H. P., & Mobley, W. H. (1973). Construct validation of an instrumentality–expectancy–task–goal model of work motivation. *Journal of Applied Psychology, 58*(3), 397–418.

Dachler, H. P., & Wilpert, B. (1978). Conceptual dimensions and boundaries of participation in organizations: A critical evaluation. *Administrative Science Quarterly, 23*, 1–39.

Daft, R. L. (1983). *Organization theory and design.* St. Paul, MN: West.

Dahl, R. A. (1957). The concept of power. *Behavioral Science, 2*(3), 201–215.

Dahl, R. A. (1986). Power as the control of behavior. In S. Lukes (Ed.), *Power* (pp. 37–58). Worcester, England: Blackwell.

Dalal, R. (2005). A meta-analysis of the relationship between organizational citizenship behavior and counter-productive work behavior. *Journal of Applied Psychology, 90*(6), 1241–1255.

Dalton, D. R. (1981). Turnover and absenteeism: Measures of personal effectiveness. In R. S. Schuler, D. R. Dalton, & J. M. McFillen (Eds.), *Applied readings in personnel and human resource management.* St. Paul, MN: West.

Dalton, D. R., & Todor, W. D. (1973). Turnover turned over: An expanded and positive perspective. *Academy of Management Review, 4*, 225–235.

Dalton, D. R., & Todor, W. D. (1982a). Turnover: A lucrative hard dollar phenomenon. *Academy of Management Review, 7*, 212–218.

Dalton, D. R., & Todor, W. D. (1982b). Antecedents of grievance filling behavior: Attitude/behavioral consistency and the union steward. *Academy of Management Journal, 25*(1), 158–169.

Dalton, M. (1959). *Men who manage: Fusions of feeling and theory in administration.* New York: John Wiley & Sons.

Damasio, A. R. (1994). *Descartes' error.* New York: Putnam.

Damon, W. (1977). *The social world of the child.* San Francisco: Jossey-Bass.

D'Andrade, R. G. (1992). Schemas and motivation. In R. G. D'Andrade & C. Strauss (Eds.), *Human motives and cultural models* (pp. 23–44). Cambridge: Cambridge University Press.

Daniels, D., & Mitchell, T. R. (1995). *Differential effects of self-efficacy, goals, and expectations on task performance.* Unpublished manuscript, School of Business Administration, University of Washington at Seattle.

Dastmalchian, A. (in press). Industrial relations climate. In P. Blyton, N. Bacon, J. Fiorito & E. Heery (Eds.), *Handbook of industrial relations.* London: Sage.

Davenport, T. H. (2006). *Thinking for a living: How to get better performance and results from knowledge workers.* Cambridge, MA: Harvard Business School Press.

Davidson, D., Suppes, P., & Siegel, S. (1957). *Decision making: An experimental approach.* Stanford, CA: Stanford University Press.

Davidson, O. B., & Eden, D. (2000). Remedial self-fulfilling prophecy: Two field experiments to prevent Golem effects among disadvantaged women. *Journal of Applied Psychology, 85*(3), 386–398.

Davis, L. E., & Taylor, J. C. (Eds.). (1979). *Design of jobs.* Santa Monica, CA: Goodyear.

Davis, T. R. V., & Luthans, F. (1980). A social learning approach to organizational behavior. *Academy of Management Review, 5*(2), 281–290.

Dawes, R. M., & Smith, T. L. (1985). Attitude and opinion measurement. In G. Lindzey & E. Aronson (Eds.), *Handbook of social psychology* (3rd ed., Vol. 1, pp. 509–566). New York: Random House.

Dawis, R., & Lofquist, L. H. (1984). *A psychological theory of work adjustment: An individual differences model and its applications.* Minneapolis, MN: University of Minnesota Press.

De Boer, E. M., Bakker, A. B., Syroit, J. E., & Schaufeli, W. B. (2002). Unfairness at work as a predictor of absenteeism. *Journal of Organizational Behavior, 23*(2), 181.

de Charms, R. (1968). *Personal causation.* New York: Academic Press.

de Cremer, D., Tyler, T. R., & den Ouden, N. (2005). Managing cooperation via procedural fairness: The mediating influence of self–other merging. *Journal of Economic Psychology, 26*(2005), 393–406.

de Leo, P. J., & Pritchard, R. D. (1974). An examination of some methodological problems in testing expectancy-valence models with survey techniques. *Organizational Behavior and Human Performance, 12*, 143–148.

de Luque, M. S., & Javidan, M. (2004). Uncertainty avoidance. In R. J. House, P. J. Hanges, M. Javidan, P. W. Dorfman, & V. Gupta (Eds.), *Culture, leadership, and organizations* (pp. 602–653). Thousand Oaks, CA: Sage.

de Waele, M., Morvel, J., & Sheitoyan, R. G. (1992). *Self-management in organizations.* Seattle, WA: Hogrefe & Huber.

Deans, R. C. (1973). Productivity and the new work ethic. In *Editorial Research Reports on the American Work Ethic* (pp. 1–20). Washington, DC: Congressional Quarterly, Inc.

Deci, E. L. (1971). Effects of externally mediated rewards on intrinsic motivation. *Journal of Personality and Social Psychology, 18*, 105–115.

Deci, E. L. (1972). Intrinsic motivation, extrinsic reinforcement and inequity. *Journal of Personality and Social Psychology, 22*, 113–120.

Deci, E. L. (1975). *Intrinsic motivation.* New York: Plenum Press.

Deci, E. L. (1976). Notes on the theory and meta-theory of intrinsic motivation. *Organizational Behavior and Human Performance, 15*, 130–145.

Deci, E. L. (1980). *The psychology of self-determination.* Lexington, MA: D.C. Heath.

Deci, E. L., Connell, J. P., & Ryan, R. M. (1989). Self-determination in a work organization. *Journal of Applied Psychology, 74*(4), 580–590.

Deci, E. L., Koestner, R., & Ryan, R. M. (1999). A meta-analytic review of experiments examining the effects of extrinsic rewards on intrinsic motivation. *Psychological Bulletin, 125*(6), 617–668.

Deci, E. L., & Porac, J. (1978). Cognitive evaluation theory and the study of human motivation. In M. R. Lepper & D. Greene (Eds.), *The hidden costs of reward* (pp. 149–176). Hillsdale, NJ: Lawrence Erlbaum Associates, Inc.

Deci, E. L., & Ryan, R. M. (1985). *Intrinsic motivation and self determination in human behavior*. New York: Plenum Press.

Deci, E. L., & Ryan, R. M. (1987). The support of autonomy and the control of behavior. *Journal of Personality and Social Psychology, 53*, 1024–1037.

Deci, E. L., & Ryan, R. M. (2000). The "what" and "why" of goal pursuits: Human needs and the self-determination of behavior. *Psychological Inquiry, 11*(4), 227–268.

Degoey, P. (2000). Contagious justice: Exploring the social construction of justice in organizations. In B. M. Staw & R. I. Sutton (Eds.), *Research in organizational behavior* (Vol. 22, pp. 51–102). New York: JAI Press.

Dempster, F. N. (1988). The spacing effect. *American Psychologist, 43*, 627–634.

Dempster, F. N. (1989). Spacing effects and their implications for theory and practice. *Educational Psychology Review, 1989*, 309–330.

Den Hartog, D. N. D. (2004). Assertiveness. In R. J. House, P. J. Hanges, M. Javidan, P. W. Dorfman, & V. Gupta (Eds.), *Culture, leadership, and organizations: The GLOBE study of 62 societies* (pp. 395–436). Thousand Oaks, CA: Sage.

Denison, D. R. (1996). What is the difference between organizational culture and organizational climate? A native's point of view on a decade of paradigm wars. *Academy of Management Review, 21*, 619–654.

Derryberry, D., & Tucker, D. M. (1994). Motivating the focus of attention. In P. M. Niedenthal & S. Kitayama (Eds.), *The heart's eye* (pp. 167–196). San Diego, CA: Academic Press.

Deutsch, M. (1983). Current social psychological perspectives on justice. *European Journal of Social Psychology, 13*, 305–319.

Dickson, D., Saunders, C., & Stringer, M. (1993). *Rewarding people: The skill of responding positively*. London: Routledge.

Diener, E., Larsen, R., Levine, S., & Emmons, R. A. (1985). Intensity and frequency: Dimensions underlying positive and negative affect. *Journal of Personality and Social Psychology, 48*, 1253–1265.

Dietz, J., Robinson, S. L., Folger, R., Baron, R. A., & Schulz, M. (2003). The impact of community violence and an organization's procedural justice climate on workplace aggression. *Academy of Management Journal, 46*(3), 317–326.

Digman, J. M. (1990). Personality structure: Emergence of the five-factor model. *Annual Review of Psychology, 41*(1), 417–440.

d'Iribarne, P. (2002). Motivating workers in emerging countries: Universal tools and local adaptations. *Journal of Organizational Behavior, 23*(3), 243–256.

Dittrich, J. E., & Carrell, M. R. (1979). Organizational equity perceptions, employee job satisfaction, and departmental absence and turnover rates. *Organizational Behavior and Human Performance, 24*, 29–40.

Dobie, K. (2005). AWOL in America. *Harper's, 310*(1585), 33–44.

Dobrow, S. (2004). *Extreme subjective career success: A new integrated view of having a calling*. Paper presented at Academy of Management, New Orleans, LA.

Dollard, J., Doob, L. W., Miller, N. E., Mowrer, O. H., & Sears, R. R. (1939). *Frustration and aggression*. New Haven, CT: Yale University Press.

Donahue, T. R. (1982). *Labor looks at quality of work life programs*. Paper presented at the Conference on Labor Participation, Amherst, MA: Labor Relations and Research Centre, University of Massachusetts.

Donovan, M. A., Drasgow, F., & Munson, L. J. (1998). The perceptions of fair interpersonal treatment scale: Development and validation of a measure of interpersonal treatment in the workplace. *Journal of Applied Psychology, 83*(5), 683–692.

Dooley, D., & Prause, J. (1995). Effect of unemployment on school leavers' self-esteem. *Journal of Occupational and Organizational Psychology, 68*, 177–192.

Dormann, C., & Zapf, D. (2001). Job satisfaction: A meta-analysis of stabilities. *Journal of Organizational Behavior, 22*(5), 483–504.

Douglas, M. (2002, October 17). Shooting took two minutes. *Kamloops Daily News*, 1.

Douglas, S. C., & Martinko, M. J. (2001). Exploring the role of individual differences in the prediction of workplace aggression. *Journal of Applied Psychology, 86*(4), 547–559.

Dowling, W. F. (1973). Job redesign on the assembly line: Farewell to blue-collar blues? *Organizational Dynamics, 2*(1), 51–67.

Downey, H. K., Hellriegel, D., & Slocum, J. W. (Eds.). (1977). *Organizational behavior: A reader*. St. Paul, MN: West.

Downey, H. K., Sheridan, J. E., & Slocum, J. W. (1976). The path–goal theory of leadership: A longitudinal analysis. *Organizational Behavior and Human Performance, 16*, 156–176.

Drake, J. A. (1974). Planner looks at job enrichment. *Planning Review, 2*(4), 30–31.

Dreher, G. F. (1982). The role of performance in the turnover process. *Academy of Management Journal, 25*(1), 137–147.

Dreher, G. F., & Ash, R. A. (1990). A comparative study of mentoring among men and women in managerial, professional, and technical positions. *Journal of Applied Psychology, 75*(5), 539–546.

Drever, J. (1952). *A dictionary of psychology*. Harmondsworth: Penguin Books.

Drory, A., & Romm, T. (1990). The definition of organizational politics: A review. *Human Relations, 43*(11), 1133.

Drucker, P. (1954). *The practice of management*. New York: Harper.

Dubin, R. (1956). Industrial workers' worlds: A study of the central life interests of industrial workers. *Social Problems, 3*, 131–142.

DuBois, P. (1979). *Sabotage in industry*. Harmondsworth: Penguin Books.

Dullard, J. P., & Miller, K. L. (1988). Intimate relationships in task environments. In S. W. Duck (Ed.), *Handbook of personal relationships* (pp. 449–466). New York: John Wiley & Sons.

Duncan, W. J., Smeltzer, L. R., & Leap, T. L. (1990). Humor and work: Applications of joking behavior to management. *Journal of Management, 16*(2), 255–278.

Dunham, R. B. (1977). Reactions to job characteristics: Moderating effects of the organization. *Academy of Management Journal, 20*(1), 42–65.

Dunnette, M. D. (1972). *Performance equals ability and what? (Tech. Rep. 4009: ONR Contract No. N00014-68-A-0141)* (No. Tech. Rep. 4009: ONR Contract No. N00014-68-A-0141). Minneapolis, MN: University of Minnesota, Center for the Study of Organizational Performance and Human Effectiveness.

Dunnette, M. D., Arvey, R. D., & Banas, P. A. (1973). Why do they leave? *Personnel, May–June*, 25–39.

Dunnette, M. D., & Kirchner, W. K. (1965). *Psychology applied to industry*. New York: Appleton-Century-Crofts.

Dwek, C. S. (1986). Motivational processes affecting learning. *American Psychologist, 41*, 1040–1048.

Dyer, L., & Parker, D. F. (1975). Classifying outcomes in work motivation research: An examination of the intrinsic–extrinsic dichotomy. *Journal of Applied Psychology, 60*, 455–458.

Eagly, A. H., & Chaiken, S. (1993). *The psychology of attitudes*. San Diego, CA: Harcourt Brace Jovanovich.

Eagly, A. H., & Johnson, B. T. (1990). Gender and leadership style: A meta-analysis., *Psychological Bulletin, 108*, 233–256.

Eagly, A. H., & Karau, S. J. (2002). Role congruity theory of prejudice toward female leaders. *Psychological Review, 109*(3), 573–598.

Earley, P. C. (2001). Understanding social motivation from an interpersonal perspective: Organizational face theory. In M. Erez, U. Kleinbeck, & H. Thierry (Eds.), *Work motivation in the context of a globalizing economy* (pp. 369–380). Mahwah, NJ: Lawrence Erlbaum Associates, Inc.

Earley, P. C. (2002). Redefining interactions across cultures and organizations: Moving forward with cultural intelligence. In B. M. Staw & R. M. Kramer (Eds.), *Research in organizational behavior* (Vol. 24, pp. 271–300). Oxford: JAI Press.

Earley, P. C., Connelly, T., & Ekegren, G. (1989). Goals, strategy development, and task performance: Some limits on the efficacy of goal setting. *Journal of Applied Psychology, 74*, 24–33.

Eckblad, G. (1981). *Scheme theory*. New York: Academic Press.

Economist. (1996, June 8). A wealth of working women. *The Economist*, 27–28.

Economist. (2005, May 14). Doctor's salaries: Practice makes perfect. *The Economist*, 61.

Economist. (2006, November 11). Single market blues. *The Economist*, 61.

Eden, D. (1984). Self-fulfilling prophesy as a management tool: Harnessing Pygmalion. *Academy of Management Review, 9*, 64–73.

Eden, D. (1988). Pygmalion, goal setting, and expectancy: Compatible ways to boost productivity. *Academy of Management Review, 13*, 639–652.

Eden, D., & Kinnar, J. (1991). Modeling Galatea: Boosting self-efficacy to increase volunteering. *Journal of Applied Psychology, 76*, 770–780.

Ediger, B. (1991). *Coping with fibromyalgia*. Toronto, Ontario, Canada: LRH.

Edstrom, A., & Galbraith, J. R. (1977). Transfer of managers as a coordination and control strategy in multinational organizations. *Administrative Science Quarterly, 22*, 248–263.

Edwards, J. R. (1994). The study of congruence in organizational behavior research: Critique and proposed alternative. *Organizational Behavior and Human Decision Processes, 58*, 51–100.

Edwards, J. R., Scully, J. A., & Brtek, M. D. (1999). The measurement of work: Hierarchical representation of the multimethod job design questionnaire. *Personnel Psychology, 1999*(52), 305–334.

Edwards, J. R., Scully, J. A., & Brtek, M. D. (2000). The nature and outcomes of work: A replication and extension of interdisciplinary work-design research. *Journal of Applied Psychology, 86*(6), 860–868.

Edwards, P. K. (1979). Attachment to work and absence. *Human Relations, 32*, 1065–1080.

Ehrenreich, B. (2007). Pathologies of hope. *Harper's Magazine, 314*, 9–11.

Eimer, D. (2007, June 17). Slavery scandal shocks China: Kidnapping of youngsters, appalling conditions shine spotlight on brutal side of country's economic boom. *Victoria Times-Colonist*, C10.

Eisenberger, R., & Cameron, J. (1996). Detrimental effects of reward. *American Psychologist, 51*(11), 1153–1166.

Eisenhardt, K. M. (1989). Building theories from case study research. *Academy of Management Review, 14*, 532–550.

Ekman, P., & Davidson, R. J. (Eds.). (1994). *The nature of emotion*. New York: Oxford University Press.

Ekman, P., & Friesen, W. V. (1975). *Unmasking the face*. Englewood Cliffs, NJ: Prentice-Hall.

Elangovan, A. R., Auer-Rizzi, W., & Szabo, E. (2007). Why don't I trust you now? An attributional approach to erosion of trust. *Journal of Managerial Psychology, 22*(1), 4–24.

Elangovan, A. R., Pinder, C. C., & McLean, M. (2008). *Resurrection of callings in organizational behavior: Interpretations and implications for inquiry and practice*. Unpublished manuscript, Victoria, BC.

Elangovan, A. R., & Shapiro, D. (1998). Betrayal of trust in organizations. *Academy of Management Review, 23*(3), 547–566.

Elfenbein, H. A., & Ambady, N. (2002). On the universality and cultural specificity of emotion recognition: A meta-analysis. *Psychological Bulletin, 128*(2), 203–235.

Elkouri, F., & Aspa-Elkouri, E. (1985). *How arbitration works* (4th ed.). Washington, DC: BNA.

Elliott, R. H., & Jarrett, D. T. (1994). Violence in the workplace: The role of human resource management. *Public Personnel Management, 23*(2), 287–299.

Ellsworth, P. C., & Smith, C. A. (1988). Shades of joy: Patterns of appraisal differentiating pleasant emotions. *Cognition and Emotion, 2*, 301–331.

Emerson, R. E. (1962). Power–dependence relations. *American Sociological Review, 27*, 31–41.

Emmons, R. A. (2003). Acts of gratitude in organizations. In K. S. Cameron, J. E. Dutton, & R. E. Quinn (Eds.), *Positive organizational scholarship: Foundations of a new discipline* (pp. 81–93). San Francisco: Berrett-Koehler.

Emrich, C. G., Denmark, F. L., & Den Hartog, D. N. (2004). Cross-cultural differences in gender egalitarianism. In R. J. House, P. J. Hanges, M. Javidan, P. W. Dorfman, & V. Gupta (Eds.), *Culture, leadership, and organizations* (pp. 282–342). Thousand Oaks, CA: Sage.

Encarta. (1993a). *Galatea*.

Encarta. (1993b). *Pygmalion*.

Endler, N. W. (1975). The case for person–situation interactions. *Canadian Psychological Review, 16*, 12–21.

England, G. W. (1991). The meaning of work in the U.S.A.: Recent changes. *European Work and Organizational Psychologist, 1*(2/3), 111–124.

England, P., & McLaughlin, S. D. (1979). Sex segregation of jobs and male–female income differentials. In R. Alvarez & K. G. Lutterman (Eds.), *Discrimination in organizations* (pp. 189–213). San Francisco: Jossey-Bass.

Ephlin, D. F. (1973). The union's role in job enrichment programs. In G. G. Somers (Ed.), *Proceedings of the 26th Annual Winter Meeting*. Madison, WI: Industrial Relations Research Association.

Erez, A., & Isen, A. M. (2002). The influence of positive affect on the components of expectancy motivation. *Journal of Applied Psychology, 87*(6), 1055–1067.

Erez, A., & Judge, T. A. (2001). Relationship of core self-evaluations to goal setting, motivation, and performance. *Journal of Applied Psychology, 86*(6), 1270–1279.

Erez, M. (2000). Make management practice fit the national culture. In E. A. Locke (Ed.), *Handbook of principles of organizational behavior* (pp. 418–434). Oxford: Blackwell.

Erez, M., & Arad, R. (1986). Participative goal-setting: Social, motivational, and cognitive factors. *Journal of Applied Psychology*, *71*(4), 591–597.

Erez, M., & Earley, P. C. (1993). *Culture, self-identity, and work*. New York: Oxford University Press.

Erez, M., & Kanfer, F. H. (1983). The role of goal acceptance in goal setting and task performance. *Academy of Management Review*, *8*(3), 454–463.

Erez, M., Kleinbeck, U., & Thierry, H. (2001). *Work motivation in the context of a globalizing economy*. Mahwah, NJ: Lawrence Erlbaum Associates, Inc.

Erikson, K., & Vallas, S. P. (Eds.). (1990). *The nature of work*. New Haven, CT: Yale University Press.

Evans, M. G. (1970). The effects of supervisory behavior on the path–goal relationship. *Organizational Behavior & Human Performance*, *5*(3), 277–298.

Evans, M. G. (1974). Extensions of a path-goal theory of motivation. *Journal of Applied Psychology*, *59*(2), 172–178.

Evans, M. G. (2002). Path-goal theory of leadership. In L. L. Neider & C. Schriesheim (Eds.), *Leadership* (pp. 115–138). Greenwich, CT.: Information Age Publishers.

Eylon, D. (1994). *Empowerment: A multi-level construct*. Unpublished doctoral dissertation, University of British Columbia, Vancouver, British Columbia, Canada.

Eylon, D., & Pinder, C. C. (1995). *Experimental test of a process model of employee empowerment*. Unpublished manuscript, Faculty of Commerce & Business Administration, University of British Columbia, Vancouver, BC, Canada.

Farrell, D. (1983). Exit, voice, loyalty, and neglect as responses to job dissatisfaction: A multidimensional scaling study. *Academy of Management Journal*, *26*(4), 596–607.

Farrell, W. (2005). *Why men earn more*. New York: AMACOM.

Fassel, D. (1992). *Working ourselves to death*. New York: HarperCollins/Thorsons.

Faunce, W. A. (1982). The relation of status to self esteem: Chair saw sociology at the cutting edge. *Sociological Focus*, *15*(3), 163–178.

Faunce, W. A. (1989). Occupational status-assignment systems: The effect of status on self-esteem. *American Journal of Sociology*, *95*, 378–400.

Fedor, D. B., & Ferris, G. R. (1981). Integrating OB mod with cognitive approaches to motivation. *Academy of Management Review*, *6*(1), 115–125.

Fehr, B., & Russell, J. A. (1991). The concept of love viewed from a prototype perspective. *Journal of Personality and Social Psychology*, *60*, 425–438.

Fein, M. (1974). Job enrichment: A reevaluation. *Sloan Management Review*, *15*(2), 69–88.

Feldman, D. C. (1977). The role of initiation activities in socialization. *Human Relations*, *30*(11), 977–990.

Feldman, D. C. (1981). The multiple socialization of organization members. *Academy of Management Review*, *6*(2), 309–318.

Feldman, D. C., & Brett, J. M. (1983). Coping with new jobs: A comparative study of new hires and job changers. *Academy of Management Journal*, *26*(2), 258–272.

Feldman, D. C., & Leana, C. R. (1989). Managing layoffs: Experience at the *Challenger* disaster site and the Pittsburgh steel mills. *Organizational Dynamics*, *18*(1), 52–64.

Feldman, J. M., Reitz, H. J., & Hiterman, R. J. (1976). Alternatives to optimization in expectancy theory. *Journal of Applied Psychology*, *61*(6), 712–720.

Fellenz, M. R. (1996). *Control theory in organizational behavior: Review, critique, and prospects*. Unpublished manuscript, University of North Carolina at Chapel Hill.

Fennel, T. (1996). The high price of salary disclosure. *Maclean's*, *109*(16), 50.

Feshbach, S., & Zagrodska, J. (Eds.). (1997). *Aggression: Biological, developmental and social perspectives*. New York: Plenum Press.

Festinger, L. A. (1954). A theory of social comparison processes. *Human Relations*, *7*, 117–140.

Festinger, L. A. (1957). *A theory of cognitive dissonance*. Evanston, IL: Row, Peterson.

Fields, D. (2002). *Taking the measure of work: A guide to validated scales for organizational research and diagnosis*. Thousand Oaks, CA: Sage.

Fields, D., Pang, M., & Chiu, C. (2000). Distributive and procedural justice as predictors of employee outcomes in Hong Kong. *Journal of Organizational Behavior*, *21*(5), 547–562.

Fineman, S. (Ed.). (1993). *Emotion in organizations*. London: Sage.

Fineman, S. (2000). Commodifying the emotionally intelligent. In S. Fineman (Ed.), *Emotion in organizations* (2nd ed., pp. 101–114). Thousand Oaks, CA: Sage.

Fineman, S. (2006). On being positive: Concerns and counterpoints. *Academy of Management Review, 31*(2), 270–291.

Fiol, C. M., & Lyles, M. A. (1985). Organizational learning. *Academy of Management Review, 10*(4), 803–813.

Firebaugh, G., & Harley, B. (1995). Trends in job satisfaction in the United States by race, gender, and type of occupation. In R. L. Simpson & I. H. Simpson (Eds.), *Research in the sociology of work: The meanings of work* (pp. 87–104). Greenwich, CT: JAI Press.

Fischer, A. (1994). Emotion concepts as a function of gender. In J. A. Russell, J. M. Fernandez-Doles, A. S. R. Manstead, & J. C. Wellenkamp (Eds.), *Everyday conceptions of emotions* (pp. 457–474). Dordrecht, The Netherlands: Kluwer.

Fishbein, M. (1967). Attitude and the prediction of behavior. In M. Fishbein, *Readings in attitude theory and measurement*, 477–491.

Fishbein, M. (1980). A theory of reasoned action: Some applications and implications. In M. M. Page (Ed.), *Nebraska Symposium on Motivation, 1979 BF683, N4*. Lincoln, NE: University of Nebraska Press.

Fishbein, M., & Ajzen, I. (1975). *Belief, attitude, intention and behavior: An introduction to theory and research.* Reading, MA: Addison-Wesley.

Fisher, A. B. (1988). The downside of downsizing. *Fortune, 117*(11), 42–52.

Fisher, A. B., & Welsh, T. (1994). Getting comfortable with couples in the workplace. *Fortune, 130*(7), 138–144.

Fisher, C. D. (1980). On the dubious wisdom of expecting job satisfaction to correlate with performance. *Academy of Management Review, 5*, 607–612.

Fisher, C. D. (2002). Antecedents and consequences of real-time affective reactions at work. *Motivation and Emotion, 26*(1), 3–30.

Fisher, C. D. (2003). Why do lay people believe that satisfaction and performance are correlated? Possible sources of a commonsense theory. *Journal of Organizational Behavior, 2003*(24), 753–777.

Fisher, C. D., & Locke, E. A. (1992). The new look in job satisfaction research and theory. In C. U. Cranny, P. C. Smith, & E. F. Stone (Eds.), *Job satisfaction* (pp. 165–194). New York: Lexington Books.

Fisher, C. D., & Noble, C. S. (2004). A within-person examination of correlates of performance and emotions while working. *Human Performance, 17*(2), 145–168.

Fisher, H. (2004). *Why we love: The nature and chemistry of romantic love.* New York: Henry Holt & Co.

Fisher, H. E. (1992). *The anatomy of love.* New York: Norton.

Fisher, W. A. (1984). Predicting contraceptive behavior among university men: The role of emotions and behavioral intentions. *Journal of Applied Psychology, 14*, 104–123.

Fiske, D. W., & Maddi, S. R. (1961). *The functions of a varied experience.* Homewood, IL: Dorsey.

Fiske, S. T. (1993). Social cognition and perception. *Annual Review of Psychology, 44*, 155–194.

Fiske, S. T., & Taylor, S. E. (1991). *Social cognition* (2nd ed.). New York: McGraw-Hill.

Fitness, J. (2000). Anger in the workplace: An emotion script approach to anger episodes between workers and their superiors, co-workers and subordinates. *Journal of Organizational Behavior, 21*, 147–162.

Fleishman, E. A. (1958). A relationship between incentive motivation and ability level in psychomotor performance. *Journal of Experimental Psychology, 56*, 78–81.

Flowers, V. S., & Hughes, C. L. (1973). Why employees stay. *Harvard Business Review, 51*(4), 40–60.

Foley, S., & Powell, G. N. (1999). Not all is fair in love and work: Coworkers' preferences for and responses to managerial interventions regarding workplace romances. *Journal of Organizational Behavior, 20*(7), 1043–1056.

Folger, R. (1977). Distributive and procedural justice: Combined impact of voice and improvement on experienced inequity. *Journal of Personality and Social Psychology, 35*, 108–119.

Folger, R. (1986). Rethinking equity theory: A referent cognitions model. In H. W. Bierhoff, R. L. Cohen, & J. Greenberg (Eds.), *Justice in social relations* (pp. 145–162). New York: Plenum Press.

Folger, R. (1987). Distributive and procedural justice in the workplace. *Social Justice Research, 1*(2), 143–159.

Folger, R. (1993). Reactions to mistreatment at work. In J. K. Murnighan (Ed.), *Social psychology in organizations*. Englewood Cliffs, NJ: Prentice-Hall.

Folger, R. (2001). Fairness as deonance. In S. W. Gilliland, D. D. Steiner, & D. P. Skarlicki (Eds.), *Research in social issues management* (Vol. 1, pp. 3–33). New York: Information Age Publishers.

Folger, R., & Cropanzano, R. (1998). *Organizational justice and human resource management.* Thousand Oaks, CA: Sage.

Folger, R., & Cropanzano, R. (2001). Fairness theory: Justice as accountability. In J. Greenberg & R. Cropanzano (Eds.), *Advances in organizational justice* (pp. 1–55). Stanford, CA: Stanford University Press.

Folger, R., & Greenberg, J. (1985). Procedural justice: An interpretative analysis of personnel systems. In K. M. Rowland & G. R. Ferris (Eds.), *Research in personnel and human resources management* (Vol. 3, pp. 141–184). Greenwich, CT: JAI Press.

Folger, R., & Skarlicki, D. P. (1998). A popcorn metaphor for workplace violence. In R. W. Griffin, A. M. O'Leary-Kelly, & J. Collins (Eds.), *Dysfunctional behavior in organizations: Violent and deviant behavior* (pp. 43–81). Greenwich, CT: JAI Press.

Ford, C. (1996). A theory of individual creative action in multiple social domains. *Academy of Management Review, 21,* 1112–1142.

Ford, C. H. (1979). MBO: An idea whose time has gone? *Business Horizons, 22*(12), 48–55.

Ford, M. E. (1992). *Motivating humans.* Newbury Park, CA: Sage.

Ford, R., & McLaughlin, F. (1987). Should Cupid come to the workplace? *Personnel Administrator, 53*(1), 100–110.

Ford, R. N. (1973). Job enrichment lessons from AT&T. *Harvard Business Review, 51*(1), 96–106.

Forgas, J. P. (1995). Mood and judgement: The affect infusion model (AIM). *Psychological Bulletin, 117*(1), 39.

Forgas, J. P., & George, J. M. (2001). Affective influences on judgments and behavior in organizations: An information processing perspective. *Organizational Behavior and Human Decision Processes, 86*(1), 34.

Forgas, J. P., Williams, K. D., & Laham, S. M. (2005). Social motivation: Introduction and overview. In J. P. Forgas, K. D. Williams, & S. M. Laham (Eds.), *Social motivation: Conscious and unconscious processes* (pp. 1–17). Cambridge: Cambridge University Press.

Forgas, J. P., Williams, K. D., & Wheeler, L. (2001). The social mind: Introduction and overview. In J. P. Forgas, K. D. Williams, & L. Wheeler (Eds.), *The social mind: Cognitive and motivational aspects of interpersonal behavior* (pp. 1–24). Cambridge: Cambridge University Press.

Fox, S., & Spector, P. E. (1999). A model of work frustration–aggression. *Journal of Organizational Behavior, 20*(6), 915–931.

Frankl, V. (1946). *Man's search for meaning.* New York: Pocket Books.

Frayne, C. A., & Geringer, J. M. (1994). A social cognitive approach to examining joint venture general manager performance. *Group & Organization Management, 19*(2), 240–262.

Frayne, C. A., & Geringer, J. M. (1997). *Self-management training and sales performance: A field experiment.* Paper presented at the Western Academy of Management, Squaw Valley, CA.

Frayne, C. A., & Geringer, J. M. (2000). Self-management training for improving job performance: A field experiment involving salespeople. *Journal of Applied Psychology, 85*(3), 361–372.

Frayne, C. A., & Latham, G. P. (1987). Application of social learning theory to employee self-management of attendance. *Journal of Applied Psychology, 72*(3), 387–392.

Frederickson, L. W., & Lovett, S. B. (1980). Inside organizational behavior management. *Journal of Organizational Behavior Management, 2,* 193–203.

Fredericksen, N. (1972). Toward a taxonomy of situations. *American Psychologist, 27,* 114–123.

Fredericksen, N., Jenson, O., Beaton, A. E., & Bloxom, B. (1972). *Prediction of organizational behavior.* Elmsford, NY: Pergamon Press.

Fredrickson, B. L. (1998). What good are positive emotions? *Review of General Psychology, 2*(3), 300–319.

Fredrickson, B. L. (2001). The role of positive emotions in positive psychology. *American Psychologist, 56,* 218.

Fredrickson, B. L. (2003). Positive emotions and upward spirals in organizations. In K. S. Cameron, J. E. Dutton, & R. E. Quinn (Eds.), *Positive organizational scholarship: Foundations of a new discipline* (pp. 163–175). San Francisco: Berrett-Koehler.

Freeman, R. B., & Medoff, J. L. (1984). *What do unions do?* New York: Basic Books.

Freeman, R. B., & Rogers, J. (1999). *What workers want.* Ithaca, NY: Cornell University Press and Russell Sage Foundation.

French, E. G. (1957). Effects of interaction of achievement, motivation, and intelligence on problem solving success. *American Psychologist, 12,* 399–400.

French, J. R. P., & Raven, R. (1959). The bases of social power. In D. Cartwright (Ed.), *Studies in social power* (pp. 150–167). Ann Arbor, MI: University of Michigan, Institute for Social Research.

Frese, M., Kring, W., Soose, A., & Zempel, J. (1996). Personal initiative at work: Differences between East and West Germany. *Academy of Management Journal, 39*(1), 37–63.

Freund, W. C. (1981). Productivity and inflation. *Financial Analysts Journal, 37*(4), 36–30.

Fried, Y., & Slowik, L. H. (2004). Enriching goal setting theory with time: An integrated approach. *Academy of Management Review, 29,* 404–422.

Friedman, S. D., & Lobel, S. A. (2003). The happy workaholic: A role model for employees. *Academy of Management Executive, 17*(3), 87–98.

Friel, D. (2005). Transferring a lean production concept from Germany to the United States: The impact of labor laws and training systems. *Academy of Management Executive, 19*(2), 50–58.

Frieze, I. H., & Boneva, B. S. (2001). Power motivation and motivation to help others. In A. Y. Lee-Chai & J. A. Bargh (Eds.), *The use and abuse of power: Multiple perspectives on the causes of corruption* (pp. 75–89). Philadelphia: Psychology Press.

Frijda, N. H. (1986). *The emotions.* Cambridge: Cambridge University Press.

Frijda, N. H., Mesquita, B., Sonnemans, J., & van Goozen, S. (1991). The duration of affective phenomena on emotions, sentiments and passions. In K. T. Strongman (Ed.), *International review of research on emotion* (Vol. 1, pp. 187–225). Chichester: John Wiley & Sons.

Fromm, E., & Xirau, R. (Eds.). (1968). *The nature of man.* New York: Macmillan.

Frone, M. R., Russell, M., & Cooper, M. L. (1994). Relationship between job and family satisfaction: Causal or noncausal covariation? *Journal of Management, 20*(3), 565–579.

Frost, P. J. (1980). Toward a radical framework for practicing organization science. *Academy of Management Review, 5*(4), 501–507.

Frost, P. J. (2003). *Toxic emotions at work: How compassionate managers handle pain and conflict.* Boston, MA: Harvard Business School Press.

Frost, P. J., & Hayes, D. C. (1979). An exploration in two cultures of a model of political behavior in organizations. In G. W. England & B. Wilbert (Eds.), *Organizational functioning in a cross-cultural perspective* (pp. 251–272). Kant, OH: Kent State University.

Frost, P. J., Moore, L. F., Louis, M. R., Lundberg, C. C., & Martin, J. (Eds.). (1985). *Organizational culture: The meaning of life in the workplace.* Beverly Hills: Sage.

Frost, P. J., Moore, L. F., Louis, M. R., Lundberg, C. C., & Martin, J. (1991). *Reframing organizational culture.* Newbury Park, CA: Sage.

Fry, L. W., & Smith, D. A. (1987). Congruence, contingency, and theory building. *Academy of Management Review, 12*(1), 117–132.

Fulmer, W. E., & Casey, M. A. W. (1990). Employment at will: Options for managers. *Academy of Management Executive, 4*(2), 102–107.

Fusilier, M. R., Ganster, D. C., & Middlemist, R. D. (1984). A within-person test of the form of the expectancy theory model in a choice context. *Organizational Behavior & Human Performance, 34*(3), 323–342.

Gagné, M., & Deci, E. L. (2005). Self-determination theory and work motivation. *Journal of Organizational Behavior, 26*(4), 331–362.

Galbraith, J. K. (1958). *The affluent society.* Toronto, Ontario: The New American Library of Canada Limited.

Galbraith, J. K., & Cummings, L. L. (1967). An empirical investigation of the motivational determinants of task performance: Interactive effects between instrumentally-valence and motivation-ability. *Organizational Behavior & Human Performance, 2*(3), 237–257.

Galsworthy, J. (1927). *The inn of tranquility.* London: Heinemann.

Galt, V. (2006, February 4). "Working retired" in demand as work force ages. *The Globe and Mail,* B11.

Gannon, M. J., & Hendrickson, D. H. (1973). Career orientation and job satisfaction among working wives. *Journal of Applied Psychology, 57,* 339–340.

Gardner, D. G., & Cummings, L. L. (1988). Activation theory and job design: Review and conceptualization. In B. M. Staw & L. L. Cummings (Eds.), *Research in organizational behavior* (Vol. 10, pp. 81–122). Greenwich, CT: JAI Press.

Garland, H. (1984). Relation of effort–performance expectancy to performance in goal-setting experiments. *Journal of Applied Psychology, 69*(1), 79–84.

Garner, W. R. (1972). The acquisition and application of knowledge: A symbiotic relationship. *American Psychologist, 27,* 941–946.

Gay, E. R., Weiss, D. J., Hendel, D. H., Dawis, R. V., & Lofquist, L. H. (1971). *Manual for the Minnesota importance questionnaire* (Vol. XXVIII). Minneapolis, MN: The Minnesota Studies in Vocational Rehabilitation.

Geddes, J. (1998). A case of procedural confusion. *Maclean's, 111,* 20.

Geen, R. G. (1991). Social motivation. *Annual Review of Psychology, 42*(1), 377–399.

Gelfand, M., Nishii, L. H., & Raver, J. L. (2006). On the nature and importance of cultural tightness–looseness. *Journal of Applied Psychology, 91*(6), 1225–1244.

Gelfand, M. J., Bhawuk, D. P. S., Nishii, L. H., & Bechtold, D. J. (2004). Individualism and collectivism. In R. J. House, P. J. Hanges, M. Javidan, P. W. Dorfman, & V. Gupta (Eds.), *Culture, leadership, and organizations: The GLOBE study of 62 societies* (pp. 437–502). Thousand Oaks, CA: Sage.

George, J. M. (1989). Mood and absence. *Journal of Applied Psychology, 74*(2), 317–324.

George, J. M. (1991). State or trait: Effects of positive mood on prosocial behaviors at work. *Journal of Applied Psychology, 76*(2), 299–307.

George, J. M. (1992). The role of personality in organizational life: Issues and evidence. *Journal of Management, 18*(2), 185–213.

George, J. M. (1995). Asymmetrical effects of rewards and punishments: The case of social loafing. *Journal of Occupational and Organizational Psychology, 68*, 327–338.

George, J. M., & Brief, A. P. (1996). Motivational agendas in the workplace: The effects of feelings on focus of attention and work motivation. In B. M. Staw & L. L. Cummings (Eds.), *Research in organizational behavior* (Vol. 18, pp. 75–109). Greenwich, CT: JAI Press.

George, J. M., & Jones, G. R. (1997). Experiencing work: Values, attitudes, and moods. *Human Relations, 50*(4), 363–392.

George, J. M., & Jones, G. R. (2000). The role of time in theory and theory building. *Journal of Management, 26*(4), 657–684.

George, L. (2006). What we believe. *Maclean's, 119*(27, 28), 34–45.

George, L., Demont, J., Geddes, J., Bryden, J., & Treble, P. (2005). Belinda and Peter: The whole story. *Maclean's, 118*(22), 22–27.

Georgopoulos, B. C., Mahoney, G. M., & Jones, N. W. (1957). A path-goal approach to productivity. *Journal of Applied Psychology, 41*, 345–353.

Gerhart, B. (2005). The (affective) dispositional approach to job satisfaction: Sorting out the policy implications. *Journal of Organizational Behavior, 26*, 79–97.

Ghoshal, S. (2005). Bad management theories are destroying good management practices. *Academy of Management Learning & Education, 4*(1), 75–91.

Giacalone, R. A., & Greenberg, J. (Eds.). (1997). *Antisocial behavior in organizations.* Thousand Oaks, CA: Sage.

Giacalone, R. A., Riordan, C. A., & Rosenfeld, P. (1997). Employee sabotage: Toward a practitioner–scholar understanding. In R. A. Giacalone & J. Greenberg (Eds.), *Antisocial behavior in organizations* (pp. 109–129). Thousand Oaks, CA: Sage.

Giles, W. F. (1977). Volunteering for job enrichment: A test of expectancy theory predictions. *Personnel Psychology, 30*(3), 427–435.

Gioia, D. A., & Pitre, E. (1990). Multiparadigm perspectives on theory building. *Academy of Management Review, 15*(4), 584–602.

Gist, M. E. (1987). Self-efficacy: Implications for organizational behavior and human resource management. *Academy of Management Review, 12*(3), 472–485.

Gist, M. E., & Mitchell, T. R. (1992). Self-efficacy: A theoretical analysis of its determinants and malleability. *Academy of Management Review, 17*, 183–211.

Gladwell, M. (2000). *The tipping point: How little things can make a big difference.* Boston: Little, Brown, & Company.

Glaser, R. C., & Strauss, A. L. (1967). *The discovery of grounded theory.* Chicago, IL: Aldine.

Glick, P., & Fiske, S. T. (in press). Sex discrimination: The psychological approach. In F. J. Crosby, M. S. Stockdale, & S. A. Ropp (Eds.), *Sex discrimination in the workplace.* Malden, MA: Blackwell.

Glomb, T. M., Steel, P. D. G., & Arvey, R. D. (2002). Office sneers, snipes, and stab wounds. Antecedents, consequences, and implications of workplace violence and aggression. In R. Lord, R. Klimoski, & R. Kanfer (Eds.), *Frontiers of industrial and organizational psychology: Emotions at work* (pp. 227–259). San Francisco: Jossey-Bass.

Gloria, J. D. (1984). Frustration, aggression, and the sense of justice. In A. Mummendey (Ed.), *Social psychology of aggression* (pp. 127–141). Berlin: Springer-Verlag.

Goffman, E. (1972). *Strategic interaction.* New York: Ballantine Books.

Gold, M. E. (1983). *A dialogue on comparable worth.* Ithaca, NY: ILR Press.

Goleman, D. (1995). *Emotional intelligence.* New York: Bantam Books.

González-Romá, V., Peiró, J. M., & Tordera, N. (2002). An examination of the antecedents and moderator influences of climate strength. *Journal of Applied Psychology, 87*(3), 465–473.

Goodall, K. (1972, November). Shapers at work. *Psychology Today*, 53–132.

Goodman, P. (1974). An examination of the referents used in the evaluation of pay. *Organizational Behavior & Human Performance, 12*, 170–195.

Goodman, P. A., & Friedman, A. (1971). An examination of Adams' theory of inequity. *Administrative Science Quarterly, 16*, 271–288.

Goodstadt, B., & Kipnis, D. (1970). Situational influences on the use of power. *Journal of Applied Psychology, 54*, 201–207.

Gopinath, C., & Becker, T. E. (2000). Communication, procedural justice, and employee attitudes: Relationships under conditions of divestiture. *Journal of Management, 26*(1), 63–83.

Gorn, G. J., & Kanungo, R. N. (1980). Job involvement and motivation: Are intrinsically motivated managers more job involved? *Organizational Behavior & Human Performance, 26*, 265–277.

Gouldner, A. W. (1960). The norm of reciprocity: A preliminary statement. *American Sociological Review, 25*, 161–179.

Gowing, M. K. (2001). Measurement of emotional competence. In C. Cherniss & D. Goleman (Eds.), *The emotionally intelligence workplace* (pp. 83–131). San Francisco: Jossey-Bass.

Graen, G. (1969). Instrumentality theory of work motivation: Some experimental results and suggested modifications. *Journal of Applied Psychology Monograph, 53*(2, Pt. 2), 38–39.

Graen, G. (1976). Role making processes within complex organizations. In M. D. Dunnette (Ed.), *Handbook of industrial and organizational psychology* (pp. 1201–1246). Chicago, IL: Rand McNally.

Grandey, A. A., Tam, A. P., & Brauburger, A. L. (2002). Affective states and traits in the workplace: Diary and survey data from young workers. *Motivation and Emotion, 26*(1), 31–55.

Granovetter, M. (1985). Economic action and social structure: The problem of embeddedness. *American Journal of Sociology, 91*(3), 481–510.

Grant, A. M. (2007). Relational job design and the motivation to make a prosocial difference. *Academy of Management Review, 32*(2), 393–417.

Greco, P. A., & Woodlock, B. K. (1989). Downsizing the organization. *Personnel Administrator, 34*(5), 105–108.

Greenberg, J. (1984). On the apocryphal nature of inequity distress. In R. Folger (Ed.), *The sense of injustice: Social psychological perspectives* (pp. 167–183). New York; Plenum Press.

Greenberg, J. (1987). A taxonomy of organizational justice theories. *Academy of Management Review, 12*, 9–22.

Greenberg, J. (1988a). Equity and workplace status: A field experiment. *Journal of Applied Psychology, 73*, 600–613.

Greenberg, J. (1988b). Cultivating an image of justice: Looking fair on the job. *Academy of Management Executive, 2*, 155–157.

Greenberg, J. (1990a). Looking fair vs. being fair: Managing impressions of organizational justice. In B. M. Staw & L. L. Cummings (Eds.), *Research in organizational behavior* (Vol. 12, pp. 111–158). Greenwich, CT: JAI Press.

Greenberg, J. (1990b). Employee theft as a reaction to underpayment inequity: The hidden cost of pay cuts. *Journal of Applied Psychology, 75*, 561–568.

Greenberg, J. (1990c). Organizational justice: Yesterday, today, and tomorrow. *Journal of Management, 16*, 399–432.

Greenberg, J. (1993a). Stealing in the name of justice: Informational and interpersonal moderators of theft reactions to underpayment inequity. *Organizational Behavior & Human Decision Processes, 54*(1), 81–103.

Greenberg, J. (1993b). The social side of fairness: Interpersonal and informational classes of organizational justice. In R. Cropanzano (Ed.), *Justice in the workplace: Approaching fairness in human resource management* (pp. 79–103). Hillsdale, NJ: Lawrence Erlbaum Associates, Inc.

Greenberg, J. (2001). The seven can(n)ons of organizational justice. In J. Greenberg & R. Cropanzano (Eds.), *Advances in organizational justice* (pp. 245–271). Stanford, CA: Stanford University Press.

Greenberg, J. (2002). Who stole the money, and when? Individual and situational determinants of employee theft. *Organizational Behavior & Human Decision Processes, 89*, 985–1003.

Greenberg, J. (2006). Losing sleep over organizational injustice: Attenuating insomniac reactions to underpayment inequity with supervisory training in interactional justice. *Journal of Applied Psychology, 91*(1), 58–69.

Greenberg, J., & Cropanzano, R. (2001). *Advances in organizational justice*. Stanford, CA: Stanford University Press.

Greenberg, J., & McCarty. (1990). Comparable worth: A matter of justice. In G. R. Ferris & K. M. Rowland (Eds.), *Research in personnel and human resource management* (Vol. 8, pp. 265–301). Greenwich, CT: JAI Press.

Greenberg, J., & Ornstein, S. (1983). High status job title as compensation for underpayment: A test of equity theory. *Journal of Applied Psychology, 68*, 285–297.

Greenberg, J., Roberge, M.-E., Ho, V. T., & Rousseau, D. M. (2004). Fairness in idiosyncratic work arrangements: Justice as an I-deal. In J. J. Martocchio (Ed.), *Research in personnel and human resources management* (Vol. 23, pp. 1–34). Amsterdam: Elsevier.

Greenberg, J., & Scott, K. S. (1996). Why do workers bite the hand that feeds them? Employee theft as a social exchange process. In B. M. Staw & L. L. Cummings (Eds.), *Research in organizational behavior* (Vol. 18, pp. 111–156). Greenwich, CT: JAI Press.

Greenberg, L., & Barling, J. (1999). Predicting employee aggression against coworkers, subordinates and supervisors: The roles of person behaviors and perceived workplace factors. *Journal of Organizational Behavior, 20*(6), 897–913.

Greene, D., & Lepper, M. R. (1974). Effects of extrinsic rewards on children's subsequent intrinsic interest. *Child Development, 45*, 1141–1145.

Greene, R. (1998). *The 48 laws of power*. New York: Penguin Books.

Greenhaus, J. H., & Powell, G. N. (2003). When work and family collide: Deciding between competing role demands. *Organizational Behavior & Human Decision Processes, 90*(2003), 291–303.

Greenspan, D. S. (2000). Downsizing with dignity. *Employment Relations Today, 29*(3), 39–48.

Greenwald, A. G. (1976). Within-subjects designs: To use or not to use? *Psychological Bulletin, 83*, 314–320.

Greenwood, R. G. (1981). Management by objectives: As developed by Peter Drucker, assisted by Harold Smiddy. *Academy of Management Review, 6*, 225–230.

Grieff, B. S., & Munter, K. (1980). *Tradeoffs: Executive, family and organizational life*. New York: New American Library.

Griffeth, R. W., Hom, P. W., & Gaertner, S. (2000). A meta-analysis of antecedents and correlates of employee turnover: Update, moderator tests, and research implications for the next millennium. *Journal of Management, 26*(3), 463–488.

Griffin, R. W. (1982). A longitudinal investigation of task characteristics relationships. *Academy of Management Journal, 24*, 99–113.

Griffin, R. W. (1987). Toward an integrated theory of task design. In L. L. Cummings & B. M. Staw (Eds.), *Research in organizational behavior* (Vol. 9, pp. 79–120). Greenwich, CT: JAI Press.

Griffin, R. W., Bateman, T. S., Wayne, S. J., & Head, T. C. (1987). Objective and social factors as determinants of task perceptions and responses: An integrated perspective and empirical investigation. *Academy of Management Journal, 30*, 501–524.

Griffin, R. W., Welsh, A., & Moorehead, G. (1981). Perceived task characteristics and employee performance: A literature review. *Academy of Management Review, 6*, 655–664.

Grigaliunas, B., & Weiner, Y. (1974). Has the research challenge to motivation-hygiene theory been conclusive? An analysis of critical studies. *Human Relations, 27*, 839–871.

Gross, B. (1965). What are your organization's objectives? *Human Relations, 18*, 215.

Guilford, J. P. (1967). *The nature of human intelligence*. New York: McGraw-Hill.

Guion, R. M. (1965). *Personnel testing*. New York: McGraw-Hill.

Guppy, N., & Goyder, C. (1984). Consensus on occupational prestige: A reassessment of the evidence. *Social Forces, 62*, 709–725.

Gutek, B. A., Cohen, A. G., & Konrad, A. M. (1990). Predicting social-sexual behavior at work: A contact hypothesis. *Academy of Management Journal, 33*, 560–577.

Guzzo, R. A. (1979). Types of rewards, cognitions, and work motivation. *Academy of Management Review, 4*, 75–86.

Gyllenhammar, P. G. (1977). How Volvo adapts work to people. *Harvard Business Review, 55*, 102–113.

Hackett, R. D., & Guion, R. M. (1985). A re-evaluation of the absenteeism–job satisfaction relationship. *Organizational Behavior and Human Decision Processes, 35*, 340–381.

Hackman, J. R. (1975). On the coming demise of job enrichment. In E. L. Cass & F. G. Zimmer (Eds.), *Man and work in society*. New York: Van Nostrand Reinhold.

Hackman, J. R. (1977). Work design. In J. R. Hackman & J. L. Suttle (Eds.), *Improving life at work* (pp. 96–159). Santa Monica, CA: Goodyear.

Hackman, J. R., & Lawler, E. E. (1971). Employee reactions to job characteristics. *Journal of Applied Psychology, 55,* 259–286.

Hackman, J. R., & Oldham, G. R. (1975). Development of the job diagnostic survey. *Journal of Applied Psychology, 60*(2), 159–170.

Hackman, J. R., & Oldham, G. R. (1976). Motivation through the design of work: Test of a theory. *Organizational Behavior and Human Performance, 16,* 250–279.

Hackman, J. R., & Oldham, G. R. (1980). *Work redesign.* Reading, MA: Addison-Wesley.

Hackman, J. R., Oldham, G. R., Janson, R., & Purdy, K. (1975). A new strategy for job enrichment. *California Management Review, 17*(4), 57–71.

Hall, C. S., & Lindzey, G. (1957). *Theories of personality.* New York: John Wiley & Sons.

Hall, C. S., & Lindzey, G. (1970). *Theories of personality* (2nd. ed.). New York: John Wiley & Sons.

Hall, D. T. (1976). *Careers in organizations.* Pacific Palisades, CA: Goodyear.

Hall, D. T., & Associates. (1996). *The career is dead – long live the career: A relationship approach to careers.* San Francisco: Jossey-Bass.

Hall, D. T., & Associates. (1997). *Integrative life planning: Critical tasks for career development and changing life patterns.* San Francisco, CA: Jossey-Bass.

Hall, D. T., & Chandler, D. E. (2005). Psychological success: When the career is a calling. *Journal of Organizational Behavior, 26,* 155–176.

Hall, D. T., & Isabella, L. A. (1985). Downward movement and career development. *Organizational Dynamics* (Summer), 5–23.

Hall, J. (1994). Americans know how to be productive if managers will let them. *Organizational Dynamics, 22*(3), 33–46.

Hall, R. E., & Jones, C. I. (1999). Why do some countries produce so much more output per worker than others? *The Quarterly Journal of Economics, 114*(1), 83–116.

Hall, R. H. (1991). *Organizations: Structures, processes, and outcomes.* Englewood Cliffs, MJ: Prentice-Hall.

Hallberg, U. E., & Schaufeli, W. B. (2006). "Same" but different? Can work engagement be discriminated from job involvement and organizational commitment? *European Psychologist, 11*(2), 119–127.

Halpern, D., & Osofsky, S. (1990). A dissenting view of MBO. *Public Personnel Management, 19,* 321–330.

Hamilton, V. L. (2000). (In)Justice in waiting: Russian officers' organizational commitment and mental distress during downsizing. *Journal of Applied Social Psychology, 30*(10), 1995–2027.

Hammond, K. R., McLelland, G. H., & Mumpower, J. (1980). *Human judgment and decision processes: Theories, methods, and procedures.* New York: Praeger.

Hamner, W. C., & Hamner, E. P. (1976). Behavior modification on the bottom line. *Organizational Dynamics, 4*(4), 3–21.

Hanisch, K. A., & Hulin, C. L. (1990). Job attitudes and organizational withdrawal: An examination of retirement and other voluntary withdrawal behaviors. *Journal of Vocational Behavior, 37,* 60–78.

Hannah, D. R. (2006). Keeping trade secrets secret. *Sloan Management Review, 47*(3), 17–20.

Hanser, L. M., & Muchinsky, P. M. (1978). Work as an information environment. *Organizational Behavior and Human Performance, 13,* 244–256.

Hanson, R., Porterfield, R. I., & Ames, K. (1995). Employee empowerment at risk: Effects of recent NLRB rulings. *Academy of Management Executive, 9*(2), 45–54.

Harackiewicz, J. M., & Stone, C. (1991). Goals and intrinsic motivation: You can get there from here. In M. L. Maehr & P. R. Pintrich (Eds.), *Advances in motivation and achievement* (Vol. 7, pp. 21–49). Greenwich, CT: JAI Press.

Harlos, K. P. (1998). Organizational injustice and its resistance using voice and silence. *Dissertation Abstracts International–A, 59/05,* 1660.

Harlos, K. P., & Pinder, C. C. (1999). Patterns of organizational injustice: A taxonomy of what employees regard as unjust. In J. A. Wagner (Ed.), *Advances in qualitative organizational research* (Vol. 2, pp. 97–126). Stamford, CT: JAI Press.

Harlos, K. P., & Pinder, C. C. (2000). Emotion and injustice in the workplace. In S. Fineman (Ed.), *Emotions in organizations* (2nd ed., pp. 255–276). London: Sage.

Harlow, H. R, Harlow, M. K. & Meyer, D. R. (1950). Learning motivated by a manipulation drive. *Journal of Experimental Psychology, 40,* 228–234.

Harré, R. (1986). An outline of the social constructivist viewpoint. In R. Harré (Ed.), *The social construction of emotions* (pp. 2–14). New York: Basic Blackwell.

Harrell, A., Caldwell, C., & Doty, E. (1985). Within-person expectancy theory predictions of accounting students' motivation to achieve academic success. *The Accounting Review*, *60*, 724–735.

Harris, H. (1995). Rethinking heterosexual relationships in Polynesia: A case study of Mangaia, Cook Island. In W. Jankowiak (Ed.), *Romantic passion* (pp. 95–127). New York: Columbia University Press.

Harris, R. (2002, December). With its strong heritage and high-quality food, A&W is the clear choice of the baby-boom generation. *Food Service and Hospitality Magazine*.

Harrison, D. A., Newman, D. A., & Roth, P. L. (2006). How important are job attitudes? Metal-analytic comparisons of integrative behavioral outcomes and time sequences. *Academy of Management Journal*, *49*(2), 305–326.

Hart, P. M. (1999). Predicting employee life satisfaction: A coherent model of personality, work and nonwork experiences, and domain satisfactions. *Journal of Applied Psychology*, *84*(4), 564–584.

Harter, J. K., Schmidt, F. L., & Hayes, T. L. (2002). Business-unit-level relationship between employee satisfaction, employee engagement, and business outcomes: A meta-analysis. *Journal of Applied Psychology*, *87*(2), 268–279.

Harvey, J. B., & Albertson, D. R. (1971). Neurotic organizations: Symptoms, causes, and treatment (Part 1). *Personnel Journal*, *50*, 694–699.

Hawthorne, N. (1986). *The scarlet letter*. New York: Chelsea House Publishers.

Haynes, R. S., Pine, R. S., & Fitch, H. G. (1982). Reducing accident rates with organizational behavior modification. *Academy of Management Journal*, *25*, 407–416.

Hebb, D. O. (1955). Drives and the C.N.S. (central nervous system). *Psychological Review*, *62*, 243–254.

Heckscher, C. C. (1988). *The new unionism*. New York: Basic Books.

Heider, F. (1958). *The psychology of interpersonal relations*. New York: John Wiley & Sons.

Heiman, G. W. (1975). A note on operant conditioning principles extrapolated to the theory of management. *Organizational Behavior & Human Performance*, *13*, 165–170.

Heller, D., Judge, T. A., & Watson, D. (2002). The confounding role of personality and trait affectivity in the relationship between job and life satisfaction. *Journal of Organizational Behavior*, *23*(7), 815–835.

Heller, D., Watson, D., & Ilies, R. (2006). The dynamic process of life satisfaction. *Journal of Personality*, *75*(5), 1421–1450.

Hendrix, W. H., & Stahl, M. J. (1986). Effects of need for power on job stress for managers and non-managers. *Journal of Social Behavior and Personality*, *1*(14), 611–619.

Heneman III, H. G., & Schwab, D. P. (1972). Evaluation of research on expectancy theory predictions of employee performance. *Psychological Bulletin*, *78*, 1–9.

Henri, R. (1923). *The art spirit*. Philadelphia, PA: Lippincott.

Henry, R. A. (1994). The effects of choice and incentives on the overestimation of future performance. *Organizational Behavior and Human Decision Processes*, *57*, 210–225.

Herrbach, O. (2006). A matter of feeling? The affective tone of organizational commitment and identification. *Journal of Organizational Behavior*, *27*, 629–643.

Herrnstein, R. J., & Murray, C. (1994). *The bell curve*. New York: Free Press.

Hershey, R. (1973). Coming – A locked in generation of workers. *Personnel*, *50*(6), 23–29.

Herzberg, F. (1966). *Work and the nature of man*. Cleveland, OH: World Publishing.

Herzberg, F. (1968). One more time: How do you motivate employees? *Harvard Business Review*, *46*(1), 53–62.

Herzberg, F. (1976). Motivational type: Individual differences in motivation. In F. Herzberg (Ed.), *The managerial choice* (pp. 1059–1076). Homewood, IL: Dow Jones-Irwin.

Herzberg, F. (1981). Motivating people. In P. Mali (Ed.), *Management handbook*. New York: John Wiley & Sons.

Herzberg, F., Mausner, B., Peterson, R. O., & Capwell, D. F. (1957). *Job attitudes: Review of research and opinion*. Pittsburgh, PA: Psychological Service of Pittsburgh.

Herzberg, F., Mausner, B., & Snyderman, B. B. (1959). *The motivation to work*. New York: John Wiley & Sons.

Hewstone, M. (1983). *Attribution theory: Social and functional extensions*. Oxford: Blackwell.

Hewstone, M., & Young, L. (1988). Expectancy-value models of attitude: Measurement and combination of evaluations and beliefs. *Journal of Applied Social Psychology*, *18*, 958–971.

Hill, C. A. (1987a). Affiliation motivation: People who need people . . . but in different ways. *Journal of Personality and Social Psychology*, *52*, 1008–1018.

Hill, C. A. (1987b). Social support and health: The role of affiliative need as a moderator. *Journal of Research in Personality*, *21*, 127–147.

Hill, C. A. (1991). Seeking emotional support: The influence of affiliative need and partner warmth. *Journal of Personality and Social Psychology, 60,* 112–131.

Hill, P. C., & Pargament, K. I. (2003). Advances in the conceptualization and measurement of religion and spirituality: Implications for physical and mental health research. *American Psychologist, 58*(1), 64–74.

Hill, R. B. (1999). *Historical context of the work ethic,* from www.coe.uga.edu/workethic/historypdf.pdf

Hirschman, A. O. (1970). *Exit, voice, and loyalty: Response to decline in firms, organizations, and states.* Cambridge, MA: Harvard University Press.

Hochschild, A. R. (1983). *The managed heart.* Berkeley, CA: University of California Press.

Hofstede, G. (1978). The poverty of management control philosophy. *Academy of Management Review, 3,* 450–461.

Hofstede, G. (1997). *Culture and organizations.* New York: McGraw-Hill.

Hollenbeck, J. R. (1979). A matrix method for expectancy research. *Academy of Management Review, 4,* 579–587.

Hollenbeck, J. R., & Klein, H. J. (1987). Goal commitment and the goal-setting process: Problems, prospects, and proposals for future research. *Journal of Applied Psychology, 72*(2), 212–220.

Hollenbeck, J. R., & Wagner III, J. A. (2002). *Organizational behavior: Securing competitive advantage* (4th ed.). Fort Worth, TX: Harcourt College Publishers.

Hollenbeck, J. R., Williams, C., & Klein, H. (1989). An empirical examination of the antecedents of commitment to difficult goals. *Journal of Applied Psychology, 74*(1), 18–23.

Holmes, T., & Rahe, R. H. (1967). The social readjustment rating scale. *Journal of Psychosomatic Research, 12,* 213–218.

Holtom, B. C., Lee, T. W., & Tidd, S. T. (2002). The relationship between work status congruence and work-related attitudes and behaviors. *Journal of Applied Psychology, 87*(5), 903–915.

Holtom, B. C., Mitchell, T. R., Lee, T. W., & Inderrieden, E. J. (2005). Shocks as causes of turnover: What they are and how organizations can manage them. *Human Resource Management, 44*(3), 337–352.

Hom, P. W., & Griffeth, R. W. (1995). *Employee turnover.* Cincinnati, OH: South-Western.

Homans, G. C. (1961). *Social behavior: Its elementary forms.* New York: Harcourt Brace and World.

Horibe, F. (1999). *Managing knowledge workers: New skills and attitudes to unlock the intellectual capital in your organization.* Toronto, ON: John Wiley & Sons.

Hormuth, S. E. (1986). The sampling of experiences *in situ. Journal of Personality, 54*(1), 262–293.

Hotelling, K. (1991). Sexual harassment: A problem shielded by silence. *Journal of Counseling and Development, 69*(6), 497–501.

House, R. J. (1971). A path–goal theory of leadership. *Administrative Science Quarterly, 16,* 321–338.

House, R. J. (1975). The quest for relevance in management education: Some second thoughts and undesired consequences. *Academy of Management Journal, 18,* 323–333.

House, R. J., Hanges, P. J., Javidan, M., Dorfman, P. W., & Gupta, V. (2004). *Culture, leadership, and organizations: The GLOBE study of 62 societies.* Thousand Oaks, CA: Sage.

House, R. J., & Mitchell, T. R. (1974). Path–goal theory of leadership. *Journal of Contemporary Business, 3*(Autumn), 81–98.

House, R. J., Shapiro, H. J., & Wahba, M. A. (1974). Expectancy theory as a predictor of work behavior and attitude: A reevaluation of empirical evidence. *Decision Sciences, 5,* 481–506.

House, R. J., Spangler, W. D., & Woyke, J. (1991). Personality and charisma in the US presidency: A psychological theory of leadership effectiveness. *Administrative Science Quarterly, 35,* 364–396.

House, R. J., & Wigdor, L. A. (1967). Herzberg's dual-factor theory of job satisfaction and motivation: A review of the evidence and a criticism. *Personnel Psychology, 20,* 369–389.

Hsee, C. K., & Abelson, R. P. (1991). Velocity relation: Satisfaction as a function of the first derivative of outcome over time. *Journal of Personality and Social Psychology, 60,* 341–347.

Huang, X., & Van De Vliert, E. (2003). Where intrinsic job satisfaction fails to work: National moderators of intrinsic motivation. *Journal of Organizational Behavior, 24*(2), 159–179.

Huberman, J. (1964). Discipline without punishment. *Harvard Business Review, 42*(4), 62–68.

Hughes, M. A., Price, R. L., & Marrs, D. W. (1986). Linking theory construction and theory testing: Models with multiple indicators of latent variables. *Academy of Management Review, 11*(1), 128–144.

Hughey, J. B., Sundstrom, E., & Lounsbury, J. W. (1985). Attitudes toward nuclear power: A longitudinal analysis of the expectancy-value models. *Basic and Applied Social Psychology, 6,* 75–91.

Huizinga, G. (1970). *Maslow's need hierarchy in the work situation*. Groningen, The Netherlands: Wolters-Noordhoff.

Hulin, C. L. (1990). Adaptation, persistence, and commitment. In M. D. Dunnette & L. M. Hough (Eds.), *Handbook of industrial and organizational psychology* (2nd ed., Vol. 2). Palo Alto, CA: Consulting Psychologists Press.

Hulin, C. L., & Blood, M. R. (1968). Job enlargement, individual responses, and worker responses. *Psychological Bulletin, 69*, 41–55.

Hulin, C. L., & Judge, T. A. (2003). Job attitudes. In W. C. Borman, D. R. Ilgen, & R. J. Klimoski (Eds.), *Handbook of psychology* (pp. 255–276). New York: John Wiley & Sons.

Hull, C. L. (1943). *Principles of behavior*. New York: Appleton-Century-Crofts.

Hunt, J. M. (1965). Intrinsic motivation and its role in psychological development. *Nebraska Symposium on Motivation, 13*, 189–282.

Hunter, J. E., Schmidt, F. L., & Jackson, G. B. (1982). *Meta-analysis: Cumulating research findings across studies*. Beverly Hills, CA: Sage.

Huseman, R. C., Hatfield, J. D., & Miles, E. W. (1985). Test for individual perceptions of job equity: Some preliminary findings. *Perceptual and Motor Skills, 61*, 1055–1064.

Huseman, R. C., Hatfield, J. D., & Miles, E. W. (1987). A new perspective on equity theory: The equity sensitivity construct. *Academy of Management Review, 12*(2), 222–234.

Hyland, M. E. (1988). Motivational control theory: An integrative framework. *Journal of Personality and Social Psychology, 55*, 642–651.

Ilgen, D. R. (1971). Satisfaction with performance as a function of the initial level of expected performance and the deviation from expectations. *Organizational Behavior & Human Performance, 6*(3), 345–361.

Ilgen, D. R., Fisher, C. D., & Taylor, M. S. (1979). Consequences of individual feedback on behavior in organizations. *Journal of Applied Psychology, 64*(4), 349–371.

Ilgen, D. R., & Hollenbeck, J. H. (1977). The role of job satisfaction in absence behavior. *Organizational Behavior & Human Performance, 19*(1), 148–161.

Ilgen, D. R., Nebeker, D. M., & Pritchard, R. D. (1981). Expectancy theory measures: An empirical comparison in an experimental simulation. *Organizational Behavior & Human Performance, 28*(2), 189–223.

Ilies, R., & Judge, T. A. (2002). Understanding the dynamic relationships among personality, mood, and job satisfaction: A field experience sampling study. *Organizational Behavior & Human Decision Processes, 89*, 1119–1139.

Ilies, R., & Judge, T. A. (2003). On the heritability of job satisfaction: The mediating role of personality. *Journal of Applied Psychology, 88*(4), 750–759.

Ilies, R., & Judge, T. A. (2005). Goal regulation across time: The effects of feedback and affect. *Journal of Applied Psychology, 90*(3), 453–467.

Inglehart, R. (1981). Aggregate stability and individual-level flux in mass belief systems: The level of analysis paradox. *American Political Science Review, 79*, 97–116.

Isen, A. M., & Baron, R. A. (1991). Positive affect as a factor in organizational behavior. In L. L. Cummings & B. M. Staw (Eds.), *Research in organizational behavior* (Vol. 13, pp. 1–54). Greenwich, CT: JAI Press.

Ivancevich, J. M., & McMahon, J. T. (1982). The effects of goal setting, external feedback, and self-generated feedback on outcome variables: A field experiment. *Academy of Management Journal, 25*(2), 359–372.

Jablonsky, S. F., & DeVries, D. L. (1972). Operant conditioning principles extrapolated to the theory of management. *Organizational Behavior & Human Performance, 7*(2), 340–358.

Jaccard, J. (1981). Attitudes and behavior: Implications of attitudes toward behavioral alternatives. *Journal of Experimental Social Psychology, 17*, 286–307.

Jaccard, J., King, G. W., & Pomazal, R. (1977). Attitudes and behavior: An analysis of specificity of attitudinal predictors. *Human Relations, 30*(9), 817–824.

Jackofsky, E. F. (1984). Turnover and job performance: An integrated process model. *Academy of Management Review, 9*, 74–83.

Jackofsky, E. F., Ferris, K. R., & Breckenridge, B. G. (1986). Evidence for a curvilinear relationship between job performance and turnover. *Journal of Management, 12*, 105–111.

Jackson, J. M., & Harkins, S. G. (1985). Equity in effort: An explanation of the social loafing effect. *Journal of Personality and Social Psychology, 49*, 1199–1206.

Jacobs, J. A., & Powell, B. (1985). Occupational prestige: A sex-neutral concept. *Sex Roles, 12*(9/10), 1061–1071.

Jacques, E. (1961). *Equitable payment*. New York: John Wiley & Sons.

Jacques, R. (1992). Critique and theory building: Producing knowledge "from the kitchen". *Academy of Management Review, 17*(3), 582–606.

Jamal, M. (1984). Job stress and job performance controversy: An empirical assessment. *Organizational Behavior & Human Performance, 33*(1), 1–21.

Jamal, M., & Mitchell, V. F. (1980). Work, nonwork, and mental health: A model and a test. *Industrial Relations, 19*(1), 88–93.

Jamieson, B. D. (1973). Behavioral problems with management by objectives. *Academy of Management Journal, 16*(3), 496–505.

Jamieson, J. (2005, October 11). Employee theft plagues small business. *CanWest News Service*.

Jankowiak, W. (1995). *Romantic passion*. New York: Columbia University Press.

Jankowiak, W., & Fischer, E. (1992). A cross-cultural perspective on romantic love. *Ethnology, 31*(2), 149–155.

Jaros, S. J., Jermier, J. M., Koehler, J. W., & Sincich, T. (1993). Effects of continuance, affective, and moral commitment on the withdrawal process: An evaluation of eight structural equation models. *Academy of Management Journal, 36*(5), 951–995.

Javidan, M. (2004). Performance orientation. In R. J. House, P. J. Hanges, M. Javidan, P. W. Dorfman, & V. Gupta (Eds.), *Culture, leadership, and organizations* (pp. 239–281). Thousand Oaks, CA: Sage.

Jenkins, D. (1975). Beyond job enrichment. *Working Papers for a New Society, 2*, 51–57.

Jenkins, S. R. (1994). Need for power and women's careers over 14 years: Structural power, job satisfaction, and motive change. *Journal of Personality and Social Psychology, 66*(1), 155–165.

Jermier, J. M. (1988). Sabotage at work: The rational view. In N. Di Tomaso & S. B. Bacharach (Eds.), *Research in the sociology of organizations* (Vol. 6, pp. 101–134). Greenwich, CT: JAI Press.

Joad, C. E. M. (1957). *Guide to philosophy*. New York: Dover.

Johns, G. (1981). Difference score measure of organizational behavior variables: A critique. *Organizational Behavior & Human Performance, 27*(3), 443–463.

Johns, G. (2006). The essential impact of context on organizational behavior. *Academy of Management Review, 31*(2), 386–408.

Johns, G., & Nicholson, N. (1982). The meanings of absence: New theories for theory and research. In B. M. Staw & L. L. Cummings (Eds.), *Research in organizational behavior* (Vol. 4, pp. 127–172). Greenwich, CT: JAI Press.

Johns, G., Xie, J. L., & Fang, Y. Q. (1992). Moderating and mediating effects in job design. *Journal of Management, 18*, 657–676.

Johnson, P. R., & Indvik, J. (1994). Workplace violence: An issue of the nineties. *Public Personnel Management, 23*(4), 515–523.

Jones, E. E. (1964). *Ingratiation*. New York: Appleton-Century-Crofts.

Jones, M. R. (Ed.). (1955). *Nebraska Symposium on Motivation*. Lincoln, NE: University of Nebraska Press.

Journal of Vocational Behavior. (1993). Special issue on the theory of work adjustment. *Journal of Vocational Behavior, 43*(1).

Judge, T. A. (1992). The dispositional perspective in human resource management. In G. R. Ferris, & K. M. Rowland (Eds.), *Research in personnel and human resources management* (Vol. 10, pp. 187–232). Greenwich, CT: JAI Press.

Judge, T. A., & Bono, J. E. (2001). Relationship of core self-evaluation traits – self-esteem, generalized self-efficacy, locus of control, and emotional stability – with job satisfaction and job performance: A meta-analysis. *Journal of Applied Psychology, 86*(1), 80–93.

Judge, T. A., & Bretz Jr., R. D. (1992). Effects of work values on job choice decisions. *Journal of Applied Psychology, 77*(3), 261–271.

Judge, T. A., & Cable, D. M. (2004). The effect of physical height on workplace success and income: Preliminary test of a theoretical model. *Journal of Applied Psychology, 89*(3), 428–441.

Judge, T. A., Erez, A., & Bono, J. E. (1998). The power of being positive: The relation between positive self-concept and job performance. *Human Performance, 11*(2/3), 167–187.

Judge, T. A., Erez, A., Bono, J. E., & Thoresen, C. J. (2003). The core self-evaluations scale: Development of a measure. *Personnel Psychology, 56*(2), 303–331.

Judge, T. A., Heller, D., & Mount, M. K. (2002). Five-factor model of personality and job satisfaction: A meta-analysis. *Journal of Applied Psychology, 87*(3), 530–541.

Judge, T. A., & Larsen, R. (2001). Dispositional affect and job satisfaction: A review and theoretical extension. *Organizational Behavior & Human Decision Processes, 86*(1), 67–98.

Judge, T. A., Locke, E. A., & Durham, C. C. (1997). The dispositional causes of job satisfaction: A core evaluations approach. In L. L. Cummings & B. M. Staw (Eds.), *Research in Organizational Behavior, 19*, 151–188.

Judge, T. A., Locke, E. A., Durham, C. C., & Kluger, A. N. (1998). Dispositional effects on job and life satisfaction: The role of core evaluations. *Journal of Applied Psychology, 83*(1), 17–34.

Judge, T. A., Thoresen, C. J., Bono, J. E., & Patton, G. K. (2001). The job satisfaction–job performance relationship: A qualitative and quantitative review. *Psychological Bulletin, 127*(3), 376–407.

Judge, T. A., & Watanabe, S. (1993). Another look at the job satisfaction–life satisfaction relationship. *Journal of Applied Psychology, 78*(6), 939–948.

Jussim, L. (1986). Self-fulfilling prophesies: A theoretical and integrative review. *Psychological Review, 93*, 429–445.

Kabasakal, H., & Bodur, M. (2004). Humane orientation in societies, organizations, and leader attributes. In R. J. House, P. J. Hanges, M. Javidan, P. W. Dorfman, & V. Gupta (Eds.), *Culture, leadership, and organizations* (pp. 564–601). Thousand Oaks, CA: Sage.

Kacmar, K. M., Bozeman, D. P., Carlson, D. S., & Anthony, W. P. (1999). An examination of the perceptions of organizational politics model: Replication and extension. *Human Relations, 52*(3), 383–416.

Kacmar, K. M., Carlson, D. S., & Bratton, V. K. (2004). Situational and dispositional factors as antecedents of ingratiatory behaviors in organizational settings. *Journal of Vocational Behavior, 65*(2), 309–331.

Kahn, W. A. (1989). Toward a sense of organizational humor: Implications for organizational diagnosis and change. *Journal of Applied Psychology, 25*(1), 45–63.

Kalimo, R., Taris, T. W., & Schaufeli, W. B. (2003). The effects of past and anticipated future downsizing on survivor well-being: An equity perspective. *Journal of Occupational & Organizational Psychology, 8*(2), 91–109.

Kane, K., & Montgomery, K. (1998). A framework for understanding disempowerment in organizations. *Human Resource Management, 37*(3–4), 263–275.

Kane, K., Montgomery, K., & Vance, C. (1996, April 1996). *A theoretical framework for understanding the empowering and disempowering nature of social exchanges in employee involvement efforts.* Paper presented at the Western Academy of Management, Banff, Alberta, Canada.

Kanfer, F. H. (1970). *Learning foundations of behavior therapy.* New York: John Wiley & Sons.

Kanfer, F. H. (1971). The maintenance of behavior by self-generated stimuli and reinforcement. In A. Jacobs & J. B. Sachs (Eds.), *The psychology of private events.* New York: Academic Press.

Kanfer, F. H. (1980). Self management methods. In F. H. Kanfer & A. P. Goldstein (Eds.), *Helping people change* (2nd ed., pp. 334–389). New York: Pergamon Press.

Kanfer, R. (1990). Motivation theory in industrial/organizational psychology. In M. D. Dunnette & L. M. Hough (Eds.), *Handbook of industrial and organizational psychology* (2nd ed., Vol. 1, pp. 75–170). Palo Alto, CA: Consulting Psychologists Press.

Kanfer, R. (2005). Self-regulation research in work and I/O psychology. *Applied Psychology: An International Review, 54*(2), 186–191.

Kanfer, R., & Ackerman, P. L. (1989). Motivation and cognitive abilities: An integrative/aptitude-treatment interaction approach to skill acquisition. *Journal of Applied Psychology, 74*(4), 657–690.

Kanfer, R., & Ackerman, P. L. (2000). Individual differences in work motivation: Further explorations of a trait framework. *Applied Psychology: An International Review, 49*(3), 470–482.

Kanfer, R., Ackerman, P. L., Murtha, T. C., Dugdale, B., & Nelson, L. (1994). Goal setting, conditions of practice, and task performance: A resource allocation perspective. *Journal of Applied Psychology, 79*, 826–835.

Kanfer, R., & Heggestad, E. D. (1997). Motivational traits and skills: A person-centered approach to work motivation. *Research in Organizational Behavior, 19*, 1–56.

Kanter, R. M. (1977). *Men and women of the corporation.* New York: Basic Books.

Kanter, R. M. (1979). Power failure in management circuits. *Harvard Business Review, 57*(4), 65–75.

Kanter, R. M. (2005). What theories do audiences want? Exploring the demand side. *Academy of Management Learning & Education, 4*(1), 93–95.

Kapstein, E. B. (2006). The new global slave trade. *Foreign Affairs, 85*, 103–115.

Karau, S. J., & Williams, K. D. (1993). Social loafing: A meta-analytic review and theoretical integrations. *Journal of Personality and Social Psychology, 65*, 681–706.

Karmel, B. (1980). *Point and counterpoint in organizational behavior.* Hillsdale, IL: Dryden Press.

Karoly, P. (1993). Mechanisms of self-regulation: A systems view. *Annual Review of Psychology, 44*(1), 23–52.

Karp, H. B., & Nickson, J. W. (1973). Motivato-hygiene deprivation as a predictor of job turnover. *Personnel Psychology, 26,* 377–384.

Katerberg, R., & Blau, G. J. (1983). An examination of level and direction of effort and job performance. *Academy of Management Journal, 26*(2), 249–257.

Katz, D. (1964). The motivational basis of organizational behavior. *Behavioral Science, 9,* 131–146.

Katz, D., & Kahn, R. F. (1966). *The social psychology of organizations.* New York: John Wiley & Sons.

Katz, D., & Kahn, R. F. (1978). *The social psychology of organizations* (2nd ed.). New York: John Wiley & Sons.

Katz, R. (1977). Job enrichment: Some career considerations. In J. Van Maanen (Ed.), *Organizational careers* (pp. 133–148). Chichester: John Wiley & Sons.

Katz, R. (1978). Job longevity as situational factor in job satisfaction. *Administrative Science Quarterly, 28,* 204–223.

Katz, R. (1980). Time and work: Toward an integrative perspective. In B. M. Staw & L. L. Cummings (Eds.), *Research in organizational behavior* (Vol. 2, pp. 81–128). Greenwich, CT: JAI Press.

Katzell, R. A., Thompson, D. E., & Guzzo, R. A. (1992). How job satisfaction and job performance are and are not linked. In C. J. Cranny, P. C. Smith, & E. F. Stone (Eds.), *Job satisfaction* (pp. 195–217). New York: Lexington Books.

Kavanagh, M. J., Hurst, M. W., & Rose, R. (1981). The relationship between job satisfaction and psychiatric health symptoms for air traffic controllers. *Personnel Psychology, 34*(4), 691–707.

Kazdin, A. E. (1975). *Behavior modification in applied settings.* Homewood, IL: Dorsey.

Kazdin, A. E. (1978). *History of behavior modification.* Baltimore, MD: University Park Press.

Keeley, M. (1983). Values in organizational theory and management education. *Academy of Management Review, 8*(3), 376–386.

Keeley, M., & Graham, J. W. (1992). Hirschman's loyalty construct. *Employee Responsibilities and Rights Journal, 5,* 191–200.

Kelley, H. H., & Michela, J. L. (1980). Attribution theory and research. *Annual Review of Psychology, 31,* 457–501.

Kelly, E. (2007, October 17). *Naval Academy unveils sexual harassment prevention program,* from www.hometownannapolis.com/cgi–bin/read/2007/10_26–37/NAV

Kelly, J. E. (1978). A reappraisal of sociotechnical systems theory. *Human Relations, 31*(12), 1069–1099.

Kelly, R. M., & Bayes, J. (1988). Comparable worth and pay equity: Issues and trends. In R. M. Kelly & J. Bayes (Eds.), *Comparable worth, pay equity, and public policy.* New York: Greenwood Press.

Kelman, H. C. (1958). Compliance, identification, and internalization: Three processes of attitude change. *Journal of Conflict Resolution, 2,* 51–60.

Kennedy, C. W., Fossum, J. A., & White, B. J. (1983). An empirical comparison of within-subjects and between-subjects expectancy theory models. *Organizational Behavior & Human Performance, 32*(1), 124–142.

Kennedy, M. M. (1992). Romance in the office. *Across the Board, 29*(3), 23–27.

Keren, G. B., & Raaijmakers, J. G. W. (1988). On between-subjects versus within-subjects comparisons in testing utility theory. *Organizational Behavior & Human Decision Processes, 41*(2), 233–247.

Kernis, M. H. (2003). Toward a conceptualization of optimal self-esteem. *Psychological Inquiry, 14*(1), 1–26.

Kerr, N. L. (1983). Motivation losses in small groups: A social dilemma analysis. *Journal of Personality and Social Psychology, 45,* 819–828.

Kerr, N. L., & Brunn, S. E. (1981). Ringelmann revisited: Alternative explanations for the social loafing effect. *Personality and Social Psychology Bulletin, 7,* 224–231.

Kerr, S. (1975). On the folly of rewarding A, while hoping for B. *Academy of Management Journal, 18*(4), 769–783.

Kidwell, R. E., & Bennett, N. (1993). Employee propensity to withhold effort: A conceptual model to intersect three avenues of research. *Academy of Management Review, 18*(3), 429–456.

Kierein, N. M., & Gold, M. A. (2000). Pygmalion in work organizations: A meta-analysis. *Journal of Organizational Behavior, 21*(8), 913–928.

Killinger, B. (1991). *Workaholics: The respectable addicts.* Toronto, Ontario, Canada: Key Porter Books.

Killingsworth, M. R. (1990). *The economics of comparable worth.* Kalamazoo, MI: W.E. Upjohn Institute for Employment Research.

Kilmann, R. H. (1981). Toward a unique/useful concept of values for interpersonal behaviour: A critical review of the literature on value. *Psychological Reports, 48,* 939–959.

King, N. (1970). Clarification and evaluation of the two-factor theory of job satisfaction. *Psychological Bulletin, 74,* 18–31.

King, S. (2007). Of inhuman bondage. *The Economist, 64 (The World in 2007).*

King Jr., W. C., Miles, E. W., & Day, D. D. (1993). A test and refinement of the equity sensitivity construct. *Journal of Organizational Behavior, 14*(4), 301–317.

Kinicki, A. J., McKee-Ryan, F. M., Schriesheim, C., & Carson, K. P. (2002). Assessing the construct validity of the job descriptive index: A review and meta-analysis. *Journal of Applied Psychology, 84,* 14–32.

Kinicki, A. J., Prussia, G. E., Wu, B. J., & McKee-Ryan, F. M. (2004). A covariance structure analysis of employees' response to performance feedback. *Journal of Applied Psychology, 89*(6), 1057–1069.

Kipnis, D. (1972). Does power corrupt? *Journal of Personality and Social Psychology, 24,* 33–41.

Kipnis, D. (2001). Using power: Newton's second law. In A. Y. Lee-Chai, & J. A. Bargh (Eds.), *The use and abuse of power* (pp. 3–18). Philadelphia, PA: Psychology Press.

Kipnis, D., Castell, P. J., Gergen, M., & Mauch, D. (1976). Metamorphic effects of power. *Journal of Applied Psychology, 61*(2), 127–135.

Kitayama, S., & Niedenthal, P. M. (1994). Introduction. In P. M. Niedenthal & S. Kitayama (Eds.), *The heart's eye* (pp. 1–14). San Diego, CA: Academic Press.

Kivimäki, M., Ferrie, J. E., Brunner, E., Head, J., Shipley, M. J., Vahtera, J., et al. (2005). Justice at work and reduced risk of coronary heart disease among employees: The Whitehall II Study. *Archives of Internal Medicine, 165*(19), 2245–2251.

Klein, H. J. (1989). An integrated control theory model of work motivation. *Academy of Management Review, 14*(2), 150–172.

Klein, H. J. (1991a). Further evidence on the relationship between goal setting and expectancy theories. *Organizational Behavior & Human Decision Processes, 49*(2), 230–257.

Klein, H. J. (1991b). Control theory and understanding motivated behavior: A different conclusion. *Motivation and Emotion, 15,* 29–44.

Klein, H. J., Wesson, M. J., Hollenbeck, J. R., & Alge, B. J. (1999). Goal commitment and the goal-setting process: Conceptual clarification and empirical synthesis. *Journal of Applied Psychology, 84*(6), 885–896.

Klein, K. J., Conn, A. B., Smith, D. B., & Sorra, J. S. (2001). Is everyone in agreement? An exploration of within-group agreement in employee perceptions of the work environment. *Journal of Applied Psychology, 86*(1), 3–16.

Kleinbeck, U., Quast, H. H., Thierry, H., & Hacker, H. (Eds.). (1990). *Work motivation.* Hillsdale, NJ: Lawrence Erlbaum Associates, Inc.

Kleinbeck, U., Wegge, J., & Schmidt, K.-H. (2001). Work motivation and performance in groups. In M. Erez, U. Kleinbeck, & H. Thierry (Eds.), *Work motivation in the context of a globalizing economy* (pp. 181–196). Mahwah, NJ: Lawrence Erlbaum Associates, Inc.

Kleinginna, P. R., & Kleinginna, A. M. (1981). A categorized list of motivation definitions with a suggestion for a consensual definition. *Motivation and Emotion,* 263–292.

Klimoski, R. (2005). Introduction: There is nothing as dangerous as a bad theory. *Academy of Management Learning & Education, 4*(1), 74.

Klinger, M. R., & Greenwald, A. G. (1994). Preferences need no inferences? The cognitive basis of unconscious mere exposure effects. In P. M. Niedenthal & S. Kitayama (Eds.), *The heart's eye* (pp. 67–85). San Diego, CA: Academic Press.

Kluger, A. N., & DeNisi, A. S. (1996). The effects of feedback interventions on performance: A historical review, a meta-analysis, and a preliminary feedback intervention theory. *Psychological Bulletin, 119*(2), 254–284.

Kluger, A. N., & Tikochinsky, J. (2001). The error of accepting the "theoretical" null hypothesis: The rise, fall, and resurrection of commonsense hypotheses in psychology. *Psychological Bulletin, 127*(3), 408–423.

Knowles, H. P., & Saxberg, B. O. (1967). Human relations and the nature of man. *Harvard Business Review, 45,* 22–24, 28, 30, 32, 34, 36, 38, 40, 172, 176, 178.

Kochan, T., Lansbury, R., & MacDuffie, J. (1997). Conclusion: After lean production? In T. Kochan, R. Lansbury, & J. MacDuffie (Eds.), *After lean production: Evolving employment practices in the world auto industry* (pp. 303–324). Ithaca, NY: ILR Press.

Kohlberg, L. (1981). *The philosophy of moral development.* New York: Harper & Row.

Kohlberg, L. (1984). *The psychology of moral development.* New York: Harper & Row.

Kohn, A. (1993). Why incentive plans cannot work. *Harvard Business Review, 71*(5), 54–63.

Komaki, J. L. (1986). Applied behavior analysis and organizational behavior: Reciprocal influence of the two fields. In B. M. Staw & L. L. Cummings (Eds.), *Research in organizational behavior* (Vol. 8, pp. 297–334). Greenwich, CT: JAI Press.

Komaki, J. L. (2003). Reinforcement theory at work: Enhancing and explaining what employees do. In L. W. Porter, G. A. Bigley, & R. M. Steers (Eds.), *Motivation and work behavior* (7th ed.). New York: McGraw-Hill Irwin.

Komaki, J. L., Barwick, K. D., & Scott, L. R. (1978). A behavioral approach to occupational safety: Pinpointing and reinforcing safe performance in a food processing plant. *Journal of Applied Psychology, 63*(4), 434–445.

Komaki, J. L., Coombs, T., Redding Jr., T. P., & Schepman, S. (2000). A rich and rigorous examination of applied behavior analysis research in the world of work. In C. L. Cooper & I. T. Robertson (Eds.), *International review of industrial and organizational psychology* (pp. 265–367). Chichester: John Wiley & Sons.

Komaki, J. L., Coombs, T., & Schepman, S. (1991). Motivational implications of reinforcement theory. In R. M. Steers & L. W. Porter (Eds.), *Motivation and work behavior* (5th ed., pp. 87–107). New York: McGraw-Hill.

Komaki, J. L., Heinzmann, A. T., & Lawson, L. (1980). Effect of training and feedback: Component analysis of a behavioral safety program. *Journal of Applied Psychology, 65*(3), 261–270.

Komaki, J. L., Waddell, W. M., & Pearce, M. G. (1977). The applied behavior analysis approach and individual employees: Improving performance in two small businesses. *Organizational Behavior & Human Performance, 19*(2), 337–352.

Kondrasuk, J. N. (1981). Studies in MBO effectiveness. *Academy of Management Review, 6*(3), 419–430.

Konovsky, M. (2000). Understanding procedural justice and its impact on business organizations. *Journal of Management, 26*(3), 489–511.

Konrad, A. M., & Langton, N. (1991). Sex differences in job preferences, workplace segregation, and compensating earning differentials: The case of Stanford MBA's. *Academy of Management Proceedings,* 368–372.

Kopelman, R. E. (1977). Across individual, within-individual and return on effort versions of expectancy theory. *Decision Sciences, 8*(4), 651–662.

Kopelman, R. E. (1979). A causal-correlational test of the Porter and Lawler framework. *Human Relations, 32*(7), 545–556.

Kopelman, R. E. (1986). *Managing productivity in organizations.* New York: McGraw-Hill.

Kopelman, R. E., Brief, A. P., & Guzzo, R. A. (1990). The role of climate and culture in productivity. In B. Schneider (Ed.), *Organizational climate and culture* (pp. 282–318). San Francisco: Jossey-Bass.

Kopelman, R. E., & Thompson, P. H. (1976). Boundary conditions for expectancy theory predictions of work motivation and job performance. *Academy of Management Journal, 19,* 237–258.

Koper, G., Van Knippenberg, D., Bouhuijs, F., Vermunt, R., & Wilke, H. (1993). Procedural fairness and self-esteem. *European Journal of Social Psychology, 23,* 313–325.

Korman, A. K. (1970). Toward an hypothesis of work behavior. *Journal of Applied Psychology, 54*(1), 31–41.

Korman, A. K. (1971). *Industrial and organizational psychology.* Englewood Cliffs, NJ: Prentice-Hall.

Korman, A. K. (1974). *The psychology of motivation.* Englewood Cliffs, NJ: Prentice-Hall.

Korman, A. K. (1976). Hypothesis of work behavior revisited and an extension. *Academy of Management Review, 1*(1), 50–63.

Korman, A. K., Greenhaus, J. H., & Badin, I. J. (1977). Personnel attitudes and motivation. *Annual Review of Psychology, 28,* 175–196.

Korsgaard, M. A., Meglino, B. M., & Lester, S. W. (1997). Beyond helping: Do other-oriented values have broader implications in organizations? *Journal of Applied Psychology, 82*(1), 160–177.

Korsgaard, M. A., Meglino, B. M., & Lester, S. W. (2004). The effect of other orientation on self-supervisor rating agreement. *Journal of Organizational Behavior, 25*(7), 873–892.

Korsgaard, M. A., Roberson, L. & Rymph, R. D. (1998). What motivates fairness? The role of subordinate assertive behavior on manager's interactional fairness. *Journal of Applied Psychology, 83,* 731–744

Kouzes, J. M., & Posner, B. A. (1995). *The leadership challenge.* San Francisco: Jossey-Bass.

Kovach, K. A. (1987). What motivates employees? Workers and supervisors give different answers. *Business Horizons, 30*(5), 58–64.

Kovach, K. A., & Millspaugh, P. E. (1990). Comparable worth: Canada legislates pay equity. *Academy of Management Executive, 4*(2), 92–101.

Kram, K. E. (1985). *Mentoring at work: Developmental relationships in organizational life.* Glenview, IL: Scott, Foresman.

Kramer, R. M., & Tyler, T. R. (1996). *Trust in organizations.* New York: Sage.

Kraut, A. I. (1975). Predicting turnover of employees from measured job attitudes. *Organizational Behavior & Human Performance, 13*(2), 233–243.

Kravitz, D., & Martin, B. (1986). Ringelmann rediscovered: The original article. *Journal of Personality and Social Psychology, 50,* 936–941.

Kray, L. J., & Lind, E. A. (2002). The injustices of others: Social reports and the integration of others' experiences in organizational justice judgments. *Organizational Behavior & Human Decision Processes, 89,* 906–924.

Kreitner, R., & Luthans, F. (1984). A social learning approach to behavioral management: Radical behaviorists "mellowing out". *Organizational Dynamics, 13*(2), 47–65.

Kristof, A. L. (1996). Person–organizational fit: An integrative review of its conceptualizations, measurement, and implications. *Personnel Psychology, 49,* 1–49.

Kristof-Brown, A. L., Jansen, K. J., & Colbert, A. E. (2002). A policy-capturing study of simultaneous effects of fit with jobs, groups, and organizations. *Journal of Applied Psychology, 97,* 985–993.

Kruger, J., & Dunning, D. (1999). Unskilled and unaware of it: How difficulties in recognizing one's own incompetence lead to inflated self-assessments. *Journal of Personality and Social Psychology, 7*(6), 1121–1134.

Kruglanski, A. W., & Mayseless, O. (1990). Classic and current social comparison research: Expanding the perspective. *Psychological Bulletin, 108*(2), 195–208.

Kruml, S. M., & Geddes, D. (2000). Catching fire without burning out: Is there an ideal way to perform emotion labor? In N. M. Ashkanasy, C. E. Hartel, & W. J. Zerbe (Eds.), *Emotions in the workplace: Research, theory, and practice.* Westport, CT/London: Quorum Books.

Kuhl, J., & Atkinson, J. W. (1984). Perspectives in human motivational psychology: A new experimental paradigm. In V. Sarris & A. Parducci (Eds.), *Perspective in psychological experimentation: Towards the year 2000* (pp. 235–252). Hillsdale, NJ: Lawrence Erlbaum Associates, Inc.

Kuhn, T. (1970). *The structure of scientific revolutions.* Chicago, IL: University of Chicago Press.

Kulik, J. A., Mahler, H. I. M., & Moore, P. J. (2003). Social comparison affiliation under threat: Effects on recovery from major surgery. In P. Salovey & A. J. Rothman (Eds.), *Social psychology of health* (Vol. xii, pp. 199–226). New York: Psychology Press.

Kurman, J. (2001). Self-regulation strategies in achievement settings. *Journal of Cross-Cultural Psychology, 32*(4), 491–503.

Lakoff, G. (1987). *Women, fire, and dangerous things: What categories reveal about the mind.* Chicago, IL: University of Chicago Press.

Lam, S. S. K., Schaubroeck, J., & Aryee, S. (2002). Relationship between organizational justice and employee work outcomes: A cross-national study. *Journal of Organizational Behavior, 23*(1), 1–18.

Lamertz, K. (2002). The social construction of fairness: Social influence and sense making in organizations. *Journal of Organizational Behavior, 23,* 19–37.

Landy, F. J., & Becker, W. S. (1987). Motivation theory reconsidered. In L. L. Cummings & B. M. Staw (Eds.), *Research in organizational behavior* (Vol. 9, pp. 1–38). Greenwich, CT: JAI Press.

Lang, P. J. (1988). What are the data of emotion? In V. Hamilton, G. H. Bower, & N. H. Frijda (Eds.), *Cognitive perspectives on emotion and motivation* (pp. 173–191). Dordrecht, The Netherlands: Kluwer.

Lansberg, I. (1984). Hierarchy as a mediator of fairness: A contingency approach to distributive justice in organizations. *Journal of Applied Social Psychology, 14,* 124–135.

LaNuez, D., & Jermier, J. M. (1994). Sabotage by managers and technocrats. In J. M. Jermier, D. Knights, & W. R. Nord (Eds.), *Resistance and power in organizations.* New York: Routledge.

Larwood, L., & Wood, M. M. (1977). *Women in management.* Lexington, MA: Lexington Books.

Laschinger, H. K. S., Finegan, J. E., Shamian, J., & Wilk, P. (2001). Impact of structural and psychological empowerment on job strain in nursing work settings: Expanding Kanter's model. *Journal of Nursing Administration, 31,* 260–272.

Laschinger, H. K. S., Finegan, J. E., Shamian, J., & Wilk, P. (2004). A longitudinal analysis of the impact of workplace empowerment on work satisfaction. *Journal of Organizational Behavior, 25,* 527–545.

Latané, B., Williams, K. D., & Harkins, S. G. (1979). Many hands make light the work: The causes and consequences of social loafing. *Journal of Personality and Social Psychology, 37,* 822–832.

Latham, G. P. (2001a). The reciprocal effects of science on practice: Insights from the practice and science of goal setting. *Canadian Psychology, 42*(1), 1–11.

Latham, G. P. (2001b). The reciprocal transfer of learning from journals to practice. *Applied Psychology: An International Review, 50*(2), 201–251.

Latham, G. P. (2003). Goal setting: A five-step approach to behavior change. *Organizational Dynamics, 32*(3), 309–318.

Latham, G. P. (2004). The motivational benefits of goal-setting. *Academy of Management Executive, 18*(4), 126–129.

Latham, G. P. (2007). *Work motivation: History, theory, research, and practice.* Thousand Oaks, CA: Sage.

Latham, G. P., & Baldes, J. J. (1975). The "practical significance" of Locke's theory of goal setting. *Journal of Applied Psychology, 60*(1), 122–124.

Latham, G. P., & Dossett, D. L. (1978). Designing incentive plans for unionized employees: A comparison of continuous and variable ratio reinforcement schedules. *Personnel Psychology, 31*(1), 47–61.

Latham, G. P., Erez, M., & Locke, E. A. (1988). Resolving scientific disputes by the joint design of crucial experiments by the antagonists: Application to the Erez–Latham dispute regarding participation in goal setting. *Journal of Applied Psychology [monograph], 73*(4), 753–772.

Latham, G. P., & Frayne, C. A. (1989). Self-management training for increasing job attendance: A follow-up and a replication. *Journal of Applied Psychology, 74*(3), 411–416.

Latham, G. P., & Kinne, S. B. (1974). Improving job performance through training in goal settings. *Journal of Applied Psychology, 59*(2), 187–191.

Latham, G. P., & Latham, S. D. (2003). Facilitators and inhibitors of the transfer of knowledge between scientists and practitioners in human resource management: Leveraging cultural, individual, and institutional variables. *European Journal of Work and Organizational Psychology, 12*(3), 245–256.

Latham, G. P., & Locke, E. A. (1975). Increasing productivity with decreasing time limits: A field replication of Parkinson's law. *Journal of Applied Psychology, 60*(4), 524–526.

Latham, G. P., & Locke, E. A. (1991). Self-regulation through goal setting. *Organizational Behavior & Human Decision Processes, 50*(2), 212–247.

Latham, G. P., Mitchell, T. R., & Dossett, D. L. (1978). Importance of participative goal setting and anticipated rewards on goal difficulty and job performance. *Journal of Applied Psychology, 63*, 163–171.

Latham, G. P., & Pinder, C. C. (2005). Work motivation theory and research at the dawn of the twenty-first century. *Annual Review of Psychology, 56*, 485–516.

Latham, G. P., & Saari, L. M. (1979a). The effects of holding goal difficulty constant on assigned and participatively set goals. *Academy of Management Journal, 22*(1), 163–168.

Latham, G. P., & Saari, L. M. (1979b). Importance of supportive relationships in goal setting. *Journal of Applied Psychology, 64*(2), 151–156.

Latham, G. P., Seijts, G. H., & Crim, D. (2006). *The effects of learning goal difficulty level and cognitive ability on strategies and performance.* Paper presented at the annual meeting of Academy of Management, August 11–16, Atlanta, Georgia.

Latham, G. P., & Steele, T. P. (1983). The motivational effects of participation versus goal setting on performance. *Academy of Management Journal, 26*(3), 406–417.

Latham, G. P., Steele, T. P., & Saari, L. M. (1982). The effects of participating and goal difficulty on performance. *Personnel Psychology, 35*(3), 677–686.

Latham, G. P., & Wexley, K. N. (1981). *Increasing productivity through performance appraisal.* Reading, MA: Addison-Wesley.

Latham, G. P., Winters, D. C., & Locke, E. A. (1994). Cognitive and motivational effects of participation: A mediator study. *Journal of Organizational Behavior, 15*(1), 49–63.

Latham, G. P., & Yukl, G. A. (1975). A review of research on the application of goal setting in organizations. *Academy of Management Journal, 18*(4), 824–845.

Lawler, E. E. (1965). Managers' perception of their subordinates' pay and of their superiors' pay. *Personnel Psychology, 18*(4), 413–430.

Lawler, E. E. (1966). The mythology of management compensation. *California Management Review, 9*(1), 11–22.

Lawler, E. E. (1967). Secrecy about management compensation: Are there hidden costs? *Organizational Behavior & Human Performance, 2*(2), 182–189.

Lawler, E. E. (1971). *Pay and organizational effectiveness: A psychological view.* New York: McGraw-Hill.

Lawler, E. E. (1972). Secrecy and the need to know. In H. Tosi, R. J. House, & M. D. Dunnette (Eds.), *Managerial motivation and compensation* (pp. 455–476). East Lansing, MI: MSU Business Studies.

Lawler, E. E. (1973). *Motivation in work organizations.* Monterey, CA: Brooks/Cole.

Lawler, E. E. (1976). Individualizing organizations: A needed emphasis in organizational psychology. In H. Meltzer & F. R. Wickert (Eds.), *Humanizing organizational behavior.* Springfield, IL: Charles C. Thomas.

Lawler, E. E. (1992). *The ultimate advantage: Creating the high-involvement organization.* San Francisco: Jossey-Bass.

Lawler, E. E., & Hall, D. T. (1970). Relationship of job characteristics to job involvement, satisfaction, and intrinsic motivation. *Journal of Applied Psychology, 54*(4), 305–312.

Lawler, E. E., & Mohrman, S. A. (1991). High-involvement management. In R. M. Steers & L. W. Porter (Eds.), *Motivation and work behavior* (5th ed., pp. 468–477). New York: McGraw-Hill.

Lawler, E. E., & Suttle, J. L. (1972). A causal correlational test of the need hierarchy concept. *Organizational Behavior & Human Performance, 7*(2), 265–287.

Lawler, E. E., & Suttle, J. L. (1973). Expectancy theory and job behavior. *Organizational Behavior & Human Performance, 9*(3), 482–503.

Lawrence, P. R. and Lorsch, J. W. (1969). *Organization and environment: Managing differentiation and integration.* Homewood, IL: Irwin.

Layard, R. (2005). *Happiness: Lessons from a new science.* London: Penguin Books.

Lazarus, R. S. (1966). *Psychological stress and the coping process.* New York: McGraw-Hill.

Lazarus, R. S. (1984). On the primacy of cognition. *American Psychologist, 39,* 124–129.

Lazarus, R. S. (1991). *Emotion and adaptation.* New York: Oxford University Press.

Lazarus, R. S. (1999). Hope: An emotion and a vital coping resource against despair. *Social Research, 66,* 665–669.

Lazarus, R. S., & Lazarus, B. N. (1994). *Passion and reason: Making sense of our emotions.* New York: Oxford University Press.

Leana, C. R., & Feldman, D. C. (1994). The psychology of job loss. In G. R. Ferris (Ed.), *Research in personnel and human resource management* (Vol. 12, pp. 271–302). Greenwich, CT: JAI Press.

Leana, C. R., Feldman, D. C., & Tan, G. Y. (1998). Predictors of coping behavior after a layoff. *Journal of Organizational Behavior, 19,* 85–97.

Leary, M. R., Kowalski, R. M., Smith, L., & Phillips, S. (2003). Teasing, rejection, and violence: Case studies of the school shootings. *Aggressive Behavior, 29,* 202–214.

LeBlanc, M. M., & Kelloway, E. K. (2002). Predictors and outcomes of workplace violence and aggression. *Journal of Applied Psychology, 87*(3), 444–453.

Leck, J. D. (2005). Violence in the Canadian workplace. *Journal of American Academy of Business, Cambridge, 7*(2), 308–315.

Ledford Jr., G. E., (1999). Comment: Happiness and productivity revisited. *Journal of Organizational Behavior, 20,* 25–30.

Lee, F., & Tiedens, L. Z. (2001). Is it lonely at the top? The independence and interdependence of power holders. In B. M. Staw & R. I. Sutton (Eds.), *Research in organizational behavior* (Vol. 23, pp. 43–91). Amsterdam: Elsevier.

Lee, T. W., Ashford, S. J., Walsh, J. P., & Mowday, R. T. (1992). Commitment propensity, organizational commitment, and voluntary turnover: A longitudinal study of organizational entry processes. *Journal of Management, 18*(1), 15–32.

Lee, T. W., & Mitchell, T. R. (1994). An alternative approach: The unfolding model of voluntary employee turnover. *Academy of Management Review, 19*(1), 51–89.

Lee, T. W., Mitchell, T. R., Sablynski, C. J., Burton, J. P., & Holtom, B. C. (2004). The effects of job embeddedness on organizational citizenship, job performance, volitional absences, and voluntary turnover. *Academy of Management Journal, 47,* 711–722.

Lee, T. W., Mitchell, T. R., Wise, L., & Fireman, S. (1996). An unfolding model of voluntary employee turnover. *Academy of Management Journal, 39*(1), 5–36.

Lee-Chai, A. Y., Chen, S., & Chartrand, T. L. (2001). From Moses to Marcos: Individual differences in the use and abuse of power. In A. Y. Lee-Chai & J. A. Bargh (Eds.), *The use and abuse of power* (pp. 57–74). Philadelphia, PA: Psychology Press.

LePine, J. A., Erez, A., & Johnson, D. E. (2002). The nature and dimensionality of organizational citizenship behavior: A critical review and meta-analysis. *Journal of Applied Psychology, 87*(1), 52–65.

Lepper, M. R., & Greene, D. (Eds.). (1978). *The hidden costs of reward*. Hillsdale, NJ: Lawrence Erlbaum Associates, Inc.

Lepper, M. R., Henderlong, J., & Gingras, I. (1999). Understanding the effects of extrinsic rewards on intrinsic motivation – Uses and abuses of meta-analysis: Comment on Deci, Koestner, and Ryan (1999). *Psychological Bulletin, 125*(6), 669–676.

Leung, K. (2001). Different carrots for different rabbits: Effects of individualism–collectivism and power distance on work motivation. In M. Erez, U. Kleinbeck, & H. Thierry (Eds.), *Work motivation in the context of a globalizing economy* (pp. 329–340). Mahwah, NJ: Lawrence Erlbaum Associates, Inc.

Leung, K., Tong, K.-K., & Ho, S. S.-Y. (2004). Effects of interactional justice on egocentric bias in resource allocation decisions. *Journal of Applied Psychology, 89*(3), 405–415.

Leventhal, G. S. (1976). Fairness in social relationships. In J. W. Thibaut, J. T. Spence, & R. C. Carson (Eds.), *Contemporary topics in social psychology* (pp. 211–239). Morristown, NJ: General Learning Press.

Leventhal, G. S. (1980). What should be done with equity theory? In K. J. Gergen, M. S. Greenberg, & R. H. Willis (Eds.), *Social exchange: Advances in theory and research* (pp. 27–55). New York: Plenum Press.

Leventhal, G. S., & Scherer, K. (1987). The relationship of emotion to cognition: A functional approach to a semantic controversy. *Cognition and Emotion, 1*(1), 3–27.

Leventhal, H., & Tomarken, A. J. (1986). Emotion: Today's problems. *Annual Review of Psychology, 37*, 565–610.

Levin, I., & Stokes, J. P. (1989). Dispositional approach to job satisfaction: Role of negative affectivity. *Journal of Applied Psychology, 74*(5), 752–758.

Levine, F. M. (Ed.). (1975). *Theoretical readings in motivation*. Chicago, IL: Rand McNally.

Levine, J. M., Resnick, L. B., & Higgins, E. T. (1993). Social foundations of cognition. *Annual Review of Psychology, 44*(1), 585–612.

Levy, L. H. (1970). *Conceptions of personality*. New York: Random House.

Lewin, K. (1938). The conceptual representation and the measurement of psychological forces. *Contributions to Psychological and Theory, 1*(4).

Lewin, K. (1945). The Research Center for Group Dynamics at Massachusetts Institute of Technology. *Sociometry, 8*, 126–135.

Lewis, C. S. (1960). *The four loves*. New York: Harcourt Brace Jovanovich.

Lewis, H. B. (1992). *Shame: The exposed self*. New York: Free Press.

Liden, R. C., Wayne, S. J., & Sparrowe, R. T. (2000). An examination of the mediating role of psychological empowerment on the relations between the job, interpersonal relationships, and work outcomes. *Journal of Applied Psychology, 85*(3), 407–416.

Lieberman, S. (1956). The effects of changes in roles on the attitudes of role occupants. *Human Relations, 9*, 385–402.

Liker, J. K., & Morgan, J. M. (2006). The Toyota way in services: The case of lean product development. *Academy of Management Perspectives, 20*(2), 5–19.

Likert, R. (1961). *New patterns of management*. New York: McGraw-Hill.

Likert, R. (1967). *The human organization: Its management and value*. New York: McGraw-Hill.

Lind, E. A., Kray, L., & Thompson, L. (1998). The social construction of injustice: Fairness judgments in response to own and others' unfair treatment by authorities. *Organizational Behavior and Human Decision Processes, 75*, 1–22

Lind, E. A., & Tyler, T. R. (1988). *The social psychological of procedural justice*. New York: Plenum Press.

Lind, E. A., & Van den Bos, K. (2002). When fairness works: Toward a general theory of uncertainty management. In B. M. Staw & R. M. Kramer (Eds.), *Research in organizational behavior* (Vol. 24, pp. 181–224). Oxford: JAI Press.

Lindell, M. K., & Brandt, C. J. (2000). Climate quality and climate consensus as mediators of the relationship between organizational antecedents and outcomes. *Journal of Applied Psychology, 85*(3), 331–348.

Lindsey, B. (2007). *The age of abundance: How prosperity transformed America's politics and culture*. New York: HarperCollins.

Lindsley, D. H., Brass, D. J., & Thomas, J. B. (1995). Efficacy-performing spirals: A multilevel perspective. *Academy of Management Review, 20*(3), 645–678.

Litwin, G. H., & Stringer, M. (1968). *Motivation and organizational climate*. Boston, MA: Harvard Business School Press.

Lobel, S. A., Quinn, R. E., St. Clair, L., & Warfield, A. (1994). Love without sex: The impact of psychological intimacy between men and women at work. *Organizational Dynamics, 23*(1), 4–16.

Locke, E. A. (1965). Interaction of ability and motivation in performance. *Perceptual and Motor Skills, 21*, 719–725.

Locke, E. A. (1968). Toward a theory of task motivation and incentives. *Organizational Behavior & Human Performance, 3*(2), 157–189.

Locke, E. A. (1969). What is job satisfaction? *Organizational Behavior & Human Performance, 4*(4), 309–336.

Locke, E. A. (1975). Personnel attitudes and motivation. *Annual Review of Psychology, 26*, 457–480.

Locke, E. A. (1976). The nature and causes of job satisfaction. In M. D. Dunnette (Ed.), *Handbook of industrial and organizational psychology* (pp. 1297–1350). Chicago, IL: Rand McNally.

Locke, E. A. (1977). The myths of behavior mod in organizations. *Academy of Management Review, 2*(4), 543–553.

Locke, E. A. (1978). The ubiquity of the technique of goal setting in theories of and approaches to employee motivation. *Academy of Management Review, 3*(3), 594–601.

Locke, E. A. (1979). Myths in "The myths of the myths about behavior mod in organizations". *Academy of Management Review, 4*(1), 131–136.

Locke, E. A. (1991). Goal theory vs. control theory: Contrasting approaches to understanding work motivation. *Motivation and Emotion, 15*, 9–28.

Locke, E. A. (1997). The motivation to work: What we know. In M. L. Maehr & P. R. Pintrich (Eds.), *Advances in motivation and achievement* (Vol. 10, pp. 375–412). Greenwich, CT: JAI Press.

Locke, E. A., Alavi, M., & Wagner, J. (1997). Participation in decision-making: An information exchange perspective. In G. Ferris (Ed.), *Research in personnel and human resources management* (Vol. 15, pp. 293–331). Greenwich, CT: JAI Press.

Locke, E. A., Cartledge, N., & Knerr, C. S. (1970). Studies of the relationship between satisfaction, goal-setting, and performance. *Organizational Behavior & Human Performance, 5*(2), 135–158.

Locke, E. A., & Latham, G. P. (1990a). *A theory of goal setting and task performance.* Englewood Cliffs, NJ: Prentice-Hall.

Locke, E. A., & Latham, G. P. (1990b). Work motivation and satisfaction: Light at the end of the tunnel. *Psychological Science, 1*(4), 240–246.

Locke, E. A., & Latham, G. P. (2002). Building a practically useful theory of goal setting and task motivation. *American Psychologist, 57*(9), 705–717.

Locke, E. A., & Latham, G. P. (2004). What should we do about motivation theory? Six recommendations for the twenty-first century. *Academy of Management Review, 29*(3), 388–403.

Locke, E. A., McClear, K., & Knight, D. (1996). Self esteem and work. In C. L. Cooper & I. T. Robertson (Eds.), *International review of organizational psychology* (Vol. 11, pp. 1–32). New York: John Wiley & Sons.

Locke, E. A., Motowidlo, S. J., & Bobko, P. (1986). Using self-efficacy theory to resolve the conflict between goal setting theory and expectancy theory in organizational behavioral and industrial/organizational psychology. *Journal of Social and Clinical Psychology, 4*, 328–338.

Locke, E. A., Shaw, K. N., Saari, L. M., & Latham, G. P. (1981). Goal setting and task performance: 1969–1980. *Psychological Bulletin, 90*, 125–152.

Locke, E. A., Smith, K. G., Erez, M., Chah, D.-O., & Schaffer, A. (1994). The effects of intra-individual goal conflict on performance. *Journal of Management, 20*(1), 67–91.

Locke, K. D. (2003). Status and solidarity in social comparison: Agentic and communal values and vertical and horizontal directions. *Journal of Personality and Social Psychology, 84*(3), 619–631.

Lodahl, T. M., & Kejner, M. (1965). The definition and measurement of job involvement. *Journal of Applied Psychology, 49*(1), 24–33.

Lofquist, L. H., & Dawis, R. V. (1969). *Adjustment to work.* New York: Appleton-Century-Crofts.

Lord, R. G., & Hanges, P. J. (1987). A control system model of organizational motivation: Theoretical development and applied implications. *Behavioral Science, 32*, 161–178.

Lord, R. G., & Kernan, M. C. (1987). Scripts as determinants of purposeful behavior in organizations. *Academy of Management Review, 12*(2), 265–277.

Lord, R. G., Klimoski, R., & Kanfer, R. (Eds.). (2002). *Frontiers of industrial and organizational psychology: Emotions at work.* San Francisco: Jossey-Bass.

Loughlin, C., & Barling, J. (2001). Young workers' work values, attitudes, and behaviors. *Journal of Occupational and Organizational Psychology, 74*, 543–558.

Louis, M. R. (1980a). Surprise and sense making: What newcomers experience in entering unfamiliar organizational settings. *Administrative Science Quarterly, 25*, 226–251.

Louis, M. R. (1980b). Career transitions: Varieties and commonalities. *Academy of Management Review*, 5(3), 329–340.

Lounsbury, J. W., Gibson, L. W., & Hamrick, F. L. (2004). The development and validation of a personological measure of work drive. *Journal of Business and Psychology*, 18(4), 427.

Luthans, F. (2003). Positive organizational behavior (POB): Implications for leadership and HR development and motivation. In L. W. Porter, G. A. Bigley, & R. M. Steers (Eds.), *Motivation and work behavior* (7th ed., pp. 178–195). New York: McGraw-Hill Irwin.

Luthans, F., & Kreitner, R. (1974). The management of behavioral contingencies. *Personnel*, 51, 7–16.

Luthans, F., & Kreitner, R. (1975). *Organizational behavior modification*. Glenview, IL: Scott, Foresman.

Luthans, F., & Ottemann, R. (1977). Motivation vs. learning approaches to organizational behavior. In F. Luthans (Ed.), *Contemporary readings in organizational behavior* (2nd ed., pp. 206–274). New York: McGraw-Hill.

Luthans, F., & Reif, W. E. (1974). Job enrichment: Long on theory, short on practice. *Organizational Dynamics*, 2(3), 30–38.

Lyubomirsky, S. (2001). Why are some people happier than others? *American Psychologist*, 56(3), 239–249.

MacCorquodale, K., & Meehl, P. E. (1948). On a distinction between hypothetical constructs and intervening variables. *Psychological Review*, 55, 95–107.

Mace, C. A. (1935). *Incentives: Some experimental studies* (No. 72): Report 72. Industrial Health Research Board (Great Britain).

MacEvoy, G. M., & Cascio, W. F. (1987). Do good and poor performers leave? A meta-analysis of the relationship between performance and turnover. *Academy of Management Journal*, 30, 744–762.

Machlowitz, M. (1980). *Workaholics: Living with them, working with them*. Reading, MA: Addison-Wesley.

Maclean's. (2006, May 22). A smashing way to feel better. *Maclean's, 119*, 41.

Maddi, S. R. (1976). *Personality theories: A comparative analysis* (3rd ed.). Homewood, IL: Dorsey.

Maddi, S. R. (1980). *Personality theories: A comparative analysis* (4th ed.). Homewood, IL: Dorsey.

Maehr, M. L. (1987). Managing organizational culture to enhance motivation. In M. L. Maehr & D. A. Kleiber (Eds.), *Advances in motivation and achievement: Vol.5, Enhancing motivation* (pp. 287–320). Greenwich, CT: JAI Press.

Maehr, M. L., & Braskamp, L. (1986). *The motivation factor: A theory of personal investment*. Lexington, MA: Lexington Books.

Maertz, C. P., & Campion, M. A. (2004). Profiles in quitting: Integrating process and content theories in turnover theory. *Academy of Management Journal*, 47, 566–582.

Mahoney, M. J. (1974). *Cognition and behavior modification*. Cambridge, MA: Ballinger.

Mahoney, T. A. (1979). Another look at job satisfaction and performance. In T. A. Mahoney (Ed.), *Compensation and reward perspectives* (pp. 1979). Homewood, IL: Irwin.

Mahoney, T. A. (1987). Understanding comparable worth: A societal and political perspective. In L. L. Cummings & B. M. Staw (Eds.), *Research in organizational behavior* (Vol. 9, pp. 209–246). Greenwich, CT: JAI Press.

Mahoney, T. A. (1988). Productivity defined: The relativity of efficiency, effectiveness, and change. In J. P. Campbell, R. J. Campbell, & Associates (Eds.), *Productivity in organizations: New perspectives from industrial and organizational psychology* (pp. 13–39). San Francisco: Jossey-Bass.

Maich, S. (2005). The workers' paradise: Why is organized labour in so much trouble? Everybody's too happy. *Maclean's*, September 19, 38.

Maier, N. R. F. (1946). *Psychology in industry: A psychological approach to industrial problems* (2nd ed.). Boston, MA: Houghton-Mifflin.

Maier, N. R. F. (1961). *Frustration: The study of behavior without a goal*. Ann Arbor, MI: University of Michigan Press.

Maier, N. R. F. (1973). *Psychology in industrial organizations* (4th ed.). Boston, MA: Houghton-Mifflin.

Mainiero, L. A. (1986). A review and analysis of power dynamics in organizational romances. *Academy of Management Review*, 11(4), 750–762.

Mainiero, L. A. (1989). *Office romance: Love, power and sex in the workplace*. New York: Rawson Associates.

Mainiero, L. A. (2003). *On the ethics of office romance: Developing a moral compass for the workplace*. Unpublished manuscript.

Malkiel, B. G. (1979). Productivity: The problem behind the headlines. *Harvard Business Review*, 57(3), 81–90.

Man, D. C., & Lam, S. S. K. (2003). The effects of job complexity and autonomy on cohesiveness in collectivistic and individualistic work groups: a cross-cultural analysis. *Journal of Organizational Behavior*, *24*(8), 979–1001.

Mandel, M., Hamm, S., Matlack,C., Farrell, C., & Therese Palmer A. (2005). The real reasons you're working so hard . . . and what you can do about it. *Business Week*, 3 October, Cover story.

Mann, F. C., & Williams, L. K. (1972). Organizational impact of white-collar automation. In L. E. Davis & J. C. Taylor (Eds.), *Design of jobs* (pp. 83–90). Harmondsworth: Penguin Books.

Manz, C. C. (1986). Self-leadership: Toward an expanded theory of self-influence processes in organizations. *Academy of Management Review*, *11*(3), 585–600.

March, J. G., & Simon, H. A. (1958). *Organizations*. New York: John Wiley & Sons.

Marini, M. M. (1989). Sex differences in earnings in the United States. *Annual Review of Sociology*, *15*, 343–380.

Markus, H., & Kitayama, M. K. (1991). Culture and the self: Implications for cognition, motivation and emotion. *Psychological Review*, *98*, 224–253.

Maroda, K. J. (2004). A relational perspective on women and power. *Psychoanalytic Psychology*, *21*(3), 428–435.

Martens, M. (1995). *Locating the measurement of emotion*. Unpublished manuscript, Faculty of Commerce and Business Administration, University of British Columbia, Vancouver, British Columbia, Canada.

Martin, L. L., Tesser, A., & McIntosh, J. (1993). Wanting but not having: The effects of unattained goals on thoughts and feelings. In D. M. Wegner & J. W. Pennebaker (Eds.), *Handbook of mental control* (pp. 552–572). Englewood Cliffs, NJ: Prentice-Hall.

Martocchio, J. J., & Judge, T. A. (1994). A policy-capturing approach to individuals' decisions to be absent. *Organizational Behavior & Human Decision Processes*, *57*(3), 358–386.

Maslow, A. H. (1943). A theory of human motivation. *Psychological Review*, *50*, 370–396.

Maslow, A. H. (1954). *Motivation and personality*. New York: Harper & Row.

Maslow, A. H. (1955). Deficiency motivation and growth motivation. In M. R. Jones (Ed.), *Nebraska Symposium on Motivation*. Lincoln, NE: University of Nebraska Press.

Maslow, A. H. (1962). *Toward a psychology of being*. New York: Van Nostrand Reinhold.

Maslow, A. H. (1968). *Toward a psychology of being* (2nd ed.). New York: Van Nostrand Reinhold.

Massie, J. L. (1965). Management theory. In J. G. March (Ed.), *Handbook of organizations* (pp. 387–422). Chicago, IL: Rand McNally.

Mathieu, J. E., & Farr, J. L. (1991). Further evidence for the discriminant validity of measures of organizational commitment, job involvement, and job satisfaction. *Journal of Applied Psychology*, *76*(1), 127–133.

Mathieu, J. E., Hofmann, D. A., & Farr, J. L. (1993). Job perception–job satisfaction relations: An empirical comparison of three competing theories. *Organizational Behavior & Human Decision Processes*, *56*(3), 370–387.

Mathieu, J. E., & Zajac, D. M. (1990). A review and meta-analysis of the antecedents, correlates, and consequences of organizational commitment. *Psychological Bulletin*, *108*(2), 171–194.

Matsui, T., Kagawa, M., Nagamatsu, J., & Ohtsuka, Y. (1977). Validity of expectancy theory as a within-person behavioral choice model for sales activities. *Journal of Applied Psychology*, *62*(6), 764–767.

Matsui, T., & Ohtsuka, Y. (1978). Within-person expectancy theory predictions of supervisory consideration and structure behavior. *Journal of Applied Psychology*, *63*(1), 128–131.

Matthews, G., Zeidner, M., & Roberts, R. D. (2002). *Emotional intelligence: Science and myth*. Cambridge, MA: MIT Press.

Mawhinney, T. C. (1975). Operant terms and concepts in the description of individual work behavior: Some problems of interpretation, application, and evaluation. *Journal of Applied Psychology*, *60*(6), 704–712.

Mawhinney, T. C. (1979). Intrinsic and extrinsic work motivation: Perspectives from behaviorism. *Organizational Behavior & Human Performance*, *24*(3), 411–440.

Mayberry, P. (1985). *Congruencies among organizational components and their relationship to work attitudes*. Unpublished doctoral dissertation, University of Illinois, Urbana.

Mayer, J. D., & Salovey, P. (1997). What is emotional intelligence? In P. Salovey & D. Sluyter (Eds.), *Emotional development and emotional intelligence: Educational implications* (pp. 3–31). New York: Basic Books.

Mayer, J. D., Salovey, P., & Caruso, D. R. (2004). Emotional intelligence: Theory, findings, and implications. *Psychological Inquiry*, *15*(3), 197–215.

Mayes, B. T. (1978a). Incorporating time-lag effects into the expectancy model of motivation: A reformulation of the model. *Academy of Management Review*, *3*(2), 374–379.

Mayes, B. T. (1978b). Some boundary considerations in the application of motivation models. *Academy of Management Review*, *3*(1), 51–58.

Mayhew, G. L. (1979). Approaches to employee management: Policies and preferences. *Journal of Organizational Behavior Management, 2*, 103–111.

Mayhew, L. (1971). *Society: Institutions and activity*. Glenview, IL: Scott, Foresman.

Mayo, E. (1933). *The human problems of an industrialized civilization*. New York: Macmillan.

McAdams, D. P. (1988). Personal needs and personal relationships. In S. Duck (Ed.), *Handbook of personal relationships* (pp. 7–22). Chichester: John Wiley & Sons.

McCall Jr., M. W., Lombardo, M. M., & Morrison, A. M. (1988). *The lessons of experience: How successful executives develop on the job*. Lexington, MA: Lexington Books.

McClelland, D. C. (1961). *The achieving society*. Princeton, NJ: Van Nostrand Reinhold.

McClelland, D. C. (1962). Business drive and national achievement. *Harvard Business Review, 40*(4), 99–112.

McClelland, D. C. (1965). Achievement motivation can be developed. *Harvard Business Review, 43*(6), 6–24, 178.

McClelland, D. C. (1970). The two faces of power. *Journal of International Affairs, 24*, 29–47.

McClelland, D. C. (1975). *Power: The inner experience*. New York: Irvington.

McClelland, D. C. (1985). How motives, skills, and values determine what people do. *American Psychologist, 40*(7), 812–825.

McClelland, D. C., & Boyatzis, R. E. (1982). Leadership motive pattern and long-term success in management. *Journal of Applied Psychology, 67*(6), 737–743.

McClelland, D. C., & Burnham, D. H. (1976). Power is the great motivator. *Harvard Business Review, 54*(2), 100–110.

McClelland, D. C., & Winter, D. G. (1969). *Motivating economic achievement*. New York: Free Press.

McConkie, M. L. (1979). A clarification of the goal setting and appraisal processes in MBO. *Academy of Management Review, 4*(1), 29–40.

McCune, J. T., Beatty, R. W., & Montagno, R. V. (1988). Downsizing: Practices in manufacturing firms. *Human Resource Management, 27*(2), 145–161.

McDonald, L. (1977). Wages of work. In M. Stephenson (Ed.), *Women in Canada* (rev. ed., pp. 181–191). Don Mills, Ontario, Canada: General Publishing.

McDonald, P., & Gandz, J. (1992). Getting value from shared values. *Organizational Dynamics, 20*(3), 64–77.

McDougall, W. (1923). *Outline of psychology*. New York: Scribner.

McElroy, J. C., Morrow, P. C., & Rude, S. N. (2001). Turnover and organizational performance: A comparative analysis of the effects of voluntary, involuntary, and reduction-in-force turnover. *Journal of Applied Psychology, 86*(6), 1294–1299.

McFarlin, D. B., & Rice, R. W. (1991). Determinants of satisfaction with specific job facets: A test of Locke's model. *Journal of Business and Psychology, 6*(1), 25–38.

McFarlin, D. B., & Rice, R. W. (1992). The role of facet importance as a moderator in job satisfaction processes. *Journal of Organizational Behavior, 13*(1), 41–54.

McFarlin, D. B., & Sweeney, P. D. (1992). Distributive and procedural justice as predictors of satisfaction with personal and organizational outcomes. *Academy of Management Journal, 35*, 626–637.

McGillicuddy-DeLisi, A. V., Watkins, C., & Vinchur, A. J. (1994). The effect of relationship on children's distributive justice reasoning. *Child Development, 63*, 1694–1700.

McGregor, D. M. (1957a). The human side of enterprise. *Management Review, 46*(11), 22–28, 88–92.

McGregor, D. M. (1957b). An uneasy look at performance appraisal. *Harvard Business Review, 35*(3), 89–94.

McGregor, D. M. (1960). *The human side of enterprise*. New York: McGraw-Hill.

McKelvey, W. W. (1982). *Organizational systematics*. Berkeley, CA: University of California Press.

McNatt, D. B., & Judge, T. A. (2004). Boundary conditions of the Galatea effect: A field experiment and constructive replication. *Academy of Management Journal, 47*(4), 550–565.

Mead, M. (1980). A proposal: We need taboos on sex at work. In D. A. Neugarten & J. M. Shaftitz (Eds.), *Sexuality in organizations: Romantic and coercive behaviors at work*. Oak Park, IL: Moore Publishing.

Meglino, B. M., & Korsgaard, M. A. (2004). Considering rational self-interest as a disposition: Organizational implications of other orientation. *Journal of Applied Psychology, 89*(6), 946–959.

Meglino, B. M., Ravlin, E. C., & Adkins, C. L. (1989). A work values approach to corporate culture: A field test of the value congruence process and its relationship to individual outcomes. *Journal of Applied Psychology, 74*, 424–432.

Meglino, B. M., Ravlin, E. C., & Adkins, C. L. (1991). Value congruence and satisfaction with a leader: An examination of the role of interaction. *Human Relations, 44*, 481–495.

Mehri, D. (2006). The darker side of lean: An insider's perspective on the realities of the Toyota production system. *Academy of Management Perspectives, 20*(2), 21–42.

Meltzer, H., & Nord, W. R. (Eds.). (1981). *Making organizations humane and productive: A handbook for practitioners.* New York: John Wiley & Sons.

Mento, A. J., Cartledge, N. D., & Locke, E. A. (1980). Maryland vs. Michigan vs. Minnesota: Another look at the relationship of expectancy and goal difficulty to task performance. *Organizational Behavior & Human Performance, 25*(3), 419–440.

Merrens, M. H., & Garrett, J. B. (1975). The protestant ethic scale as a predictor of repetitive work performance. *Journal of Applied Psychology, 60*(1), 125–127.

Merton, R. K. (1968). *Social theory and social structure.* New York: Free Press.

Merton, R. K. (1973). *The sociology of science.* Chicago, IL: University of Chicago Press.

Meyer, D. K., & Turner, J. C. (2002). Discovering emotion in classroom motivation research. *Educational Psychologist, 37*(2), 107–114.

Meyer, J. P., & Allen, N. J. (1987). A longitudinal analysis of the early development and consequences of organizational commitment. *Canadian Journal of Behavioral Sciences, 19*, 199–215.

Meyer, J. P., & Allen, N. J. (1988). Links between work experiences and organizational commitment during the first year of employment: A longitudinal analysis. *Journal of Occupational Psychology, 61*(3), 195–209.

Meyer, J. P., & Allen, N. J. (1991). A three-component conceptualization of organizational commitment. *Human Resource Management Review, 1*(1), 61–89.

Meyer, J. P., & Allen, N. J. (1997). *Commitment in the workplace.* Thousand Oaks, CA: Sage.

Meyer, J. P., Becker, T. E., & Van Dick, R. (2006). Social identities and commitments at work: Toward an integrative model. *Journal of Organizational Behavior, 27*, 665–683.

Meyer, J. P., Paunonen, S. V., Gellatly, I. R., Goffin, R. D., & Jackson, D. N. (1989). Organizational commitment and job performance: It's the nature of the commitment that counts. *Journal of Applied Psychology, 74*(1), 152–156.

Meyer, J. P., Stanley, D. J., Herscovitch, L., & Topolnytsky, L. (2002). Affective, continuance, and normative commitment to the organization: A meta-analysis of antecedents, correlates, and consequences. *Journal of Vocational Behavior, 61*(1), 20–52.

Miles, E. W., Hatfield, J. B., & Huseman, R. C. (1994). Equity sensitivity and outcome importance. *Journal of Organizational Behavior, 15*(7), 585–596.

Miles, J. A., & Greenberg, J. (1993). Using punishment threats to attenuate social loafing effects among swimmers. *Organizational Behavior & Human Decision Processes, 56*(2), 246–265.

Milkovich, G. T., & Anderson, P. H. (1972). Management compensation and secrecy policies. *Personnel Psychology, 25*(2), 293–302.

Miller, G. A., Galanter, E., & Pribram, K. H. (1960). *Plans and the structure of behavior.* New York: Henry Holt.

Miller, J. G. (1978). *Living systems.* New York: McGraw-Hill.

Miller, L. E., & Grush, J. E. (1988). Improving predictions in expectancy theory research: Effects of personality, expectancies, and norms. *Academy of Management Journal, 31*(1), 107–122.

Miller, V. D., & Jablin, F. M. (1991). Information seeking during organizational entry: Influences, tactics, and a model of the process. *Academy of Management Review, 16*(1), 92–120.

Mills, P. K. (1983). Self-management: Its control and relationship to other organizational properties. *Academy of Management Review, 8*(3), 445–453.

Miner, J. B. (1984). The validity and usefulness of theories in an emerging organizational science. *Academy of Management Review, 9*(2), 296–306.

Miner, J. B. (2003). The rated importance, scientific validity, and practical usefulness of organizational behavior theories: A quantitative review. *Academy of Management Learning & Education, 2*(3), 250–268.

Miner, M. G. (1974). Pay policies: Secret or open? And why? *Personnel Journal, 53*(2), 110–115.

Miniard, P. W., & Cohen, J. B. (1983). Modeling personal and normative influences on behavior. *Journal of Consumer Research, 10*(2), 169–180.

Minton, J. W., Lewicki, R. J., & Sheppard, B. H. (1994, November). Unjust dismissal in the context of organizational justice. In S. Henry (Ed.), *The annals of the American Academy of Political and Social Science* (Vol. 536, pp. 135–148). Thousand Oaks, CA: Sage.

Mintzberg, H. (1973). *The nature of managerial work.* New York: Harper & Row.

Mirvis, P. H., & Lawler, E. E. (1977). Measuring the financial impact of employee attitudes. *Journal of Applied Psychology*, *62*(1), 1–8.

Mischel, W. (1968). *Personality and assessment*. New York: John Wiley & Sons.

Mishra, A. K., & Spreitzer, G. M. (1998). Explaining how survivors respond to downsizing: The roles of trust, empowerment, justice and work redesign. *Academy of Management Review*, *23*(3), 567–588.

Mitchel, J. O. (1981). The effect of intentions, tenure, personal, and organizational variables on managerial turnover. *Academy of Management Journal*, *24*(4), 742–751.

Mitchell, J. J. (Ed.). (1972). *Human nature: Theories, conjectures, and descriptions*. Metuchen, NJ: Scarecrow Press.

Mitchell, T. R. (1973). Motivation and participation: An integration. *Academy of Management Journal*, *16*(4), 670–679.

Mitchell, T. R. (1974). Expectancy models of satisfaction, occupational preference and effort: A theoretical, methodological and empirical appraisal. *Psychological Bulletin*, *81*, 1053–1077.

Mitchell, T. R., & Biglan, A. (1971). Instrumentality theories: Current uses in psychology. *Psychological Bulletin*, *76*, 432–454.

Mitchell, T. R., Green, S. G., & Wood, R. E. (1981). An attributional model of leadership and the poor performing subordinate: Development and validation. In L. L. Cummings & B. M. Staw (Eds.), *Research in organizational behavior* (Vol. 3, pp. 197–234). Greenwich, CT: JAI Press.

Mitchell, T. R., Holtom, B. C., & Lee, T. W. (2001). How to keep your best employees: Developing an effective retention policy. *Academy of Management Executive*, *15*(4), 96–108.

Mitchell, T. R., Holtom, B. C., Lee, T. W., Sablynski, C. J., & Erez, M. (2001). Why people stay: Using job embeddedness to predict voluntary turnover. *Academy of Management Journal*, *44*, 1102–1121.

Mitchell, T. R., & James, L. H. (1989). Introduction and background. *Academy of Management Review*, *14*(1), 331–332.

Mitchell, T. R., & James, L. R. (2001). Building a better theory: Time and the specification of when things happen. *Academy of Management Review*, *26*, 530–547.

Mitchell, T. R., & Kalb, L. S. (1981). Effects of outcome knowledge and outcome valence on supervisors' evaluations. *Journal of Applied Psychology*, *66*(5), 604–612.

Mitchell, T. R., & Lee, T. W. (2001). The unfolding model of voluntary turnover and job embeddedness: Foundations for a comprehensive theory of attachment. *Research in Organizational Behavior*, *23*, 189–246.

Mitchell, T. R., & O'Reilly, C. A. (1983). Managing poor performance and productivity. In K. Rowland & G. R. Ferris (Eds.), *Research in personnel and human resource management* (Vol. 1, pp. 201–223). Greenwich, CT: JAI Press.

Mitchell, V. F., & Moudgill, P. (1976). Measurement of Maslow's need hierarchy. *Organizational Behavior & Human Performance*, *16*(2), 334–349.

Mitroff, I. I. (1983). *Stakeholders of the organizational mind*. San Francisco: Jossey–Bass.

Mobley, W. H. (1982). *Employee turnover: Causes, consequences and control*. Reading, MA: Addison-Wesley.

Mobley, W. H., & Meglino, B. M. (1977). A behavioral choice model analysis of the budget allocation behavior of academic deans. *Academy of Management Journal*, *20*(4), 564–572.

Moore, M. V., & Abraham, Y. T. (1992). Comparable worth: Is it a moot issue? *Public Personnel Management*, *21*(4), 455–472.

Moore, M. V., & Abraham, Y. T. (1994). Comparable worth: Is it a moot issue? Part II: The legal and juridical posture. *Public Personnel Management*, *23*(2), 263–286.

Morin, W. J., & Yorks, L. (1992). *Dismissal: There is no easy way, but there is a better way*. San Diego, CA: Harcourt Brace Jovanovich.

Morris, D. (1969). *The human zoo*. London: Vintage.

Morris, J. A., & Feldman, D. C. (1996). The dimensions, antecedents, and consequences of emotional labor. *Academy of Management Review*, *21*(3), 986–1010.

Morris, J. H., & Sherman, J. D. (1981). Generalizability of an organizational commitment model. *Academy of Management Journal*, *24*(3), 512–526.

Morrison, E. W. (1993). Newcomer information seeking: Exploring types, modes, sources, and outcomes. *Academy of Management Journal*, *36*(3), 557–589.

Morrison, E. W., & Milliken, F. J. (2000). Organizational silence: A barrier to change and development in a pluralistic world. *Academy of Management Review*, *25*(4), 706–725.

Morrison, E. W., & Robinson, S. (1997). When employees feel betrayed: A model of how psychological contract violation develops. *Academy of Management Review, 22*(1), 226–56.

Morrow, P. C. (1983). Concept redundancy in organizational research: The case of work commitment. *Academy of Management Review, 8*(3), 486–500.

Morrow, P. C. (1993). *The theory and measurement of work commitment.* Greenwich, CT: JAI Press.

Morrow, P. C., McElroy, J. C., Laczniak, K. S., & Fenton, J. B. (1999). Using absenteeism and performance to predict employee turnover: Early detection through company records. *Journal of Vocational Behavior, 55*, 358–374.

Mortimer, T. J., & Lorence, J. (1989). Satisfaction and involvement: Disentangling a deceptively simple relationship. *Social Psychology Quarterly, 52*, 249–266.

Mossholder, K. W., Bennett, N., & Martin, C. L. (1998). A multilevel analysis of procedural justice context. *Journal of Organizational Behavior, 19*, 131–141.

Mount, M. K., & Barrick, M. R. (1995). The big five personality dimensions: Implications for research an practice in human resources management. In G. R. Ferris (Ed.), *Research in personnel and human resources management* (Vol. 13, pp. 153–200). Greenwich, CT: JAI Press.

Mowday, R. T. (1998). Reflections on the study and relevance of organizational commitment. *Human Resource Management Review, 8*(4), 387–401.

Mowday, R. T. (1991). Equity theory predictions of behavior in organizations. In R. M. Steers & L. W. Porter (Eds.), *Motivation and work behavior* (5th ed., pp. 111–130). New York: McGraw-Hill.

Mowday, R. T., Porter, L. W., & Steers, R. M. (1982). *Employee–organization linkages.* New York: Academic Press.

Mowday, R. T., & Sutton, R. I. (1993). Organizational behavior: Linking individuals and groups to organizational contexts. *Annual Review of Psychology, 44*(1), 195–229.

Muchinsky, P. M. (1977). A comparison of within- and across-subject analysis of the expectancy-valence model for predicting effort. *Academy of Management Journal, 20*(1), 154–158.

Muchinsky, P. M. (2000). Emotions in the workplace: The neglect of organizational behavior. *Journal of Organizational Behavior, 21*(7), 801–905.

Muchinsky, P. M., & Monahan, C. J. (1987). What is person–environment congruence? Supplementary versus complementary models of fit. *Journal of Vocational Behavior, 31*, 268–277.

Muczyk, J. P. (1978). A controlled field experiment measuring the impact of MBO on performance data. *Journal of Management Studies, 15*(3), 318–329.

Muraven, M., & Baumeister, R. F. (2000). Self-regulation and depletion of limited resources: Does self-control resemble a muscle? *Psychological Bulletin, 126*(2), 247–259.

Murphy, G. C., & Remnyi, A. G. (1979). Behavioral analysis and organizational reality: The need for a technology of program implementation. *Journal of Organizational Behavior Management, 2*, 121–131.

Murphy, S. A. (2004). *The sounds of silence: Toward a theory of organizational shunning.* Paper presented at the Administrative Sciences Association of Canada (ASAC), Quebec City.

Murray, H. (1938). *Explorations in personality.* New York: Oxford University Press.

Murray, H. A., & Kluckhohn, C. (1953). Outline of a conception of personality. In C. Kluckhohn, H. A. Murray, & D. Schneider (Eds.), *Personality and nature, society and culture* (2nd ed.). New York: Knopf.

Murstein, B. (1988). A taxonomy of love. In R. Sternberg & M. Barnes (Eds.), *The psychology of love* (pp. 13–37). New Haven, CT: Yale University Press.

Namie, G., & Namie, R. (2003). *The bully at work: What you can do to stop the hurt and reclaim your dignity on the job.* Naperville, IL: Sourcebooks, Inc.

Naylor, J. D., Pritchard, R. D., & Ilgen, D. R. (1980). *A theory of behavior in organizations.* New York: Academic Press.

Nealey, S. M. (1963). Pay and benefit preference. *Industrial Relations, 3*, 17–28.

Nebeker, D. M., & Mitchell, T. R. (1974). Leader behavior: An expectancy theory approach. *Organizational Behavior & Human Performance, 11*(3), 355–367.

Nebeker, D. M., & Pon, G. G. (2004). *Self-efficacy and expectancy: Comparing measures and constructs.* Unpublished manuscript, National University, San Diego, California.

Nehbrass, R. G. (1979). Ideology and the decline of management theory. *Academy of Management Review, 4*(3), 427–431.

Neiss, M. B., Sedikides, C., & Stevenson, J. (2002). Self-esteem: A behavioural genetic perspective. *European Journal of Personality, 16*, 351–367.

Neuman, J. H., & Baron, R. A. (1997). Aggression in the workplace. In R. A. Giacalone & J. Greenberg (Eds.), *Antisocial behavior in organizations* (pp. 37–67). Thousand Oaks, CA: Sage.

Newman, L. (1988, February). Good-bye is not enough. *Personnel Administrator, 33*(2), 84–86.

Nicholson, N., Wall, T., & Lischeron, J. (1977). The predictability of absence and propensity to leave from employees' job satisfaction and attitudes toward influence in decision-making. *Human Relations, 30*(6), 499–514.

Nickerson, C. A., & McLelland, G. H. (1989). Across-persons versus within-persons test of expectancy value models: A methodological note. *Journal of Behavioral Decision Making, 2*, 261–270.

Niedenthal, P. M., Setterlund, M. B., & Jones, D. E. (1994). Emotional organization of perceptual memory. In P. M. Niedenthal & S. Kitayama (Eds.), *The heart's eye* (pp. 87–143). San Diego, CA: Academic Press.

Niehoff, B. P., Paul, R. J., & Bunch, J. F. S. (1998). The social effects of punishment events: The influence of violator past performance record and severity of the punishment on observers' justice perceptions and attitudes. *Journal of Organizational Behavior, 19*, 5889–5602.

Noel, T. W., & Latham, G. P. (2006). The importance of learning goals *versus* outcome goals for entrepreneurs. *Entrepreneurship and Innovation, 7*(4), 213–220.

Noon, M., & Blyton, P. (2007). *The realities of work*. Basingstoke: Macmillan Business.

Nord, W. R. (1969). Beyond the teaching machine: The neglected area of operant conditioning in the theory and practice of management. *Organizational Behavior & Human Performance, 4*(4), 375–401.

Nord, W. R. (1974). The failure of current applied behavioral science: A Marxian perspective. *Journal of Applied Psychology, 32*(12), 1026–1035.

Nord, W. R. (1977). Job satisfaction reconsidered. *American Psychologist, 32*, 1026–1035.

Nord, W. R., Brief, A. P., Atieh, J. M., & Doherty, E. M. (1988). Work values and the conduct of organizational behavior. In B. M. Staw & L. L. Cummings (Eds.), *Research in organizational behavior* (Vol. 10, pp. 1–42). Greenwich, CT: JAI Press.

Nord, W. R., & Durand, D. E. (1978). What's wrong with the human resources approach to management. *Organizational Dynamics, 6*(3), 13–25.

Northcraft, G. B., & Ashford, S. J. (1990). The preservation of self in everyday life: The effects of performance expectations and feedback inquiry. *Organizational Behavior & Human Decision Processes, 47*(1), 42–64.

Nunnally, J. C. (1967). *Psychometric theory*. New York: McGraw-Hill.

Nyhus, E. K., & Pons, E. (2005). The effects of personality on earnings. *Journal of Economic Psychology, 26*(3), 363–384.

Oates, W. (1971). *Confessions of a workaholic*. New York: World.

Oatley, K. (1992). *Best laid schemes: The psychology of emotions*. Cambridge: Cambridge University Press.

Oatley, K., & Duncan, E. (1992). Structured diaries for emotions in daily life. In K. T. Strongman (Ed.), *International review of studies on emotion* (Vol. 2). Chichester: John Wiley & Sons.

Oatley, K., & Jenkins, J. M. (1992). Human emotions: Function and dysfunction. *Annual Review of Psychology, 43*(1), 55–85.

Oatley, K., & Johnson-Laird, P. N. (1987). Towards a cognitive theory of emotion. *Cognition and Emotion, 1*(1), 39–50.

Odiorne, G. S. (1979). *MBO II*. Belmont, CA: Fearon-Pitman.

O'Donohue, W. T. (1997). *Sexual harassment: Theory, research, and treatment*. Boston, MA: Allyn & Bacon.

Office of the Inspector General. (1993). *The tailhook report*. New York: St. Martin's Press.

O'Hara, J. (1998a, May 25). Rape in the military. *Maclean's*, 15–21.

O'Hara, J. (1998b, May 25). Breaking ranks. *Maclean's*, 24.

O'Hara, K., Johnson, C. M., & Beehr, T. A. (1985). Organizational behavior management in the private sector: A review of empirical research and recommendations for further investigation. *Academy of Management Review, 10*(4), 848–864.

Oldham, G. R., & Hackman, J. R. (1980). Work design in the organizational context. In B. M. Staw & L. L. Cummings (Eds.), *Research in organizational behavior* (Vol. 2, pp. 247–278). Greenwich, CT: JAI Press.

Oliver, R. L., & Bearden, W. O. (1985). Crossover effects in the theory of reasoned action: A moderating influence attempt. *Journal of Consumer Research, 12*(3), 324–340.

Olson, J. M., & Zanna, M. P. (1993). Attitudes and attitude change. *Annual Review of Psychology, 44*(1), 117–154.

Ondrack, D. A. (1974). Defense mechanisms and the Herzberg theory: An alternate test. *Academy of Management Journal, 17*(1), 79–89.

O'Reilly, C. A. (1991). Organizational behavior: Where we've been, where we're going. *Annual Review of Psychology*, *42*(1), 427–458.

O'Reilly, C. A., & Caldwell, D. F. (1981). The commitment and job tenure of new employees: Some evidence of postdecisional justification. *Administrative Science Quarterly*, *26*(4), 597–616.

O'Reilly, C. A., Caldwell, D. F., & Mirable, R. (1992). A profile-comparison approach to person–job fit: More than a mirage. In J. L. Wall & L. R. Jauch (Eds.), *Academy of Management best paper proceedings* (pp. 237–241). Las Vegas, NV: Briarcliff Manor Academy of Management.

O'Reilly, C. A., & Chatman, J. (1986). Organizational commitment and psychological attachment: The effects of compliance, identification, and internalization on prosocial behavior. *Journal of Applied Psychology*, *71*(3), 492–499.

O'Reilly, C. A., & Chatman, J. A. (1994). Working smarter and harder: A longitudinal study of managerial success. *Administrative Science Quarterly*, *39*(4), 603–627.

O'Reilly, C. A., Chatman, J., & Caldwell, D. F. (1991). People and organizational culture: A profile comparison approach to assessing person–organization fit. *Academy of Management Journal*, *34*, 489–516.

Organ, D. W. (1990). The motivational basis of organizational citizenship behavior. In B. M. Staw & L. L. Cummings (Eds.), *Research in organizational behavior* (Vol. 12, pp. 43–72). Greenwich, CT: JAI Press.

Organ, D. W., & Konovsky, M. (1989). Cognitive versus affective determinants of organizational citizenship behavior. *Journal of Applied Psychology*, *74*(1), 157–164.

Orpen, C. (1979). The effects of job enrichment on employee satisfaction, motivation, involvement, and performance: A field experiment. *Human Relations*, *32*(3), 189–117.

Ostroff, C. (1992). The relationship between satisfaction, attitudes, and performance: An organizational level analysis. *Journal of Applied Psychology*, *77*(6), 963–974.

Ostroff, C. (1993). The effects of climate and personal influences on individual behavior and attitudes in organizations. *Organizational Behavior & Human Decision Processes*, *56*(1), 56–90.

O'Toole, J. (1981). *Making America work*. New York: Continuum.

Oxford English Dictionary. (1961). Oxford: Clarendon Press.

Park, N., & Peterson, C. M. (2003). Virtues and organizations. In K. S. Cameron, J. E. Dutton, & R. E. Quinn (Eds.), *Positive organizational scholarship: Foundations of a new discipline* (pp. 33–47). San Francisco: Berrett-Koehler.

Parker, D. F., & Dyer, L. (1976). Expectancy theory as a within-person behavioral choice model: An empirical test of some conceptual and methodological refinements. *Organizational Behavior & Human Performance*, *17*(1), 97–117.

Parker, S. K. (1998). Enhancing role breadth self-efficacy: The roles of job enrichment and other organizational interventions. *Journal of Applied Psychology*, *83*(6), 835–852.

Parker, S. K. (2003). Longitudinal effects of lead production on employee outcomes and the mediating role of work characteristics. *Journal of Applied Psychology*, *88*(4), 620–634.

Parker, S. K., & Wall, T. D. (1998). *Job and work design: Organizing work to promote well-being and effectiveness*. Thousand Oaks, CA: Sage.

Parker, S. K., & Wall, T. D. (2001). Work design: Learning from the past and mapping a new terrain. In N. Anderson, O. S. Ones, H. K. Sinangil, & C. Viswesvaran (Eds.), *Handbook of industrial work and organizational psychology* (Vol. 1). London: Sage.

Parker, S. K., Wall, T. D., & Cordery, J. L. (2001). Future work design research and practice: Towards an elaborated model of work design. *Journal of Occupational and Organisational Psychology*, *74*, 413–440.

Parker, S. R. (1981). Industry and social stratification. In S. R. Parker, R. K. Brown, J. Child, & M. A. Smith (Eds.), *The sociology of industry* (pp. 56–64). London: George Allen & Unwin.

Parkinson, C. N. (1957). *Parkinson's law and other studies in administration*. Boston, MA: Houghton-Mifflin.

Parrott, W. G. (1994). The head and the heart. In J. A. Russell, J. M. Fernandez-Doles, A. S. R. Manstead, & J. C. Wellenkamp (Eds.), *Everyday conceptions of emotions* (pp. 73–84). Dordrecht, The Netherlands: Kluwer.

Parsons, T., & Shils, E. A. (1951). *Toward a general theory of action*. Cambridge, MA: Harvard University Press.

Patchen, M. (1961). *The choice of wage comparisons*. Englewood Cliffs, NJ: Prentice-Hall.

Paterson, J. M., & Cary, J. (2002). Organizational justice, change anxiety, and acceptance of downsizing: Preliminary tests of an AET-based model. *Motivation and Emotion*, *26*(1), 83–103.

Patterson, D. G., Darley, J. G., & Elliott, R. M. (1936). *Men, women, and jobs*. Minneapolis, MI: University of Minnesota Press.

Patrick, B. C., Skinner, E. A., & Connell, J. P. (1993). What motivates children's behavior and emotion? Joint effects of perceived control and autonomy in the academic domain. *Journal of Personality and Social Psychology, 65*(4), 781–791.

Paul, W. J. J., Robertson, K. B., & Herzberg, F. (1969). Job enrichment pays off. *Harvard Business Review, 47*(2), 61–78.

Paulin, M., Ferguson, R. J., & Bergeron, J. (2006). Service climate and organizational commitment: The importance of customer linkages. *Journal of Business Research, 69*(2006), 906–915.

Pava, M. L., & Primeaux, P. (Eds.). (2004). *Spiritual intelligence at work: Meaning, metaphor, and morals* (Vol. 5). Oxford: Elsevier.

Payne, R. L. (2000). Climate and culture: How close can they get? In N. M. Ashkanasy, C. P. M. Wilderom, & M. F. Peterson, (Eds.). (2000). *Handbook of organizational culture & climate*. Thousand Oaks, CA: Sage.

Peak, H. (1955). Attitude and motivation. In M. R. Jones (Ed.), *Nebraska Symposium on Motivation*. Lincoln, NE: University of Nebraska Press.

Pearce, J. A., & David, F. (1987). Corporate mission statements: The bottom line. *Academy of Management Executive, 1*(2), 109–116.

Pearce, J. L. (2004). What do we know and how do we really know it? *Academy of Management Review, 29*(2), 175–179.

Pearson, C. M., & Porath, C. L. (2005). On the nature, consequences, and remedies of workplace incivility: No time for "nice"? Think again. *Academy of Management Executive, 19*(1), 7–18.

Pelled, L. H., & Xin, K. R. (1999). Down and out: An investigation of the relationship between mood and employee withdrawal behavior. *Journal of Management, 25*(6), 875–895.

Penner, L. A., Dovidio, J. E., Piliavin, J. A., & Schroeder, D. A. (2005). Prosocial behavior: Multilevel perspectives. *Annual Review of Psychology, 56*, 365–392.

Pennings, J. M., Barkema, H., & Douma, S. W. (1994). Organizational learning and diversification. *Academy of Management Journal, 37*(3), 608–640.

People 1st (Company). (2007). Catering for employer needs. *Personnel Today, 1/2/2007*, 19.

Peredo, A. M. (2004). Democracy, poverty and local responses. *Humanity and Society, 28*(3), 322–329.

Peredo, A. M., & Chrisman, J. J. (2006). Toward a theory of community-based enterprise. *Academy of Management Review, 31*(2), 309–328.

Pervin, L. A. (1968). Performance and satisfaction as a function of individual–environment fit. *Psychological Bulletin, 69*, 56–68.

Pervin, L. A. (1991). Self-regulation and the problem of volition. In M. L. Maehr & P. R. Pintrich (Eds.), *Advances in motivation and achievement* (Vol. 7, pp. 1–20). Greenwich, CT: JAI Press.

Peter, L. J., & Hull, R. (1969). *The Peter principle*. New York: Bantam.

Peters, L. H., & O'Connor, E. J. (1980). Situational constraints and work outcomes: The influences of a frequently overlooked construct. *Academy of Management Review, 5*(3), 391–397.

Peters, L. H., O'Connor, E. J., & Eulberg, J. R. (1985). Situational constraints: Sources, consequences, and future considerations. In K. R. Rowland & G. R. Ferris (Eds.), *Research in personnel and human resources management* (Vol. 3, pp. 79–114). Greenwich, CT: JAI Press.

Peters, T. J., & Waterman, R. (1982). *In search of excellence*. New York: Harper & Row.

Petrie, H. L. (1991). *Motivation: Theory, research, and applications*. Belmont, CA: Wadsworth.

Petrock, F. (1978). Analyzing the balance of consequences for performance improvement. *Journal of Organizational Behavior Management, 1*, 196–205.

Petrock, F., & Gamboa, V. (1976). Expectancy theory and operant conditioning: A conceptual comparison. In W. R. Nord (Ed.), *Concepts and controversies in organizational behavior* (2nd ed., pp. 175–187). Pacific Palisades, CA: Goodyear.

Pfautz, H. W. (1953). The current literature on social stratification: Critique and bibliography. *American Journal of Sociology, 58*, 391–418.

Pfeffer, J. (1981a). *Power in organizations*. Marshfield, MA: Pitman.

Pfeffer, J. (1981b). Management as symbolic action: The creation and maintenance of organizational paradigms. In L. L. Cummings & B. M. Staw (Eds.), *Research in organizational behavior* (Vol. 3, pp. 1–52). Greenwich, CT: JAI Press.

Pfeffer, J. (1994). *Competitive advantage through people: Unleashing the power of the work force.* Boston, MA: Harvard Business School Press.

Pfeffer, J. (1998). *The human equation: Building profits by putting people first.* Boston, MA: Harvard Business School Press.

Pfeffer, J., & Salancik, G. R. (1974). Organizational decision making as a political process: The case of a university budget. *Administrative Science Quarterly, 19*(2), 135–151.

Pierce, C. A., Byrne, D., & Aguinis, H. (1996). Attraction in organizations: A model of workplace romance. *Journal of Organizational Behavior, 17,* 5–32.

Pierce, J. L., & Dunham, R. B. (1976). Task design: A literature review. *Academy of Management Review, 1*(4), 83–97.

Pierce, J. L., Gardner, D. G., Cummings, L. L., & Dunham, R. B. (1989). Organization-based self-esteem: Construct definition, measurement, and validation. *Academy of Management Journal, 32*(3), 622–648.

Pieters, R. G. M., & Van Raaij, W. F. (1988). Functions and management of affect: Applications to economic behavior. *Journal of Economic Psychology, 9*(2), 251–282.

Pinder, C. C. (1977). Concerning the application of human motivation theories in organizational settings. *Academy of Management Review, 2*(3), 384–397.

Pinder, C. C. (1978). The marginal utility of the marginal utility criterion: A reply to Bobko. *Academy of Management Review, 3*(4), 910–913.

Pinder, C. C. (1982). Mutualism between management and behavioral science: The case of motivation theory. In J. Kelly & V. V. Baba (Eds.), *The new management scene: Readings on how managers manage* (pp. 133–160). Englewood Cliffs, NJ: Prentice-Hall.

Pinder, C. C. (1983). The role of transfers and mobility experiences in employee motivation and control. In H. Meltzer & W. R. Nord (Eds.), *Making organizations humane and productive: A handbook for practitioners* (pp. 281–294). New York: Wiley Interscience.

Pinder, C. C. (1984). *Work motivation: Theory, issues, and applications.* Glenview, IL: Scott, Foresman.

Pinder, C. C. (1989). The dark side of executive relocation. *Organizational Dynamics, 17*(4), 48–58.

Pinder, C. C. (1998). *Work motivation in organizational behavior.* Upper Saddle River, NJ: Prentice-Hall.

Pinder, C. C., & Harlos, K. P. (2001). Employee silence: Quiescence and acquiescence as responses to perceived injustice. In G. R. Ferris (Ed.), *Research in personnel and human resources management* (Vol. 20, pp. 331–369). Kidlington: Elsevier.

Pinder, C. C., & Moore, L. F. (Eds.). (1980). *Middle range theory and the study of organizations.* Boston, MA: Martinus Nijhoff.

Pinder, C. C., Nord, W. R., & Ramirez, C. (1984). *An experimental test of Deci's cognitive evaluation theory.* Unpublished manuscript, University of British Columbia, Vancouver, British Columbia, Canada.

Pinder, C. C., & Schroeder, K. G. (1987). Time to proficiency following job transfers. *Academy of Management Journal, 30*(2), 336–353.

Pinder, C. C., & Walter, G. A. (1984). Personnel transfer and employee development. In K. M. Rowland & G. R. Ferris (Eds.), *Research in personnel and human resource management* (Vol. 2, pp. 187–218). Greenwich, CT: JAI Press.

Pine, G. J., & Innis, G. (1987). Cultural and individual work values. *Career Development Quarterly, 35,* 279–287.

Pirola-Merlo, A., Hartel, C. E., Mann, L., & Hirst, G. (2002). How leaders influence the impact of affective events on team climate and performance in R&D teams. *The Leadership Quarterly, 13,* 561–581.

Pittman, T. S., & Heller, J. F. (1987). Social motivation. *Annual Review of Psychology, 38,* 461–489.

Pondy, L. R., Frost, P. J., Morgan, G., & Dandridge, T. C. (Eds.). (1983). *Organizational symbolism.* Greenwich, CT: JAI Press.

Popper, K. R. (1968). *The logic of scientific discovery* (2nd ed.). New York: Harper Torchbooks.

Popper, K. R. (1976). *Unended quest.* London: Fontana.

Porath, C. L., & Bateman, T. S. (2006). Self-regulation: From goal orientation to job performance. *Journal of Applied Psychology, 91*(1), 185–192.

Porter, E. H. (1962). The parable of the spindle. *Harvard Business Review, 40*(3), 58–66.

Porter, L. W. (1962). Job attitudes in management: I. Perceived deficiencies in need fulfillment as a function of job level. *Journal of Applied Psychology, 46,* 375–384.

Porter, L. W. (1963). Job attitudes in management: II. Perceived importance of needs as a function of job level. *Journal of Applied Psychology, 47,* 144–148.

Porter, L. W., Bigley, G. A., & Steers, R. M. (2003). *Motivation and work behavior* (7th ed.). New York: McGraw-Hill Irwin.

Porter, L. W., & Lawler, E. E. (1968). *Managerial attitudes and performance*. Homewood, IL: Dorsey.

Porter, L. W., Steers, R. M., Mowday, R. T., & Boulian, P. V. (1974). Organizational commitment, job satisfaction, and turnover among psychiatric technicians. *Journal of Applied Psychology, 59*(5), 603–609.

Posner, B. Z., & Munson, J. M. (1979). The importance of values in understanding organizational behavior. *Human Resource Management, 18*(3), 9–14.

Powell, B., & Jacobs, J. A. (1983). Sex and consensus in occupational prestige ratings. *Sociology and Social Research, 67*, 392–404.

Powell, B., & Jacobs, J. A. (1984). Gender differences in the evaluation of prestige. *Sociological Quarterly, 25*(2), 173–190.

Powers, W. T. (1973). *Behavior: The control of perception*. Chicago, IL: Aldine.

Pratkanis, A. R., & Greenwald, A. G. (1989). A sociocognitive model of attitude structure and function. *Advances in Experimental Social Psychology, 22*, 245–285.

Pratt, M. G. (1998). To be or not to be? Central questions in organizational identification. In D. A. Whetten & P. C. Godfrey (Eds.), *Identity in organizations* (pp. 171–208). Thousand Oaks, CA: Sage.

Premack, D. (1971). Catching up with common sense or two sides of a generalization: Reinforcement and punishment. In R. C. Glaser (Ed.), *The nature of reinforcement* (pp. 121–150). New York: Academic Press.

Pringle, C. D., & Longenecker, J. C. (1982). The ethics of MBO. *Academy of Management Review, 7*(2), 305–312.

Pritchard, M. (1976). On taking emotions seriously. *Journal for the Theory of Social Behavior, 6*(2), 211–232.

Pritchard, R. D. (1969). Equity theory: A review and critique. *Organizational Behavior & Human Performance, 4*(2), 176–211.

Pritchard, R. D., Campbell, K. M., & Campbell, D. J. (1977). Effects of extrinsic financial rewards on intrinsic motivation. *Journal of Applied Psychology, 62*(1), 9–15.

Pritchard, R. D., Paquin, A. R., DeCuir, A. D., McCormick, M. J., & Bly, P. R. (2002). The measurement and improvement of organizational productivity: An overview of ProMes, the productivity measurement and enhancement system. In R. D. Pritchard, H. Holling, F. Lammers, & B. D. Clark (Eds.), *Improving organizational performance with the productivity measurement and enhancement system: An international collaboration* (pp. 3–50). Huntington, NY: Nova Science.

Pritchard, R. D., & Payne, S. C. (2002). Performance management practices and motivation. In D. Holman, T. D. Wall, C. W. Clegg, P. Sparrow, & A. Howard (Eds.), *The new workplace: A guide to the human impact of modern working practices* (pp. 219–244). New York: John Wiley & Sons.

Prue, D. M., & Fairbank, J. A. (1980). Performance feedback in organizational behavior management: A review. *Journal of Organizational Behavior Management, 3*, 1–16.

Prussia, G. E., & Kinicki, A. J. (1996). A motivational investigation of group effectiveness using social-cognitive theory. *Journal of Applied Psychology, 81*(2), 187–198.

Quinn, R. E. (1977). Coping with Cupid: The formation, impact, and management of romantic relationships in organizations. *Administrative Science Quarterly, 22*(1), 30–45.

Rabinowitz, S., & Hall, D. T. (1977). Organizational research on job involvement. *Psychological Bulletin, 22*, 30–45.

Rafaeli, A., & Sutton, R. I. (1987). Expression of emotion as part of the work role. *Academy of Management Review, 12*(1), 23–37.

Rafaeli, A., & Sutton, R. I. (1989). The expression of emotion in organizational life. In L. L. Cummings & B. M. Staw (Eds.), *Research in organizational behavior* (Vol. 11, pp. 1–42). Greenwich, CT: JAI Press.

Rafaeli, A., & Worline, M. (2001). Individual emotion in work organizations. *Social Science Information, 40*(1), 95–123.

Raghunathan, R., & Pham, M. T. (1999). All negative moods are not equal: Motivational influences of anxiety and sadness on decision making. *Organizational Behavior and Human Decision Processes, 79*(1), 56–77.

Ragins, B. R. (2004). Sexual orientation in the workplace: The unique work and career experiences of gay, lesbian and bisexual workers. In J. J. Martocchio (Ed.), *Research in personnel and human resources management* (Vol. 23, pp. 35–120). Amsterdam: Elsevier.

Raia, A. (1974). *Managing by objectives*. Glenview, IL: Scott, Foresman.

Ralston, D. A. (1985). Employee ingratiation: The role of management. *Academy of Management Review, 10*(3), 477–487.

Ramarajan, L., Barsade, S. G., & Burack, O. R. (2006). *What makes the job tough? The influence of organizational respect on burnout in the human services.* Unpublished manuscript.

Randall, D. M. (1987). Commitment and the organization: The organization man revisited. *Academy of Management Review, 12*(3), 460–471.

Randstad. (2004). *Randstad's 2004 employee review.* Atlanta, GA: Randstad.

Rauschenberger, J., Schmitt, N., & Hunter, J. E. (1980), A test of the need hierarchy concept by a Markov model of change in need strength. *Administrative Science Quarterly,* 654–670.

Rawls, J. (1971). *A theory of justice.* Cambridge, MA: Harvard University Press.

Rayner, C., Hoel, H., & Cooper, C. L. (2002). *Workplace bullying: What we know, who is to blame, and what can we do?* London and New York: Taylor & Francis.

Reddin, W. J. (1971). *Effective management by objectives.* New York: McGraw-Hill.

Ree, M. J., Earles, J. A., & Teachout, M. S. (1994). Predicting job performance: Not much more than g. *Journal of Applied Psychology, 79*(4), 518–524.

Rees, A. (1980). On interpreting productivity change. In S. Maital & N. M. Meltz (Eds.), *Lagging productivity growth* (pp. 1–6). Cambridge, MA: Ballinger.

Reichers, A. E. (1985). A review and reconceptualization of organizational commitment. *Academy of Management Review, 10*(3), 465–476.

Reichers, A. E., & Schneider, B. (1990). Climate and culture: An evolution of constructs. In B. Schneider (Ed.), *Organizational climate and culture* (pp. 5–39). San Francisco: Jossey-Bass.

Reif, W. E., & Luthans, F. (1972). Does job enrichment really pay off? *California Management Review, 15*(1), 30–37.

Reinharth, L., & Wahba, M. A. (1976). A test of alternative models of expectancy theory. *Human Relations, 29*(3), 257–272.

Reis, H. T. (1986). Levels of interest in the study of interpersonal justice. In H. W. Bierhoff, R. L. Cohen, & J. Greenberg (Eds.), *Justice in social relations* (pp. 187–209). New York: Plenum Press.

Reis, H. T., Sheldon, K. M., Gable, S. L., Roscoe, J., & Ryan, R. M. (2000). Daily well-being: The role of autonomy, competence, and relatedness. *Personality and Social Psychology Bulletin, 26*(4), 419–435.

Repucci, N. D., & Saunders, J. T. (1974). Social psychology of behavior modification: Problems of implementation in natural settings. *American Psychologist, 29,* 649–660.

Reykowski, J. (1982). Social motivation. *Annual Review of Psychology, 33,* 123–154.

Reynolds, G. S. (1975). *A primer of operant conditioning.* Glenview, IL: Scott, Foresman.

Rhoades, L., & Eisenberger, R. (2002). Perceived organizational support: A review of the literature. *Journal of Applied Psychology, 87*(4), 698–714.

Rhodes, S. R., & Steers, R. M. (1981). Conventional vs. worker-owned organizations. *Human Relations, 34*(12), 1013–1035.

Rice, R. W., Gentile, D. A., & McFarlin, D. R. (1991). Facet importance and job satisfaction. *Journal of Applied Psychology, 76*(1), 31–39.

Rifkin, J. (1995). *The end of work.* New York: Putnam.

Rigby, C. S., Deci, E. L., Patrick, B. C., & Ryan, R. M. (1992). Beyond the intrinsic–extrinsic dichotomy: Self-determination in motivation and learning. *Motivation and Emotion, 16,* 165–185.

Riketta, M., & Van Dick, R. (2005). Foci of attachment in organizations: A meta-analytic comparison of the strength and correlates of workgroup versus organizational identification and commitment. *Journal of Vocational Behavior, 67,* 490–510.

Ringelmann, M. (1913). Researches sur les moteurs animes: Travail de l'homme [Research on animate sources of power: The work of man]. *Annales de l'Institut National Agronomique, XII,* 1–40.

Ritti, R. R. (1994). *The ropes to skip and the ropes to know* (4th ed.). New York: John Wiley & Sons.

Roberts, K. H., & Glick, W. (1981). The job characteristics approach to task design: A critical review. *Journal of Applied Psychology, 66*(2), 193–217.

Roberts, L. M. (2006). Shifting the lens on organizational life: The added value of positive scholarship. *Academy of Management Review, 31*(2), 292–305.

Robinson, S. L., & Bennett, R. J. (1995). A typology of deviant workplace behaviors: A multidimensional scaling study. *Academy of Management Journal, 38,* 555–572.

Robinson, S. L., & Rousseau, D. M. (1994). Violating the psychological contract: Not the exception but the norm. *Journal of Organizational Behavior, 15*(3), 245–259.

Rodgers, R., & Hunter, J. E. (1991). Impact of management by objectives on organizational productivity. *Journal of Applied Psychology*, *76*(2), 322–336.

Rodgers, R., Hunter, J. E., & Rogers, D. L. (1993). Influence of top management commitment on management program success. *Journal of Applied Psychology*, *78*(1), 151–155.

Roe, R. A., Zinovieva, I. L., Diebes, E., & Ten Horn, L. A. (2000). A comparison of work motivation in Bulgaria, Hungary, and the Netherlands: Test of a model. *Applied Psychology: An International Review*, *49*, 658–687.

Roethlisberger, F. J., & Dickson, W. J. (1939). *Management and the worker*. Cambridge, MA: Harvard University Press.

Rofe, Y., & Lewin, I. (1988). Social comparison or utility: An experimental examination. *Social Behavior and Personality*, *16*(1), 5–10.

Rogers, C. R. (1959). A theory of therapy, personality, and interpersonal relationships as developed in the client-centered framework. In S. Koch (Ed.), *Psychology: A study of a science* (Vol. 3, pp. 184–256). New York: McGraw-Hill.

Rogers, C. R., & Skinner, B. F. (1956). Some issues concerning the control of human behavior: A symposium. *Science*, *124*, 1057–1066.

Rokeach, M. (1967). *Value survey*. Palo Alto, CA: Consulting Psychologists Press.

Rokeach, M. (1969). *Beliefs, attitudes and values*. San Francisco: Jossey-Bass.

Rokeach, M. (1973). *The nature of human values*. New York: Free Press.

Rokeach, M. (1979). From individual to institutional values: With special reference to the values of science. In M. Rokeach (Ed.), *Understanding human values*. New York: Free Press.

Rokeach, M., & Ball-Rokeach, S. J. (1989). Stability and change in American value priorities: 1968–1989. *American Psychologist*, *44*, 775–785.

Romzek, B. S. (1989). Personal consequences of employee commitment. *Academy of Management Journal*, *32*(3), 649–661.

Ronen, S. (1994). An underlying structure of motivational need taxonomies: A cross-cultural confirmation. In M. D. Dunnette & L. M. Hough (Eds.), *Handbook of industrial and organizational psychology* (Vol. 4, pp. 241–269). Palo Alto, CA: Consulting Psychologists Press.

Ronen, S. (2001). Self-actualization versus collectualization: Implications for motivation theories. In M. Erez, U. Kleinbeck, & H. Thierry (Eds.), *Work in the context of a globalizing eEconomy* (pp. 341–369). London: Lawrence Erlbaum Associates, Inc.

Rosen, B., & Jerdee, T. H. (1974a). Effects of applicant's sex and difficulty of job on evaluations of candidates for managerial positions. *Journal of Applied Psychology*, *59*(4), 511–512.

Rosen, B., & Jerdee, T. H. (1974b). Influence of sex role stereotypes on personnel decisions. *Journal of Applied Psychology*, *59*(1), 9–14.

Rosen, B., & Jerdee, T. H. (1974c). Factors influencing disciplinary judgements. *Journal of Applied Psychology*, *59*(3), 327–331.

Rosen, B., & Jerdee, T. H. (1976). The influence of age stereotypes on managerial decisions. *Journal of Applied Psychology*, *61*(4), 428–432.

Rosenberg, M., Schooler, C., Schoenbach, C., & Rosenberg, F. (1995). Global self-esteem and specific self-esteem: Different concepts different outcomes. *American Sociological Review*, *60*, 141–156.

Rosener, J. B. (1990). Ways women lead. *Harvard Business Review*, *68*(6), 119–125.

Rosenthal, R. (1976). *Experimenter effects in behavioral research* (2nd ed.). New York: John Wiley & Sons.

Ross, L., & Nisbett, R. E. (1991). *The person and the situation: Perspectives on social psychology*. New York: McGraw-Hill.

Ross, S. L. (1977). The intuitive psychologist and his shortcomings. In L. Berkowitz (Ed.), *Advances in experimental social psychology* (Vol. 10, pp. 174–220). Orlando, FL: Academic Press.

Rotondi, T., Jr. (1975). Organizational identification: Issues and implications. *Organizational Behavior & Human Performance*, *13*(1), 95–109.

Rotter, J. B. (1955). The role of the psychological situation in determining the direction of human behavior. In M. R. Jones (Ed.), *Nebraska Symposium on Motivation*. Lincoln, NE: University of Nebraska Press.

Rousseau, D. M. (1989). Psychological and implied contracts in organizations. *Employee Responsibilities and Rights Journal*, *2*, 121–139.

Rousseau, D. M. (1995). *Psychological contracts in organizations: Understanding written and unwritten agreements*. Thousand Oaks, CA: Sage.

Rousseau, D. M. (2001). The idiosyncratic deal: Flexibility versus fairness? *Organizational Dynamics*, *29*(4), 260–271.

Rousseau, D. M. (2006a). Presidential address: Is there such a thing as "evidence-based management"? *Academy of Management Review*, *31*(2), 256–269.

Rousseau, D. M. (2006b). Keeping an open mind about evidence-based management. *Academy of Management Review*, *31*, 1089–1091.

Rousseau, D. M., & Fried, Y. (2001). Location, location, location: Contextualizing organizational research. *Journal of Organizational Behavior*, *22*, 1–13.

Rousseau, D. M., Ho, V. T., & Greenberg, J. (2006). I-Deals: Idiosyncratic terms in employment relationships. *Academy of Management Review*, *31*(4), 977–994.

Rousseau, D. M., & McCarthy, S. (2007). Educating managers from an evidence-based perspective. *Academy of Management Learning & Education*, *6*(1), 84–101.

Rousseau, D. M., & Parks, J. M. (1993). The contracts of individuals and organizations. In L. L. Cummings & B. M. Staw (Eds.), *Research in organizational behavior* (Vol. 15, pp. 1–44). Greenwich, CT: JAI Press.

Roy, D. (1952). Quota restriction and gold bricking in a machine shop. *American Journal of Sociology*, *57*, 427–442.

Royce, J. R. (1975). Psychology is multi: Methodological, variate, epistemic, work view, paradigmatic, systematic, theoretic, and disciplinary. In H. E. Howe (Ed.), *Nebraska Symposium on Motivation* (Vol. 23). Lincoln, NE: University of Nebraska Press.

Rudman, L. A., Borgida, E., & Robertson, B. A. (1995). Suffering in silence: Procedural justice versus gender socialization issues in university sexual harassment grievance procedures. *Basic and Applied Social Psychology*, *17*(4), 519–541.

Rudman, L. A., & Glick, P. (1999). Feminized management and backlash toward agentic women: The hidden costs to women of a kinder, gentler image of middle managers. *Journal of Personality and Social Psychology*, *77*(5), 1004–1010.

Rudman, L. A., & Kilianski, S. E. (2000). Implicit and explicit attitudes toward female authority. *Personality and Social Psychology Bulletin*, *26*(11), 1315–1328.

Runkel, P., & McGrath, J. (1972). *Research on human behavior: A systematic guide to method*. New York: Holt, Rinehart, & Winston.

Russell, J. A. (1991). In defense of a prototype approach to emotion concepts. *Journal of Personality and Social Psychology*, *60*, 337–347.

Russell, J. A., Fernandez-Doles, J. M., Manstead, A. S. R., & Wellenkamp, J. C. (Eds.). (1994). *Everyday conceptions of emotions*. Dordrecht, The Netherlands: Kluwer.

Ryan, R. M., Connell, J. P., & Deci, E. L. (1985). A motivational analysis of self-determination and self-regulation in education. In C. Ames & R. E. Ames (Eds.), *Research on motivation in education: The classroom milieu* (pp. 13–51). New York: Academic Press.

Ryan, R. M., & Deci, E. L. (2000). Self-determination theory and the facilitation of intrinsic motivation, social development, and well-being. *American Psychologist*, *55*(1), 68–78.

Ryan, T. A. (1970). *Intentional behavior*. New York: Ronald Press.

Ryan, T. A., & Smith, P. C. (1954). *Principles of industrial psychology*. New York: Ronald Press.

Saari, L. M., & Latham, G. P. (1982). Employee reactions to continuous and variable ratio reinforcement schedules involving a monetary incentive. *Journal of Applied Psychology*, *67*(4), 506–508.

Sackman, S. A. (1992). Culture and subcultures: An analysis of organizational knowledge. *Administrative Science Quarterly*, *37*(1), 140–161.

Salancik, G. R. (1977). Commitment and the control of organizational behavior and belief. In B. M. Staw & G. R. Salancik (Eds.), *New directions in organizational behavior* (pp. 1–54). Chicago, IL: St. Clair Press.

Salancik, G. R., & Pfeffer, J. (1974). The bases and use of power in organizational decision making: The case of a university. *Administrative Science Quarterly*, *19*(4), 453–473.

Salancik, G. R., & Pfeffer, J. (1977). An examination of need–satisfaction models of job attitudes. *Administrative Science Quarterly*, *22*(3), 427–456.

Salancik, G. R., & Pfeffer, J. (1978). A social information processing approach to job attitudes and task design. *Administrative Science Quarterly*, *23*(2), 224–253.

Saleh, S. D., & Hosek, J. (1976). Job involvement: Concepts and measurements. *Academy of Management Journal*, *19*(2), 213–224.

Salovey, P. (Ed.). (1991). *The psychology of jealousy and envy*. New York: Guilford Press.

Salovey, P., Brackett, M. A., & Mayer, J. D. (Eds.). (2004). *Emotional intelligence: Key readings on the Mayer and Salovey model*. Port Chester, NY: Dude Publishing.

Salovey, P., Hsee, C. K., & Mayer, J. D. (1993). Emotional intelligence and the self-regulation of affect. In D. M. Wegner & J. W. Pennebaker (Eds.), *Handbook of mental control* (pp. 258–277). Englewood Cliffs, NJ: Prentice-Hall.

Salovey, P., & Mayer, J. D. (1990). Emotional intelligence. *Imagination, Cognition, and Personality, 9*(3), 185–211.

Sandelands, L. E., & Boudens, C. J. (2000). Feeling at work. In S. Fineman (Ed.), *Emotion in organizations* (2nd ed., pp. 46–63). London/Thousand Oaks, CA/New Delhi: Sage.

Sandelands, L. E., & Buckner, G. C. (1989). Of art and work: Aesthetic experience and the psychology of work feelings. In L. L. Cummings & B. M. Staw (Eds.), *Research in organizational behavior* (Vol. 11, pp. 105–132). Greenwich, CT: JAI Press.

Sandler, B. E. (1974). Eclecticism at work: Approaches to job design. *American Psychologist, 29*, 767–773.

Sanna, L. J. (1992). Self-efficacy theory: Implications for social facilitation and social loafing. *Journal of Personality and Social Psychology, 62*, 744–786.

Sarbin, T. R. (1986). Emotion and act: Roles and rhetoric. In R. Harré (Ed.), *The social construction of emotions* (pp. 83–97). New York: Blackwell.

Sashkin, M., & Williams, R. L. (1990). Does fairness make a difference? *Organizational Dynamics, 19*(2), 56–71.

Sayles, L., & Strauss, G. (1977). *Managing human resources*. Englewood Cliffs, NJ: Prentice-Hall.

Schacter, H., & Singer, J. (1962). Cognitive, social, and physiological determinants of emotional states. *Psychological Review, 69*, 397–399.

Schaef, A. W., & Fassel, D. (1988). *The addictive organization*. San Francisco: Harper & Row.

Schaffer, R. H. (1953). Job satisfaction as related to need satisfaction at work. *Pyschological Monographs, 364*.

Schein, E. H. (1985). *Organizational culture and leadership*. San Francisco: Jossey-Bass Publishers.

Schein, V. E. (1973). The relationship between sex role stereotypes and requisite management characteristics. *Journal of Applied Psychology, 57*(2), 95–100.

Schein, V. E. (1975). Relationships between sex role stereotypes and requisite management characteristics among female managers. *Journal of Applied Psychology, 60*(3), 340–344.

Schlenker, B. R., & Leary, M. R. (1982). Social anxiety and self-presentations: A conceptualization and model. *Psychological Bulletin, 92*, 641–669.

Schlesinger, L. A., & Walton, R. E. (1976). Work restructuring in unionized organizations: Risks, opportunities, and impact on collective bargaining. In J. L. Stern & B. D. Dennis (Eds.), *Proceedings of the 29th annual winter meeting*. Madison, WI: Industrial Relations Research Association.

Schmidt, F. L. (1973). Implications of a measurement problem for expectancy theory research. *Organizational Behavior & Human Performance, 10*(2), 243–251.

Schmidt, F. L., & Hunter, J. E. (1977). Development of a general solution to the problem of validity generalization. *Journal of Applied Psychology, 62*(5), 529–540.

Schmidt, F. L., & Hunter, J. E. (1984). A within-setting empirical test of the situational specificity hypothesis in personnel selection. *Personnel Psychology, 37*(2), 317–326.

Schmidt, L. D., & Frieze, L. H. (1997). A mediational model of power, affiliation and achievement motives and product involvement. *Journal of Business and Psychology, 4*, 425–446.

Schmitt, N., & Bedeian, A. G. (1982). A comparison of LISREL and two-stage least squares analysis of a hypothesized life–job satisfaction reciprocal relationship. *Journal of Applied Psychology, 67*(6), 806–817.

Schmitt, N., & McCune, J. T. (1981). The relationship between job attitude and the decision to retire. *Academy of Management Journal, 24*(4), 795–802.

Schmitt, N., & Pulakos, E. D. (1985). Predicting job satisfaction from life satisfaction: Is there a general satisfaction factor? *International Journal of Psychology, 20*(2), 155–167.

Schneider, B. (1983). Interactional psychology and organizational behavior. In L. L. Cummings & B. M. Staw (Eds.), *Research in organizational behavior* (Vol. 5, pp. 1–32). Greenwich, CT: JAI Press.

Schneider, B. (Ed.). (1990). *Organizational climate and culture*. San Francisco: Jossey-Bass.

Schneider, B., & Bowen, D. E. (1995). *Winning the service game*. Boston, MA: Harvard Business School Press.

Schneider, B., Bowen, D., Ehrhart, M., & Holcombe, K. (2000). The climate for service. In N. Ashkanasy, C. Wilderom, & M. Peterson (Eds.), *Handbook of organizational culture and climate* (pp. 21–36). Thousand Oaks, CA: Sage.

Schneider, B., Ehrhart, M. G., Mayer, D. M., Saltz, J. L., & Niles-Jolly, K. (2005). Understanding organization–customer links in service settings. *Academy of Management Journal, 48*(6), 1017–1032.

Schneider, B., Salvaggio, A. N., & Subirats, M. (2002). Climate strength: A new direction for climate research. *Journal of Applied Psychology, 87*(2), 220–229.

Schneider, B., Smith, D. B., & Paul, M. C. (2001). P-E fit and the attraction–selection–attrition model of organizational functioning: Introduction and overview. In M. Erez & U. Kleinbeck (Eds.), *Work motivation in the context of a globalizing economy* (pp. 231–246). Mahwah, NJ: Lawrence Erlbaum Associates, Inc.

Schneider, B., Smith, D. B., Taylor, S., & Fleenor, J. (1998). Personality and organization: A test of the homogeneity of personality hypothesis. *Journal of Applied Psychology, 83*, 462–470.

Schneider, B., White, S. S., & Paul, M. C. (1998). Linking service climate and customer perceptions of service quality: Test of a causal model. *Journal of Applied Psychology, 83*(2), 150–163.

Scholz, U., Dona, B., Sud, S., & Schwarzer, R. (2002). Is general self-efficacy a universal construct? Psychometric findings from 25 countries. *European Journal of Psychological Assessment, 18*, 242–251.

Schor, J. B. (1991). *The overworked American*. New York: Basic Books.

Schroeder, K. G. (1988). *Mentoring as work-related support: Relationship with employee outcomes*. Unpublished manuscript, Vancouver, British Columbia, Canada.

Schuster, F. E., & Kindall, A. F. (1974). Management by objectives: Where we stand – A survery of the Fortune 500. *Human Resource Management, 13*(1), 8–11.

Schuster, J. R. (1969). Another look at compensation preferences. *Industrial Management Review, 10*(3), 1–18.

Schutte, N. S., Malouff, J. M., Hall, L. E., Haggerty, D. J., Cooper, J. T., Golden, C. J., et al. (1998). Development and validation of a measure of emotional intelligence. *Personality and Individual Differences, 25*, 167–177.

Schutz, A. (2001). Self-esteem and interpersonal strategies. In J. P. Forgas, K. D. Williams, & L. Wheeler (Eds.), *The social mind: Cognitive and motivational aspects of interpersonal behavior* (pp. 157–176). Cambridge: Cambridge University Press.

Schwab, D. P. (1980). Construct validity in organizational behavior. In B. M. Staw & L. L. Cummings (Eds.), *Research in organizational behavior* (Vol. 2, pp. 3–44). Greenwich, CT: JAI Press.

Schwab, D. P., & Cummings, L. L. (1976). A theoretical analysis of the impact of task scope on employee performance. *Academy of Management Review, 1*(2), 23–35.

Schwab, D. P., Olian-Gottlieb, J. D., & Heneman, H. G. (1979). Between-subjects expectancy theory research: A statistical review of studies predicting effort and performance. *Psychological Bulletin, 86*(1), 139–147.

Schwartz, H. S. (1982). Job involvement as obsession–compulsion. *Academy of Management Review, 7*(3), 429–432.

Schwartz, S. H. (1992). Universals in the content and structure of values: Theoretical advances and empirical tests in 20 countries. In M. P. Zanna (Ed.), *Advances in experimental social psychology* (Vol. 25, pp. 1–65). New York: Academic Press.

Schwartz, S. H., & Bilsky, W. (1987). Toward a universal psychological structure of human values. *Journal of Personality and Social Psychology, 53*, 550–562.

Schwartz, S. H., & Tessler, R. C. (1972). A test of a model for reducing measured attitude–behavior discrepancies. *Journal of Personality and Social Psychology, 24*, 225–236.

Schwartzer, R. (Ed.). (1992). *Self-efficacy: Thought control of action*. Bristol, PA: Hemisphere.

Schweitzer, M. E., Ordonez, L., & Douma, B. (2004). Goal setting as a motivator of unethical behavior. *Academy of Management Journal, 47*(3), 422–432.

Schwyhart, W. R., & Smith, P. C. (1972). Factors in the job involvement of middle managers. *Journal of Applied Psychology, 56*, 227–233.

Scott, M. B., & Lyman, S. M. (1968). Accounts. *American Sociological Review, 33*, 46–62.

Scott, S. (2007, September 3). Bullying bosses beware: Threaten or even intimidate employees and your company could face $1-million payouts. *Maclean's*, 40–43.

Scott Jr., W. E. (1966). Activation theory and task design. *Organizational Behavior & Human Performance, 1*(1), 3–30.

Seijts, G. H., & Latham, G. P. (2005). Learning versus performance goals: When should each be used? *Academy of Management Executive, 19*(1), 124–131.

Seijts, G. H., Latham, G. P., Tasa, K., & Latham, B. W. (2004). Goal setting and goal orientation: An integration of two different yet related literatures. *Academy of Management Journal, 47*(2), 227–239.

Seijts, G. H., Latham, G. P., & Whyte, G. (2000). Effect of self-and group efficacy on group performance in a mixed-motive situation. *Human Performance, 13*(3), 279–298.

Seligman, M. E. P., & Csikszentmihalyi, M. (2000). Positive psychology. *American Psychologist, 55,* 5.

Senge, P. M. (1990). *The fifth discipline: The art and practice of the learning organization.* New York: Currency Doubleday.

Senger, J. (1971). Managers' perceptions of subordinates' competence as a function of personal value orientations. *Academy of Management Journal, 14*(4), 415–423.

Seo, M.-G., Barrett, L. F., & Bartunek, J. M. (2004). The role of affective experience in work motivation. *Academy of Management Journal, 29*(3), 423–439.

Settles, M. F. (1988). Humane downsizing: Can it be done? *Journal of Business Ethics, 7*(12), 961–963.

Seybolt, J. W. (1976). Work satisfaction as a function of the person–environment interaction. *Organizational Behavior & Human Performance, 17*(1), 66–75.

Shaikh, T., & Kanekar, S. (1994). Attitudinal similarity and affiliation need as determinants of interpersonal attraction. *Journal of Social Psychology, 134*(2), 257–259.

Shalof, T. (2004). *A nurse's story: Life, death and in-between in an intensive care unit.* Toronto: McClelland & Stewart Ltd.

Shamir, B. (1991). Meaning, self and motivation in organizations. *Organization Studies, 12*(3), 405–424.

Sheldon, K. M., Elliott, A. J., Kim, Y., & Kasser, T. (2001). What is satisfying about satisfying events? Testing 10 candidate psychological needs. *Journal of Personality and Social Psychology, 80*(2), 325–339.

Sheldon, K. M., & King, L. (2001). Why positive psychology is necessary. *American Psychologist, 56*(3), 216–217.

Shepard, H. A. (1956). Nine dilemmas in industrial research. *Administrative Science Quarterly, 1*(3), 295–309.

Sheppard, B. H., Hartwick, J., & Warshaw, P. R. (1988). The theory of reasoned action: A meta-analysis of past research with recommendations for modifications and future research. *Journal of Consumer Research, 15*(3), 325–342.

Sheppard, B. H., Lewicki, R. J., & Minton, J. W. (1992). *Organizational justice: The search for fairness in the workplace.* New York: Lexington Books.

Sherman, S. J. (1980). On the self-erasing nature of errors of prediction. *Journal of Personality and Social Psychology, 39,* 211–221.

Shetzer, L. (1993). A social information processing model of employee participation. *Organization Science, 4*(2), 252–268.

Shimp, T. A., & Kavas, A. (1984). The theory of reasoned action applied to coupon usage. *Journal of Consumer Research, 11*(3), 795–809.

Shingledecker, P. (1983). *Disciplinary equity: Employee perceptions, evaluations, and reactions.* Unpublished manuscript.

Shumaker, S. A., & Brownell, A. (1984). Toward a theory of social support: Closing the conceptual gaps. *Journal of Social Issues, 40,* 11–36.

Siegel, A. L., & Ruh, R. A. (1973). Job involvement, participation in decision making, personal background and job behavior. *Organizational Behavior & Human Performance, 9*(2), 318–327.

Siegel, P. A., Brockner, J., & Tyler, T. R. (1995, August). *Revisiting the interactive relationship between procedural and distributive justice: The role of trust.* Paper presented at the 55th Annual Meeting of Academy of Management, Vancouver, British Columbia, Canada.

Sikula, A. F. (1971). *Conflict via values and value systems.* Champaign, IL: Stipes.

Simmel, G. (1950). The sociology of Georg Simmel (translated, edited, and with an introd. by Kurt H. Wolff). Glencoe, IL: Free Press

Simon, H. A. (1957). *Administrative behavior* (2nd ed.). New York: Macmillan.

Simon, H. A. (1995). The information-processing theory of mind. *American Psychologist, 50*(7), 507–508.

Simons, T., & Roberson, Q. (2003). Why managers should care about fairness: The effects of aggregate justice perceptions on organizational outcomes. *Journal of Applied Psychology, 88*(3), 432–443.

Sims Jr., H. P., & Szilagyi, A. D. (1976). Job characteristic relationships: Individual and structural moderators. *Organizational Behavior & Human Performance, 17*(2), 211–230.

Singer, M. A. (1992). Procedural justice in managerial selection: Identification of fairness determinants and associations of fairness perceptions. *Social Justice Research, 5,* 49–70.

Sirota, D., & Wolfson, A. (1972). Job enrichment: What are the obstacles? *Personnel, 49*(3), 8–17.

Skarlicki, D. P., Ellard, J. H., & Kelln, B. R. C. (1998). Third-party perceptions of a layoff: Procedural, derogation, and retributive aspects of justice. *Journal of Applied Psychology*, *83*, 119–127.

Skinner, B. F. (1953). *Science and human behavior*. New York: Macmillan.

Skinner, B. F. (1969). *Contingencies of reinforcement: A theoretical analysis*. New York: Appleton-Century-Crofts.

Skinner, B. F. (1971). *Beyond freedom and dignity*. New York: Knopf.

Skinner, B. F. (1974). *About behaviorism*. New York: Knopf.

Skinner, B. F. (1995). *Perceived control, motivation, and coping*. Thousand Oaks, CA: Sage.

Smith, A. (1937). *The wealth of nations: Inquiry into the nature and causes of the wealth of nations* (Canadian ed.). New York: Random House.

Smith, F. J. (1977). Work attitudes as predictors of attendance on a specific day. *Journal of Applied Psychology*, *62*(1), 16–19.

Smith, P. C. (1992). In pursuit of happiness: Why study general job satisfaction? In C. J. Cranny, P. C. Smith, & E. F. Stone (Eds.), *Job satisfaction* (pp. 5–19). New York: Lexington Books.

Smith, P. C., Kendall, L. M., & Hulin, C. L. (1969). *The measurement of satisfaction in work and retirement*. Chicago: Rand McNally.

Smith, R. H. (1991). Envy and the sense of injustice. In P. Salovey (Ed.), *The psychology of jealousy and envy*. New York: Guilford Press.

Snyder, C. R. (2002). Hope theory: Rainbows in the mind. *Psychological Inquiry*, *13*(4), 249–275.

Snyder, R. A., Howard, A., & Hammer, T. H. (1978). The predictive power of within- versus across-subjects scores in expectancy research. *Journal of Psychology*, *100*(2), 285–292.

Somers, M. J. (1995). Organizational commitment, turnover and absenteeism: An examination of direct and interaction effects. *Journal of Organizational Behavior*, *16*(1), 49–58.

Spangler, W. D., & House, R. J. (1991). Presidential effectiveness and the leadership motive profile. *Journal of Personality & Social Psychology*, *60*(3), 439–455.

Spector, P. E. (1978). Organizational frustration: A model and review of the literature. *Personnel Psychology*, *31*(4), 815–829.

Spector, P. E. (1997). The role of frustration in antisocial behavior at work. In R. A. Giacalone & J. Greenberg (Eds.), *Antisocial behavior in organizations* (pp. 1–17). Thousand Oaks, CA: Sage.

Spencer, H. (1870). *The principles of psychology* (Vol. 1, 2nd ed.). New York: Appleton.

Spreitzer, G. M. (1995a). Psychological empowerment in the workplace: Dimensions, measurement and validation. *Academy of Management Journal*, *38*(5), 1442–1465.

Spreitzer, G. M. (1995b). An empirical test of a comprehensive model of intrapersonal empowerment in the workplace. *American Journal of Community Psychology*, *23*(5), 601–630.

Spreitzer, G. M. (1996). Social structural characteristics of psychological empowerment. *Academy of Management Journal*, *39*(2), 483–504.

Spreitzer, G. M., & Mishra, A. K. (2002). To stay or to go: Voluntary survivor turnover following an organizational downsizing. *Journal of Organizational Behavior*, *23*, 707–729.

Sprott, D. E., Spangenberg, E. R., & Fisher, R. (2003). The importance of normative beliefs to the self-prophecy effect. *Journal of Applied Psychology*, *88*(3), 423–431.

Stackman, R. W., Pinder, C. C., & Connor, P. E. (2000). Values lost: Redirecting research on values in the workplace. In N. M. Ashkanasy, C. P. M. Wilderom, & M. F. Peterson (Eds.), *Handbook of organizational culture & climate*. Thousand Oaks, CA: Sage.

Stagner, R. (1956). *Psychology of industrial conflict*. New York: John Wiley & Sons.

Stajkovic, A. D. (2006). Development of a core confidence-higher order construct. *Journal of Applied Psychology*, *91*(6), 1208–1224.

Stajkovic, A. D., & Luthans, F. (1997). A meta-analysis of the effects of organizational behavior modification on task performance, 1975–95. *Academy of Management Journal*, *40*(5), 1122–1149.

Stajkovic, A. D., & Luthans, F. (1998). Self-efficacy and work-related performance: A meta-analysis. *Psychological Bulletin*, *124*(2), 240–261.

Stajkovic, A. D., & Luthans, F. (2001). Differential effects of incentive motivators on work performance. *Academy of Management Journal*, *4*(3), 580–590.

Stajkovic, A. D., & Luthans, F. (2003). Behavioral management and task performance in organizations: Conceptual background, meta-analysis, and test of alternative models. *Personnel Psychology*, *56*(1), 155–194.

Standing, T. E. (1973). *Satisfaction with the work itself as a function of cognitive complexity.* Proceedings, 81st Annual Convention, American Psychological Association (pp. 603–604).

Statistics Canada. (2004). *Study: Criminal victimization in the workplace* (No. 4504): Government of Canada.

Statistics Canada. (2006). *Women in Canada: A gender-based statistical report* (No. 89–503–X): Government of Canada.

Statistics Canada. (2007). *Study: Gender differences in quits and absenteeism 1983 to 2003* (No. 11–001-XIE): Government of Canada: The Daily.

Staw, B. M. (1976). *Intrinsic and extrinsic motivation.* Morristown, NJ: General Learning Press.

Staw, B. M. (1977). Motivation in organizations: Toward synthesis and redirection. In B. M. Staw & G. A. Salancik (Eds.), *New directions in organizational behavior* (pp. 55–96). Chicago, IL: St. Clair Press.

Staw, B. M. (1984). Organizational behavior: A review and reformulation of the field's outcome variables. *Annual Review of Psychology, 35,* 627–666.

Staw, B. M., & Boettger, R. D. (1990). Task revision: A neglected form of work performance. *Academy of Management Journal, 33*(3), 534–559.

Staw, B. M., Sutton, R. I., & Pelled, L. H. (1994). Employee positive emotion and favorable outcomes at the workplace. *Organization Science, 5*(1), 51–71.

Steel, P., & König, C. J. (2006). Integrating theories of motivation. *Academy of Management Review, 31*(4), 889–913.

Steers, R. M. (1977). Antecedents and outcomes of organizational commitment. *Administrative Science Quarterly, 22*(1), 46–56.

Steers, R. M., & Mowday, R. T. (1981). Employee turnover and the post-decision accommodation process. In B. M. Staw & L. L. Cummings (Eds.), *Research in organizational behavior* (pp. 235–281). Greenwich, CT: JAI Press.

Steers, R. M., & Porter, L. W. (Eds.). (1979). *Motivation and work behavior* (2nd ed.). New York: McGraw-Hill.

Steers, R. M., & Porter, L. W. (Eds.). (1991). *Motivation and work behavior* (5th ed.). New York: McGraw-Hill.

Steers, R. M., & Rhodes, S. R. (1978). Major influences on employee attendance: A process model. *Journal of Applied Psychology, 63*(4), 391–407.

Steers, R. M., & Sanchez-Runde, C. J. (2002). Culture, motivation, and work behavior. In M. J. Gannon & K. L. Newman (Eds.), *The Blackwell handbook of cross-cultural management* (pp. 190–216). Oxford: Blackwell.

Stein, A. H., & Bailey, M. M. (1973). The socialization of achievement motivation in females. *Psychological Bulletin, 80,* 345–366.

Stevens, J. M., Beyer, J. M., & Trice, H. M. (1978). Assessing personal, role, and organizational predictors of managerial commitment. *Academy of Management Journal, 21*(3), 380–396.

Stewart, A. J. (Ed.). (1982). *Motivation and society.* San Francisco: Jossey-Bass.

Stewart, A. J., & Chester, N. L. (1982). Sex differences in human social motives: Achievement, affiliation, and power. In A. Stewart (Ed.), *Motivation and society* (pp. 172–220). San Francisco: Jossey-Bass.

Stone, E. F. (1992). A critical analysis of social information processing models of job perceptions and job attitudes. In C. J. Cranny, P. D. Smith, & E. F. Stone (Eds.), *Job satisfaction.* New York: Lexington Books.

Strauss, G. (1982). Workers participation in management: An international perspective. In B. M. Staw & L. L. Cummings (Eds.), *Research in organizational behavior* (Vol. 4, pp. 173–266). Greenwich, CT: JAI Press.

Striker, L. J. (1988). Measuring social status with occupational information: A simple method. *Journal of Applied Social Psychology, 18,* 423–437.

Stumpf, S. A., & Dawley, P. K. (1981). Predicting voluntary and involuntary turnover using absenteeism and performance indices. *Academy of Management Journal, 24*(1), 148–163.

Sturman, M. C. (2006). Using your pay system to improve employees' performance: How you pay makes a difference. *CHR Reports, 6*(13), 6–16.

Sullivan, J. J. (1986). Human nature, organizations and management theory. *Academy of Management Review, 11*(3), 534–549.

Sussman, M., & Vecchio, R. P. (1985). Conceptualizations of valence and instrumentality: A fourfold model. *Organizational Behavior & Human Decision Processes, 36*(1), 96–112.

Sutherland, J. W. (1975). *Systems: Analysis, administration, and architecture.* Princeton, NJ: Princeton University Press.

Sweeney, P. D., & McFarlin, D. B. (1993). Workers' evaluations of the "ends" and the "means": An examination of four models of distributive and procedural justice. *Organizational Behavior & Human Decision Processes*, *55*(1), 23–40.

Taber, T. D., & Alliger, G. M. (1995). A task-level assessment of job satisfaction. *Journal of Organizational Behavior*, *16*(2), 101–121.

Tait, M., Padgett, M. Y., & Baldwin, T. T. (1989). Job and life satisfaction: A reevaluation of the strength of the relationship and gender effects as a function of the date of the study. *Journal of Applied Psychology*, *74*(3), 502–507.

Tallarico, C. M., & Gillis, D. (2007, April 4). *Catalyst Canada: Latest count of women in Canada's largest businesses shows marginal progress*, from www.catalyst.org

Tannenbaum, S. I., Mathieu, J. E., Salas, E., & Cannon-Bowers, J. A. (1991). Meeting trainees' expectations: The influence of training fulfillment on the development of commitment, self-efficacy, and motivation. *Journal of Applied Psychology*, *76*(6), 759–769.

Tausky, C. (1995). The meanings of work. In R. L. Simpson & I. H. Simpson (Eds.), *Research in the sociology of work: The meaning of work* (5th ed., pp. 15–27). Greenwich, CT: JAI Press.

Tavris, C. (1982). *Anger: The misunderstood emotion*. New York: Simon & Schuster.

Taylor, E. K., & Griess, T. (1976). The missing middle in validation research. *Personnel Psychology*, *29*(1), 5–11.

Taylor, F. W. (1967). *The principles of scientific management*. New York: Norton (originally published 1911).

Taylor, L., & Watson, P. (1971). Industrial sabotage: Motives and meanings. In S. Cohen (Ed.), *Images of deviance* (pp. 219–245). Harmondsworth: Penguin Books.

Taylor, P. S. (2007, March 19). In pursuit of prosperity. *Maclean's*, 32–36.

Tead, O. (1918). *Instincts in industry*. New York: Arno and The New York Times.

Tead, O. (1929). *Human nature and management*. New York: McGraw-Hill.

Telly, C. S., French, W. L., & Scott, W. C. (1971). The relationship of inequity to turnover among hourly workers. *Administrative Science Quarterly*, *16*(2), 164–171.

Tepper, B. J. (2000). Consequences of abusive supervision. *Academy of Management Journal*, *43*(2), 176–190.

Tepper, B. J. (2001). Health consequences of organizational injustice: Tests of main and interactive effects. *Organizational Behavior & Human Decision Processes*, *86*(2), 197–215.

ter Doest, L., Maes, S., Gebhardt, W., & Koelewijn, H. (2006). Personal goal facilitation through work: Implications for employee satisfaction and well-being. *Applied Psychology: An International Review*, *55*(2), 192–219.

Terborg, J. R. (1977). Validation and extension of an individual differences model of work performance. *Organizational Behavior & Human Performance*, *18*(1), 188–216.

Terpstra, D. E., & Rozell, E. J. (1994). The relationship of goal setting to organizational profitability. *Group & Organization Management*, *19*(3), 285–294.

Tesser, A., & Shaffer, D. R. (1990). Attitudes and attitude change. *Annual Review of Psychology*, *41*(1), 479–523.

Thibault, J., & Walker, L. (1975). *Procedural justice: A psychological analysis*. Hillsdale, NJ: Lawrence Erlbaum Associates, Inc.

Thibault, J., & Walker, L. (1978). A theory of procedure. *California Law Review*, *66*, 541–566.

Thierry, H. (1990). Intrinsic motivation reconsidered. In U. Kleinbeck, H. H. Quast, H. Thierry, & H. Hacker (Eds.), *Work motivation* (pp. 67–82). Hillsdale, NJ: Lawrence Erlbaum Associates, Inc.

Thomas, J. G., & Griffin, R. W. (1989). The power of social information in the workplace. *Organizational Dynamics*, *18*(2), 63–75.

Thomas, K. M., & Mathieu, J. E. (1994). Role of causal attributions in dynamic self-regulation and goal processes. *Journal of Applied Psychology*, *79*(6), 812–818.

Thomas, K. W., & Tymon, W. G., Jr. (1982). Necessary properties of relevant research: Lessons from recent criticisms of the organizational sciences. *Academy of Management Review*, *7*(3), 345–352.

Thomas, K. W., & Velthouse, B. A. (1990). Cognitive elements of empowerment: An "interpretive" model of intrinsic task motivation. *Academy of Management Review*, *15*(4), 666–681.

Thompson, J. D. (1967). *Organizations in action: Social science bases of administrative theory*. New York: McGraw-Hill.

Thoresen, E., & Mahoney, M. (1974). *Behavioral self control*. New York: Holt, Rinehart, & Winston.

Thorkildsen, T. A., & White-McNulty, L. (2002). Developing conceptions of fair contest procedures and the understanding of skill and luck. *Journal of Educational Psychology*, *94*(2), 316–326.

Thorndike, E. L. (1911). *Animal intelligence*. New York: Macmillan.

Thurow, L. C. (1980). *The zero–sum society*. New York: Penguin Books.

Tice, D. M., & Baumeister, R. F. (1993). Controlling anger: Self-induced emotion change. In D. M. Wegner & J. W. Pennebaker (Eds.), *Handbook of mental control* (pp. 393–409). Englewood Cliffs, NJ: Prentice-Hall.

Tice, D. M., Bratslavsky, E., & Baumeister, R. F. (2001). Emotional distress regulation takes precedence over impulse control: If you feel bad, do it! *Journal of Personality and Social Psychology, 80*(1), 53–67.

Tiedens, L. Z. (2000). Powerful emotions: The vicious cycle of social status positions and emotions. In N. M. Ashkanasy, C. E. Hartel, & W. J. Zerbe (Eds.), *Emotions in the workplace: Research, theory and practice* (pp. 6–81). Westport, CT/London: Quorum Books.

Tien, E., & Frankel, V. (1996). *The I hate my job handbook*. New York: Fawcett Columbine.

Tierney, P., & Farmer, S. M. (2002). Creative self-efficacy: Potential antecedents and relationship to creative performance. *Academy of Management Journal, 45*(6), 1137–1148.

Tolman, E. C. (1959). Principles of purposive behavior. In S. Koch (Ed.), *Psychology: A study of a science* (Vol. 2). New York: McGraw-Hill.

Toneatto, T., & Binik, Y. (1987). The role of intentions, social norms, and attitudes in the performance of dental flossing: A test of the theory of reasoned action. *Journal of Applied Social Psychology, 17*, 593–603.

Torbert, W. R. (1994). The good life. *Journal of Management Inquiry, 3*(1), 58–66.

Tornow, W. W. (1971). The development and application of an input–outcome moderator test on the perception and reduction of inequity. *Organizational Behavior & Human Performance, 6*(5), 614–638.

Toscano, G. A., & Windau, J. A. (1998). Profile of fatal work injuries in 1996. *Compensation and Working Conditions*, Spring, 37–45.

Trevino, L. K. (1992). The social effects of punishment in organizations: A justice perspective. *Academy of Management Review, 17*(4), 647–676.

Trevor, C. O., Gerhart, B., & Boudreau, J. W. (1997). Voluntary turnover and job performance: Curvilinearity and the moderating influences of salary growth and promotions. *Journal of Applied Psychology, 82*, 44–61.

Trice, H. M., Belasco, J., & Alutto, J. A. (1969). The role of ceremonials in organizational behavior. *Industrial and Labor Relations Review, 23*(1), 40–51.

Troyer, L. (2003). The role of social identity processes in status construction. In S. R. Thye & J. Skvoretz (Eds.), *Advances in group processes* (Vol. 20, pp. 149–172). Amsterdam: Elsevier.

Tsui, A. S., & Ashford, S. J. (1994). Adaptive self-regulation: A process view of managerial effectiveness. *Journal of Management, 20*(1), 93–121.

Tubbs, M. E. (1986). Goal setting: A meta-analytic examination of the empirical evidence. *Journal of Applied Psychology, 71*(3), 474–483.

Tubbs, M. E., & Ekeberg, S. E. (1991). The role of intentions in work motivation: Implications for goal-setting theory and research. *Academy of Management Review, 16*(1), 180–199.

Tuckman, B. W. (1968). Personality and satisfaction with occupational choice: Role of environment as a mediator. *Psychological Reports, 23*, 543–550.

Tulgan, B. (1995). *Managing generation X: How to bring out the best in young talent*. Santa Monica, CA: Merritt Publishing Co.

Turillo, C. J., Folger, R., Lavelle, J. J., Umphress, E. E., & Gee, J. O. (2002). Is virtue its own reward? Self-sacrificial decisions for the sake of fairness. *Organizational Behavior & Human Decision Processes, 89*, 839–865.

Turner, A. N., & Lawrence, P. R. (1965). *Industrial jobs and the worker*. Boston, MA: Harvard University, School of Business Administration.

Turner, A. N., & Miclette, A. L. (1962). Sources of satisfaction in repetitive work. *Occupational Psychology, 36*, 215–231.

Tyler, T. R., & Blader, S. L. (2002). Autonomous vs. comparative status: Must we be better than others to feel good about ourselves? *Organizational Behavior & Human Decision Processes, 89*, 813–838.

Tyler, T. R., & Blader, S. L. (2005). Can businesses effectively regulate employee conduct? The antecedents of rule following in work settings. *Academy of Management Journal, 48*, 1143–1156.

Universum Communications Inc. (2006). *The Universum Survey: Canadian undergraduate edition* (Trend Report). Philadelphia, PA: Universum Communications, Inc.

Unsworth, K. L., & Parker, S. K. (2003). Proactivity and innovation: Promoting a new workforce for the new workplace. In D. Holman, T. D. Wall, C. W. Clegg, P. Sparrow, & A. Howard (Eds.), *The new workplace: A guide to the human impact of modern working practices*. New York: John Wiley & Sons.

Urwick, L. F. (1967). Organization and theories about the nature of man. *Academy of Management Journal*, *10*(1), 9–15.

Van Der Merwe, S. (1978). What personal attributes it takes to make it in management. *Business Quarterly*, *43*(4), 28–35.

Van Dick, R., Becker, T. E., & Meyer, J. P. (2006). Commitment and identification: Forms, foci, and future. *Journal of Organizational Behavior*, *27*, 545–548.

van Dierendonck, D., Schaufeli, W. B., & Buunk, B. P. (1998). The evaluation of an individual burnout intervention program: The role of inequity and social support. *Journal of Applied Psychology*, *83*(3), 392–407.

Van Eerde, W., & Thierry, H. (1996). Vroom's expectancy models and work-related criteria: A meta-analysis. *Journal of Applied Psychology*, *81*, 575–586.

Van Knippenberg, D., & Sleebos, E. (2006). Organizational identification versus organizational commitment: Self-definition, social exchange, and job attitudes. *Journal of Organizational Behavior*, *27*, 571–584.

Van Maanen, J. (1977). Experiencing organization notes on the meaning of careers and socialization. In J. Van Maanen (Ed.), *Organizational careers: Some new perspectives* (pp. 15–45). New York: John Wiley & Sons.

Van Maanen, J., & Kunda, G. (1989). "Real feelings": Emotional expression and organizational culture. In L. L. Cummings & B. M. Staw (Eds.), *Research in organizational behavior* (Vol. 11, pp. 43–50). Greenwich, CT: JAI Press.

Van Maanen, J., & Schein, E. H. (1979). Toward a theory of organizational socialization. In B. M. Staw (Ed.), *Research in organizational behavior* (Vol. 1, pp. 209–264). Greenwich, CT: JAI Press.

Van Sommers, P. (1988). *Jealousy*. London: Penguin Books.

Van Yperen, N. W., & Janssen, O. (2002). Feeling fatigued and dissatisfied or fatigued but satisfied? Goal orientations and responses to high job demands. *Academy of Management Journal*, *45*(6), 1161–1171.

Vancouver, J. B., & Day, D. V. (2005). Industrial and organizational research on self-regulation: From constructs to applications. *Applied Psychology: An International Review*, *54*(2), 155–185.

Vancouver, J. B., & Scherbaum, K. L. (2002). *Self-efficacy and resource allocation planning: A discontinuous model*. Poster presented at the 17th annual conference of the Society for Industrial and Organizational Psychology, Toronto.

Vancouver, J. B., Thompson, C. M., & Williams, A. A. (2001). The changing signs in the relationships among self-efficacy, personal goals, and performance. *Journal of Applied Psychology*, *86*(4), 605–620.

Vancouver Province. (1996, June 27). Medal 78 years later. *Vancouver Province*, A26.

Vancouver Sun. (1994, September 19). Toilet toll angers workers as meat plant targets bathroom-break abusers. *Vancouver Sun*.

Vandenberg, R. J., & Lance, C. E. (1992). Examining the causal order of job satisfaction and organizational commitment. *Journal of Management*, *18*(1), 153–167.

VandeWalle, D., Brown, S. P., Cron, W. L., & Slocum, J. W., Jr. (1999). The influence of goal orientation and self-regulation tactics on sales performance: A longitudinal field test. *Journal of Applied Psychology*, *84*(2), 249–259.

Veblen, T. (1904). *The theory of business enterprise*. New York: Charles Scribners Sons.

Vecchio, R. P. (1995). It's not easy being green: Jealousy and envy in the workplace. In G. R. Ferris (Ed.), *Research in personnel and human resource management* (Vol. 13, pp. 201–244). Greenwich, CT: JAI Press.

Vroom, V. H. (1964). *Work and motivation*. New York: John Wiley & Sons.

Vroom, V. H., & Yetton, P. (1973). *Leadership and decision making*. Pittsburg, PA: University of Pittsburg Press.

Wagner, J. A. (1994). Participation's effects on performance and satisfaction: A reconsideration of research evidence. *Academy of Management Review*, *19*(2), 312–330.

Wahba, M. A., & Bridwell, L. G. (1976). Maslow reconsidered: A review of research on the need hierarchy theory. *Organizational Behavior and Human Performance*, *15*(2), 212–240.

Waldron, V. (2000). Relational experiences and emotion at work. In S. Fineman (Ed.), *Emotion in organizations* (2nd ed., pp. 64–82). London/Thousand Oaks, CA/New Delhi: Sage.

Walsh, J. P., & Ungson, G. R. (1991). Organizational memory. *Academy of Management Review*, *16*(1), 57–91.

Walster, E., Berscheid, E., & Walster, G. W. (1976). New directions in equity research. In L. Berkowitz & E. Walster (Eds.), *Advances in experimental social psychology* (Vol. 9, pp. 1–38). New York: Academic Press.

Walter, G. A., & Marks, S. E. (1981). *Experimental learning and change*. New York: John Wiley & Sons.

Walter, G. A., & Pinder, C. C. (1980). Ethical ascendance or backsliding? *American Psychologist*, *35*, 936–937.

Waluchow, W. (1988). Pay equity: Equal value to whom? *Journal of Business Ethics*, *7*(3), 185–189.

Wanberg, C. R., Glomb, T. M., Song, Z., & Sorenson, S. (2005). Job-search persistence during unemployment: A 10-wave longitudinal study. *Journal of Applied Psychology, 90*(3), 411–430.

Wanberg, C. R., Welsh, E. T., & Hezlett, S. A. (2003). Mentoring research: A review and dynamic process model. In J. J. Martocchio & G. R. Ferris (Eds.), *Research in personnel and human resources management* (Vol. 22, pp. 90–124). Amsterdam: Elsevier.

Wanous, J. P. (1974). Individual differences and reactions to job characteristics. *Journal of Applied Psychology, 59*(5), 616–622.

Wanous, J. P. (1980). *Organizational entry: Recruitment, selection and socialization of newcomers.* Reading, MA: Addison-Wesley.

Wanous, J. P., Keon, T. L., & Latack, J. C. (1983). Expectancy theory and occupational/organizational choices: A review and test. *Organizational Behavior and Human Performance, 32*, 66–86

Wanous, J. P., & Lawler III, E. E. (1972). Measurement and meaning of job satisfaction. *Journal of Applied Psychology, 56*(2), 95–105.

Warburton, W. A., & Williams, K. D. (2005). Ostracism: When competing motivations collide. In J. P. Forgas, K. D. Williams, & S. M. Laham (Eds.), *Social motivation* (pp. 294–313). Cambridge: Cambridge University Press.

Warr, P., Barter, J., & Brownbridge, G. (1983). On the independence of positive and negative affect. *Journal of Personality and Social Psychology, 44*, 644–651.

Warr, P., & Conner, M. (1992). Job competence and cognition. In B. M. Staw & L. L. Cummings (Eds.), *Research in organizational behavior* (Vol. 14, pp. 91–127). Greenwich, CT: JAI Press.

Warwick, J., & Nettlebeck, T. (2004). Emotional intelligence is . . .? *Personality and Individual Differences, 37*, 1091–1100.

Watanabe, T. (1996, July 17). Beneath orderly surface, Japanese life turns ugly. *Los Angeles Times*, reported in the *Vancouver Sun*, A10.

Watson, D., Clark, L. A., & Tellegen, A. (1988). Development and validation of brief measures of positive and negative affect: The PANAS scales. *Journal of Personality and Social Psychology, 54*, 1063–1070.

Watson, D., & Slack, A. K. (1993). General factors of affective temperament and their relation to job satisfaction over time. *Organizational Behavior & Human Decision Processes, 54*(2), 181–202.

Watson, D., Wiese, D., Vaidya, J., & Tellegen, A. (1999). The two general activation systems of affect: Structural findings, evolutionary considerations, and psychobiological evidence. *Journal of Personality and Social Psychology, 76*, 805–819.

Watson Wyatt Worldwide. (1995). *Measuring change in the attitudes of the Canadian workplace.* Toronto: WWW.

Webb, E. J., Campbell, D. T., Schwartz, R. D., & Sechrest, L. (1966). *Unobtrusive measures: Nonreactive research in the social sciences.* Chicago, IL: Rand McNally.

Weber, M. (1904/1930). *The Protestant ethic and the spirit of capitalism* (T. Parsons, trans.). New York: Scribner.

Webster, M. J. (2003). Working on status puzzles. In S. R. Thye & J. Skvoretz (Eds.), *Advances in group processes* (Vol. 20, pp. 173–215). Amsterdam: Elsevier.

Weick, K. E. (1969). *The social psychology of organizing.* Reading, MA: Addison-Wesley.

Weick, K. E. (1989). Theory construction as disciplined imagination. *Academy of Management Review, 14*(4), 516–531.

Weick, K. E., & Nesset, B. (1968). Preferences among forms of equity. *Organizational Behavior & Human Performance, 3*(4), 400–416.

Weil, F. A. (1979, December 3). Management's drag on productivity. *Business Week, 2614,* 14.

Weil, M., & Kruzich, J. (1990). Empowerment issues in administrative and community practice. *Administration in Social Work, 14*(2), 1–12.

Weiner, Y. (1982). Commitment in organizations: A normative view. *Academy of Management Review, 7*(3), 418–428.

Weiner, Y., & Vardi, Y. (1980). Relationships between job, organization, and career commitments and work outcomes–an integrative approach. *Organizational Behavior & Human Performance, 26*(1), 81–96.

Weiss, H. M. (2001). Introductory comments. *Organizational Behavior and Human Decision Processes, 86*(1), 1–2.

Weiss, H. M., & Cropanzano, R. (1996). Affective events theory: A theoretical discussion of the structure, causes and consequences of affective experiences at work. In B. M. Staw & L. L. Cummings (Eds.), *Research in organizational behavior* (Vol. 18, pp. 1–74). Greenwich, CT: JAI Press.

Welsh, D. H. B., Luthans, F., & Sommer, S. M. (1993). Managing Russian factory workers: The impact of US based behavioral and participative techniques, *Academy of Management Journal*, *36*(1), 58–79.

Whalen-Miller, S. (2006, August 7). Why wasn't I invited? Rejection, bullying. Why one school banned birthday invitations. *Maclean's*, 39.

Wharton, A. S. (1993). The affective consequences of service work. *Work & Occupations*, *20*(2), 205–232.

Wharton, A. S., & Erickson, R. J. (1993). Managing emotions of the job and at home: Understanding the consequences of multiple emotional roles. *Academy of Management Review*, *18*(3), 457–486.

Whetten, D. A., & Cameron, K. S. (2007). *Developing management skills* (7th ed.). Upper Saddle River, NJ: Prentice-Hall.

Whetten, D. A., & Godfrey, P. C. (Eds.). (1998). *Identity in organizations*. Thousand Oaks, CA: Sage.

White, J. K. (1978a). Individual differences and the job quality–worker response relationship: Review, integration, and comments. *Academy of Management Review*, *3*(2), 267–280.

White, J. K. (1978b). Generalizability of individual difference moderators of the participation in decision making–employee response relationship. *Academy of Management Journal*, *21*(1), 36–43.

White, R. (1959). Motivation reconsidered: The concept of competence. *Psychological Review*, *66*, 297–333.

Whitsett, D. A., & Winslow, E. K. (1967). An analysis of studies critical of the motivator-hygiene theory. *Personnel Psychology*, *20*(4), 391–415.

Whyte, G., Saks, A. M., & Hook, S. (1997). When success breeds failure: The role of self-efficacy in escalating commitment to a losing course of action. *Journal of Organizational Behavior*, *18*, 415–432.

Whyte, W. F. (1948). *Human relations in the restaurant industry*. New York: McGraw-Hill.

Whyte, W. F. (1956). *The organization man*. Garden City, NY: Doubleday Anchor Books.

Whyte, W. F. (1972). Pigeons, persons and piece rates. *Psychology Today*, *5*(11), 66–68, 96, 98, 100.

Wicker, F. W., Brown, G., Wiehe, J. A., Hagen, A. S., & Reed, J. L. (1993). On reconsidering Maslow: An examination of the deprivation/domination proposition. *Journal of Research in Personality*, *27*, 118–133.

Wiener, N. (1948). *Cybernetics*. New York: John Wiley & Sons.

Wiersma, U. J. (1992). The effects of extrinsic rewards in intrinsic motivation: A meta-analysis. *Journal of Occupational and Organizational Psychology*, *65*, 101–114.

Wiesenfeld, B., Raghuram, S., & Garud, R. (2001). Organizational identification among virtual workers: The role of need for affiliation and perceived work-based social support. *Journal of Management*, *27*(2), 213–230.

Wilcoxon, H. C. (1969). Historical introduction to the problem of reinforcement. In J. T. Tapp (Ed.), *Reinforcement and behavior* (pp. 1–46). New York: Academic Press.

Wilderom, C. P. M., Glunk, U., & Maslowski, R. (2000). Organizational culture as a predictor of organizational performance. In N. M. Ashkanasy, C. P. M. Wilderom, & M. F. Peterson (Eds.), *Organizational culture and climate* (pp. 193–209). Thousand Oaks, CA: Sage.

Williams, C. R., & Livingstone, L. P. (1994). Another look at the relationship between performance and voluntary turnover. *Academy of Management Journal*, *37*, 269–298.

Williams, D. E., & Page, M. M. (1989). A multi-dimensional measure of Maslow's hierarchy of needs. *Journal of Research in Personality*, *23*, 192–213.

Williams, L. K., Whyte, W. F., & Green, C. S. (1966). Do cultural differences affect workers' attitudes? *Industrial Relations*, *5*(3), 105–117.

Williams, M. A., & Mattingley, J. B. (2006). Do angry men get noticed? *Current Biology*, *16*(11), 402–404.

Winell, M. (1987). Personal goals: The key to self-direction in adulthood. In M. E. Ford & D. H. Ford (Eds.), *Humans as self-constructing living systems: Putting the framework to work* (pp. 261–287). Hillsdale, NJ: Lawrence Erlbaum Associates, Inc.

Winter, D. G. (1973). *The power motive*. New York: Free Press.

Winter, D. G. (1988). The power motive in women – and men. *Journal of Personality and Social Psychology*, *54*, 510–519.

Winter, D. G., & Stewart, A. J. (1978). Power-motivated actions in everyday life. In H. London & J. E. Exner (Eds.), *Dimensions of personality* (pp. 400–412). New York: John Wiley & Sons.

Winters, D., & Latham, G. P. (1996). The effect of learning versus outcome goals on a simple versus a complex task. *Group & Organization Management*, *21*(2), 236–250.

Wolf, G., & Connolly, T. (1981). Between-subject designs in testing expectancy models: A methodological note. *Decision Sciences*, *12*(1), 39–45.

Wolfe, M. (1994). Dr. Fabrikant's solution. *Saturday Night, 109*(6), 11–13, 16–18, 56–59.

Wollack, S., Goodale, J. G., Wijting, J. P., & Smith, P. C. (1971). Development of the survey of work values. *Journal of Applied Psychology, 55*(4), 331–338.

Womack, J. P., Jones, D., & Roos, D. (1990). *The machine that changed the world: Based on the Massachusetts Institute of Technology 5-million dollar 5-year study on the future of the automobile.* New York: Rawson Associates.

Wong, P. T. P. (1979). Frustration, exploration, and learning. *Canadian Psychological Review, 20*, 133–144.

Wood, R., & Bandura, A. (1989). Social cognitive theory of organizational management. *Academy of Management Review, 14*(1), 361–384.

Wood, R. E., & Locke, E. A. (1990). Goal setting and strategy effects on complex tasks. In B. M. Staw & L. L. Cummings (Eds.), *Research in organizational behavior* (Vol. 12, pp. 73–109). Greenwich, CT: JAI Press.

Wood, R. E., Mento, A. J., & Locke, E. A. (1987). Task complexity as a moderator of goal effects: A meta-analysis. *Journal of Applied Psychology, 72*(3), 416–425.

Woodcock, M., & Francis, D. (1989). *Clarifying organizational values.* Aldershot: Gower.

Woodworth, R. S. (1918). *Dynamic psychology.* New York: Columbia University Press.

Wortman, C. B., & Linsenmeier, J. A. W. (1977). Interpersonal attraction and techniques of ingratiation in organizational settings. In B. M. Staw & G. A. Salancik (Eds.), *New directions in organizational behavior* (pp. 133–178). Chicago, IL: St. Clair Press.

Wright, L., & Smye, M. (1996). *Corporate abuse.* Toronto, Ontario, Canada: Key Porter.

Wright, T. A., & Bonett, D. G. (1993). Role of employee coping and performance in voluntary employee withdrawal: A research refinement and elaboration. *Journal of Management, 19*(1), 147–161.

Wright, T. A., & Doherty, E. M. (1998). The incubator: Organizational behavior "rediscovers" the role of emotional well-being. *Journal of Organizational Behavior, 19*(5), 481–485.

Wright, T. A., & Staw, B. M. (1999). Affect and favorable work outcomes: Two longitudinal tests of the happy–productive worker thesis. *Journal of Organizational Behavior, 20*, 1–23.

Wrzesniewski, A. (2002). "It's not just a job": Shifting meanings of work in the wake of 9/11. *Journal of Management Inquiry, 11*(3), 230–234.

Wrzesniewski, A., McCauley, C., Rozin, P., & Schwartz, B. (1997). Jobs, careers, and callings: People's relations to their works. *Journal of Research in Personality, 31*, 21–33.

Yang, J., Mossholder, K. W., & Peng, T. K. (2007). Procedural justice climate and group power distance: An examination of cross-level interaction effects. *Journal of Applied Psychology, 92*, 681–692.

Yerkes, R. M., & Dodson, J. D. (1908). The relation of strength of stimulus to rapidity of habit formation. *Journal of Comparative and Neurological Psychology, 18*, 459–482.

Ying, X. (2007, June 21). How the reporter found the Shanxi brick kiln slaves: The reporter describes his experience in uncovering the illegal child laborers in Shanxi. *EastSouthWestNorth.*

Yorks, L. (1979). *Job enrichment revisited.* New York: AMACOM.

Youngblood, S. A., & Bierman, L. (1994). Employment-at-will: New developments and research implications. In G. R. Ferris (Ed.), *Research in personnel and human resources management* (Vol. 12, pp. 303–324). Greenwich, CT: JAI Press.

Yukl, G., Wexley, K. N., & Seymore, J. D. (1972). Effectiveness of pay incentives under variable ratio and continuous reinforcement schedules. *Journal of Applied Psychology, 56*(1), 19–23.

Yukl, G. A., & Latham, G. P. (1975). Consequences of reinforcement schedules and incentive magnitudes for employee performance: Problems encountered in an industrial setting. *Journal of Applied Psychology, 60*(3), 294–298.

Yukl, G. A., Latham, G. P., & Pursell, E. D. (1976). The effectiveness of performance incentives under continuous and variable ratio schedules of reinforcement. *Personnel Psychology, 29*(2), 221–231.

Zajonc, R. B. (1960). The concepts of balance, congruity, and dissonance. *Public Opinion Quarterly, 24*, 280–296.

Zajonc, R. B. (1965). Social facilitation. *Science, 149*, 269–274.

Zajonc, R. B. (1980). Feeling and thinking: Preferences need no inferences. *American Psychologist, 35*, 151–175.

Zajonc, R. B. (1984). On the primacy of affect. *American Psychologist, 39*, 117–123.

Zajonc, R. B. (2000). Feeling and thinking: Closing the debate over the independence of affect. In J. P. Forgas (Ed.), *Feeling and thinking: The role of affect in social cognition* (pp. 31–58). Cambridge: Cambridge University Press.

Zalkind, S. S., & Costello, T. W. (1962). Perception: Some recent research and implications for administration. *Administrative Science Quarterly, 7*(2), 218–235.

Zaltman, G., & Duncan, R. (1977). *Strategies for planned change*. New York: John Wiley & Sons.

Zedeck, S. (1977). An information processing model and approach to the study of motivation. *Organizational Behavior & Human Performance, 18*(1), 47–77.

Zeithaml, V. A., Parasuraman, A., & Berry, L. L. (1990). *Delivering quality service: Balancing customer perceptions and expectations*. New York: Free Press.

Zeldich, M. (1968). Social status. In *International encyclopedia of the social sciences* (pp. 250–256). New York: Free Press.

Ziman, J. M. (1987). The problem of "problem choice". *Minerva, 25*, 92–106.

Zoglin, R., & Thompson, M. (1996). A question of honor. *Time, 147*(22), 30–32.

Zohar, D. (2002). The effects of leadership dimensions, safety climate, and assigned priorities on minor injuries in work groups. *Journal of Organizational Behavior, 23*(1), 75–92.

Zurbriggen, E. L., & Sturman, T. S. (2002). Linking motives and emotions: A test of McClelland's hypotheses. *Personality and Social Psychology Bulletin, 28*(4), 521–535.

Zweig, D., & Webster, J. (2004). What are we measuring? An examination of the relationships between the big-five personality traits, goal orientation, and performance intentions. *Personality and Individual Differences, 36*, 1693–1708.

Author index

Subject index

Page entries for headings with subheadings refer to general aspects of that topic.
Page entries in **bold** refer to figures/tables.